THE OXFORD
LITERARY GUIDE
TO THE
BRITISH ISLES

THE OXFORD
LITERARY GUIDE
TO THE
BRITISH ISLES

Compiled and edited by
DOROTHY EAGLE
HILARY CARNELL

OXFORD
AT THE CLARENDON PRESS

Oxford University Press, Walton Street, Oxford OX2 6DP

OXFORD LONDON GLASGOW
NEW YORK TORONTO MELBOURNE WELLINGTON
KUALA LUMPUR SINGAPORE JAKARTA HONG KONG TOKYO
DELHI BOMBAY CALCUTTA MADRAS KARACHI
IBADAN NAIROBI DAR ES SALAAM CAPE TOWN

ISBN 0 19 869123 8

This edition first issued as an
Oxford University Press paperback 1980
ISBN 0 19 285098 9

Printed in Great Britain
at the University Press, Oxford
by Vivian Ridler
Printer to the University

PREFACE

THERE is a fascination about places associated with writers that has often prompted readers to become pilgrims: to visit a birthplace and contemplate the surroundings of an author's childhood, to see with fresh eyes places that inspired poems or books, to pay homage at a graveside or public memorial. Many books have described such pilgrimages and this one has had some enjoyable predecessors, in particular John Freeman's admirable work *Literature and Locality* (1963) and the *Great Britain and Ireland* volume of Margaret Crosland's *A Traveller's Guide to Literary Europe* (1966).

The *Oxford Literary Guide* was originally planned to refer only to those places where something relevant to literature—a house, a school, a garden—could be seen, but so many buildings have been demolished or replaced that it has been necessary to add the word 'gone' after the description of an author's home or workplace and leave the rest to the reader's imagination. The editors have, within the last five years, visited nearly all the places listed in the text, checking the location of buildings, signposts, and footpaths. Where it was not possible to check places at first hand, libraries and local authorities were consulted for the latest information. The opening times given for places that can be visited by the public were correct at the time of going to press.

The book is divided into two main sections. In the List of Place-Names in the British Isles the headword for each place is followed by a reference to specially drawn maps at the end of the book, and a brief description of its geographical position. (Fictitious names of real places are entered as cross-references.) The Index of Authors, which includes over 900 writers (living writers have been excluded), provides a key to the entries in the main text, enabling the reader to follow a writer's career from place to place and to discover which of his works are linked to specific localities. Whenever possible it has been indicated where writers met and talked and struck sparks off each other—in one another's houses or at the salons of patrons, London coffee houses, the Poetry Bookshop, Garsington Manor, Tibbie Shiel's Inn, or the 'Court of Poetry' at Ráthluirc.

The list of places is a selection from an almost limitless source and we are aware that we may have overlooked some interesting literary associations. We should be grateful for any suggestions for new entries to include in future editions and for any corrections of error.

We should like to thank all those—our kind friends and the people we met on our way—who helped in the preparation of this book, and we are only sorry that lack of space prevents our doing so individually.

We are particularly grateful to librarians throughout the British Isles, who, from central libraries in the cities to the smallest branch libraries in country districts, gave unfailing help and encouragement. We are indebted also to independent libraries, cathedral libraries, local historians, and incumbents, who frequently combine the care of their parishes with the keeping of local history records. In the Republic of Ireland the Irish Tourist Board helped greatly with information about local writers and places that could be visited, answered hard questions, and offered useful suggestions.

We should like to acknowledge certain books on which we have drawn for information on specific subjects: *The Oxford Companion to English Literature*, the *Dictionary of National Biography*, *Literary Liverpool* by William Amos (1971), *Literary and Artistic Landmarks of Edinburgh*, by Andrew Pennycook (1973), 'Bournemouth's Associations with Literature' in *The Story of Bournemouth*, by D. S. Young (1970), *The Early Life of Sean O'Casey*, by Martin B. Margulies (1970), *Jonathan Swift and Contemporary Cork*, by Gerald Y. Goldberg (1967), and *Nuneham Courtenay: an Oxfordshire 18th-century Deserted Village*, by Mavis Batey (*Oxoniensa*, xxxiii, 1968); also the many excellent county magazines, in particular *Lancashire Life* (for an article on Spenser by Kenneth Fields), *Cambridge, Huntingdon and Peterborough Life* (for an article on J. R. Withers by Enid Porter), and *Hampshire, the county magazine* (for articles on Titchfield by Ivor Cook, Compton Mackenzie by Albert Morris, and George Wither by W. K. Seymour). Dr. Richard Berleth of Brooklyn, New York, very kindly let us have details from his researches on Spenser's Kilcolman and the surrounding country in relation to *The Faerie Queene*, *Colin Clouts come home againe*, and *Epithalamion*, and we should like to thank him for information that would not otherwise have been available. We also acknowledge permission to quote from various works: Constable & Co., Ltd. for an extract from *The Stricken Deer*, by

David Cecil (1929); William Heinemann, Ltd., Laurence Pollinger, Ltd., the Estate of the late Mrs. Frieda Lawrence, and the Viking Press Inc. for an extract from Vol. I of *The Collected Letters of D. H. Lawrence*, ed. Harry T. Moore (1962); Faber & Faber, Ltd. and Harcourt Brace Jovanovich Inc. for extracts from *Rupert Brooke*, by Christopher Hassall (1964); the Estate of Lord Tweedsmuir for an extract from *Memory Hold the Door*, by John Buchan (1940); The Hogarth Press and Mr. Gavin Muir for extracts from *An Autobiography*, by Edwin Muir (1954) and *Selected Letters of Edwin Muir*, ed. P. H. Butter (1974); A. P. Watt & Son, M. B. Yeats, Miss Anne Yeats, the Macmillan Company of London and Basingstoke, and Macmillan in New York for quotations from *The Collected Poems of W. B. Yeats*; and the Oxford University Press by arrangement with the Society of Jesus for quotations from the fourth edition of *The Poems of Gerard Manley Hopkins*, ed. W. H. Gardner and N. H. MacKenzie (1967).

Finally, our thanks are due to our proof-readers, Professor J. A. W. Bennett, who made many valuable suggestions, Patience Bradford, and Sandra Raphael, and to Vicki Asher who typed the manuscript and helped to prepare the book for press. The maps were drawn by the Technical Graphics Department of the Oxford University Press.

D. S. E.

H. C.

October 1976

CONTENTS

ABBREVIATIONS

Aberdeens.	Aberdeenshire	Jan.	January
Apr.	April	Kincardines.	Kincardineshire
Argylls.	Argyllshire	Kinross.	Kinross-shire
Aug.	August	Kirkcudbrights.	Kirkcudbrightshire
A.V.	Authorized Version	Lanarks.	Lanarkshire
	(of the Bible)	Lancs.	Lancashire
Ave.	Avenue	Leics.	Leicestershire
Ayrs.	Ayrshire	Lincs.	Lincolnshire
b.	born	m.	marries
Banffs.	Banffshire	m.	mile(s)
Beds.	Bedfordshire	Mar.	March
Berks.	Berkshire	Mon.	Monday
Berwicks.	Berwickshire	Mt.	Mount
Bldg(s).	Building(s)	N.	north
Bucks.	Buckinghamshire	n.d.	no date
c.	*circa*, about	NE.	north-east
c.	century	N.G.S.	National Gardens Scheme
cc.	centuries	N.M.	National Monument
Cambs.	Cambridgeshire	NNE.	north-north-east
ch.	chapter	Norf.	Norfolk
Ches.	Cheshire	Northants	Northamptonshire
C.I.	Church of Ireland	Northumb.	Northumberland
Cres.	Crescent	Notts.	Nottinghamshire
Ct.	Court	Nov.	November
d.	died, dies	nr.	near
Dec.	December	N.T.	National Trust
Derbys.	Derbyshire	N.T.S.	National Trust for Scot-
Dumfriess.	Dumfriesshire		land
Dunbartons.	Dunbartonshire	NW.	north-west
E.	east	Oct.	October
ed.	edited, editor	Oxon.	Oxfordshire
edn.	edition	P	plaque
educ.	educated	Peebles.	Peeblesshire
ENE.	east-north-east	Perths.	Perthshire
ESE.	east-south-east	Pk.	Park
est.	established	Pl.	Place
Feb.	February	pr.	pronounced
fl.	flourished	prob.	probably
Fri.	Friday	pub.	published
Gdns.	Gardens	q.v.	*quod vide*, which see
Glos.	Gloucestershire	qq.v.	*quae vide*, both, or all,
Hants	Hampshire		which see
Herts.	Hertfordshire	Renfrews.	Renfrewshire
Inverness.	Invernesshire	Rd.	Road
I.O.M.	Isle of Man	Roxburghs.	Roxburghshire
I.O.W.	Isle of Wight	S.	south

ABBREVIATIONS

Sat.	Saturday	Ter.	Terrace
SE.	south-east	Thurs.	Thursday
Selkirks.	Selkirkshire	trans.	translated
Sept.	September	Tues.	Tuesday
Som.	Somerset	TV	television
Sq.	square	U.S.	United States
SSE.	south-south-east	vol.	volume
SSW.	south-south-west	W.	west
St.	Saint	Warwicks.	Warwickshire
St.	Street	Wed.	Wednesday
Staffs.	Staffordshire	Wilts.	Wiltshire
Stirlings.	Stirlingshire	WNW.	west-north-west
Suff.	Suffolk	WSW.	west-south-west
Sun.	Sunday	yd(s).	yard(s)
SW.	south-west		

PRONUNCIATION

Occasionally where a place-name has an unexpected pronunciation this is given in parentheses after the headword, using the following symbols:

ă	as in	bat	ŏ	as in	hot
ā	as in	make	ō	as in	bold
ĕ	as in	red	ŏŏ	as in	book
ē	as in	feet	ōō	as in	roof
ĭ	as in	bit	ŭ	as in	nut
ī	as in	kind	ū	as in	mute

A

ABBERLEY, Hereford and Worcester. [3 Ge] Village off the B4202, SW. of Stourport-on-Severn, home of the poet William Walsh, friend of Dryden and Addison, and encourager of the young Pope. All three may have stayed here; Pope was invited in 1707 and a tree-lined path at Abberley Hall[1] is called Addison's Walk. Walsh, an M.P., is buried in the Saxon church; his library was auctioned in *c.* 1790 (see Stanford-on-Teme), and the house, formerly Abberley Lodge, was rebuilt in the 19th c. and is now a school. Walsh collaborated with Vanbrugh in an adaptation of Molière, and his poems, of which the best known is 'The Despairing Lover', were published in 1716.

[1] Gardens occasionally open for N.G.S.

ABBEYDALE. See SHEFFIELD.

ABBOTSFORD, Roxburghs. (Borders). [6 Fd] Home (1812–32) of Sir Walter Scott who transformed the little farm of Clartyhole, once belonging to the monks of Melrose who forded the Tweed near by, into the large estate. When Maria Edgeworth, who first met Scott in Edinburgh, stayed here in August 1823 the new house, started in 1818, was almost complete. Lockhart, in the *Memoirs* (1837–8) of his father-in-law, recalls their enjoyment of the picnic at Thomas the Rhymer's waterfall in the glen. Scott in his General Preface to the Waverley novels (1829), written here, said he tried to introduce 'Scotland's natives in a more favourable light than hitherto' as Maria Edgeworth had done for Ireland. He entertained many literary friends here, including Washington Irving, Thomas Moore, who, in 1825, was flattered to be the sole guest, and Wordsworth. The house contains Scott's library, family portraits, a large collection of weapons and armour, much of his furniture, and miscellaneous items relating to Scottish history donated by friends, including Joseph Train of Castle Douglas (q.v.). Scott was cared for in the dining-room during his long illness and he died there in 1832. N. P. Willis, the American writer, visited soon afterwards, and asked in *Pencillings by the Way* (1835) 'why does not Scotland buy Abbotsford?'

The house is now carefully tended by Scott's descendants.

Open 24 Mar.–31 Oct.: weekdays 10 a.m.–5 p.m.; Sun. 2–5 p.m.

ABERDARE. See CWMAMAN.

ABERDEEN, Aberdeens. (Grampian). [7 Hf] The 'granite city' on the Don and the Dee, a cathedral and university city and prosperous port on the NE. coast of Scotland. William Dunbar, who accompanied Queen Margaret on her tour of the north, described her visit here in 1511 in *The Queenis Progress at Aberdeen*. She was Margaret Tudor, the 'Rose' of his *Thrissil and the Rois* (1503), which he wrote on her marriage to James IV. Thomas Urquhart was (*c.* 1628) at King's College (founded 1494) in Old Aberdeen before leaving on a long tour of the Continent. Arthur Johnston, 'the Scottish Ovid', who had spent over 20 years studying in Italy and France, was appointed (1637) Rector of the University soon after his return. He wrote *Musae Aulicae* (1637), translated the Psalms, and edited *Delitiae Poetarum Scotorum* (1637), Latin poems by Scots. He died in 1641. John Arbuthnot went to Marischal College aged 14 in 1682, before attending medical school in St. Andrews. John Skinner was only 13 when he obtained a bursary (1735) to Marischal College. When Burns was here on his tour in 1787 he met Skinner's son, who was the Bishop of Aberdeen. The encounter led to a correspondence, sometimes in rhyme, between Burns and the elder Skinner which resulted in some of Skinner's songs, which Burns thought among the best in Scotland, being published. Skinner retired to stay with his son at the medieval Bishop's Gate, where he died 12 days later (1807).

James Beattie was at Marischal College (1749–53) and returned to study divinity there. He taught at the Grammar School from 1758, and in 1760 was invited to become Professor of Moral Philosophy and to join the select literary society called the Wise Club. *Original Poems and Translations* (1761) led to a correspondence and friendship with Gray in 1765. His *Essay on*

Truth (1770) and the poem *The Minstrel* (Bk. I, 1771) brought him the acquaintance of Dr. Johnson, whom he visited in London. Boswell successfully enlisted Beattie's help in persuading Johnson to undertake their tour of the Highlands, though Beattie was not in Aberdeen when they arrived. Johnson found the professors disappointing, 'they had not started a single mawkin [hare] for us to pursue', and he and Boswell were relieved to sit quietly at the New Inn (gone), where they were staying. They were also disappointed at not being able to find a single copy of Arthur Johnston's poems in the bookshops. Beattie, whom Mrs. Thrale said she would have chosen if she were to marry again, died in Crown Court, Upper Kirkgate, and is buried in St. Nicholas's churchyard. James Macpherson, a contemporary of Beattie's at the University, came under Johnson's censure for not handing to the professors the manuscripts from which he said he translated *Fingal* (1762). The 6-year-old Byron attended the Grammar School in Old Town (1794–8) after his father had died and his mother, whose fortune had been dissipated, took lodgings in the town. Byron said later that his love of mountainous country stemmed from his childhood here. A statue in Skene St. in the gardens of the Grammar School commemorates him. William Thom was born (1798?) in Sinclairs Close, Justice Port (gone), and he became a weaver. After hard times he settled at Inverurie and had 'The Blind Boy's Pranks' accepted by *The Aberdeen Herald* in 1841. This created enough interest for the publication of *Rhymes and Recollections* (1844), after which he enjoyed a brief period of acclaim in London. George Macdonald went to 'Byron's old school' and King's College (1840–5). Most of his life was spent in England but he occasionally returned to the area to collect legends and Gaelic tales, which he used in his fairy stories. Marion Angus lived with her sister and invalid mother at Zoar, a cottage with a corner fireplace in Springfield Rd., Hazlehead, after her father's death. She was over 50 when she published her first collection *The Lilt and Other Verses* (1922) here. Many of her poems have the sadness of old ballads like 'Mary's Song':

> My beloved sall hae this he'rt tae break,
> Reid, reid wine and the barley cake,
> A he'rt tae break, and a mou' tae kiss
> Tho' he be nae mine, as I am his.

Other poems were collected in *Tinker's Road* (1924), *Sun and Candlelight* (1927), and *Lost Country and Other Verses* (1937).

Eric Linklater was at the Grammar School before the First World War in which he served in the Black Watch. In 1919 he returned to his medical studies and then changed to read English. After some years abroad he became an assistant lecturer (1927–8) until he gained a bursary to America. After his success as a novelist he was elected Rector of the University (1945–8).

ABERFELDY, Perths. (Tayside). [6 Ea] Town on the A826 and the A827, 10 m. SW. of Pitlochry. Robert Burns is thought to have written 'The Birks of Aberfeldy', beginning 'Now summer blinks on flowery braes', at the Falls of Moness (1 m. SW.) on the Urlar Burn. A footpath (signposted) leads to the spot and the Scottish Wildlife Trust has laid out a 3 m. nature trail.

ABERFOYLE, Perths. (Central). [6 Dc] Village off the A81, 27 m. N. of Glasgow, at the entrance to The Trossachs. A plough hangs in a tree opposite a hotel to recall the incident in Scott's *Rob Roy* (1817), when Bailie Nichol Jarvie (after whom the hotel is named) met the outlaw.

ABERGLASNEY HOUSE. See LLANGATHEN.

ABERGWILI, Dyfed. [3 Cf] Little village on the A40, 2 m. NE. of Carmarthen. A minor road leads steeply up to the N. and circles round Merlin Hill, where the enchantress Nimue ('The Lady of the Lake') is said to have lured the aged Merlin and buried him deep under a rock. A finger-post shows the way to Merlin's Grove.

ABERYSTWYTH, Dyfed. [3 Dd] Seaside resort and university town on Cardigan Bay, on the A487. The National Library of Wales (founded 1907) on a hill E. of the town, contains a unique collection of books in the Welsh language or relating to Wales. Among its treasures are the manuscript of the 12th-c. *Black Book of Carmarthen*, the *White Book of Roderick*, and the *Book of Taliesin*. As a copyright library (since 1911) it is entitled to receive new publications issued in Great Britain and Ireland. Alun Lewis went to the University in 1932 and while there published his first poems (*The Wanderers*) in the *Argosy*.

ABINGDON, Oxon. [1 Cb] Old town on the Thames, once the county town of Berkshire, 7 m. S. of Oxford on the A34. It was the birthplace of Edward Moore (1712–57), a minor dramatist who lived and died in poverty, author of the comedy *Gil Blas* (1751) and the tragedy *The Gamester* (1753). Ruskin, who had been appointed the first Slade Professor of Art at Oxford in 1869, moved to the Crown and Thistle at Abingdon in the New Year of 1871. He stayed here some months, coming to Oxford almost daily to work on illuminated manuscripts at the Bodleian Library, and then moved to rooms at Corpus Christi College. Abingdon was also the birthplace of the novelist Dorothy Miller Richardson.

ABINGER HAMMER, Surrey. [1 Dd] Village on the A25, 5 m. SW. of Dorking. West Hackhurst, the house on the brow of the steep hill N. of the village, was E. M. Forster's home from 1902 to 1945, though he spent some years in Italy, which provided him with the background for two novels, and he made two visits to India, which gave him material for *A Passage to India* (1924), thought by many to be his finest novel. Many of his essays collected as *Abinger Harvest* (1936), and his short stories *The Celestial Omnibus* (1914) and *The Eternal Moment* (1928), were written here. Piney Copse, near the house, which he describes buying in 'My Wood' was bequeathed by him to the N.T.

ABNEY, Derbys. [4 Ab] Village off the A625, 3 m. SW. of Hathersage. Cockey Farm (¼ m. S.) was the birthplace in 1750 of William Newton, who became a machinery carpenter. He was known as the 'Peak Minstrel' after his verses came to the attention of the curate of Eyam (q.v.).

ACOL (pr. Aycole), Kent. [1 Hc] Village on the B2044 in the Isle of Thanet, NE. of the county. The chalk-pit here features in R. H. Barham's 'The Smuggler's Leap' from the *Ingoldsby Legends* (1840–7). Baroness Orczy, who leased (1908–9) Cleve Court, on the Minster road, after finishing *Beau Brocade* (1908), set her next adventure story *Nest of the Sparrowhawk* here. She and her husband,

the painter Montagu Barstow, imported three horses from her home in Hungary and drove them abreast in their carriage.

ADDERBURY, Oxon. [1 Ba] Village 4 m. S. of Banbury on the A41 and the A423. The dark ironstone Adderbury House (built 1624) was inherited by John Wilmot, 2nd Earl of Rochester, who lived there intermittently after his marriage (1667) to the heiress Elizabeth Malet. Pepys records that she was expected to be the bride of the son of his patron Lord Sandwich. Wilmot, who wrote to Elizabeth

> When wearied with a world of woe,
> To thy safe bosom I retire,
> Where love, and peace, and truth does flow,
> May I contented there expire.

spent much time at the profligate court hoping for an appointment from the King. He was portrayed by Etheredge as Dorimant in *The Man of Mode* (1676). Pope stayed here in 1739, when the house belonged to the Duke of Argyle, and wrote 'Verses left by Mr. Pope, on his lying in the same bed which . . . Rochester slept in'. The narrow entrance to the drive is on the E. side of the road opposite the green and immediately above the steep hill S. of the village. It is now an Oxfordshire County Council Old People's Home and visitors are welcome, but an appointment must be made with the Warden.

ADLESTROP, Glos. [1 Ba] Stone village 1 m. N. of the A436, 6 m. W. of Chipping Norton. Jane Austen stayed at the rectory in August 1806 with her uncle. Edward Thomas (1878–1917) remembered the station by the main road

> because one afternoon
> Of heat the express train drew up there
> Unwontedly. It was late June.
>
> No one left and no one came
> On the bare platform. What I saw
> Was Adlestrop—only the name . . .

This nameplate has been moved from the station (now closed) to the village bus shelter.

ADSCOMBE, Som. [2 Fc] Village 1 m. W. of Over (Upper) Stowey, off the A39, well known to Coleridge, who hoped to rent a cottage here before he found one at Nether Stowey (1796). The family of his friend

Thomas Poole lived at Marshmills, Over Stowey. In 'The Foster-Mother's Tale' in the *Lyrical Ballads* (1798) Coleridge mentions 'the hanging wall of that old chapel' which stood in a field near Adscombe Corner. The ruined Norman chapel, in which occasional services were held, was demolished in the 1960s, though the site is still visible.

ALDBURY, Herts. [1 Db] Old village off the A41, 3 m. NE. of Tring. Mrs. Humphry Ward lived (1892–1920) at (Great) Stocks, visible behind the Tudor house and barn of Stocks Farm. The 18th-c. house with its long lime avenue, chosen for its seclusion, had a walled garden where she wrote. A brutal killing which took place in the village was woven into her novel *Marcella* (1894). She entertained large parties on Sundays; Henry James was a visitor and her young relatives Julian and Aldous Huxley spent many holidays here. In 1908 she moved into her cottage, which she had let to friends, including Bernard Shaw, while Stocks was repaired and altered. Mrs. Ward died in London but is buried in the churchyard near the NW. corner of the church.

ALDEBURGH, Suff. [4 Hf] Coastal resort, with a music festival in June, on the A1094, 17 m. NE. of Woodbridge. George Crabbe, son of a collector of salt taxes, was born (1755) here, but the house and Slaughden quay, where he worked as a boy in his father's warehouse, have been swallowed up by the sea. He was apprenticed to an apothecary, who lived in the house (now a hotel) opposite the church porch. Later he practised unrewardingly as a surgeon. The publication of his poems *Inebriety* (1775) and *The Candidate* (1780) brought him little money and many times he went hungry, so he set out for London, where Burke's timely help saved him from starvation. After his ordination in December 1781 he returned to Aldeburgh as curate and then accepted the chaplaincy at Belvoir Castle in 1782. *The Village* (1783), praised by Dr. Johnson, who read and revised the manuscript, is a satire on the idealized picture of rural delights popular in drawing-rooms and it gives a realistic account of the harsh and squalid lives of the working people of Aldeburgh. After many years away from the town Crabbe returned to the same theme in *The Borough* (1810). In an article in *The Listener* of 29 May 1941, E. M. Forster wrote of Crabbe's preoccupation with Aldeburgh and the sea. It was this article which led Benjamin Britten, whose own childhood was spent by the sea at Lowestoft to the N., to compose the opera *Peter Grimes* (1945), based on a character in *The Borough*. Forster himself was librettist with Eric Crozier of another of Britten's operas, *Billy Budd* (1951), based on the story by Herman Melville. Both operas have been performed at the annual Festival in June. Crabbe is commemorated by a bust by Thomas Thurber erected in the church in 1947. Visitors in the 19th c. include Wilkie Collins, whose novel *No Name* (1862) has a local setting, and M. R. James, writer of ghost stories, who stayed at Wyndham House, near the church. Others were guests at Strafford House, home of the sociable banker, Edward Clodd (1840–1930), founder of the Johnson and Omar Khayyám Clubs. Anthony Hope recounts in *Memories and Notes* (1927) how he, Hardy, and James Frazer sailed in Clodd's yacht to visit Fitz-Gerald's grave (see Bredfield).

ALDERTON, Suff. [4 Hf] Village on the B1083, 2 m. from the coast between the Deben and the Ore. Giles Fletcher the Younger was rector here from *c.* 1618 to his death in 1623. He is buried in the church.

ALDINGTON, Kent. [1 Gd] Small village off the B2067, 5 m. W. of Hythe. Thomas Linacre was rector in 1509, the year he became one of Henry VIII's doctors, and probably spent some time at the parsonage, now a farm, S. of the church. Erasmus followed as rector in 1511 but is not thought to have lived here, preferring Cambridge, where he was Greek Reader from 1511 to 1514. Reproductions of old portraits of both men are in the tower. Aldington Knoll, a small farmhouse overlooking Romney Marsh, was the home of Ford Madox Hueffer (later Ford Madox Ford), who collaborated with Conrad at Postling on *The Inheritors* (1901) and *Romance* (1903). From 1909 to 1910 Conrad took over the house and, restless with overwork on *Under Western Eyes* (1909), suffered a nervous breakdown.

ALDWINKLE, Northants. [4 De] Village off the A605, 5 m. SW. of Oundle, made up of two parishes. The church of Aldwinkle St. Peter has a commemorative window to

4

Thomas Fuller, born (1608) in the rectory (gone). At the other end of the village John Dryden was born (1631) in the Old Rectory, opposite the church of Aldwinkle All Saints. This, seldom used now, has a memorial tablet. Dryden, whose maternal grandfather held the living here for 40 years, often visited the village.

ALDWORTH. See HASLEMERE.

ALEXANDRIA, Dunb. (Strathclyde). [6 Dc] Village in the Vale of Leven on the A812, NW. of Dumbarton, called after a member of the Smollett family of Bonhill near by. Cameron House,[1] at the S. end of Loch Lomond, became the family home after 1763 and one room is now the Tobias Smollett Museum, which contains portraits of the author, first editions of his works, and a photograph of the plane tree at Dalquharn House (gone) under which tradition says he was born (1721). In 1766 Tobias Smollett stayed with his cousin James at Bonhill, which he had last seen in 1739, and he took pleasure in revisiting the scenes of his youth. The house eventually fell into disrepair and was demolished. In 1773 Johnson and Boswell stayed at Cameron House on their Highland tour and Johnson said 'We have had more solid talk here than any place that we have been'. Their host was the same James Smollett, who was preparing to erect an ornate classical column to commemorate his cousin, who had died in Italy in 1771. The first design, a painting of which is in the Museum, proved too costly and a simpler Tuscan column, brought from Glasgow, was erected at Renton (1 m. S.), where it now stands behind the railings on the site of the school playground on the main road. The square plinth carries a Latin obituary, which Johnson helped to revise.

[1] Open Easter–late Sept.: daily 11 a.m.–6 p.m.

ALFOXTON (or ALFOXDEN) PARK, Som. [2 Fc] House, now a hotel (residential licence), off the A39 near Holford, rented by the Wordsworths on their visit (1797) to Coleridge at Nether Stowey (q.v.). Dorothy Wordsworth's *Alfoxden Journal* records her impressions of the area from the Quantocks to the Culbone Hills which inspired *The Lyrical Ballads* (1798) on which Wordsworth and Coleridge collaborated. 'There is everything here; sea, woods wild as fancy ever

painted, brooks clear and pebbly as in Cumberland, villages so romantic.' But 'Our principal inducement was Coleridge's society'. Coleridge himself said Alfoxden dell 'is rather a place to make man forget there is any necessity for treason'. Lamb and Hazlitt were also among the visitors. The only drawback was the local people's suspicions. The Wordsworths' north-country accents and Dorothy's brown complexion, as well as the long walks they took, often at night, with camp stools, telescopes, and notebooks, led to an investigation of spying for the French revolutionaries. After a year here, the Wordsworths left with Coleridge for Germany.

ALL CANNINGS, Wilts. [1 Ac] Village off the A342, 4 m. N. of Chirton. In 1817 Coleridge stayed at the Old Rectory opposite the church with the Revd. Anthony Methuen.

ALLINGTON, Kent. [1 Fc] Village off the A20, 1½ m. NW. of Maidstone. The poet Sir Thomas Wyatt was born (1503?) at Allington Castle[1] beside the Medway. He and the Earl of Surrey were the first in England to write sonnets in the Italian form, and many of these were published in *Tottel's Miscellany* (1557). The castle, now a Retreat Centre for the Carmelite order, has been restored.

[1] Open daily, conducted visits, 2–4 p.m.

ALLINGTON, Wilts. [1 Bd] Village on the A338, 8 m. NE. of Salisbury. Jane Austen's sister Cassandra became engaged to Tom Fowle, the vicar, who died in 1797 of yellow fever in the W. Indies before they could be married. The two sisters had known Tom Fowle since he had been their father's pupil at Steventon. A copy of a marriage certificate, witnessed by Jane Austen at Steventon, is in the church.

ALLOWAY, Ayrs. (Strathclyde). [6 Dd] Village on the B7024, 1½ m. S. of Ayr. Robert Burns was born (1759) in the thatched single-room cottage[1] with the barn and cowshed, built by his father. The museum[2] at the rear has original Burns letters, songs, and other relics. Just S. the monument, built in 1820 by public subscriptions raised by Boswell's son, stands in gardens overlooking the old Brig' o' Doon, where Burns's Tam o' Shanter on his grey

5

mare outstripped the warlocks and hags. When Burns was 6 the family moved to Mt. Oliphant Farm (1½ m. S.) where he became his father's main help and an efficient ploughman. He was taught at Alloway School by John Murdoch and followed him to the Grammar School at Ayr when he moved there.

[1] Open summer: weekdays 9 a.m.–7 p.m.; Sun. 2–7 p.m.; winter: weekdays 9 a.m.–5 p.m.; Sun. 2–5 p.m.
[2] Open as above.

ALPHINGTON, Devon. [2 Ed] Village on the Plymouth road 1½ m. out of Exeter, now almost a suburb. On the W. side of the road, opposite the post office, is Mile End Cottage (P), once the home of Dickens's parents and interesting as a record of his care for his improvident father. Early in 1839 this Micawber-like character, who had previously been imprisoned for debt, was again in serious financial difficulties and Dickens decided that it would be better for his parents to live in the country, remote from London. He found 'a little white cottage with . . . a splendid view of Exeter', signed the agreement for its modest rent, arranged its furnishings, and installed his father and mother, their youngest child Augustus, and the dog, Dash. For a few years they seemed contented with their country life, but when Dickens returned from a visit to America in 1843 he found his parents tired of being immured in the 'little doll's house' and reluctantly agreed to their return to London.

ALRESFORD. See NEW ALRESFORD.

ALSTONEFIELD. See BERESFORD DALE.

ALTHORP, Northants. [4 Ce] Country house 6 m. NW. of Northampton on the A428, altered in the late 18th c. Ben Jonson wrote the masque for the entertainment in 1603 of James I's queen on her way south from Scotland after his accession. She was the guest of the Spencer family, whose home it has been since 1508.

Open May: Sun.; June–Sept.: Sun., Tues., and Thurs.; Easter Sun. and Mon., Spring and Summer Bank Holidays 2.30–6 p.m.

ALTON, Hants. [1 Cd] Market town at the junction of the A31 and the A32. A plaque of uncertain date records that Edmund Spenser lived at 1 Amery St., near the market place, in 1590. This may have been his home for a short time after he returned from Ireland with Sir Walter Ralegh to visit the court and to arrange for the publication of the first three books of *The Faerie Queene*. According to A. C. Judson (*Life of Spenser*, 1945) he probably spent the later months of 1590 writing, revising, and assembling material for *Complaints, containing sundrie small poems of the worlds vanitie* (1591), and perhaps did some of this work in Hampshire, visiting during the same period his friend Sir Henry Wallop at Farleigh Wallop, 6 m. from Alton. When Cardinal Newman was an undergraduate at Oxford he stayed at Swarthmore, 59 High St. (P).

Sir Compton Mackenzie, who stayed at Beech (q.v.) as a young man, knew Alton well and in 1925 he presented the Curtis Museum,[1] High St., with the manuscript of his story for children, 'Mabel in Queer Street'. Alton is the 'Galton' of his novels, *The Altar Steps* (1921), its sequel *The Parson's Progress* (1922), and *Buttercups and Daisies* (1931).

[1] Open Mon., Tues., Thurs., Fri. 2–5 p.m.; Sat. 10 a.m.–1 p.m., 2–6 p.m. (closed Sun. and Bank Holidays).

ALTON TOWERS, Staffs. [3 Hb] Park and pleasure grounds in hilly, wooded country, *c.* 6 m. W. of Ashbourne, well signposted from the B5032 and the B5417. The vast, ornate mansion, now partly ruined and partly converted to entertainment rooms, was a former seat of the Earl of Shrewsbury. Thomas Moore was staying there as Lady Shrewsbury's guest when he visited his old home at Mayfield in September 1835. In Disraeli's novel, *Lothair* (1870), it becomes the magnificent 'Muriel Towers', the hero's chief seat, where he celebrated his coming of age with boundless pomp and extravagance.

ALTRIVE LAKE, Selkirks. (Borders). [6 Fd] Valley of a former lake, now drained, joining the Yarrow Water, where the B709 runs S. from the Gordon Arms (q.v.) on the A708. James Hogg, after earlier unsuccessful attempts at farming, followed by some years in Edinburgh, was granted Moss End Farm, now called Eldinhope, here (1815) at a nominal rent by the Duke of Buccleuch. After his marriage (1820) to Margaret Phillips he took a 9-year lease of Mount

Benger Farm, a little further N., on the strength of her promised dowry, but this turned out to be disastrously expensive to run. He spent the rest of his life at Altrive, farming and writing. His best-known novel, *The Confessions of a Justified Sinner*, was published in 1824.

AMBLESIDE, Cumbria. [5 Bb] Little town in the vale of the Rothay, ¾ m. N. of the head of Lake Windermere, on the A591 and the A593, a busy centre for visitors in the southern Lake District. When William and Dorothy Wordsworth lived at Grasmere (q.v.) they frequently walked the 12 miles there and back, calling for letters at the post office and taking their own to the post. Mrs. Hemans lived at Dove Nest (1829–31), a house *c.* 1½ m. S., signposted up a steep road just N. of the Low-wood Hotel and recognizable by its golden dove weathercock, overlooking Windermere, with the woods (N.T.) on the Wansfell slopes above. She came to know Wordsworth and stayed at Rydal Mount (q.v.) in 1830 for a fortnight, which his wife Mary and her sister Sara found '*long*'. 'Her affectation', said Sara, 'is perfectly unendurable', but Wordsworth defended her and when she died, in the same year as James Hogg, commemorated her in the 'Extempore Effusion upon the Death of James Hogg' (1835) as

that holy Spirit,
Sweet as the spring, as ocean deep;

Matthew Arnold lived for a time at Fox How, a pleasant house built by his father, Dr. Arnold of Rugby, on an estate below Loughrigg Fell, on the far side of the Rothay. Wordsworth, a quarter of an hour's walk away at Rydal Mount, had encouraged the Arnolds to settle here and had negotiated the purchase of the land and helped with building plans. Later on Harriet Martineau used to find it a pleasant walk across the fields to visit the Arnolds from her own house, The Knoll, which she had built in 1845. Wordsworth, who was 76 when she first met him, took a great interest in the house, saying that the building of it was the wisest step of her life, 'for the value of the property will be doubled in ten years'. He planted two stone pines in the garden and helped to choose the motto for the sundial, 'Come, Light! Visit me !'. The house (preserved as a historic monument) is on the W. side of Rydal Rd., down a turning just before Haven Cottage. Charlotte Brontë, who had greatly admired Harriet's novel, *Deerbrook* (1839), stayed here for a week in 1850, between the publication of *Shirley* and *Villette*, and met the Arnold family. Matthew Arnold in 'Haworth Churchyard, 1855', his lament for Charlotte's early death, remembers how he 'saw the meeting / Of two gifted women'. Crabb Robinson, who gave Harriet a marble-mounted sideboard, also visited. She lived here until her death in 1876, a tireless advocate of social reform and an active journalist. She contributed to Dickens's *Household Words*, from its beginning in 1849 until 1857, stories and articles on health and sanitation and various industries, 'grimly bent', as Dickens said, 'on the enlightenment of mankind'. She continued writing for many other periodicals, notably the *Westminster Review* and the *Edinburgh Review*, the *National Anti-Slavery Standard* of New York, and above all the *Daily News*. Her *Complete Guide to the Lakes* was published in 1855.

AMESBURY, Wilts. [1 Ad] Town on the A303 and the A345, 8 m. N. of Salisbury. In *Guinevere* (1859), Tennyson describes the Queen's flight from the court of King Arthur to the 'holy house of Almesbury' where she dies. Lancelot is said to have led her funeral cortège over the hills to Glastonbury for burial. The early abbey at Amesbury was destroyed by invaders and the Saxon foundation which replaced it was given by King Alfred to his biographer Asser (d. 909 ?), the scholar from St. David's. The *Amesbury Psalter*, a mid-13th-c. illuminated manuscript, is now in All Souls Library, Oxford. Joseph Addison (1672–1719) went to school here before going to Charterhouse. In the early 18th c. Amesbury Abbey (now apartments) was a home of the Duke and Duchess of Queensberry who befriended Gay. He often stayed here and wrote *The Beggar's Opera* (1728), from an idea of Swift's, in the Diamond Room.

AMHUINNSUIDHE (pr. A´vīnsuey), N. Harris (Western Isles). [7 Bd] House on the N. shore of West Loch Tarbert, on the B887, which J. M. Barrie rented in the spring of 1912. He heard here the Kilmeny legend of the girl who was taken and then returned by the fairies. He said that this was the place 'where we caught Mary Rose', the heroine of his play *Mary Rose* (1920), where the second act is set on an island in the Hebrides.

AMPTHILL, Beds. [4 Df] Old market town on the A418, 8 m. S. of Bedford. Horace Walpole, who told one of his correspondents, the Countess of Upper Ossory, 'I dote on Ampthill', often stayed with her at Ampthill Park[1] (entrance to the public park off the westbound A418) where, in the former castle, Catherine of Aragon had been held pending her divorce. Walpole wrote the inscription for the ornate cross erected on the site in the park:

In days of old, here Ampthill's towers were seen
The mournful refuge of an injur'd Queen.
Here flow'd her pure but unavailing tears
Here blinded Zeal sustained her sinking years.

Hale White, who wrote as 'Mark Rutherford', called the town 'Cowfold' in *The Revolution in Tanner's Lane* (1887). Houghton House,[1] 1 m. N. off the A418, was built in 1615 and improved by Inigo Jones for the Countess of Pembroke, patron of many poets. Henry Luttrell, a fashionable wit, in his 'Lines written at Ampthill Park' (1818) mentions the 'roofless walls' and 'Chambers now tenantless'. The three-storey house makes an imposing ruin today on the sandstone ridge. It is said to have been Bunyan's House Beautiful in *The Pilgrim's Progress* (1678).

[1] Ruin open to the public.

AMPTON, Suff. [4 Fe] Village E. of the A134, 5 m. N. of Bury St. Edmunds. The flint church opposite the red-brick hall has a tablet reading 'Remember Jeremy Collier, M.A. rector of this parish 1679–1684 Divine, Historian, Controversialist, Outlaw, Nonjuring Bishop. Born 23 Sept. 1650, Buried at Old St. Pancras, London 26 Apr. 1726. "He was in the full force of words, a Good Man". Macaulay.'

ANNAMOE, Wicklow. [9 Hb] Village on the T61 between Bray and Rathdrum. Laurence Sterne had a remarkable adventure here as a child, which he describes in *Memoirs of the Life and Family of the late Rev. Laurence Sterne* (1775). During the frequent travelling of his childhood he stayed in 1721 with Mr. Fetherston, a relation of his mother's, at his parsonage at Annamoe ('Animo'), and fell into the mill-race while the mill was working and was rescued unhurt, to the amazement of 'hundreds of the common people [who] flocked to see me'. The mill, now ruined, is just N. of the bridge.

ANNAN, Dumfriess. (Dumfries and Galloway). [6 Ff] Small town at the mouth of the Annan which flows into the Solway Firth. Thomas Carlyle was educated at Annan Academy (now the Old Grammar School), described later by him as Hinterschlag Gymnasium in *Sartor Resartus*, a partly autobiographical work, which first appeared in *Fraser's Magazine* in 1833–4.

ANNESLEY, Notts. [4 Bc] Village on the A611, 2 m. SW. of Newstead Abbey. Byron at 15 fell desperately in love with his cousin Mary Chaworth who lived at Annesley Hall, 1 m. S., and was already engaged. He used to ride over from Southwell (q.v.), and sometimes spent the night here. In 'The Dream' (1816) he tells of his unrequited love and how it ended:

... the one
To end in madness—both in misery

His attachment was more poignant because, as he relates in 'The Duel' (1818), his great-uncle killed her grandfather. Byron used to keep his great-uncle's sword by his bed and it is still at Newstead. Her descendants still live at the Hall.

ANNINGSLEY PARK, Surrey. [1 Dc] Country house off the Castle Inn turn on the A320, 1 m. S. of Ottershaw. When Thomas Day moved here in 1781 it was a small, remote, early 18th-c. farmhouse in the middle of desolate heathland. Day had legal training but had inherited money and married a rich wife, and therefore was able to lead a frugal life as a disciple of Rousseau, bent on improving the lot of the poor. *The History of Sandford and Merton*, a humourless tale depicting his ideal of manliness, by which he is best remembered, was written here (1783–9). His friends the Edgeworths (he had hoped to marry Honora), whose methods of education he admired and used in bringing up two orphans, visited him here.

ANSFORD, Som. [2 Hc] Village on the A371, E. of Castle Cary. James Woodforde (1740–1803), the diarist, was born at the rectory at the corner of Tucker's Lane. When he became his father's curate he lived at Lower Ansford Manor (burned down 1892), called the Lower House in his *Diary*. His niece Nancy, who kept house for 24 years at his rectory at Weston Longville, is buried in the church, since rebuilt.

ANSTRUTHER (pr. Anster), Fife (Fife). [6 Gb] Fishing port on the N. bank of the Firth of Forth. William Tennant (1784–1848) was born in the High St. of Anstruther Easter, probably in an easterly extension of the present street, demolished in the late 19th c. It was a narrow building next door to an old tavern known as the Smugglers Howff. Tennant, later Professor of Oriental Languages at St. Andrews, was schoolmaster here and wrote *Anster Fair* (1812), a long poem on the courting of Maggie Lauder, who lived in East Green in the 16th c. He is buried in the churchyard near the NE. corner of the church; the obelisk has a Latin inscription. R. L. Stevenson spent some time (1868) at Cunzie House (P) in Crail Rd. (by the garage). In 'Random Memories' from *Across the Plains* (1892) he says 'he lodged with Bailie Brown in a room filled with dry rose-leaves' during his practical training to be an engineer, and in the evenings wrote 'Voces Fidelium', dramatic verse dialogues.

APPLETON ROEBUCK, North Yorkshire. [5 Fd] Village off the A64, 6 m. E. of Tadcaster. Andrew Marvell was tutor (1650–2) to General Fairfax's daughter, Mary, at Nunappleton House (1½ m. S., rebuilt). In his poem on the house Marvell refers to its origins as a nunnery, where in Tudor times the orphaned heiress, soon to marry the general's great-grandfather, was living. At the Dissolution the nunnery was handed over to the Fairfax family by the Abbess who had tried to prevent the marriage, and rebuilt with two long wings. Marvell also wrote 'The Garden' here and a poem on the house at Billborow (Bilbrough, N. of the A64), where the family lived when the Wharfe and the Oare flooded. Mary became the wife of the Duke of Buckingham, the 'Zimri' of Dryden's *Absalom and Achitophel* (1681). In 1810 the poet Francis Hastings Doyle was born in the house, the home of his grandfather, Sir William Milner. Doyle in his *Reminiscences* (1878) calls it an 'ugly place', much altered since Marvell's time.

ARAN ISLANDS, Galway. [9 Ba] Three islands, Inishmore (Great Island), Inishmaan (Middle Island), and Inisheer (Eastern Island), lying NW.–SE. across the mouth of Galway Bay, c. 30 m. from Galway. They are rich in archaeological remains from Pre-Christian, Early Christian, and Medieval times. Although communication with the mainland is easier than it used to be, much of the traditional way of life continues and the majority of the inhabitants are Irish-speaking. J. M. Synge came here in 1898 at the suggestion of W. B. Yeats and returned for several weeks at a time each summer or autumn till 1902. He used to live in a cottage on Inishmaan, with a family named Mac-Donagh, whose son Martin helped to teach him Irish. The account of his life there and the stories of islanders who became his friends was published in *The Aran Islands*, with illustrations by Jack B. Yeats, in 1907. Synge regarded the book as his first serious piece of work. 'In writing out the talk of the people and their stories', he said, '. . . I learned to write the peasant dialect and dialogue which I use in my plays . . . The Aran Islands throws a good deal of light on my plays.' His play *Riders to the Sea* (1905) is set in Inishmaan. The islands can be reached from Galway by the motor vessels *Naomh Eanna* and *Galway Bay*, daily in the height of the season and on a more limited schedule in the off-season. There are also daily sailings on *The Queen of Aran* from Rossaveel, 23 m. W. of Galway (can be reached by minibus). Visitors may take their bicycles across or hire them at Kilronan, Inishmore. There are also daily flights by Aer Arann from Galway.

ARBROATH, Angus (Tayside). [6 Gb] Old port and resort on the A82, 17 m. NE. of Dundee. Scott called it 'Fairport' in *The Antiquary* (1816), 'the chief favourite among all his novels', and it was 'Redlintie' in J. M. Barrie's *Sentimental Tommy* (1896). Marion Angus spent the early part of her life here, while her father was the United Presbyterian minister. After his death she moved to Aberdeen, where her first poems were published, but she returned here at the end of her life to live with a friend. She died aged 80 in 1946, and her ashes were scattered in the sea off Elliot's Point. *Selected Poems*, which has a personal memoir by Helen B. Cruikshank, was published in 1950.

ARBURY HALL. See NUNEATON.

ARBUTHNOTT, Kincardines. (Grampian).
[6 Ga] Village on the B907, 10 m. SW. of
Stonehaven. John Arbuthnot, creator of
John Bull and the close friend of Swift, was
born (1667) here, 2 years after his father
became the minister of the 13th-c. church.
His family were from the Aberdeenshire
branch of the Arbuthnotts of Arbuthnott
House[1] and spelt their name with one 't'.

[1] Open by appointment with Lord Arbuthnott.

ARDAGH, Longford. [8 Ee] Village in
pleasant wooded country, 4 m. SW. of
Edgeworthstown, on a minor road between
the T31 and the L18. Ardagh House, now
a convent, is reputedly the place where
Goldsmith, returning home from school at
the age of 16, put up for the night under the
misapprehension that it was an inn. The
owner, Mr. Fetherston, and his wife and
daughter deliberately played up to his mistake and it was not until the next morning
that the truth was revealed. The incident
suggested the plot for *She Stoops to Conquer,
or The Mistakes of a Night* (1773).

ARDOCH, Dunb. (Strathclyde). [6 Dc]
Estate on the Clyde, N. of Dumbarton, inherited in 1772 by Robert Graham. He had
lived in Jamaica for some years and had
married a Scots girl there, and he found
the massive walls and small windows of the
17th-c. house uncomfortable, so he built the
present Ardoch House, which looks over
the Firth of Clyde (on the A814) in the Georgian Colonial style. It was their home until
after his father's death when he moved back
to his birthplace at Gartmore in 1777. His
grandson, Robert Cunninghame Graham,
who wrote his biography called *Doughty
Deeds*, after his best-remembered ballad,
came to live in the house in 1903. He had
spent his youth in S. America and his
adventures there, and later in N. America,
formed the background of many of his books
written here. His friend A. F. Tschiffely, who
wrote (1933) an account of his own journey
on horseback from Buenos Aires to Washington, which was later called *Tschiffely's Ride*,
visited him here and wrote his biography
Don Roberto (1937). A plaque on the house
was given by his S. American friends and
a bronze of him riding Pampa, one of his
favourite horses, stands in the garden. On
the W. outskirts of Dumbarton (1 m. E.) a
small park next to a school contains the
mound where King Robert the Bruce had
a palace in which he died. Cunninghame
Graham is commemorated here (now N.T.S.)
by a cairn surmounted by a medallion with
the head of Pampa in relief.

**ARELEY KINGS (or ARLEY REGIS), Hereford
and Worcester).** [3 He] Village just SW. of
Stourport-on-Severn on the A451. Layamon
mentions that he was priest here (*c.* 1200)
in *The Brut*, a poem about early Britain
retelling the stories of Arthur, Lear, and
Cymbeline from Geoffrey of Monmouth's
history. A memorial tablet is in the church.

ARUN, West Sussex. [1 Dd, De] River which
runs from the N. of the county through
Arundel to Littlehampton on the coast.
Charlotte Smith's sonnet in its praise recalls
that Otway, Collins, and Hayley were all
inspired in its vicinity. In Hilaire Belloc's
The Four Men (1912) it was 'a valley of
sacred water'.

ASHBOURNE, Derbys. [4 Ac] Old town
where the A52 and the A515 cross. Viator
and Piscator who converse in Walton's
The Compleat Angler rested at the Talbot
Inn, formerly on the site of the Town Hall.
Dr. Johnson often stayed with his friend Dr.
John Taylor at The Mansion, a large red-
brick house with a pillared porch opposite
the old buildings of the Elizabethan Grammar
School. He and Boswell stayed later at the
Green Man, the inn with two signs. St.
Oswald's church has a peal, which still
rings on Sundays, that inspired Tom Moore
at Mayfield 2 m. W. to write the lines for
his song 'Those Evening Bells'. Mrs. Gaskell
stayed during the 1850s at the 18th-c. Ashbourne Hall, her cousin's home, now the
County Library.

ASHBURTON, Devon. [2 Ee] Market town
on the A38, 19 m. SW. of Exeter, birthplace
of William Gifford, the shoemaker's apprentice who became a poet and satirist, translator of Juvenal, and first editor of the
Quarterly Review. With the help of the local
physician, William Cookesley, who had
noticed his early efforts at writing poetry,
Gifford was able to leave his apprenticeship
and attend Ashburton Grammar School
(whose old gateway and Tower Room—the
oldest schoolroom in England—are still
preserved). The Ashburton Museum[1] has an

engraved portrait of Gifford in middle age and a framed cutting from an old journal (n.d.) giving the story of his life and a picture of him as a youth at the shoemaker's bench.

[1] Open 15 May–30 Sept.: Tues., Thurs., Fri., Sat., or by arrangement with the Hon. Curator, tel. 52298.

ASHBY-DE-LA-ZOUCHE, Leics. [4 Bd] Small town and former spa on the A50, 8 m. SE. of Burton-upon-Trent. The castle,[1] a ruin comprising the remains of a Norman keep and 14th- and 15th-c. manor houses, was the scene in 1607 of George Marston's masque, an entertainment given by the Countess of Huntingdon in honour of her mother, the Dowager Countess of Derby, who had arrived from Harefield (see London). The Tournament Field, where many scenes in Scott's *Ivanhoe* (1819) take place, is 1 m. N.

[1] Open daily: Sun. from 2 p.m.

ASHE. See STEVENTON.

ASHEHAM (pr. Asham), East Sussex. [1 Ee] Hamlet 4 m. SE. of Lewes on the B2109. The Regency–Gothic Asham House, at the end of the tree-lined road opposite the cement works, was leased (1912–17) by Virginia and Leonard Woolf after they saw it on a walk from Firle along the Ouse. The front of the house was 'flat, pale, serene, yellow-washed' and it was said locally to be haunted. Virginia Woolf describes the ghostly couple who restlessly open and shut doors in *A Haunted House* (1943), a collection of short pieces. The Woolfs drew water from the well and used oil lamps on their weekend and holiday visits, often with other members of the Bloomsbury Group.

ASHFORD, Hants. See STEEP.

ASHFORD, Wicklow. [9 Hb] Village 4 m. NW. of Wicklow on the T7. About 2 m. W. in the Devil's Glen are the extensive ruins of Glanmore Castle (part of which has been restored as a restaurant), built by Francis Synge, J. M. Synge's great-grandfather, at the beginning of the 19th c. It was the family seat, built to resemble a castle, on an estate which stretched for 10 m. across County Wicklow. Synge was taken there when a year old and visited again in the summer of 1889 when his uncle's widow owned it and it was already falling into

decay–a symbol of the decline of a once proud class.

ASHIESTIEL, Selkirks. (Borders). [6 Fd] The house which Sir Walter Scott rented (1804–12) when he was Sheriff of Selkirk stands among trees on the slopes of Ashiestiel Hill, overlooking the Tweed. While he was here he published his first important original work, *The Lay of the Last Minstrel* (1805), a romantic poem in six cantos, followed by *Marmion, A Tale of Flodden Field* (1808), and *The Lady of the Lake* (1810). He also began *Waverley* (1814), his first novel. The house is not open to the public, but can be seen from across the river where the A72 from Peebles turns NE. for Clovenfords.

ASHTON, Devon. [2 Ed] Village *c.* 6 m. SW. of Exeter, on a minor road off the B3193. Lady Mary Chudleigh (1656–1710) lived here after her marriage to Sir George Chudleigh and caused a stir by the publication of her poem *The Ladies' Defence* (1701) in answer to a sermon preached locally on 'Conjugal Duty'. Her *Poems on Several Occasions* (1703) was dedicated to Queen Anne, and her last work, *Essays upon several Subjects* (1710), to the Electress Sophia. She was buried at Ashton without a monument or inscription.

ASHTON-UPON-MERSEY, Greater Manchester. [3 Ga] Suburb of Manchester, just S. of the Mersey on the A56. Stanley Houghton, author of the play, *Hindle Wakes* (1912), was born here (1881), probably in Doveston Rd., though the exact location is uncertain.

ASHURST. See SHERMANBURY.

ASKEATON, Limerick. [9 Cc] Small market town 16 m. W. of Limerick on the T68, medieval stronghold of the Earls of Desmond. In the graveyard of the Protestant parish church, which is built into the remains of the ruined St. Mary's Augustinian priory, is the grave of the poet Aubrey de Vere, who lived at Curragh Chase (q.v.) 5 m. away.

ASTHALL. See SWINBROOK.

ASTON, South Yorkshire. [4 Ba] Large village on the A57, 6 m. E. of Sheffield. William Mason became rector (1754) and was host to Thomas Gray, who wrote to a friend that he was in 'a wilderness of sweets, an Elysium among the coal-pits, a terrestrial heaven', adding slyly that this was Mason's description, not his own. Mason rebuilt the rectory facing the hills, and Gray, whose pet name for his friend was Skroddles or Scroddles, complained that this sounded as if he was settling in the north and he would burn the rectory down when he came. However, on that visit (1770), his last, he spent an uneventful fortnight with his friend Dr. Thomas Wharton. Walpole stayed with Mason in 1792 and visited Roche Abbey (7 m. NE.) as Gray too had done. The house, now the Old Rectory, is opposite the church (tablet).

ASTON CLINTON, Bucks. [1 Db] Large village on the A41 between Aylesbury and Tring. Evelyn Waugh was a schoolmaster here from September 1925 to April 1927. He had previously taught in N. Wales, where he sets the school in his first satirical novel *Decline and Fall* (1928), begun here. The master in Wales, on whom he bases his character 'Captain Grimes', visited him here.

AUCHINLECK (pr. Awkinlek), Ayrs. (Strathclyde). [6 Dd] Mining village on the A76, 12 m. SE. of Kilmarnock. The 17th-c. Auchinleck House (3 m. W.) was Boswell's family home till 1762, when his father's new house was finished. This, sometimes called Place Affleck, was where he spent some time after his marriage to Margaret Montgomerie in 1769, and where he entertained Dr. Johnson on his tour in 1773. Boswell and his wife are buried in the family mausoleum next to the church in the village. The Auchinleck Boswell Society, which has literature about the village, is at 131 Main St., Auchinleck. Tel. Cumnock 2382.

AUDLEY END, Essex. [4 Ef] Country House on the A11, W. of Saffron Walden, maintained by the Dept. of the Environment. Sir Philip Sidney accompanied Queen Elizabeth on a progress and stayed with Lord Thomas Howard in 1578 when Gabriel Harvey gave an entertainment. Evelyn, the diarist, who came three times, described the style of the architecture as mixed, on his visit in 1654. Pepys played the flageolet in the cellars in 1677, and the portrait of Lord Sandwich on the staircase is his copy of a Lely by de Critz, which he mentions in his *Diary* in 1660. Vanbrugh made alterations to the Great Hall in 1721 and recommended

the pulling down of three sides of the outer court. The Library contains a French *caquetoire* armchair, once belonging to Pope.

Open Apr.–early Oct.: 11.30 a.m.–5.30 p.m. Closed Mon. and Good Friday.

AULT HUCKNALL, Derbys. [4 Bb] Village S. of the A617 at Glapwell. Thomas Hobbes (1588–1679), the philosopher, who was tutor to two Dukes of Devonshire, and spent the last years of his life at Hardwick Hall (1 m. S.), is buried in the church. A Latin memorial on the floor of the S. chapel records that he was famous at home and abroad.

AVOCA, VALE OF, Wicklow. [9 Hb] 2 m. N. of the village of Avoca on the T7 between Rathdrum and Woodenbridge is the First Meeting of the Waters, where the Avonmore and Avonbeg rivers join. Steps lead down beside the Lion Bridge to a paved garden with an enchanting view, and a bust of Thomas Moore, 'Ireland's National Poet', stands near the stump of the old tree under which he is said to have composed his poem 'The Meeting of the Waters' in 1807.

AWBEG RIVER, Cork. [9 Dd] A clear, shallow river that rises in the Ballyhoura Hills (the ridge continuing W. of the Galtee Mountains) and flows by Kilcolman Castle and Doneraile (q.v.) to join the Blackwater E. of Mallow. The Awbeg is Spenser's Mulla in *Colin Clouts come home againe* (written at Kilcolman 1591, published London 1595), where Colin Clout sat

Under the foote of *Mole* that mountain hore,
Keeping my sheepe amongst the cooly shade,
Of the greene alders by the *Mulla's* shore:

The name 'Mulla' was suggested by the 'Mullach' of Cill na Mullach, the Irish name of Buttevant, a small market town beside the Awbeg, *c.* 2 m. from Kilcolman Castle:

Mulla, the daughter of old Mole so hight
The nymph which of that water course hath charge,
That springing out of Mole, doth run down right
To Buttevant, where spreading forth at large
It giveth name unto that auncient cittie
Which Kilnemullah clepéd is of old.

The Mole represents the Ballyhouras in general, and in Spenser's story the Mulla was loved by the Bregog River, which also rises there and so far as can be traced empties into the Awbeg and the Blackwater.

The name 'Bregog' means 'deceitful' and is appropriate to the river's way of disappearing underground and reappearing as a meandering stream, broken by pools and scattered across the countryside. This accounts for the legend of the Bregog hiding and then visiting the Mulla secretly, in defiance of her father, old Mole, who forbade the marriage and in his rage threw down stones from the hills into Bregog's course. Wherever the Bregog may be found today, its banks are littered with rocks. The Mulla is mentioned again in *Epithalamion* (1595), written at Kilcolman to celebrate the poet's marriage with Elizabeth Boyle.

> Ye nymphs of Mulla, which with careful heed
> The silver scaly trouts do tend full well,
> And greedy pikes which use therein to feed
> Those trouts and pikes all others do excel.

AYNHO, Northants. [1 Ca] Stone village on the A41, birthplace of Shakerley Marmion (1603), author of *The Antiquary* (1641) and other plays. He contributed, with Ben Jonson and Drayton, to *Annalia Dubrensia* (see Dover's Hill).

AYOT ST. LAWRENCE, Herts. [1 Eb] Village 3 m. NW. of Welwyn Garden City, between the A600 and the B651. G. B. Shaw lived here from 1906 till the end of his life, and the way to his home, Shaw's Corner (N.T.),[1] is well signposted. The house is unchanged since Shaw's time and the ground-floor rooms contain his working equipment as well as many personal relics and pictures of friends and fellow-writers such as Sean O'Casey, W. B. Yeats, and Lady Gregory. Hidden from view at the bottom of the garden is the summer-house where Shaw used to write, sheltered from noise and interruptions. His ashes, with those of his wife, were scattered in the garden.

[1] Open daily (except Tues.) 11 a.m.–1 p.m., 2–6 p.m. or sunset if earlier. Closed Good Friday, last two weeks Dec. and first two weeks Jan.

AYR, Ayrs. (Strathclyde). [6 Dd] Large West-coast resort 12 m. SW. of Kilmarnock. Robert Burns, who was born $1\frac{1}{2}$ m. S., was baptized at the Auld Kirk. He mentions the old and new (rebuilt 1877) bridges in his poem 'The Brigs of Ayr'. The Tam O'Shanter Museum[1] in the High St. was formerly a brewhouse to which Burns's Tam, really Douglas Graham of Shanter, supplied malted grain. George Douglas Brown, who went to Ayr Academy in the 1880s, and made his name (as 'George Douglas') with the realistic novel *The House with the Green Shutters* (1901), is buried here.

[1] Open Apr.–Sept.: Mon.–Sat. 9.30 a.m.–5.30 p.m.; Oct.–Mar.: daily noon–4 p.m.

B

BABBACOMBE BAY. See TORQUAY.

BABLOCKHYTHE, Oxon. [1 Bb] Hamlet of caravan homes off the A4449 Eynsham–Standlake road, 2 m. SE. of Stanton Harcourt. A ferry used to ply across the river and it was there that Matthew Arnold said the scholar-gipsy had been seen

> In hat of antique shape, and cloak of grey
>
> Crossing the stripling Thames at Bab-lock-hithe,
> Trailing in the cool stream thy fingers wet
> As the slow punt swings round.

BACH-Y-GRAIG. See TREMEIRCHION.

BACTON, Norf. [4 Hc] Village on the B1159. The miller's wife in 'The Reeve's Tale' in *The Canterbury Tales* and Avarice in Lang-land's *Piers Plowman* invoke the holy cross of Bromholm, once in the 12th-c. Priory, now a ruin on the Keswick road. The *Paston Letters* give details of the funeral feast and burial of John Paston (1421–66). Panes of glass had to be removed to let out the 'reke of the torches'. His table tomb was later taken to Paston (2 m. NW.).

BAGBER. See RUSH-HAY.

BAG ENDERBY, Lincs. [4 Eb] Small village where Tennyson's father was rector jointly with Somersby ($\frac{1}{2}$ m. W.). The tall box pews, including the squire's pew where the family sat, have gone.

BALAVIL, Aberdeens. (Grampian). [7 Ef] Mansion, formerly called Belleville, built

$2\frac{1}{2}$ m. NE. of Kingussie on the site of Raits Castle by James Macpherson after the success of his long poems *Fingal* (1762) and *Temora* (1763), which purported to be translations from the Gaelic bard Ossian.

BALLAUGH, I.O.M. [5 Jg] Village on the A3, 7 m. E. of Ramsey. Hall Caine spent much of his childhood here with his uncle, who was a farmer and butcher, and his grandmother, who told him stories and folk tales of the island, which he later depicted in *The Deemster* (1887) and *The Manxman* (1894).

BALLINCOLLIG, Cork. [9 De] Village on the L39 *c.* 5 m. W. of Cork, just S. of the Lee. James Thomson (1834–82) came here to teach in 1851 and met Charles Bradlaugh (1833–91), the controversial advocate of free thought, who became his lifelong friend. Thomson's most famous poem, 'The City of Dreadful Night', was published (1874) in Bradlaugh's weekly paper, *The National Reformer.*

BALLINDERRY, Antrim. [8 Gc] The village of Lower Ballinderry is near the SE. corner of Lough Neagh, on the B12 Lurgan–Glenavy road, and 1 m. WNW., by Lough Beg (or Portmore Lough), are the remains of Ballinderry First Church (or Portmore Church), where Jeremy Taylor used to preach to a small congregation before he became Bishop of Dromore. He had taken refuge from the Cromwellians in Lord Conway's house of Portmore, near by, and it was here that he wrote (1659) the preface to *Ductor Dubitantium*, dedicated to Charles II. Sallow Island in the lough was one of his favourite retreats. Ballinderry Middle Church, $1\frac{1}{2}$ m. E., was built (1666–8) for him at the end of his life and, thanks to 19th-c. restoration, contains well-preserved original church furniture.

BALLITORE, Kildare. [9 Gb] Village near the W. edge of the Wicklow Mountains, on a minor road W. off the T51, 8 m. N. of Castledermot. It was once a Quaker settlement and its school (now demolished), founded in 1726 by Abraham Shackleton, a Yorkshireman, had Edmund Burke among its pupils from 1741 to 1744.

BALLYHOURA HILLS. See AWBEG RIVER.

BALLYLANEEN, Waterford. [9 Fd] Village on the L155, half-way between Kilmac-

thomas and the coastal village of Bunmahon. The Gaelic poet Tadhg Gaelach Ó Súilleabháin (1715–95) is buried in the churchyard, with a Latin epitaph by his friend Donnchadh Rua Mac Conmara.

BALLYLEE. See GORT.

BALLYSHANNON, Donegal. [8 Dc] Town on the T18, situated on the Erne where the estuary opens on to Donegal Bay. William Allingham, poet and editor (1874–9) of *Fraser's Magazine*, remembered especially for 'Up the airy mountain, / Down the rushy glen' (see Killybegs) and 'Four ducks on a pond', was born here when his father was a busy merchant and ship-owner. He describes his birthplace (P), in the Mall, as 'a little house, the most westerly of a row of three, in a street running down to the harbour'–not greatly altered since his time. He went to Wray's School, Church Lane, and then to boarding-school in 1837 at Killieshandra, Cavan, until he was 14, when he began working at the Provincial Bank where his father had become manager. A commemorative bust by Vincent Breen was unveiled outside the bank (now the Allied Irish Bank) in 1971. He left in 1846 to train as a Customs Officer and had various appointments in Ireland and England before leaving the Service in 1870. He died in London and his ashes were brought to Ballyshannon for burial in the Church of Ireland cemetery. The bridge, named after him, has a memorial tablet.

BALMAGHIE. See LAURIESTON.

BALNAKEIL BAY, Suth. (Highland). [7 Eb] Bay near the NW. tip of the British Isles reached by the A838. An obelisk by the ruined Durness Old Church commemorates Robert Mackay, the Gaelic poet known as Rob Donn, who died in 1778.

BALQUHIDDER (pr. Bälkidder), Perths. (Central). [6 Db] Small village 2 m. from the A84 SW. of Loch Earn. Near the ruins of two earlier churches is the family grave of Robert Campbell or Macgregor (1671–1734), Scott's *Rob Roy* (1817). He and his wife and two sons lie under three stone slabs roughly cut with patterns looking older than the 18th c. After a career embellished over the years like Robin Hood's, he died in his bed at Inverlochlarig (house gone) 6 m. W. His son Robin Oig, who married here in 1751, confronts Alan Breck in a duel in Stevenson's *Kidnapped* (1886), both agreeing to a contest with pipes in place of weapons. Alasdair Alpin MacGregor (1889–1970), who wrote many books on the Highlands and Islands, is commemorated on his father's tombstone here, which states that his ashes were scattered in the Hebrides.

BANAGHER, Offaly. [9 Ea] Village on the E. bank of the Shannon, 8 m. NW. of Birr, on the L116. Anthony Trollope was stationed here in 1841 (his lodgings have gone), when he first came to Ireland as a Post Office surveyor, and decided to try his hand at novel writing in order to supplement his income. His first two novels, *The Macdermots of Ballycloran* (1847) and *The Kellys and the O'Kellys* (1848), were realistic stories of Irish life, but achieved little success. Charlotte Brontë, who married her father's curate, the Revd. Arthur Bell Nicholls, in 1845, spent part of her honeymoon here. Mr. Nicholls, who had been brought up at Cuba House by a schoolmaster uncle, stayed on at Haworth after Charlotte's early death, but eventually returned to Ireland when her father died. He held several curacies, remarried, and finally settled at Banagher for the rest of his life (d. 1906).

BANDON, Cork. [9 De] Market town on the T65, 19 m. SW. of Cork. William Hazlitt came here at the age of 18 months when his father, an outspoken advocate of American Independence, came to Ireland and was Presbyterian minister in Bandon for 3½ years, before taking his family to America in 1783. Lennox Robinson, dramatist and a manager and then director of the Abbey Theatre, Dublin, was educated at Bandon Grammar School.

BARBARY CAMP. See COATE.

BARCHESTER. See SALISBURY.

BARNACK, Cambs. [4 Dd] Village on the B1443, 3 m. SE. of Stamford. Charles Kingsley lived at the rectory from 1824 to 1830, the year his brother Henry was born, and the family moved to Devon. Only part of their house remains by the side of the Victorian rectory (now Kingsley House).

BARNARD CASTLE, Durham. [5 Db] Old town 11 m. NW. of Scotch Corner, on the A67. Dickens and his illustrator Hablot Browne stayed at the King's Head in 1838 when they were investigating abuses in cheap boarding-schools to give authenticity to Dotheboys Hall in *Nicholas Nickleby* (1839). Dickens is said to have been influenced by the clockmaker's shop, then opposite the hotel, in choosing the title *Master Humphrey's Clock* (1840) for his new weekly in which *The Old Curiosity Shop* (1840–1) and *Barnaby Rudge* (1840–1) appeared.

BARNINGHAM WINTER, Norf. [4 Gc] Village near Matlask between the A140 and the A148. The manor was a home of the Paston family rebuilt in Jacobean times. The church in the park has memorials.

BARNS HOUSE, Peebles. (Borders.) [6 Fd] Old mansion, 3 m. SW. of Peebles, reached by a rough signposted road from Kirkton in the Manor valley. The house, situated by the river, near a ruined tower, was the setting for John Buchan's first novel, *John Burnet of Barns* (1898).

BARNSTAPLE, Devon. [2 Dc] Town in N. Devon of importance since Saxon times (formerly a seaport), on the A39 and the A361, at the head of the Taw Estuary. John Gay was born (1685) at 35 High St. (supermarket on site on Joy St. corner; P on Joy St. side) and educated at the Grammar School (formerly St. Anne's Chapel) near the parish church; the 14th-c. building, a school from 1547 to 1908, is now a museum.[1]

[1] Open Whitsun–Sept.

BARRA, Outer Hebrides (Western Isles). [7 Af] Island named after St. Finnbar, where Sir Compton Mackenzie lived during the Second World War. He set the scene of his novel *Whisky Galore* (1947) on Eriskay, a smaller island NE. across the Sound of Barra. Compton Mackenzie's body was brought here for burial after his death in 1972.

BARSHAM, Suff. [4 He] Village on the A1116. The dramatist Sir John Suckling (1609–42) chiefly remembered for 'Why so pale and wan, fond lover ?', and other lyrics, inherited the estate and lived briefly at the Hall (gone). Soldiers he recruited were housed in his banqueting hall (now a barn) before going to the Scottish war; their gaudy clothes were later derided in the ballad 'Sir John Suckling's Campaign'. The site of the Hall is down the sandy track between the houses W. of the church.

BATH, Avon. [2 Hb] City on the Avon, the Roman *Aquae Sulis*, rebuilt in Palladian style in the 18th c., frequented by the fashionable and the ailing who came to drink the waters. Chaucer's Wife of Bath probably lived in the parish of St. Michael without the Walls, today the area around Northgate St. Evelyn in 1654, and Pepys in 1668, comment in their diaries on the fine stone houses and narrow streets. Joseph Glanvill was appointed rector of the Abbey Church the year his book on witchcraft was published, generally known as *Sadducismus Triumphatus* (1666). He died here in 1680 and is buried in the Abbey. Celia Fiennes, who visited in 1687, describes in her *Journeys* (1947) the stiff canvas garments worn by men and women in the baths to conceal their 'shape', a refinement on the earlier nude mixed bathing. Congreve was here with Gay and Arbuthnot in 1721 and spent the season in the second Duchess of Marlborough's train in 1722. Arbuthnot and Gay came again in 1724. Richardson, whose wife's family lived here, visited in the 1740s.

Burke stayed at Circus House in 1756 with his physician, whose daughter he married. Sterne, never robust, put up at Three Black Birds Inn (gone). Goldsmith visited Bath in 1762 for his health and wrote his *Life of Richard Nash, of Bath, Esquire* ('Beau Nash'). Catharine Macaulay, author of a popular History of England (8 vols. 1763–83), and a friend of Dr. Johnson, lived at 2 Alfred St. for a short time. Horace Walpole stayed in Chapel Court (P) in 1766, when he met the Millers of Batheaston (q.v.). He wrote that he was tired of the place and only came for his health.

Anstey, whose satirical *New Bath Guide* (1766) describes the fashionable round in verse, lived (1770–1805) at 5 Royal Cres. at the top of the town. His contemporary Thomas Whalley, whose wife's fortune enabled him to devote himself to poetry and

travel, exchanged views on sensibility with Anna Seward when she visited his house in the centre of Royal Cres. (now a hotel) where, he said, 'the wind blew in a manner, really frightful'.

In 1772, Sheridan, living with his father at 9 New King St. (P), escorted the singer Elizabeth Linley to France from 11 Royal Cres. (to evade her persistent suitor Major Matthews) and became engaged to her in Calais. Foote's play *The Maid of Bath* (1771) satirizes another of the singer's suitors, a sexagenarian, and Sheridan's comedy, *The Rivals*, also takes place here. One of the duels Sheridan fought with Matthews took place on Lansdown Hill. He revisited the scene years later, when taking his wife, dying of consumption, to Bristol Hotwells. Goldsmith stayed with his patron Lord Clare at 11 North Parade in 1771. Smollett, who had earlier tried to practise medicine here, often came to drink the waters. He stayed in Gay St. in the 1760s. In *Humphry Clinker* (1771) Matthew Bramble stays on the Parade.

Dr. Johnson came with his friends the Thrales in 1776 and Boswell at his invitation put up at the Pelican (gone). In 1780 the Thrales brought Fanny Burney, delighted to be recognized as the author of *Evelina*, published anonymously in 1778. They stayed at 14 South Parade (P), and Elizabeth Carter, Mrs. Montagu, and Christopher Anstey called. In 1783 Mrs. Thrale, then a widow, lived in Russell St. She married Mr. Piozzi at St. James's Church (gone) early in the next year. Some years after his death she settled (1814–20) at 8 Gay St. (P). A large party gathered in the Lower Assembly Rooms (gone) for her eightieth birthday—at which she danced. Lady Miller of Batheaston died in 1781 and her memorial in the Abbey was written by Anna Seward, whom she had first encouraged to write. Gibbon, who had benefited from the waters as a youth, stayed at 10 Belvedere (P) in 1793, a few months before his death. William Lisle Bowles, recovering from ill-health on the Parade in 1795, wrote 'Elegiac Stanzas' within the sound of the 'river rapids', now a weir.

Southey, who as a boy stayed with an aunt at 108 Walcot St. (P), spent his vacations from Balliol (1792–5) with his mother at her boarding-house at 9 Duke St. De Quincey lived at 6 Green Park Buildings while at the Grammar School (*c.* 1796–9). Mary Martha Butt (Mrs. Sherwood) lodged in South Parade with her sister and widowed mother in 1801. She sold her successful novel *Susan Grey* (1869) while here. She attended a *bas bleu* evening at the lodgings of Elizabeth Hamilton, author of *Memoirs of Modern Philosophers* (1800), and used the experience in a later novel. Her detailed memoirs describe her meeting with Hannah More at 76 Gt. Pulteney St.; the future author of *The Fairchild Family* (1818–47) was not pleased by the condescension in her welcome. Jane Austen, who had often spent holidays here with members of her family, lived with her parents after her father's retirement (1801) at 1 The Paragon, then at 4 Sidney Pl. (P), previously Sidney Ter. She wrote *Lady Susan* there and began *The Watsons*. In *Persuasion* (1818), largely set in Bath, the Lady Dalrymple takes a furnished house in Laura Pl. near by. *Northanger Abbey* (1818) (like *Persuasion* written earlier but not published until after her death) satirizes Bath society as well as the Gothic novel. Both have scenes in the Pump Room[1] and in the Assembly Rooms[2] in Alfred St. (interior rebuilt), then known as the Upper Rooms. Elizabeth Inchbald's *Lovers' Vows* (1798), which caused such problems when rehearsed by the amateur actors in *Mansfield Park* (1814), was a popular play at the old Theatre Royal in Orchard St. (now the Masonic Hall). Sarah Siddons, who often acted there, lived at 33 The Paragon (P). Jane Austen was living at 27 Green Park Buildings, continuing *The Watsons*, when her father died (1804). It remained unfinished. She moved with her mother and sister to 25 Gay St. and her last lodgings here were in Trim St. (1806). Christopher Anstey, who died in 1805, was buried in St. Swithin's, Walcot St. (key available). Shelley and Mary Godwin lodged at 4 Roman Pavement and 6 Queen Sq. briefly in 1816. Fanny Burney came back to Bath with her husband General D'Arblay. They lived for a short time in Rivers St. before moving to 23 Gt. Stanhope St. (1815–18), where he died. They and their son who predeceased his mother are buried in St. Swithin's. The lines on the General's monument were composed by his wife. Harrison Ainsworth spent part of his honeymoon at 7 South Parade in 1826. Crabbe, who later spent many holidays with Mrs. and Miss Hoare, was first introduced to them during his stay at 26 Brock St. in 1826. For many years he

carried on a sentimental correspondence from Trowbridge Rectory with Elizabeth Charter of 11 Gt. Pulteney St. Landor married Julia Thullier in 1811, falling in love at first sight at a ball here. After their separation in 1835, he lived at 35 St. James Sq. (P), where he was visited by Dickens, who created the character of Little Nell there in 1840, and had his host in mind when creating Boythorn in *Bleak House* (1852–3). The much-travelled Mr. Pickwick spent some time in Bath, first at the White Hart (gone) and then in Royal Cres., where 'an extraordinary calamity befel Mr. Winkle'. Longfellow, Hawthorne, and Wordsworth also visited Landor here. Wordsworth and his sister Dorothy were guests of Miss Fenwick, their friend from Ambleside, at 9 North Parade in 1841 for his daughter's wedding. Wordsworth had opposed the match for some time as he distrusted Quillinan's ability to provide for Dora. He was too overwrought to attend the service, but gave her his blessing. Froude in 1848 and Thackeray in 1857 stayed at 16 Lansdown Pl. East. William Beckford lived at 20 Lansdown Cres. (1822–44) and linked this by an arched bridge with 1 Lansdown Pl. West, where many of his books from Fonthill were housed. He built a tower on the top of Lansdown Hill and it was from there that he is said to have seen Fonthill Tower crash to the ground 25 miles away. He had a secluded path built by his gardener (who transplanted well-grown trees) from the stables to the tower, where he spent most of his days. He revised *Dreams, Waking Thoughts and Incidents* in 1834 and wrote another book about his travels, *Recollections of an Excursion to the Monasteries of Alcobaça and Batalha* (1835). The avenue to Kingswood School, the plantation, and the grotto tunnel remain. He wished to be buried near the tower but this was not possible until some time after his death, when his daughter bought back the tower in its surrounding gardens, and part of the ground was consecrated. His tomb there has the inscription

> Eternal Power
> Grant me through obvious clouds one transient gleam
> Of Thy bright essence in my dying hour.

Bulwer-Lytton stayed at 9 Royal Cres. in 1866 and George Saintsbury lived from his retirement in 1915 to his death (1933) at no. 1, now the Georgian House Museum.[3]

As well as *History of Criticism* he wrote the entertaining *Notes on a Cellar Book* and *A Scrap Book*.

[1] Open summer: daily 9 a.m.–6 p.m.; winter: 9 a.m.–5 p.m.; Sun. 11 a.m.–5 p.m.
[2] Open as above.
[3] Open Mar. to Oct. inclusive: Tues.–Sat. 11 a.m.–5 p.m.; Sun. 2–5 p.m.

BATHEASTON, Avon. [2 Hb] Former village, now a suburb, NE. of Bath on the A4. Horace Walpole in 1766 mentions in his *Letters* dining with the agreeable Miller family in their 'new built house [Bath Easton Villa]' now 172 Bailbrook Lane, a steep turning up a hill N. of the A365. He describes the view across the Avon from their bow-window and their pretty garden with several small rivulets. In 1773 Lady Miller returned from a tour of Italy and France, where she had acquired a Tuscan vase and a passion for bouts-rimés. These she connected into a ceremony for the poetical assemblies at her fashionable breakfasts (on one occasion four duchesses were present and the line of coaches stretched back to Bath). Fortified by chocolate and macaroons the guests put their verses in the vase, which stood in the bow-window, and the author of those judged the best was crowned with laurel. Fanny Burney, who found that 'the business of the vase' was 'over for this season' when she visited, said that Lady Miller was 'an ordinary woman in very common life, with fine clothes on' but was flattered when the 10-year-old Miss Miller talked to her of Evelina as if she were a real person. The minor poets of Bath often visited the villa and William Hayley sent a poem with his wife, who found Batheaston no more ridiculous than other assemblies.

BATTLEFIELD, Salop. [3 Gc] Village on the A53, 3½ m. N. of Shrewsbury. The church, built in 1408, commemorates the battle of Shrewsbury (1403) when Henry IV defeated the rebel Earl of Northumberland, his son Hotspur, and the Earl of Worcester. In Shakespeare's version of the battle in *1 Henry IV* Falstaff plays the valiant braggart when he pretends to have slain Hotspur in single combat.

BAWDESWELL, Norf. [4 Gd] Village on the A1067 and the B1145, Chaucer's Baldeswelle where the Reeve Oswald in *The Canterbury Tales* lived.

BAYMOUTH. See SIDMOUTH.

BEACONSFIELD, Bucks. [1 Db] Old town on the A40. The poet Edmund Waller, who became an M.P. in his youth, inherited (1624) the estate of Hall Barn (rebuilt) and it was his main home until his death. After being detected in a Royalist plot, for which, having betrayed his friends, he was fined and banished, he managed to steer a safe course between Cromwell and Charles II, writing poems to both. Many of his early poems are addressed to 'Sacharissa', Lady Dorothy Sidney, whom he courted unsuccessfully after becoming a widower at 25. Waller died in 1687 and his ornate tomb is in the churchyard. Edmund Burke, who bought (1768) the two-storeyed house with a pedimented front called Gregories, invited the impoverished poet, George Crabbe, there in 1781. Burke entertained many literary friends here, including Sheridan, Garrick, and Murphy. Dr. Johnson was brought by Mrs. Thrale, who commented on the dust and the cobwebs. The house was rebuilt after a fire in 1813. Burke's memorial is in the parish church. In 1809 William Hickey, the son of one of Burke's friends, took 'a pretty cottage called Little Hall Barn . . .' near Hall Barn, then the seat of a descendant of Edmund Waller. Hickey, who brought with him his elderly sisters, an Indian servant, and a large dog, decided to fill the vacuum surrounding him after returning from his exciting life in India by 'setting his memories in order and writing down his life-story'. *The Memoirs of William Hickey* (ed. A. Spencer 1913–25, ed. P. Quennell 1960 and 1975) tell of the uproarious escapades of his youth, both amorous and felonious, his banishment to a cadetship in the East India Company and his success at the Indian Bar, which gained him a small fortune. St. Teresa's Catholic church commemorates G. K. Chesterton, who lived (1909–35) at Overroads, Grove Rd. (P), and wrote his best work there, including the Father Brown crime stories, *Collected Poems* (1915) which includes 'Lepanto', and the critical studies, *Thackeray* (1910), and *Bernard Shaw* (1909; enlarged edn. 1935).

BEAMINSTER (pr. Bĕmister), Dorset. [2 Gd] Village on the A3066 and the B3163, 5 m. N. of Bridport. It is celebrated in the lines by William Barnes, the Dorset dialect poet:

Sweet Be'mi'ter that bist a bound
By green an' woody hills all round.

The Manor House, off North St., has a painted ceiling from Fonthill (q.v.).

BEARSTED, Kent. [1 Fc] Large village on the A2020, on the eastern outskirts of Maidstone. Edward Thomas lived (1901–4) at two cottages here; the first, Rose Acre, damp and ugly and with no roses until he planted them, was 1 m. from the village at the foot of the N. Downs, and the second, which he also called Rose Acre, was on the village green next to a wheelwright's shop. He published two volumes of essays, *Horae Solitariae* (1902) and *Rose Acre Papers* (1904), and some reviews, but his financial position, with a wife and son to support, was precarious. In 1921 Sinclair Lewis spent 2 months at the Bell House at the end of the green. He was writing *Babbitt* (1922), and he left for Paris at the end of September.

BEAUCHAMP COURT. See WARWICK.

BEAUVALE PRIORY, Notts. [4 Bc] Ruin off the B600 NW. of Eastwood, the setting for D. H. Lawrence's historical short story 'A Fragment of Stained Glass'.

Permission to visit should be obtained from the farm near by.

BECCLES, Suff. [4 He] Small town on the A146, 16 m. SE. of Norwich. Crabbe, who first met Sarah Elmy, the 'Mira' of his poems, when he was an apprentice surgeon, often visited her at Beccles where she lived with her mother. On his visit in 1780 he worked on *The Village*, a satire on pastoral happiness. Crabbe and Sarah were married at St. Michael's Church in 1783. The *émigré* Chateaubriand, calling himself M. de Combourg, was rescued from penury by the Society of Antiquaries, who employed him to decipher early French manuscripts. He stayed at the inn here and spent a romantic interlude at Bungay (q.v.).

BECKHAMPTON, Wilts. [1 Ac] Village on the A4, 5 m. W. of Marlborough. The Wagon and Horses, though slightly altered, is thought to be the inn where the bagman tells his story in *Pickwick Papers* (1837). He describes his arrival 'in the snug, old parlour

before the roaring fire' after his journey across the bleak, windswept Marlborough Downs, the pleasure of successive glasses of hot punch and the consequences of the extremely odd behaviour of his bedroom chair.

BECKINGTON, Som. [2 Hb] Village on the A36 and the A361. Samuel Daniel returned to live (1610–19) in his native county. He is thought to have built a farmhouse on the right bank of the Frome and called it Cliffords after his former pupil Lady Anne. As well as farming he continued to write masques which were acted in London and Bristol. Some time before his death (1619), he moved to Rudge (then called Ridge), 2 m. W., where he made his will. He was buried in St. George's Church here, where the Lady Anne, then Dowager Countess of Pembroke, erected a memorial, renovated in 1778 by the poet William Mason.

BECKLEY, Oxon. [1 Cb] Village 4 m. NE. of Oxford. Beckley Park, with its three gables, is said to be a model for the house in Aldous Huxley's *Crome Yellow* (1921), which has 'three projected towers'. Evelyn Waugh wrote much of *Rossetti: His Life and Works* (1928) in the village at the Abingdon Arms. He also spent his honeymoon there after his marriage in June 1928 to Evelyn Gardner.

BEDFORD, Beds. [4 Df] County town on the Ouse, where John Bunyan was imprisoned from 1660 to 1672 for preaching without a licence and where he wrote *The Pilgrim's Progress*, *Grace Abounding*, and other works. His spirit lives in the Bunyan Meeting (the Congregational–Baptist Church) in Mill St., where he was minister from the end of 1671 till his death in 1688. The present church (built 1849) is the third on the site. Its doors have bronze panels with scenes from *The Pilgrim's Progress* in low relief. Attached to the church, on the site of the barn where Bunyan preached, is an excellent museum[1] containing personal relics and a collection of his works in over 150 languages. The Mott Harrison Collection (library and exhibition devoted to Bunyan) is at the Public Library in Harpur St.[2] A bronze statue by Sir Joseph Boehm, given by the 9th Duke of Bedford in 1874, stands at the corner of St. Peter's St. and the Broadway. The words of the inscription are taken from *The Pilgrim's Progress*:

> It had its eyes lifted up to heaven
> The best of books in his hand . . .

Bedford was also the birthplace of William Hale White ('Mark Rutherford'). He attended Bedford Modern School and the Bunyan Meeting. Though he left the district as a young man, his books, *The Autobiography of Mark Rutherford* (1881) and *Mark Rutherford's Deliverance* (1885) are interesting accounts of the dissenting community in which he grew up. The town also appears as 'Eastthorpe' in his novel *Catharine Furze* (1893).

¹ Open Tues.–Fri. 10 a.m.–noon; 2.30–4.30 p.m.; or by arrangement.
² Open weekdays 10 a.m.–6 p.m.

BEDHAMPTON, Hants. [1 Ce] Town on the A27 adjoining Havant. Mill Lane, near the parish church in old Bedhampton, leads to the Old Mill House facing the wide stream and reached by a small iron footbridge. Keats and his friend Charles Armitage Brown spent some time here after visiting Chichester in January 1819. They were present at the consecration of the much discussed new Gothic chapel at Stansted (q.v.) built by Lewis Way. Robert Gittings's *John Keats: The Living Year* (1967) describes how Keats used his experience there in 'The Eve of St. Agnes' (1820), begun in Chichester but finished here when his stay was extended because of illness. A plaque on the back of the house, placed there in 1959 by the Keats–Shelley Memorial Associations of England and America, records also that Keats spent his last night in England in the mill house when his ship put into Portsmouth because of a storm.

BEECH, Hants. [1 Cd] Village just off the A339, 1½ m. W. of Alton. Sir Compton Mackenzie lived at Canadian Cottage (demolished in the 1960s) in the holidays and at week-ends from 1896 to 1900. Although he said this was 'long, long before I wrote anything', he drew on his memories of the place for three of his novels: *The Altar Steps* (1921) and its sequel, *The Parson's Progress* (1922), are partly founded on Alton Abbey, Beech, which is run by Benedictines; *Buttercups and Daisies* (1931), written with lively humour, contains thinly-veiled portraits of local characters of recent memory.

BELDOVER. See EASTWOOD.

BELFAST, Antrim. [8 Hc] Capital of N. Ireland (since 1921), seaport, shipbuilding, industrial, and university city, situated on the Lagan, at the head of Belfast Lough. Its literary connections are mainly with those writers who were born here, but there is a dearth of monuments or places of pilgrimage. The earliest writer of interest was Dr. William Drennan (1754–1820), a poet and the first president of the United Irishmen, as well as a founder of the Belfast Academical Institution. He was a native of Belfast, the son of a minister of the First Presbyterian Church, Rosemary St., and is remembered as the first to call Ireland 'the Emerald Isle', in a poem of 1795. A collection of his verse and prose, *Fugitive Pieces*, was published in 1815. A memorial inscription above his grave can be seen in the Clifton St. cemetery (the New Burying Ground (1797) of the Belfast Charitable Society), on the N. edge of the city centre.

Robert Anderson (1770–1833), a poet from Carlisle, came to Belfast in 1808 to work as a pattern drawer in Brookfield, near the grange of Doagh, on the Islekelly, a little N. of Belfast. After 2 years he went to the Carnmoney (now Mossley) Cotton Printing Works, where he worked until the death of his employer, David Bigger, in 1818. He lived with Thomas and Andrew Stewart, at Springtown, in the townland of Ballyearl, and during this time wrote a number of verses, of which many appeared in the *Belfast News-Letter* and *Commercial Chronicle*, as well as in a collection of *Poems on Various Subjects* (Belfast, 1810). The poet and antiquary, Sir Samuel Ferguson (1810–86), was born at 23 High St. (site now occupied by a restaurant), but later moved to Dublin. When Anthony Trollope was working for the Post Office in Ireland he was promoted to the position of surveyor in 1853 and sent to Belfast for 18 months to take postal charge of the northern counties. He and his family took lodgings in Belfast (possibly in Lisburn Rd.) for a while and then moved to Whiteabbey, a suburban coastal town N. of the city, where he completed *The Warden* (1855), the first of the Barsetshire novels and the first of his novels to meet with success. Canon J. O. Hannay ('George A. Birmingham') (1865-1950) was born at 75 University Rd. (P), now owned by Queen's University.

Forrest Reid (1875–1947) was born at 20 Montcharles and was educated at the Royal Belfast Academical Institution. He lived at 13 Ormiston Cres. (P) from 1924 to the end of his life. C. S. Lewis (1898–1963), was born at 47 Dundela Ave. (now replaced by a block of flats), and recounts in his autobiography, *Surprised by Joy* (1955), that he and his elder brother grew up in a semi-detached villa where they wrote and illustrated stories of 'Animal-Land'. In 1905 they moved to a new house, 54 (now 76) Circular Rd., on the outskirts of the city, which 'looked down over wide fields to Belfast Lough and across it to the long mountain line of the Antrim shore'. Louis MacNeice (1907–63) and W. R. Rodgers (1909–69) were also natives of Belfast.

BELVOIR (pr. Beever) CASTLE, Leics. [4 Cc] Seat of the Duke of Rutland, 7 m. WSW. of Grantham. Crabbe was chaplain (1782–8) and he published the realistic *The Village* (1783) while here, though it stemmed from his experiences at Aldeburgh, and *The Newspaper* (1785). After his marriage (1783) he had an apartment in the castle, which was rebuilt by Wyatt in 1816 after a fire.

Open Easter to Sept.: Wed., Thur., Sat., noon–6 p.m.; Sun. 2–7 p.m.; Oct.: Sun. 2–6 p.m.

BEMBRIDGE SCHOOL, I.O.W. [1 Cf] School on the B3395, on the E. coast, where John Howard Whitehouse (Warden 1919–54) established the Ruskin Galleries,[1] which contain the largest single collection of Ruskin's work. Whitehouse, who edited (with J. Evans) *The Diaries of John Ruskin* (1956–9), also helped establish Ruskin's home, Brantwood (q.v.), as his national memorial.

[1] To view, apply to the Curator.

BEMERTON, Wilts. [1 Ad] Former village, now a suburb of Salisbury, where George Herbert was rector (1630–2) of the little church of St. Andrew. He supervised the repair of the rectory and the verse he placed over his hearth is now above the door of the Victorian addition. Izaak Walton and John Aubrey mention his love for his garden and tradition credits him with the planting of the medlar by the Nadder along whose bank he walked to Salisbury Cathedral services. Herbert died of consumption and is buried in the church (P). The E. window commemorates him and his friend Nicholas Ferrar of the Little Gidding community, to whom he sent his religious verse, entitled *The Temple* (1634), which contains 'Teach me, my God and King'. Charles I, in prison, and Cowper, recovering from depression, found solace in these poems and through Ferrar's connection with the Virginia Plantation they were well known there.

BEN NEVIS, Inverness-shire (Grampian). [6 Da] Highest peak in the British Isles, a few miles SE. of Fort William. Keats climbed it on his tour in 1819 with his friend Charles Armitage Brown and wrote a sonnet on the summit.

BENTWORTH, Hants. [1 Cd] Village on a minor road S. of the A339, c. 3½ m. W. of Alton. George Wither, one of the most famous of Hampshire poets, was born here (11 June 1588), the son of a well-to-do farmer. He received his 'grammatical learning' from a local schoolmaster and went to Magdalen College, Oxford when he was 16. Many years later he wrote of his carefree boyhood days when 'hounds, hawks and horses were at my command', and at the age of 79 he wished to return to his birthplace but died instead 'in streaming London's central roar'.

BERE REGIS, Dorset. [2 Hd] Village on the A35, half-way between Bournemouth and Dorchester. The fine church contains the Turberville window and vault referred to in *Tess of the d'Urbervilles* (1891). The village is Hardy's 'Kingsbere-sub-Greenhill', Woodbury Hill rising behind being 'Greenhill'.

BERESFORD DALE, Derbys. [4 Ab] Part of the Dove Valley approached by public footpath from Hartington on the B5023, 10 m. NE. of Ashbourne, or by the narrow no-through-road off the Hulme End–Alstonefield road (parking limited). The Beresford family owned land here for centuries and Charles Cotton, a descendant, was born (1630) in the gabled Tudor Hall with the Elizabethan wing (now all demolished) where he entertained Izaak Walton. Together they fished the Dove, resting in the little temple where their initials are entwined in a monogram over the door. This, built in 1674, is dedicated to the river and its sportsmen. This private temple is obscured by trees but can be seen in winter from the public footpath. Cotton wrote the second part, on fly-fishing, of the 5th edition of *The Compleat Angler* (1676), *Wonders of the Peak* (1681), and translated Montaigne's *Essays* (1685). Collections of his other works appeared posthumously. He sold the hall, which he called by the local name, Basford Hall, in his poems, when in debt but was able to live there again when it was bought by a Beresford cousin. The parish church at Alstonefield 2 m. S. has the pew, now painted, with the Cotton arms where the two men worshipped. It and the other oak pews were carved in Cotton's father's time.

BERKHAMSTED, Herts. [1 Db] Old town on the A41. Cowper was born at the rectory on the site of the modern one. It was red brick and had chimneys as tall as the Old Rectory (still standing) which was built behind it in 1840. Cowper was 7 when his mother died and he was sent away to school.

BERRYNARBOR, Devon. [2 Dc] Village *c.* 3½ m. E. of Ilfracombe, just S. of the A399. John Jewel, Bishop of Salisbury (1560–71) and author of the celebrated defence of the Church of England, *Apologia Ecclesiae Anglicanae* (1562), which Queen Elizabeth I ordered to be read in churches throughout the kingdom, was born (1522) at Bowden, a farmhouse in the parish.

BESTWOOD. See EASTWOOD.

BEVISHAMPTON. See SOUTHAMPTON.

BIBURY, Glos. [1 Ab] Village on the A433, 6 m. NE. of Cirencester. Pope writing to Swift in 1726 recalls their recent visit, 'I shall never more think of . . . the woods of Ciceter, or the pleasing prospect of Byberry, but your Idea must be join'd with 'em'. John Byng mentions his stay here in 1794 (*Torrington Diaries*, 1934). 'After breakfast and two fine basins of snail tea which allways is of sovereign use to my lungs, we walked down the village, by the side of a pastoral trout stream full of fish, (for this place is a famous spot for fly-fishing . . .). We procured the key of the church (a key the size of Dover Castle), and admired it as lightsome, and well-glazed.'

BIDEFORD (pr. **Biddyford**), **Devon.** [2 Dc] Ancient seaport on the estuary of the Torridge, where the A39 crosses the river by a bridge of twenty-four arches (built 1460; widened 1925). The Royal Hotel embodies, at its N. end, the original town house of John Davie, a merchant (1688), and Kingsley is said to have written part of *Westward Ho!* (1855) when staying here in 1854. He is commemorated by a statue at the N. end of the promenade.

BIEL, East Lothian (Lothian). [6 Gc] Mansion, on Biel Water, *c.* 4 m. SW. of Dunbar, in a private estate off the B6370. It has been held in some accounts that this was the birthplace of William Dunbar (*c.* 1460–*c.* 1520), known as 'the chief of ancient Scottish poets' or 'the Scottish Chaucerian', author of *The Thrissil and the Rois* (1503) and *The Twa Maryit Women and the Wedo* (*c.* 1508), but there is no strong evidence that he was of the family of the Dunbars of Biel or, as has been suggested, the grandson of Sir Patrick Dunbar, who came into possession of the lands in 1420. It is, however, extremely likely that he was a native of East Lothian.

BIGGAR, Lanarks. (Strathclyde). [6 Ed] Town on the A702, 18 m. SW. of Peebles. John Brown, essayist and author of *Rab and his Friends* (1859), an essay about a dog, was born (1810) at the manse here.

BIGNOR PARK, West Sussex. [1 De] Country house, 2 m. W. of the A29 at Bury, not visible from the road. Charlotte Smith (*née* Turner) spent her childhood here at her father's house and her family arranged the unhappy marriage to Benjamin Smith, the spendthrift son of a West India merchant. Her sonnets 'Bignor Park' and 'To the Arun' recall the pleasures of her childhood and her love for the county where she spent most of her life.

BILSTON, West Midlands. [3 Hd] Industrial town on the A463 on the SE. edge of Wolverhampton. Sir Henry Newbolt, elder son of the vicar of St. Mary's, the Revd. H. F. Newbolt, was born (1862) in Baldwin St., Bradley (area demolished and rebuilt), and baptized at his father's church. The family later moved into St. Mary's Vicarage, but the father died in 1866.

BILTON, Warwicks. [4 Be] Former village, now a suburb SW. of Rugby. Joseph Addison bought the country estate of Bilton Hall in 1713, the year of the success of his tragedy *Cato*. He started to plan gardens and plant avenues, one of which ended at wrought-iron gates (now at Magdalen College, Oxford) ornamented with his initials and those of his wife, the former Countess of Holland and Warwick. A small summer-house overlooking the stream, where Addison used to sit with his friends to eat the produce of the gardens, was destroyed (*c.* 1968) by vandals.

BINFIELD, Berks. [1 Dc] Village on the B3034, *c.* 3 m. NE. of Wokingham, on the edge of Windsor Forest, now widely developed on both sides of the main road. A house called Pope's Manor is thought to be an extension of a 17th-c. brick house bought by Pope's father in 1698 and known successively as Whitehill House, Binfield Lodge, Pope's Lodge, The Firs, and Arthurstone, before its present name. Pope was brought here from London at the age of 12 (1700) and stayed until the house was sold in 1713. During this time he planned his own method of study and began his literary career, his first published work being *Pastorals*, written when he was 16 (published in Tonson's *Poetical Miscellanies*, pt. vi, 1709); followed by *An Essay on Criticism*, a didactic poem in heroic couplets (1711), which introduced him to Addison's circle; *The Messiah*, a sacred eclogue, published in *The Spectator* (May 1712); *The Rape of the Lock*, a mock-heroic poem (published in Lintot's *Miscellanies*, 1712, enlarged 1714); and *Windsor Forest*, a pastoral poem (1713). By the time he left Binfield Pope had begun the translation of Homer's *Iliad* (6 vols., 1715-20). The row of fine Scotch firs from which one of the modern names of the house was taken probably existed in Pope's time and it has been thought that he alludes to the house and its surroundings in the lines:

> My paternal cell,
> A little house, with trees a-row,
> And like its master very low.

The original house could well have been 'little' and 'low' before the extensive 19th-c. alterations and additions were made. It is interesting to compare the aspect of the present house with a print entitled 'Pope's

House, Binfield (Adjoining Windsor Forest) Berkshire' (n.d.), on the wall of the Cottage Inn at Winkfield, *c.* 4 m. E. of Binfield.

BINSEY, Oxon. [1 Cb] Small Thames-side village reached by car from the Botley Rd. in Oxford, or on foot, from the tow-path, or across Port Meadow. The poem by G. M. Hopkins, 'Binsey Poplars felled 1879', describes his sense of loss in the lines

> My aspens dear, whose airy cages quelled,
> Quelled or quenched in leaves the leaping sun,
> All felled, felled, are all felled;
> Of a fresh and following folded rank
> Not spared, not one
> That dandled a sandalled
> Shadow that swam or sank
> On meadow and river and wind-wandering
> weed-winding bank.

A. E. Coppard, when working (1907-19) at the Eagle Ironworks in Walton Well Rd., Oxford, often visited the Perch during the midday break. Dylan Thomas, Louis Mac-Neice, and W. R. Rodgers also used to come here on week-end visits to Oxford.

BIRCHINGTON, Kent. [1 Hc] Seaside resort on the A28, adjacent to Margate. Dante Gabriel Rossetti, who spent the last months of his life as an invalid in a bungalow (gone) lent by the architect J. P. Seddon, was buried (1882) near the porch of the parish church, where a large Celtic cross marks the grave. Hall Caine looked after him and Watts-Dunton was at his death-bed. Inside the church is a Pre-Raphaelite memorial window.

BIRMINGHAM, West Midlands. [4 Ae] Second largest city in England and centre of an industrial region, Birmingham has two universities and an Anglican and a Catholic cathedral. Dr. Johnson lived here for a short while (*c.* 1734) and contributed essays to the *Birmingham Journal*. It was through Edmund Hector, who lived in a house (gone) in Old Square, that Johnson came to translate a French version of Father Lobo's *Voyage to Abyssinia*. This appeared anonymously in 1735, the year he married Mrs. Porter, whom he met here. Panelling from Hector's house has been re-erected in Aston Hall[1] (the Jacobean home of the Holte family until the 19th c. and now owned by the city). It is thought to be the original of Washington Irving's *Bracebridge Hall* (1822), the title of a collection of his essays which followed his original *Sketch-Book* (1820), which contained 'Rip Van Winkle'. This story was written while he was visiting his brother-in-law in 1818 as a diversion from the worries of a business failure. The house where he stayed has been demolished.

J. H. Newman established the Oratory of St. Philip Neri in the Hagley Rd. in the SW. suburb of Edgbaston in 1847, and a tablet to him is in the memorial church of the Immaculate Conception.

J. H. Shorthouse, born in 1834 in Great Charles St. and educated at a Quaker school here, wrote the novel *John Inglesant*, influenced by Ruskin, at 6 Beaufort Rd. (gone) before moving in 1876 to 60 Wellington Rd. He died (1903) there and is buried in Old Edgbaston cemetery.

Harriet Martineau, who died in Ambleside, was buried (1876) in the cemetery on Key Hill. Louis MacNeice, who was Lecturer in Classics at the University of Birmingham (1930–5), published a collection of *Poems* in his last year here.

¹ Open Mon.–Sat. 10 a.m.–5 p.m.; Sun. 2–5 p.m. In winter closed on Sun. and at dusk on weekdays.

BIRSTALL, West Yorkshire. [5 Ee] Town on the A62 and the A643, 6 m. SW. of Leeds. Oakwell Hall, now a museum,¹ an old stone house with mullioned windows, was 'Fieldhead' in *Shirley* (1849), the home of Charlotte Brontë's heroine Shirley Keeldar. The Rydings with its castellated roof, now in the premises of the Birstall carpet factory and visible from the gates, was the home of Ellen Nussey, the correspondent and confidante of Charlotte Brontë, whom she first met at school. In *Jane Eyre* (1847) the Rydings became 'Thornfield Hall'. Ellen Nussey is buried in the churchyard here, the 'Briarfield' church of *Shirley*.

¹ Open 2–7 p.m., except Fri.

BISHOP AUCKLAND. See OLD PARK.

BISHOPSBOURNE, Kent. [1 Hd] Quiet village off the A2 S. of Canterbury, where Richard Hooker became rector in 1595. Much of *Ecclesiastical Polity* was written here, Book V being published in 1597. A memorial on the S. side of the chancel states he was buried in 1600. The 12-ft.-long stone slab over his remains is thought to have been the old altar. He left £3 in his will for a 'newer and sufficient pulpitt'. His rectory has gone but the old yew hedge is still called Hooker's Hedge. Near the church is a late-Georgian successor to Hooker's rectory (now called Oswalds); it was Conrad's home from 1920 until his death in 1924.

BISHOPSGATE, Berks. [1 Dc] Hamlet on a minor road just W. of the A328, 3 m. S. of Windsor. Shelley and Mary Godwin stayed here in the summer of 1815, in a low-roofed cottage near the Rhododendron Walk of Windsor Park, 'so secluded that even the tax-collector didn't know it'. Bishopsgate Heath lay in front and Chapel Wood and Virginia Water to the W. A garden provided flowers. Shelley loved walking in the forest, and Peacock, whom he later joined at Marlow (q.v.), was a frequent visitor. During this time Shelley wrote *Alastor, or The Spirit of Solitude* (1816), his first important work.

BISHOP'S TACHBROOK, Warwicks. [4 Be] Village on the A452, 3 m. S. of Leamington Spa. The church has a tablet to W. S. Landor (d. 1864 in Italy), author of *Imaginary Conversations* (1824), whose family lived here. The E. window commemorates Charles Kingsley's widow, who lived at Grove House.

BISHOPSTONE, East Sussex. [1 Fe] Village off the A259 W. of Seaford. James Hurdis (1763–1801) was born here, spent his vacations from Oxford here, and in 1791 became the vicar. He lived at Hallands, a long, low, flint house with Gothic windows, in the hamlet of Norton (½ m. N.), where he set up a printing press in the cellar and produced *The Favourite Village* (1800). He was a friend and correspondent of Cowper, and of Hayley, who wrote memorial verses on his sudden death in 1801. He is buried in the church with his sister Catherine, whose gradual decline and early death he lamented in a long poem. Memorial tablets to them both are in the church together with Hayley's lines.

BISHOPSTONE, Hereford and Worcester. [3 Fe] Village S. of the A480, 6 m. W. of Hereford. Wordsworth wrote a sonnet 'Roman Antiquities Discovered at Bishopstone' (1835) on the uncovering of 'this time-buried pavement'.

BLACK BOURTON, Oxon. [1 Bb] Little village *c.* 5½ m. N. of Faringdon, on a minor road off the B4042. Maria Edgeworth was born (1 Jan. 1768) at her mother's family home, the old hall, which once stood just NW. of the church, but of which no trace remains.

BLACKDOWN. See HASLEMERE.

BLACK DWARF'S COTTAGE, Peebles. (Borders). [6 Fd] Cottage on a narrow road beyond Kirkton, overlooking the Manor Water, *c.* 3½ m. SW. of Peebles off the A72. This was the home of David Ritchie, the sinister-looking dwarf of legendary strength who was the hero of Scott's *The Black Dwarf* (1816). The present cottage, bearing the inscription 'D.R. 1802', was built by the laird of Woodhouse to replace the original one where Ritchie lived when Scott visited him in 1797. His 3 ft 10 in-high doorway has been preserved (one of normal size having been added when his sister came to live with him). He died in 1811 and was buried in Kirkton Manor graveyard. An inscribed gravestone was put up in 1845 by W. and R. Chambers of Peebles.

BLACKSTABLE. See WHITSTABLE.

BLADESOVER. See UPPARK.

BLAENAU FFESTINIOG, Gwynedd. [3 Db] Town on the A496, 13 m. NW. of Portmadoc. John Cowper Powys moved to 1 Waterloo in 1955. Among the works published while he was here, are the novels *Atlantis* (1956), and *All or Nothing* (1960). *Poems* (1964), selected by Kenneth Hopkins, was published the year after his death here.

BLAEN-Y-COED. See CYNWYL ELFET.

BLAGDON, Avon. [2 Gb] Village on the A368, 14 m. SW. of Bristol. In 1795 Hannah More started a school in Church St. (now Hannah More Cottage), for which she wrote moral tales. The popularity of these then led to the start of the Religious Tract Society which aided mass literacy. Resistance by some clergy and farmers to the education of the poor resulted in the action known as the Blagdon Controversy (1800–2) which accused Hannah More of allowing her school to be used for Nonconformist meetings.

BLAISE CASTLE. See BRISTOL, suburb of Henbury.

BLAKESWARE. See WIDFORD.

BLASKET ISLANDS, Kerry. [9 Ad] Group of islands off the SW. tip of the Dingle Peninsula, the most westerly point of Europe. The largest, the Great Blasket, was inhabited until the mid 20th c. by a hardy, independent, Irish-speaking line of men and women, whose way of life is vividly described by Robin Flower in *The Western Island* (1944) and in Maurice O'Sullivan's *Twenty Years A-Growing* (1953), Tomás Ó Crohan's *The Islandman* (1937), and Peig Sayers's *An Old Woman's Reflections* (1962), autobiographies written in Irish (later translated) by people born and bred on the island. The population supported themselves by fishing and on the produce of their fields and flocks, but as the islanders made more contact with the mainland, so their numbers diminished by emigration and those that remained found it impossible to make a living. In 1953 the last inhabitants left. The Great Blasket can be visited by curragh from the quay at Dunquin on Blasket Sound, just N. of Dunmore Head, but the island village is deserted and only the wild life remains.

BLATHERWYCKE, Northants. [4 Dd] Village off the A43, 8 m. SW. of Stamford. Thomas Randolph died, aged 30, while on a visit to his friend Anthony Stafford. While in London, Randolph had written 'An Ode to Anthony Stafford to hasten him into the Country' which contains the lines

> Come, spur away
> I have no pleasure for a longer stay,
> But must go down
> And leave the chargeable noise of this great town
>
> > I will the country see
> > Where old simplicity
> > Though hid in gray
> > Dost look more gay
> Than Foppery in plush and scarlet clad.
> > Farewell you city wits that are
> > Almost at civil war—
> 'Tis time that I grow wise, when all the world grows mad.

Randolph is buried in the Stafford family vault in the church, where there is a memorial.

BLENHEIM PALACE. See WOODSTOCK.

BLEWBURY, Oxon. [1 Cc] Village in the downs, a few miles S. of Didcot, on the A417. Kenneth Grahame, who lived here from 1910 to 1924, described it as 'the heart of King Alfred's country', hardly changed since Saxon times except for William the Conqueror's Curfew bell, which still rings during the winter. Grahame's house, Boham's, a Tudor brick farmhouse, can still be seen, but its farmland has been developed as a housing estate.

BLUNDERSTONE. See BLUNDESTON.

BLUNDESTON, Suff. [4 Hd] Village off the B1074, 3¼ m. NW. of Lowestoft, the birthplace of David Copperfield, though Dickens calls the place 'Blunderstone'. The round church tower has been restored as a memorial to the author, though the high-backed pews, from which Clara Peggotty could look through the window and make sure the house was safe during the service, are no longer there. Thomas Gray, who first met the Revd. Norton Nicholls in 1761, used to visit him at the rectory here.

BLUNHAM, Beds. [4 Df] Village off the A1, 2 m. NW. of Sandy. John Donne, rector (1622–31) while also Dean of St. Paul's, paid a yearly visit and stayed in the manor house at the entrance to Park Lane, opposite the church, then used as the rectory. Village tradition tells that he returned to London with a load of cucumbers in his carriage. The church chalice, marked 1626, was Donne's gift.

BLUNTISHAM, Cambs. [4 Ee] Village on the A1123, 3 m. NE. of St. Ives. Dorothy Sayers lived (1898–1917) at her father's Georgian rectory on the main road. In 1916, after university, she published her first verse *Op. 1*, followed two years later by *Catholic Tales*.

BOCKING, Essex. [1 Fa] Village just N. of Braintree. John Gauden was given the living (called a deanery here) in 1641 and retained it throughout the Commonwealth in spite of losing his seat at the Westminster Assembly. He claimed to be the author of *Eikon Basilike*, the account of Charles I's ordeal in 1649, which many thought to be by the King himself.

BODMIN, Cornwall. [2 Ce] County town, on the A30, on the SW. edge of Bodmin Moor. Sir Arthur Quiller-Couch was born here (21 Nov. 1863) in Pool St. (gone). The area is now known as Church Square and a free-standing pillar there, erected on the centenary of his birth, commemorates the site of the house. St. Petroc's Church contains, in the W. end, a replica of part of the Bodmin Gospels as a memorial to Joseph Frank Trewarne Warne, a sub-deacon (d. 1949). This consists of a leather cover holding two pages of written manuscript and one page of illuminated manuscript of the 9th-c. Gospels, now in the British Museum, thought to have been produced by Frankish monks.

BOLDRE, Hants. [1 Be] Village just N. of Lymington, off the A337. Its most celebrated vicar was William Gilpin, whose travels in the New Forest, the Lakes, and Scotland were recorded in *Picturesque Tours* (1882), illustrated by his own drawings. The proceeds of his *Remarks on Forest Scenery* (1791), illustrated by scenes of the New Forest, enabled him to found a school for poor children. He was vicar from 1777 until his death in 1804 and there is a tablet to his memory in the N. chapel and an engraving of his only known portrait at the W. end of the S. aisle. His tomb in the churchyard bears an inscription composed by himself. Southey married his second wife, Caroline Bowles, in Boldre church (1839).

BOLTON ABBEY, North Yorkshire. [5 Dd] Augustinian Priory established on the banks of the Wharfe in 1151. The nave is used as the parish church but the choir and the monastic buildings are now in ruins. Wordsworth, who came here first in 1807, wrote *The White Doe of Rylstone* (1815) about a tradition connected with the area.

BONCHURCH, I.O.W. [1 Cf] Coastal resort on the A3055, 1 m. E. of Ventnor. In 1849 Dickens rented Winterbourne (now a hotel, residents only), a large house on the side of the steep hill overlooking the sea. He had first seen this when staying with his friend the Revd. James White at Woodlynch (now a private hotel). Dickens wrote part of *David Copperfield* here and the story of the donkeys and some incidents from the later novel *Great Expectations* are thought to have originated here (see *Dickens on an Island*, 1970, by Richard J. Hutchings). Dickens's sons played with 'the golden haired lad of the Swinburnes', who lived at East Dene (now a guest house), a little way up the hill. Swinburne, who often signed himself Redgie, spent his childhood and many vacations here until his parents moved in 1868 when he was 31. In his *Letters* he mentions being revived from a faint by a sheep licking his face, after succeeding at the second attempt in scaling the steep Culver Cliff (3 m. NE.). H. de Vere Stacpoole (d. 1951), who lived at Cliff Dene, donated the pond to the village in memory of his wife. He made his name as a novelist with *The Blue Lagoon* (1909). A collection of his poems is called *In a Bonchurch Garden* (1937). Stacpoole and Swinburne are buried in the new church (built 1847). In 1910 Hardy wrote 'A Singer Asleep' by Swinburne's grave.

BONHILL. See ALEXANDRIA.

BOOKHAM. See GREAT BOOKHAM.

BOOTON, Norf. [4 Gd] Village 1 m. E. of Reepham, off the B1145. Whitwell Elwin (1816–1900), born at Thurning Hall, 6 m. NW., was rector (1849–1900). He contributed to the *Quarterly Review*, which he edited from 1853 to 1860. He also edited Pope's works in five volumes (1871–2). The twin-towered Gothic church with carved angels in the roof was built by him after a fire had destroyed the old church.

BORGUE, Kirkcudbrights. (Dumfries and Galloway). [6 Ef] Village on the B727, 4 m. SW. of Kirkcudbright, birthplace of William Nicholson (1782–1849) the pedlar known as the 'Galloway Poet'. Encouragement from Hogg led to the publication of *Tales in Verse and Miscellaneous Poems* (1814). A relief portrait at the school he attended shows him playing the pipes.

BOROUGH FARM, Surrey. [1 Dd] 18th-c. farmhouse now in a Nature Reserve, N. of the A3, 3 m. SW. of Milford. Mrs. Humphry Ward saw the house when staying at Peper Harrow (q.v.) and rented the major part of it (1883–90). Here she wrote her most famous novel *Robert Elsmere* (1888), which Gladstone reviewed.

BORROWDALE, Cumbria. [5 Bb] Valley of the Derwent, one of the most beautiful of the Lake District dales, which runs 5 m. S. from Derwent Water to the village of Seathwaite. Sir Hugh Walpole spent much of the latter part of his life at Brackenburn, an estate on the W. side of the valley, and died there on 1 June 1941. His romantic 'saga' of a Lakeland family, *The Herries Chronicle* (*Rogue Herries*, 1930; *Judith Paris*, 1931; *The Fortress*, 1932; and *Vanessa*, 1933) is set in and around Borrowdale.

BOSBURY, Hereford and Worcester. [3 Ge] Village on the A4154, 4 m. N. of Ledbury. The ashes of Ada Ellen Bayly, who wrote as 'Edna Lyall' and who often stayed with her brother, the vicar, were buried (1903) here. The churchyard is thought to be the one which features in her novel *In Spite of All* (1901).

BOSCASTLE, Cornwall. [2 Cd] Small village on the NW. coast, on the B3263. The little harbour at the foot of the steep main street, and the surrounding cliffs are N.T. property. It figures in Hardy's *A Pair of Blue Eyes* (1873) as 'Castle Boterel'.

BOSCOMBE, Wilts. [1 Bd] Village on the A338, 7 m. NE. of Salisbury. Richard Hooker, rector from 1591 to 1595, was said to have written the first four books of *Laws of Ecclesiastical Polity* in the former vicarage near the Close. However, it is thought that he was resident as a minor prebend in Salisbury at this time.

BOSTON, Lincs. [4 Ec] Port and market town on the Witham. A plaque on the Rum Puncheon Inn states that John Foxe, martyrologist, was born there in 1516. His *Actes and Monuments* (1563), a history of the church, has become known as the Book of Martyrs. St. Botolph's Church, whose tall tower, a landmark in the fens, is popularly known as the Boston Stump, has a stained-glass window commemorating Anne Bradstreet and Jean Ingelow. The former, her husband, and her father were part of the Puritan community who formed the Massachusetts Bay Company in 1629 and planned to settle there. They left in 1630 in the *Arbella*, formerly Kenelm Digby's privateer. Anne was the first English woman to write poetry in America and her verses were published in

London without her knowledge as *The Tenth Muse lately Sprung up in America* (1650). Jean Ingelow was born (1820) in South St. near the Haven bridge. Part of the foundations of her birthplace forms a low wall round a shrub garden in her memory. 'High Tide on the Coast of Lincolnshire 1571' from *Poems* (1863) is one of her most popular ballads. Mark Lemon spent his youth at South Place, the home of his uncle, a hop grower. Some of *Tom Moody's Tales* (1863) and his first novel, about a farmer, stem from his experience here. He left for London in 1836.

BOTALLACK, Cornwall. [2 Af] Old tin-mining village on the extreme W. coast, just over 1 m. N. of St. Just, on the B3306. Wilkie Collins visited the mines during a summer holiday in 1851 and made use of this experience as well as impressions of the surrounding country in his stories (see *Rambles Beyond Railways: or Notes in Cornwall taken A-foot*, 1851). The mines also feature in *Deep Down* (1868), a story by R. M. Ballantyne, who visited in 1868.

BOTHWELL, Lanarks. (Strathclyde). [6 Ed] Village N. of Hamilton on the A74, 12 m. SE. of Glasgow. Joanna Baillie, whose father was the minister, was born here in 1762.

BOTLEY, Hants. [1 Ce] Large village on the A334 and the A3051, just E. of Southampton. William Cobbett lived from 1804 to 1817 at Botley House with 4 acres of productive garden, and he acquired Fairthorn Farm in 1807, and Raglinton the next year. He thought Botley, where he organized single-stick matches, 'the most delightful village in the world', and here he, as the epitome of an Old English yeoman, was a generous host to his many visitors. Cobbett's *Weekly Political Register* was published from 1802 to his death in 1835 and when addressing meetings, he frequently asked the company to drink to it, raising his glass to 'Trash', the name given it by his opponents.

BOUGHTON MALHERBE, Kent. [1 Gd] Small village on a high ridge 2 m. S. of the A20 at Lenham. The early 15th-c. manor (often called Bocton in the past) was the birthplace (1568) of the poet Henry Wotton, younger son of the retired diplomat who was visited here by Queen Elizabeth I when his son was 5. Wotton left to attend Winchester College but later visited his niece and her children here. Walpole mentions the manor in his letters when his friend Galfridus Mann bought the estate in 1750.

BOULGE. See BREDFIELD.

BOURNEMOUTH, Dorset. [1 Af] Large sea-side resort on the A35, set among gardens, pine trees, and steep ravines, where the Bourne enters Poole Bay. The town only came into being in the early 19th c.; when Southey was living at Burton (q.v.) in 1797 he used to walk on Poole Heath, where the town was later built, 'through desolation', but as it began to develop it attracted visitors and residents who came to enjoy the beautiful scenery and benign climate. John Keble, author of *The Christian Year* (1827), came here for his wife's health in the winter of 1865/6 and stayed at Brookside, a boarding-house in Exeter Lane, from which he used to walk daily across the Pleasure Gardens to morning service at St. Peter's. He died here in March 1866 and is commemorated by a memorial window in the S. transept (now Keble Chapel) of St. Peter's. Disraeli came for a visit (Nov. 1874–Jan. 1875) on Queen Victoria's recommendation of 'the very salubrious air' and stayed at the Bath Hotel. While considering the New Year's Honours he wrote to the Queen recommending a baronetcy for Tennyson and the Grand Cross of the Bath, with a pension, for Carlyle, then 'old and childless and poor . . . but very popular and respected by the nation'. The Queen agreed, but Tennyson and Carlyle both declined (the former was persuaded by Gladstone to accept a peerage 10 years later). Francis Kilvert visited in the winter of 1875, but unfortunately the volume of his *Diary* (1870–9) for this period is missing. Later he wrote of 'wild sad sweet trysts in the snow and under the pine trees, among the sandhills on the East Cliff and in Boscombe Chine'. In September 1876 Paul Verlaine came to teach French and Latin at St. Aloysius' School, a small Catholic school run by the Revd. Frederick Remington (now 24 Surrey Rd.). He lived with Mr. Remington and his wife and sister at 2 Westburn Ter. (now part of the Sandbourne Hotel in Poole Rd.) and out of school hours he wrote much poetry, notably 'La mer est plus belle . . .' (originally 'La Mer de Bourne-mouth') and 'Bournemouth', the impression of the town which appeared later in *Amour* (1888). Many other poems written at this time were published in *Sagesse* (1881), *Amour, Bonheur* (1891), and *Liturges Intimes* (1892). He left at Easter 1877, with a 'splendid testimonial' (see his account of the time in the *Fortnightly Review*, July 1894). Max Beerbohm drew a cartoon of him (1904) with his scholars as he imagined them in 1877. Galsworthy was at a prep school (1876–81) called Saugeen, near St. Swithun's Church, where he sang in the choir. He travelled to and from his home in Surrey with Joseph Ramsden, his father's confidential clerk, the original of Soames Forsyte's clerk, Thomas Gradman, in *To Let* (1921). R. L. Stevenson came to Bourne-mouth in August 1884 and after staying at various addresses finally (Apr. 1885–Aug. 1887) dug himself in 'like a weevil in a biscuit' at Skerryvore in Alum Chine Rd. The site of the house (demolished by enemy bombing in 1940) is now a memorial garden, opposite the end of R. L. Stevenson Ave., containing a model of the Skerryvore Light-house, copied from the original built by the Stevenson family firm on the Argyll coast. During his 3 years in Bournemouth Steven-son published *A Child's Garden of Verses*, *More Arabian Nights*, and *Prince Otto* (1885); *The Strange Case of Dr. Jekyll and Mr. Hyde* and *Kidnapped* (1886); and *The Merry Men* and *Underwoods* (1887). In 1887 he left for the South Seas and made his home in Samoa for the rest of his life. Olive Schreiner, whose best-known work, *The Story of an African Farm*, was published in 1883, stayed here from February to April 1886, but her visit was clouded by illness. John Eglinton (pseudonym of William Kirkpatrick Magee, 1868–1961), friend and intended biographer of George Moore, was closely associated, with Joyce, Yeats, and 'AE' (George William Russell), with the Irish literary movement. While living at Bournemouth he wrote *Irish Literary Portraits* (1935) and edited *Letters of George Moore* (1942). He also wrote a memoir of 'AE' (1937), who came here in his last years and died on 17 July 1935. John Eglinton appears in Moore's auto-biographical *Hail and Farewell* (1911–14) and in Joyce's *Ulysses* (1922).

In St. Peter's churchyard an impressive tombstone marks the grave of Mary Shelley (author of the enduringly popular *Franken-stein*, 1818, a horror story written while on holiday in Switzerland), buried with Shelley's heart, which had been saved from the funeral pyre after his drowning at Viareggio, and with her parents, William Godwin, author of *Political Justice* (1793) and Mary Wollstonecraft Godwin, author of *A Vindica-tion of the Rights of Women* (1792), their bodies having been brought here from St. Pancras churchyard in 1851. In Hardy's *Tess of the d'Urbervilles* (1891) Bournemouth figures as 'Sandbourne', a 'fashionable watering-place, with its eastern and western stations, its piers, its groves of pine, its promenades, and its covered gardens'.

BOWDEN, Roxburghs. (Borders). [6 Gd] Vil-lage on the B6398, 2 m. S. of Melrose and 6 m. E. of Selkirk (N. of the A699). The poet Thomas Aird was born here (1802), under the shadow of the Eildon Hills, and educated first by his father and then at the village school before going on to study in Edinburgh.

BOWDON, Greater Manchester. [3 Ga] Dis-trict adjacent to Altrincham, on the A556, *c.* 10 m. SW. of Manchester. Mrs. Juliana Horatia Ewing, writer of books for children, came here from Aldershot in 1877 and stayed 1½ years while her husband, Major Ewing, was stationed at Manchester. They lived in the higher part of the town in a semi-detached house which Mrs. Ewing refers to as Downs Villa (one of a pair called Downs Villas), now 14 Higher Downs. Mrs. Ewing, who began by writing stories for *Aunt Judy's Magazine* (started by her mother, Mrs. Gatty), had recently made her name with three long novels written in army quarters at Aldershot: *A Flat Iron for a Farthing* (1870–1), *Six to Sixteen* (1872), and *The Miller's Thumb* (1872–3; later published as *Jan of the Windmill*, 1876).

BOWEN'S COURT, Cork. [9 Dd] Former 18th-c. mansion, home of the Bowen family who were granted land by Cromwell, 1½ m. W. of Kildorrery on the T38 and NW. of Farahy village. Elizabeth Bowen was brought up here but went to school in England. She inherited the house from her father in 1928 and wrote its history *Bowen's Court* (1942). In 1952, after her husband's death, she returned to live here but the house was too large for her and she sold it in 1960 to a neighbour. He later demolished it.

BOWES, North Yorkshire. [5 Db] Village on the A66 and the A67, 4 m. SW. of Barnard Castle. The boarding-school run by William Shaw was one of the places visited by Charles Dickens, when investigating the conditions of pupils housed and taught for the pittance paid by their parents and guardians. Shaw, though no worse than many school owners, becomes Wackford Squeers in *Nicholas Nickleby* (1838–9). His school (now apartments) was the last building in the main street W. of the village, where through the courtyard, a pump, such as described by Dickens at Dotheboys Hall, can still be seen.

BOX HILL, Surrey. [1 Ed] Wooded down (N.T.) E. of the A24, 2 m. NE. of Dorking, named from the box trees once prevalent there. Jane Austen, who probably visited from Great Bookham (q.v.), chose the hill for the scene in *Emma* (1816) of one of Mrs. Elton's 'exploring parties'. This was even more unsuccessful than the picnic at Donwell as everyone was upset by someone and Emma was unkind to Miss Bates. In a letter from Burford Bridge (q.v.), Keats wrote that he 'went up Box Hill this evening after the moon'.

BRADENHAM, Bucks. [1 Db] Village with a large green off the A4010, where Isaac D'Israeli wrote *Curiosities of Literature* (1791). His son Benjamin Disraeli described the Manor and 'the glade-like terrace of yew trees' in the gardens[1] with poetic licence in *Endymion* (1880).

[1] Open occasionally for N.G.S.

BRADFIELD COMBUST, Suff. [4 Ff] Village on the A134, 5 m. SE. of Bury St. Edmunds. Arthur Young (1741–1820), the agricultural theorist, lived at Bradfield Hall (rebuilt 1857), which was described by Fanny Burney, a relative, in *Camilla* (1796). She also wrote in her *Diary* (1842) how wretched Young's life was made by his wife, whose language was violent and whose face was so red she looked like a fiend.

BRAINTREE, Essex. [1 Fa] Formerly a wool town, now a nylon weaving centre on the A131 and the A120. Nicholas Udall (or Uvedale), vicar here from 1537 to 1544, was the author of the earliest-known English comedy, *Ralph Roister Doister*, printed in 1566, but probably first acted by the boys at Eton, where Udall was a harsh headmaster from 1534 to 1541, when he was dismissed for misconduct.

BRAMPTON, Cambs. [4 De] Village between the A604 and the A1, 2 m. W. of Huntington. Pepys House,[1] on the E. outskirts of the village, was the home of Samuel Pepys's uncle, a cousin of Lord Sandwich, through which connection Pepys had his post at the Admiralty. Pepys's father lived here on his brother's death and Pepys in his *Diary* mentions his visits here.

[1] Open if owner at home: weekdays 11.30 a.m.– 12.30 p.m. and 3–4 p.m. Appointments can be made.

BRANTWOOD, Cumbria. [5 Bc] House and 200-acre estate $1\frac{1}{2}$ m. from the head of Coniston Water, on the E. shore, on an unclassified road off the B5285, the home of John Ruskin from 13 September 1872 until the end of his life (20 Jan. 1900). In the summer of 1871 when he was recovering from a serious illness he heard that Brantwood was for sale and bought it at once without even seeing it. When he came to inspect the property in September he found 'a mere shed of rotten timber and loose stone', but the view was splendid, 'on the whole', he said, 'the finest I know in Cumberland or Lancashire', and he put in hand extensive repairs, enabling him to occupy his new home the following year. From now on his time was full of intense activity: tours, lectures, writing, sketching. In 1871 when he began *Fors Clavigera*, a series of monthly letters 'to the Workmen and Labourers of Great Britain', he decided to publish the work himself and by 1873 had transferred all his books to George Allen, a carpenter-wood engraver who became sole publisher, acting directly under him and greatly improving the style and appearance of his works. In 1885 Ruskin began *Praeterita*, his autobiography, and with its completion (on a diminished scale from the original plan) in 1889 his literary and artistic work ended. The house, now owned by Education Trust Ltd., is used as an adult residential centre and contains a large number of pictures by Ruskin and his contemporaries together with some of his furniture and part of his library. Also on view are his boat and coach and the harbour which he built with some of his friends. A nature trail through the grounds is divided into three sections, each returning via Ruskin's stone seat overlooking a small waterfall.

Open Sun.–Fri. 10 a.m.–5.30 p.m. (1 Nov.–1 Mar. by appointment only); closed Sat.

BRAY, Wicklow. [9 Ha] Busy town and seaside resort 13 m. SE. of Dublin on the T7. James Joyce's family home from 1888 to 1891 was 1 Martello Ter., next to a disused public bath-house, one of a row of three-storeyed balconied houses at right angles to the Promenade at the far end from Bray Head. Joyce's father had settled here in the hope, as he used to say, that the train fare would keep his wife's relatives away. It was here that the young Joyce used to spend his school holidays from Clongoweswood College (q.v.) and his memories of the surrounding area, the sea and the high sea wall, and the walks round Bray Head, were used in the early part of his autobiographical novel *A Portrait of the Artist as a Young Man* (1914–15). The dining-room, where Joyce was first allowed to join his elders for dinner while the younger brothers and sisters waited in the nursery, was the setting for the famous Christmas dinner and the fierce argument over Parnell.

BREACHWOOD GREEN, Herts. [1 Da] Village on an unclassified road between Whitwell and Luton, 2 m. S. of King's Walden. The Baptist Chapel has John Bunyan's pulpit, dated 1658 (originally at near-by Coleman's Green, Bendish). Near the pulpit is a copy of the Geneva Bible (the 'Breeches Bible', 1562), described as 'the Bible of Shakespeare, Milton, Bunyan, and Cromwell . . . [translated by Puritan scholars who fled from this country to Geneva when Mary came to the throne]'.

BREDE, East Sussex. [1 Ge] Village on the A28, 6 m. N. of Hastings. The church, which was presented with Swift's cradle by the vicar in 1895, is opposite the lane to Brede Place (1 m.), a 14th-c. manor with Elizabethan alterations. The American Stephen Crane, author of *The Red Badge of Courage* (1895), and Lady Stewart (Cora), rented it in January 1899 after his visit to

Cuba. The rambling house was damp and unmodernized and Crane, who was consumptive, became gravely ill. Visitors, who included Conrad and Henry James, found Cora cheerful until the end of the year, when she took Crane abroad. He died soon after and was buried in the family grave in New Jersey.

BREDFIELD, Suff. [4 Hf] Village 3 m. N. of Woodbridge, off the A12. Edward FitzGerald was born (1809) at The White House (later Bredfield House and then demolished), and he lived until 1838 with his parents at Boulge Hall (1 m. E.; burnt 1923 and demolished 1946) of which only the stables near Boulge church remain. Boulge can be reached by a concrete track leading off the Debach road. FitzGerald then lived (1838–58) in the single-storeyed thatched cottage (now Boulge House, altered) where many of his friends visited him. He is buried in Boulge churchyard where the latest successor of the rose tree from the tomb of Omar Khayyám, planted by his friends in the Omar Khayyám Club in 1893, grows over his grave.

BREDON, Hereford and Worcester. [1 Aa] Village on the B4080, 3 m. NE. of Tewkesbury. The church, dating from c. 1180, has a tall, graceful spire, immortalized by Masefield in 'All the land from Ludlow Town / To Bredon Church's spire'. In A. E. Housman's 'In summertime on Bredon' (*A Shropshire Lad*, xxi) the bells ring out over Bredon Hill, which rises 2½ m. E. The village is the setting for John Moore's novel, *Brensham Village* (1946).

BREDWARDINE, Hereford and Worcester. [3 Fe] Village on the B4352, 12 m. NW. of Hereford. Francis Kilvert was vicar here from 1877 until his death 2 years later. His grave in the churchyard is marked with a white marble cross. Selections from the notebooks which he kept from 1870 were published in three volumes (*Diary*, ed. William Plomer, 1938–40; new edn. 1969).

BREGOG RIVER. See AWBEG RIVER.

BREMHILL, Wilts. [1 Ac] Village off the A4, 4 m. E. of Chippenham. The poet, William Lisle Bowles, vicar from 1804 to 1850, lived at the 17th-c. vicarage, now Bremhill Court.

31

Thomas Moore, a frequent visitor, wrote that Bowles 'had frittered away its beauty with grottos, hermitages, and Shenstonian inscriptions'. Lamb and Wordsworth stayed with Bowles at the house which he Gothicized. His verse included epitaphs on some of the parishioners, and a poem on the planting of the two cedars in the churchyard.

BRENSHAM VILLAGE. See BREDON.

BRENTHAM. See TRENTHAM GARDENS.

BRIARFIELD. See BIRSTALL.

BRIDEKIRK, Cumbria. [5 Aa] Small village 2 m. N. of Cockermouth, on a minor road off the A595. Thomas Tickell, poet and editor of Addison's works, was born (1686) at the vicarage.

BRIDGNORTH, Salop. [3 Gd] Old market town on the A442 and the A458, picturesquely situated on the Severn, which divides it into the Low Town on the E. bank and the High Town on the W., connected by a steep winding road (the Cartway), flights of steps, and a short inclined railway. The town's earliest literary association is the Hermitage legend (recorded in *The Reliquary*, Oct. 1878) concerning Ethelward (d. 924), brother of King Athelstan and grandson of Alfred the Great. Tradition has it that Ethelward, known only for his love of literature, retired from the world and lived with his books in some sandstone caves till his death. His retreat was originally entered through a small door and seems to have consisted of four rock chambers, one apparently a chapel. The caves can be reached by a footpath near the top of Hermitage Hill on the right side of the A454 above the Low Town (there is parking space over the brow of the hill). Traces of gable roofing and brick-work indicate other caves that were still used for human habitation in the late 19th c. In the High Town near St. Leonard's Church is the small black-and-white timbered house (P) where 'the learned and eloquent' Richard Baxter lived when he was assistant minister. He dedicated *The Saint's Everlasting Rest* (1650) to the people of Bridgnorth. Thomas Percy was born (1729) in a handsome house (now a boys' club) near the bridge, his home until 1756, formerly called Foster's or Forester's Folly, now Bishop Percy's

House. He was baptized at St. Leonard's Church and at eight went to Bridgnorth School, then in the School Building (the predecessor of the present Old Grammar School erected 1784) in the High Churchyard. His publication of *Reliques of Ancient English Poetry* (1765) was instigated by his discovery of an old manuscript, containing ballads, songs, and metrical romances, in the house of Humphrey Pitt in Shifnal. The books of the Stackhouse Library, formerly housed in the vestry of St. Leonard's, were found to be affected with damp in the 1960s and were transferred to the County Library at Shrewsbury, but Bishop Heber's chair, where he used to write his well-known hymns, is still in the vestry and may be seen by arrangement with the churchwardens.

BRIDGWATER, Som. [2 Gc] Market town on the A38 and the A39, where Coleridge often stayed with John Chubb, a merchant, whose house (gone) was on the riverside. Coleridge preached in 1797 and 1798 at Christ Church, the Unitarian Chapel (locked) in Dampiet St. The (Admiral) Blake Museum near by has paintings of the town by John Chubb. In 1807 De Quincey, who had expected to find Coleridge at Tom Poole's house in Nether Stowey, rode to Bridgwater and met Coleridge in the main street. He gave him a rare Latin pamphlet when they arrived at Chubb's house. Coleridge talked far into the night, dwelling on the horror of the opium habit. De Quincey thought it a strange conversation for a first meeting, and on his ride back through the night decided to arrange for £300 to be given to Coleridge from 'an unknown friend'.

BRIDLINGTON, Humberside. [5 Hd] Coastal resort on the A165 and the A166. Charlotte Brontë and her friend Ellen Nussey hoped to spend a holiday by the sea here in 1839, but Ellen's brother Henry arranged their accommodation with his friends at Easton House Farm, 2 miles inland. However, the young women walked to Burlington, as Bridlington was then called, and Charlotte Brontë was so overcome at her first sight of the sea that she burst into tears and had to sit down. 'Our visit to Easton was extremely pleasant' she wrote, and she especially enjoyed the final week when her host and hostess arranged for their stay in lodgings on the cliff opposite the pier (now the Esplanade). She visited Easton again after her sister Anne's death (1849) and funeral at Scarborough, and for solace spent many hours writing her novel *Shirley* (1849) in the summer-house.

BRIDPORT, Dorset. [2 Gd] Small town on the A35, 15 m. W. of Dorchester and 1½ m. N. of its little harbour at West Bay. It appears as 'Port Bredy' in Hardy's Wessex novels.

BRIERY CLOSE, Cumbria. [5 Bb] Large house and estate (now a stud farm) c. 1¾ m. SE. of Ambleside, on a narrow road leading up from the A591, near the Low-wood Hotel on the NE. shore of Lake Windermere. It was formerly the home of Sir James and Lady Kaye-Shuttleworth, where Charlotte Brontë was staying when Mrs. Gaskell first met her, in August 1850. The meeting is vividly described in Mrs. Gaskell's *Letters* (1966).

BRIGHTON, East Sussex. [1 Ee] Large resort on the S. coast, formerly the fishing village of Brighthelmstone, chosen by the Prince Regent for his home and subsequently fashionable. Dr. Johnson was so much a part of the Thrale household that he usually accompanied them in the 1770s to their seaside home in West St. Their house was replaced by a concert hall (where Dickens gave some of his readings) which lost favour when the Dome was opened, and is now a dance hall (P erected by the Regency Society). Dr. Johnson worked on the *Lives of the Poets* here and Mrs. Thrale read the proofs. Fanny Burney also stayed with the Thrales and her *Diary* records her visits to Shergolds or the New Assembly Rooms in the Castle Inn (gone) in Castle Sq. (site now the Electricity showroom). They also went to the Assembly Rooms, known as Hicks, attached to the Old Ship in Ship St. Mr. Thrale played cards and his wife and Fanny Burney danced. In the mornings they patronized Mr. Thomas's bookshop on the Steine. The Thrales and their guests attended St. Nicholas's Church, where a tablet to Dr. Johnson is on a N. wall window-ledge.

In 1791, Wordsworth, waiting for a boat to France, called on Mrs. Charlotte Smith, whose nostalgic descriptions of the countryside he had admired in her *Elegiac Sonnets* bought at Cambridge two years before. Her last volume *Beachy Head and Other Poems* (1807) appeared posthumously. One of

Robert Anderson's sonnets in *Poetical Works* (1820) was addressed to Charlotte Smith. Charles and Mary Lamb spent a holiday here in 1817 'in sight of the sea' with their friends the Morgans. Dickens stayed here many times from 1837, at the Old Ship, at 148 Kings Rd., and at 62 East St. He also stayed at the Bedford Hotel (P) in 1848, when writing *Dombey and Son* (1847-8), where he lodged Captain Cuttle and other characters. Dr. Blimber's school is said to have been at Chichester House, Chichester Ter. His friend Harrison Ainsworth spent many months here with his family in the 1840s, first at 38 Brunswick Ter., then at 25 Oriental Pl. He and Dickens visited Horace Smith at 12 Cavendish Pl., where the Misses Smith welcomed their father's literary friends, including Thackeray, Thomas Hood, and Samuel Rogers. Smith was contributing to Ainsworth's *New Monthly Magazine*. Thackeray gave his lecture on 'The Four Georges' at the Town Hall in 1851. Ainsworth was at 6 Brunswick Sq. while alterations were made to Kensal Manor. Then (1853-67) he moved to 5 Arundel Ter. (P), where he wrote *Cardinal Pole* (1863) and *Constable de Bourbon* (1866).

Robert Surtees, whose sporting Cockney grocer, John Jorrocks, enjoyed himself on the Downs, died in Brighton (1864) but was buried at his family home. Richard Jefferies lived here for a short time (1885) at 5 (now 87) Lorna Rd., Hove, adjoining Brighton to the W. Thomas Hughes died here in 1896 and Herbert Spencer died at 5 Percival Ter. in 1903. A. E. Coppard (1872-1957), who went to the Board School in Fairlight Pl., leaving at the age of 9, lived with his parents in lodgings in Melbourne St. and Gladstone Pl. When he worked as a book-keeper at the Engineering Works near the barracks, he educated himself at the former public library. He married here in 1906. The short stories 'Ninepenny Flute' and 'Pomona's Babe' are about Brighton, although written after he left in 1907. John Cowper Powys taught at a girls' school in the west of the town for a short time. Conan Doyle's *Rodney Stone* (1896) and Thackeray's *Vanity Fair* (1847-8) have scenes of Regency Brighton; Henry James's short story 'Sir Edmund Orme', Arnold Bennett's *Clayhanger* (1910) and its sequel *Hilda Lessways* (1911), Maugham's *Of Human Bondage* (1915), and A. S. M. Hutchinson's

If Winter Comes (1920) also have scenes set here.

Ivy Compton-Burnett lived in Hove from 1892 to 1916. In 1897 her parents and their large family moved to 20 The Drive, a mid-Victorian double-fronted house. She published her first novel *Dolores* in 1911 and five years later moved to the first of her London flats.

BRIG O'TURK. See GLEN FINGLAS.

BRINKLEY, Cambs. [4 Ff] Village on the B1052, 5 m. S. of Newmarket. Christopher Anstey, poet and satirist, was born (1724) at the rectory, at the end of Lammas Lane, near the Hall.

BRINSOP, Hereford and Worcester. [3 Fe] Village on the A480, 6 m. NW. of Hereford. Dorothy and William Wordsworth sometimes stayed with his wife's brother at Brinsop Court (1 m. N.), and when there in 1843, their maid and friend, Jane, fell ill and died. Wordsworth's poems on Bishopstone and Ledbury (qq.v.) were written here. The Revd. Francis Kilvert came over from Bredwardine (q.v.) in 1879. In his *Diary* (1938–40; new edn. 1969), he mentions 'the grand old manor house and the lawn and the two snow-white swans on the flowing water of the Moat'. He also saw the cedar on the lawn planted by Wordsworth.

BRISTOL, Avon. [2 Hb] Cathedral and university city, and port on the Avon:

> . . . a street of masts
> And pennants from all nations of the earth,
> Streaming below the houses, piled aloft
> Hill above hill; . . .

wrote William Bowles in *Banwell Hill* (1829) when both the Avon and the Frome were crowded city waterways.

Pepys's *Diary* tells of his visit in 1668 with his wife, and her servant Deb (born in Marsh St.). Deb's uncle, a merchant, took Pepys to the Customs House in Queen Sq. and entertained them afterwards with venison, strawberries, and Bristol Milk. Burke, whose statue stands in the Centre, stayed in 1774 during his successful month-long election campaign at 19 Queen Sq., the house built by Capt. Rogers, commander of the ships *Duke* and *Duchess*. Rogers's *Voyage Round the World* (1712) relates the rescue of Alexander Selkirk from his 'Robinson Crusoe' existence. Coleridge lodged at 2 Queen Sq. when

lecturing. The Customs House and half Queen Sq. were burned in the 1831 riots and rebuilt. Crabbe in Clifton, and Charles Kingsley at school in St. Michael's Hill, witnessed the great fires. Kingsley came back in 1858 and gave a graphic account to the Mechanics' Institute. Coleridge and Southey lectured at the Assembly Rooms Coffee House (gone) in Prince St.

Defoe, whose *Tour through Great Britain* (1724–7) brought him to Bristol, is said to have met Selkirk in Ye Llandoger Trow, the old tavern in King St. and to have based *Robinson Crusoe* (1719) on his adventures. The Almshouses for Merchant Seamen was the home for some years of a Mr. Williams whose manuscript about the experiences of a young sailor marooned on a W. Indian island for 27 years was published after his death as *The Journal of Llewellin Penrose* (1815). Byron wrote that Penrose 'kept me up half the night, and made me dream of him the other half. It has all the air of truth, and is most entertaining.'

The Theatre Royal in King St. opened in 1766 with Steele's *The Conscious Lovers* for which Garrick wrote the Prologue. Sarah Siddons often acted here and Elizabeth Inchbald, novelist and dramatist, made her début as an actress in 1772 as Cordelia. Combe's *The Flattering Milliner* played here in 1775. Macready, whose father leased the theatre in 1819, often acted here, his last performance being in 1850. It is now the Bristol Old Vic, the interior having been altered. The Bristol Library in King St. (now an Employment Office) was where Coleridge, Southey, and Landor read, and the registers they signed can be seen at the Central Library. Maria Edgeworth was unable to get a ticket, though her father was a reader, as 'No ladies go to the Library'.

Thomas Chatterton (1752–70) 'the Marvellous Boy' was born at the Schoolhouse[1] in Pile St., now Redcliffe Way. He spent many hours in St. Mary Redcliffe Church, where his uncle was sexton, reading in the muniment room over the N. porch the old manuscripts which inspired his medieval-style poems. He started writing these while still at school and managed to sell some under the name of a fictitious 15th-c. monk, Thomas Rowley. At 15 he went to Corn St. as a scrivener and, as his indentures allowed him only one hour's absence in the day, it was there that he wrote the Rowley poems. But the recognition he craved never came. His satirical Will written after a dispute with his employer caused the cancelling of his indentures and at 17 he set out for London with a small subscription from his friends. A memorial was put up in the church in 1967 but his statue in the long gown of a Colston schoolboy is no longer on the green. The Colston Hall now stands on the site of his old school. More attention was paid to the question of the authenticity of Rowley's poems (1777) than to their merit. Johnson and Boswell made a special visit to look into the matter 'upon the spot' 6 years after Chatterton had died in poverty. Cottle and Southey published the *Collected Works* (1803) to help Chatterton's family. Two sisters married in St. Mary Redcliffe in 1795, Sara Fricker to Coleridge in October, and Edith to Southey in November. After some months in Clevedon the Coleridges rented rooms in Redcliffe Hill where Sara had lived before her marriage.

Southey was born (1774) in Wine St. and spent his boyhood at no. 9 (gone). A plaque is fixed where the new buildings join Christ Church. The Plume of Feathers where Coleridge gave lectures has also gone. The narrow junction here was once the main crossroads and Pepys mentions the old cross there, now at Stourhead, being 'like the one at Cheapside'.

Chatterton was an apprentice opposite the Exchange in Corn St. in 1767. Lloyds Bank is on the site of the Bush Inn where Burke's election-day celebrations took place and where Dickens's Mr. Winkle stayed while searching for Arabella Allen.

Richard Savage, befriended by Johnson, who wrote his life, died (1743) in poverty in the prison (gone) in Newgate, and was buried in the bombed churchyard of St. Peter's near by. His instability thwarted his wellwishers as Pope complained to him in a letter in 1742.

Joseph Cottle, poet, publisher, and friend of Southey, Coleridge, and Wordsworth, had his bookshop (gone) on the corner of Corn St. and High St., where they all visited him. He gave Southey and Coleridge advances on their poems which enabled them to marry, and when Southey sailed for Portugal he left his wife with Cottle and his sisters. Coleridge often used Cottle's address for his correspondence and tickets for his and Southey's lectures could be bought at his shop. Southey

never forgot Cottle's kindness and years later recalled how he was indebted to him even for his wedding ring. Wordsworth, whose 'Tintern Abbey' lines were not written down until he and Dorothy reached Bristol, took them at once to Cottle and finished them in his parlour. After the failure of the Pantisocracy scheme, Coleridge planned *The Watchman*, his short-lived periodical, from the Rummer Tavern near the flower market entrance in High St.

The Bishop's Palace near the Cathedral, where Addison stayed with his old schoolfriend Bishop Smallridge in 1718, was burned down in the 1831 riots; only a 14th-c. doorway near the Chapter House remains.

Hakluyt was made a prebend of the Cathedral in 1586 having already published two books of his Voyages (1582 and 1587). His *Principall Navigations* followed (1589 and 1598). Sydney Smith occupied the same prebendal stall in 1828. His house (gone) in Lower College Green, he wrote to Lady Holland, was large enough to take her entourage as he had a seven-stall stable and room for four carriages. He could see the masts of the East Indiamen from his window. In the Cathedral the silver candlesticks in the E. Lady Chapel were a thanksgiving gift after the safe return in 1711 of the two ships *Duke* and *Duchess*. In the E. cloister is the memorial stone to Sterne's correspondent Eliza Draper (d. 1778). When William Mason's wife died in 1767, their friend Gray added the last lines to her epitaph in the N. aisle. Lady Hesketh, Cowper's cousin to whom he wrote many of his *Letters* (1803), is buried in the Cathedral. Southey wrote the inscription for the memorial to Bishop Butler in the N. transept. His own bust, to which his friend Landor contributed, stands in the N. choir aisle near the tablet to Hakluyt.

No. 48 College St. where Coleridge and Southey lodged before their marriages is now a garage (the plaque once there has gone). De Quincey refers to the unsolved murders of Mrs. Ruscombe and her maid on College Green in his essay 'Murder considered as one of the Fine Arts' in *Blackwoods* (1827).

St. Mark's, the Lord Mayor's Chapel, at the foot of Park St. has some French and Flemish glass from Fonthill Abbey (q.v.), collected by Beckford on his travels. The large window at the E. of the S. aisle was designed by Benjamin West for the Becket room.

Hannah More, whose first school that she ran with her sisters started in Trinity St., moved in 1762 when Park St. was being built, into no. 43, where the new shop on the site has a commemorative inscription over the doorway. She helped Burke, who visited her there, with his election campaign. One pupil was 'Perdita' Robinson, the actress and novelist, who was born at the Old Minster house (gone).

Wordsworth first met Coleridge at 7 Great George St., now the Georgian House Museum.[2] This was the home of John Pinney, a W. Indies sugar merchant, who lent the Wordsworths Racedown Lodge (q.v.) and with whom they often stayed.

F. J. Fargus, author (under the pen-name Hugh Conway) of many songs and the popular novel Called Back (1885), was born in Bristol in 1847. Ambrose Bierce lived here during 1872, writing the sardonic sketches published in The Fiend's Delight and Nuggets and Dust in 1873.

[1] Open Wed. and Sat. 3–5 p.m.
[2] Open weekdays 11 a.m.–5 p.m.

Suburbs:

Clifton, to the W., was considered a health resort in the 18th and 19th centuries. Maria Edgeworth lodged in Princes Buildings in 1791 with her family as her young brother Lovell was consumptive. They walked on the Downs near by hunting for fossils. She came again in 1799 and some of her children's stories in The Parent's Assistant (1796–1800) and Moral Tales (1806) were set in Bristol. Her nephew Thomas Lovell Beddoes was born (1803) at 3 Rodney Pl., where a plaque also commemorates Humphry Davy's stay in the house. Lady Hesketh (d. 1807) wrote some of her last letters to her cousin Cowper (d. 1800) from Clifton Hill, where she spent many months during the last decade of her life. Harriet and Sophia Lee, authors of popular romances, lived in Clifton for many years. Sophia came here after retiring from her school in Bath in 1803. The last stories in their joint Canterbury Tales (1805) were written by her. They were buried in the parish church of St. Andrew's on Clifton Hill (bombed and later demolished) and commemorated by wall tablets.

York Hotel (gone) in Gloucester Pl., overlooking the Downs and Leigh Woods, was where the exploring party in Northanger Abbey (1818) dined on their abortive visit to Blaise Castle. It was closed by 1819. Mrs. Piozzi stayed for some months before her death in 1821 at 10 Sion Row near the Avon gorge. This house was one belonging to Mrs. Rudd, mother of the young actor William Conway, whom Mrs. Piozzi was befriending during his unhappy love affair. His situation was made more appealing by his belief that he was the son of a lord. Mrs. Rudd was having 36 Royal York Cres., a larger house with fine views, prepared for Mrs. Piozzi but it was not ready in time. Her will was, however, read there to her daughters who were with their mother when she died.

The frail Hannah More (d. 1833), imposed on by her servants at Barley Wood, came to spend her last years in Windsor Ter. Macaulay stayed at 16 Caledonia Pl. (P) in 1832 and Frances Trollope, mother of Anthony Trollope and herself author of over a hundred books, lived at no. 7 in 1843. Dickens, in 1851, brought a group of friends including Douglas Jerrold, John Forster, Mark Lemon, and Wilkie Collins to the Victoria Rooms, where they acted Lytton's Not so Bad as We Seem and Mr. Nightingale's Diary to such an enthusiastic audience that they repeated the performance. J. Addington Symonds, born (1840) at 7 Berkeley Sq., moved to Clifton Hill House (built 1749) as a boy and it remained his family home until 1880. He spent an increasing time abroad as he was consumptive but he was at 7 Victoria Sq. for some time after giving up his London home in 1868 until he moved back to Clifton Hill House after his father's death in 1871. He left finally in 1880 and writes (Letters, 1907) of the difficulty of clearing up accumulations of family papers. He wrote of his home in his essay 'Clifton and a Lad's Love', published in In the Key of Blue (1893). Clifton Hill House is now a university residential hall. The Manx poet T. E. Brown was a housemaster at the new Clifton College from 1864 to 1893, and it was here that he wrote the tales of Manx men and women, Betsy Lee (1873) and Fo'c's'le Yarns (1881). The lines in 'Clifton'

I'm here at Clifton grinding at the mill
My feet for thrice nine barren years have trod,
But there are rocks and waves at Scarlett still,
And gorse runs riot in Glen Chass—thank God.

show that his native island had strong ties for him, but one of the three places he asks a friend to visit for him after his death, is the Clifton gorge. In 'Epistola ad Dakyns' he writes:

> There come, and pause upon the edge,
> And I will lean on every ledge,
> And melt in grays and flash in whites,
> And linger in a thousand lights;
> And you shall feel an inner sense,
> A being kindred and intense;
> And you shall feel a strict control,
> A something drawing at your soul,
> A going out, a life suspended,
> A spirit with a spirit blended.
> And you shall start as from a dream,
> While I, withdrawing down the stream,
> Drift vaporous to the ancient sea,
> A wraith, a film, a memory—

Brown had retired to the Isle of Man but died here on a visit in 1897 and he was buried in the cemetery at Redland Green Chapel (1 m. NE.) where the tombstone also commemorates his wife and his young son. Quiller-Couch, Newbolt, who wrote the poem 'Clifton Chapel', and Robert Hichens, who also lived in Bristol, were pupils at Clifton in the 1870s, and Joyce Cary in the early years of this century.

Fishponds, to the NE. Hannah More, whose popular poems and dramas provided the money for her philanthropy, was born in the house (P) near the church, facing the park. Her father was a schoolmaster, and she and her elder sisters opened a successful school in the centre of the town.

Henbury, to the NW. Blaise Castle, an 18th-c. Gothic ruin in the grounds of Blaise Castle House (built 1795), now a Folk Museum,[1] was the place the young people in Jane Austen's *Northanger Abbey* hoped to visit but lacked time. In 1774 Burke stayed with Richard Champion here during the election campaign. He admired the view from the dining-room so much that it was afterwards called Burke's window.

[1] Open Mar.–Nov.: weekdays 2–4.30 or 5.30 p.m.; Sun. 3–4.30 or 5 p.m.

Hotwells, to the W., where the curative spring was discovered at the foot of St. Vincent's Rocks on the N. bank of the Avon, and the pump and assembly rooms rose dramatically from the water. The diarist Evelyn described climbing about on the rocks in 1654 looking for Bristol diamonds, the crystals that Spenser called adamants. Addison wrote to Swift of his visit in 1718

and Pope came in November 1739 and described the 'vast rock of an hundred feet of red, white, green, blue and yellowish marble' in his *Letters* to Martha Blount. William Combe (1741–1823) was born in Bristol and often visited Hotwells. He wrote a poem to Clifton and *The Philosopher in Bristol* (1775). He was known as Count Combe for his ostentatious living which resulted in many years spent in a debtors' prison. Fanny Burney on a visit with her father in 1767 walked down the zigzag path from Clifton Hill to the Well below where she set some scenes in *Evelina* (1778). Lydia Melford in *Humphry Clinker* (1771) described 'the enchanting variety of moving pictures' to be seen when the ships passed 'close under the windows'. The building was destroyed in the 19th c. to continue the road but the colonnade remains. Here Ann Yearsley, a milk woman, set up her Circulating Library with the money from her *Poems* which Hannah More had got published with her friends as subscribers. Ann Yearsley resented being given the proceeds as an annuity; Hannah More regarded this as ingratitude. The feud ended in the failure of the library and Ann Yearsley's insanity. The spring was excavated back into the rock, making a grotto until 1912, when river water seeped through and it was closed. De Quincey was staying in the district in 1807, writing to Cottle to arrange his first meeting with Coleridge. Soon after, he wrote to his sister that he and Hartley Coleridge had gone walking in Leigh Woods endangering their necks on the tangled paths.

The small Dowry Sq. Chapel was built to save the invalids the climb up Granby Hill to the parish church in Clifton. Hannah More wrote the epitaph there on Sir John Stonhouse (d. 1795), her 'Shepherd of Salisbury Plain', who was ordained after being cured by the waters. This chapel was demolished in 1878. Dowry Sq. was the home of the Pneumatic Institute founded in 1799 by Dr. Beddoes, who married Maria Edgeworth's sister Anna. He brought the young Humphry Davy to be its superintendent, whose use of nitrous oxide so impressed Southey and Coleridge. A young doctor helping Beddoes with the outpatients was Peter Mark Roget, later author of the *Thesaurus* (1852). Sheridan's *Letters* (1966) recount his tragic visits in 1787 and 1792 when his wife and her sister died from consumption. Bowles staying here in 1789 wrote an 'Elegy' on his dead friends. In 1845 the ailing R. H. Barham stayed at 9 Dowry Sq. but died a month later.

Kingsdown, to the N., where Coleridge and his wife took lodgings in Oxford St., when they found Clevedon too isolated. Hartley, their first child, was born here (1796), while Coleridge was visiting his friend Charles Lloyd in Birmingham.

Stoke Bishop, to the NW. Katharine Bradley and her niece Edith Cooper moved here in 1878, writing *Bellerophon* (1881) as Arran and Isla Leigh. Their joint pseudonym 'Michael Field' came into being in 1885 with *Callirrhoë.*

The Portuguese novelist Eça de Queiroz lived at 38 Stoke Hill[1] from 1878 to 1888 after his marriage when consul in Bristol. While here *O Primo Basilio, Os Maias, A Reliquia,* and *Letters from England* were published. It was known that he lived away from the consulate in Queen Sq. but the exact house then called Vashni was only located after a long search for the original of a contemporary sketch. A commemorative plaque was unveiled by the Portuguese Ambassador in 1963 and the sketch and a page in manuscript were presented to the owner of the house by the novelist's son.

[1] Appointments to visit may be made through the University Department of Spanish and Portuguese, tel. 027 24161.

Westbury on Trym, to the NW. In 1798 Southey settled with his wife in a one-time ale-house, which they called Martin Hall because of the birds nesting under the eaves. Supported by advances from his publisher, Cottle, he devoted himself to writing; he completed the first draft of *Madoc* (1805), prepared the 2nd edition of *Letters from Spain and Portugal* (1797), and wrote 'The Holly Tree', 'Ebb Tide', and the sonnet 'Winter'. He wrote later 'I have never before or since produced so much poetry in the same space of time'. The house (gone) had large rooms, a productive garden, and splendid views. He was also preparing the *Annual Anthology* (1799–1800) by getting poems from Coleridge, Lamb, 'Perdita' Robinson, Amelia Opie, and Cottle. He thought the year here one of the happiest of his life.

BRIXHAM, Devon. [2 Ee] Fishing port that became a pioneer of deep-sea trawling, S. of Tor Bay, on the A3022. Henry Francis Lyte came here in 1824 as curate-in-charge of All Saints' Church and was instituted as first incumbent in 1826. The church, built 1814–16 as a chapel of ease to accommodate the growing population of Lower Brixham, or 'Brixham Quay', was enlarged in 1825–7 and 1872 and finally rebuilt (1884–1907) in memory of Lyte. When he arrived with his wife and family they lived in Burton St., at a house now called Whitegates, until 1833, when they moved to Berry Head House (now a hotel). It was at Berry Head, a short time before his death from tuberculosis, that he wrote 'Abide with Me' after watching the sun set over Tor Bay in the late summer of 1847 (he died in Nice on 20 Nov.). The carillon of All Saints' plays his three best-known hymns daily: 'When at Thy footstool, Lord, I bend', 'Praise, my soul, the King of Heaven', and 'Abide with Me', at 8 a.m., noon, and 8 p.m. respectively.

Francis Brett Young had his first medical practice here (1907–14), when he lived at Cleveland House. His first novel, *Deep Sea* (1914), makes Brixham its background. It was followed by *The Dark Tower* (1914). Flora Thompson came here in 1940, when her husband retired from the post office in Dartmouth, and lived in Higher Brixham till her death in 1947 at a house called Lauriston, in New Rd. It was here that she wrote *Candleford Green* (1943) and *Still Glides the Stream* (1948), with difficulty, as her heart had become affected by a serious illness. She was not much moved by her success as a writer as she said it had come too late.

BROAD CHALKE, Wilts. [1 Ad] Village between the A30 and the A354, 8 m. SW. of Salisbury. John Aubrey lived here in the Old Rectory, part of a former nunnery, which has a 15th-c. entrance arch. He was churchwarden and described the church as having 'one of the tunablest ring of bells in Wiltshire'. Maurice Hewlett lived in the Old Rectory where he was visited by Ezra Pound at Christmas in 1911. His verse epic *The Song of the Plow* (1916) and *Wiltshire Essays* (1921) were written here. He died in 1923 and is commemorated by a tablet in the church.

BROAD CLYST, Devon. [2 Fd] Village on the A38, 6 m. NE. of Exeter. Eden Phillpotts, prolific writer of novels and plays, mainly of the West Country, spent his last years at his home, Kerswell, dividing his time between writing and gardening.

BROADFORD. See SKYE.

BROADHEMBURY, Devon. [2 Fd] Small village 5½ m. NW. of Honiton, off the A373. A tablet on the S. wall of the church chancel records that Augustus Montague Toplady, author of the hymn 'Rock of Ages', was vicar here 1768–78.

BROADSTAIRS, Kent. [1 Hc] Coastal resort on the A255, in the NE. of the county, popular since the 19th c. Charles Dickens spent holidays here between 1836 and 1850. He wrote part of *Pickwick Papers* (1836) while lodging at 12 High St. (gone, but P on the site of no. 31 near Woolworths). *Nicholas Nickleby* (1839) was written at 40 Albion St., now the Royal Albion Hotel (P). *The Old Curiosity Shop* (1840) and *Barnaby Rudge* (1841) were written at Lawn House, now called Archway House, which spans the walk leading from Bleak House on the cliff above to 'The Old Curiosity Shop'. Bleak House,[1] where the study, bedroom, and dining-room are furnished with Dickens's possessions, was originally called The Fort and was where he completed *David Copperfield*. The original Betsey Trotwood is said to have lived at the end of Victoria Parade; this house is now called Dickens House (P).
    The beginning of the chapter 'A Summer's Day' in Elizabeth Bowen's novel *Eva Trout* (1969), has a description of the study of Bleak House with the lantern window, which hangs out in the air overlooking the sea and, in Dickens's day, the cornfields all around.

[1] Open daily 2–4 p.m.

BROADWATER. See WORTHING.

BROCKENHURST, Hants. [1 Be] Village on the A337, halfway between Lymington and Lyndhurst. Roydon Manor, a house of mellowed brick among the trees, can be seen from a bridle path which leads off an unclassified road to the SE. W. H. Hudson lodged here when he wrote *Hampshire Days* (1903), an account of local natural history

and people, 'Inscribed to Sir Edward and Lady Grey, Northumbrians with Hampshire written in their hearts'.

BROCKLEBRIDGE. See TUNSTALL.

BROMHAM, Wilts. [1 Ac] Village off the A342, 5 m. NW. of Devizes. Thomas Moore lived at Sloperton Cottage, now on the B3102 S. of the junction with the A342, from 1818 to 1852. It was then thatched and smaller with a pretty garden and a gravelled walk, and was within walking distance of Bowood. He was visited here by Samuel Rogers and Washington Irving, who wrote later to say he was living near Sleepy Hollow, which would amuse Moore's wife, who used to laugh at his habit of falling asleep after dinner. William Lisle Bowles came from Bremhill to baptize the children, Sydney Smith and Capt. Marryat called, and William Napier walked from Battle House in the village to read them chapters of his *History of the Peninsular War*. Moore himself collected his popular songs and ballads and wrote *Captain Rock* (1824) and lives of Sheridan (1825) and Byron (1830). He spent musical evenings and accompanied his wife to archery picnics. He died here in 1852, having outlived all his children, and a large Celtic cross marks his grave in the churchyard. The W. window of the church commemorates him and the E. window by William Morris and Burne-Jones is dedicated to Elizabeth Morris.

BROMHOLM PRIORY. See BACTON.

BROMPTON-BY-SAWDON, North Yorkshire. [5 Gc] Village on the A170, 9 m. SW. of Scarborough, where Wordsworth married Mary Hutchinson at the parish church in 1802. His sister Dorothy accompanied him. Mary was acting as housekeeper for her uncle at Gallows Hill Farm, now screened by trees from the main road a mile towards Scarborough. A copy of the banns and marriage certificate is in the vestry.

BROMSGROVE, Hereford and Worcester. [4 Ae] Town SW. of Birmingham. A. E. Housman lived with his parents from 1860 to 1873 at Perry Hall (P), now a hotel, on the Kidderminster road. He was educated at Bromsgrove School.

BROUGHTON, Peebles. (Borders). [6 Fd] Village on the A701, W. of Peebles. John Buchan and his sister Anna, who wrote as 'O. Douglas', spent many holidays at The Green, their grandparents' home. It was 'Woodilee' in his novel *Witch Wood* (1927), and she wrote *Penny Plain* (1913) while staying here.

BRUISYARD, Suff. [4 He] On the B1120, 2¾ m. NE. of Framlingham, is the turning to the village of Bruisyard. A drive on the W. leads to Oakenhill Hall, a tall red-brick house with old chimneys and pointed finials. Recently modernized, this was 'Crakenhill', 'the best farm in Bruisyard' of H. W. Freeman's novel of a farming family, *Joseph and his brethren* (1928).

BUCKLAND, Glos. [1 Aa] Village off the A46, 2½ m. SW. of Broadway. Mrs. Delany describes in her *Autobiography* (1861–2) the dramatic start to her journey in 1715 to the manor,[1] which she calls The Farm. She was 15 and her uncle, Lord Lansdowne, was in the Tower for his Jacobite sympathies. Government officers arrived early in the morning before the family was dressed to prevent their leaving the capital. Her mother fainted, her father was distracted, the children cried, and only the arrival of her indomitable aunt set the cavalcade rumbling on its 5-day journey here. The medieval Buckland Rectory[2] was visited by John Wesley.

[1] Garden open occasionally in Apr. and July.
[2] Open May–Sept.: Mon. 11 a.m.–4 p.m.

BUCKLEBURY, Berks. [1 Cc] Village 5 m. from Newbury, between the B4009 and the A4. Richard Aldington's novel, *The Colonel's Daughter* (1925), had its origins in this village, where he lived (c. 1921) before going to France.

BUDMOUTH. See WEYMOUTH.

BUNGAY, Suff. [4 He] Small town on the A1143, 14 m. SE. of Norwich. In 1794 Chateaubriand, a penniless *émigré* calling himself M. de Combourg, taught French to the young ladies of the district, including Charlotte Ives, the vicar's daughter here. Injured in a fall from his horse he was carried into the vicarage (a red-brick house by the bridge) and cared for by the Ives family.

He fell in love with the 15-year-old Charlotte and Mrs. Ives suggested they should marry and make their home at the vicarage. His confession that he was already married broke the idyll: Mrs. Ives fainted and M. de Combourg left the house. He and Charlotte met once more. In 1822 Charlotte, then Lady Sutton, sought an audience with Chateaubriand, then French Ambassador in London, to ask a favour for her elder son.

BURDEROP PARK. See COATE.

BURFORD, Oxon. [1 Bb] Picturesque little Cotswold market town 20 m. W. of Oxford, on the A40. John Wilmot, 2nd Earl of Rochester, who was born at Ditchley (q.v.), was educated at the old Grammar School before going to Wadham College, Oxford. Across the bridge over the Windrush, at the foot of the wide main street, there are one or two old houses on the river bank. Compton Mackenzie stayed in one of these some time before the First World War and drew a delightful portrait of Burford as 'Wychford' in his novel, *Guy and Pauline* (1915). John Meade Falkner, author of *Moonfleet* (1898), contributed to the restoration of the church, and is buried in the churchyard.

BURFORD BRIDGE, Surrey. [1 Ed] Bridge over the Mole, 1 m. N. of Dorking. Anna Barbauld, in her poem on the bridge, wrote in 1796

From the smoke and the din, and the hurry of town
Let the care wearied cit to this spot hasten down.
Here may Industry, Peace, Contentment reign still
While the Mole softly creeps at the foot of the hill.

In late November and early December 1817 Keats spent 2 weeks in a small back room of the Fox and Hounds (now the larger Burford Bridge Hotel) consistently writing about eighty lines a day to finish *Endymion* (1818). He climbed Box Hill (q.v.) by the path behind the inn. During the second week he composed the song 'In a drear-nighted December'. Stevenson also stayed at the hotel, once when walking in the hills near by and again in 1878 when he visited Meredith at Mickleham (q.v.). He wrote part of *The New Arabian Nights* (1882) here.

BURGHLEY HOUSE, Northants. [4 Dd] Elizabethan country house on the SE. outskirts of Stamford, built for the Cecil family. The 5th Earl, John Cecil, was host to Dryden during the summer and autumn of 1696, when he was translating the Seventh Book of the *Aeneid*, which he finished here. Celia Fiennes, who visited *c.* 1700, was impressed with the carvings and tapestries but affronted by the pictures as 'they were all without garments . . .'. In 1809 John Clare was taken on for a 3-year gardener's apprenticeship. In his short *Autobiography* (1831) he tells how some servants managed to get out of their locked quarters to drink the strong beer in Tant Baker's Hole in the Wall tavern. He also saved his meagre wages to buy one of Abercrombie's popular gardening manuals but before the year was out he had left the drunken head-gardener and was on his way to Newark. After the publication of his poems in 1820 the Marquis, whom Clare had often seen fishing or shooting in the park when they were both boys, sent for him to give him a pension of fifty pounds. In 1833 Tennyson wrote 'The Lord of Burleigh', a true though fairy-story-like tale of Sarah Hoggins, 'a village maiden', who married 'a poor landscape painter' expecting to live in a cottage, only to find herself above her station. Sarah pined away after 6 years, but Tom Moore in 'You remember Ellen' from *Irish Melodies* (1822), gives her a happy ending. Hazlitt also told her story in the *New Monthly Mazagine* (1822). Her portrait is in the house.

Open Apr.–Oct.: Tues.–Thurs., Sat. and Bank Holidays 11 a.m.–5 p.m.; Good Friday and Sun. 2–5 p.m.

BURITON (pr. Berriton), Hants. [1 Ce] Quiet village on an unclassified road, 3 m. S. of Petersfield. The historic manor house on the N. side of the church was the home of Edward Gibbon, when he returned from Switzerland in 1758, where he spent as much time as possible in the library, 'although occasionally compelled to visit horse races, entertain country squires, or canvas at elections'. He joined the South Hampshire Militia and was called out for active service —'most disagreeably active', he recorded, '—a wandering life of military servitude', which ended at Christmas 1762, but which proved useful experience of military matters when he came to write the *History of the*

Decline and Fall of the Roman Empire (1776–88).

BURRANE. See KILLIMER.

BURRINGTON COMBE, Som. [2 Gb] Limestone gorge on the B3134, where Augustus Toplady (1740–78), sheltering in a cave from the storm, was inspired to write 'Rock of Ages, cleft for me' (1775).

BURSLEM. See STOKE-ON-TRENT.

BURTON, Hants. [1 Ae] Village on the B3347, 1½ m. N. of Christchurch. Southey and his wife found lodgings here in 1797 for the summer while he was studying law in London and pining for country air. He delighted in the sea and the rivers of the New Forest—'the clearest you ever saw'—and returned to London in September with reluctance. Two years later he came back to Burton and acquired a pair of adjoining cottages which he converted into the thatched house as it exists today, 'small . . . and somewhat quaint', with a fish-pond and a garden and a book-room 'that, like the Chapter House at Salisbury . . . requires a column to support the roof'. He was working at the time on 'Thalaba the Destroyer' and his letters sounded cheerful, but no sooner was the work on the house finished than he became ill and had to leave. The house, called Burton Cottage, is at the S. end of the green, shielded from the road by trees and bushes.

BURWASH, East Sussex. [1 Fd] Village on the A265, 7 m. W. of Hawkhurst. James Hurdis, who lived at The Friars (Burwash Place) was a correspondent of William Cowper, and William Hayley who, when Hurdis was in distress at the death of his sister, persuaded him to visit Eartham (q.v.). Hurdis's long poem *The Village Curate* (1788) stems from the years (1785–91) of his curacy here. The tall-chimneyed, 17th-c. house called Bateman's (N.T.),[1] ½ m. S. of the village, was the home (1902–36) of Rudyard Kipling who, on first looking over the house, felt 'her Spirit—her Feng Shui—to be good'. *Puck of Pook's Hill* (1906)—the hill of the title is visible from the house, *Rewards and Fairies* (1910), and the unfinished autobiography *Something of Myself* (1937), are among the books written in the study, which remains as he left it. He redesigned the garden, planted yew hedges, and had plans for further alterations. The lines from his poem 'Sussex' show his pleasure in the county:

God gives all men all earth to love,
But since man's heart is small,
Ordains for each one spot shall prove
Beloved over all.
Each to his choice, and I rejoice
The lot has fallen to me
In a fair ground—in a fair ground—
Yea, Sussex by the sea!

[1] Open Mar.–Oct.: daily except Fri. 2–6 p.m., but open Good Friday; June–Sept.: also Mon.–Thur. 11 a.m.–12.30 p.m.

BURY, West Sussex. [1 De] Village off the A29, 4 m. N. of Arundel. John Galsworthy bought Bury House, the Tudor-style stone house at the top of the village, at first sight in 1920, and divided his time between Bury and his Hampstead home. The house has extensive views across farmland to the South Downs, where he used to ride and where, after his death in Hampstead in 1933, his ashes were scattered.

BURY ST. EDMUNDS, Suff. [4 Fe] Town on the A45 and the A134. The translation in 1840 of Jocelin de Brakelond's 12th-c. chronicle of the abbey prompted Carlyle to describe the town in *Past and Present* (1843). John Lydgate entered the monastery at the age of 15 and was ordained in 1397. Although he became a court poet and was granted lands through the patronage of the 'Good Duke Humphrey' of Gloucester, who died in custody at St. Saviour's Hospital (ruined gatehouse in Northgate St.), Lydgate returned to spend many years in the abbey, whose library was one of the largest in the country. The massive Abbey Gateway is now the entrance to public gardens amid the ruins. Celia Fiennes visited the newly built Cupola House (now an inn in the Traverse) on her rides and a plaque records Defoe's stay a few years later in 1704. Crabb Robinson, a native, lived in Westgate St., where at 15 he first met Catherine Buck, his lifelong correspondent. She married Thomas Clarkson, the abolitionist, and she introduced

Crabb Robinson to the literary circle of the Lambs and the Lake Poets, whose activities fill his diary. Edward FitzGerald was at the King Edward VI School (1821–6) with James Spedding, a lifelong friend. Ouida, author of *Under Two Flags* (1867), was born (1839) at 14 Hospital Rd. (P). Her friends put up a commemorative drinking fountain for animals (now dry and neglected) at the foot of West St., opposite the Spread Eagle. Dickens stayed at the Angel Hotel in 1859 and 1861 on reading tours, and his Sam Weller first met Job Trotter there.

BUXTON, Norf. [4 Gc] Village off the B1150, 4 m. SE. of Aylsham. Dudwick House (rebuilt) in its park opposite the Black Lion, was the home of Anna Sewell's aunt and uncle, and is thought to be the original of Birtwick Park in *Black Beauty* (1877). Anna Sewell (1820–78) learned to ride when staying as a child with her grandparents at Dudwick Farm.

BYFLEET, Surrey. [1 Dc] Large village off the A245, 3 m. NE. of Woking. In 1749 Joseph Spence, author of the well-known *Anecdotes* about Pope and others, was given a house here by his former pupil Lord Lincoln. Spence in turn obtained the living for Stephen Duck, brought to prominence by his poem 'The Thresher's Labour'. Duck moved here in 1752 (rectory rebuilt) and in 1755 published *Caesar's Camp or St. George's Hill* which contains the lines

Remote from giddy crowds and noisy strife
Yet near the few whose converse sweeten life
Here let me live. Be mindful of my end,
Adore my Maker and enjoy my friend.

However, Duck, who began to suffer from depression after his second wife's death in 1749, enjoyed Spence's company for a few years only, before drowning himself in Reading on returning from a visit to his native village in 1756. Spence suffered a similar fate, though his death in a pond in his grounds was accidental. A memorial tablet is in the church and Spence's Point on St. George's Hill, marked by the firs he planted, perpetuates his name.

C

CAERLEON, Gwent. [2 Ga] Town on the Usk, 3 m. NE. of Newport. The name means 'Camp of the Legion' and the extensive remains of the amphitheatre and barracks of the Roman stronghold of A.D. 80 are still there. The town is probably the Carlion of Malory's *Le Morte Darthur* (1485), where Arthur was crowned and held his court. Tennyson stayed here while gathering material for the Arthurian legends of *Idylls of the King* (1859). Arthur Machen, writer of mystical, romantic, and macabre stories, who made his name in the First World War as the author of 'The Angels of Mons' in *The Bowmen and Other Legends* (1915), was born in Caerleon (1863).

CAISTER CASTLE, Norf. [4 Hd] A 15th-c. castle 5 m. NW. of Great Yarmouth, built by Sir John Fastolf (Shakespeare's Falstaff) on whose death (1459) it passed to John Paston (1421–66) by a will disputed by other claimants. Many of the *Paston Letters* were written from the castle by John's wife Margaret, during his absence in London.

CALLINGTON, Cornwall. [2 De] Quiet market town on the A390 and the A388, 8 m. NE. of Liskeard. It has been traditionally claimed as one of the sites of King Arthur's palace.

CALNE, Wilts. [1 Ac] Market town on the A4. Coleridge lodged (1814–16) with the Morgan family, friends of Charles and Mary Lamb, who also stayed here for a month in 1816. Coleridge, who was taking laudanum, was working intermittently on *Biographia Literaria*. 'Calne is a sepulchre in a desert', he wrote to a friend in Devizes asking for a good brewer. When John Morgan became insolvent Lamb and Southey contributed an allowance.

CALVERLEY, West Yorkshire. [5 Ee] Town between Shipley and Leeds on the A657. Frederick Faber, the hymn-writer who established the London Oratory in 1849, was born (1814) in his grandfather's vicarage (rebuilt) here.

CAMBO. See CAPHEATON HALL.

CAMBRIDGE, Cambs. [4 Ef] University town on the A10, founded in the 12th c. on a site first settled by the Romans. Michael Drayton mentions Cambridge as 'my most beloved town' in *Polyolbion* (1622) and Celia Fiennes, on one of her journeys in 1697, comments on all the 'walks with rows of trees and bridges over the river'. She was also interested that the Fellows and Gentlemen Commoners could have 'a large dining room, a good Chamber and good studdy for £8 a year'. Daniel Defoe in *Tour through Great Britain* (1724–7) honours the University for giving no encouragement to those who would hold scandalous assemblies at unseasonable hours: 'nor is there want of mirth and good company of other kinds'. The River Granta is called the Cam as it flows through the town and the tree-covered ground connected to the colleges by elegant bridges has become known as the Backs. Charles and Mary Lamb walked here with Crabb Robinson who mentions it in his *Diary*; Mary Lamb wrote that they were 'walking the whole time—out of one college into another' on their visit in 1815, when they lodged at 11 King's Parade (P). Charles Lamb, sad that he had missed a university education, wrote a sonnet in which he imagined himself walking about in a gown. The Lambs first met Emma Isola here, whom they later adopted.

Lamb's 'Oxford in the Vacation' was written on his visit to Cambridge in 1820 and combines his memories of both universities. The G. D. of the essay is his friend George Dyer of Emmanuel. Trollope's novel *John Caldigate* (1879) is set partly in Cambridge and partly in the near-by village of Chesterton.

Henry James wrote in *Portraits of Places* (1883), that the Backs show 'the loveliest confusion of gothic windows and ancient trees, of grassy banks and mossy balustrades, of sun-chequered avenues and groves, of lawns and gardens and terraces, of single arched bridges spanning the little stream, which . . . looks as if it had been "turned on" for ornamental purposes'. In 1907 he accepted the invitation to revisit Cambridge by the young men whom he addressed as 'My dear Cambridge Three', and he stayed two nights at 8 Trumpington St., a tall narrow house with a walled garden where they sat after meals as the June days were warm, and from where he was taken on a tour of the University. His youthful hosts introduced him to Rupert Brooke, who poled the punt on their excursion on the Cam, and though James later recalled that he was introduced to 'hundreds and hundreds of undergraduates all exactly alike', he was aware at Brooke's death 'of the stupid extinction of . . . so exquisite a being'.

Rose Macaulay, who was born (1881) here, was the daughter of a Fellow of Trinity. The second chapter of *Orphan Island* (1924) describes a don's household in Grange Rd. and most of *They Were Defeated* (1932), in which John Cleveland of Christ's and Abraham Cowley of Trinity (see below) appear, is set in 17th-c. Cambridge.

As a child Frances Cornford often visited her Darwin cousins (see Darwin College). After her marriage in 1908 she lived at Conduit Head, off Madingley Rd., and Rupert Brooke, whom she described as 'A Young Apollo golden haired', was one of the undergraduates who visited there. Her first collection of poems was published in 1910, and she mentions the poets at Cambridge over the centuries in 'In the Backs' from *Travelling Home* (1948). One of her most widely known poems was 'To a Fat Lady Seen from a Train' from *Collected Poems* (1954). Her son John Cornford was killed (1936) in the Spanish Civil War, the subject of many of his poems.

University:

Christ's College (1505). John Leland (or Leyland), who claimed to have saved the manuscripts of 'many good authors' from the monasteries after their dissolution, graduated here in 1522. Gabriel Harvey left after his B.A. in 1570 to become a Fellow of Pembroke. John Milton is said to have had rooms (1625–32) in the first court (refaced). Here he wrote 'Hymn on the Morning of Christ's Nativity' and the sonnet to Shakespeare. His memories of the University are reflected in 'Il Penseroso', written soon after he went down

> But let my due feet never fail
> To walk the studious cloister's pale,
> And love the high embowéd roof,
> With antique pillars massy-proof,
> And storied windows richly dight
> Casting a dim religious light.

The death of Edward King, whose friend he became here, inspired 'Lycidas' (1638). The mulberry tree, traditionally associated with Milton, is still in the Fellows' Garden.[1] John Cleveland, an undergraduate 1627–31, also wrote an elegy on his friend Edward King. Wordsworth, when at St. John's (q.v.), visited Milton's rooms and drank to his memory, as he records in *The Prelude*. C. S. Calverley came here from Oxford in 1852 and was elected a Fellow in 1858. His 'Ode on Tobacco' from *Verses and Translations* (1862) is written on a bronze plaque on Bacon's Tobacconist's shop (rebuilt 1934), which he patronized, on Market Hill. His friends were Walter Besant (1856–9), and W. W. Skeat, Professor of Anglo-Saxon (1878–1912) and editor of *Piers Plowman* (1886) and *Chaucer* (1894–7). There is a plaque to Skeat in the library. Forrest Reid, a novelist influenced by Henry James, was at Christ's College *c.* 1894

[1] Open daily 2–4 p.m.

Clare College (1326), with its picturesque bridge over the Cam, is one of the colleges thought to be Soler Hall of Chaucer's 'The Reeve's Tale' (cf. Trinity College). Hugh Latimer, who first came to the University in 1500 and was elected a Fellow here in 1511, became noted for his sermons. He was one of the young men bent on reforming the Church (see Jesus College). Robert Greene received an M.A. here (1583) after graduating at St. John's College. William Whitehead, who was born (1715) in St. Botolph's parish and baptized in the 14th-c. church of that name in Trumpington St., studied here and became a Fellow in 1742.

Siegfried Sassoon started to write poetry as an undergraduate (1904–8). He enlisted on the outbreak of the war in 1914. *Collected Poems 1908–1956* was published in 1961.

Corpus Christi (1352) was formerly called Bene't College from the partly Saxon church of St. Bene't (i.e. Benedict), which was used as the college chapel. Christopher Marlowe had first-floor rooms (*c.* 1578) on the right of 'P' staircase. He graduated M.A. in 1587, by which time he had already written *Tamburlaine* (1590). John Fletcher, who came up (1593) the year Marlowe was killed in a tavern, is commemorated with him on the wall plaque at the foot of 'O' staircase. Thomas Fuller, perpetual curate of St. Bene't's from 1630, preached the funeral sermon on Thomas Hobson, the well-known carrier, who operated his business from the inn later called The George (gone). Hobson, who appears in Fuller's *Worthies of England* (1662) and is also the subject of two epitaphs by Milton, let out his horses in strict rotation whatever his customer's preference, which gave rise to the phrase 'Hobson's Choice'. John Cowper Powys and his youngest brother Llewellyn were undergraduates here at the turn of the 20th c.

Darwin College (1964). A graduate college housed partly in Newnham Grange, the name given to a prosperous corn-merchant's house bought by Charles Darwin's son, after his marriage in 1884. *Period Piece* (1952), an entertaining account by Gwen Raverat of her childhood in Newnham Grange, where she was born (1895), gives a picture of her eccentric Darwin uncles and aunts, and her cousin Frances (later Cornford), in Cambridge in the decades before and after 1900.

Emmanuel College (1584). William Law, author of *A Serious Call to a Devout and Holy Life* (1729), a work of great influence in the 18th and 19th cc., became a sizar in 1705 and a Fellow in 1711. He stayed here briefly as he refused to take the oath of allegiance. Richard Hurd, who was elected a Fellow after taking his M.A. in 1742, wrote *The Polite Arts: or, a dissertation on poetry, painting, music, etc.* (1749). Thomas Percy was granted a D.D. in 1770, 5 years after he published the *Reliques*. George Dyer, the friend who often appears in Lamb's *Essays of Elia*, and who wrote a *History of the University and Colleges* (1814), graduated in 1778. Hugh Walpole was an undergraduate here from 1902 to 1905.

Fitzwilliam Museum. Museum built (1837–47) to house the bequests of Viscount Fitzwilliam. The picture galleries contain works by Joseph Highmore, the friend of Samuel Richardson, who illustrated his novel *Pamela* (1740), illustrations by Blake, and portraits of Hardy and Shaw. The library has many autograph manuscripts, some of which, including Keats's 'Ode to a Nightingale' and Brooke's 'Grantchester', are shown in cases in the galleries. M. R. James, while Director (1893–1908), catalogued the manuscripts of the museum and the colleges.

Open Tues.–Sat. 10 a.m.–5 p.m.; Sun. 2–5 p.m. Closed Bank Holidays.

Gonville and Caius (pr. Keys) College (1348 and 1557). Jeremy Taylor, who was born (1613) in the town and baptized in Holy Trinity Church, Market St., was elected a Fellow in 1633, but was summoned to Oxford in 1635. Thomas Shadwell entered in 1656, but left without a degree.

Charles Doughty, chiefly remembered for *Travels in Arabia Deserta* (1888), was an undergraduate from 1861 to 1863. After transferring to Downing and some months studying in Norway, he returned to take his degree in 1865.

J. E. Flecker studied (1908–10) Oriental Languages before entering the Consular Service.

Jesus College (1496). Thomas Cranmer was made (1515) a Fellow after studying here. It is said that he, William Tyndale, and Hugh Latimer of Clare, used to meet at the Old White Hart Inn (demolished), to discuss the reforms they hoped to make in the practices of the Church. Wordsworth begins his sonnet to them with

Aid, glorious Martyrs, from your fields of light
Our mortal ken!

Laurence Sterne, who came up in 1733 (M.A. 1740), met here his lifelong friend, John Hall (later John Hall-Stevenson, 1718–85), whom he afterwards depicted as Eugenius. S. T. Coleridge came up in 1791 and after a short interval, when he enlisted in the Dragoons in 1793, remained until 1794. In *Biographia Literaria* (1817) he writes of the 'friendly cloisters, and the happy grove of quiet, ever honoured Jesus College . . .'. The ceiling of the chapel was decorated by William Morris and the glass is by Morris, Burne-Jones, and Madox Brown (late 1860s–1870s). Sir Arthur Quiller-Couch became a Fellow in 1912 when elected to the Chair of English Literature. His published lectures, *On the Art of Writing* (1916), and *On the Art of Reading* (1920), reached a wide public beyond the University.

King's College (1441). The view of the chapel and Fellows' Building, familiar from 18th-c. prints, can still be seen from the Backs. Thomas Preston, author of *Cambises, King of Persia* (1569), became a Fellow of King's in 1556 (LL.D. 1576) before becoming the Master of Trinity Hall. Giles Fletcher the Elder, an undergraduate from 1565 to 1569, became a Fellow in 1568, and John Harington studied here *c.* 1575. Fletcher's *Licia, or*

Poemes of Love was published in 1593. His elder son Phineas, a student from 1605 to 1608, was elected Fellow in 1611. Edmund Waller stayed here for a short time (1620–2) before entering Lincoln's Inn. Horace Walpole studied here (1735–9) and then left for a tour of the Continent with Thomas Gray of Peterhouse, whom he had first met at Eton. Christopher Anstey, a former scholar, became a Fellow *c.* 1743. Most visitors admire the chapel,[1] and John Evelyn in his *Diary* mentions, as well as the beauty of the inside, the wide view that he saw from the roof. Wordsworth, who wrote three sonnets in its praise, describes

. . . the branching roof
Self poised, and scooped into ten thousand cells
Where light and shade repose, where music dwells
Lingering—and wandering on as loth to die;

William Johnson won the Chancellor's Medal, by a single vote, in 1843 with his poem 'Plato'. He became a Fellow in 1845 and held his Fellowship while he was master (1846–72) at Eton. On his retirement he took the additional name of Cory. Percy Lubbock was an undergraduate here *c.* 1898. M. R. James was elected Provost of his old college in 1905. His *Ghost Stories of an Antiquary* (1905) and its sequel (1911) reached a wide public. He became Vice-Chancellor in 1913. Rupert Brooke had rooms in the Fellows' Building in 1906, but found his first year unexciting. Later he became one of the Apostles (see Trinity College), contributed poems and reviews to the *Cambridge Review*, and joined the Fabian Society. After acting in *Dr. Faustus*, he was instrumental in forming the Marlowe Society, still in being as an undergraduate dramatic society. In 1909 he found rooms above the Orchard Tea Rooms in Grantchester (q.v.). He wrote a thesis on Webster and was elected a Fellow in 1913. G. Lowes Dickinson, an undergraduate and Fellow (1886–1920), lived here when he retired. His friend E. M. Forster, who read Classics and History here (1897–1901), became a Fellow in 1927 and had rooms on 'A' staircase from 1946 to his death in 1970. In Forster's novel *The Longest Journey* (1907) he writes of the main character that Cambridge 'had taken and soothed him, and warmed him and had laughed at him a little, saying that he must not be so tragic yet awhile'; a pleasant fate after the rigours of a public school, an institution Forster thought responsible for 'the undeveloped heart', a constant thread in his novels. Lowes Dickinson and Forster were both elected to the Society of Apostles. The happiness that both men found at the University was described by Forster when he used Lowes Dickinson's autobiographical material to write his *Life* (1934). 'As Cambridge filled up with friends it acquired a magic quality . . . People and books reinforced one another, intelligence joined hands with affection, speculation became passion, and discussion was made profound by love.'

The college is the setting for two novels by King's men: E. F. Benson's *David of King's* (1924) and Shane Leslie's *The Cantab* (1926).

[1] Open in term, weekdays 9 a.m.–4 p.m.; Sun. 2–3 p.m. (extended hours in vacation).

Magdalene (pr. Mawdlin) College (1542). Samuel Pepys came here from Trinity Hall in 1651 and graduated in 1653. In his *Diary* he writes of his later visits. On one occasion he spent the afternoon drinking immoderately at the Three Tuns and in 1667 he walked into 'the butterys, as a stranger, and there drank my bellyful of their beer, which pleased me as the best I ever drank'. The original diary is one of the manuscripts, books, and prints bequeathed by Pepys to his college and housed in his own bookcases in the Pepys Library[1] in the Second Court. Percy Lubbock, Curator of the Pepys Library (1906–8), wrote a study of Pepys (1909).

Charles Kingsley, an undergraduate here from 1838 to 1842, became Professor of Modern History in 1860. His novel *Alton Locke* (1850) has many scenes in Cambridge. A. C. Benson, Fellow from 1904, was Master 1915–25 and did much to beautify the College, where he wrote *From a College Window* (1906). Vernon Watkins, an undergraduate 1922–5, started writing early, but the first poems he considered of value were published in the new magazine *Wales* in 1936. C. S. Lewis became a Fellow here, when elected Professor of Medieval and Renaissance English (1954–63). One of his popular children's books, *The Magician's Nephew* (1955), and *Studies in Words* (1960) and *An Experiment in Criticism* (1961), were published during his years here. He died here in 1963.

The Old Library[2] (First Court) contains the Ferrar Papers (see Trinity) and manuscripts of Hardy, Kipling, and T. S. Eliot, Hon. Fellows whose portraits hang in the Hall.

[1] Open Mon.–Sat. 11.30 a.m.–12.30 p.m. and 2.30–4.30 p.m. in summer term and July and Aug. vacation. Other terms 2.30–3.30 p.m.

[2] Open Mon.–Sat. summer term and 8 July–31 Aug. 11.30 a.m.–12.30 p.m. and 2.30–3.30 p.m. Other terms 2.30–3.30 p.m.

Newnham College (1875). Katharine Bradley, who later collaborated with her niece to write as 'Michael Field', was one of the first students here. Virginia Woolf's *A Room of One's Own* (1929) is based on the papers she read to the Arts Society at Newnham and the Odtaa at Girton in 1928. The J— H— who appears in the garden of the imaginary college 'Fernham', is Jane Harrison, a Fellow and author of *The Religion of Ancient Greece*.

Pembroke College (previously Pembroke Hall, 1347). Nicholas Ridley, who may have helped Thomas Cranmer with the Prayer Books of Edward VI, became a Fellow here (c. 1524) and is commemorated by Ridley's Walk, a path S. of the Master's Lodge. Edmund Spenser came up c. 1566 and by 1569 had written sonnets on themes of Petrarch and Du Bellay and 'Hymnes in honour of Love and Beauty', which he said he wrote in his 'green youth'. Gabriel Harvey, the Fellow lecturing in rhetoric, became his friend and appeared as Hobbinol in *The Shepheards Calender* (1579). Harvey, who also helped Spenser get a place in Leicester's household, carried on fierce disputes with Robert Greene and Richard Nash, and he and Nash came under the wrath of the authorities. Lancelot Andrewes, a student contemporary with Spenser, became Master (1589–1605). Richard Crashaw was a student here (1632–4) before going to Peterhouse as a Fellow. Christopher Smart, who entered under the Duchess of Cleveland's patronage, became a Classics Scholar in 1742, graduated in 1743, and was elected a Fellow in 1745. His play *A Trip to Cambridge*, acted by his fellow undergraduates, called forth the scorn of Thomas Gray in his *Letters* (1935), 'he acts five parts himself, and one is only sorry that he can't do all the rest'. However, Smart's translation into elegant Latin of Pope's 'Ode for Music on St. Cecilia's Day' pleased the author, and his entries for the Seatonian Prize twice saved him from his creditors, whose presence at one time barricaded him in his room. These poems on a sacred subject also tempered the wrath of the college, who found that while holding a Fellowship for a single man, Smart had not told them of his marriage. His Fellowship was renewed but he sank further into debt and left his college rooms in 1749 and Cambridge in 1755. Gray, who had come to Pembroke from Peterhouse, disapproved of Smart's drinking and extravagance and foretold his end. William Mason, whom Gray had helped to a Fellowship in 1749, also disapproved but collected money for his relief, though he thought Smart's poem *Song to David* (1763) proved he was still mad. Gray spent most of his life in Cambridge and became Professor of History and Modern Languages (1768). In 'Ode to Music' (1769), Gray describes the 'Willowy Camus', 'the level lawn', and 'the cloister dim'. In his *Letters* he emphasizes how much more enjoyable the place is without people. 'It is they, I assure you, that get it an ill name and spoil it all.' Gray had rooms in the Hitcham Building in the Second Court from 1756 to 1771 when he died.

Peterhouse (1281), the oldest college. John Skelton is thought to have been attached to Peterhouse. He graduated M.A. in 1484 and in 1493 became 'poet laureate', at that time a title given to an outstanding student. He is also known to have been at Cambridge in 1504–5. Richard Crashaw, an undergraduate at Pembroke, became a Fellow here (1637–43), but was expelled for refusing to accept the Solemn League and Covenant. Thomas Gray was here (1734–8) and again from 1743 to 1756, when a practical joke by some students, who were amused by his dread of fire, caused him to find quarters at Pembroke. His rooms in the Fellows' Building still have the bars he placed at his windows.

Queens' College (1448). Erasmus Tower in Pump Court contains the rooms occupied (1511–14) by the Dutch humanist, Desiderius Erasmus, while Lady Margaret Reader in Greek. His *Colloquia* and his *Letters* are the source for details in Scott's *Anne of Geierstein* (1829) and *The Cloister and the Hearth* (1861) by C. Reade. Thomas Fuller, who studied here (1621–8), wrote *History of the University of Cambridge* (1655).

47

St. Catharine's College (1473). James Shirley came from Oxford to Cats (as it is familiarly known) and graduated (*c.* 1618), when his poem *Narcissus*, written in the style of Shakespeare's *Venus and Adonis*, was published as *Eccho*.

After an interval spent travelling Malcolm Lowry, an undergraduate 1929-32, came up from The Leys School, where he had written precocious articles for the school magazine. He had visited America, staying with Conrad Aiken to whom he had written after reading his novel *The Blue Voyage*. Lowry first had rooms in Bateman St. and frequented Roebuck House where Charlotte Haldane kept open house for aesthetes. His friends drank with him at the Red Cow, the Bath, and the Eagle and he spent the long vacations with Aiken in Rye (q.v.). Lowry's novel *Ultramarine* (1933), which he worked at intermittently here, was accepted in lieu of a thesis by his tutor.

St. John's College (1511). Thomas Wyatt came here at the then usual age of 12 and graduated in 1518, M.A. 1520. Robert Greene entered as a sizar and graduated in 1579. Thomas Nash wrote that he spent 'seven yere altogether lacking a quarter' in 'the sweetest nurse of learning in all the University', perhaps from 1581 to 1587. He developed an antipathy to Gabriel Harvey of Pembroke, which resulted in a spate of satires on both sides. Nash defended Greene, whom Harvey in *Foure Letters* had called 'The Ape of Euphues', in *Strange Newes* (1593). Robert Herrick was a student here (1613-16) but graduated from Trinity Hall. John Cleveland came here after graduating at Christ's in 1631. He became a Fellow in 1635 and appears in Rose Macaulay's *They Were Defeated* (1932), in which Herrick also features. Many of Cleveland's poems relate to Cambridge. Matthew Prior studied here from 1682 to 1686 and became a Fellow in 1688, but soon left for diplomatic service on the Continent. Charles Churchill is thought to have left the college after it was discovered that he had made a Fleet marriage (see London, City) at the age of 18 in 1749. The same year William Mason became an M.A. and was elected to a Fellowship at Pembroke. William Wordsworth, an undergraduate from 1787 to 1790, wrote his impressions of coming up in *The Prelude* (1850) as he roamed

> Delighted through the motley spectacle;
> Gowns grave, or gaudy, doctors, students, streets,
> Courts, cloisters, flocks of churches, gateways, towers:
> Migration strange for a stripling of the hills,
> A northern villager.

An inscription can be seen in the college kitchen. Henry Kirke White, whose poems impressed Southey and other friends who raised money for him to come up in 1805, died in his rooms in October 1806. He was buried in All Saints' Church (site an open space opposite the gate) but when this was demolished (1865) his memorial was removed to the chapel.[1]

William Barnes kept his name on the college roll for 10 years from 1838 as a 'ten-year-man' and graduated B.D. in 1850. Samuel Butler entered in 1854, like Barnes intended for the Church, but he quarrelled with his father and emigrated to New Zealand. His first accounts of the country were published in *The Eagle*, the college magazine. Butler's self-portrait is in the Hall, where there are also portraits of Matthew Prior and Wordsworth.

[1] Open Mon.–Sat. 9 a.m.–12 noon, 2–4 p.m.

Sidney Sussex College (1589). Thomas Rymer, author of *A Short View of Tragedy*, and Thomas Fuller from Queens', were educated here.

Trinity College (1546). This, the largest college, has an ornate fountain (1602) in the Great Court, which was the source of the college's drinking water. The Library,[1] designed by Wren, has manuscripts of works by Milton, Byron, Tennyson, Thackeray, and A. E. Housman, and busts of Bacon (Roubiliac) and Tennyson (Woolner), and the statue of Byron (Thorvaldsen) refused by Westminster Abbey. Celia Fiennes praised Grinling Gibbons's work as 'the finest carving in wood in flowers, birds, leaves, figures of all sorts, as ever I saw'. In the ante-chapel of the chapel[2] there are statues of Macaulay and Tennyson.

Soler Hall, of Chaucer's 'The Reeve's Tale', may have been King's Hall, one of the three colleges amalgamated by Henry VIII in his foundation of Trinity College (cf. Clare). King Edward III's Gate and King's Hostel remain, W. of the chapel. One of the earliest Fellows was Dr. John Dee, whose reputation as a magician began with his startling stage effects for a production of Aristophanes's *Peace* in 1546. Shakespeare is thought to have had Dee in mind in creating Prospero in *The Tempest*, written probably *c.* 1611, a few years after Dee's death. George Gascoigne was one of the earliest students and Francis Bacon (1573–5), William Alabaster (*c.* 1582), and Henry Peacham (*c.* 1590) followed before the end of the century. Giles Fletcher the Younger, a student from 1603 to 1606, became Reader in Greek Grammar (1615) and Literature (1618). *Christ's Victory and Triumph* (1610) and many of his allegories were written here. George Herbert entered in 1609, became a Fellow in 1616, and was Public Orator 1619–27. His friend Nicholas Ferrar, of Clare, prompted his decision to leave university life for the Church. The more flamboyant John Suckling was a student (*c.* 1625) for a short time before entering Gray's Inn. Thomas Randolph spent most of his adult life here, first as a student and then (1629–32) as a Fellow, when his reputation as a writer of verse both in English and Latin was made. He left Cambridge for London (1632) and died 3 years later. His *Aristippus or the Jovial Philosopher* (1630) includes an amusing sketch on the rival merits of ale and sack. Andrew Marvell, an undergraduate from 1633 to 1638, contributed to *Musa Cantabrigiensis* (1637), the year Abraham Cowley came up. Cowley lived here for 6 years until ejected from his Fellowship by the Parliamentarians in 1644. One of his comedies was acted before Prince Charles in 1641 and he speaks of Cambridge with affection in his poem 'On the Death of Mr. William Harvey'.

> Ye fields of Cambridge, our dear Cambridge, say
> Have ye not seen us walking every day?
> Was there a tree about, which did not know
> The love betwixt us two?
> Henceforth, ye gentle trees, for ever fade,
> Or your sad branches thicker join
> And in some darksome shades combine
> Dark as the grave wherein my friend is laid.

John Dryden (B.A. 1654) and Nathaniel Lee (B.A. 1668) were both scholars, who drew on their classical studies for their later dramatic works. Zacharias Conrad von Uffenbach, whose diary was edited, with others, in *Cambridge under Queen Anne* by J. E. B. Mayor in 1911, visited Richard

Bentley, the Master, whom he found 'as well lodged as the queen at St. James's . . .'. Bentley became Master in 1699 at the time his *Dissertation on the Letters of Phalaris* silenced his critics by proving the letters spurious. Echoes of the long controversy occur in Swift's *The Battle of the Books* written in 1697. Bentley, who was satirized by Pope in *The Dunciad*, held the Mastership, in spite of opposition to his despotism which nominally deprived him of it, until his death in 1742. Laurence Eusden became a Fellow of this, his own college, in 1712, and in 1717 wrote verses celebrating the marriage of the Duke of Newcastle, who had the gift of the Poet Laureateship. Eusden became the Laureate and Pope sharpened his pen to include him in *The Dunciad* (1728). Richard Cumberland, who was born (1732) in the Master's Lodge, became a Fellow for a short while before his marriage. Lord Byron, who entered in 1805 and had rooms in Nevile's Court, published *Juvenilia* (1807), later called *Hours of Idleness*, which did not find favour in the *Edinburgh Review*. In his *Letters* Byron writes 'I like a College Life extremely . . . I am now most pleasantly situated in Super-excellent Rooms, flanked on one side by my Tutor, on the other by an Old Fellow, both of whom are rather checks to my vivacity'.

Dorothy and William Wordsworth stayed (1820) at the Master's Lodge to see their brother Christopher, who had recently been elected Master and who was then Vice-Chancellor. 'All is so quiet and stately both within and without doors', wrote Dorothy Wordsworth. One evening 'a small but zealous band' of undergraduates was invited to meet the poet, and one of them, John Moultrie (1799–1874), wrote verses about his impressions of Wordsworth, which are quoted in Mary Moorman's biography. Wordsworth later wrote a sonnet on the portrait of Henry VIII by Holbein, then in the Master's Lodge. T. B. Macaulay, who came up in 1818, became a Fellow in 1824. His first essay, on Milton, was published in the *Edinburgh Review* in 1825. Macaulay's rooms were on 'E' staircase where Thackeray also lived (1829–30), as did the hero of his novel *Henry Esmond* (1852). Edward FitzGerald, an undergraduate 1827–30, had lodgings at 20 King's Parade (P). In *Euphranor* (1851), a dialogue on educational systems set in Cambridge, he describes the 'sluggish current' of the Cam, 'which seem'd indeed fitter for the slow merchandise of coal, than to wash the walls and flow through the groves of Academe'. He was a contemporary of Thackeray, Tennyson, Kinglake, and Monckton Milnes. Tennyson, who won the Chancellor's Medal (1829) with the poem 'Timbuctoo', met Arthur Hallam here, the friend whose death inspired *In Memoriam*. Hallam had rooms in New Court and Tennyson lodged at 59 Trumpington St., now incorporated in Corpus Christi College. Tennyson, Hallam, and Monckton Milnes were among the earliest members of the Society of Apostles, which met weekly in Trinity. Henry Sidgwick, Knightbridge Professor of Philosophy, elected in 1856, wrote:

Absolute candour was the only duty that the tradition of the Society enforced . . . The greatest subjects were continually debated, but gravity of treatment . . . was not imposed, though sincerity was.

F. W. Farrar, who came up in 1852, also won the Chancellor's Medal and was an Apostle. He was elected a Fellow in 1856 and he based his novel, *Julian Home* (1859), on his life at Cambridge. F. C. Burnand, an undergraduate 1853–6, founded the Cambridge Amateur Dramatic Club in 1855, now in Park St., and wrote humorous sketches and burlesques. In May 1873 F. W. H. Myers, a Fellow interested in psychical research, invited Marian Evans (George Eliot) to visit him. Their conversation in the Fellows' Garden was recounted later in Bertrand Russell's *Autobiography*:

George Eliot told F. W. H. Myers that there is no God, and yet we must be good; and Myers decided that there is a God and yet we need not be good.

James Frazer came to Trinity in 1875 (Fellow 1879) and remained here, with the exception of a short stay as Professor of Social Anthropology in Liverpool, until his death in 1941. His *Golden Bough* (12 vols., 1890–1915) is a comparative study of the beliefs and religions of mankind.

Lytton Strachey, an undergraduate from 1899 to 1903, settled in attic rooms on 'K' staircase, called mutton-hole corner. After an uncomfortable time at school he found he enjoyed Trinity. With his friends Clive Bell, Leonard Woolf, A. J. Robertson, and Saxon Sydney-Turner he formed a group called the Midnight Society, which met on Saturdays, at midnight, in Clive Bell's rooms. The group, later joined by Thoby

Stephen (brother of Virginia, later Woolf), was the precursor of the Bloomsbury Group. Strachey, who won the Chancellor's English Medal, had his first poems published in *The Granta*.

A. E. Housman became a Fellow here when appointed Professor of Latin in 1911. *A Shropshire Lad* (1896) was followed by *Last Poems* in 1922 and, in the year of his death, by *More Poems* (1936). He published a Cambridge lecture, *The Name and Nature of Poetry*, in 1933.

G. M. Trevelyan, who made history a pleasure for the general reader with *English Social History* (1942), was Master from 1927 to 1940 and wrote a history of the college.

[1] Open Nov.–Mar.: Mon.–Fri. 2.15–3.45 p.m.; Apr.–Oct. 2.15–4.45 p.m., Sat. 10.45 a.m.–12.45 p.m. Closed Bank Holidays.
[2] Open daily 8 a.m.–dusk.

Trinity Hall (1350). Raphael Holinshed, the chronicler from whom Shakespeare took the plots of many of his plays, is thought to have spent some time here. He died (*c.* 1580) the same year as Thomas Tusser, whose *Stanzas* (1580) contain the lines about his return to his college

When gains were gone, and years grew on,
And death did cry, from London fly,
In Cambridge then I found again
A resting plot;
In college best of all the rest,
With thanks to thee, O Trinity!
Through thee & thine, for me and mine
Some stay I got.

Many proverbs can be traced to Tusser's *Hundreth Good Pointes of Husbandrie* (1557). Thomas Preston, author of *A Lamentable Tragedy . . . of the Life of Cambises King of Persia* (1569), became Master in 1584. He died here in 1598 and is buried in the chapel. William Hayley was at Trinity Hall from 1763 to 1767. His 'Ode on the Birth of the Prince of Wales', the first of his then popular poems, was published in Cambridge and then reprinted in the *Gentleman's Magazine*. Edward Bulwer-Lytton came here after a few months at Trinity College. He won the Chancellor's Medal (1825) for a poem 'Sculpture'. F. J. Furnivall (B.A. 1847) was later founder of the Chaucer Society and the Early English Text Society. Leslie Stephen (an undergraduate 1850–4) was a Fellow from 1854 to 1867. In his *Life* (1885) of his friend and colleague, Henry Fawcett, he gives a description of the Fellows'

Garden 'which Mr. Henry James—a most capable judge—pronounces to be unsurpassed in Europe'.

Ronald Firbank, whose artificial conversation pieces were published between 1915 and 1926, was an undergraduate from 1907 to 1909. He left, without a degree, to spend some years travelling about the Mediterranean.

University Library. This copyright library includes a large number of manuscripts and early printed books including Caxton's first book, *Recuyell of the Historyes of Troye*. Exhibitions are held regularly.

Open to visitors who are shown round at 3 p.m. weekdays and 12 noon on Sat.

CAME, Dorset. [2 Hd] Hamlet 2 m. SE. of Dorchester, on the A352. The thatched rectory (now Old Came Rectory), set back from the road in a pleasant garden, was the home of William Barnes when he was rector of the combined parish of Whitcombe and Winterborne Came. The little church of Whitcombe can be seen from the main road; that of Winterborne Came is hidden among trees and not signposted, but can be reached by the road to Came House, a turning W. between Whitcombe and the old rectory, and it is here that Barnes is buried, his grave marked by a high cross of Celtic design.

CAMELFORD, Cornwall. [2 Ce] Busy little town on the A39, between the NW. edge of Bodmin Moor and the sea. According to tradition it was the site of King Arthur's Camelot, and Slaughter Bridge, 1 m. N., is said to be the scene of his last battle.

CAMELOT. See CAMELFORD.

CAMPTON, Beds. [4 Df] Village off the A507. Robert Bloomfield is buried outside the E. window of the church which has Dorothy Osborne's family monuments.

CANONS ASHBY, Northants. [4 Bf] Country house, on the B4525, built (1551) by the Dryden family on the ruins of an Augustinian Priory. Spenser was thought to have written part of *The Faerie Queene* in a room now called after him. His 'Rosalynde' was a kinswoman of the wife of the owner, Erasmus Dryden, according to John Aubrey. John Dryden was related to the owners but

it is not thought he visited often, although his son Erasmus lived here and is buried in the church. This, with its massive ironstone tower, is all that remains of the monastic buildings. Samuel Richardson used Ashby-Canons as the address Lucy Selby gives in *Sir Charles Grandison* (1754).

CANTERBURY, Kent. [1 Hc] Cathedral city on the Roman roads, the A2, A28, and the B2068. Chaucer stayed here (1360–1) as part of the Royal Household, and he makes *The Canterbury Tales* a collection of stories to beguile the journey of pilgrims, coming to do penance at the ornate shrine of St. Thomas à Becket, originally to the E. of the High Altar, in the Trinity Chapel of the cathedral, but wrecked in 1538. Becket's murder was the subject of dramas by George Darley in 1840, by Tennyson in 1884, and of Eliot's *Murder in the Cathedral* (1935), first staged in the Chapter House. John Bale, whose persecution after leaving the Catholic Church sent him abroad during Mary's reign, was made a prebend by Elizabeth I and spent his remaining years here. He wrote *King John* (1548) and morality plays. The poet Alexander Barclay wrote the *Life of St. Thomas* (1520) and joined the Franciscans here before becoming a rector in London in 1552. Part of their Grey Friars buildings can still be seen and the dorter (built 1267) was for a time the home of Richard Lovelace, who, though heir to estates in the county, fell on hard times during the Commonwealth after presenting the Kentish Petition. The birthplace of John Lyly (1569) is unknown, and that of Christopher Marlowe (1564) in George St. was destroyed in 1942. Like the playwright Stephen Gosson in 1554, Marlowe was baptized in St. George's Church, of which only the tower remains (P) in the new shopping area. A Victorian tribute representing the four main characters in his plays acted by Irving, Forbes Robertson, Alleyn, and James Hackett, stands in Dane John gardens by the old city wall. Near by, off the busy Rheims Way, is the church (locked) of St. Mildred with St. Mary de Castro, where Izaak Walton married in 1626. Anne Finch, Countess of Winchilsea, lived at The Moat (gone) off the Littlebourne road, where she was visited by Celia Fiennes. In their verses Pope addressed her as 'Ardelia' and Rowe as 'Flavia'.

Richard Barham was born (1785) in the Burgate at the corner of Canterbury Lane (P on site of former house). Some of his *Ingoldsby Legends* (1840) are set in the city, where the sisters Harriet and Sophia Lee chose to keep their travellers snowbound long enough to recount their improbable *Canterbury Tales* (1797–1805). Dickens set many scenes in *David Copperfield* (1850) here and the House of Agnes Hotel in St. Dunstan St. is said to have been Agnes Wickfield's home. The Sun (built 1503), now a shop near the cathedral, has a plaque listing Dickens's associations with the inn. Conrad (d. 1924) was buried in the cemetery (memorial stone) after a service in St. Thomas's R.C. Church, attended by many of his friends including Cunninghame Graham, who described the scene in 'Inveni Portum', published in *Redeemed* (1927).

Linacre, Marlowe, Hugh Walpole, and Maugham were at King's School in the cathedral precincts. Walpole and Maugham left bequests to the school. In 1961 Maugham returned to open the Maugham Library, which houses his own books, and manuscripts of *Liza of Lambeth* (1897) and *Catalina* (1948), his first and last novels. In *Of Human Bondage* (1915), his autobiographical novel, Philip Carey goes to school in Tercanbury, his name for Canterbury.

CAPHEATON HALL, Northumberland. [6 He] Country house 12 m. SW. of Morpeth, off the A696, home of the Swinburne family. Algernon Swinburne often spent holidays here at his grandfather's house in the mid-19th c. He used to ride his pony to Cambo, where he was tutored by the rector, and to Wallington, where his friends Sir Walter and Lady Trevelyan lived. Memories of Capheaton occur in *Lesbia Brandon* (1952), the unfinished novel in which Swinburne explores the state of mind of young Bertie at Ensdon, whose library the boy falls upon with 'miscellaneous voracity'.

CARISBROOKE, I.O.W. [1 Cf] Village on the B3223, just SW. of Newport. In 1648, when Charles I was imprisoned in the castle, ½ m. S., Dorothy Osborne and her brother, who had just met William Temple on the journey, stayed at the inn near by. Young Osborne, who had Royalist sympathies, scratched a biblical quotation on the window which was considered seditious, and they were taken before the Governor. Dorothy Osborne, trusting his chivalry, confessed that she was the culprit and they were released, to Temple's admiration. Dorothy Osborne's *Letters* to Temple during their long courtship were published in 1888 and 1928. John Keats stayed here in April 1817. In a letter to his friend John Reynolds from 'Mrs. Cook's, new village' (now Canterbury House, Castle Rd.) he writes that he has unpacked his books, pinned up the picture by their friend Haydon, but is apprehensive as he has not yet written a word of the long poem he has planned. His room has a view of the castle (now obscured by trees) and he has walked about the island, 'which should be called Primrose Island', and found just the place where they can read their poems aloud when Reynolds comes. He has been reading *King Lear* and he includes the sonnet 'On the Sea' which he wrote as a result. Keats visited the island again but he and Reynolds never met here though Reynolds lived in Newport (q.v.) later.

The castle figures in Meade Falkner's *Moonfleet* (1898).

CARLION. See CAERLEON.

CARLISLE, Cumbria. [5 Ba] City on the Eden, just S. of Hadrian's Wall, on the A6 and the A7, once the Roman camp of Luguvallium and former capital of NW. England. Thomas Percy, later Bishop of Dromore, was Dean here from 1778 to 1782. Robert Anderson, the Cumbrian dialect poet, was born (1 Feb. 1770) at Down Side in St. Mary's parish and educated first at the charity school run by the dean and chapter and then at the Quaker school under Isaac Ritson. He began to earn his living at 10 as assistant calico printer for his brother and was later apprenticed to a pattern drawer. After 5 years in London he returned to Carlisle in 1796, fired with ambition to be a poet, and in 1805 published *Cumbrian Ballads*, based on subjects from real life. His 'Lucy Gray', a poetic rendering of a rustic Northumbrian story, probably suggested Wordsworth's poem, 'She dwelt among the untrodden ways'. Anderson's *Poetical Works* with his autobiography was published in 1820. He died in Carlisle in 1833 and is buried in the cathedral yard, where a tombstone erected by public subscription marks his grave. There is a marble monument to him in the cathedral, with a portrait bust in high relief. Sir Walter Scott married Margaret Charlotte Charpentier (known as Charlotte Carpenter) in the cathedral in December 1797, having met her only a few months earlier when staying at Gilsland (q.v.). The house, 81 Castle St., where she was living with her companion, Miss Jane Nicholson, can still be seen.

CARMARTHEN, Dyfed. [3 Cf] Town on the estuary of the Towy. The name is connected with the legendary Merlin, first popularized in Arthurian lore by Geoffrey of Monmouth in his *Historia Regum Britanniae* (1136), the name 'Merlinus' being a latinized form of the Welsh Merddin or Myrddin, a prophet or seer after whom Carmarthen (or Caerfyrddin) was named. A Welsh version can be found in the *Black Book of Carmarthen*, a book of poetry written at the Priory of St. John's (now gone) in the 13th c., consisting of dialogues on mythology, theology, history, and literature. A facsimile copy, edited by J. Gwenogvryn Evans (1904–6) is in the Public Library. Merlin's Oak, at the E. end of the town, said to have grown from an acorn planted on 19 May 1659 to mark the town's proclamation of Charles II as king, was killed by poison by an early 19th-c. tradesman who disapproved of people gathering under it at all hours of the day and night. The old stump, patched and supported by cement, stands at a road junction and carries the prophecy traditionally ascribed to Merlin:

> When Merlin's Tree shall tumble down,
> Then shall fall Carmarthen Town.

Sir Richard Steele moved to Carmarthen from Hereford in 1724 and lived in King St. in a house belonging to the Scurlocks, the family of his second wife Mary ('dear Prue'). After her death he moved to near-by Llangunnor, returning to Carmarthen after a seizure. He died in King St., in the house which is now the Ivy Bush Hotel, and was buried in the Scurlock vault in St. Peter's Church. Sir Lewis Morris, a 19th-c. poet, best remembered for *The Epic of Hades* (1876–7), was born in Spilman St.

CARRA LOUGH, Mayo. [8 Be] Lake lying to the E. of the T40, between Castlebar and Ballinrobe. On the NE. shore, off an unclassified road, are the burnt-out ruins of Moore Hall, where George Moore was born (1852) and spent most of his early life. The

scenes of his boyhood are vividly depicted in his novel, *The Lake* (1905). After his death in London his ashes were brought to Ireland and buried in a cist on Castle Island, within sight of his birthplace, with a memorial tablet on a cairn built of stones from the ancient castle on the island.

CARRICKFERGUS, Antrim. [8 Hb] Small port and market town of great antiquity on the A2, 11 m. NE. of Belfast on the N. shore of Belfast Lough, renowned for its magnificent castle. William Congreve came to live here when he was 8, when his father, who had been stationed as an infantry lieutenant at Youghal, was transferred to the garrison at Carrickfergus for 3 years (1678–81). At that time it was a busy port, 'filled with English sailors, rough and jovial fellows', remembrance of whom may have accounted for the character of Sailor Ben, the 'absolute Sea-Wit' of *Love for Love* (1695). Louis MacNeice spent his childhood here at his father's rectory, as he relates in his unfinished autobiography, *The Strings are False* (1965).

CASKIEBAN CASTLE. See INVERURIE.

CASTERBRIDGE. See DORCHESTER.

CASTLE BOTEREL. See BOSCASTLE.

CASTLEDERG, Tyrone. [8 Eb] Small woollen-manufacturing town on the B72, 12 m. SW. of Strabane, on the Derg. After her marriage in 1850 Mrs. Cecil Frances Alexander lived at Derg Lodge in the remote parish of Trienamongan (or Termonamongan), 6 m. W. In 1853 she published *Narrative Hymns for Village Schools*, which included the well-known 'Jesus calls us o'er the tumult'.

CASTLE DOUGLAS, Kirkcudbrights. (Dumfries and Galloway). [6 Ef] Small town, a farming and tourist centre, at the N. end of Carlingwark Loch, 13 m. SW. of Dumfries. Joseph Train, the antiquary, who gave Scott much material for his historical novels, lived here and is commemorated by a plaque in the Town Hall. Lockhart, in his *Life of Scott* (1837–8), quotes Scott as saying 'if ever a catalogue of the museum of Abbotsford shall appear, no single contributor, most assuredly, will fill so large a space as Mr. Train'. Train heard the ballad 'Durham Garland' sung here by a woman whose family kept the words in their memory by singing it frequently. He was buried in 1852 at Kirton, 2 m. S.

CASTLEGREGORY, Kerry. [9 Bd] Village on the N. side of the Dingle Peninsula, overlooking Tralee Bay, 19 m. W. of Tralee. It takes its name from Gregory Hoare, a tenant-in-chief of the Desmonds, who built a castle here in the early 16th c. In 1580 his son, Black Hugh, deeming it prudent to show loyalty to the English queen, entertained Sir Walter Ralegh and Edmund Spenser, who were leading a company of Lord Grey's army to attack the Spanish and Italian garrison at Fort-del-Oro at Smerwick. An account of the feast is given in *In the Kingdom of Kerry*, by Richard Hayward (1950). The castle stood at the SE. end of the village, but nothing is left except some stones built into several of the houses and the remains of an inscribed arch from the castle doorway.

CASTLETOWNSHEND, Cork. [9 Cf] Village at the end of the L60, 5 m. SE. of Skibbereen, on the W. shore of Castle Haven. When Swift was staying at Unionhall (q.v.) in 1723 he used to come over by rowing-boat from Glandore Harbour and tradition has it that he composed the Latin poem *Carberiae Rupes* in the ruined tower near the harbour, and that he named one of the houses in the village Laputa (now called Ahakista). Castletownshend was the home of Edith Œnone Somerville, who collaborated with her cousin Violet Martin ('Martin Ross') in writing travel books, essays, sporting and children's picture books, and is remembered especially for *Some Experiences of an Irish R.M.* (1899) and *Further Experiences of an Irish R.M.* (1908), entertaining stories written in the ascendancy tradition of the big house and foxhunting, and for the sensitive novel, *The Real Charlotte* (1894). Edith Somerville lived nearly all her life at Drishane, the Georgian family mansion at the entrance to the village, and died at Tally House, a little further on. The main street goes steeply down to the harbour, circumventing two tall sycamores which she referred to as 'walled in their barbaric stone flower pot, the distraction of the village'. The Protestant church of St. Barrahane, on a hill overlooking the estuary, contains memorials to Edith Somerville, including bronze chandeliers and a tablet on the N. wall presented by American admirers. The holy table was given by her in memory of Violet Martin, who predeceased her by 34

years. They are buried in the churchyard in adjacent graves.

CASTLEWOOD. See CLEVEDON.

CATFIELD, Norfolk. [4 Hd] Village 13 m. NE. of Norwich, on the A149. William Cowper spent childhood holidays at the rectory with his uncle, Roger Donne, whose daughter Ann became the recipient of many of his letters after her marriage to Thomas Bodham.

CATTAWADE (or CATTIWADE), Suff. [4 Gf] Village on the A137, 9 m. N. of Colchester. Thomas Tusser, while farming here, wrote *Hundreth Good Pointes of Husbandrie* (1557) which, though full of maxims to which many of our proverbs can be traced, proved to have been of little help to him, as he died (1580) a prisoner for debt in London. He is commemorated by a tablet in Manningtree Church (1 m. S.).

CAVERSHAM, Berks. [1 Cc] Suburb of Reading, 2 m. NE. on the Henley road. Caversham Park is on the site of Lord Knollys's house (originally 'Cawsome-House') where Queen Anne of Denmark, wife of James I, was entertained by revels and a masque by Thomas Campion in April 1613. The house, which has since been twice rebuilt, was then 'fairely built of brick, mounted on the hillside of a Parke within view of Redding', and the Queen was so pleased with her entertainment that after supper 'she vouchsafed to make herselfe the head of their revels and graciously to adorn the place with her personall dancing'. A full description of the masque is given in *The Works of Thomas Campion*, ed. W. R. Davis, 1967, pp. 235 ff. The house is now the headquarters of the B.B.C. Monitoring Service and permission to visit must be obtained through the B.B.C.

CEIRIOG VALLEY. See GLYN CEIRIOG.

CELBRIDGE, Kildare. [8 Gf] Village on the L2, 13 m. W. of Dublin, situated on the Liffey. Celbridge Abbey (now owned by a religious order)[1] was the home of Swift's 'Vanessa', Esther Vanhomrigh (1690–1723), the daughter of a Dutch merchant who came over with William III and provisioned his troops. After meeting and falling in love with Swift in London she returned to Celbridge to be near him when he was in Dublin, and built a rustic bower where they could meet. Swift often rode over to see her, but on the last occasion (in 1723), enraged by her suspicion that he had secretly married Stella (Esther Johnson), he bade her an angry farewell. She died soon afterwards and was buried at Celbridge. Swift's poem 'Cadenus and Vanessa', the story of their relationship (written in 1713) was published after her death, at her request. A seat under the rocks by the river is known as 'Swift's Seat'.

[1] The house and garden may be seen by permission.

CHADWELL ST. MARY, Essex. [1 Fc] Village on the A1089, 2 m. N. of Tilbury. Daniel Defoe had a part interest in a tile works at West Tilbury (1 m. E.) from 1694 to his imprisonment in Newgate in 1703. He is thought to have lived for part of this time, when he was managing the business, at Sleepers (now a scheduled building), a thatched, wattle and daub farmhouse opposite the church. The house got its name from the days of the pilgrims, who slept here before crossing the Thames at Tilbury. Defoe is also thought to have returned, when in hiding to escape more charges of sedition, as he is traditionally thought to have written part of *Robinson Crusoe* (1719) here. The parish registers list the family name as Foe: Daniel called himself Defoe after 1703.

CHAGFORD, Devon. [2 Ed] Little market town on the edge of Dartmoor, 4 m. NW. of Moretonhampstead, reached by several minor roads W. of the A382 or N. of the B3212. Sidney Godolphin was killed (1643) during the civil war in a skirmish here, traditionally at the Three Crowns Inn, an early 16th-c. building facing the churchyard.

Evelyn Waugh wrote *Brideshead Revisited* (1945) while staying at Chagford in the spring and summer of 1944.

CHALDON HERRING (or EAST CHALDON), Dorset. [2 He] Little village on a minor road in a fold of the downs, S. of the A352 from a turning *c.* 7 m. SE. of Dorchester and 1½ m. N. of the sea. Theodore Francis Powys (1875–1953), after farming for a time in Suffolk, settled here in 1905 for most of his life, at a red-brick Victorian house called Beth Car. His

writing, almost all published between 1923 and 1935, consists of novels and short stories with allegorical themes of love and death, God and evil, mostly set in a Dorset rural background. Chaldon Herring is portrayed as 'Folly Down' in *Mr. Weston's Good Wine* (1927) and Chaldon Hill as 'Madder Hill'. His other titles include *Black Bryony* (1923), *Mr. Tasker's Gods* (1925), and *Unclay* (1931) (novels), and *The Left Leg* (1923), *The House with the Echo* (1928), and *Penitent* (1931) (short stories). He moved to Mappowder (q.v.) in 1940. His brother Llewelyn (1884–1939), after living abroad for health reasons, came to Chaldon Herring with his wife in 1925 and lived at Chydyok Farm, sharing the property with two of his sisters. While here he published *The Pathetic Fallacy* (a study of Christianity, 1930), *Dorset Essays* (1935), and the novels *Apples be Ripe* (1930) and *Love and Death* (an imaginary autobiography, 1939). Finally, illness made it necessary for him to move to Switzerland, where he died in December 1939. After the war his ashes were brought to Dorset as he had wished, and scattered on the cliff top near Chaldon, where a Portland stone memorial, carved by Elizabeth Muntz, now stands.

CHALFONT ST. GILES, Bucks. [1 Db] Large village off the A413. Milton's Cottage, where he came with his family in 1665 to escape the plague, was found for him by a former pupil, the Quaker Thomas Ellwood. Now a museum,[1] it contains many relics of the poet and rare editions of *Paradise Lost*, completed here before he returned to London in 1666. The popular novel *Deborah's Diary* (1859) by Anne Manning is an account of Milton's life here as told by his daughter.

[1] Open Feb.–Oct. inclusive: weekdays, except Tues. 10 a.m.–1 p.m., 2.15–6 p.m.; Sun. 2.15–6 p.m.; Nov.–Jan. inclusive: weekends only.

CHALK, Kent. [1 Fc] Village on the E. outskirts of Gravesend, on the A226. Charles Dickens spent his honeymoon (1836) here in a house at the end of the village on a corner of the lane leading to Shorne and Cobham. He often passed the house, when he was living at Gad's Hill, on his extensive walks. The house has gone and a plaque has been fixed to a weatherboard-house near by. The forge in the village is traditionally that of Joe Gargery in *Great Expectations* (1860–1), which is set in the neighbourhood. A photograph of the honeymoon cottage is at The Dickens House, Doughty St. (see London, Holborn).

CHAPELIZOD, Dublin. [8 Gf] Suburban village on the Liffey, 3 m. W. of Dublin, on the T3. The name is said to derive from Iseult (or Isolde, or Isoud), in Arthurian legend the sister (or daughter) of Moraunt, King of Ireland, slain by Tristram. The village is the scene of Le Fanu's novel, *The House by the Churchyard* (1863), and the place where the Liffey becomes Anna Livia Plurabelle in Joyce's *Finnegans Wake* (1939).

CHARLECOTE PARK, Warwicks. [4 Af] Country house (N.T.) off the B4086, 4 m. NE. of Stratford-upon-Avon. A tradition grew up that Shakespeare, as a young married man, was caught poaching deer on the Lucy estate, and when brought before Sir Thomas Lucy who imposed severe penalties, retaliated with satirical verses, and prudently left the district (*c*. 1585). Sir Thomas Lucy is said to be the model for Justice Shallow. The tradition suffered a setback when it was realized that Charlecote did not have a park in Shakespeare's time but rallied again as a warren, which Charlecote did possess, could have contained roe deer.

Open Apr.–Sept.: daily, except Mon. (open Bank Holiday Mon.) 11.15 a.m.–5.15 p.m.

CHARLES, Devon. [2 Ec] Village 6 m. NW. of S. Molton, off the B3226. In the small church a tablet commemorates R. D. Blackmore's holidays in the village where his grandfather was curate-in-charge.

CHARLTON, Wilts. [1 Ab] Village on the B4040, 2½ m. NE. of Malmesbury. Dryden stayed at the Jacobean Charlton Park (burnt down 1962), seat of his wife's father, during 1665–6 to escape the plague. He wrote *Annus Mirabilis* and *Essay of Dramatic Poesy* while here with friends including his brother-in-law Robert Howard, the dramatist, and Charles Sedley.

CHARLTON ST. PETER, Wilts. [1 Ac] Small village on the A342 near the junction with the A345. Stephen Duck, a self-educated farm labourer, was born (1705) here, and

became known as the thresher-poet from his long poem on the labourer's work which includes the lines

> From the strong planks our crab-tree staves rebound,
> And echoing barns return the rattling sound.
>
> . . . .
>
> In briny streams our sweat descends apace,
> Drops from our locks, or trickles down our face.
> No intermission in our work we know;
> The noisy threshal must for ever go.

He married here and six years later in 1730 his wife was buried in the churchyard. In the same year Joseph Spence recommended him to Pope. The village remembers him at the June Duck feast at the Charlton Cat (Ducks are married farm workers who have lived in the village for at least a year). Costs are met from the rent of Duck's acre, a field given to the threshers by the first Lord Palmerston, to whom a toast is also drunk at the feast. The Chief Duck's tall silk hat, adorned with feathers and a picture of a thresher, is kept on view in the pub.

CHARTERHOUSE SCHOOL. See LONDON (City).

CHATHAM, Kent. [1 Fc] One of the Medway towns on the A2. Cobbett arrived here in 1784 intending to enlist as a marine but found himself a foot soldier on sixpence a day instead. He spent the year here educating himself in grammar which earned him a corporal's extra twopence a day before he embarked for Nova Scotia. Many scenes in Dickens's works stem from his early years when he lived (1817–21) with his parents in Ordnance Ter. (P), now opposite the station but then covered with Virginia creeper and surrounded by fields. Later (1821–3), due to money troubles which so often embarrassed his father, they moved to the smaller House on the Brook, St. Mary's Pl. (gone), off Military Rd. Dickens went to Mr. Giles's School in Clover Lane and spent many hours at the genial parties in the Mitre Inn and Clarence Hotel in the High St., which he describes in 'The Holly Tree' from *Christmas Stories*. In *David Copperfield* (1849–50) the young hero spends a night listening to the sentries' feet after selling his jacket to buy food. Members of the Pickwick Club attended a military review, and the fields about Fort Pitt, a naval hospital, were to be the scene of Mr.

Winkle's duel until it was so happily avoided. In *The Uncommercial Traveller* (1860) Dickens describes his arrival at the railway station which had swallowed up the 'departed glories' of the fields where he had played the imaginative games of his youth.

CHATTERIS. See EXETER.

CHAWTON, Hants. [1 Cd] Village 1 m. S. of Alton, now by-passed by the A32, but well signposted. Jane Austen and her sister, Cassandra, came with their mother, following her father's death in 1805, to Chawton in July 1809 after several moves and settled in the house then known as Chawton Cottage:

> Our Chawton Home, how much we find
> Already in it to our mind:
> And now convinced, that when complete
> It will all other houses beat
> That ever have been made or mended,
> With rooms concise or rooms distended.

Thus Jane wrote to her brother, Captain (later Admiral) Francis Austen, R.N., while they were still settling in. She wrote the final versions of her six novels here and lived here until her last move, to Winchester in 1817. Now called Jane Austen's House,[1] it is beautifully cared for by the Jane Austen Memorial Trust, and has many treasures to delight her admirers: furniture, clothes, pictures, books (including an American 1st edition of her novels, 1832).

[1] Open Apr.–Oct. inclusive: daily 11 a.m.–4.30 p.m.; Nov.–Mar. inclusive: closed Mon. and Tues.

CHEDDAR, Som. [2 Gb] Small town on the A371. In 1788 Hannah More and her sisters, determined to open a school for the illiterate of the wild Mendip Hills, stayed at the George Hotel (gone). They found 'an old vicarage house, empty for years' and in spite of opposition from farmers who thought education would unsettle their labourers, opened the school (now Hannah More Cottage, Lower North St., an Old People's Club), writing their own instructional tracts to resemble the popular penny tales sold by pedlars. In 1794 Coleridge and Southey walking to Huntspill to visit George Burnett and Tom Poole were locked in the garret of the inn as though they were footpads, but Southey said, 'the cliffs amply repaid us'.

CHELTENHAM, Glos. [3 Hf] Market and light-industrial town on the A40 and the A46, 9 m. NE. of Gloucester, made popular as a spa after George III's visit in 1788. Fanny Burney, whose official post in the Royal Household made her part of the entourage, wrote a lively account in her *Diary* of their 5 weeks at Fauconberg House (rebuilt).

Tennyson stayed for a short time in 1843, while taking a cure for his nervous illness, at 6 Belle Vue Place and 10 St. James's Sq., part of the terraces, crescents, and squares, waspishly called by Cobbett 'white tenements with green balconies', which give the town its Regency flavour. At this time Tennyson was writing the elegies later called *In Memoriam* (1850). Sydney Dobell leased (1848–53) Coxhorne House at Charlton Kings (2 m. SE.), a square Georgian house in a large garden. He finished the dramatic poem *The Roman* (1850), published under the name Sydney Yendys, and began *Balder* (1854), the tragedy of a poet who kills his wife when she becomes mad after the death of their son. A. C. Bradley, the Shakespearian scholar, was educated at Cheltenham College in Bath Rd. in the 1860s. James Elroy Flecker lived from 1886, when he was 2, at Dean Close School, where his father was the first headmaster. He spent his vacations from Uppingham and Oxford here and his room, at first his nursery and then his study, looked S. across the roses and elms in the garden to the Cotswolds in the distance. In 'November Eves' he remembers the damp evenings that

> Used to cloak Leckhampton Hill
>
> . . .
>
> And send queer winds like Harlequins
> That seized our elms for violins
> That struck a note so sharp and low
> Even a child could feel the woe . . .

Flecker, who died (1915) in Davos, is buried in the cemetery here near two 'gossip pines'. A granite cross marks the grave on which an Alexandrian laurel and an *Olearia haastii* were planted to represent the trees of his poem 'Oak and Olive' in *The Old Ships* (1915). His parents erected a plaque over the door of the school chapel and this has been moved to the new War Memorial Chapel. Margaret Kennedy, who made her name with her novel *The Constant Nymph* (1924), was educated at Cheltenham Ladies College just before the First World War.

C. Day-Lewis, who was English master at Cheltenham College from 1930 to 1935, lived (1932–8) at Box Cottage, in Charlton Kings, which joins Cheltenham to the SE. He published the revolutionary poem *The Magnetic Mountain* in 1933. In 1935 he wrote a detective story, *A Question of Proof*, under the pseudonym 'Nicholas Blake', to pay for the repair of the roof. The school in the story is based partly on Cheltenham Junior School. He gave up teaching the same year. *Collected Poems 1929–36* was published in 1938.

CHEPSTOW, Gwent. [2 Ga] Old market town and former port on the A48, on the W. bank of the Wye, 2 m. above its junction with the Severn. Robert Bloomfield stayed at the Beaufort Arms when he was touring with friends along the Wye and into Wales in the summer of 1807. He describes in *The Banks of Wye* (1811) the 'delightful and social evening' spent after visiting the castle by moonlight and hearing an owl hooting lustily from the battlements.

CHERTSEY, Surrey. [1 Dc] Town on the A320. Abraham Cowley, who, as Evelyn records in his *Diary*, was considered the best poet of his day, was given an estate here by the Duke of Buckingham. His house in Guildford St. (altered in 1883) was an irregular, gabled, Tudor building with a room above the porch which jutted out into the road. This porch, with a plaque reading 'Here the last accents flowed from Cowley's tongue', was taken down in the 18th c. and the plaque has gone. The low-gabled shops in front of the Victorian building are all that remain.

Thomas Peacock lived at Gogmoor Hall with his widowed mother and grandfather, Thomas Love. In *Recollections of Childhood* (1837) he gives an idealized description of Abbey House (gone), the home of a schoolfriend. After working in a merchant's office in London, he returned here and in 1807 met Fanny Faulkner at Newark Priory (q.v.). Opposite Cowley House was Beomonds, an 18th-c. house visited by Dickens, who used the Black Swan (gone) near Chertsey Bridge in *Oliver Twist* (1838) and modelled Mr. Pecksniff in *Martin Chuzzlewit* (1843) on a local resident. The car park and public library are on the site of Beomonds, which was later the home of Ernest Coleridge, who edited

extracts from his grandfather's notebooks, *Anima Poetae* (1895). Dickens was a friend of Albert Smith, the son of a doctor, born (1816) in a house opposite the church. He was a journalist and wrote the play *Blanche Heriot or the Chertsey Curfew* (1842) and many humorous novels, some illustrated by Phiz, which were popular in the 1850s. J. Maddison Morton, son of the creator of Mrs. Grundy, wrote the popular farce *Box and Cox* (1847) at his home Laburnum Cottage in Bridge Rd.

CHESTER, Ches. [3 Fb] Ancient cathedral city on the right bank of the Dee, on the A41. The first literary connection is with William of Malmesbury, the 12th-c. historian who spent most of his life in Malmesbury, but also travelled widely in England. He writes (*c.* 1125): 'Chester is called the City of the Legions because the veterans of the Julian legions were settled there . . . The natives greatly enjoy milk and butter; those who are richer live on meat . . . Goods are exchanged between Chester and Ireland, so that what the nature of the soil lacks, is supplied by the toil of the merchants.' Ranulf Higden, a monk at St. Werburgh's, wrote the *Polychronicon* (*c.* 1342) here, a Latin universal history from the Creation to his own time. He is buried in the cathedral. Another monk of St. Werburgh's, Henry Bradshaw (d. 1513), was born in Chester and wrote (*c.* 1500) a lost chronicle of the city and a verse life of St. Werburgh, of which five known copies of a 1521 edition survive. Celia Fiennes enjoyed her visit here in 1698 and gives a good description of the city and its principal buildings and the 'wall all aboute with battlements and a walke all round paved with stone;' (*Journeys*, 1947), and Defoe was also interested in the walls, which he found in very good repair, commenting that 'it is a very pleasant walk round the city, upon the walls, and within the battlements, from whence you may see the country round' (*Tour*, 1724–7).

Swift used to travel to and from Ireland by way of Chester and his letters to Esther Johnson (*Journal to Stella*, complete edn. 1948) began in 1710, when he stayed at the Yacht Inn on the corner of Nicholas St. His friend Thomas Parnell, poet and archdeacon of Clogher, died (1718) in Chester after falling ill on his journey to Ireland, and is buried at Holy Trinity Church (rebuilt 1865), opposite the corner of Watergate St. and Weaver St. Boswell, writing to Dr. Johnson in 1779, expressed his delight in Chester and especially in its feminine society: '. . . here again I am in a state of much enjoyment. . . . Chester pleases my fancy more than any town I ever saw.'

When De Quincey ran away from Manchester Grammar School in July 1802 he made his way, on foot, to his mother's house, The Priory (gone), 'a miniature priory attached to the walls of the very ancient Anglo-Saxon Church to St. John', once owned by Sir Robert Cotton, the antiquary. After staying here a while he left to wander through Wales, on an allowance from his uncle of a guinea a week, and eventually reached London. In March 1803 he came back briefly 'to rest after the storms' before going to Worcester College, Oxford. The site of The Priory, at the bottom of Nicholas St., is occupied by the Police Headquarters. A. H. Clough was educated at the King's School (founded by Henry VIII in 1541; formerly in Northgate St.; removed to Wrexham Rd., 1962). There is an evocative description of Chester in Henry James's *The Ambassadors* (1903).

CHEVELEY, Cambs. [4 Fe] Village off the B1063, 4 m. SE. of Newmarket. When Crabbe was a young apprentice (1768–70) to the surgeon apothecary of Wickhambrook (6 m. S.), he delivered some medicines to Cheveley Park, a country house of the Duke of Rutland. Crabbe was amazed at this first contact with riches and elegance. In 'Silford Hall' published posthumously, he writes of a boy's delight at being shown round the house with its picture gallery and other splendours, and in being given a good meal by the housekeeper.

CHICHESTER, West Sussex. [1 De] Cathedral city on the A27 and the old Stane St. Reginald Pecock when Bishop (1450) wrote three works in English instead of the usual Latin, which united the differing sections of church opinion against him. These, *The Repressor of over much blaming of the Clergy* (1455), *Book of Faith* (1456), and *Provoker*, resulted in his resigning the bishopric and being sent into retirement. The Gateway and the Bishop's Palace itself date from the 14th c. Part of the palace is now the Pre-

bendal (choir) School, which has a frontage in the flint building and adjoining 18th-c. houses in West St. John Selden (b. 1584), who later disputed the legality of Charles I's privileges, was educated there by the lawyer Hugh Barker (d. 1632). Then known as the Free Grammar School, it had been reformed by Bishop Story (d. 1503), who built the ornate market cross. James Hurdis was a pupil in the 1770s. Defoe mentions the 'great hole big enough for a coach and six' made when the cathedral spire was struck by lightning.

William Collins, whose father was three times mayor, was born (1721) at 21 East St. (now a bank). He lived, after returning from London, at 11 Westgate St., which he had inherited, but he became mentally ill and was cared for by his sister until his death at the Royal Chantry in the cloisters. He is buried in St. Andrew Oxmarket, reached by a passage from East St., which has a memorial. A marble monument by Flaxman with lines by William Hayley, a native, was erected (1795) in the SW. tower of the cathedral. This shows Collins, head on hand, reading the Bible. The chapel of the Four Virgins, now the Treasury, off the N. transept, contains books with the signatures of Thomas Cranmer and John Donne, salvaged when the library was pillaged in 1643.

Charlotte Smith, who had been sent to school here at the age of 6, rented a house in the town after separating from her husband (c. 1787). Her sonnets had been printed in the town at her expense in 1784, five editions following in as many years. Her novels, which were admired by Sir Walter Scott, who wrote her biography, were so popular that she was able to keep her twelve children on the proceeds. Blake, who had been arrested in Felpham (q.v.), was tried for high treason and acquitted in 1804 at the Guildhall in Priory Park (now an archaeological museum), once the choir of Greyfriars.

A plaque on no. 11, one of the remaining houses in Eastgate Sq. (formerly Hornet Sq.), commemorates Keats's stay in 1819 with the Dilkes. 'Hush, hush! tread softly!' was written at this time, perhaps in the coach on his way down from London. He visited the old Vicars Close with its crypt, then a wine store, and Robert Gittings's *John Keats: The Living Year* gives the source of the imagery of 'The Eve of St. Agnes' which he started to write here. Charles Crocker (1797-1861) was born here and apprenticed to a shoemaker. He then worked for a bookseller and his first poem appeared in the *Brighton Herald*. A collection was published by subscription. Crocker became sexton at the cathedral in 1845 and then Bishop's verger. He was buried in the Subdeanery graveyard. Cobbett, in his *Rural Rides*, was pleased with the well-attended meeting he addressed at the Swan.

CHICKSANDS, Beds. [4 Df] An R.A.F. station shared by the U.S.A.F. on the A418 near Shefford. The priory, within the camp, was the home and perhaps the birthplace in 1627 of Dorothy Osborne, whose *Letters* to William Temple tell of the long engagement forced on them by their disobliging families. They met by chance in 1648 in Carisbrooke on their way to St. Malo, but were not married until 1654. Recounting her uneventful life at Chicksands, with nothing to look forward to but his letters, she asks him if he remembers the little house on the island of Herm which they saw from the ship on their way to St. Malo. 'Shall we go thither? thats next to being out of the world. There we might live like Baucis and Philemon, grow old together in our little cottage, and for our charity to some ship-wrecked strangers, obtain the blessing of dying both at the same time.' S. of the priory is the church at Campton with the family chapel where her father was buried. She sometimes wrote her letters while sitting at his bedside during his long illness. The priory was improved by Wyatt in 1813; the cloisters glazed 'with ancient stained glass' and fashionably rough cast. John Byng was reminded of a dairy when he visited in 1791, and feared that in place of meditation he would now think of cream. The grounds were ornamented by a ruined chapel and a cascade.

CHICKSGROVE, Wilts. [1 Ad] Hamlet 11 m. W. of Salisbury off the A30. Sir John Davies (1569-1626) was born at the manor house (rebuilt).

CHIGWELL, Essex. [1 Eb] Outer suburb NE. of London. James Smith (1775-1839), returning here, recalled the area known to him as a schoolboy:

> Abridge her tank and waterfall
> The path beneath Sir Eliab's wall
> I once again am stepping,
> Beyond that round we rarely stirred;
> Loughton we saw—but only heard
> Of Ongar and of Epping.

Ye Olde King's Head is the Maypole in Dickens's *Barnaby Rudge* (1841).

CHILVER'S COTON. See NUNEATON.

CHIPPING ONGAR. See ONGAR.

CHRISTCHURCH, Cambs. [4 Ed] Village in Upwell Fen off the A1101, 8 m. S. of Wisbech. Dorothy Sayers spent vacations at the rectory, her parents' home after 1917. Upwell Fen was probably the setting for her detective story involving campanology, *The Nine Tailors* (1934), in which the church of Fenchurch St. Paul has an angel roof resembling that of Upwell (4 m. N.). On the NE. of Upwell Fen, near Denver, she set the imaginary village of Denver Ducis, ancestral home of her detective, Lord Peter Wimsey.

CHRISTCHURCH, Dorset. [1 Be] Town on the A337, at the head of Christchurch Harbour, between the Avon and the Stour. John Marston, playwright and poet, who renounced the theatre *c.* 1607 and took holy orders, was rector here 1616-31: his name can be seen on the list of incumbents in the magnificent Priory Church. Under the tower of the church there is an elaborate sculptured monument to Shelley, erected by his son, Sir Percy Florence Shelley, who lived at Boscombe, near by. A very different literary figure is remembered in connection with the Catholic church in Purewell Rd. F. W. Rolfe ('Baron Corvo'), author of *Hadrian the Seventh* (1904), stayed in Christchurch in 1889 and 1891 and, according to A. J. A. Symons in *The Quest for Corvo* (1934), executed a number of frescoes in the R.C. church of St. Michael's, and as recently as 1960 a letter in *Country Life* states 'Corvo's fresco is still at St. Michael's'. But there are two discrepancies to confuse the story: the church is named after the Immaculate Conception and St. Joseph, and the painting at the E. end is a mural, on canvas, not a fresco. The painting, 'The Assumption', was restored in 1965, but there is considerable doubt as to whether the original was the work of the strange, enigmatic man who was author, schoolmaster, artist, and failed priest.

CHRIST'S HOSPITAL, West Sussex. [1 Ed] Public school off the A24, S. of Horsham, which moved from Newgate St. in the City (see London) in 1902. Middleton Murry mentions having a year at the old site in *Between Two Worlds* (1934). Edmund Blunden, who won an entrance scholarship here and also in 1914 a scholarship to The Queen's College, Oxford, published two short collections of verse in his last year, *Poems* and *Poems translated from the French*. Keith Douglas came here in 1931 and at 16 had one of his poems accepted in *New Verse*. He won a scholarship to Oxford in 1938.

CHUDLEIGH, Devon. [2 Ee] Village on the A38, *c.* half-way between Exeter and Ashburton. Ugbrooke Park, formerly the seat of Lord Clifford, contains a grove of beech trees known as 'Dryden's Walk'. There is a tradition that Dryden, who was a close friend of the first Lord Clifford, completed his translation of Virgil's *Aeneid* while staying here, or, alternatively, that he may have written part of *The Hind and the Panther* in the winter or spring of 1686–7.

CHURCH STRETTON, Salop. [3 Fd] Small town below the Long Mynd, 12 m. S. of Shrewsbury on the B4370. In the S. transept of the church there is a memorial to Sarah Smith, author under her pen-name 'Hesba Stretton' of *Jessica's First Prayer* (1866), who spent her childhood in the neighbourhood. The lancet window above has a stained-glass picture of Jessica. The background of her less-known novel *The Children of Claverley* is set in the near-by valley. Church Stretton is the 'Shepwardine' of Mary Webb's novels.

CIRENCESTER, Glos. [1 Ab] Roman Corinium and market town on the Fosse Way, A429, and Ermine Way, A417. In 1718 Gay and Pope spent the summer at Oakley House in the absence of Lord Bathurst, the owner. His old house had been demolished and the new Cirencester Park not yet built. Pope wrote that Oakley Wood was inspiring Gay 'like the cave of Montesinos'. His letter to Martha Blount said 'we draw plans for houses and gardens, open avenues, cut glades, plant firs, contrive water-works, all very fine and beautiful in our imagination'. He was there again in 1719 and in 1726 visited with Swift. They lodged with a tenant farmer and walked 2 miles to dinner, as Swift reminded Bathurst in a letter in 1735. Mrs. Delany, writing to Swift, recalled seeing the cottage rebuilt after it had 'burst with pride . . . after entertaining so illustrious a person'. Some of Pope's plans were used when the House in the Wood or Alfred's Hall was renovated and Gothicized. Mrs. Delany later wrote 'it is now a venerable castle and has been taken by an Antiquarian for one of King Arthur's'. She was referring to a translation (in reality a fabrication) by Charles Bertram in 1757 of an 11th-c. monk's history of Roman antiquities.

The 18th-c. theatre in Gloucester St., now Barton Hall and part of Powell School, was dismantled in the 1850s. It stood behind the old Volunteer Inn, now no. 27; Mrs. Siddons, Kean, and Kemble acted, and Cobbett lectured there.

CLANDEBOYE, Down. [8 Hc] Seat of the Marquess of Dufferin and Ava, just S. of the A2 Belfast–Bangor road and 1 m. S. of Crawfordsburn. At the S. end of the demesne is Helen's Tower, erected (1861) by the first Marquess in memory of his mother, Helen, Lady Dufferin. The top storey contains verses by Lady Dufferin to her son on his coming of age, inscribed in gold, and lower down are plaques with verses by Tennyson, Browning, and Kipling. Lady Dufferin is remembered by her poem 'The Lament of the Irish Immigrant', published with her songs in 1894. The stile referred to in the poem is at Killyleagh graveyard on Strangford Lough, *c.* 30 m. S.

CLANE, Kildare. [8 Ff] Village on the L2 and the L25, 21 m. W. of Dublin. Blackhall House, 1 m. S., was the birthplace of the Revd. Charles Wolfe, author of 'The Burial of Sir John Moore'.

CLAVERING ST. MARY. See OTTERY ST. MARY.

CLAVERTON, Avon. [2 Hb] Village 2 m. E. of Bath on the A36. Richard Graves, rector here from 1749 to his death in 1804, was the author of *The Spiritual Quixote* (1772), a gentle satire on the Methodists, in which

Whitefield and Shenstone, with whom he was at Oxford, are depicted. He also wrote *Columella, or the Distressed Anchoret* (1776), in which Shenstone again appears, *Eugenius, or Anecdotes of the Golden Vale* (1785), and *Plexippus or the Aspiring Plebian* (1790).

CLEOBURY MORTIMER, Salop. [3 Gd] Market town on the River Rea, on the A4117 between Ludlow and Kidderminster. A strong claim has been made for it as the birthplace of the 14th-c. poet William Langland, the reputed author of the allegorical poem *The Vision of Piers Plowman*. A panel in the church porch has the quotation:

> Holy Church am I, quoth she,
> Thou oughtest me to know
> 'Twas I received thee first
> And then, the Faith, didst teach.
>
> To me, they brought your sureties
> My bidding to fulfil
> That thou wouldst love me loyally
> Thy whole life through.

and records that, according to tradition, Langland was born at Cleobury Mortimer and educated at the near-by Augustinian monastery of Woodhouse (now a farm) and later at Great Malvern Priory. The stained glass in the E. window was the gift of the Vicar Prebendary Baldwyn Childe in 1875 and shows biblical and allegorical figures and the dreaming poet reclining by the Rea, with the Malvern Hills in the background. A detailed description of the window is given at the W. end of the nave.

CLEVEDON, Avon. [2 Gb] Coastal town 12 m. SW. of Bristol on the B3130. Coleridge and his wife Sara set up house here after their marriage in 1795, and a two-storey stone cottage (P) in Old Church Rd., near the junction with Coleridge Vale Rd. North, is claimed as his. He was soon writing to his publisher for further help in equipping it and Cottle drove from Bristol with a cart-load of necessities. Many years later he recalled that the cottage was only one storey high. The town was then secluded and peaceful and Coleridge liked the walk along Dial Hill, but he and Sara returned to Bristol before the birth of their first child. Thackeray, who often stayed at the 14th-c. Clevedon Court (N.T.),[1] and wrote part of *Vanity Fair* (1847) there, portrayed it as Castlewood in *Henry Esmond* (1852), but set it in Hampshire.

A commemorative tablet to Arthur Hallam, Tennyson's friend, whose early death inspired the long poem *In Memoriam*, is in the parish church of St. Andrew's. Tennyson and his wife, who had suggested the title of the poem, visited the church on their honeymoon (1850). The seashore here is traditionally the setting for 'Break, break, break, / On thy cold grey stones, O sea!'. The vicarage in Coleridge Rd. is thought to be the one rented by Rupert Brooke's parents in 1909 where he invited his friends from Cambridge for the summer vacation.

[1] Open Apr.–Sept.: Wed., Thurs., Sat., and Bank Holiday Mon.: 2.30–5.30 p.m.

CLIFFORD CHAMBERS, Warwicks. [4 Af] Village off the A46 2 m. S. of Stratford-upon-Avon. The half-timbered Manor House was the home of Anne Goodere on her marriage to Sir Henry Rainsford. She was Michael Drayton's 'Idea' and welcomed him to

> deere Cliffords seat (the place of health and sport)
> Which many a time hath been the Muses' quiet port.

He 'yearly used to come in the summertime to recreate himself' and was treated with syrup of violets by Shakespeare's son-in-law, who prescribed for Lady Rainsford. It is thought Ben Jonson and Donne, who visited her father and sister at Polesworth, came here too. The Manor was burnt down in 1918 and the present red-brick house was designed by Lutyens. Village tradition says that Shakespeare was born in the black-and-white rectory next to the church, his mother staying here because of plague in Stratford. There were certainly Shakespeares in the village, as a John Shakespeare gave a bier to the church in 1608.

CLIFTON, Notts. [4 Bc] Suburb S. of Nottingham on the B679. Clifton Grove, formerly a country estate, now a public park with a tree-lined walk above the Trent, gives the title to a collection of poems (1803) by Henry Kirke White. He died (1806) soon after entering Cambridge. His hymn 'Oft in danger, oft in woe' is still sung.

CLIFTON HAMPDEN, Oxon. [1 Cb] Village on the A415, 8 m. S. of Oxford. The Thames-side inn, the Barley Mow (badly damaged by fire in 1975), was one of the halts chosen by the characters in *Three Men in a Boat* (1889) by Jerome K. Jerome, who had also stayed there himself.

CLIVE HALL. See PRESTON BROCKHURST.

CLOGHER, Tyrone. [8 Fc] Village on the A4, at the head of the Clogher Valley. Thomas Parnell (1679–1718), poet and scholar, was archdeacon of the cathedral (rebuilt in 1818) from 1706 to 1716. He was a friend of Swift and of Pope (to whose *Iliad* he contributed an introductory essay) and author of 'The Night Piece on Death', 'The Hymn to Contentment', and 'The Hermit', published in *Poems on Several Occasions* (ed. Pope, 1722). His lines in 'Elegy to an Old Beauty' have become proverbial:

> And all that's madly wild, or oddly gay
> We call it only Pretty Fanny's way.

CLOISTERHAM. See ROCHESTER.

CLONFERT, Galway. [9 Ea] Ancient ecclesiastical settlement 5 m. NW. of Banagher, off the L2. St. Brendan the Navigator (484–577) founded a monastery here in 558–64, destroyed and rebuilt several times since, and finally transformed into an Augustinian priory. St. Brendan's roving life gave rise to many legends in medieval literature, based on the *Navigatio Sancti Brendani*, of which *The Voyage of St. Brendan* is a versified Anglo-Norman form. He is buried at Clonfert, and the partly ruined Protestant cathedral, renowned for its magnificent Romanesque west door, is named after him. In 1771 Richard Cumberland, son of the Bishop of Clonfert, stayed at the palace (burned down in the 20th c.) while he was writing *The West Indian*, a sentimental comedy produced at Covent Garden the same year, which had a long and outstandingly successful run.

CLONGOWESWOOD COLLEGE, Kildare. [8 Ff] Jesuit boarding-school (founded 1814), *c.* 1½ m. N. of Clane, off the L25 Kilcock–Naas road. Francis Sylvester Mahony ('Father Prout') was educated here, as was James Joyce, who portrayed some of his school experiences in *A Portrait of the Artist as a Young Man* (1914–15).

CLONMEL, Tipperary. [9 Fd] Ancient, formerly walled town on the T6 and the end of the T49, situated in the beautiful valley

of the Suir. Laurence Sterne was born here (24 Nov. 1713), traditionally in Mary St. (formerly Our Lady's St.), when his father, an army subaltern, was temporarily stationed in the town. Marguerite Power, later Countess of Blessington (1789–1846), came to live here at the age of 8, and a secluded part of the river near the weir where she used to bathe, known as 'Lady Blessington's bath', can be seen from the path S. of the river, a little E. of Old Bridge Rd. She spent much time on the Continent and wrote travel books and novels, but is remembered especially for her *Journal of Conversations with Lord Byron* (1832). George Borrow attended former Grammar School (now the County Engineering H.Q.), just outside the West Gate, for a few months in 1815, when his father was stationed in the town as an army officer, and it was here that he first began to learn Irish. Anthony Trollope lived in lodgings in Anne St. in 1844–5 while working as a Post Office inspector. The former Post Office building is now a chemist's shop, next to the Provincial Bank in O'Connell St.

CLOUDS HILL, Dorset. [2 Hd] T. E. Lawrence's cottage (N.T.), on an unclassified road N. of Bovington Camp, reached either from the B3390, from Bere Regis on the A35, or from East Burton on the A352. Lawrence rented the cottage first in 1923 when he was stationed at the camp as Private Shaw, and later bought it, to be a retreat where he could come to read or write or play the gramophone, and it was here that he worked on *Seven Pillars of Wisdom* (1926). He finally retired to live here in 1935.

Open Apr.–Sept.: Wed., Thurs., Sun., and Bank Holiday Mon.: 2–6 p.m.; Oct.–Mar. 12–4 p.m.

CLOUGHJORDAN, Tipperary. [9 Eb] Village on the T21a and the L34, 6 m. SE. of Borrisokane. Thomas MacDonagh, poet and co-founder of Edward Martyn's Irish Theatre (1914), was born in a house in the main street. He was one of the signatories of the Proclamation of the Irish Republic in 1916 and was executed after the Easter Rising.

CLOVELLY, Devon. [2 Dc] Picturesque village on the NW. coast, at the end of the B3237. Charles Kingsley lived here as a boy when his father was rector (1830–6) and is commemorated by a tablet in the church.

He describes the village in *Westward Ho!* (1855). Dickens came here in 1861 with Wilkie Collins and wrote about it in 'A Message from the Sea', a story written in collaboration with Collins, first published in *Household Words* (later in *Christmas Stories*). Clovelly appears as 'Steepway'.

CLOVENFORDS, Selkirks. (Borders). [6 Fd] Village on the A72, 3 m. W. of Galashiels. There is a statue of Sir Walter Scott outside the inn where he used to stay after he was appointed Sheriff of Selkirkshire (Dec. 1799) and before he moved to Ashiestiel (q.v.). The church has a memorial window to him.

CLUN, Salop. [3 Fd] Small town in the Clun Valley, on the A488 and the B4368, 5 m. N. of Knighton. The ruined Norman castle on the hill is thought to be Scott's Garde Doloureuse in *The Betrothed* (1825), where the scene is laid in the Welsh Marches. He possibly wrote part of the novel while staying here. The town is immortalized in A. E. Housman's *A Shropshire Lad* (1896):

> Clunton and Clunbury,
> Clungunford and Clun,
> Are the quietest places
> Under the sun.

though this is probably just Housman's chosen version of a traditional jingle with various alternative adjectives, such as 'prettiest' or 'wickedest'. In the novels of Mary Webb, Clun appears as 'Dysgwlfas-on-the-Wild-Moors'.

CLYRO, Powys. [3 Fe] Village on the A4153, 2 m. NW. of Hay-on-Wye. Francis Kilvert, while curate here (1865–72), kept notebooks (*Diary*, 1938–40, new edn. 1969) in which he recorded the events of the day, his journeys to outlying farms, his grief at the many lives cut short by fatal illness, and his pleasure in the beauties of the countryside.

COATE, Wilts. [1 Bc] Hamlet off the A419, 2 m. SW. of Swindon. Richard Jefferies, a farmer's son, was born (1848) and spent his early life in the house[1] (P) above the inn, which he describes in *The Old House at Coate* (1948). Cuttings from the russet apple and mulberry trees planted there by his father were taken in 1973 by the Richard Jefferies Society to perpetuate those trees he mentioned. Two of the naturalist's favourite

walks were to Barbary Camp (5 m. S.) on the Marlborough Downs and to Burderop Park (2 m. S.), the subject of *Round about a Great Estate* (1880) and the location of many scenes in *Bevis* (1882), a novel about his boyhood. Coate Reservoir, where he skated and idled hours away, also features in *Bevis*.

[1] Open Wed., Sat., Sun., 2–6 p.m.

COBH (pr. Cove), Cork. [9 Ee] Cathedral town (called Queenstown, 1849–1922) on Great Island on the N. side of Cork Harbour, the principal port for transatlantic liners, reached by the T12a from Carrigtohill on the T6 from Cork. John Tobin (1770–1804), a dramatist whose first successful play, *The Honey Moon*, was produced a few weeks after his death, is buried in the churchyard near the crossroads, ¾ m. N., in an unmarked grave. Tobin had sailed for the West Indies in search of health, but died on the first day out and was brought back to Cobh for burial. The Revd. Charles Wolfe, author of 'The Burial of Sir John Moore' (1817), is buried in the same churchyard, in the NW. corner of the ruined church, in a flat-topped grave overgrown with brambles.

COBHAM, Kent. [1 Fc] Village on the B2009, 4 m. W. of Rochester. One of Dickens's favourite walks from Gad's Hill was through Cobham Park (now a girls' school). The owner Lord Darnley, who had given him a key, arranged for the small Swiss chalet, used by Dickens as a study at Gad's Hill, to be re-erected in the grounds of the park after Dickens's death. In *Pickwick Papers* (1837), the disappointed Mr. Tupman retires to the Leather Bottle Inn, but when his friends arrive after a hot walk, they manage to persuade him to rejoin them. Part of the inn was damaged by a fire in the 1880s but it has many mementoes of Dickens.

COBHAM, Surrey. [1 Dc] Large village on the A3 and the A245, 5 m. NW. of Leatherhead. Matthew Arnold lived from 1873 until his death in 1888 at Pain's Hill Cottage (gone), now commemorated by Matthew Arnold Close on the site near the bridge over the Mole. While here he published collections of essays including a second volume of literary criticism. His letters refer to the country around and to the lake in the ornamental park of Pain's Hill, where he used to skate, and to the family pets who died here, including the canary Matthias, the subject of a short poem.

COCKERMOUTH, Cumbria. [5 Ab] Market town on the A594 and the A595, at the confluence of the Derwent and the Cocker. William Wordsworth and his sister Dorothy were born (7 Apr. 1770 and 25 Dec. 1771 respectively) in a handsome double-fronted house, now called Wordsworth House (N.T.),[1] at the W. end of the wide High St. The Derwent, flowing past the terrace-walk at the foot of the garden, was Wordsworth's lifelong happy memory of his earliest days, the river that in *The Prelude* (1850)

> . . . loved
> To blend his murmurs with my nurse's song . . .
> And from his fords and shallows sent a voice
> That flowed along my dreams.

He attended the Grammar School, a small building (gone) in the churchyard, for a time in 1776, though regular schooling did not begin until the early summer of 1779, when he went to Hawkshead (q.v.) Grammar School, but the foundations of a love of poetry were laid at home in his father's library and in learning by heart 'large portions of Shakespeare, Milton, and Spenser'.

[1] Open 1 Apr.–31 Oct.: daily except Thurs. and Sun. 10.30 a.m.–12.30 p.m., 2–5 p.m.

COCKFIELD, Suff. [4 Gf] Village off the B1070, 7 m. SE. of Bury St. Edmunds. While R. L. Stevenson was staying with his cousin and her husband Churchill Babington (rector 1866–89) he met a Cambridge colleague of his, Sidney Colvin. It was to Colvin that Stevenson addressed his *Vailima Letters* (1895) from Samoa.

COLCHESTER, Essex. [1 Ga] Old town on the A12. Crabb Robinson, the diarist, was articled to an attorney here in 1790. Jane and Ann Taylor lived (1796–1811) at 11–12 West Stockwell St. (P), off the High St. by the Town Hall. They wrote *Original Poems for Infant Minds* (1804), *Rhymes for the Nursery* (1806), which included 'Twinkle, twinkle, little star', and *Hymns* (1810).

COLEMAN'S HATCH, East Sussex. [1 Ed] Village S. of the A264, 6 m. SE. of East Grinstead. Yeats spent December and Janu-

ary of 1913–14 at Stone Cottage, 'four rooms . . . on the edge of the heath and our backs to the woods'. He returned again the next year for January and February. Ezra Pound and his wife were with him.

COLEORTON HALL, Leics. [4 Bd] Mansion (now offices of the National Coal Board) on the B587, 1 m. NW. of the village, the country home of Sir George Beaumont (1753–1827), patron of painters and poets. He lent his new farmhouse, Hall Farm, (visible from the road NW. of the Hall) to Wordsworth, from November 1806 to June 1807, as Dove Cottage was too small for his growing family. The mansion was being built by Dance the Younger, and Wordsworth, who walked daily in the grounds, was soon occupied in planning a winter garden of hollies, cypresses, yews, and box for Lady Beaumont. Dorothy Wordsworth's letters describe the farmhouse with its coal fires from Sir George's pits (mentioned in Corbett's 'Iter Boreale'), their walks to Grace Dieu, ancestral home of the Beaumonts, and recount that her brother 'composes frequently in the grove'. Coleridge, long awaited, arrived in December with Hartley, but the easy productive friendship of Alfoxton was not recaptured here. Their last guest was Walter Scott. Under the limes, painted by Constable, is a decorative urn with lines to Joshua Reynolds who stayed here, and the terrace walk has an inscription to Francis Beaumont (d. 1616), brother of Sir John whose poems were edited (1810) by Sir George, his direct descendant. Many of Wordsworth's poems were illustrated by Sir George.

COLESHILL, Bucks. [1 Db] Village off the B473, 3 m. N. of Beaconsfield. Edmund Waller was born at the Manor House (gone). Foundations of an old house thought to be the Manor were uncovered when a garage was built at Stock Place, a privately owned timber and plaster house known locally as his birthplace. In the next-door garden is 'Waller's Oak', under which he is reputed to have sat.

COLLOONEY, Sligo. [8 Dd] Village on the T3, 7 m. S. of Sligo, at the junction of the Owenmore and the Unshin. Yeats's 'Ballad of Father O'Hart' (published in *Crossways*, 1889) commemorates Father John, the 'old priest of Collooney', who died in 1793, whose story he learnt from Father O'Rorke of nearby Ballysadare and Kilvarnet.

COLTHOUSE, Cumbria. [5 Bc] Hamlet ½ m. E. of Hawkshead (q.v.), where Wordsworth lodged with Anne Tyson while he was attending Hawkshead Grammar School (1779–87). Although it was formerly thought that the Tysons' cottage, referred to in *The Prelude* (1850), was in Hawkshead, investigations initiated by Mrs. Heelis of Sawrey (Beatrix Potter) indicate that Ann Tyson and her husband moved from Hawkshead, where they had kept a shop, to Colthouse *c.* 1773 and made their living by taking schoolboy boarders. It is not certain whether the cottage still exists, but it may have been the present Green End Cottage, and the brook of *The Prelude* (IV, 50–1), which ran 'boxed within our garden', may be the little stream which runs in a channel through the orchard.

COLWICH (pr. Collich), Staffs. [3 Hc] Village 6¼ m. SE. of Stafford on the A51 near its junction with the A513. William Somerville, author of *The Chace*, was born at the manor house on 2 September 1675, but the house (which had been rebuilt) was demolished in the 1960s and only the wall and the park gates are left.

COMBE, Oxon. [1 Bb] Village 1 m. N. of the A4095 at Long Hanborough. The short-story writer A. E. Coppard moved here *c.* 1914 from Islip, to return to writing. In his autobiography (1957) he says that 'Piffing Cap' from *Pearsons Magazine* and *Clorinda walks in Heaven* (1922) have 'vague traces of Combe'.

COMBE FLOREY, Som. [2 Fc] Village off the A358, 8 m. NW. of Taunton. Sydney Smith was rector here (1829–45) and wrote that his Georgian house (now the Old Rectory) was 'like the parsonages described in novels'. 'My neighbours look very much like other people's neighbours; their remarks are generally of a meteorological nature.' The church has a memorial E. window to him. The manor house, rebuilt on the site of an Elizabethan house in the park, was the home (1956–66) of Evelyn Waugh, who wrote here the last volume of his war trilogy, *Unconditional Surrender* (1961).

CONGHAM. See SWAFFHAM.

CONGREVE, Staffs. [3 Hc] Hamlet a little W. of Penkridge, 5 m. S. of Stafford on the A449, reached by a minor road turning left beyond Cuttlestone Bridge over the Penk. This was the birthplace of Richard Hurd (1720–1808), the farmer's son who became a critic and divine and Bishop of Lichfield and Worcester.

CONINGSBY, Lincs. [4 Db] Village on the A153 near Tattershall Castle. Laurence Eusden (1688–1730), whose appointment as Poet Laureate in 1718 after he had written a flattering poem to the appointer, caused ridicule, was rector here (1725–30). Pope called him a drunken parson in *The Dunciad*. John Dyer, the poet, was rector from 1752 to his death. In the introduction to Dyer's poems in *British Poets* (1820) John Aikin suggests he was ordained and 'sat down' on the livings of Coningsby and Kirkby-on-Bane as a relief from a dissolute life. The rectory, now Church Close, where he wrote *The Fleece* (1757), is next to the church and has a medieval core. The 'fenny country' did not agree with him and he complained 'of a lack of books and company'. He died of a 'gradual decline' in 1758 and was buried in the church, but no memorial remains.

CONISBROUGH, South Yorkshire. [4 Ba] Town off the M1, 5 m. SE. of Doncaster. The Norman castle[1] in Scott's *Ivanhoe* was the home of Athelstane, whom Cedric was disappointed not to find more zealous for the Saxon cause.

[1] Open daily, Sun. from 2 p.m.

CONISTON, Cumbria. [5 Bc] Village near the head of Coniston Water, on the A593 and the B5285. Ruskin is buried in the churchyard, his grave marked by a tall cross of Tilberthwaite stone, designed by his friend W. G. Collingwood. The Ruskin Museum in the village contains a collection of drawings, letters, and other relics.

COOKHAM DEAN, Berks. [1 Dc] Village in the Thames Valley between Marlow and Maidenhead, where Kenneth Grahame stayed with his maternal grandmother ('Granny Ingles') at The Mount after his mother's death in 1864. He used to go on the river with his uncle, the Revd. David Ingles, who probably first inspired his passion for 'messing about in boats'. Later, when he was Secretary of the Bank of England and famous for *The Golden Age* (1895) and *Dream Days* (1898), he came back with his wife and son Alistair ('Mouse') and lived at Mayfield from 1906 to 1910. *The Wind in the Willows*, begun as bedtime stories for Alistair, gradually took shape as a book and was published in 1908.

COOLE PARK, Galway. [9 Db] The woods and lake of Coole lie 2½ m. NW. of Gort, off the T11. The house, where Lady Gregory lived from the time of her marriage in 1880 until her death in 1932, was pulled down in 1941 and only the garden walls and ruins of the stable block are left. The grounds are in the care of the Forestry and Wild Life Service, and the Autographed Tree, a copper beech inscribed with the initials of distinguished visitors, including those of G. B. Shaw and W. B. Yeats, still stands beside a box-hedged walk in the garden. In *Coole* (MS. 1931, ed. C. Smythe 1971) Lady Gregory describes the house in detail, especially the drawing-room, where she wrote plays, journals, articles, and folktales, and typed to Yeats's dictation, and where she kept her letters from writers and artists. She tells how Shaw used to play the piano and sing little folk-songs, and how Masefield stayed for a while, 'a shy devotee of Yeats, a maker of ballads of the sea'; but, most of all, the writer connected with Coole is Yeats, who came first in 1898 and was nursed back to health from sickness, making it his home for many years and working in a room looking towards the lake, a time remembered in his poem 'The Wild Swans at Coole' (1919). In 'Coole Park, 1929' Yeats anticipates the passing of the house and its owner:

I meditate upon a swallow's flight,
Upon an aged woman and her house,

. . . .

Here, traveller, scholar, poet, take your stand
When all those rooms and passages are gone,
When nettles wave upon a shapeless mound
And saplings root among the broken stone,
And dedicate—eyes bent upon the ground,
Back turned upon the brightness of the sun
And all the sensuality of the shade—
A moment's memory to that laurelled head.

COOLING, Kent. [1 Fc] Village off the B2000, in the marshes, N. of Rochester. The castle, once the home of Sir John Oldcastle (d. 1417), though ruined, still has a 14th-c. gatehouse. The play *The First Part of Sir John Oldcastle* (1600), though included in the 3rd and 4th folios, is not by Shakespeare. The opening scenes of *Great Expectations* (1860–1) are set in the area, and Dickens is said to have written of Pip's little brothers and sisters in the churchyard after seeing the coffin-shaped stones above the graves of thirteen children here.

COOPER'S HILL. See EGHAM.

CORK, Cork. [9 De] Port, university, and cathedral city, situated on the Lee at the head of a long and beautiful estuary on the S. coast. The river flows through the city in two main channels, spanned by several bridges, described by Spenser, who was appointed High Sheriff of Cork in 1598, as

The spreading Lee, that like an island fayre
Encloseth Corke with his divided flood.
(Faerie Queene, IV. ii.)

The Protestant church of Christ Church, between Grand Parade and South Main St., is on the site of the city's second medieval church (demolished 1717), where in 1594 Spenser is thought to have married Elizabeth Boyle, for whom he wrote *Epithalamion* (1595) in celebration of the occasion. Arthur Murphy, playwright, actor, and friend of Dr. Johnson, worked as a merchant's clerk in Cork in 1747 before going to London, where he settled. Several distinguished writers have been born in Cork, though many of their birthplaces are not recorded. They include James Sheridan Knowles (1784–1862), a dramatist who studied medicine before turning to literature, author of several plays and a popular ballad, *The Welsh Harper*, which attracted the attention of Hazlitt; William Maginn (1793–1842), one of the early contributors (under the pen-name 'Ensign O'Doherty') to *Blackwood's Edinburgh Magazine* and the founder of *Fraser's Magazine* (1830), in which he published his 'Homeric Ballads'; Thomas Crofton Croker (1798–1854), antiquarian and friend of Maginn, born in Buckingham Sq. In spite of a lack of formal education Croker devoted himself from an early age to the study of Irish songs and legends which he collected in rambles in S. Ireland, published in *Researches in the South of Ireland* (1824),

The Fairy Legends and Traditions of the South of Ireland (1825), his best-known work, which was admired by Scott, and *Legends of the Lakes* (1829), later republished as *A Guide to the Lakes* (1831) and *Killarney Legends* (1876). After an apprenticeship at 16 to Lecky and Marchant, a firm of Quaker merchants, he went to London (1818) to work as an Admiralty clerk, made his name as a folklorist, and in 1827 became a member of the Society of Antiquaries. He helped to found the Camden and Percy Societies. Scott remembered him as 'little as a dwarf, keen-eyed as a hawk, and of easy, pre-possessing manners'. Francis Sylvester Mahony (1804–66), author, under his pen-name 'Father Prout', of many entertaining papers and poems contributed to *Fraser's Magazine* (1834–6) and *Bentley's Miscellany* (1837), was also a native of Cork. He is best remembered for his lines on the celebrated bells of the church of St. Anne's, Shandon (C.I.)[1]

> With deep affection,
> And recollection,
> I often think of
>   Those Shandon bells.
> 'Tis the bells of Shandon,
> That sound so grand on
> The pleasant waters
>   Of the River Lee.

The bells hang in the elegant clock tower of St. Anne's Church, which stands on the hillside N. of the river, above Pope's Quay. Mahony, who lived nearly all his life in Cork, is buried in the churchyard. Justin McCarthy (1830–1912), historian and novelist, was born in Cork, the son of the clerk to the city magistrates, and at 17 was a reporter on the *Cork Examiner*. He is best remembered for his historical works, especially *A History of Our Own Times* (1879; with additions, 1905). He also wrote novels, of which the best known are *Dear Lady Disdain* (1875) and *Miss Misanthrope* (1878). Edward Dowden (1843–1913), poet and Shakespearian scholar, also a native, was the son of a Cork merchant and landowner, and went to Queen's College (now University College) before going to Dublin. Daniel Corkery (1878–1964), dramatist, was born at 2 Auburn Villas, near the top of Gardiner's Hill, on the NE. side of the city. His plays include *The Labour, The Yellow Bittern,* and *Fohnam the Sculptor,* but he is remembered principally for his literary studies, *The Study*

of *Irish Literature* and *The Hidden Ireland* (1925). He also wrote a novel, *The Threshold of Quiet* (1917). He spent most of his life in Cork and was Professor of English Literature at University College until he retired (1947). Michael O'Donovan (1903–66), widely known by his pen-name, 'Frank O'Connor', was born in Douglas St., but his earliest memories were of 251 Blarney St., a small cottage at the top of the hill, where he lived until he was 5 or 6, when his parents moved to 8 Harrington's Sq., near Dillon's Cross, NW. of Gardiner's Hill. He was educated at the Christian Brothers School, where he was taught by Daniel Corkery, who inspired him to learn Gaelic. His work includes novels, plays, and criticism, but he is best known for his short stories: *Bones of Contention* (1936), *The Common Chord* (1947), *Traveller's Samples* (1950), and others. He was also a Gaelic scholar and *Kings, Lords, and Commons* (1961) is an anthology of translations from the Irish. His autobiography, *An Only Child* (New York, 1958; London, 1961), gives a vivid picture of Cork in the early 1900s. A portrait bust of him stands in the public library in Grand Parade.

Visitors to the city have praised or abused it. Arthur Young found it reminiscent of a Dutch town with its pleasant waterways, and Thomas Moore delighted in the 'sort of sea avenue up to the town, with beautiful banks on either side studded over with tasteful villas'. Thackeray thought it disappointing and was dismayed by its shabbiness and idle populace. Sir Walter Scott, however, on his Irish tour of 1825, was very favourably impressed by his visit and the city reciprocated by presenting him with the freedom of Cork.

[1] Open Apr.–May: Mon. to Sat. 10 a.m.–6.30 p.m.; June–Sept.: Mon. to Sat. 9.30 a.m.–9 p.m.; Oct.–Mar.: Mon. to Sat. 10.30 a.m.–5 p.m.

CORSTON, Avon. [2 Hb] Village on the A39, 3 m. W. of Bath. Southey's first school kept by the Flowers was at the Manor Farm (track opposite the village school). 'The Retrospect', written at Oxford after his return in 1793 to find the school had closed, contains the lines,

> Silent and sad the scene: I heard no more
> Mirth's honest cry, and childhood's cheerful roar
> No longer echo'd round the shout of glee . . .

CORWEN, Clwyd. [3 Eb] Town on the A494, 11 m. E. of Llangollen. John Cowper Powys moved here from Dorset late in 1934 and the novel *Maiden Castle*, which he had begun there, was published in 1937. He also wrote the historical novel *Owen Glendower* (1941), *Porius* (1951), a romance of the Dark Ages, *Up and Out* (1957), which contained the short story 'The Mountains of the Moon', and many works of philosophy and criticism. He moved to Blaenau Ffestiniog (q.v.) in 1955.

COSSALL, Notts. [4 Bc] Village 4 m. SE. of Eastwood off the B6096. Church Cottage was the home of Louie Burrows, for a short time D. H. Lawrence's fiancée and a possible model for Ursula Brangwen of *Women in Love* (1920). It was the honeymoon cottage of the Brangwens, but Marsh Farm is no longer there. Will Brangwen was modelled on Louie's father Alfred, whose carvings are in the church with the family memorial windows.

COTTERSTOCK, Northants. [4 De] Village off the A605, 1½ m. N. of Oundle. Cotterstock Hall,[1] a 17th-c. house with rounded gables, was the home of Mrs. Elmes Steward, the daughter of Dryden's first cousin. In 1698 and 1699 Dryden spent the summers here writing *Fables Ancient and Modern* (1700), adaptations from Boccaccio and Chaucer. He was in failing health and she fed him on venison and marrow puddings.

[1] Apply in writing for appointment to visit.

COTTISFORD, Oxon. [1 Ca] Village off the A43, 6 m. S. of Brackley. In the 1880s Flora Thompson (then Timms) walked with the other children from Juniper Hill to school here, which she depicted as Fordlow in her trilogy *Lark Rise to Candleford* (1945). The school, now a private house, is on the triangle at the cross roads.

COVENTRY, West Midlands. [4 Be] Cathedral and manufacturing town 15 m. SW. of Birmingham. The Coventry Plays of the 15th and 16th centuries are thought to have been named after the town where they were performed. The legend telling of Lady Godiva's sacrifices for the people of Coventry is mentioned in Drayton's *Polyolbion* (1612–22), and is the subject both of Tennyson's poem, written after a visit in 1840, and of one of Landor's *Imaginary Conversations*. There is a statue of Lady Godiva in Broadgate.

Mary Ann Evans ('George Eliot'), who went to boarding school at 29 Warwick Row, returned (1841–9) when her father retired and moved to Bird Grove, Foleshill Rd. She was often invited to Rosehill, Radford Rd., the home of Charles Bray, a manufacturer. He was a free-thinker and Miss Evans met other well-educated women there including Rufa Brabant, whose father was acquainted with the publisher, John Chapman. Emerson stayed with the Brays on his way from London to Liverpool to return to America and was most impressed with his first meeting with Miss Evans, who surprised him with her decided praise for Rousseau's *Confessions*. The Brays took Mary Ann Evans on a holiday to the Continent as a diversion after her father's death in 1849. Bray was asked to find a translator for Strauss's *Life of Jesus* and when Rufa Brabant was unable to continue with it after her marriage the task came to Mary Ann Evans, who was to have help from Charles's sister-in-law Sara Hennell. Mary Ann Evans completed her own translation in 1846.

COWAN BRIDGE, Lancs. [5 Cc] Village on the A65, 2 m. SE. of Kirkby Lonsdale. Just N. of the old bridge over the Leck is a row of cottages (P), once part of the Clergy Daughters' School, where Charlotte and Emily Brontë were pupils (1824–5). Their elder sisters, Maria and Elizabeth, had died of typhus contracted there and Charlotte gives a gloomy picture of the school as 'Lowood' in *Jane Eyre* (1847). The school was moved to Casterton in 1833.

COWES, I.O.W. [1 Ce] Town on the N. coast, divided by the estuary of the Medina. West Cowes is noted for the Royal Yacht Squadron built on the site of the castle where in 1650 William D'Avenant was imprisoned. A staunch Royalist, active in Charles I's cause, he left France for Virginia on Queen Henrietta Maria's behalf but was intercepted by a Parliamentarian ship. While in prison he continued his poem of chivalry, *Gondibert* (1651) which, when he was taken to the Tower, he said was 'interrupted by so great an experiment as dying', though this fate was happily delayed and he was released on bail in 1652. Charles and Mary Lamb spent a holiday here in 1803 with Fanny Burney's nephew, Martin. 'We do everything that is idle, such as reading books from the circulating library, sauntering, hunting little crabs among the rocks, reading churchyard poetry, which is as bad at Cowes as any churchyard in the Kingdom can produce.'

COWFOLD. See AMPTHILL.

COWSLIP GREEN, Avon. [2 Gb] Hamlet at the Butcombe turn off the A38 near the Paradise Motel. Hannah More lived here (1785–1802) (house now called Brook Lodge) after her successful dramas provided the money for her Sunday schools for the poor. She designed the house herself, sending the 'plan and drawing' to her friends. Horace Walpole wrote that he thought Cowslip Green sounded a sort of cousin to Strawberry Hill. Anna Seward visited in 1791. When Southey visited with his publisher and friend Cottle, the Misses More wrote that 'he was brimful of literature, and one of the most elegant and intellectual young men they had seen'.

COXHOE HALL. See KELLOE.

COXWOLD, North Yorkshire. [5 Fc] Village off the A19, 8 m. SE. of Thirsk. Laurence Sterne acquired the living here in 1760 and divided his time between Shandy Hall[1] (P), his name for the cottage he improved (the last house in the village well beyond the church), and London society. He finished *Tristram Shandy* (1760–7), and wrote *A Sentimental Journey* (1768) and the *Letters to Eliza* (1775) here. He and his wife often visited Newburgh Priory[2] (1 m. E.) as guests of Lord Fauconberg, the patron of the living. Shandy Hall, where his works are on sale, is owned by the Laurence Sterne Trust, who in 1969 had Sterne's body removed from London and reburied outside the S. wall of the nave where his original tombstone now stands.

[1] Open June–Sept.: Wed. 2–6 p.m. or by appointment.
[2] Open 4 June–24 Sept.: Wed. 2–5.30 p.m.

CRABBETT PARK. See WORTH.

CRAIGENPUTTOCK, Dumfriess. (Dumfries and Galloway). [6 Ee] Moorland farm, 7 m. W. up the glen from Dunscore, inherited by Carlyle's wife, Jane Welsh, and lived in by them (1828–34). He contributed articles on German Literature to periodicals and wrote *Sartor Resartus* (1833–4) while here.

CRANBROOK, Kent. [1 Fd] Village off the A229, 12 m. S. of Maidstone. Phineas Fletcher (1582–1650) and his brother Giles (1558?–1623), who both became poets and who were the cousins of the dramatist John Fletcher (1579–1625), were perhaps both born at their grandfather's rectory (site now part of Cranbrook School). Phineas was certainly baptized here, but Giles's birthplace, which some think was in London, has not been confirmed. In 1760 Edmund Gibbon, then in the Militia, was billeted at the George Inn while guarding French prisoners of war at Sissinghurst Castle (2½ m. N.). Sydney Dobell was born here in 1824, but his father, a wine merchant, moved to Cheltenham shortly afterwards. One of this extensive family erected the Union Mill (restored).

CRANFORD. See KNUTSFORD.

CRANHAM. See PAINSWICK.

CREDENHILL, Hereford and Worcester. [3 Fe] Village on the A480, 3 m. W. of Hereford. Thomas Traherne, rector here from 1657 to 1667, but not resident until 1661, was the author of meditations known as the *Centuries*, published soon after his death (1674), but written for a community in Kington (12 m. NW.). Manuscripts containing his poems were discovered (1896 or 1897) by Bertram Dobell, who edited the first edition in 1903. Ten years later further poems were found in British Museum manuscripts and published as *Poems of Felicity* (1910).

CRIEFF, Perths. (Tayside). [6 Eb] Town on the Earn and the A85, 17 m. W. of Perth, birthplace (1705) of David Mallet (really Malloch) who spent most of his life in London. Charles Reade spent many holidays at his brother's house from 1838 to 1848. His love affair here is thought to have inspired the romance *Christie Johnson* (1853).

CROFT-ON-TEES, North Yorkshire. [5 Eb] Village on the A167, 3 m. S. of Darlington. C. L. Dodgson ('Lewis Carroll') lived at the rectory (now the Old Rectory) opposite the church as a boy when his father was rector. The garden, where tea was often laid on a long table, is mostly unchanged, though the acacia tree has grown a new trunk. The boy used to do conjuring tricks and write plays for his marionettes while on holiday from Richmond Grammar School (1844–5) and Rugby (1845–50). A bronze tablet has been erected in the church by the village to commemorate him as the author of *Alice's Adventures in Wonderland* (1865). Also in the church is the curtained Milbanke pew, like a small gallery up a winding stair, where tradition says Byron and Annabella Milbanke worshipped on their honeymoon at Halnaby (pr. Hannaby) Hall. The lodge gates and the drive can be seen $1\frac{1}{2}$ m. along the Middleton Tyas road, but the house has gone.

CROMARTY, Ross and Cromarty (Highland). [7 Ee] Town at the E. of the Firth of Cromarty, on the A832, NE. of Inverness. Cromartie House is on the site of Cromarty Tower, birthplace of Thomas Urquhart (b. 1611, and where he was living (1645–50) when he joined the rising at Inverness to proclaim Charles II king in 1649. The next year Charles landed in the Firth and Urquhart followed him to Worcester, and after the battle was imprisoned in the Tower of London. He was allowed to return here on parole (1652–3) and some of his translations of Rabelais were published in 1653, and others posthumously in 1693. He died abroad in 1660. *Collections of Miscellaneous Treatises* was published in 1774 and 1834. One, 'Ekskubalauron', includes his account in 'Vindication of the Honour of Scotland' of the 'Admirable Crichton'.

CROOM, Limerick. [9 Dc] Small market town on the T11, 10 m. N. of Ráthluirc, situated on the Maigue. Seán Ó Tuama, a Gaelic poet who had been a member of the 'Court of Poetry' that was held at the farm of Seán Clárach Mac Domhnaill (see Ráthluirc), was an innkeeper at Mungret Gate, near the Fair Green. After Mac Domhnaill's death in 1754 he invited local poets, including Aindrias Mac Craith, to his own 'Court', which continued to meet at intervals. He is buried in Croom churchyard.

CROSTHWAITE, Cumbria. [5 Bb] Village on the A591, just NW. of Keswick. Robert Southey is buried in the churchyard, his grave and tombstone recently restored at the expense of the Brazilian Government in memory of his *History of Brazil* (1810–19). In the church he has a marble effigy, carved by a young local sculptor, with a poem thought to be by Wordsworth.

CROWBOROUGH, East Sussex. [1 Fd] Small town on the A26, 7 m. SW. of Tunbridge Wells. Richard Jefferies spent the winter of 1885–6 at Downs Cottage (P) in London Rd., where he wrote his last essays, *Field and Hedgerow* (1889). Sir Arthur Conan Doyle lived at Windlesham Manor in Sheep Plain (now a nursing home) and died (1930) there. He was buried in the garden but his body was later moved to Minstead. Edwin Muir and his wife Willa, who brought Franz Kafka's novels to English readers with their translations, lived (1929–32) at The Nook, Blackness Rd., where they translated *Das Schloss* (*The Castle*, 1930). A. S. M. Hutchinson's last home was New Forest Lodge in Beacon Rd., where he died in 1971.

CROWLAND (or CROYLAND), Lincs. [4 Dd] Small town off the A47, 10 m. NE. of Peterborough where the half-ruined Norman abbey towers above the fens. Some consider *Gesta Herewardi* to have been a 15th-c. forgery and not written by the 10th-c. monk Ingulf of Croyland as was supposed. It gives an account of the Saxon outlaw Hereward and his resistance to the Normans. Charles Kingsley's novel *Hereward the Wake* (1866) also tells the story of Hereward and his horse Swallow.

CUCKFIELD (pr. Cookfield), West Sussex. [1 Ed] Small town on the A272, 1 m. W. of Haywards Heath. The physician and traveller Andrew Boorde (or Borde) was born near here (*c.* 1490) but the family who built the 17th-c. Borde Hill[1] is not thought to be his. Harrison Ainsworth stayed at Cuckfield Park in 1830 with his friend William Sergison, who had changed his name and been ordained on marrying the Sergison heiress. In 1831 Ainsworth started *Rookwood* (1834), modelling the house of that name on Cuck-field Park, which has a 16th-c. wing, and describing it in the language of the Gothic novelist Mrs. Radcliffe. The 'omen' tree that he mentions, which foretells the death of a member of the family by shedding a branch, was recently felled, but a new shoot is springing from the stump. Henry Kingsley lived at Attrees (now Kingsleys), a half-timbered house in High St. named after a 17th-c. churchwarden. He died (1876) here and is buried in the churchyard on the slope below the church, where his grave is marked by a tall obelisk.

¹ Open (garden and woodlands only) Apr.–Aug.: Sun. and Wed. 2–7 p.m.; Sept. 2–5 p.m.

CULLEN, Banffs. (Grampian). [7 Ge] Small fishing port on the A98, E. of Lossiemouth. In 1773, on their tour of Scotland, Dr. Johnson and Boswell breakfasted here; dried haddock was served but Johnson refused the dish. George Macdonald stayed in a house in Grant St. (now a tea room) in 1873 and he called the place 'Portlossie' in his novel *Malcolm* (1875).

CULMSTOCK, Devon. [2 Fd] Village on the B3391, off the A38, situated in the Culm Valley below the Black Down Hills. R. D. Blackmore, who had been brought up by his aunt after his mother's death, came to live here when his father married again and accepted the curacy in 1831. He grew to love the surrounding country and referred to Devon as 'my (almost) native land'.

CUMNOR, Oxon. [1 Bb] Village WSW. of Oxford. The site of the medieval Cumnor Place, where in 1560 Amy Dudley was found dead at the foot of 'a paire of staires', is W. of the church. The first written account of rumours of her murder, *The Secret Memoirs of Robert Dudley*, published on the Continent, accused Dudley of poisoning not only her but his second wife's husband too. Aubrey in *Brief Lives* and Anthony à Wood in *Athenae Oxonienses* (1691–2) drew on the *Memoirs*, and Ashmole told the story in *Antiquities of Berkshire* where Scott saw it. Scott also read Mickle's ballad 'Cumnor Hall' (1784), the title he preferred for his novel but changed to *Kenilworth* (1821) at his publisher's wish.

The church has a small collection relating to Amy Dudley, and the ornate tomb of Anthony Foster, her host, who was suspected as her husband's agent in her murder. A few heavy stones in the church-yard wall are all that remain of the house, but 3 m. N. at Wytham some windows and doorways of the ruin it had become were put in when the church was renovated in 1810.

CUMNOR HILL. See OXFORD (Oriel College).

CURRAGH CHASE, Limerick. [9 Dc] Demesne 5 m. SE. of Askeaton, on a minor road between the T68 and the T28. The poet Aubrey de Vere was born (10 Jan. 1814) in the family house (burned down in 1941). He was educated privately and at Trinity College, Dublin, and made many literary friends in England, where he often stayed. Tennyson, whom he visited several times, at Farringford and Haslemere (qq.v.), spent a month with him at Curragh Chase in 1848. De Vere published *The Waldenses and other poems* in 1842, and his voluminous works include *The Legends of St. Patrick* (1872), *Critical Essays* (1887–9), and *Recollections* (1897). He died here (21 Jan. 1902) and was buried at Askeaton (q.v.).

CURTISDEN GREEN, Kent. [1 Fd] Village on the B2079, 4 m. NW. of Sissinghurst. Richard Church, poet and novelist, lived (1939–65) near the post office at The Oast House, converted by his wife and near a large cherry orchard. *The Solitary Man and other poems* (1941), some essays, two volumes of autobiography, *Over the Bridge* (1955) and *The Golden Sovereign* (1957), and a guidebook, *Kent* (1948), were all published during his time here.

CWMAMAN (pr. Coŏmă'man), Mid Glamorgan. [2 Fa] Mining village in a valley just S. of Aberdare, off the A4059. Alun Lewis, poet of promise who was killed in the Second World War, was born here (1 July 1915) and grew up in a time of depression in the mining valleys of S. Wales. He went to Glynhafod Elementary School and obtained a scholarship as a boarder at Cowbridge Grammar School. There is a memorial low-relief bust of him in the reference department of Aberdare public library.

CYNWYL ELFET (or CONWYL ELFED), Dyfed. [3 Cf] Village 5 m. NW. of Carmarthen, on the A484. A signpost by the bridge shows the way to Y Gangell, the birthplace of Dr. Elvet Lewis, minister, poet, and hymnwriter, crowned bard of the National Eisteddfod of Wales. The tiny cottage is preserved as a national memorial and contains his portrait, bardic chair, and other personal relics. He is buried at Blaen-y-coed, about 1 m. W.

D

DALKEY, Dublin. [8 Gf] Coastal resort and residential district on the T44, 9 m. SE. of Dublin, for which it was formerly the port and centre of commerce. At the top of the hill, commanding views of Dublin Bay from Dalkey Island to Howth Head and of Killiney Bay from the Island to Bray Head, is Torca Cottage (P), the summer home of Bernard Shaw and his family from 1866 to 1874. G.B.S. was happy to get away from the dull surroundings of their Dublin house and remembered later: 'I had a moment of ecstatic happiness in my childhood when my mother told me that we were going to live in Dalkey.' He learnt to swim in Killiney Bay. The Shaws were poor and would not have been able to rent such a pleasant place if it had not been for the financial help given by George Vandaleur Lee, a colourful member of the Shaw ménage at that time, who taught Mrs. Shaw singing and influenced the musical taste of the young G.B.S.

DALQUHARN HOUSE. See ALEXANDRIA.

DALSWINTON, Dumfriess. (Dumfries and Galloway). [6 Ee] Village 8 m. N. of Dumfries, off the A76. Burns visited the progressive landowner Patrick Miller here and dined both in the old and the improved new mansion. He rented Ellisland (1789) from Miller through his factor, whose son, the poet Alan Cunningham, was born (1784) at Blackwood (rebuilt), visible from the bridge at Auldgirth. Cunningham was apprenticed to a stonemason brother but devoted his time to literature, educating himself at the library of the pastor at Quarrelwood (1½ m. E., manse and church now a private house), a village of weavers with independent minds. In 1804 he walked to Mitchelstack and met Hogg, the 'Ettrick Shepherd'. His first ballads were published in Cromek's *Remains of Nithsdale and Galloway Song* (1810). His best-remembered poem is 'A Wet Sheet and a Flowing Sea' from *Songs of Scotland, Ancient and Modern* (1825), collected when he was in London.

DARESBURY (pr. Darzbry), Ches. [5 Cf] Village *c.* 3 m. S. of Warrington, on the B5356 between the A49 and the A56. Charles Lutwidge Dodgson ('Lewis Carroll') was born (27 Jan. 1832) and lived until 1843 at the Old Parsonage, Newton-by-Daresbury, when his father was vicar of Daresbury. The house, situated on the Glebe Farm *c.* 2 m. S. of the church, was burnt down in 1883 and not rebuilt, the site, still in open fields, being now marked by a pillar with a plaque bearing a quotation from Dodgson's poem 'The Three Sunsets':

An island farm 'mid seas of corn
Swayed by the wandering breath of morn
The happy spot where I was born.

The place can be reached by turning S. from the village, crossing over the M56, bearing left and then right, almost to the end of Morphany Lane. The church has a Lewis Carroll memorial window (1934) at the E. end of the Danniell Chapel, depicting the Adoration of the Babe and including the figures of Lewis Carroll and Alice and illustrations from *Alice's Adventures in Wonderland* as heraldic supports. An album listing Lewis Carroll's works and the names of subscribers to the memorial from Great Britain and the U.S.A. stands below the window on a table made from some of the original oak beams of the church.

DARFIELD, South Yorkshire. [4 Ba] Small town on the A635, 5 m. SE. of Barnsley. The churchyard on the hill has the railed tomb of Ebenezer Elliott (d. 1849), the ironfounder and author of *The Village Patriarch* (1829).

DARLINGTON, Durham. [5 Eb] Industrial town, terminus of the first railway (1825). Ralph Hodgson was born (1871) in Garden St., ran away from school, and later lived in America and Japan. His poems first appeared in the anthologies called *Georgian Poetry*. He also published short collections entitled *The Last Blackbird and other Lines* (1907), *Poems* (1917), and *The Skylark and Other Poems* (1958).

DARTFORD, Kent. [1 Fc] Old manufacturing town where the A2 crosses the Darent. Jane Austen stayed twice at the Bull and George (now the premises of a chemist) in the High St. She shared a room with her mother 'up two pairs of stairs' as they wanted 'a sittingroom and chambers' on the same floor. They dined on 'beef steaks and a boiled fowl but no oyster sauce'. They were going to Godmersham Park.

Sidney Keyes, the young poet who died (1943) as a prisoner of war in N. Africa, was born (1922) at The Dene in Dene Rd., his grandfather's home. Keyes, orphaned early, lived with his grandfather, a mill-owner who wrote a history of the town, and went (1931–4) to the Grammar School until leaving for Tonbridge.

DARTINGTON, Devon. [2 Ee] Village in the Dart Valley, 2 m. NW. of Totnes, on the A384. J. A. Froude, the historian, was born (1818) at his father's rectory, now the Old Postern, at the entrance to Dartington Hall School, of which it has become a part.

DARTMOOR, Devon. [2 De, Ee] High tract of open country over 300 sq. m. in area, of which the main part, anciently the royal Forest of Dartmoor, is a National Park. The scenery is wild and hilly, with numerous streams among the moors, and occasionally wooded. Two main roads, the A384 (Tavistock–Ashburton) and the B3212 (Yelverton–Moretonhampstead), cross the moor, intersecting at Two Bridges. In 1826 a poem entitled 'Dartmoor' by N. T. Carrington, a schoolmaster and poet of Plymouth, narrowly missed a prize (offered by the Royal Society of Literature and won by Mrs. Hemans) because it was late, but it pleased George IV, who awarded the author 50 guineas. R. D. Blackmore gives an excellent description of the country in one of his lesser-known novels, *Christowell: a Dartmoor Tale* (1881), and Conan Doyle makes the most of its wildness and mystery in his detective thriller, *The Hound of the Baskervilles* (1902). Eden Phillpotts, the most prolific and versatile of Devon writers, wrote eighteen Dartmoor novels, a cycle planned to cover the whole area, begun with *Children of the Mist* (1898) and completed with *Children of Men* (1923). Of these, the tragic tale *The Secret Woman* (1905) is probably the best known.

DARTMOUTH, Devon. [2 Ef] Ancient seaport on the W. bank of the beautiful Dart estuary, reached by the A379 from Torquay and the ferry from Kingswear or by the B3207 from the Plymouth road. In the chancel of St. Saviour's Church is the brass of John Hawley (d. 1408), the chief shipowner in Dartmouth in his day and possibly the model for Chaucer's Shipman in *The Canterbury Tales* (*c.* 1387–1400) ('For aught I woot, he was of Dertemouthe'). Certainly Chaucer was here on business during Hawley's lifetime, and the description of the Shipman in the Prologue could fit the type of man he was. The brass is protected by a cover and permission must be obtained to see it. Defoe, in his *Tour* (1724–7), describes the sight of many small fish skipping and playing on the surface of the water and was told it was a school of pilchards. His servant bought seventeen on the quay for $\frac{1}{2}d$. and he, a friend, and the servant had them for dinner, dressed by the cook for $\frac{1}{4}d$. Defoe recorded, 'We really din'd for three farthings, and very well too'. Flora Thompson lived here from 1928 to 1940 at The Outlook, 126 Above Town, a semi-detached house on the high side of a narrow street running S. from just above the church. She began *Lark Rise* (1939) in 1937 and followed it by *Over to Candleford* (1941). She is buried in Long Cross Cemetery.

DAUNTSEY, Wilts. [1 Ac] Village off the A420, 7 m. NE. of Chippenham. In 1628 George Herbert, who suffered from consumption, went to recuperate at Dauntsey Park, the home of Lord Danby, elder brother of Herbert's mother's second husband. Here he met Jane Danvers, a young relative of his host, and Izaak Walton declared he married her after a three-days' acquaintance.

DAWLISH, Devon. [2 Fe] Seaside resort on the A379. Jane Austen spent a holiday here in 1802. In *Sense and Sensibility* (1811) Robert Ferrars, on meeting Elinor Dashwood, presumes that as she lives in a cottage in Devonshire it must be near Dawlish. When she sets him right (the Dashwoods' cottage was 4 m. N. of Exeter) 'it seemed rather surprising to him that anybody could live in Devonshire, without living near Dawlish'. In *Nicholas Nickleby* (1838–9) Nicholas is born on a small farm near Dawlish, the inherited property of his unworldly father, which is sold up at his death, and bought again by Nicholas at the very end of the story, as his first act when he becomes rich and prosperous.

DEAL, Kent. [1 Hd] E. coast resort 8 m. N. of Dover. Elizabeth Carter, whose father was perpetual curate, was born in South St., now the Carter House Hotel (P). A linguist, she published her early poems in 1738, but it was her translation of *Epictetus* (1758) which brought her a wide public, friendship with Samuel Richardson and Dr. Johnson, and entry into the select band of bluestockings. The £1,000 she received enabled her to buy a property on the S. outskirts of the town, where she took her father on his retirement, and to spend every winter in London. She was one of the last women to assume the customary title of 'Mrs.' though unmarried. Cobbett hurried through the town in 1823 and wrote in *Rural Rides* (1830) that he found it a 'villainous' place, 'full of filthy-looking people'.

DEAN PRIOR, Devon. [2 Ee] Small village on the A38, a few miles S. of Ashburton. Robert Herrick, a Londoner who regarded himself as an exile in Devon, was vicar here from 1629 to 1647 and from 1662 to the end of his life (having been ejected by Parliament and reinstated after the Restoration). Most of his poetry—over 1,000 poems of great diversity and charm—was written during the first period and published under the title *Hesperides* (1648), a tribute to the West Country in spite of his avowed dislike of Devon, and although he missed the literary circles of London he wrote contentedly of simple things, as in *Noble Numbers*,

a collection of devotional verse published with *Hesperides*:

> Lord, Thou hast given me a cell
>   wherein to dwell;
> A little house, whose humble roof
>   Is weather-proof;
> Under the spars of which I lie
>   Both soft and dry.

He wrote many love-lyrics, but never married, being cared for by his servant Prudence Baldwin ('faithful Prew'), who, like himself, was buried in the churchyard. He is commemorated by a tablet and a stained-glass window in the church, and a show-case near the door contains his *Poetical Works*, edited by L. C. Martin, and various books of essays concerning his life and work. Parts of the old vicarage are incorporated in the back of the present building.

Herrick figures in Rose Macaulay's novel *They Were Defeated* (1932), the first part of which is set in Dean Prior.

DEEPDENE. See DORKING.

DENTON, Kent. [1 Hd] Village 8 m. SE. of Canterbury on the A260. Gray stayed here with his Cambridge friend, William Robinson, who rented Denton Court (rebuilt). After his visit in 1768 some verses on Lord Holland's villa at Kingsgate were found in his dressing-table drawer and returned to him. Egerton Brydges, brought up at Wootton (1 m. SE.), married Robinson's daughter and bought the Court in 1792, spending large sums to repair and enlarge it. He was able to entertain the troop of yeomanry he had raised against an invasion, in the galleried great hall. His *Censura Literaria* (1805) was started here before he moved to Littlebourne in 1810. The house fell into disrepair while Brydges was on the Continent and in 1822 it was demolished and replaced by a smaller building. The inn, formerly the Red Lion, changed its name to the Jackdaw after one of Barham's *Ingoldsby Legends* (see Tappington Hall Farm).

DERBY (pr. Darby), Derbys. [4 Bc] Industrial town on the Derwent, formerly a Roman settlement, and an important Saxon town on Ryknild St. (A38) and the Roman road (A6006). Dr. Johnson married Mrs. Elizabeth Porter at St. Werburgh's Church in Friar Gate in 1735, and he and Boswell made later visits. Maria Edgeworth attended Mrs. Latuffiere's school here (1775-81) and learned handwriting, French, and embroidery, lessons augmented in the holidays by her father's advanced ideas on education. She accompanied her father in 1813, when he stayed with his friend William Strutt, the inventor of the Belper Stove. Herbert Spencer, who was born (1820) in Exeter St., went to school here until 1833, and then returned as an assistant master (1837), with more interest in natural science than classics. Derby is 'Stoniton' in George Eliot's *Adam Bede* (1859).

DERG LODGE. See CASTLEDERG.

DERREEN HOUSE. See LAURAGH.

DEVIL'S BEEF TUB, Dumfriess. (Dumfries and Galloway). [6 Fe] Deep depression in the hills, 4 m. N. of Moffat, visible from the A701. Scott uses this hollow for the scene of the daring escape of the Laird of Summertrees in *Redgauntlet* (1824).

DEVIZES, Wilts. [1 Ac] Market town on the A361 and the A342. Fanny Burney and her friend Mrs. Thrale stayed at the Bear Hotel on their way to Bath in 1780. They were interested in Mrs. Lawrence, the innkeeper's wife, who seemed 'something above her station'. They heard singing and the piano, and met her two accomplished daughters and 'the wonder of the family' Thomas, her 10-year-old son, whose skill in drawing was so impressive. They planned to return but their fear of mobs increased by tales of riots in London led them to avoid the towns.

DEWSBURY, West Yorkshire. [5 Ee] Town on the A638, 8 m. SW. of Leeds. Healds House on Dewsbury Moor (1 m. W.) was the new site of Miss Wooler's school on its move from Mirfield (q.v.). Charlotte Brontë was a teacher here, and Emily was a pupil but missed her home so much that she left and Anne came in her place. Charlotte remained until 1838.

DINTON, Wilts. [1 Ad] Village on the B3089, 9 m. W. of Salisbury. It is thought that the Old Rectory, near the church, was built (1725) on the site of the house where Edward Hyde, later Lord Clarendon, was born (1609). His family is said to have lived in other houses in the area, including the 14th-c. Wardour Castle, blown up after the siege of 1643. A tradition also arose that Edward Hyde lived for a time in the Elizabethan house which is now called Little Clarendon (N.T.).[1] This is next to the birthplace of Henry Lawes (1596-1662), the musician who suggested to Milton the idea of the masque *Comus* (1637) and who wrote the music for it.

[1] Open by appointment only.

DISS, Norf. [4 Ge] Town on the A143 and the A1066, 22 m. NE. of Bury St. Edmunds, where the poet Skelton was rector from 1498 to his death in 1529. He made his will here but was not permanently resident. The church is the setting of his poem 'Ware the Hawk'.

DITCHINGHAM, Norf. [4 Hd] Village on the B1332 (ex A144), 2 m. N. of Bungay. Rider Haggard's wife inherited the square, red-brick Ditchingham House, set back behind a paddock on the main road. He wrote many of his novels here including *Dawn* (1884) and *Eric Brighteyes* (1888), and they settled here from 1889. He is commemorated by a window in the N. aisle of the church and the porch was rebuilt by him.

DITCHLEY, Oxon. [1 Ba] Country house of the Lee family built by Gibbs in 1722, now a conference centre, 1 m. SW. of the A34 at Kiddington. A print of the earlier house, described by Thomas Hearne (1678-1735) shortly before it was pulled down, is in the library. The poet John Wilmot, 2nd Earl of Rochester, was born in 1648 and spent his childhood there—his mother's first husband was a Lee. The Velvet Room has a Gheeraerts portrait of an Elizabethan Sir Henry Lee, with his faithful hound Bevis, who both appear in *Woodstock* (1826), a novel by Scott set in the Civil War. A series of prints illustrating Saint-Pierre's *La Chaumière Indienne* (1791) is upstairs.

Open last week of July and first week of Aug.

DONAGHMORE, Tyrone. [8 Fc] Village on the B43, 2½ m. NW. of Dungannon. The Revd. Charles Wolfe was rector here (1818-21), but resigned on account of ill-health. He is remembered for his poem 'The Burial of Sir John Moore', published anonymously

76

in the *Newry Telegraph* (1817) and immediately acclaimed. It was attributed to Byron, among others, before its authorship was known.

DONEGORE, Antrim. [8 Gb] Hamlet 3 m. E. of Antrim on the N. side of the B95. Sir Samuel Ferguson (1810–86), poet and antiquary, is buried in the old churchyard, once the site of an ancient ecclesiastical settlement.

DONERAILE, Cork. [9 Dd] Attractive small town on the L40, 3 m. E. of Buttevant off the L37, situated on the Awbeg. It was part of the 3,000-acre estate granted to Edmund Spenser after the crushing of the Desmond rebellion in 1586, together with the ruined stronghold of Kilcolman (3 m. N.). Spenser came from Dublin, where he had been Clerk to the Irish Court of Chancery, to live at Kilcolman in 1587 and was visited 2 years later by Sir Walter Ralegh, who encouraged him to bring the newly completed first three books of *The Faerie Queene* to London, for publication in 1590. Spenser returned to Kilcolman the following year and wrote the pastoral allegory *Colin Clouts come home againe* (printed 1595), dedicated to Ralegh. In 1594 he married Elizabeth Boyle, for whom he wrote the *Amoretti* sonnets and *Epithalamion* (both printed in 1595). After another visit to London, when he published the next three books of *The Faerie Queene* (1596), he was back once more at Kilcolman, but was forced to leave when his home was attacked and burnt down, and it is possible that some unpublished manuscripts of *The Faerie Queene* were lost in the fire. The ruined tower of Kilcolman Castle, near the 'rushy lake' of *Epithalamion,* is now in the grounds of the Kilcolman Wildfowl Refuge, reached by a minor road off the L40, and access is restricted. It is probable that Spenser did not live in the castle itself, but in a house near by, all trace of which has gone.

Canon Sheehan, author of *Luke Delmege, My New Curate, Lisheen,* and other novels of Irish life, especially in Co. Cork, was parish priest of Doneraile from 1895 until his death in 1913. He lived at a house overlooking the river and is commemorated by a statue by Francis Doyle-Jones in front of his church.

DONNINGTON, West Sussex. [1 De] Village off the A286, 1½ m. S. of Chichester. Ellen Nussey hoped her brother Henry, curate-in-charge of Earnley (4 m. S.) and settled in the rectory (now the Old Rectory) here, would marry her friend Charlotte Brontë, but when he proposed in 1839 after first offering for another woman, he received a 'decided negative'. Charlotte wrote to Ellen 'I had not, and could not have, that intense attachment that would make me willing to die for him; and, if ever I marry, it must be in that light of adoration that I will regard my husband . . .'.

DONNYBROOK, Dublin. [8 Gf] SE. suburb of Dublin, on the T7. See Dublin (Trollope).

DOONE VALLEY. See OARE.

DORCHESTER, Dorset. [2 Hd] County town overlooking the valley of the Frome. William Barnes, the Dorset poet, is remembered by a statue outside St. Peter's Church in High West St. with a dialect rhyme below it:

> Zoo now I hope his kindly face
> Is gone to vind a better place
> But still wi'vo'k a left behind
> He'll always be a-kept in mind

Barnes spent much time in Dorchester. He ran a little school in Durngate St., which later moved to South St. When he was rector of Came during the last 24 years of his life he frequently walked to and from the town and was greatly respected as a local historian. He was one of the founders of the County Museum, run by the Dorset Natural History and Archaeological Society, which now has a Thomas Hardy Memorial Room, with a reconstruction of Hardy's study and a collection of material concerning his life and work. A bronze statue of Hardy seated, hat on knee, looks westward from a grassy bank in Colliton Walk. He was educated at the village school, and after an apprenticeship as an architect and a period in London he lived in various places in the county, finally settling in 1885 at Max Gate, a house of his own design, about a mile out of Dorchester on the Wareham Road. Opposite this house a field path leads to Old Came Rectory, the home of William Barnes when he was rector of Whitcombe and Winterborne Came. Dorchester figures as 'Casterbridge' in Hardy's *The Mayor of Casterbridge* (1886) and other Wessex novels. A detailed tour guide for Casterbridge (and for other settings of Hardy's novels) can be obtained from the Secretary, The Thomas Hardy Society Ltd., The Vicarage, Haselbury Plucknett, Crewkerne, Somerset.

Llewelyn Powys was born in Dorchester in 1884 when his father was curate of St. Peter's, and his brother, Theodore Francis, was educated at the Grammar School. After his return from America in 1934 the eldest brother, John Cowper Powys, stayed for a short time in the town working on his novel *Maiden Castle* (1937), before moving to Corwen (q.v.).

DORKING, Surrey. [1 Ed] Town on the A24 and the A25. Anna Barbauld, who came to live with her brother John Aikin in 1796, wrote of her delight in the countryside in her poem on Burford Bridge (q.v.). Disraeli dedicated *Coningsby* (1844) to Henry Hope, owner of Deepdene, as it was 'conceived and partly executed amid the glades and galleries' there. The house on the eastern outskirts, which was later a hotel, has been replaced by a modern office block but the wooded terrace on the hill behind the house is N.T. (footpath only). George Gissing lived at 7 Clifton Ter. in 1895, the year that *Eve's Ransom*, *Paying Guest*, and *Sleeping Fires* were published. Meredith, whom Gissing visited, was buried in the cemetery in 1907.

DOUGLAS, Cork. [9 De] Suburban village on the L66, 3 m. SE. of Cork. This was the birthplace of Esmé Stuart Lennox Robinson (1886–1958), playwright, director of the Abbey Theatre, and co-editor of *The Oxford Book of Irish Verse* (1958).

DOUGLAS, I.O.M. [5 Jg] Port and chief town, on the wide bay SE. of the island. Wordsworth, accompanied by Crabb Robinson, spent a few days here in 1833. Of the many sonnets he wrote on his tour, three were inspired by the sight of the island from the sea, and one was called 'On Entering Douglas Bay, Isle of Man'. Matthew Arnold enjoyed holidays here, as many thousands have later, and in 1843 wrote 'To a Gipsy Child by the Sea-shore'. T. E. Brown was born (1830) at the Old Grammar School house (gone) in New Bond St., when his father was chaplain of St. Matthew's Church (gone) in North Quay. When he was 2 the family moved to Kirk Braddan Vicarage (gone), a simple, long, low, whitewashed house, 2½ m. S. of

Douglas. It was here that he met the men and women from whom he drew the characters in his stories in *Fo'c's'le Yarns* (1881): his father's gardener became 'Old John', and the Revd. William Corrin, vicar of Kirk Christ in Rushen near by, became 'Pazon Gale'. Brown's poem on 'Braddan Vicarage', written in England, has the lines

> I wonder if in that far isle
> Some child is growing now, like me
> When I was child: care pricked, yet healed the while
> With balm of rock and sea.

The Manx Museum[1] in Crellin's Hill has manuscripts and other memorials of T. E. Brown.

[1] Open weekdays 10 a.m.–5 p.m.

DOUNBY. See ORKNEY ISLANDS.

DOUNE, Perths. (Central). [6 Ec] Small town on the A84. The 14th-c. castle was owned later by the 'Bonnie Earl of Moray' of the ballad. He died mysteriously at Donibristle in 1592.

> Oh! lang will his Lady
> Look o'er the Castle Doune,
> Ere she see the Earl of Moray
> Come sounding thro' the toon.

Scott, who stayed at Newton of Doune, the house known locally as 'Old Newton', describes in *Waverley* (1816), traditionally written in the top room of the tower, the escape of prisoners captured during the Forty-five uprising. One of the seven, still confined in February 1746, was John Home, later author of the romantic tragedy *Douglas* (1756), who got safely away carrying a companion injured when their improvised rope broke.

DOVE COTTAGE. See GRASMERE.

DOVEDALE, Derbys. [4 Ab] Narrow wooded valley NW. of Ashbourne, stretching for 2¾ m. N. from Thorpe (footpath only) through limestone crags. Izaak Walton and Charles Cotton, who both fished the Dove, praised its beauty. Dr. Johnson's Happy Valley in *Rasselas* (1759), and George Eliot's Eagle Valley in *Adam Bede* (1859), are thought to have been modelled on Dovedale.

DOVER, Kent. [1 Hd] Chief of the Cinque Ports on the SE. coast, where Watling Street, the A2, starts. On the E. cliff, the castle[1] was visited by Celia Fiennes, whose ancestors had been Hereditary Constables. To the W. is Shakespeare's Cliff over which the blind Gloucester in *King Lear* tried to jump.

The parish church of St. Mary's has a wall tablet to the actor and dramatist, Samuel Foote, who died (1777) here on his way to recuperate in France. Another tablet commemorates Charles Churchill, who died at Boulogne nursed by Wilkes, and was brought back for burial in the old churchyard. Byron, waiting for a favourable wind to escape from his creditors, spent 2 days here, his last in England. He visited the churchyard with his friend Hobhouse and measured himself against the grave of Churchill 'who blazed / The comet of a season', afterwards paying the sexton to turf it. His tombstone inscribed 'Life to the last enjoyed, here Churchill lies' has been removed but will be re-erected when the road development is complete.

Many 18th- and 19th-c. visitors stayed at the Ship Inn (gone), sometimes called the Shipwright, near the harbour. Chateaubriand was given a very respectful reception when he arrived in 1822 as the new ambassador, in contrast to his previous visit as a penniless *émigré*. Fenimore Cooper, author of *The Last of the Mohicans* (1826), remarked on the 'solid unpretending comfort' of the hotel and 'the perfect order in which everything was kept' in *England, with Sketches of Society in the Metropolis* (1837). Another American, the journalist and poet, N. P. Willis, also listed the comforts of the place, adding that 'a greater contrast than this to the things that answer to them on the Continent could scarcely be imagined'. He also noted with relief that as well as being 'kind and civil' his landlady 'spoke English' (*Pencillings by the Way*, 1835). The Ship Inn was demolished *c.* 1907.

In 1851 Matthew Arnold spent some days here after his marriage in June, and 'Dover Beach' with the lines:

> on the French coast the light
> Gleams and is gone; the cliffs of England stand,
> Glimmering and vast, out in the tranquil bay.

was probably written then, though he also spent a night here on his way back from his Continental honeymoon in October. In 1852 Wilkie Collins stayed with Dickens at 10 Camden Cres. (within a few minutes' walk of baths and bathing-machines). Dickens read *Bleak House* there to Collins

and Augustus Egg. In 1884 Henry James lodged on Marine Parade where he wrote the first part of *The Bostonians*. In the dedication to his *Cruelle Énigme* (1885) James Paul Bourget mentions staying here with James.

[1] Open weekdays 9.30 a.m.–4.30 p.m., Sun. 2–4.30 p.m. Later closing in spring and summer.

DOVER'S HILL, Glos. [4 Af] Hill (N.T.) W. of Chipping Camden, the scene of the Cotswold Games revived by Robert Dover in 1612, held every Whitsun until stopped by enclosures in 1852, and revived again in the 1960s. Endymion Porter (1587–1649) of Mickleton Manor 2 m. N., friend and patron of many poets, brought a party of courtiers to the games, and *Annalia Dubriensia* (1636) was a collection of poems by Ben Jonson, Drayton, Randolph, Heywood, and Marmion in their praise. The first exploit of Wildgoose in Richard Graves's *The Spiritual Quixote* (1772) is also about the games. A memorial to Dover, with a relief portrait, stands in the car park.

DOWNE, Kent. [1 Ec] Village between the A21 and the A233, 8 m. NW. of Sevenoaks. Samuel Butler often visited Charles Darwin at his home, Down House.[1] In *Unconscious Memory* (1880) Butler describes the disagreement between them, which prevented further visits. Charles Darwin's grandchild, Gwen Raverat, born (1885) 3 years after his death, describes the idiosyncrasies of her five Darwin uncles and captures the flavour of family holidays here in the 1890s in *Period Piece* (1952). Though when she 'was eleven Grandmamma died and it all came to an end', Down House (owned by the Royal College of Surgeons) remains much as it was in Darwin's lifetime and one room is devoted to exhibits relating to his work.

[1] Open daily except Fri. and Mon. 11 a.m.–5 p.m.

DOWN HALL, Essex. [1 Fb] The estate in Matching Green, S. of the A414 from Hatfield Heath, bought by Matthew Prior in 1720 partly with money from the folio edition of his poems (1719) and partly with a gift from Lord Oxford, who owed his liberty in some measure to Prior's loyalty to him when under interrogation in prison. The ballad *Down Hall* (1721), admired by Lamb, is an amusing account of Prior's adventures on his first visit there. He spent his last two years of failing health improving the house and gardens and died while visiting Lord Oxford. Pope spent the Christmas of 1725 at Down Hall, staying on with Bridgman to discuss plans for the landscaping of Marble Hill at Twickenham. Down Hall was rebuilt by Pepys Cockerell in 1870, and has indented panels decorated in the Mogul style. Later a girls' school, it is now a managerial college. It overlooks a great expanse of Epping Forest. A thatched summerhouse has a quotation from Fitz-Gerald cut into the panelling.

DOWNIE, Argylls. (Strathclyde). [6 Cc] Estate on Loch Crinan on the Sound of Jura, W. of Lochgilphead, where in 1796 Thomas Campbell stayed as tutor to Sir William Napier's 8-year-old son. His favourite walk was to the opposite end of the bay, called Poet's Hill. He started to write his long poem *The Pleasures of Hope* (1798) here, which has the lines

What though my wingèd hours of bliss have been,
Like angel-visits, few and far between?

DOZMARY POOL, Cornwall. [2 Ce] Lonely expanse of water, high on Bodmin Moor, reached by a minor road *c.* $1\frac{1}{2}$ m. SE. of Bolventor, a tiny hamlet on the A30, 10 m. NE. of Bodmin. By some accounts this is the lake into which Sir Bedivere threw King Arthur's sword Excalibur (see 'The Passing of Arthur' in Tennyson's *The Idylls of the King*, 1869).

DROMORE, Down. [8 Gc] Cathedral and market town on the A1 and the B2. Jeremy Taylor (1613–67), appointed Bishop of Down and Connor in 1660, received the further See of Dromore in 1661 and built the core of the present cathedral, to replace the medieval cathedral burnt down in 1641. He was buried in a vault beneath the altar. Thomas Percy, editor of *Reliques of Ancient English Poetry* (1765), was Bishop from 1782 until his death in 1811 and carried out a major restoration and enlargement of the cathedral in 1808. He is buried in the transept.

DRUMCLIFF, Sligo. [8 Dc] Hamlet on the T18, at the head of Drumcliff Bay, SW. of Ben Bulben and $4\frac{1}{2}$ m. N. of Sligo. W. B. Yeats is buried in the graveyard of the

Protestant church where his grandfather was rector (1811–46), in the heart of the countryside he loved so much. He died in France on 28 January 1939, but in 1948 his remains were brought back and buried, as he had wished, 'under bare Ben Bulben's head'. His epitaph is from his poem 'Under Ben Bulben', written at the very end of his life:

Cast a cold Eye
On Life, on Death.
Horseman pass by!

DRYBURGH ABBEY, Berwicks. (Borders). [6 Gd] Ruined abbey set in a bend of the Tweed among beautiful trees, 4 m. SE. of Melrose, signposted from the B6404 N. of St. Boswells and from the B6356 *c.* 5 m. S. of Earlston. The abbey lands belonged to Sir Walter Scott's great-grandfather, but the inheritance passed from his descendants, leaving them only the right to 'stretch their bones' in the abbey. Scott is buried in St. Mary's aisle. Near Bermeyside, *c.* 2 m. N. on the B6356 is 'Scott's View', where he often went to look across the Tweed to the Eildon Hills, and where it is said that on the day of his funeral his hearse rested briefly when his horses stopped as they had so often done before.

J. G. Lockhart, Scott's son-in-law and first biographer, is also buried here.

DUBLIN, Dublin. [8 Gf] Capital of the Republic of Ireland, a cathedral and university city and port situated on the Liffey at the head of Dublin Bay. Its site as a human settlement dates from prehistoric times and it was a community of some consequence when the Vikings invaded and established themselves in the 9th and 10th centuries. It was enlarged and fortified by the Anglo-Normans in the 12th c. and acknowledged Henry VIII as King of Ireland in the 16th c. But its chief heritage of architecture and literature dates from the early 18th c. and in spite of recent changes it is this that gives it its predominant character. Because of its richness in literary associations the following account has been planned in three parts in order to make reference easy. First come the writers who were natives, regardless of whether they stayed or left; second, the writers who came as schoolboys or students or professional men or visitors, however long or short their stay, insofar as it was significant; and third, the buildings and institutions which have some connection with literature or literary people. Detailed locations are not given in the text as all streets referred to can be found on map 13.

Natives of Dublin

The first distinguished literary native to write in English is Richard Stanyhurst (1547–1618), historian and translator of Virgil, son of the Recorder of Dublin. After graduating at Oxford he studied law for a time and then, diverted by history and literature, returned to Ireland accompanied by Edmund Campion, the Jesuit, as his tutor. He contributed a general description of Ireland and a history of Ireland during the reign of Henry VIII to Holinshed's *Chronicles* (vol. i, 1577). He emigrated to the Low Countries in 1579, where he translated the first four books of the *Aeneid* (Leiden, 1582), a grotesquely prosaic paraphrase of the Latin. Sir John Denham (1615–69), poet and playwright, remembered especially for his topographical poem *Cooper's Hill* (1642), was born in Dublin when his father was chief Baron of the Exchequer in Ireland, but after his education at Oxford does not appear to have returned to his birthplace. He served the Royalist cause in the Civil War and spent some years abroad before the Restoration. Thomas Southerne (1660–1746), dramatist, author of the successful plays *The Fatal Marriage* (1694) and *Oroonoko* (1695), was born in the Oxmantown Rd. area and educated at Trinity College, but went to the Middle Temple to study law and spent the rest of his life in London.

Dublin's greatest citizen, Jonathan Swift, was born (30 Nov. 1667) at 7 Hoey's Court (gone), at the corner of Werburgh St. and Ship St. The pub that once displayed his bust has also gone, but a plaque at the corner of Ship St. near the castle gate records the position of his birthplace. He was educated at Kilkenny Grammar School before entering Trinity College, where he was publicly censured for bad behaviour and neglect of study, obtaining his degree only by 'special grace'. After some years in England as secretary to Sir William Temple (see Farnham) he returned to Ireland and was ordained (1694), receiving the small prebend of Kilroot and later, after

Temple's death in 1699, the living of Laracor (qq.v.). In 1713, disappointed in his hopes of an English bishopric, he became Dean of St. Patrick's Cathedral and spent the remaining 32 years of his life in Dublin. This was the period of his major literary output: in addition to his immortal satire, *Gulliver's Travels* (1726), he wrote a great number of tracts and pamphlets on politics, Irish affairs (such as *The Drapier's Letters* of 1724, which prevented the introduction of 'Wood's Half-pence', a supply of copper coins which could have ruined the Irish economy), religious matters, and social life (satirized in *A Complete Collection of Polite and Ingenious Conversation*, 1738), as well as miscellaneous verses, and letters to Bolingbroke, Pope, Gay, Arbuthnot, and others. In *Verses on the Death of Dr. Swift* (1731) he imagines how the news of his death will be received:

> Poor POPE will grieve a Month; and GAY
> A Week; and ARBUTHNOT a Day . . .,

and reviews his life and principles:

> Fair LIBERTY was all his Cry;
> For her he stood prepared to die;

Towards the end of his life he suffered acutely from a form of vertigo (now thought to be Menière's syndrome) which was followed by periods of insanity. He died in 1745 and was buried in St. Patrick's Cathedral (see below). His Deanery is now part of a police station in Bride St., and its successor, built in 1781, is entered from Upper Kevin St. and contains a few Swift relics.

Richard Steele, whose English father was married to a woman of an old Irish family, was born (1672) in Bull Alley, just N. of St. Patrick's Cathedral. He left Dublin at the age of 13, to be educated at Charterhouse and Oxford, and later to follow a literary career in London, but the effect of his early upbringing was apparently evident enough for Thackeray to describe him as 'undoubtedly an Irishman'. Thomas Parnell (1679–1718), poet and scholar, who became Archdeacon of Clogher (q.v.), was born in Dublin, but his birthplace is not recorded. He was educated at Trinity College. Edmund Burke was born (1729) at 12 Arran Quay (house demolished), the son of a Protestant father and a Catholic mother. After attending a Quaker school at Ballitore (q.v.) he went to Trinity College and subsequently to the Middle Temple (1750).

Among the causes he espoused was the emancipation of Irish Trade, the Irish parliament, and the Irish Catholics. His statue, by John Foley, stands in the forecourt of Trinity College. Edmond Malone (1741–1812), critic and Shakespearian scholar, was born in Dublin and educated at Trinity College. He studied law in London and was called to the Irish Bar soon after 1767, but gave up a promising legal career for a life in London, where he joined Dr. Johnson's circle and devoted himself to literature. Richard Brinsley Sheridan was born (1751) at 12 Upper Dorset St. (P). His father was Thomas Sheridan, an actor and manager of the old Theatre Royal, and his mother, Frances, a playwright. He received his basic education from his father and from the age of 7 till 8½ attended Samuel Whyte's Academy, which formerly stood on the site of 79 Grafton St. He then joined his parents, who had moved to London, and never returned to his native city, though it always remained a cherished memory. Thomas Moore, poet and song-writer, was born at a house on the site of 12 Aungier St., at the corner of Little Longford St. (P). He too attended Whyte's Academy and then proceeded to Trinity College, being one of the first Catholics to be admitted. He began writing poetry at an early age and made a name for himself in Dublin society as a singer and musician. After graduating in 1799 he went to London to study law. He published a volume of Poetical Works in 1801 and won himself the title of Ireland's national song-writer with the publication of Irish Melodies (1807–35). A statue of him (regarded as 'utterly unworthy') stands on College Green, at the junction of Westmoreland St. and College St. A collection of his manuscripts can be seen at the Royal Irish Academy Library, Dawson St.

George Croly (1780–1860), author and divine, was born in Dublin (the site is unrecorded) and educated at Trinity College, which he entered at 15. He was ordained in 1804 and after holding a curacy in the North of Ireland went to London c. 1810, where he made his name with a tragedy, Catiline (1822), and a romance, Salathiel (1829), based on the legend of the Wandering Jew. Byron called him 'the Revd. Rowley Powley' (Don Juan, xi. 57). Charles Robert Maturin (1782–1824), writer of novels of mystery and horror, was born in Dublin of Huguenot descent. He was educated at Trinity College, took orders, and for a time kept a school. He combined a clerical career with the writing of stories and plays, and his first novel, The Fatal Revenge (1807), excited the admiration of Scott and was followed by The Wild Irish Boy (1808) and The Milesian Chief (1811). In 1816 his tragedy, Bertram, sponsored by Byron, was successfully produced at Drury Lane, but later plays were failures and he returned to novel-writing. His 'Gothic' novel, Melmoth the Wanderer (1820), is a masterpiece of the genre. Maturin was curate of St. Peter's, Aungier St., and lived at 37 York St., where he gained a reputation for bizarre behaviour and eccentric dress that increased with the years.

Mrs. Anna Brownell Jameson (1794–1860) was a Dubliner by birth, but left the city when she was only 4, when her family moved to England. Her father, D. Brownell Murphy, was a miniature painter and when she turned to literature after her marriage she specialized to a great extent on subjects connected with art (Hand Book to the Galleries of Art in London, 1842; Early Italian Painters, 1845; Sacred and Legendary Art, 1848), but the book by which she is best remembered is Shakespeare's Heroines (formerly entitled Characteristics of Women, 1832). George Darley (1795–1846), poet, critic, and mathematician, was born and educated in Dublin. He spent 5 years at Trinity College (1815–20), but became estranged from his family, who opposed his wish for a literary career, and came to London in 1822, in which year his blank verse poem, The Errors of Ecstasie, was published. He wrote for the London Magazine and later joined the staff of the Athenaeum. He edited the plays of Beaumont and Fletcher.

Samuel Lover, novelist and song-writer, was born (24 Feb. 1797) at 60 Grafton St. He was educated privately and lived for a time at 9 D'Olier St., having left home to become an artist. He also developed a gift for writing songs and was befriended by Thomas Moore, in whose honour he had sung a tribute of his own composition at a banquet. He went to London in 1835 and in addition to painting and song-writing began to write novels, later returning to live in Dublin. He is remembered especially for the novels Rory O'More (developed from a ballad, 1836) and Handy Andy (1842), a rollicking burlesque of Irish life. He published his *Songs and Ballads* in 1839, and was associated with Dickens in the founding of *Bentley's Miscellany* (1837).

Anna Maria Hall (*née* Fielding, 1800–81), novelist, was born and brought up in Dublin and though she left Ireland at 15 she turned her early experiences to good account in several of her successful books, such as *Sketches of Irish Character* (1829), *Lights and Shadows of Irish Life* (1838), and *The White Boy* (1845), which were widely enjoyed in England. Her style in describing rural life has been compared to Miss Mitford's. James Clarence Mangan, poet, was born (1 May 1803) at 3 Fishamble St. (house gone, but P on site), the son of a poor shopkeeper. He was brilliant at school, receiving most of his education from a priest who encouraged him to learn several languages, but he had to earn money from an early age to help to support his family and his life was shadowed by poverty. He worked as a lawyer's clerk and in Trinity College library, and contributed poems and translations to the *Dublin University Magazine* and *The Nation*. He wrote versions of old Irish songs by studying prose translations of the Gaelic and his hymn to Ireland, 'My Dark Rosaleen', is still remembered. He never achieved the success and recognition that might have been his, and his death from cholera on 20 June 1849 was probably hastened by an addiction to opium. He lived for much of his life at 3 Lord Edward St. (P on the Castle Inn). A bust of him by Oliver Sheppard stands in St. Stephen's Green Park. Charles James Lever, novelist, was born on 31 August, 1806 in the North Strand (now Amiens St.) at the corner of North Cope St. (now Talbot St.) and studied medicine at Trinity College and Steven's Hospital. He practised as a doctor in various parts of Ireland and turned to literature as an extra source of income. He published his first novel, *Harry Lorrequer* in the *Dublin University Magazine* (which he later edited) in 1837 and thereafter wrote a novel a year, gaining great popularity for the vogue of breezy stories of Irish squires and peasants, the English garrison, and the sporting life. He spent much of his time abroad, but was frequently in Dublin and entertained his literary friends at Templeogue House, his home for many years, now in the suburb of Templeogue, S. of Dublin on the Terenure–Tallaght road. Lever was parodied

by his friend Thackeray in *Novels by Eminent Hands* (1856). Joseph Sheridan Le Fanu, great-grand-nephew of R. B. Sheridan, was born (23 Aug. 1814) at the Royal Hibernian Military School (now St. Mary's Chest Hospital), on the S. side of Phoenix Park, above the Liffey, where his father was chaplain. He was educated privately and at Trinity College, where he began contributing to the *Dublin University Magazine*, which he eventually owned. He was called to the Bar in 1839 but did not practise, having already begun to make his name as a writer especially of ballads (such as *Shamus O'Brien*, 1837), which became immensely popular. But he is remembered as a master of the macabre and the supernatural, especially in the novels *The House by the Churchyard* (1863), and *Uncle Silas* (1864), and the collection of stories in *In a Glass Darkly* (1872). He lived at 45 Lower Dominick St. and later at 18 (now 70, P) Merrion Sq., where he died (7 Feb. 1873).

Mrs. Cecil Frances Alexander (*née* Humphreys), author of 'All things bright and beautiful' and other hymns, was born (1818) at 25 Eccles St. and lived in Dublin until her family moved to Redcross (q.v.) in 1825. Another Dublin native who left at an early age was Dionysius ('Dion') Lardner Boucicault (*c.* 1820–90), who was educated at University College School, London, and became a skilful adapter of plays and novels by other hands. His early play, *London Assurance* (1841), was a great success and was followed by many others including adaptations from the French and those with Irish settings, such as the famous *The Colleen Bawn* (1860), adapted from Gerald Griffin's *The Collegians* (1829), *Arrah-na-Pogue* (1864), and *The Shaughraun* (1874). The historian William E. H. Lecky was born in Newtown Park, near Dublin, and educated at Trinity College, where his statue (by Sir William Goscombe John) stands beside the campanile. His principal work is *The History of England in the Eighteenth Century* (1878–90), in which the last volumes concern the history of Ireland and are designed to refute the misstatements of Froude. Lecky was M.P. for the University from 1895 to 1902, strongly pro-Irish in his sympathies, though an opponent of Home Rule. Alfred Perceval Graves (1846–1931), school inspector who published many volumes of Irish songs and ballads, was born at 12 Fitzwilliam Sq. and educated at Trinity College. He was the author of the popular song 'Father O'Flynn', written in 1875 and first published in the *Spectator*. Bram (Abraham) Stoker (1847–1912), author of the supreme horror story, *Dracula* (1897), was born at 15 Marino Cres. in the NE. suburb of Clontarf. He worked as a Civil Servant in Dublin (1867–77) and published *The Duties of Clerks of Petty Sessions* (1878) before becoming touring manager and secretary to Henry Irving.

Oscar Wilde was born (16 Oct. 1854) at 21 Westland Row (P) and later moved to 1 Merrion Sq. (P) with his father, Sir William, an eye surgeon, and his mother, who contributed patriotic poems to *The Nation* under the name 'Speranza'. Wilde was at Trinity College before going on to Magdalen College, Oxford in 1874. Bernard Shaw was born (1856) at 3 (now 33, P) Synge St. The plaque was erected by a local dustman at his own expense, with the wording by Shaw himself. He was baptized at St. Bride's Church (now secularized) by the Revd. W. G. Carroll, his uncle by marriage, who, when the sponsor arrived for the ceremony drunk and incapable, ordered the sexton to take his place, just as though, according to Shaw, 'he would have ordered him to put coal on the fire'. His education began with a governess at home and was continued at the Wesley Connexional School (now Wesley College) on St. Stephen's Green, then at a school in Aungier St., and lastly (for 6 months only) at the Central Model School (where instruction is now in Irish only) in Marlborough St., opposite St. Mary's Pro-Cathedral. He took a job at 15 in an estate agency in Molesworth St. and 5 years later (1876) left Dublin to join his mother in London, where she had settled to follow her musical career. He did not return to Ireland for *c.* 30 years, and then only for occasional visits. W. B. Yeats, one of the great figures of the Irish literary revival, was born (13 June 1865) at Georgeville, 5 Sandymount Ave., ½ m. from Sandymount Castle, where his uncle was then living. His family moved to London when he was 3 and he did not return to Dublin till he was 15, when he attended the High School at 40 Harcourt St. and then studied art at the National College of Art in Kildare St. After a few years at 10 Ashfield Ter. in the suburb of Harold's Cross the Yeats family went back to London again and he had no settled home in Ireland

until after his marriage in 1917, when he bought the old tower at Ballylee (see Gort). After 1922 he lived for a few years at 82 Merrion Sq. (P) and later at a flat at 42 Fitzwilliam Sq. His last move was to Riversdale House in the suburb of Rathfarnham, S. of Dublin.

J. M. Synge was born (16 Apr. 1871) at 2 Newtown Villas, Rathfarnham. His father died the following year and his mother moved with her five children to 4 Orwell Park, Rathgar, *c.* 2 m. nearer the city. Synge was a delicate boy and after 4 years of irregular schooling, first at Mr. Herrick's Classical and English School at 4 Leeson St. and then at Bray, he was taught by a tutor at home. He studied at Trinity College (1888–92), but said that he gained little as his time was almost wholly devoted to playing the violin and attending lectures at the Royal Academy of Music. He went to Coblenz in 1893 to study music, but gave up the idea of a musical career and turned instead to literature. After writing and studying in Paris he took Yeats's advice and visited the Aran Islands and the West of Ireland and drew on his experiences for his prose writings and his plays. By the time *The Aran Islands* was published (1907) he had already made his name as a dramatist with *In the Shadow of the Glen* (1903), *Riders to the Sea* (1904), *The Well of the Saints* (1905), and his great comedy, produced in the teeth of opposition and rioting at the Abbey Theatre, *The Playboy of the Western World* (1907). His last years, spent in or near Dublin, were clouded by illness and he died at 130 Northumberland Rd. on 24 March 1909.

Oliver St. John Gogarty, surgeon, poet, and writer of entertaining memoirs, was born (17 Aug. 1878) at 5 Parnell Sq. (P). He studied medicine at Trinity College and became a fashionable surgeon in Dublin. Yeats had a high opinion of his poetry, and included seventeen of his poems in the *Oxford Book of Modern Verse*, but he is best remembered for his autobiographical account of Ireland in the 1920s, *As I was going down Sackville Street* (1937; taking his title from an old ballad—the 18th-c. Sackville St., originally Drogheda St., is now O'Connell St.). Gogarty was at one time a friend of James Joyce and figures as the 'Stately, plump Buck Mulligan' in *Ulysses*. He lived at 25 Ely Pl., formerly the home of John

Wilson Croker (1780–1857), editor of Boswell's *Life of Johnson*, and now rebuilt to house the Royal Hibernian Academy and art gallery. Gogarty spent much of the latter part of his life in the United States. Patrick Pearse, poet, short-story writer, patriot, and schoolmaster, was born (10 Nov. 1879) at 27 Pearse St. (P). He was educated at University College and after qualifying as a barrister devoted himself to encouraging the development of literature in Irish. He was active in the Gaelic League and established a school for teaching the Irish language, St. Enda's College (Coláiste Éinne), which he moved to Rathfarnham in 1910, at the Hermitage, down Whitechurch Rd. Pearse was executed on 3 May 1916 for his part in leading the Easter Rising.

Sean O'Casey was born (30 Mar. 1880) at 85 Upper Dorset St. (P on site now occupied by the Hibernian Bank), a large house, which his father, Michael Casey, a clerk in the Society for Church Missions, rented and probably sublet. The boy was baptized 'John' in St. Mary's Church (C.I.) by the Revd. T. R. S. Collins, who appears in O'Casey's autobiographies as part of the composite figure, the Revd. T. R. S. Hunter. The family moved *c.* 1881 or 1882 to 9 Innisfallen Parade, and when Sean was 5 he went to St. Mary's Infant School, 20 Lower Dominick St., where his sister Bella taught. After his father's death in 1886 the family moved twice, coming to 25 Hawthorne Ter. in 1889, a small but pleasant cottage in NE. Dublin from which Sean probably attended St. Barnabas's School, though his autobiographical *I Knock at the Door* (1939) is rather obscure about his schooling. His school attendance was irregular on account of an eye disease which afflicted him from an early age and dogged him throughout his life, but Bella used to help him out at home. Then, at 14, he began work as a labourer, as described in his autobiography (though dates are lacking and proper names are altered). In 1897 he moved with his mother and three brothers to a flat at 18 Abercorn Rd., near St. Barnabas's Church (C.I.), which he attended for many years. He taught himself Irish, joined the Gaelic League, and was inducted into the Irish Republican Brotherhood. His mother died in 1918 and he left the flat 2 years later. His early plays, *The Shadow of a Gunman* (1925), *Juno and the Paycock* (1925), and

The Plough and the Stars (1926), based on his experience of Dublin in the years of the 'Troubles', show a strong sense of tragic irony as well as humour, but the fierce critical attacks aroused by the last play drove him from Ireland and from 1926 he spent the rest of his life in England.

James Joyce was born (2 Feb. 1882) at 41 Brighton Sq. (P), between Rathgar and Terenure, to the S. of Dublin. His family were constantly moving house and only a few of the more significant addresses are recorded here. They were at 23 Castlewood Ave., Rathmines (1884–7) before moving to Bray (q.v.), while Joyce was a boarder at Clongoweswood College (q.v.). In 1893 he went to Belvedere College for 5 years, a Jesuit school in Gt. Denmark St., where he contemplated but abandoned a vocation to the priesthood. The school figures in *A Portrait of the Artist as a Young Man* (1914–15). Part of this time the family were living at 17 North Richmond St. and many of their neighbours turn up in Joyce's writings: 'North Richmond Street was a quiet street . . . the houses, conscious of decent lives within them, gazed at one another with brown imperturbable faces. . . .' Joyce went on to University College, where he graduated in modern languages in 1902. No. 8 Royal Ter. (now Inverness Ter.), Fairview, was one of a number of houses in that area in which the Joyce family lived about that time. Although Joyce began his writing career while still an undergraduate his works were not published until after he left Dublin. After graduating he went to Paris, returning in 1903 when his mother was dying, and then, except for one or two brief visits later, spent the rest of his life in Paris, Trieste, and Zürich. His first published work was a volume of verse, *Chamber Music* (1907), followed by *Dubliners* (1914), shrewd and often touching short stories of unheroic Dublin people. *Ulysses*, his most widely read novel, with its minutely detailed picture of Dublin in 1904, was published in Paris in 1922. A map showing the setting of the eighteen episodes of the book can be obtained from the Regional Tourism Organization, Eastern Region, Moran Park, Dun Laoghaire, Co. Dublin. Joyce boasted that if Dublin were destroyed it could be rebuilt in detail from his works. His friend and contemporary, the poet and novelist James Stephens, was born in a poor part of Dublin (his birthplace is not recorded) in 1882 (or possibly earlier) and was largely self-educated. His talent for writing was discovered by 'AE' (G. W. Russell), who helped him to publish his first book of poems, *Insurrections* (1909). Stephens helped to found the *Irish Review* in 1911 and the following year published *The Crock of Gold*, the prose fantasy by which he is best remembered. He was Registrar of the National Gallery from 1919 to 1924. Brendan Behan (1923–64), author in Irish and English, was born at 14 Russell St. (P) and educated by the French Sisters of Charity, North William St. He joined the I.R.A. in 1937 and was arrested in Liverpool and sentenced to 3 years in Borstal and, on his return to Dublin, to 14 years (of which he served 6) by a military court in 1942. He depicts life in an Irish prison in his first play, *The Quare Fellow* (1956) and his own early life in the autobiographical novel *Borstal Boy* (1958). The London success of *The Hostage* (1959), the English version of his Irish play, *An Giall* (1958), won him an international reputation.

People who came to Dublin

Edmund Spenser arrived in Dublin in November 1580 as secretary to Lord Grey de Wilton, newly appointed Lord Deputy, and the following year was made Clerk of the Irish Court of Chancery, a post which he held for nearly 6 years before becoming 'undertaker' for the settlement of Munster and moving to his estate of Kilcolman near Doneraile (q.v.). He had just begun writing *The Faerie Queene*, of which the first three books were completed at Kilcolman and taken to London in 1589 for printing. John Davies (1569–1626), barrister and poet, came to Ireland as Solicitor-General in November 1603 and was knighted in December. In 1606 he was promoted to Attorney-General for Ireland and Sergeant-at-Arms, and became Speaker of the Irish Parliament in 1613. During this time he wrote *A Discourse of the true reasons why Ireland has never been entirely subdued till the beginning of His Majesty's reign* (1612). He returned to England in 1619. The playwright James Shirley (1596–1616) came to Dublin in 1636 when London theatres were closed on account of the plague. He wrote plays (*St. Patrick for Ireland*, *The Royal Master*, and others) for the newly opened St. Werburgh Theatre before returning to London in 1640.

William Congreve came to Trinity College from school at Kilkenny (as did Swift, just before him) in 1686, leaving for England in 1689 when James II was persecuting the Protestants and so caused Trinity to be closed for a time. George Farquhar entered Trinity in 1694 as a sizar (a student receiving an allowance in exchange for menial duties), but the story goes that he was expelled for making a profane joke. He then served in the army for a time before becoming an actor, but gave up the latter career after accidentally wounding a fellow player in a duelling scene. He turned instead to writing comedies (of which *The Recruiting Officer* (1706) and *The Beaux' Stratagem* (1707) were the most successful), living mostly in London, where he died in poverty.

Thomas Tickell (1686–1740), a poet who enjoyed the patronage of Addison, first visited Dublin in 1710 with him when the latter was secretary to Wharton, the newly appointed Lord Lieutenant of Ireland. Addison lost office the next year with the fall of the Whigs, but after the death of Queen Anne he was restored to his old secretaryship (1715) and provided Tickell with employment under him. After Addison's death in 1719 Tickell edited his works (4 vols., 1721), prefacing the first volume with his finest poem, 'On the Death of Mr. Addison', and c. 1723 he migrated to Ireland for good, settling at Glasnevin. He became secretary to the Lords Justices of Ireland, and enjoyed the friendship of Swift. His house is now the residence of the director of the beautiful Botanic Gardens[1] (founded 1795) which occupy his former demesne. Tickell is buried at Glasnevin and has a memorial in the church. Mrs. Delany (1700–88), whose letters and diaries brilliantly reflect the literary and social circles of the 18th c., first came to Ireland in 1731, being then Mrs. Pendarves, the young widow of Alexander Pendarves. She stayed at the newly built house of Dr. Clayton, Bishop of Killala, 80 St. Stephen's Green (now part of Iveagh House), from which she made many excursions, entertainingly described, and one in particular that affected her future life–to Delville at Glasnevin. This was Dr. Delany's house, which became her home after her marriage to him in 1743. The house, where Swift was a frequent visitor, has gone, as have its once characteristic adjuncts: the orange trees, bowling green, grotto, temples, rustic bridges, and paddocks of deer and cattle, and the site is now occupied by the Bon Secours Hospital.

Henry Brooke (1703–83), author of the curious, Rousseau-inspired novel, *The Fool of Quality* (1766–72), was educated at a school in Dublin run by Dr. Thomas Sheridan, grandfather of R. B. Sheridan and friend of Swift. He entered Trinity in 1720, studied law in London, and returned to Dublin as a practising lawyer. Later he spent some more time in London and then came back to settle in Dublin for the rest of his life. Oliver Goldsmith entered Trinity in 1744 as a sizar. He was short of money, especially after his father's death in 1747, but his tutor was unsympathetic and beat him when he broke in on a party with which the young man was celebrating his winning of a 30-shilling-a-year exhibition. Humiliated and hopeless, Goldsmith ran away to Cork, where his brother helped him to adjust to his problems, so that he eventually returned to take his degree in 1749. His statue by John Henry Foley stands at the entrance to Trinity.

In 1800 De Quincey visited Dublin with his friend Lord Westport. They stayed at the latter's house in Sackville (now O'Connell) St. and attended the last sitting of the House of Lords, described by De Quincey in his *Autobiographic Sketches* (1853–4). After the Act of Union (1800) the handsome 18th-c. Parliament House on College Green was adapted for use as the Bank of Ireland. Marguerite Power, who married Charles John Gardiner, Earl of Blessington, in 1818 after the end of her first unhappy marriage, lived for a time in Dublin. The Gardiner family house in Henrietta St. (now part of a convent) where she held her salons is one of a number of especially fine Georgian houses which distinguish this once fashionable district. A woman writer of a very different kind was her contemporary, Mrs. Felicia Hemans (1793–1835), a poet greatly extolled in her day, who came to Dublin in 1831 to live with her brother, first at 36 Merrion Row and then at 21 Dawson St., where she died. She is buried at St. Anne's Church (C.I.). Sir Samuel Ferguson (1810–86), distinguished poet and antiquary, was educated at Trinity College and lived in Dublin after being called to the Bar in 1838. He contri-

buted poetry to the *Dublin University Magazine*, and lived for many years at 20 North Great George's St., hospitably receiving writers and their friends. In 1867 he became Deputy Keeper of the Records of Ireland and lived latterly at Howth (q.v.).

Sir Walter Scott visited Dublin briefly but memorably at the outset of his tour of Ireland in July 1825. He stayed in St. Stephen's Green with his son, an army officer, and was surprised and touched by the warmth of the public welcome he received. He visited St. Patrick's Deanery and other places as a pilgrim paying homage to Swift and found that wherever he went he himself was the object of honour and acclaim. Notables called on him, he was cheered in the streets, and almost mobbed in the theatre. Thackeray stayed with his friend Charles Lever at Templeogue House (see above) during his Irish tour of 1842, and his *Irish Sketch Book* (under the pseudonym 'Michael Angelo Titmarsh', 1843) gives a most readable account of his experiences in Dublin as well as the rest of Ireland. His admirer, Anthony Trollope, who had had various Post Office appointments in Ireland and was making his name as a novelist, came in 1854 from Belfast to Dublin, where he met his future wife. After their marriage and the birth of two sons they settled at 5 Seaview Ter. (off Ailesbury Rd.), Donnybrook (now a suburb on the Dublin–Bray road), until their departure for England in 1859.

George Moore was a visitor to Dublin before settling there in 1901. He stayed in St. Stephen's Green at the Shelbourne Hotel, which figures in his novel *A Drama in Muslin* (1886). After some years in London he returned to Ireland and, encouraged by Yeats and Edward Martyn to take part in the Irish literary revival, he settled at 4 Ely Pl., with a small garden across the street. House and garden both figure in his trilogy of Dublin reminiscences, *Hail and Farewell* (1911–14), written largely at his later house, 4 Upper Merrion St. George William Russell (1867–1935) (known as 'AE' or 'Æ', because of an early pseudonym 'Æon', which a printer's compositor contracted to the diphthong alone), poet, journalist, and painter, came to Dublin with his family from the north of Ireland when he was about 10 and was educated at Rathmines School and at the Metropolitan School of Art, where he met Yeats. He worked for Sir Horace Plunkett in the Irish Agricultural Organization, 84 Merrion Sq., and for many years was editor of *The Irish Homestead* (merged with *The Irish Statesman* in 1923), his office becoming a well-known port of call for literary visitors. His first poems, *Homeward: Songs by the Way* (1894), combine mysticism and Irish mythology and were well received. His play, *Deirdre* (1902), was a forerunner of the poetic drama associated with the Irish National Theatre. 'AE' lived in a modest house in Rathgar, famous for his literary evenings. He left for England in 1932.

[1] Open summer: weekdays 9 a.m.–6 p.m., Sun. 11 a.m.–6 p.m.; winter: weekdays 10 a.m.–dusk, Sun. 11 a.m.–dusk.

Institutions and famous buildings

Abbey Theatre, Marlborough St. Erected by Miss A. E. Horniman of Manchester, a friend and admirer of W. B. Yeats, to provide a permanent home for the Fays' National Theatre Co., which had been producing his plays. It incorporated the hall of the Mechanics' Institute in Abbey St. (formerly the site of the old Theatre Royal, burnt down in 1880) and an adjoining building, and opened in 1904 with Yeats's *On Baile's Strand* and Lady Gregory's *Spreading the News*. Yeats and Lady Gregory were the initial directors, and dramatists whose plays helped to make the theatre world-famous include J. M. Synge, Lennox Robinson (who succeeded Yeats as manager in 1910 and became director in 1923), and Sean O'Casey. In 1951 the theatre was accidentally burnt down and the company played in the Queen's Theatre until the rebuilt Abbey was opened in 1966.

Archbishop Marsh's Library, St. Patrick's Close. Built in 1701 by Archbishop Marsh, the first public library in Ireland and one of the earliest in the British Isles. There are four main collections, consisting of 25,000 books relating to the 16th, 17th, and early 18th centuries, the most important being that of the library of Edward Stillingfleet (1635–99), Bishop of Worcester, which contains books printed by some of the earliest English printers. There are also *c.* 300 manuscripts, including a volume of the Lives of the Irish Saints (*c.* 1400) in Latin. A small book of Elizabethan poetry contains a poem to Queen Elizabeth by Sir Walter Ralegh. There are interesting mementoes

of Jonathan Swift, who was a governor of the library, including his copy of Clarendon's *History of the Rebellion*, with extensive annotations. Swift's death mask and some of his autograph writings are also on view, and the table at which he wrote *Gulliver's Travels* and *The Drapier's Letters*. James Joyce's signature can be seen for 19 and 22 October 1902 and the *Ulysses* reference to the 'stagnant bay in Marsh's Library'.

Open Mon. 2–4 p.m., Wed., Thurs., Fri. 10.30 a.m.–12.30 p.m., 2–4 p.m., Sat. 10.30 a.m.–12.30 p.m.

Charlemont House, in Palace Row, on the N. side of Parnell Sq., formerly the mansion of the Earl of Charlemont, since 1930 the Municipal Gallery of Modern Art. The portraits include those of 'AE', Lady Gregory, and Douglas Hyde. Yeats's poem 'The Municipal Gallery Revisited', evoking the period of Ireland's political and literary revival, can be bought at the bookstall.

Open Tues.–Sat. 10 a.m.–6 p.m., Sun. 11 a.m.–2 p.m.

Chester Beatty Library, 20 Shrewsbury Rd., established in 1952 by Sir Alfred Chester Beatty (1875–1968). The library contains Oriental and Western manuscripts, bindings, colour-prints, etc., housed in two galleries. Its treasures include the earliest known manuscripts of the New Testament (A.D. 200–50) and the 1259–60 manuscript of Omar Khayyám.

Open Apr.–Sept.: Wed. 2.30–5 p.m., Sat. 3–6 p.m.

Mount Jerome Cemetery, Harold's Cross, a suburb S. of the Grand Canal, between Rathmines and Kimmage. It includes Dublin's largest Protestant burial ground, where the following are buried: Thomas Davis (1814–45), Joseph Sheridan Le Fanu (1814–73), William E. H. Lecky (1838–1903), Edmund Dowden (1843–1913), G. W. Russell ('AE', 1867–1935), and J. M. Synge (1871–1909).

National Gallery, Merrion Sq., erected in memory of William Dargan (1799–1867), benefactor of the arts. Bernard Shaw, whose statue by Troubetzkoy stands near the entrance, bequeathed one-third of his estate to the gallery. The portraits include those of James Joyce, George Moore, James Stephens, and W. B. Yeats.

Open Mon.–Wed. 10 a.m.–6 p.m., Thurs. 10 a.m.–9 p.m., Sat. 10 a.m.–6 p.m., Sun. 2–5 p.m.

National Library, Kildare St. (built 1885–90). It has important collections of books, manuscripts, prints, drawings, and historical archives.

Open weekdays 10 a.m.–10 p.m., Sat. 10 a.m.–1 p.m. Closed Aug.

Royal Irish Academy, Academy House, 19 Dawson St. (founded 1783; royal charter 1785). The library of the Academy, Ireland's foremost learned society, houses a noteworthy collection of Irish manuscripts, which includes the *Cathac*, a 6th–7th c. manuscript of the Psalter, possibly by St. Columcille; *Lebor na hUidre*, the *Book of the Dun Cow*, an 11th–12th-c. codex; and the Stowe Missal, an 8th–9th-c. Mass book.

Open Mon.–Fri. 9.30 a.m.–5.30 p.m.; Sat. 9.30 a.m.–1 p.m. Closed Aug.

St. Patrick's Cathedral, Patrick St. (a church rebuilt 1191 on the site of a pre-Norman church, granted cathedral status 1213, and generally restored 1864–9). Swift's grave is in the S. aisle, beside that of 'Stella' (Esther Johnson, 1681–1728) and near by is his monument to her and a bust of him by Patrick Cunningham (1775), the gift of Swift's publisher. Swift's famous Latin epitaph composed by himself is over the door of the robing-room, accompanied by Yeats's translation and lines by Pope. His pulpit stands in the NW. corner of the N. transept. Other monuments include those to Samuel Lover (N. aisle), Charles Wolfe (S. transept), and Sir Samuel Ferguson (S. aisle).

St. Patrick's Hospital, Bow Lane, James's St. (1749–57). The hospital, now a psychiatric centre, was founded by Swift:

> He gave the little wealth he had
> To build a house for fools and mad;
> To show by one satiric touch,
> No nation wanted it so much.

It has an interesting collection of Swift relics.

Trinity College, College Green (founded 1592 by Elizabeth I). 'The College of the Holy and Undivided Trinity' was a Protestant establishment from which Catholics were excluded from taking degrees until 1793. On the S. side of Library Sq. is the library (1712–32), which houses Ireland's greatest collection of books, manuscripts, and historical papers. The many treasures on view in the splendid Long Room on the first floor include the *Book of Durrow*, a 7th-c. illuminated gospel book; the *Book of Kells* (later 8th c.), the most famous of the illuminated gospel books, from the monastery of Kells, Co. Meath, but possibly compiled at St. Columba's monastery at Iona; and the *Garland of Howth* (8th–9th c.), a gospel book from Ireland's Eye, a little island just N. of Howth (q.v.). Among the many busts lining the aisle is one of Swift by Roubiliac. Apart from the scholars mentioned above, the list of distinguished writers who attended the college includes the following: James Ussher (1581–1656), a foundation scholar who later became Archbishop of Armagh, and bequeathed his collection of books and manuscripts to the college; Roger Boyle, 1st Earl of Orrery (1621–79); Nahum Tate (1652–1715); George Berkeley (1685–1753); Charles Wolfe (1791–1823); William Maginn (1793–1842); John Wilson Croker (1780–1857); Thomas Davis (1814–45); Aubrey de Vere (1814–1902); John Mitchel (1818–75); Edward Dowden (1843–1913), who became professor of English literature here in 1867; and James Owen Hannay (1865–1950), ('George A. Birmingham') who became a canon of St. Patrick's.

University College, Belfield, Stillorgan Rd., 3 m. SE. of the city centre. The main part of the College has moved from Earlsfort Ter. (which houses the faculties of medicine and architecture). The College is part of the National University of Ireland, tracing its origin to the Catholic University of 1851, founded at nos. 82–7 College Green. Nos. 85 and 86 were joined together in 1853 to form the Catholic University of Ireland, with John Henry Newman as the first rector. In 1852 the college was administered by the Jesuit Fathers and, as University College, housed at nos. 84–6. It was here that Gerard Manley Hopkins, S.J. was Classics professor, 1884–9 (he died of typhoid fever in 1889 and was buried in the Jesuit plot at Glasnevin cemetery). Patrick Pearse and James Joyce were students here. In 1908 it became a college of the new undenominational National University of Ireland. Thomas MacDonagh, poet and co-founder of Edward Martyn's Irish Theatre, was a lecturer in English literature here in 1914.

DUDDON, Cumbria. [5 Bc] River which rises on Wrynose Fell and flows S. to the sea near

Barrow-in-Furness. Wordsworth wrote, between 1806 and 1820, a series of thirty-four sonnets to the river, which he had first explored in childhood, when staying with cousins at Broughton. The sonnets proved 'wonderfully popular' and, as Wordsworth realized later, were 'more warmly received' than some of his other work.

DULLBOROUGH TOWN. See ROCHESTER.

DUMBARTON. See ARDOCH.

DUMBLE. See MANCHESTER.

DUMFRIES, Dumfriess. (Dumfries and Galloway). [6 Ee] Old county town on the A75, where Burns settled in 1791 after giving up farming. He lived first in Bank St. (house gone) and then in Mill Vennel, renamed Burns St., where his house is now a museum.[1] During his last years, which he spent collecting Scottish songs, he was worried over the health of his children and his own increasing weakness for which strenuous remedies were recommended by his doctor. He frequented the Globe and the Hole in the Wall in Queensberry Sq. with his friends, and his pew in St. Michael's Church is marked with a tablet. He died of rheumatic fever in 1796 and was buried in St. Michael's churchyard. Wordsworth's 'At the Grave of Burns' describes it as 'grass grown' and his sister Dorothy in her *Journal* writes in 1803 'The churchyard is full of . . . expensive monuments in all sorts of fantastic shapes—obelisk wise, pillar wise . . .' and these are still there today. In 1808 Robert Anderson made a detour on his way to work in Ireland and visited Burns's widow, who let him sit in the poet's chair. He wrote 'The Mountain Boy' and the 'Vale of Elva' on the journey. In 1815 Burns was reinterred in a mausoleum like a little domed temple which Keats wrote was 'not very much to my taste'. He wrote a sonnet 'On visiting the tomb of Burns', and 'Meg Merrilees' about the gipsy 'tall as Amazon', also mentioned by Scott in *Guy Mannering*. Thomas Aird became editor (1835–63) of the *Dumfriesshire and Galloway Herald* and lived in the town until his death in 1876. He was buried near Burns's tomb. J. M. Barrie (1860–1937) was educated at the Academy and the Burgh Museum in the

Observatory has some of his and Burns's manuscripts.

[1] Open Apr.–Sept.: weekdays 10 a.m.–1 p.m. and 2–5 p.m.; Sun. 2–7 p.m. Oct.–Mar.: weekdays 10 a.m.–noon and 2–5 p.m.

DUMPLING GREEN, Norf. [4 Gd] Hamlet between East Dereham and Yaxham on the B1135. The lane opposite the Jolly Farmers, a thatched house (once a pub) at right angles to the road, leads to the red-brick house, traditionally known as George Borrow's birthplace, said to be his grandparents' farm. However, research reveals a house 400 yards away was their small-holding.

DUNCTON HILL, West Sussex. [1 De] Hill on the N. of the South Downs, one of the many places in Sussex mentioned by Hilaire Belloc in *The Four Men* (1912). The four, Grizzlebeard, Sailor, Poet, and Belloc as Myself, converse as they walk through the county. Belloc then sets off for his home at Terra Regis or King's Land at Shipley (q.v.), certain that after his death

> The passer-by shall hear me still,
> A boy that sings on Duncton Hill.

DUNDEE, Angus (Tayside). [6 Fb] Port on the Firth of Tay, 22 m. E. of Perth. Robert Fergusson was educated at the Grammar School, leaving in 1765. In 1815 Thomas Hood, emaciated after a series of illnesses, came by sea to recuperate at his aunt's house in Nethergate. His uncle was the owner of the brig *Hope*, and the 16-year-old boy spent much time with the sailors on Craig Pier. Alexander Elliot in *Hood in Scotland* (1885) tells how his sense of fun enabled him to entertain his aunt during an illness. The imaginary side-glances and hand-claspings that he described while watching the churchgoers from her window may have outraged her sense of decorum but she was soon asking him to 'keek oot again, Tam'. Later he had lodgings in Overgate, and he may have worked as an engraver. The manuscript of *The Dundee Guide* which he wrote in imitation of Anstey's *New Bath Guide* was lost, and *The Bandit*, also written here, is reminiscent of Scott. Hood returned home, his health temporarily improved, in 1817. William Thom died in poverty here in 1848. His grave has a memorial in the Western Cemetery. William McGonagall lived for many years in Paton's Lane and worked as a carpet weaver. His first collection of verses appeared in 1877 and *Poetic Gems* (1890) includes 'Tay Bridge'. Bathos, irrelevant material, and disjointed rhythms have caused him to be known as the best bad poet.

DUNGIVEN, Londonderry. [8 Fb] Village on the A6, 9½ m. S. of Limavady. John Mitchel (1815–75), nationalist, journalist, and author, was born at Camnish, near by, where his father was Unitarian minister.

DUNMOW. See GREAT DUNMOW.

DUNOON, Argylls. (Strathclyde). [6 Cc] Resort on the W. shore of the Firth of Clyde, on the A885. A statue on the front commemorates Mary Campbell, the subject of Burns's poems 'Highland Mary' and 'To Mary—in Heaven'. She was born at Auchnamore near by, met Burns while she was a dairymaid at the house he called 'the castle of Montgomery', and died of typhus before she could accompany him in emigrating to the West Indies.

DUNVEGAN CASTLE. See SKYE.

DUNWICH, Suff. [4 He] Coastal resort off the B1125, an important port before erosion by the sea. FitzGerald, who took Carlyle there in 1855, also visited when translating Omar Khayyám (1859). Jerome K. Jerome, who spent annual holidays at the turn of the century at Mrs. Scarlet's lodgings (she also kept a shop), found that FitzGerald had stayed there. Swinburne's 'By the North Sea' from *Studies in Song* (1880) was inspired by his visit, and Henry James visited in 1879.

Edward Thomas finished the first draft of his biography of Richard Jefferies in a coastguard cottage at Minsmere in 1907, high up on 'a heaving moor of heather and close gorse' half a mile away from where the ruined church had half fallen over the eroded cliff. He often walked on the sands below, sometimes picking up shells and coloured pebbles with a 17-year-old girl who showed him her poems, until he was suddenly confronted by her irate father.

DURHAM, Durham. [5 Ea] Cathedral and university city which began on the high peninsula made by the Wear's horseshoe bend, with the building of a church in 995 to safeguard the coffin of St. Cuthbert. This coffin (now restored and in the Chapter Library) was carried with them by the monks driven from the monastery at Lindisfarne by fear of Danish raids. The cathedral, which replaced this church, still retains the Norman 'solidity' remarked on by Dr. Johnson. It became the burial place in 1020 of the Venerable Bede, who died (735) at Jarrow (q.v.). The words 'Hac sunt in fossa Baedae venerabilis ossa' were carved on his 16th-c. tomb in the Lady Chapel called the Galilee in 1831, but he was first described as venerable in the 9th c.

Dobson's Drie Bobbes, edited by E. A. Horsman (1955), gives a lively account of Dobson's pranks at school and in the town in the middle of the 16th c.

The bishops, once Princes Palatine, lived in the castle[1] (part of the University since 1836), where it is possible that Barnabe Barnes spent some time while his father was bishop (1577–87). Barnes, a younger son, published soon after his return from one of the Earl of Essex's expeditions *Parthenophil and Parthenope, Sonnettes, Madrigals, Elegies and Odes* (1593), which made his reputation as a poet, and as one who used the recently introduced sonnet form. His last publication, an anti-popish tragedy, *The Devil's Charter* (1607), is said to have influenced some scenes in Shakespeare's *The Tempest* and *Cymbeline*. Barnes was buried (1609) in the church of St. Mary-le-Bow (rebuilt 1668), North Bailey, now disused and dwarfed by university buildings.

Christopher Smart attended Durham School in the 1730s and came to the notice of Henrietta, Duchess of Cleveland, of Raby Castle (off the A688 just E. of Staindrop). She invited him to the castle, secured his entry to Cambridge in 1739, and gave him a pension. Robert Surtees, born (1779) in South Bailey, spent most of his life gathering material for his *History of Durham* (1816–40). The Surtees Society, founded in 1834, the year of his death, concentrates on the literature of the old kingdom of Northumbria. Robert Smith Surtees, a younger son of another family, was educated at Durham School, which he left in 1819 to work in a solicitor's office. The death of his elder brother changed his fortune and he became High Sheriff in 1856. Thomas Jefferson Hogg, whose grandfather had made a fortune in Durham, also attended Durham School, and left for Oxford in 1810. Sir Walter Scott visited Durham in 1827 and dined at the castle hall at the banquet given by the bishop to honour the Duke of Wellington, when, as Lockhart relates in the *Life*, Scott was also toasted. The old ballad 'Durham Garland' gave Scott the story for his novel *Guy Mannering* (1815). Edward Bradley was at University College (1843–7) and he took the pseudonym Cuthbert Bede, when he wrote his satire of Oxford University life, *The Adventures of Mr. Verdant Green, an Oxford Freshman* (1853–7). John Meade Falkner, whose post as tutor took him to Newcastle in 1883, after leaving Oxford, was drawn to the city, which he later made his home, by his interest in church architecture, archives, and heraldry. He combined these interests with a mystery in his novel *The Nebuly Coat* (1903). He became hon. librarian to the Dean and Chapter and was appointed hon. reader in palaeography. He died here in 1932 but was buried in Burford (q.v.).

¹ Open Apr. first 3 weeks, weekdays. July–Sept.: weekdays 10 a.m.–12.30 p.m., 2–5 p.m. May–June and winter: Mon., Wed., and Sat. 2–4 p.m.

DURRAS HOUSE, Galway. [9 Da] House, now a Youth Hostel (P), on the W. side of Kinvarra Bay, off the T69, 2½ m. NW. of Kinvarra. At the end of the 19th c. it was the property of Count Florimond de Basterot (1836–1904), a friend of W. B. Yeats and Lady Gregory, who joined him and his cousin Edward Martyn here in talks which first broached the idea of a national theatre.

DUTON HILL. See THAXTED.

DYMCHURCH. See ST. MARY IN THE MARSH.

DYMEIRCHION. See TREMEIRCHION.

DYMOCK, Glos. [3 Gf] Village on the B4215, 4 m. S. of Ledbury. John Kyrle, the 'Man of Ross', was born (1637) at the White House. In 1911 Lascelles Abercrombie settled at Gallows, two cottages joined together (now partly ruined in a neglected garden) at Ryton (2 m. E.). 'Ryton Firs' in *Emblems of Love* (1913) describes the daffodils

> tumbling in broad rivers
> Down sloping grass under the cherry trees
> And birches.

In 1913 Rupert Brooke and John Drinkwater joined him for a time at Gallows, and Wilfrid Gibson came to stay at the Old Nail Shop at Greenway Cross, a red-brick cottage with exposed timbers which then had a thatched roof. The four poets contributed to *New Numbers*, a quarterly published from Ryton in 1914. It contained some of Brooke's poems on the Pacific, also 'The Great Lover' and the prophetic 'The Soldier', and Gibson's 'The Old Nail Shop'. In the summer the American poet, Robert Frost, rented the black-and-white labourer's cottage, Little Iddens, then in the middle of a vegetable garden, which his wife and children cultivated. Edward Thomas came to Old Fields, a cottage in a field near by, where Frost persuaded him to try writing verse as well as the essays he had written formerly. Though the group dispersed at the end of the year, Gibson still remembered in *The Golden Room* (1928) the friends who had met in the Old Nail Shop. Frost returned to England for honorary degrees in 1957, and visited the four cottages. *Dymock down the Ages* (1951) by Canon J. E. Gethyn-Jones contains a chapter on the poets and has photographs of their homes.

DYSART CASTLE, Kilkenny. [9 Fc] The site of the now ruined castle is on the W. bank of the Nore, 2 m. SE. of Thomastown, a small market town on the T20 Kilkenny–New Ross road. This was once the home of the Berkeley family and the birthplace of the philosopher and bishop, George Berkeley (1685–1753).

DYSGWLFAS-ON-THE-WILD-MOORS. See CLUN.

E

EARLHAM HALL, Norf. [4 Gd] Country house 1½ m. W. of Norwich, now the administrative building of the University of East Anglia, was the home of the Gurney family. *Earlham* (1922) is Percy Lubbock's account of his childhood among his eccentric aunts, uncles, and other relations at the end of the 19th c., which is considered his masterpiece.

EARL'S CROOME. See STRENSHAM.

EARTHAM, West Sussex. [1 De] Village W. of the A285, 6 m. NE. of Chichester. Eartham House (rebuilt 1904 and now Great Ballard School) was the home of William Hayley, a popular poet, though Southey wrote 'everything about the man is good except his poetry'. In 1792 Cowper and the invalid Mrs. Unwin were brought by John Johnson, with his servants and Beau his dog, to spend a holiday with Hayley with whom he had corresponded over his life of Milton. The scheme that Cowper should live at Eartham after Mrs. Unwin's death came to nothing as 'the melancholy wildness of the scenes' near by soon became more than he could bear. He enjoyed the company of Mrs. Charlotte Smith, then writing *The Old Manor House* (1793, reprinted 1969), and another frequent visitor, Romney, who drew sketches of them both to hang either side of the fireplace in the billiard-room. Cowper met here his correspondent of many years, James Hurdis, whom Hayley invited when after his sister's death at Burwash Hurdis felt he could no longer live in the house there. Anna Seward also visited that year. Hayley had praised her *Louisa* (1782) but offended her with his *Essay on Old Maids*. However, she came again in 1796 and was also painted by Romney, who after hints presented the portrait to her father. The red-brick and flint orangery remains. The church has a marble tablet to Hayley's son Thomas by Flaxman, whose pupil he had been.

EASTBOURNE, East Sussex. [1 Fe] Resort on the A22 and the A259. Lewis Carroll spent his summer vacations from Oxford (1877-87) at 7 Lushington Rd., where a plaque 'to perpetuate his memory with gratitude'

as the author of *Alice in Wonderland*, was placed by the Eastbourne Literary Society in 1954. Edna Lyall lived at 6 Osbourne Rd., in Old Town from 1884 to her death in 1903. Her reputation had been made with *We Two* (1884) and after moving here she showed sympathy with Irish Home Rule and the Boers in her later novels *Doreen* (1889) and *The Hinderers* (1902). In the essay 'Such, such were the Joys', published posthumously in *The Partisan Review* (1952), George Orwell discusses the guilt and bewildering incomprehension he felt at the crimes, often nameless, of which he was accused at his preparatory school. Cyril Connolly, a friend of Orwell's at St. Wulfric's, describes his time here in *Enemies of Promise* (1938). In 1970 he returned to the town and lived at 48 St. John's Rd. till his death in 1974.

EAST BUDLEIGH, Devon. [2 Fe] Village 1½ m. N. of Budleigh Salterton on the A376. Sir Walter Ralegh's birthplace, the thatched Tudor farmhouse of Hayes Barton,[1] can be reached by Hayes Lane, a narrow turning on the W. side of the village.

[1] Open June–mid-Sept.: daily except Sat. and Sun. 2.15-5 p.m.

EASTBURY, Berks. [1 Bc] Little village in the Lambourn Valley, 10 m. NW. of Newbury on the B4000. In the S. wall of the church there is a window by Laurence Whistler, provided by people from all over the world, in memory of Edward Thomas and his wife Helen, who spent the last years of her life here. The window is of clear glass engraved with scenes of hills and sea and trees, interspersed with lines from Thomas's poetry.

EAST CHALDON. See CHALDON HERRING.

EAST COKER, Som. [2 Gd] Village off the A37, 3 m. S. of Yeovil. The ashes of T. S. Eliot (d. 1965), whose ancestors left the village for America, are buried as he requested in the church (tablet). The second section of his *Four Quartets* (1944) is named after the village.

EAST DEREHAM, Norf. [4 Gd] Town on the A47. Cowper, ill with depression, was brought here by his cousin the Revd. John Johnson, with Mrs. Unwin (d. 1796) helpless after strokes. They lived in a red-brick house in the market place, now replaced by the 19th-c. Memorial Congregational Chapel (P). Cowper died in 1800 and his memorial in the church has lines by his friend William Hayley.

George Borrow's parents (married here in 1793) were tenants in Norwich St. (now the Co-op) at the time of his birth but tradition holds that his mother returned to her parents in Dumpling Green (q.v.) for the event.

EAST ENDELSTOW. See ST. JULIOT.

EASTHAMPSTEAD, Berks. [1 Dc] Village on the A3095, just S. of Bracknell. There is an epitaph in the church by Pope on his friend Elijah Fenton, a minor 18th-c. poet (recorded in Dr. Johnson's *Lives of the Poets*), who assisted him in the translation of *The Odyssey*. Reeds Hill Farm, near Church Hill House Hospital, is thought to be the house rented by Shelley and his first wife, Harriet, in 1814.

EAST MERSEA, Essex. [1 Gb] Straggling village in the marshes at the mouth of the Colne, where Baring-Gould was rector from 1870 to 1881. His novel *Mehalah* (1880, reprinted 1969) is set in the local marshes and the main character has been compared to Heathcliff in *Wuthering Heights* (1847).

EASTON, Dorset. [2 He] Village on the E. side of the Isle of Portland. On the Wakeham Rd., near the turning down to Church Ope, is the Hardy and Portland Museum, housed in Avice's Cottage,[1] a low thatched building made famous by Hardy as the home of Avice in *The Well-Beloved* (1897). Dr. Marie Stopes, who lived at the Old Lighthouse, restored the cottage from a state of disrepair and founded it as a museum in 1929.

[1] Open summer: Mon.–Sat. 10 a.m.–5 p.m.; winter: Mon., Wed., Thurs., Sat., 10 a.m.–5 p.m.

EASTON, Humberside. See BRIDLINGTON.

EASTON MAUDIT, Northants. [4 Cf] Village off the A509, 9 m. E. of Northampton, where Thomas Percy lived as vicar (1756–78). His collection of old ballads was published as *Reliques of Ancient English Poetry* (1765). His house (now the Old Rectory) was visited by Goldsmith, of whom he wrote a memoir (1801), and by Garrick and Dr. Johnson, who are commemorated by a brass in the front pew of the church where they worshipped with other members of the Garrick Club.

EASTON PIERCY or PERCY. See KINGTON ST. MICHAEL.

EAST STOUR, Dorset. [2 Hc] Village on the A30, *c.* 4 m. W. of Shaftesbury. Henry Fielding came here at the age of 3 with his family and lived at the Manor House, which stood on the site of the farm by the church, formerly known as Fielding's Farm, now Church Farm. After an education at Eton and at Leyden, where he studied law, he supported himself in London for a few years by writing for the stage, and then in 1734 married Charlotte Cradock, his model for Sophia Western in *Tom Jones* (1749), and brought her to East Stour. They lived here for a short time and he then decided to take up the study of law again and returned to London, where he was called to the Bar in 1740. Parson Adams, the amiable curate of Fielding's *Joseph Andrews* (1742), is thought to have been modelled on the Revd. William Young, rector of the adjoining parish of West Stour, with whom Fielding collaborated in the translation of the *Plutus* of Aristophanes.

EAST TUDDENHAM, Norf. [4 Gd] Village S. of the A47, 6 m. E. of East Dereham, where Parson Woodforde dined with his friend the Revd. John Du Quesne in the Hall he bought as his vicarage, now Berries Hall on the Weston road.

EASTWOOD, Notts. [4 Bc] Small hilltop mining town 8 m. NW. of Nottingham. D. H. Lawrence, a miner's son born (1885) at 8A Victoria St. (P), transposed many local scenes into his novels and called the town 'Bestwood' in *Sons and Lovers* (1913), 'Woodhouse' in *The Lost Girl* (1920), and 'Beldover' in *Women in Love* (1920). The Lawrences lived (1887–91) at 28 Garden Rd.,[1] the 'Bottoms' of *Sons and Lovers*, restored (1973) by the Association of Young Writers. While living (1891–1902) at 12 Walker St., then on the edge of cornfields, Lawrence attended Beauvale School and in 1898 was its first pupil to win a scholarship to a grammar school. Lawrence described the view from Walker St. as 'the country of my heart'. There was the small Moorgreen colliery where Walter Morel worked in *Sons and Lovers*, Lambclose House, off the B600, the probable model for many of Lawrence's middle-class homes, and Moorgreen Reservoir, then much deeper than today, where a real drowning fatality led to the similar tragedy in Willey Water in *Women in Love*. The reservoir becomes 'Nethermere' in *Sons and Lovers* and *The White Peacock* (1911). His family moved to 97 Lyncroft in 1902, where Lawrence and his friends, who were training as teachers, often met while they were at the British School here. They called themselves the Pagans and no. 97 was the Pagan Headquarters. *A Visitors' Guide to Eastwood and the Countryside of D. H. Lawrence* by Michael Bennett, the Eastwood Librarian, is available at the Library.

[1] Open Sat., Sun., Bank Holidays, and weekdays in July and Aug. 10 a.m.–6 p.m.

EATANSWILL. See SUDBURY.

EBCHESTER. See HAMSTERLEY HALL.

ECCLEFECHAN, Dumfriess. (Dumfries and Galloway). [6 Fe] Village off the A74, 6 m. S. of Lockerbie. Thomas Carlyle's birthplace[1] (N.T.S.) has many relics of the historian and his parents. Carlyle (1795–1881) was at school here before going to Annan Academy. He is buried beside his parents and a statue to him was erected in the village in 1927.

[1] Open Mar.–Oct.: 10 a.m.–6 p.m., except Sun.

ECCLESFIELD, South Yorkshire. [5 Ef] Town on the Sheffield–Chapeltown road, N. of the ring road. Margaret Gatty, wife of the incumbent, created *Aunt Judy's Magazine* (1866) and wrote the improving *Parables from Nature* (1855–71). Her daughter Juliana (later Mrs. Ewing), was born at the vicarage (gone) and contributed to *Aunt Judy's Magazine*. A tablet in the church commemorates them.

EDGEWORTHSTOWN (or MOSTRIM), Longford. [8 Ee] Small town in the Irish mid-

lands at the junction of the T3 and the T31. Goldsmith went to school here (1741–5) under the Revd. Patrick Hughes, an old friend of his father's, and learnt to enjoy the Latin poets and historians. From this school (demolished) he went to Dublin for his entrance examinations to Trinity College. Edgeworthstown was the ancestral home of Maria Edgeworth, where she came with her father and stepmother in 1782 and settled for the rest of her life. It was here that she wrote her early stories for children (*The Parent's Assistant*, 1796) and, with her father, educational books such as *Practical Education* (1798), followed by novels of which the first and most famous was *Castle Rackrent* (1800). Sir Walter Scott in his tour of Ireland enjoyed a happy visit here in the summer of 1825, and Wordsworth stayed for two days in September 1829, when he found 'the authoress . . . very lively'. Edgeworthstown House, still with its original pillared porch and square entrance hall, has been modernized and extended to form a nursing home run by the Sisters of Mercy. Maria Edgeworth and her father Richard Lovell Edgeworth are buried in St. John's churchyard, and there are memorials inside the church (P at the church gate).

EDIAL, Staffs. [4 Ad] Village c. 3 m. SW. of Lichfield, on the B5012. Edial House (somewhat altered in the early 19th c.) was Dr. Johnson's home when he married in 1735 and the place where he opened a private school with the help of his wife's money. The school was not successful and in 1737, accompanied by the young David Garrick, one of his pupils, he set out for London, which was henceforth to be his home.

EDINBURGH, Midlothian (Lothian). [6 Fc] Capital of Scotland, cathedral and university city on the S. bank of the Firth of Forth, named after the 6th-c. king of Northumbria, Edwin, who built his fortress high on the precipitous crag of volcanic rock which underlies the city. The castle dominates historic Old Edinburgh, or the Royal Mile, which stretches E. to Holyrood Palace and Abbey at the foot of the slope. Above Princes St. in the valley the elegant and spacious 18th-c. New Town rises northwards. The literary associations of the city are so manifold that only its distinguished native writers and the more significant of its vast number of residents and visitors can be accounted for here. Streets referred to can be found on map 12.

Natives and residents

Gavin Douglas (1474?–1522), poet and bishop, was provost of St. Giles in 1501 and lived at a palace in the Cowgate. He wrote two allegorical poems, *The Palice of Honour* (1553?) and *King Hart* (first printed 1786), and, with his translation of the *Aeneid* (1553), was the earliest translator of the classics into English. William Drummond of Hawthornden (1585–1649), sometimes called 'the Scottish Petrarch', was educated at the High School and at the University. His library is housed in the University Library, George Sq. Allan Ramsay (1686–1758) came to Edinburgh in 1701 as a wig-maker's apprentice and stayed to make his name as a poet and bookseller. In 1718 he opened a bookshop and by 1720 was publishing books for sale 'at the sign of the Mercury, opposite the head of Niddry's Wynd [now Niddry St.]', the house (gone) where he lived and carried on his business until 1726. While he was here he began the *Tea Table Miscellany* (1724–32), a collection of new Scots songs set to old melodies, and his best-known work, *The Gentle Shepherd* (a pastoral drama, 1725). He moved to another shop in 1726, in the Luckenbooths (gone) in the High St., near St. Giles, and here changed his sign of Mercury to that of the heads of Ben Jonson and Drummond of Hawthornden. Two years later he began the first circulating library in Scotland, which was looked at askance by certain sober-minded people as a potential source of lewd and profane reading for the young. Ramsay retired to a house of his own design on Castle Hill, nicknamed the 'Goose Pie' on account of its curious octagonal shape, now (somewhat altered by his son, Allan Ramsay the painter, 1713–84), part of a picturesque group of houses beneath the Castle Esplanade. There is a statue of the elder Ramsay in Prince's St. Gardens and a monument to him in Greyfriars Churchyard, on the S. wall of the church. John Gay (1685–1732) enjoyed Ramsay's acquaintance when he came to Edinburgh in 1729 as secretary to the eccentric Duchess of Queensberry. Gay's musical play, *Polly* (a sequel to *The Beggar's Opera*), had just been banned in London by the Lord Chamberlain, and 'her mad Grace'

had swept him up to Edinburgh to stay at Queensberry House (now a home for the elderly) in the Canongate. Gay and Ramsay used to meet at an inn called Jenny Ha's Change House (gone) for wine and conversation.

Dr. Johnson (1709–84) first visited Edinburgh in August 1773 at the outset of his tour of the Hebrides with James Boswell. He stayed 4 days at the White Horse Inn (P on site) in Boyd's Close (gone), St. Mary's Wynd (now St. Mary's St.), and was shown the sights by Boswell. On their return from the Hebrides Johnson stayed about a fortnight with Boswell and his wife and met and enjoyed the hospitality of many distinguished members of society. Boswell's father, Lord Auchinleck, failed to appreciate his qualities, however, and was scathing about his son's attachment to 'an auld dominie', and Mrs. Boswell felt provoked to utter her famous comment, 'I have often seen a bear led by a man but never till now have I seen a man led by a bear'.

David Hume (1711–76), historian and philosopher, was born in Edinburgh and educated at the University. At the age of 40 he moved into the first home of his own, in Riddle's Close, 322 High St. He was appointed Keeper of the Advocates' Library in 1752, the year he wrote his *Political Discourses*, and while here probably began the *History of Great Britain* (1754–61), which he continued after his removal to Jack's Land (now 229), Canongate, an old four-storeyed building entered from Little Jack's Close. In 1762 he had apartments in James Court (destroyed by fire) off the Lawnmarket (later occupied by Boswell) and finally built himself an imposing house at the corner of St. Andrew Sq. and St. David St., where he ended his days. He was buried in the Calton Old Burial Ground, by the SE. corner of Waterloo Pl., in a tomb designed by Robert Adam, visible from many parts of the city.

Tobias Smollett (1721–71) stayed with his sister in 1766, in the second flat of 182 Canongate, over the archway leading into St. John St. The apartments are reached by a turret staircase in the house now 22 St. John St. (P). Smollett, in the character of Matthew Bramble, describes the city and its notable authors in *Humphry Clinker* (1771). William Falconer (1732–69) was born in Edinburgh, the son of a barber, and became a sailor. He wrote *The Shipwreck* (1762, revised 1764 and 1769), a poem in three cantos recounting the wreck of a ship off the coast of Greece, which had considerable vogue in its day. He also compiled a useful *Universal Marine Dictionary* (1769).

James Boswell (1740–95), Dr. Johnson's biographer, was the son of Lord Auchinleck, a judge of the Court of Session, and was born in Blair's Land, Parliament Sq., where he lived till he was 9. He was educated at a private school and then the High School, and entered the University at 13. He studied law in Edinburgh, Glasgow, and Utrecht, and practised as an advocate, but his interest lay in the direction of politics and literature. Having made the acquaintance of Dr. Johnson in London he received him on the latter's arrival in Edinburgh in 1773 (see above). Boswell had apartments in James Court, off the Lawnmarket, previously occupied by David Hume (see above), and for a time he rented the house of his uncle, Dr. Boswell, S. of the Meadows, for £15 a year, now 15A Meadow Pl. and the only one of his Edinburgh homes still standing. The entrance is in a narrow lane behind a derelict church, but the house is obscured by a high wall. He inherited the family house at Auchinleck (q.v.) on his father's death in 1782.

Henry Mackenzie (1745–1831), author of the once popular novel, *The Man of Feeling* (1771), cherished by Burns as one of his 'bosom favourites' books, was born in Libberton Wynd, which ran between the Lawnmarket and the Cowgate, where George IV Bridge now stands. He was educated at the High School and the University, and lived in many different places in Edinburgh, ending his days at 6 Heriot Row, facing Queen St. Gardens. He is buried in the Greyfriars Churchyard on the N. side of the terrace. Robert Fergusson (1750–74) was born at Cap Feather Close off the High St. (site now built over on the E. side of the N. Bridge). He was educated at a small school in Niddry's Wynd and then at the High School before going on to the Grammar School at Dundee and St. Andrews University, with the object of reading for the ministry. After his father's death, however, he left the University without a degree and turned his thoughts to literature. He took a job in a law office to help to support his mother, and began writing poetry, and it was as a writer of Scots poetry, especially of the life and manners of his contemporary

Edinburgh, that he excelled. In 1773 *Poems by Robert Fergusson* was published, containing his best Scots poems to date and a promise of even better to come. But he began to suffer fits of depression, aggravated by bouts of dissipation, and was removed to the Bedlam (or Mad House, as it was known) of the city, where he died on 16 October 1774. Burns's tribute to him was

> My elder brother in misfortune
> By far my elder brother in the Muse.

Fergusson was buried in the Canongate cemetery, in a grave on the W. side of the church, not far from the gateway, marked by a headstone erected and inscribed by Burns 12 years later.

George Crabbe (1755–1832) visited Edinburgh in August 1822 at the invitation of Sir Walter Scott. He arrived during the preparations for the visit of George IV, met the Highland chieftains at Scott's house, and attended a levee on 17 August at which the King appeared in a 'Stewart tartan'. Crabbe, like Scott, composed lines in honour of the royal occasion. Elizabeth Hamilton (1756–1816), a novelist who was brought up in Stirlingshire and later moved to London, stayed for a time in Edinburgh in the West Lodge, where she wrote her most notable book, *The Cottagers of Glenburnie* (1808). Maria Edgeworth, who had corresponded with her after reading her *Memoirs of Modern Philosophers* (1800), met her here during her visit in the winter of 1803/4.

Robert Burns (1759–96) came to Edinburgh in 1786 after the success of the Kilmarnock edition of his poems published that August, in order to arrange for a second impression. He set out from Kilmarnock on a borrowed pony and arrived 2 days later at his lodgings in Baxter's Close (house long ago demolished, but P over the Lawnmarket entrance to Lady Stair's Close). He had a letter of introduction to the Earl of Glencairn, who proved to be an ideal patron and helped to launch him in fashionable and literary circles. Burns played up to his role of 'ploughman poet' and charmed society with his conversation and vitality. The Edinburgh edition of his poems sold 3,000 copies and early the next year Burns toured the Borders with some of his new friends, returning the following winter to stay in the house of a schoolmaster on the SW. corner of St. James's Sq. in the New

Town. Here he worked on the production of the second volume of the *Scots Musical Museum*, a collection of songs including many written by himself. In December he met Mrs. Maclehose, a young society woman of poetic aspirations, whose husband was abroad, and fell deeply in love. She became the 'Clarinda' of a passionate correspondence and the subject of his poem 'Ae fond kiss', and treasured the memory of their relationship long after his letters had dwindled away after his return home in February 1789. There is a monument to Burns on the S. side of Regent Rd.

Sir Walter Scott was born on 15 August 1771 in a house at the top of College Wynd, which led from the Cowgate to the college buildings and has now become part of Guthrie St. (P on 8 Chambers St. records the site as 'near this spot'). The family moved in 1774 to 25 George Sq. (P) and here Walter lived until 1797. He and his brothers received their early education from a tutor and in October 1779 he went to the High School for 4 years, before entering the University to study law. He passed his final examinations and qualified as an advocate in 1792. After his marriage to Charlotte Carpenter in December 1797 he brought her to lodgings at 108 George St., moving from there to 10 South Castle St., and a few months later to 39 Castle St. (P and statuette of his seated figure above the door), where they lived for the next 28 years and where Scott wrote most of the *Waverley* novels. After the crash of J. M. Ballantyne's bookselling business in which he was a partner Scott left the house on 15 March 1826 and, apart from the time spent at his home at Abbotsford (q.v.), stayed in various lodgings in the city when he needed to be at the court. He retired from the court in 1830 and settled at Abbotsford for the last 2 years of his life. The Scott Monument[1] (1844) in East Prince's St. Gardens has a statue of Scott and his dog Maida by Steell under the canopy of a 200-ft-high spire, with niches containing sixty-four figures of characters from his works.

James Hogg (the 'Ettrick Shepherd', 1770–1835) had first met Scott when the latter was collecting material for his *Minstrelsy of the Scottish Border* in 1802, as he and his mother knew many of the old Border ballads, and in 1803 he came to Edinburgh as Scott's guest and astonished Mrs. Scott by his unsophisticated manners. Scott remained his friend till the end of his life, encouraging and advising him in his literary work and finding help for him when he was short of money. Hogg later returned to stay in lodgings in Ann St. (obliterated by the building of Waverley Bridge) and then at the Harrow Inn near the Grassmarket (the remains of which constitute an irregular row of old gabled houses, 46–54 Candlemaker Row). He wrote 'The Forest Minstrel' in 1810, dedicated to the Countess of Dalkeith, who gave him £100. In 1812 he was living in Deanhaugh St. in the NW. suburbs, where he completed *The Queen's Wake* (1813), a poem about Mary Queen of Scots and a bardic competition at Holyrood, which made his reputation as a poet. But he is best remembered today for the strange and terrifying novel, *The Private Memoirs and Confessions of a Justified Sinner* (1824), published at first anonymously because, said Hogg, 'it being a story replete with horrors, after I had written it I durst not venture to put my name to it', but more probably because he guessed it would offend the Calvinists. The setting is largely in Calvinist Edinburgh of the late 17th and early 18th centuries and there is a vivid description of the Brocken spectre, seen from the summit of Arthur's Seat.

Francis Jeffrey, Lord Jeffrey (1773–1850), advocate, judge, and a leading literary figure of his time, was born at 7 Charles St. and educated at the High School and University. He began married life (1801) at 18 Buccleugh Pl. (P) and it was here that he and Henry Brougham discussed Sydney Smith's proposal for a liberal magazine, the *Edinburgh Review*, launched in 1802. The *Review* was an immediate success and, under Jeffrey's editorship (1803–29), reached the status of an institution. Jeffrey moved in 1802 to 62 Queen St., then to 92 George St. (1810), and finally to a mansion at 24 Moray Pl. Jeffrey's friend, the Revd. Sydney Smith (1771–1845), who persuaded him and Brougham to take up his suggestion of the *Edinburgh Review*, came to Edinburgh in 1798 as a private tutor and lodged at 38 Hanover St. for about a year. He stayed in the city until 1803, moving to 19 Queen St. for a while and then, after his marriage in 1800, to 46 George St. After he returned to London he continued to keep up his connection with the *Review*.

Thomas Campbell (1777–1844), one of Scott's regular correspondents, studied law at the University in 1796, but only briefly, as he found it 'dull and unprofitable'. He spent the winter of 1797 teaching Greek and Latin to private pupils, and taking long walks over Arthur's Seat while completing his poem *The Pleasures of Hope*, which had tremendous success when published in Edinburgh the following year. The familiar line, ''Tis distance lends enchantment to the view', is supposed to have been written on Calton Hill. Campbell at that time had lodgings in Alison Sq. (now demolished). He settled his parents in a house that he bought on St. John's Hill and, after leaving for London in 1802, used to return there for later Edinburgh visits.

Susan Edmonstone Ferrier (1782–1854) was born in Edinburgh, the daughter of James Ferrier, Writer to the Signet and a colleague of Scott. She lived in her parents' home between Morningside and Edinburgh town, keeping house for her father after her mother's death in 1797. Her home at 25 George St. is now part of the George Hotel. She began writing at an early age, her first novel, *Marriage*, being written in 1810 though not published till 1818. It was followed by *The Inheritance* (1824) and *Destiny* (1831), and all three give entertaining accounts of the friction of fashionable and literary Scottish middle-class society. She was a frequent visitor at Scott's home, where she was always welcome. She is buried in St. Cuthbert's churchyard, behind St. John's Church, at the W. end of Prince's St.

Thomas De Quincey (1785–1859) had already contributed to *Blackwood's Magazine* (the Tory rival to the *Edinburgh Review*) when he moved to Edinburgh in 1828. *Blackwood's* published the first part of his 'On Murder as one of the Fine Arts' in 1827 and De Quincey continued to be an occasional contributor till 1849. He also wrote for the *Edinburgh Literary Gazette*. He lived in Great King St., in Forres St., and at Duddingston, before settling till the end of his days at 42 Lothian St. (recently demolished). But he was improvident and had a large family to support and the necessity of evading his creditors drove him from time to time to take up residence in the Sanctuary in Holyrood, in one of the 'houses of refuge' where debtors could live,

situated within 100 yds. of the front of Holyrood Palace. The little community within the Sanctuary was under the jurisdiction of the Baron Bailie of Holyrood, appointed by the Hereditary Keeper of the Palace. With the abolition of imprisonment for debt in 1880 the need for sanctuary ended, although the privilege still exists. One of the Sanctuary houses, at the foot of Abbey Hill and the end of the Royal Mile, is now occupied by tea-rooms. De Quincey was a regular opium-taker, but he was well liked for his quiet manner, the excellence of his conversation, and his beautiful voice. He was a friend of John Wilson (see below) from their Lake District days and when he called on him one evening at 29 Ann St. he was invited to stay the night—and remained, a welcome addition to the household, for nearly a year. He is buried in St. Cuthbert's churchyard.

John Wilson (1785–1854), a distinguished scholar and athlete, came to Edinburgh from Windermere in 1812 and was called to the Bar, but never practised. He wrote verse, which was well received, and as 'Christopher North' contributed regularly to *Blackwood's Magazine* until the mid 1830s, and is remembered especially for the *Noctes Ambrosianae*, a series of topical, critical, poetical, and convivial dialogues which were supposed to take place in Ambrose's tavern (long gone and whereabouts not known). James Hogg in particular became famous as the 'Ettrick Shepherd' in the *Noctes*. Wilson became Professor of Moral Philosophy in the University in 1820. He lived at 53 Castle St. and in 1819 moved to 29 Ann St., a house of great charm, near the Water of Leith. In 1826 he moved to 6 Gloucester Pl. (P, now the Christopher North House Hotel), where he died.

Thomas Carlyle (1795–1881) first came to Edinburgh in 1809 to study for the ministry, walking from his home at Ecclefechan (q.v.) in 3 days. He left the University in 1813 without taking a degree and returned to teach mathematics at his old school at Annan. In 1817 he came back to Edinburgh to begin his theological course, but had doubts about his vocation and abandoned it for a literary career, which started with contributing articles to an encyclopedia. After his marriage to Jane Welsh (1826) he lived at 21 Comely Bank (P) for two years, where Francis Jeffrey was a frequent visitor, 'much taken', Carlyle wrote, 'with my little Jeannie, as well he might be, one of the brightest, cleverest creatures in the whole world'. Carlyle was elected Lord Rector of the University 1865-6.

William Motherwell (1797-1835), poet and collector of ballads, was educated at the High School. With Hogg he issued an edition of Burns's works in 1834-5. Robert Chambers (1802-71), publisher, editor, and miscellaneous writer, founded with his brother William (1800-83) the publishing firm of W. and R. Chambers of Edinburgh and in 1832 issued a popular weekly educational magazine, *Chambers's Edinburgh Journal*. They also published *Chambers's Encyclopaedia* (begun 1859, completed 1868, and followed by numerous later editions). Robert became Lord Provost, 1865-9. Marjory Fleming (1803-11), the child prodigy born at Kirkcaldy (q.v.), wrote some of her Journals while staying at 1 North Charlotte St. with her aunt, Mrs. Keith, and the cousin (her 'dear Isa') who acted as her teacher and corrected her work. George Borrow (1803-81) went to the High School at the time his father was quartered at the castle as an army officer, and *Lavengro* (1851) recounts the fights that used to occur between boys of Old Edinburgh and the New Town.

Dr. John Brown (1810-82), physician and author of *Rab and his Friends* (1859), was educated at the High School and the University. He practised medicine in Edinburgh for most of his life and from 1850 till his death lived at 23 Rutland St. The house, now offices, has a memorial to him carved in the stonework of the wall to the left of the front window.

William Aytoun (1813-65), poet and humorist, was born in Edinburgh and educated at the Academy and the University. He divided his time between law and literature, joining Blackwood's staff in 1844, and becoming Professor of Belles-Lettres at the University in 1845 and Sheriff of Orkney in 1850. He is remembered chiefly for the *Bon Gaultier Ballads* (1845), a collection of parodies and light verse which he published jointly with Sir Theodore Martin (1816-1909), another Edinburgh native. Martin was educated at the High School and University and practised as a solicitor in Edinburgh before going to London in 1846. He contributed to *Tait's* and *Fraser's* maga-

zines before collaborating with Aytoun. Robert Michael Ballantyne (1825-94), also a native of Edinburgh, went to Canada as a young man and worked as a clerk in the Hudson's Bay Company before turning to literature. He returned to take up a partnership with the publishing firm of Thomas Constable, and wrote one of the best known of his popular stories for boys, *The Young Fur Traders* (1855), while living in Edinburgh. Alexander Smith (1829-67), poet and essayist, was made secretary to the University in 1854. He met Sydney Dobell in the same year and collaborated with him on 'Sonnets on the War'. He is buried in Warriston Cemetery on the N. side of the city, his grave marked by a tall Celtic cross with his portrait in low relief. Andrew Lang (1844-1912), a native of Selkirk (q.v.), was educated at the Edinburgh Academy before going to St. Andrews University. George Edward Bateman Saintsbury (1845-1933), critic and author of many works on English and European literature, was Professor of Rhetoric and English Literature at the University from 1895 to 1915. He lived at Murrayfield House and from 1900 until he retired at 8 Eton Ter.

Robert Louis Stevenson (1850-94) was a native who grew up in Edinburgh and in spite of long absences abroad retained his memories and love of the city to the end of his life. He was born at 8 Howard Pl. (P; the mementoes formerly kept here when the house was a museum have been transferred to Lady Stair's House—see below) and was baptized Robert Lewis Balfour Stevenson after his maternal grandfather (he adopted Louis as his middle name while he was a student). In 1857 the Stevensons moved to 17 Heriot Row on the N. side of the New Town, their home for the next 30 years. Incidents and scenes of his childhood, including 'Leerie', the lamplighter, are contained in *A Child's Garden of Verses*, published in 1885 while he was in Bournemouth (q.v.), and dedicated to 'Cummy', his pet name for Alison Cunningham, his beloved nurse and life-long mentor. Robert was a delicate boy and his attendance at various schools was irregular on account of frequent illness. He went to the Academy for a time between the ages of 11 and 12, but his education was mainly at Mr. Robert Thompson's school in Frederick St. He entered the University in 1867 to study engineering at his father's wish, but later changed to law and qualified as an advocate. He was called to the Bar in July 1875, but left for France shortly after, and gradually turned to literature as a career. *Treasure Island* (1883), his most popular work, began as a story told to his stepson on holiday at Braemar and was first published as a serial. Two unfinished novels, his masterpiece, *Weir of Hermiston* (1896), and *St. Ives* (1898), were set largely in Edinburgh. Stevenson came back to Edinburgh in 1880, but ill-health took him away again, and after his father's death in 1887 he returned briefly for the last time, before sailing for America with his wife and mother. He finally settled in Samoa, where he died. There is a commemorative tablet in St. Giles's Cathedral bearing the lines from his tomb on Mount Vaea:

> Under the wide and starry sky
> Dig the grave and let me lie.

Kenneth Grahame (1859–1932) was an Edinburgh native whose ties with the city were broken at an early age. He was born at 30 Castle St. (P records him simply as the author of *The Golden Age*—the book that first made his name), but after his mother's death when he was a young child he went to live with his grandmother at Cookham Dean (q.v.) and spent the rest of his life in England. His contemporary, Sir Arthur Conan Doyle (1859–1930), was born at 11 Picardy Pl. (demolished 1969) and in 1876 went to the University to study medicine. He attended the lectures of Dr. Joseph Bell, a man of remarkable deductive powers who inspired the creation of the inimitable Sherlock Holmes. Conan Doyle went to Southsea (see Portsmouth) in 1882 to practise as a doctor, and at the same time began his career as a writer. James Matthew Barrie (1860–1937) entered the University in 1878 and lodged with a Mrs. Edwards at 3 Great King St. (P). After taking his M.A. in 1882 he worked as a journalist on the *Nottingham Journal* before going to London to make his career. In 1930 he became Chancellor of the University. Sir Compton Mackenzie (1883–1972), prolific novelist and writer on many topics, spent much of his last decade at 31 Drummond Pl., wintering in Edinburgh and spending summers in the south of France. He completed the last volumes of his autobiography, *My Life and*

Times (1963–71), during this time. He was Lord Rector of the University 1931–4.

¹ Open Apr.–Sept.: daily 10 a.m.–7 p.m.; Oct.–Mar.: weekdays 10 a.m.–3 p.m. Closed Sun.

Transient visitors

Edinburgh's reputation as a seat of learning and home of philosophers, poets, novelists, and critics has attracted an endless stream of visitors with literary interests, and it seems a matter of chance that some visits have been recorded and others forgotten. A few writers who came only briefly, such as Johnson, and Crabbe, who was the guest of Scott, have been mentioned above: one or two others are added here.

Maria Edgeworth (1768–1849) met Elizabeth Hamilton (see above) when she visited Edinburgh with her father in 1803, and kept in touch with her afterwards by correspondence. She came again 20 years later and visited Sir Walter Scott before setting out on a tour of the Highlands.

Percy Bysshe Shelley (1792–1822) married the 16-year-old Harriet here in 1811, just after he had been sent down from Oxford. They stayed for a short time at 60 George St. and, returning the following year, at 36 Frederick St.

Charlotte Brontë (1816–55) was charmed by her brief visit in July 1850. She contrasted Edinburgh with London in two of her letters: 'Edinburgh compared to London is like a vivid page of history compared to a huge dull treatise on political economy'; and London to her is 'a great rumbling, rambling, heavy Epic—compared to Edinburgh, a lyric, brief, bright, clear and vital as a flash of lightning'.

Sydney Dobell (1824–74), one of the members of the so-called 'Spasmodic School' of poets ridiculed by William Aytoun, visited Edinburgh with his wife while they were staying at Lasswade in 1854. They went out to Granton by the Firth of Forth, on the N. edge of the city, and were amazed at the violence of the storm: 'The great waves charged the parapet above the beach in long separate lines and came over like a regiment of white lions, all mane and tail.'

During the First World War Wilfred Owen and Siegfried Sassoon met as patients at the Craiglockhart War Hospital, *c.* 3 m. S. of Prince's St. Owen had been sent back from the front in France in June 1917, suffering from nervous exhaustion, and was transferred from a hospital in Southampton to Craiglockhart for treatment and observation. Sassoon arrived a few weeks later, a medical board having found him in need of medical attention after he had made public a protest to his commanding officer against the prolongation of the war. An account of their meeting and friendship and of Owen's poetry written at this time can be found in *Wilfred Owen* (1974), by Jon Stallworthy. Craiglockhart, originally built as a Hydro in 1880, became a military hospital in 1916 and is now a teacher training college of the Convent of the Sacred Heart.

Institutions and famous places

Lady Stair's House Museum, Lady Stair's Close, between the Lawnmarket and the Mound. The house was built in 1622 by Sir William Gray and became the home of Elizabeth, first Countess of Stair in 1719. It was presented to the city by the Earl of Rosebery in 1907 and now houses collections concerning the lives and works of Burns, Scott, and Stevenson.

Open June–Sept.: Mon.–Sat. 10 a.m.–6 p.m.; Oct.–May: Mon.–Sat. 10 a.m.–5 p.m. During Festival, also Sun. 2–5 p.m. Parties at other times by arrangement.

National Library of Scotland, E. side of George IV Bridge, one of the largest libraries in Britain, developed from the Advocates' Library (founded 1682). It became a copyright library in 1710 and took its present name in 1925. It possesses an extensive collection of illuminated manuscripts and specimens of early printing, and, among papers illustrating Scottish history, literature, and life, are letters and papers of Hume, Boswell, Burns, Stevenson, Scott, and Carlyle.

Open Mon.–Fri. 9.30 a.m.–8.30 p.m.; Sat. 9.30 a.m.–1 p.m.

Old Tolbooth, Parliament Sq. The site of this historic building (1466–1817) which finally became a prison known as the 'Heart of Midlothian' is marked by decorative cobbles on the pavement near St. Giles's Cathedral. It was the setting for the opening of Scott's novel, *The Heart of Midlothian* (1818).

Royal High School. The school traces its origin from the Abbey School founded in 1128, though the first actual building was not recorded until 1503. It became a grammar school in 1517 and later a 'hie schule', housed in the garden of the Blackfriars monastery, at the end of Infirmary St. near the High School Wynd. This school, which became known as the Royal High School in 1590, was superseded in 1777 by the new High School (the building is known as the Old Infirmary and is now part of the University Geography Dept.), which in turn moved to new premises (1825–9) in Regent Rd. (now the City Art Centre), and in 1968 to East Barnton Ave. in the NW. of the city.

University of Edinburgh (Old College), South Bridge, founded in 1583 by the town council as the 'Town's College' and later known as the 'College of James VI', and eventually the 'University of Edinburgh'. The present building was designed by Robert Adam in 1789 and completed by W. H. Playfair in 1834. SW. are the New University Buildings of 1884, and mid 20th-c. buildings occupy the S. and E. sides of George Sq. The University Library in George Sq. contains manuscripts of Scottish literature, and two important collections of books: Drummond of Hawthornden (16th-c. literature) and Halliwell-Phillipps (Shakespeare). Alexander Anderson, the railway poet known as 'Surfaceman' was assistant librarian 1880–3 and 1886–1909.

Apart from the scholars mentioned above, the list of distinguished writers who attended the University includes the following: James Thomson (1700–48), who came to study divinity, but cared more for poetry and left for London; David Mallet (or Malloch, 1705?–65); Mark Akenside (1721–70), a brilliant medical student; Oliver Goldsmith (1730?–74), who also studied medicine (1752–4) and is said to have lived in College Wynd (now Guthrie St.); James Macpherson (1736–96); Thomas Aird (1802–76), poet and friend of Carlyle; Alexander Balloch Grosart (1857–1909); William Archer (1856–1924); and John Davidson (1857–1909). Oliver Wendell Holmes (1809–94) received an honorary degree here in 1886.

EDNAM, Roxburghs. (Borders). [6 Gd] Village on the A699, *c.* 2 m. N. of Kelso. James Thomson was born (1700) in the former manse and is commemorated by a monument on Ferney Hill near by.

The bridge over the Eden Water has a plaque (1952) commemorating Henry Francis Lyte, author of 'Abide with me', who was born (1793) in a near-by house.

EDSTONE. See WOOTTON WAWEN.

EGHAM, Surrey. [1 Dc] Town on the A30. Sir John Denham, the poet who became Surveyor-General over Wren, lived in the family home (gone) near the church (rebuilt 1817) in which one of the few memorials transferred from the old building is to his father, and another, which shows him kneeling, holding a book, is to his mother. His lines on the Thames

O, could I flow like thee, and make thy stream
My great example as it is my theme,
Though deep, yet clear, though gentle yet not
   dull,
Strong without rage, without o'erflowing full.

from *Cooper's Hill* (1642), the topographical poem by which he is best remembered, were inspired by the view from the local hilltop of that name, where the Commonwealth Air Forces Memorial now stands, which overlooks the meadow of Runnymede. Dr. Johnson wrote of Denham's translations of Virgil which influenced Dryden and Pope, that he was 'one of the first that understood the necessity of emancipating translation from the drudgery of counting lines and interpreting single words'. F. J. Furnivall, the son of a successful doctor, was born (1825) at Great Fosters, the Tudor house (now a hotel). He founded the Early English Text Society (1864).

ELAN VALLEY, Powys. [3 Ee] Narrow valley SW. of Rhayader, traversed by the B4518, now flooded by the building of a reservoir. In the summer of 1811 Shelley spent some weeks here at Cwm Elan, a house owned by his cousins, the Grove family. Shelley returned the next year with his wife Harriet and in 'The Retrospect' contrasts the sad time he had the year before with the happiness of this visit with her. Shelley was also writing part of *Queen Mab* (1813) here. Thomas Grove helped them in their negotiations for a house of their own: this was Nantgwillt, a large house with a ghost and 200 acres, in which they lived while the negotiations were under way, but the lease proved too expensive and they left.

ELLASTONE, Staffs. [4 Ac] Village on the B5032, 5 m. SW. of Ashbourne, the 'Hayslope' of George Eliot's *Adam Bede* (1859). Half-way to Ashbourne and S. of the road are the ruins of Calwich Abbey, now farm buildings, a contender with Wootton Lodge on the Farley Rd. for her 'Donnithorne Chase'. Calwich (pr. Callich) had been the home of Bernard Granville who entertained his sister, Mrs. Delany, and also Rousseau from Wootton Hall (q.v.). Rousseau, Byron's 'self-torturing sophist', walked in the gardens with his host's niece, the pretty Mary Dewes, who received a stern warning from her aunt about the danger of his ideas. A memorial to Granville (d. 1775) composed by Mrs. Delany is on the end wall outside the church.

ELLEN'S ISLE, Perths. (Central). [6 Db] Island at S. end of Loch Katrine where Scott set some of *The Lady of the Lake* (1810). N. P. Willis tells in his *Pencillings by the Way* (1835) how his coach party was entertained by its guide:

There . . . gentlemen and ladies, is where Fitz-James blow'd his bugle, and waited for the light Shallop of Ellen Douglas; and here where you landed and came up them steps, is where she brought him to the bower, and the very tree's still there—as you see me tak' hold of it—and over the hill yonder, is where the gallant gray giv' out, and breathed his last, and (will you turn round if you please, them that likes) yonders where Fitz-James met Red Murdoch that killed Blanche of Devon, and right across the water swim young Greme that disdained the regular boat, and I s'pose on the lower step set the old Harper and Ellen many—a time, a—watching for Douglas . . .

The island is passed by the S.S. *Sir Walter Scott* on its way from Trossachs pier to Stronachlachar.

ELLERAY. See WINDERMERE.

ELLISLAND, Dumfriess. (Dumfries and Galloway). [6 Ee] Farm on the A76, 6 m. N. of Dumfries, on the bank of the Nith. In 1789 Robert Burns leased the farm, which he intended to improve with new methods, but when these proved unprofitable he was forced to work as an exciseman. The poem 'To Mary—in Heaven', about the dead Mary Campbell, and 'Tam o' Shanter' were written here, and he also collected here many songs for James Johnson's *Scots Musical Museum*

(1787–1803), including 'Auld Lang Syne' and 'A Red, Red Rose'. Burns's health was not improved by the bizarre medical methods of the time or by his anxiety about the frailty of his children. It is thought his heart was affected by rheumatic fever in his childhood: he died in 1796 and was buried in Dumfries. Part of the farmhouse now contains Burnsiana.

Open at reasonable hours.

ELPHIN, Roscommon. [8 De] Small town on the L43, 9 m. SW. of Carrick-on-Shannon. Oliver Goldsmith's maternal grandmother lived at Ardnagowan near by, the finest house in the district except for the Bishop's Palace, and it was here that he may have been born (10 Nov. 1730?) (though other accounts of his birth maintain that his mother was at Pallas (q.v.) at that time). At 8 years old he attended the Diocesan School under the Revd. Michael Griffin for a short while, staying with his uncle John at Ballyoughter, near Ardnagowan, before being transferred to another school, at Athlone.

ELSFIELD, Oxon. [1 Cb] Small village on northern outskirts of Oxford off the A40. R. D. Blackmore, who lived as a child with his aunt at the vicarage, used many local scenes in his woodland tale *Cripps the Carrier* (1876). Cripps Cottage, the carrier's home, is on the road in Beckley leading to Otmoor 2 m. NE. John Buchan lived at the Manor House from 1919 to 1935, when he was appointed Governor-General of Canada. Many of his novels were written here, including *Midwinter* (1923), which opens with a scene on Otmoor near by. In his autobiography, *Memory hold the Door* (1940), he recalls that the Manor House was the home of Francis Wise, the antiquary, when he was Librarian at the Bodleian in Oxford (1748–67). Buchan's grave is in the churchyard.

ELSTON, Notts. [4 Cc] Quiet village E. of the A46, 5 m. SW. of Newark. Erasmus Darwin was born in 1731 at the Hall (rebuilt in 1837). There are family monuments in the church and his mother built the almshouses in 1744.

ELSTOW, Beds. [4 Df] Village on the A6, 1½ m. S. of Bedford, the home of John Bunyan, who lived here with his parents and, after a brief period of service in the Parliamentary Army at Newport Pagnell, as a young married man, practising the trade of tinker. His birthplace, often described as 'at' or 'near' Elstow, is in fact nearer to the hamlet of Harrowden and can be approached from the Harrowden Road out of Bedford. A granite block in the fields marks the site of the cottage, and the determined pilgrim can reach it by turning down Old Harrowden Lane and following the signpost beside the brook. Except in dry weather the going is heavy and the mud can be a chastening reminder of the Slough of Despond.

The village church dates from the foundation of Elstow Abbey in 1078. It was extensively restored in 1880, but the Perpendicular font in which Bunyan was baptised on 30 November 1628 is still there. The Bunyan Memorial windows in the N. and S. aisles illustrating *The Holy War* and *The Pilgrim's Progress* were added in 1880. The Moot Hall[1] on the green, a medieval market hall and manorial court, houses a collection of furniture, books, and documents associated with Bunyan and his time. In the upper room there is a beautiful Chinese lacquer cabinet in which Sir William Temple cherished the letters of Dorothy Osborne, written mainly between 1648 and 1655, before their marriage.

[1] Open Tues.–Sat. 11 a.m.–5 p.m.; Sun. 2.30–5.30 p.m.; Bank Holidays, except Christmas Day and Good Friday.

ELY, Cambs. [4 Ee] Cathedral city on the A10. Alexander Barclay, a Benedictine monk here, translated the *Life of St. George* from Latin, and wrote his *Eclogues* (c. 1515), moral pastorals anticipating Spenser. Tradition says the monastery, where Hereward the Wake sought sanctuary, was saved in return for his surrender and he was killed outside.

ENNIS, Clare. [9 Cb] Busy market town on the Fergus, on the T11 and the T41. The poet Thomas Dermody, called by his biographer J. G. Raymond 'Ireland's most erratic genius', was born here (17 Jan. 1775; house gone), the son of a schoolmaster. He was a precocious boy, taught classics in his father's school from the age of 9, and wrote much poetry, including 'Monody on the Death of Chatterton', before he was 12. A born rebel, he ran away to Dublin, worked in a bookshop, and published his first book of poems in 1792, but rejected a chance of going to Trinity College, and enlisted in the army. Later he lapsed into irregular ways which led to his early death in London. Lines from his poem 'Enthusiast' match his uneven personality:

> He who such polish'd lines so well could form,
> Was Passion's slave, was Indiscretion's child:
> Now earth-enamour'd, grov'ling with the worm;
> Now seraph-plum'd, the wonderful, the wild.

The Harp of Erin (2 vols., 1807) contains his complete poetical works.

ENNISKILLEN, Fermanagh. [8 Ec] County town, on the A4 and the A46, situated on an island in the Erne, between Upper and Lower Loughs Erne. Portora Royal School, ¾ m. NW., is an 18th-c. building incorporating the school founded by James I in 1608. Among its pupils were Henry Francis Lyte and Oscar Wilde.

ENNISTYMON, Clare. [9 Cb] Small market town and holiday resort on the Cullenagh, on the T69 and the T70. Brian Merriman, author of *The Midnight Court*, is thought to have been born here *c.* 1749, but the exact place is unrecorded. (See Feakle.)

EPSOM, Surrey. [1 Ec] Former spa whose therapeutic waters were first discovered *c.* 1639, according to John Aubrey, who tried them in 1654. In a letter to her future husband Dorothy Osborne mentions staying here for 3 weeks to take the waters which 'agreed' with her. Pepys, whose failing eyesight was causing concern, got leave to come here in 1668. He stayed at the King's Head (site now entrance to shopping precinct) in the High St. In his diary he says 'Lord Buckhurst and Nell are lodged in the next house, and Sir Charles Sedley with them; and keep a merry house. Poor girl! I pity her.' This house, formerly Nell Gwynne's Café, is now a jeweller's. Shadwell's comedy *Epsom Wells* (1673) mentions the 'impertinent, ill-bred City wives', who flocked to the well on the Downs, which Celia Fiennes on her travels described as 'unpaved', 'dirty', and 'the wooden building, dark'. This old well (P) still stands in a small railed enclosure, reached by a footpath at the end of Wells Rd. (off the A24 Dorking Rd.). Wells House near by stands on the site of a later well.

EPWORTH, Humberside. [4 Ca] Small town on the A161, 16 m. E. of Doncaster. The Old Rectory[1] (owned by the World Methodist Council) was the boyhood home of John and Charles Wesley. Built in 1709, it replaced the house where they were born, burned down earlier in the year.

[1] Open Mon.–Sat. 10 a.m.–noon, 2–4 p.m., Sun. 2–4 p.m. Paying guests and large parties should consult the Warden in advance.

ERISKAY. See BARRA.

ESHER, Surrey. [1 Ec] Town on the A3. The sisters Jane and Anna Maria Porter lived (1823–32) at Alderlands, a house with a pillared porch, at 85 High St. The historical novels *The Hungarian Brothers* (1807) by the latter and *The Scottish Chiefs* (1810) by Jane were very popular both in English and in translation. William and Mary Howitt lived (1835–40) at West End Cottage (West End Gardens now on the site), which had a 'well-stocked orchard, and a meadow to the Mole with rights of fishing and grazing'. William wrote *Rural Life in England* (1836) and *Visits to Remarkable Places*. They also lived (1866–70) at The Orchard, Hare Lane (on the corner of Rayleigh Drive), Claygate.

In 1859 Meredith, on the advice of his friend Capt. Maxse, the original of the Radical parliamentary candidate in *Beauchamp's Career* (1874), became the tenant of Fairholme, once the Bunch of Grapes, an old posting inn, now The Grapes, a private house. By chance he met again the Duff Gordons of Belvedere House, which their hospitality led to his calling the Gordon Arms. They were the originals of Lady Jocelyn and Rose in *Evan Harrington* (1861), the novel he finished after his move to Copsham Cottage on the Oxshott Rd., Esher Common. The gipsies he met on the common appear in *Poems of the English Roadside* (1862). Swinburne visited him and read *The Rubáiyát of Omar Khayyám* (1859), newly published, and wrote 'Laus Veneris' on the Round Hill behind the cottage, a favourite place of Meredith's which he dubbed the Mound. Meredith divorced his first wife, and he explores the 'dusty answer' to the question why in the poems in *Modern Love* (1862). Meredith moved soon after his happy marriage (1864) to Marie Vulliamy whom he met here.

ESSENDON, Herts. [1 Eb] Village on the B158, 4 m. E. of Hatfield. Beatrix Potter, as a child, used to stay with her grandmother at Camfield Place. She describes the house as 'the place I love best in the world' in her *Journal* (1966), which is illustrated with photographs and some of her drawings.

ESTHWAITE LODGE, Cumbria. [5 Bc] White Georgian house on a minor road near the W. shore of Esthwaite Water, *c.* 2 m. S. of Hawkshead. Francis Brett Young spent his summers here between 1928 and 1933 and wrote *The House under the Water* (1932). Hugh Walpole stayed with him and his wife and finished the Paris section of *Judith Paris* (1931).

ETON, Berks. [1 Dc] Small town to the N. of Windsor, dominated by Eton College, the public school founded in 1440 by Henry VI. One of the earliest headmasters was Nicholas Udall (or Uvedale) (1534–41). He was notorious for flogging and he was also dismissed for misconduct in 1541. His play *Ralph Roister Doister* (1566), the earliest English comedy, was probably acted by the boys during his time here. John Harington, translator of *Orlando Furioso* (1591), and the ingenious inventor of a perfumed water-closet, was a pupil in the 1570s.

Sir Henry Wotton became Provost in 1624 after many years of being 'an honest man sent to lie abroad for the good of his country'. He died here in 1639 and is buried in the chapel. Giles Fletcher the Elder left in 1565, his son Phineas in 1600, and Edmund Waller in 1620. Henry Fielding was here *c.* 1720 and Horace Walpole and Thomas Gray were contemporaries (1727–34). Gray's *Ode on a Distant Prospect of Eton College* was written *c.* 1742 and contains the lines:

Alas! regardless of their doom
The little victims play!
No sense have they of ills to come
Nor care beyond to-day

. . . . .

Yet, ah! why should they know their fate,
Since sorrow never comes too late,
And happiness too swiftly flies?
Thought would destroy their paradise.
No more—where ignorance is bliss
'Tis folly to be wise.

Christopher Anstey was a pupil 1738–42, and John Hookham Frere was here 1784–8.

Shelley, who arrived in 1804, was considered an eccentric, attracted to scientific experiments. He had started to write at home and before he left in 1810 had published two novels in the style of 'Monk' Lewis, *Zastrozzi* and *St. Irvyne*. John Cornewall Lewis and Alexander Kinglake were contemporaries *c.* 1820, and Kinglake later gave a portrait of their Provost, Dr. Keate, in *Eōthen* (1844). William Johnson, who assumed the name Cory on his retirement in 1872, became an assistant master here at his old school in 1845. One of his best-remembered poems is the translation of the epitaph to Heraclitus by his friend Callimachus. Cory writes in *Letters and Journals* (1897)

I could not get to sleep last night, being engaged in making a half-humorous, half-sentimental boating song for the 4th of June; . . . I do a song with a tune in my head, or perhaps two; last night it was 'Waiting for the Wagon' and 'A health to the outward-bound'.

Swinburne came here in 1849, overlapping with Robert Bridges who came in 1854. Bridges became a friend of D. M. Dolben, whose poems, some written here, he edited years later in 1915. Dolben was drowned in 1867 soon after leaving Eton. Edward Plunkett (Lord Dunsany) and Percy Lubbock were pupils in the 1890s. Lubbock published *Shades of Eton* in 1929. Julian Grenfell, Ronald Knox, and G. H. Tyrwhitt-Wilson (Lord Berners) were pupils at the turn of the century. Lord Berners's *A Distant Prospect* (1945), an account of his childhood, includes the story of his leaving the college in a high fever to be treated at home.

Aldous Huxley was at Eton from 1908 to 1911 when he left because of serious eye trouble. After Oxford he returned to teach from the autumn of 1917 until April 1919, while working on *Leda and Other Poems* (1920). M. R. James became Provost in 1918, while Eric Blair (George Orwell) was a scholar. Cyril Connolly gives a picture of his years here (1918–21) at the end of *Enemies of Promise* (1938), an appraisal of writers and the pitfalls awaiting them. He sums up with his 'Theory of Permanent Adolescence' in which he claims that public schools intensify 'the glories and disappointments' of experiences so that they dominate boys' lives and arrest their development. Eric Parker, later a writer on natural history and sport, gives an account of his years here in *Eton in the*

Eighties (1914) and in the novel *Playing Fields* (1922). Like Connolly he discusses the all important election to the society 'Pop'.

School yard and cloisters, open weekdays in holidays 10 a.m.–5 p.m., more restricted in term. Chapel, Upper School, and Lower School guided tour 11.30 a.m.–12.30 p.m. and 2.30–5 p.m. Closed Sun.

ETTRICK, Selkirks. (Borders). [6 Fe] Hamlet on Ettrick Water, on a minor road turning off the B709 at Ramseycleuch. A 20-ft red Corsehill monument carrying a bronze portrait medallion marks the birthplace (long demolished) of James Hogg, 'the Ettrick Shepherd'. He is buried in the churchyard, near the grave of Tibbie Shiel (see Tibbie Shiel's Inn).

EUSTON, Suff. [4 Fe] Village 4½ m. SE. of Thetford on the A1088. The Duke of Grafton's estate here was described by Robert Bloomfield in *The Farmer's Boy* (1800):

> Round Euston's water'd vale and sloping plains,
> Where woods and groves in solemn grandeur rise,
> Where the kite brooding unmolested flies;
> The woodcock and the painted pheasant race,
> And skulking foxes destined for the chase.

EVERSLEY, Hants. [1 Cc] Village SE. of Reading where the A327 crosses the Blackwater. Lying back from a minor road a little to the S. is the church where Charles Kingsley was rector from 1844 to 1875. Most of his books including *The Water Babies* (1863) were written in the rectory. Inside the church there is a plaque of Kingsley in high relief below a Latin inscription, and a memorial window in the chancel shows St. Elizabeth of Hungary (the subject of one of his poems) and two water babies. Kingsley's grave in the churchyard is marked by a marble cross, with the inscription 'Amavimus, Amamus, Amabimus'.

EWELME, Oxon. [1 Cb] Village on the B4009. Chaucer is traditionally said to have visited his granddaughter Alice (effigy in the church), wife of William de la Pole (1396–1450) who built the almshouses. Jerome K. Jerome after the success of *Three Men in a Boat* (1887), lived at Gould's Grove (or Troy), an old farmhouse on the hill (1½ m. SE.) near the junction with the A423. He worked in a summer-house called The Nook which was surrounded by a thick yew hedge. Israel Zangwill, on a visit, wrote *Children of the Ghetto* (1892) here in between digging up worms with his pen to feed a young blackbird. H. G. Wells, W. W. Jacobs, and Eden Phillpotts were other visitors. Jerome worshipped at Ewelme Church, where he was buried (1927).

EXETER, Devon. [2 Ed] Cathedral and university city and county town of Devon, on the NE. bank of the Exe, the Isca Dumnoniorum of the Romans and the Escancestre of the Saxons. Defoe in his *Tour through the Whole Island of Britain* (1724–7) describes the city as 'famous for two things which we seldom find united in the same town, viz., that it is full of gentry and good company, and yet full of trade and manufactures also'. Its distinguished natives include Sir Thomas Bodley (1545–1613) and Richard Hooker (1553– or 1554–1600, born in Heavitree, now an E. suburb). Thomas Fuller (1608–61) came here with the Royalists when they moved from Oxford in 1643 and was made chaplain to Charles I's infant daughter the next year. During his time here he was a popular preacher and was working on *The Worthies of England* (1662). Thomas D'Urfey (1653–1723), a poet and dramatist of Huguenot descent, was born here and went to London to make his name, his most popular work being *Wit and Mirth, or Pills to purge Melancholy* (1719), a collection of songs and ballads. Sabine Baring-Gould (1834–1924), theologian and prolific writer in many fields, was born in Exeter, but spent a great part of his life as rector of Lew Trenchard (q.v.). Patrick Sheehan came to work in Exeter shortly after he was ordained in 1875 and stayed till 1877, when he returned to his native Mallow. George Gissing came in 1891 for 2 years, staying first at 24 Prospect Park and then at 1 St. Leonard's Ter. He enjoyed the peace after London: 'Every morning when I wake', he said, 'I thank heaven for silence.' *Born in Exile* (1892) is set partly in the city and its environs, and part of the setting of *The Private Papers of Henry Ryecroft* (1903) also derives from his knowledge of the surrounding countryside.

The Turk's Head in the High St. is a 15th-c. inn where Dickens found the original of his Fat Boy for *Pickwick Papers* (1837). In Thackeray's *Pendennis* (1848–50) Exeter is portrayed as 'Chatteris'.

The cathedral, dating from Norman times, was substantially rebuilt between *c.* 1270 and *c.* 1360. Miles Coverdale was bishop in 1551–3 and John Gauden in 1660–2. It suffered bomb damage in the Second World War, but this has been repaired. Just inside the W. entrance there is a memorial tablet to R. D. Blackmore, unveiled by Eden Phillpotts in 1904. A statue of Richard Hooker stands on the N. side of the Close.

The Cathedral Library,[1] now housed principally in the Bishop's Palace adjoining, claims a history of over 900 years, beginning with the gift of sixty-six books from Leofric, the first Bishop of Exeter, between 1050 and his death in 1072. These include the 10th-c. *Exeter Book*, the largest known collection of Anglo-Saxon poems, including 'The Wanderer', 'The Seafarer', and 'Deor'. There is also the Exeter Domesday Book, and many medieval manuscripts, including the beautiful 13th-c. Psalter probably written for the Church of St. Helen at Worcester, and the 14th-c. manuscript of the *Polychronicon* of Ranulf Higden of Chester. An interesting example of early printing (1492) is a fragment of Chaucer's *Canterbury Tales*, the opening of the 'Franklin's Tale'.

[1] Open Mon.–Fri. 2–5 p.m.

EYAM (pr. Eem), Derbys. [4 Ab] Village off the A623, 4 m. SW. of Hathersage, which volunteered to isolate itself to contain the plague in 1665. Anna Seward was born (1747) and lived at the vicarage near the church until her father became prebend of Lichfield as well, and they moved there. His curate Peter Cunningham, author of the poems 'Britannia's Naval Triumph' and 'Russian Prophecy', recognized the merit of William Newton, a young machinery carpenter of Abney (q.v.). Cunningham introduced Newton to Anna Seward when she visited the parish and she encouraged his writing and got him a mill partnership. The poet Richard Furness (b. 1791), son of a small farmer of Eyam, set up his own business as currier in 1813. After a runaway marriage he moved to Dore (8 m. NE.) as a schoolmaster, where he also practised medicine and surgery and superintended the design and building of a new chapel. The satirical *Rag Bag* (1832) was followed by *Medicus-Magus* (1836), a long poem with a glossary, on local village life, which was later called *The Astrologer*. He was buried (1857) at Eyam.

F

FAILFORD, Ayrs. (Strathclyde). [6 Dd] Village on the A758, 2 m. E. of Mauchline. A path from the bridge leads to the monument marking the spot where Burns and Mary Campbell took their last farewell of each other on 14 May 1786.

> That sacred hour can I forget
> Can I forget the hallowed grove
> Where by the winding Ayr we met
> To live one day of parting love.

FAIRPORT. See ARBROATH.

FALLS OF BRUAR, Perths. (Tayside). [6 Ea] Falls 3 m. W. of Blair Atholl on the A9. Robert Burns visited the scene in 1787 and, finding the water falling through bare rocks, wrote 'The Humble Petition of Bruar Water' to the Duke of Atholl, who responded by planting firs. Though these trees have now

gone, later plantings still keep the place green.

FALLS OF LEDARD, Perths. (Central). [6 Dc] Falls at the W. of Loch Ard, off the B829, which Scott describes in his novel *Waverley* (1814).

FALMOUTH, Cornwall. [2 Bf] Port and holiday resort at the end of the A39, overlooking a sheltered harbour opening off the Carrick Roads. Howard Spring moved here from Mylor (q.v.) in 1947 and settled at The White Cottage, Fenwick Rd. Here he finished *There Is No Armour* (1948), a novel which begins in Didsbury and moves on to Falmouth and the neighbouring country, and continued writing until the end of his life. His last novel was *Winds of the Day* (1964).

FARINGDON, Oxon. [1 Bb] Market town on the A417 and the A420, between Oxford and Swindon. Faringdon House,[1] an elegant 18th-c. house replacing the former Elizabethan building, standing in beautiful grounds to the N. of the church, was built by George III's Poet Laureate, Henry James Pye, c. 1770—a more lasting memorial to his good taste than his undistinguished poetry. Having been dedicated to writing poetry from the age of 10, when he read Pope's translation of the *Odyssey*, he published his first poem when he was 17 and continued to write for the rest of his life, combining this occupation with the affairs of a country gentleman and election as an M.P. in 1784. Election expenses together with inherited debts compelled him to sell the estates and leave Faringdon some time in the 1780s. He was made Poet Laureate by Pitt in 1790 and, according to Southey (his successor in the office), went on rhyming 'doggedly and dully'. There is a copy of his self-portrait in the Pye Chapel in the church. The grounds of the house are said to be haunted by the headless ghost of Hampden Pye, an earlier member of the family, who was serving abroad as a midshipman when his stepmother, in collusion with the ship's captain, arranged for his death so that her own son could become heir. His head was blown off during an action at sea, seemingly by accident, but his ghost came back to haunt his stepmother. The story, told to Richard Barham by Mrs. Mary Ann Hughes (grandmother of Thomas Hughes of Uffington), was the source of 'The Legend of Hamilton Tighe' in *The Ingoldsby Legends* (1840).

In the 1930s Faringdon House became the home of Lord Berners, musician, author, painter, and wit. He wrote some whimsical novels, including *The Camel* (1936) and *Far from the Madding War* (1941). *First Childhood* (1934) and *A Distant Prospect* (1945) are two volumes of autobiography. He was Nancy Mitford's 'Lord Merlin' in *The Pursuit of Love* (1945), with his telegraphic address 'Neighbourtease'. Across the road to the E. is Faringdon Hill, celebrated in verse by Henry Pye and planted by him (or by his successor, William Hallet) with clumps of Scots pine. On top of this Lord Berners built a folly tower, culminating in a Gothic octagonal lantern, in 1935, the last folly of any size to be built in England.

[1] Grounds open annually for the N.G.S.

FARNHAM, Surrey. [1 Dd] Old town on the A287 and the A325. The castle,[1] on a hill to the N., was garrisoned in swift succession by the Parliamentarian George Wither and the Royalist John Denham in 1642. Wither, a convert to puritanism, raised a troop of horse for the cause. In 1643 he wrote *De Defendendo* to refute charges of cowardice at the Royalist onslaught. The domestic buildings were a residence[2] of the bishops of Winchester, including William of Wykeham and William Waynflete. Izaak Walton, who had been George Morley's steward in his previous See, accompanied him here in 1662 and is thought to have written part of the lives of Hooker (1665) and Herbert (1670) in the palace.

Waverley Lane, by the station, leads to an entrance to the ruins in the fields of Waverley Abbey, the first Cistercian house in England, from which Scott is said to have taken the title of his series of novels. Opposite the lodge, along Moor Park Lane, is the much altered 17th-c. house, bought in 1680 by Sir William Temple, the diplomat, and his wife, Dorothy Osborne. He renamed the house (previously Compton Hall) after Moor Park (q.v.) in Herts., and replanned the gardens on similar lines (site today is the field below the house). It is now Moor Park College[3] for Adult Christian Education. Swift, whose mother is thought to have been a family connection of Temple's, came here (c. 1690), acting as secretary while waiting for a post in Ireland which he hoped Temple would secure for him. While he was here Swift met the young Esther Johnson (a daughter of a servant or companion to Temple's sister), later the recipient of many of his intimate letters (collected as *Journal to Stella*, 1948). Disappointed in the extent of Temple's patronage, Swift returned to Ireland in 1694 but came back in 1696 and again stayed here. He wrote in 1696 and 1697 *A Tale of a Tub* and *The Battle of the Books*, satires on 'corruptions in religion and learning' published together in 1704. When Temple died in 1699, Swift returned to Ireland.

Cobbett, who described his first reading of *A Tale of a Tub* as the 'birth of intellect', was born (1762) at his father's inn, the Jolly Farmer, in Bridge Sq. (now the William Cobbett with a plaque erected by the Farnham Society). A column with his bust in the riverside Gostrey Meadow near by calls him the 'champion of Democracy, master of English Prose and enemy of cant in public affairs'. He left Farnham when 11 to walk to Kew to find work but he often visited the town, as he relates in *Rural Rides*. In 1835 he was buried at the parish church, which has a tablet with his portrait in relief on the S. wall of the tower. The museum,[4] 38 West St., has mementoes of him.

Augustus Toplady, author of 'Rock of Ages' (1775), was born (1740) at 10 West St., which has a plaque of stone from Burrington Coombe (q.v.). Ada Ellen Bayly, who wrote as 'Edna Lyall', spent her holidays from the age of 4 (1861) with her cousins in West St., where she began *We Two* (1884). *To Right the Wrong* (1894), a novel about the Civil War, which has scenes in the town, came to her mind in the church.

George Sturt, who wrote as 'George Bourne', was born (1863) at 44 The Borough and was at the Grammar School (1876–84), where he became a pupil-teacher. He describes the family business which he entered after his father died (1884) in *The Wheelwright's Shop* (1923). His family lived on the premises at 84 East St. but in 1891 he moved to Vine Cottage in a large garden at Lower Bourne (now a suburb). The old man he engaged as gardener and handyman there provided the subject of *The Bettesworth Book* (1901) and *Memoirs of a Surrey Labourer* (1907), and often appears in *The Journals of George Sturt* (ed. 1941 by Geoffrey Grigson and 1967 by E. D. Mackerness). Sturt, who was looked after by his unmarried sisters, was disabled by strokes and he died at Vine Cottage in 1927. J. M. Barrie wrote *Peter Pan* (1904) in the pinewoods behind his country home Black-lake Cottage (now Lobs Wood Manor) in Tilford Lane (1 m.) where his Newfoundland dog, the original of Nana, is buried.

[1] Open daily from 2 p.m.
[2] Open Wed. 2–4.30 p.m.
[3] Open for residential courses on general subjects, details from the Education Secretary.
[4] Open Tues.–Sat. 11 a.m.–5 p.m.; Sun. 2–5 p.m.

FARRINGFORD, I.O.W. [1 Bf] Georgian house (now a hotel), off Bedbury Lane, Freshwater, leased by Alfred Tennyson in 1853 and bought with the proceeds from *Maud* (1855). It was then ivy-covered, secluded from the village by its park and farmland, and had a view across the sea. Tennyson's many visitors included Charles Kingsley, Edward FitzGerald, Arthur Hugh Clough, Edward Lear, and Swinburne. It is possible that Charles Dodgson got the idea of the Mouse's Tale in *Alice's Adventures in Wonderland* (1865) from a dream Tennyson related on his visit. Works written here include *The Charge of the Light Brigade* (1854), *Maud* (1855), *The Idylls of the King* (1859), and *Enoch Arden* (1864). Some were written in the attic which he called the 'fumitory', some in the garden arbour, or in his study in the newly added west wing, where his later poems were written, including *Locksley Hall Sixty Years After*. Tennyson started to build Aldworth (see Haslemere) in 1868 and then usually spent the winters here. Freshwater Church, where his wife is buried, has a stone commemorating him with the lines

Speak, living voice, with thee death is not death;
Thy life outlives the life of dust and breath.

Much of Tennyson's life was spent out of doors and his favourite walk was along the Downs to the Needles. This is now called Tennyson Down, where a large memorial cross has been erected on the site of the beacon 'by the People of Freshwater and other friends in England and America'.

FAVERSHAM, Kent. [1 Gc] Old town off the A2, 8 m. NW. of Canterbury. The timber and plaster 80 Abbey St. (P), with its overhanging storeys, once part of the abbey buildings, was the home of Richard Arden, mayor in 1547. Holinshed in his *Chronicles* (1577) records the murder in 1559 on which the unknown author, thought by some to be Shakespeare, bases his play *The Tragedy of Mr. Arden of Feversham* (1592). In this, Arden, after many attempts, is murdered by his wife and her lover who are both caught and executed. George Lillo also used this subject for his play *Arden of Feversham* published posthumously in 1762.

FAWLEY, Berks. [1 Bc] Village off the A338, 4 m. S. of Wantage. Thomas Hardy, whose maternal grandmother came from the village, calls it 'Marygreen' in *Jude the Obscure* (1895), which is partly set here. Aunt Drusilla's house cannot be identified but the large green with the school and the rectory are still there.

FEAKLE, Clare. [9 Db] Secluded little village on the L194, near the foothills of the Slieve

Aughty Mountains. Brian Merriman (Brian Mac Giolla-Meidhre, 1749? or 1757?–1805), poet and schoolmaster, is buried in the old churchyard. His grave is unmarked, but there is a bronze plaque, designed by Seamus Murphy, on the outer wall (unveiled 1967). He was a native of Clare, possibly of Ennistymon, and lived at Feakle, earning his living as a hedge-school teacher and working a small farm (for which he won a premium in 1796 for the quality of his flax). The work for which he is remembered is *The Midnight Court* (*Cúirt an mheádhon oídhche*, 1780), a long poem that has been described as 'a rhythmical bacchanalia' and has been published in several English translations from the Irish, notably by Frank O'Connor (1945), Lord Longford (1949), and David Marcus (1953).

FELIXSTOWE, Suff. [1 Ha] Port and resort on the coast between the Orwell and the Deben. The sea by the long esplanade was the scene of the swim in Meredith's *Lord Ormont and his Aminta* (1894).

FELPHAM, West Sussex. [1 De] Resort on the A259 adjoining Bognor Regis. Limmer Lane by the post office leads to the site of Turret House where the poet Hayley lived when Felpham was a small village. He gave up his estate at Eartham in the 1790s and called the house his marine cottage. Flaxman, the sculptor, who had designed the memorial to Hayley's son, may have introduced him to Blake as an illustrator for his *Ballads founded on Anecdotes of Animals* (1805). Hayley in 1800 provided Blake with a cottage (now Blake's House, behind the Thatch Inn). Blake enjoyed this at first and wrote that 'the voices of winds, trees and birds . . . make it a dwelling for immortals'. He began the poem *Milton* (1804) and composed *Jerusalem* for the place, and made some illustrations for Hayley's life of Cowper (1803). But the local people, and even Hayley too, thought him strange and his ideas incomprehensible. In 1804 a disturbance in his garden led him to eject a drunken soldier, who retaliated by accusing him of sedition. He was arrested and taken to Chichester, accused of high treason, but found not guilty. Hayley is buried in the churchyard.

FIVE TOWNS. See STOKE-ON-TRENT.

FLADBURY, Hereford and Worcester. [4 Af] Village *c.* 3 m. NW. of Evesham, just S. of the B4084. E. of the cross-roads a drive leads uphill among orchards to Craycombe House, a dignified Georgian building restored by Francis Brett Young, who lived there from 1932 till the end of the war, when he moved to South Africa. Many of his books were written here, including *White Ladies* (1935).

FLEET, Dorset. [2 He] Village consisting of East and West Fleet: a few scattered cottages, a church, and Moonfleet House (now the Moonfleet Manor Hotel), lying between Chesil beach and the B3157 from Weymouth to Bridport. The house, formerly Fleet House, belonging to the Moone or Mohun family and dating from the 17th c., stands on the edge of the water at the end of a minor road, *c.* 1½ m. from Chickerell, and was the setting for Meade Falkner's *Moonfleet* (1898), a novel of adventure and smuggling, based on local tradition.

FLEETWOOD, Lancs. [5 Bd] Large seaside resort at the end of the A587, at the mouth of the Wyre. Mrs. Molesworth spent several summers there in her childhood, when it was only a small, quiet place, and describes it as 'Sandyshore' in *The Rectory Children* (1889).

FLETCHING, East Sussex. [1 Ed] Village off the A272, 4 m. NW. of Uckfield. Edward Gibbon first met his friend Holroyd in Lausanne. In 1793, though in ill-health, he again made the journey to England to be with his friend after his wife's death. Holroyd was then Lord Sheffield and had inherited Sheffield Park[1] (1½ m. W. on the A275). Gibbon spent the rest of the year there but went to London in the New Year and died suddenly a few days later. Sheffield, who had Gibbon's body interred in his family mausoleum in the parish church, collected his friend's memoirs, which were published with his *Miscellaneous Works* in 1796.

[1] Garden (N.T.) open Apr.: Wed., Sat., and Sun. 11 a.m.–7 p.m.; May–Sept.: daily 11 a.m.–7 p.m.; Oct.–19 Nov.: daily 11 a.m.–5 p.m.

FLODDEN FIELD, Northumb. [6 Gd] The site, 3 m. SE. of Coldstream off the A697, was where the battle (1513) took place in the wars between the Scots and the English. It was made the subject of poems and ballads, including *Ballade of the Scottysshe Kynge* (1513) by John Skelton, a ballad by Thomas Deloney, and 'The Flowers of the Forest' by Jane Elliot—a Scottish lament beginning 'I've heard them lilting at the ewe-milking'. Scott's *Marmion, A Tale of Flodden Field* (1808), a poem in six cantos, ends with the battle in which Marmion is killed.

FOCKBURY, Hereford and Worcester. [3 Hd] Hamlet *c.* 1½ m. NW. of Bromsgrove, between the A491 and the A448. A. E. Housman was born (1859) in Valley House (now Housmans), a pleasant Georgian building in sheltered grounds. When still an infant he moved with his parents to Bromsgrove (q.v.), returning to Fockbury *c.* 1873 to live at the Clock House (called at that time Fockbury House).

FOLKESTONE, Kent. [1 Hd] S. coast resort 7 m. W. of Dover. Dickens rented 3 Albion Villas (now Copperfield House) from mid July to October 1855. He was at first unable to concentrate on the writing of *Little Dorrit* as his sons made such a noise on the wooden staircase during their holidays. His exercise was in climbing 'a precipitous cliff in a lonely spot overhanging the wild sea-beach'. Wilkie Collins, who often joined Dickens on his holidays, visited him here. H. G. Wells and his wife Catherine moved into their new home, The Spade House, looking over the terraced garden to Sandgate Bay in 1900. He wrote here *Mankind in the Making* (1903), *The Food of the Gods* (1904), *Kipps* (1905), *Tono-Bungay* (1909), and *The History of Mr. Polly* (1910), using first a small study, then enlarging it and later building a garden study where he could be undisturbed. He entertained his friends, among them Shaw, Conrad, Henry James, and Kipling, and played exciting floor games with his sons. The house, little altered, is now a Vegetarian Guest House and Retreat.[1] A. E. Coppard was born in lodgings here in 1878 and he recalls his childhood in *It's Me, O Lord* (1957).

[1] Visits can be made by appointment.

FOLLY DOWN. See CHALDON HERRING.

FONTHILL ABBEY, Wilts. [1 Ad] The remains of William Beckford's extravagant and fantastic mansion are in private grounds in Fonthill Abbey Wood, Fonthill Gifford, on a minor road *c.* 1 m. S. of Fonthill Bishop on the B3089, 15 m. W. of Salisbury. Beckford, a man of vast wealth, remembered for his oriental romance, *Vathek* (1787, reprinted 1970), inherited the house from his father and in 1790 employed James Wyatt to rebuild it in the Gothic style, complete with a high wall round the grounds to keep out unwanted visitors. Here he housed his great collection of curios, works of art, and books, and spent visits between his tours of the Continent. The building took nearly 20 years to complete (the Great Tower was too hurriedly erected in 1799 and collapsed soon after), but Nelson and Sir William and Lady Hamilton were entertained there in 1800, and in 1807 Beckford moved into the S. wing. Eventually his fortune dwindled and in 1822 he sold the abbey and moved to Bath (q.v.). In October 1823 Thomas Moore, who was staying near by, walked over for the sale and brought back a cup and saucer as a memento for his wife, Bessy. Today all that remains is some 60 ft of the Lancaster Tower, the dismantled Duchess's Bedroom, the Oratory, and the Steward's room with adjoining bedrooms.

FORDHAM, Cambs. [4 Fe] Large village on the A142 and the B1102, 14 m. NE. of Cambridge. James Withers came here in 1824 to work for a market gardener and, with the exception of a few years, lived here until his death in 1892. He had been writing for many years before his *Poems* were published (1854), after coming to the notice of his employer. Two other collections followed in 1856 and 1860, and the three volumes were issued as one in 1863. This resulted in a visit to London and an offer of employment there, but Withers refused to live in a town and settled with his wife and four children in a riverside cottage at the foot of the hill below the church, now known as the Poet's Cottage. One of his longer poems was 'Wicken Fen' about a village 4 m. W., which now has the fen preserved in its natural state by the N.T. His grave is marked by a tombstone, and a stained-glass window in the church was inscribed to his memory.

FOREMARK, Derbys. [4 Bc] Village 2 m. E. of Repton. William Stevens became chaplain (1778) to Sir Robert Burdett of Foremark Hall[1] (built 1759–61), now the Preparatory

Department of Repton School. Stevens's *Journal* (1965), kept from 1792–1800, tells of his weekly journeys from Repton to preach and his irksome dependence on his patron. He met Fanny Coutts here and they fell in love, but her parents prevented their marriage. A miniature of Stevens is in the school and the three-decker pulpit he used is still in the church.

[1] Open 15 June–4 July: 2.30–4.30 p.m.

FOREST HILL, Oxon. [1 Cb] Small village on the eastern outskirts of Oxford, off the A40. Milton, whose grandfather had lived at Stanton St. John, came here in 1643 possibly to collect a debt from Richard Powell of the manor house. A month later he returned to London married to the 17-year-old Mary Powell. Many scenes in Robert Graves's novel, *Wife to Mr. Milton* (1943), are set in the village, and the novelist Anne Manning wrote a popular account, *Mistress Mary Powell* (1851). The house they describe has been rebuilt, the ornate gateway seen over the churchyard wall, and the mounting block now outside the main gate were there in Milton's time.

William Mickle, who lived at the old manor and married here, was a corrector at the Clarendon Press (1765–71), translator of the *Lusiads* (1775), and author of 'Cumnor Hall' (1784) among other ballads. His gravestone is in the church vestry.

FORGNEY, Longford. [8 Ef] Village on the L121, 2½ m. E. of Ballymahon. The village church has a memorial window to Oliver Goldsmith, who was baptized there.

FORT AUGUSTUS. See LAGGAN.

FOSTON-LE-CLAY, North Yorkshire. [5 Fd] Village off the A64, 9 m. NE. of York, where Sydney Smith was rector from 1806 to 1828. He might have appointed a curate-in-charge of the parish, but conditions of residence in livings were tightened, so he left London, where he had lectured on moral philosophy to an appreciative audience, and arrived in 1809. Finding the rectory ruinous he stayed at Heslington, York, until his new one[1] was finished in 1814. A brass in the N. aisle of the church, erected by public subscription, calls him 'Friend and Counsellor of his parishioners'.

[1] The Old Rectory. Open June–Sept.: Sun. and Aug. Bank Holiday 2.30–6 p.m.

FOULSHIELS, Selkirks. (Borders). [6 Fd] Hamlet on the A708, *c.* 3 m. W. of Selkirk, in the Yarrow Valley. On the opposite side of the road to Newark Castle is the dilapidated cottage (P) where Mungo Park was born (1771). It was here that he compiled most of the narrative of *Travels in the Interior of Africa* (1799).

FOWEY (pr. Foy), Cornwall. [2 Cf] Picturesque seaport situated near the mouth of the Fowey, at the end of the A3082. The road comes steeply down into the narrow ways of the town and it is advisable to leave a car at the top of the hill and walk down the paths and steps to the waterfront. Celia Fiennes, visiting in 1698, wrote of the road 'dropping at breakneck speed' and that

Near the road were many holes and sloughs wherever there was clay ground, and when, by the rain, these were filled with water it was difficult to sheer danger. My horse was quite down in one of these holes, head and all, but by the good hand of God's providence, I giving him a sharp strap, he floundered up again, and retrieved his feet and got clear of the place with me on his back.

A short way along the Esplanade, just above Polruan Ferry, is The Haven (P), the home of Sir Arthur Quiller-Couch ('Q') from 1892 to 1944. Here he wrote many of his novels and short stories, immortalizing Fowey as 'Troy Town' in *The Astonishing History of Troy Town* (1888). He also edited *The Oxford Book of English Verse* (1899) and other anthologies. He was mayor of Fowey in 1937–8 and is commemorated by a memorial on Hall Walk, overlooking the harbour. Kenneth Grahame, who became friends with 'Q' in 1899, used to come and stay and they enjoyed sailing together. Grahame married Elspeth Thomson at St. Fimbarrus's Church on 22 July 1899, with his cousin Anthony Hope Hawkins as best man (the entry in the marriage register may be seen at the County Archivist's Office, Truro). *The Wind in the Willows* (1908), begun as bedtime stories for his young son, Alistair, *c.* 1904, was continued in letters to him during visits to Fowey, which inspired much of the idyllic river setting of 'messing about in boats'.

FOX HOW. See AMBLESIDE.

FRAMLINGHAM, Suff. [4 He] Market town at the junction of the B1116 and the B1120.

The ruined flint castle[1] with its moat and thirteen towers, some having red-brick Tudor chimneys, was the home of the Howards, hosts to Mary Tudor when Jane Grey was declared queen. Henry Howard, Earl of Surrey, who with Thomas Wyatt first used the Italian sonnet form, and, in his translation of the *Aeneid*, blank verse, has an ornate painted alabaster tomb in the church; he was beheaded by Henry VIII. Under Elizabeth, William Alabaster was confined to the castle after having been interrogated in the Tower for being a Catholic.

Open summer: daily from 9.30 a.m.; winter: Sun. from 2 p.m.

FRENCHPARK, Roscommon. [8 De] Hamlet on the T77 and the L11, 9 m. NE. of Castlerea. Douglas Hyde, poet and Gaelic scholar and one of the founders of the Abbey Theatre, was born (1860) at the rectory. After an academic life in Dublin he retired from his professorship of Modern Irish at University College and came to live at Ratra House, which had been bought for him by public subscription, but he was recalled to Dublin to become first President of the Republic of Ireland (1938–45). He is buried in Frenchpark churchyard.

FRESHWATER. See FARRINGFORD.

FRIMLEY, Surrey. [1 Dc] Town on the A325, 3 m. SW. of Bagshot. Francis Bret Harte, the American author of *The Luck of Roaring Camp* (1870), was buried (1902) in St. Peter's churchyard. The low red-marble tombstone surrounded by chains is near the churchyard wall.

FRINGFORD, Oxon. [1 Ca] Village off the A421, 4 m. NE. of Bicester. In 1890 when she was 14, Flora Thompson (then Timms) was driven by her father in a borrowed cart to take up work as assistant to Mrs. Whitton, the postmistress, who also kept the forge (now a private house called The Forge) on the large green. She stayed until she was nearly 20 when she chose the more varied positions offered as a relief clerk, for which she was thought flighty by her family. Later she drew on her life here for her autobiographical novel *Candleford Green* (1943) in which Mrs. Whitton appears as Miss Lane.

FROME ST. QUINTIN, Dorset. [2 Hd] Village off the A37, 10 m. NW. of Dorchester. George Crabbe occasionally visited here after he had been presented to the living together with Evershot (3 m. NW.) in 1783. He brought his wife in 1784 and stayed at Frome St. Quintin House. His host was George Baker, who had just completed the classic portico (with 'Geo. Baker A.D. 1782' cut in the stone above).

G

GAD'S HILL, Kent. [1 Fc] Hamlet on the A226, 3 m. NW. of Rochester, haunt of robbers who preyed on travellers on the old Dover road. The coaching inn is named after Falstaff, who robbed with his cronies and was robbed in turn in *1 Henry IV*. Dickens, who had looked with envy at the 18th-c. Gad's Hill Place when a boy, realized his ambition to buy the house in 1856. The owner was Eliza Lynn (later Mrs. Lynn Linton, the novelist) who had spent her girlhood there. The main road runs through the property and Dickens had a tunnel made to link the garden with the wilderness and shrubbery in which he set the little Swiss chalet given him by the actor Fechter. *Great*

Expectations (1860), *The Uncommercial Traveller* (1860), *Our Mutual Friend* (1865), and the unfinished *Edwin Drood* (1870) were largely written in the chalet or in the study on the ground floor, which was the setting for the drawing *The Empty Chair* by Fildes after Dickens's death here in 1870.

GAINSBOROUGH, Lincs. [4 Ca] Manufacturing and market town on the Trent and the A361, 16 m. NW. of Lincoln. Marian Evans, who wrote as George Eliot, searching for a river capable of producing a flood to cause the tragedy in the novel she was writing, visited the town in 1859. George Lewes wrote 'We took a boat from Gainsborough and rowed down to the Idle [a tributary joining the Trent at Stockwith, 4 m. N.] which we ascended on foot some way, and walked back to Gainsborough'. The title of the novel, *The Mill on the Floss*, was chosen by John Blackwood, the publisher, but though 'St. Ogg's' was set on a tributary of the tidal River Trent, descriptions of life at the mill come from Marian Evans's memory of Arbury Mill near her childhood home.

GALASHIELS, Selkirks. (Borders). [6 Fd] Town on the A6091 and the A72, 6 m. N. of Selkirk. A plaque erected in the wall on the outskirts E. of the town, on the road to Abbotsford, states that Sir Walter Scott's carriage, bringing him home in 1832 after a journey abroad in search of health, paused at its usual stopping place to let the paralysed man see his favourite view of his home across the Tweed.

GALTON. See ALTON.

GALWAY, Galway. [9 Ca] Cathedral and university town, situated at the NE. corner of Galway Bay, at the end of the T4 and several other main roads. Frank Harris (1856–1931), journalist, biographer, and miscellaneous writer, was born in Galway of Welsh parentage, but after being educated at the Royal School, Armagh, ran away to America at the age of 16 and became a cowboy. Later he went to London (*c.* 1883) and began his journalistic career on the *Evening News*. Another native of the city, Pádraig Ó Conaire (1882–1928), writer in Irish of essays and short stories, is commemorated in Eyre Sq. by a statue by Albert Power, which shows him seated informally in a setting of rocks and plants.

The modern cathedral, on the W. bank of the Corrib, was built on the site of the old county gaol where Wilfrid Scawen Blunt was imprisoned in 1887 for organizing a mass protest meeting of the oppressed tenants on the notorious Clanricarde estates (near Portumna). He described his experiences in *In Vinculis* (1889).

There are regular sailings from the harbour to the Aran Islands (q.v.).

GARDENLEIGH. See ORCHARDLEIGH PARK.

GARINISH ISLAND (or ILNACULLIN), Cork. [9 Be] Island off the W. shore of Glengarriff

Harbour, accessible by boat from the T65 or the L61. Formerly privately owned and landscaped (1910–13) and containing attractive Italian and Japanese gardens, classical temples, and exotic plants, it is now State property. Bernard Shaw visited the island when he was staying at Glengarriff in 1923, and wrote part of *Saint Joan* (1924) there. 'During that year', he said, 'I was at Glengarriff from the 18th July to the 15th August, and at Parknasilla [Kerry] from the 15th August to the 18th September, working at the play all the time . . . But the play was neither begun nor finished in Eire. A good deal of it was written in rapidly moving trains between King's Cross and Hatfield . . .'

GARSINGTON, Oxon. [1 Cb] Village 5 m. SE. of Oxford, on a minor road off the B480 from Cowley. Rider Haggard was sent to the Revd. H. J. Grahame's school at the rectory when he was 10 (1866), as he seemed to be learning nothing from his day schools in London. He made friends with a farmer called Quatermain, who let him help to feed the pigs and gave him walnuts from whose shells the boy made little boats. Haggard used the name in *King Solomon's Mines* (1885) and other romances with African settings.

The Manor[1] was the home of Lady Ottoline and Philip Morrell from 1915 to 1928, and a place of unflagging hospitality to young writers and artists, though sometimes regarded with suspicion as a pacifist centre during the war. Aldous Huxley, then an undergraduate at Balliol, described his first visit in a letter to his father (8 Dec. 1915): '. . . out to Garsington for luncheon to the Philip Morrells, who have bought a lovely Elizabethan manor there. Lady Ottoline . . . is a quite incredible creature—arty beyond the dreams of avarice and a patroness of literature and the modernities.' Later, as a frequent guest, he was writing that the household was among the most delightful he knew: 'always interesting people there and v. good talk'. He stayed for an amusing Christmas, when Middleton Murry and Katherine Mansfield, Lytton Strachey, Carrington, and Clive Bell were of the party. 'We performed a superb play invented by Katherine, improvising as we went along.' Other visitors included Siegfried Sassoon, on leave in 1916, who found it 'enchanting', D. H. Lawrence, who discovered a keenly sympathetic friend in Lady Ottoline, and T. S. Eliot. When the conscientious objectors became too many for the Manor they overflowed into the bailiff's house across the road. A portrait of a typical house-party , is given in Aldous Huxley's first novel, *Crome Yellow* (1921), and the house is possibly a model for Breadalby in D. H. Lawrence's *Women in Love* (1920). Lady Ottoline's own account of the Manor appears in vol. ii of her memoirs, *Ottoline at Garsington* (1974).

[1] Gardens open for N.G.S.

GARTMORE, Perths. (Central). [6 Dc] Village off the A81, 4 m. S. of Aberfoyle. Gartmore House (visible from the A81) looking over Flander's Moss to the Lake of Menteith, was the birthplace of Robert Graham (1735–97) who, having gone at 17 to Jamaica, returned on inheriting Ardoch (q.v.) in 1772. His father and elder brother having died, he moved to Gartmore in 1777, where he wrote the lyrics, including 'If doughty deeds my lady please', for which he is best remembered. He became M.P. for Stirlingshire, was twice elected Rector of Glasgow University, and in 1791, on inheriting Finlaystone across the Clyde, the seat of the Glencairns, his mother's family, added Cunninghame to his name. He was buried with his wife and young son in the walled burial ground.

His grandson, R. B. Cunninghame Graham, often known as 'Don Roberto' from his Spanish upbringing in S. America, came here on inheriting the encumbered estate in 1885, and wrote *Father Archangel of Scotland* (1896), a collection of short stories, with his wife Gabriela de la Balmondière, the poet. He left here for Ardoch in 1903 and later sold the house, which is now owned by the local authority.

GASK HOUSE, Perths. (Tayside). [6 Eb] Country house ½ m. E. of the A9, 6 m. NE. of Gleneagles, in the Strathearn area. Caroline Nairne, *née* Oliphant, was born (1766) here and her family had Jacobite sympathies. She married (1806) a cousin, whose rights were restored to him a few years before his death when he became Lord Nairne of Nairne. Lady Nairne, the author of numerous popular ballads including 'The Land o' the Leal', 'Will ye no come back again?', and 'Caller Herrin', which were

published in *Lays from Strathearn* (1846), came back to live in her family home after the death of her husband and only son, and was buried in the chapel (1845).

GATEHOUSE OF FLEET, Kirkcudbrights. (Dumfries and Galloway). [6 Df] Small town on the A75 at the head of Fleet Bay, 6 m. NW. of Kirkcudbright. In 1793, on an August evening walk, Robert Burns composed the lines beginning 'Scots wha hae wi' Wallace bled' to the tune of Bruce's marching song at Bannockburn. The air, which he said always brought tears to his eyes, warmed him to such 'a pitch of enthusiasm on the theme of Liberty and Independance' that he wrote the words with the struggle for liberty then taking place in France also in mind. Burns is traditionally said to have written down the lines in a room, still pointed out, at the Murray Arms Hotel here.

GAYHURST, Bucks. [4 Cf] Village on the B52, 2 m. NW. of Newport Pagnell. The mansion, which was given by Queen Elizabeth I to Francis Drake, was the birthplace in 1606, of Kenelm Digby, whose father was hanged for his part in the Gunpowder Plot. The initials KD appear on columns in the main hall. The house, which underwent major repairs in 1973 and can be seen from the church (1728), was owned by the Wrighte family in the 18th c. In 1779 Cowper drove over with Mrs. Unwin from Olney and praised the gardens with the hothouse and orange trees. He also walked here (it took him 55 minutes) to discuss plants and seeds which he exchanged with the gardener.

GIBRALTAR OF WESSEX. See PORTLAND, ISLE OF.

GIGGLESWICK, North Yorkshire. [5 Cd] Village off the A65, 1 m. NW. of Settle. Near here, 1¼ m. NW. of Settle, on the A65 opposite a turning to a farm, is the Ebbing and Flowing Well, which is called a fountain in Drayton's *Polyolbion* (1612–22).

At Giggleswick where I a Fountain can you show,
That eight times in a day is sayd to ebb and flow.

The water comes from under the limestone Giggleswick Scar, which towers above the road.

GILSLAND, Cumbria. [6 Gf] Village in the Irthing Valley, on the B6318, c. 5 m. NE. of Haltwhistle. The young Walter Scott, on a tour of the Lakes with his brother and a friend in the summer of 1797, made it (then a sequestered little watering-place) their headquarters. One September day they noticed an attractive young woman on horseback and at a ball that night they vied with each other to get presented. She was Charlotte Mary Carpenter, daughter of Jean Charpentier of Lyons who had died early in the Revolution, and was under the guardianship of Lord Downshire. Scott took her in to supper, fell in love, and after a whirlwind courtship married her in December in Carlisle. The surrounding country forms much of the background to *Guy Mannering* (1815).

GLASGOW, Lanarks. (Strathclyde). [6 Dc] Ancient, industrial, university city and port on the Clyde. The site of the University, founded in the 15th c., probably with Robert Henryson among the founders, and moved to Gilmorehill in 1870, is now covered by the Goods Station in the High St. Adam Smith, a student here, became Professor of Logic in 1751 and of Moral Philosophy the next year. His studies here culminated in his great work *The Wealth of Nations* (1776), written after he retired to Kirkcaldy (q.v.). He was elected Lord Rector in 1787. Near by is Gallowgate, where Dr. Johnson and Boswell stayed at an inn (no. 203 on the site) at the end of their tour of the Highlands in 1773. They were presented to some of the professors at the University but Boswell says in his account that 'we had not much conversation' because they 'did not venture to expose themselves much to the battery of cannon' they knew Johnson would use.

In 1772 Joanna Baillie, daughter of the minister at Hamilton near by, was sent to school in Glasgow when she was about 10. In 1776 her father became Professor of Divinity at the University, where the family lived. Soon after her father's death in 1778, she moved to her brother's house in London with her mother and sisters, where she began her writing career.

Thomas Campbell was born (1777) at 215 High St. (P on site). He attended the University of which he was subsequently elected Lord Rector three times. William Motherwell, who wrote the popular ballad 'Jeanie Morrison' at the age of 14, was born (1797) at 117 High St. (P). He left the city after university but settled here again in 1830, when he became editor of *The Courier. Poems, Narrative and Lyrical* (1832) in which 'Jeanie Morrison' was published, was followed in 1835 by the edition of Burns's works in which he collaborated with James Hogg. He died in the same year and his grave in the Necropolis is marked with a monument. J. G. Lockhart lived here as a child while his father was minister of the College Kirk. He went to the High School for a short while and at 13 in 1809 he entered the University. He is commemorated by a plaque at no. 40 Charlotte St.

In 1816 Carlyle made the acquaintance of Edward Irving, founder of the Catholic Apostolic Church, who lived at 34 Kent St. (P). Carlyle's wife Jane Welsh, whom he married in 1826, had been a pupil of Irving's. David Wingate, born (1828) at Cowglen, followed his father into the mines at the age of 9. He published *Poems and Songs* (1862) and *Annie Weir* (1866) and then studied at the Glasgow School of Mines. Later he became manager at collieries near by. He contributed to *Blackwood's*, and published two more collections of poems. He died at Mount Cottage, Tollcross, in 1892. William Black, who was born (1841) in Trongate and went to the School of Art, became a clerk with a firm of bookbinders in Jamaica St. He wrote his first novel *James Merle* here, but it was not published until he went to London in 1864. Some parts of his novel *A Daughter of Heth* (1871) are set in the city.

De Quincey rented rooms at 79 Renfield St. from 1841 to 1847 though he rarely used them. He had first stayed with Professor John Nichol at The College and then took rooms in the High St. opposite. Nichol remembered that he often visited the Observatory and that he was 'writing for all sorts of things'. In 1848 his landlady at Rotten Row had nothing to complain about apart from his poor appetite. He was then contributing to *Tait's Magazine*.

Robert Buchanan lived with his parents at 9 Oakfield Ter. and went to the High School and the University (1856–8). In 1859 his father, who was editor of the *Sentinel* (which had offices in Howard St.), went bankrupt and the next year the 19-year-old Robert Buchanan set out for London with a few pounds in his pocket. Hugh MacDonald, who lived at Bridgeton, wrote dialect verses for *The Citizen*, *The Sentinel*, and the *Glasgow Times* while on their staffs (1849–58). He became editor (1858) of the *Morning Journal* until his death in 1860. Articles in these journals were collected as *Rambles round Glasgow* and *Days at the Coast*. He is commemorated by a fountain on Glasgow Green. MacDonald was a friend of Alexander Smith, a young lace pattern designer whose poetry, first published in *The Weekly Citizen*, soon reached a wider public. *A Life Drama and other poems* (1853), published when he was 23, procured him the post of Secretary to the University of Edinburgh and the entrée to the literary world, where he was satirized in *Firmilian* by William Aytoun, who dubbed him a member of the 'Spasmodic School'. In Smith's chapter on Glasgow in *A Summer in Skye* (1865), he writes of Tannahill's indelible association with Gleniffer Braes (q.v.) and of MacDonald's with the Clyde. In his own poem 'Glasgow' in *City Poems* (1857) he uses country images to describe the town

> Instead of shores where ocean beats
> I hear the ebb and flow of streets.

and thinks of the Clyde

> Between the huddled gloom of masts
> Silent as pines unvexed by blasts.

In *Alfred Hagart's Household* (1866), a largely autobiographical novel, Glasgow is 'Hawkhead'. After Bret Harte's exciting days in the gold-fields were over he became American consul at 35 Burnbank Gardens from 1880 until his appointment came to an end with a change of administration in 1885. William Sharp attended Glasgow Academy and the University (1866–74) and then worked in a lawyer's office (1874–6). He went abroad for health reasons and visited Scotland rarely but wrote many mystical novels and Celtic tales under the name Fiona Macleod. This secret was kept until after his death in Sicily in 1905.

A. C. Bradley, the Shakespearian scholar, was Professor of English from 1890 to 1900.

John Buchan and his sister Anna lived in Queen Mary Ave. with their parents in the 1880s and 1890s, and went to the Hutcheson Grammar Schools. The Gorbals Diehards, who appear in his novels, were based on some boys in the Sunday-school class he took at his father's church. Anna Buchan, who wrote as O. Douglas, gives a

picture of a Glasgow family in *The Setons* (1917).

J. J. Bell, whose book *I Remember* (1932) describes the Glasgow of his youth in the 1880s, was born (1871) at Bothwell Ter. (gone), Hillhead, and went to Kelvinside Academy and the University. The sketches he wrote in the Glasgow dialect for the *Evening Times* became best sellers when they appeared in book form as *Wee MacGreegor* (1902), and successive volumes.

John Watson, the pastor who wrote as 'Ian Maclaren', published *St. Jude's* (1907), Glasgow sketches. He died on a lecture tour of the U.S.A. after being elected President of the National Free Church Council in 1907.

Neil Munro, best remembered for his historical novels of the Highlands, was also editor (1918–27) of the *Glasgow Evening Times* and author of *The Clyde: River and Firth* (1907). *The Brave Days* is an account of Edwardian Glasgow. Catherine Carswell was born (1879) in Renfrew St. and, after University, studied music abroad. In 1907 she became dramatic and literary critic of the *Glasgow Herald* until she reviewed D. H. Lawrence's novel *The Rainbow* (1915), then banned as obscene. She wrote two novels in the twenties and two controversial studies, a life of Burns (1930) and *The Savage Pilgrimage* (1932) about her friend D. H. Lawrence. Her unfinished autobiography *Lying Awake* (1950) was published after her death in 1946. In *One Way of Living* (1939) O. H. Mavor, who took the pseudonym 'James Bridie' from his grandparents, describes his childhood at the then countrified East Kilbride, and his schooldays at Miss Carter's, the High School and Glasgow Academy, while living at 110 Armadale St., Dennistoun. After qualifying as a doctor at the University and subsequent war service, he settled in Langside Ave. and bought a practice near by. His popular plays written in Glasgow include *The Anatomist* (1931), *Tobias and the Angel* (1931), and *A Sleeping Clergyman* (1933). Among the statues in George Sq. in the centre of the city are those of Robert Burns, Thomas Campbell, and Sir Walter Scott.

GLASTONBURY, Som. [2 Gc] Town on the A39, 6 m. SW. of Wells. Legends of King Arthur, whose Isle of Avalon is traditionally placed here, were a favoured theme of medieval poets and chroniclers including

Layamon, Geoffrey of Monmouth, Huchoun, and Malory. Their works inspired Tennyson's *Idylls of the King* (1859), John Masefield's novel *The Badon Parchments* (1948), and J. C. Powys's *A Glastonbury Romance* (1933) with its modern setting. The site (P) where the monks claimed to have found (1191) the remains of Arthur and Guinevere and where the re-interment took place in 1278 is S. of the Lady Chapel in the ruined monastery.

GLEN AFFRIC, Inverness-shire (Highland). [7 Df] Valley at the end of the A831, *c.* 40 m. SW. of Inverness. Neil Gunn, whose novels *Morning Tide* (1931), *Highland River* (1937), *Young Art and Old Hector* (1942), and *The Well at World's End* (1951), describe the Highland way of life, lived at the end of a mountain road in this valley after resigning from the Civil Service in 1937.

GLEN COE, Argylls. (Highland). [6 Ca] Valley through steep mountains traversed by the A82 from the village of Glencoe to the desolate Rannoch Moor. The legendary Gaelic bard Ossian (Oisin), son of Fingal (Finn), is said to have been born here in the 3rd c. In 1763 James Macpherson published *Temora*, an epic in eight books purporting to be translations of Ossian. The work was much admired, though some, including Dr. Johnson, were sceptical about the existence of originals of such antiquity. After Macpherson's death in 1796 an investigation found he had embellished his free translation of old Gaelic legends with additions of his own.

The sudden massacre in 1692 of Macdonalds by Campbells, who had been living in their midst, called forth the poem by Scott, written in 1814, which begins

> O tell me Harper, wherefore flow
> Thy wayward notes of wail and woe,
> Far down the desert of Glencoe,
> Where none may list their melody?

Thomas Campbell's *Pilgrim of Glencoe*, a long poem about the reconciliation between a Campbell and a Macdonald in 1715, and William Aytoun's 'Widow of Glencoe', also tell of the treachery.

Much of Stevenson's *Kidnapped* (1886) takes place in this area and 'Rannoch by Glencoe' is the title of a poem by T. S. Eliot.

GLENCORSE OLD CHURCH, Midlothian (Lothian). [6 Fc] Little ruined church with a frail wooden steeple and remarkable 17th- and 18th-c. gravestones, reached by a steep lane off a minor road beside the Glencorse Burn, *c.* 7 m. S. of the centre of Edinburgh, between the A701 and the A702. R. L. Stevenson used to worship here and set his novel *The Body Snatchers* (1881) in the church.

GLENDALOUGH, Wicklow. [9 Hb] 'The Valley of the Two Lakes', reached by the L107, 1½ m. W. of Laragh on the T61. This picturesque glen is associated with the life and legends of St. Kevin, who came as a hermit in the 6th c. Beyond the ruins of the Seven Churches there is a hole in the rock, near the shore of the upper lake, known as 'St. Kevin's Bed', which Sir Walter Scott visited on his tour of Ireland in 1825. According to Lockhart, who accompanied him, he insisted on making his way to it, where a fall of 30 or 40 ft would mean plunging into deep water, '. . . in spite of all remonstrances, crawling along the precipice. He succeeded and got in—the first lame man that ever tried it.'

GLEN FINGLAS, Perths. (Central). [6 Db] Valley N. of Brig o' Turk on the A821, scene of Scott's ballad 'Glenfinlas or Lord Ronald's Coronach'. The striking scenery in this glen was the background for the portrait of Ruskin painted by Millais in 1853.

GLENGARRIFF. See GARINISH ISLAND.

GLENIFFER BRAES, Renfrews. (Strathclyde). [6 Dd] These hills near Paisley, reached by the B775, were a favourite walk of the weaver poet Robert Tannahill, who wrote the lines:

> Keen blows the wind on the braes o' Gleniffer
> The auld castle turrets are covered wi' snaw.
> How changed frae the time when I met wi' my lover.
> Among the broom bushes on Stanley green shaw.

Stanley Castle no longer has a wooded hillside, as it now rises from the dammed loch forming the waterworks. Open-air concerts held here by the Tannahill Choir from 1876 to 1883 provided money for his memorial statue in Paisley Abbey grounds. Hugh Macdonald (1817-60), whose popular verses appeared first in Glasgow papers, is commemorated at the well in Robertson Park here. A medallion with his head in relief is on the fountain erected in 1883, which has the verse:

The bonnie wee well on the Breist of the Brae
Where the hare steals to drink in the gloamin'
    sae gray
Where the wild moorlan' birds dip their nebs
    and tak' wing
And the lark weets his whistle ere mounting to
    sing.

GLENMALURE, Wicklow. [9 Hb] Deep gorge through which the Avonbeg flows from the SE. slopes of the Wicklow Mountains to join the Avonmore in the Vale of Avoca (q.v.). This wild and picturesque place was the setting for Synge's play *In the Shadow of the Glen* (1903).

GLENSHIEL, Inverness-shire (Highland). [7 Df] Valley traversed by the A87, *c.* 15 m. SW. of Lochalsh. In 1773 Dr. Johnson rode through with Boswell on their way to Skye. Soon after passing the site of the battle of 1719, they stopped to let the horses feed on the rich grass. Johnson describes the scene in his *Journey to the Western Islands* (1775), where he wrote that he 'first conceived the thought of this narration' at this spot.

GLOUCESTER, Glos. [3 Hf] County town on the A40, the A38, and the A417. The poet and traveller John Taylor (1580–1653), who later became one of the King's Watermen in London, was born here and educated at the Grammar School before being pressganged for the Cadiz expedition. William D'Avenant, poet and dramatist, was knighted during the siege of 1643 for his services in importing arms from France for the Royalists. William Lisle Bowles wrote the sonnet 'On Hearing the Messiah Performed in Gloucester Cathedral' in 1835. The Manx poet T. E. Brown (1830–97) was headmaster of the Crypt School for a short time when W. E. Henley (born in 1849 at 2 Eastgate St., now rebuilt), who edited his *Collected Poems* in 1900, was a pupil. The illustrations in Beatrix Potter's *The Tailor of Gloucester* (1901) show the little house (now selling antiques and curios) in College Court off Westgate St., where the tailor lived.

GLYN CEIRIOG, Clwyd. [3 Fb] Village *c.* 2 m. S. of Llangollen, reached by a minor road or by the B4500 from Chirk (on the A483). The Institute and Library are a memorial to John Ceiriog Hughes (1832–87), poet, farmer, and station-master on the Cambrian Railway. He wrote lyrics in Welsh, many for setting to traditional airs, and was the author of 'God Bless the Prince of Wales'. His poem *Owain Wyn* (1856) has been acclaimed as the best Welsh pastoral. Adjoining the Institute there is a memorial to George Borrow, who praised the Ceiriog Valley in *Wild Wales* (1862).

GODMERSHAM, Kent. [1 Gd] Small village off the A28, 6 m. SW. of Canterbury. Jane Austen's brother Edward, adopted by the Knights, inherited the estate here in 1797. Jane and her sister Cassandra often stayed here and many of Jane's letters were written from the 18th-c. Godmersham Park.[1] The church has the chancel window and a wall memorial to Edward and Elizabeth Knight.

[1] Grounds open in the summer.

GODOLPHIN HOUSE, Cornwall. [2 Af] Mansion ½ m. NW. of Godolphin Cross, a village on a minor road between Breage (A394) and Townshend (B3280). It was a former home of the Earls of Godolphin and the birthplace of Sidney Godolphin (1610–43), a poet of promise who was killed at Chagford (q.v.) in the Civil War. He was the 'little Sid' of Sir John Suckling's works.

Open June–July: Thurs. 2–5 p.m.; Aug.–Sept.: Tues. and Thurs. 2–5 p.m.

GOLANT, Cornwall. [2 Ce] Small village on the W. bank of the Fowey, 2 m. N. of Fowey town, reached either by boat, or by car from a turning off the B3269, the Lostwithiel road. This was traditionally the setting of the romance of Tristram and Iseult of Arthurian legend, and the ancient grass-grown mound of Castle Dore, 1 m. inland, is reputedly the palace of King Mark, legendary king of Cornwall.

GOLDEN GROVE, Dyfed. [3 Df] Village *c.* 3½ m. SW. of Llandeilo, just S. of the B4300 (also signposted from the A40, 3 m. W. of Llandeilo). Jeremy Taylor, who had been Charles I's chaplain and imprisoned after the Royalist defeat at Cardigan, retired here in 1645 and stayed until he moved to Lisburn (q.v.) in 1658. Many of his best works were written at this time, including

Holy Living and *Holy Dying* (1650-1) and *The Golden Grove* (a manual of daily prayers, 1655). The mansion on the site of the original building in which he lived is now owned by the Carmarthen Technical and Agricultural College.[1]

[1] Appointments to visit may be made only through the Principal, tel. Dryslwyn 341/2.

GOLDSHAW. See WHALLEY.

GOMERSAL, West Yorkshire. [5 Ee] Town, 5 m. SE. of Bradford, on the A643. The Red House (1660) in Oxford Rd., now a museum,[1] was the home of Charlotte Brontë's friends at Roe Head School, Mary and Martha Taylor, whose family appear in *Shirley* (1849) as the Yorkes and their house as Briarmains. Charlotte Brontë often stayed here between 1831 and 1840 and described the house and local scenes in her novel. Oakwell Hall, Birstall (q.v.), was the home of her heroine, and Hartshead and Kirklees Park (where tradition places Robin Hood's grave) were Nunnely. One room in the museum is devoted to the Brontës and *Shirley*, and the guide lists many places connected with them. Mary Taylor (Rose Yorke) is buried in the churchyard. Herbert Knowles (1798-1817), who sent his poem 'The Three Tabernacles' (known as 'Stanzas in Richmond Churchyard', and written when he was at school there in 1816) to Southey, was born here, lived with his parents at Pollard Hall, and died of a decline a month after Southey had obtained a sizarship for him at St. John's Cambridge. He is buried at Heckmondwike, 2 m. S.

[1] Open Tues.-Sat. 10 a.m.-noon, 2-5 p.m.; Sun. 2-5 p.m.

GOODNESTONE (pr. Gŏoneston), Kent. [1 Hc] Village off the A257, 2½ m. S. of Wingham. Jane Austen spent holidays with her brother Edward when, after his marriage (1791) to the daughter of Sir Brook Bridges of Goodnestone Park, he lived at Rowling House (1 m. E.). She mentions in her *Letters* leading the dancing at the evening parties at the Park, and also that Edward has changed his name to that of his aunt Knight, who had made him her heir, an expedient that Frank Churchill was to use in *Emma* (1816). The Edward Knights left Rowling for their aunt's estate at Godmersham.

Montague Rhodes James, author of *Ghost Stories of an Antiquary* (1905), was born at the rectory and baptized in the church.

GORDON ARMS, Selkirks. (Borders). [6 Fd] Hotel (formerly an inn) at the crossroads of the A708 and the B709, in the Yarrow Valley. It was here and hereabouts that Sir Walter Scott traditionally met James Hogg, 'the Ettrick Shepherd', who spent most of his life at Altrive and Mount Benger near by. A plaque records that they met and parted here for the last time in the autumn of 1830.

GORING-BY-SEA, West Sussex. [1 De] South-coast resort W. of Worthing on the A259. The southbound side of the dual Sea Lane, by the parish church, leads to Jefferies Lane, a short cul-de-sac, where Jefferies House has a plaque stating that 'Richard Jefferies, Naturalist and prose writer lived and died here'. When Jefferies died (1887) the house was called Sea View House, but later development has blocked the view.

GORT, Galway. [9 Db] Market town in the plain, on the T11, 15 m. SW. of Loughrea. On a minor road a few miles NE., signposted from the L11, is Thoor Ballylee,[1] the 16th-c. castle keep beside a river bridge, formerly the property of Lady Gregory of Coole, which Yeats bought for £35 in 1917, soon after his marriage, and restored as a summer home. It was here that he wrote *The Tower* poems (1928) and *The Winding Stair* poems (1933). On the wall are inscribed his lines:

I, the poet William Yeats,
With old mill-boards and sea-green slates,
And smithy work from the Gort forge,
Restored this tower for my wife George;
And may these characters remain
When all is ruin once again.

After his death the tower did in fact become ruinous, but has since been repaired by Bord Failte Eireann and was opened by Padraic Colum in 1965 as a Yeats museum. Near the castle was the home of Mary Hynes, the miller's daughter loved by Blind Raftery, whom Yeats speaks of in 'The Tower'.

[1] Open Apr., May, June, Sept., Oct.: daily 10 a.m.-6 p.m.; July, Aug.: 10 a.m.-7 p.m. (or 9 p.m. on request).

GRACE DIEU, Leics. [4 Bd] Ivy-clad ruin of an Augustinian Priory on the A512, 3 m. E.

of Coleorton. Francis Beaumont, the dramatist brother of Sir John Beaumont the poet, was born (1584) at the manor house built in the secularized Priory after the Dissolution. His friend Michael Drayton visited him here. The Wordsworths walked here in 1807 while staying at Coleorton (q.v.), where they would have liked a stream 'bustling through the rocks' as they found here.

GRANTCHESTER, Cambs. [4 Ef] Village 2½ m. SW. of Cambridge on a cutting of the Granta. Chaucer, who may have been in Cambridge on a parliamentary visit, places 'The Reeve's Tale' from *The Canterbury Tales* at Trumpington Mill on the Granta itself. The mill and its successor (burned down in 1928) stood above the mill pond, now known as Byron's Pool, signposted from the Trumpington Rd. Skelton, while at Cambridge, is thought to have often walked to Trumpington (1 m. E.), where the vicar's daughter is said to have copied out his poems for him. Wordsworth visited Chaucer's mill and Tennyson is thought to have had Trumpington Mill in mind as the setting for his poem 'The Miller's Daughter'.

Rupert Brooke, while an undergraduate, found lodgings at The Orchard (now tea rooms) in 1909 with an indulgent landlady.

I have a perfectly glorious time, seeing nobody I know day after day. The room I have opens straight out onto a stone verandah covered with creepers, and a little old garden full of old-fashioned flowers and crammed with roses. I work at Shakespeare, read, write all day, and now and then wander in the woods or by the river. I bathe every morning and sometimes by moonlight, have all my meals (chiefly fruit) brought to me out of doors, and am as happy as the day's long.

The popular bathing place was Byron's Pool, named after the poet, who visited from Cambridge. E. M. Forster and Lytton Strachey also stayed at The Orchard when visiting him. He had offered Strachey a room at The Old Vicarage next door where he wrote

The garden is a great glory. There is a soft lawn with a sundial and tangled antique flowers abundantly; and a sham ruin, quite in a corner; . . . There are trees rather too closely all round; and a mist.

In 1910 Brooke moved into The Old Vicarage, a three-storeyed house with dormer windows, where his landlady was Mrs. Neeve, whose husband kept bees. Brooke's friends (some of whom later were members of the Bloomsbury Group), with whom he used to spend camping holidays, visited him here and Christopher Hassall's biography (1964) has illustrations of the large breakfast parties on the lawn. While holidaying in Germany his nostalgia for Grantchester led him to write 'The Sentimental Exile', a poem better known as 'The Old Vicarage, Grantchester', which contains the lines

Oh! there the chestnuts, summer through,
Beside the river make for you
A tunnel of green gloom, and sleep
Deeply above; and green and deep
The stream mysterious glides beneath
Green as a dream and deep as death.

On his return he was surprised to be greeted by his landlady with the assurance that there was 'honey still for tea'. She had read the poem published in his College magazine.

GRASMERE, Cumbria. [5 Bb] Village on the W. side of the A591, c. ¼ m. N. of Grasmere Lake. On the E. side of the main road is Town End, where Wordsworth and his sister Dorothy came in December 1799 to 'live in retirement' among their native mountains. Their cottage, formerly an inn known as the Dove and Olive Branch, now called Dove Cottage,[1] at the foot of the hill on the old road to Ambleside, consisted of two rooms downstairs and four upstairs (of which two were very small). At that time there were no buildings between the cottage and the lake and from the 'little nook of mountain-ground' that rose steeply behind they had a view, as Wordsworth wrote to Coleridge, 'of the lake, the church, Helm Crag, and two thirds of the vale'. The little garden was soon stocked with vegetables and flowers; in May, when Dorothy began her *Grasmere Journals*, she spoke of hoeing the first row of peas, transplanting radishes, and bringing back wild plants from the woods. The *Journals* record the day-to-day life of herself and her beloved William, their walks and observations of everything around them, the local people, the visits of Coleridge and William's sailor brother John, until January 1803, soon after William's marriage to Mary Hutchinson (October 1802). William drew on Dorothy's writings for many of his themes, sometimes for the very words, as in her descriptions of the daffodils near Ullswater, beyond Gowbarrow Park: 'I never saw daffodils so beautiful they grew among the mossy stones about and about them, some rested their heads upon these stones as on a pillow for weariness and the rest tossed and reeled and danced and seemed as if they verily laughed with the wind that blew upon them over the lake, they looked so gay ever glancing ever changing.', which echoes in 'I wandered lonely as a cloud':

When all at once I saw a crowd,
A host of golden daffodils;
Beside the lake, beneath the trees,
Fluttering and dancing in the breeze.

. . . .

Ten thousand saw I at a glance,
Tossing their heads in sprightly dance.

The waves beside them danced; but they
Out-did the sparkling waves in glee:

Wordsworth was writing poetry almost from the day they moved in, and Dorothy noted down the details, together with the weather and her domestic chores, as in these entries for March 1802: 'A mild morning. William worked at the Cuckow poem ['To the cuckoo']. I sewed beside him.'; 'While I was getting into bed he wrote the Rainbow ['My heart leaps up']'; 'A divine morning. At Breakfast Wm wrote part of an ode [*Ode: Intimations of Immortality*]. Mr. Olliff sent the dung and Wm went to work in the garden.'

On 4 November 1807 they had a memorable visit from De Quincey, who arrived as escort to Sara Coleridge and her three children. He had already written (at the age of 18) to Wordsworth in admiration of the *Lyrical Ballads*, and was now meeting his hero for the first time. He was 'so modest,' wrote Dorothy later, 'and so very shy, that even now I wonder how he ever had the courage to address himself to my brother by letter'. He stayed in the best bedroom of the humblest house he had known as a guest, and was wakened by the eldest Wordsworth child (aged 3), who became a devoted friend. The cottage, small enough on any account for accommodating three people and their frequent visitors, became too cramped when Wordsworth's children numbered three, and the family moved to Allan Bank (N.T.) in May 1808. This house, on high ground at the foot of Easedale, *c.* 1½ m. NW. of Grasmere, was more spacious for their needs—Dorothy wrote of 'the comfort of each having a room of our own'—and in spite of chronically smoking chimneys they settled in happily, with Coleridge and De Quincey as their

guests for the first winter. In March 1809 the Wordsworths took Dove Cottage for the latter and he kept the tenancy till 1834, long after he had moved to Edinburgh with his family.

Opposite Dove Cottage a converted barn houses the Wordsworth Museum,[2] containing manuscripts, notebooks, and personal relics.

The Wordsworths left Allan Bank in June 1811 and moved into the old vicarage, a more manageable house, though it turned out to be sadly damp. It stood by the bridge opposite the church. During his last years in Grasmere Wordsworth completed *The Excursion*. But after the deaths of his two children, Catherine and Thomas, in 1812, the nearness to the graveyard became too painful and in 1813 they moved to Rydal Mount (q.v.). Wordsworth is buried in Grasmere Churchyard, near Dorothy (d. 1855), his wife Mary (d. 1859), and Sara Hutchinson (Mary's sister, d. 1835), and other members of the family lie close by. There is also the grave of Hartley Coleridge and a memorial to Arthur Hugh Clough (who died in Florence, 1861). Eight of the yew trees near the path by the Rothay, which runs by the churchyard wall, were planted by Wordsworth.

There is a monument in the church to Wordsworth, with a profile head by Woolner and a translation of Keble's Latin dedication to Wordsworth of his *Oxford Lectures on Poetry*.

[1] Open weekdays 10 a.m.–6 p.m.; winter 10 a.m.–12.45 p.m., 2–4.15 p.m.; closed Jan.–Mar.
[2] Open as above.

GRAVESEND, Kent. [1 Fc] Thameside town on the A226. Dr. R. Austin Freeman settled (1902–21) at 2 Woodville Ter. (site now of the Woodville Halls) where he started to write the detective stories solved by Dr. Thorndyke, the expert on medical jurisprudence. *The Red Thumb Mark* (1907) features the then new technique of fingerprint identification. He lived most of his life here and was at 94 Windmill St. from 1930 until his death in 1943. He is buried in the cemetery. Conrad's story, *Heart of Darkness*, is told on board a ship lying off Gravesend.

GREAT BOOKHAM, Surrey. [1 Dc] Village on the A246, 2 m. SW. of Leatherhead.

Fanny Burney and her husband General D'Arblay, lived at The Hermitage, on the corner of East St., after their marriage in 1793. She wrote her third novel *Camilla* (1796) here, with 'no episode' as she told the King, 'but a little baby'. They had lived frugally, as the General was in exile and had no money, but they were able to build their own house from the proceeds of this novel. Jane Austen's *Letters* show she spent holidays at the vicarage (gone, the cedar tree seen through the gap in the line of shops near the church marks the site), where her cousin Cassandra was married to the Revd. Samuel Cooke (tablet in the chancel of the church), Jane Austen's godfather. One of her visits was in 1814, the year she began *Emma* (1816), which has a scene on the near-by Box Hill.

GREAT CASTERTON, Leics. [4 Dd] Village once on the Great North Rd., now by-passed by the A1. John Clare, who called it Bridge Casterton, 'a lovely little town', worked (1817–18) here as a lime-burner, sometimes more than the usual 14 hours a day. He spent his wages on buying books and his free time writing verses, collected in 1820 as *Poems descriptive of Rural Life*. He drank with other lime-burners at the Flower Pot (now Stonecroft, a private house) at Tickencote ($\frac{1}{2}$ m. N.). Clare described the banks of the Gwash as 'very stunt', giving flat-country dwellers the fancy of mountains. He first met Patty Turner, later his wife, here.

GREAT DUNMOW, Essex. [1 Fa] Market town at the junction of the A130 and the A120. Harrison Ainsworth's novel *The Flitch of Bacon* (1854) caused the revival, in the Town Hall in 1855, of the ceremony (which he attended) mentioned in *Piers Plowman* and *The Canterbury Tales*, of the award of a side of bacon to a married couple who could swear to have lived in complete harmony for a year and a day. In Chaucer's time the oath was taken at Dunmow Priory, $2\frac{1}{4}$ m. SE., but the custom lapsed in the 18th c. Now a jury awards the prize every fourth year at a ceremony in the park below the Foakes Memorial Hall.

GREAT GLEMHAM, Suff. [4 He] Village 3 m. SW. of Saxmundham off the A12. Crabbe and his wife accepted the offer of

Dudley North's large house (gone) in 1796 and remained until 1801. They had hoped to live in Parham (q.v.) but his wife's relatives resented them.

GREATHAM (pr. Grettam), West Sussex. [1 De] Hamlet E. of the A29, 6 m. NE. of Arundel. Shed Hall, the long low cottage adapted from cowsheds at Humphreys Homestead on the Rackham road, was lent by Viola Meynell to Padraic Colum for his honeymoon in 1912, and to D. H. Lawrence in 1915, when he was finishing *The Rainbow*. Shed Hall was the setting for the title story in Lawrence's *England, My England* (1922).

GREAT LIVERMERE, Suff. [4 Fe] Village E. of the A134, 5 m. NE. of Bury St. Edmunds. M. R. James, antiquary and writer of ghost stories, was brought up at the vicarage, now Livermere Hall, a large house in grounds opposite the war memorial. The thatched church has carved bench ends of animals similar to those he makes come alive and furry under the hands of the horrified parson in his story in *Collected Ghost Stories* (1931).

GREAT MALVERN, Hereford and Worcester. [3 Ge] Spa on the A449, 8 m. SW. of Worcester. William Langland, traditionally the author of the late 14th-c. poem *Piers Plowman*, is thought to have been born at Colwall to the SW., and educated at the Benedictine monastery here, of which the Abbey Church remains. The Malvern Hills at Colwall were perhaps the scene of the dream that inspired his poem.

The mineral waters of the town attracted many visitors but Defoe was more interested in the gold which 'this idle generation' seemed to him too lazy to mine. Thomas Gray, who stayed for a week in 1770, first read *The Deserted Village* here and immediately recognized Goldsmith's worth as a poet. Lord Lytton came for the water cure many times, as did Sydney Dobell, who brought his wife and had 'a charming stroll on the hills with Carlyle'. M. R. James, author of *Ghost Stories of an Antiquary*, initiated the restoration of the Abbey glass (1910). Dikrān Kouyoumdjian (Michael Arlen, 1895–1956) and C. S. Lewis (1898–1963) were at school here.

GREAT TORRINGTON, Devon. [2 Dc] Village situated above the Torridge, 7 m. SSE.

of Bideford, on the A386. William Johnson (who later assumed the surname Cory) was born (7 Jan. 1823) at Palmer House. He was a great-nephew of William Johnson, who was three times mayor of Torrington and brother-in-law of Sir Joshua Reynolds. Reynolds and his friend Dr. Johnson visited Palmer House together in 1762.

GREAT WIGBOROUGH, Essex. [1 Gb] Village on the B1026, 4 m. E. of Tiptree. Stephen Gosson was rector from 1591 to 1600, during which time Philip Sidney's *Apologie for Poetry* was published (1595). This essay, probably written *c.* 1580, was in reply to Gosson's *Schoole of Abuse* (1579), dedicated to Sidney and containing 'a pleasant invective against Poets, Pipers, Players, Jesters and Such like Caterpillers of a Commonwealth'. His church tower was rebuilt after the earthquake in 1884.

GREAT YARMOUTH, Norf. [4 Hd] East-coast port and resort on the A47. Thomas Nash's *Lenten Stuffe* (1599) is a satire on the town and the smoked herrings for which it is famous. The Royalist poet John Cleveland was imprisoned in 1655, possibly in the gaol in Middlegate St., but was released after appealing to Cromwell. The actor and playwright Arthur Murphy (1727–1805), who became a barrister, wrote *The Raffle* while holidaying here after being on the Norfolk circuit (*c.* 1780). John Aikin, perhaps to be near his sister Mrs. Barbauld at Palgrave, settled here in 1784 to practise medicine. He wrote *England Delineated* on national character and a memoir on John Howard whom he had helped with the appendix to his book on prison reform. He had also given up eating sugar as a protest against the slave trade, but he found the Yarmouth people against his liberal ideas and left for London in 1792. James Woodforde (1740–1803) mentions staying at the Wrestlers in Church Plain with his nephew in *Diary of a Country Parson* (1924–31). They walked on the quay and saw the sailors from a Dutch ship wearing 'monstrous large trousers'. They drank wine and gin on a collier, and his nephew was 'highly pleased' with the place. Anna Sewell, author of *Black Beauty* (1877), was born (1820) next door to the Fisherman's Hospital (now called Sewell House; P). George Borrow lived here for his wife's health, first (1853–5) at 169 King St.

and then (1856–9) at 37–9 Camperdown Place, now a hotel. Watts Dunton in his autobiography mentions first meeting him swimming in the sea. Dickens set many scenes in *David Copperfield* (1850) in the neighbourhood. Mr. Peggotty lived on the shore.

GREEBA CASTLE, I.O.M. [5 Jg] Large house on the slopes of Greeba Hill, off the Douglas-Peel road, A1, near Crosby. Hall Caine, the novelist, recommended to write about the Isle of Man by D. G. Rossetti, rented the house, after his success with *The Deemster* (1887), and here started *The Manxman* (1894), which was finished in a boarding house on Marine Parade in Peel. Caine then bought Greeba Castle, which was his home, though he made frequent journeys, until his death here in 1931. For a short while (1901–8) he was a Member of the House of Keys but his reforming zeal, which had appealed to the voters, was short-lived.

GREENOCK, Renfrews. (Strathclyde). [6 Dc] Clydeside shipbuilding town and port on the A8. Jean Adam, daughter of a ship's captain, was born (1710) at Cartsdyke, now part of the town. She is said to have become interested in poetry with the help of the minister, whose children she was teaching. *Poems* (1734) was published by subscription and she then set up a school for girls. This failed, and after becoming a pedlar she was forced to beg. She was admitted to the workhouse hospital in Glasgow two days before she died (1765). She is thought by some to have written the ballad, 'The Sailor's Wife', because of her acquaintance with Collin and Jean Campbell, a ship's captain and his wife from Cartsdyke, and because of the descriptions of the housewife's many tasks, which might spring more readily to the thoughts of a woman than a man. However, the poem is more often said to be by William Mickle. In 1786 Mary Campbell, Burns's 'Highland Mary', whom he hoped to marry before emigrating, died here of typhus and was buried in the churchyard at the West Kirk with her brother from whom she caught the disease. The church was rebuilt in the 19th c. and the coffins re-interred in the new cemetery at Nelson St. West, where a monument stands among the rhododendrons and pines on the hillside. John Galt arrived in the town with his parents when he was 10. After some years as a clerk in the Customs House he went to London in 1804. He returned in 1834 and lived in West Blackhall St. (P), where he became paralysed and died (1839). He is buried in the old cemetery in Inverkip St. (P, over the locked gate).

GRESHAM, Norf. [4 Gc] Village off the A148, 3 m. SE. of Sheringham. The tree-covered hill, once a moated island, ¼ m. S. of the church is the site of the castle (built *c.* 1319) inherited by the Pastons, who withstood a siege here in the 15th c.

GRETA BRIDGE, North Yorkshire. [5 Db] Village on the A66, 10 m. NW. of Scotch Corner. In 1809 and 1812 Sir Walter Scott stayed at Rokeby Hall here with his friend the Member of Parliament, classical scholar, and traveller in Greece and Turkey, J. B. Morritt. Scott set *Rokeby* (1813) here, his long poem about the Civil War, which contains the songs 'A weary lot is thine, fair maid', and 'Brignal Banks'. Brignall (1 m. SW.) is a village on the N. side of the river Greta.

GRETNA GREEN, Dumfriess. (Dumfries and Galloway). [6 Ff] Village on the Scottish side of the border, 10 m. NW. of Carlisle, off the A74, formerly famous for its instant marriages. Scottish law recognized that a declaration of intent to marry made by two people before witnesses constituted a legal marriage. This appealed to runaway couples from England for whom lengthy negotiations were not desired, especially after 1753, when an Act of Parliament made such marriages in the Fleet prison illegal. In *Pride and Prejudice* (1813) Lydia's sisters are torn between the worry of her future if she had indeed gone to Gretna with such a feckless extravagant as Wickham, and the shame her present association with him was bringing on the family if she had not. In *Mansfield Park* (1814) the conduct of Julia, who had 'gone to Scotland' with Yates was a mere imprudence in contrast with her sister's adultery.

GREY MARE'S TAIL, THE, Dumfriess. (Dumfries and Galloway). [6 Fe] Waterfall (N.T.S.) *c.* 8 m. NE. of Moffat, near the A708, where the waters of Loch Skeen fall over 200 ft to flow into Moffat Water. It is described by

Scott in the introduction to Canto II of *Marmion* (1805), and the wild scenery of the mountainous tract above Moffat, which he loved to explore by hill pony, features in *Old Mortality* (1816). A good footpath leads from a car park beside the road to the foot of the falls, and a more hazardous one on the other side goes to the top.

GRIMSBY, Humberside. [4 Ea] Important fishing port on the S. bank of the Humber and on the A18. It takes its name from Grim, a Danish fisherman who, in the early 14th-c. verse romance *The Lay of Havelok the Dane*, saves the young prince of Denmark by escaping with him to England. Grim figures in the port's seal.

GRONGAR HILL. See LLANGATHEN.

GROOMBRIDGE, Kent. [1 Fd] Village on the A264, 5 m. SW. of Tunbridge Wells. A public footpath from St. John's Church passes in front of the moated 17th-c. Groombridge Place, where Evelyn helped the owner Philip Packer design the gardens. W. Hale White lived (1903–13) at The Cottage, set back in its gardens from the A264, N. of the village. He wrote here a biography of John Bunyan (1904), under whose influence he grew up in Bedford, and, as a tribute to Dr. Johnson, *Selections from the Rambler* (1907). In the same year he met Dorothy Horace Smith, the young author of a first novel, and they were married in the parish church in 1911 after his recovery from an operation. He was buried in the churchyard there in 1913.

GUILDFORD, Surrey. [1 Dd] Large town, on the A3, thought by Malory to be the Astolat of Arthurian Legends. The 12th-c. poem *The Owl and the Nightingale* refers to a Nicholas of Guildford in terms suggesting that he was the author. The popular Gothic novelist Charlotte Smith was buried (1806) in St. John's Church, Stoke, where her family erected a monument in the chancel to her 'talents and virtues'. Cobbett in *Rural Rides* (1830) thought this 'the most agreeable and happy looking town'. C. L. Dodgson ('Lewis Carroll') often stayed at his family home with his sisters at The Chestnuts (P) in Castle Hill, a three-storey house with a birdcage-like trellis over the front steps. He occasionally preached at St. Mary's, which he always attended when staying here. He died here (1898) and his grave under a pine tree in the cemetery at the top of the Mount has a marble cross. Some of his letters and other relics are in the Museum and Muniment Room,[1] Castle Arch.

[1] Open weekdays 11 a.m.–5 p.m.

GWENNAP, Cornwall. [2 Bf] Village c. 2½ m. SE. of Redruth, just off the A393. Gwennap Pit is a stepped amphitheatre, c. 300 yds. in circumference, perhaps originally caused by mining subsidence. John Wesley preached here on several occasions to large congregations of miners, first in 1762 and lastly in his 85th year.

H

HAGLEY, Hereford and Worcester. [3 Hd] Village 5 m. NE. of Kidderminster, bypassed by the A456. Hagley Hall, the home of the Lyttelton family since 1564, rebuilt as a Palladian mansion in the 18th c., is at the end of a cul-de-sac, opposite the church. James Thomson stayed here in 1743 and added lines on Lord Lyttelton and Hagley Park to the text of *Spring* in his revised edition of *The Seasons* (1744). Horace Walpole visited in 1753 and praised the garden ecstatically: '. . . all manner of beauty; such lawns, such woods, rills, cascades, and a thickness of verdure quite to the summit of the hill, and commanding such a vale of towns and meadows, and woods extending to the Black Mountains in Wales, that I quite forgot my favourite Thames!' Addison, Pope, and Shenstone, all specialists in landscape gardening, visited at one time or another. Dr. Johnson came with Mr. and Mrs. Thrale in 1774 as the guests of the young Lord Lyttelton's uncle, but unhappily they were coldly received and made to feel uncomfortable and unwanted.

There is a good view of the Hall and estate from a track beyond the church that leads uphill for ½ m. to 'Milton's Seat', a bench in a clearing on the hillside, inscribed with lines from *Paradise Lost*, Book V, perhaps in memory of Walpole's statement that Milton's description of the Garden of Eden was direct inspiration for Hagley Park.

HALESOWEN, West Midlands. [4 Ae] Town on the A456, c. 9 m. W. of Birmingham. William Shenstone, a minor 18th-c. poet, was born at the Leasowes, an estate on Mucklow Hill, 1½ m. NE. of the town, which he inherited in 1745. He spent most of the rest of his life here, writing poetry, corre-

sponding with his friends, and, for which he is best remembered, beautifying his estate in the 'picturesque' manner. The grounds are now partly a golf-course and partly a public park, and the club-house occupies the 'new house' on the site of Shenstone's home, mentioned by John Byng in the *Torrington Diaries* on his visit in 1781. In the shrubbery near the front door is the grave of Rajah, a favourite dog. There is a memorial to Shenstone in the parish church, in the form of a large urn beside the N. wall and an inscription praising his 'native elegance of mind' and 'wit that never gave offence'. A plain tombstone in the church-yard marks his grave. Francis Brett Young, the novelist, is commemorated by a tablet on one of the church pillars, recording his birth (1884) and baptism.

HALNABY HALL. See CROFT-ON-TEES.

HALSTEAD, Kent. [1 Fc] Village off the A21, 5 m. NW. of Sevenoaks. E. Nesbit spent the years 1871 to 1877 at The Hall, 'a long low red-brick house, that might have been commonplace but for the roses and the ivy that clung to the front of it, and the rich, heavy jasmine that covered the side', as she described it later. The games that she and her brothers and sisters played on the new railway line at Knockholt probably gave her the idea for her novel *The Railway Children* (1906). Family fortunes deteriorated and the Nesbits moved to London where Edith married in 1880.

HAM, Wilts. [1 Bc] Small village off the A338, 4 m. S. of Hungerford. Lytton Strachey lived from 1924 to the end of his life at Ham Spray House, a pleasant Georgian building sheltered by trees at the end of a long avenue and looking S. to the Newbury Downs. The Mill House at Tidmarsh (q.v.) had become too damp for him in winter and after the move to higher ground his health improved. In December 1925 he began work on *Elizabeth and Essex* (1928), and followed this with collections of shorter writings in *Portraits in Miniature* (1931) and *Characters and Commentaries* (1933). The devoted Carrington kept house as before, and her husband, Ralph Partridge, completed the strange trio. When Strachey died in 1932 Carrington took her own life.

HAMBLETON HILLS, North Yorkshire. [5 Fc] The Wordsworths paused when they reached the highest point on the road (A170) over the hills, where the view inspired William's sonnet 'Dark and more dark the shades of evening fell', and Dorothy's entry in her *Journal*, both describing the same objects silhouetted against the western sky. It was Wordsworth's wedding day, 4 October 1802.

HAMSTERLEY HALL, Durham. [5 Da] Estate off the A694, 12 m. SW. of Newcastle, inherited by R. S. Surtees from his father in 1838. Surtees was the creator of Jorrocks, the sporting grocer who became an M.F.H., and the Hall was probably the original of that described in his novel *Hillingdon Hall* (1845). He was buried (1864) in Ebchester church near by.

HANLEY. See STOKE-ON-TRENT.

HARDWICK HALL. See AULT HUCKNALL.

HARE HATCH. See WARGRAVE.

HARRINGTON HALL, Lincs. [4 Eb] Large mansion in the village N. of the A158, 7 m. NW. of Horncastle. In 1834 Alfred Tennyson became acquainted with Rosa Baring, stepdaughter of Admiral Eden, the tenant of the Hall. Her companionship was a solace to him when he and his sister at Somersby (1 m. NE.) were suffering after the death of Arthur Hallam. Years later he recalled the walled garden with the raised walk round the walls in *Maud* (1855) and also in 'Roses on the Terrace' from *Demeter and Other Poems* (1889).

HARROGATE, North Yorkshire. [5 Ed] Town on the A59 and the A61, 17 m. N. of Leeds. From the late 16th to the 19th centuries the sulphur and iron in the many springs made the place a fashionable health resort, which was visited by the characters of Smollett's *Humphry Clinker* (1771). In 1816 Elizabeth Hamilton, persuaded that a warmer climate than Edinburgh would benefit her health, came south but was taken ill on the journey and died here. She was buried in Christ Church (rebuilt 1831), High Harrogate (on the A59, Knaresborough Rd.), where the marble tablet placed by her sister to 'one who was the ornament, the instructress and the example of her sex' still remains on the wall of the N. aisle.

HARROWDEN. See ELSTOW.

HARTINGTON. See BERESFORD DALE.

HARTLEBURY, Hereford and Worcester. [3 He] Village 4 m. S. of Kidderminster on the A449. The dark sandstone castle[1] has been a seat of the bishops of Worcester for over a thousand years. Izaak Walton lived here (1660–2) as Bishop Morley's steward, probably fishing in the moat and near-by rivers. John Gauden, bishop after Morley was translated to Winchester in 1662 taking Walton with him, claimed authorship of *Eikon Basilike* (1649), thought to be by Charles I. Richard Hurd, bishop (1781–1808), whose writings include *Letters on Chivalry and Romance* (1762), left a lasting memorial in his library opened in the Castle in 1782. This contains a number of books that once belonged to Pope, including a copy of Chaucer, which he was given at the age of 13.

[1] State Rooms open first Sun. in the month and Bank Holidays 2.30–5.30 p.m. County Museum open Mon.–Thurs. 10 a.m.–6 p.m.; Sat. and Sun. 2–6 p.m.

HARTLEPOOL (pr. Hartlipool), Cleveland. [5 Fa] Industrial town and port *c.* 17 m. SE. of Durham. Compton Mackenzie was born (1883) in theatrical lodgings in Adelaide St., West Hartlepool. His parents were appearing at the Gaiety Theatre.

HARTSHILL, Warwicks. [4 Bd] Hilltop village on the B4111, 3 m. N. of Nuneaton. A shelter, built (1972) in granite from the quarry near by, stands on the green to commemorate the birthplace of Michael Drayton (1563–1631). He is thought to have become page at the age of 7 to Sir Henry Goodere at Polesworth. Later he dedicated a series of sonnets, *Ideas Mirror* (1594), to Anthony Cooke, 'his everkind Maecenas' who lived in the manor here.

HASLEMERE, Surrey. [1 Dd] Town on the A3 and the A286. In 1868 Tennyson started to build Aldworth, his new home, situated on a heather-covered ledge near the top of Blackdown (N.T., 1 m. SE.). The house has stone-mullioned windows, a balustraded projecting central bay, tall pinnacled dormers, and a large hall. The name came from his wife's family home in Berkshire, and he describes her pleasure in the view eastward over the Weald in the lines

> You came, and looked and loved the view
> Long known and loved by me,
> Green Sussex fading into blue
> With one gray glimpse of sea.

One of his favourite walks was to Chase Pond, and another to the Temple of the Four Winds, his name for a group of firs on the exposed SE. corner of Blackdown, where a stone seat was placed in 1954 to commemorate him. The road along the crest of the down (now tree-covered) is called Tennyson's Lane. He wrote many of the Arthurian poems here, including *The Holy Grail* (1869) and *Gareth and Lynette* (1872), and his collection, *Ballads* (1880). After refusing many honours, he accepted a barony in 1883. He died here in 1892 and was buried in Westminster Abbey. Friends in the town erected a stained-glass window depicting Sir Galahad (from a design by Burne-Jones) in the parish church of St. Bartholomew in 1899. Another window in the N. aisle commemorates Gerard Manley Hopkins, who died (1889) in Dublin (q.v.) and is buried in Glasnevin Cemetery. Hopkins used to visit his parents, who lived after 1885 at Court's Hill Lodge.

HASTINGS, East Sussex. [1 Ge] Resort on the A21 and the A259. Leigh Hunt started the long poem *The Story of Rimini* when on holiday here with his wife and first child in 1812. Two years later Byron stayed with his half-sister Augusta near All Saints' Church at Hastings House (gone). He swam,

drank smuggled Hollands, and ate the local turbot. Keats spent short holidays here in 1815 and 1817. He was a friend of Haydon the painter, who lodged on his visit at the New England Bank, a weatherboarded tavern at the hamlet of Bo-Peep (site now West Marina station) where Keats may also have stayed. The 'lively Lady from Hastings' was Isabella Jones, whose friendship inspired 'The Eve of St. Agnes' (1820) and other poems.

The first scheme for a new resort adjoining Hastings, later carried through (1828–34) by James and Decimus Burton and called St. Leonard's, is thought to have influenced Jane Austen's unfinished novel *Sanditon*. Charles and Mary Lamb lodged at 4 York Cottages near the Priory (gone) in 1823. They bathed and Charles was dipped three times by the attendants before his stutter enabled him to say 'once'. They also tried the local turbot and the smuggled Hollands. They walked to Lovers' Seat (footpath from Fairlight Rd.), Mary's favourite place, and to Hollington Church, which Charles preferred. His description of this 'protestant Loretto' led his friend Thomas Hood (1799–1935) to honeymoon here on his marriage (1825) to John Reynolds's sister. Hood wrote that 'the small Christian dovecote' gave him the sentimental desire to be buried there. Hollington Wood, where he killed an adder, he thought romantic enough for even the lovers in Boccaccio. Like the Lambs they enjoyed walking and a sprained ankle on the shingle brought on a fit of punning. The elderly George Crabbe was knocked down by a phaeton as he got out of the coach to stay at 34 Wellington Sq. in 1830, causing his friends, the Hoares, great concern.

Thomas Campbell took a house and stayed for almost a year in South Colonnade (site near Marine Court) from the summer of 1831; he wrote to his sister that his 'small neat house hung over the sea almost like the stern of a ship'. He also visited Lovers' Seat and 'Lines on a view from St. Leonards' and 'Lines on the Camp Hill' were written at this time.

In 1854 Rossetti took rooms in the Old Town at 12 East Parade (now the saloon bar of the Cutter Hotel) on the front, while Elizabeth Siddal, the model for many preRaphaelite portraits, stayed at 5 High St. She was lodging at 12 Beach House (now probably East Beach St.) when they were married in 1860 at St. Clement's Church. The sanctuary light and the framed sonnet on the W. wall are donations in Rossetti's memory. In 1857 George Macdonald lived with his wife at Providence House on East Hill, once a rope-walk called the Tackleway. He renamed the house Huntly Cottage (P) after his birthplace. His friendship with Lewis Carroll, who was having treatment for a stammer, started here. Macdonald, whose health was precarious, returned to the town in 1871 after the publication of *At the Back of the North Wind* and stayed at Halloway House (next to Huntly Cottage).

Carlyle spent some months in 1864 at 117 Marina (P). In the same year John Addington Symonds married Catharine North at St. Clement's Church. Her family, with whom they stayed during the early years of their marriage, lived in a red-brick Queen Anne house, Hastings Lodge (gone), in Old London Rd.

Coventry Patmore lived in the Mansion House between High St. and Old London Rd. (1875–91). He had liked the house when he visited the resort with his young family and his pleasure in settling there was increased as his daughter was in a convent near by. Patmore was the chief contributor to the Catholic church, St. Mary Star-of-the-Sea, dedicated in memory of his second wife in 1883. His house was renamed Old Hastings House in 1892. Olive Schreiner spent some winters in Hastings during her years in England (1882–9).

Matilda Betham-Edwards (1838–1919) lived at 1 High Wickham (P). Author of the popular novel *Kitty* (1870) and many others, she was visited by Henry James and Mrs. Humphry Ward and she was a friendly neighbour of Hale White, who lived at 9 High Wickham from 1892 and in 1895 moved to the larger no. 5 until 1900. There he wrote *Catharine Furze* (1893), which has many scenes taken from his childhood home of Bedford, and *Clara Hopgood*. He spent many hours in the observatory he had had constructed in the garden (1896). Henry James gives his view of Hastings as a place to retire to in *Portraits of Places* (1883). 'There amid the little shops and the little libraries, the bath-chairs and the German bands, the Parade and the long Pier, with a mild climate, a moderate scale of prices, and the consciousness of a high civilisation,

I should enjoy a seclusion which would have nothing primitive or crude.'

In 1860 Augustus Hare (1834–1903) moved to Little Ridge, Ore, with the aunt who had adopted him. He called her 'the Mother' and wrote her biography, *Memorials of a Quiet Life* (1872–6). The house, which overlooked the sea, they renamed Holm-hurst (now St. Mary's Convent School). Soon after the 1914–18 War, Rider Haggard bought North Lodge on Maze Hill. He spent the winters there, writing in the room above the archway spanning the road. Mary Webb died at a nursing home in West Hill in 1927. Henry Handel Richardson wrote *The Young Cosima* while living (1930–46) at Green Ridges, Tilekiln Lane, Fairlight, a modern house looking over the Old Town to the sea.

HATHERSAGE, Derbys. [5 Ef] Village on the A625, 9 m. SW. of Sheffield. In 1845 Charlotte Brontë spent a short holiday with her friend Ellen Nussey, who was house-keeping at the vicarage for her brother away on his honeymoon. He had proposed to Charlotte some years before. The Eyre family memorials in the church may have prompted her to choose that name for the heroine of *Jane Eyre* (1847). Opposite the church porch is the grave tended by the Ancient Order of Foresters of Little John of the Robin Hood legends. Tradition says he died in a cottage near by.

HAVERTHWAITE, Cumbria. [5 Bc] Small village in the Leven Valley, 2½ m. SW. of Newby Bridge, on the A590. Arthur Ransome spent the last years of his life at Hill Top, a house (now a kennels) on a minor road on the edge of the woods, with a splendid view of Furness Fells, *c.* 1½ m. NW. of the village.

HAWKHEAD. See GLASGOW.

HAWKSHEAD, Cumbria. [5 Bc] Village on the B5285, NW. of the head of Esthwaite Water. Although the village has become much enlarged and caters for many visitors, the heart of it, consisting of picturesque narrow streets and footpaths, is virtually unspoilt. Below the church is the Free Grammar School, founded by Edwin Sandys (later Archbishop of York) of Esthwaite Hall and attended by Wordsworth (1779–87) before he went to Cambridge. The school is now a museum,[1] housing what is believed to be the finest extant library of a medieval grammar school. Wordsworth's desk, with his name carved on it, is still there, and among objects of particular interest is the housekeeping ledger of Ann Tyson, with whom he lodged after she moved to Colthouse (q.v.) and to whom reference is made in *The Prelude*. Her cottage near the centre of the village has a plaque that later research has made out of date.

[1] Open May–Sept.: daily except Mon. and Thurs. 2–5 p.m.

HAWORTH (pr. Howarth), West Yorkshire. [5 De] Moorland village off the A6033, 4 m. SW. of Keighley. Patrick Brontë brought his wife and young family to the parsonage (now the Brontë Parsonage Museum[1]) at the top of the village on the edge of the moor in 1820. Mrs. Brontë died the next year and her sister took over the care of the six children. After short-lived and unhappy absences for schooling and teaching, the parsonage was their home until their early deaths. The first publication of the three surviving girls (the oldest two died as a result of privations at a school which later emerged as Lowood) was a collection of poems (1846) which did not sell, under the pseudonym of 'Currer, Ellis, and Acton Bell'. Charlotte then wrote *The Professor*, refused by the publishers, based on her stay in Brussels, where she and Emily were equipping themselves to open their own school at the parsonage. This failed, as no pupils applied. Charlotte's next book, *Jane Eyre* (1847), was an immediate success. Emily's *Wuthering Heights* and Anne's *Agnes Grey* written at the same time were then published; Anne's second novel, *The Tenant of Wildfell Hall*, followed in 1848. A few months later Emily died before the worth of *Wuthering Heights* was acknowledged. Anne died at Scarborough 6 months after Emily. Charlotte, left alone with her father, finished *Shirley* (1849) and *Villette* (1853) and made the acquaintance of her biographer Mrs. Gaskell. She also received a proposal of marriage from Mr. Nicholls, the curate, but was only allowed to accept him after 2 years of opposition by her father. They were married in Haworth Church (their certificate is on view), but Charlotte died 9 months later (1855). The Brontë Society (founded 1893), whose museum started in one room

over the Pennybank, was given the parsonage in 1927 and transferred there the next year, which also saw the arrival of Henry Houston Bonnell's collection of Brontëana from Philadelphia. The Society's annual periodical, *Transactions*, contains the first printing of many Brontë documents. Its comprehensive guide to the house, which has been restored to resemble the Brontë home, contains a short history of the family. A leaflet lists the places which influenced their work, including a favourite walk to the Brontë waterfall, Ponden Hall (setting of Thrushcross Grange), and High or Top Withens (ruins), the possible site of *Wuthering Heights*. Mrs. Gaskell, who visited in 1853, contrasted the bleak aspect of the house outside with the 'snugness and comfort' of the interior. She walked on the moor with Charlotte, who told her stories of the families there which made her think *Wuthering Heights* tame in comparison.

Matthew Arnold's poem 'Haworth Churchyard', written after Charlotte's death, says in error the grass

> Blows from their graves to thy own.

as the Brontës (with the exception of Anne) were buried in the family vault in the church (rebuilt 1881), where a plaque marks the site. A stained-glass window is an American tribute to Charlotte Brontë, and the Memorial Chapel has been added.

[1] Open weekdays 11 a.m.–4.45 or 5.45 p.m.; Sun. from 2 p.m.

HAWSTEAD, Suff. [4 Fe] Village off the A134, 4 m. S. of Bury St. Edmunds. John Donne wrote *An Anatomie of the World* (1611), the funeral elegy on the 12-year-old daughter of Sir Robert Drury of Hawstead Place (demolished 1827), who died in London and was buried here. Though it is thought Donne never saw Dorothy he may have heard of her from his sister, who might have been living in the village as her husband was attached to the Drury household. He may also have heard of the family from his friend, Joseph Hall, who was urging him to become ordained and who had been chaplain (1601–8) to Lady Drury. The elegy was thankfully accepted by the now childless couple and Donne was asked to join them on their tour of the Continent. The church has the alabaster tomb of the Drury children with an effigy of Dorothy above. There is also a memorial window to Joseph Hall.

HAWTHORNDEN, Midlothian (Lothian).
[6 Fc] Mansion on the banks of the North
Esk, the 'cavern'd Hawthornden' of Scott's
ballad 'Rosabelle', *c.* 7 m. S. of Edinburgh,
reached from the A768. William Drummond
of Hawthornden was born (1585) in the
old 15th–16th-c. manor and in 1638 restored
it for his own use 'that he might rest in
honourable leisure', as recorded on a panel
on the main S. wall. Ben Jonson, who had
journeyed from London to Edinburgh on
foot in 1618, paid him a visit at the old
house, staying for 3 weeks and draining
his cellar dry. Drummond, author of *The
History of Scotland, 1423–1542* (1655), *The
Cypresse Grove*, a prose meditation on death
(1623), and a number of poems, left a
manuscript record of the visit, *Ben Jonson's
Conversations with William Drummond, 1619*
(published 1833).

HAYES BARTON. See EAST BUDLEIGH.

HAYSLOPE. See ELLASTONE.

HAYWARDS HEATH, West Sussex. [1 Ed]
Town on the A272, 12 m. N. of Brighton.
Margaret Ashford was educated at The
Priory in the 1890s. As Daisy Ashford, she
was the author of *The Young Visiters* (1919),
an unintentionally comic view of the adult
world written at the age of 9 in 1890, which
has been compared with Jane Austin's *Love
and Freindship*.

HEAVITREE. See EXETER.

HELENSBURGH, Dunbartons. (Strathclyde).
[6 Dc] Town and resort, at the entrance to
Gare Loch, on the Firth of Clyde. Neil Munro,
author of popular dialect tales including
The Vital Spark (1906), and of the historical
novel *John Splendid* (1898), lived at Craig-
endoran, S. of the town.

C. Day-Lewis mentions in his autobiography, *The Buried Day* (1960), his
arrival at Larchfield School in the autumn
of 1928 to teach English. After a little over
a year he was succeeded by W. H. Auden.

Marion Angus, Scots poet and ballad-
writer, spent the winter of 1931 here and
invited Auden to visit her. She wrote to a
friend that he read 'yards and yards' of his
poems, 'not one line of which I could under-
stand. I thought to myself, is this the new
poetry? It sounds like a voice from another

planet.' George Blake, who succeeded Neil
Munro as literary editor of the *Glasgow
Evening News*, settled here in 1932 and used
the town as the background for *Down to
the Sea* (1937) and other novels about the
shipbuilders of the Clyde. O. H. Mavor, who
wrote as 'James Bridie', lived at Rockbank
after retiring from his medical practice in
Glasgow. His later plays include *Mr. Bolfry*
(1943) and *Daphne Laureola* (1949).

HELPSTON, Cambs. [4 Dd] Village on the
A1443, 6 m. E. of Stamford. John Clare,
born (1793) in a thatched farm labourer's
cottage in Woodgate (P erected in 1921 by
the Peterborough Museum Society), spent
his early years on the land. He went to
school in the church vestry at Glinton (1 m.
E.), tried unsuccessfully to become a lawyer's
clerk, and in 1809 was hired by the proprietor of the inn next door to the cottage
to help in his small-holding. The young men
of the village met at a cottage where the
Billings brothers lodged in Woodgate, which
they called Bachelors' Hall. Clare, whose
poems show his close observation of the
countryside, transplanted many of the local
wild flowers into the garden of the cottage
next door to his birthplace, where he made
his home with Patty after their marriage
in 1820. *Poems Descriptive of Rural Life*
(1820) was popular, but though Clare continued to write he was never able to keep
his family solvent for long. He suffered many
attacks of mental distress, and in 1832 a
cottage and small-holding were provided for
him in Northborough (q.v.). After his death
(1864) at Northampton asylum, his body
was buried in the churchyard at Helpston
as he had wished. A monument was erected
opposite the Buttermarket.

HENLEY, Oxon. [1 Cc] Thames-side town
on the A423. The Red Lion Hotel, an old
coaching inn by the bridge, put up the poet
Shenstone in 1750 and Johnson and Boswell
in 1776. Bedrooms have been named after
these three visitors and a replica of the
verse said to have been scratched on a
window-pane by Shenstone can be seen in
the room he occupied.

HEREFORD, Hereford and Worcester. [3 Gf]
Ancient cathedral and former county town
on the Wye. The poet who called himself
John Davies of Hereford, his 'loving and

deere mother', was born in the town some time between 1560 and 1565. He was probably educated at the Grammar School as he went to Oxford. Thomas Traherne was born (1638) here, the son of a shoemaker. It is thought that after his father's death he was brought up by Philip Traherne, a prosperous innkeeper who became mayor of the town, and sent him to Oxford. The cathedral, built from the 11th to the 13th centuries, still retains a large part of the monastic library in the Archive Chamber.[1] This includes 8th- and 9th-c. manuscripts and thousands of chained books in their old presses, a collection said to be the largest in the world. Walter Map or Mapes (fl. 1200), who is thought to have been born in the old county of Herefordshire, was a canon here. A plaque on the wall of the bishop's garden in Gwynne St. marks the site of the traditional birthplace of Nell Gwynne, who is often mentioned by Pepys in his *Diary*.

[1] Open weekdays 11 a.m.–1 p.m., 2–4 p.m.

HERGEST, Hereford and Worcester. [3 Fe] Village off the A44, 1 m. SW. of Kington. The Red Book of Hergest compiled from legends and Welsh folk tales in the 14th and 15th centuries was found at Hergest Court (built 1430), the home of the Vaughan family, by Lady Charlotte Guest, who had learned Welsh after her marriage in 1833. She published the tales (exploits of Welsh knights) together with other legends, including some of King Arthur, as the *Mabinogion* (1839–49), from the Welsh 'instruction to young bards'.

HEXHAM, Northumb. [6 Gf] Market town on the A69, 21 m. W. of Newcastle and just S. of Hadrian's Wall. W. W. Gibson, friend of Rupert Brooke and the Georgian poets, was born in a bow-windowed Georgian house on Battle Hill. Only the room above the archway, which led to the stables, now remains—next to the post office. He wrote the lines for the fountain (now dry), erected in the market place in 1901.

HEYTESBURY (pr. Hātisbry), Wilts. [1 Ad] Village on the A36, *c.* 3½ m. SE. of Warminster, on the edge of Salisbury Plain. At the E. end of the village a drive leads from the main road through informal parkland to Heytesbury House, the home for many years of Siegfried Sassoon. In 'Awareness of

Alcuin' (*Collected Poems 1908–1956*, 1961) he wrote:

> At peace in my tall-windowed Wiltshire room
> (Birds overhead from chill March twilight's close)
> I read, translated Alcuin's verse, in whom
> A springtide of resurgent learning rose.

T. E. Lawrence (remembered in the village as T. E. Shaw) used to come over for visits when he was stationed at Bovington Camp. Sassoon died here and was buried at Mells, *c.* 3 m. W. of Frome.

HIGHAM FERRERS, Northants. [4 De] Small market town on the A6 and the A45. The heroine of H. E. Bates's novel *The Sleepless Moon* (1956) lives in the small house on the edge of the churchyard near the 15th-c. Grammar School, and she walks to her wedding in the church. Bates, in his autobiography *The Vanished World* (1969), mentions the prisoner-of-war he saw here which gave him the idea for the short story 'The Hessian Prisoner'.

HIGH BEECH, Essex. [1 Eb] Village off the A11 in Epping Forest. Tennyson lived at Beech House (rebuilt 1850) at the foot of Wellington Hill with his mother and siblings from 1837 to 1840. He was described as 'wandering weirdly up and down the house in the small hours, murmuring poetry to himself; the sisters fond, proud, cultivated, appreciative'. His engagement to Emily Sellwood was accepted by her parents in 1837 though his lack of means and employment caused doubts. Perhaps to allay these Tennyson invested a legacy in a scheme to carve wood by machinery, an enthusiasm of the owner of the asylum, Fairmead (gone), where John Clare was sent in 1837. Tennyson often visited the 'earnest-frothy' Dr. Allen there, where Thomas Campbell had found a refuge (1828) for his deranged son, and probably remembered the inmates when writing *Maud* (1855). The wood-carving venture was not successful and the engagement was broken off in 1840, his unhappiness appearing in 'Love and Duty'. Though Clare felt compelled to escape to his family in 1840 he had written

> I love the breakneck hills, that headlong go,
> And leave me high, and half the world below.
> I love to see the Beech Hill mounting high,
> The brook without a bridge and nearly dry,
> There's Buckets Hill, a place of furze and clouds,
> Which evening in a golden blaze enshrouds.

Edward Thomas was stationed here in the army in 1915. About his poem to his younger daughter he wrote 'All the place names are from this part of Essex—which I like more and more'. A year later he installed his family in a cottage where he spent his last Christmas with them before he was killed in France; the novelist Arthur Morrison (1863–1945) was his neighbour.

HIGHER BOCKHAMPTON, Dorset. [2 Hd] Hamlet 3 m. NE. of Dorchester, ½ m. S. of the A35, along Cuckoo Lane. A turning at the top of the hill leads to Hardy's Cottage (N.T.),[1] but cars must be left in the Thorncombe Wood car park and the rest of the way made on foot up the lane or through the wood (c. 10 minutes). Thomas Hardy was born in the cottage on 2 June 1840 and lived there for most of the first 30 years of his life. His earliest-known poem, 'Domicilium', written in his early teens, describes the cottage as he knew it:

It faces west, and round the back and sides
High beeches, bending, hang a veil of boughs,
And sweep against the roof. . . .

Red roses, lilacs, variegated box
Are there in plenty, and such hardy flowers
As flourish best untrained. Adjoining these
Are herbs and esculents; and farther still
A field; then cottages with trees, and last
The distant hills and sky.

Behind the scene is wilder. Heath and furze
Are everything that seems to grow and thrive
Upon the uneven ground. . . .

and as his grandmother described it when she first lived there:

Our house stood quite alone, and those tall firs
And beeches were not planted. . . .

Heathcroppers
Lived on the hills, and were our only friends;
So wild it was when we first settled here.

Another poem, 'The Self-Unseeing' (1901), describes a return visit and childhood memories.

A detailed picture of the cottage, as Tranter Dewy's House, appears in *Under the Greenwood Tree* (1872), written in the deep window-seat of Hardy's bedroom, where he also wrote *Far From the Madding Crowd* (1874). (For tour guides for these and other novels see note under Dorchester.) A gate near the cottage leads to 'Egdon Heath', Hardy's 'untamed and untameable wild', now considerably modified by forestry plantations. Near by is a stone memorial

to Hardy, erected by 'a few of his American admirers' (1931).

[1] The garden can be seen from the lane. Appointments to visit the cottage should be made by writing to the tenant or telephoning Dorchester 2366.

HIGHER DENHAM, Bucks. [1 Db] Quiet village off the A412, 2 m. E. of Gerrard's Cross. John Dryden stayed (1692) with his wife's relatives, the Bowyers, at Denham Court,[1] down a mile-long avenue leading from the church. He wrote *Alexander's Feast* (1697) under the cedar tree by the river. The house is owned by the London Borough of Hillingdon.

[1] Appointments to visit should be made by telephoning Denham 2144.

HIGH LAVER, Essex. [1 Fb] Village on a minor road E. of Harlow on the A11, and W. of Fyfield on the B184. John Locke, author of *Essay concerning Human Understanding* (1690), lived from 1691 to his death in 1704 at Oates, the home of Sir Francis and Lady Masham. Damaris Masham, educated by her father, a Regius Professor of Hebrew at Cambridge, was influenced by Locke's philosophy and was a writer of religious works. She read to Locke in his last illness and published an account of him in the *Great Historical Dictionary*. Locke was buried, by his desire with little pomp, in the churchyard. His tomb was enclosed by a railing in 1866 and his epitaph, which he wrote in Latin, is on the churchyard wall.

HIGH ONGAR. See ONGAR.

HILGAY, Norf. [4 Fd] Village on the A10, S. of Downham Market, where Phineas Fletcher was rector from 1621 to his death in 1650. His chief work was *The Purple Island or the Isle of Man* (1633), a poem in ten books in imitation of Spenser. His rectory and much of the church have been rebuilt.

HITCHIN, Herts. [4 Df] Market town at the junction of the A505 and the A600. George Chapman, poet, playwright, and translator of Homer, is traditionally thought to have been born in or near the town and a plaque at 35 Tilehouse St. records that he lived there. Also in Tilehouse St. is the Baptist Church (rebuilt in 1844) established in 1674 'under the pastoral care of John Bunyan', which contains his chair and a letter written by him.

HODNET, Salop. [3 Gc] Small hill town, with many half-timbered houses, c. 12 m. NE. of Shrewsbury, on the A53 and the A442. The church contains an illustrated Bible printed at Nuremberg in 1479, also Erasmus's New Testament of 1522, and a copy of Bishop Jewel's attack on the Catholic Church (edited by his friend John Garbrand, 1582). A tile in the chancel commemorates Reginald Heber (later Bishop), author of 'From Greenland's Icy Mountains' and other hymns, who was vicar here from 1807 to 1823. In the town a lamp post at the crossroads also serves as a memorial to Heber.

HOGHTON (pr. Hawton), Lancs. [5 Ce] Small village c. 5 m. SE. of Preston, on the A675. On the E. side of the road a long, straight drive runs up the hill to Hoghton Tower, a fortified 16th-c. mansion in which Harrison Ainsworth set the last episodes of his novel, *The Lancashire Witches* (1848). He deplored its then ruinous condition, but it has since been restored. It is no longer open to visitors.

HOLLESLEY (pr. Hōzli), Suff. [4 Hf] Village 12 m. E. of Ipswich, near the mouth of the Ore. Brendan Behan was arrested in 1939 in connection with I.R.A. activities and was subsequently sent to a Borstal school here. He tells of his experiences in *Borstal Boy* (1958), which was dramatized and first played at the Abbey Theatre in 1967.

HOLNE, Devon. [2 Ee] Little village high above the Dart Valley, 2¼ m. SW. of the medieval Holne Bridge on the A384 and 4 m. NW. of Buckfastleigh on the A38. Charles Kingsley was born (12 June 1819) at the old vicarage, a short way from the village, off the Hexworthy road, while his father was curate-in-charge for a few months. A memorial window in the N. transept of the church includes a portrait medallion of Kingsley in middle age.

HOLT, Norf. [4 Gc] Large village on the A148, 10 m. SW. of Cromer. W. H. Auden was at Gresham's School (founded 1555) from 1920 to 1925. He called himself a 'typical little highbrow and difficult child'

in an essay in *The Old School* (1934) edited by Graham Greene.

HOLYBOURNE, Hants. [1 Cd] Village off the A31, 2 m. NE. of Alton. In 1865 Mrs. Gaskell bought The Lawns, a large house still in the main street here. She was writing *Wives and Daughters*, which was being published in instalments in *The Cornhill*, and she intended to give the house to her husband, a Unitarian minister in Manchester, as a present on completion of the novel. However, she died suddenly here in November and the novel remained unfinished.

HOLYWELL, Clwyd. [3 Fa] Town on the A55, 10 m. E. of St. Asaph, named after the Holy Well of St. Winefride, the most famous healing well in the British Isles and a place of pilgrimage from the 7th c. to the present day. According to legend, Prince Caradoc attempted to seduce Winefride and struck off her head when she ran from him. She was miraculously restored to life by St. Beuno, her uncle, and a spring of water gushed from the place where her head had fallen. In the late 15th c. a fine perpendicular Gothic chapel was built over the well, which was housed in the lofty fan-vaulted crypt. Celia Fiennes described her visit in 1698:

I saw abundance of devout papists on their knees all round the well . . . there are stone steps for the persons to descend who will bathe themselves in the well; and so they walk along the stream to the other end and then come out but there is nothing to shelter them but are exposed to all the company that are walking about the well; . . . they tell of many lamenesses and aches and distempers which are cured by it. . . . They come also to drink the water which they take up where the spring rises . . . (*Journeys*, 1947).

Defoe in 1724 remarked on the 'fine chapel dedicated to this holy Virgin . . . [under which] the water gushes out in a great stream, and the place where it breaks out is formed like a cistern, in which [the pilgrims] bathe . . .', and Dr. Johnson, visiting with the Thrales in 1774, noted, like Celia Fiennes, the lack of privacy for bathing: 'the bath is completely and indecently open: a woman bathed while we all looked on'; as well as the copious flow of water that 'yields a 100 tuns of water a minute and all at once becomes a great stream . . . turning a mill within 30 yards of its eruption and in the course of 2 miles 18 mills more'.

G. M. Hopkins's poem 'St. Winefride's Well' extols the curative power of the water of

> This dry dene, now no longer dry nor dumb, but moist and musical
> With the uproll and the downcarol of day and night delivering
> Water, which keeps thy name, (for not in rock written,
> But in pale water, frail water, wild rash and reeling water,
> That will not bear a print, that will not stain a pen,
> Thy venerable record, virgin, is recorded)
> Here to this holy well shall pilgrimages be.

Frederick Rolfe lived here from 1895 to 1898 under the name of 'Fr. Austin' (the abbreviation stood for his Christian name—not, as he might have wished to suggest, 'Father'). He wrote for the local magazine, the *Holywell Record*, in which he aired his views and his grievances, and he obtained a commission to paint banners for the shrine. Five of these, representing St. Augustine of Canterbury, St. George, St. Gregory, St. Winefride, and St. Ignatius of Loyola, may be seen at the Presbytery on request. His emblem of a crow (with reference to his pseudonym 'Baron Corvo') appears as a background detail in the first two.

HONINGHAM (pr. **Hunningam**), **Norf.** [4 Gd] Village off the A47. 'Parson' Woodforde dined with the M.P. for Great Yarmouth, Charles Townshend, at the Hall (gone). His *Diary* records that the meal was 'too frenchified in dressing' but 'the drawing room in which we drank Tea etc. was hung with Silk and there were elegant gilded chairs and expensive mirrors'. He won a shilling at loo. The smugglers, John and Robert Buck, who supplied 'coniac' and gin to Woodforde, lived at the inn, which was renamed after them.

HONINGTON, Suff. [4 Ge] Village on the A1088, 7 m. SE. of Thetford. Robert Bloomfield, author of *The Farmer's Boy* (1800), was born in the cottage, now called after him, at the corner of Mill Lane, near the church, in which he is commemorated with a bronze plaque. Bloomfield also wrote 'On visiting the place of my nativity' and a poem on vaccination, his father having died of smallpox when he was a year old. His mother is buried in the churchyard.

HOPE, Salop. [3 Fd] Little village on the A488, *c.* 12 m. SW. of Shrewsbury. It lies under the Stiperstones, with ancient Roman lead mines in the vicinity, and was chosen by Mary Webb as the background to her novel *Gone to Earth* (1917).

HOPE END, Hereford and Worcester. [3 Gf] Estate 1¾ m. N. of Ledbury, off the A4154, where Elizabeth Barrett lived from 1809 when she was 3. Her father improved the house (now rebuilt) in the Gothic style to the admiration of fashionable tourists (Princess Victoria was a visitor), until forced to sell in 1832. All but the three eldest of his large family were born here. Elizabeth rode her pony to visit her Greek tutor, the blind Hugh Boyd, subject of some of her poems, and in her *Diary* (1969) tells how much her visits meant. Her father paid for the publication of her poem, *Battle of Marathon* (1820), when she was 14. Many of her early poems were inspired by the district and 'The Lost Bower' set in the wood above the house 'by an actual fact of my childhood'. In a letter to Miss Mitford in December 1842 she recalled her feelings as 'our old serene green stilness was trodden under foot' when Hope End was open to view before the auction. That house has gone but the stables with minarets and crescent moons remain.

HORSHAM. See CHRIST'S HOSPITAL.

HORTON, Berks. [1 Dc] Small village off the B3378, now within the sound of Heathrow though once 'far from the city's noise'. In the partly Norman church which can be unlocked on request is the memorial window to John Milton, who lived here from 1632, after leaving Cambridge, till 1640. In the chancel is the tomb of his mother Sara (d. 1637). The traditional site of the Milton home is Berkin Manor, but the building is later. Milton wrote 'L'Allegro' and 'Il Penseroso' here, also the sonnets 'Now the Bright Morning-Star . . .' and 'O Nightingale . . .', and 'Lycidas', the elegy on his Cambridge friend Edward King.

HOTHFIELD, Kent. [1 Gd] Village S. of the A20, 3 m. W. of Ashford. Alfred Austin, editor (1883–94) of the *National Review*, lived (1867–1913) at Swinford Old Manor, ½ m. S. He recounts in *The Garden that I Love* (1894) how he found the house and restored the neglected garden. A prolific writer, he produced twenty volumes of verse between 1871 and 1908. He became Poet Laureate in 1896.

HOUGHTON HALL, Norf. [4 Fc] Country house, c. 14 m. NE. of King's Lynn, N. of the A148 at the New Houghton turn, built by Sir Robert Walpole (1722–31). In the park (no admittance except to the church) is the parish church of St. Martin where Sir Robert and Horace Walpole are buried without memorials. (Inquire at the lodge for church key.)

HOUGHTON HOUSE. See AMPTHILL.

HOVE. See BRIGHTON.

HOWTH (pr. **Hōth**), **Dublin.** [8 Gf] Fishing port and pleasant suburban resort 9½ m. NE. of Dublin, on the N. side of Howth Head, the great hilly promontory guarding the E. approach to Dublin Bay. Sir Samuel Ferguson (1810–86) lived here at Strand Lodge in the latter part of his life and was profoundly interested in local archaeology and legends. His poem 'Aideen's Grave' concerns the fine dolmen in the castle demesne, and 'The Cromlech of Howth' describes the cairn on Shelmartin (or Hill of Howth), supposedly the burial place of the 1st-c. King Crimthan. W. B. Yeats lived here with his family on their return to Ireland in 1880, first at Balscadden Cottage and later at Island View.

HUCCLECOTE, Glos. [3 Hf] Village 2 m. E. of Gloucester on the A436. Sydney Dobell, having spent the first 2 years after his marriage in 1844 in Gloucester, moved to Lark Hay to recuperate from rheumatic fever. He started his most popular poem *The Roman* (1850) here, published under the pseudonym 'Sydney Yendys', after he left in 1848.

HUCKNALL, Notts. [4 Bc] Small town, once called Hucknall Torkard, 6 m. N. of Nottingham. The church contains the Byron family vault where the body of Lord Byron, brought back from Greece, was buried in 1824. A high relief of his head surmounts the memorial in the chancel erected by his half-sister Augusta. Thomas Moore, visiting in 1827 while writing the Life of his friend, found the church locked but a small boy climbed through a window and let him in.

The King of Greece presented a marble slab in 1881, in recognition of Byron's efforts for Greek freedom. An account of Byron's funeral and the opening of the vault in 1938 is obtainable in the church. A statue of Byron erected in 1903 stands on the front of the Co-operative Building near the church.

HUGHENDEN, Bucks. [1 Db] Small village off the A4128, 1½ m. N. of High Wycombe. The Manor House[1] (N.T.) was Gothicized by Benjamin Disraeli, whose home it was from 1848 to his death in 1881. He bought Hughenden the year after the publication of *Tancred* (1847), the third novel in the trilogy publicizing his 'Young England' policy, which he hoped would impress the rich with the necessity of caring for the poor, 'the two nations' of the country. *Lothair* (1870) and *Endymion* (1880), written here, though about political circles, have no political purpose. He was buried in the church in the grounds, which has a large memorial donated by Queen Victoria.

[1] Open Feb.–Oct.: weekdays except Tues. 2–6 p.m. or sunset if earlier; Sat. and Sun. 12.30–6 p.m.

HUGHLEY, Salop. [3 Gd] Small village off the B4371, in the valley below the N. end of Wenlock Edge. Those who know A. E. Housman's poem

> The vane on Hughley steeple
> Veers bright, a far-known sign,

will look in vain, as did the poet's brother, Laurence, for the steeple and the suicides' graves. A. E. Housman explained that the place he really meant had an ugly name, so he substituted Hughley: 'I did not apprehend,' he wrote, 'that the faithful would be making pilgrimages to these holy places'.

HULL. See KINGSTON UPON HULL.

HUNSTANTON, Norf. [4 Fc] Summer resort on the A149, on the Wash, 16 m. N. of King's Lynn. It is the seaside where children play in *The Shrimp and the Anemone* (1944), the first novel of the trilogy *Eustace and Hilda* by L. P. Hartley.

HUNTINGDON, Cambs. [4 De] Town 3 m. E. of the A1. Hinchinbrooke,[1] the mansion bought from the Cromwell family by the Montagu who married Pepys's great-aunt, became the home of Sir Edward Montagu (later Lord Sandwich) who employed Pepys in his household and later at the Admiralty. As a boy (*c.* 1644) the diarist spent a short time at the Free School in the High St. (now the Cromwell Museum[2]). Pepys, who often visited his relatives in the neighbourhood, records being choked by the dust of the re-building at Hinchinbrooke, now part of the Comprehensive School which incorporates the old Free Grammar School.

Cowper lodged in the town in 1765, bringing with him the servant who had looked after him at Dr. Allen's asylum. At the end of the year he was rescued from house-keeping difficulties by the Unwin family who invited him to join them in their house (P) in the High St. (opposite Hartford Rd.). Cowper stayed here happily until the sudden death of the Revd. Morley Unwin from a riding accident led him to move with Mrs. Unwin, the Mary of his poems, to Olney in 1767. John Clare, making his first journey from his village to London, passed through the town in the coach and was shown Cromwell's birthplace at one end and Cowper's house with its 'melancholy looking garden' at the other. This garden is now obscured by other houses.

[1] Open May: Sun. 2–5 p.m.; Aug.: Wed., Thurs., Sat., and Sun. 2–5 p.m.
[2] Open Tues.–Sat. 11 a.m.–1 p.m., 2–5 p.m.; Sun. 2–4 p.m.

HUNTINGFIELD, Suff. [4 He] Village off the B1117, 4 m. SW. of Halesworth. John Paston, who lived at the Hall after marrying the owner's widow, was buried (1575) in the church, which has a painted hammer-beamed roof with gilded angels. A long rhyme commemorates this 'gentele man by birth and deedes' which, though difficult to read, is given in full in the church guide.

HUNTLY, Aberdeens. (Grampian). [7 Ge] Town on the A96, 39 m. NW. of Aberdeen. George Macdonald was born (1824) at Upper Pirriesmill, a farmhouse just beyond the level crossing by Bleachfield St. This was the home of his grandparents, who appear as characters in his novels *Alec Forbes* (1865) and *Robert Falconer* (1868). The river Bogie runs near by and the old mill still stands by the bridge. Macdonald, who describes the surroundings in his poem 'The Hills', often returned and his fairy stories owe much to the tales, half remembered

from his childhood, which he sought out on these visits.

HURSLEY, Hants. [1 Bd] Village on the A31, 5 m. SW. of Winchester. Thomas Sternhold (d. 1549), who with John Hopkins made metrical translations of the psalms, lived here and was buried in the churchyard. There is a brass on the W. wall of the church tower in memory of his wife. John Keble, founder of the high Anglican Oxford Movement, was vicar 1836–66 and was responsible for the building of the present church on the old foundations, chiefly from the proceeds of *The Christian Year* (a volume of sacred verse published 1827). He is buried in the churchyard and there is a memorial brass on the chancel floor.

HURSTBOURNE TARRANT, Hants. [1 Bd] Village on the A343, 6 m. N. of Andover. William Cobbett, who rode about the countryside recording the worsening plight of the agricultural workers, often came here. In *Rural Rides* (1830) he writes that Up-husband, the local name, is 'a great favourite' with him 'not the less so certainly on account of the excellent free quarter that it affords'. His host was a Mr. Blount, who lived in the red-brick farmhouse by the bridge. Cobbett's initials (WC 1825) are still to be seen where he scratched them on the brick wall to the left of the front gate.

HURSTPIERPOINT, West Sussex. [1 Ee] Large village W. of the A23, 8 m. N. of Hove. Harrison Ainsworth lived (1869–78) at Little Rockley, a house then on the edge of the village, with his unmarried daughter. He occasionally visited his mentally ill brother whom he had installed in a house in Reigate, but compared with former times his life was a solitary one. Novels written here include *Boscabel* (1872), and *The Manchester Rebels* (1874) about the 1745 rebellion, which proved one of his most popular.

HURSTWOOD, Lancs. [5 De] Hamlet at the end of a minor road 2½ m. SE. of Burnley (or 1½ m. NE. of a turning to Walk Mill off the A646 SSE. of Burnley), lying below Worsthorne Moor and Black Hameldon Hill. Past the Hall a farm track leads to a gabled Elizabethan cottage known as 'Spenser's House'. This was the home of the grandparents of Edmund Spenser, who, though born in London, probably spent much of his boyhood in the district of Burnley, where his father had numerous relatives. After getting his M.A. at Cambridge in 1576 Spenser came to live at Hurstwood for two years, during which time he fell deeply in love with a beautiful girl who rejected him for a rival. Although her identity is uncertain it has been thought that she was Rose Dyneley, the daughter of

a Clitheroe yeoman. She became the Rosalynd of *The Shepheards Calender* (1579), in which Spenser laments his unrequited love, and of *Colin Clouts come home againe* (1595). In 1578 Spenser sadly took a friend's advice to 'quit the bleak and shelterless hills to go down to the warmer and softer south', and left for London, taking the manuscript of *The Shepheards Calender* with him.

I

IFIELD, West Sussex. [1 Ed] Former village, 1 m. E. of Crawley, now part of the town. Mark Lemon moved from London in 1858 to Vine Cottage (demolished 1970s) which later, because of boundary changes, became part of Crawley High St. He was a close friend of Dickens and was known as 'Uncle Porpoise' to the Dickens children, who sometimes visited with their mother. When John Tenniel was illustrating *Through the Looking-glass* he used the 8-year-old Kate Lemon as a model for Alice. She disliked having to wear striped stockings for the occasion. Lemon, who was editor of *Punch*, entertained the contributors at Vine Cottage. He and his family attended St. Margaret's Church, Ifield, where he was buried in 1870. His grave, SE. of the church, has a plain stone border. Crawley Church has a window, donated by his family, commemorating his charitable works in the town.

ILAM, Staffs. [4 Ac] Small village 4 m. NW. of Ashbourne, between the A515 and the A52. The 19th-c. Ilam Hall, now a Youth Hostel, is on the site of an earlier house where Izaak Walton and his friend Charles Cotton often visited Robert Port, who is buried in the church where his memorial has verses by Cotton. Congreve also stayed with the Port family and is said to have written *The Old Bachelor* (1693) in a grotto in the extensive grounds (N.T.). Dr. Johnson visited Ilam with the Thrales in 1774, and again in 1779 when he and Boswell walked to see the Manifold rise from its underground journey from Thor's Cave (footpath), but in spite of the evidence of the gardener, who had experimented with corks, Dr. Johnson was not convinced. He thought

it 'a place that deserves a visit' even if the stream was too small to come up to his expectation.

ILCHESTER, Som. [2 Gc] Village on the A303 and the A37, 6 m. NW. of Yeovil. A brass tablet, erected in the church to commemorate the seven-hundredth anniversary of Roger Bacon's birth here (1214), calls him 'Doctor Mirabilis' and 'a free enquirer into true knowledge'. Though his scientific experiments led people to believe him a necromancer and his Franciscan colleagues kept him under surveillance for years, the Pope commissioned his treatises which led him to be called the founder of modern philosophy.

ILSINGTON, Devon. [2 Ee] Village on the E. edge of Dartmoor, *c.* 2½ m. SW. of Bovey Tracey, on a minor road off the A382. John Ford, the dramatist, was born at the Manor of Bagtor, 1½ m. SW., and baptized in the village church (22 Apr. 1586). Little is known of his life, though after living and working in London he probably spent his last years in Devon. His plays, some of which were written in collaboration with Dekker and Rowley, include the tragedies *'Tis Pity She's a Whore* (1633) and *The Broken Heart* (1633).

INCHCAILLOCH, Stirlings. (Central). [6 Dc] Wooded island, whose name means Island of the Old Women, at the SE. end of Loch Lomond opposite the village of Balmaha. In Scott's *The Lady of the Lake* (1810), the poem about an escapade of the disguised James V, a fiery cross is made from sacred yew trees growing here.

INCHCAPE ROCK, North Sea. [6 Gb] Lighthouse rock E. of the Tay estuary, also known as the Bell Rock. Robert Southey's poem 'The Inchcape Rock' recounts the exploits of Sir Ralph the Rover. R. M. Ballantyne spent two weeks on the rock before writing his adventure story, *The Lighthouse* (1865).

INCH KENNETH. See MULL.

INCHMAHOME, Perths. (Central). [6 Dc] Ruined priory on the largest island in the Lake of Menteith, off the A81, 7 m. SW. of Callander. R. B. Cunninghame Graham, who could see the island (which can be reached by ferry) from his home at Gartmore, chose to be buried here and his body was brought from Buenos Aires, where he died (1936).

INNERLEITHEN, Peebles. (Borders). [6 Fd] Busy little town on the A72, 6 m. SE. of Peebles. Scott, who knew it as a straggling village of thatched and whitewashed cottages, is said to have laid the scene of *St. Ronan's Well* (1823) here, and soon afterwards it gained a reputation as a popular watering-place. The Well is reached by a steep road above the car park on the N. side of the High St. and the waters can be drunk on a terrace overlooking the Tweed Valley.

INNISFREE, Sligo. [8 Dd] Small island near the SE. shore of Lough Gill, the beautiful 5-m.-long lake SE. of Sligo. The island, immortalized in Yeats's 'The Lake Isle of Innisfree', can be reached by boat from the shore, at the end of a narrow lane leading N. from the L117, 2 m. W. of the little town of Dromahair. Further W., near the SW. end of the lake, where the main road runs by the shore, is Dooney Rock, also celebrated by Yeats, in 'The Fiddler of Dooney', which commands a splendid view of Lough Gill and its many islands.

INVERARAY, Argylls. (Strathclyde). [6 Cb] Town at the NW. of Loch Fyne, on the A83 and the A819. Inveraray Castle[1] ($\frac{1}{2}$ m. N.), the seat of the Campbells, Earls and later Dukes of Argyll, is described by Boswell in *Journal of a Tour of the Hebrides* (1785), an account of his journey with Dr. Johnson in 1773. Matthew Lewis, often called 'Monk' Lewis after his Gothic novel *The Monk*, which became very popular in 1796, stayed at the castle on many occasions. It was here in 1798 that he first met Scott, whose poetry

he influenced. He dedicated *Romantic Tales* (1808) to Lady Charlotte Campbell, the daughter of his host. Alexander Smith stayed here on his visits to Skye (q.v.) and in *A Summer in Skye* (1865) he wrote that he climbed a near-by hill and saw the town appear like a miniature. Scott's *A Legend of Montrose* (1819), a novel about Montrose and his rival the Covenanter Archibald Campbell, the 8th Earl, was said by Smith 'to haunt you at Inveraray', where a fierce battle took place in 1644. Neil Munro, who was born (1864) in the town, set here part of his novel *John Splendid* (1898) which also relates the Covenanters' struggle against the Highland clans. He is commemorated by a memorial in Glen Aray, N. of the town. In Stevenson's *Catriona* (1893) David Balfour attends the trial here of James of the Glens.

[1] Open first Sat. in Apr. to last Sat. in June: daily except Fri. 10 a.m.–12.30 p.m., 2–6 p.m. June to second Sun. in Oct.: daily 10 a.m.–6 p.m. Sun. 2–6 p.m.

INVERSNAID, Stirlings. (Central). [6 Db] Village at the NW. end of Loch Lomond, landing stage of the Inveruglas ferry. Wordsworth, his sister Dorothy, and Coleridge, set out in 1803 to walk to Loch Katrine, 7 m. E. On their return they were given dinner in the ferryman's house by his young daughter, Wordsworth's 'Highland Girl'.

> For I methinks, till I grow old
> As fair before me shall behold
> As I do now the Cabin small
> The Lake, the Bay, the Waterfall
> And thee, the spirit of them all.

Crabb Robinson, finding his arrangements for the ferry had broken down, was rowed across by Old Andrew, a frail old man. On mentioning this to Wordsworth later he was amazed to find that he had inspired Wordsworth's poem on the Brownie. Gerard Manley Hopkins's poem 'Inversnaid' begins

> This darksome burn, horseback brown,
> His rollrock highroad roaring down,
> In coop and in comb the fleece of his foam
> Flutes and low to the lake falls home.

INVERURIE, Aberdeens. (Highland). [7 Hf] Town on the A96, 16 m. NW. of Aberdeen. Arthur Johnston, the 'Scottish Ovid', was born (1587) at Caskieban Castle (now part of Keith Hall). He left the town as a youth for the Medical School at Padua. William Thom settled here in 1840, though it is not certain whether he worked at a loom in the cottage where he lived in North St. (rebuilt, P removed to the Public Library) or in a weaving shop near by. He had been out of work for 3 years following a slump in America and had taken to the road with his family. He earned a few pence by playing a flute but they often had to sleep by the roadside where he also had to bury the baby that died in its mother's arms. In 1841 his poem 'The Blind Boy's Pranks' was accepted by *The Aberdeen Herald* and was well received. His *Rhymes and Recollections of a Handloom Weaver* (1844) led to his leaving for London, where for a time he was befriended by Lady Blessington.

IONA, Argylls. (Strathclyde). [6 Bb] Small island, off the SW. of Mull, where Columba founded a monastery *c.* 563 in which it is thought the 8th-c. *Book of Kells* (see Kells) was compiled, and where subsequently many kings and princes were buried, including Duncan, according to *Macbeth*. In St. Oran's Chapel (built 1080 and restored) is the Tomb of Lord Ronald, the subject of Scott's poem, *The Lord of the Isles* (1815), about Bruce's campaign in 1307. Johnson and Boswell both recorded their visits to Iona, to which they give the Gaelic name Icolmkill. Boswell quotes Johnson's 'sublime passage'

That man is little to be envied, whose patriotism would not gain force upon the plain of Marathon, or whose piety would not grow warmer among the ruins of Iona.

IPSDEN, Oxon. [1 Cc] Small village on the Icknield Way, 3 m. SE. of Wallingford, on a minor road off the B479. Charles Reade was born (8 June 1814) in the manor house, on the S. side of the village.

IPSWICH, Suff. [4 Gf] Market town and port on the Orwell, visited by Defoe, who abhorred the 'noisome cookery of whaling'. Clara Reeve, author of Gothic romances, was born (1729) here, daughter of the perpetual curate of St. Nicholas Church. Cobbett visited in 1830 and Dickens stayed at the Great White Horse Hotel in Tavern St., where he set Mr. Pickwick's encounter with the lady in yellow curl-papers. *Margaret Catchpole* (1845, reprinted 1930) is the story of a girl who becomes involved with smugglers while in service with the family of the author, Richard Cobbold. Edward FitzGerald was introduced by the vicar of

Flowton (5 m. W.) to the oriental scholar E. B. Cowell, who had joined his father's business in the town in 1842. Cowell, who went to India in the 1850s, sent FitzGerald the *Rubáiyát* of Omar Khayyám which he translated so successfully into English. Christchurch Mansion,[1] a museum in a park, has relics of FitzGerald. Jeremy Collier in the 1660s and Rider Haggard in the 1860s were pupils at Ipswich School.

[1] Open weekdays 10 a.m.–6 p.m.; Sun. 3–5 p.m.; earlier closing in winter.

IRONGRAY, Kirkcudbrights. (Dumfries and Galloway). [6 Ee] Village 1½ m. S. of the B729, 4 m. NW. of Dumfries. A flat stone near the E. porch of the church was donated 'by the author of Waverley' to Helen Walker (d. 1791), who had the qualities Scott invested in his imaginary character, Jeanie Deans.

IRVINE, Ayrs. (Strathclyde). [6 Dd] Port on the W. coast, 12 m. N. of Ayr. James Montgomery was born (1771) in the house later called Montgomery House, in Montgomery St. and now demolished. He was the son of a pastor of the Moravian Brethren and his hymns remain popular today. Burns lodged (1781–2) at 4 Glasgow Vennel (P) while learning flax dressing, and then moved to lodgings in the High St. where he became very ill with pleurisy. He lost all his possessions when the house caught fire after he had celebrated Hogmanay with his friends and he moved back to Glasgow Vennel. He spent 7 months here and is commemorated by a statue on Irvine Moor. John Galt, whose father was a sea-captain, was born (1779) in the High St. (site now the Bank of Scotland where the P with a relief portrait of his head has been reaffixed). The scene of Galt's novel *Annals of the Parish* (1821, reprinted 1967) is set in Dreghorn (2 m. E.) and the surrounding villages. Galt's family moved to Greenock when he was 10 and other Galt relatives moved into the house. It was with them that their young cousin, Edgar Allan Poe, came to stay in 1815, and attended the Royal School.

ISLINGTON, Norf. [4 Fd] Village 4 m. SW. of King's Lynn off the A47. A turn off the main road near Tilney leads to Church Farm, traditionally the home of the heroine of the ballad 'The Bailiff's Daughter of Islington'.

J

JARROW, Tyne and Wear. [6 Hf] Industrial town on the Tyne, with shipyards and oil installations, formerly the site of the monastery where Bede spent much of his life. The partly 7th-c. St. Paul's Church has a chair traditionally said to be his. Bede's Latin history, *Historia Ecclesiastica Gentis Anglorum*, finished in 731, contains the simile likening a man's life to the short span of a sparrow's flight from the dark of the night through a lighted room into the night again, which Wordsworth mentions in 'Persuasion', one of his *Ecclesiastical Sonnets* (1822).

JEDBURGH, Roxburghs. (Borders). [6 Gd] Ancient royal burgh, on the A68, situated on the Jed Water. James Thomson was educated at the Grammar School, at that time (early 18th c.) part of the old abbey. Burns stayed at 27 Canongate on a visit in 1787, but the house has gone. Scott was a frequent visitor and it was here that he made his first appearance as an advocate, successfully pleading for a noted poacher and sheepstealer. He visited the Wordsworths in September 1803, when they were staying at 5 Abbey Close (P) and read to them in the evening from the unpublished manuscript of *The Lay of the Last Minstrel*.

JUNIPER HILL, Oxon. [1 Ca] Hamlet 5 m. S. of Brackley, off the A43. Flora Thompson (*née* Timms) was born in 1876 at 'the end house' of a still unmetalled lane. The thatched cottage (now slated) looked out over the field called Lark Rise (still the haunt of larks today), from which she took the title of her first autobiographical novel, or social history, about the hard life of country working people, observed and written as one of them. The village children walked 3 miles to the school at Cottisford (q.v.), which she left at 14 to work in the post office at Fringford (q.v.). Her three novels, based mainly on her life in the neighbourhood, published in one volume as *Lark Rise to Candleford* (1945), were written in Devon but their success came too late for her to enjoy it.

JURA, Argylls. (Strathclyde). [6 Bc] Island of the Inner Hebrides, S. of Mull. George Orwell (Eric Blair) lived at Barnhill from 1946 to 1949, the year his novel *Nineteen Eighty-Four* on the horrors of totalitarianism was published. He left the island to go into hospital as he was ill with tuberculosis, and he died in 1950.

K

KEGWORTH, Leics. [4 Bc] Village off the A6, 12 m. SW. of Nottingham. Tom Moore lived on the London Rd. (now The Cedars) from the spring of 1812 to 1813. He got the house through Lord Moira, from whom he had expected a substantial government post. When he returned in 1827, he called the place 'our wretched barn of a house' but his wife Bessy was pleased with the large garden.[1] Moore often walked to Donington Park, Moira's house, where he read in the library.

[1] Open occasionally for N.G.S.

KELLOE, Durham. [5 Ea] Village off the A177, 6 m. SE. of Durham. Elizabeth Barrett

was born (1806) at Coxhoe Hall, an 18th-c. mansion (demolished, site now in the conifers E. of the Kelloe–Coxhoe road near the junction with the B6291) where her parents stayed before moving to their estate at Hope End. A tablet in Kelloe Church states she was 'a great poetess, a noble woman, a devoted wife'.

KELLS (or CEANANNUS MÓR), Meath. [8 Fe] Market town near the Blackwater, on the T9 and the T35. It is celebrated especially for the Columban monastery, which for long treasured the *Book of Kells*, an illuminated gospel book of the late 8th c., probably written in Iona and brought to Kells when the monks of Iona sought refuge here from the Norse invaders of the early 9th c. The *Book of Kells* is now in Trinity College, Dublin, and of the monastery there survive only five high crosses, St. Columcille's House, a round tower, and a few other fragments.

KELMSCOTT (or KELMSCOT), Oxon. [1 Bb] Small village off the B449 about 2½ m. E. of Lechlade. The Manor, a gabled Cotswold-stone house dating from the late 16th c., was the home of William Morris from 1871 till his death in 1896 and contains relics of his work as writer, artist, and designer. In his Utopian story *News from Nowhere* (1891) the travellers end their journey here, and Morris's woodcut frontispiece depicts the house. At first he shared the tenancy with Dante Gabriel Rossetti, but a lack of sympathy between the two, exacerbated by Rossetti's love for Morris's wife, Jane, gradually made the situation intolerable and Rossetti left in 1874. W. T. Watts-Dunton wrote part of the once-popular novel *Aylwin* (1898) here, portraying Kelmscott as 'Hurstcote' and Rossetti as the painter. The house is now owned by the Society of Antiquaries, London W.1.[1] Morris died at his London home, Kelmscott House, Hammersmith, but is buried in the village churchyard.

[1] Visits can be arranged by post through the Secretary, Burlington House, London W.1.

KELSO, Roxburghs. (Borders). [6 Gd] Town with a fine Georgian market square, on the banks of the Teviot and the Tweed. In 1783 Walter Scott attended the old Grammar School then on the site of the nave of the Norman abbey, which still has impressive ruins. Part of his family lived at Garden Cottage, later added to and renamed Waverley Lodge, but he lived with his favourite uncle, Captain Robert Scott, at Rosebank near by, a property that he inherited on his uncle's death. Scott invested the money from the sale of Rosebank in the printing business of his old schoolfellow here, James Ballantyne.

KELSTON, Avon. [2 Hb] Village on the A431, 3 m. NW. of Bath. Sir John Harington, godson of Queen Elizabeth I, inherited the manor built by James Barozzi of Vignola for his father. He translated *Orlando Furioso* (1591) at the Queen's suggestion and enter-

tained her at Kelston (1592) when he was Lord Lieutenant of Somerset. His collection of anecdotes, *Nugae Antiquae* (1769), which contains information about Queen Elizabeth I's last illness, was published by a descendant. The house, on the site of Tower House gardens, was demolished after the 18th-c. Kelston Park was built. It is said that the perfumed water-closet Harington invented was erected in the garden. An old carved chimney-piece was recovered and is now in the Old School House.

KENILWORTH, Warwicks. [4 Be] Town on the A46 and the A452. The 12th-c. castle, now ruined, was improved by John of Gaunt and when lived in by the Earl of Leicester was often visited in his school holidays by his nephew, Philip Sidney, who was 11 when Queen Elizabeth I paid her first visit. George Gascoigne describes the Queen's last stay (1575) in *The Princely Pleasures of the Court of Kenilworthe*. Scott stayed at the Kings Arms Hotel while writing *Kenilworth* (1821), and the four-poster bed in which he slept is still in use. Edith Cooper, the poet, who wrote in collaboration with Katharine Bradley as 'Michael Field', was born in the town in 1862.

KENNINGHALL, Norf. [4 Ge] Village on the B1113, 7 m. NW. of Diss. Place Farm, 2 m. past the church, is the remaining wing of Kenninghall Palace, a home of the Howards, and birthplace of Henry Howard, Earl of Surrey (1517-47). Ploughing uncovered foundations to the N., and the banqueting hall to the S., then used as a barn, was demolished in living memory. Parts of the moat still drain the fields.

KESSINGLAND, Suff. [4 He] Coastal resort on the A12, 5 m. S. of Lowestoft. Rider Haggard bought (*c.* 1900) The Grange, a large house on the cliffs formerly a coastguard station (the lane there from Wash Lane is called after him). He named each room after an admiral and made a garden, preventing erosion of the cliff top by planting marram grass. He continued his successful novels with *Pearl-Maiden* (1903) and *Ayesha* (1905), but he also wrote *Rural England* (1902) and *The Poor and the Land* (1905), detailed surveys of the plight of the agricultural workers, for which he was knighted in 1912. He let the house to Kipling for the summer of 1914.

KESWICK, Cumbria. [5 Bb] Market town and holiday centre on the A591, in the heart of the Lake District, situated on the Greta near the NE. shore of Derwent Water. Thomas Gray came here on a Lakeland tour in September 1767 and again 2 years later, when his letters take the form of a *Journal* written to amuse his friend Dr. Thomas Wharton, who had been prevented by illness from accompanying him. He spent 6 days at Keswick, 'lap'd in Elysium', before proceeding slowly by Ambleside to Kendal.

In the spring of 1794 William and Dorothy Wordsworth stayed *c.* 6 weeks at Windy Brow, a farm-house on Latrigg lent by their friends William and Raisley Calvert. Dorothy, enraptured to be with her brother after long separation, recalls how they travelled by coach from Halifax to Kendal and thence on foot: 'I walked with my brother at my side, from Kendal to Grasmere, eighteen miles, and after from Grasmere to Keswick, fifteen miles, through the most delightful country that ever was seen.' After Dorothy left in June to stay with cousins at Rampside on the Furness coast, William spent most of the rest of the year at Keswick, probably at Windy Brow, where Raisley Calvert became seriously ill with the consumption from which he died in the following January.

Later, Coleridge, who was staying with the Wordsworths at Town End, near Grasmere (q.v.), in April 1800, found a house to let on the hillside on the W. of Keswick, high above the river, with a magnificent view. This was Greta Hall (P), now the boarding-house of the girls' school, and he brought his family to live here until 1803, when the damp climate at last proved too much for his tendency to severe colds. He was in constant touch with Wordsworth, the two keeping up a frequent interchange of visits, discussing poetry and preparing a new edition of *Lyrical Ballads*. During this time Coleridge completed 'Christabel' and wrote 'Dejection: an Ode'. In 1802 Charles Lamb, who only tolerated the country for the sake of his friends, brought his sister Mary to visit Coleridge and they spent 3 'delightful weeks'. In the same year Southey came to Keswick and for a time shared Greta Hall with Coleridge, whose wife, Sara, was his sister-in-law. After Coleridge's departure in 1803 Southey stayed on with his family and in 1809 took possession of the house, where he remained until his death on 21 March 1843. (He is buried in the churchyard of Crosthwaite (q.v.), near by.) During these years he wrote an immense amount of verse and prose, and was a regular contributor to the *Quarterly Review*. He became Poet Laureate in 1813 after Sir Walter Scott had generously declined the honour in his favour. His longer poems include *Madoc* (1805), *The Curse of Kehama* (1810), and *Roderick, the last of the Goths* (1814), and his *History of Brazil* (1810–19) is still valued. In the winter of 1811–12 Shelley came with Harriet, shortly after their marriage, to stay with Southey and his wife, but found Southey lacking in his earlier reforming enthusiasms, and his wife dull. Shelley returned to Keswick in 1813 and stayed at a house (now called Shelley's Cottage) in Chestnut Hill, where (as on so many other occasions) he alarmed his neighbours by performing chemistry experiments.

Sir Hugh Walpole, who lived at Brackenburn, Borrowdale (q.v.), is buried in the SW. corner of St. John's churchyard, which occupies a commanding position SW. of the market-place.

The Fitz Park Museum[1] in Station Rd., opposite the entrance to Fitz Park, contains manuscripts of Southey, Wordsworth, and Hugh Walpole, some personal relics, and a bust of Walpole by Epstein.

A short walk from the town along the E. shore of Derwent Water leads to the Ruskin Memorial at Friar's Crag (N.T.), where a plinth bears a low-relief portrait bronze by Lucchesi. When Ruskin was $5\frac{1}{2}$ he spent a few days in the Lake District when travelling with his parents to Scotland, and long after recorded his vivid memory of the spot:

> The first thing which I remember, as an event in life, was being taken by my nurse to the brow of Friar's Crag on Derwent Water; the intense joy mingled with awe, that I had in looking through the hollows in the mossy roots, over the crag into the dark lake, has ever associated itself more or less with all twining roots of trees ever since.

Beatrix Potter stayed near Keswick with her family in 1903 and sketched the lake and St. Herbert's Island (the sanctuary of a 7th-c. hermit (N.T.)), which is pictured as Owl Island in *The Tale of Squirrel Nutkin* (1903). The island can be reached by regular boats from Keswick.

[1] Open Mon.–Sat. 10 a.m.–12 noon, 2–5 p.m.

KETTERING, Northants. [4 Ce] Manufacturing town on the A6 and the A43, 14 m. NE. of Northampton. H. E. Bates was educated at the Grammar School (1916-21). In his autobiography, *The Vanished World* (1969), he writes that the arrival of a wounded ex-officer as his teacher and his reading of *The Red Badge of Courage* (1895) by Stephen Crane, combined to give him the desire to write for a living. He left school at 16 to become a reporter on a local newspaper, and he published his first novel at 20.

KIDDERMINSTER, Hereford and Worcester. [3 Hd] Manufacturing town on the Stour, 14 m. N. of Worcester. Richard Baxter, the Presbyterian minister, lectured here in 1641 before becoming a chaplain to Parliamentary troops. He returned here after writing in retirement *Aphorisms of Justification* (1649) and *The Saint's Everlasting Rest* (1650). He moved to London *c*. 1660. His statue, which stood in the main square, now stands in a garden next to the parish church.

KIDDINGTON, Oxon. [1 Ba] Village off the A34, 12 m. NW. of Oxford. Thomas Warton, the rector here from 1771 to his death in 1790, wrote a *History of Kiddington* (1783). He combined his duties here with a Fellowship at Trinity College, Oxford (q.v.).

KILCOLMAN CASTLE. See DONERAILE.

KILKENNY, Kilkenny. [9 Fc] Historic cathedral and market town and capital of the county, situated on the Nore, on the T6, the T19, and the T20. Kilkenny College (the Grammar School), a Protestant boarding-school founded (1666) by the first Duke of Ormonde, is on the E. side of Lower John St., across the river from the Castle. Among many distinguished literary men educated here were Jonathan Swift, William Congreve, George Farquhar, and George Berkeley. The original building, superseded by the present one, which dates from 1782, is described in John Banim's novel, *The Fetches* (1825), as being of irregular and straggling design, 'having partly a monastic physiognomy'. John Banim (1798-1842), novelist, dramatist, and poet, is remembered chiefly for his pictures of Irish life in *Tales by the O'Hara Family* (1825), in some of which he collaborated with his brother Michael (1796-1874), who was also a novelist. They were both natives of Kilkenny.

In the Parade, opposite the Castle, the

Revenue Commission offices occupy the premises of the old Private Theatre, where Gay's musical play *Polly* (1729) was first performed (it had been banned by the Lord Chamberlain in England), and where Thomas Moore acted in 1808, 1809, and 1810. Moore's roles were chiefly singing ones, but he also wrote and spoke the prologues. He fell in love with Bessy Dyke, a 14-year-old actress who played Lady Godiva in a farce in which he acted, and whom he married in London in 1811. He returned in 1823, when he wrote that he 'dined and slept at Kilkenny, at our old club-house now turned into an inn' and 'walked with Lord L[ansdowne] about the town, and recollected the days of my courtship, when I used to walk with Bessy on the banks of the river'.

The castle, splendidly situated above the W. bank of the Nore, was the seat of the powerful Butler family from the 14th c. until 1935, when it became the property of the city. It was the home of Lady Eleanor Butler, who, with her friend, the Hon. Sarah Ponsonby, emigrated to Wales in 1778 in the teeth of family opposition (see Llangollen).

KILKENNY WEST, Westmeath. [8 Ef] Small village *c*. 7 m. NE. of Athlone, off the T31, where Oliver Goldsmith's father, the Revd. Charles Goldsmith, was first assistant and then successor to his wife's uncle, the Revd. Mr. Green, the curate-in-charge. The church is usually taken to be 'The decent church that topt the neighbouring hill' in *The Deserted Village* (1770).

KILLARNEY, Kerry. [9 Cd] Market town and tourist centre on the T29 and the T65, situated near lakes and mountains of great beauty. Many writers, from the early 19th c. on, have visited the town and made expeditions in the surrounding country. Sir Walter Scott, on his tour of Ireland in 1825, considered the Upper Lake (*c*. 5 m. SW. of the town) the grandest sight he had ever seen, and Tennyson, who visited Killarney while he was staying with Aubrey de Vere at Curragh Chase (q.v.), wrote the lyric 'The splendour falls on castle walls' (for the 3rd edn. of *The Princess*, 1853) when he heard a bugle blown beneath 'The Eagle's Nest' and 'eight distinct echoes'. Hugh Kelly, author of the comedies, *False Delicacy* (1768),

A Word for the Wise (1770), and *The School for Wives* (1773), was born (1739) in Killarney, but went to London (1760) to make his name.

A memorial to the Four Kerry Poets, designed by Seamus Murphy, was unveiled at Martyr's Hill on 15 August 1940 (a further ceremony following at Muckross (q.v.) on the same day). The memorial, moved for road redevelopment, has been re-erected at the old entrance to the railway, near by. The statue symbolizes the tradition of the free spirit of Ireland which was handed from one to another of these poets who wrote between the early 17th and late 18th centuries: Pierce Ferriter (d. 1653), who 'stands for all that is heroic in Irish history'. He was said to have 'composed poetry with one eye on Irish character, Irish manners and customs; the other on the Catholic refinement which distinguished the poetical literature of Europe in the Middle Ages. . . . He lamented with great dignity the Cromwellian transplantation and transportation decrees which affected rich and poor in Ireland.' Geoffrey O'Donoghue (d. 1677) is remembered for 'his lofty courage and intelligent verse which kept alive the spirit of independence among a people fast becoming entangled in a web of slavery'. He was succeeded by Aodhgan O'Rahilly (d. 1728), who flourished in the early 18th c., in whose verse 'the noble qualities of Ireland's chieftains and people' were kept alive at a time when the Catholic Church was suppressed and had to work in secret. Eoghan Ruadh O'Sullivan (d. 1784) was a popular poet of noble birth. It was said of him that 'he dignified labour by his sparkling genius, his wit and humour relieved the tedium of the winter nights'.

KILLEAGHY HILL. See MUCKROSS.

KILLEENEN, Galway. [9 Da] Hamlet 3 m. W. of Craughwell, off the T21 (Galway–Loughrea road). In the neglected cemetery is the grave of Antoine Ó Reachtabhra (1784–1834), the poet known as 'Blind Raftery'.

KILLIMER (pr. Kil̃mer), Clare. [9 Cc] Small village on the N. shore of the Shannon estuary, the terminus of the car ferry from Tarbert on the S. shore. About 1 m. E., on the road to Knock, is the little churchyard of Burrane, the burial place of Ellen Hanley, the 'Colleen Bawn', on whose tragic story Gerald Griffin based his novel *The Collegians* (1829). She is buried in the same grave as Peter O'Connell, a professor of languages and literature, who found her body after she had been drowned in the Shannon by her husband in 1819. The flat gravestone, protected from souvenir hunters by a concrete casing, lies in the old churchyard *c.* 8 ft above the road and opposite the gate to the new churchyard below. The facts and the fiction of the story of the Colleen Bawn are told by William MacLysaght in *Death Sails the Shannon* (1953, new edn. 1970).

KILLYBEGS, Donegal. [8 Dc] Fishing port on an inlet of Donegal Bay, on the T72a. It was here in January 1849, while on Customs duty, that William Allingham wrote 'The Fairies':

> Up the airy mountain,
> Down the rushy glen,
> We daren't go a-hunting,
> For fear of little men.

KILLYLEAGH. See CLANDEBOYE.

KILMACTHOMAS, Waterford. [9 Fd] Village on the Mahon, *c.* 14 m. SW. of Waterford, off the T12. The Gaelic poets Tadhg Gaelach Ó Súilleabháin (1715–95) and Donnchadh Rúa Mac Conmara (d. 1814) lived and worked here for some time and are strongly associated with the neighbourhood.

KILMALLOCK, Limerick. [9 Dc] Small market town on the T36, 6 m. NW. of Ráthluirc (Charleville). Aindrias Mac Craith (An Mangaire Súgach), a celebrated 18th-c. Gaelic poet, is buried in the graveyard of the ruined collegiate parish church of SS. Peter and Paul (N.M.), in the grave of the Hawthorne family, at the W. side of the S. door.

KILMARNOCK, Ayrs. (Strathclyde). [6 Dd] Manufacturing town, bypassed by the A77, 12 m. NE. of Ayr. *Poems Chiefly in the Scottish Dialect* (1786), Burns's collection of poems which first brought him recognition, was published here. The site of Wilson's printing shop in Star Inn Close is marked with a granite slab. The Laigh Kirk near the Cross was the setting for 'The Ordination', but Tam Samson's house in London Rd. and the Angel Inn (Begbies) in Market Lane have gone. In Kay Park a Victorian tower commemorates Burns and has a fine view. The spiral stair climbs past two rooms containing books, tapes, and portraits. One portrait is of the poet and essayist Alexander Smith, born here (1829, site unknown). In Smith's autobiographical novel, *Alfred Hagart's Household* (1866), Kilmarnock is called Spiggleton.

KILROOT, Antrim. [8 Hb] Village near the coast, c. 2½ m. NE. of Carrickfergus, just off the A2. Jonathan Swift had his first living here after his ordination in 1695 and stayed until 1696. His home, where he wrote *A Tale of a Tub* (1704), was demolished after a fire in 1959 and the church is now ruined.

KINGSBERE-SUB-GREENHILL. See BERE REGIS.

KINGSBRIDGE, Devon. [2 Ef] Busy little market town on the A379 and the A381 at the head of the Kingsbridge estuary. Pindar Lodge, at the beginning of the Promenade, is the house (now a hotel) where John Wolcot (the satirist 'Peter Pindar') was born. The house, which has been largely rebuilt, is in the parish of Dodbrooke and originally faced on to Ebrington St., now its back entrance. Wolcot attended Kingsbridge Free School before going to Bodmin Grammar School.

KINGSBURGH. See SKYE.

KINGSGATE, Kent. [1 Hc] Village 3 m. E. of Margate, N. of North Foreland, where Lord Holland built a villa in 1760 (now divided into flats). It was an imitation of Cicero's villa at Baiae and had a vast Doric portico with twelve columns of Portland stone. Thomas Gray wrote some satirical lines about it and the sham ruins built in the gardens:

Now mould'ring fanes and battlements arise
Arches and turrets nodding to their fall,
Unpeopled palaces delude his eyes
And mimick desolation covers all.

KINGSHOUSE INN, Argylls. (Highland). [6 Da] Inn on the old road through Glen Coe, now just off the A82. Campbell soldiers are said to have met here before the massacre in 1692. Neil Munro describes the place in his novel *John Splendid* (1898).

KING'S LYNN, Norf. [4 Fd] Port on the Great Ouse, 3 m. S. of the Wash, formerly called Lynn and Lynn Episcopi. The mystic Margery Kempe, daughter of John Burnham, a prominent man, was born in Lynn c. 1373. She sailed from the port on her travels to the Continent and to Jerusalem in her search for true faith. She dictated *The Book of Margery Kempe*, an account of her spiritual journey through life, part of which was printed by Wynken de Worde in 1501. It was published by the Early English Text Society in 1940. John Capgrave was also born (1393) in Lynn and spent many years in the Augustinian Friary here, eventually becoming Provincial of the Order in England. His chronicle of English history, and lives of St. Gilbert of Sempringham and St. Catharine of Alexandria, unlike his other works, were written in English.

Eugene Aram was arrested (1758) for murder while a master at the Grammar School, which at that time was in St. John's Chapel adjoining St. Margaret's Church. His tragedy was the subject of a poem by Thomas Hood in 1831 and of a novel by Lytton in 1832. One of his pupils was Charles Burney, whose sister Fanny was born (1752) either at St. Augustine's House in Chapel St., or at 84 High St. (rebuilt). Fanny, who started writing at the age of 10, spent holidays with her stepmother at The Dower House, near St. Margaret's Church where her father was organist (1751–60), and she wrote in a little cabin in the garden which bordered the river. She recalls in her *Diary* how she was sometimes driven indoors by the damp air or 'the annoying oaths of the watermen'.

KINGSTON LISLE. See UFFINGTON.

KINGSTON UPON HULL (or HULL), Humberside. [5 Ge] Port on the Humber, visited by John Taylor, 'the water-poet', who travelled extensively, on his 'merry-wherry-ferry voyage'. Andrew Marvell spent his youth at the vicarage of Holy Trinity Church, where his father was 'lecturer' from 1624 until his death by drowning in the Humber in 1641. Marvell was educated at the Grammar School, then near by, under his father who was the Master. Marvell, who left for Cambridge in 1638, was later three times elected M.P. for Hull. William Mason, who had a poetical interest in gardens, was born (1724) at Holy Trinity Vicarage while his father was incumbent. A large bronze plaque, erected in Queen's Gardens in 1973, depicts the hero of Defoe's *Robinson Crusoe* (1719), who sailed from the port on his adventures.

The poet Stevie Smith (1902-71) was born here but left for London when she was 5.

KINGTON ST. MICHAEL, Wilts. [1 Ac] Village *c.* 2½ m. NW. of Chippenham, off the A429. A memorial window in the church commemorates two natives of the parish, distinguished by their writings on the antiquities of Wiltshire: John Aubrey, F.R.S. (1625-97), whose works include the unfinished manuscripts of *Topographical Collections of Wiltshire, 1659-70*, with illustrations (corrected and enlarged by J. E. Jackson, 1862), and John Britton, F.S.A. (1771-1857), author of *Beauties of Wiltshire* (1801) and other works. John Aubrey was born at Easton Piers (now Easton Piercy or Percy), a hamlet in the parish of Kington St. Michael to the NW. of the village. He inherited the house, Lower Easton Piers (illustrated in the *Collections of Wiltshire*), from his mother's family, but pecuniary troubles compelled him to sell it in 1671 and from then on he had no settled home. The site of the house (long demolished) is occupied by Easton Percy Farm, opposite the site of the old Priory Chapel.

KING WILLIAM'S COLLEGE, I.O.M. [5 Jg] Public school (founded 1668), on the A12. F. W. Farrar and T. E. Brown were contemporaries here in the 1840s. Farrar's school story, *Eric, or Little by Little* (1858), written while he was a master at Harrow, is thought to have been loosely based on his experiences here. Brown, who was a day-boy and lived with his mother and family at Castletown near by, became Vice-Principal (1858-61).

KIRKANDREWS, Kirkcudbrights. (Dumfries and Galloway). [6 Df] Hamlet 2 m. W. of Borgue (q.v.) on the Carrick road. William Nicholson, 'the Galloway poet', was buried (1849) in the old churchyard overlooking Wigtown Bay.

KIRKBY-ON-BANE. See CONINGSBY.

KIRKCALDY, Fife (Fife). [6 Fc] Port on the A92. Adam Smith (1723-90), son of the Comptroller of Customs, was born at 220 High St. (P on site) and educated at the burgh school. He returned to the town in 1766 and devoted his time to the study of economic theory, supported by a pension from the Duke of Buccleuch, whom he had tutored on the Continent. *The Wealth of Nations* was published 10 years later.

Marjory Fleming (1803-11) was born at 130 High St. (rebuilt), then a three-storey house with a garden through an archway. Her journal, written while staying with an aunt and corrected by her cousin, was first edited by H. B. Farnie as *Pet Marjorie* (1858), and later popularized (1863) by Dr. John Brown, who drew a sentimental picture of her sitting on Scott's knee. Though neither Scott nor Marjory mention each other, their meeting was not denied by her sister. *The Complete Marjory Fleming*, with a facsimile of the journals, was edited by Frank Sidgwick in 1934. She died after an attack of measles and is buried in Abbotshall churchyard; her life-sized effigy shows the journal open on her knee. Raith Park where she often played is now a public park.

Carlyle lived in Kirk Wynd off the High St. in 1816, when appointed a master at the burgh school. A plaque on the wall of the Fife Free Press car park near by commemorates him and Adam Smith on the site of the school. Anna Buchan ('O. Douglas'), younger sister of John Buchan, was born at the manse at Pathhead, now joined to Kirkcaldy but then a separate town. Her autobiography *Unforgettable, Unforgotten* (1943) describes her happy childhood with her brothers, their large garden (now built over), and their delight in Scott's 'Rosabelle'. The heroine of this ballad lived in Ravenscraig Castle, just N. of the town, and was drowned crossing 'the stormy firth'.

KIRKCONNEL, Dumfriess. (Dumfries and Galloway). [6 Ee] Mining village on the A76. Alexander Anderson (1845-1909), born here, became a platelayer (1862) and published *A Song of Labour and Other Poems* (1873) under the pseudonym 'Surfaceman'. Encouraged by Carlyle, he became assistant librarian at Edinburgh University. There is a monument in the churchyard at the top of the village, where he is buried.

KIRKOSWALD, Ayrs. (Strathclyde). [6 De] Village on the A77, 10 m. SW. of Ayr. Burns studied surveying and mensuration here (1775), sleeping at Ballochniel Farm (1 m. S.), where his uncle worked. The Shanter Hotel, on the site of the school, has a pewter tankard said to be the poet's. The nightmare ride in 'Tam O' Shanter' ended here. Tam and his 'ancient drouthy cronie' were modelled on Douglas Graham and John Davidson, who are both buried in the churchyard. They were all friends of the souter (cobbler) and met at his house (Souter Johnnie's House (N.T.S.)[1]), which now contains Burnsiana and cobbler's tools.

[1] Open Apr.–Sept. daily 2.30–8 p.m.

KIRKTON MANOR. See BLACK DWARF'S COTTAGE.

KIRRIEMUIR, Angus (Tayside). [6 Fa] Town on the A926, 12 m. N. of Dundee. J. M. Barrie was born (1860) at 9 Brechin Rd.[1] (N.T.S.), which now houses personal relics and mementoes. His father was a handloom weaver like the occupants of many of the other houses in the road. Most of his stories of the town, which he called 'Thrums', a weaving term, came from his mother, whose life he told in *Margaret Ogilvy* (1896). Her family had been members of the Auld Licht Kirk (demolished 1893) in Bank St., from which he took the name of his first collection of sketches *Auld Licht Idylls* (1888). Her pastor there became Mr. Carfrae in *The Little Minister* (1891). In 1872 after 2 years in Forfar, the Barries settled at the ivy-covered Strathview (now modernized), but it was the cottage opposite that became known as the House on the Brae of *A Window in Thrums* (1889). The Den, a ravine now a public park, is mentioned in *Sentimental Tommy* (1896). Barrie, who went to London in 1884, often visited his parents here. He is buried with them on the W. side of the cemetery near the manse.

[1] Open Apr.–Oct.: weekdays 10 a.m.–12.30 p.m., 2–6 p.m., Sun. 2–6 p.m.

KIRROUGHTREE, Kirkcudbrights. (Dumfries and Galloway). [6 Df] Former country house now a hotel on the A712, 2 m. NE. of Newton Stewart. It was the home of Patrick Heron, the M.P., with whom Burns

stayed in 1794 and 1795. He had expectations that Heron would help to further his career and he wrote the verses known as the 'Heron Election Ballads'.

KNEBWORTH, Herts. [1 Ea] Tudor mansion,[1] 3 m. S. of Stevenage, off the A1, mostly rebuilt in the Regency Gothic style by the novelist Sir Edward Bulwer-Lytton (1st Baron Lytton) and his mother. He was portrayed as the Hon. Bertie Tremaine in Disraeli's *Endymion* (1880). He and Dickens took part in Jonson's *Everyman in his Humour* performed here in 1850, and also in his own *Not so Bad as We Seem* (1851). Lytton's later works were written here, including the futuristic *The Coming Race* (1871), published anonymously.

[1] Park open Apr.–Oct.: daily 11 a.m.–6 p.m. House and gardens open Apr.: Sat., Sun., Good Fri., and Easter Mon.; May–Sept.: daily except Mon. or except Tues. after spring and late summer Bank Holidays when house and gardens are also open 2–5 p.m.

KNOCKBRIT, Tipperary. [9 Ec] Village on the L154, halfway between Cashel and Fethard, 1 m. from the L111. Marguerite Power, later Countess of Blessington, was born here (1 Sept. 1789), the daughter of a farmer and agent, and spent her first 8 years here before moving to Clonmel (q.v.).

KNOCKNAREA, Sligo. [8 Cd] Mountain (1,078 ft high), 5 m. W. of Sligo, crowned by Miosgán Meva (N.M.), traditionally the tomb of Queen Maeve, a passage-grave-type cairn 200 ft in diameter and 34 ft high, Yeats's 'cairn-heaped grassy hill / Where passionate Maeve is stony-still.' On the S. side is Knocknarea Glen, a deep wooded ravine ⅔ m. long. The mountain and many of the surrounding features celebrated in legend are referred to by Yeats in many of his early poems, e.g. 'The Wanderings of Oisin' (1889).

KNOLE, Kent. [1 Fc] Country house (N.T.) approached by the road opposite St. Nicholas Church in Sevenoaks. It is the setting for *Orlando* (1928), the novel by Virginia Woolf, who gave the manuscript to Victoria Sackville-West, born here in 1892. She bequeathed it to the house as she 'felt there was so much about Knole in it, that it was the right place'. The manuscript is now shown in the Great Hall. In Victoria Sackville-West's own novel the house is Chevron, the background for the family in *The Edwardians* (1930). In *Knole and the Sackvilles* (1923) she tells how her ancestor Thomas Sackville (later 1st Earl of Dorset), part author of *The Mirror for Magistrates* (1559) and *Gorboduc* (1565), was given the house by his cousin Queen Elizabeth I in 1566. The 3rd Earl was a friend of Jonson, Fletcher, Drayton, and Donne, who preached in the chapel (not shown) on his annual visits to his parish church of St. Nicholas (P) in Sevenoaks, where he was rector (1616–31). The countess moved to tears by Donne's sermons was the unhappily-married Anne Clifford, a pupil, as a girl, of the poet Samuel Daniel, and the subject of many poems. The 6th Earl (1638–1706), author of some satires and the lyric 'To all you ladies now at land', was a friend and companion of Charles Sedley at Charles II's court. He was also a friend and patron of Dryden, who dedicated his *Essay on Satire* and *Essay on Dramatic Poesy* to him, and of Prior, who owed his years at Cambridge to him. Prior also wrote that 'A freedom reigned at his table which made every one of his guests think himself at home'. The dining-room became known as the Poets' Parlour (not shown) because it had portraits of the poets on the wall.

Open Apr.–Sept.: Wed.–Sat. and Bank Holidays (except Good Friday, Christmas and Boxing Day) 10 a.m.–12 noon, 2–5 p.m.; Oct.–Dec. and Mar. closing at 3.30 p.m.

KNOWSLEY HALL, Merseyside. [5 Bf] Country seat of the Earl of Derby, 6 m. E. of Liverpool, just N. of the A57. When Shakespeare was a member of the Earl of Leicester's company, which gave two performances at Latham House, near Ormskirk in July 1587, he probably played here about the same time. Edward Lear was engaged by Lord Stanley (later the 13th Earl) in 1832 to make coloured drawings of the rare birds and animals in his menagerie. Lear became a friend of his patron's grandchildren and entertained them with limericks and other verse which he illustrated himself and published as *A Book of Nonsense* (1846, anonymously; 1861, with more limericks and his own name). Adult society was formal and distinguished. Lear wrote to a friend: 'Nothing I long for half so much as

to giggle heartily and to hop on one leg down the Great Gallery–but I dare not.'

KNOWSTONE (pr. Nowston), Devon. [2 Ec] Small village 7 m. ESE. of South Molton, on a minor road between the A361 and the B3221. Parson Froude, the infamous, bad-tempered vicar here for nearly 50 years, died in 1853 in a fit of rage and is buried in the churchyard. He is portrayed as Parson Chowne in R. D. Blackmore's *Maid of Sker* (1872).

KNUTSFORD, Cheshire. [3 Ga] Quiet town on the A50 and the A537. Mrs. Elizabeth Cleghorn Gaskell (*née* Stevenson) came here from London when she was just over 1 year old, after her mother's death, and was brought up by her aunt, Mrs. Hannah Lumb, at Heath House (now Heathwaite House, P), a double-fronted brick house on the S. side of Knutsford Heath (now Gaskell Ave.). She lived here until her marriage to the Revd. William Gaskell in 1832, in the parish church (where the marriage certificate may be seen), and attended the Brook St. Unitarian Chapel, which is described in her novel, *Ruth* (1853). She is buried in the Chapel graveyard, with her husband and two of her daughters. Her best-known novel, *Cranford* (first published in *Household Words*, 1851–3), is a sympathetic portrait of the little town she grew up in and the idiosyncrasies of its inhabitants.

A memorial tower in King St., erected (1907) on the 150th anniversary of her birth, displays a bust of Mrs. Gaskell as a young woman, on the wall facing the street, and a high-relief plaque of her in later life on another side, and gives a list of her works, accompanied by quotations from Job, Thomas à Kempis, Milton, Gladstone, and King Alfred. The King's Coffee House next door, designed in the rural Italian 18th-c. style, was also built to commemorate Mrs. Gaskell, with a suitable inscription referring to *Cranford*. The interior, decorated in the contemporary 1907 style, a blend of the Arts and Crafts Movement and *Art Nouveau*, was a favourite haunt of Galsworthy and other literary and artistic celebrities of the day.

Tatton Park (N.T.),[1] 3½ m. N., with over 1,000 acres of deer park and a 19th-c. mansion containing collections of pictures, furniture, and silver, was the original of Cumnor Towers in Mrs. Gaskell's *Wives and Daughters* (1864–6). It can be entered on foot from the Knutsford gate or by car from the main entrance in Ashley Rd., off the Manchester road.

¹ Open 25 Mar.–3 May, 31 Aug.–19 Oct.: Sun., Tues.–Sat., Bank Holidays: house

2–5.15 p.m., gardens 2–6 p.m., park 11 a.m.–6.30 p.m.; 4 May–30 Aug.: Sun., Tues.–Sat., Bank Holidays: house 2–5.45 p.m., gardens 2–6.30 p.m., park 11 a.m.–8 p.m.; winter months: park open to pedestrians from Knutsford gate, Sun., Tues.–Fri., closed Christmas Day.

KNYPE. See STOKE-ON-TRENT.

L

LACEY GREEN, Bucks. [1 Db] Village off the A4010, 2 m. S. of Princes Risborough. Pink Rd., a left turn at the beginning of the village by the Whip, leads to the Pink and Lily, an inn where Rupert Brooke spent week-ends with his friends. There are photographs of him and a copy of one of his poems over the old fireplace.

LAGGAN, Inverness-shire (Highland). [7 Df] Village N. of Loch Lochy on the A82. In 1779 the minister, James Grant, who was also chaplain at Fort Augustus, married Anne, the daughter of the barrack-master at the garrison there. Her *Letters from the Mountains* (1803), published after his death to enable their son to join the E. India Company, were in the Romantic tradition and proved popular. Anne Grant had spent her adolescence in Albany, America and was friendly with Dutch settlers there and her *Memoirs of an American Lady* (1808) stems from that time.

LAKE DISTRICT, Cumbria. [5 Bb and Bc] Area in the Cumbrian Mountains *c.* 35 m. square, occupying large parts of the former counties of Cumberland and Westmorland and the former N. part of Lancashire. Its mountains, dales, and lakes form a pattern of great beauty and variety and offer endless scope to naturalists, climbers, and walkers. They were both an inspiration and a way of life to the 'Lake Poets', Wordsworth, Coleridge, and Southey, who lived and wrote in Grasmere, Keswick, and Ambleside. The terms 'Lake Poets' and 'Lake School' derive from the *Edinburgh Review*, which used 'Lake School' in August 1817, in a derisory context (later the scorn was modified and the terms became current without a derogatory

sense). But before these poets were writing Thomas Gray recorded his impressions of the Lake District in his *Journal of a tour in the Lakes*, embodied in his *Correspondence* (ed. P. Toynbee and L. Whibley, 3 vols., 1935), and William Gilpin, in his series of *Picturesque Tours*, published a *Guide to the Lakes* (1789), which became one of Wordsworth's treasured possessions. Wordsworth's own *Guide through the Lakes* (1835) was originally written in 1810 as an introduction to T. Wilkinson's *Select Views in Cumberland*.

Wordsworth and his sister Dorothy were natives who stayed for a time in the south of England, but were irresistibly drawn back to the county of their early days and settled there for life, first at Grasmere and then at Rydal Mount, near Ambleside. Coleridge, on the other hand, was drawn there more by devotion to Wordsworth, and after a few years found the climate too damp and left for the south. Southey joined them and put down roots at Keswick for the rest of his life. De Quincey came at 18 as a visitor to Grasmere, a wholly dedicated worshipper of Wordsworth, and maintained his attachment to the district for many years, marrying, acquiring property, writing, but never really settling. He made friends with the ebullient John Wilson of Elleray at Windermere and when the latter moved to Edinburgh he joined him and abandoned the Lakes for good. Later literary figures have included Harriet Martineau and Matthew Arnold at Ambleside, Ruskin at Brantwood, on Coniston Water, Sir Hugh Walpole at Borrowdale, Beatrix Potter at Near Sawrey, near Esthwaite Water, and Arthur Ransome at Newby Bridge and Haverthwaite. Large areas of the Lake District have become the property of the National Trust, thanks to the tireless efforts of Canon H. D. Rawnsley (1851–1920), vicar of Crosthwaite, 1883–1917. Beatrix Potter (later Mrs. William Heelis) was a strong supporter and generous benefactor.

LAKE OF MENTEITH. See INCHMAHOME.

LALEHAM, Surrey. [1 Dc] Village on the B377 and the B376, 2 m. NE. of Chertsey. Matthew Arnold was born here in 1822, but the house, where his father tutored before becoming headmaster of Rugby, has been demolished. He spent his last years at Cobham (6 m. SW.), but was buried (1888) in the churchyard here. A brass tablet commemorates him in the church where he worshipped.

LAMAS, Norf. [4 Hd] Village E. of the B1354, 10 m. N. of Norwich. The grave of Anna Sewell, author of *Black Beauty* (1877), is still tended among the Irish yews by the chapel (closed).

LANCASTER, Lancs. [5 Bd] Historic town on the tidal Lune, where the A6 crosses by Skerton Bridge. No. 1 High St. was the birthplace (1869) of Laurence Binyon, poet and authority on Far Eastern art, who is remembered especially for his poem 'For the Fallen' (1914):

> They shall grow not old, as we that are left grow old:

LANGAR, Notts. [4 Cc] Village S. of the A52, 10 m. SE. of Nottingham. Samuel Butler was born (1835) at the rectory (now Langar House). *The Way of all Flesh* (1903), a satirical and autobiographical novel, paints a grim picture of his youth here before the differences with his father reached the point where he emigrated to New Zealand.

LANGHAM, Norf. [4 Gc] Village on the B1388, 14 m. W. of Cromer. Captain Frederick Marryat moved here after publishing *Masterman Ready* (1841) and lived (1843–8) at Manor Cottage (rebuilt) in Cocksthorpe Rd. He is buried in the churchyard, and a tablet in the church commemorates him.

LANGHOLM, Dumfriess. (Dumfries and Galloway). [6 Fe] Small town 17 m. NW. of

Gretna Green, where the A7 crosses the Esk. William Mickle (1735–88), poet and translator, was born at Wauchope Manse, the last house in the town on the Lockerbie road. A tablet on the town hall recalls that he was the author of 'Cumnor Hall' and 'There's Nae Luck aboot the Hoose'. It is said that at 13 he read *The Faerie Queene* and decided to be a poet.

LANGLEY, Berks. [1 Dc] Expanding town off the A4, merging with the suburbs of Slough. The beautifully restored parish church is in the old village centre. Prominent treasures are the unusual Kedermister pew and library. An early reader of the old leather-bound ecclesiastical books was John Milton, who often walked over from Horton (q.v.); some of the marginal annotations are said to be in his hand. The founder Sir John Kedermister, whose portrait hangs near his books, was descended from his namesake, Edward IV's Ranger of Langley Forest. The poet Waller's daughter married into the family.

LANGLEY BURRELL, Wilts. [1 Ac] Village E. of the A420, 1 m. N. of Chippenham. Francis Kilvert was curate here from 1872 to 1876 after leaving his curacy at Clyro (q.v.). His parents' house, now called Kilvert's Parsonage, has been restored. Among the entries in the notebooks that he kept from 1870 to 1877 (*Diary*, 3 vols., 1938–40; new edn. 1969), he records his parish work, his pleasure in the countryside, and the election at Chippenham, when a secret ballot was used for the first time. The pages of his notebooks were ornamented with his own drawings. The church is on the A420 (½ m. NW.).

LANGPORT, Som. [2 Gc] Small town on the A372 and the A378, 13 m. W. of Taunton. Walter Bagehot (1826–77) was born at a stone house (P) near the Langport Arms. He was editor of *The Economist* from 1860 to the end of his life. He died at Herds Hill, a large house on the hill W. of the town on the A378. His critical essays, *Literary Studies* (1879), were published posthumously.

LANGTON BY SPILSBY, Lincs. [4 Eb] Small village 9 m. E. of Horncastle, off the A158, the home of the Langton family for 800 years. When Johnson visited his friend

Bennet Langton in 1764 he stayed in the Elizabethan manor, which was demolished in 1845. The church, built in 1725, was recently restored, and the Langton pew where Johnson sat now contains the organ.

LARACOR, Meath. [8 Ff] Village on the L25, 2 m. S. of Trim. Swift came here in 1700 as rector of the parish and remained, with frequent absences in London and Dublin, until his appointment as Dean of St. Patrick's in Dublin. Only fragments of his Glebe House remain, NW. of the church which replaced his, but which still has the altar plate he used. Many of his tracts and satires were written here, including the *Argument to Prove the Inconvenience of abolishing Christianity* (1708) and also part of the *Journal to Stella* (1766; 1768). Stella (Esther Johnson) came in 1701 to be near him and lived with her friend Mrs. Dingley at a house (now ruined, known as 'Stella's Cottage') a little N., near the gates of Knightsbrook House. The willows bordering the stream where the three of them used to walk are the descendants of those planted by Swift. He kept the living till the end of his life, but seldom returned after he had become Dean.

LARGO, Fife (Fife). [6 Fc] Village on the A915, comprising Upper and Lower Largo. The latter, on the coast, was the birthplace of Alexander Selkirk (1676). His thatched cottage on the shore has given way to a street of houses, and on one a statue of Robinson Crusoe (whose prototype he was) stares out to sea.

LARK RISE. See JUNIPER HILL.

LASSWADE, Midlothian (Lothian). [6 Fc] Village in the Esk Valley, c. 10½ m. SE. of Edinburgh. William Drummond of Hawthornden, who lived in the mansion 2½ m. SW., is buried in the churchyard. Sir Walter Scott used to stay at Lasswade Cottage (enlarged) in the summers of 1798–1804, and the village is possibly the 'Gandercleugh' of Jedediah Cleishbotham, the fictitious schoolmaster and parish clerk who was supposed to have sold *Tales of My Landlord* (1817–31) for publication.

In 1840 De Quincey settled at Mavis Bush (now De Quincey Cottage), Polton, 2 m. SW. of Lasswade, on the Hawthornden road, and this, apart from periods in Edinburgh and

Glasgow, became his home for the rest of his life.

LAUGHARNE (pr. Larn), Dyfed. [2 Da] Small town on the A4066, on the Taf estuary, the home of Dylan Thomas, who came here with his wife in 1938 at the invitation of Richard Hughes, the novelist, and lived first in a two-roomed cottage in Gosport St. and then at Sea View, near the town hall. They left in October and after returning briefly in 1939 and 1940 came back for good in 1949, to live at The Boathouse, a whitewashed, slate-roofed house below the cliff, where Thomas worked in the blue-painted garden shed. The house can be seen from the end of Cliff Rd. called Dylan's Walk. When he first came to Laugharne Thomas was writing the short stories later published as *Portrait of the Artist as a Young Dog* (1940), and *Quite Early One Morning*, from which his best-known work, *Under Milk Wood* (1954), a play for voices, developed. The town of 'Llaregyb' is traditionally associated with Laugharne, where the play has been performed periodically since 1958. Dylan Thomas died on a lecture tour in the United States in November 1953 and was brought home for burial in the hillside graveyard of St. Martin's Church, where his grave is marked by a plain white wooden cross.

LAURAGH, Kerry. [9 Be] Village on the L62 on the S. side of the Kenmare River, near the turning for the Healy Pass. Derreen House,[1] on a small peninsula where the coast road for Kenmare turns off the main road, was rented by J. A. Froude, the historian, from the 5th Marquis of Lansdowne in 1867 and 1869–70, when he began his controversial work, *The English in Ireland in the Eighteenth Century* (3 vols., 1872–4). 'Froude's Seat', above the Middle Walk in the beautiful grounds planted by Lord Lansdowne about this time, commands a fine view of the estuary and distant mountains. While he was here Froude gathered information and local colour for his romance, *The Two Chiefs of Dunboy* (1889).

[1] Garden open Apr.–Sept.: Sun., Tues., Thurs. 2–6 p.m.

LAURENCEKIRK, Kincardines. (Grampian). [6 Ga] Chief town in the district of Howe of the Mearns. James Beattie, the poet who became Professor of Moral Philosophy, was born (1835) near the town, where his father was a farmer and shopkeeper. Dr. Johnson and Boswell stopped here on their Highland journey (1773) while Boswell arranged a visit to Lord Monboddo. In *The Journal of a Tour of the Hebrides* (1774) Boswell writes of the town and the improvements that Lord Gardenston is making by 'building a manufacturing village', a project of which he approves, though he remarks that Lord Gardenston is as fond of it as if he had 'founded Thebes'.

LAURIESTON, Kirkcudbrights. (Dumfries and Galloway). [6 Ef] Village on the A762, 8 m. SE. of New Galloway. A tall cairn at the N. of the village commemorates Samuel Rutherford Crockett, poet and novelist of the Kailyard School, admired by R. L. Stevenson, whose poem dedicated to Crockett is quoted on the cairn. Crockett was born (1859) at the farmhouse of Little Duchrae on the A762, 1 m. S. of Mossdale. His first two novels *The Lilac Sunbonnet* and *The Raiders*, both published in 1894 and set locally, were so successful that he gave up the ministry and devoted himself to writing. He died at Tarascon in France and is buried at Balmaghie churchyard (a left turn by the bridge 3 m. E. on the B795). His memorial is included at the foot of a tombstone to Isabella Young, 20 yds from the gate.

LAVENHAM, Suff. [4 Gf] Village on the A1141 and the B1071, 6 m. NE. of Sudbury. The Grange in Shilling St., one of the old timbered houses with an overhanging storey, was the childhood home of Jane and Ann Taylor, authors of verses and tales for the young. Their father, Isaac Taylor, author and engraver, published *Specimens of Gothic Ornaments selected from the Parish Church of Lavenham* in 1796, the year they left for Colchester.

LAW HILL, West Yorkshire. [5 De] House 1,000 ft up on Southowram Bank, 1½ m. ESE. of Halifax. Emily Brontë was a teacher here in 1837 when the house was an efficiently run school for girls. She is thought to have been employed for 6 months but it is possible that she stayed for 18. Many of

her poems written here have a nostalgia for Haworth, including the lines:

Awaken on all my dear moorlands
The wind in its glory and pride,
O call me from valleys and highlands
To walk by the hill-river's side!

. . . .

But lovelier than cornfields all waving
In emerald and scarlet and gold
Are the slopes where the north wind is raving
And the glens where I wandered of old.

The history of the family who previously owned Law Hill and the near-by Walterclough Hall furnished her with the story of *Wuthering Heights* (1847), and one of her fellow teachers was called Earnshaw. Her description of the façade of Wuthering Heights closely resembles High Sutherland Hall, 1½ m. N.

LEADHILLS, Lanarks. (Strathclyde). [6 Ee] Village on the B797 in the Lowther Hills, 5 m. SW. of Crawford. Allan Ramsay, author of *The Gentle Shepherd* (1725), was born near here. His father was manager of Lord Hopetoun's lead mines, and after his death his mother married a farmer in the same neighbourhood. Allan Ramsay was sent to Crawford School and then, after his mother's death, was apprenticed (1701) to a wigmaker in Edinburgh.

LEAMINGTON (pr. Lemmington) SPA, Warwicks. [4 Be] Fashionable health resort in Georgian and Victorian times, 13 m. S. of Coventry. Camden, whose family held land here, mentions the medicinal well in *Britannia* (1586).

Ruskin, whose parents were worried about his tubercular symptoms, came here in 1841 to consult Dr. Henry Jephson, who subjected him to a regimen of baths and exercise. He stayed first at The Bedford, a fashionable hotel at 15 Leamington Parade, and then moved to 53 Russell Ter. a 'small square brick lodging-house'. He amused himself by writing a fairy tale, *The King of the Golden River*, for the 12-year-old Effie Gray (later his wife), who had been staying with his family.

Dickens gave readings here in 1855 and 1862. The local paper hoped he might attract large audiences, which they regretted were 'not common things in this town'. In *Dombey and Son* (1846–8), Dombey and

Major Bagstock meet Mrs. Skewton at the pump rooms. Nathaniel Hawthorne in 1858 stayed at 10 Lansdowne Circus, 'one of the coziest nooks in England, or in the World', while writing *Our Old Home* (1863). Ambrose Bierce wrote *The Lantern* (1874), a short-lived satirical magazine, while staying here. This was subsidized by the Empress Eugénie to help refute attacks on the Emperor.

LEATHERHEAD, Surrey. [1 Ec] Old town on the A24 and the A245. The Running Horse, part of which dates from the 15th c., is thought to be the inn of the ale-wife in Skelton's poem *The Tunning of Elynour Rummyng*, written *c.* 1517, which describes the brewing (tunning) of 'noppy ale' for 'travellers and tynkers, for sweters and swynkers, and all good ale drynkers'. Skelton was attached to Prince Henry's household and may have been staying at the royal palace at Nonsuch, 5 m. NE. (foundations visible in the park).

In 1808 Sheridan rented Randall's Farm (opposite the cemetery entrance) from his friend Richard Iremonger for 15 months. Sheridan wrote inviting a friend to a fishing party 'on our river Mole' near by.

Sir Anthony Hope Hawkins, author as Anthony Hope of *The Prisoner of Zenda* (1894), was buried (1933) in the parish churchyard.

LECHLADE, Glos. [1 Bb] Small market town where the A361 joins the A417, 11 m. NE. of Swindon. In 1815 Shelley, with Peacock, Mary Godwin, and Charles Clairmont, rowed up the Thames from Windsor and stayed at the inn here. Shelley had been listless on the journey, which Peacock put down to a diet of bread and butter. He recommended 'three mutton chops, well peppered', which so raised Shelley's spirits that he made exuberant plans to row the length and breadth of Britain. But unable to get the boat to the source of the river they stayed another night at the inn before rowing back. Shelley wrote 'Stanzas in a Summer Evening Churchyard' and a stone set in the churchyard wall in 1968 at the beginning of Shelley's Walk, leading from the church to the river, quotes from the poem.

LEDBURY, Hereford and Worcester. [3 Gf] Market town on the A449, 7 m. SW. of Great Malvern, which has a claim (cf. Great Malvern) to be the birthplace of William Langland. Wordsworth's sonnet, 'St. Catherine of Ledbury' (1835), describes the saint's rapture on hearing the bells peal out without human ringers, which she took to be a sign for her to settle here 'Till she exchanged for heaven that happy ground'. John Masefield was born (1878) at The Knapp, but he ran away to sea at an early age. Some of his *Collected Poems* (1946) refer to the country near by and to the church, which has 'a golden vane surveying half the shire'.

LEIGHTON, Salop. [3 Gc] Village on the B4380, S. of The Wrekin and above the valley of the Severn. Leighton Lodge was the birthplace of Mary Webb, author of country novels in a Shropshire setting (*Gone to Earth*, 1917, *Precious Bane*, 1924, etc.).

LEIGHTON BROMSWOLD, Cambs. [4 De] Village off the A604, 6 m. NW. of Huntingdon. The church was rebuilt during the time George Herbert was prebend, though it is not known whether he ever visited it. His family crest is on one of the lead rainwater pipes. A copy of his poem 'The Elixir', now a popular hymn, is in the church.

LEVENS HALL, Cumbria. [5 Bc] Tudor mansion[1] 5 m. S. of Kendal, on the A6. Mrs. Humphry Ward, granddaughter of Thomas Arnold of Rugby, stayed here during the winter of 1896/7 while writing her novel *Helbeck of Bannisdale* (1898). She used the Hall and Sizergh Castle[2] (2 m. N.) as models for 'Bannisdale'.

[1] Open May–Sept.: Sun., Tues., Wed., Thurs. 2–5 p.m. Guided tours: Sat. 2–4.30 p.m. Garden: daily 10 a.m.–5 p.m.
[2] Open Apr.–Sept.: Wed. 2–5.45 p.m.; gardens only: Tues. and Thurs. 2–5.45 p.m.

LEVERINGTON, Cambs. [4 Ed] Village 1 m. NW. of Wisbech off the B1169. Tradition holds that Oliver Goldsmith stayed at Park Farm on the Gorefield Rd. with the Lumpkin family, when writing *She Stoops to Conquer* (1773). There is still a pond by the roadside, and a tablet in the church commemorates an Anthony Lumpkin, two points of evidence for the tradition.

LEWES, East Sussex. [1 Ee] Town on the A27. Evelyn in his *Diary* mentions staying here with his grandparents, the Stansfields, for his schooldays, first with Mr. Potts in the Cliffe and then at the Grammar School. He records laying one of the stones at the foundation of the church his grandfather was building at South Malling (1 m. N.), and the solemnity of his grandfather's funeral in 1627 at All Saints Church (monuments). When Evelyn attended the Grammar School, in 1630, it adjoined the grounds (now public gardens) of Southover Grange, his new home after his grandmother's remarriage. This house, now owned by the council, can be rented for receptions and meetings. One room is called after Evelyn and another after Harrison Ainsworth, who portrays the house as Mock Beggars Hall in *Ovingdean Grange* (1860), a novel set in the Civil War.

Thomas Rickman was born (1761) in the Cliffe at the bottom of the town; his forceful satires written under the pseudonym 'Clio' appeared in the *Black Dwarf* and other periodicals. An early friend of his was Tom Paine, who lodged at the Bull House near the former Westgate in the High St. Paine drew up a petition about the grievances over pay and conditions of his fellow excisemen. This was circulated in London and, when the demand failed, he lost his post. He had married the daughter of his landlord, a tobacconist, and helped run the business for a time, but he separated from his wife and set out for America in 1774. Rickman, who became a bookseller in London, sold Paine's works and the two met again at his shop.

LEW TRENCHARD, Devon. [2 Dd] Village c. 10 m. SW. of Okehampton, just S. of the A30. The Revd. Sabine Baring-Gould, antiquarian and expert on West Country folklore and legend, theologian, hymn-writer, novelist, and musician, was rector and squire here from 1881 till his death in 1924. He is buried in the churchyard. His numerous works include *The Gaverocks: A Tale of the Cornish Coast* (1887), the thriller, *In the Roar of the Sea* (1892), folklore, *A Book of the West* (1899), and *A Book of Dartmoor* (1900). His best-known hymn is 'Onward, Christian Soldiers'.

LICHFIELD, Staffs. [4 Ad] Cathedral city at the junction of the A38 and the A51. Joseph Addison lived here when his father became Dean in 1683, and was one of the many distinguished pupils of the Grammar School, an ancient foundation originally situated in St. John's St. The building was replaced by the present structure in 1849, but the school itself was moved in 1903 to Borrowcop Hill, to the S. of the city. The 16th-c. Headmaster's House (now offices) still exists. George Farquhar stayed at the George Inn in Bird St. (P) in 1705, when he was a lieutenant in the Grenadiers, recruiting troops in Lichfield. The inn is mentioned in *The Beaux' Stratagem* (1707) as the place where Aimwell and Archer arrive to seek the rehabilitation of their fortunes.

Samuel Johnson, the city's most famous son, was born above his father's bookshop in the house at the corner of Breadmarket St. on the Market Sq. and was baptized in St. Mary's Church across the way. The house, hardly altered since his father built it in 1707-8, is now an admirable museum[1] containing books and personal relics of Dr. Johnson and portraits of relatives and friends. There is a statue of Johnson in the Square, erected in 1838, with three bas-reliefs on the base depicting scenes from his life, and another statue, of later date, of James Boswell, his biographer. Johnson had his first English lessons in 1714 at Dame Oliver's School in Dam St., where the site is marked by an inscription. He later went to the Grammar School. He kept a close attachment to Lichfield throughout his life, and he and Boswell used to return for visits and stay at the Three Crowns Inn (P on the site), two doors from his birthplace. Johnson also frequently stayed at Redcourt House, the 'stately house with a handsome garden' built by his step-daughter, Lucy Porter, in Tamworth St., but this has now been demolished and the site is occupied by a medical centre. His parents and his brother Nathaniel are buried in St. Michael's Church on Greenhill on the E. side of the city and the tombstone bears the eloquent Latin epitaph he wrote.

Erasmus Darwin, botanist, physician, and author of the poem *The Botanic Garden* (1789-91), written in heroic couplets in imitation of Pope, lived in a house at the W. end of the Close (P) from 1756 to 1781 and established a botanical garden near by. Although his poem, once popular, was later ridiculed, it contains lines of not wholly fantastic prophecy:

Soon shall thy arm, Unconquered Steam, afar
   drag the slow barge, or drive the rapid car;
Or on wide waving wings expanded bear
   the flying chariot through the fields of air.

Anna Seward, a poet known as 'the Swan

of Lichfield', lived from 1754 to 1809 at the Bishop's Palace, for a long time the residence of her father, Canon Seward. She was the centre of a literary coterie which included Erasmus Darwin, and was visited by Sir Walter Scott, who published her poems in 1810 with a memoir. She knew Johnson (her portrait is in the birthplace museum) and was able to supply Boswell with information for his *Life of Samuel Johnson* (1791). Miss Mitford, however, was less than charitable in a letter of April 1818:

I wonder [she wrote] by what accident Miss Seward came by her fame. Setting aside her pedantry and presumption, there is no poet male or female who ever clothed so few ideas in so many words. She is all tinkling and tinsel—a sort of Dr. Darwin in petticoats.

Nathaniel Hawthorne came to Lichfield in the mid 19th c. partly to see the cathedral and partly to visit Johnson's birthplace. The agreeable account of his visit can be read in *Our Old Home* (1863). Richard Garnett, one-time Keeper of Printed Books at the British Museum and author of *The Twilight of the Gods* (1888), a series of classical and oriental fables, was born (1835) in Lichfield.

The city is dominated by 'The Ladies of the Vale', the three graceful spires of the cathedral, which stands in the quiet Close, surrounded by courtyards and historic buildings of great charm and elegance. Among the numerous statues and memorials in the cathedral the literary pilgrim can find monuments to Lady Mary Wortley Montagu (discovered with delighted surprise by Hawthorne) and Anna Seward near the W. door, and in St. Michael's chapel a bust of Johnson by Westmacott and Johnson's epitaph on Garrick. Richard Hurd, critic and divine, best known for his *Letters on Chivalry and Romance* (1762), was Bishop of Lichfield 1775–81.

¹ Open weekdays (except Mon. and Public Holidays), apart from Late Summer Holiday) 10 a.m.–1 p.m., 2–4 p.m. (5 p.m. May–Sept.); Sun. (May–Sept.) 2.30–5 p.m.

LIDGATE, Suff. [4 Ff] Village on the B1063, 5½ m. SE. of Newmarket. John Lydgate (1370?–1451?), court poet for a time under the patronage of Humphrey of Gloucester, was born at Suffolk House (rebuilt) on the main street. Known as 'the Monk of Bury' (see Bury St. Edmunds), he is shown wearing a habit in the brass on the chancel floor.

LIMPSFIELD, Surrey. [1 Ed] Village on the A25. Edward Garnett (reader for the publishers Fisher, Unwin) and his wife Constance, translator of many Russian classics, built in 1896 The Cearne, a house in the woods overlooking the valley, off the B269 at Limpsfield Chart. They entertained many writers here including Hudson, Cunninghame Graham, Belloc, Edward Thomas, W. H. Davies, and Galsworthy, whose character Bosinney in *The Man of Property* was partly based on Garnett. In 1898 when Conrad visited he met F. M. Hueffer (later Ford) and his wife who lived near by. Hueffer introduced D. H. Lawrence to the hospitable Garnett and many of Lawrence's dialect poems, including the long 'Whether or not', were written by the log fire at The Cearne. A young generation, including Rupert Brooke, used to meet at Champions, the home of their neighbours, the Oliviers, where Shaw, E. V. Lucas, and other friends were at one time the audience for Garnett's play *Robin Hood*, which the young people acted.

Florence Barclay (*née* Charlesworth), born (1862) at the vicarage, was the author of the popular novel *The Rosary* (1909). She was buried in the churchyard (1921).

Richard Church married in 1916 and rented a Georgian cottage in the High St. of Limpsfield village, next door to a grocer's shop (now a bookshop opposite the Bull Inn), which features in his first novel *Oliver's Daughter*, written 10 years later, where the heroine is a grocer's daughter. In 1927 Church leased the 14th-c. Comfort's Cottage in a clearing in Staffhurst Wood for a year before moving to London. W. H. Davies, who met Church there, bought a cottage in the High St. near the parish church.

LINCOLN, Lincs. [4 Db] Cathedral city at the junction of Ermine St. (A15) and Fosse Way (A46). Walter Map or Mapes (fl. 1200), author of *De Nugis Curialium*, a collection of essays and tales giving a contemporary account of life in the 12th c., was a canon of the cathedral. The child martyr, 'Little St. Hugh' (?1246–55), whose shrine is in the S. aisle of the cathedral, was a favoured subject of poets. He is mentioned in 'The Prioress's Tale' in Chaucer's *The Canterbury Tales*, in Marlowe's *The Jew of Malta*, and in 'The Jew's Daughter', a ballad in Percy's *Reliques*. Robert Grosseteste, notable philosopher and scientist, and author of *Le Chasteau d'Amour*, was Bishop 1235–53. He was buried in the SE. transept of the choir.

The Norman castle[1] figures in the Early English verse romance *Havelock the Dane*.

Elizabeth Penrose (1780–1837), who as 'Mrs. Markham' wrote popular histories for young people, died in Minster Yard and was buried in the Cloister Garth. Ada Bayly, the novelist 'Edna Lyall', lived with her sister at 5 Minster Yard, where *Donovan* (1882) and its popular sequel *We Two* (1884) were written; she left Lincoln in 1884.

Tennyson, a native of Lincolnshire, is commemorated by a statue on the green outside the cathedral. The Tennyson Research Centre[2] in the City Library houses a large collection of family books and papers. Catalogues (vols. I and II, ed. N. Campbell) are being prepared by the Tennyson Society. There is an Exhibition Room at the Usher Gallery,[3] which contains manuscripts, letters, and personalia.

[1] Open daily; Sun. from 2 p.m.
[2] Open Mon.–Fri. 9.30 a.m.–7 p.m.; Sat. 9.30 a.m.–5 p.m.; closed Sun. and Bank Holidays.
[3] Open weekdays 10 a.m.–5.30 p.m.; Sun. 2.30–5 p.m.

LINDLEY, Leics. [4 Bd] Hamlet 3 m. N. of Nuneaton, approached by a gated track on the eastbound carriageway of the A5, E. of the A444 junction. A modern house (hidden in trees behind Motor Industries Research Association's building) has replaced the 18th-c. Lindley Hall built on the site of the manor where Robert Burton was born (1577) and spent his childhood. He went away to school and spent most of his life in Oxford.

LISBURN, Antrim. [8 Gc] Cathedral and manufacturing town on the Lagan, 8 m. SW. of Belfast, on the A1. In Christ Church, cathedral (C.I.) of the diocese of Connor, there is a memorial to Jeremy Taylor, Bishop of Down and Connor (1661–7), who spent the last 6 years of his life here.

LISSOY, Westmeath. [8 Ef] Small village on the T31, 6 m. SW. of Ballymahon. Goldsmith grew up here after his father had moved from Pallas to become curate-in-charge of Kilkenny West, and the ruined parsonage at the end of a broad tree-lined avenue may still be seen. Goldsmith's first lessons began when he was 3, with Mrs. Elizabeth Delap, who thought him one of the dullest pupils she had ever taught, though she lived to be proud of him. At the age of 6 he went to the village school, under Thomas Byrne, a veteran of the Peninsular Wars, identified as the schoolmaster of *The Deserted Village* (1770) in the lines:

A man severe he was, and stern to view;
I knew him well, and every truant knew.

It was at this time that Goldsmith contracted smallpox, which left him scarred for life. Lissoy has been regarded as the 'sweet Auburn' of *The Deserted Village* and many of the features, such as 'the never-failing brook', 'the busy mill', and 'the decent Church that topped the neighbouring hill', can be matched with local landmarks. It is possible that Goldsmith drew on happy childhood memories for the idyllic scenes in the poem (see also Nuneham Courtenay).

LITTLE BARFORD, Beds. [4 Df] Hamlet on the B1043, 3 m. S. of St. Neots, birthplace of Nicholas Rowe (1674–1718), dramatist and Poet Laureate, who lived chiefly in London.

LITTLEBOURNE, Kent. [1 Hc] Village on the A257, 4 m. E. of Canterbury. Lee Priory, on the E. of the village over the bridge, was rebuilt in the Gothic style for Thomas Barrett, a friend of Horace Walpole, who after a visit in the summer of 1790 wrote to Mary Berry 'I think that if Strawberry were not its parent, it would be jealous'. On Barrett's death in 1803 the ownership of the priory passed through Samuel Egerton Brydges's wife to his eldest son. After his wife's death Brydges lived at the priory from 1810 to 1818, when he went abroad. The printers, Johnson and Warwick, set up a press here to print poems of Breton, Browne, Ralegh, and other Elizabethans, which had been collected by Brydges from many sources. Jane Austen was one of those unimpressed by his novels, but his many bibliographical works have been highly regarded, including *The British Bibliographer* (1810–14), and *Restituta* (1814–16). He became an M.P. in 1812 and was made a baronet in 1814. After alterations to the house, one of the rooms was re-erected at the Victoria and Albert Museum as an example of neo-Gothic architecture.

LITTLE CHART, Kent. [1 Gd] Village off the A20 and the B2077, 5 m. NW. of Ashford. H. E. Bates in his autobiography, *The Vanished World* (1969), *The Blossoming World* (1971), and *The World in Ripeness* (1972), describes how in 1931 he found the barn, which he and his wife converted to The Granary, in a garden made from a wilderness, that was his home until his death in 1974. He wrote here *The Fallow Land* (1932) and *The Poacher* (1935), which, like the later *Love for Lydia* (1952), stem from his youth in the Nene Valley in Northamptonshire, the war novels, which include the first part of *Fair Stood the Wind for France* (1944) written while on leave, *The Purple Plain* (1947), and *The Jacaranda Tree* (1949), also the 'Chaucerian' tales of the Larkin family. He is the author of the short stories written by 'Flying Officer X'.

LITTLE DUCHRAE. See LAURIESTON.

LITTLE DUNHAM, Norf. [4 Fd] Village off the A47, 4 m. NE. of Swaffham. The Revd. John Johnson took his cousin, the poet Cowper, and Mrs. Unwin to Dunham Lodge, a large 18th-c. house in a park, in 1795. They stayed here a short time only before moving to East Dereham.

LITTLE EASTON, Essex. [1 Fa] Village off the A130, 2 m. NW. of Great Dunmow. The road to the church leads beyond the two lakes to The Glebe, the large Georgian house where H. G. Wells lived in the First World War, and where he wrote *Mr. Britling Sees it Through* (1916).

LITTLE GADDESDEN, Herts. [1 Db] Village 5 m. N. of Berkhamsted on the B5406. The house, traditionally the home of John of Gaddesden (d. 1361), is near the war memorial on the green (P) opposite the entrance to Ashridge Park. He was an eminent 14th-c. medical writer, who may have been known to Chaucer. In the Prologue to *The Canterbury Tales* (written c. 1387–1400), the Doctor of Physic refers to him as 'Gatesden'.

LITTLE GIDDING, Cambs. [4 De] Hamlet 7 m. SW. of Norman Cross, off the B660, where Nicholas Ferrar (1592–1637) founded, at the Manor House (gone) in 1625, a family community devoted to prayer and practical works of charity. He was a friend of George Herbert, who sent him the manuscript of his collection of poems before he died. These were published as *The Church* (1633), later becoming known as *The Temple*. The Little Gidding Community worshipped three times a day in the church, which resembles a small college chapel. T. S. Eliot in *Four Quartets* (1944) commemorates the place 'Where prayer has been valid'. Both poets are remembered in the church.

LITTLEHAMPTON, West Sussex. [1 De] S. coast resort at the mouth of the Arun. John Galsworthy often spent working holidays at the Beach Hotel. At Christmas in 1918, when writing *Saint's Progress* (1919), he received the offer of a knighthood. His letter of refusal was somehow delayed and he found his name in the New Year's honours list and had to write again to correct the mistake.

LITTLE WENHAM, Suff. [4 Gf] Small village 6 m. SW. of Ipswich, off the A12 W. of Capel St. Mary. Jane Brewis (*née* Scrope) for whom Skelton wrote *Phylyp Sparowe*, a lamentation on her pet killed by a cat, lived after her marriage in the old moated manor down the narrow lane by the inn. She died in 1514 and her tomb is in the church here (key at Capel St. Mary Vicarage).

LIVERPOOL, Merseyside. [3 Fa] Second seaport of England, on the N. bank of the estuary of the Mersey. The earliest known reference to Liverpool in a dramatic work occurs in *Fair Em, the Miller's Daughter of Manchester: With the Love of William the Conqueror*, a 'pleasant comedie' containing the lines: 'Since fortune hath thus spitefully crost our hope, let us leave this quest and harken after our King, who is at this daie landed at Lirpoole' (c. 1590, anon., though it has been attributed to Shakespeare, who was a member of Lord Strange's company which performed it). Defoe, always ready for new experiences in his travels, describes his arrival by ferry from the Wirral:

You land on the flat shore on the other Side, and must be content to ride thro' the water for some length, not on Horseback, but on the shoulders of some Lancashire Clown, who comes knee-deep to the Boat's side, to truss one up; and then runs away more nimbly than one desires to ride, unless his Trot were easier.

Having arrived dryshod, he was favourably impressed with all he saw, noting not only the 'prodigious Increase of Trade' but also that 'there is no town in England, except London, that can equal Liverpoole for the Fineness of the Streets and Beauty of the Buildings' (*A Tour through the Whole Island of Great Britain*, 1724–7).

William Roscoe, author of *The Life of Lorenzo de' Medici* (1795) and *The Life and Pontificate of Leo the Tenth* (1805), as well as poems, including the piece for children, *The Butterfly's Ball and the Grasshopper's Feast* (1807), was born (8 Mar. 1753) in Mount Pleasant (the subject of another poem), and later lived at 51 Lord St., Islington, Alberton Hall, and Lodge Lane, where he died.

Another native was Mrs. Felicia Dorothea Hemans (*née* Browne), the daughter of a merchant, who began writing poetry at an early age and achieved great popularity in her day. She was born (25 Sept. 1793) at 118 Duke St. (P) and lived there until the family moved to N. Wales c. 1800. She had already made her name as a poet (*The Forest Sanctuary*, 1826, was one of her best works) when she returned to Liverpool in 1827 to further the education of her five sons (her husband having settled permanently abroad). She lived in a Georgian house (demolished 1958) on the N. side of Wavertree High St., near the junction of Sandown Lane, leaving finally for Dublin in 1831.

Hazlitt briefly visited Liverpool in 1790 and, while staying with a Mrs. Tracy, the wife of a West India merchant, saw his first play, *Love in Many Masks*, with the farce, *No Song, No Supper*, and wrote his first drama criticism in a letter to his father. In 1801 De Quincey stayed with his mother at Mrs. Best's Cottage, Everton (at that time a pleasant little village), and again in 1803, when he first wrote to Wordsworth (31 May), a letter of homage and praise of *Lyrical Ballads*, to which the latter replied briefly and self-deprecatingly (though he wrote again, more fully, the following year when De Quincey was at Oxford). Liverpool fascinated De Quincey by its concourse of strangers from overseas: he called it 'the many-languaged town'.

Washington Irving's literary connection with Liverpool was tenuous, but it could be claimed that a business failure there c. 1818 led to the writing of 'Rip Van Winkle' (*The Sketch-Book*, 1820). Irving had joined his brother in the Goree Arcade as a merchant, but the venture failed and he sank into acute depression, which was relieved only by a visit to his brother-in-law at Birmingham (q.v.), where he took to writing. Arthur Hugh Clough was born (1 Jan. 1819) at 9 Rodney St. (P), the son of a cotton merchant, but went to America with his family at the age of 4. He returned to England to be educated at Rugby and Oxford, and was back in Liverpool in 1836 for a time, living at 51 Vine St.

When William Cobbett returned in November 1819 from his second visit to America he caused great excitement at the Custom House by having the bones of Tom Paine in his luggage. He had exhumed these from a patch of unconsecrated ground near New York, where Paine had been buried (1809), with the intention, advertised in the *Political Register*, of raising money to build a mausoleum to house them in England as an object of pilgrimage, but instead of subscriptions he received only ridicule, as in Byron's lines:

> In digging up your bones, Tom Paine,
> Will. Cobbett has done well;
> You visit him on earth again,
> He'll visit you in hell.

Transatlantic visitors continued to come and go throughout the 19th c. Ralph Waldo Emerson, American philosopher and poet came (1848) to lecture on his second visit to England. His six lectures on 'Representative Men', given at the Mount St. Mechanics Institute, were published in 1850. Herman Melville, American writer of stories of the sea, stayed here for a time in 1837 when a cabin boy on a sailing ship, drawing on his experiences later in his novel *Redburn* (1849). He was back again in 1856 for 10 days, *en route* for Constantinople, when he stayed at the White Bear Hotel, Dale St., and visited Nathaniel Hawthorne, who was U.S. Consul (1853–7). In *Our Old Home* (1863) Hawthorne describes the Consulate, which he detested, as

located in Washington Buildings, (a shabby and smoke-stained edifice of four stories high, thus illustriously named in honour of our national establishment) at the lower corner of Brunswick St., contiguous to the Goree Arcade, and in the neighbourhood of some of the oldest docks.

His landlady, Mrs. Blodget, lived at 153 (formerly 133) Duke St. Mrs. Harriet Beecher Stowe came on a visit in 1853 and stayed with Mr. Cropper, a brother-in-law of Matthew Arnold, at Dingle Bank—'a beautiful little retreat on the banks of the Mersey'.

Dickens was a frequent visitor to the city. He first came in 1838 with Hablot K. Browne ('Phiz', his illustrator), whose son was an oculist in Rodney St. At one time Dickens enrolled as a special constable in order to investigate the 'home industry' of separating the sailors from their money. This, and a description of a workhouse he visited (demolished), are recorded in *The Uncommercial Traveller* (1860). He appeared as an actor in benefit performances at various premises, including the Theatre Royal (now the Union Gold Store, Williamson Sq.), and over the years, until almost the end of his life, he gave readings of his works to packed houses in the Philharmonic Hall, St. George Hall Concert Room, the Theatre Royal, and elsewhere. *Nicholas Nickleby* (1839) and *Martin Chuzzlewit* (1844) have references to a famous Liverpool character, Sarah Biffin, an armless artist who painted miniatures with a brush in her mouth (she was not legless, as Dickens believed). The Scottish-born novelist Mrs. Margaret Oliphant spent her adolescence in Liverpool, where her father was a Customs official. Her first novel, *Passages in the Life of Mrs. Margaret Maitland* (1849), was written here. Augustine Birrell, critic and essayist, was born (1850) in Wavertree, the son of a Baptist minister, but the house is not recorded. Richard Le Gallienne was born (1866) at 55 Prescot St. and later moved with his family to Birkenhead. According to one of his publishers 'he looked more like a poet than any man has ever looked before or since'.

Matthew Arnold was in Liverpool in 1888 to meet his daughter on her return from the U.S., when he died suddenly of a heart attack, but there are different accounts of the place and manner of his death: in one it was thought that he collapsed as he was running to catch a tram to the landing-stage, where he was to meet his daughter's ship; in another that he strained his heart by jumping over a gate or fence while staying with his brother-in-law at Dingle Bank and died suddenly on his way back from church, but it seems that records are confused. The primary school at Dingle Lane is called after him.

John Masefield was a cadet (1891-4) on the training ship *Conway* (see the description of Liverpool in his semi-autobiographical

New Chum, 1942). He wrote many poems connected with Liverpool, among them 'The Valediction (Liverpool Docks)' (1902); 'The Wanderer of Liverpool' (about a four-masted 3,000-ton barque laid down in 1890) and 'A Masque of Liverpool' (both 1930); and a poem to mark the opening of the cathedral's new doors in 1949 (he had a stall in the cathedral as a member of the College of Counsel). In 1911 the production of John Galsworthy's play *Strife* at Kelly's Theatre (destroyed 1941) led to the emergence of the Liverpool Playhouse, the oldest repertory theatre in the country. When George Orwell was touring in the N. of England in 1935, gathering material for *The Road to Wigan Pier* (1937), he was interested to see some blocks of workers' flats in corporation housing estates (St. Andrew's Gardens, Brownlow Hill), which struck him as being modelled on the contemporary pioneer flats in Vienna.

Two distinguished men of letters had chairs at the University: A. C. Bradley, remembered chiefly as a Shakesperian scholar (*Shakespearean Tragedy*, 1904), was Liverpool's first Professor of Literature and History (1882-9), and Sir James Frazer, author of *The Golden Bough* (1890-1915), was Professor of Social Anthropology (1907-22). Lytton Strachey was an undergraduate (1897-9), lodging at 80 Rodney St., but was lonely and unhappily self-conscious about his appearance—he wanted to be a superman, but felt he was a freak. Professor Walter Raleigh, under whom he studied English Literature, recommended him to Trinity College, Cambridge, as a student of remarkable distinction.

The Brown, Picton, and Hornby Libraries, containing together more than 200,000 volumes, are housed in the Public Library (largely rebuilt since the Second World War) in William Brown St. The Hornby Library has a fine autograph collection, including poems by Johnson and Cowper. The Walker Art Gallery next door has a link with D. H. Lawrence. He corresponded at one time with a Liverpool girl called Blanche Jennings, who, in return for a photograph of himself, sent him a reproduction of Maurice Greiffenhagen's *The Idyll*, which belongs to the gallery. The picture is discussed in *The White Peacock* (1911).

Liverpool has had two M.P.s who were also literary figures: Sir Francis Bacon (1588-92) and William Roscoe (1806-7).

LLANARMON DYFFRYN CEIRIOG, Clwyd.
[3 Fc] Quiet little village in the depths of
the Berwyn Mountains, *c.* 6 m. SW. of
Llangollen, at the end of the B4500. John
Ceiriog Hughes (1832–87), the lyric writer
who is commemorated at Glyn Ceiriog
(q.v.), was born at Penybryn (P), a long,
low farmhouse, high above the bridge.

LLANDAFF, South Glamorgan. [2 Fb] Cathedral town 2¼ m. NW. of Cardiff, of which it
is practically a suburb. Geoffrey of Monmouth (1100?–54), chronicler and author
of *Historia Regum Britanniae* (first printed
1508), the principal source of the stories of
King Arthur and the Knights of the Round
Table, was made archdeacon of the 12th-c.
cathedral *c.* 1140. He was appointed Bishop
of St. Asaph in 1152, but died at Llandaff
before entering his diocese.

Many of the windows and decorations in
the cathedral are Pre-Raphaelite, and Swinburne, Burne-Jones, and William Morris and
his wife were models for the figures in the
Rossetti Triptych (1856–64), illustrating the
Seed of David.

LLANDOVERY, Dyfed. [3 Df] Market town
on the A40, 13 m. NE. of Llandeilo, in the
Vale of Towy. George Borrow stayed at the
Castle Hotel on his travels through Wales,
recounted in *Wild Wales* (1862), and his
four-poster bed in the room named after him
is still in use.

LLANDUDNO, Gwynedd. [3 Da] Popular
seaside resort in N. Wales on the A496 and
the A546. When Matthew Arnold took his
family there for a holiday in 1864 he found
inspiration for his essay *On the Study of
Celtic Literature* (1864). 'All interests are
here', he wrote, '–Celts, Romans, Saxons,
Druidism, Middle Ages, Caer, Castle, Cromlech, Abbey,–and this glorious sea and
mountains with it all.' He stayed at 10 St.
George's Cres. (4–24 Aug.), his visit coincid-
ing with the Eisteddfod, which he describes
in the essay. About the same time C. L.
Dodgson ('Lewis Carroll') is believed to have
visited Dean Liddell of Christ Church, Oxford,
at his summer residence, Pen Morfa, on the
West Shore, now part of the Gogarth Abbey
Hotel. Sir William Richmond (1842–1921),
whose portrait of the three Liddell daughters,
The Three Graces, hangs in the Tate Gallery,
said that part of *Alice in Wonderland* (1865)

was written at Pen Morfa and read aloud in
the evenings to the family and guests including M. Arnold and Gladstone. Dodgson
is commemorated by a statue of the White
Rabbit at the end of the Model Yacht Pond
and by a marble font, given by children, in
the Church of Our Saviour.

LLANFYNYDD, Dyfed. [3 Df] Village on a
tributary of the Towy, *c.* 5 m. NW. of
Llandeilo, approached by narrow twisting
roads through wooded country. John Dyer,
who later lived at Aberglasney House,
Llangathen, was born (1699) here and
baptized in the parish church.

LLANGATHEN, Dyfed. [3 Df] Village in the
Vale of the Towy, off the A40 *c.* 3 m. W.
of Llandeilo. Aberglasney House, below the
village, was the home of the 18th-c. poet
John Dyer, whose poem *Grongar Hill* (1726)
celebrates the near-by hill and the surrounding country seen from the summit.
The landmarks in the poem can be recognized today and one can still

> Hear the thrush, while all is still
> Within the groves of Grongar Hill,

but the blackthorn tree under which Dyer
wrote, pictured in the frontispiece to the
1941 edition, has disappeared. The house,
probably built around portions of a 16th-c.
mansion belonging to Bishop Anthony Rudd
of St. David's, has long been derelict. It may
be visited by permission of the owner of
Aberglasney Farm.

LLANGOLLEN, Clwyd. [3 Fb] Picturesque
resort in the valley of the Dee, on the A5.
Hazlitt describes his visit to 'this delightful
spot' in the essay 'On Going a Journey' in
Table-Talk (1821–2), when he dined at the
inn on his birthday (10 Apr. 1798) off a
bottle of sherry and a cold chicken. For
50 years it was the home of the eccentric
'Ladies of Llangollen', Lady Eleanor Butler
(1739–1829) and the Hon. Sarah Ponsonby
(1755–1831), who lived at Plas Newydd,[1]
an elaborately decorated house standing in
extensive grounds on the hillside above the
town. They were ardent admirers of Rousseau and read *La Nouvelle Héloïse* aloud, but
their literary interests also ranged widely
and they constantly sought to 'improve'
themselves. Among their many visitors were
Southey and his wife and Hannah More and
her sister Patty in 1811, Wordsworth (who

wrote a sonnet in the grounds) in 1824, and Sir Walter Scott and his son-in-law John Lockhart in 1825. Lockhart, writing to his wife Sophia, says

'your papa was waylaid by the celebrated 'Ladies', ... who having been one or both crossed in love, foreswore all dreams of matrimony in the heyday of youth, beauty, and fashion, and selected this charming spot for the repose of their now time-honoured virginity.

Borrow was too late to see the Ladies, but was shown round the house in 1854 by a guide who remembered them well. Browning spent the autumn of 1886 at the Hand Hotel with his sister Sarianna (who was convalescing), to be near his old friends Sir Theodore and Lady Martin of Bryntisilio, 3 m. away. Sir Theodore had said that 'a word to the hostess of the Hand Hotel was scarcely needed to secure every attention for the poet and his sister, for she was one of his readers'.

[1] Open May–Sept.: Mon.–Sat. 10.30 a.m.–7.30 p.m.; Sun. 11 a.m.–4 p.m.

LLANGUNNOR, Dyfed. [3 Cf] Scattered parish *c.* 1 m. E. of Carmarthen, on the B4300. Richard Steele retired here and lived at a farmhouse called Ty-Gwyn (or White House), a property belonging to his wife's family on the slope of the hill. From here he could look up the Towy Valley to the distant view of Grongar Hill, celebrated by his friend John Dyer. *The Conscious Lovers* is traditionally supposed to have been written, at least in part, in an arbour in the orchard and first acted at Ty-Gwyn by friends of Steele. The house was demolished in the early 19th c., but a farmhouse of the same name occupies the site. The little church on the top of the hill commemorates Steele in an eloquent stone tablet above the font.

Sir Lewis Morris, a 19th-c. poet, born at Carmarthen, is buried in the churchyard according to his wish:

Let me at last be laid
On that hillside I know, which scans the vale,
Beneath the thick yew's shade
For shelter, when the rains and winds prevail.

LLANSANTFFRAED, Powys. [3 Ef] Village on the A40, 6 m. SE. of Brecon. Henry Vaughan was born (1621) in the parish at a house called Newton (sometimes Newton-by-Usk; in Welsh Trenewydd), near Sceth-

rog. The present-day Newton Farm was probably built out of the ruins and on the site of his birthplace. This was his life-long home, except for the years (1632–8) at Oxford and London, and probably a short period of soldiering, and from here he practised medicine both locally and further afield. In *Silex Scintillans* (1650; 1655), his collection of religious and mystical poetry, he calls himself 'Silurist', by association with his beloved country of Brecon, anciently inhabited by the Silures tribe. He is buried outside the E. wall of the church, with a tombstone bearing a Latin epitaph composed by himself. The church (rebuilt in the 19th c.) has a memorial tablet. Siegfried Sassoon writes movingly in 'At the Grave of Henry Vaughan' (*Collected Poems 1908–1956*)

Here sleeps the Silurist; the loved physician;
The face that left no portraiture behind;
· · ·
Here faith and mercy, wisdom and humility
(Whose influence shall prevail for evermore)
Shine. And this lowly grave tells Heaven's tranquillity.

LLANTHONY, Gwent. [3 Ff] Small village in the Honddu Valley, 9 m. N. of Abergavenny, reached by turning off the A465 at Llanvihangel Crucorney. The ruined Augustinian priory, now in the care of the Department of the Environment, was bought *c.* 1807 by Walter Savage Landor, who planned to develop the estate and live as a model country gentleman. He was refused permission to restore the priory, but managed to live in the building occupying the W. range, now a hotel. He married Julia Thuillier in 1811 and they frequently entertained Southey and his wife, but in 1814, having quarrelled with his neighbours and the country people, Landor left Llanthony and his mother took over the management of the estate.

LLANTYSILIO, Clwyd. [3 Fb] Small village off the A5, 2 m. NW. of Llangollen (q.v.). The church, in the fields above the river, has a brass tablet on the S. wall in memory of Browning, who, though not usually a regular churchgoer, attended services here during his stay at Llangollen in 1886.

LLAREGYB. See LAUGHARNE.

LOCH KATRINE. See TROSSACHS and ELLEN'S ISLE.

LOCHLEA, Ayrs. (Strathclyde). [6 Dd] Farm 2½ m. NW. of Mauchline, off the B744, where Burns and his brothers and sisters lived with their parents from 1777 to their father's death in 1784. Some of the poems and songs he wrote here were collected in *Poems Chiefly in the Scottish Dialect* (1786). Burns left to study flax dressing in 1781 as the farm could not provide a living for so many people, and on his return he found his father gravely ill and the farm failing.

LOCH LEVEN CASTLE, Kinross. (Central). [6 Fc] Ruined 14th-c. castle on an island in the loch. Mary Queen of Scots was imprisoned here in 1567 and escaped in 1568. Scott's novel *The Abbot* (1820) is based on this episode and the battle which followed.

LOGIEALMOND (pr. Lōgīahmond), Perths. (Tayside). [6 Eb] District by the River Almond, NW. of Perth. John Watson, Free Church minister here (1875–7), who wrote as 'Ian Maclaren', calls the area 'Drumtochty' in his stories of rural life, *Beside the Bonnie Brier Bush* (1894). These tales in the Kailyard tradition were popular in America and in translation on the Continent.

LONDON. [10, 11] The capital of the United Kingdom (situated on the tidal Thames), consisting, since 1965, of an area of 610 sq. m., known as Greater London, and including parts of Essex, Kent, Surrey, Hertfordshire, and most of the former county of Middlesex. The historic centre from which the great metropolis has grown is the City of London, known as 'the square mile', which maintains its independence under the control of the Corporation entitled 'The Mayor and Commonalty and the Citizens of the City of London'. The City, established by the Romans in A.D. 43 as Londinium and described by Tacitus as 'a busy emporium for trade and traders', remained an outpost of the Roman Empire for nearly 400 years, until the Romans finally left Britain. During the Middle Ages it began to expand beyond the City walls and by the 16th c. men of wealth and influence were building great houses on the river banks all the way to the village of Westminster, where the Court was, and to quiet country places further out.

The literary associations of London from Chaucer's time to the 20th c. are so dense that only a selection can be given here. These are listed alphabetically under the names of recognizable areas, such as Chelsea or Highgate, and references from the index of authors indicate the relevant headings. These areas are shown on two maps: one for the whole of Greater London (11) and the other for central London (10).

Literary guides to London are listed in the selective bibliography at the end of the book. As well as guides to particular areas (such as the City, Hampstead, etc.), George G. Williams's *Guide to Literary London* (1973) and Geoffrey Fletcher's *Pocket Guide to Dickens* (1976) are useful general guides.

Adelphi [10 Gc], area S. of the Strand developed (1768–74) by the Adam brothers. **Adelphi Ter.** (rebuilt 1938, P), which overlooked the river, was the home of Garrick, the actor-manager, who lived at no. 5, the centre house, until his death in 1779. He was visited here by Dr. Johnson and other members of the Literary Club and by the young Hannah More. Thomas Hardy was employed (1862–7) in an architect's office at no. 8, where he found the marble fireplaces useful to make quick sketches on. Bernard Shaw lived from 1899, soon after his marriage, until 1927 at his wife's flat at no. 10. *Man and Superman* (1903) and *Major Barbara* (1905) were written here. After 1906 he divided his time between this apartment and his house at Ayot St. Lawrence (q.v.).

Thomas Hood, who married his friend John Reynolds's sister Jane in 1825, moved 2 years later to 2 **Robert St.** (P), their first real home together. Their friend Charles Lamb wrote 'On an Infant Dying as soon as Born' about their daughter.

> Riddle of destiny, who can show
> What thy short visit meant, or know
> What thy errand here below.

The plaque on nos. 1–3 (rebuilt) also commemorates John Galsworthy, who lived here from 1912 to 1918, and J. M. Barrie, who had an apartment on the top floor. It was here, in 1919, that Barrie received the adult Daisy Ashford, who as a child of 9 had written *The Young Visiters*, for which her publisher then hoped Barrie would write a foreword. His appreciation of the child's unerring eye for the quirks of her characters led some people to think he, himself, was the author.

Anerley [11 Ee], district in the SE. Walter de la Mare lived (1899–1908) at 195 **Mackenzie Rd.** when working in London for an oil company. He wrote here *Songs of Childhood* (1902) and a novel *Henry Brocken* (1904) under the name 'Walter Ramal'. He then lived (1908–12) in **Worbeck Rd.** where he wrote more novels and *The Listeners and Other Poems* (1912), which combines images of dreams and childhood. From 1912 to 1925 he lived at 14 **Thornsett Rd.**, where he published two other collections of poems and *Memoirs of a Midget* (1921), the novel that won (1922) the James Tait Black Memorial Prize.

Artillery Row. See Finsbury.

Arundel House. See Highgate.

Astley's Amphitheatre. See Lambeth.

Barnes [11 Cd, Dd], district to the SW. Abraham Cowley lived (1663–5) in the old mansion where Walsingham had entertained Queen Elizabeth I, in **Barn Elms Park.** Philip Sidney married Walsingham's daughter Frances in 1583 and lived here until he sailed for the Netherlands (1585). Jacob Tonson (1656–1736), publisher of Addison and Steele, had a house (gone) in the park where he entertained the Kit-Cat Club, whose members also included Congreve and Vanbrugh, when he was its secretary and moving spirit. The promenade in the park, fashionable in the 17th and 18th cc. and mentioned by Congreve in *Love for Love* (1695) was also the scene of duels.

Fielding lived (1748–53) in failing health at Milburne House (altered) on **Barnes Green.** Matthew Lewis, nicknamed 'Monk' from his successful Gothic novel, bought in 1798 Hermitage Cottage (gone) in Goodenough's Lane (site now at the head of **Nassau Rd.** near the church). He was living there in 1801 and he owned the cottage throughout his life but was not a permanent resident.

William Cobbett, who leased (1828–30) the home farm on the Barn Elms estate, continued to edit his *Weekly Political Register* while he was living there, and wrote *Advice to Young Men* (1830).

Battersea [11 Dd], district to the S. William Blake married Catherine Boucher, daughter of a market gardener in Battersea,

at the parish church in 1772. G. A. Henty, whose roving life as a war correspondent led him over many of the scenes he used in his adventure stories, lived at 33 **Lavender Gdns.** (P). His many stories include *With Clive in India* (1884), *With Moore at Corunna* (1898), and *With Buller in Natal* (1901). Edward Thomas and his wife lodged at 61 **Shelgate St.** (P) for a short time in 1900 before moving into the country at Bearsted (q.v.). *The Happy-Go-Lucky Morgans* (1913), his only novel, is partly set in the area.

Bayswater [10 Ac, Bc, Cc, Dc], district NW. of Hyde Park. Sir James Barrie lived (1902–9) at 100 **Bayswater Rd.** (P), one of a pair of pleasant Regency houses standing in their own gardens above the main road, on the corner of Leinster Ter. It was here that he wrote the plays *Peter Pan* (1904; also partly written at Farnham, q.v.) and *What Every Woman Knows* (1908).

In **Hyde Park Pl.**, Bayswater Rd., behind a group of flats (St. George's Fields) is a disused graveyard, now the playground of the Hyde Park Nursery School. This was the burial place of Laurence Sterne, whose bones were twice disturbed: the first time apparently by body-snatchers for dissection purposes, but recognized and re-interred; second time (1969) removed more reverently, by the Sterne Trust for re-burial at Coxwold (q.v.). Ann Radcliffe, author of Gothic novels, was buried here (1823) and her tombstone is one of those lining the walls.

Lytton Strachey came at the age of 4 to 69 **Lancaster Gate**, just N. of the Lancaster Gate entrance to Kensington Gdns., when his parents moved from Clapham Common in 1884. The house, now part of Douglas House (nos. 66–71), was his home for the next 25 years.

Ivy Compton-Burnett lived (1916–29) at 59 **Leinster Sq.**, where she wrote *Pastors and Masters* (1925) and *Brothers and Sisters* (1929), set between 1885 and 1910.

Alice Meynell was a daughter of T. J. Thompson, a friend of Dickens, who visited the family in Italy where she spent her childhood. She lived (1890–1905) at 47 **Palace Ct.** (P) and her first volume of poems was published before her marriage to Wilfrid Meynell in 1877. The Meynells rescued Francis Thompson from destitution and were friends of Meredith and Coventry

Patmore. Alice Meynell published three volumes of poems here and the essays, *The Rhythm of Life* (1893), *The Colour of Life* (1896), and *The Spirit of Peace* (1898).

In 1849 Harriet Martineau, then highly esteemed for her novel *Deerbrook* (1839), was staying at 17 **Westbourne St.** She mentions in her *Autobiography* (1877) receiving a copy of *Shirley* (1849) and a short letter from the new author 'Currer Bell' hoping that a meeting might be arranged. Charlotte Brontë's usual nervousness had been increased when she had been introduced to Thackeray at her publisher's house, 4 **Westbourne Pl.** (gone), where she was staying, but her meeting with Harriet Martineau passed without any awkwardness, and she had easily distinguished her from the other women present, by her ear-trumpet. It was on this visit to London, where she met again a family she had known in Brussels, that the idea came for her next novel *Villette* (1853).

Beckenham. See Bromley.

Belgravia [10 Dd, De, Ee], district between Buckingham Palace Rd. and Knightsbridge. Margaret Oliphant, novelist and biographer, spent her last years at 85 **Cadogan Pl.**, on the E. side of Sloane St. Her *Autobiography* published posthumously (1899), describes her efforts to provide an education for her own and her brother's children by writing novels.

Dickens lived at 1 **Chester Row** in 1846, the year he founded, and was for a short time the editor of, *The Daily News*.

Shelley's second wife, Mary (*née* Godwin), spent her last years at 24 **Chester Sq.**, and died there in 1851. Matthew Arnold lived at no. 2 (P) for 10 years until 1868. *Schools and Universities on the Continent* (1868) was written after visits made in connection with his post as Inspector of Schools (1851–83). *New Poems* (1867) contains 'Rugby Chapel', and 'Thyrsis' in memory of Arthur Hugh Clough, who died in Florence in 1861.

Algernon Charles Swinburne was born at 7 **Chester St.** in 1837.

Edward Trelawny, author of *Adventures of a Younger Son*, and *Records of Shelley, Byron, and the Author* (1858), lived at 17 **Eaton Sq.** during 1838. Sir W. S. Gilbert lived (1907–11) at no. 90 and, after a successful series of operas in collaboration with Sir Arthur Sullivan, wrote *Fallen Fairies* (1909) with

Edward German and a serious sketch *The Hooligans* (1911).

George Meredith lived (1849) at 153 **Ebury St.** (gone). George Moore lived from 1911 to his death in 1933 at no. 121 (P). He was visited here by many literary friends including Yeats and Shaw. He wrote the novels *The Brook Kerith* (1916) and *Ulick and Soracha* (1924) here, also the autobiographical *Hail and Farewell* and *Conversations in Ebury St.* Victoria Sackville-West and her husband Harold Nicolson lived for a short time at no. 182 (gone) in the 1920s.

No. 17 **Gerald Rd.** was the London home of Noël Coward from the mid 1930s to the mid 1950s. As well as his earlier plays, which caught the mood of the 1920s, Coward wrote *Cavalcade* (1931), and *This Happy Breed* (1943), whose patriotism was popular in wartime, and two volumes of autobiography, *Present Indicative* (1937) and *Future Indefinite* (1954).

Swinburne lived at 18 **Grosvenor Pl.** for a short time (1860–1) while working on *The Queen Mother. Rosamond. Two Plays* (1861) (chiefly written at Oxford). Mrs. Humphry Ward lived (1891–1919) at no. 25, while engaged in her many philanthropic works. Her novels were written in the country.

Walter Bagehot, editor of *The Economist* from 1860, lived at 12 **Upper Belgrave St.** (P) for many years. *Literary Studies* was a posthumous collection of articles which had appeared first in the *National Review*.

Swinburne lived at 36 **Wilton Cres.** in 1865 when *Atalanta in Calydon*, a drama with Greek-style choruses, and *Chastelard*, a romantic drama about Mary, Queen of Scots, were published.

Bethnal Green [11 Fc], a parish in the East End. This former village just outside London was the home of the heroine of the ballad 'The Blind Beggar's Daughter of Bednall-Green'. Israel Zangwill, journalist, novelist, and playwright, prominent in Jewish cultural circles, is commemorated by a plaque at 288 **Old Ford Rd.** He published his first novel in 1881. *Children of the Ghetto* (1892), written at the invitation of the Jewish Publication Society of America, and dramatized by him in 1899, was followed by other humorous and realistic stories of Jewish life. His play *The Melting Pot* (1908) is about immigrants to America. He was a friend of Jerome K. Jerome and W. W. Jacobs.

Bexleyheath [11 Hd], district to the SE. From 1860 to 1865 William Morris lived at The Red House[1] in **Red House Lane**, off Upton Rd., formerly in the village of Upton in Kent. Morris met the architect Philip Webb, who designed the house, when he himself was studying to be an architect in Oxford. The two, who were lifelong friends, became partners in a firm to establish good decoration and design as a fine art. The only poetry Morris wrote here was the unfinished 'Scenes from the Fall of Troy'.

[1] Open first Sat. and Sun. each month 2.30–4.30 p.m.

Blackheath [11 Fd], district to the SE. Nathaniel Hawthorne, who gives an account of his Puritan ancestors in the introduction to *The Scarlet Letter* (1850), lived at 4 **Pond Rd.** (P) during his visit in 1856. He describes Blackheath in 'A London Suburb' in *Our Old Home* (1863).

In the spring of 1928 Malcolm Lowry's father made him an allowance of £7 a week and found him a room at 5 **Woodville Rd.** Lowry started writing *Ultramarine* (1933) here.

Bloomsbury [10 Ea, Fa, Fb, Ga, Gb], district N. of St. Giles High St., between the City and Marylebone. When Carlyle and his wife first came to London they lodged (1831–2) at 33 (formerly 4) **Ampton St.** (P), on the E. side of Gray's Inn Rd.

Sir Anthony Hope Hawkins (author, as 'Anthony Hope', of *The Prisoner of Zenda*, 1894) lived at 41 **Bedford Sq.** from 1903 to 1917.

Dr. Peter Mark Roget, physician and scholar, came to London in 1808 and lived at 39 **Bernard St.** (gone) until 1843. He did not begin to devote his time to the compilation of the *Thesaurus* (his best-known work) until he retired from medical practice in 1840. Two of his autograph letters, dated 4 June 1825 and 23 May 1859, can be seen at the Holborn Central Library in Theobald's Rd.

The British Museum[1] (built 1823–1938 on the site of Montagu House), main entrance in Great Russell St., houses in its many galleries, as well as Greek, Oriental, and other Antiquities, the Reference Library, now part of the copyright national library of the United Kingdom, the British Library (1973).

The museum, founded in 1753 and opened in Montagu House (gone) in 1759, had as its nucleus the collection of Sir Hans Sloane and the Cottonian Library, state papers and other manuscripts, collected by Sir Robert Bruce Cotton (d. 1631) and presented to the nation by his grandson in 1702. The Harleian Manuscripts, added in 1754, were the collections of the 1st and 2nd Earls of Oxford. George II's and George III's bequests are housed in the King's Library. Garrick donated the statue of Shakespeare by Roubiliac in this gallery. Keats wrote a sonnet on the Elgin Marbles, the sculptures from Athens which Robert Haydon persuaded the nation to buy for the museum. Keats's 'Ode on a Grecian Urn' was also written after he had seen the sculptures. The E. wing contains the Grenville Library bequeathed by Thomas Grenville (d. 1846), and the large collection of early printed books and manuscripts. Treasures displayed in the galleries include the manuscripts *Beowulf* (*c.* 1000), the *Winchester Psalter* (*c.* 1060), an 11th-c. *Anglo-Saxon Chronicle*, *Booke of Sir Thomas More*, 15th-c. *Froissart's Chronicles*, 15th-c. *The Canterbury Tales*, the first folio edition of Shakespeare's plays (1623), and the 15th-c. manuscript of Malory's *Le Morte Darthur*, predating Caxton's edition, bought from Winchester College in 1976. Holograph letters, poems, and manuscripts of more recent works are also displayed.

Richard Garnett was an official here from 1875 to 1899, and Laurence Binyon for 40 years until his retirement in 1933. Binyon's *Collected Poems* (two vols. 1931) contains 'For the Fallen', first published in *The Times* on 21 September 1914, by which he is best remembered. Lines from the poem are carved on the wall at the entrance to the museum as a war memorial to the staff.

Brunswick Sq., N. of Guildford St. and now mainly occupied by University buildings, was the home of Virginia Stephen shortly before her marriage to Leonard Woolf. She and her brother Adrian moved in 1911 into no. 38 (gone), a 4-storeyed house which they shared with J. M. Keynes, Duncan Grant, and Leonard Woolf. She and Leonard left when they married in 1912. Their friend E. M. Forster came here later and lived at no. 26 from 1929 to 1939.

Isabella, in Jane Austen's *Emma* (1816), gives a spirited defence of the healthiness of Brunswick Sq., after her father's complaint of the general sickliness and bad air of the capital.

> Our part of London is so very superior to most others. You must not confound us with London in general, my dear sir. The neighbourhood of Brunswick Square is very different from all the rest. We are so very airy. I should be unwilling, I own, to live in any other part of the town; there is hardly any other that I could be satisfied to have my children in; but we are so remarkably airy. Mr. Wingfield thinks the vicinity of Brunswick Square decidedly the most favourable as to air.

George Gissing lived at 22 **Colville Pl.**, near the S. end of Tottenham Court Rd., from January to September 1878. His days of poverty and hardship here are described in *The Private Papers of Henry Ryecroft* (1903).

Thackeray brought his young wife to live at 13 **Coram St.** (then Great Coram St.), which runs from Woburn Pl. to Brunswick Sq., in 1837 and it was here that his first child, Anne Isabella, was born. After the birth of a third child, in 1840, Mrs. Thackeray suffered a mental breakdown from which she never recovered and a few years later Thackeray gave up the house. Mr. Todd, the junior partner in the firm of Osborne & Todd in *Vanity Fair*, lived in Great Coram St.

In 1896 to 1906 Dorothy Richardson had a top-floor room at a lodging house kept by a Mrs. Baker at 7 **Endsleigh St.** She was working as the assistant to a Harley St. dentist and in her spare time reading at the British Museum. She started to write reviews and was introduced to H. G. Wells after a chance meeting with his wife, who had been a school friend of hers. She came back to a room here from 1907 to 1911. The young Jewish friend who became her fiancé for a short time becomes Michael in *Pilgrimage* (1915–38), her long autobiographical novel, begun after she left Endsleigh St., which she calls Tansley St.

Fitzroy Sq., off Fitzroy St. a little S. of Euston Rd., is now a well-cared-for pedestrian precinct. No. 39 (PP) was the home of Bernard Shaw from 1887, when he moved in with his mother from 36 Osnaburgh St., to 1898, when he married Charlotte Payne-Townshend. He was music and drama critic for several papers, writer of political and economic tracts for the Fabian Society, which he had joined in 1884, and the author of several unsuccessful novels, when

in 1892 he began to make his name as a dramatist with the production of *Widowers' Houses*, written in collaboration with William Archer, his friend and neighbour at no. 27. This play was followed by *Mrs. Warren's Profession* (1893), *Arms and the Man* (1894), and *Candida* (1894). In May 1898, when he was suffering from a foot injury and general debilitation, he received a visit from Charlotte Payne-Townshend, the fellow-Fabian whom he had first met at the house of Sidney and Beatrice Webb in 1896 and whom he gradually became deeply attached to. Charlotte, his 'green-eyed Irish millionairess', who had called at Beatrice Webb's suggestion, was shocked at his poor state of health and invited him to her home at Haslemere to be looked after. Shaw liked the idea but considered it outside the bounds of propriety, so he promptly arranged for their marriage, which took place on 1 June at the Strand Register Office, he still hobbling on crutches. He was restored to health and, after visits to Surrey and Cornwall and a Mediterranean cruise, he settled at 10 Adelphi Ter. (see Adelphi) for the next 28 years.

Virginia Woolf (*née* Stephen) lived at no. 29 with her brother Adrian from 1907 to 1911, when her sister Vanessa, married to Clive Bell, took over their former family house at 46 Gordon Sq. Virginia and Adrian began to entertain and to revive the 'Thursday evenings' started by Thoby Stephen and interrupted by his untimely death. Their circle of friends expanded to include Cambridge contemporaries of Thoby's and by the end of 1907 they had embarked on regular Friday evening readings—of authors ranging from the Restoration dramatists and Shakespeare to Swinburne and Ibsen. In 1909 Lytton Strachey proposed to Virginia Stephen and was accepted. But the engagement was short-lived and was broken to the relief of both parties. When their lease expired Virginia and Adrian moved to 38 Brunswick Sq.

Gordon Sq., in the heart of London University buildings, was once the centre of the 'Bloomsbury Group', whose members lived in or near the Square in the early 20th c. The prime movers of the Group were the children of Sir Leslie Stephen, Thoby (who died young), Vanessa and her husband Clive Bell, Virginia and her husband Leonard Woolf, their brother Adrian, and their friends

Lytton Strachey, E. M. Forster, Roger Fry, J. M. Keynes the economist, and G. E. Moore the philosopher, among many others in the world of art and letters who met 'for the pleasures of human intercourse and the enjoyment of beautiful objects'. Their headquarters was at no. 46, which became the home of the Stephen brothers and sisters in 1905 after the death of their father. The Thursday evening 'at homes', which soon became an institution, were started by Thoby, and his friend Leonard Woolf was one of the first to be invited. Others who soon became regulars included Clive Bell, Desmond MacCarthy, and Lytton Strachey. Thoby died in 1906 and soon afterwards Vanessa married Clive Bell. Virginia and Adrian left for Fitzroy Sq. in 1907, but kept in close touch with the others.

Lytton Strachey made no. 51 (P) his London base when his family moved there in 1909 after his father's death, and it was here that he wrote *Queen Victoria* (1921). The house is now the University publications department.

Swinburne lived in rooms at 3 **Great James St.**, running N. off Theobalds Rd., from 1872 to 1875 and from 1877 to 1878. Edmund Gosse has described taking Mallarmé there in 1875 to effect a much-desired introduction, 'where that extraordinary man of genius lived in a dignified mediocrity'. Swinburne, for his part, was quick to praise 'the almost miraculous beauty' of Mallarmé's translation of Poe's *The Raven*.

Theodore Watts-Dunton, who later took Swinburne to live with him at Putney (q.v.), first got to know him when he was living near by, at no. 15 in 1872-3.

No. 24 was the London home of Dorothy Sayers.

Great Russell St. runs from Tottenham Court Rd. to Southampton Row, past the main entrance to the British Museum. The poet Harold Monro, founder of the quarterly *Poetry Review* (1912–), opened the Poetry Bookshop at no. 38 in 1913 and ran it till the end of his life (1932) as a centre for anyone interested in poetry and a place for poetry readings. It was here that Edward Marsh introduced W. H. Davies to him. Davies, a poet and wanderer, had made his name with *The Autobiography of a Super-Tramp* (1908) and had been granted a civil pension in 1911. He lived at no. 14 from 1916 to 1922.

Anthony Trollope was born (1815) in **Keppel St.**, N. of the British Museum. The house, believed to have been no. 6 (though unnumbered when his father was living there), was demolished for University development.

Virginia Woolf's last London home was at 37 **Mecklenburgh Sq.** (gone), where she and Leonard Woolf ran the Hogarth Press from 1939 until the bombing in September 1940 necessitated its evacuation and it was moved to Letchworth until the end of the war.

Russell Sq., one of London's largest squares, off Southampton Row, was once an exclusive residential area, with an uninterrupted view of the Hampstead Hills. Thomas Gray had lodgings (the Imperial Hotel occupies the site) in 1759-61 so that he could be within easy reach of the reading-room of the newly-opened British Museum. William Cowper lodged at no. 62 when he was a law student in the early 1750s. Henry Crabb Robinson, whose *Diary* is a remarkable source of facts and anecdotes about his literary contemporaries, lived at no. 30 (gone) from 1839, first as a lodger and then, from 1864 till his death in 1867, as the householder. Mary Russell Mitford lived at no. 56 in 1836 and left an account of a literary dinner party that she gave:

Mr. Wordsworth, Mr. Landor and Mr. White dined here. I like Mr. Wordsworth, of all things, Mr. Landor is very striking-looking and exceedingly clever. Also we had a Mr. Browning, a young poet, . . . and quantities more of poets.

Ralph Waldo Emerson, American philosopher and poet, stayed at no. 63 when he visited England in 1833. Mrs. Humphry Ward and her husband lived at no. 61 (the first house adjacent to Southampton Row) from 1881 till 1891, when they moved to Grosvenor Pl. T. S. Eliot used no. 24, where he worked in the editorial office of Faber and Faber, as his London address.

In Thackeray's *Vanity Fair* the Osbornes lived at no. 96 and the Sedleys at no. 62.

St. Giles-in-the-Fields Church (rebuilt 1731-3 by Henry Flitcroft, the third since its foundation in 1101) is on the S. side of **St. Giles High St.**, which leads from St. Giles Circus to High Holborn. The dramatist James Shirley died after shock and exposure in the Great Fire and is buried with his wife in the church. George Chapman, translator of Homer, is buried in the S. side of the churchyard and has a monument by Inigo Jones. Andrew Marvell is also buried here and there is a memorial tablet to him on the N. wall.

Colley Cibber, actor, playwright, and Poet Laureate, was born (1671) in **Southampton Pl.**, facing Southampton House (later Bedford House, which Evelyn says he saw being built in 1664). Pope made him the hero of the last edition (1743) of his satirical poem *The Dunciad*.

Jerome K. Jerome lodged at 33 (gone) **Tavistock Pl.** with his friend George Wingrave in 1889. Wingrave was the 'George' of *Three Men in a Boat* (1889). Jerome's *Idle Thoughts of an Idle Fellow* (1889) was written here. His play *The Passing of the Third Floor Back* (1907) is set in a Bloomsbury boarding-house.

Tavistock House (rebuilt; now B.M.A. House) in **Tavistock Sq.**, was Dickens's home from 1851. He wrote *Bleak House* (1852-3), *Hard Times* (1854), *Little Dorrit* (1855-7), *A Tale of Two Cities* (1859), and started *Great Expectations* (1860-1) here. He was also able to stage the theatrical entertainments he loved in the schoolroom at the back of the house, where he used a platform outside the window as a prop for the scenic effects. Friends taking part included Mark Lemon, Wilkie Collins, and Alfred Ainger, and the plays included Collins's *Frozen Deep* and *The Lighthouse*, Lemon's and Dickens's *Mr. Nightingale's Diary*, and a farce *Tom Thumb* by Henry Fielding. Hans Andersen was a guest in 1857. Dickens moved to Gad's Hill (q.v.) in 1860.

Virginia and Leonard Woolf took the lease of no. 52 in 1924 and ran the Hogarth Press there until 1939. The site is now occupied by the Tavistock Hotel.

University College, London, in Gower St., founded in 1826, opened in 1828 as the University of London. Thomas Campbell and Crabb Robinson were among the group who first advocated a university for London and saw the project through. The library has a James Joyce centre and letters and manuscripts of George Orwell.

Dr. Peter Mark Roget lived at 18 **Upper Bedford Pl.**, now Bedford Way, to the N. of Russell Sq., from 1843 till his death in 1869. His *Thesaurus of English Words and Phrases*, was published in 1852 and has been through many subsequent editions.

A plaque at 5 **Woburn Pl.** commemorates

Yeats's lodgings from 1895 to 1919 at what was then 18 Woburn Buildings. During this time he published the poems *The Wind among the Reeds* (1899), *The Green Helmet and other poems* (1910), and the plays *Cathleen ni Hoolihan* (1902), *On Baile's Strand* (1904), and *Deirdre* (1907). He married Georgie Hyde-Lees in 1917 and moved to Oxford 2 years later. Dorothy Richardson, while living (1906) at 2 Woburn Buildings, often saw him working by candlelight across the street.

[1] Open weekdays 10 a.m.–5 p.m.; Sun. 2.30–6 p.m. Closed Good Friday, Christmas Day, and Boxing Day.

Bromley [11 Fe], district to the SE. H. G. Wells was born (1866) above his father's crockery shop at 47 **High St.** (site now Medhursts, P). Wells first went to school at Morley's Academy (gone) also in the High St. but later went on to the Grammar School at Midhurst (q.v.). His father became bankrupt and his mother, who had been in service, became the housekeeper at Uppark (q.v.). Dinah Mulock lived at Chilchester Lodge, **Wickham Rd.**, Beckenham, after her marriage in 1865 to George Craik, and in 1870 they moved to the Corner House, Shortlands, near by. She attended St. Mary's Church there and a brass commemorating her as the author of *John Halifax, Gentleman* was put up after her death (1887).

Camberwell [11 Ed], district to the SE. Robert Browning, who was born (1812) in Southampton St. (gone), is commemorated by a plaque at 179 **Southampton Way**, adjacent to the house where he next lived with his parents. He was baptized in the Congregational Chapel at Walworth (S. of Camberwell) and is commemorated there by Browning Rd. (formerly York St.).

Camden Town [11 Ec], district to the N. Charles Dibdin, who published a *History of the Stage* (1795) and produced several plays at the Lyceum Theatre, lived in Arlington Row (gone). He is best remembered by his nautical songs, of which 'Tom Bowling' was the most popular. His last songs, including 'The Round Robin', were written here.

But the standing toast that pleased the most
Was—The wind that blows, the ship that goes,
And the lass that loves a sailor!

Charles Dickens lived (1823–4) at 16 **Bayham St.** (gone) when his father was transferred to Somerset House from Chatham. The family were often in financial difficulties and Charles was sent to work in 1824 at Warren's Blacking Factory in the City, just before his father was arrested for debt. Camden Town and its neighbourhood feature in his novels as the homes of Bob Cratchit, Jemima Evans, Traddles, and Micawber. After John Dickens's release from gaol, the family moved to Little College St. and then to Somers Town to the N.

Carshalton [11 Df], district to the S. William Hale White, who wrote as 'Mark Rutherford', lived in three houses here. The first was demolished to make way for a railway; he lived (1865-6) then at Stream or Spring House (now Honeywood, the Citizens' Advice Bureau). His sons liked the stream which ran through the garden and under the kitchen, but White was concerned about the damp. He wrote to the *Telegraph* in reply to Ruskin's letter about poor standards, asking where good, simple styles of houses could be found cheaply. This led to an introduction to Ruskin and through him to Philip Webb, who designed a new house for White on **Park Hill** (now no. 19). It was red-brick, tile-hung, dry, and sound-proof, and had interior designs by William Morris. White lived here for 21 years (1868-89) while working at the Admiralty, and moved only when his wife's paralysis made more ground-floor rooms necessary. He wrote here *The Biography of Mark Rutherford* (1881), *Mark Rutherford's Deliverance* (1885), and *The Revolution in Tanner's Lane* (1887).

Catford. See Lee.

Chalk Farm [11 Dc], district to the NE. of Regent's Park. W. B. Yeats came to London with his family in 1867 and lived at 23 **Fitzroy Rd.** (P) until 1874, when they moved to West Kensington.

'Henry Handel Richardson' (Ethel Florence Richardson) lived (1910-34) at 90 **Regent's Park Rd.**, where she wrote the trilogy *The Fortunes of Richard Mahoney* (1930).

Chelsea [10 Bf, Cf, Dd, De, Df], district between Kensington and the river. Arnold Bennett spent his latter years (1923-30) at 75 **Cadogan Sq.** (P), on the W. side of Sloane St.

Jerome K. Jerome wrote *Three Men in a Boat* (1889) when he was living in **Chelsea Gdns.**, in a block of flats at the corner of Chelsea Bridge Rd. and Ebury Bridge Rd.

He described his 'little circular drawing-room' on the top floor as 'nearly all windows, suggestive of a lighthouse', from which he looked down upon the river and over Battersea Park to the Surrey Hills beyond.

Thomas Carlyle came to Chelsea with his wife Jane when they left Scotland for London in 1834, and lived at 24 **Cheyne Row**[1] (N.T.) until the end of his life. His two most famous works, *The French Revolution* (1837) and *Frederick the Great* (1857-65), were written in his 'sound-proof' study at the top of the house. The house contains the original furnishings and many personal relics. His dog, Nero, is buried in the garden. There is a statue of Carlyle, 'Sage of Chelsea', between the foot of Cheyne Row and Chelsea Embankment, sheltered by trees and shrubs.

Cheyne Walk is an irregular street of houses overlooking the river, running from Royal Hospital Rd. to Lots Rd. Power Station, W. of Battersea Bridge. No. 4 (P) was George Eliot's last home, where she lived with her husband John Cross, a few weeks only until her death. D. G. Rossetti lived at no. 16 (P) from 1862 to 1882 and his house became a meeting-place for artists and writers. Swinburne stayed there intermittently (1862-4), writing poetry in the first-floor drawing-room, and other visitors included George Meredith, William Morris, and Oscar Wilde, coming and going in a house filled with immense collections of furniture and bric-à-brac and a garden inhabited by all manner of exotic birds and beasts. A memorial to Rossetti stands in the shrubbery between Cheyne Walk and the Embankment, a bust in high relief showing him with quill pen and palette, carved by Ford Madox Brown, on a base designed as a drinking fountain by John Seddon.

No. 18, called 'Don Saltero's', stands on the site of Don Saltero's Coffee House, which was originally opened by James Salter c. 1695 at the corner of Lawrence St. Salter had been valet to Sir Hans Sloane (1660-1753) on his travels abroad and acquired from him a strange assortment of unwanted curiosities from the collection which became the nucleus of the British Museum. These exhibits added to the fame of the establishment, which he finally moved to no. 18 c. 1717, describing it as 'My Museum Coffee-House', and which became a meeting-place for literary men from London as well as local Chelsea people: Addison, Steele,

Goldsmith, Sterne, Dr. Johnson. Steele, who is believed to have nicknamed him 'Don Saltero', gave him welcome publicity in the *Tatler*, 1709-10. Fanny Burney refers to 'Saltero's Coffee House' in *Evelina* (1778). **Carlyle Mansions**, on the E. corner of Lawrence St., is a block of flats where Henry James had his winter quarters from 1912 till his death there in 1916 (a bust of him, carved in 1914, is in the public library in Manresa Rd.). A children's hospital now stands on the other corner of Lawrence St., on the site of no. 59 where the Welsh poet Ernest Rhys lived for a time from 1886. **Chelsea Old Church** (mainly rebuilt after bomb damage in the Second World War) is at the corner of Old Church St. In the More Chapel (which escaped the bombing) is a tomb designed by Sir Thomas More, but there is no evidence that he was buried there. John Donne preached here at the funeral of Magdalen Herbert, mother of George Herbert, and his friend Izaak Walton was among those who attended. Thomas Shadwell, 17th-c. Poet Laureate and dramatist, who lived in the vicinity, was buried in the churchyard, but the exact site is unknown. On the S. wall there is a memorial plaque to Henry James. Between the church and the Embankment there is a statue of Sir Thomas More, whose manor house, once situated in extensive grounds a little further W., was a centre of learning and culture from *c.* 1524 until 1534 when he was committed to the Tower on a charge of high treason. At no. 91 Margaret Fairless Barber ('Michael Fairless') lived for a time with her friends the Dowsons and began the essays later published as *The Roadmender* (1901). William Bell Scott, poet and artist, lived at no. 92, celebrated in his poem 'Bellevue House', and Mrs. Elizabeth Gaskell, *née* Stevenson, was born at no. 93 (P), but only lived there just over a year before being taken to Knutsford after her mother's death. No. 104 (P) was the home of Hilaire Belloc and his wife from *c.* 1900 to 1906.

Bram Stoker, author of *Dracula* (1897), lived at 4 **Durham Pl.**, a dignified row of houses dated 1790, lying back from Ormonde Gate near the corner of St. Leonard's Ter.

George Meredith lived at 8 **Hobury St.** (P) for a time (1858-9) after being separated from his first wife. Here he wrote *The Ordeal of Richard Feverel* (1859) and the first chapters of *Evan Harrington* (1861). He often came across Carlyle in his walks and longed to speak to him, a wish that was fulfilled when Carlyle himself made contact with him through his publisher and encouraged him to call at Cheyne Row.

John Gay was secretary to the Duchess of Monmouth when she lived at the 'great house' *c.* 1714, on the site of 16 **Lawrence St.** Tobias Smollett lived (1750-62) in apartments in the present house (P), where he wrote *Peregrine Pickle* (1751), *Ferdinand Count Fathom* (1753), and the less successful *Sir Launcelot Greaves* (1760-2). Among his visitors were Goldsmith, Sterne, and Dr. Johnson (whom he called 'The Great Cham of Literature').

George Gissing lived at 33 **Oakley Gdns.** (P) as a young man.

Ranelagh Gardens,[2] formerly belonging to the Earl of Ranelagh (site now part of the Chelsea Royal Hospital grounds), were opened to the public in 1742 for entertainments of singing and dancing known as *ridottos*. Many of Christopher Smart's songs were sung here, some set to music by Thomas Arne (employed at Ranelagh from 1745), whom Smart had probably met through Charles Burney, his friend at Cambridge. Gray, who refused to desert Vauxhall Gardens at first, spent many evenings here later, as did Lord Chesterfield and Horace Walpole. Matthew Bramble and Lydia Melford in Smollett's *Humphry Clinker* (1771) give, as usual, widely divergent views on the entertainments. Karl Moritz, visiting England in 1782, compared the gardens unfavourably with Vauxhall at first, but was entranced on entering the Rotunda (gone) to be reminded of his childhood idea of fairyland. Robert Bloomfield's poem 'A Visit to Ranelagh' comments on the visitors incessantly walking round and round. The gardens closed in 1803, and were completely remodelled in 1860.

St. Luke's Church in Sydney St., between King's Rd. and Fulham Rd., is the parish church of Chelsea (built in Gothic Revival style, 1820-4). Dickens married Catherine Hogarth here in 1836, and Charles Kingsley served for a short time as curate to his father (who was rector, 1836-60) before going to Eversley (q.v.).

The Royal Court Theatre (formerly the Court Theatre, rebuilt 1888 after an earlier theatre) stands on the E. side of **Sloane Sq.** In the foyer was a bust (which has disappeared) of Bernard Shaw (by Michael Werner, 1955), commemorating the production of eleven of his plays from 1904 to 1907. These included *Candida, John Bull's Other Island* (which had a 'special evening performance for H.M. the King' on 11 Mar. 1905), *Man and Superman*, and *The Doctor's Dilemma* (which has a programme note saying '*The Doctor's Dilemma* is the title of a story by Miss Hesba Stretton, who has been kind enough to allow the Author to use it for his tragedy'). The plays, produced by Harley Granville-Barker (1877–1946), ran to 701 performances. Since 1956 the theatre has been the home of the English Stage Company.

Sloane St., a long, straight thoroughfare which runs from Knightsbridge to Sloane Sq., was named after Sir Hans Sloane (1660–1753), the physician and naturalist whose collection of books, manuscripts, prints, coins, and other treasures formed the nucleus of the British Museum. Edgar Allan Poe, who was brought to England from Boston, Mass. in 1815, went to a boarding school at no. 146 in 1816–17 before going to Stoke Newington (q.v.). Mrs. Mary Louisa Molesworth, author of children's books, lived in Sloane St. for the last 20 years of her life (1901–21).

Mark Twain lived at 23 **Tedworth Sq.** (P) in 1897. He describes in his autobiography how the publishing firm of Webster & Co., New York, which he had founded, had failed in the early 1890s, its liabilities exceeding its assets by 66 per cent. Feeling morally bound to repay the debts, he decided to write a book and return to the lecture platform, with the result that he set off on a world tour in 1895, wrote *Following the Equator* (1897) while staying in London, and paid off the debts in full at the end of 1898 or the beginning of 1899.

No. 34 **Tite St.** (P) was Oscar Wilde's home from the time of his marriage in 1884 until his disastrous trial and imprisonment brought his career to an end in 1895. His principal work was written here, including *The Happy Prince* (fairy-tales, 1888), *The Picture of Dorian Grey* (novel, 1891), and the social comedies, *Lady Windermere's Fan* (1892), *A Woman of No Importance* (1893), *An Ideal Husband* (1895), and the brilliant and enduring *The Importance of Being Earnest* (1895).

Leigh Hunt lived with his wife and seven children (1833–40) at 22 **Upper Cheyne Row** (P).

Thomas Wolfe, the American novelist, lodged in a room at 32 **Wellington Sq.** in 1926 when writing his first book, *Look Homeward, Angel*, published, after being rejected many times, in 1929.

¹ Open Wed.–Fri. 11 a.m.–1 p.m., 2–6 p.m. or dusk if earlier, Sun. 2–6 p.m. or dusk if earlier (closed Good Friday and Dec.).
² Open to visitors.

Chessington [11 Cf], district to the SW. Chessington Hall (site in **Garrison Lane**, near the church) was often visited by Fanny Burney in the 1770s. Her host was her father's friend, the embittered author of the unsuccessful tragedy *Virginia* (1754) whom she called 'Daddy Crisp'. She was staying here when Mrs. Thrale reported Dr. Johnson's praise of *Evelina* (1778) and she danced with joy round the mulberry tree on the lawn. The epitaph to Samuel Crisp, on the N. wall of the church, with its rhyming tribute to his 'enchanting powers of brightening social and convivial hours' was written by Dr. Burney. The house, partly 16th-c., which Fanny Burney called 'Liberty Hall' was rebuilt (1830–40) and this was in turn demolished in the 1960s.

Chislehurst [11 Ge], district to the SE. Ronald Firbank's parents bought the 18th-c. house, Coopers (now part of a school), in **Hawkwood Lane** in 1886. The artificial romance *Lady Appledore's Mésalliance* (1907), in which someone sits up all night with a sick orchid, was written when 'dear Home', as Firbank called the hundred-acre estate, had to be sold.

Chiswick [11 Cd], riverside district to the W. of Hammersmith. Pope came here with his parents in 1716 and lived at the corner house of Dr. Matthias Mawson's New Buildings in Chiswick Lane, now the Fox and Hounds (or the Mawson Arms), **Chiswick Lane South**. While he was here he wrote 'Elegy on the Death of an Unfortunate Lady' and 'Epistle of Eloisa to Abelard'. He moved to Twickenham (q.v.) in 1718. Rousseau stayed in Chiswick as an exile from France in 1765–6 and lodged with 'an honest grocer', probably in Church St., before going to Wootton (q.v.) in early 1766. Thackeray received his early education at the Preparatory School for Young Gentlemen, at

Walpole House in Chiswick Mall, and later turned it into Miss Pinkerton's Seminary for Young Ladies, attended by Becky Sharp and Amelia Sedley in *Vanity Fair* (1847–8). In 1876 W. B. Yeats moved with his family to 8 **Woodstock Rd.**, one of the new houses in Bedford Park built by Norman Shaw under the influence of William Morris. They spent 4 years here before returning to Ireland and Yeats remembered the distinction of having a bathroom, Morris wall-paper, and a garden with apple trees. He went to the Godolphin Boys' School in Hammersmith (q.v.).

City [10 Hb, Hc, Jb, Jc, Kc], district from the Tower to Holborn and the Strand, including the old City of London. The garden at the corner of **Aldermanbury** and Love Lane replaces the church of St. Mary Aldermanbury, bombed in the Second World War and removed in 1966 to Westminster College, Fulton, Missouri, as a memorial to Sir Winston Churchill. The foundations of the church showing the round pillars of the nave remain. Shakespeare, who is thought to have lived near by in Silver St. (gone), has a memorial bust on a pedestal which also commemorates his friends and fellow-actors Henry Condell and John Heminge. They edited the *First Folio* (1623) of his plays (the book is depicted open showing their foreword) and are buried here.

A plaque on the post office at 2 **Aldgate High St.** records that Geoffrey Chaucer lived in 1374 in the rooms over Aldgate, a medieval gate into the City (removed 1760). Chaucer is thought to have lived here from 1374 to 1386 except when his duties in the King's service took him to embassies abroad or to oversee customs at the ports. Chaucer wrote *Troylus and Cryseyde* during the time he was living here, and one of the two men named in the dedication was Ralph Strode, the philosopher, who at one time was living over Aldersgate (*c.* 1 m. W.).

Blackfriars, an area between Queen Victoria St. and the river, was the site of Blackfriars' Monastery, rented out after the Dissolution as apartments, houses, and shops. In 1596 James Burbage adapted some of the buildings including the Frater for the second Blackfriars' Theatre (Playhouse Yard now on the site). This was a small indoor theatre seating about 700 and intended for performances in the winter

months. Disputes between Burbage and the City authorities resulted in the theatre being used by another company, the Children of Paul's, boy actors from the Cathedral School, but in 1608 Burbage's company, the King's Men (formerly the Lord Chamberlain's Men) were granted a lease. Shakespeare had a profitable share in this company which also played in Southwark (q.v.). *Cymbeline* (1610) was performed at both theatres. Ben Jonson lived in Blackfriars from 1607 to 1616 and Shakespeare bought a house here in 1613 to use on his visits from Stratford-upon-Avon (q.v.).

David Copperfield spent a miserable time as a boy in Blackfriars after his mother's death when he was sent to wash and label bottles at Murdstone and Grinby's warehouse, 'a crazy old house with a wharf of its own, abutting on the water when the tide was in, and on the mud when the tide was out, and literally overrun with rats'. His first day there was not auspicious.

No words can express the secret agony of my soul as I sunk into this companionship; compared these henceforth everyday associates with those of my happier childhood—not to say with Steerforth, Traddles, and the rest of the boys; and felt my hopes of growing up to be a learned and distinguished man crushed in my bosom.

He made the acquaintance of Mr. Micawber and lodged at his house. After Micawber's arrest for debt, David decided to run away.

Harrison Ainsworth wrote most of *The Tower of London* (1840) at the Sussex Hotel in **Bouverie St.**, off Fleet St., where on completion of the novel he gave a large dinner for friends including Dickens, Forster, and Barham, and he sang the popular ballad 'Lord Bateman'. In the 1840s and 1850s the contributors to *Punch* (founded 1841) met at no. 10 and dined at a large deal table known as the Mahogany Tree. Mark Lemon, founder and editor (1841–70), first published Hood's *The Song of the Shirt* (1843) in *Punch*.

The Mermaid Tavern stood on the E. side of **Bread St.** near the junction with Cheapside. It was frequented by Marlowe (d. 1593), Shakespeare, Donne, Beaumont, Fletcher, Drayton, Selden, Browne, and Coryate, most of whom were members of one of the earliest clubs, established by Sir Walter Ralegh *c.* 1603, which met here on the first Friday of the month. Beaumont writing to Ben Jonson exclaims

> What things have we seen,
> Done at the Mermaid! heard words that have been
> So nimble, and so full of subtle flame,
> As if that every one from whence they came,
> Had meant to put his whole wit in a jest,
> And had resolv'd to live a fool, the rest
> Of his dull life.

And Keats in 'Lines on the Mermaid Tavern' asks the dead poets whether even Elysium can compare with the place. The houses where Donne (1571 or 1572) and Milton (1608) were born are gone.

The 14th-c. Carthusian Priory in **Charterhouse Sq.** was re-established in 1611 as a school for boys and a refuge for old lay brothers. Elkanah Settle, whose dramas had vied in popularity with Dryden's, spent his last years from 1718 here and died in 1724. Pupils at **Charterhouse** included Crashaw, Lovelace, Joseph Addison and his contemporary Richard Steele, John Wesley, Thomas Day, F. T. Palgrave, and Thackeray. In *The Newcomes* (1853–5) Thackeray's Colonel Newcome, a pupil here in his youth, has a last refuge here in old age. The manuscript of this novel is in the library of the school's new buildings at Godalming. Max Beerbohm was a pupil there. The Charterhouse, restored after Second World War damage, again houses the brothers.

At the end of 1816 Keats moved into lodgings with his brothers at **76 Cheapside**, where their sitting-room overlooked the street. He was still working as a dresser at Guy's Hospital but stimulated by his friendship with Charles Cowden Clarke which led to his meeting Leigh Hunt, John Reynolds, and the painter Robert Haydon, he was writing more. His first collection of *Poems* (1817) contained the sonnet on Chapman's Homer which he had looked at with Clarke, that on the Elgin Marbles which he had seen with Haydon, others addressed to Hunt, Reynolds, and his brothers, and also the longer 'Sleep and Poetry' suggested by the Chaucer lent him by Clarke. Keats and his brothers moved to Hampstead in the summer of 1817.

F. W. Rolfe ('Baron Corvo') was born (1860) at no. 112 (rebuilt). The family moved to Camden Town when he was a young child.

Clifford's Inn, Fetter Lane, is a block of flats built on the site of the oldest of the Inns of Chancery, to which Selden was admitted in 1602. George Dyer, the myopic subject of one of Charles Lamb's essays, 'Amicus Redivivus', lived here (1792–1841). Samuel Butler settled at no. 15 after his return from New Zealand in 1864. He wrote the satirical novel *Erewhon* (1872) and its sequel, *Erewhon Revisited* (1901), which contains the Professors Hanky and Panky. The autobiographical novel *The Way of all Flesh* (1903), published the year after Butler's death, gives an embittered account of paternal tyranny.

Horace Smith, parodist and novelist, was a clerk in a merchant's office at 39 **Coleman St.**, near Moorgate. He had published some novels when he made his name with *Rejected Addresses* (1812), parodies written with his brother James.

Thomas Gray was born (1716) at 39 **Cornhill** (rebuilt), near St. Michael's Church, where his father is buried. One of the carved panels on the door at no. 32 (site of former no. 65) commemorates the first visit of Charlotte and Anne Brontë to their publishers in 1848 and shows them meeting Thackeray, though this meeting took place the next year. 'We found 65 Cornhill to be a large bookseller's shop, in a street almost as bustling as the Strand', Charlotte Brontë wrote in her letter home, and after managing to accost and ask one of the 'many young men and lads' in the shop if she might see Mr. Smith, she allayed her nervousness during the interval by looking 'at some books on the counter'. Mr. Smith, who had not met 'Currer Bell', showed sharp surprise for a moment when Charlotte Brontë advanced with his opened letter to Currer Bell in her hand. She said they had come to give him 'ocular proof' that Currer and Acton Bell were different people, to refute the rumour that the pseudonyms hid merely one writer. Another panel at no. 32 shows Garraway's Coffee House (gone) established at 3 Exchange Alley, off Cornhill, in 1670 and mentioned in the *Tatler* (1709–10), in *Amelia* (1751), and in many novels by Dickens, whose Mr. Pickwick writes the short letter requesting 'chops and tomato sauce' from there. Garraway's (demolished *c.* 1873) is thought to have been built over an old monastery, whose crypt made a fine cellar. Mr. Pickwick, attended by Sam Weller, stayed on many occasions at the

George and Vulture, an inn in Castle Court, Birchin Lane, another alley off Cornhill.

Crane Court, Fleet Street is a narrow entry leading to the hall (gone) where the Philosophical Society invited Coleridge to give a series of lectures on Shakespeare in 1813. Byron, Rogers, and Godwin were among the audience which Crabb Robinson reported was usually about 150. Mark Lemon helped to inaugurate *Punch* at no. 9 in 1841. Douglas Jerrold, who wrote as 'Q', and Thackeray who wrote *Jeames's Diary* and *The Snobs of England*, were both contributors.

Crosby Sq., **Bishopsgate** was the site of Crosby Place, built in the 1460s for a rich merchant and then the home of Richard III, mentioned by Shakespeare in his play on the King. Thomas More lived here soon after returning from Flanders, where he started *Utopia* (1516), until he moved to his riverside house in Chelsea (c. 1524). *Utopia* had been translated from Latin into German, French, and Italian before an English version was made in 1551. Crosby Place, home of the Countess of Pembroke in 1609, was demolished c. 1908 except for the timbered Hall, which was re-erected near the site of More's Chelsea home in 1910, and is now the dining-hall of the British Federation of University Women. Stephen Gosson, author of *Schoole of Abuse* (1579), was rector of **St. Botolph's Bishopsgate**, from 1600 till his death in 1624.

The site of the Fleet Prison, from medieval times until its demolition in 1846, was near the entrance to Fleet Lane in **Farringdon St.** Thomas Nash was imprisoned here after his play *The Isle of Dogs* (1597) caused a furore by exposing abuses. John Donne spent a short time here in 1601, when it became known that he had secretly married a minor. While John Cleland was imprisoned for debt (1748–52), he wrote *Fanny Hill: Memoirs of a Woman of Pleasure* (1748–9), which caused a further rift with his family. Charles Churchill made a Fleet marriage dispensing with licence or banns, but this practice, whereby imprisoned clergy officiated, was stopped by the Marriage Act of 1753. Walter Besant's novel *The Chaplain of the Fleet* (1881) is about the abuses of the marriages.

Dickens sets scenes in the Fleet in *Pickwick Papers* (1837), when Mr. Pickwick, incarcerated after refusing to pay his fine, treats Mr. Jingle with charity and secures his release from poverty and squalor.

Fleet St. is a street of publishers, printers, booksellers, and journalists. No. 1 (P) marks the site of the Devil Tavern, where Ben Jonson and his friends established the Apollo Club which had the rules engraved in marble over the chimneypiece. Thomas Randolph is said to have made Ben Jonson's acquaintance here after writing some verses about having no money. The verses were accepted as payment for his bill. No. 10 is the site of Richard Tottel's printing house at the sign of the Hand and Bar, where the *Songs and Sonnets* of Wyatt and Surrey, which came to be known as *Tottel's Miscellany* (1557), were published. Later, rooms above became Dick's Coffee House, which Addison and Steele, who gathered there, mention in the *Tatler*. Dryden lived (1673–82) in this street. His best-known play *All for Love* (1678) and the poem *Absalom and Achitophel* were written at this time. John Murray founded the *Quarterly Review* in 1809 at his publishing offices (site of no. 32).

William Tyndale was a preacher at **St. Dunstan-in-the-West** (rebuilt in 1833 and restored after bomb damage in 1950) before he went to the Continent in 1524. John Davies of Hereford (d. 1618), Thomas Campion (d. 1620), and Thomas Carew (d. 1639?) were buried there. John Aubrey in *Brief Lives* records that Michael Drayton lived at 'the bay-window house next the east end of St. Dunstan's' and Izaak Walton, who was a vestryman (or parish officer) lived 'two doors west of Chancery Lane'. He is commemorated by a tablet on the wall outside the church and by a stained-glass window (visible behind the Romanian icon-screen), donated by 'Anglers and other admirers' in 1895. Walton's *Compleat Angler* (1653) was published by the press at St. Dunstan's churchyard. John Donne was rector here from 1624 to his death in 1631. Dickens is said to have written *The Chimes* (1844) about St. Dunstan's. Two Mitre Taverns have disappeared from the street: the Elizabethan tavern frequented by Shakespeare, Ben Jonson, and their circle, was at the corner of Old Mitre Court; the Mitre that became the special haunt of Dr. Johnson and Boswell was farther west. Goldsmith was often at the Mitre and Boswell, who wrote that Fleet St. was Dr. Johnson's favourite street, records that Johnson also said here that 'Goldsmith should not be for ever attempting to shine in conversation'. Cobbett lived in Fleet St.

during the time he was a journalist with Tory leanings. He started the weekly *Political Register* (1802–35) here. The publishers Taylor and Hessey had their offices at no. 93. This was the rendezvous for Hazlitt, William Cary, John Reynolds, Lamb, De Quincey, and Landor. Keats stayed here and Clare, who first came to London in 1821 in the company of Taylor's cousin, stayed here then and on his later visit. In the winter of 1833 Dickens posted his first story 'in a dark letter-box in a dark office in a dark court in Fleet St.' Ye Old Cocke Tavern at no. 22 is said to have been Dickens's favourite tavern. **St. Bride's Church**, just S. of the E. end of Fleet St., was rebuilt 1670–84 by Wren and again in 1956–7 to Wren's plans after bomb damage. Thomas Sackville, co-author of *Gorboduc*, was buried in the old church in 1608. Samuel Pepys, born (1633) in Salisbury Ct. (P) near by, was baptized in St. Bride's and Richard Lovelace, who died in Gunpowder Alley (now Shoe Lane), was buried in the old church in 1658. Samuel Richardson, who employed Goldsmith for some months in his printing works in Salisbury Sq., was buried in the Wren building in 1761.

Oliver Goldsmith had two rooms (1760–2) in Mrs. Carnan's house, 6 Wine Office Ct., Fleet St. (bombed and rebuilt as the House of Goldsmith), where Dr. Johnson visited him for the first time in 1761. Thomas Percy, who went with him, was surprised into commenting on his unusual neatness and Johnson replied that Goldsmith defended his own slovenliness by quoting Johnson's, and so he intended to set a better example. Goldsmith, whose *Memoirs of M. Voltaire* was being serialized in the *Ladies' Magazine*, and whose income was precarious, asked Johnson for help when he became seriously in debt. Johnson sold the manuscript of a novel of Goldsmith's that he had laid aside, the landlady was paid, and some years later *The Vicar of Wakefield* (1766) was published. Newbery, the publisher, then made plans to help Goldsmith with his finances by paying him an allowance and housing him near his own country apartments in Islington.

Ye Olde Cheshire Cheese (or the Cheese) in Wine Office Ct. was rebuilt after the Fire of London in 1666 and claims associations with Johnson, Boswell, and Goldsmith, though Boswell does not mention the name. The seat in the restaurant on the ground floor where it is said they sat is marked with a plaque and a copy of Reynolds's portrait of Johnson hangs above it. In the 1890s the Rhymers' Club met here. It was founded in 1891 by Yeats and Ernest Rhys; Lionel Johnson, Ernest Dowson, John Davidson, and Richard Le Gallienne used to drink and read their poems aloud here. Davidson published a collection of poems as *Fleet Street Eclogues* in 1893. A second volume followed in 1896. Le Gallienne's *The Romantic Nineties* (1926, reprinted 1951) gives a first-hand account of the literary and artistic scene.

Grub St., which Dr. Johnson in his *Dictionary* said was 'much inhabited by writers of small histories . . . whence any mean production is called Grub St.', used to lead N. from **Fore St**. It was renamed Milton St. (Milton died near by) and disappeared in the redevelopment in the 1960s. George Gissing's novel, *New Grub Street* (1891), has powerful descriptions of a writer struggling to make his way in London.

John Foxe (d. 1587) and Milton (d. 1674) are buried in **St. Giles Cripplegate Church**, Fore St. Milton's grave is marked by a tablet near the pulpit.

Dr. Johnson's House,[1] 17 **Gough Sq**. (spelt 'Goff' by Dr. Johnson), on the N. side of Fleet St., is reached by the narrow alleyway off Johnson's Ct. (well signposted). Dr. Johnson lived here from 1749 to 1759, the only one of his many London residences to have survived. In 1750 he began *The Rambler*, a twice-weekly periodical, written almost entirely by himself, which ran until 1752, the year his beloved wife Tetty died. By this time he was fully occupied on the *Dictionary* (1755), which had been commissioned by a syndicate of booksellers and was compiled in the garret, a room running the full length of the house, where he employed six clerks —five of whom were Scots. In 1758 he began *The Idler*, a series of papers contributed over 2 years to *The Universal Chronicle or Weekly Gazette*, and it is possible that he wrote *Rasselas* (1759) here, although he may have done so after moving to Staple Inn (see Holborn).

The house, now the property of Dr. Johnson's House Trust, contains portraits of Johnson and his contemporaries, personal relics, and a copy, which may be handled, of the first edition of the *Dictionary*. In the parlour there is a copy of 'In the Shades—

1915', an imaginary conversation by Max Beerbohm (one of the original governors of the Trust), with portraits of Johnson and Boswell, celebrating the opening of the house after its restoration in 1911.

After several other moves Johnson lived in Johnson's Ct. (rebuilt, P on E. side) from 1765 to 1776, and finally at Bolt Ct. (demolished) near by, where he died (1784). The last house had a garden which, though no gardener, he delighted to water. 'I have three bunches of grapes', he wrote to a friend, 'on a vine in my garden.'

Green Arbour Ct., Old Bailey, was a small enclosed square formerly at the corner of Seacoal Lane and Green Arbour Lane. Oliver Goldsmith lodged (1759-60) here with Mrs. Martin and he was popular with her children and with the other poor families in the court. When Thomas Percy visited he was surprised to find only one chair so that his host was obliged to sit on the window sill. Goldsmith finished *Enquiry into the present State of Polite Learning* (1759) here and was writing regularly for *The Bee*, the *Ladies' Magazine*, and the *Critical Review*. The publisher and philanthropist John Newbery also interested him in his new *Public Ledger* for which Goldsmith wrote his 'Chinese Letters'. By the middle of 1760 he had found new lodgings, probably through Newbery, whose wife had been a connection of the new landlady, but Goldsmith still continued to help Mrs. Martin and the children. Nathaniel Hawthorne described the 'miserable houses' in the square in *Our Old Home* (1863) and commented on the washing hanging from every window.

Guildhall, centre of the administration of the City, has a 15th-c. crypt although much of the building suffered in the Fire of London in 1666 or in the Second World War and has been rebuilt. The trial of Henry Howard, Earl of Surrey, was held in the Great Hall in 1547. He was condemned to death for treason on slender evidence. Pepys in his *Diary* mentions attending a banquet in 1663 when the French Ambassador was 'in a discontent', and being present at a trial later in the year about a ship's insurance. Elkanah Settle, as City poet from 1691, wrote plays and pageants for the Lord Mayor's Show. Dickens sets the Bardell and Pickwick trial here in *Pickwick Papers* (1836-7). The Guildhall Library[2] has many books and manuscripts relating to the City,

including Stow's *Chronicles* and *A Survey of London*. It also has the deed signed by Shakespeare in 1613 for the purchase of a house in Blackfriars. The stained-glass window depicts Stow and Milton and there are busts of Chaucer and Tennyson on the stairs.

Stained-glass windows in **St. Lawrence Jewry Church**, by Guildhall, commemorate William Grocyn (d. 1519), the scholar who introduced Greek studies to Oxford University, and Thomas More, his pupil, author of *Utopia* (1516). The church was rebuilt, by Wren after the Fire of London in 1666, and after bomb damage in the Second World War.

In **King William St.** Thomas Kyd was baptized (1558) at the **Church of St. Mary Woolnoth**. John Newton, author with Cowper of the *Olney Hymns*, was rector from 1780 to his death in 1807. He was buried here beside his wife and their remains were moved to Olney in 1893.

In **Leadenhall St.** an early 16th-c. church, **St. Andrew Undershaft**, possibly derives its name from the large maypole which used to be put up at the church on May Day. John Stow, born near by in the parish of Cornhill, has a memorial erected by his wife at the end of the N. aisle. He published many chronicles as *The Annales of England*, the second edition of Holinshed's *Chronicle* (1585-7), and wrote the fascinating *Survey of London* (1598) with its details of the customs of the day. At the annual church service commemorating him the quill pen in his memorial is renewed.

The East India House which stood on the corner of **Lime St.** and Leadenhall St. was where Charles Lamb worked as a clerk for over 30 years. In a letter to Crabb Robinson at the end of March 1825 he wrote, 'I have left the d—d India House for Ever'.

The certainty of the bet 'All Lombard Street to a china orange' shows the riches of **Lombard St.**, named after the medieval merchant bankers from Lombardy. Alexander Barclay became rector of All Hallows Church (site at entrance to Ball Alley) in 1552, the last year of his life. Joseph Addison married the Dowager Countess of Warwick and Holland in **St. Edmund's Church** in 1716.

Pontacks (gone), the fashionable eating-house of the late 17th and early 18th cc., is mentioned in Evelyn's *Diary* and in plays by Congreve, Southerne, and Susannah Centlivre. T. S. Eliot, who settled in England in 1915 and worked (1919–22) in Lloyds Bank here, wrote *The Waste Land* (1922), which contains realistic images of London.

Miles Coverdale, rector of **St. Magnus the Martyr** in **Lower Thames St.** from 1563 until his resignation in 1566, is buried near the altar. The church was rebuilt by Wren in 1666.

The Stationers' Hall, off **Ludgate Hill**, is the home of the Stationers' Company, founded in 1403 and incorporated by royal charter in 1557, which decreed that all work intended for publication had to be registered here. The registers contain titles and dates of works from the middle of the 16th c. The Hall was rebuilt after the Fire of London and refronted in 1800, and the Stationers' Company is now joined by the Newspaper Makers' Company.

Samuel Purchas was rector of **St. Martin-within-Ludgate**, rebuilt after the Fire of London, by Wren, from 1614 to his death in 1626. He wrote *Purchas his Pilgrim, Microcosmus or the Histories of Man* (1619) and *Hakluytus Posthumus, or Purchas his Pilgrimes, containing a History of the World in Sea Voyages and Land Travell by Englishmen and Others* (1625), partly based on papers which came to Purchas after the death of Richard Hakluyt, Archdeacon of Westminster. Richard Barham, who died at Amen Corner (see St. Paul's) in 1845, is commemorated by a tablet in the porch.

John Keats was born (1795) on the site of 85 **Moorgate** (P), then a prosperous livery stable owned by his father at the Swan and Hoop at Finsbury Pavement (gone). Keats went to school from the age of 8 at Enfield and his parents both died while he was there. He and his brothers and sister were put in charge of a guardian and at 16 he was apprenticed to a surgeon.

The Central Criminal Court on the corner of **Newgate St.** and Old Bailey stands on the site of Newgate Prison. Sir Thomas Malory, imprisoned for murder as well as other crimes, is thought to have written *Le Morte Darthur* to while away the many years spent here. He was perhaps allowed to read in the fine library of Grey Friars Monastery (gone) opposite, and he finished (1469–70) the work which was printed by Caxton in 1485. He is said to have died (1471) in prison and been buried in Grey Friars.

George Wither, the Puritan, was imprisoned here 1660–3 after his manuscript *Vox Vulgi* was considered seditious. Defoe's *The Shortest Way with Dissenters* (1702) led to his being imprisoned here after being pilloried, when he was cheered by the passers-by, and wrote *Hymn to the Pillory* (1704) as a result. He also started *The Review* in prison, a thrice-weekly paper about foreign and commercial affairs which lasted until 1713. Richard Savage spent one of his many periods of imprisonment here, this time (1727) not for debt, but for killing a man in a brawl. He was pardoned soon afterwards. *The Newgate Calendar* (1774) is an account of the inmates' crimes from 1700 and a later series was edited in 1826. Borrow mentions the chronicles of Newgate in *Lavengro* (1851). The original building of **Christ's Hospital**, often called The Bluecoat School, was on the site of Grey Friars. Camden, Richardson, Dyer (b. 1755), Coleridge, Lamb, and Leigh Hunt were pupils here, and Middleton Murry had a year here before the school moved in 1902. A plaque formerly on the site of the school and now on the E. wall of **St. Sepulchre's Church** in Giltspur St. (leading N. from Newgate St.) commemorates Charles Lamb 'Perhaps the most loved name in English Literature, who was a Bluecoat boy here for 7 years'. Lamb's *Essays* recount his impressions of Coleridge at Christ's Hospital, and his *Letters* mention the evenings he spent with the adult Coleridge and Southey at the Salutation and Cat, a coaching inn (burned 1883) opposite the school where they drank egg-hot, a hot drink made from beer, eggs, sugar, and nutmeg, and smoked oronooko, a Virginian tobacco.

Paternoster Row was a street famous for its booksellers and publishers until its destruction in the Second World War. The Chapter Coffee House stood at the entrance to Paul's Alley (gone), an opening off Paternoster Row. Thomas Chatterton, who in 1770 when 17 had come to London to make his literary fortune, wrote to his mother from here sending trifling gifts, saying 'I am quite familiar at the Chapter Coffee House and know all the geniuses there', but within 3 months he was dead. In 1848 Charlotte and Anne Brontë made an overnight train journey to visit their publishers. They stayed at the Chapter Coffee House, where they had been with their father, as they knew nowhere else.

A plaque at the entrance to **Plough Ct.**, Lombard St., states that Alexander Pope was born (1688) here. The house (gone) faced up the alley. His father was a prosperous linen-draper and Pope a precocious child, who suffered a crippling illness when he was 12.

Thomas Hood was born (1799) at 31 **Poultry**, now the Midland Bank (P), near Queen Victoria St. His family moved shortly afterwards, so it is more likely that his poem 'I remember, I remember | The house where I was born' refers to Islington (q.v.). Sir John Vanbrugh was buried (1726) at **St. Stephen Walbrook**, near the Mansion House. In 1731 Defoe died 'of lethargy' in lodgings in Ropemaker's Alley, now **Ropemaker St.**

The G.P.O. in **St. Martin's le Grand** stands on the site of the old Northumberland House, home of Shakespeare's 'Hotspur', where Thomas Percy lodged when in London in the late 1760s and 1770s. Boswell recalls that he and Dr. Johnson 'passed many an agreeable hour' there with Percy, who was also a frequent companion when they dined at the near-by taverns. Percy's antiquarian interests led him to publish *The Northumberland Household Book of 1512* (1768). A fire in 1780 burned £100-worth of Percy's clothes and movables but did not cause him a 'literary loss'.

St. Paul's Cathedral,[3] at the top of Ludgate Hill, was built (1675–97) by Wren on the site of the church destroyed in the Fire of London, 1666. Sir Philip Sidney, who died of wounds at Zutphen in 1586, was buried with great pomp in Old St. Paul's. The monument in the S. choir aisle to John Donne, Dean of St. Paul's from 1621 to his death in 1631, is one of the few surviving. He sat in a shroud to the sculptor Nicholas Stone. (One of the best known of Harrison Ainsworth's historical novels is *Old St. Paul's*, 1841.) There are statues in the Wren church of Dr. Johnson (in a toga) and his friend Joshua Reynolds under the dome to the N. The S. choir aisle has a monument to H. H. Milman, Dean from 1849 to his death in 1868 and author of *Annals of St. Paul's Cathedral* (1868). The crypt contains memorials to William Blake (d. 1827), R. H. Barham (d. 1845), Charles Reade (d. 1884), Walter Besant (d. 1901), W. E. Henley (d. 1903), and T. E. Lawrence (d. 1935). Sydney Smith was a canon from 1831 to his death in 1845. The ashes of Max Beer-

bohm (d. 1956) and W. de la Mare (d. 1956) are buried here.

John Newbery, a bookseller and publisher, established himself in **St. Paul's Churchyard** in 1744. Richard Barham, who had been appointed a minor canon of St. Paul's in 1821, came to know Mary Ann Hughes, the wife of a canon residentiary who lived in Amen Corner, a precinct near the cathedral. She was a mine of information on legends, ghost stories, and ballads and she encouraged him to write verse. Barham himself lived (1824–39) at 4 St. Paul's Churchyard (gone) and much of his collection, *The Ingoldsby Legends* (1840–7), which first appeared in periodicals, originated from her. She also was visited by Harrison Ainsworth, and Scott, who wove her account of Wayland's Smithy into *Kenilworth* (1821). Mrs. Hughes moved to Kingston Lisle in the 1830s after her husband died. In 1839 Barham himself moved into Sydney Smith's house in Amen Corner, as he was leaving for Green St. Barham's comic description of his garden, which contained 'eight broken bottles' and 'a tortoiseshell cat asleep in the sunniest corner', appears in his *Life* (1870) written by his son. He wrote 'As I lay a thinking', his last poem, shortly before his death (1845), and he was buried at St. Mary Magdalene, Old Fish St., where he had been rector. After the church was burned down in 1885, the commemorative tablet was re-erected in St. Martin-within-Ludgate.

St. Paul's School was founded by Dean Colet in 1509 with William Lily as first High Master. They collaborated on a book to help the pupils and this became known later as the *Eton Latin Grammar*. Literary Old Paulines include William Camden, Milton, Pepys, J. H. Reynolds, R. H. Barham, L. Binyon, G. K. Chesterton, and Edward Thomas. The school moved to new buildings in Hammersmith in 1884.

Merchant Taylors' School (founded 1561), in **Suffolk Lane** until 1875, had Spenser, Thomas Kyd, Thomas Lodge, James Shirley, and John Byrom among its pupils.

A plaque on Kent House in **Telegraph St.**, across Moorgate on the E. side, marks the site of a house where Robert Bloomfield lived. In 1781 he came from a farm in his native Suffolk to be apprenticed to his uncle, a tailor in Pitcher's Ct. (gone), off Bell Alley (now **Great Bell Alley**). He read the newspaper to the men as they worked and one, seeing his interest in literature, lent him *Paradise Lost* and *The Seasons*. He married in 1790 and continued to work in Bell Alley where he wrote *The Farmer's Boy* (1800), a long poem which proved popular, about the life he was not strong enough to follow.

The Temple consists of the Inner Temple and the Middle Temple, two of the four Inns of Court (q.v.), situated between the Victoria Embankment and Fleet St., which have occupied the site of the buildings of the Order of Knights Templars since the 14th c. Maps, fixed to the walls of buildings throughout the area, are numerous and helpful, indicating places with literary and other associations. Many of the buildings suffered from bombing in the Second World War, but much restoration has been carried out, as far as possible with the use of the original materials.

Middle Temple Hall,[4] an assembly hall on the S. side of Fountain Ct., opened by Elizabeth I in 1576, was the setting for the first presentation of *Twelfth Night*. It was acted before the Queen in 1601, probably by Shakespeare's own company. One of the stained-glass windows contains the coat of arms of Sir Walter Ralegh. John Evelyn, the diarist, lived in Essex Ct. (off Fountain Ct.) in 1640, but stayed less than a year. Oliver Goldsmith took a room in Garden Ct. (also off Fountain Ct.), above the Middle Temple Library, for a short time in 1764, when he was living in the country at Canonbury. This year saw the publication of *The Traveller*, a long poem begun years before in Scotland, which established him as a poet. In 1765 he took more comfortable rooms on the second floor of 2 Brick Ct. (demolished) and after the death of his friend John Newbery in 1767 he lived there, except for intervals in the country, for the rest of his life. He was able to furnish his rooms very well from the proceeds of his successful comedy *The Good Natur'd Man* (1768). He was writing *The Deserted Village* (1770) when he heard of the death of his brother, to whom he dedicated the poem, in which many references to their childhood in Ireland can be detected.

Anthony Hope Hawkins ('Anthony Hope') was called to the Bar in 1887. The story of *The Prisoner of Zenda* (1894) came to him as he was walking back to his chambers in Brick Ct. after winning a case at Westminster county court.

Fountain Ct. itself, a wide, tree-shaded court W. of Middle Temple Lane, is described by Dickens in *Martin Chuzzlewit* (ch. XLV) as the accustomed meeting place of Tom Pinch and his sister Ruth, where for once Tom is late and it is the ardent John Westlock instead who encounters Ruth and overtakes her in the sanctuary of Garden Ct.

The Temple Church,[5] which takes its name from the crusading Order of Knights Templars (founded 1118), has belonged to the lawyers of the Inner Temple and the Middle Temple since 1608, when the Benchers secured the freehold by charter from James I. John Marston, playwright and divine, who was a student at the Middle Temple but apparently found legal studies distasteful, returned to London after giving up his living at Christchurch, Hants, and was buried (26 June 1634) beside his father in the church. His gravestone, which bore the inscription 'Oblivioni sacrum', has disappeared. On the left of the entrance from the S. porch the gravestone of John Selden, jurist, legal antiquary, and scholar, may be seen through a glass panel on the floor. The basement apartment under the S. aisle containing his coffin is reached by a stair in the porch. Beside the W. porch there once stood the music shop of John Playford, Clerk of the Temple Church, whom Pepys used to visit to buy the latest songs. On the upper level of the graveyard on the N. side an inscribed stone marks the vicinity of Goldsmith's grave. Charles Lamb, like the rest of his brothers and sisters, was baptized in the church.

Members of the Middle Temple (in addition to those already mentioned) include: Sir Walter Ralegh (1552?-1618); Sir John Davies (1569-1626), barrister and poet, who entered in 1587 and after returning to Oxford to take his B.A. (1590) was called to the Bar in 1595, but was expelled the following year for attacking his friend Richard Martin at dinner in Hall (he was restored to his position and reconciled to Martin 6 years later); John Ford (1586?-1640?), who entered in 1603 but was never called to the Bar; Thomas Carew (1598?-1639?), who entered in 1612; John Evelyn (1620-1706); John Aubrey (1626-97), who entered in 1646 but was not called to the Bar; Thomas Shadwell (1642?-1692); Thomas Southerne (1660-1746), who came from Trinity College, Dublin, to study law and spent the rest of his life in London; William Congreve (1670-1729), who entered in 1691 and stayed 3 years, but made little progress towards the Bar, preferring the playhouse and the literary society of Will's Coffee House; Nicholas Rowe (1674-1718); William Somerville (1675-1742), who entered in 1696; Henry Brooke (1703-83), who entered in 1724 but was recalled to Ireland by the death of an aunt, who made him guardian of her daughter Catherine, whom he later married; Henry Fielding (1707-54), who was called to the Bar in 1740; Edmund Burke (1729-97), who entered in 1750; William Cowper (1731-1800), who entered in 1748, but spent more time visiting his cousins Theodora and Harriet Cowper in Southampton Row than studying law; he was called to the Bar in 1754, but never practised; William Hayley (1745-1820), who entered in 1766, when he was still at Cambridge, but preferred poetry to law; Thomas Moore (1779-1852), who entered in 1799, after being at Trinity College, Dublin; W. M. Thackeray (1811-63), who entered in 1831, but soon abandoned the legal profession.

Charles Lamb was born (10 Feb. 1775) at 2 Crown Office Row (rebuilt; P), opposite the gates of the Inner Temple Gardens (private). His father was confidential clerk to Samuel Salt, one of 'The Old Benchers of the Inner Temple' portrayed in Lamb's 'Elia' essay of that name (1821), which also has an affectionate portrait of his father as 'Lovel'. It was in Mr. Salt's chambers, remembered by Lamb as the 'place of my kindly engendure' in 'cheerful Crown Office Row', that he and his elder sister Mary grew up and 'tumbled into a spacious closet of good old English reading, and browsed at will on that fair and wholesome pasturage'. They lived there until Mr. Salt's death in 1795, when they moved into lodgings at 7 Little Queen St. (see Holborn, Kingsway). Charles had entered the East India Company as a clerk at the age of 17 (where he remained for 30 years) and had just begun writing. Near the Embankment end of the Gardens there is a fountain commemorating Lamb and a stone figure of a boy inscribed with a quotation from one of his Essays: 'Lawyers were children once.'

Members of the Inner Temple included: Francis Beaumont (1584-1616), who entered in 1600 but does not seem to have pursued his legal studies; William Browne (1591-1643), who entered in 1611, wrote an elegy on Prince Henry (printed 1613), and superintended the masque here of Ulysses and Circe in 1615; William Wycherley (1640-1716), who entered in 1659, but found the fashionable and literary circles of London more attractive than the study of law; James Boswell (1740-95), who, after studying law at Edinburgh, Glasgow, and Utrecht, came to the Inner Temple in 1775 and was called to the English Bar in 1786; Sir Francis Doyle (1810-88), who entered in 1832 and was called to the Bar in 1837, but found that his marriage in 1844 required him to take a more remunerative job—in Customs and Excise; John Forster (1812-76), who entered in 1828, was called to the Bar in 1843, but gave up law for literature; Thomas Hughes (1822-96), who was called to the Bar in 1848, became a Q.C. in 1869 and a Bencher in 1870; Sir Compton Mackenzie (1883-1972), who studied law for a time, and then turned to writing.

Charles Lamb remembers in Essays of Elia the idiosyncrasies of the clerks, who toiled at 'worm-eaten tables . . . with tarnished gilt-leather coverings' at the South-Sea House (gone), **Threadneedle St.**, 'a melancholy looking, handsome brick and stone structure to the left where Threadneedle St. abuts upon Bishopsgate'. Here Lamb himself, when 17, was a clerk for a short time before going to the East India House in 1792. Kenneth Grahame, while working (1898-1908) at the Bank of England, wrote The Wind in the Willows (1908), which began as stories for his young son.

The Tower of London was built as a fortress and a palace by William the Conqueror on the N. bank of the river. Among those imprisoned here were James I of Scotland, a political prisoner for many years, and author of The Kingis Quair; Sir Thomas More in 1534-5 for refusing to recognize Henry VIII as the Pope's superior; Thomas Wyatt in 1536 for complicity in Anne Boleyn's adultery: he was released on that charge, and was imprisoned again (1540-1) as an ally of Thomas Cromwell, and again released. Sir Walter Ralegh was imprisoned by Elizabeth I (1592) and by James I for treason (1603-16). Much of his poetry that is lost is said to have been written here.

William D'Avenant was transferred to the Tower (1650–2) from Cowes (q.v.) after being captured by the Parliamentarians. John Wilmot, 2nd Earl of Rochester was imprisoned for a short time in 1665 by Charles II for abducting the heiress, Elizabeth Malet, who later became his wife. The site on Tower Hill where More was executed is commemorated by a plaque on the pavement to the last victims to die here in 1746. More was buried in St. Peter's ad Vincula within the Tower. Scenes from Scott's *Peveril of the Peak* (1823) and Harrison Ainsworth's *The Tower of London* (1840) are set in the Tower. **All Hallows Barking**, NW. of the Tower, has the grave of William Thynne (d. 1546), friend of Skelton and first editor of Chaucer's works.

Pepys lived for many years N. of the church in Seething Lane near the Navy Office where he was employed from 1659 to 1673. His *Diary*, written from 1660 to 1669, and given up because of failing eyesight, describes the plague, the Fire of London, and intrigues at Court, as well as political and domestic events. During the Fire, having got his wife, her servant, and his gold safely away, he climbed 'to the top of Barking Steeple and there saw the saddest sight of desolation that I ever saw'. He and his wife went to church at St. Olave's in Seething Lane where, after her death (1669), he set up a bust that he could see from his pew. He died at Clapham Common (q.v.) and is buried in the crypt at St. Olave's in the same grave as his wife.

The Mermaid Theatre in Puddle Dock, **Upper Thames St.**, opened there by Bernard Miles in 1959, was the first theatre to be built in the City for three hundred years.

Chaucer, the son of a vintner, was born (1345?) on the site of this street.

Dante Gabriel Rossetti lived (1852–62) at 14 Chatham Pl. (gone), at the Blackfriars Bridge end of the **Victoria Embankment**. Elizabeth Siddal, whom he married in 1860, was the subject of his poems as well as the model for his paintings. Grief at her death, from an overdose of chloral some months after the birth of a still-born child, led Rossetti to bury with her the manuscript of these poems (which he later retrieved).

Robert Herrick was apprenticed for 10 years (c. 1604–14) to his uncle, the goldsmith Sir William Herrick (or Hericke), who lived in **Wood St.**, Cheapside.

Wordsworth in 'Reverie of Poor Susan' mentions the old clump of trees where

At the corner of Wood Street, when daylight appears,
Hangs a thrush that sings loud, it has sung for three years.

A single plane tree in a small paved courtyard raised above the street is all that remains now of the churchyard of St. Peter Cheap, destroyed in the Fire of London, 1666.

¹ Open Mon.–Sat. winter: 11 a.m.–5 p.m.; summer: 11 a.m.–5.30 p.m.
² Open Mon.–Sat. 9.30 a.m.–5 p.m.
³ Open daily 7.45 a.m.–7 p.m. (5 p.m. in winter), except during services.
⁴ Open (when not in use) Mon.–Fri. 10 a.m.–12 noon, 3–4.30 p.m.
⁵ Open weekdays 10 a.m.–5 p.m.; Sun. for services.

Clapham Common [11 Dd, Ed], district to the S. A plaque on The Elms, 29 North Side, Clapham Common commemorates Sir Charles Barry, the architect whose house is on the site of Pepys's last home (1700–3). Pepys lived at the house of William Hewer, his former servant. In 1700 Evelyn writes in his *Diary* 'I went to visit Mr. Pepys, at Clapham, where he has a very noble and wonderfully well-furnished house, especially with India and China curiosities. The offices and gardens well accommodated for pleasure and retirement.' Pepys died here in 1703 and was buried in the City.

Harriet Westbrook was at a school in Clapham run by Miss Hawkes. Her fellow pupils included the sisters of Shelley, who introduced her to their brother, with whom she eloped to Scotland in 1811.

A plaque at 5 **The Pavement** commemorates Zachary Macaulay, the philanthropist, and his son Thomas Babington, later Lord Macaulay. T. B. Macaulay grew up here, rambled over the Common, and attended Mr. Greaves's day school. He frequently visited Hannah More, who started his library by her presents of books. Macaulay went to Cambridge in 1818 and his father moved to Gt. Ormond St. in 1823.

Lytton Strachey was born (1880) at Stowey House, but his family moved to Lancaster Gate when he was 4.

Covent Garden [10 Gc], area to the NE. of Trafalgar Sq. A plaque on the Broad Ct. side of 19–20 **Bow St.** mentions Sackville, Wycherley (who died here in 1716), and

Fielding among others who lived here. This is the site of the Magistrates House, where Fielding officiated. Near by was the Cock Tavern frequented (*c.* 1670) by Sedley and Sackville. At no. 1 Will Urwin or Unwin established Will's Coffee House *c.* 1660 and it was probably 'the Great Coffee House' that Pepys looked into in 1668, commenting, 'there I perceive is a very witty and pleasant discourse', but he could not stay long as he had to collect his wife. Here, a few years before Samuel Butler's death in 1680, a Dr. Yonge saw 'the famous old Mr. Butler, an old paralytick claret drinker, a morose surly man except elevated with claret, when he becomes very brisk and incomparable company'. Dryden frequented Will's, having his own seat by the fireside in winter and by the window in summer. Wycherley, Addison, Steele, Congreve, and the young Pope were all visitors. Addison forsook Will's for Button's *c.* 1712 and the name the Wits' Coffee House by which Will's had been known, went with him. Will's closed in 1739 and the site was then used as 20-1 Russell St. Boswell, who wrote that in 1763 he drank at the Will's mentioned in the *Spectator*, must have visited one of the many other Will's Coffee Houses.

The Theatre Royal in **Catherine St.** is the fourth on the site; it took the name Drury Lane as it originally opened on to that street. Dramatists who have been associated with the management include D'Avenant, Killigrew, Dryden, Hill, Cibber, and Sheridan. Adjoining the theatre and on the corner of Russell St. and in 1766 overrun by its extensions, was the Rose Tavern (established 1651), where Pepys dined alone in 1668 'on a breast of mutton off the spit'. The duel in 1712 between Lord Mohun and the Duke of Hamilton which ended fatally for both, and which Thackeray in *Henry Esmond* (1852) uses to deprive Beatrix of a coronet, was actually arranged here by the seconds. The Rose Tavern is often mentioned in Restoration plays, in the *Tatler*, and in Gay's song 'To Molly Mog of The Rose', though the Rose at Wokingham (q.v.) claims her as the landlord's daughter there.

Covent Garden itself was once a convent garden developed by Inigo Jones (1573-1652) as a colonnaded square. **St. Paul's Church** (W. side), rebuilt after a fire in 1795 to Jones's designs, is the burial place of Samuel Butler (d. 1680), author of *Hudibras*

(1663-78), Wycherley (d. 1716), and John Wolcot (d. 1819). Lady Mary Wortley Montagu was baptized there (1689). The churchyard is now a garden with seats. The opening scene of Shaw's *Pygmalion* (1916) is set outside St. Paul's where Professor Higgins meets the flower seller, Eliza Doolittle.

In the 16th and 17th cc. the fruit and flower market (removed 1974) was surrounded by fashionable houses. William Alexander (d. 1640) and Thomas Fuller (d. 1661) both died in the Square. Aubrey in *Brief Lives* writes that after 1660 Sir Kenelm Digby (d. 1665) 'lived in the last fair house westward in the north portico . . . I think he died in this house'. Thomas Killigrew lived 1636-40 on the N. side. At the W. end of this N. side was the Great Piazza Coffee House where Boswell dined in 1773, where in 1809 Sheridan drank 'a glass of wine at his own fireside' (after the fire at his Drury Lane theatre near by), and where the lonely Jos Sedley 'dined with nobody' in *Vanity Fair*. Dickens stayed at the Great Piazza Hotel in 1844 and 1846, and characters in Thackeray's *The Newcomes* (1855) join a supper club in the Tavistock Hotel. This end of the N. side was rebuilt in the 1890s and became part of the market.

At the N. of the E. side the Shakespeare's Head Tavern (gone), frequented by Boswell, stood next to the Bedford Coffee House (fl. 1730-1837) haunt of actors, dramatists, and their audiences: Pope, Collins, Fielding, who met Arthur Murphy here and made him his assistant on *The Covent Garden Journal* (1752), Churchill, Horace Walpole, and Sheridan. Hummums Hotel (established 1699), S. of Russell St., was visited by Dr. Johnson and Boswell. Gibbon, however, in his *Autobiography* (first published in 1796 as *Memoirs of my Life and Writings*) remembers that, as a young man, he was 'too bashful to enjoy, like a manly Oxonian in town, the taverns and bagnios of Covent Garden'.

The young Hannah More stayed in **Henrietta St.** on her first visit to London with her sisters in 1774. She was introduced to Dr. Johnson by Sir Joshua Reynolds. Jane Austen, who often visited her brother Henry, stayed with him at no. 10 in 1813. He helped her in dealings with her publisher.

Rules Restaurant in **Maiden Lane** was patronized by Dickens. One of his *Sketches by Boz* is called 'Covent Garden'.

Samuel Butler spent his last years in Rose Alley (now **Rose St.**) which led from the NE. corner of Covent Garden piazza. He died there and Aubrey was one of the pall-bearers at his funeral in St. Paul's Church near by. Dryden, on his way in 1679 from Will's Coffee House to his home in Long Acre, was assaulted in Rose Alley by a masked gang thought to have been in the pay of the Earl of Rochester, who supposed Dryden responsible for the *Essay on Satire* (written by the Earl of Mulgrave, but published anonymously) in which Rochester was derided.

Addison and his friends Steele, Philips, and Cibber, visited Button's Coffee House (gone) established near the SW. end of **Russell St.**, in 1712. Pope, who derided Philips's 'namby-pamby' verses and Addison's rule over his 'little senate', came with Gay, Swift, and Arbuthnot. Button's, also called the Wits' Coffee House, was closed by 1751, and Elizabeth Inchbald wrote the successful play *Such Things Are* (1788) in lodgings on the floor above.

Tom's Coffee House (gone) was established at no. 8 in 1700 above a bookshop. It was a rendezvous of Dr. Johnson and the following 'clubable' men: Arthur Murphy and Goldsmith who first met Johnson in the 1760s; George Colman the Elder, who collaborated with Garrick in 1766 and dramatized Fielding's *Tom Jones* as *The Jealous Wife* (1761); and Fielding who in his *Covent Garden Journal* (1752) attacked Smollett over *Peregrine Pickle* (1751). Boswell first met Dr. Johnson at Thomas Davies's bookshop below the Coffee House in 1763.

Charles and Mary Lamb lived (1817–21) at '20 Russell Court, Covent Garden East, half way up, next the corner, left hand side' (now 20–1) as he replied to a letter from the painter Haydon who had given him similar directions to a dinner. Many of the *Essays of Elia* (1820–3) were written here and Wednesday evening parties of 'not silent whist' were attended by their many friends.

Tavistock St. was the site of York St., where at no. 4 De Quincey lodged for some years till 1824 and wrote *Confessions of an English Opium Eater* (1822).

Cranford [11 Bd], parish to the W. Thomas Fuller, whom Pepys called a 'great cavalier parson', became rector of the village of Cranford in 1658, combining this after the Restoration with again resuming the lectureship at the Savoy Chapel. In 1661 Pepys mentions in his *Diary* that Fuller had talked to him about his 'last and great new book' which was to be 'the History of all the Families of England'. However, when Pepys read 'England's Worthys' (*The Worthies of England*, 1662) after Fuller's death and burial here (1661), he found that 'he says nothing at all, nor mentions us either in Cambridgeshire or Norfolke'.

Crayford [11 He], parish to the SE. Algernon Blackwood, the novelist interested in the occult, was born (1869) at the Manor House (now an Adult Education Centre). He is best remembered for his first long novel *John Silence* (1908), and for his short stories, including *Tales of the Uncanny and Supernatural* (1949).

Croydon [11 Ef], district to the S. D. H. Lawrence taught (1908–12) at the newly-built **Davidson High School** in East Croydon, from where he could see the 'fairy-like, . . . blue bubble of the Crystal Palace'. His pupils, 'my pack of unruly hounds', are mentioned in his few poems on the school written at his lodgings with the Jones family at 12 **Colworth Rd.** They all lived in the kitchen, 'small bare, and ugly, because the electric isn't connected up—all too poor to have it done'. 'Jones' he wrote to an Eastwood friend 'is just jawing me how to make my fortune in literature.' He often 'worked all night at verse' published by Hueffer in the *English Review* and he was able to give his mother a copy of his first novel *The White Peacock* (1911), but she died before she could read it. He also entered into his short-lived engagement to Louie Burrows on one of his vacations. After an absence through ill-health Lawrence resigned from the school in 1912.

Denmark Hill [11 Ed], area to the S. John Ruskin lived (1842–72) at 163 **Denmark Hill**, an imposing house, with a veranda and portico, standing in seven acres. In his autobiography *Praeterita* (1885–9) he writes that there was 'a stable, and a farmyard, and a haystack and a pigstye and a porter's lodge, where undesirable visitors could be stopped before startling us with a knock'. Ruskin wrote *Modern Painters* (1843), later volumes (1846–60), and *The Stones of Venice* (1851–3) in his study on the first floor, though from 1852 to 1854 he was married and officially living elsewhere. In 1854 after the breakdown of his marriage he made his home again here with his parents. After the death of his father (1864) and mother (1871) he moved (1872) to Brantwood (q.v.). No. 163 became a hotel, called Ruskin Manor, and was demolished in 1947. Ruskin is commemorated by Ruskin Park, almost directly opposite the site of his house. A drawing of the house can be seen at Brantwood.

Deptford (pr. Detford) [11 Fd], parish to the SE. **St. Nicholas's Church** (rebuilt in 1697 and, after bombing, in 1957) contains a new tablet to Christopher Marlowe, who died in 1593. He was thought to have been killed as a result of an argument over the bill in a tavern here, but is now said to have been deliberately murdered for political reasons while employed as a government agent. He is buried in the churchyard. Marlowe's plays include *Tamburlaine* (1590), *The Tragedy of Dr. Faustus* (1604), and *Edward II* (1594), and he wrote the lyric so often parodied, 'Come live with me and be my love' in *The Passionate Pilgrim* (1599). He influenced Shakespeare, who pays tribute to him in *As You Like It* written after Marlowe's death, and he is said to have written part of Shakespeare's *Titus Andronicus*. Michael Drayton praises him in the lines:

Next Marlow, bathed in the Thespian Springs,
Had in him those brave translunary things,
That the first poets had.

John Evelyn settled at Sayes Ct. (site now Sayes Ct. Gardens, off Evelyn St.) in 1653 after many years of Continental travel on which he was Edmund Waller's companion. His *Diary* (1818, new edn. 1955) gives details of his life here, the visit of his friend Samuel Pepys, the beginnings of the Royal Society, and in 1694 his removal to the family home at Wotton (q.v.) on becoming his brother's heir.

Dulwich (pr. Dullidge) [11 Ee], district to the S. Edward Alleyn (1566–1622), the actor-manager, bought the manor here in 1605 and in 1619 founded **Dulwich College**, rebuilt in 1870 on the edge of the common. The school possesses the *Diary* of his stepfather-in-law, Philip Henslowe, manager of the Rose and Fortune Theatres. The *Diary*, kept between 1592 and 1609, gives miscellaneous information and the

accounts of the actors and playwrights employed by Henslowe. Alleyn is buried in the chapel, between College Rd. and Gallery Rd., where the Old College stood.

P. G. Wodehouse, author of the 'Jeeves' novels, was educated at Dulwich and had a lifelong affection for his old school. His Memorial Study, containing his desk and personal belongings bequeathed by him, can be seen in the library.

East Sheen. See Richmond.

Edmonton [11 Ea], parish to the N. After his mother's death in 1810 Keats was articled to a surgeon and lived with his grandmother in a house on the site of **Keats Parade**, a row of shops at the SE. end of **Church St.**, near the railway. At no. 7 a plaque over a chemist's shop commemorates the former cottage belonging to the surgeon Thomas Hammond, where Keats served his apprenticeship (1811–15). Some of his early poetry written at this time was published in *Poems by John Keats* (1817).

A short distance further W., near the corner of Lion Rd. and up a narrow garden path, is Lamb's Cottage (P), formerly Bay Cottage, where Charles Lamb brought his sister Mary in May 1833, when she was suffering from severe and prolonged depressions, to be in the care of a Mr. and Mrs. Walden, who took in patients. This year saw the publication of *Last Essays of Elia*, the work that marked the end of his literary life. He died on 27 December 1834, following a fall that bruised his face and led to a fatal attack of erysipelas. He was buried in the churchyard near by, where Mary, as they had both wished, was buried beside him, 13 years later. Much of the churchyard has been grassed over and the headstones removed to the sides, but the Lambs' tombstone still stands in its place, in a paved enclosure SW. of the church. Inside the church, near the entrance, there are two mural tablets side by side, each with a portrait medallion; the first in memory of Lamb, 'the gentle Elia', bearing Wordsworth's lines:

At the centre of his being lodged
A soul by resignation sanctified.
O, he was good, if e'er a good man lived.

and the second in memory of William Cowper, whose *Diverting History of John Gilpin* (1782) immortalized the Bell at Edmonton.

Eltham [11 Gd, Ge], parish to the SE. The 18th-c. red-brick Well Hall (gone) in **Well Hall Rd.**, covered with Virginia creeper, was the home (1899–1922) of E. Nesbit. She wrote here the stories for children which appeared regularly in the *Strand Magazine*, *The Wouldbegoods* (1901), *Five Children and It* (1902), *The Phoenix and the Carpet* (1904), and *The Railway Children* (1906). The old moat, part of the Tudor house of Sir Thomas More's daughter Margaret Roper (who tradition says buried her father's head here after his execution), gave its name to The Moat House, home of E. Nesbit's fictitious family, the Bastables. She and her husband, both founder members of the Fabian Society, entertained many literary friends here including Wells, Chesterton, and Frederick Rolfe, some of whom played her favourite games of charades and hide-and-seek. Extra participants made from clothes padded with paper came to life as the Ugly Wuglies in *The Enchanted Castle* (1907). E. Nesbit, who married again in 1917, found the house too large after her family had grown up, and left in 1922. The site of the house is now Well Hall Pleasaunce, a public garden. The renovated outbuilding is now the Tudor Barn Restaurant with an art gallery above.

Enfield [11 Ea], district to the N. Captain Frederick Marryat, author of novels about the sea, was at school at Holmwood (demolished), at the NW. corner of Baker St. by the turning into Clay Hill. He often tried running away, with the idea of going to sea. **Chase Side** is a road running N. and S. from Windmill Hill and Church St. to Lavender Hill and Lancaster Rd. Charles and Mary Lamb moved here from Islington in 1827, having previously made excursions and visits ever since Charles first came with Crabb Robinson to see friends in 1814. They lived first at a house originally called The Manse (later The Poplars), now Clarendon Cottage (P), no. 85. Lamb had hoped they were settled for life, but housekeeping proved too heavy a burden for Mary and in 1829 they moved next door, to a house now called Westwood Cottage, to lodge with a retired haberdasher and his wife, where they stayed until they moved to Edmonton in 1833. These were not happy years. Lamb missed his friends, though Hazlitt, Leigh Hunt, and Thomas Hood came occasionally and the faithful Crabb Robinson often

walked over for tea or a stroll, on one occasion, as he records in his *Diary*, bringing with him 'the mighty Walter Savage Landor'. Lamb did little serious literary work during this period, apart from the completion of the *Last Essays of Elia* (1833), but some of his best writing appears in his *Letters* (ed. E. V. Lucas, 3 vols., 1935). Clarendon Cottage and Westwood Cottage are part of Gentlemen's Row, a group of houses lying back from the main road.

A plaque in the booking hall of Enfield Town Station, **Southbury Rd.**, commemorates Keats's first school, which occupied a house built on the site in the late 17th c. In 1849 it became the station house and was demolished in 1872.

Erith [11 Hd], parish S. of the river to the E. William Thynne (d. 1546) was granted a house and tithes here by Henry VII. Thynne, an admirer of Chaucer, is thought to have been host to John Skelton, when he was writing his satirical attack on Cardinal Wolsey, *Why Come ye nat to Courte*. Both men had Court appointments and, after Skelton's death, Thynne edited *Chaucer's Works* (1532).

Finsbury [10 Ja, Jb], district to the N. **Bunhill Fields**, City Rd., a burial ground, called the 'Campo Santo of Nonconformity' by Southey, was used from 1685 to 1852. It contains the graves of John Bunyan (d. 1688), Daniel Defoe (d. 1731), marked by an obelisk erected by the boys and girls of England in gratitude for their enjoyment of *Robinson Crusoe* (1719), Isaac Watts (d. 1748), and William Blake (d. 1827).

After going into hiding at the Restoration, Milton lived (1662–74) in a house (gone) in **Bunhill Row**, then called Artillery Row, where he finished *Paradise Lost* (1667) and wrote the sequel *Paradise Regained* (1671). He left London with his family during the plague years.

Fortune St. commemorates the Fortune Theatre built outside the City wall here by Henslowe and his stepson-in-law Edward Alleyn in 1600 for performances by the Lord Admiral's Men. The building and design are described in Henslowe's *Diary*. Alleyn took the chief parts in Marlowe's *Tamburlaine the Great*, *The Jew of Malta*, and *The Tragedy of Doctor Faustus*.

Fulham [11 Dd], parish N. of the river to the SW. **Elysium Row**, between nos. 128

and 154 (P above nos. 144-6) **New King's Rd.**, was Horace Smith's home after his second marriage. He lived here from 1818 to 1821.

Samuel Richardson, 'the father of the English novel', had already had a successful career as a printer in Fleet St. before he turned to writing. He came to 40 **North End Cres.**, North End Rd., in 1739 and developed an idea of making a novel based on a series of letters, which he published in 1740, with immediate success, under the title *Pamela, or Virtue Rewarded*. He wrote this and its successors, *Clarissa* (1747-8) and *Sir Charles Grandison* (1753-4), in a little grotto in the garden. He moved to Parson's Green in 1754.

As a boy, Kipling used to spend his holidays here with his aunt, Lady Burne-Jones. The house has been superseded by a block of flats (Samuel Richardson House), but part of the garden remains, with another block of flats, The Grange, at the end of it.

Great Stanmore. See Harrow Weald.

Greenwich (pr. Grinidge) [11 Fd], district on the S. bank of the river to the E. The Tudor palace, predecessor of Charles II's palace which became Greenwich Hospital, was the scene of performances before Queen Elizabeth I of two Shakespeare plays in the winter of 1594.

In 1851 Harrison Ainsworth gave a whitebait dinner for his friends at The Trafalgar Inn at the N. end of **Park Row** near the Royal Naval College. This was to celebrate the completion of his novel *Mervyn Clitheroe*. Dickens and Ainsworth often attended each other's completion dinners.

The Royal Observatory in Greenwich Park was the objective of the anarchist who blew himself up there in 1894. Conrad is said to have admitted that this incident was the source of his novel *The Secret Agent* (1907).

C. Day-Lewis lived (1958-72) in **Crooms Hill**, W. of Greenwich Park. He was made Poet Laureate in 1968. He published *Pegasus* (1957), *The Buried Day* (1960) his autobiography, *The Room and Other Poems* (1965), *Whispering Roots* (1970), and many detective stories, under the pseudonym Nicholas Blake, during this time. He died in 1972 while visiting friends.

Grub St. See City, Fore St.

Hackney. See Stoke Newington.

Ham [11 Ce], riverside parish to the SW. Sarah Smith, author, as 'Hesba Stretton', of *Jessica's First Prayer* (1866), the popular tale of a waif finding Christianity, lived (1890-1911) at Ivy Croft. She is buried in the churchyard.

Hammersmith [11 Dd], district N. of the river to the W. Coleridge lived at 7 **Addison Bridge Pl.** (P) from 1811 to 1812. It was at this time that he was working on *The Friend*, 'a literary, moral, and political weekly paper' which was subsequently rewritten and published as a book (1818).

Rider Haggard lived at 69 **Gunterstone Rd.** from mid 1885 till *c*. April 1888. He completed *King Solomon's Mines* (published in Sept. 1885), his first, and immensely successful, African romance.

Arthur Murphy, playwright, actor, and friend of Dr. Johnson, lived from 1795 to 1799 at 16 **Hammersmith Ter.** after leaving the Bar. He is buried in the churchyard of St. Paul's, but the commemorative tablet has disappeared.

When W. B. Yeats was living with his family in Chiswick he attended the **Godolphin Boys' School** (founded 1856) in **Iffley Rd.** as a day boy. Yeats described the school, which catered for the sons of struggling professional men, as 'a Gothic building of yellow brick, with a separate house for boarders, all built *c*. 1860 or 1870'. He found it 'rough' and 'cheap' and disliked being teased for his 'Irishness'. He was there from 1876 to 1880, when the family returned to Ireland. The school was closed in 1900 and from 1906 the premises have housed the **Godolphin and Latymer School for Girls.**

Marie Louise de la Ramée, who achieved international fame as a romantic novelist under the name 'Ouida' (a childish pronunciation of 'Louisa'), came to London from Bury St. Edmunds (q.v.) in 1857, when she was 18, and after a short stay at 41 Lansdowne Rd., Kensington Park, moved to Bessborough House, 11 **Ravenscourt Sq.** (P). Here she lived with her mother, Mme de la Ramée, and her grandmother, Mrs. Sutton, who had bought the house, until the latter's death in 1866. After the house was sold Ouida and her mother took apartments at 51 Welbeck St. before moving to the Langham Hotel. In 1870 they left England and finally settled in Italy.

Ouida first made her name in 1859 when Harrison Ainsworth, her doctor's cousin, arranged for a series of her short stories to be published in *Bentley's Miscellany*, a periodical which introduced many notable writers to the public. Ouida's first long novel, *Granville de Vigne*, was published in 1863 and was followed in rapid succession by many others, of which the best known is probably *Under Two Flags* (1867). Her stories dealt with high life and stirring action, her style was flamboyant, and her popularity immense. A parody in *Punch* of her novel *Strathmore* (1865) helped to establish her reputation.

Leigh Hunt spent his last years (1853–9) at 7 (now 16, P) **Rowan Rd.**, formerly Cornwall Rd. Nathaniel Hawthorne describes in *Our Old Home* (1863) how he visited him here, 'a beautiful and venerable old man, buttoned to the chin in a black dress-coat', occupying 'a very plain and shabby little house'. The plaque was unveiled in September 1973 by his great-great-grandson, Mr. John Leigh Hunt.

Kelmscott House (PP), 26 **Upper Mall**, stands 100 yds upstream of the river creek which formerly separated the Upper and Lower Malls. George Macdonald, poet and novelist, came to live here in 1868, the house then being known as The Retreat, and wrote *Robert Falconer* (1868), a novel of the Aberdeenshire countryside, and the fairy tales *At the Back of the North Wind* (1871) and *The Princess and the Goblin* (1872). His wide circle of friends included Browning, Ruskin, Tennyson, the Carlyles, and Morris, and it was to the last named that he sold the house in 1878. Morris moved in with his family at the end of October and renamed the property Kelmscott House after his country home at Kelmscott (q.v.). His Utopian story, *News from Nowhere* (1891), begins in Kelmscott House, as he envisaged it as a guest-house of the 21st c. In 1890 he set up the Kelmscott Press, for which he designed founts of type and ornamental letters and borders, and from which he published his own works, reprints of the English classics, and various smaller books. The coach-house, which bears an inscription over the lintel, taken from *News from Nowhere*, was used for weaving Morris Hammersmith carpets. Morris was happy to think of his country home up the river and twice rowed the 130 miles upstream to visit it. He died in Hammersmith and was buried in Kelmscott churchyard.

The William Morris Society now owns Kelmscott House and has undertaken the foundation of a Centre there for the study of Morris and his ideals.

Charles Reade lived at 3 Blomfield Villas, **Uxbridge Rd.**, from 1882 to 1884 and died here.

Hampstead [11 Db, Dc], district to the N. on the W. of Hampstead Heath. John Galsworthy lived at Grove Lodge, **Admiral's Walk** (P), a secluded, tree-lined street off Hampstead Grove, from 1918 till his death in 1933. He wrote much of *The Forsyte Saga* (1922) and its sequel *A Modern Comedy* (1929) here, and his study overlooking the garden can be seen from Windmill Hill, at the other side of the house.

Joanna Baillie, poet and dramatist, came to Hampstead in 1802 from her native Scotland with her mother and sister. After her mother's death in 1806 she and her sister moved to **Bolton House** (P), one of a group of four tall houses between the S. end of Hampstead Grove and the S. end of Windmill Hill, facing Holly Bush Hill, and lived here until her death in 1851. Scott was introduced to her in 1806 by Southey, at his own request, and became a good friend, and Wordsworth used to walk over from London across the fields to stroll on the Heath with the lady he considered 'the ablest authoress of the day'. She wrote three volumes of *Plays on the Passions* (1798, 1800, and 1812), the most successful drama being *The Family Legend* (1810), and collections of poems published as *Fugitive Verses* (1790) and *Metrical Legends* (1821).

Aldous Huxley lived with his father and stepmother at 16 **Bracknell Gdns.**, between Frognal Lane and Heath Drive, in 1917, while a clerk at the Air Board. He began work on his second collection of wartime poems, published the following year as *Defeat of Youth*.

In September 1899 Frederick Rolfe rented an attic room at 69 **Broadhurst Gdns.**, West Hampstead (demolished in the Second World War), which appears in *Hadrian the Seventh* (1904), the work by which he is best known—part autobiography, part fantasy, written while he lived here.

Downshire Hill runs from Rosslyn Hill to the edge of Hampstead Heath, lined on its N. side with pleasant early-19th-c. houses. Olive Schreiner lived at no. 30 in 1885, and

Edwin Muir at no. 7 in the 1930s. Muir's *Autobiography* (1954) gives a description of the contemporary literary set in Hampstead, which 'was filled with writing people and haunted by young poets despairing over the poor and the world, but despairing together, in a sad but comforting communion'. He also describes how he and his wife Willa were still translating from the German, mainly from Hermann Broch and Franz Kafka: 'At one stage Kafka's stories continued themselves in our dreams, unfolding into slow serpentine nightmares, immovably reasonable.'

Katherine Mansfield and John Middleton Murry lived at 17 **East Heath Rd.** (P) after their marriage in 1918. They called it the Elephant. In an entry in her *Journal* (1927), headed *October, Hampstead: Geraniums*, she writes 'I went to London and married an Englishman, and we lived in a tall grave house with red geraniums and white daisies in the garden at the back'.

In **Frognal**, just N. of the Frognal Way turning, opposite Frognal Lane (formerly West End Lane), stood Priory Lodge (demolished 1925), sometimes called Dr. Johnson's House. In 1745 Dr. Johnson used to come out from London and stay with his wife, who lodged here for a time for the sake of her health, and it was here that he wrote most, if not all, of *The Vanity of Human Wishes* (1749).

At 18 **Frognal Gdns.**, a secluded road leading from Church Walk to Frognal, is a private drive to Frognal End (P), the house where Sir Walter Besant spent his last years (1896–1901). He died here and was buried close by in the cemetery N. of the parish church.

Aldous Huxley rented a flat from June 1919 to December 1920 at 18 **Hampstead Hill Gdns.**, a quiet street curving round from Rosslyn Hill to Pond St. Here he completed *Leda and other poems*, his third collection of wartime poems, and *Limbo*, short stories, both published in 1920.

Hampstead Parish Church has near the lectern a marble bust of Keats, erected (1894) by a group of American admirers. There is also a memorial tablet to Joanna Baillie, whose grave is in the SE. corner of the churchyard.

The Load of Hay at 94 **Haverstock Hill** was rebuilt (1863) on the site of an old coaching inn where Addison used to alight

from the London coach to visit Steele, who, in the summer of 1712, was living in a cottage beyond a high bank at the other side of the road. Steele had come here to find a rural retreat, partly to escape the attention of his creditors, and he described the cottage (the last home of Sir Charles Sedley, d. 1701) as 'in a solitary spot between London and Hampstead'. The cottage was the subject of many paintings, notably by Constable, and reproductions from these illustrate Steele's *Correspondence* (ed. R. Blanchard, 1941), *Annals of Hampstead* (T. J. Barratt, 1912), *Northern Heights of London* (W. Howitt, 1869), etc.; it was demolished in 1867, the site being commemorated by **Steele's Rd.** (not by the Sir Richard Steele further up the Hill).

Heath House, a handsome Georgian house at the junction of North End Way and Spaniards Rd., was once the home of Sir Samuel Hoare, a 19th-c. Quaker banker and hospitable friend of many poets. His frequent guests included Crabbe, Cowper, Campbell, and Wordsworth.

Heath St. is one of the two principal streets of the old village running from the top of High St. to Whitestone Pond and the Heath. The Kit-Cat Club, said by Vanbrugh to have been the best club that ever was, held its summer meetings in the early 18th c. at the Upper Flask Tavern, which stood on the site of no. 124 (now occupied by Queen Mary's Maternity Hospital). Members (each of whom had his portrait painted for the Club) included Steele, Addison, Congreve, and Vanbrugh, as well as artists and leading society figures. These portraits are now in the National Portrait Gallery, north of Trafalgar Sq.

Evelyn Waugh, whose first novel was the satirical *Decline and Fall* (1928), was born (1903) at 11 **Hillfield Rd.**, West Hampstead. His father was Arthur Waugh, publisher and man of letters.

Keats Grove is a road near the SE. corner of Hampstead Heath. Keats lived (1818–20) with Charles Armitage Brown in one of a pair of semi-detached houses built in 1815 by Brown and Charles Wentworth Dilke and known as Wentworth Pl. Keats's fiancée, Fanny Brawne, lived next door with her widowed mother. A nightingale that sang in the garden inspired his 'Ode to a Nightingale' written in May 1819. Wentworth Pl. is now a museum[1] containing relics of

Keats and his friends. Next door is the Heath Branch Library housing the Keats Memorial Library.

In the garden of **Kenwood House**, an 18th-c. mansion in the N. part of Hampstead Heath, converted into an art gallery and museum, entered from Hampstead Lane, it is a pleasant surprise to come upon Dr. Johnson's summer-house, in which he and Mrs. Thrale used to sit and talk in the garden at Streatham Park (q.v.). After the house was demolished the summer-house was moved to Ashgrove, Knockholt, Kent, and in 1968 was refurbished and transferred to its present site.

George Orwell lived at 10A **Mortimer Cres.**, South Hampstead, from 1943 to 1944, when he was bombed out. The newly-completed manuscript of *Animal Farm* (1945) was sent to the publishers somewhat crumpled and dusty, but otherwise unscathed.

Wilfrid Gibson, whose early work was published in *Georgian Poetry* (ed. Edward Marsh, 1912–22), lived at 26 **Nassington Rd.**, off Parliament Hill, from 1934 to 1939. His volume of *Collected Poems* (1905–25) was published in 1926 and he continued to publish other volumes of poetry throughout the war and up to 1950, the last title being *Within Four Walls*.

New End Hospital, between Rosslyn Hill and Pond St., was built (as the Hampstead General Hospital) on the site of The Green, 'the pretty, old-fashioned house at Hampstead' which was Francis Turner Palgrave's boyhood home.

Dinah Mulock came in 1857 to **North End**, formerly a village N. of Hampstead, and settled at Wildwood Cottage, where she became the centre of a large literary coterie. The work by which she is chiefly remembered, *John Halifax, Gentleman*, was published the year she arrived and was immensely successful, 250,000 copies being sold in her lifetime. Abel Fletcher, the mill-owner, is believed to have been based on a Hampstead resident. In 1865 she married George Lillie Craik, a partner in Macmillan's publishing house, and soon after went to live at Beckenham (see Bromley).

Parliament Hill runs up from South End Rd. to Hampstead Heath. In the autumn of 1932 Malcolm Lowry became a frequent visitor at no. 68, a large house known as 'Bourgeois Towers', where the Australian poet Anna Wickham lived with her three sons, James, John, and George Hepburn. James, a Cambridge friend of Lowry's, had found him living in squalor in the Bloomsbury area, moving from one dreary room to another, and took him home, where he was made welcome and taken care of. His first novel, *Ultramarine*, begun in 1928 and written mainly during his Cambridge years, was accepted about this time and (after a series of misadventures) published in 1933.

At **South End Green** a coffee bar on the corner of Pond St. and South End Rd. stands on the site of a bookshop where George Orwell worked in return for his lodging (1934–5) and wrote *Keep the Aspidistra Flying* (1936). He is commemorated by a plaque with a portrait bust.

The Vale of Health is a cul-de-sac in Hampstead Heath on the N. side of East Heath Rd., overlooking a pond where Shelley used to sail paper boats. Leigh Hunt lived here in 1815, possibly in one of the three Villas of the Heath (Hunt Cottage) or, now thought more probably, at Vale Lodge, and was visited by Keats and Shelley. Ernest Rhys stayed at Hunt Cottage in the 1880s, believing it to have been Hunt's home. The Indian poet and dramatist, Rabindranath Tagore (1861–1941) lived in one of the Villas (P) in 1912, the year he published *Gitanjali*, a collection of poems for which he was awarded the Nobel Prize (1913). D. H. Lawrence and his wife took a ground-floor flat at 1 **Byron Villas** (P) in 1915. They were full of plans for forming a community of like-minded people, such as Katherine Mansfield and John Middleton Murry, and when Lawrence's newly-published novel, *The Rainbow*, was suppressed in November as obscene, they decided that they must emigrate to America. 'It is the end of my writing for England', said Lawrence bitterly, and he posted a pack of his manuscripts (including *The Rainbow*) to his friend Lady Ottoline Morrell, at Garsington (q.v.), for her to keep until they were worth selling. He and Frieda gave up the flat in December, hoping (though vainly) to sail for Florida.

Well Walk, off East Heath Rd., took its name from the chalybeate spring which was a source of health-giving waters drunk by the fashionable in the 18th c. Keats had lodgings here next door to the Wells Hotel (formerly the Green Man) before moving to Wentworth Place (Keats Grove) in 1818.

John Masefield lived at no. 14 from 1913 to 1916. Thomas Sturge Moore lived from c. 1914 to 1919 in Constable's house, no. 40, which became a meeting-place for artists and writers and their friends.

¹ Open Mon.–Sat. 10 a.m.–6 p.m., Sun. 2–5 p.m.

Hampstead Garden Suburb [11 Db], district N. of Hampstead. Old Wyldes (P), **Hampstead Way**, a 17th-c. farmhouse owned by Sir Raymond Unwin, the Suburb's architect and 'father of British town planning', from 1907 until his death in 1940, was once a retreat and a meeting place for artist and writers. William Blake was a frequent visitor when his friend John Linnell, a successful landscape and portrait painter, rented the house from 1824 to 1830. Linnell commissioned Blake to engrave illustrations to the Book of Job and to produce a new series of illustrations from Dante. Dickens spent some time here in 1832, and later visitors included Walter Besant and Bernard Shaw.

Hampton [11 Be], riverside district to the SW. Richard Steele bought a house in Hampton Wick, 2 m. E., in 1707. It is thought he lived here for a short time only, with his wife, the 'dear Prue' to whom he apologizes so often in his letters. The house, which he called the Hovel, is thought to be the place Addison had sold to get repayment for a loan he made Steele.

Garrick's Villa (now flats) which he bought in 1754, with the Grecian temple in the garden of 'syringas and lilacs' sloping to the Thames, was visited by his many friends, including Hannah More and Dr. Johnson. Garrick discussed details here for the first night of Richard Cumberland's *The West Indian* (1771), a successful play for many years.

Harefield [11 Ab], parish to the NW. The parish church has the painted, canopied tomb of Alice, Dowager Countess of Derby, who seems to have retained this title when she came to Harefield Place (gone, site near the church) with her second husband Sir Thomas Egerton (later Lord Ellesmere). He was Jonson's 'grave and great orator' and was also eulogized by Samuel Daniel. In *Colin Clouts come home againe* Spenser, who calls her Amaryllis, reminds her that he is a member of her 'noble familie'. Sir John

Davies (1569–1626) wrote *The Lottery* as part of the entertainment given by the newly married couple to Queen Elizabeth I in 1602. Milton is thought to have met the Dowager Countess here, perhaps through an introduction by his friend Henry Lawes, who was attached to the household of her stepson (who was also her son-in-law), the Earl of Bridgwater. Lawes wrote the music for 'Arcades', the masque Milton wrote to entertain the Dowager Countess here. It was probably performed in 1633 with some of her grandchildren among the actors. Entertainments for the Dowager Countess and her family were also given at Ashby de la Zouche and Ludlow (qq.v.).

Harrow on the Hill [11 Cb], parish to the NW. Harrow School (founded 1572) has had many distinguished literary men among its pupils. R. B. Sheridan was there from 1762 to 1768 and left his name carved on a panel of the old Fourth Form Room. He came back to live in Harrow at the end of 1781, a married man and a successful playwright (*The Rivals* had been produced in 1775 and *The School for Scandal* in 1777), and his house, The Grove, by the N. side of the churchyard, is now a school boarding-house. Byron was a pupil from 1801 to 1805 and his name can also be seen on the same panel as Sheridan's. He used to spend many hours in the churchyard near the tomb of John Peachey (now protected with iron casing), which he mentions in a letter from Italy in 1822 as 'my favourite spot'. A marble plaque near the tomb is engraved with a verse from his 'Lines written beneath an elm' (2 Sept. 1807) in which he considers being buried there:

Here might I sleep where all my hopes arose,
Scene of my youth, and couch of my repose;
For ever stretch'd beneath this mantling shade,
Press'd by the turf where once my childhood play'd;

Anthony Trollope came in 1827 and stayed till he was nearly 19, but he was looked down on by the other boys because he was a day-boarder. His home from 1817 to 1827 had been at Julians, a big house (now altered) S. of the Hill, and then a farmhouse (demolished c. 1901) near by called Julians Hill (which appears in *Orley Farm*, 1862). A later move was to a farmhouse at Harrow Weald, from which Trollope had to tramp 3 miles of muddy lanes to school. This was believed to be Durrant's Farm, at the corner of Weald Lane and High Rd. (demolished in the 1930s).

Other literary Harrovians include C. S. Calverley, R. B. Cunninghame Graham, J. A. Symonds, H. A. Vachell, author of *The Hill* (1905), a novel about the school, John Galsworthy, G. M. Trevelyan, and L. P. Hartley. F. W. Farrar was a master here (1855–70) and wrote *Eric, or Little by Little* (1858, about schooldays in the Isle of Man), and *Julian Home, A Tale of College Life* (1859, about Cambridge).

Byron House, at the foot of **Byron Hill** on the right-hand side going up, was the home of Matthew Arnold (1868–73) when he was inspector of schools for a country area including Harrow, as well as for Westminster. The grounds have been broken up for housing development, but one of the new gardens preserves Arnold's treasured and still flourishing vine. Charles Kingsley lived for a few months in 1873 in a large Victorian house (now flats) in **London Rd.**, known as Kingsley House. A little further south R. M. Ballantyne spent the later part of his life (1880–93) at Duneaves, **Mount Park Rd.**, not far from South Harrow underground station.

Harrow Weald [11 Cb], district N. of Harrow on the Hill. Sir W. S. Gilbert bought a house and estate (now a country hotel) on the edge of the common in 1890 and lived there until his death from heart failure, after rescuing a young woman from the lake. His ashes are buried in the churchyard at Great Stanmore.

Hendon [11 Db], parish to the NW. Church Farm House Museum,[1] the oldest surviving dwelling-house in the ancient parish or manor of Hendon, is next to the church and Greyhound Inn. Mark Lemon, editor of *Punch* and friend of Dickens, lived at the 200-acre farm with his grandparents after the age of 8 and local people and incidents inspired some of his *Tom Moody's Tales* (1863), which were often autobiographical.

[1] Open Mon., Wed.–Sat. 10 a.m.–12.30 p.m., 1.30–5.30 p.m.; Tues. 10 a.m.–1 p.m.; Sun. 2.30–6 p.m.

Herne Hill [11 Ed], area to the S. John Ruskin lived (1823–42) at 28 **Herne Hill**, a large semi-detached villa, from the age of 4 until his parents moved to Denmark Hill

(q.v.) to the N. Ruskin writes of the house, its garden, the almond blossom, the country walks and views in his autobiography *Praeterita* (1885–9). In 1852, 4 years after his marriage, his father bought no. 30, adjacent to their former home, for his son and daughter-in-law. Ruskin's mother, who was excessively possessive about her only child and worried about his health, wished to have him near her. He was able to work in his old study at Denmark Hill every day, and his wife was expected to drive over to join the family for dinner. But in 1854 Ruskin's wife, who was in love with the painter Millais, got an annulment of her marriage. Ruskin, after travelling abroad, rejoined his parents at Denmark Hill. No. 28 was let from 1852 and was demolished in 1906. A plaque which had been on the house was re-erected in the front garden on the site in 1925. Door plates and a drawing of the house can be seen at Brantwood (q.v.).

Highgate [11 Db, Eb], district to the N. on the NE. of Hampstead Heath. Coleridge lived for 19 years in Highgate and at 3 **The Grove** (P) with his friends James and Ann Gillman from 1823 until his death. Lamb visited him in 1831 and put up at the Gate House Inn near by.

Highgate Cemetery is in two parts, the principal gates opposite each other in Swain's Lane. The older part, to the W., which was closed to the public in the 1970s because of vandalism, is to be reopened for restricted times. It is a fantastic and beautiful place on the hillside below St. Michael's Church, the sunlight penetrating with difficulty through a tangle of trees and shrubs on mourning cherubs and broken columns. The newer part is more formal, though its regularity is pleasantly broken by glades and shaded paths. Here George Eliot's obelisk (not far from Karl Marx's monument) is easily found, but the graves of Crabb Robinson, Christina Rossetti, and Leslie Stephen take time to discover. Mrs. Henry Wood's massive family tomb is in the old part.

When Gerard Manley Hopkins was at Highgate School (1856–63) he boarded at Elgin House (now commercial premises) in **Highgate High St.** He won the school Poetry Prize in 1860.

A. E. Housman wrote *A Shropshire Lad* (1896) while he was living at 17 **North Rd.** (P) from 1886 to 1905. The house (formerly

Byron Cottage) is one of a row set back from the road behind sycamore trees and has been little altered since Housman's day.

St. Michael's Church was built on the site of Arundel House ¶parts of the cellar are incorporated in the undercroft), which was demolished in 1825, the place where Francis Bacon died from a chill after stuffing a chicken with snow to test the preservation of meat by refrigeration.

Coleridge was reburied here, after having been removed from a grave in Old Highgate Chapel. A fine memorial to the 'poet, philosopher and theologian' was erected on the N. wall of the nave by his friends James and Ann Gillman, whose own memorial of similar design accompanies it.

On the outside wall of **Waterlow Park** on the W. side of Highgate High St., just N. of Lauderdale House, a weather-beaten plaque records the site of the cottage where Andrew Marvell once lived. The inscription reads:

Four feet below this spot is the stone step formerly the entrance to the cottage in which lived

ANDREW MARVELL

poet, wit and satirist

colleague with John Milton in the Foreign or Latin Secretaryship during the Commonwealth and for about twenty years MP for Hull. Born at Winstead, Yorkshire, 31st March 1621. Died, in London, 18th August 1678, and buried in the church of St.-Giles-in-the-Fields.

Holborn (pr. Hoebern) [10 Ga, Gb, Hb], district between the City and Bloomsbury. In 1770 the 17-year-old Thomas Chatterton lodged in the attic at 39 **Brooke St.** (P erected in 1928 on site) kept by Mrs. Angel, a sack maker. He wrote a burletta (a musical farce) for the entertainments in Marylebone Gdns. and spent some of the money he received on presents for his mother and sister in Bristol. A letter to them boasts of the amount of work he has had accepted and that he has 'a deal of business now'. However, the works that he mentioned never appeared, his second burletta was not performed, and his money ran out. His death from arsenic poisoning was thought to be due to poverty and despair; his landlady had offered him food but a baker had refused him a loaf on credit and Chatterton might have thought his landlady, to whom he owed rent, would expect payment too. The possibility that he died as a result of trying to cure himself of a venereal disease has also been put forward.

He was buried in the workhouse cemetery (gone) in Shoe Lane on the day his second burletta was performed.

Sydney Smith, having arrived with his wife from Edinburgh, lived (1803–6) at 14 (formerly 8) **Doughty St.** (P). In March 1837 Dickens, with his wife Catherine and their baby son Charles, came to live at no. 48 (P), now The Dickens House[1] (signposted from Theobalds Rd. and Guilford St.). Here he finished the last five monthly numbers of *The Pickwick Papers* (Apr.–Oct. 1837) and wrote *Oliver Twist* (1837–8) and *Nicholas Nickleby* (1838–9). He also began *Barnaby Rudge*, but its publication did not begin until 1841. This pleasant 18th-c. house, where his reputation became established, was the scene of the lively dinner parties that he delighted to give, where the guests included many literary and artistic celebrities, notably Harrison Ainsworth, Leigh Hunt, and John Forster, who became Dickens's lifelong friend and biographer. By October 1839 Dickens had become the father of two more children, both daughters, and as the family needed a larger house they moved to 1 Devonshire Ter. (see Marylebone).

The Dickens House is owned by the Dickens Fellowship (founded 1902) and contains a library and museum of wide-ranging interest. Pages of the original manuscripts of Dickens's early books are on view, as well as a large collection of his letters and personal relics. Of particular interest is the velvet-topped portable desk designed by himself, from which he gave dramatic readings from his works in many parts of Britain and America.

Gray's Inn, one of the four Inns of Court (q.v.), and known to have existed as a school of law since the 14th c., is situated between High Holborn and Theobalds Rd. and is bounded on the E. by Gray's Inn Rd. The main entrance is through the 17th-c. gateway in High Holborn and leads to South Sq., where the statue of Sir Francis Bacon, Lord Verulam (by F. W. Pomeroy, 1912) stands at the E. end of the lawn. Bacon, regarded by many as the Inn's greatest figure, entered as a student in 1576, became a Bencher in 1586, and treasurer in 1608. He retained his chambers here, on the site of the present Verulam Buildings on the NE. corner of Gray's Inn Sq., until his death in 1626, and laid out the Gardens,[2] entered from Field Ct. At least one ancient catalpa tree which he planted there is alleged to have been grown from a slip brought by Sir Walter Ralegh from America. The gardens and walks were once fashionable places for meeting and talking; Pepys mentions strolling there, Bacon and Ralegh paced arm-in-arm, Sir Philip Sidney, Addison, Macaulay, all knew them well, and Charles Lamb called them 'the best gardens of any in the Inns of Court, my beloved Temple not forgotten'.

The Hall, on the N. side of South Sq., was built in 1556–60, bombed in 1941, and rebuilt in its original style in 1951. It was the scene of many royal occasions and the setting for the first production of Shakespeare's *The Comedy of Errors* in 1594. The 16th–17th-c. stained glass includes the arms of Bacon. T. B. Macaulay, called to the Bar in 1826, took chambers in 1829 at 8 South Sq. (library on site). Dickens, aged 15, worked as a clerk for Ellis and Blackmore, solicitors, at 1 South Sq., then Holborn Ct. The desk he used here is preserved at The Dickens House in Doughty St.

Other distinguished members include: George Gascoigne (1525?–1577), who entered before 1548; Thomas Campion, who entered in 1586 but withdrew before 1595, was probably connected with the Gray's Inn masque of 1594–5, which included some of his songs. He was an authority on music and published some books of airs; Thomas Middleton (1570?–1627), who probably entered 1593; James Shirley (1596–1666), who was a resident *c.* 1625 and compiled the text for the Inns of Court masque *The Triumph of Peace* (1634); Robert Southey (1774–1843), who entered in February 1797, but found the study of law 'laborious indulgence' and gave it up. He published *Minor Poems* the same year, completed 'Madoc', and planned 'Thalaba the Destroyer'.

William Hayley, who studied law at the Middle Temple, lived (*c.* 1770) at 55–6 **Great Queen St.**, off Kingsway (near Lincoln's Inn Fields). William Blake, who became his friend, served his apprenticeship as an engraver with James Basire at no. 31 from 1771–8, and R. H. Barham, who was appointed a minor canon of St. Paul's in 1821, lived at no. 51 from 1821 till 1824.

Henry Crabb Robinson moved to 56 **Hatton Garden** in 1810 when his landlord changed houses. Dorothy Wordsworth, one of the many literary friends mentioned in Robinson's *Diary*, dined with him here when he accompanied her in the coach from Bury St. Edmunds to stay with the Lambs.

On the N. side of **Holborn**, between Brooke St. and Leather Lane, the Prudential Building occupies the site of Furnival's Inn (demolished 1897; P), where Dickens lived in 1836. Inside the covered entrance on the left is a bust of Dickens by Percy Fitzgerald, commemorating the writing of *The Pickwick Papers*, which first appeared in twenty monthly instalments beginning in April 1836. Thackeray met Dickens here for the first time, having called with the idea that he might illustrate Dickens's stories. The drawings that he offered, however, were unsuitable and this disappointment (so he said) caused him to direct his attention to another form of art. John Macrone, who published Dickens's sketches in book form, *Sketches by Boz* (1836–7), brought N. P. Willis, the American littérateur, to call on Dickens here. Willis described the poverty of 'the young paragraphist' in his rooms, his 'three-pair-back' as Dickens called them.

Hazlitt married Sarah Stoddart in 1808 at **Holborn Circus** at **St. Andrew's**. Charles and Mary Lamb were groomsman and bridesmaid and Charles wrote that he was nearly turned out of the church during the ceremony as 'anything awful makes me laugh'.

John Ruskin was born (1819) at 54 **Hunter St.** (demolished 1969) and lived there until his parents moved to Herne Hill in 1823. The drawing-room door and shutter knobs and the front-door chain were preserved and can be seen in Ruskin's study at Brantwood (q.v.).

Holy Trinity Church (P), **Kingsway**, was built (1831) on the site of 7 Little Queen St., where Charles and Mary Lamb and their family had lodgings when they left the Temple in 1795. It was here in the following year that Mary, in a fit of insanity, stabbed her mother to death and was temporarily confined to an asylum at Hoxton. Charles, who had moved with his father after the tragedy to 45 Chapel St. (gone), Pentonville, was determined that Mary should not stay in hospital, and for the rest of his life took the responsibility of caring for her and helping her over the recurrent attacks of her congenital mental illness.

Lincoln's Inn, one of the Inns of Court (q.v.), is situated between Chancery Lane and Lincoln's Inn Fields. It was named after Henry de Lacy, Earl of Lincoln (d. 1311), whose house stood in the vicinity and whose lion crest is on a shield over the Gothic gateway in Chancery Lane. The Old Hall (1506), opposite the gatehouse, was for centuries the centre of the Inn's communal life, where the members took their meals, performed masques, and danced, activities conducive 'to the making of gentlemen more fit for their books at other times'. The New Square (17th c.), which has housed many eminent members of the Bar and legal profession, is reached through an archway between the Hall and the Chapel. Arthur Murphy, dramatist and actor and friend of Dr. Johnson, lived at no. 1 from 1757 to 1788, having been accepted by Lincoln's Inn after being refused at Gray's Inn and the Middle Temple because he had been an actor at Covent Garden and Drury Lane. He was called to the Bar in 1762. Dickens worked as a clerk in a solicitor's office here for a short time when he was 14. On the N. side of the Square are the Inn gardens,[3] mentioned by Pepys in his *Diary* and by Steele in the *Tatler*, and the 19th-c. Hall and Library, the latter containing the oldest collection of books in London (founded 1497).

Distinguished members of the Inn include: Sir Thomas More (1478–1535), who entered in 1496 and was called to the Bar within a very short time; during this period he devoted his leisure to studying literature; Richard Edwards (1523?–66), who entered after leaving Oxford in 1547, but does not appear to have followed the legal profession; Thomas Lodge (1558?–1625), who entered in 1576; John Donne (1571/2–1631), who entered in 1592 and shared chambers with Christopher Brooke, another poet; later he was the Chapel's first chaplain; George Wither (1588–1667), who entered in 1606, but preferred to be a writer; Sir John Denham (1615–69), who entered in 1634 after leaving Oxford, and was called to the Bar in 1639; Lord Macaulay (1800–59), who was called to the Bar in 1826 and in 1829 took chambers in 8 South Sq. (demolished to make room for the Library); Benjamin Disraeli (Lord Beaconsfield) (1803–81), who entered in 1824 and kept nine terms, but removed his name in 1831. He began his literary career by writing poetry, but made his name with his successful first novel,

Vivian Grey (1826–7); Charles Reade (1814–84), who entered in 1835 and was called to the Bar in 1842; Thomas Hughes (1822–96), who entered in 1845 and migrated to the Inner Temple in 1848; Rider Haggard (1856–1925), who was called to the Bar in 1884 but left after his success as a novelist; Sir Henry Newbolt (1862–1938), who was called to the Bar in 1887 and practised for 12 years, gradually spending more time on writing. He spoke of his 'real claim to immortality' as having contributed largely to the *Law Digest*. His first novel, *Taken from the Enemy*, a tale of the Napoleonic wars, appeared in 1892; John Galsworthy (1867–1933), who was called to the Bar in 1890, but did not practise for long.

Lincoln's Inn Fields, a spacious square, laid out by Inigo Jones in 1618, between Lincoln's Inn and Kingsway. The poet Thomas Campbell lived at no. 61 from c. 1828 to 1832. John Forster, biographer and critic, moved into chambers at no. 58 in 1832 after studying law at the Inner Temple. He was called to the Bar in 1843, but gave up a legal career for literature and became a close friend of Lamb, Leigh Hunt, and Dickens. His works include biographies of Goldsmith, Landor, and Dickens, and the first volume of a life of Swift. Dickens portrays Forster's house as the home of Mr. Tulkinghorn in *Bleak House* (1852–3).

William Cowper worshipped at the church of **St. George-the-Martyr, Queen Sq.** when he was a law student. Frederick Walker's picture, *Thanksgiving*, was drawn here, showing the family in church, to illustrate Thackeray's novel, *The Adventures of Philip* (1861–2). William Morris and his family lived in the upper part of no. 26 from 1865 to 1872, above the workshops of the manufacturing and decorating firm of Morris, Marshall, Faulkner & Co. He published the poems, *The Life and Death of Jason* (1867) and *The Earthly Paradise* (1868–70), while he was living here.

Charles Churchill taught for a short time at a boarding school at no. 24 run by a Mrs. Dennis and known as the 'Ladies' Eton'. Fanny Burney was a pupil here, and after her father's second marriage in 1770, she lived with him and her stepmother for the next 4 years at a house in the Square with a pleasant prospect of Hampstead and Highgate.

Staple Inn in Holborn, opposite the end

of Gray's Inn Rd., was a former Inn of Chancery and consists of sets of chambers round two courtyards erected in 1545–89, and largely rebuilt in the 18th c. The Inn suffered extensive bomb damage in the Second World War and has been faithfully restored. Dr. Johnson stayed at no. 2 in the first court in 1759–60 and is believed to have written *Rasselas* here, in the evenings of a single week, in order to pay the expenses of his mother's funeral. Alternatively, he may have written it before leaving Gough Sq. (see City).

Benjamin Disraeli was born (1803) at 22 **Theobalds Rd.** (P, formerly 6 King's Rd., Bedford Row).

[1] Open weekdays 10 a.m.–5 p.m. (closed Bank Holidays, Easter Sat., and a week at Christmas).
[2] Open May–July: 12 noon–2 p.m.; Aug.–Sept.: 9.30 a.m.–5 p.m.
[3] Open Mon.–Fri. 12 noon–2.30 p.m.

Holloway [11 Ec], district to the N. **Bowman's Mews** turns off the SW. end of Seven Sisters Rd. near its junction with Holloway Rd. A plaque there records that in Elizabethan times it was a favourite spot for archery contests and that near-by Bowman's Lodge (gone) was the birthplace and childhood home (1812–22) of Edward Lear.

Hornsey [11 Eb], district to the N. In 1817 Thomas Moore took a furnished cottage at the foot of **Muswell Hill** in order to be near London while he was correcting the proofs of *Lalla Rookh* (1817), a series of oriental tales in verse connected by a prose narrative. At first he disliked the cottage because it abounded in rats and the chimneys smoked, but later the family was happy enough until the tragic death, after a fall, of his little daughter, Barbara. He left Muswell Hill in the autumn, returning only to visit Barbara's grave in Hornsey churchyard. The house, later called Lalla Rookh Cottage, has gone (site behind the houses in Etheldene Ave.) and its garden has been incorporated in Alexandra Park.

Hungerford Stairs. See Strand, Charing Cross Station.

Hyde Park [10 Cc, Dc], 360-acre public park to the W. of Mayfair and N. of Belgravia. The bird sanctuary in the NW. part is a memorial to W. H. Hudson, author of *Birds in London* (1898), *Birds and Man* (1901),

and *Adventures among Birds* (1913), and Epstein's sculpture *Rima* portrays the heroine of *Green Mansions* (1904), the spirit of the forest.

Ezra Pound remembers 'our London, my London, your London' in *Pisan Cantos* LXXX (1949)

and the Serpentine will look just the same
and the gulls be as neat on the pond
and the sunken garden the same unchanged

In 1974 a short ceremony at Byron's statue at Hyde Park Corner celebrated the hundred and fiftieth anniversary of his death.

Charles Reade lived (1869–79) at 2 **Albert Ter.** (later 19 Albert Gate, gone) opposite Sloane St. The American actress Rose Eytinge, who played in the stage version of Reade's *Griffith Gaunt* (1866), described the house on her visit in the late 1870s as

distinguished from its neighbours by the courtyard, which is full of foliage, underbrush, and a 'rockery' and 'fernery', while an arbor covers the walk leading up to the doorway. Inside the house is a perfect treasure house of objects. . . . Mr. Reade's study is at the back of the house in a room on the first floor, which he had built himself. It extends clear across the house, some thirty or forty feet, and has an enormous window in the centre, which commands a view of the gardens and Hyde Park. . . .

Reade's novel *A Terrible Temptation* (1871), written like the earlier *Hard Cash* to highlight the need for reform of the laws regarding lunacy, also shows how the author assembled the evidence needed in all his novels advocating change.

Inns of Court. Groups of buildings belonging to the four legal societies having the exclusive right to admit persons to practise at the English Bar: the Inner Temple and Middle Temple (see City), Lincoln's Inn and Gray's Inn (see Holborn). These societies, formed in the 14th and 15th cc., became wealthy and powerful, and governed themselves by elected bodies of Benchers (senior members). Students training to become barristers used to receive a general education at the Inns, including subjects such as history and music as well as law.

Islington [11 Ec], former riverside village to the N. In 1683 Thomas Sadler built a music hall and entertainment centre round a medicinal spring which became a popular spa, called Sadler's Wells (now in Roseberry Ave.). 'The Morning Ramble', a burlesque of 1684, though praising Epsom and Tunbridge Wells says

> Those are but good for one disease,
> To all distempers this gives ease.

In 1753 the wooden building became a theatre with a regular company and in 1765 a new stone theatre was built.

In Smollett's *Humphry Clinker* (1771), Winifred Jenkins, who had been enchanted by the tumbling and dancing upon ropes and wires, was molested in a dark passage by 'a fine gentleman' who began to show 'his cloven futt'. She hardly knew how she was rescued 'being in such a flustration'. The actor-manager Samuel Phelps, who lived at 8 **Canonbury Sq.** (P), made Shakespeare's plays popular at Sadler's Wells for nearly 20 years. The theatre was rebuilt in 1931. Evelyn Waugh was living in Canonbury Sq. when his first satirical novel *Decline and Fall* (1928) was published.

Canonbury Tower (now a theatre), built originally as part of the country house of the priors of St. Bartholomew's, was rebuilt in Queen Elizabeth I's reign and later (1616–25) leased to Sir Francis Bacon. In the 1760s the first floor of this tower with its two wings became the country home of the publisher, John Newbery, and his family, and he installed (1762) Oliver Goldsmith in one of the apartments above. Goldsmith, who wrote *The Traveller* (1764) here, often took a room in the city for short periods until Newbery's death in 1767.

Charles and Mary Lamb lived (1823–7) at Colebrook Cottage (now 64 **Duncan Ter.**, P), 'a detached, whitish house, close to the New River, end of Colebrook Ter., left hand from Sadler's Wells'. Lamb, who retired from the India Office in 1825, mentions in his *Letters* the pleasure of his first garden with his vegetables and his vine. They were visited by a large number of friends including Crabb Robinson, Mary Russell Mitford, Mary Shelley, Barry Proctor, the young Harrison Ainsworth and their near-neighbour Thomas Hood. Their publisher Edward Moxon helped carry books into their new quarters and later married their adopted daughter, Emma Isola. Their friends left safely except the myopic George Dyer, who walked straight into the New River (now safely under the gardens dividing Duncan Ter. from Colebrook Row). His rescue gave Lamb the subject for 'Amicus Redivivus', in

Essays of Elia (1823). Lamb's friend Thomas Hood moved to no. 5 Lower St. (now 50 **Essex St.**) as a child and it is probably this house that he was thinking of in his poem beginning

> I remember, I remember,
> The house where I was born,

A plaque on no. 3 **Terrett's Pl.**, off Upper St., mentions 'A Singular Little Old Fashioned House' where Tom Pinch in Dickens's *Martin Chuzzlewit* (1843–4) goes looking for lodgings.

In 'Sursum Corda' in *Success* (1902), Cunninghame Graham tells of his two months imprisonment in Pentonville Prison following his arrest during a demonstration in Trafalgar Sq. in 1887.

Kensal Green [11 Dc], district to the NW. Harrison Ainsworth lived (1835–41) at Kensal Lodge, **Harrow Rd.**, a white, two-storeyed house overlooking woods and fields to Willesden. He describes the view as 'A superb panorama . . . a vast and beautiful prospect . . .' in *Jack Sheppard* (1839), the story of a young criminal, John Sheppard (1702–24), subject of many 18th-c. plays and ballads, who was hanged at Tyburn. Ainsworth's book, set mainly in the Willesden area near by, started the myth that Sheppard was buried in Willesden cemetery, whereas he had a pauper's grave in St. Martin-in-the-Fields. Ainsworth also wrote the major parts of *Crichton* (1837) and *The Tower of London* (1840) here. He lived next door (1841–53) at the larger Kensal Manor to make a home for his daughters. He entertained his many friends at both these houses, including John Macrone his publisher, Francis Mahony, William Maginn, Daniel Maclise who painted his portrait, Cruikshank who illustrated his novels, Richard Barham, John Forster, Dickens who brought his 'conjuring apparatus' for the winter evenings, and Mrs. Hughes, Thomas Hughes's grandmother, who brought her fund of ghost stories and legends. Thackeray walked across the fields with the family to Willesden Church where Harrison Ainsworth was churchwarden. In the summer the guests sat on the seat round the old oak tree in the garden where they could hear nightingales. *Windsor Castle* (1843), *The Lancashire Witches* (1848), and *Mervyn Clitheroe* (1851) were mainly written here.

The main entrance to **Kensal Green Cemetery** is in Harrow Rd., near its junction with Ladbroke Grove. It contains the graves of many distinguished writers, including Thomas Hood (d. 1845. 'He sang the Song of the Shirt'), Sydney Smith (d. 1845), Douglas Jerrold (d. 1857), Leigh Hunt (d. 1859), Thackeray (d. 1863), Samuel Lover (d. 1868), John Forster (d. 1876), Harrison Ainsworth (d. 1882), Trollope (d. 1882), Wilkie Collins (d. 1889), and Francis Thompson (d. 1907), in the R.C. cemetery. The area of the cemetery is extensive and a newcomer would find it best to consult the office,[1] where a numbered map indicates the location of every grave.

[1] Open Mon.-Fri. 9 a.m.-5 p.m., Sat. 9 a.m.-12 noon, Sun. 2-6 p.m.

Kensington [10 Ab, Ac, Ad, Ae, Af, Bd, Be], district W. and SW. of Hyde Park. Sir Edwin Arnold, author of *The Light of Asia* (1879), a poem in eight books of blank verse about the life and philosophy of the Buddha, made his last home at 31 **Bolton Gdns.**, South Kensington (P) and died there (1904). Beatrix Potter was born at no. 2 and lived there, apart from visits to Scotland and the Lake District, until her marriage to William Heelis in 1913. The house (together with many of its neighbours) has been demolished, and the site is occupied by Bousefield Primary School; only nos. 7 and 8, of similar design, remain to give an idea of what it looked like. Beatrix Potter's *Journal, 1881-97* (ed. L. Linder, 1966), gives an insight into her conventional middle-class upbringing which nevertheless allowed scope for the growth of her vigorous and independent mind.

Brompton Cemetery, N. of Fulham Rd., has the graves of Lady Morgan, author of *The Wild Irish Girl* (1806), Borrow, who died at Oulton in 1881 and is buried with his wife, and G. A. Henty, who died on his yacht in Weymouth in 1902.

Brompton Oratory, or the London Oratory of St. Philip Neri, a Roman Catholic church founded (1849) principally by the efforts of Cardinal Newman, was built on its present site in Brompton Rd. in 1854. A statue of Newman stands at the W. end. Frederick Faber, author of many hymns and devotional books, was its first head.

Stéphane Mallarmé, at the age of 21, married Marie Gherard here on 10 August 1863, and in 1927 Alfred Noyes married his second wife, Mary Weld-Blundell.

Mallarmé, who had come to London in the autumn of 1862 in order to improve his English and study the life and works of Edgar Allan Poe, stayed at 6 **Brompton Sq.** (P), on the N. side of Brompton Rd., from April to the end of August in the following year. He later made French translations of Poe's poems that delighted Swinburne (whom he addressed as 'Cher Monsieur et Maître').

Lord Macaulay spent his last years (1856-9) at Holly Lodge (gone), at the upper end of **Campden Hill**, near the narrow way to Holland Walk. The original plaque commemorating his death was placed there in 1903 and re-erected in 1968 on Atkins Building, an extension of Queen Elizabeth College.

Ford Madox Hueffer lodged at South Lodge, 80 **Campden Hill Rd.** (P), the home of the novelist Violet Hunt, from *c.* 1912 until he enlisted in the army. He changed his name to Ford Madox Ford after joining up.

Ivy Compton-Burnett lived (1934-69) at 5 Braemar Mansions, **Cornwall Gdns.**, at first with Margaret Jourdain, but alone after her death in 1951. Most of her novels, including *Daughters and Sons* (1937), *Parents and Children* (1941), and *Mother and Son* (1955) which won the James Tait Black Memorial Prize, were written here. After the Second World War Ivy Compton-Burnett invited her friends to Saturday afternoon tea-parties, formal meals where unpunctuality was censured. She was made a D.B.E. in 1957 and given an honorary degree by Leeds University in 1960. She died in 1969 and after cremation her ashes were buried at Putney Vale cemetery.

Henry James lived at 34 **De Vere Gdns.** (P) from 1886. Among the novels he wrote here are *The Tragic Muse* (1890), *What Maisie Knew* (1897), and *The Sacred Fount* (1901). From 1896 he spent the winters here until in 1902 he bought a house in Rye. No. 22 (P) was Robert Browning's last home (1888-9) in England before he returned to Italy where he died (1889).

W. B. Yeats stayed with his family at 14 **Edith Rd.**, West Kensington from 1874 to 1876, when they moved to Bedford Park (see Chiswick).

G. Lowes Dickinson, pacifist, critic, and

Fellow of King's College, Cambridge (q.v.), is commemorated at 11 **Edwardes Sq.** (P), his London home.

J. M. Barrie lived 1895-8 at 133 **Gloucester Rd.** He wrote here *Sentimental Tommy* (1896) and *Margaret Ogilvy* (1896), the life of his mother, both set in his home town of Kirriemuir (q.v.).

W. S. Gilbert lived (1883-90) at 39 **Harrington Gdns.** (P), a house he designed himself. His operas, containing satires on topics of the day and with music by Arthur Sullivan, include *Princess Ida* (1884), *The Mikado* (1885), *Ruddigore* (1887), *The Yeomen of the Guard* (1888), and *The Gondoliers* (1889).

George Borrow, after many travels, lived at 22 **Hereford Sq.** (P), on the W. side of the Old Brompton Rd. end of Gloucester Rd., from 1860 until his return to Oulton (q.v.) in 1874. *Wild Wales*, an account of his wanderings in Wales, was published in 1862. His wife Mary died in 1869.

Holland House (P on site), a 17th-c. mansion, was famous under the third Lord Holland as a centre of influence in the Whig Party. Addison, who married the Dowager Countess of Warwick and Holland in 1716, lived here until his death in 1719. The first Lord Holland, who acquired the house in 1767, often entertained Horace Walpole.

The imperious wife of the third Lord Holland (1773-1840), Carlyle's 'proud old dame', welcomed men of promise in political and literary circles so long as they reached her exacting standards of wit and worldly knowledge. Sheridan, Thomas Campbell, Sydney Smith, Tom Moore, Rogers, Crabbe, Washington Irving, Fenimore Cooper, Mackintosh, Monckton Milnes, Dickens, and Macaulay succeeded in entertaining her.

The house was demolished after damage in the Second World War. One wing has been rebuilt and is now a Youth Hostel.

Ford Madox Hueffer (later Ford) lived 1908-10 at 84 **Holland Park Ave.**, where he edited the *English Review*.

Dickens had lodgings in 1862 (gone) at 16 **Hyde Park Gate**, off Kensington Rd., when he came to London from Gad's Hill (q.v.).

Sir Leslie Stephen, scholar and original editor of *The Dictionary of National Biography*, lived at no. 22 (P), from 1879 till his death in 1904. His daughter Virginia (later Virginia Woolf) was born here in 1882.

Ezra Pound rented the first-floor front room at 10 **Kensington Church Walk**, a paved cul-de-sac off Holland St., near St. Mary Abbott's Garden, from Mrs. Langley, his 'unique and treasured landlady'. It had 'a cast-iron fireplace with a hob either side of the bars and a pair of good windows looking south'. His bath, which he used to supply with cans of hot water from the kitchen boiler, was kept under his bed—see his poem 'The Bathtub'. He lived here from 1909 till his marriage with Dorothy Shakespear in 1914.

Gore House in **Kensington Gore** (site now the Royal Albert Hall) was the home of Lady Blessington, whose salon, first at Seamore Pl. (gone), Mayfair, and here after 1836, was the scene of brilliant gatherings. The American N. P. Willis wrote, in *Pencillings by the Way* (1835), that she was 'one of the most lovely and fascinating women I have ever seen'. After her husband's sudden death she turned to writing to augment her income. Her first novel, *Grace Cassidy, or the Repealers* (1833), was followed by *Conversations with Lord Byron* (1834), first published in the *New Monthly Magazine*. She wrote other novels and edited *The Keepsake* for ten years from 1841. *The Belle of the Season* (1840) was in verse. She was acquainted with many of the literati of her day and among those who frequented her salon at Gore House, where she was living with Count D'Orsay, were Samuel Rogers, Landor, Thomas Campbell, Horace and James Smith, joint authors of *Rejected Addresses* (1812), Tom Moore, Disraeli, Harrison Ainsworth, Dickens, Monckton Milnes, Forster, Dickens's first biographer, and Thackeray.

Though Lady Blessington's income from her writing was considerable she became bankrupt in 1849 and fled to Paris whither D'Orsay had preceded her. Gore House was sold and in 1851 it became the restaurant attended by the thousands of visitors to the Great Exhibition (1851). Thackeray described the scene in an article in *Punch*.

When Sir James Barrie lived in Bayswater Rd. (1902-9) he used to walk in **Kensington Gdns.** with his Newfoundland dog, Luath, the prototype of Nana in *Peter Pan, or the Boy who wouldn't grow up* (the popular play for children, produced 1904). The Peter Pan statue, near the Westbourne Gate entrance, was designed by Sir George Frampton in 1912 at Barrie's expense. The near-by stretch of the Serpentine, the 'Long Water', was the place where Shelley's first wife, the tragic young Harriet, drowned herself (1816).

Marie Corelli lived at 47 **Longridge Rd.** (P) from 1883 to 1900. After her father had had a stroke she moved with him from their home at Mickleham (q.v.) and began her writing career. Her first novel, *A Romance of Two Worlds*, was published in 1886 and was followed by the successful *Barabbas* (1893) and the immensely popular *The Sorrows of Satan* (1895). In 1900 she decided to settle in Stratford-upon-Avon (q.v.).

James Russell Lowell, American poet and essayist, lived at 37 **Lowndes St.** in 1880 and at nos. 10 and 31 **Lowndes Sq.** (1881–5), when an American Minister in England.

Andrew Lang lived from 1875 at 1 **Marloes Rd.** (P). He wrote here the poems *Ballades in Blue China* (1880) and *Helen of Troy* (1882), the anthropological *Custom and Myth* (1884), some historical works, essays, including *Letters to Dead Authors* (1886), *Books and Bookmen* (1887), and the *Life and Letters of J. G. Lockhart* (1896). Lang returned to St. Andrews at the end of his life.

The historian J. A. Froude lived from 1862 to 1892 at 5 **Onslow Gdns.** (P), leading off Onslow Sq. W. E. H. Lecky, another historian, lived at no. 38 (P) after his marriage in 1871, and died here.

No. 36 **Onslow Sq.** (P), just S. of South Kensington Station, became Thackeray's home in 1853 after his return from his first American lecture tour. His daughter, Anne Ritchie, described the house as 'a pleasant, bowery sort of home, with green curtains and carpets, looking out upon the elm trees'. They lived there for 7 years, next door to Thackeray's friend, Baron Marochetti, who subsequently made his bust for Westminster Abbey. Here Thackeray completed *The Newcomes* (1853–5) and wrote *The Virginians* (1857–9), *The Adventures of Philip* (his last complete novel, 1861–2, published serially in the *Cornhill Magazine*, of which he was the first editor in 1860), and many of *The Roundabout Papers* (also published in the *Cornhill Magazine*, 1860–3).

No. 57 **Palace Gardens Ter.** (P), off Bayswater Rd., a little W. of Kensington Gdns., was the birthplace of Sir Max Beerbohm, essayist and caricaturist. The tree-lined terrace is known as 'Cherry Mile'.

At the S. end of Kensington Palace Gdns., a quiet private road shaded by tall trees, is **Palace Green**. Thackeray lived at no. 2 (P),

designed by himself, for the last 2 years of his life (1861–3) and died there.

Kenneth Grahame lived (1901–8) at 16 **Phillimore Place** (P) when he was Secretary to the Bank of England (he retired in 1908). It was here that he wrote most of *The Wind in the Willows* (1908), which began as bedtime stories for his son Alistair (known as 'Mouse').

No. 40 **St. Luke's Rd.**, North Kensington was the home from 1886 to 1922 of W. H. Hudson, naturalist and writer, whose best remembered work is *Green Mansions* (1904), a romance of the S. American forest. A plaque placed on the house by the Hudson's Friends Society of Quilmes, near Buenos Aires, has a bronze bas-relief showing the house where he was born.

G. K. Chesterton was born (1874) at 32 **Sheffield Ter.** (P), between Campden Hill Rd. and Kensington Church St. He spent his early years (1879–99) at 11 **Warwick Gdns.** (P), S. of Kensington High St. His first book of poems, *The Wild Knight* (1900), was written here.

On the S. side of Kensington High St., nearly opposite the end of Kensington Church St., is **Young St.**, where Thackeray lived at no. 13 (now no. 16, P) from 1846 to 1853. He wrote *Vanity Fair* (1847–8), *Pendennis* (1848–50), and *The History of Henry Esmond* (1852) here, and began *The Newcomes* (1853–5). In May 1850 he met Charlotte Brontë again at her publisher's house and she discussed his literary shortcomings with 'decent amity'. Though George Smith, her publisher, had told Thackeray that she was shy and did not wish to be recognized as the author of *Jane Eyre*, he arranged an evening party for her to meet a large gathering including the Carlyles and Adelaide Proctor. Thackeray's daughter, then aged 13, observed that Charlotte Brontë 'enters in mittens, in silence, in seriousness . . .'. The evening was insipid and Thackeray left for his club in the middle of the party.

Keston [11 Ff], district to the SE. Mrs. Craik, author of the popular *John Halifax, Gentleman* (1856), was buried (1887) in Keston churchyard, on the A233, 1¼ m. S. of the junction with the A232. Her grave with a tall Celtic cross is near the hedge bordering the triangular green.

Kew [11 Cd], riverside district to the SW.

Stephen Duck, whose long poem 'The Thresher's Labour' later included in *Poems on Several Occasions* (1736), found favour with Queen Caroline, was consequently made a Yeoman of the Guard. In 1733 he married the Queen's housekeeper at Kew and lived in the Palace[1] but his life there was not happy. He became librarian in 1735 and, after taking Orders, was made preacher at Kew Palace Chapel. He may have met James Thomson, author of *The Seasons*, at Richmond as they exchanged volumes of their verse. Duck left on becoming rector of Byfleet (q.v.) in 1752.

In 1773 Cobbett, aged 11, worked in Kew Gardens[2] after walking here from Farnham (q.v.).

Fanny Burney, through Mrs. Delany, became (1786) Second Keeper of the Robes to Queen Charlotte and she describes her unhappy life at Kew and the other royal palaces in her *Journal*. She was able to resign only because of a breakdown in health. Walpole commented on the menial task of folding muslins and Macaulay wondered that a writer of her calibre should have accepted such a post.

[1] Open Apr.–Sept.: weekdays 11 a.m.–5 p.m., Sun. 2–6 p.m.
[2] Open all the year, except Christmas and New Year's Day, from 10 a.m.

Kingsbury [11 Cb], district to the NW. In 1771, when **Edgware Rd.** still led from village to village, Oliver Goldsmith first spent the summer at a cottage, belonging to a farmer called Selby, on a hill between the villages of Edgware and Hyde. He wanted to be uninterrupted while writing and also to save himself the expenses of the city. He was here when *The History of England* (1771) was published and when he mentioned that he was writing a new comedy. This, when the difficulty of deciding on a title was resolved, became *She Stoops to Conquer* (1773). He also wrote part of *History of the Earth and Animated Nature* (1774) here and friends, finding him away, were amused to see that he had drawn subjects for this on the walls of his room. He was making plans to retire here but was taken ill in London and died in 1774.

Kingston upon Thames [11 Ce], district S. of Richmond Park to the SW. John Galsworthy was born (1867) at Parkfield, **Kingston Hill**, where his parents were wait-

ing for their new house to be finished on the twenty-four acres they had bought. This was Coombe Warren (gone), the first of their houses on Coombe Hill. The best remembered home of his childhood was Coombe Leigh, where he lived from 1875 to 1878, and again from 1881 to 1886 when the family returned to London. The estate with its spinney, cricket field, and large garden was the model for the surroundings of Forsyte House. The area has been developed and Coombe Leigh is now Coombe Ridge, a school in **George Rd.**

Lambeth [10 Gd, Hd], district S. of the river. When Arthur Rimbaud and Paul Verlaine came back to London in early 1874 (after their first visit in 1872–3) they shared a room in a boarding-house at 178 **Stamford St.**, near Waterloo Station. They were both hard up and lived in considerable squalor, ready to take any available job (such as employment in a cardboard-box factory) to make ends meet. Rimbaud probably composed the poem *Jeunesse* during this time. He left London, possibly for Scotland, at the end of July, was briefly in Reading in November, and finally returned to his home at Charleville at the end of the year.

The site of Astley's Amphitheatre (est. 1794 and given the prefix Royal in 1798), the most popular equestrian entertainment of the showman, Philip Astley, was at 225 **Westminster Bridge Rd.** Jane Austen herself visited in 1796 and in *Emma* (1816) tells how Harriet Smith and Robert Martin, at last, come to an understanding here, well out of reach of Emma's interference. A spectacle based on the ride in Byron's *Mazeppa* (1819) was one of the popular events taken on tour after the amphitheatre was burned down. It was often performed by the actress Ada Menken, author of the poems *Infelicia* (1868) and a friend of Dickens, who mentions Astley's in *Sketches by Boz*.

Lee [11 Fd, Fe], district to the SE. Ernest Dowson was born (1867) at The Grove, **Belmont Hill**, in Lee, then a village. After Oxford, which he left after a short time without a degree, and some years in the 1890s when he was a member of the Rhymers' Club, he went abroad. 'Non sum qualis eram . . .', the poem with the refrain 'I have been faithful to thee, Cynara! in my fashion', was published in *Poems* (1896). In 1900 he was found destitute by a friend who cared for him at 26 Sandhurst Gdns., Catford (a few miles SW.). He died 6 weeks later and was buried in the Catholic cemetery at Lewisham to the NW.

Lewisham. See Lee.

Leytonstone [11 Fb], district to the NE. John Drinkwater, Georgian poet and author of the play *Abraham Lincoln* (1918), was born (1882) at Dorset Villa, 105 **Fairlop Rd.**, the son of a schoolmaster who became an actor. Drinkwater Towers in Browning Rd., a tower-block of flats, is called after him.

Marylebone (or St. Marylebone) (pr. Măril'b'n) [10 Ca, Da, Db, Eb, Fb], district between Regent's Park and Oxford St. Edward Bulwer, later Lord Lytton, was born (1803) at 31 **Baker St.**

Sherlock Holmes, the amateur sleuth whose amazing powers of deduction solved the crimes in the ingenious stories of Sir Arthur Conan Doyle, lived at 221B Baker St., though no such number can now be found. Here hansom cabs deposited the clients who called for his help, and here, aided by the faithful Dr. Watson, he evaded many attacks from would-be murderers. Holmes's tweed cape and deer-stalker hat, his meerschaum pipe and magnifying glass, and the habit attributed to him of saying 'Elementary, my dear Watson' became known to a wide public.

Gibbon, after disposing of his Buriton estate and putting up with lodgings including that over 'a stinking apothecary's', leased (1773–83) 7 **Bentinck St.** (rebuilt, P). He wrote to his mother of the comfort of his library, '*my* gardens at Kensington', and the friends 'who are chained to London'. These included Goldsmith, Joshua Reynolds, and his friends in the House of Commons, one of whom wrote 'I have seldom met with a more agreeable party or more profitable subjects of conversation' than at Gibbon's house. In February 1773 Gibbon wrote in his *Autobiography*

No sooner was I settled in my house and library than I undertook the composition of the first Volume of my history. At the outset all was dark and doubtful: . . . and I was often tempted to cast away the labour of seven years.

Dickens lived (1833–4) at no. 18 (rebuilt) while writing *Sketches by Boz* (1835–6).

Coleridge lodged at 17 **Berners St.** (rebuilt, P) for 18 months (1812–13) with his friends the Morgan family. He wrote *Remorse*

(1813) here. Charles Lamb was a frequent visitor.

Henry Taylor, who worked in the Colonial Office, lived for some years in **Blandford Sq.** In 1828 he started to write the play *Philip van Artevelde* (1834), after a suggestion by Southey, with whom he had made a tour of Belgium and France (1824–5).

From the late 1840s to 1850 Wilkie Collins lived with his mother and brother at no. 38. He wrote here a *Memoir* (1848) of his father, a painter and a friend of David Wilkie, and also his first novel *Antonina* (1850).

Marian Evans (George Eliot) and George Lewes took the lease (1860–3) of no. 16. She heard here that Queen Victoria had praised her novel *Adam Bede* (1859), and she wrote *Silas Marner* (1861). After a visit to Italy to research into the background of her new novel, she began *Romola*, set in the Italy of Savonarola, in January 1862.

George Gissing lived from 1884 to 1890 at 7K **Cornwall Residences**, a block of flats near Baker St. Station, behind Madame Tussaud's. While he was here he published *The Unclassed* (1884), *Isabel Clarendon* (1886), *Demos: A Story of English Socialism* (1886), *Thyrza* (1887), *A Life's Morning* (1888), *The Nether World* (1889), and *The Emancipated* (1890).

Conan Doyle moved with his wife in 1890 from Southsea to London and he then found a consulting room at 2 **Devonshire Pl.**, where he set up his plate as an oculist. Every day he walked from Montagu Pl. and waited from ten o'clock until four, but as no patients appeared and the conditions were ideal he used the time to write. The 'first fruits of a considerable harvest' enabled him to give up the surgery and, as he wrote in *Memories and Adventures* (1930) 'to trust for ever to my power of writing'.

Swinburne lived (1865–70) at the two-storeyed 22 **Dorset St.**, where *Poems and Ballads* (1866), including 'Laus Veneris', 'Dolores', and 'A Litany', and *A Song of Italy* (1867) were written. His irregular life at this time often resulted in illness, when he was cared for at Shiplake by his mother. Elizabeth and Robert Browning spent 1855 at no. 13 (rebuilt), where she was writing *Aurora Leigh*. This was her last home in England. Rose Macaulay, author of the satirical novels, *Potterism* (1920), *Dangerous Ages* (1921), and *Told by an Idiot* (1923), lived in St. Andrew's Mansions here for many years after 1926. She also wrote the historical novel *They Were Defeated* (1932) and the novel of London at the end of the war, *The World my Wilderness* (1950).

John Byng (later Lord Torrington), who summed up his military service and civilian appointment in the lines:

His early days were spent in camps
His latter days were passed at stamps

lived at 29 **Duke St.**, near Manchester Sq., after retiring from the army and becoming a Comptroller of Stamps. He set out from here, sometimes accompanied for part of the journey by his wife, on the sight-seeing tours he describes in the *Torrington Diaries* (1934, reprinted 1970).

Thomas Moore lodged at 44 **George St.** on coming from Dublin in 1799 to the Middle Temple, and later at no. 85. He dedicated *Anacreon* (1800), a verse translation of 6th-c. B.C. odes, to the Prince of Wales, and was dubbed 'Anacreon Moore' by Byron, whose friend he became. A plaque from Moore's lodgings in Bury St. was re-erected on no. 85 in 1963.

Charles and Mary Lamb, Wordsworth, Coleridge, Tom Moore, and Samuel Rogers were guests of the M.P. Thomas Monkhouse at 34 **Gloucester Pl.** in 1823. Lamb wrote that he 'dined in Parnassus'. Elizabeth Barrett, one of a large family, lived at no. 99 (P, previously 74) from 1835 to 1838. Dickens lodged at no. 57 in 1865.

Wilkie Collins lived at no. 65 (P, previously 90) from 1867 to 1888. *The Moonstone* (1868), written here, was dictated as he was being given laudanum to relieve pain. Sergeant Cuff, one of the earliest detectives in fiction, appears in this novel.

James Boswell lived from 1790 until his death in 1795 at 122 **Great Portland St.** (P). He had outlived the friends who liven the pages of his *London Journal*.

Rossetti House (P) at nos. 106–10 **Hallam St.**, is on the site of 38 Charlotte St., where Christina Rossetti was born (1830), when her brother Dante Gabriel was 2. Six years later the family moved to no. 50.

Barry Cornwall (pseudonym of Bryan Procter, the friend of Lamb and Dickens) lived with his daughter, the poet Adelaide Procter, at 38 **Harley St.** in the 1840s and 1850s. Katherine Mansfield lived (1903–6) at no. 41 while at Queen's College (founded 1848) near by. At this time she was hoping

to make music her career. Arthur Pinero, whose plays *The Second Mrs. Tanqueray* (1893) and *Trelawny of the Wells* (1898) are still revived, lived at no. 115A (P) for some years after 1910.

George Gordon Byron was born (1788) in **Holles St.**, off Cavendish Sq.

Marie Louise de la Ramée (Ouida) lived at the Langham Hotel, in **Langham Pl.**, 1867–70. She was visited by a number of writers and painters, including Millais, Browning, and Lord Lytton. The hotel was also a favourite of many Americans, including the poet H. W. Longfellow and the novelist Samuel Clemens ('Mark Twain'). It became part of the B.B.C. in the 1930s and it was here that Max Beerbohm arranged his broadcasts, collected as *Mainly on the Air* (1946, 1957), that were such a feature of wartime Britain.

Edmond Malone, a member of Dr. Johnson's Club, lived from 1779 to his death in 1812 at 40 **Langham St.** (P). He edited Shakespeare's *Works* in 1790 and gave his friend Boswell scholarly assistance with the *Life of Samuel Johnson* (1791). Boswell spent many days with Malone here, though there were occasions when he wrote 'Malone was busy with his Shakespeare, so I could not get any of his time'. The Malone Society (founded 1906), which publishes early dramatic texts and other documents, is named after him.

Ezra Pound took lodgings next to the Yorkshire Grey in 1908. He wrote 'Night Litany', 'The Goodly Fere', and 'Sestina Altaforte'. He was also working on a 'damn bad novel' which he burnt here.

Leigh Hunt lived at 15 **Lisson Grove** (gone) *c.* 1815–17 and was visited by Byron, Wordsworth, and Shelley. In 1817 the painter Haydon gave a dinner at no. 116 (P) for friends, including Charles Lamb, and Keats who wished to be introduced to Wordsworth. The company talked of their favourite poets and Keats had asked a young surgeon, who was about to explore the Niger, to fling a copy of his *Endymion* into the Sahara, when they were joined by a Comptroller of Stamps who said he was a correspondent of Wordsworth. Lamb, who took exception to the interruption and became impolite, was led out to the next room but his protests remained audible and the pleasant atmosphere was ruined. Haydon painted Amelia Opie here.

Near the N. end of **Marylebone High St.** a little garden marks the site of the 15th-c. **Marylebone Parish Church,** where Francis Bacon was married in 1606. In the church built on the site in 1741, displaced as the parish church by the new building (see below), and destroyed by bombs in the Second World War, Sheridan married the beautiful singer, Elizabeth Linley, in 1773, the year after he had escorted her to France from Bath, where she had been plagued by an unwanted suitor. In 1788 Byron was baptized here. Thomas Holcroft, actor, novelist, and playwright, friend of Tom Paine and Charles Lamb, who lived in **Marylebone St.** during the 1780s, died in 1809 in Clipstone St. and was buried here. There are memorials to Allan Ramsay and Charles Wesley, who were buried in the churchyard.

St. Marylebone Parish Church (built 1812–13), in **Marylebone Rd.** opposite York Gate, has a window commemorating Robert Browning and Elizabeth Barrett, who were married here secretly in 1846 a week before their elopement. There is also a bronze tablet to Browning erected on the W. wall in 1887.

Ferguson House, a little further E., stands on the site of 1 Devonshire Ter., Charles Dickens's home from 1839 to 1851. The villa with a double bow-front and dormer windows above had a walled garden. Ferguson House has a panel with Dickens's characters in low relief. Dickens wrote here part of *The Old Curiosity Shop* (1841), *Barnaby Rudge* (1841), *American Notes* (1842) and *Martin Chuzzlewit* (1843–4), written after his visit to America, *A Christmas Carol* (1843), the first of his Christmas books, and *Dombey and Son* (1848), which has many scenes in Marylebone. Longfellow was among Dickens's visitors in 1842. Dickens kept ravens here, prototypes of Grip in *Barnaby Rudge.*

Arnold Bennett moved to 97 Chiltern Court Mansions, a large block of flats on the Baker St. corner, in 1930 and died here (1931) a few months later. H. G. Wells also lived here from 1930 to 1937, during which time he wrote the science fiction novel *The Shape of Things to Come* (1933).

Wilkie Collins lived at 9 **Melcombe Pl.,** between Marylebone Rd. and Marylebone Station, from the end of 1864 to 1867, and wrote his novel *Armadale* (1866).

Anthony Trollope lived (1872–80) at 39 **Montagu Sq.** (P), W. of Gloucester Pl.

The Eustace Diamonds (1873), which appeared first in the *Fortnightly Review,* was written here. John Forster, friend of Harrison Ainsworth and Dickens and the latter's first biographer, lived at no. 46 in the 1850s.

Sheridan lived at 22 **Orchard St.,** the S. end of Baker St., after his marriage in 1773, and wrote *The Rivals* and *The Duenna,* comedies acted in 1775. Sydney Smith lived (1806–9) at no. 18 while he was lecturing on moral philosophy to a large audience, which needed the addition of a gallery in the lecture room. The witty *Letters of Peter Plymley* (1807–8) were written here.

Coventry Patmore, author of poems collectively called *The Angel in the House,* and an assistant in the printed books department of the British Museum (1848–62), is commemorated by a plaque at 14 **Percy St.**

John Buchan, who lived until 1919 in the house he bought, 76 **Portland Pl.,** in 1913, wrote the spy story *The Thirty-nine Steps* (1914) while recuperating from an illness.

In 1781 the fashionable Mrs. Elizabeth Montagu moved to her new house, now 22 **Portman Sq.,** designed by 'Athenian' Stuart. It had a room decorated with 'roses and jessamine', the delight of Cowper and Mrs. Delany, and another adorned with the feathers of brightly coloured birds. Mrs. Montagu's salon was attended by other 'blue stockings' and by Burke, Horace Walpole, Dr. Johnson, and Boswell. She was the author of three of Lyttleton's *Dialogues of the Dead* and an essay on Shakespeare which attacked Voltaire's views. She was the patron of London's chimney-sweeps and gave them an annual dinner.

The French poet, André de Chénier, lived (1787–90) at no. 31 while Secretary to the Ambassador. He made few friends in England but visited Richard and Maria Cosway, the miniature painters whom he had known in Paris. He was working on his *Bucoliques* and he bought many English editions of the classics while here. He was guillotined shortly before the fall of Robespierre.

Boswell worked on his *Life of Samuel Johnson* (1791) in **Queen Anne St.** Richard Cumberland lived at the corner of Wimpole St. and Queen Anne St. when finishing *The West Indian* (1771) begun at his father's house in Clonfert. His later work did not enjoy the same high degree of success as this play.

Edward Lear lived at 30 **Seymour St.** (P). He needed to be near the Regent's Park Zoo in order to study parrots for his commission from the Royal Zoological Society.

Plaques at 3 **Spanish Pl.** commemorate both Captain Marryat, who wrote *Masterman Ready* (1841) when living here, and the comedian George Grossmith. George and his brother Weedon were joint authors of *The Diary of a Nobody* (1894), which catalogues with poignant irony the domestic and social gaucheries of Mr. Charles Pooter of The Laurels, Holloway, an assistant in a mercantile business.

Letitia Elizabeth Landon, who lived at 28 **Upper Berkeley St.**, wrote, as 'L.E.L.', novels and poems, including her first poem 'Rome', published in the *Literary Gazette* in 1820, *The Fate of Adelaide* (1821), another poem, *Ethel Churchill* (1837) considered her best novel, and *Traits and Trials of Early Life* (1837), which may be autobiographical. She died (1838) from poisoning soon after her marriage to George MacLean, a provincial governor, and her arrival in West Africa.

Max Beerbohm lived at no. 48 with his family from the early 1890s, when he was at Oxford, to 1910 when he married and went to live in Italy. He wrote here the essays collected as *The Works of Max Beerbohm* (1896), *More* (1899), and *Yet Again* (1909), and also *Zuleika Dobson* (1911), the fantasy about Oxford which he began in 1898.

The Brownings spent part of the summer of 1852 at 58 **Welbeck St.**, now a hotel. Marie Louise de la Ramée lived with her mother at no. 51 for a short time in 1867, when her popular novel *Under Two Flags* was published. Trollope died (1882) at no. 33, now part of the rebuilt Welbeck Mansions, where he was being nursed after a stroke.

Elizabeth Barrett, who was a semi-invalid perhaps as a result of a fall from her pony, lived at 50 **Wimpole St.** (rebuilt, P) from 1838 to 1846. The publication of her poems and *Prometheus Bound* (1833) began a correspondence with Robert Browning which resulted in his offer of marriage. The ceremony took place in secret in 1846 to prevent her father from banning the marriage because of her precarious state of health. The popular play by Rudolph Besier (1878–1942), *The Barretts of Wimpole Street* (1930), presents Mr. Barrett as a parent whose zealous care of his daughter becomes a tyranny. On her elopement to Italy Elizabeth Barrett took with her the spaniel that Mary Mitford had given her. The dog's story is told in *Flush: a Biography* (1940) by Virginia Woolf.

Wilkie Collins spent the last months of his life at no. 82 (rebuilt) and died there in 1889.

Mayfair [10 Dc, Eb, Ec, Ed, Fb], district between Oxford St. and Piccadilly. **Albany**, just E. of Burlington House, is a private enclave (P near by) where in 1802 the mansion of the Duke of York and Albany was divided into fashionable sets of rooms or chambers. Byron lived here for a short time and Matthew Gregory Lewis, known as 'Monk' Lewis after his Gothic novel, lived here from *c.* 1812. Lewis made two journeys in 1815–16 and 1817–18 to look into the running of his plantation in Jamaica and his *Journal of a West Indian Proprietor* (1834) was published after his death from a fever on the voyage home in 1818. Lord Lytton had a *pied-à-terre* here when he was living at Knebworth (q.v.) and Lord Macaulay lived here from 1841 to 1856.

Soon after moving to new offices at 50 **Albemarle St.**, John Murray published Byron's successful *Childe Harold* (1812), and introduced the young author to Scott here. The *Quarterly Review*, founded by Murray in 1809 and edited by Gifford, contained the article on Keats's *Endymion* (1812) to which Byron replied with the lines:

> Who killed John Keats?
> 'I' says the Quarterly,
> So savage and Tartarly,
> ''Twas one of my feats.'

Scott, who tried to temper Gifford's bitterness to new-style authors, praised Jane Austen's *Emma* (1816) and reviewed his own *Tales of My Landlord* (1817). Murray recounts in his *Autobiography* how the booksellers' messengers filled the streets and made 'obstreperous demands' for copies of Byron's *Don Juan* on publication day in 1819. It was at no. 50 that Murray angrily refused to jeopardize Byron's reputation by publishing his memoirs. Tom Moore, to whom the memoirs had been bequeathed, reluctantly acquiesced, and the manuscript was burnt in the grate in 1824.

Berkeley Sq., a residential square built in the 1740s, is now chiefly office blocks. Colley Cibber, a popular actor turned dramatist, who became Poet Laureate in 1730, and was satirized by Pope in *The*

Dunciad, died here (on the site of no. 19) in 1757. Horace Walpole stayed (1779–97) at his town house, no. 11 (gone), when visiting from Strawberry Hill, and he died here. Thackeray called the square, then the finest in London, Buckley Sq. in *Yellowplush Papers* (1837) and Gaunt Sq. in *Vanity Fair* (1847–8).

Charles Reade lodged (1856–68) with Laura Seymour, an actress, who with her husband kept a boarding-house at 6 **Bolton Row** (gone, formerly at the end of Bolton St.). Reade's novel *It is Never too Late to Mend* (1856), part of which is set in the gold-fields of Australia, exposes the harshness of the penal system. Its realism was also popular when dramatized. *The Cloister and the Hearth* (1861), a historical novel often considered his best work, *Hard Cash* (1863), propaganda against the lunacy laws, and *Griffith Gaunt* (1866), which raised a storm because of its alleged immorality, were also written here. Reade spent part of the year in Oxford where he was a Fellow of Magdalen.

A plaque on 11 **Bolton St.** commemorates Fanny Burney, who lived here (1818–28) after the death of her husband General D'Arblay.

Henry James, the American who called himself an 'observant stranger', moved into lodgings on the first floor at no. 3 in December 1876 and stayed until 1885. *The Europeans* (1878), *Daisy Miller* (1879), *Washington Square* (1881), and *The Portrait of a Lady* (1881) are among the works he wrote partly here and partly on visits to Italy and the south coast of England. He said that *The Princess Casamassima* (1886) originated in his habit of walking through the London streets.

Somerset Maugham is commemorated at 6 **Chesterfield St.** (P). His plays include *The Circle* (1921), *The Breadwinner* (1930), and *For Services Rendered* (1932). He made his own selection of his works, *Collected Plays* (3 vols., 1931), *Complete Short Stories* (3 vols., 1951), and *Far and Wide* (2 vols., 1955), novels.

Ronald Firbank, author of novels that are mainly conversations, was born (1886) at 40 **Clarges St.** (site now Fleming's Hotel).

Benjamin Disraeli's last novel *Endymion* was published in 1880, the year he resigned as Prime Minister. He died at 19 **Curzon St.** (P) in 1881.

Evelyn's town house (gone) was 'nine doors up' in **Dover St.** and he died there in 1706. Dr. Arbuthnot, Queen Anne's physician, lived in Dover St. (1714–21) after her death. His friends, including Swift, Pope, Gay, and Congreve, formed (*c.* 1713) the Scriblerus Club, whose memoirs, written mainly by Arbuthnot, were published in 1741. Edward Moxon, who helped his friend Lamb move books to his Islington cottage and who married Lamb's adopted daughter, moved to new premises in this street in 1832. Later he became Wordsworth's publisher. Brown's Hotel, nos. 17–24, has a Kipling room to commemorate his frequent visits. Mark Twain stayed at Brown's when on his lecture tour (*c.* 1895), and Alphonse Daudet was also staying there on his short visit (1895) to meet Henry James and Meredith.

Sydney Smith lived at 56 **Green St.** from 1839 to his death in 1845. He was made a canon of St. Paul's in 1831 and held a country living but he is better known for his droll wit, which made him a popular dinner guest and an amusing letter writer and reviewer, than for his interest in religious dogma.

General John Burgoyne, whose home when not on active service was at 10 **Hertford St.** (P), near the S. end of Park Lane, wrote the comedies *The Maid of the Oaks* (1774) and the very successful *The Heiress* (1786). He and Sheridan were prominent in the impeachment of Warren Hastings (*c.* 1788) and after the death here of Burgoyne, the 'Gentlemanly Johnny' of Shaw's *The Devil's Disciple* (1900), Sheridan bought (1795) the house (P), soon after the opening of the newly built theatre in Drury Lane of which he was manager. Bulwer-Lytton wrote the popular historical novels *The Last Days of Pompeii* (1834) and *Rienzi* (1835) at no. 36. His son, the poet who wrote as Owen Meredith, was born there (1831).

Contributors to *Bentley's Miscellany* (founded 1837), who included Dickens, Tom Moore, Richard Barham, and Harrison Ainsworth, met for dinners in the Red Room at the publisher's house (gone) in **New Burlington St.** Dickens, as editor, had an uneasy time with Richard Bentley and wrote that the magazine had always been Bentley's in deed as well as in name. His 'A Familiar Epistle from a Parent to a Child aged Two Years, Two Months' appeared on his handing over the editorship to his friend Harrison Ainsworth in 1839.

Mark Akenside had a prosperous medical practice in Burlington St., now **Old Burlington St.**, from 1760 until his death in 1770. He is said to have died in the bed, given him by a friend 9 years before, in which Milton had died. He was buried in St. James's Church, Piccadilly.

John Gay died (1729) at the home of the Duke and Duchess of Queensberry (site at the corner of Old Burlington St. and Burlington Gdns.).

The Café Royal, near **Piccadilly Circus**, with red-plush seats, gilded mirrors, and chandeliers, was a haunt of literary and artistic coteries in the decades at the turn of the 19th c. In the 1880s and 1890s it was the special rendezvous for Oscar Wilde and others in the Aesthetic Movement who believed in 'Art for Art's sake'. Ernest Dowson and some of his friends from the Rhymers' Club also came here. In 1913–14 Ronald Firbank, one of the later aesthetes, dined here.

Contributors to *Fraser's Magazine* (1830–82) formed a literary club, the Fraserians, which met for dinners at the publisher's at 215 **Regent St.** Maclise's sketch of the diners shows Maginn (co-founder with Hugh Fraser), Coleridge, Southey, Carlyle, Hogg, Egerton Brydges, Mahony, Ainsworth, and Thackeray. R. M. Ballantyne spent some time at a fire station in Regent St. when collecting material for his novel *Fighting the Flames* (1867).

St. George's Church, Hanover Sq. is an early 18th-c. church where the following were married: Shelley and Harriet Westbrook in 1814 after a ceremony in Scotland following their elopement, Disraeli to Mrs. Wyndham Lewis in 1839, Marian Evans (George Eliot) to John Cross in 1880, and John Galsworthy to Ada Galsworthy in 1904.

Sheridan, author of *The Rivals* and *The School for Scandal*, lived for 5 years until his death in 1816 at 14 **Savile Row** (P). His speech of nearly 6 hours at Warren Hastings's trial and that upholding the freedom of the Press are among his collected *Speeches* (1816).

Thomas Holcroft worked in his father's cobbler's shop in **South Audley St.** as a boy. He acted at Covent Garden as Figaro in his translation of Beaumarchais's *Le Mariage de*

Figaro, which he had seen in Paris in 1784. Ambrose Philips (d. 1749), a member of Addison's circle, and Lady Mary Wortley Montagu, a toast as a child of the Kit-Cat Club, letter-writer, and an early advocate of vaccination, are buried in the Grosvenor Chapel in South Audley St. Also buried here are David Mallet (d. 1765), author of the ballad 'William and Margaret' (1723); William Whitehead (d. 1785), dramatist and Poet Laureate; and Elizabeth Carter (d. 1806), a friend of Dr. Johnson, who admired her puddings as well as her excellent classical translations.

William Blake and his wife lived (1804–21) in one room at 17 **South Molton St.** (P). He engraved the plates, with illustrations surrounding the text, for his poem *Milton*, for Young's *Night Thoughts*, and Blair's *The Grave*.

Mitcham [11 Df], district to the S. John Donne lived (1606–10) in a two-storeyed house (gone) in **Whitford Lane**, with overhanging gables and a row of yews in the garden. His letters from 'his hospital' and sometimes his 'prison' show his anxiety at his lack of a place at Court to provide for his increasing family, and his inability to accept the only alternative, ordination. *Pseudo-Martyr* (1610), *Biathanatos*, and *Ignatius His Conclave* (1611) were written here.

Mortlake. See Richmond.

Muswell Hill [11 Eb], district W. of Hornsey. W. E. Henley lived from 1896 to 1899 at Grange Lodge, Tetherdown, which had originally been built as a public house and then refronted.

Newington [10 He], district S. of Southwark. Thomas Middleton, author of *A Chaste Maid in Cheapside*, *Women beware Women*, and many other plays, some in collaboration with other dramatists, lived in **Newington Butts** (site unknown) from 1609 to his death in 1627. He was buried in the parish church, demolished in 1720.

Paddington [10 Aa, Bb, Cb], district W. of Marylebone. Thomas Hardy married Emma Lavinia Gifford at St. Peter's Church, **Elgin Ave.** in September 1874, 4½ years after they had first met at St. Juliot (q.v.).

Olive Schreiner, author, under the pseudonym 'Ralph Iron', of *The Story of an African Farm* (1883), lived at 16 **Portsea Pl.** (P) from 1885 to 1887. This is a quiet corner near the SW. end of Edgware Rd., between Connaught St. and Kendal St.

When Robert Browning returned from Italy in 1861 after the death of his wife he lived until 1887 at 19 **Warwick Cres.** (site now a block of flats), overlooking the stretch of the Grand Union Canal called Little Venice. His sister-in-law Arabella lived close at hand, at 17 Delamere Ter., and he used to call there every evening. His long poem, *The Ring and the Book* (4 vols., 1868–9), based on the story of a Roman murder-case, was written while he was living here.

Palmer's Green [11 Ea], district to the N. Florence Margaret Smith (Stevie Smith) lived (1907–71) from the age of 5 when her parents moved from Hull, at 1 **Avondale Rd.** She went to Palmer's Green High School and later worked as secretary to a publisher. She wrote three novels: *Novel on Yellow Paper* (1936), *Over the Frontier* (1938), and *The Holiday* (1949). She attended St. John's Church and her poems reflect her desire to believe in a just God free from High Anglican dogma. She died in 1971 and after a service at Holy Trinity, Buckfastleigh, was cremated at Torquay. *Selected Poems* was published in 1972 and *Collected Poems* in 1975.

Petersham. See Richmond.

Pimlico [10 Ee, Ef, Ff], district S. of Victoria. Joseph Conrad took rooms (1889–90) in **Bessborough Gdns.**, near Vauxhall Bridge, after returning from 2 years at sea in the Merchant Navy. Soon afterwards he had the idea of writing a novel and he had begun *Almayer's Folly* when he sailed for the Congo in May 1890.

Marian Evans (George Eliot), after boarding with the publisher John Chapman, moved in September 1853 into lodgings on her own at 21 **Cambridge St.** She was translating Feuerbach's *Essence of Christianity* (1854) and editing the *Westminster Review*. By July 1854 she and George Lewes had decided to live together and they left for a holiday in Germany.

Pinner [11 Bb], district to the NW. Bulwer Lytton wrote *Eugene Aram* (1832) while he was living at Pinner Wood House, **Albury Drive** in 1831–2. The house is reached by

way of Pinner Hill, which runs E. across Pinner Woods golf course, becomes an unfenced road, and turns S. at a farm at the NE. corner of Pinner Woods, after which Albury Drive forks left (SE.) almost immediately.

A. E. Housman lived at 1 Yarborough Villas (gone), **Devonshire Rd.** after his landlady moved from 17 North Rd., Highgate (q.v.). When he left in 1911 to take up his appointment as Kennedy Professor of Latin at Cambridge his landlady is reported to have told him that, though sorry to lose him, she could not entirely regret his going, as she understood that by living in a college he would have other men's society forced upon him and 'would be taken out of himself, shaken up, made to chatter like the rest of the world . . .'.

On the wall of the S. aisle of the Parish Church there is a monument to Henry James Pye, Poet Laureate in the reign of George III. His poetry has not endured and he was subject to ridicule by his contemporaries. He is chiefly remembered in connection with the nursery rhyme 'Sing a song of sixpence' with its line 'When the Pye was opened . . .'.

Poplar [11 Fc], district to the E. Arthur Morrison, author of *A Child of the Jago* (1896), was born (1863) in one of the two John Streets here. These, rebuilt and now renamed Grundy St. and Rigden St., N. of East India Dock Rd., may have been those depicted in his introduction to *Tales of Mean Streets* (1894).

Putney [11 Dd], district to the N. of Wimbledon Common. Edward Gibbon, born in Putney in 1737, is commemorated by **Gibbon Walk.** As a child he was cared for by his aunt, Catherine Porten, and he mentions, in his *Autobiography*, 'that the house, near Putney bridge and churchyard, of my maternal grandfather, appears in the light of my proper and native home.' Leigh Hunt died at a friend's house in **Putney High St.** in 1859. In 1879 a joint tenancy was agreed between Watts-Dunton and Swinburne for no. 2 The Pines at the foot of **Putney Hill** (now no. 11, P). Swinburne's health improved under Watts-Dunton's care but his last volumes of verse *Astrophel* (1894), *A Tale of Balem* (1896), and *A Channel Passage* (1904), show a loss of power. Swinburne wrote monographs on *Shakespeare* (1880), *Ben Jonson* (1889), and other Elizabethans and also on more modern writers including Dickens and the Brontës. Max Beerbohm visited him in 1899 and describes the tamed Swinburne in his essay 'No. 2 The Pines'.

Regent's Park [10 Ca, Da], district enclosing one of the largest open spaces in London. Elizabeth Bowen lived at 2 **Clarence Ter.** from 1935 until the death of her husband in 1952. She wrote here the novel, *The House in Paris* (1935), two volumes of short stories, *Look at All Those Roses* (1941) and *The Demon Lover* (1945), and the two major novels set in London, *The Death of the Heart* (1938), and the wartime story, *The Heat of the Day* (1949). She worked in the Ministry of Information during the day and was an air-raid warden at night, and *The Heat of the Day* is considered a realistic evocation of London in wartime.

William Wilkie Collins lived at 17 **Hanover Ter.** with his mother and brother Charles from 1850 to 1859. He first met Dickens soon after coming here and he contributed many travel sketches and short stories to his *Household Words*, including the eerie tale 'A Terribly Strange Bed' in the April number of 1852. He joined the staff of this periodical in 1856, and wrote *The Woman in White* (1860), the first crime detection novel, for its successor *All the Year Round*, where it shared a place with Dickens's *A Tale of Two Cities*. Wilkie Collins, whose father was a popular Royal Academician, was often visited by his friends of the Pre-Raphaelite Brotherhood here and he and Edward Lear were among those at the dinner before Millais left for his marriage to Effie Gray. Dickens frequently invited Collins to join him on his holidays, and shared his love of amateur theatricals, and the families were further united when Dickens's daughter Kate married Charles Collins.

Edmund Gosse lived at no. 17 from 1901. His *Father and Son* (1907), first published anonymously, depicts the tyrannies of family relationships in an exclusive sect. Alfred Noyes, who had visited Gosse here, lived at no. 13 after his second marriage in 1928, but soon afterwards found the Isle of Wight home where he gradually spent more time. When he finally gave up the house, H. G. Wells moved in (1937) and it was at no. 13 (P) that he died in 1946. His last work *Mind at the End of its Tether* (1945) reflects his disillusion at yet another war.

Marian Evans (George Eliot) lived with George Lewes as his wife at The Priory, 21 North Bank, a road (gone) formerly curving S. off **Lodge Rd.** They moved into the house, secluded in its garden full of roses by the Regent's Canal, in November 1863 after an interior designer had made 'an exquisite thing of it'. Hampstead Heath was a favourite place for long walks together. The play George Eliot was writing, set in Spain, was put aside for *Felix Holt* (1866), the novel about a Radical and the Reform Bill, but it appeared later as the dramatic poem *The Spanish Gypsy* (1868). Lewes, who called her Polly, wrote for the *Pall Mall Gazette*, became editor of *The Fortnightly*, and made hard bargains with her publishers. George Eliot began *Middlemarch* here in January 1869 but this was interrupted by the illness of Lewes's son, at whose deathbed she wrote the first part of her poem *The Legend of Jubal* (1870). Emanuel Deutsch, a friend who taught her Hebrew, inspired her novel *Daniel Deronda* (1874–6). These like her other works were partly written elsewhere. Though George Eliot's situation was considered immoral, an increasing number of literary friends came to her parties, including Wilkie Collins, Trollope, Browning, Tennyson, Henry James, and in 1878 Turgenev. George Lewes died here in 1878 and George Eliot married their friend John Cross in May 1880, and moved to Chelsea in November.

Cyril Connolly, founder and editor (1939–50) of *Horizon*, lived at 25 **Sussex Pl.**

Richmond [11 Cd, Ce], riverside district to the SW. In 1736 James Thomson, with a government sinecure, moved into a small cottage in **Kew Foot Lane.** He was in love with 'Amanda' (Elizabeth Young who refused his offer of marriage), for whom he had described the view from **Richmond Hill** in the lines beginning 'Which way, Amanda, shall we steer our course', which he added to *Summer* when it was published in *The Seasons* (1744). Thomson was often visited by William Collins, who sometimes lodged at the Castle Inn where Thomson was to be found when not at his cottage. Collins said this was Thomson's real Castle of Indolence. In 1739 Thomson moved to a larger cottage in the same lane, which became known as Rossdale, then Rosedale, and was incorporated into the Royal Hospital. (Fanny

Burney was a visitor and saw the garden alcove where Thomson wrote.) He collaborated with Thomas Arne on the masque *Alfred* (1740) which contains 'Rule Britannia'. Thomson died in August 1748 after contracting a chill on a river trip.

Richard Burton boarded at Charles de la Fosse's school on **Little Green** for a short time in his youth. His last years were spent in translating *The Lusiads* (1880–4), *The Arabian Nights* (1885–8), and the *Pentamerone*, published posthumously. He was buried (1890) in the cemetery of St. Mary Magdalen at Mortlake (1½ m. NE.) in a large tomb resembling an Arab tent (restored 1975). Some books and relics (many of his papers were burned by his wife) can be seen at East Sheen district library near by.

Virginia and Leonard Woolf moved to 17 **The Green** in 1914, and then lived (1915–24) at Hogarth House, **Paradise Rd.**, from which they took the name of their hand-printing press. Virginia Woolf, recovering from depression when they first arrived, contributed 'The Mark on the Wall' to the first publication *Two Stories*. Other Hogarth Press works were T. S. Eliot's *The Waste Land* (1921) and V. Woolf's *Kew Gardens* (1919). The house, which was divided during their occupation, has been restored to its original appearance but is now offices.

Marian Evans and G. H. Lewes lived at 7 **Clarence Row**, East Sheen (probably the site of the Bull Inn), during the summer of 1855, and after a short holiday settled (1855–9) at 8 **Park Shot** (site now The Courthouse) where Marian first used the pseudonym George Eliot when writing *Amos Barton* (1857), the first part of *Scenes of Clerical Life*. The house was ivy-clad and secluded though near the railway. A long narrow walled garden was at the back. She started *Adam Bede* (1859) here.

John Gay, who from 1720 became part of the Duke and Duchess of Queensberry's household, often lived with them at Douglas House, off **Petersham Rd.**, Petersham, to the S.

Dickens was on holiday here in 1836. His address, Mrs. Denman's, was probably the Dysart Arms, whose proprietor had that name. He returned in 1839 to rent Elm Cottage (now Elm Lodge) in Petersham Rd., where he was visited by the artist Maclise, and Forster, whose biography of Dickens comments on his prowess at athletic games

performed in the extensive grounds, and his frequent swims from the cottage to Richmond Bridge. Both *Pickwick Papers* and *Oliver Twist*, which he was writing on these visits, have scenes in the vicinity, and in the later *Nicholas Nickleby*, Morleena Kenwigs dines, as did her creator, on a 'cold collation, bottled-beer, shrub, and shrimps' at Eel Pie House. From 1838 Dickens frequently stayed at the old Star and Garter Hotel on Richmond Hill, to celebrate his birthday, a new novel, or, as in 1844, the birth of his third son. In 1850 Tennyson and Thackeray were his guests there when *David Copperfield* was published. The Misses Berry, in their youth friends of Horace Walpole, spent the summer months at Devonshire Lodge after 1820. They invited Dickens to dine and when he declined, they called upon Sydney Smith to add weight to their invitation. Dickens had just finished *Nicholas Nickleby* and Sydney Smith wrote that the Misses Berry and their other guests would have 'not the smallest objection to be put into a Number, but on the contrary would be proud of the distinction; and Lady Charlotte, in particular, you may marry to Newman Noggs'.

Richmond Park is the remaining part of royal lands surrounding Henry VII's palace, which replaced the earlier palace at Sheen. James Thomson's favourite walks are commemorated by a board, at the entrance to Pembroke Lodge here, which has a verse by John Heneage Jesse. Jeanie Deans, in Scott's *The Heart of Midlothian* (1818), meets Queen Caroline here and obtains her sister's pardon. Harriet Beecher Stowe (1811–96), author of *Uncle Tom's Cabin*, paid a short visit to Byron's widow in 1859, and was invited to meet Lord John Russell (1st Earl Russell) at Pembroke Lodge. She thought the household 'so New England-like'.

Thomson was buried (1748) near the font in **Richmond Parish Church**, where a tablet was erected in 1792. Other tablets commemorate Norton Nicholls (d. 1809) with whom Gray stayed at Blundeston, the actor Edmund Kean (d. 1833), John Heneage Jesse (d. 1874), and Mary Braddon (d. 1915), author of the popular *Lady Audley's Secret* (1862). She lived at Lichfield House (site now Lichfield Court), **Sheen Rd.**, where most of her novels were written. She married the publisher John Maxwell in 1874, but they had lived together for some years and had a child, which helped her critics dub her and her novels sensational. Many of her novels, including *The Conflict* (1903), have scenes set in the neighbourhood. She died at Lichfield House.

George Colman the Elder, manager of Covent Garden and the Haymarket, lived in **The Vineyard** (house gone). Soon after 1764, when he inherited money from the Earl of Bath, he built Bath House, a villa by the river, a short distance from Garrick at Hampton, with whom he was collaborating on *The Clandestine Marriage* (1766). Bath (later Northumberland) House was demolished in 1968. It was in a bookshop in the town that the 11-year-old William Cobbett, on the way to find work in Kew Gardens, bought Swift's *Tale of a Tub* (1704) with his last threepence. Reading that work, he said, was 'the birth of intellect'.

St. James's [10 Ec, Ed, Fc, Fd], district between Piccadilly and St. James's Park. Horace Walpole, who was born (1717) in **Arlington St.** (P on no. 22 commemorates his father Robert Walpole), wrote many of the vast collection of his *Letters* from a house (gone) opposite, which his father bought in 1742 and bequeathed to him at his death in 1745. Walpole stripped it of all but the essentials to furnish Strawberry Hill, Twickenham (q.v.) in 1766, but continued to use it as his town house until 1779 when he moved to Berkeley Sq.

Byron lodged (1813–14) at 4 **Bennet St.** In January 1813 he started to write *The Giaour*, published in June, and he also wrote here *The Bride of Abydos* and *The Corsair* before moving to Albany.

William Gifford, editor of the *Anti-Jacobin* and first editor of the *Quarterly Review*, died at his house, 6 **Buckingham Gate**, on 31 December 1826.

Steele lived (1707–12) in **Bury St.** 'at the third door, right hand, turning out of Jermyn Street' with his second wife, 'dear Prue', while writing for the *Tatler* and the *Spectator*. He was troubled by debts and was indignant to find his wife upset after the landlady had approached her for payment. Swift lodged here on his visits to London in 1710, 1713, and 1726. Tom Moore often lodged here and after his marriage he and Bessy lived here for a short time (1811–12). The plaque at no. 28, where he also stayed when he visited from Bromham, has been

moved to George St. Crabbe lodged at no. 37 while arranging publication of *Tales of the Hall* (1819). Sinclair Lewis stayed at no. 10 for a short time in 1922 when writing *Babbitt*, and on his visits in 1924 and 1927.

Thomas Campbell lived (1832–40) on the top floor of the site of 10 **Duke St.**, above the headquarters of the Polish refugees from the 1831 revolution. Campbell's patriotic verses gave him the introduction to Niemcewicz, the poet and former aide-de-camp to their national hero Kosciousko, whom he met here.

Matthew Prior, poet and moderate Tory, lived, from 1706 until sent as a diplomat to Paris in 1711, at the end of **Great George St.** near St. James's Park.

Pall Mall was a street associated with chocolate houses, taverns, and clubs. The Cocoa Tree, established in the 1690s as a chocolate house, was frequented by Steele, Swift, and his friend Rowe, who was made Poet Laureate in 1715, 3 years before he died. It became a private club in 1745 and Gibbon, who lodged at 'Mr. Taylor's Grocers' at no. 29 during 1769, found the Cocoa Tree 'served now and then to take off an idle hour'. He also frequented White's and Boodle's, clubs which are still in being. Byron, who fell in love with his cousin Mary Chaworth, wrote 'The Duel' about the fatal quarrel at the Star and Garter Tavern (gone) where his great-uncle killed her grandfather in 1769. The miniature painters, Richard and Maria Cosway, held musical evenings at their home, Schomberg House, Pall Mall (the W. wing survives at no. 80). André de Chénier, who had known them in Paris, frequented their salon while he was at the French Embassy (1787–90). Horace Walpole, who also attended the salon, wrote slightingly of Richard Cosway. Lockhart, who married Scott's elder daughter in 1820, lived for the next decade at no. 25, where he wrote several novels including *Adam Blair* (1822), and his adaptations of *Ancient Scottish Ballads* (1823). He was the first biographer of his father-in-law, who visited them here. Richard Monckton Milnes gave fashionable parties for literary and political figures at no. 26, where he lived from 1837. *Tribute*, which he inaugurated in 1836 as a Christmas annual, contained his friend Tennyson's verses which were later included in *Maud* (1855). Monckton Milnes published the *Life and Letters of Keats* (1848) using material from Charles Armitage Brown.

Milton lived (1652–60) at a house (gone) on the N. side of **Petty France** where the gardens extended to St. James's Park, soon after becoming Latin Secretary (1649) to the new Council of State. The state papers he read provoked the sonnet 'On the Late Massacre in Piedmont'. Also written here were the sonnets on the death of his second wife and 'On his Blindness'. In 1658 he turned again to an early draft of *Paradise Lost*, but at the Restoration in 1660 he was deprived of his office by the Royalist government and went into hiding.

Aaron Hill lived in this street until 1738. He wrote the words for Handel's opera *Rinaldo* (1711), re-wrote an earlier play of his own *Elfrid* as *Athelwold* (1732), and translated and adapted Voltaire's *Zaïre* as *Zara* (1736). Correspondence with Pope, which followed the satirical exchanges in *The Dunciad* and Hill's *Progress of Wit*, eventually became more friendly.

John Cleland, author of *Fanny Hill* (1748–9) and *Memoirs of a Coxcomb* (1751) died in a house (gone) here in 1789. Hazlitt rented (1812–19) Milton's house from Jeremy Bentham, who lived near by. Hazlitt's friend, the painter Robert Haydon, mentions in his *Autobiography* (1853) that he 'and I often looked with a longing eye from the windows of the room at the white-haired philosopher in his leafy shelter'. Haydon was invited here to the christening of Hazlitt's son and complained that nothing was arranged and the parson not ordered, yet Charles and Mary Lamb remained unperturbed.

St. James's Church, Piccadilly, with modern wrought-iron gates, was rebuilt to Wren's original plan after being burnt out in the Second World War. Charles Cotton (d. 1687), Thomas D'Urfey (d. 1723), Dr. Arbuthnot (d. 1735), and Mark Akenside (d. 1770) are buried here. The white marble font and the Grinling Gibbons altarpiece were saved after the bombing.

St. James's Palace in **The Mall** was built by Henry VIII. Thomas Coryate, who came to London after his father's death in 1607, became part of Prince Henry's household here, perhaps as a Court buffoon. It is thought that the distinguished foreigners he met at Court first gave him the ambition to travel. Dr. John Arbuthnot, physician (1709–14) to Queen Anne, was a member with Pope, Gay, Swift, Congreve, and Atter-

bury of the Scriblerus Club (formed *c.* 1713) which met in his rooms here.

Addison had lodgings in **St. James's Pl.** in 1710 when he was contributing to his friend Steele's *Tatler*. William Whitehead, Poet Laureate and dramatist who became Garrick's reader of plays, lived (1768–72) at no. 3. In 1769 Gibbon, who was slowly preparing his long *History of the Decline and Fall of the Roman Empire*, had 'an indifferent lodging' at Miss Lake's at no. 2. The widowed Mrs. Delany lived in this street from 1770 until her move to Windsor *c.* 1785. She mentions in her *Autobiography and Letters* (1861–2) that her friends Mrs. Carter and Mrs. Chapone called her house The Dove and Olive Branch from the painted window there which she had brought from Ireland. Samuel Rogers, who inherited his banker father's fortune, moved to no. 22, which backed on St. James's Park, in 1803 and instituted here the famous breakfasts to which the majority of the literary figures for the next 50 years were invited. His *The Pleasures of Memory* (1792) and his verse tales were popular and he was offered the Laureateship in 1850 but declined. *Recollections of the Table Talk of Samuel Rogers* (1856) edited by Dyce and his own *Recollections* (1859) were both published after his death in 1855.

The publisher John Macrone had his office at 3 **St. James's Sq.** He met Dickens at Ainsworth's house in Kensal Green (q.v.) after having published Ainsworth's first novel *Rookwood* (1834), which became immediately popular, and he later published Dickens's sketches in book form, *Sketches by Boz* (1836–7). Thackeray sketched Dickens, Maclise, Mahony, and himself in Macrone's office in 1837.

Many of the taverns and chocolate houses in **St. James's St.** eventually became private clubs. Steele (knighted in 1714) lodged (1714–16) next to White's Chocolate House, where in 1709 he had written many numbers of the thrice-weekly *Tatler*, which set out to record acts of 'Gallantry, Pleasure and Entertainment' in the house. Steele wrote the weekly *Town Talk* (1715–16) here but his authorship was sometimes disputed. Letitia Pilkington, abandoned by her husband and with no income, managed to set up a bookshop in this street. Swift, who had helped her husband before their separation, became severely critical of them both and she retaliated in her *Memoirs* (1748), which Colley Cibber arranged to get published. Steele and Swift patronized the Thatched House Tavern (gone), on the W. of the street, which was popular into the 19th c., when Scott attended meetings there of the Literary Club, founded by Dr. Johnson. After the death (1768) of Dr. Delany, who had introduced the Pilkingtons to Swift, Mrs. Delany took lodgings (1769) in Thatched House Court (gone).

Gibbon, who was in poor health, stayed at the house of his friend Elmsley (site of no. 74) during the Christmas and New Year of 1793/4. The surgeons recommended an operation and he was thought, at first, to be recovering but he died after two more operations. The first cantos of *Childe Harold* were published in March 1812, when Byron was lodging at no. 8 (rebuilt and now Byron House), near his friend Hobhouse. He said later 'I awoke one morning, and found myself famous'. Thackeray lived at no. 88 when he assumed the character of Fitz-Boodle to contribute *The Luck of Barry Lyndon* (1844) to *Fraser's Magazine*.

St. John's Wood [11 Dc], district NW. of Regent's Park. Katherine Mansfield and John Middleton Murry rented a house at 5 **Acacia Rd.** in July 1915, partly to be near D. H. Lawrence, who had just arranged to live in Hampstead and with whom they were planning to launch a magazine called *The Signature*. The house had a gracious atmosphere that suited Katherine, and a garden with a lovely pear-tree, and Lawrence and Frieda both liked it. Katherine's brother 'Chummie', to whom she was deeply attached, had just finished his military training and was a frequent visitor. It was from here that he left for the Front in September. A few days later the news came that he had been killed and Katherine felt that she could not go on living in the house. She and Murry gave it up and went to the South of France in November.

Thomas Hood lived (1841–5) at 17 **Elm Tree Rd.** (rebuilt), where he edited (1841–3) the *New Monthly* and his own *Hood's Magazine* (1843–4). The poem *The Song of the Shirt*, a powerful description of the sweated labour of seamstresses, was published in *Punch* in 1843. Hood's health gave way under the constant worry over money and he died soon after the efforts of his friends

to get him a pension were successful. He had just moved to Devonshire Lodge, 28 **Finchley Rd.** (P).

Dorothy Richardson lived (1916–38) in a top-floor room at 32 **Queen's Ter.** (rebuilt). When writing *Honeycomb* (1917), the third of her autobiographical novels, collectively called *Pilgrimage*, she married the painter Alan Odle, a fellow lodger, who a medical board said was dying of tuberculosis. Her Impressionist novels, to which the critics first applied the term stream-of-consciousness, were written partly here and partly in cottages in Cornwall.

Sayes Court. See Deptford.

Shadwell [11 Ec], district in the East End. Colley Cibber was buried in the family vault at the Danish Church, **Wellclose Sq.**, built by order of the King of Denmark for Danes in the Port of London. Cibber's father, the sculptor Caius Cibber, who had worked on the church, was also buried there. The building was demolished in 1870 and St. Paul's School is now on the site. Dickens visited Shadwell to see the emigrant Mormons in their ship the *Amazon*. His essay 'Bound for the Great Salt Lake' describes them and life along the waterfront.

Shoreditch [10 Ka, Kb], district in the East End. In 1576 James Burbage, one of Lord Leicester's players, leased a site (now 86–8 **Curtain Rd.**, P) for the first building to be used specifically for play acting. It was called the Theatre (opened 1577) and was next door to the Priory of St. John the Baptist, Holywell. Burbage lived with his sons in Holywell Lane near by. Shakespeare, a friend of the Burbages, acted at the Theatre and the Curtain and lodged near Norton Folgate, S. of Shoreditch High St. Theatres were closed in 1592 because of the plague and he is thought to have written *Venus and Adonis* and *The Rape of Lucrece* at this time. In 1594 he joined the Lord Chamberlain's Company as actor and playwright with Burbage as manager. After Burbage's death in 1597, his son, Richard, dismantled the Theatre and rebuilt it in Southwark (q.v.) with Shakespeare as co-partner in the company. **St. Leonard's**, the parish church, whose steeple and columned portico remain from the 18th-c. rebuilding, was restored after bomb damage and the churchyard is now a garden. James and

Richard Burbage and George Lillo, playwright and friend of Fielding, are buried here.

Old Nichol St., off Shoreditch High St. was the setting for Arthur Morrison's novel *A Child of the Jago* (1896). He came to stay with Arthur Osborne Jay, vicar of Holy Trinity parish (which included Old Nichol St.), who had been impressed with the realism of his *Tales of Mean Streets* (1894). In this area, with the highest incidence of crime and infant mortality, Morrison found the setting for which he had been searching. *A Child of the Jago* was 'the story of a boy who, but for his environment, whould have been a good citizen'. Jay's work led to the building of a church, a social club, and a gymnasium, and eventually to large slum clearance. When the new housing estate was opened (1900), the publicity given by Jay's writings and *A Child of the Jago* led to the ceremony being performed by the Prince of Wales.

Shortlands. See Bromley.

Smithfield [10 Hb], district in the N. of the City. This large open space ('smooth field'), just outside the medieval walls, was used for tournaments, pageants, cattle markets, and fairs from the 12th c. Stow describes the main way there, Giltspur St., getting its name from the knights passing by. It was also used as a place of execution. William Wallace (d. 1305) and Wat Tyler (d. 1381) were killed here. Rahere, a prebendary of St. Paul's and a counsellor of Henry I, founded (1123) the Augustinian Priory dedicated to St. Bartholomew, and became its first prior. The priory's hospital was refounded by Henry VIII after the Dissolution and has become the teaching hospital familiarly called 'Barts' today. A plaque (erected 1956) on the wall commemorates William Wallace and the Protestant martyrs. Robert Bridges became a medical student in 1869 and held appointments there after qualifying but retired because of ill health in 1881. During this time he published three volumes of *Poems*. The Lady Chapel of the Priory church of **St. Bartholomew-the-Great** (Rahere's choir still stands) was used in the 18th c. by a printing works and Benjamin Franklin, who had set up his own press in Philadelphia, worked there for a time after he came to England in 1757.

Smithfield was also the site of the Cloth Fair, instituted by Rahere, the largest fair for clothiers and drapers in the country. It attracted entertainers and Ben Jonson in his play *Bartholomew Fayre* (1614) depicts these and the bawds, cutpurses, and tricksters, who preyed on the stallholders and their customers. Evelyn and Pepys were visitors and Pepys writes in his *Diary* of the re-introduction of the old custom of wrestling. He also saw Jonson's play 'with puppets'. Elkanah Settle, whose changes of allegiance left him with little support after the Revolution, wrote farces and other short pieces for the Fair. In 1707 his play *The Siege of Troy* was staged at the booth of Mrs. Mynn, a show-woman. The Fair, which continued as an entertainment until 1855, appealed to rich and poor, as George Stevens's lines in *Songs* (1772) state:

While gentle folks strut in their silver and satins
We poor folk are tramping in straw hat and
pattens.

Lamb took William and Dorothy Wordsworth after their return from France in 1802 and in *The Prelude* (1850) Wordsworth remembers the 'chattering monkeys', 'the hurdy gurdy', and the 'children whirling in their roundabouts' at

The Fair
Holden where martyrs suffered in past time.

A brass in the church of **St. Bartholomew-the-Less** shows John Shirley (d. 1456) and his wife in the habit of pilgrims. They were buried in the church. Shirley, said to have travelled in many countries, translated from Latin and French and transcribed the works of Chaucer, Lydgate, and others. It is on his authority that some poems are said to be Chaucer's. Thomas Watson, author of *The Tears of Fancie* (1593), sonnets inspired by Ronsard, and by Petrarch whose equal some consider him, was buried here in 1592. He also wrote Latin versions of Tasso's *Aminta* which were translated into English without his knowledge. He is Spenser's 'Amyntas' in *Colin Clouts come home againe* (1595). John Lyly, author of *Euphues* (1578) and other works, was buried here in 1606.

Soho [10 Ec, Fb, Fc], district between the E. end of Oxford St. and Leicester Sq. A plaque on Dickins and Jones's store commemorates Mme de Staël who lived (1813–14) at 30 **Argyll St.** She was visited by Crabb Robinson who was helping her with the publication of *De l'Allemagne* (1813), the book which provoked her exile by Napoleon. When Byron visited he met de Rocca, the young Swiss cavalry officer she had married secretly in 1811. Thomas Campbell also visited her here and wrote a sonnet to her.

In *Light on a Dark Horse* (1951), Roy Campbell writes of his escapades at 50 **Beak St.**, off Regent St., where he lived (1920-2) after his marriage at the age of 19. He began *The Flaming Terrapin* (1924) here and reviewed for the *Daily Herald* and the *New Statesman*.

William Blake was born (1757) at 28 Broad St. (now **Broadwick St.**). Most of the street has been rebuilt. An inscription on the wall on the left of steps leading to William Blake House, 8 Marshall St., states that the house is on the site of his birthplace.

In 1810 Crabb Robinson visited an exhibition of Blake's paintings and engravings in **Carnaby St.** This street was restyled in the 1960s as a pedestrian precinct and became a symbol of 'swinging London'.

Charles Dibdin, dramatist and songwriter, lived at 30 **Charlotte St.** (now the Étoile Restaurant) from 1805 to 1810.

William Collins lived (1744-9) in the old Kings Square Court, site now part of **Dean St.**, with his mistress. Hester Chapone had lodgings in this street and in 1791 was at no. 17. Thackeray's Lamberts in *The Virginians* (1859) lived here and Dickens's Dr. Manette in *A Tale of Two Cities* (1859) lived at no. 10.

Elizabeth Inchbald, actress and dramatist, finished her first novel *A Simple Story* (1791) in a second-floor room of a house in **Frith St.** The two main characters are based on herself and Kemble the actor. Maria Edgeworth was able to forget the author and believe 'in the real existence of all the people' in the novel. Hazlitt died (1830) at no. 6 (P) and opposite was later the site of the Commercio (gone), the restaurant where plans for the *Criterion*, a quarterly, were worked out. Richard Church, in his autobiography, mentions dining there in 1921 with T. S. Eliot the editor, Herbert Read, and Bonamy Dobrée, when Richard Aldington came in and said he had decided to leave England.

Dryden, after moving (1686) from Long Acre, lived at 43 **Gerrard St.** (rebuilt, P). He had become a Catholic and was out of favour after the Revolution, when he lost the Laureateship and a government post. His last years were devoted to translations of the classics and to *Fables Ancient & Modern* (1700), a collection of tales from Chaucer, Boccaccio, and Ovid, partly written while staying with friends in the country. He died here in 1700. Dr. Johnson's Club, which included Burke, Joshua Reynolds, Goldsmith, Garrick, and Boswell among its members, met (1764-83) at the Turk's Head (gone) at no. 9. Burke lived later at no. 37 (P, now a restaurant). Dickens, who, as a boy, visited his uncle in lodgings over Manson's bookshop, wrote about the characters he met there in *Sketches by Boz* (1836-7). His uncle's barber remembered the Napoleonic war and Mrs. Manson lent him books. At the beginning of the 20th c. the Mont Blanc Restaurant was one of the meeting places for the Tuesday literary lunches when Edward Thomas, Galsworthy, Norman Douglas, Belloc, and W. H. Davies assembled from the country. Conrad first met Hudson here in 1902.

Nearly all the houses in **Golden Sq.** have been refaced. Swift dined at no. 21 with Lord Bolingbroke, to whom Pope dedicated his *Essay on Man* (1733). Lady Mary Wortley Montagu lived at no. 19 and John Reynolds lived at no. 27 in 1832. Smollett's Matthew Bramble lodged here and the hero of Thackeray's *Henry Esmond* visits General Webb here, a vain man who regarded the Churchills as upstarts. Dickens's Ralph Nickleby of *Nicholas Nickleby* also lived in the square and Newman Noggs, who had 'once been a gentleman', lived near by 'at the Crown in Silver St.' (gone).

The painter, Benjamin Haydon, had a studio (1808-17) at 41 **Great Marlborough St.** In his *Autobiography* (1853), published posthumously, he writes of Leigh Hunt, whom he visited in gaol, and of Hazlitt, who invited him with Charles and Mary Lamb to the christening of his son. He invited Keats, whom he had met at Leigh Hunt's, to dine here with Cowden Clarke and John Reynolds. On his way home Keats composed the sonnet

'Great spirits now on earth are sojourning'

meaning Wordsworth, Hunt, and Haydon. Haydon later took Keats to see the Elgin Marbles (which the nation bought through Haydon's persuasion). Keats, who admired his robust directness, enclosed the sonnet he wrote on them with one to Haydon himself. On another visit here Haydon took a mask of Keats's face. Wordsworth, whom Haydon introduced to Keats, also wrote a sonnet to him and also came here to have a plaster cast made of his head. Haydon's paintings sold at first but later he quarrelled with his patrons (even Sir George Beaumont's mansion had no space for his very large canvasses), fell into debt, and killed himself (1846). Another painter, James Northcote, lived for 40 years (1790-1831) in this street. His *Conversations* (1830), in which his literary friends appear, was edited by Hazlitt, whose merit as a painter Northcote recognized. Northcote illustrated his own *One Hundred Fables* (1828), and Sir Walter Scott sat for his portrait here in the same year. John Reynolds, Keats's friend, lived (1836-8) at no. 10.

In 1802 Thomas de Quincey was befriended at 61 **Greek St.** by Ann, the prostitute who saved him from destitution and who appears in *Confessions of an English Opium Eater* (1822). The House of St. Barnabas, at no. 1, on the corner of Soho Sq. is often wrongly thought to be the birthplace of William Beckford (cf. Soho Sq.). The first owner was Richard Beckford, a prosperous Alderman in the City, who died (1756) before his nephew, William, was born (1759). Douglas Jerrold, author of 'Mrs Caudle's Curtain Lectures' in *Punch* during 1845, was born in this street in 1803. He was the author of the plays *Black Ey'd Susan* (1829) and *The Bride of Ludgate* (1831), amusing and successful comedies, and he edited *Lloyds Weekly Newspaper* from 1852 until his death in 1857.

Arthur Rimbaud and Paul Verlaine came to London in 1872 (they were 18 and 28 respectively) and lodged at 35 **Howland St.**, off Tottenham Court Rd. They felt lonely and homesick at first and were depressed by the dreariness of the English Sunday. However, they settled down to a regular life of reading and studying English, and Verlaine, who was so happy that he wished this existence could continue for ever, finished his collection of poems, *Romances sans Paroles* (1874). They wandered from pub to pub, learning English of great variety, and they tramped throughout London (Kew, Pimlico, Whitechapel, and the City) in order to get to know it thoroughly. Rimbaud left Verlaine in February 1873 to return to his home at Charleville. They were together again the following year in lodgings near Waterloo Station.

Leicester Sq., formerly Leicester Fields, has statues to Shakespeare, Hogarth, and Joshua Reynolds in the central garden. Swift had lodgings in the square in 1711. Thomas Holcroft, the son of a shoemaker, was born (1745) in Orange Court (gone), Leicester Fields. Hannah More in 1774, and Crabbe in 1782, both met Dr. Johnson at the house (Fanum House now on site, P) in the centre of the W. side, where his friend Sir Joshua Reynolds lived for many years. Mrs. Inchbald, the actress known as the Muse, who earlier had lodgings in Leicester Court (gone) returned to the E. side opposite Reynolds's house in the late 1790s and stayed until 1803. Each of her many comedies including *Wives as they Were* (1797) and *Lovers' Vows* (1798) was written in a few weeks and their success enabled her to give up acting.

William Blake lodged (1785-91) at 28 **Poland St.** He engraved his own drawings to his *Songs of Innocence*, *The Book of Thel*, and *Tiriel* in 1789, and the next year produced his major work, *The Marriage of Heaven and Hell*.

Shelley and his friend Hogg found lodgings at no. 11 in March 1811 after their expulsion from Oxford. Shelley tried inexpertly to appease his father but the break between them proved final.

A plaque in the Central Reference Library in **St. Martin's St.** states that this was the site of Isaac Newton's house which later became the home (1774-89) of Dr. Burney. Here Fanny Burney wrote *Evelina* (1778), her most successful novel, and *Cecilia* (1782).

William Beckford, author of *Vathek* (1787), was born (1759) at 22 **Soho Sq.**, his father's town house. William Beckford senior, who was twice Lord Mayor and who possessed a colossal fortune, chose the best tutors for his son. Mozart, an 8-year-old prodigy, taught the 5-year-old boy musical exercises, and Alexander Cozens taught him painting and drawing. Cozens was the first to influence Beckford in Oriental, Persian, and Arabic studies, which inspired *Vathek*. Beckford, who inherited his father's fortune at the age of 11, spent many years travelling abroad.

Hazlitt's gravestone can still be seen in the churchyard (now a garden) of **St. Anne's, Wardour St.**, where he was buried (1830).

Hester Lynch Salusbury married Henry Thrale here, against her will, in 1763.

Southgate [11 Ea], district to the N. Eagle Hall (demolished 1940s), in the **High St.**, was the birthplace (1784) of Leigh Hunt.

Southwark (pr. Sutherk) [10 Hc, Jc, Jd, Kd], district S. of London Bridge. **Bankside**, a riverside road now dominated by the power station, was in Shakespeare's day an area of entertainment with theatres, amusement parks, and a bear garden. Philip Henslowe (d. 1616) managed the Rose Theatre, commemorated by Rose Alley, here from 1592 to 1603. Henslowe employed many dramatists, including George Chapman, John Webster, Thomas Dekker, Thomas Kyd, and Michael Drayton, and his *Diary* kept during 1592–1609 records their transactions. Shakespeare acted at the Rose. In 1599 Burbage's theatre at Shoreditch (q.v.) was assembled here as the Globe by Burbage's son, Richard, a friend of and fellow actor with Ben Jonson and Shakespeare. Richard Burbage and Shakespeare became partners in the Lord Chamberlain's Company. Many of Shakespeare's plays were acted at the Globe including *Hamlet, King Lear, Macbeth, Richard III*—one of Burbage's most popular roles, *As You Like It, A Midsummer Night's Dream*, and *Twelfth Night*. The Globe, 'the wooden O' with its thatched roof, was burnt down in 1613 by cannon-fire used as stage effects, and rebuilt the next year. Shakespeare is said to have lived near the bear-garden and Beaumont and Fletcher also lived in the vicinity. Fletcher and Peele collaborated with Shakespeare and Massinger, and Beaumont with Fletcher during this very productive time for play writing. Jonson's *Bartholomew Fayre* (1614) was first acted at the Hope Theatre, which Henslowe opened (1613) as a bear-garden where plays could be acted.

Borough High St. was the main medieval route from London to Canterbury and the Continent. Southwark is commonly known as 'the Borough'. On the W. side of the street just S. of the Thames is **Southwark Cathedral** or the Church of St. Saviour and St. Mary Overie (or Overy), one of the finest Gothic buildings in London, with many associations with the Elizabethan actors and playwrights on Bankside. In the N. aisle is the tomb of John Gower (d. 1408) whose head in the effigy rests on his three main works, *Speculum Meditantis, Confessio Amantis*, and *Vox Clamantis*, the last of which gives an account of contemporary life including the Peasant's Revolt. Gower spent his last years in the precincts. Sir Edward Dyer, who had considerable fame as a poet at the end of the 16th c., was buried in the chancel on 11 May 1607. Shakespeare is commemorated by an alabaster effigy (1912) in the S. aisle and by stained-glass windows (1954) showing characters from his plays. John Fletcher (d. 1625) and Philip Massinger (d. 1639) have inscriptions on flagstones in the choir. The tomb of Lancelot Andrewes (d. 1626), who as Bishop of Winchester lived in the 13th-c. Winchester Palace (site among the warehouses in Clink St.), is in the S. ambulatory. He was one of the translators of the Authorized Version of the Bible. Keats studied medicine from 1814 to 1816 at Guy's Hospital on the E. side of the street. At no. 77 the medieval George Inn (N.T.) with a gallery round its courtyard, was rebuilt in 1677 after an extensive fire in Southwark and became a flourishing coaching-inn in the 18th and 19th cc., and was mentioned by Dickens in *Little Dorrit* (1855–7). Shakespeare's plays are acted in the courtyard on Saturday afternoons in the summer. Near by, **White Hart Yard** marks the site of the 15th-c. White Hart Inn, mentioned in the *Paston Letters* (written 1440–86), in Shakespeare's *2 Henry VI*, and in Dickens's *Pickwick Papers* (1836–7). The Old Tabard Inn is on the corner of **Talbot Yard**, the alley where the Tabard Inn (demolished 1629), known to Chaucer's pilgrims, was situated. The Old Marshalsea, a prison (site near entrance to **Mermaid Court**), held Ben Jonson, George Chapman, and John Marston when they were imprisoned after writing *Eastward Hoe* (1605), a comedy with a mistimed slight on the Scots. They were soon released through the influence of their powerful friends. George Wither was fined and imprisoned in 1614 for the sedition in *Abuses Stript and Whipt* (1613), and while here wrote *Shepherd's Hunting*, a collection of pastorals in which he sometimes calls himself Philarete. He may also have written the lyric 'Shall I wasting in despair' here as it was first printed in *Fidelia* in 1615, soon after his release. He was again imprisoned here after the publication of *Wither's Motto* (1621), a self-eulogy on 'nec habeo, nec careo, nec curo', in which some hidden satire was suspected. King's Bench Prison stood until 1758 near the entrance to **Angel Pl.** Thomas Dekker, always poor, was confined here (1613–19) for debt and Richard Baxter, interrogated by Judge Jeffreys, was fined and imprisoned (1685–6) for libelling the Church in *Paraphrase of the New Testament* (1685). The Marshalsea Prison (P) moved into new buildings near here in 1811 and Dickens, who visited his father during his imprisonment for debt, faithfully depicted 'the crowding ghosts of many miserable years' in scenes in *Little Dorrit* (1855–7). Nahum Tate, Poet Laureate from 1692 and satirized in the *Dunciad*, was buried (1715) in the **Church of St. George the Martyr.** Little Dorrit, christened in the church, was rescued from sleeping on the steps by a kindly verger, and was later married here. She is depicted in a poke bonnet, praying, in the modern stained-glass window in the E. end. Near by in Horsemonger Lane (gone) Leigh Hunt was imprisoned for 2 years (1812–14) for libelling the Prince Regent. He was on friendly terms with the gaoler, who allowed him to walk in the garden and he wrote of his room

I papered the walls with a trellis of roses; . . . the barred windows I screened with Venetian blinds; I had the ceiling covered with clouds and sky and when my bookcases were set up with their busts, and flowers and a pianoforte made their appearance, perhaps there was not a handsomer room on that side of the water.

He was visited by Byron, Keats, and Charles Lamb who compared the room to one in a fairytale. After 1758 the King's Bench Prison was transferred to a site near **Scovell Rd.** Tobias Smollett was tried by the King's Bench in 1759 for defaming the character of Admiral Sir Charles Knowles, fined, and imprisoned for 3 months. He was visited by his friend Goldsmith, who had practised as a doctor in Southwark, by Garrick, and by the publisher John Newbery for whom he had often worked and who now arranged for him to edit *The British Magazine.* Christopher Smart was confined here for debt from *c.* 1769 to his death in 1771. His decline took the form of praying aloud, which Dr. Johnson had no difficulty in accepting, but insolvency was more generally unpalatable. Mrs. Charlotte Smith lived in the prison for some months with her children while her husband was a debtor (*c.* 1784). William Combe, who wrote the verses for

Rowlandson's satirical drawings about Dr. Syntax, was imprisoned for debt here on a number of occasions. Robert Haydon was imprisoned here for debt four times between 1822 and 1837, and John Galt on returning from an unsuccessful venture in Canada was here for debt in 1829. The prison closed *c.* 1860.

In September 1816 Keats took lodgings at 8 Dean St. (what remains of the road, now under the railway arch, is called **Stainer St.**) to be near Guy's Hospital where he was studying. Charles Cowden Clarke, son of his schoolmaster at Enfield, was now lodging at 6 Little Warren, Clerkenwell and on a visit there in October, Keats first saw the folio edition of Chapman's translation of Homer. They spent the night reading and discussing this and at dawn Keats walked back to Dean St. where he immediately wrote down the sonnet beginning 'Much have I travell'd in the realms of gold,'.

The bust on the Dickens School in **Lant St.** commemorates his stay in lodgings when his father was a debtor in the Marshalsea.

A plaque on a brewery wall at the E. end of **Park St.** commemorates the Globe Theatre on Bankside in which Shakespeare, who acted there, had a share. The brewery is a successor to that owned by Henry Thrale, who lived with his wife Hester after their marriage in 1763 to his death in 1782 at their town house in this street (formerly called Deadman's Pl.). Arthur Murphy, Hester Thrale's 'dear Mur', introduced them to Dr. Johnson, who was soon given his own room, where he wrote part of the *Lives of the English Poets* (1779–81). When Henry Thrale stood successfully for Parliament, Johnson, who enjoyed electioneering, wrote his speeches. Mrs. Thrale's diaries and notebooks, started here, were published as *Thraliana* (1942). The Anchor in near-by Clink St. has a 'Mrs. Thrale's Room' which has her portrait and a print of her house at Streatham.

Stoke Newington [11 Ec], district NE. of Islington. Daniel Defoe was educated (*c.* 1670) at the Nonconformist Academy (gone) at **Newington Green.** He was followed (1690–4) by Isaac Watts, whose first hymn, 'Behold the glories of the Lamb', was written about the time he left the school. Defoe, who led a restless life as a journalist and government agent, was at

Stoke Newington from 1709. At first he lived in a house on the N. side of **Stoke Newington Church St.** and later he built a house on the site of no. 95 (P). His wife Mary Tuffley came from Newington Green and their daughter Sophia was baptized in Hackney Church on Christmas Eve 1705. Another daughter died here. His tombstone, thought to have been removed from his grave in Bunhill Fields when a marble obelisk was erected there, is now in the entrance hall at Stoke Newington District Library.

Mary Wollstonecraft (later Godwin), her sister Eliza, and a friend, Fanny Blood, transferred their school from Islington to Newington Green (site unknown), a few months after its opening in 1783. Mary Wollstonecraft's *Thoughts on the Education of Daughters* (1787) and *Original Stories from Real Life* (1788) arose from the practical experience of teaching here and, when the school failed to provide her with a living, as governess to Lord Kingsborough's children.

John Aikin, a Unitarian who lived here from 1798 to his death in 1822, was attracted to this former village because of its long-established Dissenting community. He wrote most of the volumes of his *General Biography* (1815) in a house (gone) in Stoke Newington Church St., helped in his later years by his daughter, Lucy. His sister Anna Barbauld (her life was written by Lucy Aikin) lived at no. 113, opposite his house, from 1802. Her short tales, written for the children at her school in Palgrave (q.v.), proved popular. Charles Lamb, who wrote 'Mrs. Barbauld's stuff has banished all the old classics of the nursery', may have taken from her the idea that grew into his *Tales from Shakespear* (1807), published by the second Mrs. Godwin (whose husband wrote as 'Baldwin'). Mrs. Godwin, Mrs. Inchbald, and Mrs. Barbauld, were called 'the three bald women' by Lamb.

Edgar Allan Poe, who had come from America in 1815 to stay with cousins at Irvine (q.v.), was at Bransby's School on the N. side of Church St. from 1817 to 1820. A plaque commemorating him is in the entrance hall of Stoke Newington District Library.

William Hazlitt attended the New College for Protestant Dissenters at Hackney (founded in 1786 in a mansion in Lower Clapton and closed c. 1797), site between Tresham Ave. and Urswick Rd. at the S. of Lower Clapton Rd., 1½ m. SE.

Strand [10 Fc, Gc, Hc], district between Trafalgar Sq. and the City. Pepys lived (1679–88) at 12 **Buckingham St.** (P) but the house has been altered since his day. In 1688 he moved to no. 14 (rebuilt), which then overlooked the river. He lived here until in 1700 failing health led him to stay with his former servant at Clapham Common (q.v.).

Coleridge stayed at no. 21 during 1799 and Dickens put David Copperfield in a 'set of chambers' at no. 15 with Mrs. Crupp, the landlady.

Charing Cross Station is on the site of Hungerford Stairs, which led up from the river to the Strand. In his autobiographical novel *David Copperfield* (1849–50) Dickens's own experiences as a boy in Warren's Blacking Factory here are retold by David and set in Blackfriars (q.v.). Mr. Micawber, whom David first met there, set off with his family for their new life in Australia from Hungerford Stairs. 'The last days of the emigrants were spent in a little, dirty, tumbledown public-house, which in those days was close to the stairs, and whose protruding wooden rooms hung over the river.'

Clement's Inn was formerly one of the Inns of Chancery. Hardy worked here for a few weeks in 1870 and wrote a wistful little poem, 'To a Tree in London (Clement's Inn)'.

Heinrich Heine, who visited England for 3 months in 1827, stayed at 32 **Craven St.** (P). Benjamin Franklin, who represented the Pennsylvania Assembly (1757–62 and 1764–72) as well as other states, lived at no. 36 (P). His *Autobiography*, partly written in French, was published in 1868.

Devereux Ct., a narrow street off the Strand, was the site of the Grecian Coffee House, patronized by Addison and Steele and mentioned in the *Spectator*. Harrison Ainsworth, who lodged at no. 6 on first arriving in London in 1824, noted that it was still in existence then.

Essex St. is on the site of the Earl of Leicester's great Tudor house, where Edmund Spenser was one of the household (1578–80) before he left for Ireland. He met Leicester's nephew, Philip Sidney, here and they formed the Areopagus Club with others.

Spenser wrote the sonnets to Rosalind, published *The Shepheards Calender* (1579), and began *The Faerie Queene* here. After Leicester's death in 1588 the house became the home of the 2nd Earl of Essex, brother of Sidney's Stella. Essex, who married Sidney's widow in 1590, was a patron of literature and was praised by Daniel, Chapman, Spenser, and Jonson. On Spenser's return from Ireland (1596–7) he again stayed here and wrote *Prothalamion* (1596) and *View of the Present State of Ireland* (1596). The red-brick arch and steps at the lower end of the street is the old watergate to Essex House, where in *Prothalamion* 'the gentle knights' receive their 'fair brides'.

Essex House was the home (1712–31) of the Cottonian Library, now in the British Library in Bloomsbury. A plaque on the new Essex Hall, at the Strand end, commemorates Fielding, who lived in the street, and Dr. Johnson, who planned a club to meet at the Essex Head (rebuilt). This tavern was kept by a former servant of the Thrales, and Johnson and his friends made rules to meet thrice weekly. Eight years after Johnson's death Boswell recorded that they were still meeting there.

Northumberland St. is the site of Hartshorne Lane, thought to be the birthplace of Ben Jonson (b. 1573), who spent his early years here with his mother and stepfather, a bricklayer, who taught Jonson his trade.

Sir Arthur Conan Doyle's amateur detective, accompanied on many of his exploits by Dr. Watson, is commemorated at the Sherlock Holmes Restaurant[1] at no. 10, which has a room containing mementoes, including his deer-stalker hat and meerschaum pipes. The *Strand Magazine* published many of the Sherlock Holmes short stories from 1892.

The Queen's Chapel of the Savoy, rebuilt after a fire in 1864, is in **Savoy St.** on the site of the original chapel burned by the peasants in 1381 and rebuilt in 1505, and again in the 19th c. Gavin Douglas, author of the allegorical poem *The Palice of Honour* and first translator of the *Aeneid*, who went to the English Court in 1517, died of the plague in 1522 and was buried here. Thomas Fuller was a lecturer here in 1642 and again after the Restoration. Pepys, who often met Fuller and formerly had 'a high esteem of his preaching', heard him give 'a poor dry sermon' a few months before his death of

'a sort of fever' in 1661. The Puritan George Wither, who had often been imprisoned on account of his satirical pamphlets, died (1667) in this neighbourhood and was buried here, though he had expressed a wish to return to his birthplace at Bentworth (q.v.).

The **Strand** itself is the principal thoroughfare from the West End to the City. A short way from the Trafalgar Sq. end, near Villiers St., is the site of York House, a Tudor residence of the archbishops of York. Francis Bacon, born here in 1561, was befriended by a later occupant, Sir Thomas Egerton, whose household after his second marriage included his wife's young niece Ann More, and John Donne. Donne became Egerton's secretary after his return in 1596 from the Cadiz expedition where he had been with Egerton's son, first met at Lincoln's Inn. Egerton's third marriage (1600) to the influential Dowager Countess of Derby might have improved Donne's chances of a place at Court but for his rash marriage with the 17-year-old Ann More. This caused his imprisonment and dismissal from Egerton's service. Donne's wife was the subject of many of his love poems throughout her life but at this moment he is said to have written 'John Donne, Ann Donne, Undone'. York House itself was demolished at the end of the 17th c. but Arthur Murphy, who came from school at St. Omer aged 16, lodged in the old York House buildings in 1744. Sir John Davies died (1626) at his house in the Strand, during the night after his appointment as Lord Chief Justice had been announced.

Early in the 17th c. Endymion Porter's house in the Strand (site unknown) was a centre for poets and painters including D'Avenant, Dekker, Ben Jonson, and Herrick. The area N. of **John Adam St.** is the site of Durham House, the home of the 1st Earl of Essex where *c.* 1576 Philip Sidney met Essex's daughter Penelope Devereux, thought to be the Stella of his collection of sonnets *Astrophel and Stella* (1591) published posthumously. Durham House was later granted by Queen Elizabeth I to Ralegh, who lived there before being sent to the Tower in 1592. Exeter House (site between **Exeter St.** and **Burleigh St.**) was the home of the Earl of Shaftesbury where Locke, the family physician and friend, wrote part of the *Essay concerning Human*

Understanding (1690). The Burleigh St. corner was the site of Exeter Exchange (demolished 1829), a large building with book and other stalls on the ground floor, and with a famous menagerie above. 'Parson' Woodforde paid a shilling to see the wild beasts and Mr. and Mrs. John Dashwood in *Sense and Sensibility* (1811) took little Harry (whose inheritance was safeguarded at Marianne's and Elinor's expense). Mary Lamb often heard the lions roaring when she walked home along the Strand and Charles Lamb included the Exeter Exchange in the list of places he rated higher than the Lakes.

Savoy St. and **Lancaster Pl.** are on the site of Savoy Palace, the home of John of Gaunt (Shakespeare's 'time-honoured Lancaster') which with its outbuildings and gardens stretched from the Strand to the river. Chaucer found a patron in Lancaster, married a retainer of his Duchess, and wrote *The Boke of the Duchesse* on her death.

Somerset House is on the site of an earlier royal house where Anne of Denmark, James I's queen, was entertained by a series of masques and pastoral plays by the leading dramatists, often stage-managed by Inigo Jo es.

Lamb's poem beginning 'When maidens such as Hester die' refers to Hester Savory (daughter of a goldsmith of the Strand) who died 3 months after her wedding in 1802. William Blake lived from 1821 to his death in 1827, in Fountain Ct., an alley once between 103 and 104 the Strand. Crabb Robinson, who saw only two chairs and a bed, called it squalid, but Samuel Palmer, one of the young painters influenced by Blake, disagreed. 'The millionaire's upholsterer can furnish no enrichments like those of Blake's enchanted room' he wrote, remarking on his 'delightful working corner' with the 'implements ready—tempting to the hand'. Fountain Tavern (P on site), formerly at the Strand end of the alley, was frequented by Swift and by those who opposed the policies of the Prime Minister, Walpole. Congreve, author of *Love for Love* (1695) and *The Way of the World* (1700), lived for many years in **Surrey St.** (site now Arundel Great Court). He frequented the Fountain with his friends from the Kit-Cat Club.

The publisher John Chapman, who resembled Byron, had his offices at no. 142

and lived on the floors above with his wife, his children, and their governess. He put up many of his literary friends in the house and Emerson, who visited briefly in 1847, stayed for 3 months in 1848. In 1851 Chapman persuaded Mary Ann Evans (George Eliot) to board here. She was anxious to increase the small income left her by her father and Chapman needed an assistant to edit the *Westminster Review*. She began to write her name as Marian at this time. Gordon Haight in *George Eliot and John Chapman* (1940) describes how the two women in the house reacted to the arrival of a third. In October 1851 Chapman introduced Miss Evans to George Lewes in Jeff's bookshop in Burlington Arcade (off Piccadilly), and she frequently went with Lewes when he reviewed plays for his journal *The Leader* (1850–66).

The young Hale White was another employee who boarded at no. 142. He found Marian Evans (her family still called her Mary Ann) a stimulating influence who made the menial tasks allotted to him bearable by her interest and encouragement. She was 12 years older than he and he describes her in the quiet back room, sitting 'half sideways to the fire' with her feet over the arm of a chair, correcting proofs. White met many of the literary figures of the day at Chapman's Wednesday evening parties. American visitors to no. 142 at this time included William Bryant, poet and editor of the New York *Evening Post*, and Horace Greeley, founder (1841) of the *New-York Tribune*, and of 'Go West, Young Man!' fame.

The Somerset Coffee House at no. 166 was frequented by Boswell in the 1760s.

Mrs. Inchbald, who had been living in a community, welcomed the independence of her lodgings (*c.* 1805–9) with Miss Baillie, a milliner at no. 163 (gone). She was writing the prefaces to the many volumes of *The British Theatre* (1806).

King's College (founded 1829) was attended by Charles and Henry Kingsley, W. S. Gilbert, Walter Besant, and Edwin Arnold. St. George's Coffee House (gone) between **Devereux Ct.** and **Essex St.** was visited by Shenstone, Arthur Murphy (*c.* 1752), and Walpole. Danes End behind iron gates was the home and chambers of Watts-Dunton from 1873. Guests on his sociable Wednesday nights included Swinburne and William Morris.

The Wren Church of **St. Clement Danes** (rebuilt after bombing in the Second World War) still has an oranges-and-lemons ceremony although the bells, which chimed the air, were broken. John Lyly was married here in 1583 and Nathaniel Lee (d. 1692) and Thomas Otway (d. 1685) were buried here. Dr. Johnson worshipped in the old church and a statue of him, with bas-reliefs of Boswell and Mrs. Thrale on the base, stands outside.

The largest of the maypoles set up at every street corner after the Restoration, according to John Aubrey, stood at the corner of Drury Lane, near the church of **St. Mary-le-Strand**. It was broken by a high wind in 1672 and taken down. The Revd. James Bramston (1694?-1744) wrote of it in *Art of Politics*:

What's not destroyed by Time's devouring hand?

Where's Troy, and where's the Maypole in the Strand?

Dickens often mentions the Strand. The young David Copperfield visits two pudding shops in the vicinity, one near St. Martin's Church where the pudding was dear and the other in the Strand itself where the pudding was 'heavy and flabby, with great flat raisins in it, stuck in whole at wide distances apart'. David later stays at the Golden Cross Hotel (gone) with Steerforth. Mr. Pickwick and his friends leave London in the *Commodore* coach from the same hotel. Mr. Jingle delivers a cautionary tale to the outside passengers about hitting their heads on the low archway. The *Commodore* was the stage-coach Dickens had himself travelled up in from school at Chatham in 1823. As the only inside passenger he had eaten his sandwiches 'in solitude and dreariness' while the rain lasted the whole journey.

When Baroness Orczy was waiting for a train at the **Temple underground station** in 1901, the character of Sir Percy Blakeney, the hero of *The Scarlet Pimpernel* (1905) and other romances of the French Revolution, came to her mind complete with his elegant hands, his spyglass, and his characteristic speech and laugh. In her autobiography, *Links in the Chain of Life* (1947), she writes that he was her creation alone and that he was not modelled on anyone.

Francis Bacon (b. 1561), the essayist, and Thomas Holcroft (b. 1745), actor and dramatist, were baptized, and the poet, Tom Moore, was married (1811) in **St. Martin-in-the-Fields** (rebuilt 1726), in **Trafalgar Sq.** The following were buried here: Sir John Davies (d. 1626), author of *Nosce Teipsum*, George Farquhar (d. 1707), author of *The Recruiting Officer* and *The Beaux' Stratagem*, and James Smith (d. 1839), co-author of *Rejected Addresses*.

Kipling lived (1889-91) at 43 **Villiers St.** (P) in rooms on the fifth floor, where he wrote *The Light that Failed* (1890), contributed 'Barrack-Room Ballads' to the *National Observer*, and arranged for the publication of *Life's Handicap* (1891), a collection of short stories.

Dickens published *Household Words* (1850-9) from offices at 16 **Wellington St.** This weekly had contributions from Bulwer-Lytton, Mrs. Gaskell, William and Mary Howitt, and Wilkie Collins, who collaborated on many stories with Dickens in *Household Words* and in its successor *All the Year Round* (1859-70), which was published from no. 10. *The Leader* (1850-66), founded by George Lewes and Thornton Leigh Hunt, with Spencer and Kinglake on the staff, was published in this street. George Eliot, who lived with Lewes after Mrs. Lewes had left him for Thornton Hunt, often helped with the periodical when Lewes was ill.

¹ Open 12 noon-2 p.m. and 6-8.45 p.m. Closed Sun. and Bank Holidays.

Streatham (pr. Strettam) [11 Ee], district to the S. Streatham Park was the country home (now built over) of Henry and Hester Thrale, who married in 1763 and were introduced to Dr. Johnson by the playwright Arthur Murphy soon afterwards. Johnson, who had his own room here and conducted chemistry experiments in an oven he had built in the kitchen garden (site behind Thrale Rd.), was the most frequent of the visitors, who included Goldsmith, Burke, Murphy, Garrick, Boswell, and Cumberland. Many of these had portraits painted for the library. Giuseppe Baretti was resident Italian tutor (1773-6) to Queeney Thrale, the eldest daughter. Author of an *Italian and English Dictionary* (1760), he also wrote at Johnson's suggestion an account of his travels in Spain and Portugal (1762). Dr. Charles Burney came to teach Queeney music and later his daughter Fanny was patronized by Mrs. Thrale. Dr. Johnson wrote the lines on

Henry Thrale's memorial (d. 1782) in the church. Hester married Gabriele Piozzi in 1784 and after Johnson's death wrote *Anecdotes of the late Samuel Johnson* (1786) on her honeymoon tour of Italy. She also published Johnson's letters (1788). The Piozzis left Streatham Park in 1795.

Surbiton [11 Cf], district to the SW. Richard Jefferies lived (1877–82) at 2 Woodside, now 296 **Ewell Rd.** (site now shops near the police station), where he wrote *Nature Near London* (1883).

Sydenham [11 Ee], district to the SE. Thomas Campbell lived (1804–22) at **Sydenham Common** in a house with 'green jalousies' and 'white palings' (gone, site thought to be in **Peak Hill**). After writing *Annals of Great Britain* (1807), he planned, with Scott, *Specimens of British Poets*, and, when Scott drew back from the scheme, he went on alone. The work was published in 1819. He also wrote here the poems 'Lord Ullin's Daughter', 'The Soldier's Dream', 'The Turkish Lady', and 'Battle of the Baltic'. Campbell's home life was tragic: one son died here, the other became mentally deranged, and his wife was an invalid. He had some happiness in his journeys to Paris, Germany, and Edinburgh, and in the visits of his friends, George Crabbe, Tom Moore, Samuel Rogers, and Byron. The first three thought of forming a poets' club with him, choosing the name 'The Bees'.

Teddington [11 Be], riverside district to the SW. Thomas Traherne lived (1669–74) in the house (gone) of Sir Orlando Bridgeman, Lord Keeper, as his chaplain. The manuscripts of his metaphysical poems, thought at first to be by Vaughan, were recognized and edited by Dobell in 1903. Traherne died here and was buried in St. Mary's Church, of which he was rector (1672–4).
In 1857 R. D. Blackmore, who was teaching classics at Twickenham, inherited enough money to build himself a country house in a large garden. He moved in in 1860 and called it Gomer House (site at end of **Doone Close** opposite the station) after a favourite dog. He started a market garden there, specializing in fruit growing, and wrote novels during the winter, including the most popular *Lorna Doone* (1869), *Craddock Nowell* (1866), and *Cripps*

the Carrier (1876). He was buried (1900) at Teddington cemetery.

Tooting [11 De], district to the S., near Wandsworth Common. After the publication of *The Return of the Native* (1878), Hardy lived (1878–81) at 1 Arundel Ter., **Trinity Rd.** (P on no. 172), Upper Tooting, but his stay here was marred by an illness during 1880–1, when *The Trumpet-Major* (1880) was published.

Twickenham [11 Be], riverside district to the SW. The philosopher Francis Bacon lived (1595–1605) and perhaps wrote some of his *Essays* (1597) at Twickenham Park, the Tudor house and grounds (now covered by the St. Margaret's area) which Lucy, Countess of Bedford, took over after he left. She was the centre of a brilliant circle, and patron of Jonson, Drayton, George Chapman, Samuel Daniel, and Donne, who all wrote poems to her. Donne often stayed here between 1605 and 1610. Sir John Suckling was born in 1609 in a house on the site of the present Kneller Hall at **Whitton,** which in the 19th c. was a government training college for teachers, with F. T. Palgrave its Vice-Principal (1850–5). Palgrave was a friend of Tennyson and talked with him about his plan for a volume of selections from English verse, which became known as *The Golden Treasury*.
Pope leased a villa with gardens to the river in **Crossdeep** in 1719, when he was translating the last volume of the *Iliad*, and he spent much time improving the house and embellishing the gardens. His grotto[1] (in the grounds of St. Catherine's Convent) built under the Teddington road to link his gardens on either side, was lined with rock crystals. His ideas, implemented by Kent and Charles Bridgeman, the landscape architects, impressed others. The fashion for grottoes was taken up by Samuel Richardson and Mrs. Delany. Pope's influence on the landscape was also felt at **Marble Hill,**[2] the Palladian villa built (1724–9) for Henrietta Howard, a mistress of George II. Pope advised her on the gardens and wrote to his friend Lord Bathurst for the loan of some sheep to crop the 'new springing grass'. He was often visited by his friends the Scriblerians, Gay, Arbuthnot, Congreve, and Swift, and by Voltaire (in exile 1726–9). Lady Mary Wortley Montagu's residence at Savile House (gone) in **Heath Rd.** was short-

lived, as their friendship turned to enmity. Pope, who was known as the Wasp of Twickenham, attacked many of his friends in *The Dunciad* (1728), which appeared anonymously. Henry Brooke moved here (to be near Pope who had admired his poem *Universal Beauty*, 1735) after the success of *Gustavus Vasa* (1739), which had previously been banned. However, he soon settled in Dublin. Pope, who had erected an obelisk (1732) in the garden to the memory of his mother, died in 1744 and was buried by her side in the parish church. His parents' memorial is on the E. wall. His friend William Warburton erected a monument in 1761 on the N. wall referring to Pope's desire to be buried here rather than in Westminster Abbey. Horace Walpole commented on the sorry state of the gardens in 1760, and in 1807 another owner razed the villa to the ground and 'blotted out utterly every memorial to the poet'. Today **Pope's Grove** and **Grotto Rd.** point to the site. Henry Fielding lived (1743-8) in Back Lane (now **Holly Rd.**) and is thought to have written part of his most lasting work, the novel *Tom Jones* (1749), here. He was a cousin of Lady Mary Wortley Montagu.

Colley Cibber, actor and dramatist, lived a little upstream from Pope (who lashed him in *Epistle to Dr. Arbuthnot* and *The Dunciad*, 1743) and is thought to have written *The Refusal* (1721) in the cottage later famous as Strawberry Hill (now St. Mary's College, **Strawberry Hill**).[3]

Horace Walpole rented this small coachman's cottage in five acres, three hundred yards from the river, in 1747. Two years later he bought and began to Gothicize it, after toying with other styles, including the Chinese. He continued to improve it throughout his life so that the house, once small enough to have been 'sent in a letter', eventually had twenty-two rooms and forty-six acres of gardens containing cottages, a little wood, and two cascades. His press, set up in 1757, printed *The Bard* and *The Progress of Poetry* by his friend Thomas Gray and 30 years later some verses by Hannah More. She dined here in 1783 and 'passed as delightful a day as elegant literature, high breeding, and lively wit can afford'. He also printed some copies of his own blank-verse play *The Mysterious Mother*, which has never been performed. His earlier novel *The Castle of Otranto, a Gothic Story* (1765) was

a great success, twenty-one editions appearing before the end of the century. Walpole stocked the house with curiosities and opened it to visitors. He died in London and the contents of the house were sold in 1842. The sale lasted a month, and Harrison Ainsworth wrote a preface to the catalogue. Walpole's young friends, with whom he corresponded, Agnes and Mary Berry, lived for a time at Little Strawberry Hill (gone) in the grounds.

Dickens lived (1838-9) at 2 **Ailsa Park Villas** (opposite the station) while writing *Nicholas Nickleby*.

Tennyson lived (1851-3) at Chapel House, **Montpelier Row**, bordering Marble Hill. He wrote 'Ode on the Death of the Duke of Wellington' here, and at such a short distance from London was often visited by his friends, including Thackeray and FitzGerald.

R. D. Blackmore taught classics (1853) at Wellesley House Grammar School, **Hampton Rd.** (later Fortescue House School). While here his verse *Poems by Melanter* and *Epullia* were published, both anonymously.

Walter de la Mare lived (from *c.* 1950) at the end of Montpelier Row at 4 South End House, where he died in 1956.

[1] May be viewed on Saturdays.
[2] Open daily, except Fri. 10 a.m.–5 p.m. (4 p.m. Nov.–Jan.).
[3] Appointments must be made 2 weeks in advance to visit on Wed. or Sat. p.m. Apply to the Principal.

Vauxhall Gardens (pr. Voxhall) [10 Gf], former gardens S. of the river. They were a popular resort of London citizens and the fashionable, covering the area about Vauxhall Walk and Kennington Lane, which opened in 1661 and was at first called the New Spring Gardens after the old pleasure ground at Charing Cross. The gardens contained fruit trees in a wild tangle of bushes divided by gravelled walks as well as the 'pretty-contrived plantation' mentioned by Evelyn in his *Diary*. He often visited his friend Samuel Morland whose house, where he conducted his experiments in pumping water, was near the gardens which later enveloped the site. Pepys was rowed across the Thames by watermen and landed at Vauxhall Stairs. He mentions the 'abundance of roses' and 'the cakes and powdered beef and ale' that refreshed the party before going 'home again by water, with much pleasure'. Sir Roger de Coverley with Mr. Spectator also arrived by boat (the land route before the building of Westminster Bridge was very circuitous) and he would have enjoyed himself better had there been 'more nightingales and fewer strumpets'. The popularity of the gardens was revived in 1732 by Jonathan Tyers, who arranged concerts for fashionable music-lovers and controlled the worst excesses of the bucks who caused annoyance to the heroines of both Fielding's *Amelia* and Fanny Burney's *Evelina.*

Lydia in *Humphry Clinker* thought the walks delightful and marvelled at the 'pavilions, lodges, groves, grottos, lawns, temples and cascades', which Matthew Bramble dismissed as a 'composition of baubles, overcharged with paltry ornaments'. The cascade which operated only at set times was the cause of Beau Tibbs's friend's irritation in Goldsmith's *The Citizen of the World* (1762). She wished to see the waterworks but as she feared she would appear lacking in gentility to leave before the music stopped, she waited, and so missed the spectacle. A Cruikshank sketch shows Dr. Johnson, Goldsmith, and Hester Thrale at supper in one of the booths while the Regent and Perdita Robinson stand under the orchestra's box. Tom Tyers, then proprietor, was portrayed as Tom Restless by Johnson in the *Idler.* J. H. Reynolds in his sonnet on Vauxhall calls the thinly-cut ham 'transparent'. He also mentions the 'soaked silks and wet white satin' caused by watching fireworks 'while it hardly rains'. Arias from Thomas Holcroft's operas were popular here and songs written by Robert Anderson and sung by Master Phelps earned Anderson free admission to the gardens in 1794.

Karl Moritz, a German schoolmaster, mentions in *Travels* (1795), his delight at the gardens and the music, although he thought the women over-bold. Other visitors were Leigh Hunt, and Keats, who wrote the sonnet 'To a Lady seen for a few moments at Vauxhall'. The gardens also included the Rural Downs among whose tree-studded hillocks was a statue of Milton. Nightingales had always frequented the gardens and Gilbert White, staying with his brother at Lambeth, recorded seeing a green woodpecker and commented on the noise of the owls.

In *Vanity Fair* (1847–8) Captain Dobbin, unhappily escorting two pairs of lovers, hardly noticed any of the sparkling attractions of the gardens because his Amelia went with George. Rebecca Sharp walking with Jos in the dark walks had almost flattered him into a proposal when interrupted by the bell for the fireworks. After that, a bowl of rack punch caused Jos to sing and wink and call Rebecca his 'diddle-diddle-darling' to the amusement of the onlookers, so that the chance of her becoming Mrs. Jos Sedley was lost for ever. A final gala was held in 1859 and then the gardens were dismantled.

Victoria [10 Ee], district round Victoria Station. Ann Radcliffe, whose Gothic novels combined horror, sensibility, and a love of the picturesque, lived (1815–23) at 5 Stafford Row, which was situated where **Bressenden Pl.** joins Buckingham Palace Rd. She influenced many writers including Keats, who called her Mother Radcliffe and used many of her typical adjectives in 'The Eve of St. Agnes'. Byron is said to have modelled his scowl on one of her characters, and Coleridge reviewed *Mysteries of Udolpho* (1794), the novel that Catherine Morland found was no guide to life in *Northanger Abbey* (1818). Mrs. Radcliffe made one journey to Holland and Germany but preferred to live quietly at home as her health was poor and she suffered from asthma. She died here in 1823.

Joseph Conrad took rooms (1893–6) at 17 **Gillingham St.** after returning from the voyages to Australia on which he was first mate and had made the acquaintance of John Galsworthy. While waiting for another ship he continued the novel *Almayer's Folly* (1895) and when this and *The Outcast of the Islands* (1896) were accepted he gave up the Merchant Navy. He married Jessie George in March 1896 and they spent 4 months in Brittany.

Thomas Campbell lived (1804) after his marriage, at 25 Upper Eaton St., Pimlico, as **Grosvenor Gdns.** was called before it was rebuilt. George Darley, on the staff of the *London Magazine*, published *Sylvia* (1827), a pastoral drama, the year he moved to no. 5. After an interval (1830–9) he returned to no. 27 until 1842. He was then writing for the *Athenaeum.*

Campbell also lived at 8 **Victoria Sq.** (P),

looked after by his niece Mary, for the last 4 years of his life (1841–4). He worked on *The Pilgrim of Glencoe* (1842), *Frederick the Great* (1842), *Petrarch*, and 'The Child and the Hind'. Margaret Oliphant, who wrote popular tales of Scottish life, lived at no. 14 c. 1880, when she published *A Beleaguered City*, a tale of the occult.

Walthamstow [11 Fb], district to the NE. William Morris was born in 1834 at Elm House (gone), which he left at the age of 6. A plaque commemorating him is on the Fire Station opposite the site. After the death of his father the Morris family moved to The Water House, so called from a moat in the grounds behind the house, his home from 1848 to 1856. These grounds are now **Lloyd Park**, called after Edward Lloyd, the publisher, a later owner of The Water House whose family donated it to Walthamstow in 1898. The William Morris Gallery[1] was opened in 1950, an event made possible by a gift of works of art by Sir Frank Brangwyn, R.A. (who had worked with Morris in his youth) in association with A. H. Mackmurdo, architect and founder of The Century Guild, who introduced Brangwyn to Morris. The collections contain material of all aspects of William Morris's work, including a selection of his correspondence, original manuscripts, and a complete set of books printed by the Kelmscott Press. The reference library[2] contains books and periodicals relating to the period and publications by private presses.

[1] Open weekdays 10 a.m.–5 p.m.; and Tues. and Thurs. (Apr.–Sept. only) 10 a.m.–8 p.m.; first Sun. in each month 10 a.m.–12 noon and 2–5 p.m. Closed Bank Holidays.
[2] Open by appointment.

Wanstead [11 Gb], district to the NE. Wanstead House (site on golf course), home of the Earl of Leicester, was the scene of Philip Sidney's masque *Queen of the May* written for Queen Elizabeth I's visit (1578). Pepys visited the house, and Evelyn in 1683 commented in his diary on 'the prodigious cost in planting of walnut trees . . . and making of fish-ponds' by 'the over growne and suddenly monied' Josiah Child, one time an ordinary merchant's apprentice. Thomas Hood (1799–1845) lived (1832–5) in dilapidated splendour at Lake House (gone), part of the estate, which had a Grinling Gibbons fireplace and peeling

plaster. Here he edited the *Comic Annual* and wrote the ballad *Tylney Hall* (1834). His son Tom (1835–74) was born there but soon after the family moved abroad to save money.

Westminster [10 Fd, Fe, Gd], district between Pimlico and the Strand. **Axe Yard**, Whitehall, a court which disappeared in the 18th c., was near King Charles St. Pepys, born in London in 1633, began his *Diary* here in January 1660, living in a garret with his wife and servant Jane.

Boswell mentions in his memoirs (*London Journal*) the good bargain he had in his lodgings in **Downing St.**, where he spent the year 1763.

James Macpherson, author of poems which he claimed were translations from Ossian, spent his last years in **Fludyer St.** (gone).

Spenser returned from Ireland in 1598 and lodged in **King St.** (gone, site parallel to Whitehall), where he died a month later, in January 1599, some say in poverty.

Crabb Robinson lodged with the Colliers in **Little Smith St.** from 1805 until he moved with them to Hatton Garden in 1810. His *Diary* mentions most of the writers of the time.

St. Margaret's, Westminster was built on the site of an earlier church where Caxton was buried (1491). A memorial brass was erected (1820) to him by bibliophiles, who founded a club named after the Duke of Roxburghe, collector of many volumes printed on Caxton's press. A stained-glass window to Caxton was destroyed by bombing. Skelton, who spent his last years in a house abutting on the abbey, where the right of sanctuary still existed, keeping him free from Wolsey's reprisals, was buried (1529) by the altar but his alabaster memorial has gone. Sir Walter Ralegh, beheaded near by (1618), is thought to have been buried here. A memorial window to him, with an inscription by James Russell Lowell, was donated by Americans. Milton, who married his second wife here (1656) and buried her and their infant child here a year later, also has a memorial window donated by Americans. His inscription is by John Greenleaf Whittier. In 1655 Pepys married the dowerless, 15-year-old Elizabeth St. Michel, who often appears in his *Diary*, and in 1631 Edmund Waller married an heiress here. Thomas Campbell also married here in 1803. The west porch was built in memory of Frederick Farrar, rector of St. Margaret's (1876–95), author of a number of school stories, including *Eric, or Little by Little* (1858), as well as the popular *Life of Christ* (1874).

Charles Churchill, who was born (1731) in Vine St. (gone), succeeded his father as curate of **St. John's Church, Smith Sq.** in 1758. He separated from his wife, with whom he had made a Fleet marriage while still at Westminster School, in 1761, the year he published *The Rosciad*, a satire on actors of the day. Two years later his reckless spending and improprieties caused his parishioners to demand his resignation. Churchill, whom Dr. Johnson called a 'blockhead', had become a follower of Wilkes and wrote for his *North Briton*. He was on his way to visit Wilkes in Paris when he died (1764) of a fever.

In 1895 Somerset Maugham wrote his first novel *Liza of Lambeth* (1897) when lodging at 11 **Vincent Sq.**, while a medical student.

Westminster Abbey, Collegiate Church of St. Peter, dates from the 11th c. when the Benedictine abbey on Thorney Island was refounded by Edward the Confessor. English kings and queens have been crowned here from the time of William the Conqueror in 1066 to Queen Elizabeth II in 1953, and many of them are buried here. Francis Beaumont reflects on this in 'Ode on the Tombs in Westminster Abbey'

> Mortality behold and fear
> What a change of flesh is here!
> Think how many royal bones
> Sleep within this heap of stones:
> Here they lie had realms and lands,
> Who now want strength to stir their hands.

Many writers are buried in the abbey and others have memorials; most of these are near the S. transept, an area now called Poets' Corner. There is a canopied tomb of Chaucer (d. 1400); a tablet to William Tyndale (d. 1536), translator of the Bible; a marble monument and an effigy to William Thynne (d. 1584), first editor of Chaucer's works; a monument to Spenser (d. 1599), who was buried near Chaucer at the expense of his patron, the Earl of Essex; the grave of Francis Beaumont (d. 1616), playwright and collaborator of John Fletcher; the grave of Hakluyt (d. 1616), ambassador

to Paris, Archdeacon of the Abbey, and author of *Principall Navigations, Voyages, and Discoveries of the English Nation*; a monument to Shakespeare (d. 1616) with lines from *The Tempest*; a tablet to Camden (d. 1623), the antiquary; the grave of Drayton (d. 1631) and a monument with lines ascribed by tradition to Ben Jonson; the grave of Ben Jonson (d. 1637) with a medallion; the grave of James Ussher (d. 1656), author of *Annales Veteris et Novi Testamenti*; the grave of Abraham Cowley (d. 1667), author of *The Mistress* and *Pindaric Odes*; the grave of William D'Avenant (d. 1668), said to be Shakespeare's godson; the grave of John Denham (d. 1669), author of *Cooper's Hill*; a bust of Milton (d. 1674); the grave of Edward Hyde, Earl of Clarendon, who died in Rouen in 1674; the grave of Thomas Killigrew (d. 1683), playwright and partner with D'Avenant in the monopoly controlling acting in London; a monument with the lines

> The Poets Fate is here in emblem shown:
> He asked for Bread and he received a Stone.

commemorating Samuel Butler, who died in poverty (1680); a stained-glass window to Bunyan (d. 1688) with scenes from *The Pilgrim's Progress*; the grave of Aphra Behn (d. 1689), author of *The Rover*; the grave and monument of Dryden (d. 1700); the grave of Nicholas Rowe (d. 1718), dramatist and Poet Laureate (1715–18); the grave and a statue of Addison (d. 1721), creator of 'Sir Roger de Coverley'; the grave of Matthew Prior (d. 1721), author of *Four Dialogues of the Dead*, buried, as he wished, at the feet of Spenser; the grave and a statue of Congreve (d. 1729), author of *The Way of the World*; and the grave of his friend John Gay (d. 1732), author of *The Beggar's Opera*; a statue to James Thomson (d. 1748), author of *The Seasons*; a monument to Isaac Watts (d. 1748), author of 'Our God, our help in ages past'; the grave of Aaron Hill (d. 1750), librettist of Handel's *Rinaldo*; a monument to Gray (d. 1771), author of *Elegy in a Country Churchyard*; a monument with a bust of Goldsmith (d. 1774) and lines by Johnson, erected by fellow members of the Literary Club; the grave of Samuel Foote, actor and dramatist, who died (1777) in Dover; the grave and a statue of Johnson himself (d. 1784); the grave of James Macpherson (d. 1796), author of Ossianic poems, who was buried here at his own request; a bust of Burns (d. 1796); the grave of Sheridan (d. 1816), author of *The Rivals*; tablets to Keats (d. 1821), Shelley (d. 1822), and Byron (d. 1824), who all died abroad; the grave of William Gifford (d. 1826), first editor of the *Quarterly Review*; busts of Scott (d. 1832), Coleridge (d. 1834), and Southey (d. 1843); the grave and a statue of Thomas Campbell (d. 1844), author of *The Pleasures of Hope* and 'Hohenlinden'; a tablet to Henry Francis Lyte (d. 1847), author of 'Abide with me', commemorating the centenary of his death and placed near that of Isaac Watts; a statue of Wordsworth (d. 1850); a tablet to the Brontë sisters: Emily (d. 1848), Anne (d. 1849), and Charlotte (d. 1855), with Emily's line 'with courage to endure'; the grave and bust of Macaulay (d. 1859), author of *Lays of Ancient Rome*; a bust of Thackeray (d. 1863); the grave of Dickens (d. 1870), who had wished to be buried in Rochester; a bust of the Australian Adam Lindsay Gordon (who committed suicide in 1870), author of *Bush Ballads and Galloping Rhymes*; the grave of Bulwer-Lytton, Lord Lytton (d. 1873), author of *The Last Days of Pompeii*; a tablet to Gerard Manley Hopkins (d. 1889), laid in 1975 on the centenary of the shipwreck in the Thames which had caused him to write 'The Wreck of the Deutschland'; the graves and memorials of Browning (d. 1889) and Tennyson (d. 1892); a medallion to Ruskin (d. 1900), author of *Modern Painters*; a tablet to Henry James (d. 1916); the graves of Hardy (d. 1928) and Kipling (d. 1936); and tablets to T. S. Eliot (d. 1965), John Masefield (d. 1967), and W. H. Auden (d. 1973).

Westminster Abbey Gatehouse (gone) was used as a prison in the 16th and 17th cc. The Royalist Richard Lovelace, imprisoned here in 1642 after presenting the Kentish Petition to the House of Commons, wrote the lyric 'To Althea, from Prison', which contains the lines:

Stone walls do not a prison make,
Nor iron bars a cage.

Wordsworth's sonnet beginning 'Earth hath not anything to show more fair' was written on 3 September 1802 when he and Dorothy were driving across **Westminster Bridge** in the coach early in the morning on their way to France. It is matched by her description of 'one of nature's own grand spectacles' in her *Journal*.

Westminster School, through the archway from Broad Sanctuary to **Dean's Yard,** was founded *c.* 1560 by Queen Elizabeth I, but the school attached to Westminster Abbey which it superseded was mentioned in the 14th c. Great School (restored 1950s) was the monks' dormitory. Nicholas Udall (or Uvedale), who had been the Headmaster of Eton, was Head Master here from 1554 until his death in 1556. William Camden was usher here from 1575 to 1593 when he was appointed Head Master. He collected much antiquarian material on his journeys in the vacations for *Britannia* (1586), his survey of the country, and *Annales* (1589), a panegyric on Queen Elizabeth I. Both were translated from Latin into English later. Ashburnham House in Little Dean's Yard, a 17th-c. building with interiors possibly by Inigo Jones and now part of the school, once housed the Cottonian Library. In 1731 a fire destroyed some of the manuscripts and in 1753 the library was moved to the British Museum (British Library). Literary pupils at Westminster School include: William Harrison, Richard Hakluyt, William Alabaster, Robert Bruce Cotton, Ben Jonson, Richard Corbett, Giles Fletcher the Younger, George Herbert, Thomas Randolph, William Cartwright, Abraham Cowley, John Locke, John Dryden, Elkanah Settle, Nathaniel Lee, Matthew Prior, Nicholas Rowe, Aaron Hill, John Dyer, Charles Wesley, John Cleland, John Burgoyne, William Cowper, Charles Churchill, George Colman the Elder, Richard Cumberland, Edward Gibbon, Augustus Toplady, the Hon. John Byng, George Colman the Younger, Robert Southey—expelled for writing an essay against flogging—Matthew Gregory Lewis, James Anthony Froude, George Alfred Henty.

Bernard Shaw lived 1928–45 at 4 **Whitehall Ct.,** between Horse Guards and Northumberland Ave. This was his London *pied-à-terre* while his home was at Ayot St. Lawrence.

Willesden. See Kensal Green.

Wimbledon [11 De], district to the S. Captain Marryat had a country retreat at a Gothic lodge in **Woodhayes Rd.** from 1839 to 1843. Marian Evans (George Eliot) and George Lewes lived from February 1859 to

September 1860 at Holly Lodge, South Fields, now 31 **Wimbledon Park Rd.** (P). During this time they found a suitable site for the mill in her novel *The Mill on the Floss* which she finished here.

Winchmore Hill [11 Ea], district S. of Enfield. Rose Cottage (demolished) in **Vicars Moor Lane** was the home of Thomas Hood from 1829 to 1832 when he began his *Comic Annual* (1830).

LONDONDERRY (or DERRY), Londonderry. [8 Eb] Historic port, naval base, and garrison town on the W. bank of the Foyle, on the A2 and the A40. George Farquhar was born (1678) in Shipquay St. and attended the Free School (founded 1617, and succeeded by Foyle College in 1814), formerly situated not far from Magee University College in Northland Rd. George Berkeley was appointed Dean of the Protestant cathedral (founded 1633) in 1724, but left for America with plans for founding a missionary college in Bermuda (1728–32), which he had to abandon for want of support. Mrs. Cecil Frances Alexander, author of 'All things bright and beautiful' and other hymns, came here in 1867 when her husband became bishop. She died at the palace in 1895 and is buried in the city cemetery. Joyce Cary (1888–1957), the novelist, was a native of Londonderry.

LONGLEAT, Wilts. [1 Ad] Country House[1] off the A362, 4 m. SW. of Warminster. In 1717 Mary Granville stayed with Lord and Lady Lansdowne, who arranged her marriage (which took place here) to their friend Mr. Pendarves of Roscrow, very much against her will. Later, as Mrs. Delany, she wrote a number of Journals. George Crabbe dined here in 1824, a guest of the Marquis of Bath. He had recently met Scott in Edinburgh and told Thomas Moore, a fellow guest, about his visit.

[1] Open daily in summer 10 a.m.–6 p.m.; winter 10 a.m.–4 p.m.; closed Christmas Day.

LONG MELFORD, Suff. [4 Ff] Village stretching for 2 m. along the A134, just N. of Sudbury. At the N. end the large green is dominated by the Perpendicular church. In the Clopton chantry chapel (c. 1496) the ceiling is decorated by verses on a scroll said to be by John Lydgate (d. 1450), one-

time monk at Bury St. Edmunds. Edmund Blunden, who returned from Hong Kong in 1965, lived at Hall Mill. He died in 1974 and is buried in the churchyard. A souvenir collection of his poems is on sale in the church for which he wrote a guide.

LONGSIDE, Aberdeens. (Grampian). [7 He] Village 7 m. W. of Peterhead on the A950. John Skinner, the Episcopalian minister here from 1742 until a few days before his death in 1807, lived in a cottage in Linshart, where he wrote songs, poems, and a translation of the Psalms into Latin. He had not thought of publishing the songs until his son met Burns, who proved persuasive. Burns declared 'The Reel of Tullochgorum' the 'best Scotch song Scotland ever saw'. 'Eire with the Crookit Horn' and 'Tune your Fiddle' were others included in Johnson's *Musical Museum*. Skinner's *Songs and Poems* (1859) were collected posthumously. He died in his son's house in Aberdeen, and is buried here.

LONG SLEDDALE, Cumbria. [5 Bb] Narrow valley, 7 m. long, off the A6, 4 m. N. of Kendal, in which Mrs. Humphry Ward set the first part of her novel, *Robert Elsmere* (1888), under the name 'Long Whindale'. At the head of the valley, where the road is only a rough track, is Low Sadgill, a lonely farmhouse which became 'High Ghyll', the home of Mary Backhouse, whose illness brings together Catherine and Robert Elsmere.

LONG WHINDALE. See LONG SLEDDALE.

LONG WITTENHAM, Oxon. [1 Cb] Thames-side village on the A415, 3 m. SE. of Abingdon. Robert Gibbings, whose *Sweet Thames run Softly* (1940) and *Till I End my Song* (1957) were illustrated with his own woodcuts, lived at Footbridge Cottage, by the Cross. He was buried (1958) in the churchyard.

LONGWORTH, Oxon. [1 Bb] Little village near the Thames, on a minor road N. of Kingston Bagpuize on the A420. The Old Rectory was the birthplace of Dr. John Fell (1625–86), Dean of Christ Church, Oxford, and Bishop of Oxford. He contributed greatly to the development of the Oxford University Press, for which he procured matrices and punches of the best available types (from which the 'Fell types' are still cast), and every year he arranged for the publication of a different classical author. It seems unfair that the most familiar association with his name should be Thomas Brown's lines: 'I do not love you, Dr. Fell. . . .' The Old Rectory was also the birthplace of Richard Doddridge Blackmore, author of *Lorna Doone* (1869), whose father was curate there for a short time, but it was not a home to remember as his mother died when he was 4 months old and he was taken away to live with an aunt during the years before his father remarried.

LOTHERSDALE, North Yorkshire. [5 Dd] Village off the A629, 4 m. SW. of Skipton. The painted posts and entrance gate to Stonegappe Hall are visible from the crossroads above the village. Charlotte Brontë was governess for a few months in 1839 to Mrs. Sidgwick's family here, the 'Gateshead Hall' of *Jane Eyre*.

LOUGHBOROUGH (pr. Luffbro), Leics. [4 Bd] Manufacturing town on the A60, 11 m. NW. of Leicester. John Cleveland, who was born here (*c.* 1613), was educated at the school founded by a charitable bequest, which was held in All Saints' Church. His father was the schoolmaster.

LOUGHTON (pr. Lowton), Essex. [1 Eb] Town on the A121, on the NE. outskirts of London. Loughton Hall (rebuilt), designed by Inigo Jones, was the home of Lady Mary Wroth after her marriage in 1604. She was the daughter of Robert Sidney of Penshurst (q.v.) and she wrote *Urania* (1621) in the style of *The Arcadia* of her uncle Philip Sidney. She was the subject of a poem by George Wither, and a sonnet by George Chapman which prefaced his translation of the *Iliad* (1611).

Arthur Morrison, who settled here soon after his marriage in 1892, wrote the novels of London working-class life, *A Child of the Jago* (1896), *To London Town* (1899), and *The Hole in the Wall* (1902). *Cunning Murrell* (1900), a novel about witchcraft in earlier years of the 19th c., is set in Essex. Morrison left Loughton in 1913. W. W. Jacobs, a contemporary of Morrison, lived for some years at The Outlook, Park Hill. He wrote many humorous short stories about the

Cockney crews of the barges and small coasters, including *Many Cargoes* (1896), *Short Cruises* (1907), and *Sea Whispers* (1926). He also wrote macabre tales, of which the most gripping, 'The Monkey's Paw', was dramatized.

LOUTH, Lincs. [4 Ea] Market town 25 m. NE. of Lincoln on the A16 and the A157. Tennyson was at the Grammar School from 1815 to 1820, when his father decided to teach him at home. In 1827 *Poems of Two Brothers*, by Tennyson and his brother Charles, was published by Jacksons in the Market Place.

LOWER HALLIFORD. See SHEPPERTON, Surrey.

LOWER INGLESHAM, Wilts. [1 Bb] Village on the A361, 1 m. S. of Lechlade. The small parish church was repaired in 1888–9 by William Morris, and the old pews remain. A commemorative brass to Morris is to the right of the entrance.

LOWER SAPEY, Hereford and Worcester. [3 Ge] Hamlet on the B4203, 6 m. NE. of Bromyard. Hatt House, an old farmhouse perched on the hillside on the way to Harpley, was the home of Edmund Seward, with whom Robert Southey stayed in December 1793, falling in love briefly with another guest, Augusta Roberts. 'The snow confined us for six days', he wrote.

LOWER WICK, Hereford and Worcester. [3 He] Village on the outskirts of Worcester, *c.* 2 m. along the A499 to Malvern. Mrs. Mary Martha Sherwood, best known for *The History of the Fairchild Family* (1818–47), came to live here on her return from a period spent in India, with her husband, their five children, two adopted Indian orphans, and the motherless child of a distant relative from Brussels. The house, where she said she spent the happiest years of her life, was old and 'marvellously ill-constructed', standing among orchards above the roar and whirl of the mill where the Teme joins the Severn. Henry, her little boy, thought of Worcester as Calcutta and the Teme as the Ganges. Sherwood Lane above the roundabout leads to the site of the house, demolished in 1966 to make way for a housing estate.

LOWESTOFT, Suff. [4 Hd] Port on the A146. Thomas Nash was born here in 1567; his father was the minister, probably a curate. Crabbe, a surgeon-apprentice at Woodbridge, used to ride to Normanston Park where the Misses Blackwell and Waldron and others, who had formed a small community, had agreed to 'polish' Sara Elmy, his fiancée. After his ordination and their marriage (1783) they revisited Normanston (1790) and Crabbe, who called them his 'Ladies of the Lake', after Lake Lothing, wrote

> Trees may be found and lakes as fair
> Fresh lawns and gardens green:
> But where again the Sister-pair
> Who animate the scene.

Crabbe also heard Wesley preach on this visit.

Conrad first landed in England (1878) here and served on the coaster *Skimmer of the Sea*. Part of Watts-Dunton's *Aylwin* (1898), a romance that features the East Anglian gipsies, takes place in the neighbourhood.

LOWICK, Cumbria. [5 Bc] Small village a few miles S. of Coniston Water, on a minor road between the A5084 and the A5092. Arthur Ransome was lord of the manor (1947–9) when he lived at Lowick Hall, a manorial hall dating from Norman times, which he worked on and greatly improved during his short residence.

LOWOOD. See COWAN BRIDGE.

LOW-WOOD. See BRIERY CLOSE.

LUDLOW, Salop. [3 Gd] Picturesque old town on the A49, on a hill above the junction of the Teme and the Corve. In 1634 Milton's masque, *Comus*, with music by Henry Lawes, was performed in the (now roofless) great hall of the Castle in celebration of the Earl of Bridgewater's appointment as President of Wales and the Marches. Samuel Butler (1612–80) wrote part of his satire, *Hudibras*, in his rooms above the 14th-c. castle gateway during the time he was steward to the Earl of Carbery (1661–2).

Stanley Weyman, author of many historical romances, including *Under the Red Robe* (1894), was born at 54 Broad St., where he lived until his marriage in 1895. His novel *The New Rector* (1891) is set in Ludlow.

A. E. Housman, though not a native of Shropshire, knew and loved the country near Ludlow and Much Wenlock, and his ashes are buried outside the N. door of St. Laurence's Church. A tablet on the outer wall of the church commemorates him as professor of Latin and author of *A Shropshire Lad*:

> Goodnight. Ensured release
> Imperishable peace:
> Have these for yours

LURGAN, Armagh. [8 Gc] Town on the A3 and the A26, 2½ m. SE. of Lough Neagh, an important linen centre. George William Russell (1867–1935), poet and artist, familiarly known as 'AE', was born in William St. and was educated in the town until he was *c.* 10, when he moved to Dublin with his family.

LUTTERWORTH, Leics. [4 Be] Market town on the A426, W. of the M1 intersection 20. Wycliffe was rector (1374–84) and spent his last years here working on the first English translation of the Bible. He died after being taken ill during a service in the church and was carried through what is now Wycliffe's Doorway in the S. side of the chancel. He was buried in the churchyard but in 1428 his body was exhumed and burnt, and his ashes cast into the Swift by order of a Papal Commission. Some of his works, with Foxe's *Book of Martyrs* and part of a medieval cope, reputedly his, can be seen by the S. door. A white marble memorial, erected in 1837 under the E. window in the S. aisle, shows Wycliffe preaching.

LYME REGIS, Dorset. [2 Gd] Old fishing town picturesquely situated on Lyme Bay, on the A3052, a seaside resort which began to be fashionable in the late 18th c. Jane Austen, in a letter to her sister Cassandra of 14 September 1804, describes a visit here with her parents, James the coachman, and Jenny the maid, and gives an account of an evening spent at the weekly ball at the Assembly Rooms (site now a car park) at Cobb Gate, at the E. end of the Marine Parade, and of her enjoyment of sea bathing. Eleven years later she drew on her memories of this and possibly other visits to the town when she was writing *Persuasion* (finished in 1816 but not published until 1818) and planned the expedition to Lyme of the young people. The famous Cobb (the long, curving harbour wall) is probably familiar to more people than have ever seen it as the place of Louisa Musgrove's dramatic fall, and Bay Cottage (now a café) at the W. end of the Marine Parade as the place where Captain Harville had taken rooms for the winter season and where Louisa stayed to convalesce. On the cliff-side above the cottage a pleasant little garden (P) commemorates Jane Austen's association with Lyme, its opening on 23 April 1975 being the occasion of the performance of a short play, *Miss Austen at Lyme*, by Henry Chessell, the mayor.

LYMINGTON, Hants. [1 Be] Old port and yachting station on the A337, at the mouth of the Lymington on the W. side of the Solent. Henry Francis Lyte, author of 'Abide with me', was curate here from *c.* 1820 until he went to Brixham (q.v.) in 1824. Frederick Marryat (1792–1848) lived for a time in the Brockenhurst Rd., just N. of the town, the house where he stayed being portrayed as 'Wolverley Lodge' in *The Children of the New Forest* (1847).

William Allingham was stationed here as a Customs Officer, 1863–70. He describes the Office in his *Diary* (ed. H. Allingham and D. Radford, 1907) as

. . . a small first-floor room over the Coastguard Station [demolished], looking upon the little Harbour (muddy at low water, occupied chiefly by pleasure-yachts), and the woods of Walhampton beyond. . . . in the evening after my arrival . . . I heard four nightingales.

While he was here he edited *The Ballad Book* (1864) and wrote *Laurence Bloomfield in Ireland*, a poem of over 5,000 lines (published in book form 1864), which he regarded as his most important work and which was quoted by Gladstone in the House of Commons.

Coventry Patmore (1823–96) came to Lymington in 1891 and stayed for the rest of his life.

LYMPORT. See PORTSMOUTH.

LYNDHURST, Hants. [1 Be] Village in the heart of the New Forest, 5 m. SW. of Southampton on the A35. In the churchyard is the grave of Mrs. Reginald Hargreaves, *née* Alice Liddell, who inspired Lewis Carroll's *Alice's Adventures in Wonderland* (1865). The graves of the 'Two yeomen . . . and a maiden fair' of Kingsley's 'A New Forest Ballad' cannot now be located.

LYNMOUTH, Devon. [2 Eb] Holiday resort on the N. coast, where the East and the West Lyn meet before flowing into the sea. The twin village of Lynton, situated near the edge of the cliff, 430 ft above, is reached by a steep road and a funicular railway. Coleridge took many walks here with Wordsworth when he was living (1797–8) at Nether Stowey (q.v.). Dorothy Wordsworth, who often walked with them, mentions the two men 'laying the plan of a ballad' which became 'The Ancient Mariner', published in the *Lyrical Ballads* (1798). Hazlitt also walked here with Coleridge, who was impressed with the desolate Valley of the Rocks near Lynton.

In June 1812 Shelley and his wife, Harriet, then 17, stayed at Mrs. Hooper's cottage here. Shelley's pleasure in sailing makeshift 'boats' and launching bottles containing messages, led him to be looked upon with suspicion. He and Harriet left after 9 weeks and returned to Wales. The cottage was rebuilt after a fire in 1907 and is now called Shelley's Cottage.

LYNTON. See LYNMOUTH.

M

MACKERY END, Herts. [1 Eb] Hamlet approached by the road opposite the Cherry Tree Inn in Lower Luton Rd., Wheathampstead, 3 m. E. of Harpenden. The Lambs' visits to their Great Aunt Gladman at the farmhouse, and the mansion,[1] farmyard, and the sheepshearing supper, are described by Mary Lamb in *Mrs. Leicester's School* (1808) and by Charles in his essay 'Mackery End' (1820).

[1] Garden open for N.G.S.

MACKWORTH, Derbys. [4 Bc] Village on the A52, 2½ m. NW. of Derby. Samuel Richardson was baptized in the parish church in August 1689, and spent his early years here. It is thought that he was apprenticed to a stationer in Derby before starting his own printing business in London.

MADDER HILL. See CHALDON HERRING.

MAIDENCOMBE, Devon. [2 Ee] District, now part of St. Marychurch, on the N. side of Torquay. Kipling and his wife came here in September 1896 to Rock House, Rock House Lane, a place that he said seemed 'almost too good to be true . . . with big rooms each and all open to the sun, the grounds embellished with great trees and the warm land dipping southerly to the clear sea under the Marychurch cliffs'. But gradually they were overcome by depression—'a gathering blackness of mind and sorrow of heart'—caused by 'the Feng-shui—the Spirit of the house itself' a 'Spirit of deep, deep Despondency', described by Kipling in *Something of Myself* (1937), that drove them away the following June. But while he was there Kipling first had the idea of writing 'tracts or parables on the education of the young', which developed into the series of tales called *Stalky & Co.* (1899). Rock House was the subject of a psychoanalytical story, 'The House Surgeon', written somewhat in the manner of Henry James.

MAIDSTONE, Kent. [1 Fc] Market and manufacturing town on the Medway. William Hazlitt was born (1778) in Rose Yard, Mitre Lane (house gone), near his father's Unitarian Chapel in Bullock Lane.

The Museum and Art Gallery[1] at Chillington Manor House, a 16th-c. mansion in St. Faith's St., has many relics of Hazlitt, though he left the town before he was 2.

[1] Open weekdays 10 a.m.–5 p.m.

MALAHIDE CASTLE, Dublin. [8 Gf] Castle SW. of the village of Malahide, 9 m. NE. of Dublin, between the L86 and the L87, the home of the Talbot family for over 800 years. A store of James Boswell's private papers was brought here by Emily Boswell, a direct descendant, who married the 5th Lord Talbot de Malahide. In the 1930s and 1940s further caches of documents and journals were discovered and stimulated the demand for a life of Boswell. The complicated story of the Malahide papers is told in *The Treasure of Auchinleck*, by David Buchanan (1975).

MALDON, Essex. [1 Gb] Small port and yachting resort on the Blackwater, 10 m. E. of Chelmsford. The Old English poem *The Battle of Maldon* tells of the raid in 991 by the Northmen, who were camped on an island (now Northey Island) in the estuary. The battle was delayed by the rising tide and after a stand by the ealdorman Byrhtnoth and his friend Ælfric, Byrhtnoth was slain with a poisoned spear. The end of the poem, thought to have been written before the close of the century, is missing.

MALHAM TARN, North Yorkshire. [5 Dd] Lake 3 m. N. of Malham between the B6479 N. of Settle, and the B6160. Charles Kingsley, when a guest at Tarn House (now let to the Field Studies Council), is said to have been asked why there were black streaks down the limestone cliffs near by, and jokingly replied that a chimney-sweep must have fallen over them. This gave him the idea from which he wrote *The Water Babies* (1863), where Tom goes over Harthover Fell and Lewthwaite Crag.

The area round the lake is the property of the National Trust and the public has access to the S. shore.

MALLOW, Cork. [9 Dd] Busy market town on the Blackwater, on the T11 and the T30, famous as a spa in the 18th c., when it was known as the 'Irish Bath'. People came from all over the country to drink the waters, and the notorious young gallants, the 'Rakes of Mallow', gathered here for their uproarious meetings, but by the time Sir Walter Scott visited (1825) on his Irish tour it was losing its fashionable reputation. The original Spa House (now private) can be seen on the E. side of Spa Walk, on the Fermoy road.

Thomas Osborne Davis (1814–45), poet and leader of the Young Ireland movement, was born at 72 Thomas Davis St. (P). At the age of 4 he moved with his family to live in Dublin. Canon Sheehan (1852–1913) was born in William O'Brien St., near the Main St. corner (P above Murphy's Bar), and the stained-glass windows behind the altar in St. Mary's Church are a memorial to him. Anthony Trollope lived at Bank Place when he was working here as a Post Office surveyor (1845–51). He was trying his hand at novel-writing at this time, but had not yet achieved success. Mrs. Henry Wood lived here for some time at Rock Cottage.

MALMESBURY, Wilts. [1 Ab] Small town on the A429, 14 m. W. of Swindon. William of Malmesbury (d. c. 1143) the historian, was librarian at the abbey here. Thomas Hobbes was born (1588) while his father was minister of Westport Church, though the house has gone. An old acacia tree in the garden of Abbey House is said to have been planted by him. Addison was M.P. for Malmesbury from 1710 to 1719.

MALPAS. See TRURO.

MALVERN. Area at the base and on the slopes of the Malvern Hills. See GREAT MALVERN and WEST MALVERN.

MANATON, Devon. [2 Ee] Quiet village on the B3344, 3 m. S. of Moretonhampstead. John Galsworthy spent his honeymoon (1904) at Wingstone, a house beside a farm, down an avenue off the road a little N. of the village, which he had discovered on a walking tour earlier that year. He and his wife loved the place so much that they became summer tenants of the main part of the house for 15 years. Part of the novel *The Country House* (1907) and most of *Fraternity* (1909) were written here. In

August and October of 1914 Galsworthy recorded visits from Bernard Shaw and his wife, and 'much talk'. The pleasure Galsworthy felt in living in the county of his ancestors in the peace of an unspoilt country is described in his letters (*Life and Letters*, by H. V. Marrot, 1935, which also has photographs of the house).

MANCHESTER, Greater Manchester. [3 Ha] Great commercial city and capital of the cotton-manufacturing district formerly in SE. Lancashire; since the opening of the Ship Canal in 1894 England's third port. In the Civil War it withstood a Royalist siege in 1642, but in 1715 and again in 1745 (when Prince Charles Edward Stuart occupied the town) it showed Jacobite sympathies (see Shenstone's ballad, 'Jemmy Dawson'). When it was still known as 'the largest village in the country' it was the home of John Byrom, Jacobite poet and inventor of a system of shorthand. His loyalties are discreetly worded in 'To an Officer in the Army':

> God bless the King, I mean the Faith's Defender;
> God bless—no harm in blessing—the Pretender;
> But who Pretender is, or who is King,
> God bless us all—that's quite another thing.

Byrom wrote the hymn, 'Christians awake' for his daughter, Dorothy. It was originally entitled 'Christmas Day—for Dolly' and it seems likely that it was sung in the street of the Byrom House in Hanging Ditch in 1750. Byrom was born (1692) in the house now called the Old Wellington Inn, in the old market place, lived in St. John St., and was buried in the cathedral.

There has been doubt about the birthplace of De Quincey, but according to local records he was born (15 Aug. 1785) in a small house on the corner of the former Tasle St. and Red Cross St., near his father's place of business in the city, on a site now occupied by a building on the corner of Cross St. and John Dalton St. (P above firstfloor window on Cross St. frontage). He was baptized in St. Ann's Church near by and was taken when a few weeks old to The Farm, Moss Side, 'a pretty rustic dwelling'. In 1791 he moved with his family to Green Heys, a large country house (demolished 1852), 2 m. NW. of the city centre, built and furnished by his father for c. £6,000. After his father's death in 1792 he stayed on with his mother for 4 years and then, after boarding for a short time with his tutor, the Revd. Samuel Hall, followed her to Bath. In 1800 he went to Manchester Grammar School, but found the monotonous routine irksome and, when his guardians refused to remove him, ran away in 1802 and went to Chester (travelling on foot in 2 days) to stay with his mother. He wrote 'Vision of Sudden Death' in a Manchester tavern.

Charles Swain, an engraver who wrote poetry in his leisure time, was born (1803) in Every St., off Gt. Ancoats St., and died at his house, Prestwich Park. He is buried in Prestwich churchyard, with a memorial in the church. Many of his lyrics were set to music, including the popular 'When the Heart is Young' and 'I cannot mind my wheel, mother'. He also wrote 'Dryburgh Abbey, a Poem on the Death of Sir Walter Scott' (1832). There are portraits of Swain in the Public Library and the City Art Gallery, and at Salford Museum.

William Harrison Ainsworth, the son of a solicitor, was born (4 Feb. 1805) at 21 (now 57) King St. (P on National Westminster Bank). He went to Manchester Grammar School, of which he gave an interesting and accurate account in *Mervyn Clitheroe* (1851). He was articled to a solicitor, but on his father's death in 1824 went to finish his legal education in London, and soon afterwards turned from law to literature. On 15 September 1881, near the end of a prolific writing career, he was entertained by the mayor of Manchester at a banquet in the town hall 'as an expression of the high esteem in which he was held by his fellow-townsmen and of his services to literature'.

Mrs. Elizabeth Gaskell came to Manchester in 1832 after her marriage to William Gaskell, minister of Cross Street Unitarian Chapel and lecturer on English literature at Owens College. They lived first at 14 Dover St., Oxford Rd. (gone), then (1842–9) at 121 Upper Rumford St. (gone), and finally at 84 Plymouth Grove (P; now the University Overseas Centre), a large family house where visitors were welcomed, including distinguished writers such as Charlotte Brontë, Dickens, Carlyle, and Mrs. Harriet Beecher Stowe. *Mary Barton, a Tale of Manchester Life* (1848), her first novel, which brought her immediate success, and *North and South* (published serially in *Household Words*, 1854–5) are stories of industrial life and the struggle as she saw it of the work people to obtain their rights. Dickens, who admired her work and shared her interests in social reform, also used a Manchester setting for his novel, *Hard Times* (1854). On a visit in 1837 he was introduced by Harrison Ainsworth to a solicitor named Gilbert Winter, at whose home, Stock House (gone) in Cheetham Hill Rd., he met William and Daniel Grant, on whom he is said to have modelled the Cheeryble Brothers in *Nicholas Nickleby* (1838–9). He was in Manchester again in 1852, when he visited the Gaskells and was for a time both theatrical manager and actor at the Free Trade Hall. In June 1851 Charlotte Brontë paid her first visit to the Gaskells, a couple of days on her way home from London. It was very hot and the only thing she made a point of doing was to buy a shawl as a present for Tabby, the old family servant at Haworth. Before she had met Mrs. Gaskell Charlotte Brontë had already stayed in Manchester, where she had brought her father in August 1846 for a cataract operation. They stayed in lodgings at 83 Mount Pleasant, Boundary St., Oxford Rd. (gone; P on site), then a quiet terrace of brick houses, and arranged their own board, about which Charlotte found herself excessively ignorant: 'I can't tell what to order in the way of meat', she wrote in a letter. It was here that she began *Jane Eyre* (1847), at the very time when *The Professor* (1857, posthumously) was being rejected by one publisher after another. They returned home at the end of September. In 1853 Mrs. Gaskell had a visit from Mrs. Harriet Beecher Stowe, whose anti-slavery novel, *Uncle Tom's Cabin* (1852), was creating widespread interest. Mrs. Stowe describes the visit 'to the author of *Mary Barton*' in her *Sunny Memories of Foreign Lands* (1854). Mrs. Molesworth (Mary Louisa Stewart), writer of children's books, came to Manchester when she was 2 (1841) and stayed till she was married 20 years later. She was a pupil of William Gaskell at Plymouth Grove. Her home, 92 Rusholme Rd., is described in *Little Miss Peggy* (1887) and in the beginning of *The Carved Lions* (1895).

George Macdonald, a Congregational minister who turned to literature c. 1856 and became a lay member of the Church of England, lived (from 1854) at 3 Camp Ter., Lower Broughton. It is unfortunate that he should be remembered by 'Where did you come from, baby dear?', but, although not a great poet and only a mediocre novelist, he wrote some delightful fairy stories, such as *The Princess and the Goblin* (1872), *At the Back of the North Wind* (1871), and 'The Light Princess'.

Mrs. Frances Hodgson Burnett, author of some forty books, but best remembered for *Little Lord Fauntleroy* (1886), was born (24 Nov. 1849) at 141 York St. (later Cheetham Hill Rd.) (original house probably demolished) and moved in 1852 to 9 St. Luke's Ter. (later 361 Cheetham Hill Rd.; P). After the death of her father, Edwin Hodgson, in 1853 the family fortunes declined and in 1855 she moved with her family to a house in a poorer district, 19 Islington Sq. (gone), Salford, where she lived until they all emigrated (1856) to Knoxville, Tennessee. Another native writer, of a very different kind, was Nathaniel Gould, who left school to enter the tea trade, but became a journalist and, while living in Australia (1884–95), a novelist. Nearly all his novels were about horse-racing.

Howard Spring came to Manchester from Cardiff and was a journalist on the *Manchester Guardian* from 1915 till 1931, when he moved to London. After his marriage in 1920 he lived in East Didsbury, and of this period he wrote 'I came to love Manchester as I have known and loved no other city'. His career as a novelist began with *Shabby Tiger* (1934), followed by a dozen others, of which the best known is *Fame is the Spur* (1940).

Two late-19th-c. writers were students at Owens College, incorporated (1871) in the University and transferred from its original site in Quay St. (P on County Court) in 1873; one was the novelist, George Gissing, a brilliant student (specializing in Greek and Latin) whose academic career began in 1872 and was cut short because of petty thefts to help a girl he loved; the other was the poet Francis Thompson, who studied medicine reluctantly (1877–83) and left without a degree. The University Library has a permanent exhibition of editions of their works and also those of Mrs. Gaskell.

Manchester Grammar School (founded 1515) was moved from its original site beside Chetham's Hospital in 1931 to Birchfields Rd. (a continuation of Upper Brook St.), Rusholme. As well as De Quincey and Harrison Ainsworth, mentioned above, its

distinguished pupils include William Stanley Houghton, author of the farce, *The Dear Departed* (1908) and the more famous *Hindle Wakes* (1912); and Louis Golding, a native of Manchester, whose best-known novels of life in the city were *Magnolia Street* (1931) and *Five Silver Daughters* (1934).

There are three libraries of special interest near the city centre, in addition to the Central Public Library in St. Peter's Sq. The Portico Library in Mosley St., established in 1806 as a social and literary institution, has rare first editions and was mentioned by De Quincey. A plaque records the names of famous readers, including De Quincey, Mrs. Gaskell, and Peter Mark Roget. The last-named, best known for his *Thesaurus of English Words and Phrases* (1852), was appointed physician to Manchester Infirmary in 1804 and became the Library's first secretary. He was primarily a scientist with leanings to higher mathematics and did not devote his time to the *Thesaurus* until after he retired in 1840. Chetham's Library, near the cathedral, established in 1653 under the Will of Humphrey Chetham (1580–1653), claims to be the oldest free public library in England. It has a special collection of the works of John Byrom. Harrison Ainsworth wrote much of his early work at a table in the bow window, traditionally used by Sir Walter Ralegh. The John Rylands Library, established in 1900 in Deansgate, was built and endowed by the widow of John Rylands (1801–88) in his memory. Its collection of rare bibles, books, and manuscripts, which includes the Althorp Library of the 5th Earl Spencer, is among the most valuable in the world. It became the John Rylands University Library of Manchester in 1973 and the main part is now housed in the university area.

The Shakespeare Garden in Platt Fields Park, Rusholme, near the Grangethorpe Rd. turning off Wilmslow Rd., is a quiet place of unique appeal. It is an Elizabethan-style walled garden, with narrow paths between formal beds of flowers and herbs, sheltered by shrubs and trees, and reputedly contains all the plants mentioned in Shakespeare's works and nothing that is not mentioned.

Manchester is the 'Dumble' of Mrs. Gaskell's *Cranford* (1851–3) and the 'Doomington' of Louis Golding's *Magnolia Street* (1931).

MANNINGTREE. See CATTAWADE.

MANORBIER, Dyfed. [2 Ca] Village near the coast, on the B4585, just S. of the A4139 Pembroke–Tenby road. The picturesque ruined Castle[1] was the birthplace of the chronicler and travel writer Giraldus Cambrensis (Gerald de Barri, 1146?–1200?). His most important work was *Itinerarium*, a description of the topography of Wales.

[1] Open Apr.–Sept.: daily 11.30 a.m.–12.30 p.m., 1.30–6 p.m.

MAPLEDURHAM HOUSE, Oxon. [1 Cc] Elizabethan manor house off the B4526, 4 m. NW. of Reading, built beside the Thames for the Blount family. Pope, who was a friend and correspondent of Mary and Martha Blount throughout his life, wrote some lines 'To Miss Blount, On her leaving the Town after the Coronation':

> She went, to plain-work, and to purling brooks,
> Old-fashion'd halls, dull aunts, and croaking rooks.
> She went from Op'ra, park, assembly, play,
> To morning-walks, and pray'rs three hours a day;
>
> Or o'er cold coffee, trifle with the spoon,
> Count the slow clock, and dine exact at noon;
> Divert her eyes with pictures in the fire,
> Hum half a tune, tell stories to the squire;
> Up to her godly garret after sev'n
> There starve and pray, for that's the way to heav'n.

Pope visited the house in 1713 and 1714, and in 1717 the sisters moved from the family home, which their brother had inherited, to live in London.

Open Easter to Sept.: Sat. and Sun. 2.30–5 p.m.

MAPPOWDER, Dorset. [2 Hd] Village on the N. side of the N. Dorset Downs, on an unclassified road opposite the junction of the B3143 from Dorchester and the B3146. It was the home of T. F. Powys, who lived for the last 10 years of his life near the church in the little lodge at the entrance to Newleaze House (the Old Rectory) and is buried in the churchyard. There is a detailed account in the church of other distinguished members of the Powys family.

MARGATE, Kent. [1 Hc] Resort on the NE. coast, on the A28. Gray, staying at Denton in 1766, visited 'Margate, which is Bartholomew Fair by the seaside'. Keats,

lodging here in 1816 and 1817 for a few weeks while working on *Endymion*, found it bare and treeless. Lamb, who came first when 15, returned 'with Mary, to drink sea-water and pick up shells' in 1821. One of his *Essays of Elia* (1820–3) is about 'The Old Margate Hoy', the coaster which took visitors from London to Margate.

MARKET BOSWORTH, Leics. [4 Bd] Small town on the B585, 11 m. W. of Leicester and 2 m. N. of the battlefield of Bosworth Field, 1485. In 1731 Samuel Johnson, soon after his father's death, became a master at the Grammar School for a few years. This was called Dixie School, which had been refounded in 1601 with bequests from Sir Wolstan Dixie (1525–94), a Lord Mayor of London. Johnson combined teaching with acting as secretary to a descendant of Sir Wolstan, who lived at the Hall, visible across the park. Johnson, who also lived at the Hall, often used to visit the Revd. Beaumont Dixie at the rectory.

MARKETHILL, Armagh. [8 Gd] Little market town on the A28, 7 m. SE. of Armagh. Gosford Castle, 1½ m. N., a 19th-c. Norman-style mansion, is near the site of the former Manor House where Dean Swift used to visit Sir Arthur Acheson, Bt. (later Earl of Gosford) after Stella's death. His 'walk', 'chair', and 'well', are still pointed out in the demesne.

MARKYATE, Herts. [1 Db] Village (formerly called Market Street) 2½ m. NW. of Harpenden, bypassed by the A5. William Cowper was sent at the age of 6 to a private boarding-school here and endured nearly 4 years of being teased and bullied before going to Westminster School (1741). The school, situated in the High St., was originally known as the Mermaid, later the Old Vicarage, and 'Cowper's Oak', the tree where he took refuge from being pelted with stones for being 'bookish', is near the field across the way from the Old Vicarage garden, reached by a footpath on the Dunstable side of Cavendish Rd.

MARLBOROUGH, Wilts. [1 Bc] Town on the A4 and the A345. In 1728 James Thomson wrote *Spring*, part of *The Seasons* (1730), while a guest of the Countess of Hertford. Her house later became one of the most splendid of the coaching inns and was described by Stanley Weyman in his novel

The Castle Inn (1898). In 1843 it became the main building of the new Marlborough College, and her grotto, where she and Thomson often sat, is by the Mound in the school grounds. C. S. Calverley, William Morris, J. Meade Falkner, A. Hope Hawkins, E. F. Benson, Siegfried Sassoon, Charles Sorley, and Louis MacNeice were educated at the college. F. W. Farrar, author of *Eric, or Little by Little* (1858), and an assistant master in 1854, was Master from 1871 to 1876. E. F. Benson's school story, *David Blaize* (1915) is about Marlborough College. Charles Sorley, who was killed at the battle of Loos in 1915, wrote of local places such as Barbary Camp, and Liddington Castle (the favourite places of Richard Jefferies whom he admired) in *Marlborough and other Poems* (1916). Writing from France in 'I have not brought my Odyssey' he thinks of his return here

> And soon, O soon, I do not doubt it,
> With the body or without it,
> We shall all come tumbling down
> To our old wrinkled red-capped town.
> Perhaps the road up Ilsley way,
> The old ridge-track, will be my way.

Many of his poems had appeared in the College magazine, *The Marlburian*.

MARLOW, Bucks. [1 Db] Town where the A404 crosses the Thames. Thomas Love Peacock wrote *Nightmare Abbey* at 47 West St. (once Peacock's Restaurant, now renamed). Shelley stayed with him here on returning with Mary Godwin from Switzerland. After Shelley's wife Harriet drowned herself in the Serpentine it was Peacock who counselled an immediate re-marriage. The couple moved into Albion House, two-storeyed with Gothic windows, early in 1817. Leigh Hunt on a visit found Mary transcribing *Laon and Cythna*, published later as *The Revolt of Islam* (1818), and preparing her own *Frankenstein* for publication. The friends walked, rowed, and dined in the local inns together. Shelley sold the house in 1818 before leaving England for ever. It is now divided, and not shown to the public. Izaak Walton is commemorated by 'The Compleat Angler' Hotel with its riverside gardens.

MARTLEY, Hereford and Worcester. [3 Ge] Village 6 m. NW. of Worcester on the B4204, with a red sandstone church which

has medieval wall paintings and a fine chancel screen. The poet and parodist C. S. Calverley was born in 1831 in a panelled room in one of the oldest rectories lived in by an incumbent. His father Henry Blayds, who changed his name in 1852, was a curate-in-charge here during the long absence of the rector after a riding accident. The beautiful raftered hall was 'modernized' in Elizabethan times, the addition of a floor giving a bedroom above.

MASBOROUGH. See ROTHERHAM.

MATCHING GREEN. See DOWN HALL.

MATFIELD, Kent. [1 Fd] Village on the B2162, 5 m. NE. of Tunbridge Wells. In *The Weald of Youth* (1942) the poet and novelist, Siegfried Sassoon, describes his life at Weirleigh, the tall red-brick house where before the First World War he learned to ride and arranged for his first poems to be published.

MATTISHALL, Norf. [4 Gd] Village off the A47, 4 m. SE. of East Dereham. Mattishall Hall, a red-brick Georgian house in South Green, was the home (then called South Green House) of the Bodhams. Anne Bodham (*née* Donne) sent her cousin William Cowper the miniature of his mother that inspired the poem 'On the Receipt of my Mother's Picture out of Norfolk'. The Bodhams were often visited by 'Parson' Woodforde, whose *Diary* includes a description of Thomas Bodham's funeral. The church contains memorials to the Bodhams and other members of the Donne family and to George William Smith, the curate, who took the services at Weston Longville when Woodforde went on holiday.

MAUCHLINE (pr. Moklin), Ayrs. (Strathclyde). [6 Dd] Village on the A76, 9 m. SE. of Kilmarnock, which Burns often visited when he was living (1777–89) at Lochlea and Mossgiel (qq.v.). He fell in love with Jean Armour, daughter of a master-mason who found him ineligible. He also met the lawyer Gavin Hamilton here, at whose house next to the 15th-c. Mauchline Tower he at last married Jean Armour in 1788. Burns House[1] where they rented a room is in Castle St., and Poosie Nansie's Tavern (still an inn) in Loudoun St. features in 'The Jolly Beggars'. The churchyard has a plan showing the graves of four of Burns's children and of many characters mentioned in his poems. It is also the setting for 'The Holy Fair' a satire on the annual gathering for communion. The church where Burns was often punished for his misdemeanours has been rebuilt.

[1] Open Mon.–Sat. 10 a.m.–7 p.m.; Sun. 2–7 p.m.

MAUGHOLD, I.O.M. [5 Jg] Village 4 m. SE. of Ramsey. T. E. Brown, who married his cousin here in 1858, considered it one of the three places dearest to his heart. After he retired as a schoolmaster, he settled at 10 Windsor Mount, Ramsey, a few miles to the E.

During his youth Hall Caine often stayed with his uncle in the Schoolhouse, which had a rounded end like a lighthouse. When he was 17 his uncle died and for almost a year Hall Caine took his uncle's place as schoolmaster. After his death at Greeba Castle, Hall Caine, who had once planned to be buried on the headland, was interred in the churchyard (1931), where a tall Celtic cross, engraved with characters from his novels, was later erected.

MAUTBY, Norf. [4 Hd] Village 5 m. NW. of Great Yarmouth, home of Margaret Mautby, an heiress who married (1440) John Paston. She wrote many of the *Paston Letters*, and was the mother of Margery, who was determined to marry for love in spite of punishments. Margaret Paston returned here when she became a widow. Her funeral (1484) was costly and an elaborate monument was erected in the S. aisle of the church, but this was lost when the aisle became ruined.

MAYBOLE, Ayrs. (Strathclyde). [6 De] Hilltop town on the A77, 9 m. SW. of Ayr. Walter Kennedy, the late-15th-c. poet and rival of William Dunbar, whose *The Flyting of Dunbar and Kennedy* (1508) contained some of Kennedy's poems, is thought to have been Provost of Maybole *c.* 1594. The Kennedys were Earls of Cassilis in the 15th and 16th centuries and their castle here (restored and now offices) may have been the home of the Countess of Cassilis, heroine of the ballad 'Gypsy Laddie'. This early Scottish ballad was associated with the exploits of Johnny Faa, recognized as lord and earl by James V and later hanged. It was in the 18th c. that a Countess of Cassilis was first associated with the ballad which, in an English version, has her say:

> Oh! What care I for thy goosefeather bed
> With the sheet turned down so bravely–o
> Oh! What care I for my new wedded lord,
> I'm off with the raggle-taggle gypsies–o.

MAYFIELD, Staffs. [4 Ac] Village 2 m. W. of Ashbourne on the B5032 and the A523. Mayfield Cottage (now Standcliffe Farm off Gallowstree Lane in Upper Mayfield) was the home of Thomas Moore (1813–17), where he wrote the satirical *Twopenny Postbag* (1813) and the successful *Lalla Rookh* (1817), four tales in verse to entertain a young princess on her journey across India to be married. Moore's young daughter Olivia Byron, called after his friend, Lord Byron, died here and is buried in the churchyard. He returned here in 1827 and visited her grave.

MAYLAND, Essex. [1 Gb] Small village off the B1012, 7 m. SE. of Maldon. John Gauden, bishop of Exeter and Worcester (qq.v.), was born here in 1605 while his father was rector, but the rectory and the church have been rebuilt.

MEDMENHAM ABBEY, Bucks. [1 Dc] An 18th-c. mansion on the site of a Cistercian abbey, 4 m. SW. of Marlow. Here Sir Francis Dashwood founded the Hell-fire Club, whose members, sometimes called the Monks of Medmenham, adopted as their motto 'Fay ce que voudras' after that of the community at Rabelais's Abbey of Thelema in *Gargantua* (1534). There it was expected that a carefully selected band of virtuous people with the highest qualities would need no rules to live a virtuous life, but Charles Johnstone's description of the activities of the club in *Chrysal, or the Adventures of a Guinea* (1760–5) suggests that a virtuous life was not one of the aims here.

MELBOURNE, Derbys. [4 Bc] Small town on the A514, 8 m. S. of Derby. Melbourne Hall,[1] a mainly 17th- and 18th-c. building, was a retreat during the Commonwealth for Richard Baxter, the Nonconformist minister at Kidderminster. He wrote here part of

The Saint's Everlasting Rest (1650), the book that George Eliot, in *The Mill on the Floss* (1860), makes Mrs. Glegg turn to with such relief in times of domestic crisis. Baxter, who has been called an 'irrepressible heresiarch', was a Parliamentarian who did much to restore the monarchy, and then suffered under Charles II and James II.

[1] Open Easter Sat.–Tues., Spring Bank Holiday Sat.–Tues., and June–Sept. daily, except Mon. and Fri. 2–6 p.m. Bank Holiday Mon. from 11 a.m.

MELCHESTER. See SALISBURY.

MELLSTOCK. See STINSFORD.

MEOLE BRACE, Salop. [3 Gc] Suburb of Shrewsbury on the A5 and the A49. Mary Webb lived here before her marriage at her family home, Maesbrook. In 1912 she married Henry Webb in the village church, a 19th-c. building remarkable for its stained-glass windows by Morris and Burne-Jones. A brass plate on one of the pews records that Mary Webb worshipped here, 1902–12.

MERE, Wilts. [2 Hc] Village on the A303, 9 m. SW. of Warminster. The Dorset poet, William Barnes, was a schoolmaster here from 1823 to 1835. He married Julia Miles in 1827 and transferred his school to the old Chantry House, adjoining the church-yard, which was their home until they went back to Dorchester.

MEREWORTH, Kent. [1 Fd] Village on the A228, 6 m. SE. of Maidstone. *The Torrington Diaries* (1934, reprinted 1970), twenty-four volumes about the leisurely rural rides made (1781–94) by John Byng, 5th Viscount, were left at Yotes Court (E. of Seven Mile Lane), but an auction dispersed them. Byng, a nephew of the Admiral, stayed there in 1790 with cousins.

MERTON, Norf. [4 Fd] Village 10 m. N. of Thetford, off the B1110. The Old Rectory, now called Silverdell, was often visited by Edward FitzGerald while his friend George Crabbe, grandson of the poet, was incumbent. FitzGerald visited in 1883 but was taken ill almost immediately and died here soon afterwards.

MEYLLTEYRN SARN, Gwynedd. [3 Cc] Village on the B4413, 6 m. NE. of Aberdaron.

Roy Campbell and his wife Mary lived (1922–4) at Ty Corn, an old cottage they thought had been a stable, not far from the sea. While Campbell finished *The Flaming Terrapin* (1924) and their daughter Tess was born, they were supported by his father. In *Light on a Dark Horse* (1951) Campbell writes how well he got on with the locals, who admired his bravery in rowing the doctor to an urgent case on the near-by island during a heavy storm.

MICKLEHAM, Surrey. [1 Ed] Village off the A24, 2 m. N. of Dorking. Fanny Burney often visited Norbury Park, the home of her friend Mrs. William Lock. In 1793 she made the acquaintance of a group of French *émigrés* who had taken Juniper Hall[1] (N.T.; altered, now let to the Field Studies Council). These included Talleyrand, Mme de Staël, and General D'Arblay. Many visits took place between the two households; Fanny Burney improving D'Arblay's English and he, her French, and their marriage took place at Mickleham Church in 1794. The impecunious couple took rooms at Phenice Farm, Bagdon Hill (rebuilt), and, after living at Great Bookham, returned to build (1797) their own house (gone, site near the railway station). This, called Camilla Cottage by Dr. Burney after Fanny's novel, *Camilla* (1796, reprinted 1972), which provided the money, was their home until D'Arblay returned to France in 1802.

Marie Corelli lived (1865–83) at Fern Dell, on the old London–Dorking road now by-passed by the A24, but her success as a popular novelist came later. The house above, on the winding Box Hill road below Juniper Hall, is Flint Cottage, the home of George Meredith, and his second wife (d. 1885), from 1867. One of his most popular novels, *Diana of the Crossways* (1885), was written here. The little chalet high up in the steep garden was furnished as a study bed-room, where he could work undisturbed. There was also a shed for Picnic, the donkey. Meredith was visited by George Gissing, whose work he was one of the first to praise, Stevenson, who appeared as Woodseer in *The Amazing Marriage*, Barrie, and James Russell Lowell, the American poet. In 1895 Henry James accompanied Alphonse Daudet, who describes his host and himself, both then suffering from paralysis, as two wounded seagulls. Meredith died in 1907 and was buried with his second wife in Dorking cemetery.

[1] Visitors must make an appointment with the Warden.

MICKLETON MANOR. See DOVER'S HILL.

MIDDLETON-BY-WIRKSWORTH, Derbys. [4 Bb] Hillside village on the B5023, 3 m. SW. of Matlock. D. H. Lawrence lived from April 1918 to May 1919 at the bungalow, Mountain Cottage, built overlooking the gorge. He was writing his 'never-to-be-finished *Studies in Classic American Literature*' and reading Gibbon. He wrote of the country in a letter to Katherine Mansfield in February 1919 and described the different trails in the snow around the cottage,

beautiful ropes of rabbit prints, trailing away over the brows; heavy hare marks; a fox, so sharp and dainty, going over the wall; birds with two feet that hop; very splendid straight advance of a pheasant; . . . little leaping marks of weasels, coming along like a necklace chain of berries; odd little filigree of the field mice; the trail of a mole . . .

Lawrence failed to obtain a grant to help his finances and moved south again with the idea of going abroad.

MIDDLETON STONEY, Oxon. [1 Ca] Village on the A43, 3 m. NW. of Bicester. The mansion in the park is on the site of the house where John Gay stayed with his patrons, the Duke and Duchess of Queensberry, who financed the production of his play *The Beggar's Opera* (1728), which is said to have made Gay rich, and Rich (the producer) gay.

MIDDLETON TOWER, Norf. [4 Fd] A 15th-c. gatehouse of the moated manor (rebuilt 1860), off the A47, on a minor road near the railway station, *c.* 4 m. SE. of King's Lynn. The gatehouse tower was built by Lord Scales, some of whose letters from Middleton are included in the *Paston Letters*. He had fought with Henry V and when he was killed in London he was succeeded by his daughter, whose husband, Sir Anthony Woodville (or Wydvill), translated some French works, which were printed by Caxton.

MIDHURST, West Sussex. [1 De] Old market town on the Rother, 7 m. S. of Haslemere, on the A286. H. G. Wells was briefly at the Grammar School in 1881, where he learnt Latin from Horace Byatt, the headmaster, having previously been apprenticed to a chemist in the town. In 1883, after two unhappy years apprenticed to a drapery establishment in Portsmouth, he returned at Mr. Byatt's invitation as a student assistant teacher, and the following year won a scholarship to the Normal School of Science in London. Midhurst figures as 'Wimblehurst' in *Tono-Bungay* (1909).

MILBY. See NUNEATON.

MILLAND, West Sussex. [1 Dd] Village E. of the A3, 2 m. S. of Liphook. Thomas Otway was born (1682) at the rectory (rebuilt), near the church on the A3. His father was curate of Trotton (4 m. S.), where the church has a memorial to Thomas Otway, but they moved to Woolbeding (q.v.) while he was still a child.

MILSTON, Wilts. [1 Bd] Village off the A345, 3 m. N. of Amesbury. Joseph Addison was born (1652) at his father's vicarage (rebuilt, now Addison's House) and baptized in the old flint church.

MINSTEAD, Hants. [1 Be] Little village in the New Forest, 2½ m. NNW. of Lyndhurst, on a minor road between the A31 and the A337. Sir Arthur Conan Doyle is buried on the S. side of the churchyard, near open fields, in a simple grave inscribed 'Steel true, blade straight' and, under his name, 'Patriot, physician and man of letters'. Conan Doyle knew and loved the New Forest from early days. His novel, *The White Company* (1891), set in the 14th c., when Beaulieu Abbey dominated life in the area, was written while he was staying at a cottage on Emery Down, 2 m. S. A few years before his death he bought the half-timbered house of Bignell Wood in the parish of Minstead.

MINSTER-ON-SEA, Kent. [1 Gc] Village E. of Sheerness in the Isle of Sheppey. The partly Saxon church of St. Mary and St. Sexburga contains the late-13th-c. monument to Sir Robert Shurland, whose adventures were told in 'The Grey Dolphin' in Richard Barham's *Ingoldsby Legends* (1840).

MINTO, Roxburghs. (Borders). [6 Gd] Village off the A698, 6 m. NE. of Hawick.

Minto House, in an estate to the N., was the birthplace of Jane (sometimes Jean) Elliot (1727–1805), third daughter of Sir Gilbert Elliot, and author of the most popular version of the old lament for Flodden, 'The Flowers of the Forest', which begins 'I've heard them lilting at the ewe-milking'. Robert Burns thought 'the gentry were no longer capable of writing true ballads, but they could and did write true folk-songs, as witness Jean Elliot's "The Flowers of the Forest"'.

MIRFIELD, West Yorkshire. [5 Ee] Town on the A644, 2 m. SW. of Dewsbury. Anne Brontë became a governess to Mrs. Ingham for 9 months at Blake Hall (gone). Miss Wooler's School at Roehead to the N. was attended by Charlotte (1831–2), who returned as a teacher from 1835 to the end of 1837, while first Emily, who stayed 2 months only, and then Anne were pupils. Charlotte first met Ellen Nussey and Mary Taylor here who, with the exception of her sisters, became her closest friends.

MOCKLERSHILL. See MULLINAHONE.

MOLE. See AWBEG RIVER.

MONKSHAVEN. See WHITBY.

MONTGOMERY, Powys. [3 Fd] Village, formerly the county town of Montgomeryshire, on the B4385 and the B4386, 9¾ m. S. of Welshpool. George Herbert, the brother of Edward Herbert, first Baron Herbert of Cherbury (1583–1648), was born (1593) either in the now ruined castle or in the town. Donne, who was a lifelong friend of their mother, Lady Magdalen Herbert, stayed at the castle in 1613, but his poem, 'The Primrose, being at Montgomery Castle', is thought to have been written earlier. The poem, 'Good Friday 1613 Riding Westward', was written on his way here from Polesworth (q.v.).

MOORE HALL. See CARRA LOUGH.

MOOR PARK, Herts. [1 Db] A 17th-c. mansion (altered by Leoni 1720) off the A404, SE. of Rickmansworth, now a golf club. In 1620 the Earl and Countess of Bedford (née Lucy Harington, a patron of many poets) built a new house here and planned the famous gardens. Sir William Temple, the diplomat, occasionally managed to meet Dorothy Osborne here when she visited her cousins. In his essay *Of Gardens* he describes the walks, tree-hung cloisters and parterres: 'the perfectest figure of a garden I ever saw, either at home or abroad, was that of Moor Park.' When the differences between their families were finally resolved they spent their honeymoon (1654–5) here. In 1680 he renamed the house he bought near Farnham (q.v.), Moor Park.
Open on Mondays.

MOOR PARK, Surrey. See FARNHAM.

MORETON, Dorset. [2 Hd] Little village in the Frome valley, 1 m. E. of the B3390. T. E. Lawrence is buried in the new cemetery, on the opposite side of the road from the turning to the church. He had been living at Clouds Hill (q.v.) and died (May 1935) after a motor-cycle accident.

MORETON, Oxon. [1 Cb] Village 2 m. SSW. of Thame, off the B4013. William Basse (or Bas) (1583?–1653) lived in a cottage here at one time. He was retainer to his patron Sir Richard (later Lord) Wenman of Thame Park. His first published work was *Sword and Buckler, or Serving Man's Defence* (1602), followed in the same year by *Three Pastoral Elegies*. He also wrote 'Epitaph on Shakespeare' and 'Angler's Song', which was included in *The Compleat Angler*.

MORPETH, Northumb. [6 He] Small town on the Wansbeck (or Wensbeck) and the A1. Mark Akenside, who often stayed here as a youth, praised these lines from *The Pleasures of Imagination* (1744):

O ye Northumbrian shades! which overlook
The rocky pavement and the mossy falls
Of solitary WENSBECK's limpid stream,
How gladly I recall your well-known seats,
Beloved of old; and that delightful time,
When all alone, for many a summer's day,
I wander'd through your calm recesses, led
In silence, by some powerful hand unseen.

MORWENSTOW, Cornwall. [2 Cd] Large parish comprising the scattered hamlets of Woodford, Shop, Crosstown, and others, c. 6–7 m. N. of Bude, reached by minor roads from the A39. Robert Stephen Hawker, the eccentric parson-poet, was vicar here from 1835 to 1874. He restored the church, which had had no resident incumbent for over 100 years, and built the vicarage, with an inscription in Old English lettering over the door:

A House, a Glebe, a Pound a Day,
A Pleasant Place to Watch and Pray;
Be true to Church, Be kind to Poor,
O Minister, for evermore.

His great poetic achievement was *The Quest of the Sangraal* (1863), which he is thought to have written in the hut which he built of timber from wrecks, dragged up from the rocks below, on the edge of the 450-ft Vicarage Cliff (N.T.). But his best-known work is 'The Song of the Western Men', which he wrote as an undergraduate, staying on vacation (1825) at Coombe Cottage on the S. border of the parish. He said that he wrote it 'under a stag-horned oak in Sir Bevil's Walk in Stowe Wood'. It was printed anonymously in *The Royal Devonport Telegraph and Plymouth Chronicle*, where it was noticed by Davies Gilbert, President of the Royal Society, and sent to the *Gentleman's Magazine* as a supposedly ancient traditional ballad. Scott referred to it, Macaulay quoted it, and Dickens reprinted it in *Household Words*, but the author long remained 'unnoted and unknown'.

MOSSGIEL, Ayrs. (Strathclyde). [6 Dd] The farm (rebuilt) 1 m. N. of Mauchline on the Tarbolton road, rented by Robert Burns and his brother Gilbert from Gavin Hamilton, a fellow Freemason, after their father's death in 1784. Burns wrote much of his best work at a table under the skylight in the attic he shared with his brother. The mouse he disturbed with his plough, the daisy, and 'poor Maillie', the old sheep who had fallen on her back, all encountered during his work on the farm, were the subjects of the verses he wrote down at night. *Poems Chiefly in the Scottish Dialect* (1786) was published in Kilmarnock to provide the passage money for him and Mary Campbell, 'Highland Mary', to emigrate, but its success and her death kept him in Scotland. Jean Armour, whose name had so often been linked to his in searing reproofs from the pulpit at Mauchline, became his wife in 1788, and the whole family left the farm the next year.

MOSTRIM. See EDGEWORTHSTOWN.

MOUNT BENGER FARM. See ALTRIVE LAKE.

MOUNT OLIPHANT. See ALLOWAY.

MOUNT ST. MARY'S COLLEGE, Derbys. [5 Ef] Jesuit school at Spinkhill, off the A616, 8 m. SE. of Sheffield. While Gerard Manley Hopkins was bursar here from October 1877 to April 1878, he wrote 'The Loss of the Eurydice', a long poem on a small ship that foundered in a gale.

MUCKROSS, Kerry. [9 Cd] Small village on the T65, 2 m. S. of Killarney. Muckross Abbey (N.M.) was founded for Franciscan friars in 1440 by Donald MacCarthy on the site of an earlier religious settlement. The ruins of the buildings demolished by Cromwell's troops in 1652 are preserved in a beautiful park-like setting. Among the many tombs in the church is a memorial tablet to the Four Kerry Poets of the 17th and 18th centuries: Pierce Ferriter, Geoffrey O'Donoghue, Aodhgan O'Rahilly, and Eoghan Ruadh O'Sullivan (see Killarney). Sir Walter Scott visited the abbey during his tour of Ireland in 1825.

At the other side of the main road a lane runs up behind the post office to Killeaghy Hill, where a small, tree-ringed burial ground overlooks the Killarney lakes. Somewhere in the tangle of undergrowth is the grave of Rudolph Eric Raspe, German expatriate and mineralogist, who compiled *Baron Munchausen's Narrative of his Marvellous Travels and Campaigns in Russia* (1785) while working as a mining engineer in Cornwall. Raspe subsequently went to Scotland and became estate surveyor of land that he 'planted' with samples of rich ore. On revealing his 'finds' to the landowner he was handsomely rewarded, and left for Ireland before the trickery could be exposed. He became manager of copper mines in Killarney and may well have been hatching further nefarious plans when he contracted typhoid fever and died at Muckross in 1794.

MUDEFORD (pr. Muddiford), Dorset. [1 Be] Village on the coast 2 m. E. of Christchurch. The last house in the road to Avon Beach, no. 175, was built in the style of a Persian tent by William Stuart Rose (1775–1818), M.P. for Christchurch and a poet. It is part of a complex of houses called Gundimore, the others being numbered 169–73, and Rose lived there on and off for 18 years, during which time it was a focal point for poets, artists, and politicians. The round house was named after Sir Walter Scott, who stayed there briefly in 1807 while he was writing *Marmion*. Coleridge and Southey were also visitors.

MUDFOG. See ROCHESTER.

MULL, Argylls. (Strathclyde). [6 Bb] Island off the W. coast of Scotland, visited by Dr. Johnson and Boswell on their tour in 1773. They landed at Tobermory and rode, with some difficulty as bridles were scarce and streams were high, to visit Sir Allan Maclean on Inch Kenneth.

In the summer of 1795 Thomas Campbell became a tutor at Sunipol (*c.* 8 m. W. of Tobermory) where he wrote 'The Exile of Erin'. Ulva (island off mid-west Mull) was the destination hoped for in the escape of Lord Ullin's daughter in Campbell's ballad and Lochgyle his name for Loch-na-Keal which divides it from Mull, where to Lord Ullin's horror

> The waters wild went o'er his child,
> And he was left lamenting.

Keats walked across Mull in 1818 with his friend John Reynolds, whose spectacles caused much interest in such an isolated region. They found the 37-mile-long track hard walking as it was boggy.

MULLA. See AWBEG RIVER.

MULLAGH, Cavan. [8 Fe] Village on the L17, *c.* 5½ m. SW. of Virginia. Rantavan House, *c.* 1 m. SW., is the birthplace of Henry Brooke (1703–83). In 1774 he retired to a summer house (now a stable) he had erected at Corfad (or Longfield) in Mullagh parish. He died in Dublin and was buried beside the ruined church of Teampull Ceallaigh near Mullagh (his grave is unmarked).

MULLINAHONE, Tipperary. [9 Fc] Village on the L111 and the L153, 13 m. SW. of Kilkenny. Charles Kickham (1828–82), poet, novelist, and patriot, spent the greater part of his life here. The house where he lived, in Fethard St., is marked by a plaque, and a Celtic cross stands over his grave, which bears an epitaph by the celebrated Fenian and friend of Yeats, John O'Leary. Kickham's

best novel, *Knocknagow*, is based on rural life in this part of Tipperary. He is thought to have been born at Cnoicin a' Ghabba, 'The Smith's Hillock' (now called Mocklershill), 4 m. E. of Cashel.

MUNDESLEY (pr. Munzly), Norf. [4 Hc] Coastal resort on the B1145. Cowper spent his final years (1795–1800) alternately in his cousin's house in the High St. (now Cowper's House) and at East Dereham (q.v.), as change was thought to help his depression.

MURIEL TOWERS. See ALTON TOWERS.

MUSBURY, Devon. [2 Gd] Village on the A358, 4 m. NE. of Seaton Bay. Cecil Day-Lewis moved in 1938 from Cheltenham to Brimclose here. In *The Buried Day* (1960) he describes his pleasure in the countryside. He was on the edge of Hardy country here and his pastoral poems show an affinity with Hardy. As the Second World War progressed Day-Lewis resigned from the Communist Party and left the area to spend most of the war years in London, where he worked for the Ministry of Information.

MUSCOATES, North Yorkshire. [5 Fc] Hamlet S. of the A170, on the Slingsby road, 4¼ m. S. of Kirbymoorside. Muscoates Grange, a stone farmhouse with a tiled roof, was the birthplace of Herbert Read (1893–1968), who in the 1930s published many works of literary and art criticism, and in 1940 *Annals of Innocence and Experience*, his autobiography.

MUSTON, Leics. [4 Cc] Village off the A52, 6 m. W. of Grantham. Crabbe was rector here from 1789 to 1814, with a prolonged absence (1792–1805) in Suffolk. He often combined his new calling with his old profession of doctoring and was well liked in his early days here. He was also in touch with many botanists and made a garden to help his study of rare specimens. His wife had developed a depressive illness after the loss of her two sons and she died here in 1814 and is buried in the chancel (P). Crabbe exchanged the living for Trowbridge (q.v.) in the same year. His rectory has been rebuilt.

MYLOR, Cornwall. [2 Bf] Little village on Mylor Creek, off the Truro estuary, *c.* 2 m.

ENE. of Penryn. Katherine Mansfield and John Middleton Murry took a cottage here in 1916 after leaving D. H. Lawrence and Frieda at Zennor (q.v.). It was a pleasant and peaceful place, with a kitchen garden running down to the water's edge, but Katherine was restless and made frequent trips to London as well as visiting Lady Ottoline Morrell at Garsington. Murry spent much time on his own, reading and reviewing French books for *The Times Literary Supplement*. Later in the year he was taken on as a translator in a department of the War Office in London and Katherine went to live in Chelsea, not far from where he had rooms.

Howard Spring came to live at Mylor in 1939, in a bungalow on Hooper's Hill, looking down the creek. Here he finished *Fame is the Spur* (1940) and wrote the second part of his autobiography, *In the Meantime* (1942), and *Hard Facts* (1944), a novel set mainly in Manchester. His funeral service was held in the Church of St. Mylor (after his death in Falmouth, 1965) and his ashes were laid in the churchyard.

MYROSS. See UNIONHALL.

N

NAB FARM, Cumbria. [5 Bb] Farm, also referred to as The Nab or Nab Cottage, on the N. shore of Rydal Water, on the A591, *c.* ¼ m. W. of Rydal Mount. This was the home of Margaret Simpson, whom De Quincey used to visit when he was living at Dove Cottage and whom he married in Grasmere Church in February 1817 after she had borne him a child the previous November. Although it was an enduring love-match the union incurred the strong disapproval of the Wordsworths, especially Mary and Dorothy, who thought marriage between one of the gentry and a 'low-born woman' quite unsuitable. De Quincey resented their criticism, and his former happy relationship with them, already strained by his cutting down of hedges round Dove Cottage orchard and his increasing addiction to opium, came to an end. He maintained friendly relations with his father-in-law, however, and in 1829 became owner of Nab Farm, where his family were staying, in a complicated mortgage arrangement devised for their mutual benefit. But De Quincey was unable to keep up the payment of interest on the mortgage and in 1833 the farm had to be sold.

NAILSWORTH, Glos. [2 Ha] Market town on the A46, 3½ m. S. of Stroud, the final home of the 'super-tramp', W. H. Davies, where, in his own words, he could be 'near to Wales but . . . not haunted by any sort of trail from his past'. He came here in 1931 and, after one or two moves, settled for the rest of his days in Glendower (P), a low, two-storeyed cottage overlooking the valley on the narrow road to Watledge.

NAVESTOCK, Essex. [1 Fb] Straggling village 6 m. NW. of Brentwood off the A128. After leaving Oxford, Swinburne spent the summer of 1859 as the pupil of the Revd. William Stubbs, the historian, later Bishop of Oxford, whom he called 'a very passable parson'. Swinburne showed the first draft of his play *Rosamond* (1861) to Stubbs, who persuaded him to burn it as it was erotic. Stubbs's Victorian–Gothic vicarage, renamed Marleys, is on the green.

NEAR SAWREY, Cumbria. [5 Bc] Quiet village 2 m. SE. of Hawkshead on the B5285, between Esthwaite Water and Lake Windermere. Hill Top (N.T.),[1] behind the Tower Bank Arms (pictured in *The Tale of Jemima Puddle-Duck*, p. 62) and out of sight of the road, is the 17th-c. farmhouse bought by Beatrix Potter and bequeathed by her to the National Trust. In the summer of 1896 her parents, with whom she lived in London, had rented a furnished house called Lakeland (now Ees Wyke) in the village, and she explored the neighbourhood with delight. Of Sawrey itself she wrote in her secret journal: 'It is as nearly perfect a little place as I ever lived in' (*The Journal of Beatrix Potter, 1881–1897*, transcribed from her code writings by Leslie Linder, 1966).

When Hill Top Farm came on the market a few years later the royalties from *The Tale of Peter Rabbit* (1900), the first of her series of children's books, helped her to buy it, and by degrees her visits there became longer and more frequent until she broke right away from her family and made it her own home, where for the first time in her life she was really happy. Six of the now classic *Tales* are closely connected with Hill Top and Sawrey, especially *Tom Kitten* (1907), *Jemima Puddle-Duck* (1908), and *Samuel Whiskers, or the Roly-Poly Pudding* (1908), and it is a joy to recognize their familiar features in the much-loved old house and its surroundings. After her marriage in 1913 to William Heelis, her solicitor, Beatrix Potter moved to Castle Cottage, a long, low house across the meadow at the other side of the road. Here she gave up writing and spent the next 30 years of her life concerned with farming matters, breeding sheep, and buying farm property eventually to be made over to the National Trust. Through her generosity and farsightedness over 4,000 acres in some of the most beautiful parts of the Lake District have been preserved for the nation.

[1] Open Apr.–Oct.: weekdays 11 a.m.–5.30 p.m.; Sun. 2–5.30 p.m.

NEIDPATH CASTLE, Peebles. (Borders). [6 Fd] A 13th-c. castle on the A72, 1 m. W. of Peebles, on a steep hillside above the Tweed. Walter Scott, who often visited the castle, and Thomas Campbell both wrote ballads entitled 'The Maid of Neidpath' about the tragedy of the girl so altered by illness that her lover passed her by, and broke her heart.

Open Apr.–mid Oct.: Mon.–Sat. 10 a.m.–1 p.m. and 2–6 p.m.; Sun. 1–6 p.m.

NETHERAVON, Wilts. [1 Ad] Village off the A345, 4 m. N. of Amesbury. In 1794 Sydney Smith obtained the curacy of Netheravon, and became tutor to the son of the squire, Michael Hicks-Beach, whom he subsequently accompanied to Edinburgh. The house is now a barracks.

NETHER STOWEY, Som. [2 Fc] Village on the A39, 10 m. W. of Bridgwater. In the winter of 1796 Coleridge, his wife Sara, and their son, moved to a small thatched cottage in Lime St. (now tiled, enlarged, and called

Coleridge Cottage (N.T.))[1] found for him by his friend Thomas Poole, whose garden joined the cottage garden. Coleridge visited Wordsworth at Racedown and in deciding to rent the house at Alfoxden, Dorothy Wordsworth wrote in her *Journal* that their 'principal inducement was Coleridge's society'. Wordsworth and Coleridge agreed to combine to publish a collection of their verse, the former providing simple subjects such as 'Simon Lee the old Huntsman' and 'Lines composed above Tintern Abbey' and the latter providing the 'supernatural or at least romantic' characters with 'The Ancient Mariner' and 'The Foster Mother's Tale'. Joseph Cottle, who published the collection as *The Lyrical Ballads* (1798), mentions his visit in *Early Recollections of Southey and Coleridge* (1837). During Lamb's stay in 1797, Sara spilled boiling milk over Coleridge's foot, and 'This Lime Tree Bower my Prison Is' was written in the garden while Lamb and Wordsworth were walking together; the lime tree is no longer there. Hazlitt first met Wordsworth here. The Wordsworths and Coleridge were regarded with suspicion locally because of their nocturnal walks with camp stools and notebooks. Unusual northern accents and Dorothy's brown complexion led to the belief that they were French spies, and an investigator from the Home Office arrived at the Globe Inn (now Globe House) next to Poole's house. Servants gave evidence of talk about 'Spy Noza' when the friends gathered at table, but at length the investigator told his superiors he thought them harmless cranks. The poets left Stowey in 1798 to tour Germany. Thomas Poole is commemorated in the church where a tablet states he was a friend of Coleridge, Wordsworth, and Southey. Coleridge called Poole his 'anchor'.

[1] Open Mar.–Oct.: Sun.–Thurs. 11 a.m.–1 p.m., 2–5 p.m.

NETLEY ABBEY, Hants. [1 Be] Ruined Cistercian abbey, built *c.* 1239, 3 m. SE. of Southampton, on the A336 (toll at floating bridge). Pope and Lord Peterborough, his host at Bevis Mount, set out in August 1734 to sail round the Isle of Wight. They lunched in the woods at Netley and sketched the ruins. Pope writes of this visit to Martha Blount in his *Letters*. Gray, who went by ferry, describes his two visits in 1755 and

1764 to his friends James Brown and Norton Nicholls. The ferryman told him he would never venture there at night. William Lisle Bowles wrote 'Sonnet to Netley Abbey' after his visit and N. P. Willis crossed from Ryde to picnic among the ruins with a party of friends in the 1830s. He describes, in *Loiterings of Travel* (1840), how a young man sketched the scene of 'gaily dressed ladies' and 'bright wines on the mossy grass'. He thought that the ivy enhanced the beauty of the ruins.

Open daily, Sun. from 2 p.m.

NETTLEBED, Oxon. [1 Cb] Village, 5 m. W. of Henley, on the A423. Karl Moritz, a German schoolmaster, stayed here while walking from London to Dovedale, with a change of linen and the works of Milton in his pocket. He found travellers on foot were received with suspicion but he was given a carpeted bedroom, a very good bed, and supper in the kitchen. It reminded him of Fielding's novels, which he found had given him an accurate idea of English manners. There were pewter dishes round the walls and hams, black puddings, sugar loaves, and sausages hung from the ceiling. Next morning he wore clean linen and at once was shown into the parlour. At church he noticed the ten commandments (which are still there), written above the altar, and was pleased at the instrumental accompaniment given by the villagers, who still have a good choir. Writing home he mentioned the blacksmith's tombstone in the churchyard, because of the verse:

My sledge and anvil be declined,
My bellows too have lost their wind;
My fire's extinct, my forge decayed,
My coals are spent, my iron's gone,
My nails are drove: my work is done.

NEW ALRESFORD (pr. Allsford), Hants. [1 Cd] Small market town on the A31, 8 m. E. of Winchester. The parish church has specimens of cuneiform inscriptions on two ancient bricks from Ur of the Chaldees (birthplace of Abraham) and Babylon: (1) from the Ziggurat at Ur dedicated to the Moon God Nannar, *c.* 2150 B.C.; (2) from Nebuchadnezzar's Palace at Babylon, *c.* 604–562 B.C. At 27 Broad St. a plaque marks the house where Mary Russell Mitford was born on 16 December 1787 and where she lived until she was 10, when her winning of a

£20,000 lottery prize enabled her father to move the family to a new house at Reading.

Alresford Pond, to the N. of the town, was created by Bishop Lucy in the early 13th c. in order to make the Itchen navigable from Alresford to Southampton and is celebrated by George Wither in his pastoral poem, *Fair Virtue* (1622): 'For pleasant was that pool . . .'. There is a handsome memorial window to Wither in the church of Old Alresford, 1 m. N.

Many literary men of the mid 19th c. were guests of Lady Ashburton at The Grange, an imposing mansion in a park (*c.* 3 m. NW.). On one occasion she was mockingly taken to task by Henry Taylor, author of *Philip van Artevelde*, for the heartless way previously honoured guests were displaced in favour of new writers. Lady Ashburton's hurried excuses caused wry smiles by others in the house party, which at various times included Tennyson, and Carlyle, with whom she conducted 'an affair of the heart and head' for 14 years, until her death (1857).

NEWARK CASTLE, Selkirks. (Borders). [6 Fd] The remains of this 15th-c. royal hunting seat stand in a dominating position above the Yarrow, *c.* 3 m. W. of Selkirk. The castle is in the Bowhill Estate of the Buccleuch family and is reached by a narrow road off the B7039 immediately after crossing the bridge from the A708. Here, in 'Newark's stately tower' Scott laid the scene of *The Lay of the Last Minstrel* (1805), where the minstrel recited the lay to the Duchess of Buccleuch after the execution of her husband in 1685.

NEWARK ON TRENT, Notts. [4 Cb] Ancient town on the Great North Road, now bypassed by the A1. In 1619 Richard Corbett with some Oxford friends stayed at the 14th-c. White Hart Inn on the journey he describes in 'Iter Boreale'. John Cleveland was Judge-Advocate at the Royalist garrison in Newark in 1645–6. While here he wrote *The Character of a London Diurnal* (1647). In Scott's *Heart of Midlothian* Jeanie Deans stayed a night at the Saracen's Head Inn (now a bank) on her way to London.

NEWARK PRIORY, Surrey. [1 Dc] Ruins of an Augustinian priory (*c.* 1190) visible from the B367 S. of Pyrford. Thomas Love Peacock fell in love with Fanny Faulkner and used to meet her here in 1807, when he was living at Chertsey, but through a misunderstanding the engagement was broken off, and she, thinking herself deserted, married another. She died in the following year. 'Revisiting Newark Abbey' (1842), 'Remember Me' (1809), and 'Al mio primiero amore' (1813) all relate to her and she was partly the model for Miss Touchandgo of *Crotchet Castle* (1831).

NEWBY BRIDGE, Cumbria. [5 Bc] Village on the A590 and the A592, just W. of the S. end of Lake Windermere. Arthur Ransome (1884–1967), author of a series of children's books, wrote *Swallows and Amazons* (1931) when he was staying at the Newby Bridge Hotel. He used Windermere and its neighbourhood for the setting of many of his stories.

NEWCASTLE UNDER LYME, Staffs. [3 Hb] Old industrial town on the A34, 2 m. W. of Stoke-on-Trent. Sir John Davies (1569–1626), barrister and poet, was M.P. here in 1614. Mrs. Craik (Dinah Maria Mulock, 1826–87), author of *John Halifax, Gentleman* (1857), came here with her parents in 1831 and lived first in Lower St. and later at 2 (now 7) Mount Pleasant. Arnold Bennett (1867–1931) came to the Middle School, where he became head boy, for the last stage of his education before entering his father's legal practice at 18. The town appears as 'Oldcastle' in his 'Five Towns' novels.

NEWCASTLE UPON TYNE, Tyne and Wear. [6 Hf] Port on the A1, and former county town of Northumberland, which grew up round the strategic site chosen by the Romans for a station on Hadrian's Wall and by the Normans for a castle. Local coal has been exported from here since Tudor times, hence the proverbial saying for a useless activity, 'carrying coals to Newcastle'. Mark Akenside was born (1721) in Butcher Bank (now Akenside Hill). After a short time at the free school, he was sent to a private academy kept by a dissenting minister, a calling he intended to follow, when he set out for Edinburgh at 18.

John Forster, biographer of his friend Charles Dickens, was born (1812) in Gallowgate, where his father was a dairy farmer. He began writing at an early age and while still at the Royal Grammar School had his

play *Charles at Tunbridge* performed at Newcastle Theatre in 1828. In the same year his grandfather sent him to Cambridge, where he stayed a month before leaving for London. Another native was Hugh Stowell Scott, son of a shipowner. He went away to school and spent much of his life abroad. His travels gave his historical novels, many of which have a European background, an authentic setting. He wrote as 'Henry Seton Merriman'.

NEWCHURCH-IN-PENDLE. See WHALLEY.

NEW CUMNOCK, Ayrs. (Strathclyde). [6 De] Village on the A76 where Afton Water joins the Nith. A cairn in a picnic area beside the road above the Afton, on a turn off the B741, was erected by the New Cumnock Burns Club for their Golden Jubilee 1973, to commemorate Burns's song 'Flow gently, sweet Afton'.

NEWPORT, Gwent. [2 Ga] Industrial town and seaport on the estuary of the Usk. W. H. Davies records in *The Autobiography of a Super-tramp* (1908) that he was born on 20 April 1871 at the Church House Inn, 14 Portland St. (off Commercial Rd., near the docks), and in 1938 attended the unveiling of a plaque on the house to this effect. In 1941 (soon after his death) the discovery of his birth certificate showed that his memory had been unreliable and that he had in fact been born on 3 July 1871 at 6 Portland St. (demolished). When he was 3 his father died and he went to live with his grandparents at the Church House, moving with them on their retirement first to 38 Raglan St. and later to Upper Lewis St. He disliked school and benefited more from his own wide reading than from lessons. After his grandfather's death his grandmother apprenticed him to a picture-framer, but he became restless and left for work in Bristol. He set sail for America in June 1893.

St. Julian's Parish Church, on the Caerleon side of the town, was built on a site given by Ronald Firbank. On the E. wall is a large crucifix which he presented in memory of his parents, Sir Thomas and Lady Firbank, and beneath it is a memorial stone inscribed with a request for prayers for the donor, who died (1926) 6 months before the church was finished. Firbank had visited Newport *c.* 1904 to look for the former home of his paternal grandparents, a Tudor mansion called St. Julian's, but found that it had fallen into disrepair. The grounds of the ruined house have been developed as St. Julian's Estate.

NEWPORT, I.O.W. [1 Cf] Administrative capital on the Medina, 5 m. S. of Cowes. In 1846 John Hamilton Reynolds was appointed clerk to the newly formed County Court, but his health was undermined and he died in 1852. He was buried in the old churchyard, now a rose-garden adjoining the public park on Church Litten, where his tombstone has been preserved. The inscription 'Friend of Keats' was added during renovations in 1917. Reynolds was the recipient of many of Keats's letters.

NEWPORT, Salop. [3 Gc] Small country town on the A41 and the A518, 8 m. NE. of Wellington. The Grammar School (founded 1656) numbers among its famous pupils Thomas Brown (1663–1704), the satirist remembered chiefly for his lines beginning 'I do not love you, Dr. Fell,' and Thomas Percy (1729–1811), who collected the ballads, historical songs, and metrical romances, published as *Reliques of Ancient English Poetry* (1765). They both proceeded to Christ Church, Oxford.

NEWRY, Down. [8 Gd] Seaport and manufacturing town at the head of Carlingford Lough on the A1. John Mitchel, leader of the Young Ireland movement and editor of the *Nation*, whose *Jail Journal, or Five Years in British Prisons* (1856) gives an account of his transportation for sedition, is buried in the Unitarian (First Presbyterian) churchyard, Old Meetinghouse Green, High St.

NEWSTEAD ABBEY, Notts. [4 Bb] Former Augustinian priory, on the A60, 9 m. N. of Nottingham, which became the Byron family home and was inherited by the poet in 1798. He lived here intermittently until forced by debts to sell in 1816.

> Shades of heroes, farewell! your descendant departing
> From the seat of his ancestors, bids you adieu!
> Abroad or at home, your remembrance imparting
> New courage, he'll think upon glory and you.

Thomas Moore, writing his life of Byron (1830), mentions in his *Memoirs* seeing the oak Byron planted and the grave of Boat-

swain, the favourite dog who died of rabies, subjects of two poems by Byron. Moore's host on this visit in 1827 was Colonel Wildman, Byron's successor, who also entertained Washington Irving in 1835 when he wrote his impressions in *Abbotsford and Newstead Abbey* (1835). Though the old priory church is a ruin, the visitor will no longer find that as in 'On Leaving Newstead Abbey'

> Through thy battlements Newstead, the hollow winds whistle;
> Thou, the hall of my Fathers art gone to decay;
> In thy once smiling garden, the hemlock and thistle
> Have choak'd up the rose which late bloom'd in the way.

as the abbey and grounds are well cared for by the Corporation of Nottingham.

Abbey open Good Fri.–Sept.: daily, tours conducted at 2, 3, 4, and 5 p.m. Oct.–Easter: by arrangement. Gardens open all the year: daily, 10 a.m. to dusk.

NEWTON ABBOT, Devon. [2 Ee] Market town and tourist centre at the junction of the A380 and several other main roads, c. 5 m. from the coast. Sir Arthur Quiller Couch was educated at Newton Abbot College before going to Clifton College, Bristol (q.v.).

NEWTON-BY-USK. See LLANSANTFFRAED.

NEWTON NOTTAGE, Mid Glamorgan. [2 Eb] Little village on the A4106, 1¼ m. E. of Porthcawl. R. D. Blackmore, whose mother died when he was a baby, was cared for by his aunt, Mary Frances Knight, probably at her home here before her marriage to the Revd. Richard Gordon, and later at Elsfield (q.v.).

NEWTON TONEY, Wilts. [1 Bd] Village off the A338, 9 m. NE. of Salisbury. Celia Fiennes was born at the Manor House (gone), from where she set off on many of the rides recounted in her Journal, of which an incomplete version was published in 1888 under the title *Through England on a Side Saddle in the Time of William and Mary*. A definitive edition, *The Journeys of Celia Fiennes*, edited by Christopher Morris, was published in 1947.

NEWTOWN, Waterford. [9 Fd] Little village 2 m. NE. of Kilmacthomas, just N. of the

T12. The Gaelic poet Donnchadh Rúa Mac Conmara (d. 1814) is buried in the graveyard.

NORHAM CASTLE, Northumb. [6 Gd] Ruined 12th-c. castle on the Tweed, 6 m. SW. of Berwick-upon-Tweed. This border stronghold of Durham's Princes Palatine was the setting for the opening scenes of *Marmion* (1808), Scott's long poem about the battle of Flodden in 1513.

NORMANDY, Surrey. [1 Dd] Village 7 m. NE. of Farnham, on the A323. William Cobbett farmed at Normandy Farm near the manor from 1831 to his death in 1835, when the hamlet was part of the parish of Ash. He published *Rural Rides* in 1830, an account of journeys taken from 1821 to refute the landlords' policy towards agricultural labourers with a firsthand account of the distress and mismanagement. There is a tradition, recounted in Ralph Wightman's *Rural Rides* (1957), that Cobbett brought Tom Paine's bones here instead of leaving them in Liverpool (q.v.) and that the young daughter of Cobbett's friend at the manor was frightened to pass the room where they lay. Cobbett died here and was buried at Farnham (q.v.).

NORMANSTON. See LOWESTOFT.

NORTHAMPTON, Northants. [4 Ce] Manufacturing town on the A43 and the A45. Anne Bradstreet, who became the first poet in English in N. America, is thought to have been born (c. 1613) here. George Dyer, the kindly but absent-minded friend of Charles Lamb, taught at a school here in the 1780s.

In 1841 John Clare, who had previously been cared for in a private institution, was brought to the county asylum here. At first he was able to walk the mile to the town centre where his favourite resting place was under the portico of All Saints' Church. He was well looked after by the staff and his fellow inmates, enjoyed the gardens in summer, and sat in the large window in the winter. His poems reveal the sadness he felt on being abandoned by his family, and on being far from the familiar sights and sounds of home. Some of the many poems written here were published in *Poems of John Clare's Madness*, edited by Geoffrey Grigson in 1949. Mary Mitford gives an account of her visit

to him in her *Recollections* (1852). Clare died in 1864 and was buried by his wish in his native Helpston (q.v.).

Jerome K. Jerome died (1927) here suddenly while on a motoring holiday. His ashes were buried in the churchyard at Ewelme (q.v.).

NORTHBOROUGH, Cambs. [4 Dd] Village on the A15, 6 m. NW. of Peterborough. John Clare's poor health caused his patrons to build a six-roomed stone cottage (opposite Pingle Lane beyond the church). His income was too small to stock the smallholding but friends gave him a cow and some pigs and he moved in with Patty and the children in 1832. He was irritated by sightseers and had the door put at the back from where he could escape when he saw their approach from his study window. *The Rural Muse* was published in 1835 and 2 years after Clare's mental condition caused his friends to send him to a private asylum. Clare later described his escape and the long walk back to his family. His freedom was short-lived as his mental distress again caused his removal, this time permanently.

NORTHCHURCH, Herts. [1 Db] Village 1 m. W. of Berkhamsted, on the A41. Maria Edgeworth spent her school holidays (1776–80) here with her father Richard Edgeworth and step-mother Honora. After Honora died of consumption in 1780, her father married Honora's sister Elizabeth, and brought her back to the house with the shutters, on the main road, now called Edgeworth House. Richard Edgeworth's friend Thomas Day visited here, after the awkwardness of his having been a suitor of Honora had lessened by her death and his own marriage.

NORTH HINKSEY. See OXFORD (Christ Church and Oriel College).

NORTH KESSOCK, Ross and Cromarty (Highland). [7 Ee] Village on the N. of the Firth of Beauly, with a ferry link to Inverness. Dalcraig, 2 m. W. of the B9161 on the way to Redcastle, was the last home of Neil Gunn (d. 1973), whose novels, including *The Silver Darlings* (1941) and *The Green Isle of the Great Deep* (1944), describe the harshness of the life of the coast and of the Highlands.

NORTH NIBLEY, Glos. [2 Ha] Village 10 m. SW. of Nailsworth, on the A4060, which honours William Tyndale. A tower, from which a good view can be had of the Severn estuary, was erected on the hill overlooking the village in 1866, commemorating his first translation of the Bible into English and his death at the stake in Vilvorde in 1536. The path to the tower is sign-posted and climbs through beech woods to the level turf above. It can be very muddy in wet weather.

NORTON, Cleveland. [5 Eb] Former village now joined to Stockton-on-Tees. Thomas Jefferson Hogg, friend and first biographer of Shelley, was born (1792) at Norton House.

NORWICH, Norf. [4 Gd] Cathedral, market, and manufacturing city on the Wensum. An alley off King St. leads to the church (rebuilt after war damage) of Julian or Juliana (1343–1413), the mystic recluse, whose cell is now a chapel incorporating the original roughcast stones. She wrote *XVI Revelations of Divine Love* here, and at Carrow Abbey (ruins and the rebuilt Prioress's house in Reckitt and Colman Co.'s grounds in Bracondale Rd.) was visited by Margery Kempe (b. 1373?), whose search for true belief also took her to Jerusalem. Extracts from the *Book of Margery Kempe* were printed (1501) by Wynken de Worde. John Skelton, made rector of Diss in 1498, met the young Jane Scrope at Carrow seeking refuge with her sister and mother, whose husband had been executed. Jane's pet sparrow, killed by a cat, inspired Skelton's *Phylyp Sparowe*.

The Pastons, a merchant family with many castles and manors, also had houses in the town. The Music House (so called because the waits met there) in King St., the 12th-c. home of Jewish merchants, belonged to them in the 15th c. (now called Wensum Lodge (P), where the International Club meets on Saturdays). The Pastons also lived in Crown Court, off the cobbled Elm Hill (pedestrians only). John and Margaret Paston gave money for the rebuilding of St. Peter Hungate Church, now a museum[1] of church art and craftsmanship, at the top of the hill, completing the hammerbeam roof with the carved angels in 1460. The

Maid's Head, dating from Norman times, is also mentioned in the *Paston Letters*, though the façade is 18th-c. John Bale (1495–1563) was educated by the Carmelites (site of the Friary now a printing works near Whitefriars Bridge) but later became a Protestant.

Robert Greene, dramatist, poet, and pamphleteer, was born in the city (*c.* 1560) and went to the Grammar School (founded 1250; refounded by Edward VI; enlarged and modernized by Dr. Augustus Jessopp, headmaster 1859–79).

Henry Peacham, tutor to the sons of William Howard in 1613–14, spent some time between his travels on the Continent in Howard House (P) in King St., where many of the old houses had riverside gardens. His best-known work *The Compleat Gentleman*, written for the youngest Howard son, was published in 1622. Richard Corbett, bishop in 1632, quarrelled with the Strangers, the immigrant weavers, and banned them from his chapel in 1634. His collected poems (1647) were published after his death.

Thomas Browne lived (1637–82) near the Lamb Inn (Littlewoods on site). *Religio Medici* (1643) was written before he settled here. He was knighted in St. Andrew's Hall, once the Blackfriars' church, when Charles II visited the city in 1671. John Evelyn, who stayed with him that year, described Browne's house in his *Diary* as 'A paradise and a cabinet of rarities' and wrote about the city 'The suburbs are large, the prospects sweet with other amenities, not omitting the flower gardens, in which all the inhabitants excel'. Browne was buried in St. Peter Mancroft Church (tablet); his statue stands in the little paved garden below.

George Crabbe was ordained in the cathedral in 1782. Southey in 1798 visited a group of intellectuals who attended the Octagon Chapel (built 1756) in Colegate. One of them, John Opie, who painted his portrait, was newly married, and the couple lived where Opie St. joins Castle Meadow. Amelia Opie wrote *Father and Daughter* (1801), *Poems* (1802), *Adeline Mowbray* (1804), suggested by a story of Mary Wollstonecraft, and a memoir of her husband (d. 1807). In 1825 she became a Quaker through the influence of the Gurneys, who lived at Gurney Court (P) until *c.* 1786. The Martineau family (descended from the Strangers) then lived at the Court where Harriet was born in

1802. She started writing moral tales for children, progressing to *Illustrations of Political Economy* (1832-4), after which she moved to London. William Taylor (1765-1836), an enthusiast for German literature, which he publicized by his translations, lived in Upper King St. (rebuilt) and later Surrey St. He taught George Borrow German and wrote *Historic Survey of German Poetry* (1828-30). He and Amelia Opie contributed to Southey's *Annual Anthology* (1799-1800).

George Borrow, whose parents' house in Willow Lane is now called Borrow House, attended the Grammar School, and was then articled to a solicitor for a short time before setting out on his travels. Mousehold Heath, the open space on the NE. outskirts, and the gipsies he met there, feature in *Lavengro* (1851) and *Romany Rye* (1857), both partly autobiographical. Some Borrow manuscripts are in the Central Library, which has a fine local collection.

Mary Sewell, author of popular poems for children, lived (1867-84) at 125 Spixworth Rd., Old Catton. Her daughter Anna kept bees in the garden of the L-shaped house and there wrote *Black Beauty* (1877). A horse-trough was erected in Anna's memory by her niece, at the junction of Constitution Hill and St. Clement's Hill.

Daisy Ashford, author at 9 of *The Young Visiters* (1919), lived here after her marriage. Another early work, *Love and Marriage*, short stories written with her sister, was published when she was living in Woodland Rd., Hellesdon in 1965.

¹ Open weekdays 10 a.m.–5 p.m.

NOTTINGHAM, Notts. [4 Bc] Manufacturing town on the A52 and the A60, well known to Celia Fiennes, who stayed on her rides through England at the Crown and the Blackamoor's Head (both gone). She approved of the beer and compared other towns unfavourably with Nottingham. In 1656 Charles Cotton married his cousin, Isabella Hutchinson, at St. Mary's Church and Lovelace wrote the poem 'Triumph of Philamore and Amoret' in celebration.

Henry Kirke White was born (1785) in Exchange Alley at his father's butcher's shop (P now on new Cheapside). After working at a stocking loom he was employed by lawyers, who encouraged his studies. His determination to be ordained led him to publish *Clifton Grove and other Poems* (1803) in the hope that the proceeds would pay for his education at Cambridge. The money was insufficient, but his piety and scholarship so impressed the Fellows that he was able to enter St. John's. Southey, who believed him a genius, edited his literary remains, of which many editions were published. Philip Bailey was born (1812) here (P on site of Weekday Cross) and lived at Old Basford. The founder of the 'Spasmodic School', he returned there and wrote *Festus* (1839) after practising at the Bar. Byron, who could not afford to live at Newstead Abbey, lived with his mother in Pelham St. (house gone) in 1798 and later in St. James St. (P). They worshipped in the Unitarian Chapel in High Pavement where Coleridge had preached.

Soon after collaborating on *The Forest Minstrel* (1823) William and Mary Howitt settled in the town, living first above their chemist's shop in a small house in Parliament St., then in 1822 in 'part of a fine old mansion house built by a French architect' in the market place 'opposite to the Long Row'. William Howitt wrote a poem on the occasion of Byron's lying-in-state. He and his wife had both joined the large throng but disapproved of the disorderly scenes which continued *en route* for the interment at Hucknall. In 1831, Wordsworth visited Howitt's chemist's shop when his wife was taken ill on their journey back to the Lakes. Mrs. Wordsworth was put to bed in their house and the poet also stayed the night with them. Later in the year the 6 acres of the market place were filled with rioters and 'the heaving, raging ocean of agitated life became . . . a headlong torrent leading directly to the Castle' which the Howitts then saw burning. In 1835 Howitt was elected Alderman. The next year they sold the shop and left on a tour of Scotland and the Lakes. They were friends of Joseph Gilbert and his wife Ann, author of rhymes for the young, who lived in College St. (now offices) and are buried in the cemetery.

John Drinkwater was on the staff (1898-1901) of the Northern Assurance Co. in Victoria St. (P). D. H. Lawrence was at the High School and University College (now Nottingham University) (1903-6). The riots in the town form the background of his story 'Goose Fair'.

NUNAPPLETON HOUSE. See APPLETON ROEBUCK.

NUNEATON, Warwicks. [4 Bd] Manufacturing town on the A444. Robert Burton, who was born (1577) at Lindley (q.v.) near by, went to his first school here. The novelist George Eliot (Mary Ann or Marian Evans), born (1819) at Arbury Farm 2 m. SW. (now South Farm), lived (1820–41) at Griff House (now a hotel) on the A444. She was baptized at Chilvers Coton (church rebuilt) in Avenue Rd., the 'Shepperton' of *Scenes of Clerical Life*, and attended a dame school in the double-fronted house opposite her home before going to Coventry. Many of her characters and situations were modelled on her experiences here. Her father, agent to the Newdigate family of Arbury Hall,[1] the Cheverel Manor of *Scenes of Clerical Life*, was partly the model for Adam Bede and Caleb Garth; and her mother (d. 1835) partly for Mrs. Poyser and Mrs. Hackit. Arbury Mill inspired *The Mill on the Floss* (1860), although the scene was changed to the Trent. The town, the 'Milby' in *Janet's Repentance*, has George Eliot Memorial Gardens near the library and a hospital with wards named after her characters.

[1] Open Easter Sun. to October: Sun., Bank Holidays and Tues. following 2.30–6 p.m.

NUNEHAM COURTENAY, Oxon. [1 Cb] Village on the A423, 5 m. S. of Oxford. The regularity of the matching pairs of cottages facing each other across the main road was the result of a planned removal of the entire village in 1760–1, when the 1st Earl of Harcourt required the site for his landscape-garden. The mid-18th-c. vogue for creating magnificent gardens at the cost of destroying villages which spoilt the view roused Goldsmith to take a lone stand against the practice. In *The Deserted Village* (1770) he expressed his fears that it would lead to the ruin of the peasantry, and it has been thought that he had Nuneham Courtenay in mind when he wrote the poem. The Revd. T. Mozley, referring to the time when J. H. Newman, his brother-in-law, was staying at the schoolhouse (1828, then the officiating clergyman's residence), speaks of the tradition that the village was 'the true Auburn of Goldsmith's "Deserted Village"' (*Reminiscences chiefly of Oriel College and the Oxford Movement*, 1882). In an essay 'The Revolu-

tion in Low Life' (*New Essays*, 1927) Goldsmith says that he had actually witnessed in the summer of 1761 the removal of a village and the destruction of its farms to make a new 'seat of pleasure' for a wealthy landowner, 50 m. from London, and it seems almost certain that Nuneham Courtenay was this village, and that the subject of the essay corresponds with the theme of the poem:

> The man of wealth and pride
> Takes up a space that many poor supplied;
>
> His seat, where solitary sports are seen,
> Indignant spurns the cottage from the green.

The solitary widow of 'sweet Auburn' left after the houses of the other villagers had been destroyed:

> She only left of all the harmless train,
> The sad historian of the pensive plain.

is paralleled by a real old woman at Nuneham called Barbara Wyatt, the 'Mopsa' of a poem ('The Removal of the Village at Nuneham Courtenay') by the Poet Laureate, William Whitehead, who extolled the kindness shown to her by the 'indulgent' Earl in leaving her to end her days in her 'clay-built cot'. A memorial to her can be seen on a seat on the terrace near the site of her cottage in Nuneham Park. The site of the old village is beside the present estate road. In spite of the poignancy of 'The Deserted Village' there is no evidence that (at Nuneham at any rate) any real hardship was suffered, and many villagers may have been better off after their removal, as Whitehead suggests:

> The careful matrons of the plain
> Had left their cots without a sigh,
> Well pleased to house their little train
> In happier mansions warm and dry.

Goldsmith may have woven several strands into his poem: his general concern over the practice of destroying villages to make private parks, his experience of witnessing such an occurrence at Nuneham in 1761, and his idealized childhood memories of Lissoy (q.v.).

The 2nd Earl of Harcourt was an admirer of Rousseau, who is said to have stayed in the village in 1767 and to have planted seeds of many foreign wild flowers in Nuneham Park—his favourite, the periwinkle, grows up the banks and, as in *La Nouvelle Héloïse*, trailing garlands of clematis, bryony, and creepers twine among the trees 'negligently, as they do in the forest'. A garden seat bears a quotation from Rousseau's concept of nature. Lord Harcourt entertained artists and writers, including Mason, Whitehead, Walpole, Gilpin, and Fanny Burney, who, on her visit in 1786 with George III and Queen Charlotte, recorded in her diary that she was lost for a quarter of an hour in the 'straggling, half-new, half-old, half-comfortable, half-forlorn' house which the Earl was remodelling. He encouraged Mason to lay out the flower-garden, with carefully irregular beds and inscriptions and memorial urns placed in flowery glades, embodying the theories expressed in his poem 'The English Garden'. Much is now altered and overgrown, but a fine view of the mansion and the park[1] can be had from the river.

[1] Grounds occasionally open to the public, or by application to the University of Oxford.

O

OAKINGTON, Cambs. [4 Ee] Village off the A604, 5 m. NW. of Cambridge. H. E. Bates was posted to the R.A.F. station here in the winter of 1941. In *The World in Ripeness* (1972) he describes the pilots' asides which inspired his short stories 'It's Just the Way It Is' and 'The Sun Rises Twice', published under the pseudonym 'Flying Officer X'.

OARE, Som. [2 Ec] Village off the A39, midway between Lynton and Porlock. The small church has a tablet with a relief portrait commemorating the centenary of the birth (1825) of R. D. Blackmore, author of the novel *Lorna Doone* (1869). Blackmore, whose grandfather was the rector (1809–42), set scenes in the novel in the neighbourhood. Plovers Barrows Farm, home of the hero John Ridd, is said to be Oareford. Farmer Snow is based on the 17th-c. Nicholas Snow of Oare Farm (now Manor) who is buried in Oare Church (P), where Lorna Doone was shot at her wedding. Blackmore is said to have written part of the novel at Parsonage Farm where, as well as at Yenworthy Farm, he set one of the Doone raids. A path from Malmsmead along Badgworthy (pr. Badgery) Water, passes a plaque erected in 1969 to commemorate the centenary of the publication of *Lorna Doone*, and leads to the combe now known as Doone Valley. Near-by Hoccombe Combe has ruins of houses said to have been occupied in the 17th c. by Doones.

OBAN, Argylls. (Strathclyde). [6 Cb] Resort on the A85 and W. coast port for Mull and the Islands. Dr. Johnson and Boswell landed here in 1773 after a fine crossing from Mull and next day over a leisurely breakfast they talked of Goldsmith's poem *The Traveller*.

Robert Buchanan lived (1866–74) at The White House on the Hill (now Soraba Lodge, 1 m. S.). He attacked the Pre-Raphaelite poets in 'The Fleshly School of Poetry', an article published in *The Contemporary Review* (1871) and wrote *The North Coast and Other Poems* (1868), novels, and plays.

OCHILTREE, Ayrs. (Strathclyde). [6 Dd] Hillside village on the A70, W. of Auchinleck, birthplace of George Douglas Brown. It is the 'Barbie' of his sombre novel *The House with the Green Shutters* (1901), written under the pseudonym 'George Douglas', whose realism was in sharp contrast to popular sentimental accounts of the simple life of the poor in Scotland. His house (P) in the main street at the top of the village is now the British Legion Club.

ODCOMBE, Som. [2 Gd] Village off the A3088, 3 m. W. of Yeovil. The church has a vivid modern E. window and a facsimile of the title-page of Thomas Coryate's *Crudities* (1611), the story of his travels, mainly on foot, through Europe. An account of his life hangs under the tower where the shoes he wore hung until their decay in 1702. Coryate (1577?–1617) was born in the Elizabethan rectory which stood near the church. His last journey in 1612 took him through Mesopotamia to India where he died.

OLDCASTLE. See NEWCASTLE UNDER LYME.

OLD DAILLY, Ayrs. (Strathclyde). [6 De] Hamlet on the B734, $2\frac{1}{2}$ m. E. of Girvan. The Pre-Raphaelite poet and painter William Bell Scott (1811–90) was an annual summer guest of Miss Alice Boyd at Penkill Castle, where his illustrations of James I's *Kingis Quair* decorate the stairs. The Penwhapple which runs through the grounds was the subject of his sonnets 'The Old Scottish Home', 'Outside the Temple', and 'Lost Love'. Alice Boyd, a painter herself, invited D. G. Rossetti and his sister Christina here. Rossetti, prevented by eye trouble from painting, returned to writing while staying here (1868–9) with Scott, and began 'The Stream's Secret' in a cave in the gardens. Scott designed a new hall for Penkill (*c.* 1883), where he died. He is buried in the church (P; ruins) and Swinburne contributed memorial verses to the *Athenaeum*.

OLD PARK, Durham. [5 Ea] Farm on the Wilmington road off the A6074, $3\frac{1}{2}$ m. NE. of Bishop Auckland. Thomas Gray was a visitor in the 1760s to his friend Dr. Thomas Wharton, whose experimental farm and gardens were an attraction for the tourist of his day. The house takes its name from the ground which slopes towards it.

OLNEY, Bucks. [4 Cf] Small market town on the A509, 10 m. SE. of Northampton. William Cowper and Mrs. Unwin came here in 1767, at the Revd. John Newton's suggestion, to live at Orchard Side in the Market Place (now the Cowper and Newton Museum[1]). Cowper and Newton collaborated on the *Olney Hymns* (1779) in a household, described by David Cecil in *The Stricken Deer* (1929), where

time was divided between irregular piety and unrestrained philanthropy, where masters and servants alike were liable at any time to burst out with intimate revelations about the state of their souls.

Cowper helped with parish work and taught in the Sunday School. He continued to suffer from depression and during one bout was cared for at the rectory by Newton. On his return to Orchard Side, the villagers gave him a leveret, the first of three. These, Puss, Tiney, and Bess, who had a special door from the hall to the parlour, were the subject of many of Cowper's *Letters*, considered 'divine chit-chat' by Coleridge and Lamb, two recipients. The house is furnished with

much of Cowper's furniture, including the sofa of *The Task*.

Now stir the fire, and close the shutters fast,
Let fall the curtains, wheel the sofa round,
And, while the bubbling and loud-hissing urn
Throws up a steamy column, and the cups,
That cheer but not inebriate, wait on each,
So let us welcome peaceful ev'ning in.

Poems (1782) contains the satires written at Mrs. Unwin's suggestion when Cowper was unable to garden: 'Table Talk', 'The Progress of Error', 'Truth', 'Expostulation', 'Hope', 'Charity', 'Conversation', and 'Retirement'. The ballad *John Gilpin* (1782) came from a story that Lady Austen, who lived at the rectory of Clifton Reynes, $\frac{1}{2}$ m. E., told him in order to divert his depression. A room in the house is devoted to its many editions. *The Task* (1784), also written at her suggestion, was an immediate success. The garden contains the 'Bouderie' or the 'nutshell of a summerhouse which is my verse manufactory', and Cowper's pew moved from the church in 1904 and now in a shelter here. In 1786 Orchard Side needed repairs and Cowper and Mrs. Unwin moved to Weston Underwood (q.v.). A window in the Memorial Chapel of the parish church portrays Newton, Cowper, and the hares.

[1] Open summer weekdays 10 a.m.–5 p.m.

ONGAR, Essex. [1 Fb] Village made up of Chipping Ongar on the A113 and High Ongar on the A122, 7 m. E. of Epping. Isaac Taylor, the engraver and dissenting minister, moved in 1811 with his children, including Ann and Jane, authors of popular rhymes and hymns for children, to Castle House. Soon after Ann's marriage the family moved to Peaked Farm in 1814, where Jane wrote *Display, A Tale for Young People* (1815), and other works. She was buried (1824) in the chapel graveyard.

ORCHARDLEIGH PARK, Som. [2 Hb] Mansion, home of the Duckworth family, N. of Frome. The entrance is on the A362, *c.* $1\frac{1}{2}$ m. NW. of Frome, just beyond the railway bridge. Sir Henry Newbolt is buried in the churchyard of the small island church, which is situated in a lake in the grounds. The church, probably dating from the 13th c. (restored 1879), is reached by a bridge at the W. end of a sheltered lake and contains stone carvings and 15th–16th-c. stained glass of great interest. A poem by Geoffrey Swain pays tribute to Sir Henry Newbolt:

Most English Poet of our Poets' Race!
A son of Clifton's School, where lives his fame;

and there is a memorial tablet on the N. wall to him and his wife Margaret (*née* Duckworth) of Orchardleigh. At the E. end of the churchyard, overlooking the water, two simple stones mark their graves. Orchardleigh is described in his historical romance *The Old Country* (1906), where it is called 'Gardenleigh'.

Cars are not admitted without permission, but the 2 m. walk to the church is rewarding, although sometimes muddy.

ORKNEY ISLANDS (Orkney). [7 Ga] Group of islands off the N. coast of Scotland. Edwin Muir was born (1887) at The Folly, a farm his father rented in Deerness parish on Mainland, but moved when 8 to a new farm on Wyre, a small island NW. of Deerness. Muir spent 6 happy years here before the landlord repossessed the farm and the family moved to Glasgow.

Eric Linklater was born (1899) at Dounby on the A986 in the N. of Mainland. He returned to live here after his marriage in 1933, and commanded the defences at the beginning of the Second World War. His novel *White Maa's Saga* (1929) is set in the islands.

ORLESTONE, Kent. [1 Gd] Village on the B2070, 5 m. S. of Ashford. Capel House, an old farmhouse on the Bonnington road, was where Conrad lived (1910–19) and recovered from ill health and low spirits. He found the place 'sympathetic', and his writings here included the long short-story 'A Smile of Fortune', and the novels *Chance* (1913) and *Victory* (1915).

OSWESTRY, Salop. [3 Fc] Ancient border market town on the A483. Wilfred Owen was born (18 Mar. 1893) at Plas Wilmot, the home that his parents shared with his maternal grandfather. He spent 4 happy years here before his grandfather died and the family had to sell the house and its contents and move away.

OTTERBOURNE, Hants. [1 Be] Village on the A33, 4½ m. S. of Winchester. Charlotte Mary Yonge was born and lived all her life

at Elderfield, a large white house across the road from the church. She came under the influence of John Keble (rector of Otterbourne with the neighbouring parish of Hursley, q.v.), who encouraged her to expound his religious views in her fiction. She wrote over 150 books, including novels, of which *The Heir of Redclyffe* (1853) first brought her popular success, historical romances, and a biography of Hannah More (1888). She is buried near the S. porch of the church which her father and Keble designed together.

OTTERY ST. MARY, Devon. [2 Fd] Market town on the Otter, S. of the A30 between Exeter and Honiton. Alexander Barclay (1475?–1552), poet, scholar, and divine, probably of Scottish origin, translated Sebastian Brandt's *Narrenschiff* (1494) into English as *The Ship of Fools* (1509), when a priest at the college, founded by Bishop Grandison in 1337. His version was a free adaptation of the original, which had been written first in Swabian dialect and then in Latin, and he intended it as a satire of contemporary English life and its corruptions and abuses.

Samuel Taylor Coleridge was born on 21 October 1772 at the schoolhouse, the thirteenth and youngest child of the Revd. John Coleridge, vicar 1760–81, and master of the Grammar School. After his father's death the 9-year-old boy went to Christ's Hospital, London. He wrote a sonnet 'To the River Otter' and remembered his birthplace and the music of the church bells in 'Frost at Midnight' (Feb. 1798). A memorial plaque on the churchyard wall has a low-relief bust and portrays the albatross from *The Rime of the Ancient Mariner* (1798).

A. W. Kinglake went to the Grammar School before going to Eton. Ottery St. Mary appears as 'Clavering St. Mary' in Thackeray's *Pendennis* (1848–50).

OULTON, Suff. [4 Hd] Village 2 m. NW. of Lowestoft, just N. of Oulton Broad. George Borrow settled at Oulton Cottage (gone), his wife's home on the north bank, after their marriage in 1840. He wrote *The Bible in Spain* (1843) and *Lavengro* (1851) in a summer-house in the garden. He returned to Oulton in 1874 after his many excursions and died here in 1881. There is a memorial in the church.

OVER STOWEY. See ADSCOMBE.

OVINGDEAN, East Sussex. [1 Ee] Village on the B2123. Harrison Ainsworth often walked over the Downs to church here, when living in Brighton (1853–67) 3 m. W. In his novel *Ovingdean Grange* (1860), Prince Charles spends his last night in England at the Grange (near the church in the lower village) before escaping to France. The red-brick Tudor front has been stuccoed and the oak panelling and stained glass have disappeared.

OXFORD, Oxon. [1 Cb] University and cathedral city, which grew up round the Saxon priory of St. Frideswide at the confluence of the Thames and the Cherwell. The settlement was first mentioned as Oxnaforda in the *Anglo-Saxon Chronicle* of 911. The priory church, of which Walter Map (or Mapes) was archdeacon in 1197, now serves as the cathedral and as the chapel of Christ Church, the college built by Cardinal Wolsey on the site of St. Frideswide's. Geoffrey of Monmouth, creator of King Arthur as a romantic hero, is thought to have studied at Oxford c. 1129. Grosseteste, first rector (1224) of the Franciscan order in Oxford, who became first Chancellor of the University, who made translations from Greek and wrote the long poem *Le Chasteau d'Amour*. The philosopher and man of science, Roger Bacon, lived in the Franciscan House (site now a car park in Paradise Sq.) after his return from Paris c. 1250 until c. 1257, when his researches alarmed the religious community and he was sent away. While here he is said to have studied astronomy from the roof of the New Gate, built to control the long bridge over the marshes known as Grandpont. Bacon, after writing his three major works under surveillance in Paris, is thought to have died in Oxford (1294) and to have been buried in the Franciscan burial ground. Pepys visited in 1668 and writes in his *Diary* (1970–6) that he climbed the tower to 'Roger Bacon's study'. The gate had then become a house and had an ornamented second storey. This Folly (demolished in 1779) gave to the bridge its present name, Folly Bridge.

Chaucer shows some knowledge of the town and gown, and especially of Osney, in 'The Miller's Tale' in *The Canterbury Tales* c. 1387–1400. John Skelton is thought to

have been made 'poet laureate' (before the official post existed) in Oxford c. 1490 and he himself claimed to have received the honour from Henry VII. William D'Avenant was born (1606) at the Crown Inn in Cornmarket (now no. 3), where his father was innkeeper. The Painted Room[1] on the second floor, so called when 16th-c. paintings were restored on the walls in 1927, is said to be where Shakespeare stayed on his way each year to and from Stratford. The antiquaries, John Aubrey and Anthony Wood, vary in their accounts of Shakespeare's relationship to young D'Avenant; they imply that though he admitted to being his godfather, he might perhaps have been his natural father too.

Alexander Pope often passed through Oxford. His friend, Joseph Spence, mentions meeting him at the Cross Inn (the Golden Cross) in 1735 looking 'quite fatigu'd to death'. He had just walked from Bagley Hill (3 m. S.) after giving up his coach to a young woman whose arm had been broken in an accident.

Karl Moritz, a German schoolmaster savouring the land of his favourite poet John Milton in spite of constant rebuffs from suspicious innkeepers, was taken to the Mitre by a young chaplain, who had accompanied his walk from Nuneham Courtenay. In *Travels in England* (1795), Moritz mentions the sightseeing tour he took with this guide next day. They saw the elderly Thomas Warton, whom Moritz knew as the editor of Milton's poems, and who the young chaplain said was partial to duck shooting. Moritz thought the buildings were 'much over loaded with ornaments' and deplored their 'dingy, dirty, and disgusting appearance'.

Charles Lamb's 'Oxford in the Vacation' from his *Essays of Elia* (1833) was written during his visit to Cambridge in 1820 and is a conflation of his memories of the two universities. Jane Austen and her elder sister, Cassandra, were sent to school here, for a short time, to the widow of a Principal of Brasenose. Jane Austen often mentions Oxford, where her father and brothers were educated, in her novels and she depicts three very different undergraduates in *Northanger Abbey* (1818), and in *Mansfield Park* (1814) in which the serious-minded Edmund Bertram is destined for the Church. Edward Bradley, author, as 'Cuthbert Bede', of *The Adventures of Mr. Verdant Green, an Oxford*

Freshman (1853–7), is thought to have been studying here during 1849 to enter the Church, though he was not a member of the University.

Wordsworth, a Cambridge man, wrote two sonnets on Oxford during his visit in May 1820. One ends with praise of High St.

> I slight my own beloved Cam, to range
> Where silver Isis leads my stripling feet;
> Pace the long avenue, or glide adown
> The stream-like windings of that glorious street.

William Cobbett was uncomplimentary about the University and lashed out in *Rural Rides* (1830):

> Upon beholding the masses of buildings at Oxford, devoted to what they call '*learning*', I could not help reflecting on the drones that they contain and the wasps they send forth.

Mrs. Humphry Ward lived (1872–81) at 5 (now 17) Bradmore Rd. immediately after her marriage. In 1888 she was nursing her dying mother at 2 Bradmore Rd., when she heard that Gladstone wished to discuss her recently published novel *Robert Elsmere*. She met him twice at the Warden's lodgings at Keble and defended the novel, which he said was an attack on Christianity. Gladstone's review appeared in the *Nineteenth Century* in May 1888.

Hardy set many scenes of *Jude the Obscure* (1895) in Oxford, his 'Christminster'. Jude Fawley had lodgings in Jericho, the area near Walton St., and St. Silas's Church in the novel is really St. Barnabas's, whose architect, Arthur Blomfield, employed Hardy for 5 years from 1862. Christ Church becomes Cardinal College and St. Aldate's, Cardinal St.

In *Portraits of Places* (1883) Henry James writes that Oxford

> typifies to an American, the union of science and sense—of aspiration and ease. A German university gives a greater impression of science, and an English country house or an Italian villa a greater impression of idle enjoyment; but in these cases, on the one side, knowledge is too rugged, and on the other, satisfaction is too trivial. Oxford lends sweetness to labour and dignity to leisure.

Part of the title story of James's *A Passionate Pilgrim* (1875) has scenes in Oxford and describes the cloisters of Magdalen and the gardens of New College, St. John's, and Wadham. 'The Altar of the Dead' (1895) was sketched out while James was lodging at 15 Beaumont St. in 1894.

William de Morgan's novel *Joseph Vance* (1906) describes a row from Binsey upstream to Godstow.

In his autobiography A. E. Coppard tells of his life in Oxford (1907–19), and his first lodgings in Iffley (2 m. SE.). An episode there, when he was charged with poaching while exercising his two whippets, was the origin of his story 'The Poor Man' written 15 years later. Coppard moved many times before giving up his job at the Eagle Ironworks (still in Walton Well Rd.) to devote himself to writing. He and his wife lived for a time in a fourth-floor flat in Cornmarket, the setting for 'Arabesque' and 'The Quiet Woman'. During the First World War Ronald Firbank rented rooms at 66 High St., where he wrote the novels *Inclinations* (1916), *Caprice* (1917), and *Valmouth* (1919). He chose black décor with exotic designs; cushions on the floor served as seats.

Yeats, with his wife and child, lived for some years on the corner of Broad St. opposite Balliol in a tall narrow house (gone), where many literary friends visited him. He moved to Shillingford (q.v.) in April 1921 to save money by letting the house. John Masefield lived at Boar's Hill in the 1920s and his house is now called Masefield House.

Kenneth Grahame, who was educated at St. Edward's School from 1868 to 1875, died at Pangbourne in 1932 and was buried in St. Cross churchyard in the same grave as his son for whom he wrote *The Wind in the Willows*. His epitaph was written by his cousin Anthony Hope Hawkins.

Charles Williams came to Oxford in 1940. He worked for the Oxford University Press and was the author of many poems on the Arthurian legend, including *Taliessin in Logres* (1938) and the unfinished *The Arthurian Torso* (1948), which has a commentary by his friend C. S. Lewis of Magdalen. They and other cronies, including J. R. R. Tolkien, drank in the back bar of the Eagle and Child (P) in St. Giles', where they were known as 'the Inklings'. Williams also wrote religious works, biographies, and metaphysical thrillers, his name for *War in Heaven* (1930), *The Place of the Lion* (1931), and others. He is buried in St. Cross churchyard, as is H. W. Garrod of Merton (d. 1960). St. Cross Church, described by a character in Dorothy Sayers's *Busman's Honeymoon* (1936) as 'an obscure little church in a side street', was the scene of Lord Peter Wimsey's marriage to Harriet Vane. George Santayana lodged in Beaumont St. during the First World War. In *My Host the World* (1953) he describes a visit to Robert Bridges and to Lady Ottoline Morrell at Garsington (q.v.). His novel *The Last Puritan* (1935) has scenes in Oxford and Iffley. Thomas Wolfe, the American novelist, who visited Oxford briefly, set here some scenes of his novel *Of Time and the River* (1935).

Dylan Thomas and his family spent Christmas 1945 at Holywell Ford, off St. Cross Rd., with A. J. P. Taylor and his wife. In March the Thomases moved into a summer-house on the water's edge in the Taylors' garden for a short stay which lengthened to a year. Dylan Thomas had just published *Deaths and Entrances* (1946) and he was suffering from exhaustion. While here he wrote many of the scripts for his B.B.C. broadcasts, which proved popular and brought his name to a wider audience. Thomas was one of the group of poets, including Louis MacNeice, who met at the Port Mahon in St. Clement's and the George (closed), on the corner of Cornmarket and George St., which had a restaurant upstairs cooled by *punkahs*.

Elizabeth Bowen lived in Old Headington after her marriage to Alan Charles Cameron in 1923, the year she published her first volume of short stories, *Encounters*. She wrote her first four novels here and another volume of short stories, *Joining Charles* (1929). She inherited her father's house in Ireland in 1928 and after living there for a few years following the death of her husband, returned here in 1960 for a short time before leaving for Hythe, where she had spent her childhood. She received an hon. D.Litt. from the University in 1957.

[1] Open Mon.–Fri. 9.30 a.m.–12.30 p.m., 2.30–4.30 p.m.

University:

All Souls' College (1438). Graduate college which refused a fellowship to William Camden in 1571 because of his Protestantism. Jeremy Taylor, who became a Fellow on the recommendation of Archbishop Laud, who had heard him preach at Cambridge, preached many of his outstanding sermons at St. Mary's, the University Church, near by in the High St. John Evelyn inspected the new painting over the plastered reredos in the college chapel in 1664 but wrote in his *Diary* that it 'seemes too full of nakeds for a Chapell'. Christopher Codrington, who had rich sugar estates in Barbados, was made a Fellow in 1690. The college inherited his books and a large sum of money for the rebuilding of the library, which in spite of losses at the Reformation, contains many manuscripts, including the 13th-c. Amesbury Psalter. Edward Young, who became a Law Fellow in 1708, was a friend of Thomas Tickell of Queen's and like him a member of Addison's circle in London. Richard Graves, a friend and contemporary of Shenstone at Pembroke, was made a Fellow in 1736. Francis Doyle, a Fellow from 1835 to 1844, who succeeded to the baronetcy in 1839, was Professor of Poetry (1867–77). He wrote many poems extolling courage and patriotism including 'The Private of the Buffs', and was made an hon. D.C.L. in 1877.

T. E. Lawrence was elected a Fellow in 1919 and lived in the college for a time. He started to write here *Seven Pillars of Wisdom* (1926), about his experiences in the Middle East, which earned him the name 'Lawrence of Arabia'.

Balliol College (1263). John Wycliffe, a Fellow who became the Master in 1361, was forbidden to teach here in 1381 after refuting the doctrine of transubstantiation. John Evelyn, an undergraduate (1637–40), describes in his *Diary* his years here, uneventful except for the time he was so entranced with watching a play that he fell off a table and injured his leg. He visited Oxford again in 1654, when he was made welcome at Balliol, and he showed his wife the rarities of the Bodleian.

Adam Smith came from Glasgow University as Snell Exhibitioner and graduated *c.* 1744. He stayed on for 2 years and went home to Kirkcaldy.

Robert Southey, who came up from Westminster in 1792, met Edward Seward here, after whose death he wrote 'I loved him with my whole heart, and shall remember him with gratitude and affection, as one who was my moral father, to the last moment of my life'. It was to Seward, who graduated in 1793 and died suddenly in 1795, that Southey wrote the poem 'To a Dead Friend'. Southey was visited by Coleridge in 1794 and with other friends planned to form a community on the banks of the Susquehannah in America. This, which they called a Pantisocracy, would give the minimum time to manual labour and the maximum to the improvement of the mind. While at Balliol Southey was engaged on his epic *Joan of Arc* (1796).

J. G. Lockhart came from Glasgow with a Snell Exhibition in 1809 and graduated in Classics in 1813. He was a friend of H. H. Milman of Brasenose.

Matthew Arnold, son of Thomas Arnold of Rugby, came up with a classical scholarship in 1841, and gained a reputation for a lack of seriousness and a tendency to practical jokes, indolence, and affectation, although he won the Newdigate Prize with his poem 'Cromwell' in 1843. He was a contemporary of F. T. Palgrave and intimate friend of Arthur Hugh Clough, who had also been at Rugby, and whom he followed to Oriel (q.v.) as a Fellow. C. S. Calverley, after 2 years here, left for Cambridge in 1852.

Algernon Swinburne, who came up in 1856, became acquainted with the Pre-Raphaelites when they decorated the Union with illustrations from the Arthurian legends, which inspired his poem 'Queen Yseult'. He wrote the first draft of his play *Rosamond* here, and was kindly treated by Benjamin Jowett, Professor of Greek, whose translations of Plato he read in draft. Swinburne, who was invited on Jowett's vacation reading parties, left Oxford in 1859. Jowett, Master 1870–93, was the subject of innumerable stories and the jingle

> I am Master of this college:
> What I don't know isn't knowledge.

He, with Matthew Arnold, Ruskin, Pater, and others, was satirized in W. H. Mallock's *The New Republic* (1877). T. H. Green, the idealistic philosopher on whom Mrs. Humphry Ward based Mr. Gray in *Robert Elsmere* (1888), was a Fellow here from 1860. He and Jowett are buried in St. Sepulchre's cemetery[1] in Walton St.

J. A. Symonds, Andrew Lang, and Gerard Manley Hopkins were undergraduates in the 1860s. Symonds won the Newdigate Prize with his poem 'The Escorial' in 1860. Gerard Manley Hopkins came up in 1863 with an exhibition to read Classics. He became a friend of Robert Bridges and fell under the influence of Walter Pater of Brasenose and the writings of J. H. Newman. It is thought that his Platonic dialogue 'On

the Nature of Beauty' was written for Pater. In his letters to his mother he describes his first rooms and writes 'Balliol is the friendliest and snuggest of colleges, our inner quad is delicious and has a grove of fine trees and lawns, where bowls are the order of the evening'. The *Journal*, which he began here, describes his walks to the surrounding villages. His poem 'Duns Scotus's Oxford' opens with the lines

> Towery city and branchy between towers;
> Cuckoo-echoing, bell-swarmèd, lark-charmèd,
>   rook-racked, river-rounded:

and closes with strictures on the town's 'brickish skirt'. In 1866 Hopkins wrote 'Heaven-Haven' and having had instruction, which he kept from his family, high Anglicans, was finally received into the Catholic Church. After leaving Oxford for a course of study to become a Jesuit he returned in 1878 to be a curate at St. Aloysius's, the Catholic church at the S. end of Woodstock Rd. and it was at this time that he wrote the poem 'Binsey Poplars'. The Holy Water stoup in the church was given in his memory. A. C. Bradley, an undergraduate from 1869 to 1872, was elected a Fellow in 1874 and Professor of Poetry in 1901. He is chiefly remembered as a Shakespearian critic by *Shakespearean Tragedy* (1904) and *Oxford Lectures* (1909).

Anthony Hope Hawkins was elected President of the Union, when an undergraduate (1881–4), as was Hilaire Belloc, a contemporary here of George Douglas Brown in the 1890s. Belloc's poem 'To the Balliol Men Still in Africa' contains the lines:

> Balliol made me, Balliol fed me,
> Whatever I had she gave me again;
> And the best of Balliol loved me and led me,
> God be with you, Balliol men.

C. E. Montague, author of *Rough Justice* (1926) and *Right off the Map* (1927), was an undergraduate 1885–8. Julian Grenfell, who graduated in 1909, is remembered for the poem 'Into Battle' about the First World War, in which he was killed in 1915. L. P. Hartley and Aldous Huxley were undergraduates during the war. Part of Huxley's novel *Eyeless in Gaza* (1936) describes life in N. Oxford. He lived (1915–16) with the Haldanes at Cherwell (now the site of Wolfson College). Dorothy L. Sayers's detective hero, Lord Peter Wimsey, an officer in the war, was a Balliol man. Ronald Knox, an undergraduate 1906-10, wrote sermons, essays, and detective stories. He was an hon. Fellow from 1953 to his death in 1957. Logan Pearsall Smith describes his memories of Oxford in his autobiography *The Unforgotten Years* (1938). Arnold Toynbee, author of *A Study of History*, was Fellow and Tutor (1912-15) and hon. Fellow from 1957. He includes some mention of his Oxford friends in *Acquaintances* (1967). Cyril Connolly's undergraduate years in the early 1920s are encapsulated in the letters he wrote to Noel Blakiston, a friend at Eton, who went to Cambridge. These, which show the very high goals he set for himself, were published as *A Romantic Friendship* (1975).

¹ Open 7.30 a.m.–5 p.m.

Bodleian Library (1490). The University Library as we now know it was started by a collection of manuscripts bequeathed by Duke Humphrey of Gloucester (d. 1447). Much of this collection had been dispersed when Thomas Bodley refounded the Library in 1602. He devoted the rest of his life and most of his fortune to enlarging it, and arranged (1610) that the Stationers' Company should give a free copy of every book printed in England to the Library. Bodley, who was knighted in 1604, left his own collection to the Library. Further volumes and a large number of oriental manuscripts were given by the jurist John Selden. Anthony Wood, who helped carry Selden's books into the Library in 1659, found several pairs of spectacles left between the pages. Wood was allowed to have a pair and he kept them in memory of Selden until his death. A large marble plaque on the stairs gives a list of the many benefactors to the Library. Many books and manuscripts can be seen in the 15th-c. Divinity School below, including *Tottel's Miscellany* (1557), Shakespeare's *Venus and Adonis* (1593), an autograph of a poem by Donne, Shelley's notebook containing 'Ode to the West Wind', Kenneth Grahame's original manuscript of *The Wind in the Willows*, the third manuscript of *Seven Pillars of Wisdom* by T. E. Lawrence, and Joyce Cary's papers and manuscripts.

Brasenose College (1509), familiarly known as B.N.C. John Foxe was an undergraduate here from 1533 to 1537 and then became a Fellow of Magdalen. Barnabe Barnes, who joined the Earl of Essex's

expedition in 1591 after graduating, may have written here some of the sonnets, madrigals, elegies, and odes which he published in 1593 as *Parthenophil and Parthenope*. Robert Burton was an undergraduate here from 1593, and in 1599 was elected a Student (Fellow) of Christ Church. Both John Marston, B.A. 1594, and Thomas Traherne, B.A. 1656, graduated here and later were ordained. Elias Ashmole, whose collection of curiosities, originally made by John Tradescant and his son, formed the nucleus of the Ashmolean Museum and who bequeathed his library to the Bodleian, studied physics and mathematics here after joining the Royalists.

R. H. Barham and H. H. Milman were both undergraduates in the early years of the 19th c. Milman won the Newdigate Prize in 1812 with the poem 'Apollo Belvedere' which was later considered the 'most perfect' prize poem by Dean Stanley, himself a winner of university prizes. Milman was made a Fellow in 1814 and a year later published *Fazio*, a drama, in which the main part of Bianca was acted by the principal actresses of the time. *Samor, the Lord of the Bright City* (1818), a poem about Vortigern written in a style resembling Southey's *Madoc* (1805), was considered by Southey rather 'too full of power and beauty' for anything less than a dramatic rendering. Milman, who became vicar of St. Mary's, Reading, in 1818, was elected Professor of Poetry in 1821.

Walter Pater, who became a Fellow in 1864, had a long association with Oxford. His first critical study 'Winckelmann', published in the *Westminster Review* in 1867, was included in *Studies of the History of the Renaissance* (1873), which established his reputation. *Marius the Epicurean* (1885), a philosophical romance, *Imaginary Portraits* (1887), and *Appreciations* (1889), literary criticism, were followed by posthumous publications including the unfinished *Gaston de Latour* (1896), which has portraits of Montaigne and Ronsard. Pater lived for many years at 2 Bradmore Rd., and then at 64 St. Giles', where he died (1890). He is buried in St. Cross churchyard.

John Buchan came here (1897-9) from Glasgow University and won the Stanhope Prize with an essay on Walter Ralegh, and the Newdigate Prize with a poem on the Pilgrim Fathers. Later he lived at Elsfield (q.v.), and he wrote in his autobiography, *Memory Hold the Door* (1940), that

Oxford has a cincture of green uplands and a multitude of little valleys. It is only from her adjacent heights that her charms can be comprised into one picture and the true background found to her towers.

John Middleton Murry describes his years here (c. 1909–12) in *Between Two Worlds* (1934). His fear of ordeals at the hands of the 'hearties' was dispelled by his friendly reception. His rooms looked across to the roof of the Radcliffe Camera. In 1911 he was editing the illustrated quarterly *Rhythm* with Michael Sadleir, financed by Joyce Cary, and he wrote to Katherine Mansfield for a contribution. He left Oxford in 1912 uninterested in further examinations, and later married Katherine Mansfield.

Charles Morgan came up in 1919 after serving in the navy in the war, which gave him the theme for his first novel, *The Gunroom* (1919). He became President of the University Dramatic Society, and left in 1921 to join the staff of *The Times*. He returned as Zaharoff Lecturer (French Studies) in 1948.

Edward Bradley's hero, Mr. Verdant Green, was an undergraduate here.

Christ Church (1525). This college is often called 'the House' and includes the former Canterbury Hall (site now Canterbury Quad). Thomas More studied Greek here under Linacre from 1492 to 1494, soon after Linacre and Grocyn had returned from a visit to Italy. The three scholars often met later in London. Richard Edwards, a Student (Fellow) here from 1547, composed *Palamon and Arcite* to entertain Queen Elizabeth on her visit in 1566. William Camden was at Magdalen then but transferred here soon after. His contemporary, Philip Sidney, was an undergraduate from 1568 to 1571 when he left on account of the plague. Richard Hakluyt, who later chronicled the English voyages of exploration, was another contemporary. George Peele, who graduated in 1577, was much admired as a poet while here.

Richard Corbett lived here from 1598 when he became a Student. He was Dean of the cathedral (Head of the college) in 1620 and then Bishop of Oxford until he was transferred to Norwich. In 1613 Corbett gave the funeral oration for Sir Thomas Bodley, benefactor of the University Library, and in 1619 as Senior Student was host to Ben Jonson, who received the degree of M.A., 'by their favour not his studie', by which he probably means he made no effort to get the honour. Corbett's verses, collected as *Certain Elegant Poems* (1647), include 'The Fairy's Farewell' with the line 'Farewell rewards and fairies', 'Iter Boreale', a traveller's tale, and a poem to his son Vincent on his third birthday.

Robert Burton spent 53 years in Oxford, as an undergraduate, a Student (1559–1640), and as rector of St. Thomas Martyr, a parish in the W. near the present railway station. He built the S. porch of the church, which has his arms over the door. His *Anatomy of Melancholy* (1621) on the causes, symptoms, and varieties of melancholy, written as a medical treatise, is illuminated by examples from classical and contemporary literature. Dr. Johnson said it was 'the only book that ever took him out of bed two hours sooner than he wished to rise'. Burton was buried (1640) in the cathedral, where a monument, erected by his brother, on a pillar contains a bust and lines in Latin composed by himself. William Cartwright, who became a Student in 1628, was a dramatic preacher. His play *The Royal Slave* was acted before Charles I on his visit in 1636. He became a Proctor in 1643 and died later that year. His *Comedies, Tragi-comedies, with other Poems* was published in 1651. John Fell became Dean in 1660 and Bishop of Oxford in 1676. Thomas Brown, who was an undergraduate 1678–82, is remembered as the author of the lines

> I do not love you, Dr. Fell;
> But why I cannot tell.

John Locke, who graduated in 1658, returned to live in college in 1680 but was expelled reluctantly by Dean Fell for his alleged complicity in 1684 in Shaftesbury's plot. Thomas Otway left in 1672 without taking the degree examination. Richard Steele stayed one year only before going to Merton in 1691, and John Philips, author of *The Splendid Shilling* (1701), a mock heroic poem in Miltonic blank verse, was an undergraduate in the 1690s.

John Boyle, 5th Earl of Orrery, a friend of Swift, Pope, and Dr. Johnson, who was an undergraduate in the 1720s, wrote to his son when he came up about Swift. These letters were published as *Remarks on the Life and Writings of Dr. Jonathan Swift* (1751).

George Colman, a barrister on the Oxford circuit until he became an established dramatist and a friend of David Garrick, was an undergraduate in the 1750s. His son, George Colman the Younger, spent a few years here before going to Aberdeen to study medicine in 1781. Matthew Gregory Lewis was an undergraduate from 1791 to 1794, when he became an attaché at The Hague.

John Ruskin became a gentleman commoner with rooms in Peckwater Quad in January 1837. His mother rented rooms at 90 High St. and he visited her for tea and again after dinner on most days. He won the Newdigate Prize in 1839 with his third entry, but soon after a haemorrhage necessitated recuperation abroad. He returned to graduate in 1842. His publications include *Modern Painters* (1843–60) and *The Stones of Venice* (1851–2), and his Oxford memorial is the University Museum in Parks Rd., built in Venetian Gothic with pillars and capitals ornamented with animals and flowers. The story of the difficulties Ruskin faced to get the building of the museum accepted by the authorities is told in *The Oxford Museum* (1859, reprinted 1893), by Sir Henry Acland and John Ruskin. Not least of his troubles was the prevailing thought that science was 'adverse to religion'. Ruskin's enthusiasm ensured that the workers were provided with books and started their day with 'simple prayers'. His desire to promote the dignity of manual labour led a group of undergraduates, including Oscar Wilde, to improve the road at North Hinksey. Ruskin, who established the Ruskin School of Drawing, was twice appointed Professor of Fine Art (1870–9 and 1883–4) and many of his lectures were published. In North Oxford houses built with stained-glass windows, Romeo balconies, pointed turrets, and castellated roofs, show the influence of his architectural doctrine.

T. E. Brown, a servitor here from 1850 to 1853, found himself, because of his lowly status, ineligible for a Studentship in spite of his academic attainments. He was later elected to a Fellowship at Oriel, then considered 'the blue riband' of the University.

Charles Dodgson, an undergraduate from 1851–1855, became a Student and mathematical lecturer. He suffered from a stammer and lived a retired life carrying on friendships chiefly by correspondence. He was, however, able to communicate with children and *Alice's Adventures in Wonderland* (1865) and its sequel *Through the Looking Glass* (1872) were written as a result of a story he made up for Alice Liddell, the young daughter of the Dean, during afternoon excursions in a punt up the river to Godstow (2 m. N.). He used the pseudonym 'Lewis Carroll'. Alice Liddell is said to have bought sweets at a little shop ('Alice's Shop') with stone mullions (opposite what is now the Memorial Gardens). The photographs that Dodgson took of many of his contemporaries at 'the House' survive.

Edward Martyn, who came from Dublin in the 1870s and found himself almost the only Catholic here, contributed £10 to the new organ at St. Aloysius's Church.

W. H. Auden, an undergraduate (1925–8), was one of the poets, including Louis MacNeice and Cecil Day-Lewis, who were grouped together as left-wing in the 1930s. Auden edited *Oxford Poetry* in 1926 with Charles Plumb and with Day-Lewis in 1927. A limited edition of his *Poems* (1928) was hand-printed in Oxford. In 1939 he went to the U.S. and became an American citizen. He was elected Professor of Poetry (1956–60) and an hon. Student in 1961. He came back to England in 1972 and lived in a cottage in the college grounds. He died on a visit to Vienna in 1974.

Clarendon Building. The Oxford University Press was housed from 1713 to 1829 in this building by Nicholas Hawksmoor (1661–1736) in Broad St. Profits from the *History of the Great Rebellion*, Clarendon's great work (1702–4), partly paid for the building. Edward Hyde, Earl of Clarendon, whose statue is in a niche at one end, was chief minister under Charles II and Chancellor of the University 1660–7. The Press moved from here to its present premises in Walton St. in 1829.

Corpus Christi College (1517), usually known as Corpus. Nicholas Udall (or Uvedale), a scholar here in 1520, became a Fellow in 1524 and was suspected of nonconformity in religious matters 2 years later.

Richard Edwards was here for 7 years, as undergraduate and Fellow (1544–7), before migrating to Christ Church in 1547.

Richard Hooker and Stephen Gosson were both ordained in the 1570s.

Thomas Day, author of *Sandford and Merton* (1783–9), studied here in the 1760s. In 1871 Ruskin, an hon. Fellow, had rooms in college overlooking the garden. Robert Bridges, a friend while an undergraduate here of Gerard Manley Hopkins of Balliol, whose collected poems he edited in 1918, lived (1907–30) at Chilswell House (now occupied by a religious community), Boars Hill (3 m. SW.). He became Poet Laureate in 1913 and his long philosophical poem *The Testament of Beauty* (1929), written there, was published when he was 85, the year before his death.

Henry Newbolt, whose poems, including 'Drake's Drum', have remained popular for over 50 years, was an undergraduate here in the 1880s. Bernard Spencer, an undergraduate (1927–30), edited *Oxford Poetry* (1929–30). Many of his early poems were published in *New Verse* in the late 1930s when he was working with Geoffrey Grigson.

Exeter College (1314) has associations with the West Country. John Ford studied here (*c.* 1601–2) and was followed by another Devonian, William Browne of Tavistock, who became a tutor in 1624. Joseph Glanvill, who graduated in 1655, returned in 1659, engaged on *The Vanity of Dogmatizing* (1661). This contains the first reference to the story of the scholar who left the University to join a band of gipsies, which inspired Matthew Arnold's poem 'The Scholar-Gipsy' (1853). William Gifford, a shoemaker's apprentice from Ashburton (q.v.), rewarded for his industry by the opportunity to study here (B.A. 1782), left benefactions to help other students. J. A. Froude became Devon Fellow in 1842, but resigned after a copy of his *Nemesis of Faith* (1849) was publicly burned by a former Professor of Moral Philosophy. Froude, a friend of Carlyle and Kingsley, became Regius Professor of Modern History in 1892 and lived at Cherwell Edge (now Linacre College). Three volumes of his lectures were published between 1894 and 1896. In 1846 F. T. Palgrave (best known as the compiler of *The Golden Treasury*, 1861) became a private secretary to Gladstone, then out of office, and in 1847 was elected a Fellow. When Gladstone became Oxford's M.P. later in the year,

Palgrave joined the Civil Service. He was Professor of Poetry from 1885 to 1895.

R. D. Blackmore, who spent his childhood near by at Elsfield and then in Devon, was a classical scholar here (1844–7). William Morris, a student from 1853 to 1855, became interested in the Pre-Raphaelites and with Burne-Jones painted scenes from Arthurian legends at the Union. A Morris tapestry from a painting by Burne-Jones is in the chapel.

Alfred Noyes published his first collection of poems *The Loom of Years* (1902) while an undergraduate. Noyes wrote in 1907 in 'Oxford Revisited'

> And still in the beautiful City, the river of life is no duller,
> Only a little strange as the eighth hour dreamily chimes.
> In the City of friends and echoes, ribbons and music and colour,
> Lilac and blossoming chestnut, willows and whispering limes . . .

He mentions in *Two Worlds for Memory* (1953) his surprise when he found his initials added to those of Ford and Morris on the windows of the dining hall, where those members of the college who have obtained merit, are commemorated. J. R. R. Tolkien was an undergraduate just before the First World War, in which he served from 1915 to 1918. He was later made an hon. Fellow. R. M. Dawkins, Professor of Modern Greek and Fellow (1920–39), wrote *Forty-five Stories from the Dodecanese* (1950), *Modern Greek Folk Tales* (1952), and a study (1952) of his friend Norman Douglas. He also befriended Frederick Rolfe. He was made an hon. Fellow in 1939 and spent much of his time here until his death in 1955.

Hertford College (1874) including the former Hart Hall. Samuel Daniel entered Hart Hall in 1579 and later became tutor to William Herbert at Wilton. John Donne, who came up in 1584, became acquainted with Henry Wotton and John Davies of Queen's, who remained his lifelong friends. John Selden, who like Donne went on to the Inns of Court, was an undergraduate at the turn of the 17th c.

Evelyn Waugh, an undergraduate at Hertford in the 1920s, who became a Catholic in 1930, wrote, as well as his satirical novels, a life of the Jesuit martyr, Edmund Campion, which received the Hawthornden Prize in 1936, and a Life of his friend Ronald Knox (1959). In *Brideshead*

Revisited (1945), a novel with many scenes in Oxford, Waugh describes Oxford as 'the city of aquatint' and mentions the café in Broad St. where Balliol and Trinity men shuffle in their bedroom slippers to breakfast, Dollbear and Goodall, chemists in the High famous for their pick-me-ups, and the George. His autobiography, *A Little Learning* (1964), gives an account of his years here.

John Meade Falkner, who graduated here in 1882, wrote *The Lost Stradivarius* (1895), a mystery novel in which an undergraduate finds a violin hidden behind the panelling in his room in the older part of the college, overlooking New College Lane. Falkner became an hon. Fellow in 1927.

Jesus College (1571) has a strong Welsh connection. Henry Vaughan, from Brecknock (now part of Powys), was an undergraduate from 1638.

Lewis Morris, who later helped to establish the University of Wales, won the Chancellor's Essay Prize in 1858. He was made a Fellow after the publication of *The Epic of Hades* (1876–7), an account in blank verse of his supposed encounter with some characters of Greek mythology. Frederick Rolfe spent part of 1906–7 here as secretary to Dr. Hardy. T. E. Lawrence, whose family lived in Polstead Rd. (he made his study in an outhouse), came up from Oxford High School in 1906 and graduated in 1910.

Lincoln College (1427). William D'Avenant was an undergraduate in the 1620s, and his first play *The Tragedy of Albovine* was produced in 1629. D'Avenant was a Royalist like Thomas Fuller, who came here in 1643, lived in college, and preached to Charles I.

Mark Pattison, author of the life of Isaac Casaubon (1875) was Rector (1861–84). Marian Evans (George Eliot) visited him when she was writing *Middlemarch* (1871–2), though whether her portrait of the elderly pedant Mr. Casaubon owes anything to him has been doubted. Pattison is certainly thought to be the origin of Professor Forth in Rhoda Broughton's novel *Belinda* (1883). She was a prolific novelist and was a welcome guest of Pattison's at the Rector's Lodgings. She lived at 51 Holywell St. from 1894 to 1900 and at Riverview, Headington Hill, from 1900 until her death in 1920. Edward Thomas, who lodged at 113 Cowley Rd. in 1898 as an external student, won a

scholarship here later in the year, and married before leaving the University. *Oxford* (1903) was one of the first topographical books he wrote in an effort to make a living from writing.

Magdalen College (pr. Mawdlin) (1458). John Foxe, an undergraduate in the 1530s, was elected a Fellow in 1539 but resigned in 1545 over his religious beliefs. He went abroad after the martyrdom of his friend Latimer. The English version of his long account of religious persecution, *Actes and Monuments* (1563), became known as *The Book of Martyrs*. John Lyly, who was here from 1567 to 1575, went on to Cambridge. Though in *Euphues* (1578) he thought Oxford Colleges 'more stately for the building' and Cambridge 'much more sumptuous for the houses in the town' he writes that they are equal in learning 'for out of them both do dayly proceed men of great wisdom'.

Thomas Bodley came here after some years in Geneva, where his parents had gone to escape religious persecution. He graduated B.A. in 1563 before becoming a Fellow of Merton.

John Florio, son of a refugee from religious persecution, entered the college in 1581. His great work, an Italian–English Dictionary (1598), led to his appointment as a reader in Italian to Queen Anne in 1604.

George Wither, an undergraduate from 1603 to 1605, writes in 'A Love Sonnet'

> In summer time to Medley,
> My love and I would go;
> The boatman there stood ready,
> My love and I to row.

Medley ferry (1 m. W.), now replaced by a bridge, was the nearest river crossing to Binsey (q.v.). Wither also gives snatches of his life here in *Fair Virtue* (1622), a long poem written when he was 18.

Joseph Addison became a Fellow here at his own college in 1698. He was a noted classical scholar and his Latin poems were admired by Dryden. He travelled on the Continent (1699–1703) with a scholarship to enable him to embark on a diplomatic career and, though he became an Under-Secretary of State in 1706, did not resign his Fellowship until 1711. His favourite walk by the mill where there was a ford, and along the bank of the Cherwell, then known as the Water Walk, is now called Addison's Walk after him. A young girl at the mill was later the subject of T. E. Brown's poem 'An Oxford Idyll'.

William Collins, who came up in 1741, was a friend of Gilbert White of Oriel. *Persian Eclogues* (1742), his first volume of verse, was well received, but his health was poor and he suffered a mental breakdown while he was here. Edward Gibbon became a Catholic after some 'unprofitable' months here (1752–3) and his father sent him to Lausanne. He poured much scorn on the Fellows who he said 'had absolved their conscience' from 'the toil of reading, or thinking, or writing'. H. J. Pye, an under-graduate in the 1760s, was later Poet Laureate and a constant butt for ridicule. James Hurdis, who graduated in 1782 and was made a Fellow in 1786, tried to vindicate academic life here from Gibbon's gibes. His long poem *The Village Curate* (1788) was written here but it is based on his years at Burwash (q.v.). He was made Professor of Poetry in 1793 and took a house at Temple Cowley (2 m. E.) with his two sisters during terms and lived also at Bishopstone (q.v.).

R. S. Hawker, whose studies at Pembroke had been interrupted by his marriage, trans-ferred here in 1824. 'The Song of the Western Men', published anonymously and usually referred to by the first line 'A good sword and a trusty hand', was written in the vacation in 1825 and many critics, including Scott and Dickens, thought it a 17th-c. song. Hawker won the Newdigate Prize in 1827 with 'Pompeii'. On a later visit to Oxford he was the object of a practical joke, which gave him a poor opinion of Matthew Arnold, the perpetrator.

Charles Reade, an undergraduate from 1831 to 1835, became a Fellow in 1838 but spent much of his time in London. *Masks and Faces* (1851), a popular play which he rewrote as the novel *Peg Woffington* (1852), and *The Cloister and the Hearth*, his novel about 15th-c. Europe, preceded others which he wrote to promote social change. He entertained Marian Evans (George Eliot) in his rooms, painted deep blue to simulate tropical sea and sky, though it was thought he admired her more for her unconventional life than for her writing. J. A. Symonds was elected a Fellow in 1862 and the next year won the Chancellor's Essay Prize with 'The Renaissance', but he was soon forced by ill health to go abroad, where he spent most of his life. Oscar Wilde, an undergraduate from

1874 to 1878, whose rooms faced E., over the kitchens, won the Newdigate Prize with his poem 'Ravenna'. He was the founder of an aesthetic cult whose members were caricatured as those who were 'anxious for to shine in the high aesthetic line' in the Gilbert and Sullivan opera *Patience* (1881). A. D. Godley, who was a Fellow (1883–1912) and Public Orator (1910–25), wrote three volumes of light verse, *Verses to Order* (1892), *Lyra Frivola* (1899), and *Fifty Poems* (1927). Many poems are about life in the University. T. E. Lawrence first travelled to the Middle East when he was a Senior Demy (1910–14). Compton Mackenzie, in his novel *Sinister Street* (2 vols., 1913–14), describes life in the first decade of the 20th c. when he was an undergraduate.

C. S. Lewis, a Fellow (1924–54) until he became a Professor at Cambridge, wrote here *The Allegory of Love: a Study in Medieval Tradition* (1936) and *English Literature in the Sixteenth Century*, Vol. III in the *Oxford History of English Literature* (1954). As well as literary criticism C. S. Lewis wrote works on religious and moral themes including *The Pilgrim's Regress* (1933), *The Problem of Pain* (1940), and *The Screwtape Letters* (1942). His versatility was also shown by science fiction novels one of which, *That Hideous Strength* (1945), gives an account of a college meeting, and the very popular stories for children which include *The Lion, the Witch and the Wardrobe* (1950). He lived in college and also had a house in Kiln Lane, Headington Quarry.

Magdalen Hall (*c.* 1487). Thomas Hobbes, author of *The Leviathan* (1651), was an undergraduate 1603–8. Edward Hyde, author of *History of the Great Rebellion*, graduated B.A. in 1626.

In September 1817 John Keats shared his friend Benjamin Bailey's rooms for a fort-night. He worked each morning on *Endy-mion* and in the afternoons he and Bailey took a punt on the Isis and tied up among the rushes. They named one secluded spot 'Reynolds's Cove' after their friend John Reynolds, whose sister Bailey was hoping to marry. Keats enjoyed his visit and enclosed a poem on Oxford, a parody of Wordsworth's 'The Cock is crowing', in his letter to Rey-nolds. George Gleig, who had fought in the Peninsula and in America, was a con-temporary of Bailey here. Gleig, ordained in

1820, was the author of *The Subaltern* (1826). Bailey later married his sister. Magdalen Hall was burnt down after a party in 1820 (site now St. Swithun's Quad, Magdalen College) and the student body was later incorporated in Hertford College.

Martyrs' Memorial (1841), St. Giles'. This Gothic pinnacled memorial commemorates the Protestant martyrs, Thomas Cranmer, Hugh Latimer, and Nicholas Ridley. They were held in Bocardo, a prison over Cornmarket by the North Gate in the city wall (a restored bastion of the wall can be seen behind shops at the SW. corner of Broad St.). Latimer and Ridley were burnt alive in the ditch outside the wall (site marked with a concrete cross let into the surface of Broad St.) in 1555, and Cranmer was burnt the next year.

Merton College (1264), incorporating St. Alban Hall. Thomas Bodley became a Fellow in 1564 and M.A. in 1566. He was buried in the chapel with great ceremony according to instructions in his will. A memorial by Nicholas Stone was erected in 1615. Philip Massinger and Thomas Carew followed one another, as undergraduates, in the first decade of the 17th c. Anthony Wood, who was born (1632) at his father's house near the college and attended New College School (1641–4), was an undergraduate from 1647 to 1652, when he was given a bible clerkship. He collected much information on Oxford for *Historia et Antiquitates Univ. Oxon.* (1674). He spent most of his time shut away in his father's house in a closet-like room he constructed by the chimney in the garret. There he maintained a long correspondence with John Aubrey on, as well as other topics, his biographical dictionary of Oxford scholars, *Athenae Oxonienses* (1691–2), which contained such unfavourable judgements on Lord Clarendon that his son brought an action and Wood was expelled from the University. *The Life and Times* was even more bitter and Wood complains of the vice and the 'decay of learning', the 'multitudes of ale-houses' and the 'harlots, pimps and panders, bawds and buffoons, lechery and treachery, atheists and papists' with which the place abounds. Wood, who called himself à Wood towards the end of his life, died in the garret which his father had bequeathed him and is buried

in the ante-chapel, which contains his memorial as well as Bodley's, which was moved from the chapel.

Richard Steele, who had been at Christ Church, transferred here in August 1691 but did not stay long. He left in March 1692 and the next year he was commissioned in the Duke of Ormonde's Regiment of Life Guards.

Andrew Lang, best known for his collections of fairy stories such as the *Blue Fairy Book*, was a Fellow (1868–75). George Saintsbury, an undergraduate from 1863 to 1866, who became a literary critic and historian, was elected an hon. Fellow in 1909. Max Beerbohm, who was an undergraduate from 1891 to 1894, contributed some essays to *Isis* and other university publications. Many of his drawings, letters, and books are now on show in the Beerbohm Room in Mob Quad. His novel *Zuleika Dobson* (1911) describes the disastrous effect that his beautiful heroine has on all the undergraduates in Oxford, before she asks her maid to look up the next train to Cambridge. H. W. Garrod, who educated himself and won the Newdigate Prize, was elected a Fellow in 1901 and remained here until his death in 1960. He published *Oxford Poems* in 1912, and was Professor of Poetry 1923–8. Many of his lectures were published. T. S. Eliot came here in 1914–15 after Harvard and was made an hon. Fellow in 1949.

Louis MacNeice describes his years as an undergraduate (1926–30) in *The Strings are False* (1965), his unfinished autobiography. His first volume of poems, *Blind Fireworks* (1929), was published the year before his marriage at Carfax Registry Office (gone), and his acceptance of a lectureship at Birmingham. Cantos 12 and 13 of *Autumn Sequel* (1954) are set in Oxford.

Edmund Blunden, formerly an undergraduate at Queen's, was a Fellow from 1931 to 1943. He published *Poems 1930–40* (1940) and *Shells by a Stream* (1944) while here. John Mulgan, the New Zealand novelist, read English Literature under Blunden from 1933 to 1935 and then joined the Clarendon Press in Walton St. He compiled an anthology, *Poems of Freedom* (1938), published a novel with a New Zealand background *Man Alone* (1939), and joined the Oxfordshire and Buckinghamshire Light Infantry in 1939. *Report on Experience* (1947), an autobiographical work, was published after his death in Cairo in 1945. Keith

Douglas, an undergraduate who also had Blunden as tutor from 1938 until called up in 1940 for war service, wrote many poems in Oxford, most of them published in the wartime Oxford magazine *Kingdom Come*. He edited *Cherwell*, the undergraduate journal, and helped to prepare *Augury*, an Oxford miscellany of verse and prose. He was killed in Normandy in 1944.

J. R. R. Tolkien was a Fellow and Merton Professor of English Language and Literature from 1945 to 1959. His trilogy *The Lord of the Rings* was completed in 1955.

New College (1379). William Grocyn studied here and became a Fellow in 1467. He was one of the scholars who introduced the study of Greek to the University. Henry Wotton left after 2 years (1584–6) to go to Queen's College. William Somerville, who became a Fellow when he graduated in 1693, joined the Middle Temple 3 years later. He is remembered for *The Chace* (1735), a long poem in blank verse on various aspects of hunting and management of hounds. William Harrison was elected a Fellow here at his own college in 1706 and it was probably soon after that he wrote the poem 'Woodstock Park' (see Woodstock). Harrison died young of a fever while still a Fellow and Thomas Tickell of Queen's wrote of him as 'that much lov'd youth'.

James Woodforde, an undergraduate from 1759 to 1763, was ordained deacon at Christ Church Cathedral. In *Diary of a Country Parson* (5 vols. 1924–31) he writes that he played cricket on Port Meadow, the 300-acre open space NW. of the city, and that he went to shoot in Stanton Woods (NE.) with the 'Masters'. Woodforde returned in 1773 as Fellow and Sub-Warden. His hope for a college living was answered when he was made rector of Weston Long-ville (q.v.). When on the annual journeys from his rectory to holidays in his native Somerset he stayed at the Angel Inn (site now the Examination Schools in the High St.) or at the Blue Boar (site now the Town Hall).

Sydney Smith, an undergraduate from 1789, became a Fellow in 1791 but left no witty sayings about his time here. Thomas Warton, Fellow of Trinity and Poet Laureate, wrote in 1789 'Verses on Sir Joshua Reynolds's Painted Window at New College'. This window, in the ante-chapel, has a painting of the Nativity in the upper lights, and a row of figures representing the Virtues in the lower.

Lionel Johnson and John Galsworthy were undergraduate contemporaries in the 1880s. Johnson's poem 'Oxford' from *Poems* (1895) has the lines:

> There, Shelley dreamed his white Platonic dreams;
> There, classic Landor throve on Roman thought;
> There, Addison pursued his quiet themes;
> There, smiled Erasmus, and there, Colet taught.
> That is the Oxford, strong to charm us yet:
> Eternal in her beauty and her past.
> What though her soul be vexed? She can forget
> Cares of an hour: only the great things last.

Galsworthy is commemorated by a plaque in the cloisters. R. C. Sherriff, author of the play *Journey's End* (1929), who spent 2 years here (1932–4) as a mature student, founded a scholarship in English Literature at the college.

Oriel College (1326) including St. Mary's Hall. Walter Ralegh was a member of the college (1568–9) but though Anthony Wood, the antiquary, wrote he was 'worthily esteemed', little is really known of his life here. John Taylor, 'the water-poet', lived in college during the plague in 1625 and was here again in the Civil War, when he saw the surrender of the city in 1645.

Gilbert White, an undergraduate from 1740 to 1743, was elected to a Fellowship (1744–55) and he became a Proctor and Dean of the college. His friend Mulso introduced him to his sister, Hester (later Chapone), to whom he proposed marriage but was refused. White was also a friend of William Collins of Magdalen.

J. H. Newman, who became a Fellow in 1822, was one of the founders of the Oxford or Tractarian Movement. He was appointed vicar of St. Mary's parish which included Littlemore (3 m. E.), where, until his new parsonage was built, he stayed in a cottage which later became the George Inn. His sermons at St. Mary's have been published and his *Apologia pro Vita sua* (1864), which gives an account of his spiritual history, in answer to Charles Kingsley's charges, is considered a masterpiece. His novel *Loss and Gain* (1848) contains an account of an Oxford breakfast at a tutor's, formerly a well-established institution but now generally discontinued. J. A. Froude, who won the Chancellor's Essay Prize and graduated in 1842, became a Fellow of Exeter. T. E. Brown, who was elected a Fellow in 1853 after being considered ineligible at his own college, stayed here only 5 years before returning to his native Isle of Man. Arthur Hugh Clough, who was a friend of Matthew Arnold at Rugby, and who preceded him as an undergraduate at Balliol, was a Fellow here from 1841 to 1848. His poem *The Bothie of Tober-na-Vuolich: A Long Vacation Pastoral* written in 1848 was considered by many, perhaps those satirized in it, as 'indecent & profane, immoral & (!) Communistic' as Clough himself recorded to a friend. Thomas Hughes, who also came from Rugby, was an undergraduate (1842–5) who can hardly be separated from his novel *Tom Brown at Oxford* (1861), a sequel to the hero's schooldays at Rugby. Matthew Arnold, son of the headmaster eulogized in Hughes's school story, was a Fellow here from 1845 to 1847. *Poems* (1853) contains 'The Scholar-Gipsy', based on the tale of an Oxford scholar, whom poverty 'forced to leave his studies', first recounted in Glanvill's *The Vanity of Dogmatizing* (1661). Arnold's poem describes the peaceful rural haunts of the scholar who wandered near by in North Hinksey and on Cumnor Hill in a former golden age

> O born in days when wits were fresh and clear,
> And life ran gaily as the sparkling Thames;
> Before this strange disease of modern life,
> With its sick hurry, its divided aims
> Its heads o'ertaxed, its palsied hearts, was rife.

Arnold gives another nostalgic description in his preface to *Essays in Criticism* (1865)

> Beautiful city! so venerable, so lovely, so unravaged by the fierce intellectual life of our century, so serene! . . . whispering from her towers the last enchantments of the Middle Age. . . . Home of lost causes, and forsaken beliefs, and unpopular names, and impossible loyalties!

Arnold's poem 'Thyrsis' in *New Poems* (1867), was written to commemorate his friend Clough, who died in Florence aged 42, and contains many references to the places they had visited together.

Pembroke College (1624). This college, which includes the earlier Broadgates Hall and Beef Hall, retains a connection with Abingdon School. Francis Beaumont, the dramatist, entered Broadgates Hall in 1597, but left a year later, after his father's death.

Thomas Browne studied medicine here and became an M.A. in 1629. He practised for a short while in the county, was made an M.D. in 1637, and then settled in Norwich (q.v.).

Samuel Johnson came up in 1728 and had rooms on the second floor over the gateway. He had hoped to eke out the small amount of money he had by sharing the rooms of a friend. This friend left Oxford before Johnson could benefit and, after 14 months, he was forced to leave the University. Johnson always thought of Oxford with pleasure and often returned. In 1754 he came with Hannah More, whom he showed over the college, and he stayed with his friend Thomas Warton of Trinity. He came again in 1755. It was a college tutor here whom he afterwards quoted as saying 'Read over your compositions, and where ever you meet with a passage which you think is particularly fine, strike it out'. The college still has his desk, some of his books, a portrait by Reynolds, and his teapot.

Richard Graves was a friend and contemporary of William Shenstone in the 1730s. Shenstone appears in Graves's novels *Columella* (1776) and *The Spiritual Quixote* (1772, reprinted 1967), in which another contemporary, George Whitefield, the Methodist, is satirized. Thomas Lovell Beddoes, who came up in 1820, wrote *The Improvisatore* (1821), tales in verse, followed by *The Bride's Tragedy* (1822), a drama, which like his other works has an obsession with death. Beddoes graduated in 1825, the year he began *Death's Jest Book*, a play which features such Gothic elements as a sepulchre, a charnel-house, a poisoned goblet, and a spectre. Beddoes spent most of the last 25 years of his life revising the play, mainly in Zurich. The lyrics and some of the blank-verse passages are very fine.

R. S. Hawker came up in 1823 but his studies here ended when he married. The woman of his choice was 20 years older than himself, and their marriage proved a happy one. Hawker transferred to Magdalen in 1824. J. R. R. Tolkien, Professor of Anglo-Saxon and a Fellow (1926–45), wrote during this time, as well as critical works on *Beowulf* and Beorhtnoth, the novel *The Hobbit* (1937), the first of a series, which have a strange mythology invented by himself.

The Queen's College (1341). This college elected many of its early scholars and Fellows from the old counties of Cumberland and Westmorland. Henry Wotton came to Queen's from New College in 1586. The play *Tancredo*, which he wrote for a performance in the college, was based on Tasso's *Gerusalemme Liberata* (1581), and brought him to the notice of Alberico Gentile, the Professor of Civil Law, a connection of use to him in his future diplomatic career. John Davies from Wiltshire, a student from 1585 to 1590, returned to Oxford in 1598 after attacking a colleague in the Middle Temple. He composed *Nosce Teipsum* (1599) here, a philosophical poem discussing the vanity of acquiring knowledge without also cultivating the mind and the soul. Thomas Middleton entered in 1598 and his early poems, *The Wisdom of Solomon Paraphrased* (1597), *Micro-Cynicon* (1599), and *The Ghost of Lucrece* (1600), written here, have none of the power of his later plays. Little is known of his life here but later he described, perhaps from his own experience, a poor scholar who, while servant to a rich Londoner, 'kept his study warm' while he was playing tennis 'and sucked the honey of wit from the flowers of Aristotle' by reading his employer's books.

William Wycherley, who came in 1659, stayed a short time only and left before passing the entrance requirements. Joseph Addison spent a short time here before obtaining a demyship at Magdalen in 1689. Thomas Tickell became an M.A. in 1709 after publishing his poem 'Oxford' in 1707, and in 1711 was elected Professor of Poetry over the heads, it was thought, of more worthy candidates. His *On the Prospect of Peace* (1712) was noticed by Addison and Pope, and led to his contributing to the *Guardian* and *Spectator* and to his getting a post in Ireland under Addison. William Collins spent a short time here in 1740 before going as a demy to Magdalen. William Gilpin became an M.A. here in 1748 and later wrote lives of the Oxford martyrs, *Latimer* (1755), *Wycliffe* (1765), and *Cranmer* (1784), though he is chiefly remembered for his popular illustrated tours.

Walter Pater graduated B.A. in 1862 before becoming a Fellow of Brasenose.

Edmund Blunden was an undergraduate (1919–23) after serving in the First World War. He published three volumes of verse before becoming Professor of English Literature at Tokyo University (1924–7). Thomas Hardy was made an hon. Fellow here in 1922. He had visited Oxford for a performance of *The Dynasts* by O.U.D.S. in 1920, when an hon. D.Litt. was conferred on him. Sidney Keyes, an undergraduate from 1940 to 1942, who had started to write poetry at school, published *Iron Laurel* (1942) and *Cruel Solstice* (1943) before his death in the N. African campaign in 1943. These volumes were then published as *Collected Poems* (1945).

St. Edmund Hall (13th c.). Thomas Hearne, the antiquary, was educated here (B.A. 1699, M.A. 1703) through the influence of Francis Cherry, a non-juror, who had the similar interests of a bibliophile. Hearne became a Keeper at the Bodleian Library but lost his post when he, as a Jacobite, refused to take the oath of allegiance to George I. He published *Reliquiae Bodleianae* (1703), and a large number of medieval texts and chronicles. His diaries contain diatribes on the decay of learning. His tombstone can be seen in the near-by churchyard of St. Peter in the East (now the college library).

St. John's College (1555). James Shirley came here in 1612 from the Merchant Taylors' School but soon transferred to Cambridge. Abraham Cowley, who had been at Cambridge, migrated here in the Civil War. During his 2 years here (1644–6) his friend, the physician William Harvey, was made Warden of Merton. A. E. Housman, who came up with a scholarship in 1877, took a First in Honour Moderations, but failed in his hopes of getting a good degree in 1881.

St. Mary the Virgin (13th–14th c.). St. Mary's, the University Church in the High St., has a tablet in the sanctuary to Amy Dudley, who died (1560) at Cumnor (q.v.). She was the wife of Lord Leicester, Queen Elizabeth's favourite. All three are characters in Scott's novel *Kenilworth* (1821). The martyrs Cranmer, Latimer, and Ridley were condemned as heretics after a long interrogation by the University clergy in this church in 1554.

Somerville College (1879). Rose Macaulay was the first of a group of writers who were up c. 1910 to 1915. Her satirical novel

Potterism (1920) was the first of her successes. Dorothy L. Sayers, who was born (1893) in Oxford where her father was headmaster of the Cathedral School, came up with a scholarship in 1912. Her detective novel *Gaudy Night* (1935), set in an imaginary women's college, which she places apologetically on Balliol's cricket ground, has the two main characters Oxford-educated with first class degrees like herself. The sequel, *Busman's Honeymoon* (1936), in which the two characters marry, also has some scenes in Oxford. Dorothy Sayers, who became a publisher's reader at Blackwell's, published two volumes of poetry, and edited *Oxford Poetry* from 1917 to 1919, when she left Oxford.

Vera Brittain, who described Dorothy Sayers as an 'exuberant young female', who always seemed to be preparing for parties, mentions her own years here in *Testament of Youth* (1933) and *Testament of Friendship* (1940), the latter a tribute to the friend, Winifred Holtby, whom she met here. Winifred Holtby, who is chiefly remembered by *South Riding* (1936), a novel about her native Yorkshire, also wrote the earlier novels *The Land of Green Ginger* (1927) and *Poor Caroline* (1931), as well as short stories and a study of Virginia Woolf (1932). Another contemporary was Margaret Kennedy, who made her name with *The Constant Nymph* (1924), which was also very popular when dramatized. Helen Waddell, whose novel *Peter Abelard* (1933) brought her medieval scholarship before a wide public, was a Research Fellow here (1920-2).

Trinity College (1555). Thomas Lodge, an undergraduate from 1573 to 1577, left to enter Lincoln's Inn. He returned to study medicine and became an M.D. in 1603. John Denham entered in 1631 but left soon after to study law, and 10 years later John Aubrey spent a short time here, but left in 1643 because of smallpox and civil war. In June 1697, passing through Oxford to stay with his friend Lady Long, he died suddenly and was buried in the church of St. Mary Magdalen (tablet in the S. chapel). Aubrey's short biographies of his contemporaries, first published in 1813 and now known as *Brief Lives*, were used by Anthony Wood of Merton (q.v.).

Elkanah Settle came up in 1666 but left without taking a degree. Shortly afterwards his version of the historical tragedy, *Cambyses, King of Persia*, was performed in London. After success there it was acted in Oxford.

Thomas Warton, younger son of Thomas Warton, Professor of Poetry (1718-28), came up in 1744 and was made a Fellow in 1751. He wrote *The Pleasures of Melancholy* and other verses while an undergraduate. *The Triumphs of Isis* (1749), which made his name, was a reply to the aspersions William Mason of Cambridge had made on the University in *Isis* (1748). Warton contributed poems to many Oxford periodicals, wrote an ode for the Encaenia which was set to music, and edited the Oxford anthologies, *The Union* (1753) and *The Oxford Sausage* (1764). He also wrote an amusing satire on guide books, *A Companion to the Guide* (1760). His friendship with Dr. Johnson began after the publication of *Observations on the Faerie Queene of Spenser* (1754), which Johnson thought outstanding. Warton was Johnson's host on his visit that summer and was helpful in getting him made M.A. the next year. Johnson and Boswell both came in 1776 when Johnson received an LL.D. Warton was one of the earliest to appreciate Gothic architecture again and led the way for the Romantic Movement's admiration. He wrote the life of Dr. Ralph Bathurst, a President of the College, and that of Sir Thomas Pope, the founder, though this latter was thought tedious by Horace Walpole. He died (1790) in a chair in the S.C.R. and is buried in the ante-chapel. The chair and his portrait, painted by his friend Sir Joshua Reynolds, are in the Old Library.

William Lisle Bowles, who graduated in 1792, wrote one of his many sonnets to the river Cherwell with its 'willow'd edge'. Walter Savage Landor came up in 1793 but quarrelled with the authorities and was rusticated for a year, by which time his father had died and he could not return.

J. H. Newman was an undergraduate here (1816-20) and in 1822 became a Fellow of Oriel. A bust of him is in the college garden. Richard Burton, Arabic scholar and explorer, came up in 1840 after having spent many years abroad with his parents. He left without graduating and joined the Indian Army in 1842. Sir Arthur Quiller-Couch, an undergraduate here from 1882 to 1886, became a lecturer in classics

(1886-7). He edited *The Oxford Book of English Verse* (1900) and *The Oxford Book of Ballads* (1910) and then became a Professor of English Literature at Cambridge. Laurence Binyon was here from 1887 to 1890. His first volume of verse, *Lyric Poems* (1894), was published when he took up an appointment at the British Museum.

James Elroy Flecker came up with a scholarship in 1902. Some of his poems, including 'Oxford Canal', 'I have Sung all Love's great Songs', and 'Roses and Rain', were included in *The Best Man*, a paperback volume published in 1906. Some were also included in *Bridge of Fire* (1907). He was disappointed at getting a third class degree. Joyce Cary, an undergraduate here from 1909 to 1912, returned to Oxford after resigning from the Colonial Service because of ill health in 1920. He settled at 12 Parks Rd., where he wrote a succession of novels including *Aissa Saved* (1932), *The African Witch* (1936), *Mr. Johnson* (1939), *Charley is My Darling* (1940), *The Horse's Mouth* (1944), and *Not Honour More* (1955). Cary, who became paralysed, died in 1957 and is buried in Wolvercote cemetery ($2\frac{1}{2}$ m. N.).

Ronald Knox became a Fellow here in 1910. After ordination in 1912 he was chaplain until his conversion to Catholicism. He was Catholic chaplain to the University from 1926 to 1939, and lived in the Old Palace in St. Aldate's. He wrote *Essays in Satire* (1928), *Let Dons Delight* (1939), other essays, and a number of detective stories.

University College (1249), commonly known as Univ., was reputedly founded by Alfred the Great. Dr. Johnson dined here with Boswell in 1776, on visiting Oxford to receive the honorary degree of LL.D., and later said that he drank three bottles of port without feeling the worse for it.

Percy Bysshe Shelley's year here in 1810 was described by Thomas Jefferson Hogg, his contemporary, in the *New Monthly Magazine* in 1832. As undergraduates they had written together 'Posthumous Fragments of Margaret Nicholson' and taken part in a number of hair-raising experiments, which left Shelley's hands and clothes marked with chemicals. They walked about Shotover Hill (3 m. E.), and Shelley indulged in his habit of sailing paper boats. He was sent down when he sent a copy of his pamphlet, 'The

Necessity of Atheism', to the Master and other heads of colleges, and refused to admit it was his. Hogg protested and was also expelled. Shelley's death by drowning near Spezia in Italy in 1822 was not commemorated until 1893, when a marble memorial was erected under a dome in a corner of the main quad.

Edwin Arnold, an undergraduate from 1851 to 1854, won the Newdigate Prize in 1852 with 'Belshazzar's Feast', which was published in his *Poems Narrative and Lyrical* (1853). He went to India as Principal of the College of the Deccan in 1856, and his long poem, *The Light of Asia* (1879), on the life of Buddha, coincided with an interest in Eastern religious thought, and proved very popular. After his death in 1904, his ashes were deposited in the chapel. C. S. Lewis came up in 1917 and enlisted within a short time. He resumed his studies after he was demobilized in January 1919.

Wadham College (1610). Shakerley Marmion, a young dramatist patronized by Ben Jonson, took his M.A. in 1624, and then fought in the Netherlands. Charles Sedley came up in 1656 and John Wilmot, 2nd Earl of Rochester, entered in 1660. They became intimate friends at Court later. Rochester gave the college four silver tankards. John Gauden came to Wadham after being at St. John's, Cambridge. He was made a D.D. in 1641.

L. A. G. Strong, a classical scholar during the First World War, left in 1917, before taking his degree, to join the staff of Summer Fields, a prep school in North Oxford, to replace the men who had enlisted. He graduated after the war but returned to the school to teach. During his time here he met many writers who were in Oxford, including L. P. Hartley, A. E. Coppard, Roy Campbell, and Yeats, who was living opposite Balliol. Strong was able to leave teaching when his novel *Dewer Rides* (1929) was accepted and proved successful. C. Day-Lewis came up in 1923 already writing verse and in 1927 edited *Oxford Poetry* with W. H. Auden, and published his own poems, *Country Comets*, the next year. He describes his time here in *The Buried Day* (1960). He taught (1927-8) at Summer Fields (Strong had told him of the vacancy) and lived in a room over the gate lodge. He was elected Professor of Poetry (1951-5).

Worcester College (1714), which includes the earlier Gloucester Hall, is the only college with a lake. Thomas Coryate came here in 1596 but little is known of his life until he was appointed court jester to Prince Henry's household. Kenelm Digby, whose father had been executed for treason in 1606, spent 2 years (1618–20) here before he went to Paris. Richard Lovelace, who came up in 1634, was made much of by the courtiers on Charles I's stay in 1636, and was made an M.A. by the Chancellor, Archbishop Laud, before he had finished his studies. Lovelace joined Sir John Suckling's troop to fight in Scotland in 1639. Samuel Foote, who came up in 1737, managed to dissipate a large fortune here before leaving to read for the Bar.

Thomas de Quincey, who spent his time wandering about the country and almost starved in London after running away from school, decided to study at Oxford and arrived to choose a college in December 1803. He settled on Worcester after trying Christ Church, as he found the 'caution money', a sum of money demanded as a surety of good behaviour, was lower here, and his allowance was meagre. He led an isolated life here, reading German philosophy and learning the language, and buying the latest works in English. He wrote to Wordsworth, whose *Lyrical Ballads* (with Coleridge) were 'so twisted with my heart strings'. De Quincey's health was poor, however; he felt himself doomed by consumption and while low spirited over the disappearance of his brother he bought some opium in London to relieve the pain of neuralgia. The dreams that resulted he later recorded in *Suspiria de Profundis* (1847). He left Oxford without a degree before his viva, in spite of his belief that he had written well in the examination, in May 1808.

Henry Kingsley, younger brother of Charles, led an exuberant life as an undergraduate in 1850, left the college without a degree, and spent some years in the Australian gold-fields and in the mounted police in Sydney. An early chapter of *Ravenshoe* (1861) describes the process of rustication from an Oxford college.

The family press run by Dr. Charles Daniel, Fellow from 1863 and Provost (1903–19), was active here intermittently from 1874 to 1906.

OXNEAD, Norf. [4 Gc] Hamlet 3 m. SE. of Aylsham, off the B1354, near Burgh. William Paston (1378–1444), the 'Good Judge', one of Fuller's *Worthies*, inherited the manor by marrying Agnes Berry, who wrote many of the *Paston Letters*. One low, red-brick wing of the Tudor house remains. The church has a memorial to Clement Paston, a sea-captain (d. 1597).

OXTED, Surrey. [1 Ed] Small town on the A25, 7 m. E. of Redhill. In 1897 the American novelist, Stephen Crane, and Lady Cora Stewart lived at Ravensbrook House (now flats) at the foot of Snats Hill, to the N. of the town. Crane, who had made his name with *The Red Badge of Courage* (1895), a realistic novel of the American Civil War, published two volumes of short stories, *The Open Boat* (1898) and *The Monster* (1899).

OYSTERMOUTH, West Glamorgan. [2 Ea] Village 5 m. SW. of Swansea on the road to the Mumbles. On the W. side of the churchyard is the grave of Dr. Thomas Bowdler, whose *Family Shakespeare* (1818), an expurgated edition 'in which those words and expressions are omitted which cannot with propriety be read aloud in a family', gave rise to the verb 'to bowdlerize'.

P

PADSTOW, Cornwall. [2 Be] Picturesque resort, formerly a port, on the A389, on the estuary of the Camel. On South Quay is Ralegh's Court House, where Sir Walter Ralegh held court when he was Warden of Cornwall (from 1585).

D. H. Lawrence came here after leaving London in December 1915 and stayed at his friend J. D. Beresford's house, Porthcothan, St. Merryn (2 m. W., on the B3276), until the following March. He had plans (which never materialized) to settle in Florida with a group of like-minded people, and this was meant to be the first step on the way. 'The wind blows very hard', he wrote, 'the sea all comes up the cliffs in smoke.' In January they had a visit from Dikrān Kouyoumdjian, the Bulgarian novelist who became a naturalized British citizen in 1922 and changed his name to Michael Arlen. In *Women in Love* (1920) Arlen is lampooned as a minor character.

PAIGNTON, Devon. [2 Ee] Seaside resort, with a small harbour, overlooking Tor Bay, on the A379 and the A385. The 14th-c. Coverdale Tower, which was part of the palace belonging to the bishops of Exeter, was once thought to be where Miles Coverdale stayed while working on his translation of the Bible, but this is now regarded as an exploded myth, originating in some anonymous guide book. Coverdale was appointed by Edward VI, on account of 'his extraordinary knowledge of divinity and his unblemished character', to be assistant to Vesey, the last Bishop of Exeter to hold Paignton, but it is doubtful whether he ever visited the town.

PAIN'S HILL. See COBHAM, Surrey.

PAINSWICK, Glos. [2 Ha] Village on the A46, 3 m. NE. of Stroud. Sydney Dobell, who died in 1874, spent the last years of his life at Barton End House, Horsley (8 m. SW.) and his grave in the churchyard here has a Celtic cross. James Elroy Flecker, whose home was in Cheltenham, mentions Cranham (3 m. NE.), where he spent some months in a sanatorium in 1910 after the diagnosis of tuberculosis, and Painswick Hill in the poem 'Oak and Olive' from *The Old Ships* (1915).

PAISLEY, Renfrews. (Strathclyde). [6 Dc] Industrial town on the west of Glasgow. Alexander Wilson, born here in 1766, became a weaver like his father. In 1791 he published his first volume of poems, which contained 'Watty and Meg', and then emigrated to America, where he became a schoolmaster near Philadelphia. *The Foresters* (1805), a collection of nature poems, led to his commission for *American Ornithology* (1808–14), a study unfinished at his death (1813). He is commemorated by a statue near Paisley Abbey.

Robert Tannahill, also a weaver, was born (1774) in Castle St., where the house has a plaque with the lines:

> Here Nature first wak'd me to rapture and love
> And taught me her beauties to sing.

Near by at 11 Queen St. is the thatched cottage where he lived from childhood to his death (1810). Most of *Poems and Songs* (1807) had first appeared in Glasgow journals. Tannahill founded a club with a group of friends which met to discuss poetry and music at the Sun Tavern, 12 High St., where James Hogg was their guest. A depressive illness and worry over the delay of a second edition of his poems led to his suicide in the mill stream, known now as Tannahill's Pool, just visible through the railings in Maxwelton St. He is buried in the cemetery. Open-air concerts on Gleniffer Braes, his favourite walk, raised money for his statue erected in 1883 near the abbey. John Wilson ('Christopher North'), son of a rich manufacturer, was born (1785) at 63 High St. and educated at the Grammar School. William Motherwell, while Sheriff-clerk depute of Renfrewshire (1819–29), published a collection of Scottish ballads, *Minstrelsy, Ancient and Modern* (1827), for which he wrote a historical introduction. He also became editor (1828–30) of the *Paisley Advertiser*.

PALGRAVE, Suff. [4 Ge] Village off the A143, 1 m. SW. of Diss. Palgrave House (gone), where Palgrave School had been in Tudor times, was the home of 'honest Tom

Martin' (1697–1771), the antiquary whose collections were published as *The History of Thetford* (1779). Anna Barbauld helped her husband with his school (1774–86) in the same house, which came to be called Barbauld House. She wrote *Hymns in Prose for Children* (1781) and *Evenings at Home*. One pupil was William Taylor, later author of *Historic Survey of German Poetry* (1828–30).

PALLAS, Longford. [8 Ef] Hamlet in the parish of Forgney, 2½ m. W. of Ballymahon, at the end of a minor road off the L121. The Revd. Charles Goldsmith, father of Oliver Goldsmith, rented a dilapidated farmhouse here, farmed the near-by fields, and assisted at the local church of Kilkenny West. Oliver is thought to have been born, probably in 1730, on 10 November, at Pallas, though he may have been born at his maternal grandmother's house, Ardnagowan, near Elphin, where his mother was staying about this time. When he was about 2 his family moved to Lissoy (q.v.). The Pallas building has been demolished, but the site, preserved and well signposted, can be reached by a stile and footpath.

PANGBOURNE, Berks. [1 Cc] Village on the Thames, on the A329. Kenneth Grahame spent his last years here and is commemorated by a decorative sign at the N. end of the main street. *The Wind in the Willows* (1908) shares the sign with the 9th-c. granter of Pangbourne's charter, Berhtulf King of Mercia. Church Cottage, where Grahame lived, is withdrawn from traffic, and its pleasant garden, with the old village round-house now a tool-shed, and a stretch of grass ending in a tree-shaded amphitheatre, may be seen by courtesy of the present owner. E. H. Shepard came here to plan the illustrations for *The Wind in the Willows*, with such success that Pangbourne and its stretch of river became for many readers the veritable home of Rat and Mole.

Jerome K. Jerome's heroes of *Three Men in a Boat* (1889) visited the riverside Swan Hotel.

PANTASAPH, Clwyd. [3 Fa] Village 1 m. S. of the A55, c. 2 m. W. of Holywell. Francis Thompson lived (1893–7) near the Franciscan monastery. He stayed at various places, including the old post office (gone),

the last being Aloysius Cottage (formerly Craecas), up the hill to the N. Most of the poems in *New Poems* (1897) were written here.

PARHAM, Suff. [4 Hf] Village on the B1116, 4 m. SE. of Framlingham. Crabbe, a surgeon's apprentice at Woodbridge (1771–5), first met Sara Elmey, the 'Mira' of his early poems, at Ducking Hall (rebuilt), where she was staying with her uncle, John Tovell. He returned in 1792, with Sara his wife, as Tovell's executor and intended to settle, but her relatives' resentment and the death in quick succession of two of their sons, decided their move. In 1814, after Sara's death, Crabbe spent a day here rambling round the fields and wrote:

The nightbird's song that sweetly floats
On this soft gloom—this balmy air
Brings to the mind her sweeter notes,
When those dear eyes can shine no more.

PARKGATE, Ches. [3 Fa] Village on the B5135 on the W. coast of the Dee estuary, former port for Ireland. It was after leaving here that Milton's friend, Edward King, lamented in 'Lycidas', was drowned when his ship foundered on the way to Dublin, 10 August 1637. Swift referred to his arrival from Dublin in his first letter to Stella (*Journal to Stella*, 1710–13) from Chester in September 1710: 'I got a fall off my horse riding here from Parkgate, but no hurt; the horse understanding falls very well, and lying quietly till I got up.' De Quincey, writing from Ireland to his sister Jane on 3 September 1800, said: 'We shall sail [from Dublin] by the first Parkgate packet.... Parkgate is situated near Chester, on the River Dee, twice as far from Dublin as Holyhead. This passage is very dangerous, ... in general not more than three days ... but sometimes much longer.' The long stretches of sand, subject to tidal flooding, are the scene of Kingsley's poem 'O Mary go and call the cattle home', which first appeared in his novel *Alton Locke* (1850). The hero hears an old air on the piano, 'wild and plaintive, rising and falling like the swell of an Æolian harp upon a distant breeze', and, searching for words to fit it, is inspired by a painting of the sands at the mouth of the Dee and the story of a girl who was drowned bringing home her father's cattle.

PASTON, Norf. [4 Hc] Village on the B1149, 8 m. SE. of Cromer. It was a home of the Paston family, whose letters (1872) tell of the difficulties of life in the Wars of the Roses, the castle sieges, wrangles with powerful neighbours, and a daughter determined to marry beneath her. The site of their house extends NE. of the present Hall (c. 1750), but their old flint barn is still near the church. The tomb of John Paston (d. 1466) in the chancel was brought from Bromholm Priory at Bacton (q.v.) and the ornate effigy of Katherine Paston (d. 1628) has an inscription by John Donne. The church guide includes a short family history. Selections from the letters, edited by Norman Davis, were published in 1958 and (in modern spelling) in 1963. Part I of a complete edition, *The Paston Letters and Papers of the Fifteenth Century*, edited by Norman Davis, was published in 1971 and Part II in 1976.

PEEBLES, Peebles. (Borders). [6 Fd] Quiet country town on the Tweed, on the A72 and the A703. Robert Chambers (1802–71), who with his brother William (1800–83) founded the publishing firm of W. and R. Chambers, Edinburgh, renowned for its encyclopaedia and dictionaries, and wrote a number of books on Scottish history, biography, and literature, was a native and spent his early years here. The brothers were born in a small house (P) in Biggiesknowe, over the bridge and to the right, with a garden running down to the river. The Chambers Institute, now the Peebles Museum,[1] High St., was their gift to the town. At the E. end of High St., on the S. side, a plaque records a building erected on the site of the surgery of Mungo Park (1771–1806), the surgeon, explorer, and author of *Travels in the Interior of Africa* (1799). He settled here as a surgeon in 1801 but was out of his element, and in 1805 set off again for Africa, to explore the Niger.

Bank House, on the corner of High St. near the bridge, was the home of Anna Buchan ('O. Douglas'), author of many novels. Peebles appears as 'Priorsford' in a novel of that name (1932), as well as in several others. She describes the life of her family here in *Unforgettable, Unforgotten* (1943).

[1] Open Mon. to Fri. 10 a.m.–noon, 1.30–4 p.m., 5–7 p.m.; Sat. 10 a.m.–noon, 1.30–5 p.m.

PEEL, I.O.M. [5 Jg] Fishing port and resort on the W. coast, at the mouth of the Neb. The tower known as Fenella's Tower was the place where Fenella, the beautiful girl who was pretending to be a deaf-mute, jumped into the boat in Scott's *Peveril of the Peak* (1823).

PENDOCK, Hereford and Worcester. [3 Gf] Village on the B4708, 8 m. W. of Tewkesbury. William Symonds, who became the rector in 1845 and inherited Pendock Court shortly afterwards, wrote two historical novels about the district. *Malvern Chase* (1881) is set in the Wars of the Roses, and *Hanley Castle* (1883) during the Civil War.

PENICUIK (pr. Pennycŏŏk), Midlothian (Lothian). [6 Fd] Town on the Esk, 8 m. S. of Edinburgh, on the A701. Allan Ramsay (1686–1758) is commemorated by an obelisk in the grounds of Penicuik House[1] (a modern house replacing the original Queen Anne building which was largely destroyed by fire in 1899).

Samuel Rutherford Crockett (1860–1914) was a minister of the Free Church of Scotland here from 1886 to 1895, when he relinquished the ministry to devote himself to writing. He published a book of poems, *Dulce Cor*, in 1887, which attracted the attention of R. L. Stevenson and led to a friendship between the two men. Crockett's collection of short stories of Scottish provincial life, *The Stickit Minister* (1893), dedicated to Stevenson, was immediately popular and was followed by the successful novels, *The Raiders* (1894), *The Lilac Sunbonnet* (1894), and many others. He lived at Bank House, in Penicuik Estate, overlooking the Esk, where he amassed a substantial library, and enjoyed visits from J. M. Barrie, R. L. Stevenson, and Andrew Lang. He moved to Torwood Villa, near Peebles, in 1906.

In the nave of the old church there is a memorial, surmounted by a dog's head in relief, to James Noble, the Howgate carrier, and his wife Ailie, who are buried in the churchyard. They and their dog Rab lived at Howgate, a hamlet to the SE. and are immortalized in Dr. John Brown's story *Rab and his Friends* (1859).

[1] Applications to visit must be made in writing.

PENRITH, Cumbria. [5 Cb] Old market town on the A6, bypassed by the M6. Wordsworth's mother, Ann Cookson, before her marriage to John Wordsworth, lived in her parents' house in the market square. Her father was a linen-draper and lived over his shop (still a draper's store, but rebuilt). As children, William and Dorothy and their brothers used to visit their grandparents and for a time attended a select and old-fashioned little dame school, but the atmosphere of the household was uncongenial and William, who was a high-spirited boy, found his grandparents and his Uncle Kit stern and unsympathetic. After the death of their father (1783) William and his brothers spent their school holidays at Penrith under the supervision of their uncle, who was especially unfriendly to William, with whom he had frequent clashes. Dorothy, who had been living with relations at Halifax after her mother's death in 1778, moved to Penrith in the summer of 1787 and was happy to be with her brothers, especially William, in the holidays. Together they used to explore the countryside, climb Penrith Beacon, and scramble over the ruins of Brougham Castle[1] (1½ m. SE.), and they renewed a friendship, begun in their early schooldays, with Mary Hutchinson and her sisters and youngest brother who, also orphaned, were living with an aunt at Penrith. This friendship laid the foundation of an extraordinarily happy household when William married Mary (1802), and brought her to share his home with Dorothy at Grasmere (q.v.).

[1] Open daily, Sun. from 2 p.m.

PENRYN, Cornwall. [2 Bf] Ancient town at the head of Penryn Creek, on the A39. Shortly after her marriage in 1817 Mrs. Pendarves (later Mrs. Delany) came to live at her husband's home, the manor of Roscrow (demolished 1890), overlooking Falmouth harbour and Pendennis Castle. Her marriage was not happy and the house, which she called 'Averno' because its situation made her think of Italy, was 'old, damp, and poorly furnished, with floor boards pulled up to get at the rats', but she enjoyed the company of her brother, Bunny, with whom she explored the neighbourhood on horseback. They rode together on the sands and gathered shells—a pastime which led to the making of the 'shell-pictures' for which she became renowned.

PENSHURST PLACE, Kent. [1 Fd] Country house 4 m. SW. of Tonbridge, off the A26.

The Great Hall, which has a 60-ft. high roof of chestnut beams, was begun in 1339 and added to in the 15th c. One of the owners was Humphrey of Gloucester (d. 1447), the Duke Humphrey who bequeathed his library to Oxford University. Later the estate was given by the young Edward VI to Sir William Sidney, grandfather of Philip and Robert Sidney, who were born and spent part of their youth here. As a boy Philip accompanied his father to Ireland and Wales and later attended Queen Elizabeth's court in the hope of employment, but between whiles spent his time at Penshurst or Wilton (q.v.), his sister's home. He inherited the estate while he was Governor of Flushing in the Netherlands, and died soon afterwards from wounds received in an attack on the Spaniards at Zutphen. His younger brother Robert, also employed at court and on foreign missions, spent more time here and added the Long Gallery and the Nether Gallery to the house. In 'To Penshurst' from The Forest (1612) Ben Jonson, a frequent visitor, describes the groves, the mount, the river, and the oak tree planted when Philip Sidney was born, and then comes nearer the house:

Then hath thy orchard fruit, thy garden flowers,
The early cherry with the later plum,
Fig, grape and quince, each in his turn doth come:
The blushing apricot and woolly peach
Hang on thy walls, that every child may reach.

Jonson writes that the informal hospitality of Sir Robert and his wife makes Penshurst a pleasure to visit. Their eldest daughter, Mary, married here in 1604 the newly knighted Sir Robert Wroth of Loughton (q.v.). Robert Sidney is thought by some to have written the words for A Musicall Banquet (1610) of his godson, Robert Dowland, and he is now known to be the author of a notebook containing songs, sonnets, and longer poems dedicated to his sister, which has recently been found to be in his handwriting. Robert Sidney's granddaughter, Dorothy, was courted here by Edmund Waller, who called her Dorothea, or Sacharissa, in the poems he wrote to her, addressed to her portrait, to her sister Lucy, and to her maid. While walking about the estate he wrote:

Ye lofty beeches, tell this matchless dame,
That if together ye fed all one flame,
It could not equalise the hundredth part
Of what her eyes have kindled in my heart!

However, in 1639 she married Lord Spencer, later Earl of Sunderland.

John Evelyn visited in the summer of 1652 and wrote in his *Diary* (1955) that the place was

famous once for its Gardens and excellent fruit: and for the noble conversation which was wont to meete there, celebrated by that illustrious person Sir Phil. Sidny, who there composed divers of his pieces. It stands also in a park, is finely water'd: and was now full of Company, upon the marriage of my old fellow-collegiate, Mr. Robert Smith, who married my Lady Dorothy Sidny, widdow of the Earle of Sunderland.

There are many portraits in the house, including those of Philip Sidney, Robert Sidney and his wife, their sister, the Countess of Pembroke, and Dorothy, Countess of Sunderland. Philip Sidney's helmet, carried at his funeral in St. Paul's, is displayed in the Great Hall. Monuments to other members of the family are in the small parish church near by.

Open Easter Sat. to last Sun. in Sept. daily except Mon. and Fri.: 2–6 p.m.; from 1 p.m. from July. Bank Holidays 11.30 a.m.–6 p.m.

PENZANCE, Cornwall. [2 Af] Seaport and holiday resort situated on the NW. of Mount's Bay, on the A30. In July 1820 Mrs. Piozzi, having recently celebrated her 80th birthday in Bath, came here to recoup her depleted finances, hoping to enjoy warm sea-bathing and economical living. Accommodation was hard to find and she was obliged to take a little 'nutshell of a cottage'. Although she missed the social amenities of Bath, she achieved her object of settling her debts: 'No Milliner's Shop,' she wrote, '*no* Rooms, *no* Theatre, *no* Music Meeting—*no* Pleasure, but *no* Expence. I had too much of *both* the last Winter at Bath.' The following spring she decided to return to civilization and reached Clifton (see Bristol) on 18 March.

John Davidson, Scottish poet and schoolmaster, spent his last years here. Depressed by poverty and ill-health he drowned himself near Penzance and when his body was recovered he was buried at sea.

Penzance Library in Morrab Rd. has a collection of rare Cornish books and prints.

PEPER HARROW (pr. Pepper), Surrey. [1 Dd] Village off the A3, 5 m. SW. of Guildford. Mrs. Humphry Ward stayed at the rectory (now Mulberry House, Shackle-

ford) in 1882. It became the Murewell Rectory of her most famous novel *Robert Elsmere* (1888). Henry James visited her here.

PERTH, Perths. (Tayside). [6 Fb] Large town and tourist centre on the Tay, once the capital of Scotland. The house of the heroine of Scott's *The Fair Maid of Perth* (1828), at the corner of Blackfriars Wynd, was rebuilt in its old style late in the 19th c. and is now a craft and curio shop. The City Chambers contain late 19th-c. stained-glass windows of scenes from the novel. Scott describes the Battle of the Clans (1396) fought on the North Inch (now a park) between picked warriors of two rival clans and watched by King Robert and his queen as if at a tournament. Royal guests stayed at Blackfriars Monastery (then between Athol Pl. and Carpenter St.) where Simon Glover and his daughter, the Fair Maid, worshipped. It was at Blackfriars that Robert's son, King James I, was assassinated (1437). His poem *The Kingis Quair* or King's Book, an account of his courtship of his wife, written *c.* 1424 while a prisoner in England, is used by Rossetti in 'The King's Tragedy' included in *Ballads and Sonnets* (1881). The narrator, Catherine Douglas (Kate Barlass), tells of the events leading to her vain attempt to bar the door with her arm to save the King. James was buried in the Charter House, which he had founded in 1425 (site S. of the hospital in King St.). A plaque near the corner of St. John St. and South St. states that the site of the house of Gavin Douglas, Bishop of Dunkeld (1516–20), can be seen through the archway, 'pend', there. He was the first translator of the classics into English with the *Aeneid* (1553).

John Ruskin spent many holidays as a boy with his parents in Perth, sometimes staying in Main St., Bridgend (house gone), N. of the Tay, and sometimes at 10 Rose Ter. (P), overlooking North Inch. He married Euphemia (Effie) Gray, whose parents had taken over Ruskin's grandfather's house, Bowerswell (now an old people's home), N. of the river. His mother felt unable to attend the wedding there. Ruskin's parents were first cousins; his grandfather had killed himself at Bowerswell, and his mother had an aversion for the house.

The dramatic critic William Archer was born (1856) in Perth (house unknown); his family left for Norway soon afterwards. John Buchan was born (1875) at the manse in York Pl. The house is now divided in two and a plaque marks No. 20. William Soutar was born (1898) in Perth and lived with his parents at 27 Wilson St. (P) from 1924 until his death in 1943. His poems, judged as some of the best of the Scottish revival, appeared regularly from 1931 and were published as *Collected Poems* (1948). He kept diaries from 1930, when he became bedridden, and these were published as *Diaries of a Dying Man* (1954), from the title he gave to his last one, kept from July to October 1943, when he died.

PETERBOROUGH, Cambs. [4 Dd] Industrial and cathedral city on the Nene, 11 m. SE. of Stamford. The latest version of the *Anglo-Saxon Chronicle*, to 1155, was written in the Benedictine Abbey of which the church, built in the early 12th c., has been Peterborough Cathedral since 1541.

L. P. Hartley, who was born (1895) at Whittlesea (or Whittlesey), 5 m. E., spent his youth at Fletton Towers, the family home, in the suburb of Fletton among brickfields. Hartley wrote *The Killing Bottle* (1932), short stories, and the novels *The Shrimp and the Anemone* (1944), a study of the childhood of a brother and sister, *The Go-Between* (1953), and *The Brickfield* (1964).

PICKWORTH, Leics. [4 Dd] Village E. of the A1, 5 m. NW. of Stamford. Late in 1817 John Clare worked at Mr. Clark's lime kilns, traditionally sited at the entrance to the village, W. of the church, where two ruined chimneys remain in an overgrown enclosure lined with trees. The ruins of the medieval village were the subject of Clare's 'Elegy on the Ruins of Pickworth', and the old church, whose Gothic arch near the classical building of the new church can still be seen, inspired 'On a Sunday Morning'. Clare used to cross the fields to Walk Farm (situated between the village and the Ryhall road and then called Walkherd Lodge),

> Where in youth and beauty blooming
> Lives sweet Patty of the Vale.

He married Patty in 1820 after the publication of *Poems Descriptive of Rural Life*.

PIERS COURT. See STINCHCOMB.

PILTON, Devon. [2 Dc] Village ½ m. N. of Barnstaple. Hector Hugh Munro ('Saki') was

brought up here from the age of 2. His mother had died soon after his birth in Burma, and his father, an Inspector-General of Police, took a house, Broadgate Villa, where Hector and his brother and sister lived with his paternal grandmother and two aunts. The grandmother was gentle and dignified, but Aunt Augusta and Aunt Tom, vividly described in the biography of Saki by his sister in *The Square Egg* (1924), dominated the house with their fierce quarrels and jealousies. Aunt Augusta, the autocrat, was a woman of ungovernable temper and a moral coward, the last person who should have been in charge of children. She is depicted, 'more or less', according to her niece, in 'Sredni Vashtar' (*Chronicles of Clovis*, 1911), and 'to the life' in 'The Lumber-Room' (*Beasts and Super-Beasts*, 1914). Broadgate Villa, now two houses, Fairmead and Fairview, is on the corner of Bellaire and Bellaire Drive, NW. of the church, a pleasant building with a balcony over a pillared veranda, no longer shut in by the high walls of Saki's time.

PIMPERNE, Dorset. [1 Ae] Village on the A354, 2 m. NE. of Blandford Forum. Christopher Pitt, a minor 18th-c. poet whom Dr. Johnson included in his *Lives of the English Poets* (1779–81), was rector here from 1722 till his death in 1748.

PLAYFORD, Essex. [4 Gf] Village 4 m. NE. of Ipswich, off the A12. The red-brick Tudor Hall surrounded by its moat was the home of Thomas Clarkson (1760–1846), the abolitionist. He was visited here by the diarist Crabb Robinson, who had known Catherine Clarkson since their youth in Bury. Haydon, staying here in 1840 to paint the portraits of those in the Anti-Slavery Convention, mentions in his autobiography that the date 1593 was on the house but that parts were older. One of the main rooms has a fireback with this date today.

PLOWDEN HALL, Salop. [3 Fd] Home of the Plowden family for many generations, situated *c*. 1½ m. ENE. of Lydbury North, between the A489 and the B4385. This splendid old white house is said to be the original of the Hall described at the beginning of J. H. Shorthouse's historical novel *John Inglesant* (1881).

PLYMOUTH, Devon. [2 De] One of the chief seaports of England, known as Sutton in the Domesday Book and by its present name since 1439, situated at the head of Plymouth Sound, at the mouths of the Plym and the Tamar. The adjacent towns of Stonehouse and Devonport were combined with Plymouth in 1914 and the three became a city in 1928. It suffered extensive bombing in the Second World War and rebuilding has replaced many buildings of historic interest.

The theologian Joseph Glanvill (1636–80) was born here (site unrecorded), the son of a merchant. He became rector of the Abbey Church, Bath (q.v.).

N. T. Carrington (1777–1830), a Devon poet, was born in Old-town St. (gone). His first names have sometimes been given as Noel Thomas, but according to local records he was named Nicholas Toms after his father's step-father. Soon after his birth his parents moved to Plymouth Dock (now Devonport) and here he spent his boyhood. After he left school he became a dockyard apprentice, but found it uncongenial and ran away to sea. He was present at the Battle of Cape St. Vincent and then returned to his parents, settled down as a schoolmaster, and in 1809 established his own academy. He wrote poetry as a leisure occupation and contributed occasional pieces to magazines and annuals. His poem 'Dartmoor' narrowly missed the Royal Society of Literature prize in 1826, but he was awarded 50 gns. by George IV. His popular *Teignmouth, Dawlish and Torquay Guide* (1810) has been frequently reprinted. A copy of his portrait (c. 1825) can be seen in the Public Library.

Robert Stephen Hawker, author of 'The Song of the Western Men', was born (3 Dec. 1803) at 6 Morley St., the vicarage of Charles Church (now only a shell since the bombing), where his grandfather was incumbent, and baptized (29 Dec. 1803) in the parish of Stoke Damerel (now part of the city, to the NW.), when his father was curate there. He spent most of his life as vicar of Morwenstow (q.v.), but was buried at Plymouth, in Ford Park cemetery, off Ford Park Rd. His grave, near the northern end of the cemetery, is marked by a granite cross.

Henry Austin Dobson, poet and essayist, was born (18 Jan. 1840) at Plymouth, the son of an engineer, and educated at Beaumaris Grammar School and at Strasbourg before entering the Board of Trade. Plymouth was the native town of Hardy's first wife, Emma, and he had a great affection for it. His poem 'The West-of-Wessex Girl' (begun in Plymouth, Mar. 1913, four months after her death) laments the fact that they were never there together:

> Yet now my West-of-Wessex girl,
> When midnight hammers slow
> From Andrew's, blow by blow,
> As phantom draws me by the hand
> To the place—Plymouth Hoe—
> Where side by side in life, as planned,
> We never were to go!

Other natives include J. C. Squire (1884–1958), who was educated at the Grammar School before going to Blundell's at Tiverton, and L. A. G. Strong (1896–1958), whose Devon upbringing inspired *Dewer Rides* (1929), a Dartmoor story whose success encouraged him to give up teaching for novel-writing.

POLCHESTER. See TRURO.

POLESDEN LACEY, Surrey. [1 Dd] Regency house 1½ m. S. of the A246 at Great Bookham, built on the site of the house which Sheridan bought (1796) for his second wife. He wrote 'it shall be a seat of health and happiness—where she shall chirp like a bird, bound like a fawn and grow fat as a little pig'. He also bought Yew Trees Farm near by. In 1798 he was still enjoying 'nature and retirement' but in 1802 when his wife, son, servants, and labourers, including his washerwoman's family, caught scarlet fever so badly that he feared for their lives, he wished he had never seen the place.

POLESWORTH, Warwicks. [4 Bd] Village on the B5000, 4 m. E. of Tamworth. The red-brick and timbered house (gone), built after the dissolution of the abbey, was the home of Sir Henry Goodere (1534–95), a patron of Michael Drayton, who it is thought came as a page at the age of 7 and possibly had lessons in the school over the abbey gateway (now a flat). Drayton wrote many poems to Anne the younger daughter, 8 years his junior, who, as 'Idea', was the object of his love throughout his life. Goodere was Philip Sidney's cousin, was with him when he died, and present at his funeral. Drayton's '*Lyrick* Pieces' to Sir Henry trust that

> They may become John Hewes his lyre
> Which oft at Polesworth by the fire
> Hath made us gravely merry.

One of the old stone fireplaces, with the Goodere crest of a partridge with an ear of corn in its beak, still survives at the vicarage built in 1868 on the site of the house, and John Hewes is mentioned by Hakluyt in a list of those sailing to Virginia in 1584. Drayton's 'Ode to the Virginia Voyage' may have been inspired by Hewes. The second Sir Henry (1571–1627), a nephew, married his cousin Frances, whom Drayton wrote of as 'Panape'. Goodere was the lifelong correspondent of Donne, who officiated at the marriage of his daughter Lucy to Francis Nethersole (memorial in the church) and visited him here. In 1613 Donne wrote 'Good Friday' on leaving Polesworth for Montgomery. Ben Jonson's verses to Goodere mention his 'well-made choice of books and friends'.

PONDEN HALL, West Yorkshire. [5 De] House 2 m. from Haworth (q.v.), across the moor beyond Stanbury. Emily Brontë, who found the story for her novel, *Wuthering Heights* (1847), when she was a teacher at Law Hill (q.v.), set Thrushcross Grange, the home of the Lintons, in her own well-loved moors. The Earnshaws' home, Wuthering Heights, is thought to have been placed at the small farmhouse of Top Withens (ruins), to the S., not far from the waterfall that is now called the Brontë Waterfall.

PONTERWYD, Dyfed. [3 Dd] Village on the Rheidol, 13 m. E. of Aberystwyth on the A44. George Borrow stayed at the inn (now the George Borrow Inn) on his tour of Wales in the summer and autumn of 1854. He gives an account of his travels in *Wild Wales* (1862).

PORLOCK, Som. [2 Ec] Former port, now a resort, on the A39, visited by William and Dorothy Wordsworth and Coleridge in 1797, and in 1799 by Southey, who stayed at the Ship and wrote some lines by the alehouse fire. A road off the A39 at the top of Porlock Hill leads to Ash Farm where tradition says Coleridge, after a dream, wrote *Kubla Khan* until interrupted by a 'man from Porlock' (Broomstreet Farm off the A39 also has a claim). In the novel *Lorna Doone* (1869) by R. D. Blackmore, John Ridd and his father, who was later ambushed and killed at the top of Porlock Hill, often came here.

PORT BREDY. See BRIDPORT.

PORTLAND, ISLE OF, Dorset. [2 He] Rocky limestone peninsula, $4\frac{1}{2}$ m. long by $1\frac{3}{4}$ m. wide, reached by the A354 S. of Weymouth. Hardy called it 'the Gibraltar of Wessex' and in *The Well-Beloved* (1897) it figures as 'the Isle of Slingers'. Off the rocky headland of Portland Bill in the south William Wordsworth's brother John, captain of the East Indiaman *Abergavenny*, was lost when it went down in February 1805. Wordsworth was deeply affected by the tragedy, which seems to have been one of the heaviest blows of his life. His poems 'Character of the Happy Warrior' and 'Elegiac Stanzas' commemorate his brother.

PORTSEA. See PORTSMOUTH.

PORTSMOUTH, Hants. [1 Ce] City and naval base, occupying Portsea Island, N. of Spithead. Charles Dickens was born at 1 Mile End Ter., Portsea, now the Dickens Museum,[1] 393 Commercial Rd., his father being a clerk in the Navy Pay Office. The family moved to a smaller house in Hawke St. (gone), and in 1814 to London. Dickens came back to Portsmouth in 1838 to collect local colour for *Nicholas Nickleby* (1838–9). George Meredith was born in a house (gone) on the corner of Broad St. and High St. (though for many years his biographers have been misled by his own reference to his birthplace as simply 'near Petersfield'), and baptized in St. Thomas's Church (now the cathedral). His grandfather, Melchisedek Meredith, was a prosperous tailor and naval outfitter, immortalized as Melchisidec Harrington, 'the Great Mel', in the novel *Evan Harrington* (1860), and his father, Augustus, who carried on the business, was the original of Evan Harrington. Portsmouth is the 'Lymport' of the novel and many of the characters are drawn from Meredith's relations and contemporaries. He attended St. Paul's School, Southsea (a private school which existed 1825–50) before going to boarding-school at Lowestoft in 1840.

Sir Walter Besant was born in St. George's Sq., Portsea (the house has gone). His novel *By Celia's Arbour* (1878) gives a description of the old town of his boyhood. Rudyard Kipling, who was born in India, was sent as a boy (1874–7) to live with relatives in Campbell Rd., Southsea, and went to school at Hope House. It has been thought that some of the descriptions in his novel *The Light that Failed* (1890) belong to this period of his life.

H. G. Wells served 2 years (1881–3) of an uncongenial apprenticeship at Hyde's Drapery Establishment, on the corner of St. Paul's Rd. and King's Rd. (gone), the misery of which is reflected in the early part of his novel *Kipps* (1905).

Sir Arthur Conan Doyle first set up in practice as a doctor at 1 Bush Villas, Elm Grove, Portsea (gone), in September 1882, and married in August 1885. It was here that the character of Sherlock Holmes was conceived and first appeared in the detective novel *A Study in Scarlet* (1887). Holmes was modelled on Dr. Joseph Bell, under whom Doyle had studied medicine at Edinburgh University (1876), and Dr. Watson, the narrator and Holmes's foil, on Doyle's friend Dr. James Watson, the president of the Portsmouth Literary and Scientific Society. Other novels written at Portsmouth were *Micah Clarke* (1888), *The Sign of Four* (1890), and *The White Company* (1891). Doyle left for Vienna, to study the eye, in 1889.

Portsmouth appears frequently in the seafaring novels of Captain Marryat and also as the home of Fanny Price in Jane Austen's *Mansfield Park* (1814).

[1] Open daily: summer 10 a.m.–7 p.m., winter 10 a.m.–5 p.m.

PORTSTEWART, Londonderry. [8 Fa] Pleasantly situated little seaside resort on the A2, 4 m. W. of Portrush. Charles Lever, the novelist, was employed here in 1832 as a dispensary doctor when a young married man, and rented a small house called Verandah Cottage. He soon became popular and his lively temperament and unconventional ways earned him the nickname of 'Dr. Quicksilver'. While he was here he began contributing to the *Dublin University Magazine*, which he later edited, his novel *Harry Lorrequer* first appearing there in instalments beginning in 1837. He left for an appointment in Brussels in May 1837.

POSTLING, Kent. [1 Hd] Village off the A20, 3 m. N. of Hythe. Visible from the road between the village and the junction with the B2068, Stone Street, is Pent Farm, rented from 1898 to 1907 by Conrad from Hueffer, with whom he collaborated on *The Inheritors* (1901) and *Romance* (1903). Conrad also wrote *Lord Jim* (1900), *Youth* and *Typhoon* (1902), *Nostromo* (1904), and *The Mirror of the Sea* (1906) while living here.

POXWELL, Dorset. [2 He] Village on the A353, 5½ m. NE. of Weymouth. Poxwell Manor, a stone-mullioned house built in 1654, may be seen from the churchyard gate (the church has been demolished). It was possibly Hardy's model for Squire Derriman's 'Oxwell Hall' in *The Trumpet-Major* (1880).

PRESTON, Lancs. [5 Ce] Engineering and cotton-weaving town on the A6, with docks on the Ribble. Francis Thompson, a doctor's son, was born (16 Dec. 1859) at 7 Winckley St. (a bronze plaque has a portrait head in relief and a quotation from 'The Hound of Heaven'). He spent his early childhood here before the family moved (1864) to Ashton-under-Lyme, 6 m. E. of Manchester.

PRESTON BROCKHURST, Salop. [3 Gc] Village on the A49, 8 m. N. of Shrewsbury. William Wycherley, Restoration dramatist, was born (1640) at Clive Hall, 1½ m. W. After his education in France and at Oxford he often returned to Clive Hall, which he inherited on his father's death in 1697.

PRESTWICH. See MANCHESTER.

PRILLISK. See PROLUSK.

PRIOR PARK, Avon. [2 Hb] Palladian mansion 1½ m. SE. of Bath, built (1743) by Wood for Ralph Allen. Pope, a life-long correspondent and a guest here, advised Allen on his pictures and statues, and wrote:

Let humble Allen with an awkward shame
Do good by stealth, and blush to find it fame.

Fielding, who also visited, was an early recipient of Allen's good will and made him a model for Squire Allworthy in *Tom Jones* (1749). In 1833 Tom Moore visited the house (now a Catholic school)[1] with his wife and sister.

[1] Open May–Sept.: Tues. 3–6 p.m.; Wed. 2–6 p.m.

PRIORSFORD. See PEEBLES.

PROLUSK (or PRILLISK), Tyrone. [8 Fc] Hamlet 2¾ m. NW. of Clogher (on the A4). The novelist and folklorist William Carleton was born here, the youngest of a peasant family of 14, and grew up in the district. He is remembered especially for his short stories, based on his own experiences and sympathies, which were collected under the title *Traits and Stories of the Irish Peasantry* (1830, 2nd ser. 1833), and for the novel *Fardorougha the Miser* (1837).

PUDDLETOWN, Dorset. [2 Hd] Village on the A35 and the A354, 5 m. NE. of Dorchester. This was the 'Weatherbury' of Hardy's *Far from the Madding Crowd* (1874), though the village is much changed since the date of the novel and it is rash to try to identify all the features in the story. Bathsheba Everdene's farmhouse, described as on a hill west of the church, 'not more than a quarter of a mile' away, is regarded as being modelled on Waterston Manor,[1]

Lower Waterston, an Elizabethan house nearly 2 m. NW. in the Piddle Valley, on a minor road off the B3134 to Druce.

[1] Gardens open Apr.–Sept.: Sun. 2–6 p.m.

PYRFORD, Surrey. [1 Dc] Village on the B367, 1 m. S. of West Byfleet. Pyrford Place (rebuilt) in Warren Lane was the home of a lady-in-waiting to Queen Elizabeth, who, after being widowed, became the second wife of the Lord Keeper, Sir Thomas Egerton. They used the house as their country home. On Lady Egerton's death (1600) the house passed to her son Francis Wolley, who gave refuge to his cousin Ann More and Egerton's secretary John Donne after their rash marriage in 1601. Evelyn wrote that 'the house is timber, but commodious, and with one ample dining room, and the hall adorned with paintings of fowle and hunting'. Donne's first two children, Constance and John, were born and probably christened here, but the records of the small Norman church on the hill are missing for that period.

R

RACEDOWN LODGE, Dorset. [2 Gd] Three-storeyed Georgian house (now a farmhouse) near the village of Bettiscombe on the B3165 Crewkerne–Lyme Regis road, on high ground facing westward below Pilsdon Pen (909 ft., the highest hill in Dorset). It was the property of John Pinney, a retired sugar merchant, who settled in Bristol in the 1780s and rebuilt and furnished it (it was previously called Pilsmarsh or Pylemarsh Lodge). His son John Frederick, a friend and admirer of Wordsworth, offered it, with his father's approval, as a home for William and his sister Dorothy. The Wordsworths arrived in September 1795 and stayed until June 1797 and here for the first time realized their longed-for idea of living together and sharing the experiences of daily life. They had with them Basil Montagu, the young son of a London friend of Wordsworth, whose wife had lately died. The child, who was under 3 when he arrived, benefited from Dorothy's affectionate and sensible

management and after 6 months she wrote that he was her 'perpetual pleasure . . . quite metamorphosed from a shivering half-starved plant, to a lusty, blooming, fearless boy'.

Wordsworth's time at Racedown was a vitally important stage in his career. Here, while living on money bequeathed to him by his friend Raisley Calvert, and sustained by Dorothy's faith in him, he recovered his own belief in himself as a poet, after a period of doubt and lack of self-confidence. In London he had been unsettled and had written little; now he came back to Nature, his 'first love'. In the 11th book of *The Prelude* he looks back to the Racedown years and Dorothy,

> . . . the beloved woman in whose sight
> Those days were pass'd, . . .
>
> She, in the midst of all, preserv'd me still
> A Poet, made me seek beneath that name
> My office upon earth, and nowhere else.

and the renewal of his communion with Nature:

And lastly, Nature's self, by human love
Assisted, through the weary labyrinth
Conducted me again to open day,
Revived the feelings of my earlier life,
Gave me that strength and knowledge full of peace,
Enlarged, and never more to be disturbed.

His first writing at Racedown was the revision of 'Salisbury Plain', a long narrative poem about war and poverty, a bitter indictment of social injustice. In the autumn of 1796 he began his blank verse tragedy, *The Borderers*, a play which was rejected as unsuitable for acting. By the following spring he was steadily writing poetry, including 'Lines left upon a Seat in a Yew-tree', and 'The Ruined Cottage'. There was a visit from Mary Hutchinson, who shared Dorothy's excitement and helped to copy out poems. After she left (in June) Coleridge arrived and the two poets spent much time in reading aloud each other's work. Then the Wordsworths went back with Coleridge to his cottage at Nether Stowey, from which they moved to Alfoxden Park (q.v.).

RADWINTER, Essex. [1 Fa] Village 4 m. E. of Saffron Walden on the B1053. William Harrison, rector from 1559 to his death in 1593, wrote the *Description of England*, which, with his translation of a *Description of Scotland*, was included in Holinshed's *Chronicles* (1577).

RAMSGATE, Kent. [1 Hc] Coastal resort on the A254. Wickham's attempted elopement with Darcy's sister in *Pride and Prejudice* (1813) was set here, and here Tom Bertram in *Mansfield Park* (1814) experienced the difficulties of knowing whether young ladies were 'out' or not. Jane Austen herself visited the town, probably in 1803 when her brother Frank was stationed here. Egerton Brydges, a former neighbour in Steventon, last saw her in Ramsgate. Coleridge, an enthusiastic bather, was a regular summer visitor from 1816 when he lived in Highgate.

R. M. Ballantyne, author of *Coral Island* (1858), stayed here researching for his stories *The Lifeboat* (1864) and *The Floating Light of the Goodwin Sands* (1870). The coxswain Isaac Jarman let him sail in the tug accompanying the lifeboat.

RANNOCH MOOR. See GLEN COE.

RANTAVAN HOUSE. See MULLAGH.

RATHFARNHAM, Dublin. [8 Gf] Suburban village 3½ m. S. of Dublin, on the L94. See Dublin (Pearse).

RATHGAR. See DUBLIN.

RÁTHLUIRC, Cork. [9 Dd] Market town, long known as Charleville (so named in honour of Charles II), NW. of the Ballyhoura Hills, on the T11 and the T36. In the ruined church of Ballysallagh, ¼ m. SSE., is the grave, bearing a Latin epitaph, of Seán Clárach Mac Domhnaill (1691–1754), a Gaelic poet whose works include a translation of Homer. His farm at Kiltoohig, on the west side of the town, became a meeting place (known as a 'Court of Poetry') for other poets, including Seán Ó Tuama (1706–75) and Eoghan Ruadh O'Sullivan (d. 1784).

RAVENSCRAIG CASTLE. See KIRKCALDY.

READING, Berks. [1 Cc] County town, noted for its industries and its University (1926), situated on the Kennet near its confluence with the Thames, 38 m. W. of London. Jane Austen and her elder sister, Cassandra, went to the Abbey School (1785–7), run by Mrs. Latournelle, a French émigrée. The school occupied two rooms (now used by the local authority) over the Gateway of the ruined Benedictine Abbey in Forbury Rd. and eventually overflowed into a near-by house (demolished). Jane's contemporary, Mary Martha Sherwood (remembered especially for *The History of the Fairchild Family*, 1818–47), was also a pupil, as was Mary Russell Mitford, when she came with her parents from New Alresford to Reading in 1797. A £20,000 lottery prize won when she was 10 enabled Mary's father, Dr. Mitford, a man of extravagant tastes and improvident ways, to move to a larger house, 39 London Rd. (P). This, a substantial red-brick building of the late 18th c., may not have been built for the Mitfords (as has been supposed), though it must have been quite new when they moved in. In 1802 Dr. Mitford bought Grazeley Court, a mid-16th-c. farmhouse c. 3 m. from Reading, which he pulled down and replaced with a building which he named Bertram House (demolished). The Mitfords moved here some time between 1804 and 1806 (the dates are disputed) and stayed until 1820, when they went to Three Mile Cross (q.v.).

Oscar Wilde was imprisoned in Reading gaol (rebuilt) in Forbury Rd., after being moved from Wandsworth Prison in November 1895. He served a 2-year sentence of hard labour, after a London court found him guilty of homosexual practices, and left prison in 1897, bankrupt and ruined in health. While in prison he wrote a long, bitter letter to Lord Alfred Douglas (the son of the Marquis of Queensberry, whose denunciation had initiated the proceedings against him), published in part as *De Profundis* (1905) and in full in the *Letters* (ed. R. Hart-Davis, 1962). *The Ballad of Reading Gaol* (1898), written in Paris, where he spent his last few years, is a moving account of his experience in prison.

> I never saw a man who looked
> With such a wistful eye
> Upon that little tent of blue
> Which prisoners call the sky.
>
> .   .   .
>
> All that we know who lie in gaol
> Is that the wall is strong;
> And that each day is like a year,
> A year whose days are long.

REDCROSS, Wicklow. [9 Hb] Village in the Redcross Valley, on a minor road off the L29, *c.* 6 m. S. of Wicklow. Mrs. Cecil Frances Alexander (*née* Humphreys) lived here with her family at Ballykeane House from 1825 to 1833, when they moved to Strabane (q.v.).

REDNAL, West Midlands. [4 Ae] Village, now a suburb, 8 m. SW. of Birmingham, off the A38. Cardinal Newman (d. 1890) is buried in the graveyard of the country house of the Oratory Fathers.

REIGATE (pr. Rīgate), Surrey. [1 Ed] Old town on the A25. John Foxe, the martyrologist, was tutor, by the Duchess of Richmond, to the three children of Henry, Earl of Surrey, the poet beheaded in 1547. They lived in the castle (earthworks now a public garden) until Foxe fled to the Continent on the accession of Queen Mary in 1553.

Harrison Ainsworth often stayed with his invalid brother at Hill View Lodge, now in Glovers Rd., where he wrote *Boscobel* (1872). In 1878 he moved to Belvedere, St. Mary's Rd. (both houses E. of Bell St.) where he died (1882). Katharine Bradley and her niece Edith Cooper lived here in retirement from 1888. They contributed to the American journal *The Dial* as 'Michael Field'.

RENDHAM, Suff. [4 He] Village on the B1119, 3 m. NW. of Saxmundham. Crabbe, who had left Muston to be his wife's uncle's executor, spent 1801 to 1805 at a house known locally as Lady Whincups, then opposite the new parsonage at the bottom of the hill (now at the entrance to Grove Farm and marked with a plaque).

RENISHAW, Derbys. [4 Bb] Village on the A616, 2 m. N. of Staveley. The 16th-c. Renishaw Hall, home of Edith and Osbert Sitwell, features in *Left Hand, Right Hand*, one of the five volumes of Osbert Sitwell's autobiography 1944–50, which tells of his early life here and the eccentricities of his father, Sir George Sitwell.

RENTON. See ALEXANDRIA.

RENVYLE. See RINVYLE.

REPTON, Derbys. [4 Bc] Village on the B5008, 7 m. SW. of Derby. W. B. Stevens was appointed usher at Repton School in 1776, and although teaching was 'scholastic slavery' he became Headmaster 3 years later. His second book of poems was published in 1782. His lack of money twice dashed his hopes of a wife and his *Journal* (1965) kept from 1792 to his death in 1800 reveals his obsession with independence. He died and is buried here and the lines on his monument in the church are by Anna Seward, whom he visited at Lichfield.

Vernon Watkins, poet and scholar was educated at Repton School. He left in 1922 for Magdalene College, Cambridge (q.v.).

RICHMOND, North Yorkshire. [5 Eb] Town on the A6108, 4 m. SW. of Scotch Corner, with a ruined castle above the Swale. In 1816 Herbert Knowles, a pupil at the Grammar School, wrote 'The Three Tabernacles', better known as 'Stanzas in Richmond Churchyard', which he later sent to Southey, who obtained for him a sizarship at Cambridge. C. L. Dodgson was also at the Grammar School (1844–6) before going to Rugby.

RINGMER, East Sussex. [1 Ee] Village on the A265, 3 m. NE. of Lewes. From 1745 onwards Gilbert White made annual visits to his aunt Rebecca, who lived at Delves House set among the trees across the common. Many details in *The Natural History of Selborne* (1789) were observed here, including Timothy, his aunt's tortoise. He had written under Timothy's name to his friend Heckey Mulso (later Chapone), and he took Timothy, inherited with the rest of the property, to Selborne after his aunt's death in 1780.

RINGMORE, Devon. [2 Ef] Small village *c.* $3\frac{1}{2}$ m. S. of Modbury, on a minor road off the B2392. R. C. Sherriff wrote *Journey's End*, his play about the First World War, produced in 1929, while here. The village pub, where he stayed, is named after the play.

RINVYLE (or RENVYLE), Galway. [8 Ae] Promontory on the N. coast of Connemara, reached by a minor road, 5 m. from Letterfrack, on the T71. Rinvyle House Hotel, near the beach, belonged for many years to Oliver St. John Gogarty, who entertained Yeats (who felt the spirits of the house unfriendly), Shaw, Augustus John, and other artistic and political friends.

RIPE, East Sussex. [1 Fe] Village N. of the A27, 6 m. E. of Lewes. The 17th-c. weatherboarded White Cottage, in a lane by the Lamb, was the last home of Malcolm Lowry, author of *Under the Volcano* (1947). His wife found the place, in January 1956, the 'dream cottage' of his doctor's orders, remote yet within reach of fortnightly therapy for manic-depression and alcoholism. Here Lowry was able to write again and completed *October Ferry to Gabriola*, short stories collected later as *Hear Us O Lord from Heaven Thy Dwelling Place*, poems, and the essay on the encroachments on freedom made by McCarthyism, before he died in June 1957. He is buried in the churchyard.

ROBIN HOOD'S BAY, North Yorkshire. [5 Gb] Seaside village at the foot of a steep cliff on the B1447, 5 m. SE. of Whitby. Leo Walmsley grew up in Robin Hood's Bay,

the 'Bramblewick' of his first three novels, *Three Fevers* (1932), *Foreigners* (1935), and *Sally Lunn* (1937), set in this part of his native county.

ROCHESTER, Kent. [1 Fc] Cathedral city on the Medway and the A2. Dickens, who spent his youth in neighbouring Chatham (q.v.), his honeymoon at Chalk (q.v.), and his last years at Gad's Hill (q.v.), made many references to the city. The poetic fervour of Mr. Pickwick and his friend Snodgrass at their first sight of the Norman castle is tempered by Jingles's 'Ah, fine place! . . . glorious pile —frowning walls—tottering arches—dark nooks—crumbling staircases—.' The Royal Victoria and Bull remembers that it is the Bull Hotel where Pickwick and his creator stayed and Eastgate House (P), now a museum,[1] with Dickens's chalet from Gad's Hill in the garden, resembles Westgate House. *Great Expectations* (1861) opens on the near-by marshes, Miss Havisham's house is modelled on Restoration House in Maidstone Rd., and Uncle Pumblechook's on one of the black and white Tudor houses in the High St. 'The Seven Poor Travellers' in *Christmas Stories* features Richard Watts's Hospital, also in the High St. The city becomes 'Dullborough' in the *Uncommercial Traveller* (1860), and the 'Mudfog' of *Mudfog Papers* (1880). It is also 'Cloisterham' of the unfinished *Edwin Drood* (1870), where Eastgate House is again the model for Miss Twinkleton's seminary at The Nun's House, and Uncle Pumblechook's house doubles as the house (P) of Mr. Sapsea, auctioneer and mayor. The sinister John Jasper lives over the College Gate and Edwin and Rosa sit under the trees in The Vines to discuss their future. Dickens, who wished to be buried here, has a memorial in the cathedral.

[1] Open daily except Fri. 2–5.30 p.m.

ROCK FERRY, Merseyside. [3 Fa] Suburb of Birkenhead, on the A41. Nathaniel Hawthorne lived here 1853–6 when U.S. consul at Liverpool, crossing the Mersey to his office by ferry. His house was in Rock Park, described by his son as 'a damp, winding, verdurous street, protected at each end by a small granite lodge, and studded throughout its length with stuccoed villas'. It was the starting-place for many excursions in the Wirral and N. Wales, recorded in Hawthorne's *Journal*, and here he finished

Tanglewood Tales (1853), stories from Greek mythology for children.

ROCKINGHAM, Northants. [4 Cd] Village 8 m. N. of Kettering on the A6003. Rockingham Castle,[1] a mainly Elizabethan house inside the Norman walls, was the model for Chesney Wold in *Bleak House* (1853). Part of the book was written here while Dickens was staying with his friends, the Watsons.

[1] Open Easter–Sept.: Thurs., Bank Holiday Sun. and Mon., and Sun. in Aug. 2–6 p.m.

RODMELL, East Sussex. [1 Ee] Village on the A275, 3 m. S. of Lewes. Leonard and Virginia Woolf bought Monks House, near the church, in 1919. Thought to have been a retreat for the monks of Lewes Priory it was in fact early 18th-c. At first they used oil lamps and well water, hardships mitigated by an acre of garden and a view across the Ouse to the hills that Leonard Woolf describes in his autobiography as unchanged since Chaucer's day. One of their earliest visitors was T. S. Eliot, whose *The Waste Land* they were publishing at their Hogarth Press. They divided their time between Monks House and their London home until that was bombed in 1940. In 1941 Virginia Woolf drowned herself in the Ouse on the recurrence of her manic-depressive illness. Her ashes are buried in the garden.

ROLVENDEN, Kent. [1 Gd] Village on the A28, 3 m. SW. of Tenterden. Frances Burnett, author of *Little Lord Fauntleroy* (1886), came from America and rented Great Maytham Hall, on the Rolvenden Layne road, throughout the 1890s. It is thought she based the overgrown wilderness in *The Secret Garden* (1911) on the high-walled garden here. The house was altered by Lutyens in 1910 and is now flats in carefully tended grounds. A tablet in the church commemorates her.

ROOS HALL, Suff. [4 He] Tudor house on the A1116, ½ m. from Beccles, family home of Sir John Suckling (1609–42), who lived mainly at Court.

Open May–Sept.: Wed., Fri., Sat., 2–5.30 p.m.

ROSCROW. See PENRYN.

ROSLIN CHAPEL, Midlothian (Lothian). [6 Fc] A 15th-c. chapel, between the A701 and the A6094, 7 m. S. of Edinburgh, built by Sir William Sinclair (or St. Clair), of 'the lordly line of high St Clair'. Legend states that the Sinclairs were buried in their armour instead of coffins, and that a red glare over Roslin would foretell disaster, as Scott mentions in his ballad 'Rosabelle' (see Kirkcaldy).

Seem'd all on fire that chapel proud,
Where Roslin's chiefs uncoffin'd lie,
Each Baron for a sable shroud,
Sheath'd in his iron panoply.

And each St Clair was buried there
With candle, with book, and with knell;
But the sea-caves rung, and the wild winds sung
The dirge of lovely Rosabelle.

ROSS-ON-WYE, Hereford and Worcester. [3 Gf] Market town on the A40, situated on high ground above the river, looking towards the Welsh hills. Inside the Market Hall at the end of the S. wall there is a memorial to John Kyrle (1637–1724), the 'Man of Ross', celebrated by Pope in his *Moral Essays, Epistle III, to Lord Bathurst* (1732), concerning the use of riches. Kyrle was a wealthy man who spent nearly all his life in Ross, where he lived in modest style and devoted his surplus income to the public good. Pope, whose poem holds up Kyrle's good works as an example of a rich man's liberality, wrote to a friend (7 June 1732):

A small exaggeration you must allow me as a poet; yet I was determined the groundwork at least should be *Truth*, which made me so scrupulous in my enquiries.

Kyrle's house, a half-timbered building in the market-place, became the King's Arms Inn after his death and was later converted into shops (P and low relief portrait). His garden at the back, with a summer-house and curious 'mosaic' made with horses' teeth by the poor whom he patronized, can be visited by courtesy of the proprietor of the chemist's shop. The Prospect, a public garden given by Kyrle to the people of Ross, leads off the churchyard, and the footpath, John Kyrle's Walk, offers fine views of the river and the hills. Kyrle is buried in the chancel of the church.

Coleridge stayed at the King's Arms on his tour of Wales in 1794 and wrote the lines beginning

Richer than miser o'er his countless hoards,
Nobler than kings or king-polluted lords,
Here dwelt the man of Ross.

Robert Bloomfield lodged at the Swan in the summer of 1807 when touring with friends along the Wye. Dickens met his biographer, John Forster, in the Royal Hotel (P) in September 1867 to discuss his proposed American tour of 1867-8. Forster was not in favour of the project, but Dickens decided to go nevertheless.

ROTHERHAM, South Yorkshire. [4 Ba] Industrial town, NW. of Sheffield. Ebenezer Elliott was born (1781) at the New Foundry, his father's ironworks in the suburb of Masborough. He wrote his first poem 'Vernal Walk' when 17 and his later *Tales of the Night* (1818) was praised by Southey. In 1821 he set up his own iron works in Sheffield (q.v.).

ROTHLEY, Leics. [4 Bd] Village on the B5328, 6 m. N. of Leicester. The old manor house, home of the Babingtons from 1565-1845 (now the Rothley Court Hotel), was the birthplace of Thomas Babington Macaulay (b. 1800). The hotel has a memorial on the lawn commemorating the drafting of the Treaty for the Abolition of Slavery, a cause to which Macaulay's father was dedicated. Macaulay was made Baron Macaulay of Rothley in 1857.

ROTTINGDEAN, East Sussex. [1 Ee] Coastal resort on the A259, 4 m. E. of Brighton. Kipling stayed with his uncle, Edward Burne-Jones, at North End House (P), and wrote 'Recessional' there. He then lived (1897-1902) at The Elms, across the Green, where a commemorative plaque was placed on the long garden wall by the Kipling Society. Here he wrote *Stalky & Co.* (1899), *Kim* (1901), and the *Just So Stories* (1902). Conrad was one of his visitors. The Grange, built as the vicarage in the early 19th c. and now the public library and museum,[1] has a Kipling room with portraits, letters, and early editions of his works. In 1909 D. H. Lawrence bicycled over the Downs from Croydon where he was teaching and lodged in the High St.

[1] Open daily; Sun. from 2 p.m.

ROUSHAM (pr. Rowsham) HOUSE, Oxon. [1 Ba] Country house E. of the A423, 12 m. N. of Oxford, home of the Cottrell-Dormer family. This 17th-c. house was visited by Pope, Gay, and Horace Walpole, guests of the Dormers and admirers of the gardens, terraces, and temples designed by William Kent about the Cherwell which runs through the grounds. Walpole wrote that 'The whole is as elegant and antique as if the emperor Julian had selected the most pleasing solitude about Daphne to enjoy a philosophic retirement'. Literary treasures include autograph letters of Gay, Swift, and Pope, Mrs. Caesar's copy of Pope's *Works* (1735), inscribed 'from her most obliged and faithful servant', and her volumes of Pope's translation of the *Odyssey*. Mrs. Caesar, Pope's patron and friend, whose daughter married into the family, undertook to find subscribers for this work. Portraits of the Caesars and Pope are among those here.

Open: Gardens, daily 10 a.m.-6 p.m.; House, June, July, Aug.: Wed. 2 6 p.m. and Bank Holidays.

ROWLING HOUSE. See GOODNESTONE.

ROWTON, Salop. [3 Gc] Village on a minor road W. of the A442, 7 m. N. of Wellington. Richard Baxter, the Nonconformist divine, son of Richard Baxter of Eaton-Constantine (9 m. S.) and Beatrice, daughter of Richard Adeney of Rowton, was born (1615) at his mother's home. It is thought that Mrs. Baxter was obliged to return to her parents' house because her husband had 'gambled away' his freehold property and involved himself in debts and difficulties, though he later altered his way of life.

ROYDON MANOR. See BROCKENHURST.

RUDGE. See BECKINGTON.

RUDSTON, Humberside. [5 Gd] Village on the B1253, 5 m. W. of Bridlington. Winifred Holtby, author of *South Riding* (1936), the novel set in Yorkshire by which she is best remembered, was born (1898) at the Victorian Rudston House in Long St., where she spent her youth. She is buried in the churchyard and the memorial by the font in the church was erected after her death (1935) by the Winifred Holtby Society.

RUGBY, Warwicks. [4 Be] Town 12 m. SW. of Coventry, on the A428. Rugby School, founded in 1567, came into prominence in the 19th c., when Thomas Arnold became headmaster (1828-42).

Literary Rugbeians include W. S. Landor, Thomas Hughes, Matthew Arnold the headmaster's son, Arthur Clough, C. L. Dodgson (Lewis Carroll), P. Wyndham Lewis, and Rupert Brooke, born (1887) in Hillmorton Rd., the son of a housemaster. Thomas Hughes's novel *Tom Brown's Schooldays* (1857), by 'An Old Boy', gives a picture of life in the school under Dr. Thomas Arnold. Matthew Arnold, who wrote a poem on the school chapel (replaced in 1872 by a building of Butterfield's), taught here for a term in 1845.

RUSHDEN, Northants. [4 De] Small manufacturing town on the A6, 12 m. SE. of Kettering. Robert Herrick visited Rushden Hall in 1623. He wrote 'Panegyric to Sir Lewis Pemberton', the owner, and found him 'good, hospitable and kind'. H. E. Bates was born here in 1905, and worked in the warehouse of a firm of leather and grindery factors near Rushden Hall. He had time to read at work and he also began to write, 'a conscious hunger' he developed after reading Stephen Crane's novels. His first novel, *The Two Sisters* (1926), was published when he was 20. Bates, who had visited Rushden Hall on his first job on a newspaper, noticed on his way back a tall, proud girl in a cloak lined with scarlet, and later he used this, combined with the Hall, in *Love for Lydia* (1952). Like *The Fallow Land* (1932) and *The Poacher* (1935), this is set locally in the Nene Valley.

RUSH-HAY, Dorset. [2 Hd] Small-holding in the parish of Bagber, a hamlet 2 m. W. of Sturminster Newton (q.v.), on the A357 at the Bagber Common turn. This was the birthplace of William Barnes, the Dorset poet, schoolmaster, and clergyman. He attended the village dame school until he was old enough to go to the church school at Sturminster Newton and make the daily walk there and back across the common.

RYDAL, Cumbria. [5 Bb] Little village on the A591, 2 m. NW. of Ambleside. Just above the church a steep road leads up to Rydal Mount,[1] the home of Wordsworth from 1813 until his death in 1850. Here he wrote almost half the poems published in his lifetime and established his reputation (he became Poet Laureate in 1843), and here he received

visits from countless admirers and many distinguished writers, including Matthew Arnold, Henry Crabb Robinson, Ralph Waldo Emerson, Nathaniel Hawthorne, and William and Mary Howitt. In 1848 Swinburne, aged 11, was taken to visit Wordsworth. The old man treated the boy with kindly understanding and the latter was moved to tears by his parting words: 'I do not think, Algernon, that you will forget me.' The house, originally a farmhouse on the Rydal Hall estate, was owned by the de Flemings from the time it was built (1550) until 1970 when it was purchased by the Wordsworth Trust. Much of the furniture is that used by the Wordsworth family, and William's study contains numerous first editions of his works, including that of *The White Doe of Rylstone*, published soon after he came here from Grasmere; also genealogical tables and a case containing the sword of his much loved brother John, captain of the *Abergavenny*, in whose shipwreck he was lost off Portland Bill in 1805 (a tragedy which deeply affected William). From the principal bedroom can be seen 'Dora's field', which William bought at a time when he feared he might be turned out of Rydal Mount, so that he would be able to build a house on it: however, the tenancy was renewed and he gave the field to his daughter, Dora. It was later given to the National Trust by his grandson, Gordon Wordsworth. The four acres of hillside garden, with two long terraces and beautiful vistas between the trees, are much as they were when Wordsworth designed them.

[1] Open daily 10 a.m.–12.30 p.m.; 2–5.30 p.m.

RYDE, I.O.W. [1 Ce] Resort on the NE. of the island. The American writer, Nathaniel Parker Willis, who visited the town in the early days of its popularity (c. 1830), wrote

Ryde is the most American-looking town I have seen abroad; a cluster of white houses and summery villas on the side of the hill, leaning up from the sea. It is a place of baths, boarding houses and people of damaged constitutions, with very select society, and quiet and rather primitive habits.

RYE, East Sussex. [1 Ge] Port on the Rother and the A259. John Fletcher, the dramatist, Beaumont's collaborator, was born (1579), while his father was priest-in-charge, probably in the Tudor building superseded by the Old Rectory in 1703, but traditionally in the half-timbered Ancient Rectory (P) refronted in 1701, now a shop serving luncheons and teas. In 1896, Henry James rented Point Hill in Playden (1 m. N.) as a change from his London flat. The house, almost covered by a large ash tree, looked across the red roofs of the town to the church. He finished *The Spoils of Poynton*, put aside in Torquay when it became too long for the *Atlantic Monthly*. In October he moved to the Old Rectory for a short tenancy and then in 1898 bought Lamb House (P) in West St., his home until his death (1916). *The Wings of the Dove* (1902), *The Ambassadors* (1903), and *The Golden Bowl* (1904) were written in the garden house (destroyed 1940) or the upstairs study.[1] He often bicycled in the district and was visited by many writers including Conrad, Chesterton, Stephen Crane, and Wells, who wrote in his autobiography that the house was 'one of the most perfect pieces of suitably furnished Georgian architecture imaginable'. After James's death in London, Lamb House became the home of E. F. Benson, author of the popular Lucia books, which have many scenes in Rye, and two volumes of reminiscences *As We Were* (1930) and *As We Are* (1932). He was Mayor of Rye (1934–7) and gave the W. window in the church in memory of his parents; another window commemorates his brother A. C. Benson.

The Mermaid Inn, which features in many smuggling stories, was bought by Richard Aldington's mother in 1913. It became a club, used by servicemen in the 1914–18 War, and Aldington's wartime experiences produced his novel *Death of a Hero* (1929). Jeake's House was the home of the American poet and novelist Conrad Aiken during the depression. Malcolm Lowry, whose first novel *Ultramarine* (1933) owed much to Aiken's *Blue Voyage* (1927), spent his Cambridge vacations (1929–32) with Aiken and his family. Ford Madox Ford's *The Half Moon* (1909), the early chapters of his *Some Do Not* (1924), and Thackeray's unfinished *Denis Duval* (1864–7) are set in Rye, though Thackeray intended further exploits to occur at sea.

[1] Open Mar.–Oct.: Wed. and Sat. 2–6 p.m.

RYLSTONE, West Yorkshire. [5 Dd] Village on the B6265, 5 m. N. of Skipton. *The White Doe of Rylstone* (1815) is the title of Wordsworth's poem about a tragedy of Queen Elizabeth's time, when the survivor of a persecuted Catholic family is visited by the doe she had reared in happier days.

S

SAFFRON WALDEN, Essex. [4 Ef] Town on the A130, SE. of Cambridge. Gabriel Harvey, friend of Spenser and disputant with Roger Greene and Thomas Nashe, was born (1550) in a house in the cattle market. The museum (opened in 1834) near the church, has the carved fireplace showing his father's craft of rope-making, an oak window, and part of a wall-painting (c. 1580), all from the Harvey home, now demolished.

ST. ALBANS, Herts. [1 Eb] Town on the A5 and the A6, which sprang from Roman Verulamium whose extensively excavated ruins are on view. The great Norman abbey marks the site where Alban became the first Christian martyr in Britain c. 304. Matthew Paris entered the monastery in 1217 and was its chronicler (from 1236 until his death in 1259), expanding his account to include Continental events. The Dissolution swept away all the monastic buildings except the abbey and its great Gateway, erected in 1365, where the third printing press to be set up in England was working c. 1480. *The Boke of St. Albans* (1486) printed there by an unnamed 'Scholemaster printer' is generally attributed to Dame Juliana Berners. She was thought to be a prioress at Sopwell Nunnery, which was ½ m. SE. of the abbey, though only a ruined Elizabethan house remains on the site. It is now thought more likely that the part on hawking was written by Julyan Barnes, as the name was first printed, and the rest by other hands.

Francis Bacon, Lord Chancellor, Baron Verulam, and Viscount St. Albans, inherited

Gorhambury 2 m. W., and retired there after his impeachment in 1621, to devote himself to science and literature. He reissued his famous *Essays* (1597) in a final form in 1625. He wished to be buried in St. Michael's Church and a monument of him, sitting in a characteristic pose, was erected in the chancel by his heir. The present Gorhambury, completed in 1784, has a collection of family books and portraits, but his house is a ruin in the park. James Shirley was Master of the Grammar School from 1623-5.

Cowper, during one of his fits of despondency, was looked after here in 1763 by Dr. Nathaniel Cotton who also wrote verses. On his recovery Cowper wrote that he was 'very deep in debt to my little physician of St. Albans'. Dickens often stayed at the Queen's Hotel in Chequer St. and mentions the brickmakers' cottages on Bernard's Heath in *Bleak House* (1852), but the Georgian building of that name has no connection with him. The City Council has published a comprehensive Guide.

ST. ANDREWS, Fife (Fife). [6 Fb] Ancient university town and E. coast resort, now famous for its golf course. Andrew of Wyntoun was a canon-regular of the cathedral (ruins) about the last quarter of the 14th c. and author of the *Orygynale Cronykil*, an account from the beginning of the world to the accession of James I in 1406. The chronicle, perhaps begun here, includes the stories of Macbeth and the witches and was published in 1795 from the manuscript in the Royal Library.

William Dunbar is thought to have been at the university *c.* 1480 before obtaining a place at the court of James IV. David Lindsay (or Lyndsay), who was a student here *c.* 1515, was, like Dunbar, involved with the education of Prince James, to whom after his accession as James V, many of his poems continued to give advice and exhortation. Gavin (or Gawain) Douglas, a son of the 5th Earl of Angus, studied here (1489-94) and was appointed archbishop here in 1514. Challenged by a rival faction, he was imprisoned in the castle (ruins) until allowed to accept the bishopric of Dunkeld, which he was offered by Queen Margaret. John Mair (Major) taught logic and philosophy from 1522 to 1525. In his Latin *History of Greater Britain* (1521) he advocated union of the two countries. After

returning from Paris he was appointed (1533) Provost of St. Salvator's College, where he spent the rest of his life and died in 1550. Mair, whose writings were all in Latin, was said by Rabelais to have written an account of the making of black puddings, 'De modo faciendi boudinos'. Robert Aytoun graduated from the university in 1588 and also went to Paris. His poems were written in Latin, French, or English. He is said to have written 'Old Long Syne' which may have suggested 'Auld Lang Syne' to Burns. John Arbuthnot, after deciding not to go into the Church like his father, obtained an M.D. here in 1696.

Robert Fergusson studied (1765-8) here before settling as a clerk in Edinburgh, having had to give up his hope of reading divinity after his father's death. Dr. Johnson and Boswell stayed here on their tour in 1773. They had supper at Glass's Tavern and then went in 'procession to St. Leonard's College, the landlord walking before us with a candle, and the waiter with a lantern'. Dr. Watson provided them with 'very comfortable and genteel accommodation'. They walked over the ruins of the cathedral, looked at the old castle and were well entertained at dinner by the professors. William Tennant, a schoolmaster at Anstruther (q.v.), was Professor of Oriental Languages (1834-48) at his old university. Andrew Lang, who was educated here before going to Balliol, returned here and lived at 8 Gibson Pl. He died at Banchory in 1912 and his grave in the East Cemetery at St. Andrews has a Celtic cross.

ST. ASAPH, Clwyd. [3 Ea] Small cathedral city on the A55 and the A525, 6 m. N. of Denbigh. Mrs. Felicia Hemans, a poet of great popularity in her day, and admired by Wordsworth, now perhaps best remembered for 'Casabianca', lived as a girl (1809-12) and again, after her marriage and a brief stay at Daventry, until 1825 at Bronwylfa, a large house on the hillside NE. of the town. It was replaced by a later building, which can be seen from 'Mrs. Hemans' Bridge', where she used to sit and write her poetry. The bridge, no longer spanning the diverted Elwy, can be reached by leaving St. Asaph by Chester St., crossing the dual carriage-way, and turning left along a narrow lane. Mrs. Hemans is commemorated in the cathedral by a tablet in the S. aisle and a window in the N. wall of the chancel. A lock of her hair and a book of her poems are on view in the Cathedral Museum,[1] which also contains various books of historic interest from the Cathedral Library (now mainly housed at Aberystwyth) and autograph letters from Dickens, Charles Darwin, Thackeray, and Trollope.

[1] Open Apr.–Sept. or on request to the verger.

ST. BEUNO'S (pr. Bīno's) COLLEGE, Clwyd. [3 Ea] Jesuit seminary on the E. slopes of the Vale of Clwyd, $\frac{3}{4}$ m. N. of the village of Tremeirchion (q.v.). Gerard Manley Hopkins entered the college as a theology student in August 1874, and it was here that he wrote 'The Wreck of the Deutschland', in the early part of 1876, a long, profoundly religious poem in the form of a Pindaric ode, inspired by the disaster which had occurred the previous December. In 1877, his last year at St. Beuno's, he wrote a number of sonnets concerned with objects of Nature as his discerning eye saw them, including 'The Windhover', and 'Pied Beauty', which begins 'Glory be to God for dappled things–'. He was ordained priest in September and moved to Mount St. Mary's College in Derbyshire.

ST. DAVID'S, Dyfed. [3 Af] Smallest cathedral city in Great Britain, on the westernmost bend of the A487, c. $\frac{3}{4}$ m. from the sea. Giraldus Cambrensis (Gerald de Barri), chronicler and travel writer, gives an entertaining account of the see in 1188. He was twice elected bishop (1176 and 1198) but failed to obtain consecration, probably because the English feared that he would make the Welsh Church independent of Canterbury. He was buried here c. 1223 and an effigy in the S. choir aisle of the cathedral has been suggested as possibly his.

ST. ENODOC, Cornwall. [2 Be] Hamlet on the E. side of the Camel estuary, c. 1 m. N. of the village of Rock, reached by ferry from Padstow, or from Wadebridge by a turning off the B3314. It is the setting for Sabine Baring-Gould's novel, In the Roar of the Sea (1892), a tale about wreckers on the Cornish coast. The little 15th-c. church, near the golf course, now recovered from the sanddunes which once enveloped it, is described in the opening chapter. Peter Trevisa, the rector, dies exhausted after his unavailing efforts to clear away the sand which restricts entry to the church to a hole in a window.

ST. HELIER, Channel Islands. [2 Lj] Port and resort in Jersey. Edward Hyde, later first Earl of Clarendon, stayed (1646–8) in Elizabeth Castle with the young Prince Charles, whom he had brought here for safety. The prince was soon sent to France and Hyde continued writing his History of the Rebellion, which he had begun in the Scilly Isles (q.v.).

ST. IVES, Cambs. [4 Ee] Market town on the Ouse. The critic and novelist Theodore Watts (he added his mother's name of Dunton in 1896) was born in 1832 at The Red House, Market Hill. He was a solicitor's son and after leaving school he joined his father's firm in the house (it is a solicitor's firm again now) until setting up his own practice in London (c. 1870). The gipsies he met when driving with his father near Rington and Graylingham woods appear in the romance Aylwin (1898).

ST. IVES, Cornwall. [2 Af] Holiday resort and haunt of artists, formerly a pilchardfishing town, situated on the W. side of St. Ives Bay, at the end of the A3074. Virginia Woolf spent her summers here as a child, at Talland House (now holiday flats), a large white house in Talland Rd. overlooking the harbour. Godrevy Lighthouse, on an island at the far side of the bay, was probably in her mind when she wrote To the Lighthouse (1927).

Dorothy Richardson came here in 1912 at the invitation of John and Beatrice Beresford, who gave her the use of the chapel next to their cottage to write in. She met Hugh Walpole and they all went for walks on the cliffs. She wrote Pointed Roofs (1915), a novel at first rejected, but published later with the support of Edward Garnett.

ST. JULIOT, Cornwall. [2 Cd] Church, known locally as St. Jilt, 2 m. E. of Boscastle, in the Valency Valley, reached by a minor road (signposted to Lesnewth W. of the A39) and up a steep hill N. of the river. Thomas Hardy came here as a young architect in March 1870 to advise on the restoration of the church (which dates from 1450), and some of his drawings are still there. A little further on, a grassy road leads down to the Old Rectory (now a private house), where Hardy met Emma Gifford, the rector's sister, and fell in love with her. They married in 1874 and there is a memorial plaque to her in the church. The valley and the country round are recognizable, with a few minor alterations, as the Cornish scene of *A Pair of Blue Eyes* (1873): the church becomes 'St. Agnes's' in the parish of 'West Endelstow', and Lesnewth 'East Endelstow' (although it is in fact to the south).

ST. LAWRENCE, I.O.W. [1 Cf] Village 2 m. E. of Ventnor, with the cliffs above and the sea below. Alfred Noyes lived (1929–58) at Lisle Combe, a house he described in *Orchard's Bay* (1939), and where he planted a cedar from Swainston (q.v.) and a yew from Farringford (q.v.). His *Collected Poems* were published in 1950, and a further volume of verse, *Letter to Lucian*, in 1956. His autobiography, *Two Worlds for Memory* (1953) was written here.

ST. LEONARDS. See HASTINGS.

ST. LUKE'S, Channel Islands. [2 Lj] District near St. Helier, the capital of Jersey, where Victor Hugo lived from 1852 to 1855 to escape the regime of Louis Napoleon. *Les Châtiments*, his verse satirizing the Second Empire, was published in 1853, and his house, Maison Victor Hugo, is now a hotel.

ST. MARY IN THE MARSH, Kent. [1 Gd] Small village 2 m. SW. of Dymchurch. E. Nesbit, who died at The Long Boat, Jesson St. Mary, near Dymchurch where she had spent many happy holidays with her family and friends, was buried in the churchyard here. Her second husband, whom she called The Skipper, carved the wooden name plate over her grave. John Davidson describes a visit to Dymchurch in 'In Romney Marsh' where

> Masts in the offing wagged their tops;
> The winging waves peal'd on the shore;
> The saffron beach, all diamond drops
> And beads of surge, prolonged the roar.

ST. MARY'S LOCH, Selkirks. (Borders). [6 Fd] Lake to the W. of Ettrick Forest, beside the A708 (Selkirk–Moffatt road), Scott's 'lone St. Mary's silent lake' of

Marmion (introduction to Canto II). His note on this line reads: 'This beautiful sheet of water forms the reservoir from which the Yarrow takes its source. . . . In the winter it is still frequented by flights of wild swans; hence my friend Mr. Wordsworth's lines':

> The swan on sweet St. Mary's lake
> Floats double, swan and shadow.

(written in fact before Wordsworth had been there himself, in 'Yarrow Unvisited', in *Memorials of a Tour in Scotland*, 1803).

ST. OGG'S. See GAINSBOROUGH.

ST. PETER PORT, Channel Islands. [2 Kh] Capital of Guernsey. Victor Hugo, an opponent of Louis Napoleon's regime in France, moved here from Jersey in 1855 and lived at 20 Hauteville. He then lived (1856–70) at Hauteville House, where he wrote his greatest and most popular novel, *Les Misérables* (1862), *Littérature et Philosophie Mêlées* (1864), *Chansons des Rues et des Bois* (1865), and *Les Travailleurs de la Mer* (1866), an epic of the sea, set in Guernsey. He is commemorated by a statue in Candie Gardens.

ST. SERF'S INCH, Kinross. (Tayside). [6 Fc] Island in Loch Leven with the ruins of the priory of Augustinian canons, which superseded a Celtic settlement. Andrew of Wyntoun, prior until his death *c.* 1420, probably wrote here the major part of *The Orygynale Cronykil*, a metrical record of Scottish history from the beginning of the world to the accession of James I. It includes the story of Macbeth, Macduff, and the witches, later used by Shakespeare.

ST. STEPHEN, Cornwall. [2 Cf] Village on the A3058, 4 m. W. of St. Austell. The brothers Joseph Hocking (1850–1935) and Silas Hocking (1860–1937) were born here, the sons of a mine-owner. Both were Methodist ministers and prolific novelists. Silas, whose first story, *Alec Green*, was published in 1878, achieved immense popularity with his novels, mainly on religious themes, and after holding pastorates in Liverpool, Manchester, and Southport, retired from the ministry in 1895 to devote himself to writing. Joseph spent some time in the Near East as a young man before settling as pastor in Woodford Green, Essex. He wrote about fifty novels between 1891 and 1936, some with Cornish settings, others with historical and religious themes.

SALCOMBE, Devon. [2 Ef] Resort and yachting centre at the end of the A381, beautifully situated on the steep W. side of the wooded estuary of the Avon. J. A. Froude rented The Moult as a summer residence for many years, when he was living and working in London, and built a small yacht which he sailed himself. Later he took Woodville (now Woodcot), where he retired in 1894 and died (20 Oct.) the same year. Both houses stand in extensive grounds, between North and South Sands, on the road to Bolt Head. Froude is buried in the cemetery, on the other side of the town. Tennyson's poem 'Crossing the Bar' is traditionally associated with his visit to Salcombe in May 1889. He was convalescing after an illness, cruising in a friend's yacht, which put in to the harbour so that he might stay with Froude. When he left, sitting on deck on a fine Sunday evening, the church bell was ringing for evensong, and he noticed how as the yacht reached the sandy bar the waves 'gave forth a surfy, slow, deep, mellow voice, and with a hollow moan crossed the bar on their way to the harbour'. The haunting impressions of the scene are recorded in the poem, written the following October at Farringford (q.v.).

SALFORD. See MANCHESTER.

SALISBURY (pr. Sawlzbry), Wilts. [1 Ad] Cathedral city 15 m. W. of Winchester. John Foxe, who returned to England after Queen Elizabeth's accession, published his *Book of Martyrs* (1563) in the year he was made Canon of Salisbury. Philip Massinger, whose father was employed by the Herberts of Wilton, was baptized in November 1583 at St. Thomas's Church, but the record does not survive in the Diocesan Office in The Close. In 1668 Pepys, who was guided 'all over the plain by the sight of the steeple' of the cathedral, was given a silk bed at the George Inn (gone). He thought the town 'a very brave place' and noted that the 'river runs through every street' (a system of canals for water and drainage), before going sightseeing to Stonehenge and Wilton. The heavy old timbers of the George Inn now form the entrance to Old George Mall,

where a plaque commemorating Pepys's visit is affixed. The cathedral contains the diamond-shaped stone with William Browne's epitaph to the Countess of Pembroke (d. 1631) 'Sidney's sister, Pembroke's mother' and also a bust of Richard Jefferies (d. 1887), a native and a lover of Wiltshire. Trollope in his *Autobiography* (1883) recalls how when 'wandering one midsummer evening round the purlieus of Salisbury Cathedral', he 'conceived the story of *The Warden*, from whence came the series of novels of which Barchester . . . was the central site . . .'. Although Barchester was Winchester and the county of Barset was imaginary, *The Warden* was certainly inspired by his view of the city from the 'little bridge' near the cathedral. Hardy called Salisbury 'Melchester' in his novels of Wessex.

SALTRAM HOUSE, Devon. [2 Df] Mansion (N.T.) built *c.* 1750, incorporating the remains of a Tudor house, in a landscaped park 3½ m. E. of Plymouth city centre, between the A38 and the A379. Dr. Johnson sometimes visited here when he came with Sir Joshua Reynolds, who was a native of Plympton St. Maurice near by. Fanny Burney was also a visitor, and wrote (1789) 'the house is one of the most magnificent in the kingdom, its view is noble'.

Open 29 Mar.–31 Oct.: daily 11 a.m.–1 p.m. (last admission 12.30 p.m.), 2–6 p.m. or sunset if earlier (last admission half an hour before closing). Nov.–Mar.: garden open daily during daylight hours.

SALVINGTON. See WORTHING.

SANDBOURNE. See BOURNEMOUTH.

SANDGATE BAY. See FOLKESTONE.

SANDWICH, Kent. [1 Hc] Old town on the A256 and the A257, 12 m. E. of Canterbury, once the premier Cinque Port. Tom Paine, who set up business as a staymaker in 1759, married Mary Lambert at St. Peter's Church and lived at 20 New St. (P). His business failed and he moved to Dover, where his wife died in 1760. Sandwich is the 'Sunwich Port' of W. W. Jacobs's comic stories of longshoremen.

SANDYCOVE, Dublin. [8 Gf] Coastal resort just SE. of Dun Laoghaire. Signposts to

'James Joyce's Tower' indicate the martello tower, one of a series of defences against the threat of Napoleonic invasion, which figures in the first chapter of *Ulysses* (1922). Joyce stayed there briefly in September 1904 and it now houses a small museum.[1]

[1] Open May–Sept.: Mon.–Sat. 10 a.m.–1 p.m., 2–5.15 p.m.; Sun. 2.30–6 p.m. Other times by arrangement with the Eastern Regional Tourism Organisation Ltd., Moran Park, Dun Laoghaire, Co. Dublin. Tel. (01) 808571.

SANDYMOUNT. See DUBLIN.

SANDYSHORE. See FLEETWOOD.

SAPISTON, Suff. [4 Ge] Village off the A1088, 6 m. SE. of Thetford. Robert Bloomfield worked from the age of 11 to 15 on the farm of William Austin, a connection of his mother's. Then, too puny for the work, he was apprenticed to his brother, a shoemaker, in London, where he wrote *The Farmer's Boy* (1800) about his life in this neighbourhood. On the green by the church, where the cows were milked and where Austin's farmhouse still stands, 'shadowing elms obstruct the morning ray' still. The thatched church is derelict now but Austin's tombstone and those of his infant children can still be seen in the churchyard. Fakenham near by, a favourite resort of young Bloomfield and the Austin children, is remembered in the lines:

> The moat remains, the dwelling is no more,
> Its name denotes its melancholy fall
> For village children call the spot Burnt Hall.

SAPPERTON, Glos. [1 Ab] Village off the A419, 5 m. W. of Cirencester. During the Second World War John Masefield lived at Pinbury Park, a gabled house with a yew avenue, called the Nuns' Walk. His poems, *Land Workers* (1942) and *Collected Poems* (1946), were published during this time.

SAWREY. See NEAR SAWREY.

SCALEBY CASTLE, Cumbria. [5 Ba] Castle ½ m. S. of the village of Scaleby, 5½ m. NE. of Carlisle, on a minor road between the B6264 and the A6071. William Gilpin was born here (4 June 1724), the son of Captain John Bernard Gilpin, and was educated at Carlisle and St. Bees before going to Oxford.

SCARBOROUGH, North Yorkshire. [5 Gc] Resort on the E. coast popular since the 18th c. In Smollett's *Humphry Clinker* (1771) the drowning Matthew Bramble was brought safely to the beach. But he was naked and had 'extravagant ideas of decency and decorum', so the party left next day. Sheridan set his comedy *A Trip to Scarborough* (1777) here. In 1849 Anne Brontë died at 2 The Cliff, demolished about 20 years later to make way for the Grand Hotel. She is buried not far from the castle in the detached part of St. Mary's churchyard, beyond the ruined part of the church. Charlotte visited the grave in 1852. Edith Sitwell was born in the family's seaside home, Wood End, by the Crescent, now a museum[1] containing first editions of the Sitwells' works. Osbert Sitwell's novel, *Before the Bombardment* (1926), is set in the town.

[1] Open weekdays 10 a.m.–5 p.m.; Sun. 2–5 p.m., summer only.

SCARNING, Norf. [4 Gd] Village on the A47, 3 m. W. of East Dereham, where Dr. Augustus Jessopp was rector (1879–1911). His book *Arcady for Better for Worse* (1887) has fine descriptions of the district. He lived in The Hall, next to the church. A granite cross marks his grave by the entrance from The Hall to the churchyard and there is a tablet in the church. He is still remembered in the village.

SCILLY ISLES, Cornwall. [2 Jg] Group of *c.* 150 islands, five of which are inhabited, 28 m. SW. of Land's End. Traditionally they are the remnants of the legendary Arthurian land of Lyonesse, supposed to be lying under the sea between them and the mainland.

Edward Hyde, later first Earl of Clarendon, came here on 4 March 1646 with the young Prince Charles and his council and stayed until 17 April, when they moved to St. Helier in Jersey because the Parliamentary fleet was threatening their safety. On 18 March Hyde began *The True Historical Narrative of the Rebellion and Civil Wars in England* (first published after his death by his son, 1702–4), which he continued at St. Helier.

George Eliot and George Lewes visited St. Mary's, the largest island, from March to May 1857 and lodged at the post office. She was writing *Mr. Gilfil's Love-Story* (published in *Scenes of Clerical Life*, 1858) and he was studying marine life for his *Seaside Studies at Ilfracombe, Tenby, The Scilly Isles, and Jersey* (1858).

Sir Arthur Quiller-Couch gives a graphic account of the islands in the second half of the 19th c. in his romantic novel, *Major Vigoureux* (1907).

The Scilly Isles can be reached by boat or helicopter from Penzance.

SEAGRAVE, Leics. [4 Cd] Village W. of the A46, the Fosse Way, 8 m. N. of Leicester. Robert Burton who, in the fifth edition of the *Anatomy of Melancholy* (1638), mentions that the village is more barren than neighbouring ones 'yet no place likely yields better aire', was inducted into the living here in 1632. Burton spent most of his time in Oxford but he visited this parish occasionally, perhaps because it is not far from his brother's home and his own birthplace, at Lindley. He also left some money to Seagrave in his will.

SEAHAM, Durham. [5 Ea] A coal-port off the A19, 6 m. SE. of Sunderland. Seaham Hall (now a hospital) was the home of Anne Isabella Milbanke, whose marriage ceremony to Lord Byron took place in the drawing-room in January 1815.

SELBORNE, Hants. [1 Cd] Village on the B3006, 5 m. S. of Alton. Gilbert White, 18th-c. naturalist and writer, was born at the vicarage and lived at his home, The Wakes (now the Oates Memorial Library and Museum and the Gilbert White Museum),[1] from 1751 till his death in 1793. The museum contains personal relics and editions of *The Natural History and Antiquities of Selborne* (1789), which he wrote at The Wakes, and in the grounds can be seen the pathway which he laid down to enable him to reach his bird-watching arbour, the ha-ha which he dug, and his famous sundial. He is buried in the churchyard, his grave, to the N. of the chancel, marked by a simple headstone with only his initials and the date of his death.

[1] Open Apr.–Oct.: 10.30 a.m.–12.30 p.m., 2–5 p.m.; Sun. 2–5 p.m.; Nov.–Mar.: Sat. and Sun. 2–5 p.m. (closed Fri. and during Dec.).

SELKIRK, Selkirks. (Borders). [6 Fd] Ancient Royal Burgh on the A7 and the A708, over-

looking Yarrow Water. On the hill approaching the W. side of the Market Place a wall plaque marks the site of Old Forest Inn, where Burns stayed when he wrote his 'Epistle to Willie Creech' (the publisher of the 2nd edn. of his poems) on 13 May 1787. In the High St. there is a statue of Mungo Park, the explorer and author of *Travels in the Interior of Africa* (1799), who was born at Foulshiels (q.v.). The museum has some relics of his expeditions to Sumatra and the Niger. Sir Walter Scott, who was Sheriff of Selkirkshire from 1800 until his death in 1832, is commemorated by a statue in the Market Place, outside the Court-house where he administered justice. Andrew Lang was born (1844) in a house now called Viewfield and attended the Grammar School before going to Edinburgh Academy.

SEVENOAKS. See KNOLE.

SEVENOAKS WEALD, Kent. [1 Fd] Village off the A21, 3 m. S. of Sevenoaks. Edward Thomas, with his wife and children, rented (1904–6) Else's Farm above the railway, and opposite the inn still known locally as the Shant. He often spent 16 hours a day on reviews and other commissions but was always short of money. He made fortnightly journeys to London to find work and his friends, including Edward Garnett and his young son David, came at weekends. Thomas rented Stidolph's Cottage in Eggpie Lane to write in and wore a path across the fields to its door. There he installed W. H. Davies to write *The Autobiography of a Super Tramp* (1908), which had been recounted through tobacco fumes by the fire at the farmhouse. Davies broke his wooden leg there and the village carpenter made a makeshift replacement from Thomas's design.

SHAFTESBURY, Dorset. [2 Hc] Ancient town on the A30 and the A350, situated on the edge of a 700-ft plateau, with extensive views over Blackmoor Vale. The town is well described in Hardy's *Jude the Obscure* (1895), where it appears under its old name of 'Shaston'. The railway station at Semley, c. 2 m. N. of the town, is now closed.

SHALLOWFORD, Staffs. [3 Hc] Little village on the river Meece, 5 m. NW. of Stafford, reached by a turning off the A5013 near

Great Bridgeford. The Izaak Walton Cottage, a charming half-timbered building in a pleasant garden, was originally part of Halfhead Farm, where Izaak Walton used to stay after he retired from business in London. He bequeathed the property, which he is believed to have owned from 1654 onwards, to his native Stafford for charitable uses. Eventually the farm was sold and the cottage, admirably restored, was opened as a museum.[1]

[1] Open daily, except Tues., 10 a.m.–noon, 2.30–4.30 p.m.

SHANKLIN, I.O.W. [1 Cf] Resort on the SE. coast adjacent to Sandown. John Keats lodged at Mrs. Williams's house, Eglantine Cottage, 76 High St. (P), in July and August 1819. He completed the first book of *Lamia*, and with Charles Armitage Brown started the drama, *Otho the Great*. H. W. Longfellow, the American author of the poems, *Hiawatha* (1855) and *Tales of a Wayside Inn* (1863), which contains 'Paul Revere's Ride', stayed at the Crab Inn in the Old Village in July 1868. He wrote to a friend that he was staying in 'a lovely little thatch-roofed inn, all covered with ivy'. The inscription, that he was asked to write, now embellishes the fountain outside:

> O traveller, stay thy weary feet;
> Drink of this fountain pure and sweet;
> It flows for rich and poor the same.
> Then go thy way, remembering still
> The wayside well beneath the hill,
> The cup of water in His name.

SHARPHAM, Som. [2 Gc] Hamlet N. of the A39 at Walton, ½ m. W. of Street. Sharpham Park, an old manor house (with garden walls remaining from a demolished wing) now divided into two, one part a farm, was the birthplace of Edward Dyer (date unknown), a friend of Philip Sidney. Dyer, who wrote elegies, has been regarded as the author of the lyric on contentment 'My mind to me a Kingdom is'. He held an official post in the county and died in 1607. A century later Henry Fielding was born in the same house (his mother's home) but spent only a short time there before his parents moved to East Stour.

SHASTON. See SHAFTESBURY.

SHAUGH PRIOR, Devon. [2 De] Village on a minor road, *c.* 5 m. NE. of the centre of Plymouth. The church has a memorial in white marble, an inscription set in a Gothic arch, commemorating the Devon poet, N. T. Carrington, a native of Plymouth who loved this district. One of his favourite haunts was Shaugh Bridge, *c.* 1 m. NW., where the Plym and the Meavy meet, and shortly after his death some of his admirers had his name carved on the Dewerstone, a commanding rock overlooking the Plym just above the bridge.

SHAWELL, Leics. [4 Be] Village off the M1, 4 m. NE. of Rugby. Tennyson often stayed at the rectory (now the Old Rectory) after his father's ward, Sophie Rawnsley, married the rector. The Elmhirsts built a wooden room in the rectory garden, where Tennyson could smoke and work undisturbed at his elegy on his friend Hallam. The eldest Elmhirst daughter was a bridesmaid in 1850 at Tennyson's wedding, conducted by Sophie's brother.

SHEFFIELD, South Yorkshire. [5 Ef] University, cathedral, and steel manufacturing city on the Don. James Montgomery settled here as clerk to the *Sheffield Register* in 1792. This changed its name to the *Sheffield Iris* and Montgomery became a contributor, editor, and then its owner. He was imprisoned for libel over political articles and wrote *The Wanderer of Switzerland* (1806) and other poems which have fallen into obscurity. His hymns, which include 'Songs of praise the angels sang' and 'Forever with the Lord', remain popular.

Ebenezer Elliott, owner of a successful ironworks (1821–41), took an active interest in literary and political events. His early verse, *Tales of the Night* (1818), was praised by Southey, but anger at the 'bread tax' produced *The Village Patriarch* (1829) and the *Corn-Law Rhymes* (1831) by which he is best remembered. A bronze statue (now in Weston Park) paid for by Sheffield workingmen, was erected (1854) in the market place.

In 1876 Ruskin, idealistic superintendent of the Guild of St. George, bought thirteen acres of land at Abbeydale. 'We will try to make some small piece of English ground, beautiful, peaceful and fruitful. We will have no steam engines upon it, and no railroads.' There were few supporters for this simple life and the land was run as a market garden. Today it is the Abbeydale Industrial

Hamlet[1] showing early machinery. Many of the paintings and books given by Ruskin to the Guild, and formerly to be seen in Sheffield, are now on loan to Reading University.

[1] Open 10.15 a.m.–5 p.m.

SHEFFIELD PARK. See FLETCHING.

SHEFFORD, Beds. [4 Df] Small town at the junction of the A507 and the A600. Robert Bloomfield, who lived his last years in great poverty in North Bridge St. (P), died there in 1823.

SHEPPERTON. See NUNEATON.

SHEPPERTON, Surrey. [1 Dc] Large village 2 m. E. of Chertsey. The satirical novelist T. L. Peacock bought (1823) a riverside house (P) at the entrance to Walton Lane in Lower Halliford (then a separate hamlet) for his mother, where he could spend weekends and holidays from his post in the India Office. After his marriage to Jane Griffith, whom he had met 8 years before in Wales, he bought the house adjoining his mother's and turned them into one (now Elmbank). After his retirement (1856) he settled here permanently. *Memoirs of Shelley* (1858) and *Gryll Grange* (1860) were written here. His daughter married the novelist George Meredith who joined him (1853) for a while but, after disagreements, moved to Vine Cottage across the green. Meredith was deserted by his wife in 1858. She died in 1861, and is buried in the churchyard where her tombstone has lines written by her father, who was buried (1866) in the cemetery.

As a boy the hymn-writer J. M. Neale was tutored at the rectory which he often revisited after his ordination. Author of 'Jerusalem the golden', 'Good King Wenceslas', and many other hymns as well known, he also wrote the novel *Shepperton Manor* (1844) about the village in the 17th c. Part of this was written at the rectory.

SHEPWARDINE. See CHURCH STRETTON.

SHERBORNE, Dorset. [2 Hd] Ancient stone-built town on the A30, 5 m. E. of Yeovil. It was the seat of a bishopric from 705 to 1078 and the chronicler Asser (d. 909?) was bishop here. During his episcopate he wrote a life of King Alfred in Latin (*c.* 893). In the N. transept of the Abbey Church (the church of the former Benedictine abbey, which dates from the 15th c.) is a stone which is believed to mark the grave of the poet, Sir Thomas Wyatt, who died of a fever here in the summer of 1542, when on his way to bring the imperial ambassador from Falmouth to London.

The old castle, now ruined, at the E. end of the town, was leased by Queen Elizabeth I to Sir Walter Ralegh in 1592 and given to him in 1599. He attempted to modernize the building, but abandoned it in order to build the existing castle.[1] A will made by Ralegh in July 1597 was discovered in the Digby Estate Office in Sherborne in the 1970s and reveals something of his style of living and his concern for his wife and heirs. The will and related documents are occasionally on display when the castle is open to the public. The castle is mentioned in Hardy's *The Woodlanders* (1887) and is a central feature of Dame the Seventh in his *A Group of Noble Dames* (1891). Sherborne appears as 'Sherton Abbas'.

Sherborne School (founded 1550) incorporates the 15th-c. Abbot's Hall and other monastic buildings formerly belonging to the abbey. Its distinguished pupils include Lewis (later Sir Lewis) Morris, the brothers John Cowper and Llewelyn Powys, and Cecil Day-Lewis.

[1] Open Easter Sat.–last Sun. in Sept.: Thurs., Sat., Sun., Bank Holiday Mon. 2–6 p.m.

SHERIFFHALES, Salop. [3 Gc] Village *c.* 3 m. N. of Shifnal, on the B4379, N. of the A5. In the latter part of the 17th c. an academy was held at the Manor House (down a private road W. of the village) for the advanced education of those who were barred from the university by the Test Act of 1673 on account of their Nonconformist views. The academy was run by the Revd. John Woodhouse on a plan devised by Richard Baxter.

SHERIFF HUTTON, North Yorkshire. [5 Fd] Village 10 m. NE. of York, off the A64. The ruined castle (privately owned), within a double moat and with its five storeys visible on the skyline from far away, was granted to the Earl of Surrey, victor of Flodden (1513). Skelton, who celebrated the battle in *Ballade of the Scottyshe Kynge*, spent Christmas (1522) here with Surrey's daughter-in-law Elizabeth (mother of the poet). Her ladies-in-waiting crown him among the great poets in his egotistic *Garlande of Laurell*, probably written here at this time.

SHERMANBURY, West Sussex. [1 Ee] Hamlet 2 m. N. of Henfield, on the A281. A tree-lined drive S. of the bridge over the Adur leads to Mock Bridge House, where Margaret Fairless Barber spent her last two summers (1900–1). She took the name of Dowson, the family by whom she was 'adopted' and who nursed her during her prolonged illness. She continued to write here, under the pseudonym 'Michael Fairless', the essays started in Chelsea, and later published as *The Roadmender*. 'There is a place waiting for me under the firs in a quiet churchyard' she wrote and her grave with a tall wooden cross is in Ashurst churchyard, 2 m. W.

SHERTON ABBAS. See SHERBORNE.

SHIFNAL, Salop. [3 Gc] Market town on the A464, 12½ m. NW. of Wolverhampton. Thomas Brown, the satirist, was reputed to have been born (1663) in Shifnal, but the exact location is not known. The parish was formerly a very large one, including several townships, and Brown's birthplace may have been outside the town itself. Thomas Percy owed the publication of his *Reliques of Ancient English Poetry* (1765) to the discovery, while visiting his friend Humphrey Pitt, of an old manuscript (which was being used for lighting fires) containing ballads, songs, and metrical romances. The Pitts lived at Priors Lee Hall, now the headquarters of the Ironbridge Gorge Development Corporation, in the parish (but not in the town) of Shifnal.

The town, which has many well-preserved half-timbered and Georgian houses, appealed strongly to Dickens and is described by him in *The Old Curiosity Shop* (1841).

SHILLINGFORD, Oxon. [1 Cb] Little village (formerly in Berks.) 10 m. SE. of Oxford, on the A423. W. B. Yeats stayed here with his wife and child between April and June 1921, having let their house in Oxford for the summer months. They rented Minchen's Cottage, a modest two-storeyed cottage on the W. side of the road to Warborough, hoping to go to Ireland, as Yeats said in a letter, 'at the first sign of a lull in the storm there as George [his wife] pines for Ballylee'. (The 'storm' was the outbreak of violence that had followed the meeting of the Dáil in 1919 and its subsequent suppression.) While he was in Shillingford Yeats began writing 'Meditations in Time of Civil War', the first of a series of poems finished at Thoor Ballylee in 1922, *Seven Poems and a Fragment*, which he described as 'a lamentation over lost peace and hope'. From Shillingford the Yeats family moved over to Thame (q.v.).

SHINFIELD. See THREE MILE CROSS.

SHIPBOURNE (pr. Shibbon), Kent. [1 Fd] Village on the A227, 5 m. SE. of Sevenoaks. The poet Christopher Smart was born (1722) at Fairlawn, the country house ½ m. N. of the church, where his father was steward.

SHIPLAKE, Oxon. [1 Cc] Village on the A4155, 4 m. NE. of Reading. Tennyson married Emily Sellwood here. The reconciliation after their broken engagement occurred after he had sent a copy of the elegies on the death of Arthur Hallam to his friend Rawnsley, the vicar whose wife was a cousin of Emily's and in favour of the marriage. Doubts Emily and her parents had felt about his religious beliefs were dispelled and they were married a fortnight after *In Memoriam* (1850), the title chosen by Emily for the elegies, was published. Before her wedding, Emily stayed at Holmwood, the Georgian house, visible through the iron gates at Binfield Heath, 1 m. W. In the coach to Pangbourne, the first stop on their honeymoon, Tennyson wrote a poem to Rawnsley who had performed the ceremony, and whose three children were bridesmaids.

The church, on a knoll above the Thames, has a memorial to James Granger, vicar from 1746 to his death in 1776, whose *Biographical History of England* (1769) included blank pages to be filled with illustrations to suit the owner's taste. To Grangerize became a popular pastime.

Swinburne made many visits to Holmwood, his parents' home from 1865–79, usually to recuperate from his intemperate life in London. He was working on *Tristram of Lyonesse* in 1869 and wrote 'On the Cliffs' in the summer of 1879 after a longer illness than usual had prevented his writing from the November of the previous year. The novelist, Watts-Dunton, visited Holmwood that summer, and an arrangement for the tenancy of 2 The Pines (see London, Putney) jointly with Swinburne was agreed upon. Eric Blair ('George Orwell') lived as a boy at Roselawn, Station Road.

SHIPLEY, West Sussex. [1 De] Village off the A272, 6 m. SW. of Horsham. Hilaire Belloc lived from 1906 to his death in 1953 at King's Land, a house dating from the 15th c. Much of his work, including light verse, essays, novels (some illustrated by his friend, G. K. Chesterton), and studies of the French Revolution, was written here. His love of Sussex is shown in the lines from 'The South Country'

> I never get between the pines
> But I smell the Sussex air;
> Nor I never come on a belt of sand
> But my home is there.

Shipley Mill[1] (P) near his house has been restored as a memorial to him.

[1] Open May–Oct. first Sat. and Sun. 2.30–5.45 p.m., or by written appointment from R. D. Jebb, King's Land.

SHIRLEY, Derbys. [4 Ac] Village off the A52, 9 m. NW. of Derby. John Cowper Powys and his brother, Theodore Francis, were born at their father's rectory in 1872 and in 1875 respectively. They lived here until their father returned to Dorchester in his native Dorset in 1879.

SHOREHAM, Kent. [1 Fc] Village off the A225, 5 m. N. of Sevenoaks. William Blake was often visited in London by a group of young painters including Samuel Palmer, whom he most influenced, and when Palmer moved here to the Water House in 1826 Blake, although in poor health (he died in 1827), came to stay with him. The group, known locally as the Extollagers, roamed day and night over the countryside, reciting poetry and carrying painting equipment and camp stools. Blake accompanied them on a ghost hunt to the ruined castle and demonstrated his telepathic powers by foretelling Palmer's unexpected appearance well before it occurred.

The Regency Dunstall Priory with its round tower was the childhood home of Lord Dunsany. He inherited the house in 1916 and lived here intermittently. He died at his Irish home, Dunsany Castle in Co. Meath, but was buried at his request in the churchyard here where there is a memorial. His short stories, plays, and verse are largely myth and fantasy but *The Curse of the Wise Woman* (1935) is partly autobiographical.

SHOREHAM-BY-SEA, West Sussex. [1 Ee] Port and sailing resort on the Adur, W. of Hove. Woodview, the house in George Moore's novel, *Esther Waters* (1894), is said to be modelled on Buckingham House (gonc). The grounds are now a public park. Esther visits the entertainments at Swiss Gardens and undergoes many disasters before finding peace with her former employer, widowed and impoverished, and living in a corner of the old house.

Evelyn Waugh, who was at Lancing College from 1917 to the end of 1921, gives an account of his years here in his autobiography *A Little Learning* (1964).

SHOTTERMILL, Surrey. [1 Dd] Residential district, 1 m. SW. of Haslemere, on the B2131. George Eliot rented a furnished house called Brookbank here with George Lewes from May to August in 1871. The house, not far from the railway, is now divided in two, Brookbank and Middlemarch, and the yew tree under which George Eliot sat while writing *Middlemarch* (1872) is just visible in the garden behind. Tennyson first met her here, and used to come over from Aldworth and read his poems to her. She liked being here so much, where 'there were no interruptions except welcome ones', that on leaving Brookbank she decided to prolong her stay and moved across the road to Cherrimans before returning to London in September.

SHOTTERY, Warwicks. [4 Af] Village 1 m. NW. of Stratford-upon-Avon, home of Anne Hathaway, whom Shakespeare married in 1582. A bond giving the names of two men standing surety for Shakespeare's pledge to marry Anne Hathaway can be seen at Worcester (q.v.). The Hathaways, yeomen farmers, owned the partly 15th-c. farmhouse until it was bought by the Shakespeare Birthplace Trust in 1892. Much of their furniture is still in the house, formerly larger, but known now as Anne Hathaway's Cottage.[1]

[1] Open Apr.–Oct.: weekdays 9 a.m.–6 p.m., Sun. 10 a.m.–6 p.m.; Nov.–Mar.: weekdays 9 a.m.–4 p.m., Sun. 1.30–4.30 p.m.

SHREWSBURY (pr. Shrōzbry), Salop. [3 Gc] Historic county town, strikingly situated on rising ground within an almost encircling loop of the Severn, now bypassed by the A5. The town dates from the 5th c., when it became the seat of the Princes of Powis. It was conquered at the end of the 8th c. by Offa, King of Mercia, and as a Saxon and then a Norman stronghold it suffered many sieges and plunderings by the Welsh, who were finally subjugated by Edward I in 1283. At the top of Pride Hill, opposite the post office, a modern cross (1952, replacing an earlier one) marks the place where the body of Hotspur was hanged, drawn, and quartered after the battle of Shrewsbury, 1403 (see Battlefield).

George Farquhar wrote *The Recruiting Officer* while staying (1705) at the Raven Hotel (gone) in Castle St., near the Gateway of the Council House. The play, dedicated to 'all friends round the Wrekin', gives a life-like picture of Shrewsbury at the time of the Restoration and includes an allusion to the Raven itself.

William Hazlitt, who spent most of his youth at Wem (q.v.), was within easy reach of Shrewsbury. He picked up a copy of *Paradise Lost* here, and his first 'literary production' was a letter in 1791 to the *Shrewsbury Chronicle*, protesting against the treatment of Joseph Priestley by the Birmingham mob. Hazlitt was a great admirer of Coleridge and in 1808 walked over to Shrewsbury to hear him preach at the Unitarian Chapel, the last occasion on which Coleridge did so, as he shortly afterwards gave up Unitarianism.

John Hamilton Reynolds, poet and friend of Keats, was born (1794) in the town and baptized in St. Mary's Church. He went to Shrewsbury School before going on to St. Paul's School, London. Mary Webb (1881–1927), whose novels are set in Salop, where she was born and grew up, is buried in Shrewsbury cemetery. In her stories the town is depicted as 'Silverton'.

Shrewsbury School (founded 1552 by Edward VI) stands on the hill across the river, reached by Kingsland Bridge. The present buildings (1882) superseded the old buildings on the original site opposite the castle (now occupied by the museum and library). Sir Philip Sidney (1554–86) was educated here, and entered school in 1564 on the same day as Sir Fulke Greville, Lord Brooke (1554–1628), his friend and later his biographer. A statue of Sidney was erected (1923) in front of the new school as a memorial of the First World War. Other notable pupils include Frederick William Faber (1814–63), author of devotional books and hymns, remembered especially for 'My God, how wonderful Thou art' and 'Pilgrims of the Night'; Samuel Butler (1835–1902), author of *Erewhon* (1872); and Stanley Weyman (1855–1928), author of historical romances. The school library[1] has special collections which include western medieval manuscripts, among which is a manuscript of the earliest known miracle play in English, and incunabula and other early printed books.

Shrewsbury cakes have long been famous and are celebrated in 'Bloudie Jacke' in *The Ingoldsby Legends* (1840): 'She has given him . . . a Shrewsbury cake, | Of Pailin's own make.'

[1] Can be seen by arrangement with the librarian.

SIDMOUTH, Devon. [2 Fd] Seaside resort 9 m. NE. of Exmouth, approached by the A3052 or the A375. Elizabeth Barrett came here with her family in 1832 after the sale of Hope End, her father hoping that the warm climate would help to dispel her cough. They took a house at 7–8 Fortfield Ter., previously occupied by the Grand Duchess Helena of Russia and described by Elizabeth as 'not at all *grand*, but extremely comfortable and cheerful, with a splendid sea view in front, and pleasant green hills and trees behind'. The house is now flats, but a replica of the original Russian Eagle still stands above it. The family moved to Belle Vue (now the Cedar Shade Hotel) in All Saints Rd. in 1833 and stayed there until they left for London 2 years later. While she was in Sidmouth Elizabeth translated Æschylus' 'Prometheus Bound'. She also became acquainted with the Revd. George Hunter, minister of a Nonconformist chapel, with whom she seemed to find a kindred spirit as they walked beneath the trees and talked about poetry and literature.

But he fell in love with her and became embittered by her inability to respond to his devotion, which persisted for 13 years—until he realized that Browning had won her heart (see the *Cornhill Magazine*, Spring 1951, 'Miss Barrett and Mr. Hunter'). Sidmouth is the 'Baymouth' of Thackeray's *Pendennis*.

SILVERDALE, Lancs. [5 Bc] Extensive but unspoilt village in pleasant country near Morecambe Bay, on an unclassified road *c*. 3½ m. NW. of Carnforth (A6) and *c*. 3 m. S. of Arnside (B5282). Mrs. Gaskell often came from Manchester and stayed at a house now known as Gibraltar Tower, in a secluded position next to Gibraltar Farm. Her study was at the top of the tower, commanding a magnificent view of the bay, and here she found the much-needed peace and privacy for writing many of her books. 'Abermouth' in *Ruth* (1853) is probably modelled on Silverdale. The village hall is called Gaskell Hall in her memory and contains a portrait photograph.

SILVERTON. See SHREWSBURY.

SISSINGHURST CASTLE, Kent. [1 Gd] Part of an Elizabethan manor-house (N.T.) off the A262, 2½ m. N. of Cranbrook, restored from 1930 by Victoria Sackville-West and her husband Harold Nicolson, who also planted the gardens together. They made their home in the 15th-c. South Cottage where Harold Nicolson wrote biographies including *King George V* (1953), and the essay *The English Sense of Humour* (1947). He died there in 1968. Victoria Sackville-West had her study in the Elizabethan tower (P) where she wrote the novels *The Dark Island* (1934) and *Pepita* (1937), and the biographical study *Saint Joan of Arc* (1936). On the second floor of the tower is the printing press used by Virginia and Leonard Woolf to print the first edition of *The Waste Land* (1922) and other early works of the Hogarth Press. The Turret houses diaries, letters, and a series of pictures showing the restoration of the house and gardens. Victoria Sackville-West died (1962) in the 16th-c. Priest's House by the White Garden which was also the last home of the poet and novelist Richard Church (d. 1972).

In 1760, when the house was still intact, Edward Gibbon in the Hampshire Militia was appointed to guard the 17,500 French prisoners-of-war held there. He complained in his Journal of 'the inconceivable dirtiness of the season' in which his few men walked from their 'wretched barracks' to undertake guard duty of so many.

Garden and Tower open Apr.–mid Oct.: Mon.–Fri. noon–6 p.m. Sat., Sun., Bank Holidays 10 a.m.–6.30 p.m.

SKIPTON, West Yorkshire. [5 Dd] Market town on the A59 and the A65. The Norman castle[1] was repaired (1650–8) by Lady Anne Clifford (born here 1590), who built a new entrance. The poet Samuel Daniel became her tutor here until her marriage in 1609, and she acted in some of his masques performed at Court.

[1] Open daily 10 a.m.–dusk. Sun. from 2 p.m. Also conducted parties on the hour.

SKYE, Inner Hebrides (Highland). [7 Be–Cf] Island off the W. of Scotland reached by ferries from Mallaig and Lochalsh. Dr. Johnson and Boswell both give accounts of their month's stay in 1773. They were entertained by the Macdonalds at Kingsburgh (rebuilt), when Flora Macdonald described her adventures during Prince Charles Edward's escape, and Johnson slept in the Prince's bed. Johnson and Boswell also stayed at Broadford with the Mackinnons at Coire Chatachan (now ruins), which Johnson called Coriatachan and described as being 'very pleasantly situated between two brooks, with one of the highest hills of the island behind it'. Johnson was impressed with the hospitality given without payment on the island. He and Boswell also stayed 10 days at Dunvegan Castle,[1] in the NW. of the island, home of the Macleods, which dates back to the 14th c. They saw the drinking horn (still on view) of Rory More, the 16th chief, which Boswell said held 'a bottle and a half'.

Alexander Smith often spent holidays in Skye, his wife's home, after their marriage in 1857. His *A Summer in Skye* (1865) describes the locality with digressions on the associations it recalls. R. L. Stevenson wrote the song, popularly called 'The Skye Boat Song', published in *Songs of Travel* (1896) after his death.

[1] Open Easter–mid Oct.: daily 2–5 p.m.

SLAINS CASTLE, Aberdeens. (Grampian). [7 He] Extensive ruins, off the A975, 7 m.

S. of Peterhead, of a house (built 1664) which replaced the earlier castle (site 4 m. S.). Dr. Johnson and Boswell mention staying here in 1773 with the Earl and Countess of Errol. They sat in the bow window looking out across the sea, and also made a visit to the Buller of Buchan, a collapsed sea cave near by.

SLANE, Meath. [8 Ge] Small town in the valley of the Boyne, situated under the lee of Slane Hill, which towers above it, 9 m. W. of Drogheda, on the T26. Francis Ledwidge (1891–1917), a poet of great promise, was born here and worked for a time on the land. He served with the British Forces in the First World War and was killed in Flanders. *Songs of the Field* (1915) and *Songs of Peace* (1916) were published in his lifetime; his *Complete Poems*, with a preface by Lord Dunsany, in 1919.

SLIGO, Sligo. [8 Dd] Market town and port, beautifully situated on the Garavogue, between Lough Gill and the sea, at the junction of the T3, the T17, and the T18. As a boy W. B. Yeats spent many holidays here with his maternal grandparents, the dour and difficult old merchant, William Pollexfen, and his kind and gracious wife, Elizabeth. They lived at Merville, a big house with 60 acres of land on the edge of the town, until the 1880s, when they moved, first to Charlemont, overlooking the harbour, and later to a smaller place called Rathedmond. Yeats and his brother Jack and his two sisters loved Sligo and became deeply attached to the country round—a rich store of legend and folklore for the young poet (see especially Collooney, Innisfree, and Knocknarea).

SLINGERS, ISLE OF. See PORTLAND, ISLE OF.

SMA' GLEN, Perths. (Tayside). [6 Eb] High valley between Crieff and Amulree on the A822, traditionally the burial place of Ossian, the 3rd-c. legendary bard. Wordsworth passed through the glen in 1803 and wrote:

> In this still place, remote from men
> Sleeps Ossian, in the Narrow Glen.

SMAILHOLM, Roxburghs. (Borders). [6 Gd] Village on the B6397, 6 m. NW. of Kelso.

Walter Scott came here at the age of 3 to stay at his grandfather's farm, Sandyknowe, to recuperate from an illness that left him permanently lame. Here he listened to tales of the Borders related by his grandmother and aunt, and here his lifelong attachment to the life and romance of the Border country was first formed. There is a Scott memorial window in the church.

To the SW. stands Smailholm Tower, built in 1533 on a hilltop near a small loch and commanding splendid views. It appears in the third canto of Scott's *Marmion* and in 'The Eve of St. John'. The key to the Tower may be obtained from Sandyknowe Farm.

SMERWICK, Kerry. [9 Ad] Village on the W. shore of Smerwick Harbour, an extensive and beautiful inlet at the NW. extremity of the Dingle Peninsula. In 1579 invading Spaniards, accompanied by a Papal Nuncio, built a fort (Fort-del-Oro) here, to support the Desmond rebellion. The following year the garrison, reinforced by about 600 Italians, was bombarded and ruthlessly massacred by English troops under Lord Grey. Ralegh and Spenser are said to have taken part in the affair, but this has been disputed. Kingsley describes it in *Westward Ho!* (1855), where the hero, Amyas Leigh, takes Don Guzman, a Spanish captain, prisoner. On the W. side of the little peninsula, near the Three Sisters rocks, is Ferriter's Castle, whose last owner was Pierce Ferriter, the soldier-poet, commemorated at Killarney and Muckross (qq.v.).

SNAILBEACH, Salop. [3 Fd] Hamlet in the Hope Valley, on a minor road off the A488, c. 10 m. SW. of Shrewsbury. The little chapel, frequented by the mining community, was the centre of interest in Mary Webb's *Gone to Earth* (1917).

SNARGATE. See WAREHORNE.

SNOWFIELD. See WIRKSWORTH.

SOCKBURN, North Yorkshire. [5 Eb] Village on the Tees, 8 m. N. of Northallerton, off the A167. Dorothy Wordsworth wrote that Thomas Hutchinson's home here was 'a pleasant farm on the banks of the Tees' when she, her brother William, and Coleridge stayed with him in 1799 after their tour of Germany. Wordsworth married Hutchinson's sister Mary in 1802, and on a later visit wrote much of *The White Doe of Rylstone* here after seeing Scarsdale and Bolton Abbey.

SOMERSBY, Lincs. [4 Eb] Small village between the A153 and the A158, 6 m. NW. of Horncastle. Alfred Tennyson was born (1809) at the rectory, his home until 1837. He and his brothers and sisters suffered from the peculiar position of their father, the elder son disinherited in favour of his younger brother. Tennyson, after a short time at Louth Grammar School, was educated at home by his father and at an early age had written *The Devil and the Lady* in imitation of Elizabethan drama. *Poems by Two Brothers*, a collection of his and his brother Charles's verse, was published in 1827, the year he went to Trinity College, Cambridge. *Poems Chiefly Lyrical* (1830), which contained 'Claribel' and 'Mariana', was followed by a collection in 1833, which included 'The Lotos-Eaters', 'Œnone', and 'Two Voices'. The brothers used to write in an attic reached by a separate stair. A Cambridge friend, Arthur Hallam, visited the rectory and became engaged to Alfred's sister but his sudden death soon afterwards plunged the family into despair. In 1833 Tennyson started a series of elegies to Hallam, which were published many years after the family had left Somersby. Tennyson spent some time visiting Harrington Hall (q.v.) and then became acquainted with Emily Sellwood, whom he first met in Holywell Wood on the Tetford road. The church, which had a thatched roof in Tennyson's time, has a bust of the poet. The castellated Grange next to the rectory, formerly known as Baumber's Farm, is said to have been designed by Vanbrugh.

SOULDERN, Oxon. [1 Ca] Quiet village off the A41, 8 m. SE. of Banbury. Wordsworth wrote the sonnet 'On a parsonage in Oxfordshire' when staying in 1820 with his friend Robert Jones at the rectory (gone, site below the garden of the present one).

SOUTHAMPTON, Hants. [1 Be] Historic city, seaport, and university town, situated at the head of Southampton Water, the estuary of the Test, on a peninsula bounded on the E. side by the Itchen. Isaac Watts was born here (17 July 1674), of Puritan stock. A plaque at the back entrance of Marks and Spencer's store in Vincent's Walk records that 'On this site stood the Above Bar Congregational Church founded in 1662 and destroyed by enemy action in 1940. Among those who worshipped here was Isaac Watts, author and hymn writer.' Watts was born in the first Meeting House on this spot, though shortly after his birth his family moved to 41 French St. (also bombed, and later demolished). He attended King Edward VI School and went on to the Nonconformist Academy at Newington Green. His writings include sermons, philosophical treatises, poems, and educational manuals, but he is chiefly remembered for his hymns, especially 'Our God, our help in ages past', 'When I survey the wondrous cross', and 'Jesus shall reign where'er the sun'. His statue, carved by a local sculptor, R. C. Lucas, stands in Watts Park, N. of the Civic Centre, and has panels on three sides of the pedestal, showing him as a young poet, a teacher, and a philosopher. The last panel depicts a terrestrial globe and a telescope, with a quotation from Dr. Johnson: 'He has taught the art of reasoning and the science of the stars.' The Church of the Ascension, Bitterne Park, has four memorial windows illustrating seven of his best-known hymns, and St. Andrew's Church in Brunswick Pl. contains his sculptured head and shoulders, rescued from the ruin of the Above Bar Congregational Church. The modern Isaac Watts Memorial Church (dedicated 1960) stands at the junction of Winchester Rd. with Luccomb Rd.

Charles Dibdin, dramatist and song-writer, was also a native of Southampton (born 15 Mar. 1745) and lived here till he was 11, when he became a chorister at Winchester Cathedral. After his father's death he went to London, where he wrote songs (including 'Tom Bowling', 'Poor Jack', and other sea songs), plays, and novels. He is commemorated by a stone tablet erected (1814) by the Southampton Literary and Philosophical Society on the W. front of Holy Rood Church (ruined) in Bernard St., on the E. side of High St. A portrait and a statuette of Dibdin can be seen at the Tudor House Museum.[1]

In the 18th c. Southampton became fashionable as a spa, assembly rooms were built, and many distinguished visitors came and went, including Pope, who stayed in

1734 with his friend Lord Peterborough at Bevis Mount (outside the city gates, 1 m. N., the estate now occupied by suburban houses), from which he visited Netley Abbey (q.v.); and Gray, who also stayed at Bevis Mount (1755 and 1764) and went over to Netley.

In 1806 Jane Austen came from Bath with her mother and sister, Cassandra, and stayed in lodgings with her brother Frank. They moved in 1807 to 3 Castle Sq., a roomy, comfortable house (gone), which stood near the Juniper Berry public house in modern Upper Bugle St., with a pleasant garden, bounded on one side by the city walls, on the top of which it was possible to walk and enjoy extensive views. The Austens stayed here until the spring of 1809 and during part of this time Jane looked after her two young nephews, who came to stay after their mother's death. On one occasion they had a little water party on the Itchen and the boys rowed part of the way from the ferry to Northam, where they landed and walked home. In the evening Jane introduced them to the card game, 'speculation'.

Robert Pollok (1795–1827), a Scottish poet born at the little farm of Moorhouse, 10 m. S. of Glasgow, is commemorated by a red granite obelisk in the old churchyard of St. Nicholas, Millbrook. He qualified as a minister, but ill-health prevented his taking a regular appointment. On 1 September 1827, suffering from consumption, he came to stay with his sister at Shirley Common in the hope of recuperating, but died a fortnight later. His religious/philosophical poem, *The Course of Time*, was published in ten books in 1827 and went through many editions in Britain and America.

The centenary of the death of another writer was celebrated on 5 March 1967 when a brass plate was unveiled on the London Hotel, Terminus Ter., recording that 'Charles Browne, known to the world as Artemus Ward, died in the hotel which formerly stood opposite this spot, March 6th, 1867'. The former hotel, Radley's, is now the Royal Mail House. Browne was a popular American humorous writer, well known for his comments on life in the character of Artemus Ward, the travelling showman. He was taken ill on the boat from Jersey and brought to Southampton,

where he died. His body was eventually taken back to his birthplace, Waterford, Maine.

George Saintsbury, literary historian and critic, was born (23 Oct. 1845) in a house (gone) which stood at the corner of Briton St. and Orchard Pl. After his retirement from the chair of Rhetoric and English Literature at Edinburgh in 1915 he spent a few months in Southampton before settling in Bath, where he died (1933). He is buried in the Old Cemetery at Southampton.

Southampton is the 'Bevishampton' of Meredith's *Beauchamp's Career* (1876).

[1] Open weekdays 10 a.m.–5 p.m., Sun. 2.30–4.30 p.m.

SOUTH CADBURY, Som. [2 Hc] Village off the A303, 6 m. N. of Sherborne. Charles Churchill was curate here (1754–6) until he left for Rainham, London.

SOUTHEND-ON-SEA, Essex. [1 Gc] Large town and resort on the Thames estuary. In Jane Austen's *Emma* (1816) Mrs. John Knightley stoutly declares that her family thoroughly enjoyed their holidays here and that they 'never found the least inconvenience from the mud'.

Edwin Arnold wrote *The Light of Asia* (1879), the poem on the life of Buddha which proved very popular, while living at Hamlet House.

SOUTH HARTING, West Sussex. [1 Ce] Village on the B2146, 4 m. SE. of Petersfield. Alexander Pope used to stay at Ladyholt Park (now gone), the home of his friend John Caryll. Anthony Trollope lived at the Grange, now Northend House, for 18 months during 1880–2. It is said that he wrote standing at a desk upstairs, rode every morning before breakfast, and shocked the village with his week-end parties. The church has a reproduction of his portrait in the National Portrait Gallery.

SOUTH MALLING. See LEWES.

SOUTH MARSTON, Wilts. [1 Bb] Village off the A361, 6 m. NE. of Swindon. Alfred Williams lived most of his life in this village where he was born (1877) and buried (1931). He worked in the railway works at

Swindon and his knowledge of the classics in *Nature and Other Poems* (1912) caused the reviewers great surprise. He was living at Dryden Cottage when he described rural life in *A Wiltshire Village* (1912).

SOUTHOVER GRANGE. See LEWES.

SOUTHPORT, Lancs. [5 Be] Well-built seaside resort and residential town on the A565, S. of the Ribble estuary. The sporting novelist, Nathaniel Gould (1857–1919) was educated at Strathmore House School. Mary Webb (1881–1927), author of novels set in the background of her native Salop, spent 2 years (1897–9) at Mary Walmesley's school, Longsight, 1 Albert Rd. In 1901 the Bulgarian-born Dikrān Kouyoumdjian (1895–1956) came to live at Southport, first at Rosslare, Park Rd., then Rosslare, 85 Hesketh Rd., and finally 6 Hesketh Rd. He became a naturalized British subject in 1922, taking the name Michael Arlen, and achieved outstanding success with his best-selling novel, *The Green Hat* (1924).

SOUTH QUEENSFERRY, West Lothian (Lothian). [6 Fc] Town at the S. end of the Forth road bridge. Near the ferry jetty, formerly the main way across the Firth of Forth, is Hawes Inn, which Scott mentions in *The Antiquary* (1816), and where David Balfour's abduction is planned in Stevenson's *Kidnapped* (1886).

SOUTHSEA. See PORTSMOUTH.

SOUTHWATER, West Sussex. [1 Ed] Village off the A24, 3 m. S. of Horsham. In 1895 Wilfrid Scawen Blunt took possession of Newbuildings Place,[1] which came into his family in 1757, and commissioned a tapestry illustrating Botticelli's *Spring* from William Morris. He entertained his many friends here including Yeats, who read his poems aloud, and Belloc, a good neighbour at Shipley (q.v.). In 1907 Francis Thompson visited and Blunt remarked in *My Diaries* (1920) that he was not long for this world. Padraic Colum also visited from Greatham (q.v.), where he was spending his honeymoon. Cunninghame Graham's essay on his friend in *Redeemed* (1927) mentions the ride in the woods behind the house, where Blunt chose to be buried, and the great grass mound of the grave between the row of new

yew trees that he had planted under the oaks. Today the tomb, inscribed with lines from Blunt's *Collected Poems* (1914), is overshadowed by these tall yews. The essay also mentions the Arab horses bred here, and in the house 'the newelled staircase . . . the priest's secret chamber, the prints of horses . . . from the Godolphin Arab down to his own Messaud'.

[1] Visits in the summer months by appointment.

SOUTHWELL, Notts. [4 Cc] Small cathedral city NE. of Nottingham on the A612. Byron's mother rented Burgage Manor, the white house with the pillared porch on the green, from 1803 to 1808. He spent his holidays here from Harrow, extending them at 15 when he fell so desperately in love with his older cousin at Chaworth that he wouldn't go back. The Eliza of his early poems, printed at Newark, lived opposite him at The Burgage with his mother and brothers, and told Thomas Moore, who was staying at the Saracen's Head in 1828 preparing his *Life of Byron*, that after overcoming his shyness, Byron would 'come in and go out at all hours, as it pleased him, and in our house considered himself perfectly at home'. They sang ballads together, a favourite being 'Mary Anne', the name of his cousin. His signature is preserved on the wall.

SPALDING, Lincs. [4 Ed] Market town on the Welland, 14 m. SW. of Boston. In 1709 the antiquary Maurice Johnson founded the Spalding Gentlemen's Society, modelled on the Royal Society. He lived in the Elizabethan Ayscoughfee Hall (altered), now a school and museum. The Society, which has its library and museum[1] in Broad St., had Pope and Gay among its members.

[1] Inquiries to the Hon. Secretary, the Museum.

SPELSBURY, Oxon. [1 Ba] Village on the B4026, 7 m. NW. of Woodstock. Wilmot 2nd Earl of Rochester, after the deathbed repentance avowed by Bishop Burnet, was buried (1680) in the vault beneath the church. There are memorials here to the Lees of Ditchley into which family his mother married.

SPIGGLETON. See KILMARNOCK.

SPRINGHILL, Londonderry. [8 Fb] Manor house (N.T.) 1 m. SE. of Moneymore, a

Plantation town on the A29, 5 m. NE. of Cookstown. The house was built in the latter half of the 17th c., with later additions, and is an example of the fortified manor house built by the settlers in Ulster. Formerly the home of the Lenox Conynghams, it was bequeathed to the National Trust in 1957. The library contains early editions of Gerard's *Herball* (1597), Ralegh's *History of the World* (1614), and Hobbes's *Leviathan* (1651).

Open 1 Apr.–30 Sept.: daily except Tues. but open Easter Tues. 2–6 p.m.

STAFFORD, Staffs. [3 Hc] County town on the A34 and the A518. Izaak Walton was born here on 9 August 1593, a plaque on 62/62A Eastgate St. marking the traditional site of his birthplace. He was baptized on 21 September 1593 (the entry in the register is at the County Record Office) in the strangely oriental-looking font in the parish church of St. Mary's and is commemorated by a 19th-c. bust on the N. wall of the nave.

R. B. Sheridan was M.P. for Stafford 1780–1806 and used to stay at Chetwynd House (P), a pleasant Georgian building, now a post office, on the corner of Greengate St. and Mill Bank.

The Swan Hotel seems to have been a lively place in 1825 when, according to his account in *Romany Rye* (1857), Borrow appears to have been general superintendent of the stables:

The inn, of which I had become an inhabitant, was a place of infinite life and bustle ... And often in after life, when lonely and melancholy, I have called up the time I spent there, and never failed to become cheerful from the recollection.

But with the coming of the railways the old coaching inns declined and when Dickens stayed a night in the town some time in the 1840s he gave a depressed account of what may well have been the Swan, as

the extinct town inn, the Dodo ... It provides one with a trackless desert of sitting room ... and possesses interminable stables at the back— ... horseless

(see 'A Plated Article' in *Household Words*, 1858). But the pendulum swung again and with the advent of the car it gradually recovered and is now flourishing once more.

The William Salt Library[1] (established 1872) in Eastgate St. has a valuable collec-

tion of books and manuscripts relating to Staffordshire local history.

[1] Open Tues.–Sat. 10 a.m.–12.45 p.m., 1.45–5 p.m.

STAMFORD, Lincs. [4 Dd] Market town bypassed by the A1. John Clare often walked here from Helpston. One of the books he bought for 'little or nothing' at Ned Drury's shop (site opposite the old post office in the High St.) was *The Compleat Angler*, but he caught no more fish after reading it than before. Drury's cousin, John Taylor, published Clare's first poems in 1820. Octavius Gilchrist, a grocer, editor of Corbett's *Poems* and a contributor to Leigh Hunt's *Reflector* and the *Quarterly Review*, befriended Clare and conveyed him on his first visit to London. Gilchrist's shop is thought to have been in the High St. opposite the public library.

STANFORD-LE-HOPE, Essex. [1 Fc] Village off the A13, 5 m. NE. of Tilbury. In 1896 Joseph Conrad and his wife moved to a small house which he called 'a damned jerry-built rabbit hutch'. The next year they moved into Ivy Walls, an Elizabethan farmhouse (rebuilt) on the edge of the village. Conrad felt isolated from intellectual stimulation and welcomed the visits of John Galsworthy, Edward Garnett, and Stephen Crane. On a visit to the Garnetts at Limpsfield he met Ford Madox Hueffer, who persuaded him to move to Postling in 1898.

STANFORD-ON-TEME, Hereford and Worcester. [3 Ge] Village on the B4203, 13 m. NW. of Worcester. Mrs. Sherwood, author of *The Fairchild Family* (1818–47) and numerous other novels, was the daughter of the Revd. George Butt. She was born at the rectory on the hill W. of the bridge over the Teme, and her first memory was of 'the half circular window over the hall door'. This part of the house has been demolished and the rest modernized (now the Old Rectory). She describes her happy childhood in her *Life* (1854), recording how pleased she was at her father's purchase for a guinea of a wagon-load of books at the auction of William Walsh's library at Abberley (q.v.).

STANSTED, Hants. [1 Ce] Hamlet 3½ m. NE. of Havant off the B2147 at Westbourne. Stansted Chapel was rebuilt (1817) in the

Gothic style from a 15th-c. core by the owner of Stansted House, Lewis Way, who wished to found a college to convert the Jews and then settle them in a permanent homeland. Keats attended the impressive service of dedication, driving over from Bedhampton (q.v.), and used descriptions of carvings, tapestries, and carpets in the 18th-c. house, and the stained glass of the chapel, in 'The Eve of St. Agnes' and 'The Eve of St. Mark'. Anglican services are held here and the E. window is unusual in having Jewish emblems. A short account of Lewis Way hangs in the vestibule and Lord Bessborough's *A Place in the Forest* (1958) gives the history of the house.

STANTON HARCOURT, Oxon. [1 Bb] Village on the B4449, 6 m. W. of Oxford. Near the church is a 15th-c. building known as Pope's Tower, which was part of the former manor house belonging to the Harcourt family. Alexander Pope was lent a room on the top floor by the first Viscount Harcourt, so that he could write his translation of the *Iliad* in peace, and here he finished the fifth volume in 1718. The tower can be visited when the gardens are open to the public.[1] In a letter to Martha Blount (Aug. 1718) Pope tells the story of John Hewet and Sarah Drew, young rustic lovers who were killed by lightning in the harvest field and buried together in the churchyard. Pope and John Gay were both touched by the story and persuaded Lord Harcourt to erect a little monument over the grave, with an epitaph by Pope engraved on it. Goldsmith introduces Gay's version of the story into *The Vicar of Wakefield* (1766), where Sophia Primrose says 'There is something so pathetic in the description that I have read it an hundred times with new rapture'. But Lady Mary Wortley Montagu was less touched by pathos. In reply to a letter from Pope enclosing two versions of his proposed epitaph she remarked 'I must applaud your good nature in supposing that your pastoral lovers ... would have lived in everlasting joy and harmony, if the lightning had not interrupted their scheme of happiness' and offered a more cynical epitaph of her own, ending:

For had they seen the next year's sun,
A beaten wife, and cuckold swain
Had jointly curs'd the marriage chain;
Now they are happy in their doom,
FOR POPE HATH WROTE UPON THEIR TOMB.

On the N. side of the church is Wesley's Cottage, where John and Charles Wesley and their sister Kezia used to stay when they visited the vicar.

[1] N.G.S.

STANTON ST. JOHN, Oxon. [1 Cb] Village on the B4027, 4 m. NE. of Oxford, where Milton's grandfather lived. A. E. Coppard rented (1919–22) Shepherd's Pit, a small cottage with a barn in a grassy hollow off the road to Oxford, after he had given up his job. He used to write at an old table outside his 'yaller door' that the locals laughed at, and on fine nights slept out and was awakened by whitethroats. He played cricket against Islip, watched by Garsington Manor guests, and occasionally went to the Star and the George. Few people called except the postman until Harold Taylor arrived on a bicycle to offer to publish his collected stories *Adam and Eve and Pinch Me* (1921) as the first volume for the Golden Cockerel Press. His verse *Hips and Haws*, and the stories *Clorinda walks in Heaven* followed in 1922.

STATHERN, Leics. [4 Cc] Village S. of the A52, 4 m. SW. of Belvoir Castle. In 1785 Crabbe was made curate here and lived happily with his wife in the rectory next to the church where their three children were baptized. He met Dr. Edmund Cartwright, inventor of the power-loom, rector of Goadby Marwood, 6 m. S., and author of a popular poem *Armine and Elvira* (1772), and accompanied him to Doncaster to see the looms working. In 1787 Crabbe's patron, the Duke of Rutland, died and with the help of the Duchess, who had his sermon on the Duke published, Crabbe was made rector of Muston (q.v.) in 1789.

STEEP, Hants. [1 Cd] Village at the foot of Stoner Hill on an unclassified road 1 m. N. of Petersfield. Edward Thomas lived (1913–16) at Yewtree Cottage, one of a group of semi-detached cottages on the road to the church. He had previously lived (1906–9) at Berryfield Cottage, c. 1 m. from Ashford, near Steep, so that his son, Mervyn, could go to school at Bedales, and then at Wick Green (also spelt Week Green) at the top of the hill, where a house was built for him by Geoffrey Lupton, a master at Bedales and a disciple of William Morris. The house (now the Bee House, Cockshutt Lane) was the work of local craftsmen and commanded a splendid view: 'Sixty miles of South Downs at one glance', but Thomas and his family never felt at home in it, as he explains in the poem 'Wind and Mist'. Rupert Brooke, many of whose friends had been at Bedales, spent some days at Wick Green, in the summer of 1910, reading his poems to Thomas. After Thomas moved to Yewtree Cottage he kept on the study, where he could house his books and have solitude for writing. Half the room was used as an apiary and when Ernest Rhys visited him he remarked: 'The bees seemed a natural part of his equipment on a hot day, and you could smell the honey in his own hive'. A large sarsen stone in a clearing on the slope of the Shoulder of Mutton Hill records the dedication of the hillside to Thomas's memory. The place can be found by following Cockshutt Lane as far as Old Litten Lane and then turning down the footpath to Steep.

Thomas Sturge Moore, poet and art critic, lived (1922–32) in the village at Hillcroft (P), not far from Yewtree Cottage.

STEVENAGE, Herts. [1 Ea] Town off the A1, SE. of Hitchin, expanded as one of the New Towns after the Second World War. Rooksnest, beyond the church, off Rectory Lane, Old Town, was E. M. Forster's childhood home. He lived in the large red-brick house until 1893, and the house and the wych elm in the garden are portrayed in *Howards End* (1910), the novel in which Mrs. Wilcox resembles his mother. His sole playmate was the gardener's boy. Forster's sudden removal from his home, when his mother was turned out abruptly, may have inspired his short story 'Ansell', published posthumously, in which a middle-aged academic gives up his Fellowship to make his home with a former gardener's boy.

STEVENTON, Hants. [1 Cd] Small village c. 6 m. SW. of Basingstoke, between the A30 and the B3400. Jane Austen was born in the rectory, the seventh child of James Austen, the rector of this and the neighbouring parish of Deane for over 40 years. The site of the house (demolished in the 19th c.) is marked by a metal pump, the successor of an old family pump, which stands in a field by the lane leading to the

church. Jane Austen lived here for the first 25 years of her life, as recorded in a memorial in the church, and by the time she was 23 had written *Sense and Sensibility*, *Pride and Prejudice*, and *Northanger Abbey*, although they were not published until many years later. A reproduction of a drawing of the rectory can be seen at her home at Chawton (q.v.). Ashe House, about 2 m. N. of Steventon, off the B3400, was the rectory of Ashe and home of the Lefroys, friends of the Austens. Mrs. Lefroy was the sister of Sir Egerton Brydges, who describes in his *Autobiography* (1834) the 'small parsonage-house' in the adjoining parish, where he lived for 2 years after his marriage in 1786. Jane Austen's niece, Anna, married Benjamin Lefroy, youngest son of the rector and later his successor.

STEYNING (pr. Stenning), West Sussex. [1 Ee] Village on the A283, 5 m. from the S. coast. Yeats often stayed at the Chantry House (P) above the small green in Church St. in the 1930s, the home of Miss Shackleton Heald. He began his play 'Purgatory' here and a new Crazy Jane poem.

STICKNEY, Lincs. [4 Eb] Village on the A16 between Boston and Spilsby, where Paul Verlaine spent a year (1875–6) teaching French, Latin, and drawing on an *au pair* basis at the Grammar School, where he was known as 'Mr. Mossou'. He had come from prison in Brussels where he had been sentenced to 2 years' hard labour for wounding Rimbaud, the young poet with whom he had been living, in an emotional scene. He wrote after his arrival 'my life is madly calm, and I am so happy about it . . . I have an appalling need of calm'. He found private pupils and made friends, among them Canon Coltman, the rector and a friend of Tennyson. Verlaine used to make translations from *Hymns Ancient and Modern* while walking up and down the playground and these inspired many poems in *Sagesse* (1881). He left in March 1876 as he found the climate too depressing.

STILLINGTON. See SUTTON-ON-THE-FOREST.

STINCHCOMBE, Glos. [2 Ha] Village on the B4060, 2 m. E. of Dursley. Evelyn Waugh lived (1937–56) at Piers Court after his second marriage. He wrote here *The Loved*

One (1948), *Helena* (1950), and *Men at Arms* and *Officers and Gentlemen* (1955), the first two volumes of his trilogy about the war, in which he served first in the Marines and then in the Commandos. He also experienced here the mental disturbances that preceded the hallucinations he suffered on a voyage to Ceylon, recounted in *The Ordeal of Gilbert Pinfold* (1957).

STINSFORD, Dorset. [2 Hd] Village off the A35, just over 1 m. E. of Dorchester. There is a memorial window to Hardy in the church, where he sang in the choir as a boy. His heart is buried in the churchyard, near the graves of his parents, and Cecil Day-Lewis, his devoted admirer, is buried close by. Stinsford is the 'Mellstock' of *Under the Greenwood Tree* (1872) and of the poems 'A Church Romance' (1835) and 'Afternoon Service at Mellstock' (1850).

STIRLING, Stirlings. (Central). [6 Ec] Ancient burgh on the Forth, on the A9 and the A80. William Alexander (1567?–1640), the poet, built Argyll's Lodging (*c.* 1632) in Castle Wynd, an ornate house round a courtyard seen through tall iron gates, after he became Secretary of State. It is now a Youth Hostel. He wrote *Aurora* (1604) and *Recreations with the Muses* (1637), which include love lyrics, and a number of tragedies. He was a friend of Drummond of Hawthornden and was made Earl of Stirling in 1633. Burns, visiting the Highlands, stayed at James Wingate's inn in 1787, now the Golden Lion Hotel. His statue stands in Albert Place.

George Robert Gleig (1796–1888), novelist and biographer, was born at 81 Baker St. (site now part of a small public garden) and was educated at the Grammar School. Alexander Balloch Grosart (1827–99), who edited reprints of rare works, was born here.

STISTED (pr. Stisted), Essex. [1 Ga] Village between the A120 and the A1017, 3 m. NE. of Braintree. The Revd. Charles Forster, rector 1838–71, was the grandfather of E. M. Forster, whose biography of his great-aunt, *Marianne Thornton* (1956), includes a description of the rectory (now Glebe House, opposite the school), overflowing with laundry and children. The church, restored by Charles Forster, contains a roundel to one of the children, Doanie, who died aged 16.

STOKE DAMEREL. See PLYMOUTH.

STOKE-ON-TRENT, Staffs. [3 Hb] City of The Potteries in the N. of the county, formed by the federation of the familiarly known 'Five Towns' of Tunstall, Burslem, Hanley, Stoke-upon-Trent, and Longton (immortalized by Arnold Bennett's novels and stories as Turnhill, Bursley, Hanbridge, Knype, and Longshaw), which, with Fenton, were united in 1910. Records of literary figures begin with Elijah Fenton, a poet best remembered for his collaboration with Pope in translating the *Odyssey* (1725–6), who was born (1683) at Shelton Old Hall (now an iron and steel works), Hanley. Another native was Mrs. Craik (Dinah Maria Mulock), who was born (1826) in the parish of Stoke-upon-Trent, at Longfield Cottage (gone), Hartshill, where her father was minister of a small congregation. 'Longfield' appears in *John Halifax, Gentleman* (1857). In 1831 the family moved to Newcastle under Lyme.

Arnold Bennett, Stoke's most famous author, was born (27 May 1867) in a house and shop formerly at the corner of Hope St. and Hanover St., Hanley (P on present building). Later he lived at Dain St., Burslem (1875–6), 175 Newport Lane (1876–8), and 198 Waterloo Rd. (1878–80). In 1880 his father moved the family to 205 Waterloo Rd., now the Arnold Bennett Museum,[1] with two rooms furnished with his personal effects and other objects of the period. Bennett began his education (1875) at the infants' school in the Swan Bank Methodist Sunday School (gone) and went on (1876) to the Burslem Endowed School, formerly part of the Wedgwood Institute before it was moved (1880) to Longport Hall (an event referred to in *The Old Wives' Tale*). He entered his father's legal practice at 18, but finding it uncongenial left for London in 1889. The experience and understanding of these 22 years provided the background for thirteen novels and three volumes of short stories set in 'The Five Towns', of which the best-known are probably *The Old Wives' Tale* (1908), *Clayhanger* (1910), *The Card* (1911), and *The Matador of the Five Towns* (1912). Bennett's topography centres on Burslem, and an excellent leaflet, 'Bennett Country', giving a list of landmarks, with maps and a key to his names for towns and suburbs in Stoke-on-Trent and adjacent areas, can be obtained from the Central Library,

Hanley. The site of 'The Shambles' and post office (see *The Old Wives' Tale* and *Clayhanger*) was redeveloped in 1960 as an ornamental garden, and a commemorative portrait plaque of Bennett made by the Wedgwoods was erected there in 1962. Moorland Rd. leads up the hill from Burslem to the local cemetery, where Bennett's ashes are interred in his mother's grave.

¹ Open Mon., Wed., Thurs., Sat. 2–5 p.m.

STOKE POGES, Bucks. [1 Dc] Large village on the A332. Thomas Gray often visited his mother, who in 1742 came to live with her sister at West End (now Stoke Court). Gray wrote *Ode on a Distant Prospect of Eton College* here and is thought to have begun *c.* 1742 the *Elegy in a Country Churchyard*, finished here in 1750 and inspired in part by the death of Richard West, his friend at Eton. Gray's poem 'A Long Story' is set in the Manor House where he visited Lady Cobham and Henrietta Speed. Near the church is a solid monument (N.T.) erected in 1799 and giving lines from his poems. Gray, who wrote the inscription on his mother's tomb in the churchyard, is buried with her.

STONEGRAVE, North Yorkshire. [5 Fc] Village 5 m. SE. of Helmsley, on the B1257. Stonegrave House was the home for 20 years of Sir Herbert Read (1893–1968), the literary and art critic, whose writings include *In Defence of Shelley* (1935), *Poetry and Anarchism* (1938), collected poems and essays, and his autobiography, *Annals of Innocence and Experience* (1940). His allegorical novel *The Green Child* (1935) is set in this part of Yorkshire.

STONITON. See DERBY.

STORRINGTON, West Sussex. [1 De] Small town on the A283, 8 m. NW. of Worthing. The Norbertine monks of Storrington Priory, beyond the parish church, cared for Francis Thompson after he had been rescued from vagrancy and destitution in London by Alice and Wilfred Meynell. Many of his poems, including 'The Hound of Heaven', were written here.

STOURBRIDGE, West Midlands. [3 Hd] Old market town on the A458, 8 m. W. of Birmingham. The 17-year-old Samuel John-son spent 6 months (1726–7) at King Edward VI School. This was then a long low building behind the headmaster's and usher's houses in the High St. between the two inns, the Vine and the Old Horse. Johnson is thought to have taught the younger boys in return for his board and lodging. The school had a good library and both the headmaster and the usher had been at Oxford University. Johnson's family had many connections in the town and Bishop Percy later wrote that Johnson was well entertained by his relatives, who introduced him to prominent people. Johnson wrote many poems on classical themes as well as 'Festina Lente', an exhortation in heroic couplets, and the hymn for the feast of St. Simon and St. Jude, which contains much 'extatic fury' and shows that he was experimenting with a variety of verse forms. No reason has been found for his sudden return to Lichfield. Some years later in 1731 he stayed in the town again hoping to be selected for the post of usher, but he was unsuccessful. The school has been rebuilt.

STOURCASTLE. See STURMINSTER NEWTON.

STOURHEAD, Wilts. [2 Hc] Country house (N.T.) on the B3092, 3 m. NW. of Mere, with grounds and gardens landscaped in the 18th c. for the Hoare family. The changing of the landscape into *le jardin anglais* needed the combination of philosopher, patron, poet, and architect. Locke's philosophy of Man 'in a state of Nature' appealed to patrons who, after a war against France, wished to break away from Le Notre's geometric designs which they saw as the embodiment of despotism. This wish led to the softening of line under the architects Kent and Wyatt and to the removal of whole hillsides under 'Capability' Brown. Under their influence water meandered in serpentine ways, fell into grottoes embellished with statues and overhung with shrubs, and was crossed by eye-catching bridges half hidden by trees. Temples stood out on knolls, cast reflections in lakes, or nestled in dells. Pope wrote of consulting 'the Genius of the Place' and had Claude Lorraine in mind when he thought of gardens as paintings taken from their frames and spread out over the countryside. The chief architect of the temples at

Stourhead is Flitcroft. Pope's lines embellish the curb of the basin in the grotto which has a statue of a sleeping nymph:

Nymph of the Grot these sacred springs I keep
And to the murmur of these waters sleep;
Ah! spare my slumbers, gently tread the cave,
And drink in silence or in silence lave.

The Bristol Cross, of which Pepys remarked on his visit there that it reminded him of the one at Cheapside, and which the citizens later asked to have removed as it obstructed the road, was re-erected here in 1765.

Alfred's Tower, a red-brick triangular tower, with a statue of King Alfred, was erected in 1772 on Kingsettle Hill (2 m. NW.) and commemorates his fight against the Danes in 879. 'Parson' Woodforde wrote in his *Diary* of his visit to the Tower.

House open Apr.–Sept.: daily except Mon. and Tues. but open Bank Holiday Mon. 2–6 p.m. Mar., Oct., and Nov.: Wed., Sat., and Sun. 2–6 p.m., or to sunset if earlier.
Gardens open all the year: daily 8 a.m.–7 p.m. or sunset if earlier.

STOWE, Bucks. [1 Ca] Former ducal seat, now a public school, off the A422, NE. of Buckingham. The landscaped gardens[1] here derive from the early 18th-c. desire to free design from the geometric bonds of the former age and to develop gardens similar to Milton's description in *Paradise Lost* where Man (as hoped for by Locke) would be enobled by Nature. Charles Bridgeman's design for an octagonal lake was changed, by the ideas of Sir Richard Temple and his friends at the Kit-Cat Club, into a serpentine channel. Kent introduced the ha-ha to enable wilder country to appear in vistas unbroken by hedges, and created the Elysian Fields and the Grecian Valley. The Temple of Ancient Virtue and the Temple of British Worthies are also by Kent. In the latter are busts including those of Bacon, Shakespeare, Locke, and Milton. Pope, who was a frequent visitor, addressed the first of his *Moral Essays* (1733) to his host, then Lord Cobham. He describes the aims of the designers in his *Epistle to Lord Burlington*:

Consult the Genius of the Place in all;
That tells the Waters or to rise, or fall,
Or helps th'ambitious Hill the heavens to scale,
Or scoops in circling theatres the Vale,
Calls in the Country, catches opening glades,
Joins willing woods, and varies shades from shades,

Now breaks, or now directs, th'intending Lines;
Paints as you plant, and, as you work, designs.
Still follow Sense, of ev'ry Art the Soul.
Parts answering parts shall slide into a whole,
Spontaneous beauties all around advance,
Start ev'n from Difficulty, strike from Chance;
Nature shall join you, Time shall make it grow
A Work to wonder at—perhaps a STOW.

Congreve spent many summers here and Cobham commemorated his wit by a statue, designed by Kent, showing Comedy in the guise of a monkey holding up a mirror to life.

T. H. White's novel *Mistress Masham's Repose* (1947) is set at Stowe. He was a master at the school and left in 1936.

[1] Open Easter weekend and two weeks in July 2–6.30 p.m.

STOWMARKET, Suff. [4 Gf] Town on the A45, 12 m. NW. of Ipswich. The Old Vicarage in Milton Rd. was the home from 1628 of Dr. Thomas Young, who earlier had tutored John Milton in London. Milton is thought to have visited Young here and to have planted a mulberry tree (gone) in the garden. George Crabbe went to Richard Haddon's school here in 1766, when he was 11, and learned the rudiments of Grammar and Latin, but he was mostly self-taught.

STRABANE, Tyrone. [8 Eb] Border town on the A5, situated on the Mourne near where it unites with the Finn to become the Foyle. Mrs. Cecil Frances Alexander (*née* Humphreys) lived at Milltown House (now the main building of the Grammar School) from 1833 until her marriage in 1850. She published her *Hymns for Little Children* (1848) here, which includes 'All things bright and beautiful', 'There is a green hill far away', and 'Once in Royal David's city'. In 1860 she came to live at Camus Rectory, 3 m. S., when her husband, the Revd. William Alexander, became rector. While she was here she edited *The Sunday Book of Poetry* (1864), a selection of poems by various authors, for the *Golden Treasury Series*. In 1867 she moved to Londonderry when her husband became bishop.

STRADBROKE, Suff. [4 Ge] Village on the B117, 7 m. SE. of Diss. There is a tradition that Robert Grosseteste (d. 1253), Bishop of Lincoln and first Chancellor of Oxford

University, was born here. A modern painted effigy of him is at the crossroads.

STRATFORD-UPON-AVON, Warwicks. [4 Af] Old market town on the A34, 24 m. SE. of Birmingham. Shakespeare was born (1564) in the house in Henley St. owned by his father, a glover and wool merchant, who became an alderman. His mother, Mary (née Arden), came from Wilmcote (q.v.). The birthplace,[1] half-timbered with lattice windows, has been carefully restored by the Shakespeare Birthplace Trust who bought it in 1847. The Birth Room has the signatures of Scott, Carlyle, Isaac Watts, and others scratched on a window pane. Part of the house is furnished as an Elizabethan home, and part is a museum housing books, manuscripts, and pictures relating to Shakespeare's life, and the desk he is said to have used at the Grammar School. This, now called Big School,[2] where he was probably a pupil some time in the 1570s, is a raftered room on the first floor of the Guildhall. Shakespeare could have seen plays acted here by the travelling players of Lord Leicester or Lord Danby. Shakespeare probably left Stratford in 1585, according to tradition because of deer-poaching at Charlecote Park (q.v.). In 1597 he bought the town's most important house, New Place, built for Hugh Clopton, a Lord Mayor of London, c. 1483. Shakespeare visited New Place yearly until 1610 when he settled there. He died in 1616 and is buried in the parish church by the Avon; the words on the stone over his grave in the chancel are said to be his own:

Good friend for Jesus sake forbeare
To digg the dust enclosed heare;
Blest be ye man yt spares thes stones
And curst be he yt moves my bones.

A monument with a bust by his contemporary Gerard Janssen, or Johnson, is on the wall above the grave. In the 19th c. Shakespeare's American admirers donated two stained-glass windows, one representing the Seven Ages of Man. Graves of his wife, his daughter Susanna, and her husband, the eminent physician, Dr. Hall (monument), are near by. His daughter Judith, who married a vintner and lived at the corner of Bridge St. and High St. (now Quiney House, the Information Centre), and her twin Hamnet, are buried in the churchyard. Susanna Hall and her husband, who

lived in Old Town (now Hall's Croft),[3] moved into New Place after Shakespeare's death.

In 1769, 10 years after the demolition of New Place (now a garden)[4] had angered the town, David Garrick organized a commemorative Jubilee attended by many friends, including James Boswell and Arthur Murphy, but marred by rain. Garrick declared the new Shakespeare Hall (now the Town Hall) open and donated the bust by Cheere, now over the door. The Garrick Inn in High St. commemorates his visit. Nash's House (P)[5] inherited by Shakespeare's granddaughter, contains Tudor furniture and items about local history including the Jubilee. A theatre was built in Chapel Lane in 1827, but the first permanent Shakespeare Memorial Theatre, founded by Charles Flower, opened in 1879. This burnt down in 1926 and a world-wide fund made possible the present building (opened 1932), now called the Royal Shakespeare Theatre, where his plays run from April to October each year. The theatre, which has a Library,[6] and a Picture Gallery and Museum,[7] stands in gardens and overlooks the Avon. The Gower Monument to Shakespeare is near by. The opening of the Shakespeare Centre, next to the birthplace, commemorated the 400th anniversary of Shakespeare's birth. The Centre has a library for students and is the headquarters of the Shakespeare Birthplace Trust, which administers the birthplace, Anne Hathaway's Cottage at Shottery (q.v.), the garden at New Place, Hall's Croft, and Mary Arden's House.

Washington Irving stayed (under the name of Geoffrey Crayon) at the Red Horse in Bridge St. c. 1818 and wrote about the town in *The Sketch-Book of Geoffrey Crayon, Gent.* (1819-20). His compatriot Nathaniel Parker Willis, author of two books about his visits to this country, stayed in Irving's room about 10 years later. He reported the landlady's account of her surprise when a guest told her how she had been 'immortalized' in Irving's book. She showed Willis Irving's poker, inscribed with his pseudonym, and a battered copy of the *Sketch-Book*. Irving's chair and the sexton's clock he mentions, both inscribed, can now be seen on the first-floor landing, but the poker has disappeared.

Mrs. Gaskell, who was at Avonbank School (demolished 1866) near the entrance to the church, wrote the chapter on Stratford in William Howitt's *Visits to Remarkable Places* (1840); it was her first published work. In it she describes Clopton House[8] (1 m. N.) which she visited when at school. Mary Mackay, who wrote as 'Marie Corelli', settled at Mason's Croft (P, now the University of Birmingham Shakespeare Institute) in Church St. in 1901, at the height of her popularity as a romantic novelist. Her pony-chaise drawn by Shetland ponies, her gondola, The Dream, on the Avon, and later her Daimler, became well known in the town. Her enthusiasm for rescuing old buildings from development was not always welcomed, but Samuel Clemens ('Mark Twain') appreciated her renovation of Harvard House[9] (home of the mother of the founder of Harvard University), which he asked her to show him on his visit in 1907. She died at Mason's Croft in 1924 and is buried in the cemetery.

[1] Open Nov.–Mar.: weekdays 9 a.m.–4 p.m.; Sun. 1.30–4.30 p.m.; Apr.–Oct.: weekdays 9 a.m.–6 p.m.; Sun. 10 a.m.–6 p.m.
[2] Open Easter and Summer holidays: 9 a.m.–12.30 p.m. and 2–4 p.m.
[3] Open Nov.–Mar.: weekdays 9 a.m.–12.45 p.m. and 2–4 p.m.; Apr.–Oct.: weekdays 9 a.m.–6 p.m.; Sun. 2–6 p.m.
[4] Open Nov.–Mar.: weekdays 9 a.m.–12.45 p.m. and 2–4 p.m.; Apr.–Oct.: weekdays 9 a.m.–6 p.m.; Sun. 2–6 p.m.
[5] Open Nov.–Mar.: weekdays 9 a.m.–12.45 p.m. and 2–4 p.m.; Apr.–Oct.: weekdays 9 a.m.–6 p.m.; Sun. 2–6 p.m.
[6] Open for students only, weekdays 10 a.m.–5 p.m.; Sat. 10 a.m.–12.30 p.m.
[7] Open 10 a.m.–1 p.m., 2–6 p.m.; Apr.–Nov.: Sun. 2–6 p.m.
[8] Open daily 10 a.m.–5 p.m.
[9] Open 9 a.m.–1 p.m., 2–5.15 p.m.

STRATHMORE, Angus (Tayside). [6 Fa, Fb, Ga] Valley stretching from Coupar Angus in the SW. to Howe of the Mearns in the NE. Violet Jacob (née Erskine) wrote about this area in her dialect poems including Songs of Angus (1915) and The Northern Lights (1927). She wrote about her family in The Lairds of Dun (1931), which gives an account of The House of Dun, her birthplace (4 m. W. of Montrose) built in 1730 by Robert Adam. In 'The Lang Road' she describes the men absent in the war:

> Below the braes o' heather and far alang the glen,
> The road runs southward, southward, that grips the souls of men,
> There's mony a lad will ne'er come back amang his ain to lie
> An' its lang, lang, waitin' till the time gangs by.

STRATHYRE, Perths. (Central). [6 Db] Small village on the A84, in the valley with Strathyre Forest on the hills above, described by Sir Walter Scott in The Lady of the Lake (1810) and A Legend of Montrose (1819).

STRENSHAM, Hereford and Worcester. [1 Aa] Village S. of the A4104, at the junction of the M5 and the M50. Samuel Butler was born (1612) in a long low house known later as Butler's Cot (demolished in the 1870s), which his father had leased from Sir John Russell of Strensham Court, for whom he worked, perhaps as secretary. After a few years at Worcester School and having been given his father's 'Law and Latin books', Samuel Butler went as secretary to Thomas Jefferey, a justice, who lived at Earl's Croom (2 m. NW.). Jefferey lived in the 16th-c. half-timbered house (altered) opposite the church, and there Butler started his hobby of painting. Two portraits thought to be his, in poor condition, are now at the rectory there.

STRETTON HALL, Staffs. [3 Hc] Manor house NW. of the crossing of the A5 and the A449. After leaving Trinity College, Dublin, in 1689, William Congreve came to stay here with his paternal grandfather, Richard. According to tradition, it was under one of the old oaks in the grounds that he wrote the first draft of The Old Bachelor (1693) (possibly revised later in another version written at Ilam, q.v.).

STURMINSTER NEWTON, Dorset. [2 Hd] Market town on the Stour, c. 8 m. SW. of Shaftesbury, on the B3091 and the B3092. William Barnes, who spent his early years at Rush-hay, in the near-by parish of Bagber, attended the church school, and the eagle lectern in the church is a memorial to him. Robert Young, the tailor and poet who wrote as 'Rabin Hill', was born here (1811). He left school at the age of 11 and, after working in London and Poole, returned to his native town, succeeded in business, and built his own house, The Hive, where he lived for most of the rest of his life. His poems, in Dorset dialect, include 'Rabin Hill's Visit to the Railway', composed on the opening of the Somerset and Dorset line in 1861. Young also owned Riverside Villa, at the end of Rickett's Lane, on a bluff overlooking the Stour, which Hardy rented when he was writing *The Return of the Native* (1878). Young ended his days at Riverside Villa (1908) and was buried in the cemetery.

Sturminster Newton appears as 'Stourcastle' in *Tess of the d'Urbervilles* (1891).

SUDBURY, Suff. [1 Ga] Market town on the A134 and the A133, 15 m. NW. of Colchester, thought to be 'Eatanswill', where the parliamentary election takes place in Dickens's *Pickwick Papers* (1837), and where Pickwick and his friends encounter Mrs. Leo Hunter, the hostess who likes to meet famous people.

SUNIPOL. See MULL.

SUNNINGWELL, Oxon. [1 Bb] Small village off the A34 between Oxford and Abingdon. Roger Bacon, 13th-c. philosopher and scientist, who came to Oxford *c*. 1250, is believed to have frequented the church tower to study astronomy and test his theories about making telescopes. A model of the church in its 13th-c. setting stands in the unique seven-sided Jewel Porch (built *c*. 1550–2, when John Jewel was rector) and shows Bacon at the top of the tower in the habit of a Franciscan friar, with an astrolabe in his hand.

SUNWICH PORT. See SANDWICH.

SUTTON COURT, Som. [2 Hb] Elizabethan house on the A368, ½ m. N. of Bishop's Sutton, enlarged in the 19th c. John Locke (1632–1702) visited it, as did John Addington Symonds, who wrote about the house, his sister's home, in *In the Key of Blue* (1892).

SUTTON COURTENAY, Oxon. [1 Cb] A large, straggling village on the B4016, between Abingdon and Didcot. A simple headstone in the churchyard near the end of an avenue of yews marks the grave of Eric Blair (1903–50), author, under the pen-name George Orwell, of the political satires *Animal Farm* (1945) and *Nineteen Eighty-four* (1949), and other novels and essays.

SUTTON-ON-THE-FOREST, North Yorkshire. [5 Fd] Village on the B1363, 8 m. N. of York. Laurence Sterne held the living here (1738–69), at first staying in York. In

1741 he married Elizabeth Lumley, whose money furnished and repaired the thatched vicarage (now rebuilt after a fire) next to the church, where they lived until 1759. Her influence got him the parish of Stillington (2 m. N.) to which he walked across the fields to preach in the afternoons after taking morning service here. Stephen Croft of Stillington Hall often entertained him but his other parishioners were not so friendly and were deliberately slow in saving him when he fell through the ice. Sterne went shooting with his pointer (once keeping his congregation waiting while he pursued a covey of partridges), played his fiddle, and painted portraits. His wife became deranged and had to be taken to an asylum. Sterne relieved his loneliness by writing *Tristram Shandy* (1760–7), which he paid to have printed in York and which was an immediate success. After acquiring the additional living of Coxwold (q.v.) in 1760, he spent much of his time in fashionable circles.

SWAFFHAM (pr. Swoffam), Norf. [4 Fd] Market town on the A47 and the A1065. The 15th-c. church contains the Parochial Library,[1] which includes an illuminated *Book of Hours* (*c*. 1420) and *The Black Book of Swaffham*, an inventory of church rents, donations, and possessions, compiled by Dr. John Botright, rector from 1435 to his death in 1474, whose tomb is in the chancel. In 1690 the priest's chamber above the vestry was fitted up to house almost four hundred books bequeathed by Sir Henry Spelman the antiquary, born (1560 or 1564) at Congham, a village 9 m. NW. Spelman's library includes *Holinshed's Chronicle* (1577).

[1] May be seen on application to the verger.

SWAFFHAM (pr. Swoffam) PRIOR, Cambs. [4 Ee] Village on the B1102, 8 m. NE. of Cambridge. Edwin and Willa Muir, who first translated Franz Kafka's novels, moved to Priory Cottage in 1956. In a letter to T. S. Eliot Muir wrote:

> The little house is very charming, and we have fallen in love with it. It is in a pleasant village, and looks out on two ruined church towers, each set on a little knoll of its own; one of them damaged by lightning sometime, and the other by time itself. The neighbours are kind, and the village shop is next door. I confess that some-

times I have a slightly sinking feeling, knowing that now I have nothing to do but write, and must depend upon it. But I feel it will be all right.

The poems Muir wrote here are included in *Collected Poems* (1960) published after he died in Cambridge in January 1959. He is buried in the churchyard. Willa Muir wrote *Living with Ballads* (1965), for which her husband had begun some notes, and then *Belonging* (1968), the story of their life together.

SWAINSTON HALL, I.O.W. [1 Bf] 18th-c. house (burnt in a 1941 air raid) off the B3401, with a 13th-c. oratory (now a tutorial college), home of Sir John Simeon. Tennyson often came over from Farringford (6 m. W.) and *Maud* (1855) evolved from a conversation the two men had here and the poem is set in the garden with the cedars. Tennyson called Sir John 'the prince of courtesy' in the lines 'Swainston' that he wrote after his death.

SWALLOWFIELD, Berks. [1 Cc] Village on the A33 a few miles S. of Reading. This was the last home of Mary Russell Mitford, who moved here from Three Mile Cross in 1851 and published her *Recollections of a Literary Life* the following year. She died on 10 January 1855 and was buried in the churchyard, where a tall stone cross, erected by public subscription, marks her grave. The church, peacefully withdrawn from the main road, is described in 'The Visit' in *Our Village* (1824–32), 'peeping out from amongst magnificent yew-trees'. Miss Mitford's cottage has been enlarged and altered out of recognition.

SWANBOURNE, Bucks. [1 Ca] Village on the B4032, 2 m. E. of Winslow. Swanbourne House, not to be confused with the newer house now a school, was the home of Lady Fremantle (*née* Elizabeth Wynne), the chief contributor to the *Wynne Diaries* (3 vols. 1935–40). She and her sisters spent their early lives on the Continent and Elizabeth married Captain Thomas Fremantle in 1797 at Lady Hamilton's house in Naples. The diaries include accounts given by the three sisters of their lives between 1789 and 1820, and some letters and the journal of Captain, later Admiral, Sir Thomas Fremantle, a friend of Nelson.

SWANSEA, West Glamorgan. [2 Ea] Large seaport and metal-working town on the NW. shore of Swansea Bay, at the mouth of the Tawe. Richard Savage, whose biography appears in Dr. Johnson's *Lives of the English Poets* (1781), lived here from 1739 to 1740, in Barber's Court, off Orchard St. (site now occupied by a large store), having left London to escape his creditors. He had published a moderately successful play, *The Bastard* (1728), and a long moral and descriptive poem entitled *The Wanderer* (1729), which was praised by Johnson, but his financial state was chronically precarious and he was forced to move on again, this time to Bristol (q.v.).

Walter Savage Landor wrote his epic poem *Gebir* (1798) while staying here, influenced, it seems, by his reading of an Arabian romance by Clara Reeve, which he had borrowed from the Swansea Library. During his visit he met Lord Aylmer, father of Rose, his early love, whose death at the age of 20 he lamented in the elegy 'Rose Aylmer'.

Dylan Thomas was born (27 Oct. 1914) at 5 Cwmdonkin Drive, on the west side of the town, known as the Uplands, and spent his first 20 years in Swansea. He was a delicate child and had somewhat erratic schooling before going to the Grammar School at the age of 10. (The school suffered damage by fire-bombs in 1941 and was rebuilt in another part of the town and renamed Bishop Gore School.) Much of the background of his early life is described in the semi-autobiographical *Portrait of the Artist as a Young Dog* (1940). He left school in 1931 and got a job with the *South Wales Daily Post* (now the *South Wales Evening Post*). During the next 3 years he wrote the poems published in *Eighteen Poems* in 1934, the year after his first visit to London, when his reputation as a poet was steadily growing. Although Cwmdonkin Drive remained his home for another 2 years he made frequent visits to London, meeting new people and extending his literary acquaintance. In early 1936 he completed *Twenty-five Poems*, which was published in the autumn and aroused much controversial criticism, including warm praise from Edith Sitwell. The same year he moved to London and cut his ties with Swansea. A simple carved stone monument in his memory has been erected in Cwmdonkin Park, where he played as a child.

Vernon Watkins, poet and friend of Dylan Thomas, went to school in Swansea before going to Repton. After serving in the R.A.F. he was a lecturer at University College, Swansea, and lived at Pennard Cliffs a few miles SW. of the town. His works include *Ballad of Mari Lwyd and other poems* (1941), *The Lady with the Unicorn* (1948), and an edition of letters from Dylan Thomas to himself (1957).

SWANSTON, Midlothian (Lothian). [6 Fc] Small village of tidy thatched cottages on the edge of the Pentlands, now within the city of Edinburgh, *c.* 3 m. S. from the centre, and reached by Swanston Rd. off Oxgangs Rd. (B701), ½ m. W. from Coniston Rd. (A702). Swanston Cottage, now dilapidated and screened by trees in a neglected garden, was the holiday home of R. L. Stevenson

(1867–81; 'secluded Swanston, lapped in a fold of the Pentlands'). The village figures in his unfinished novel, *St. Ives* (New York, 1897; London, 1898; completed by Sir A. Quiller-Couch), and the Pentland moorland is associated with *Weir of Hermiston*, his unfinished masterpiece (1896).

On the slope of the village green is a seat in memory of the poet and critic Edwin Muir, given by his friends to mark the place where he liked to linger and meditate.

SWINBROOK, Oxon. [1 Bb] Stone village on the Windrush, 2 m. E. of Burford. Nancy Mitford (1904–73), much of whose satirical novel *The Pursuit of Love* (1945) is set in the Jacobean manor at Asthall (1 m. SE.), is buried in the churchyard.

SWINFORD OLD MANOR. See HOTHFIELD.

T

TAGHMON (pr. Tahmōn'), Wexford. [9 Gd] Village on the L128 and the L160, 9 m. W. of Wexford. Henry Francis Lyte, remembered especially as the author of 'Abide with me', was curate here after his ordination in 1815 until 1816. A memorial tablet[1] was erected in the church on the centenary of his birth.

[1] Can be seen on application to the rector, tel. Wellington Bridge 63688.

TANGMERE, West Sussex. [1 De] R.A.F. station, off the A27, 4 m. NE. of Chichester, where H. E. Bates was stationed in 1942. He wrote the popular collections of short stories of air-force men and women under the pseudonym 'Flying Officer X'. He also finished here the novel *Fair Stood the Wind for France* (1944).

TANTALLON CASTLE, East Lothian (Lothian). [6 Gc] Massive red sandstone castle on a cliff promontory overlooking the sea, near the A198, 3 m. E. of North Berwick. The best view is obtained from the little cove to the S., reached by a tree-lined side road from Auldhame to the sea and then by a path to the N. point of the bay. The castle, which dates from *c.* 1375, was a stronghold of the Douglases and features in Scott's

Marmion (1808) and in Stevenson's *Catriona* (1893).

Open Apr.–Sept.: Mon.–Sat. 9.30 a.m.–7 p.m., Sun. 2–7 p.m.; Oct.–Mar.: Mon.–Sat. 9.30 a.m.–4 p.m., Sun. 2–4 p.m.

TAPPINGTON HALL FARM, Kent. [1 Hd] Remaining part of an Elizabethan mansion off the A260, 2 m. SW. of Denton, inherited by R. H. Barham's father. Barham's *Ingoldsby Legends* (1840), first published in *Bentley's Miscellany* and *The New Monthly Magazine*, are humorous and grotesque verses based on old legends. Many ghost stories and anecdotes are about the county and two are set in Tappington itself. 'The Spectre of Tappington' recalls a murder committed in the Hall, and Tappington Moor in 'The Hand of Glory' is Barham Downs to the N.

TARBOLTON, Ayrs. (Strathclyde). [6 Dd] Village on the B744, 5 m. W. of Mauchline, frequented by Robert Burns while living (1777–89) at Lochlea and Mossgiel (qq.v.). He joined in the social life of the village at the hall attached to an inn, now called the Bachelors' Club[1] (N.T.S.) from the literary and debating society of that name that he and his friends founded there in 1780. Burns joined the Freemasons who also met at the hall, but after a dispute their two lodges, which had united, separated again and Burns and the St. James's Lodge met at another inn, James Manson's (site near by marked with a stone). He addressed a poem to this lodge. Dr. Hornbook's house ('Death and Dr. Hornbook') is near the churchyard, and Willie's Mill ('Epitaph on William Muir') is at the E. of the village. The opening lines of 'Highland Mary'

Ye banks and braes and streams around
The castle of Montgomery

refer to the near-by Coilford House (burnt down 1960s) where Mary Campbell, who came from the Highlands, was a dairymaid when she first met Burns. He planned to emigrate to the W. Indies with her but she died of typhus.

¹ Open on request. Key with custodian, Mr. Samuel Hay, 28 Croft St.

TAUNTON, Som. [2 Fc] County town in the valley of Taunton Deane, on the A38 and the A358. It was founded c. 705 by Ine, King of the West Saxons, as a stronghold against the Celts. The castle (much restored) dates from the 12th c. and houses the County Museum. It is probable that Samuel Daniel was born (1562) near Taunton, though the exact location is not known. He was the son of a music-master, was educated at Oxford, and after a career in London (he was Spenser's 'new shepherd late up sprong' in *Colin Clout*), returned to Somerset and rented a farm near Beckington (q.v.).

In May 1798, when Coleridge was living at Nether Stowey, he walked 11 miles to conduct the service for the Unitarian minister at the Mary Street Chapel in Taunton, Dr. Toulmin. He continued to preach at the chapel from time to time, at this period of his life when he was an ardent Unitarian.

A. W. Kinglake, historian and author of *Eōthen* (1844), a narrative of his travels in the Near East, was born (5 Aug. 1809) at Wilton House, Upper High St. (now a home for the elderly). Kinglake lived here until he was sent to the Grammar School at Ottery St. Mary, and subsequently to Eton.

A. P. Graves was an inspector of schools when he came to Taunton from Huddersfield in the spring of 1882. His district was West Somerset, with headquarters at Taunton, and he and his wife and their four children settled at Haines Hill and spent 3 happy years there. They had as a near neighbour Arthur Kinglake, the eccentric brother of A. W. Kinglake, and they enjoyed the friendship of Juliana Horatia Ewing and her husband, who were living at Trull (q.v.), and gave Graves encouragement in the publication of *Songs of Old Ireland*, which was going through the press at that time. He lived for a time at West Hay in the village of Kingston St. Mary, 2 m. N. of Taunton, and in 1895 was transferred to Southwark.

TAVISTOCK, Devon. [2 De] Market town on the A384 and the A386, traditionally regarded as the western capital of Dartmoor. It was the birthplace (house not traced) of William Browne (1590–1645), whose narrative poem *Britannia's Pastorals* (Bks. I 1613, II 1616, III 1852) contains some of the earliest topographical poetry, concerning the surrounding countryside:

My muse for lofty pitches shall not roam,
But homely pipen of my native home.

Among various epitaphs he wrote the well-known lines on the Dowager Countess of Pembroke, 'Sidney's sister, Pembroke's mother'. He was educated at Tavistock Grammar School before going to Oxford. The church (restored 1845) has a window designed by William Morris.

TEALBY, Lincs. [4 Da] Village on the B1203, 4 m. NE. of Market Rasen. When Tennyson's uncle inherited Bayons Manor here in 1835, he embellished it with all the conceits of the Gothic style. There were concealed staircases, secret rooms, oriel windows, and crenellated towers, costly enough for a sly story to spread that the son would not be responsible for his father's debts. The tension between the poet's family and Bayons was increased when the novelist Edward Bulwer, later Lord Lytton, who often stayed here, labelled Tennyson a 'School-Miss' and he retaliated with the 'Literary Squabbles' verses. Lytton wrote *The Last of the Barons* (1843) in the Tapestry room. The house became a ruin after its Victorian heyday and was totally demolished in 1964. The church has family memorials.

TEIGNMOUTH (pr. Tīnmuth), Devon. [2 Fe] Seaside resort and fishing and shipbuilding centre, situated on the N. shore of the mouth of the Teign, on the A379. Fanny Burney came here on three occasions: as a young woman in 1773; in attendance on Queen Charlotte in 1778; and in 1791, shortly before her marriage. She was delighted with the country and tried sea-bathing, when her bathing machine was pushed into the sea by two sturdy women and the plunge into the water gave her a shock 'beyond expression great!'

Jane Austen visited here during her Devon holiday in 1802, and in March 1818 Keats came to stay with his brother Tom (P at 35 The Strand, but it is doubtful whether this was the actual house). While he was here he completed *Endymion*, wrote the Pre-face, and sent it to his publishers. It rained a great deal and in a letter to B. R. Haydon he called Devon 'a splashy, rainy, misty, snowy, foggy, haily, floody, muddy, slip-shod County'.

TEMPLE GROVE, East Sussex. [1 Fd] Country house at Heron's Ghyll, 2 m. NE. of Mares-field. Coventry Patmore, who had com-pleted the four parts of his long poem on married love, *The Angel in the House*, in 1862, bought the 400-acre estate, which he named Heron's Ghyll, and moved here with his family and his second wife in 1865. He was most successful in improving the estate but wrote no poetry while here. The house has stained-glass medallions representing the heroines lauded in verse throughout the ages, including Eve, Helen of Troy, Guine-vere, Laura, and Beatrice. Patmore sold the estate in 1875 and moved to Hastings (q.v.).

TEMPLEOGUE. See DUBLIN.

TENBY, Dyfed. [2 Ca] Seaside resort on the W. side of Carmarthen Bay, on the A478 and the A4139, situated on a rocky pro-montory overlooking two sandy bays. The town dates from the 12th c., when it was a settlement of Flemish cloth-workers. Giraldus Cambrensis was rector of the parish church (the predecessor of the present church of St. Mary) from 1172 to 1175.

TERCANBURY. See CANTERBURY.

TETFORD, Lincs. [4 Eb] Village 5 m. NE. of Horncastle, off the A158. Johnson when staying at Langton in 1764 came to the

White Hart Inn to address the Tetford Club, a gathering of neighbouring gentry, and it remains very much as it was then, with its high-backed oak settle.

TEWKESBURY, Glos. [1 Aa] Old town where the Severn and the Avon meet. The great Norman abbey was saved by the town at the Dissolution on the plea that it was the parish church. The Milton organ is said to have been played by John Milton while secretary to the Council of State when Crom-well installed it in Hampton Court; the town bought it in 1727. Near by is the marble memorial to Mrs. Craik, author of *John Halifax, Gentleman* (1857), the fame of which turned the Abbey Mill into 'Abel Fletcher's Mill', now a restaurant. The Pickwick Club dined at the Royal Hop Pole which has a Pickwick and a Sam Weller bar. The Tudor House Hotel, the mayor's house in *John Halifax, Gentleman*, was the boyhood home of John Moore, whose amusing novels are about the local countryside. A room in the museum in Church St. commemorates him.

THAME, Oxon. [1 Cb] Market town on the A418, between Oxford and Aylesbury. John Fell (b. 1625) and Anthony Wood (b. 1632) were pupils at the Grammar School then in the Tudor building next to the church. Yeats, with his wife and child, rented the three-storeyed Cuttlebrook House, 42 High St., in 1921. He found the furniture pleasing, especially the guns and swords on the top floor. They noticed an unseasonal smell of roses, and the doctor attending the birth of their son commented on it. The house belonged for a time to The Red House Children's Book Shop.

John Fothergill's *An Innkeeper's Diary* (1931) describes the Spread Eagle in the High St., where he was 'Pioneer Amateur Innkeeper' from 1922 to 1932. The inn was frequented by writers. Carrington, friend of Lytton Strachey and the 'Mary Bracegirdle' of Aldous Huxley's *Crome Yellow* (1921), painted the inn sign for Fothergill.

THAXTED, Essex. [1 Fa] Old wool town on the A130, birthplace in 1577 of Samuel Purchas, later rector of Ludgate Hill, London.

The silver hanging lamp in the S. chapel of the 14th-c. church is a memorial to A. E. Coppard (d. 1957), short-story writer and poet, who lived at Duton Hill, *c*. 3 m. S.

THEBERTON, Suff. [4 He] Village on the B1122, 2 m. N. of Leiston. C. M. Doughty, author of *Travels in Arabia Deserta* (1888) and *Dawn in Britain* (6 vols., 1906) was born (1843) at Theberton Hall, visible from the road, and is commemorated by a tablet in the thatched church with the round flint tower.

THERFIELD, Herts. [4 Ef] Village 3 m. SW. of Royston, off the A505. The poet William Alabaster, who had been the Earl of Essex's chaplain on the Cadiz expedition, and had been imprisoned by Elizabeth after becoming a Catholic, was given the rich living here by James I, whose chaplain he was. The Old Rectory[1] is partly medieval.

[1] Open on written application.

THETFORD, Norf. [4 Fe] Town on the A11 and the A134. The site of the birthplace of Thomas Paine (1737–1809), author of *The Rights of Man* (1791–2), is the garden of Grey Gables in White Hart St. A photograph of the original house is in the county library. A gilded statue erected by American friends of the Thomas Paine Society stands outside the Council Offices opposite the Bell Hotel. Educated at the Grammar School, Paine worked for his father, a staymaker, before leaving the town when he was 20.

THOOR BALLYLEE. See GORT.

THORNEY, Cambs. [4 Ed] Fenland village on the A46 and the B1040. Reginald Pecock was forced to resign as Bishop of Chichester (q.v.) in 1458 and was sent to live in seclusion here at the Norman abbey, where he died (1460).

Gilbert White, who visited in 1750 to help his uncle, an agent on the Duke of Bedford's estate, wrote here the verses, 'Invitation to Selborne', addressed to Hester Mulso, the sister of a friend at Oxford.

THORNTON, West Yorkshire. [5 De] Suburb 4 m. W. of Bradford. Brontë Pl., off the B6145, leads to the High St. where a plaque on no. 74 commemorates the births of Charlotte (1816), Branwell (1817), Emily (1818), and Anne (1820) Brontë.

THORPE GREEN HALL, North Yorkshire. [5 Ed] Mansion in the village of Little Ouseburn, off the A1167, 7 m. NE. of Knaresborough. In March 1841 Anne Brontë became governess to the daughters of Mrs. Robinson here. In 1843 her brother, Branwell, joined her as tutor to Edmund Robinson. Branwell, who took opium and was a drunkard, was the model for Arthur Huntingdon in Anne Brontë's novel, *The Tenant of Wildfell Hall* (1848). Anne left the Robinsons in June 1845 and Branwell was dismissed a few weeks later. Her first novel *Agnes Grey* (1847) is about the life of a governess, who suffers from both her employers, one a parsimonious manufacturer, and the other a fashionable country gentleman.

THORPE-LE-SOKEN, Essex. [1 Ha] Village on the A136, 12 m. E. of Colchester. Arnold Bennett bought Comarques, a Queen Anne house, opposite the vicarage, midway between this village and Thorpe Green, in 1913, the year *The Regent* was published. He wrote his third Clayhanger novel, *These Twain* (1916), here, bought a yacht, and kept a flat in London. He sold the house in 1920 after separating from his wife.

THREE MILE CROSS, Berks. [1 Cc] Village in the parish of Shinfield, on the A33, just S. of Reading. On the E. side of the main road stands a humble cottage, now called The Mitford, where Mary Russell Mitford spent most of her writing life. She moved here with her parents in 1820, when her father's extravagance prevented the upkeep of their larger house near Reading. The village and surrounding neighbourhood were the source of her delightful sketches of rural life, contributions to the *Lady's Magazine* later published in five volumes as *Our Village* (1824–32). Miss Mitford's devotion to her father is reflected in the dedication to her 'most cherished friend', her beloved and venerable father' of 'recollections of the beautiful scenery where they have so often wandered, and of the village home where for so many years they have dwelt together'. Her parents are buried at the parish church of St. Mary's, Shinfield.

THRUMS. See KIRRIEMUIR.

THURNING HALL. See BOOTON.

TIBBIE SHIEL'S INN, Selkirks. (Borders). [6 Fd] Old fishing inn (now a hotel) on the isthmus between St. Mary's Loch and the Loch of Lowes, 100 yards from the A708 (Selkirk–Moffatt road). It was run by Tibbie Richardson, better known as 'Shiel', from 1824, when she was widowed, until her death in 1878 in her 96th year. It owed its fame initially to Robert Chambers, who stayed there while collecting material about the Yarrow for his *Picture of Scotland* (1827), and wrote about the 'small, neat house, kept by a decent shepherd's widow, who lets her spare room . . . and can provide her lodgers with as wholesome and agreeable country fare as may anywhere be found'. The inn was a favourite haunt of James Hogg, 'the Ettrick Shepherd', whom John Wilson quotes in *Noctes Ambrosianae* as saying: 'A wren's nest round and theekit wi' moss—sae is Tibbie's', and it became famous as a meeting-place for the *literati* of Edinburgh, such as Wilson, Scott, and De Quincey. Carlyle came as a student, tramping from Edinburgh to Ecclefechan, and R. L. Stevenson as a youth in 1867. The pleasant dining-room has many mementoes and contemporary engravings, and Tibbie's visitors' book is a remarkable record of the number and character of her patrons. Across the road is a monument to Hogg, with his dog, Hector—a fulfilment of his wish for a memorial in 'a quiet spot fornent Tibbie's dwelling'.

TIDMARSH, Berks. [1 Cc] Village on the Pang, 1 m. S. of Pangbourne, on the A340. Lytton Strachey lived with his devoted friend Carrington at the Mill House, built on the end of a large weather-boarded water-mill E. of the crossroads, from December 1917 to July 1924. The house stood in 1½ acres of ground which included a small orchard and a sunken Roman bath, supplied with water from the millstream, and was an ideal headquarters for Strachey, where Carrington did the housekeeping and he could rest between excursions in the outside world. Strachey had just finished *Eminent Victorians* and was busy with proof-reading for the first months of 1918. Its publication suddenly brought him success and fame and encouraged him to set about his classic biography of Queen Victoria (published in 1921). In spite of its attractions the situation of the Mill House proved too damp in the winter and in 1924 Strachey and Carrington moved to a house at Ham (q.v.).

TILFORD, Surrey. [1 Dd] Village off the B3001, 3 m. SE. of Farnham. Charlotte Smith, who, after her husband's bankruptcy, supported her family by writing novels which proved very popular, spent her last year here. She died in 1806 and is buried at Guildford. The village was well known to William Cobbett from his youth at Farnham. In *Rural Rides* (1830) he mentions stopping on the green to show his son, Richard, the oak he had seen as a boy, which he said was 30 feet in circumference (P on seat).

TILQUILLIE CASTLE, Kincardines. (Grampian). [7 Hf] Country house off the A957, 2 m. SE. of Banchory. Norman Douglas was born here in 1868. His reminiscences, *Looking Back* (1932), state that he spent little time on the estate after leaving to study in Karlsruhe (*c.* 1886). He lived in Capri, when he left the Foreign Service, and wrote there his most successful novel *South Wind* (1917).

TINTAGEL, Cornwall. [2 Cd] Village on the Atlantic coast, on the B3263, *c.* 4½ m. NW. of Camelford. On Tintagel Head, a rocky promontory ½ m. away, jutting into the sea across a narrow causeway, are the fragmentary ruins of a castle, built partly on the mainland and partly on the so-called 'Island' and traditionally the birthplace of King Arthur. The castle, a stronghold of the Earls of Cornwall from *c.* 1145 until the 15th c., was thought to have been built on the site of Arthur's castle (*c.* 5th–6th cc.), but excavations have uncovered remains of a Celtic monastery probably occupied from *c.* 500 to *c.* 850. A path leads down to a shingle beach, on the W. side of which is Merlin's Cave, where, according to Tennyson's *Idylls of the King* (1859), Arthur appears to Merlin after his secret upbringing. King Arthur's Hall in the village was put up between the First and Second World Wars by the Fellowship of the Round Table. It has stained-glass windows picturing Arthur's knights, and a library of Arthurian literature.

Swinburne stayed at Tintagel in 1864 from the end of August to the end of October with his friend J. W. Inchbald, and wrote of visits to 'lone Camelford and Boscastle divine'. While he was here he finished *Atalanta in Calydon* (1865).

TINTERN ABBEY, Gwent. [2 Ga] Ruined Cistercian abbey (founded 1131, rebuilt 13th and 14th cc., and suppressed by Henry VIII, 1536), situated on grassland in a bend of the Wye, with wooded hills above, c. 4 m. N. of Chepstow, on the A466. Wordsworth and his sister Dorothy visited the abbey in July 1798, after leaving Alfoxton (q.v.) and before going to Germany. Wordsworth wanted to revisit the hills and valleys of Wales, which he had explored in 1793. He and Dorothy left Bristol (q.v.) after spending a few days with Joseph Cottle, crossed the Severn by ferry, and walked up the Wye Valley as far as Goodrich Castle. They spent a night at Tintern on the way and, after walking back to Chepstow, returned to Tintern for a second night before going back all the way to Bristol by boat. Wordsworth's poem, 'Lines Composed a Few Miles above Tintern Abbey, on revisiting the Banks of the Wye during a Tour, July 13, 1798', was composed after leaving Tintern, completed on his return to Bristol, and taken to Cottle for publication in *Lyrical Ballads* (1798).

Sydney Dobell made a journey to Tintern Abbey with some friends in 1858 and wrote a sonnet about it.

Open weekdays 9.30 a.m.–4, 4.30, or 7 p.m., Sun. from 2 p.m.

TIPPERARY, Tipperary. [9 Ec] Market town and manufacturing centre on the Ara, in the Golden Vale (or Vein), on the T13 and the T36. In Main St. there is a fine statue (by John Hughes, 1898) of Charles Kickham, the poet, novelist, and patriot.

TITCHFIELD, Hants. [1 Ce] Little town 10 m. SE. of Southampton, S. of the A27. Titchfield Abbey,[1] dissolved in 1536, was rebuilt as a mansion by Thomas Wriothesley, 1st Earl of Southampton, in 1542. John Florio, lexicographer and translator of Italian descent, stayed here (1590-1) as tutor to the young 3rd Earl, who lived under the care of his widowed mother. Florio's brother-in-law, Samuel Daniel, also stayed, and Thomas Nash and Shakespeare visited. It is believed that the majority of Shakespeare's sonnets were written about the abbey, most of them in the abbey itself, as well as several of the *Passionate Pilgrim* collection (1599), *Love's Labour's Lost* (1595), and the neglected poem *A Lover's Complaint*. The N. wall of the cloister was once the wall of the adjoining Great Hall, where it is possible that *Love's Labour's Lost*, *Romeo and Juliet* (1595), *A Midsummer Night's Dream* (1595 or 1596), and *Twelfth Night* (1600-1) were performed for the first time.

[1] Open daily, Sun. from 2 p.m.

TITCHMARSH, Northants. [4 De] Village off the A605, 2 m. NE. of Thrapston. John Dryden, who was born (1631) at Aldwinkle near by, spent his childhood with his mother's relatives, the Pickerings, at the manor (gone, site near Dryden's Close). The church has memorials to the Pickerings and to Dryden, composed by his cousin Elizabeth Creed.

TIVERTON, Devon. [2 Fd] Old market and lace-making town situated on the Exe, 14 m. N. of Exeter, on the A373 and the A396. Mrs. Hannah Cowley (1743-1809), the daughter of a bookseller, Philip Parkhurst, was born here. She was a prolific writer for the London stage, after her first success with *The Runaway* at Drury Lane in 1776. Other plays included *A Bold Stroke for a Husband* (1783) and *The Belle's Stratagem* (1780). She also wrote sentimental verses as 'Anna Matilda'. She died at Tiverton and is buried here.

R. D. Blackmore went to Blundell's School (founded 1604), as did John Ridd, the hero of *Lorna Doone* (1869). Old Blundell's School (N.T.)[1] was converted into dwelling-houses when the new school was built in 1882.

[1] Forecourt open at reasonable hours.

TOBERMORY. See MULL.

TONBRIDGE, Kent. [1 Fd] Old market town on the Medway and the A227, 7 m. SE. of Sevenoaks. Among the pupils of Tonbridge School (founded 1553) were E. M. Forster in the 1890s, and Sidney Keyes in the late 1930s. Some of the poems Keyes wrote here were included in *Iron Laurel* (1942), published while he was at Oxford.

TONG, Salop. [3 Hc] Little village on the A41, 11 m. NW. of Wolverhampton. The 15th-c. church is remarkable for the number and beauty of its tombs. At the W. end of the tomb of Sir Richard Vernon is the miniature effigy of his son George, later Sir George Vernon, reputed to be the 'King of the Peak' in Scott's novel, *Peveril of the Peak* (1823). The verses forming the epitaph at the head and foot of Sir Thomas Stanley's tomb were written by Shakespeare, according to Sir William Dugdale (1605–86), antiquarian, and begin

Ask who lyes heare, but do not weep,
He is not dead, he dooth but sleep.

Dickens had the village in mind when he described the place where Little Nell and her grandfather find peace at the end of their wanderings in *The Old Curiosity Shop* (1841), and Cattermole's illustrations are reminiscent of the interior of the church. Outside the S. door a sign marks the 'reputed resting-place of Little Nell'.

TOP WITHENS. See HAWORTH.

TORQUAY, Devon. [2 Ee] Large seaside resort 23 m. S. of Exeter on the A380 (or 24 m. on the A379 coast road), situated on seven hills where two valleys meet. Tennyson, who stayed here in 1838, called it 'the loveliest sea-village in England', and it was the inspiration for his poem 'Audley Court'. Elizabeth Barrett came here from London in 1838 in the hope that the mild climate would improve her health. She stayed at the Bath House, 1 Beacon Ter. (now the Hotel Regina; P), sheltered by the hills and overlooking the harbour, but the good results of her visit were ruined by the death of her favourite brother Edward in a sailing accident in Babbacombe Bay, in July 1840. She was so prostrated that although she longed to leave the sea and its painful associations she was too ill to travel until September 1841, when she went in an invalid carriage by easy stages back to Wimpole St. In the summer of 1840 she wrote in a letter that she had 'written lately (as far as manuscript goes) a good deal, only on all sorts of subjects, and in as many shapes . . . I lie here weaving a great many schemes'. After the tragedy, when she was unable to write, books were her great solace, especially the Greek classics, in spite of the doctor's advice not to tire herself with studying.

Kingsley came over from Eversleigh in the winter of 1853/4 with his wife, who had been ill, and stayed until the following spring. His house, Livermead Cottage, at the entrance to Livermead Beach, was burnt down and replaced by a villa-residence called Livermead Cliff. Kingsley enjoyed the scientific society he met in Torquay, 'a place',

he wrote, 'which should be as much endeared to the naturalist as to the patriot and the artist' and he described his wanderings among rocks and pools and 'happy evenings spent over the microscope . . . examining the wonders and labours of the day'. In the spring of 1854 he wrote the Preface to *Theologica Germanica*—the book which Martin Luther said he owed more to than any other 'saving the Bible and St. Augustine'—which was published in its first English translation (by Susan Winkworth) that year.

Edward Bulwer-Lytton first came to Torquay in August 1856 and, like his friend Disraeli, who was a frequent visitor, grew much attached to the place. He stayed for a time at the old Union Hotel before buying Argyll Hall in Warren Rd., where he used to come each winter to relax, write, and entertain his friends. He died there on 18 January 1873, just after reading the proofs of his last work, having, it is believed, caught a chill whilst watching a burning brig which had drifted on to the rocks below the hill on which his villa stood.

Eden Phillpotts, prolific author of novels and plays, especially of the West Country, lived at Eltham, Oak Hill Rd., from *c.* 1901 until 1929. During this time he wrote much of the work for which he is best remembered, including the Dartmoor novels, such as *The Secret Woman* (1905, dramatized 1912), *The Thief of Virtue* (1910, probably his own favourite), and *Widecombe Fair* (1913); also the immensely popular plays, *The Farmer's Wife* (1917) and *Yellow Sands* (with his daughter Adelaide, 1926). He was made a Freeman of Torquay in 1921. An account of his friendship with Arnold Bennett during these years is given in his autobiography, *From the angle of 88* (1951).

Margaret Fairless Barber, author of *The Roadmender* (1901) and an invalid for most of her life, lived here for some years before her death (1901). Sean O'Casey came from Totnes in 1955 and lived, with his wife Eileen, to the end of his life in a flat in a large white Victorian house, Villa Rosa, 40 Trumlands Rd., St. Marychurch, just off the Torquay-Teignmouth road. His last plays, *The Bishop's Bonfire* (1955), *The Drums of Father Ned* (1960), and *Behind the Green Curtains* (3 plays, 1961), and essays and stories entitled *The Green Crow* (1956), were published at this time.

A less positive literary association is that

of Sir Richard Burton, travel writer (especially of his *Pilgrimage to Mecca*, 1855–6) and translator from the Arabic of *The Thousand and One Nights* (1885–8). According to his own account he was born at his maternal grandparents' home, Barham House, near Elstree, Herts., but, although the Elstree parish register records his baptism on 2 September 1821, a marginal note in the same handwriting reads 'born 19th March, 1821, Torquay, Devon', so it is reasonable to regard him as a native of Torquay, although the exact place and circumstances of his birth are not known.

TORRINGTON. See GREAT TORRINGTON.

TOTNES, Devon. [2 Ee] Old town situated on a steep hill above the Dart, on the A381 and the A385. In 1938 Sean O'Casey came here from London with his wife and family so that the children could go to Dartington Hall School. They rented Tingrith, a Victorian house in Ashburton Rd., which became their home until they moved to Torquay (q.v.) 17 years later.

TREMADOC, Gwynedd. [3 Db] Village, 1 m. N. of Portmadoc on the A497, laid out by W. A. Madocks in 1810 but never developed into the town he envisaged. Madocks's philanthropy in building a causeway to reclaim land in the estuary of the Glaslyn inspired Shelley to help him to raise the money. Shelley and Harriet, his wife, lived at a house (gone) on Madocks's estate of Tan-yr-Allt, until intruders fired shots at him one evening and the Shelleys left the neighbourhood. The reasons for the attack are obscure but might have arisen out of local resentment of Shelley's political views.
    T. E. Lawrence, who became known as 'Lawrence of Arabia' after his exploits during the First World War, recounted in *Seven Pillars of Wisdom* (1926), was born at Woodlands (P) in 1888.

TREMEIRCHION, Clwyd. [3 Ea] Straggling hillside village overlooking the Vale of Clwyd, a few miles SE. of St. Asaph, off the A55. A tablet on the N. side of the chancel in the little church commemorates Hester Lynch Piozzi, 'Dr. Johnson's Mrs. Thrale', who was buried (1821) in a vault then outside the church, but since covered by the N. transept, built later. The only child of John Salusbury, she grew up at the family home, Bach-y-graig (gone), a 16th-c. mansion of pyramidal shape, topped by a cupola, which nestled at the foot of 'Dymeirchion' (now spelt Tremeirchion) Hill on the edge of a wood. When she revisited it in 1774 with her husband, Henry Thrale, and Dr. Johnson, she was saddened to find the place in a dilapidated state, as was the church, which Johnson noted was 'in a dismal condition, the seats all tumbling about, the Altar rail falling, . . .'. After her husband's death (1781) Mrs. Thrale married Gabriel Piozzi (1784) and they decided to build a house at Tremeirchion, near the top of the hill, with a fine view of the valley and distant Snowdonia. The house, built as an Italian villa, was called Brynbella (Welsh *Bryn*, hill; Italian *bella*, beautiful) and in 1795 became their home for the rest of their lives. In 1800 Gabriel Piozzi renovated Bach-y-graig for a tenant and a few years later undertook extensive additions and repairs to the church. Mrs. Piozzi wrote in September 1803 to her daughter Queeney that they were 'paving, glazing, slating it etc.' and providing a new pulpit, desk, and cloths.

TRENTHAM GARDENS, Staffs. [3 Hb] Park and pleasure grounds on the Trent, on the A34 just S. of Stoke-on-Trent. Trentham Hall, the mansion, now ruined, was described by Disraeli in his novel, *Lothair* (1870), as 'Brentham', the ducal home of the hero's college friend, where the stables had the best riding horses in England and the guests played croquet on the velvet lawn, watched by the duchess from a Turkish tent.

TRE-TALIESIN, Dyfed. [3 Dd] Village on the A487, *c.* 9 m. NE. of Aberystwyth. A footpath leads 1 m. E. to Bedd Taliesin, an ancient stone tomb traditionally regarded as the grave of Taliesin (*fl.* 550), reputedly the greatest of the Welsh bards, but probably a mythical personage. He is first mentioned in *Saxon Genealogies*, appended to the *Historia Britonum c.* 690. Much poetry, probably of later date, has been ascribed to him, and the 14th-c. *Book of Taliesin* is a collection of poems by different authors and of different dates. Taliesin figures prominently in Peacock's *The Misfortunes of Elphin* (1829) and is mentioned in Tennyson's *Idylls of the King* (1859) as a member of the Round Table.

TREVONE, Cornwall. [2 Be] Village 1½ m. W. of Padstow, on a minor road N. of the B3276. Dorothy Richardson, pioneer of the 'stream-of-consciousness' novel, lived here after her marriage to the painter Alan Odle in 1917. They rented Rose Cottage in the village and later other cottages in the Padstow area, spending the winters here when rents were low and letting their room in Queen's Ter., London. Dorothy Richardson's novels, written between 1917 and 1938, either in Cornwall or in London, form a single sequence entitled *Pilgrimage*.

TROSSACHS, THE, Perths. (Central). [6 Db] The country between Loch Achray and Loch Katrine, so called from the Gaelic word meaning 'bristly', a wild area covered with oak, birch, and rowan trees, bog-myrtle, and heather. Dorothy Wordsworth, who thought the word meant 'many hills', records in her *Journals* (1897) how she and William pleased the boatman on Loch Katrine in 1803 by exclaiming at the grandeur of the scenery as he rowed, while Coleridge strode along the lakeside to keep warm. Wordsworth, who had difficulty in finding any shelter for the night, called the area 'Untouched, unbreathed upon' in his sonnet. Parts of Scott's poem *The Lady of the Lake* (1810), and his novel *Rob Roy* (1817) are set here. One of the islands in Loch Katrine is called Ellen's Isle (q.v.) after Ellen Douglas, the heroine of *The Lady of the Lake*.

TROTTON. See MILLAND.

TROWBRIDGE, Wilts. [1 Ac] Market town on the A363, 8 m. SE. of Bath. In 1814, soon after the death of his wife, George Crabbe moved to the vicarage here (demolished in the 1960s) and eventually met his neighbouring poets William Lisle Bowles and Tom Moore. Crabbe's married son John came as his curate in 1816, and in 1819 Crabbe published *Tales of the Hall* followed the next year by his *Collected Works*. In *Romance of an Elderly Poet* (1913) A. M. Broadley and W. Jerrold tell of Crabbe's proposal of marriage to Charlotte Ridout and later his sentimental correspondence with Elizabeth Charter of Bath. Crabbe died here in 1832 and there is a memorial tablet in the chancel.

TROY TOWN. See FOWEY.

TRULL, Som. [2 Fc] Village 1¾ m. SW. of Taunton. Mrs. Ewing settled here in 1883, when her husband returned from military duties in Ceylon. She was happy here, wrote *Mary's Meadow* (1883-4) and *Letters from a Little Garden* (1884-5), and cultivated her garden, but 2 years later, after an illness that necessitated two spinal operations, she died. She is buried in the churchyard and a memorial window on the N. wall of the church testifies to the affection in which she and her husband were held. The beautiful alms dish was the gift of their nephews and godchildren.

TRUMPINGTON. See GRANTCHESTER.

TRURO, Cornwall. [2 Bf] Cathedral city and county town on the A39, situated on the Truro River. Samuel Foote (1720-77), dramatist, actor, and humorist, was born at Johnson Vivian's House (gone), formerly on the S. side of Boscawen St., and was baptized in St. Mary's Church, of which only the S. aisle survives, now forming the S. aisle of the choir of the cathedral. Foote grew up in the town residence of the Footes of Lambesso, a house on the N. side of Boscawen St., which later became the Red Lion Hotel (now a restaurant). He was educated at Worcester Grammar School and Oxford and made his name in London as a wit and writer of short topical sketches.

Sir Hugh Walpole wrote a series of novels in a Cornish setting, which include *The Cathedral* (1922), *The Old Ladies* (1924), and *Harmer John* (1926), in which the town of 'Polchester' represents Truro. In the N. aisle of the cathedral (built 1880-1910) a tablet commemorates Sir Arthur Quiller-Couch as one who 'kindled in others a lively and discriminating love of English literature'.

Kenneth Grahame's marriage certificate, bearing the signatures of Anthony Hope Hawkins and Sir Arthur Quiller-Couch as witnesses to his marriage (22 July 1899) at Fowey, may be seen at the County Archivist's Office (a new building on the outskirts of the town).

Malpas (pr. Mōpus), 1½ m. SE., can be reached by a pleasant road on the E. bank of the river. The ferry here is mentioned in the Tristram and Iseult stories, when Iseult had to make her way across the water to the palace of King Mark at Blandreland (in the parish of Kea).

TULLIRA (or TULIRA) CASTLE, Galway.
[9 Da] Mansion *c*. 5 m. N. of Gort, W. of the
T11 to Galway. The house, rebuilt (1882)
in a so-called 'Tudor' style which W. B.
Yeats found very unpleasing, was the home
of Edward Martyn, poet, playwright, and
patron of the arts, and a founder of the
Irish Literary Theatre. His many friends
included Yeats, Lady Gregory, and George
Moore (in whose autobiographical *Hail and
Farewell*, 1911–14, he figures prominently).
Martyn was a descendant of a wealthy
Catholic land-owning family and his mother
was determined that he should fulfil his
role as one of the principal local landlords.
He spent lavishly on her rebuilding projects,
but to her disappointment refused to contemplate marriage. He bequeathed his entire
library to the Carmelites in Clarendon St.,
Dublin, and gave instructions (which were
duly carried out) that after his death his
body should be used for dissection by medical
students and his remains buried in a pauper's
grave.

TUNBRIDGE WELLS, Kent. [1 Fd] Inland
spa, on the A26 and the A267, which grew
up round the chalybeate spring discovered
in 1606. The church of King Charles the
Martyr has the names of Pepys and Evelyn,
who both visited here, on the list of subscribers whose money paid for the building.

Defoe gives a picture of the resort in
A Tour through Great Britain (1724–7). He
arrived when the Prince of Wales was
visiting, which drew a larger crowd than
usual to the place.

The Ladies that appear here, are indeed the
glory of the Place; the coming to the Wells to
drink the Water is a meer matter of custom; some
drink, more do not, and few drink Physically:
But Company and Diversion is in short the main
business of the Place; and those People who have
nothing to do any where else, seem to be the only
People who have any thing to do at Tunbridge. . . .
As for Gaming, Sharping, Intrieguing; as also
Fops, Fools, Beaus, and the like, Tunbridge is as
full of these, as can be desired, and it takes off
much Diversion of those Persons of Honour and
Virtue, who go there to be innocently recreated:
However a Man of Character, and good behaviour . . . may single out such Company as
may be suitable to him.

Defoe left Tunbridge because he was short
of money, the one thing no one could do
without here, he wrote. John Gay escorted
the Countess of Burlington here in 1723.

He had been staying with Lord Burlington
in London, working on his play *The Captives*,
and he continued with it here. It was performed at Drury Lane the next year.

Edward Young, rector of Welwyn, who
never received the preferment his friends
thought he merited, often came here for
health and exercise. He believed that 'steel
water', as the chalybeate spring was called,
and riding were his 'only cure'. His long
poem *Night Thoughts on Life, Death, and
Immortality* (1742–5), with its vision of
eternity, was a popular solace to his contemporaries. Richard Cumberland, whose
sentimental comedies had introduced him
to Garrick and his circle, often visited with
his family, and after losing his post through
a change in government, chose to settle in
a house (gone) on Mt. Sion. Fanny Burney,
who stayed at the Sussex Hotel (now the
Royal Victoria Hotel) on The Pantiles with
Mrs. Thrale soon after the publication of
her novel *Evelina* (1778), mentions in her
Journal the airs his wife and daughters
assumed. She was warned that he would
refuse to speak to her as, now that his new
plays were no longer acceptable, he hated
to meet successful authors. She set some
scenes from *Camilla* (1796) on Mt. Ephraim.

The Pantiles, a paved walk shaded by
trees, and sometimes called The Walks or
The Promenade, contains the Bath House
(P, built 1804), now without its Victorian
crenellations, and the site of the Assembly
and Gaming Rooms (P on 40–6).

Horace Smith spent the last years of his
life here with his daughter Elizabeth. He died
in 1849 and is buried in Holy Trinity churchyard. Thackeray, who spent part of his
childhood (1825) at Bellevue, on the Common, recalls reading the Gothic novel,
Manfroni, or the One-Handed Monk, alone in
the drawing-room while his parents were
out and being too frightened to move. This
was one of the books from 'the well-
remembered library on the Pantiles' that he
mentions in 'Tunbridge Toys' from *Roundabout Papers* (1863), written when he was
living (1860) at another house on the
Common (now Thackeray House, P).

TUNSTALL, Lancs. [5 Cc] Village on the
A683, just over 3 m. S. of Kirkby Lonsdale.
When Charlotte and Emily Brontë were at
school at Cowan Bridge (q.v.) they used to
come the 2¼ m. by the 'exposed and hilly

road' to attend the parish church, where the Revd. William Carus Wilson, founder of the Clergy Daughters' School (1823), was vicar. After the morning service the girls were given food in the room above the porch. Charlotte depicts Tunstall as 'Brocklebridge' in *Jane Eyre* (1847).

TWYFORD, Hants. [1 Bd] Village on the A33, 3½ m. S. of Winchester. Alexander Pope came here at the age·of 8 for his first schooling away from home, and was apparently unhappy. According to a 19th-c. magazine, *Merry England*, he 'was dismissed in consequence of writing a lampoon on his tutor, and was transferred to a Roman Catholic school situated close by Hyde Park Corner, kept by another priest, where he lost nearly all that he had gained under Mr. Banisher [the headmaster]'. His schoolhouse, a beautiful old house called Seagers Buildings which stood in a quiet corner, was pulled down in the 1960s to make room for a housing estate. In 1771 Benjamin Franklin stayed at Twyford House, at the top of the hill, while he was writing the first part of his autobiography. His host was Jonathan Shipley, Dean of Winchester and later Bishop of St. Asaph.

TWYWELL, Northants. [4 De] Stone village off the A604, 3 m. W. of Thrapston, where Hester Mulso was born. The Elizabethan manor (gone) in which she wrote 'The Loves of Amoret and Melissa', when only 9, has 'numerous chimnies', trees trained up between the stone mullioned windows, and was near 'a lake overhung with trees'. She became 'nearly mistress of French and Italian' and was proficient enough in Latin to be considered a bluestocking. Dr. Johnson published her letters in *The Rambler* and Samuel Richardson treated her as one of his 'daughters'. She married a Mr. Chapone but was widowed within a year. The churchwarden is custodian of a copy of her *Letters on the Improvement of the Mind* (1774) conceived originally for a favourite niece and then highly esteemed. The house was demolished *c.* 1839.

TYNWALD HILL, I.O.M. [5 Jg] Artificial mound off the A1, near Peel, seat of the old parliament, where new laws and names of officers appointed for the year are still announced in a ceremony held formerly on Midsummer Day, now 5 July. Wordsworth wrote a sonnet on the ceremony ('Tynwald Hill'), which is also described in Hall Caine's *The Deemster* (1887), his most popular novel.

U

UFFINGTON, Oxon. [1 Bb] Village in the Vale of the White Horse (formerly in Berks.), *c.* 4½ m. S. of Faringdon, reached by minor roads off the B4508 and the B4507. Thomas Hughes, author of *Tom Brown's Schooldays* (1857), was born (20 Oct. 1822) in an old farmhouse in the village (pulled down in the later 19th c. to make way for the new school) and was baptized in the church, where his grandfather was vicar. He spent his early years here before going to a prep school at Twyford, Hants (1830), and the opening chapters of *Tom Brown's Schooldays* describe the village and the features of the Vale which he knew so well: White Horse Hill, with its white chalk galloping horse (374 ft long) revealed by the cut turf; Uffington Castle above on the Ridgeway, the ancient track running along the crest

of the Downs; the Blowing Stone, on the way from the Hill to Kingston Lisle, nearly 4 ft high and pierced with holes, which was said to have been used long ago to sound the alarm at the approach of an enemy; and, 1½ m. W., a burial place of great antiquity, known as Wayland's Smithy, whose legends Scott adapted for his novel, *Kenilworth* (1821). Tom Brown's early days are set in Uffington and before going to Rugby he attends the old schoolhouse, a small stone building dated 1617, just outside the churchyard on the corner of the Faringdon road.

Thomas Hughes returned to Uffington in 1857, after a long absence, for the scouring of the White Horse, recorded in his *The Scouring of the White Horse; or the Long Vacation Ramble of a London Clerk* (1859).

There is a memorial plaque to him in gunmetal with a portrait in low relief in the church, on the N. wall of the N. transept. The organ was dedicated to his memory on 24 January 1918. A new village hall, the Thomas Hughes Memorial Hall, was opened on 29 November 1975 by Mrs. L. Akroyd, a great-grand-niece. The foyer contains a brass plaque with an engraving of the Uffington White Horse to commemorate the 150th anniversary (1972) of his birth.

After the death of his grandfather (1833) his grandmother, Mrs. Mary Anne Hughes, moved to Kingston Lisle, 1½ m. SE., where her house (probably Kingston Lisle House) still stands. She was a friend of Scott, Dickens, Richard Barham, and Harrison Ainsworth, and, when she lived in London, had regaled them with an immense fund of legends and folklore, which frequently served as source material for novels and poems. Ainsworth stayed with her on many occasions at Kingston Lisle, and wrote the last chapters of *Jack Sheppard* (1839) and *Guy Fawkes* (1841) here. Ainsworth, who was offered every comfort, including 'your own hours for every meal; your own sitting room; your great chair;', dedicated *Guy Fawkes* to his hostess. In his story, *Old St. Paul's* (1841), some of the scenes are based on White Horse country, including an account of the Blowing Stone, and Mrs. Hughes is portrayed as 'Mrs. Compton'.

ULVA. See MULL.

UNDERWOOD, Notts. [4 Bc] Village 9 m. N. of Nottingham near the junction of the B600 (A613) and the A608, particularly associated with D. H. Lawrence. Haggs Farm up a private gated track from Felley Mill Lane was the home of his friends, the Chambers family.

Whatever I forget, I shall never forget the Haggs—I loved it so. I loved to come to you all, it really was a new life began in me there.... Oh, I'd love to be nineteen again, and coming up through the Warren and catching the first glimpse of the buildings.

Miriam in *Sons and Lovers* (1913) is partly modelled on Jessie Chambers. Felley Mill Farm, where he and his friends often walked to, becomes Strelley Mill in *The White Peacock* (1911).

UNIONHALL, Cork. [9 Cf] Village in the parish of Myross on the S. coast, half way between Skibbereen and Ross Carbery. On the E. side of a narrow road up the hill beyond the Protestant parish church of Myross double gates open on to a drive through the beautiful garden of the former Rock Cottage (now The Glebe), the rectory where Dean Swift stayed in the summer of 1723, when he left Dublin after Vanessa's death for a 3 or 4 months' visit to the south of Ireland. It is not certain with whom he stayed, but the original house still stands, with later additions, overlooking Glandore Harbour from which, Charles Smith says (in *The Ancient and Present State of the County and City of Cork*, 1750), Swift 'often diverted himself in making little voyages on the coast . . . towards Baltimore; and the excursions occasioned his Latin poem *Carberiae Rupes* ['the Rocks of Carbery']'. According to the Somerville family records Swift wrote the poem in a ruined tower, known as 'Swift's Tower', at Castletownshend (q.v.).

UPHAM, Hants. [1 Ce] Village on a minor road off the A333, *c.* 8 m. SSE. of Winchester. Edward Young, author of *Night Thoughts on Life, Death, and Immortality* (1742–5), was born (1683) at his father's rectory (now the Old Rectory). The plaque recording his birth has been moved to the New Rectory. Young grew up in Upham and was educated at Winchester before going to Oxford.

UPPARK, West Sussex. [1 Ce] Queen Anne mansion (N.T.) on the B2146, 5½ m. SE. of Petersfield. After leaving Bromley at the age of 13 H. G. Wells lived here for a time when his mother was housekeeper to Miss Fetherstonhaugh. He read voraciously from the library and a hidden store of books discovered in the attic, which included Thomas Paine's *The Rights of Man* (1791–2). The house figures as 'Bladesover' in the partly autobiographical *Tono-Bungay* (1909).

Open Wed. 2–6 p.m., Sun. 10 a.m.–7 p.m.

UPPER FAHAN, Donegal. [8 Ea] Parish, part of the little resort of Fahan on the E. shore of Lough Swilley, 7 m. NW. of Londonderry. Mrs. Cecil Frances Alexander, hymn-writer remembered especially for 'All things bright and beautiful', 'There is a green hill far away', and 'Once in Royal David's city', lived here from 1855 to 1860, when her husband, the Revd. William

Alexander, was rector. The church has a chancel in her memory.

UPPINGHAM, Leics. [4 Cd] Small market town on the A6003, 9 m. N. of Corby. Jeremy Taylor, chaplain to Archbishop Laud and to Charles I, became resident rector here early in 1638. The church still has the pulpit from which he preached and the paten that he gave. He left in the summer of 1642 to join Charles I, who was with his troops.

Uppingham School (founded 1584), which came into prominence as a public school under Edward Thring (1853–87), had Norman Douglas as a pupil in the early 1890s and James Elroy Flecker and Ronald Firbank at the turn of the century.

UPTON-ON-SEVERN, Hereford and Worcester. [1 Aa] Village on the A4104, 11 m. S. of Worcester. The White Lion in the High St. was the hotel where the characters in Henry Fielding's *Tom Jones* (1749) had such a disturbed night.

UPWELL. See CHRISTCHURCH, Cambs.

UTTOXETER, Staffs. [4 Ac] Market town on the A50 and the A518. In the centre of the market-place a bas-relief (a replica of that on the base of his statue in Lichfield) on the stone conduit depicts the scene of Dr. Johnson's 'penance'. As a youth he once refused to look after his father's bookstall at the market when the latter was ill and the remembrance of this sin of pride caused him to return 50 years later and stand in contrition at the site for a long time bareheaded in the rain. 'I trust', he said, 'I have propitiated heaven for this only instance, I believe, of contumacy towards my father.' Nathaniel Hawthorne, in *Our Old Home* (1863), tells how he made a sentimental journey to see the very spot where Johnson had stood, but had to rely on his imagination, as there was no memorial to mark it or person who could tell him. He dined at the Nag's Head (gone) on 'bacon and greens, some mutton chops, juicier and more delectable than all America could serve up at the President's table, and a gooseberry pudding, . . . besides a pitcher of foaming ale'—all for 18 pence.

V

VALE OF THE WHITE HORSE. See UFFINGTON.

VALLEY OF THE ROCKS. See LYNMOUTH.

VENTNOR, I.O.W. [1 Cf] S. coastal resort on the B3327. Pearl Craigie ('John Oliver Hobbes') wrote her first novel *Some Emotions and a Moral* (1891) here after separating from her husband. She lived with her father in London and in Springhill Castle (house gone, garden now a public park), W. of the town, where she wrote many other novels and some less successful dramas, the most popular being *The Ambassador* (1898). In 1900 she moved to St. Lawrence Lodge, a small cottage near by, where she wrote *Robert Orange* (1902), whose hero is based

on Disraeli. After her death in 1906 her father renamed the cottage Craigie Lodge.

VIRGINIA, Cavan. [8 Fe] Pleasant little market town on the T24 and the T35, on the N. shore of Lake Ramor. Quilca House, *c.* 1½ m. NE., was once the home of the Revd. Thomas Sheridan, a friend of Jonathan Swift, who spent many summers here as his guest. Swift wrote the greater part of *Gulliver's Travels* here, and it is said that his Brobdignagian farmer was modelled on a Mr. Doughty, a local man of unusually large proportions. A landmark near by is known as Stella's Bower. Richard Brinsley Sheridan, the grandson of Thomas, spent the greater part of his youth at the family home at Quilca.

W

WAIN WOOD, Herts. [1 Ea] Wood a few miles S. of Hitchin, approached by a footpath from the road from Hitchin to Preston. Among the trees is a natural amphitheatre known as 'Bunyan's Dell', where people gathered in their hundreds to hear Bunyan preach secretly, knowing that they risked fines or imprisonment or even transportation for defying the law prohibiting such meetings. Services are still held here on special occasions, attended by pilgrims from all over the world.

WAKEFIELD, West Yorkshire [5 Ee] Industrial town on the A61, 8 m. S. of Leeds. George Gissing, whose father was a chemist, was born (1857) above the shop in the market-place at 30 Westgate (P). George's father, author of two books on the flora of the neighbourhood, died when George was 13, and he and his brothers were sent away to boarding school. Wakefield appears as the heroine's home town in Gissing's novel *A Life's Morning* (1888).

WALLINGTON HOUSE, Northumb. [6 He] Country house[1] (N.T.), 10 m. W. of Morpeth, on the B6342, home of the Trevelyan family since 1777. In the mid 19th c. Ruskin made many visits here. In 1853 he came with his wife and the Pre-Raphaelite painter, Millais. His visit in 1857 coincided with that of John Bell Scott, who was painting the new hall, made by covering in the courtyard, where his *St. Cuthbert* was being displayed. Ruskin and the other guests decorated the pillars with flower paintings. Ruskin first met Swinburne here riding from his home at Capheaton (q.v.) to tuition at Cambo rectory. Swinburne looked on Wallington as a second home. Dr. John Brown of Edinburgh was another guest.

[1] Grounds open Easter–Sept.: daily 10 a.m.–6 p.m. Hall open Apr.–Sept.: daily except Tues. and Fri. 2–6 p.m.; Oct.: Sat., Sun. 2–5 p.m.

WALLYFORD, East Lothian (Lothian). [6 Fc] Village on the A5094, S. of Musselburgh. Margaret Oliphant Wilson was born (1828) here, though in her *Autobiography* (1889, reprinted 1974) she writes that she 're-membered nothing' about the place. How-ever, she returned after her marriage in 1852 to her cousin Francis Oliphant, and she set the scene of her short story 'Isabel Dysart' here.

WALMER, Kent. [1 Hd] Coastal resort, adjoining Deal, which grew up round Henry VIII's castle. This became the official residence of the Warden of the Cinque Ports, where Benjamin Robert Haydon spent a short stay when invited to paint a portrait of the Duke of Wellington. Haydon gives an account of his visit in his *Autobiography* (1853). Robert Bridges was born (1844) at Roselands (now a convent) and went to Eton.

WALSALL, West Midlands. [3 Hd] Manufacturing town E. of the M6, NW. of Birmingham. Jerome Klapka Jerome, author of the popular novel *Three Men in a Boat* (1889), was born (1859) in Bradford St., which has disappeared in recent development.

WALTHAM ABBEY, Essex. [1 Eb] Old town on the A121, surrounding the Norman abbey where King Harold was interred. John Foxe, author of *The Book of Martyrs* (1563), lived here from 1565 but the house has gone. Thomas Fuller, who admired Foxe, was perpetual curate from 1649 to 1658. He married his second wife in 1651, finished his *Church History* (1655) here, and worked on *The Worthies of England* (1662).

Sheridan stayed here from August 1772 to April 1773 between escorting Elizabeth Linley to Paris and their marriage.

WALTHAM CROSS, Herts. [1 Eb] Town on the A121 and the A1010, 2 m. E. of Waltham Abbey. Trollope lived at the brick Georgian Waltham House (gone), 'a rickety old place' near the Cross, from 1859 to 1870. This was his most settled home; he enjoyed hunting and found time to write *The Claverings* (1867), *The Last Chronicle of Barset* (1867), and other novels by rising early. On summer evenings his guests sat talking under the cedar tree while 'tobacco smoke went curling up into the night'. At Christmas the same children's games were played here as at Noningsby in *Orley Farm* (1862) and a nephew said later he had only to play commerce to imagine himself a child again.

WALTHAM ST. LAWRENCE, Berks. [1 Dc] Village on the B3024, 3 m. E. of Twyford. John Newbery, the original of Goldsmith's 'philanthropic publisher of St. Paul's Church-yard, who has written so many little books for children' in *The Vicar of Wakefield* (1766), was born here, educated at the village school, and after a prosperous career in London, buried in the churchyard at his own request. He was the first bookseller to provide books for the very young on a large scale and he probably wrote many of the stories himself, although *Goody Two Shoes* (1765) has generally been attributed to Goldsmith. As well as Goldsmith (whom he frequently helped financially), his friends included Dr. Johnson, Christopher Smart, and Smollett, and the epitaph on his imposing tombstone was written by Smart's biographer, the Revd. C. Hunter.

WALTON-ON-THAMES, Surrey. [1 Dc] Town on the A244, 3 m. E. of Chertsey. In 1717 and 1719 Congreve stayed in Ashley Park (gone), the seat of Viscount Shannon, whose large memorial by Roubiliac is in the church. William Maginn, whose intemperance dissipated the rewards of a long association with *Fraser's Magazine*, died (1842) of consumption soon after retiring here. He is buried in an unmarked grave in the parish churchyard.

WALTON ON THE HILL, Surrey. [1 Ec] Village on the B2032, 4 m. E. of Leatherhead. Sir Anthony Hope Hawkins ('Anthony Hope') lived at Heath Farm, Deans Lane, where he wrote *Memories and Notes* (1927), a volume of reminiscences. He died here in 1933.

WANTAGE, Oxon. [1 Bb] Market town in the Vale of the White Horse, on the A338 and the A417. Alfred the Great, King of the West Saxons, was born here (849) and is commemorated by a statue (1877) in the market-place. There was probably a royal palace, but no trace of it survives. Alfred is distinguished in the history of English literature for the revival of letters that he effected in the West of England. He translated Pope Gregory's *Cura Pastoralis*

and the *Historia adversus Paganos* of Orosius, a Spanish disciple of St. Augustine; and he is believed to have inspired and possibly written the earlier part of *The Anglo-Saxon Chronicle*, a record of events in England from the Christian era to the middle of the 12th c.

WARBORNE. See WIMBORNE.

WARE, Herts. [1 Eb] Old town on the A10 and the A414, 3 m. NE. of Hertford. The Great Bed of Ware, a richly-carved oak bed 10 ft square, was a well-known wonder mentioned in Shakespeare's *Twelfth Night*, Farquhar's *The Recruiting Officer*, and Ben Jonson's *Epicœne*. The bed is thought to have been made for the owner of Ware Park during Queen Elizabeth's reign, when visitors expected to share a bed, and it was rebuilt in an inn in the town in 1650. Guests carved their initials on the oak, the first dated 1653. In the 19th c. it became a spectacle at various inns where it was displayed for twopence. It can now be seen in the Victoria and Albert Museum in London.

Ware was the unexpected limit of John Gilpin's ride in William Cowper's ballad (1782).

WAREHAM, Dorset. [1 Af] Market town on the Frome, on the A351 and the A352. In St. Martin's Church there is a recumbent statue by Eric Kennington of T. E. Lawrence in Arab dress, his head resting on a camel saddle. Lawrence was living at Clouds Hill (q.v.) at the time of his death.

WAREHORNE, Kent. [1 Gd] Small village in Romney Marsh, off the B2067, SW. of Hamstreet. R. H. Barham was curate of Snargate (3 m. S.) and Warehorne, living here in the redbrick rectory (now Church Farm) next to the church. In his *Life* (1870) his son tells of his acceptance by the smugglers of Snargate, 'Good night', they'd say, 'it's only parson'.

WARESIDE. See WIDFORD.

WARGRAVE, Berks. [1 Cc] Village on the E. bank of the Thames, 3 m. S. of Henley, on the A321. Thomas Day, author of *The History of Sandford and Merton* (1783–9), is buried in the churchyard. He died on

28 September 1789, after a fall from his horse when he was visiting his mother at Bear Hill, near by. A memorial erected on the wall of the S. aisle of the church contained an epitaph thought to have been written by his friend, Richard Lovell Edgeworth, father of Maria Edgeworth, who used to live at Hare Hatch, c. 1½ m. SE. The memorial, however, is not to be seen today and it was probably destroyed in 1914 when the church was burned down by suffragettes (rebuilt 1916). The epitaph declared that Day had

promoted by the energy of his writings, and encouraged by the uniformity of his example, the unremitted exercise of every public and private virtue.

WARNHAM, West Sussex. [1 Ed] Village off the A24, 2 m. NW. of Horsham. Field Place[1] (1 m. S.) was the birthplace of Shelley, who as a boy fished and shot in the park and made up fantastic stories to tell his sisters during his holidays from Syon House Academy and Eton. *Original Poetry* (1810) by 'Victor and Cazire' contains his early poems with those of his sister Elizabeth. His expulsion from Oxford and his runaway marriage caused a permanent break with his father, although he later undertook the custody of Shelley's children after the marriage failed. Shelley's son Charles, who died aged 11, shares a memorial in the church with Elizabeth (d. 1831), in the Field Place chapel. A facsimile of Shelley's certificate of baptism (1792) can be seen in the S. aisle.

[1] Garden open for the N.G.S.

WARWICK, Warwicks. [4 Be] Ancient county town on the A41, 11 m. S. of Coventry, home of Guy of Warwick, a legendary knight of giant size, who became a hermit. *Guy of Warwick* is a verse romance of the early 14th c. about his exploits in the Holy Land and against the giant Colbrand, the monstrous dun cow, and the winged dragon. He is commemorated at Guy's Cliffe (1¼ m. N.) by a 15th-c. chantry erected by Richard de Beauchamp, Earl of Warwick, who claimed to be a descendant, and by a statue by Keith Godwin erected in 1964. In 1449 the last de Beauchamp heiress married Richard Neville, known as Warwick the Kingmaker, hero of Lytton's *The Last of the Barons* (1843). The king-

maker's large camp-kettle is in the Great Hall of Warwick Castle[1] dating from the 14th c.

Richard Corbett mentions Guy of Warwick in 'Iter Boreale' which tells of his visit to the castle in 1619. James I gave Warwick Castle to his Chancellor of the Exchequer, Fulke Greville, whom he made Baron Brooke. Corbett meets Fulke Greville and comments on the beauty of the gardens. Greville, who was born in 1554 at Beauchamp Court (gone), was a friend of Philip Sidney from their school days. They went to Queen Elizabeth's court together and were members of the Areopagus Club. *Caelica*, Greville's collected poems, were influenced by Sidney, whose *Life* (1652) Greville wrote c. 1610, though like most of his other work it was not published until after his death. Greville, assassinated by a servant who thought himself excluded from Greville's will, was buried N. of the choir in St. Mary's Church, in the former Chapter House. The Beauchamp Chapel, S. of the choir, contains the ornate tomb of Robert Dudley, Earl of Leicester (d. 1588), who features in Scott's *Kenilworth* (1821). The church also has a bust of W. S. Landor, born (1864) at Ipsley Court, below the East Gate.

[1] Open Good Friday–mid Sept.: 10 a.m.–5.30 p.m., shorter hours out of season. Closed Nov.–Feb.

WATERINGBURY, Kent. [1 Fd] Village on the A26, 5 m. SW. of Maidstone. In 1931 George Orwell, who had been sleeping in London doss-houses to share the lives of down-and-outs, set off with two tramps to find work in the hop-fields. He describes his 18 days at Home Farm here, where they lodged on straw in a barn, in the essay 'Hop Picking', and used his experience in the novel *A Clergyman's Daughter* (1935).

WATERSTON MANOR. See PUDDLETOWN.

WAVERLEY ABBEY. See FARNHAM.

WEATHERBURY. See PUDDLETOWN.

WEEDON LOIS, Northants. [4 Bf] Village off the B4525, 3 m. SE. of Moreton Pinkney. The extension to the churchyard contains the grave of Dame Edith Sitwell (1887–1964), with a tombstone by Henry Moore.

WELLBRIDGE. See WOOL.

WELWYN (pr. Wellin), Herts. [1 Eb] Village off the A1(M). Edward Young, rector 1730–65, wrote the long poem *The Complaint, or Night Thoughts, on Life, Death, and Immortality* (1742–5), which became very popular at once. The bluestocking Mrs. Chapone, who admired the man and his philosophy, wondered how he could have 'blundered so egregiously as to imagine himself a poet', but Dr. Johnson, who included him in *Lives of the English Poets*, wrote that 'with all his defects, he was a man of genius and a poet'. Young married the widowed granddaughter of Charles II, Lady Elizabeth Lee, and bought Guessons (P), the house opposite the W. door of the church. He promoted Welwyn as a spa on his arrival, building the Assembly Rooms (now the cottages behind the garden next to the White Horse in Mill St.) and laying out a bowling green at his own expense. The chalybeate spring still occasionally floods the gardens of the Mill House. John Byng, recording his tour of 1789 in the *Torrington Diaries*, states that 'The Welwyn Assembles, tho' continued, are not so frequented as formerly'. The W. wall of the church has a monument to Young.

WEM, Salop. [3 Gc] Small market town on the A5113, 10 m. N. of Shrewsbury. William Hazlitt came here when he was 8 and lived in Noble St. for most of his early years. His father was a Unitarian minister.

WEST BRADENHAM, Norf. [4 Gd] Village off the A47, 8 m. W. of Swaffham. A lane leads S. through the village of Little Fransham to a turn marked 'Wood Farm only'. This house on the family estate was the birthplace of Rider Haggard (1856).

WESTBURY ON TRYM. See BRISTOL.

WEST DEAN, Wilts. [1 Bd] Village 7 m. SE. of Salisbury, off the A36, whence Lady Mary Pierrepoint eloped to marry (1712) Edward Wortley Montagu. Nothing remains of her grandfather's house where she spent her childhood, but his ornate tomb has been restored in the 14th-c. Borbach chantry, once used as the family chapel. Part of the gardens is now a public park.

Gilbert White was curate here for a short time and mentions how lonely he felt away from Selborne.

WEST ENDELSTOW. See ST. JULIOT.

WEST GRINSTEAD, West Sussex. [1 Ee] Village off the A24, 6 m. S. of Horsham. Pope used to stay at West Grinstead Park (house gone) with his friend John Caryll and while here in 1712 wrote the satirical *The Rape of the Lock* about the origin of a family feud mentioned by his host. Pope's Oak, under which according to tradition he wrote the poem, can be seen from the public footpath through the Park. The tree is also shown in the background of a stained-glass window in the parish church. Hilaire Belloc, who died at Shipley, is buried in the Catholic churchyard here. A tablet by the church door indicates the site of the grave.

WEST HARTLEPOOL. See HARTLEPOOL.

WEST MALVERN, Hereford and Worcester. [3 Ge] Village on the B4232, to the W. of Great Malvern. Dr. Roget, author of *The Thesaurus of English Words and Phrases* (1852), died on his annual holiday at Ashfield House, now 225 West Malvern Rd. He is buried in the churchyard of St. James's Church. His gravestone records that he was 90 years old.

WESTMILL, Herts. [1 Ea] Village off the A10, 2½ m. N. of Puckeridge. The turning to Cherry Green leads to Button Snap, the little thatched cottage on the hill owned by Charles Lamb from 1812 until he sold it for £50 in 1815. A plaque states that the cottage was acquired from the Royal Society of Arts by the Charles Lamb Society and 'Dedicated to Elia's Memory' on 3 September 1949.

WESTON COLVILLE, Cambs. [4 Ff] Village on the B1052, 7 m. SW. of Newmarket. James Withers, born here in 1812, the only son of a shoemaker, was taught to read and write by his mother and started work on a farm at the age of 10. He returned here for a short time, when his mother paid for his apprenticeship as a shoemaker from a legacy, but after her death he had to take to labouring again. 'My Native Village', from his *Collected Poems* (1863), describes the annual Feast and the shoemaker's shop, where his father, and later he himself, had worked.

WESTON LONGVILLE, Norf. [4 Gd] Village off the A1067, 9 m. NW. of Norwich where 'Parson' Woodforde was rector (Old Rectory *c.* 1840 on the site) from 1776 to his death in 1803. 'I breakfasted, dined, supped and slept again at home' he prefaces many entries in his *Diary*. He fishes in his pond (recently uncovered); goes coursing; doses his household against the Whirligigousticon (malaria) and other agues; reads *Evelina* and *Roderick Random*; meets the female soldier turned pedlar at the Hart (still thatched but unlicensed) from where he also sets out to beat the bounds. He brews beer and by mischance his pigs get drunk; hears 'a thump at the front door' and finds 'Coniac' and gin. He frequently dines with the Custance family, both at Weston Hall and then after 1781 at their new Weston House, until they leave for Bath. He is buried in the chancel of the church, which has a memorial and his portrait, painted by his nephew Samuel from a crayon drawing made here. The Parson Woodforde Society,[1] which first met in 1968, aims to extend knowledge of Woodforde's life and social background and to provide an opportunity for those interested in him to meet each other. A journal is published twice yearly.

[1] Particulars can be obtained from the Society at 'Mansard', 27 Castle Hill Ave., Berkhamsted, Herts.

WESTON SUPER MARE, Avon. [2 Gb] Seaside resort on the A370, 21 m. SW. of Bristol. Mary Webb lived at 6 Landemann Circus after her marriage in 1912.

WESTON UNDERWOOD, Bucks. [4 Cf] Small village 10 m. SE. of Northampton, a favourite walk of William Cowper when he was living (1767–86) at Olney (q.v.). He was often accompanied by Mary Unwin, with whom he had shared a house since her husband's death. Sometimes he came alone

When winter soaks the field and female feet
Too weak to struggle with tenacious clay
Or ford the rivulets, are best at home.

Their goal was Weston Park (gone), the home of their friends the Throckmortons,

who gave them a key to the gardens and to the wilderness or spinney opposite the house. The gardens (known today as the Flamingo Gardens and Tropical Bird Zoo) contain Cowper's epitaphs to the spaniel Fop and the pointer, cut on stone columns surmounted by urns, which stand under the trees housing exotic birds whose plumage casts our native 'jay, the pie and e'en the boding owl' into the shade. The little temple where he used to rest is still there and ½ m. away, along the lane skirting the gardens, is the Alcove, a rather larger temple still crowning the summit and embracing the view of 'Square tower, tall spire' among other 'beauties numberless'. Behind the Alcove is a large pit where the clay is still tenacious. In 1786, at the suggestion of his cousin Lady Hesketh, Cowper and Mary Unwin moved into the Lodge, a house in the main street. His quiet life here was interrupted by Mrs. Unwin's illness, when Lady Hesketh came to look after them and solace his depression. His lines 'To Mary' were written at this time. In 1795 Cowper and Mrs. Unwin left to stay with 'Johnny of Norfolk', a younger cousin, in East Dereham. The poem 'The Yardley Oak', about a tree in Yardley Chase, gives its name to the village inn, Cowper's Oak. The church contains an inscription to Dr. Gregson, the Throckmorton's chaplain, with whom Cowper, who nicknamed him Griggy, discussed his translations of Virgil.

WESTPORT, Mayo. [8 Be] Market town and small seaport on the T39 and the T71, beautifully situated on the banks of the Carrowbeg, which flows into the SE. corner of Clew Bay. Westport House,[1] a modernized early Georgian mansion (the seat of the Marquess of Sligo), stands at the W. end of the town. De Quincey stayed here in 1800 with his friend, Lord Westport, after they had been together in Dublin.

Thackeray was delighted with his visit on his Irish tour of 1842. 'Nature', he said in *The Irish Sketch Book* (1843), 'has done much for this pretty town of Westport; and after Nature, the traveller ought to be grateful to Lord Sligo, who has done a great deal too. In the first place he has established one of the prettiest, comfortablest inns in Ireland . . . Secondly, Lord Sligo has given up, for the use of the townspeople, a beautiful little pleasure-ground about his house.' Canon J. O. Hannay ('George A. Birmingham') was rector here from 1892 to 1913 and began his prolific writing career with *The Spirit and Origin of Christian Monasticism* (1903). He then turned to novels and established his popularity with *Spanish Gold* (1908), followed by *Lalage's Lovers* (1911), *The Major's Niece* (1911), and *The Inviolable Sanctuary* (1912), the beginning of a long and steady output. Westport and scenes of Mayo provided much of his local colour.

¹ Open Apr.–mid Oct.: daily 2–6 p.m.; mid July–early Sept.: daily 10.30 a.m.–6 p.m.

WEST TARRING. See WORTHING.

WESTWARD HO!, Devon. [2 Dc] Bathing resort, named after Kingsley's novel (1855), on Barnstaple or Bideford Bay, 3 m. NW. of Bideford, on the B3236. Rudyard Kipling, who was born and had spent his childhood in India, was educated at the United Services College here from January 1878 to July 1882. He described it as 'largely a caste school . . . some 75 per cent of us had been born outside England, and hoped to follow their fathers into the army . . .'. Kipling drew on memories of his schooldays for *Stalky & Co.* (1899), stories about the exploits of Beetle (himself) and his friends, Stalky and M'Turk, which he dedicated to Cormell Price, the headmaster. The verses which form the introduction to the book include the evocative lines:

> Western wind and open surge
> Took us from our mothers;
> Flung us on a naked shore
> (Twelve bleak houses by the shore!)
> Seven summers by the shore!
> 'Mid two hundred brothers.

The twelve houses still survive, as Kipling Ter. (P), now let off as flats and guest-houses, and the school gymnasium is now an entertainment centre. The rough land to the south of the school buildings was the scene of much of the action in *Stalky & Co.* and is described in the opening of the first story, 'In Ambush'.

In summer all right-minded boys built huts in the furze-hill behind the College—little lairs whittled out of the heart of the prickly bushes, full of stumps, odd root-ends, and spikes, but, since they were strictly forbidden, palaces of delight. And for the fifth summer in succession,

Stalky, M'Turk, and Beetle (this was before they reached the dignity of a study) had built, like beavers, a place of retreat and meditation, where they smoked.

This area, 18 acres of gorse-covered hill, now called Kipling Tors, was given to the National Trust in 1938 by the Rudyard Kipling Memorial Fund.

WETHERINGSETT, Suff. [4 Ge] Village with timber and plaster houses off the A140, the old Roman Pye Rd., 8 m. S. of Diss. Richard Hakluyt was rector here from 1590 until his death in 1616, but he was also made archdeacon of Westminster in 1603 and was therefore not resident during the whole of his rectorship.

WEYMOUTH, Dorset. [2 He] Coastal town, port, and royal watering-place, overlooking Weymouth Bay and Portland Harbour, on the A353. Thomas Love Peacock was born here (18 Oct. 1785), but soon after his father's death in 1788 his mother took him to live in her father's house in Chertsey (q.v.). George III used to stay at Gloucester Lodge, the Duke of Gloucester's home on the seafront (since 1820 the Gloucester Hotel), and Fanny Burney records in her *Diary* her visits there in attendance on Queen Charlotte in the summer of 1789. 'The King bathes', she wrote, 'and with great success.'

G. A. Henty, writer of adventure stories for boys, died (1902) on board his yacht, *The Egret*, which was moored in the harbour. His body was taken to London and buried in Brompton cemetery.

Weymouth is the 'Budmouth' of Hardy's *The Trumpet-Major* (1880), a novel set in the time of the Napoleonic wars.

WHALLEY, Lancs. [5 Ce] Attractive little town on the Calder, on the A59 and the A671. The ruined Cistercian abbey¹ is depicted in Harrison Ainsworth's *The Lancashire Witches* (1848). Ainsworth stayed (1848) with Archdeacon Rushton at the vicarage at Newchurch-in-Pendle, a small village *c.* 6 m. NE., in the Forest of Pendle, while he was gathering material for the novel. Pendle appears in the story as 'Goldshaw'.

Stonyhurst College, a Roman Catholic (Jesuit) school for boys (founded at St. Omer, 1594 and transferred here in 1794), is situated 4 m. NW. of Whalley, off the B6243. The nucleus of the buildings is the Elizabethan mansion built by Sir Richard Shireburn in 1594-1606. The library contains an ancient manuscript of the Gospels, copies of Froissart's *Chronicles*, and Caxton's version of *The Golden Legend*. Alfred Austin, Poet Laureate 1896-1913, Wilfrid Scawen Blunt, who entered the Diplomatic Service from school in 1858, and Sir Arthur Conan Doyle, who went on to Edinburgh University, were educated here. G. M. Hopkins studied scholastic philosophy (1870-1) here before becoming a theology student at St. Beuno's College (q.v.). After his ordination Hopkins returned to teach Classics at Stonyhurst for a short time in 1878 and then from 1882 till 1884, when he went to Dublin (q.v.). He describes the neighbourhood in his *Journal* (1959).

¹ Open daily 10 a.m. to dusk.

WHITBY, North Yorkshire. [5 Gb] Old whaling port on the A171, 16 m. NW. of Scarborough. The cross commemorating Caedmon, an Anglo-Saxon herdsman, who in a vision suddenly received the power to compose verse, stands on the headland near the abbey he entered *c.* 670. Though other poems have been attributed to him, the hymn on Creation quoted by Bede is the only one thought to have survived.

St. Mary's Church has many memorials to the whalers, whom Mrs. Gaskell, after staying at 1 Abbey Ter. in 1859, portrayed in *Sylvia's Lovers* (1863), calling the town 'Monkshaven'. Alfred Ainger, preparing to holiday here in the 1890s with his nieces, was advised by Gerald du Maurier 'to see the forty or fifty cobles embark to herring-fish, with all the town, men women and children, pushing the boats off. . . . Tell them to walk along the cliffs westward . . . through fields and over stiles till they reach Sylvia Robson's cottage (of course they know Sylvia's Lovers by heart) . . .'.

Leo Walmsley, who grew up in Robin Hood's Bay (q.v.), called Whitby 'Burnharbour' in his novels about local fishermen.

WHITCOMBE. See CAME.

WHITEABBEY. See BELFAST.

WHITE HORSE HILL. See UFFINGTON.

WHITSTABLE, Kent. [1 Gc] Seaside resort and old fishing port, famous for oysters, on the A290, 8 m. N. of Canterbury. After his parents died, Somerset Maugham was brought up at the rectory in Canterbury Rd. by his uncle, easily recognizable as the Revd. William Carey in the novel *Of Human Bondage* (1915), in which the town is called Blackstable. *Cakes and Ale* (1930) is also said to have some scenes based on Maugham's life here. He made two visits to the Old Rectory in 1948 and in 1951 when he stayed at the Bear and Key. There is a photograph of the house in *Somerset and all the Maughams* by R. Maugham (1966).

WICK. See LOWER WICK.

WICKHAMBROOK, Suff. [4 Ff] Village off the A143, 9 m. SW. of Bury St. Edmunds. George Crabbe, after his short period of schooling, was apprenticed (1768) to Mr. Smith, a surgeon-apothecary here. He helped on the farm and with the delivery of medicines. One errand was to Cheveley Park (5 m. NW.), where he was amazed at the elegance and culture. As a diversion from the dullness of his job he had started to write verse but after 2 years he rebelled and went home to Aldeburgh (q.v.).

WIDCOMBE, Avon. [2 Hb] Former village 1½ m. SW. of, and now joining, Bath. Henry Fielding stayed for some time in 1748 at Widcombe Lodge while writing *Tom Jones* (1749). He is said to have modelled 'Squire Western' on his neighbour at Widcombe Manor. This 18th-c. house was the home (1927-52) of H. A. Vachell, author of *The Hill* (1905), a story of Harrow School, novels, plays, including *Quinney's* (1914) about an antique dealer who appears in subsequent novels, and autobiographical works including *Fellow Travellers* (1923) and *Methuselah's Diary* (1950).

WIDFORD, Herts. [1 Eb] Village on the A119 and the B180, 4 m. NE. of Ware. Blakesware at Wareside (1½ m. W.) was the mansion where Mary Field, grandmother of Charles and Mary Lamb, lived as housekeeper to the Plumer family. Charles and his sister sometimes stayed here. Mary remembers the house in some of the tales in *Mrs. Leicester's School* (1808), and Charles refers to his grandmother and

Blakesware in 'The Grandame' and his essays 'Blakesmoor in H—' and 'Dream Children'. This last also recalls his love for Ann Simmons, who lived at the cottages called Blenheims (gone, site in field opposite New Blenheims). Their grandmother is buried in the churchyard at Widford. Blakesware (demolished 1830) was on the site of The Blessed Sacrament House, and near the main drive is a road which once led to the mill (of which only a few traces remain) where Charles Lamb slept on a goosefeather bed when visiting the Misses Norris. These were the daughters of his father's friend at the Temple and they ran a school at Goddards in Widford on the Stansted Abbots road. Charles Lamb's visits—he sometimes walked here from Edmonton—used to stop work at the school for the day. The children, eager to fetch him for breakfast, arrived at the mill before he was awake.

WILMCOTE (pr. Wilmcut), Warwicks. [4 Af] Village off the A34, 3 m. NW. of Stratford-upon-Avon. Mary Arden's House,[1] part of the Shakespeare Birthplace Trust, was the birthplace and home until her marriage of Shakespeare's mother. The long, low, half-timbered farmhouse is furnished with Tudor furniture and the barns house old wooden wagons.

[1] Open Apr.–Oct.: weekdays 9 a.m.–6 p.m.; Sun. 2–6 p.m.; Nov.–Mar.: weekdays 9 a.m.–12.45 p.m., 2–4 p.m.

WILTON, Wilts. [1 Ad] Village on the A30, 3 m. W. of Salisbury. Wilton House, begun in Tudor times and added to in the 17th and 18th cc., was the home after her marriage of Mary Herbert, the Countess of Pembroke, sister of Sir Philip Sidney. She is thought to have suggested the prose romance *The Arcadia* which he began (*c.* 1580) during one of his many visits, and to have played some part in its composition, and in its revision for publication in 1590, after his early death. The Countess, who was the Urania of Spenser's *Colin Clout* (1595), was the patron of many poets including Nicholas Breton, Ben Jonson, and two local men, the Somerset-born Samuel Daniel, who tutored her son, and Philip Massinger, whose father was a member of the household. Shakespeare visited in 1603, when *As You Like It* was performed before James I. Mary Herbert's son, Philip, the 4th Earl,

who built the classical front of the house and laid out the gardens, was the patron of Massinger and William Browne who lived here for some years. The Single Cube Room contains the frieze by De Critz illustrating *The Arcadia*.

A. G. Street started writing as a recreation from farming at Ditchampton Farm where he was born (1892) and which he wrote about in 1946. The first two of his popular novels were *Farmer's Glory* (1932) and *Strawberry Roan* (1932).

WIMBLEHURST. See MIDHURST.

WIMBORNE (or WIMBORNE MINSTER), Dorset. [1 Ae] Ancient town on the Allen at its confluence with the Stour, on the A31. The splendid old Minster of St. Cuthburga (dating from the 12th c.) possesses a chained library, founded in 1686 for the free use of the citizens of Wimborne. It contains some 185 works in 240 volumes, mainly theological, including the beautiful *Regimen Animarum* (*The Direction of Souls*) written on vellum in 1343. The earliest printed book is a copy of Anselm's *Opuscula* (*Lesser Works*) of 1495. A copy of Sir Walter Ralegh's *History of the World* (1634) has 104 pages which have been damaged by apparently deliberate burning and neatly repaired with the missing words rewritten. Both the damage and the repair have been attributed to Matthew Prior, the poet and diplomatist, who was the son of a Wimborne joiner.

Thomas Hardy stayed at Wimborne from 1881 to 1883 (the house is not known) and describes it as 'Warborne' in *Two on a Tower* (1882). In his poem 'Copying architecture in an old minster (Wimborne)' he refers to the passage of time marked by the Quarter Jack or Jackman, the figure of a Grenadier who stands high on the wall of the West Tower and wields his hammer each quarter-hour when the bells of the ancient astronomical clock in the baptistery are struck:

How smartly the quarters of the hour march by
  That the jack-o'-clock never forgets;
Ding-dong; and before I have traced a cusp's eye
Or got the true twist of the ogee over
  A double ding-dong ricochetts.

WIMPOLE HALL, Cambs. [4 Ef] Mansion (built 1638–40) between the A603 and the A14, 8 m. SW. of Cambridge. The wings were added to the house by Robert Harley, Earl of Oxford, when he was patron to Matthew Prior, who often visited here from Down Hall (q.v.). Prior died here in 1721 and was buried in Westminster Abbey. Pope was another visitor here. Harley's fine library is now in the British Library in London (see Bloomsbury).

WINCHESTER, Hants. [1 Bd] Historic county town and cathedral city, situated on the Itchen and the hillside above it, on the A31 and the A34. The British settlement of Caer Gwent was developed by the Romans as Venta Belgarum, the 5th-largest town in Britain, and became the Saxon Wintanceaster, capital of Wessex, in 519. King Alfred made it his capital, and his statue (by Hamo Thorneycroft, erected in 1901 to commemorate the 1000th anniversary of his death) stands at the E. end of High St., dominating the Broadway. Near West Gate, at the top of High St., stands the Great Hall[1] of the former Norman castle. Sir Walter Ralegh was tried here and condemned to death in 1603. At the W. end, above the remains of the royal dais, hangs a representation of the Round Table of King Arthur's Knights, probably made in Tudor times or even earlier.

Izaak Walton came to Winchester in his last years and lived with his son-in-law, Prebendary Hawkins, at 7 The Close (down Dove Alley). He died here (15 Dec. 1683) and was buried in Prior Silkstede's Chapel in the S. transept of the cathedral. At the end of the 19th c. the fishermen of England added the figure of Izaak Walton to the Great Screen at the East End, and in 1914 the fishermen of England and America gave the memorial window in the chapel, above his tomb.

Jane Austen came to Winchester at the end of May, 1817. She had been suffering from ill-health for some time and had decided to place herself in the care of a Winchester doctor, Giles King Lyford. But her illness, now thought to be Addison's Disease, did not yield to treatment and on 18 July she died at the house, 8 College St. (now owned by Winchester College; P), where she was staying with her sister Cassandra. She died with her faculties unimpaired and 3 days before her death she wrote a light-hearted poem for St.

Swithin's Day, entitled 'Venta' (published in a booklet available in the cathedral). She was buried in the cathedral in the N. aisle of the nave, where an inscribed stone marks her grave, above which are a brass tablet and a memorial window. The City Museum[2] near by contains a few of her personal belongings.

In 1819 Keats stayed from 12 August until early October with his friend Charles Armitage Brown (house demolished). He wrote 'Ode to Autumn' and revised 'The Eve of St. Agnes'. He was impressed with the neatness of the town: 'The side streets here are excessively maiden-lady-like;' he wrote. He also gave a description of his daily walk:

I take a walk every day for an hour before dinner and this is generally my walk. I go out at the back gate across one street, into the Cathedral yard, along a paved path, past the beautiful front of the Cathedral, turn to the left under a stone doorway—then I am on the other side of the building—which leaving behind me I pass on through two college-like squares seemingly built for the dwelling place of Deans and Prebendaries—garnished with grass and shaded with trees. Then I pass through one of the old city gates and then you are in College Street.

The Hospital of St. Cross,[3] c. 1 m. S. of the city centre, reached by St. Cross Rd., was founded by Bishop Henry of Blois for thirteen poor brethren in 1136 and extended by an 'Almshouse of Noble Poverty' by Cardinal Beaufort in 1446. It is believed that Trollope based The Warden on St. Cross, and the scandal concerning the abuse of the Mastership in 1808.

Charlotte M. Yonge, who lived all her life at Otterbourne (q.v.), is commemorated by the reredos in the Lady Chapel of the cathedral.

The Cathedral Library[4] is housed in the oldest book room in Europe, which was added to the cathedral in the 12th c. During the Reformation and again in Cromwell's time many manuscripts and books were taken into private custody and some were probably lost, but there are many treasures to be seen, notably the beautiful Winchester Bible, written c. 1150 in 2 volumes (rebound in 4 vols., 1948), and the private library of Bishop Morley, first offered by him to the Dean and Chapter in 1667. Other items of interest include a copy of Ralegh's speech from the scaffold, an unrecorded edition of Eikon Basilike, and a copy of the first edition of Gilbert White's *Natural History and Antiquities of Selborne* (1789).

Winchester College[5] in College St. was founded by William of Wykeham in 1382 and is one of the oldest public schools in England. Distinguished literary men who were pupils include Nicholas Udall (or Uvedale) (1505–56), who became headmaster of Eton (q.v.); Sir Henry Wotton (1568–1639); Sir John Davies (1569–1626); Thomas Coryate (1577 or 1579–1617); Sir Thomas Browne (1605–82); Thomas Otway (1652–85) (P erected by William Collins and Thomas and Joseph Warton); John Philips (1676–1709); Edward Young (1683–1765); William Somerville (1675–1742); William Whitehead (1715–85); William Collins (1721–59), who later returned to live in Winchester, where he wrote *Persian Eclogues* (1742); Sydney Smith (1771–1845); Anthony Trollope (1815–82), who was here for a short time before moving to Harrow in 1827 as a day-boarder; and Matthew Arnold (1822–88), who was here before going to Rugby in 1837 under his father's headmastership.

Charles Wolfe (1791–1823) was educated at Hyde Abbey School before going to Trinity College, Dublin.

In Hardy's *Tess of the d'Urbervilles* (1891) Tess is hanged in the city gaol. Winchester is the 'Wintoncester' of the novel.

[1] Open weekdays 10 a.m.–4, 4.30, or 5 p.m.; Sun. in summer 2–4.30 p.m.
[2] Open weekdays 10 a.m.–4, 5, or 6 p.m.; Sun. 2–4 p.m.
[3] Open weekdays, summer 9.30 a.m.–12 noon, 2–5 p.m.; winter 10–11.30 a.m., 2–3.30 p.m.
[4] Open weekdays 10 a.m.–12.30 p.m., 2.30–4.30 p.m.
[5] Open Bank Holidays, except 25–6 Dec.; conducted tours, except Wed. and Sun. a.m., 10, 11.45 a.m., 2, 3, and (Apr.–Sept. only) 4.30 p.m.

WINDERMERE, Cumbria. [5 Bc] Popular tourist centre for the Lake District, comprising the combined villages of Bowness, on the E. shore of Lake Windermere, and Windermere, on the hillside 1 m. NE., on the A591 and the A592. On the N. side of Church St., nearly opposite the railway station, a public footpath leads up the hill through Elleray Wood to Orrest Head, which commands a magnificent view of the lake and mountains. The house of Elleray, now a girls' school reached by a private drive, was once the home of John Wilson (author,

under the pen-name 'Christopher North' of many of the *Noctes Ambrosianae* papers in *Blackwood's Magazine*). While still an undergraduate at Oxford Wilson inherited a fortune and bought the small estate of Elleray. He left the University in 1807 and settled in a small rustic cottage (now Christopher North's Cottage, Old Elleray, situated beside the public footpath), at that time the only dwelling on the estate. He lived here for several years while planning and building the mansion of Elleray, from which, he said, 'The whole course of a noble lake, about 11 miles long, lies subject to your view'. Wilson was a devoted admirer of Wordsworth, whom he first visited at Grasmere in 1807, and one of the first critics to do justice to his poetry. He was also a friend of Southey and Coleridge at Keswick and of De Quincey, who described their first meeting at Wordsworth's house. Wilson was a colourful and athletic figure who became well known for his prowess in sport and sailing as well as his intellectual interests. Harriet Martineau said of him 'He made others happy by being so intensely happy himself, and when he was mournful none desired to be gay'. When he was at Elleray he wrote a quantity of poetry, published under the title *The Isle of Palms and other Poems* (1812). In 1815 he suddenly lost most of his money and went to Edinburgh (q.v.), but Elleray remained in his possession until 1848, and he was able to return there from time to time. On one of his holidays, in 1825, he entertained Sir Walter Scott and J. G. Lockhart, the highlight of the visit being a regatta on the lake in honour of Scott's 54th birthday, with a procession of more than 50 gaily-decorated barges following Wilson's 'flagship'.

WINDSOR, Berks. [1 Dc] Royal Borough on the A308 and the S. bank of the Thames, dominated by Windsor Castle, chief residence of the sovereign since Norman times. Geoffrey Chaucer is thought to have lived in the Winchester Tower while Clerk of the Royal Works, *c.* 1390. The Scottish King James I, captured (*c.* 1406) as a youth by the English, spent the later years of his exile imprisoned in the castle by Henry V, a few years his senior. While here James courted Jane Beaufort, daughter of the Earl of Somerset, and married her in 1424 shortly after his release. His poem *The*

Kingis Quair, first printed in 1783, is about their courtship.

In 1786 Fanny Burney obtained the post of Second Keeper of the Robes to George III's queen through the help of Mrs. Delany. However, this independence from her stepmother was dearly bought and her health suffered, as she recounts in her *Diary and Letters*.

WINESTEAD, Humberside. [5 He] Village off the A1033, 13 m. SE. of Hull. Andrew Marvell was born (1621) at the rectory at the Rimswell turn (now the Old Rectory, rebuilt), but when he was 6 his father became 'lecturer' at Holy Trinity Church, Hull, and the family left for the town.

WINNINGTON HALL, Ches. [3 Ga] Former country house, now a guest home in a chemical factory estate, NW. of Northwich. When Ruskin was in the neighbourhood (1859–68), he often stayed here at Margaret Bell's school for girls. He enjoyed the company of the young pupils, whom he called affectionately 'the birds' and who, in spite of their flowing cotton dresses, played cricket and swung dangerously with rope swings. His correspondence with Miss Bell and the girls, some of whom called him 'Bear' or 'Papa', is edited by Van Akin Burd as *The Winnington Letters* (1969).

WINTERBORNE CAME. See CAME.

WINTERBOURNE EARLS, Wilts. [1 Bd] The most southerly of the villages, on the A338, that take their name from the river Bourne, N. of Salisbury. This village with Winterbourne Dauntsey, Winterbourne Gunner, and his favourite, Winterbourne Bishop, are mentioned by W. H. Hudson in *A Shepherd's Life* (1910), in which he recounts his impressions of the South Wiltshire Downs.

WINTERSLOW, Wilts. [1 Bd] Village off the A30, 6 m. NE. of Salisbury. Hazlitt and Sarah Stoddart lived at Middleton Cottage, which she owned, after their marriage in 1808. Sarah was a friend of Mary Lamb, who came with Charles to stay in the summers of 1809 and 1810. They walked to Wilton, Stonehenge, and Salisbury and Hazlitt mentions in 'Farewell to Essay Writing' how they had walked out 'to look at the Claude Lorraine skies over our heads

. . . to gather mushrooms that sprung up at our feet, to throw into our hashed mutton at supper'. Hazlitt edited the *Memoirs of Thomas Holcroft* (1816) here. Winterslow was a favourite place of his and after his divorce in 1823 he stayed at the Winterslow Hut (now the Pheasant Inn) on the main road (2 m. N.). The essays written here were collected by his son (born at Middleton Cottage) and called *Winterslow* (1839).

WINTONCESTER. See WINCHESTER.

WIRKSWORTH, Derbys. [4 Bb] Small market town on the B5035 and the B5023, 5 m. S. of Matlock. Marian Evans, who wrote as George Eliot, occasionally used to visit her aunt, who told her the story that became the germ of the novel *Adam Bede* (1859), in which the main characters bear a resemblance to her aunt and uncle. Marian Evans read Southey's *Life of Wesley* (1820) for help on Methodists, and drew on articles in the *Gentleman's Magazine* for her descriptions of the countryside, Poyser's Farm, and the lead miners of Derbyshire. The town is said to be the 'Snowfield' of the novel.

WISBECH, Cambs. [4 Ed] Town on the A47 and the A1101. The Wisbech and Fenland Museum,[1] near the church, houses the 17th-c. Town Library, the Literary Society's Library, and the Chauncey Hare Townshend bequest. Townshend was a friend of Southey and Dickens, and his collection contains the manuscripts of *Great Expectations* and Lewis's *The Monk*, first editions autographed by Dickens, and letters from Swift, Goethe, Burns, Keats, Lamb, Clare, Byron, and others.

William Godwin, philosopher and novelist, was born (1756) here. John Clare travelled to Wisbech by water as a boy for a brief stay when his uncle tried unsuccessfully to get him work in an attorney's office.

[1] Open Tues.–Sat. and Bank Holidays 10 a.m.–1 p.m., 2–5 p.m. (winter to 4 p.m.).

WITHAM, Essex. [1 Gb] Old town on the B1018, bypassed by the A12, 9 m. NE. of Chelmsford, possible birthplace of Thomas Campion in 1567. A tablet in the parish church commemorates William Pattisson who, on his honeymoon, was drowned with his bride in a Pyrenean lake. Crabb

Robinson, who saw it happen from the shore, recounted it in his *Diary* (1869).

Dorothy L. Sayers lived from 1929 to her death in 1957 at 24 Newland St. (listed as being of architectural interest), where a plaque was unveiled in 1975 by the Lord Peter Wimsey of the contemporary dramatizations of her detective novels, two of which, *The Nine Tailors* (1934), and *Busman's Honeymoon* (1936), have an East Anglian setting. Her plays with religious themes include *The Man Born to be King* (1943), written for the radio, and she also translated Dante's *Inferno* (1940) and *Purgatorio* (1955). The Dorothy L. Sayers Historical and Literary Society, founded in 1976 by her admirers, has its offices in the house.

WITHYHAM, East Sussex. [1 Fd] Village on the B2110, 7 m. SE. of East Grinstead. Thomas Sackville, 1st Earl of Dorset, author with Thomas Norton of the blank verse tragedy *Gorboduc* (1561), was born here. Charles Sackville, Lord Buckhurst, was a companion of Charles Sedley in his early days. His poems, including the lyric 'To all you ladies now at land', were published with Sedley's in 1701. He became the 6th Earl, died in 1706, and is buried in the Sackville chapel in the parish church where there are many family memorials. Old Buckhurst, a family home of the Sackvilles, is now flats.

Penns in the Rocks, an 18th-c. house in gardens with rocky outcrops, was the home in the 1930s of Dorothy Wellesley. Through Lady Ottoline Morrell she met W. B. Yeats and their letters on poetry were published in 1940. Yeats included many of her poems in *The Oxford Book of Modern Verse* (1936). He stayed here in 1938 and enjoyed sitting in The Folly, a small classical temple in the glade in front of the house.

WITLEY, Surrey. [1 Dd] Village on the A283, 4 m. SW. of Godalming. Mr. and Mrs. George Lewes (as George Lewes and George Eliot were called), after many holidays in hotels and furnished houses, bought in 1877 The Heights (P, now Roslyn Court opposite the National Institute of Oceanography in Wormley, ½ m. S.) which was to be their country home. Delays in the arrival of their furniture made their bedroom look as if there had been a distraint on the house, George Eliot wrote, but the view and the country walks made up for the initial discomforts. John Cross, who came from Weybridge, set up tennis equipment and taught her to play. They met their neighbours Alfred Tennyson and William Allingham, and Henry James visited. The next summer George Eliot worked on *Theophrastus Such*, but soon George Lewes became fatally ill. After his death George Eliot married John Cross, and in 1880 the couple spent the autumn here before her death in December.

WITTON LE WEAR, Durham. [5 Da] Village on the A68, 5 m. NW. of Bishop Auckland, with a camping and caravan centre in the grounds of the 15th-c. castle. Henry Taylor spent his youth with his stepmother at the square-towered Witton Hall. After some time away as a midshipman he wrote here 'The Cave of Ceada', a poem accepted by the *Quarterly Review*. Another poem, 'The Lynnburn', is about the river which runs through the village. In 1824 Taylor, then aged 24, accepted a post in the Colonial Office in London.

WOKINGHAM, Berks. [1 Cc] Busy market town on the A329 between Reading and Bracknell. The Olde Rose Inn in the Market Place was famous as a meeting-place of 18th-c. wits, and tradition has it that one wet afternoon in 1726 Pope (who had lived near by at Binfield) and his friends, Gay, Swift, and Arbuthnot, amused themselves by composing a ballad in praise of pretty Molly Mog, the landlord's daughter. A copy of the ballad, which attained great popularity when published in the contemporary *Mist's Weekly Journal*, hangs on a dining-room wall.

WOODBRIDGE, Suff. [4 Hf] Market town on the A12 and the A45. In 1771 George Crabbe was apprenticed to Mr. Page, a surgeon-apothecary who employed him chiefly in his dispensary on the bank of the Deben. Crabbe found congenial friends and first met Sara Elmy, his future wife, during this time. Edward FitzGerald, who often came here from Bredfield, met Bernard Barton (1784–1849), friend of Lamb and Southey, and wrote his life, which prefaced the collection of Barton's poems in 1849. FitzGerald married Barton's daughter Lucy in 1860, but separated from her 6 months later and moved to lodgings over a shop in the market-place. The 'Wits of Woodbridge', who included FitzGerald, Barton, and Crabbe's grandson, met at the Bull Inn. Tennyson and his son Hallam also stayed at the Bull in 1876 on their visit to Fitz-Gerald at Little Grange, Pytches Rd., his home from 1864 until his death (1883). Members of the Omar Khayyám Club, founded in 1892 by Edward Clodd, often met at the Bull. They sometimes sailed here from Aldeburgh in Clodd's yacht to visit FitzGerald's grave at Boulge.

WOODCROFT CASTLE, Cambs. [4 Dd] Private house 1 m. SE. of Helpston, on the Etton–Marholm road. Its siege by Crom-well's men inspired Clare's poem, 'Wood-croft Castle', written when he was sent 'to drive plough' here (c. 1809).

WOODHOUSE. See EASTWOOD.

WOODSTOCK, Oxon. [1 Bb] Old town on the A34, 7 m. N. of Oxford, once surrounded by the royal forest which survives today in the old oaks in Blenheim Park. Henry II tried to conceal his mistress, Rosamond Clifford, here and Deloney in his *Garland of Good Will* (1631) lists the precautions he took:

Most curiously this Bower was built of stone and timber strong,
An hundred and fifty doores did to that Bower belong,
And they so cunningly contriv'd with turnings round about,
That none but with a clew of thread could enter in or out.

But all the 'labyrinthine brickwork maze in maze', as Tennyson describes it in his play *Becket* (1884), was unable to save her. Her exact fate is uncertain; Deloney has the Queen poison her while the King is in France, where Drayton places him in *England's Heroicall Epistles* (1597) writing to tell Rosamond that his heart remains with her in 'Sweet Woodstock'; Tennyson, who makes her Henry's morganatic wife in *Becket*, has her banished to the nunnery at Godstow, where she is said to be buried.

Another bower, this time covered with green ivy, was made for Elizabeth's visit when *The Queen's Majestie's Entertainment at Woodstock* (1575), the play by George Gascoigne, which tells of a princess giving up her lover for reasons of state, was acted before the Queen and Leicester. Pope, who

came to see Fair Rosamond's Well in 1717, 'toasted her shade in the cold water' and noted that only one wall of Henry's manor remained standing. Scott tells how this destruction came about in his novel *Woodstock* (1826), set in the Civil War, when the manor was the home of the Cavalier Sir Henry Lee, Ranger of Woodstock Forest, whose daughter loved a Roundhead. The site of this old manor near Vanbrugh's bridge is marked by a stone pillar. So when John Wilmot was made Ranger by Charles II, more as a reward for his father's virtue than his own, he had to live in High Lodge near the Combe gate. This battlemented tower is now private flats but when Nathaniel Haw-thorne visited, he described in *Our Old Home* (1863) seeing the canopied bed in the ground-floor room where Rochester made his death-bed repentance. Vanbrugh de-signed Blenheim Palace in 1705, the year his plays *The Country House* and *The Con-federacy* were published. 'Woodstock Park', the poem by William Harrison, protégé of Addison and Swift, was included by Dodsley in his *A Collection of Poems by several hands* (1748–58).

Chaucer's House in Park St. is probably on the site of the Gothic house where John Aubrey, the antiquary, said Chaucer stayed with his son.

WOOL, Dorset. [2 He] Village on the Frome, 4 m. W. of Wareham, on the A352. Wool-bridge Manor (formerly the home of the Turbervilles; now a hotel) on the N. side of the main road, approached by a fine 17th-c. bridge, was Hardy's 'Wellbridge Manor-house' in *Tess of the d'Urbervilles* (1891), where Tess and Angel Clare spent their wedding night. S. of the main road and E. of the village a minor road leads to the ruins of Bindon Abbey,[1] where, in the NE. corner, there is the empty stone coffin where the sleepwalking Angel laid Tess. In the story Hardy places the abbey and the adjacent mill nearer to the manor-house than they are in fact. Wool itself appears as 'Wellbridge'.

[1] Open daily.

WOOLBEDING, West Sussex. [1 Dd] Village off the A272, 1 m. NW. of Midhurst. Thomas Otway (1652–85), the dramatist, spent his youth here; his father was rector until 1670. Charlotte Smith, who with her improvident husband and large family lived for a time (c. 1786) in the 17th-c. colonnaded Woolbeding Hall, made the decision to leave him here. When in France, she had translated *Manon Lescaut* (1785), which was withdrawn as offensive, but her *Elegiac Sonnets* (1784), although Anna Seward thought their best lines plagiarisms, were as popular as the novels she wrote later, which gave her financial independence.

WOOTTON, Kent. See DENTON.

WOOTTON, Staffs. [4 Ac] Village 5 m. SW. of Ashbourne off the B5032. Wootton Hall, of which only the entrance gates remain, was lent by Mr. Davenport to Jean-Jacques Rousseau and his mistress Thérèse le Vasseur in 1766 when he was forced to leave France. William Howitt in *Visits to Remarkable Places* (1842) reports that Rousseau dressed in 'Armenian dress, a furred cap, and caftan or long striped robe with a belt', and that he was still remembered by the local people who called him 'Roos Hall' or 'Dross Hall', and who thought his habit of roaming the hills botanizing was peculiar. Many neighbours were sociable, including the young Duchess of Portland who shared his interest in plants, Mrs. Delany's brother at Calwich Abbey who invited him there, and his host, who arranged for his servants to look after him when he himself was in London. Rousseau wrote the major part of his *Confessions* here, but left suddenly, fearing that he was about to be poisoned.

WOOTTON WAWEN (pr. Wawn), Warwicks. [4 Ae] Village on the A34, 6 m. NW. of Stratford. The church with its Saxon sanctuary and 11th- to 15th-c. additions has a memorial to the poet of *The Chace* (1735), William Somerville (1675–1742), who lived at Edstone near by. His poems are about the sports and pastimes of a country squire. The house he lived in has been replaced.

WORCESTER (pr. Wŏŏster), Hereford and Worcester. [3 He] Cathedral city on the Severn. Florence of Worcester, a Benedictine monk, wrote *Chronicon ex Chronicis*, which was continued by other monks after his death here in 1118. Near the cathedral is the city's oldest church, St. Helen's (now

the Diocesan Registrar's Office), where the bond of 1582 pledging two Stratford men to ensure the marriage of William Shagspere and Anne Hathwey can be seen (photocopies on sale).

Samuel Butler and Samuel Foote were pupils (c. 1620 and c. 1730 respectively) at King's School, whose hall is the monks' old refectory, a Decorated building on a Norman base.

Bishop Gauden, whose seat was at Hartlebury Castle (q.v.), is buried at the W. end of the S. aisle of the cathedral. Izaak Walton, who also lived at Hartlebury Castle as Bishop Morley's steward, wrote the inscription on the tablet in the Lady Chapel commemorating his wife, which contains, after a list of her virtues, the anguished aside 'Alas, that she is dead'.

Celia Fiennes writes in her journal (*The Journeys of Celia Fiennes*, edited Christopher Morris, 1947) that she visited the town on the day William Walsh, the poet from Abberley (q.v.), was elected to parliament.

Mrs. Henry Wood was born here in 1814. She was Ellen Price, the daughter of a glover, and though she seldom returned after leaving when 20, many of her novels have the city, which she disguises as 'Helstoneleigh', as their background. *Mrs. Halliburton's Troubles* (1862) is about glovemakers.

Mary Martha Sherwood, who spent most of her life in the neighbourhood with the exception of the years with her husband's regiment in India, was living in Britannia Sq., when she finished the last volume of the popular moral saga, *The Fairchild Family* (1847). Many of the novels of Francis Brett Young are set in the neighbourhood. His ashes were interred in the cathedral, which has tablets commemorating the three local novelists.

WORTH, East Sussex. [1 Ed] Village off the B2036, 2 m. E. of Crawley. Cobbett, riding round the countryside to catalogue the abuses of the 'jobbers' and landlords, often stayed at Worth Lodge (gone), the farm where his friend Samuel Brazier used Cobbett's methods and grew maize, known as Cobbett's corn. Old Mrs. Brazier, who could neither write nor read, understood well the making of bread, the brewing of beer, the keeping of cows, the rearing of pigs, the salting of meat, the rearing of poultry, the obtaining of honey . . .

so that it is not surprising that Cobbett wrote *Cottage Economy* (1821) here.

Crabbett Park (now a school of equitation) on the B2036 was inherited by Wilfrid Scawen Blunt in 1872 soon after he had retired from the Diplomatic Service and married Lady Anne Noel, the Arabic scholar. Blunt, who continued to travel in the Arab world, wrote *Sonnets and Songs of Proteus* (1875), and *Esther* (1892).

WORTHAM, Suff. [4 Ge] Village on the A143, 3 m. SW. of Diss, where the Revd. Richard Cobbold wrote about smugglers and transportation in the novel *Margaret Catchpole* (1845). The large old rectory is by the new one, on the hill above the church, where he is commemorated.

WORTHING, West Sussex. [1 Ee] Resort on the A259 and the A24. A turn S. off the A27, 1 m. W. of the A24 roundabout, leads to the Lamb at Durrington from which Salvington Rd. runs to the former village of Salvington, now a suburb. Near the inn that bears his name is the site of the birthplace (1595) of John Selden in Selden's Way. This was a small, square, brick and flint house with a thatched roof, donated to the Council in 1941, but burnt down *c.* 1957. A plaque is on the gatepost of the bungalow which replaced it. West Tarring church (just S. of Salvington) has replicas in the porch of his will and his dying testimony. In a north-eastern suburb, not far from the parish church, is the Broadwater and Worthing cemetery where Richard Jefferies (d. 1887) 'Prose Poet of England's Fields and Woodlands', is buried. The naturalist W. H. Hudson (d. 1922) was buried by his own wish in the same cemetery as the man he admired.

WOTTON (pr. Wŏŏton), Surrey. [1 Dd] Village on the A25, 2¾ m. SW. of Dorking. John Evelyn was born (1620) at his father's home, Wotton House, a large rambling house (now rebuilt) surrounding a courtyard. He writes in his *Diary* that

it was sweetly environ'd with those delicious streames and venerable Woods, as in the judgment of strangers, as well as Englishmen, it may be compared to one of the most tempting and pleasant seates in the Nation.

He would have written about 'the Gardens, Fountaines and Groves' but that everyone knew about their magnificence. Evelyn's love of gardens led him to visit the best examples on the Continent, and on his return to plan and plant the garden of his home at Sayes Court (see London, Deptford). In 1694, he returned to Wotton to live in the apartment his brother assigned to him as heir of the estate and his prayer to God that 'this solemn Remove may be to the Glory of his mercy, & the good of my family' was a timely intercession because his nieces and their husbands threatened to go to law about the entail. Evelyn spent some time with his son in London to avoid the quarrel. His brother died in 1699 and 2 years later Evelyn finished planting 'the Elm walke at the back of the Meadow'. On his 80th birthday he thanked God that he was in full possession of his faculties but asked pardon that during the sermons he was 'apt to be surprised with sleepe'. He died aged 86 in London and was buried in the parish church here where a long epitaph commends him..

WREST PARK, Beds. [1 Da] Home of the National Institute of Agricultural Engineering, 8 m. N. of Luton and S. of Silsoe on the A6. In the 1620s John Selden was steward to Henry Grey, 9th Earl of Kent, and is thought to have written *Marmora Arundelliana* (1624) at a former house here. He also came here after being released, because of the plague, from imprisonment for supporting protests about tonnage and poundage. John Aubrey's gossip relates that he married the Countess of Kent after the Earl's death. Another member of the household here was Samuel Butler (1612–80), first as page to the Countess and then as secretary.

Gardens open Apr.–Sept.: Sat., Sun., and Bank Holidays 2–7 p.m.

WRINGTON, Avon. [2 Gb] Village off the A38, 9 m. SW. of Bristol. John Locke was born (1632) at the house of his mother's brother, which he later inherited. He stayed here occasionally, perhaps between 1680 and 1690, and is commemorated by a plaque on the churchyard wall. Hannah More lived at Barley Wood from 1802 till a short time before her death in 1833. She and her sisters wrote tracts for the schools they were starting in the neighbourhood. Coleridge and Cottle, his friend and publisher, visited them in 1814 and the young De Quincey, whose mother lived at Westhay on the Congresbury road, first read *The Ancient Mariner* in the library here. Hannah More corresponded with many of the intellectuals of her day; her *Letters* were published in 1834. She is buried in the churchyard.

WYCHFORD. See BURFORD.

WYE, Kent. [1 Gd] Small town off the A28, 5 m. NE. of Ashford. The first Englishwoman to become a professional writer, Aphra Behn, was for many years thought to have been baptized at the parish church in 1640. She sailed to Surinam with her father (who died on the voyage to take up his appointment of lieutenant-governor) and remained there long enough to make the territory the background for her novel *Oroonoko or The Royal Slave*, dramatized by her friend Thomas Southerne in

1695. Swinburne wrote 'This improper woman of genius was the first literary abolitionist—the first champion of the slave in the history of fiction'. Her husband is thought to have been a city merchant who died in 1665, perhaps of the plague. She became a spy for Charles II's government, who were so dilatory in paying her that she was put in a debtors' prison. Her novels and plays, written in the robust style of the times, were very popular and she herself was a friend of Dryden, Otway, and other Restoration wits, who celebrated her in their verses.

WYMONDHAM (pr. Windam), Norf. [4 Gd] Market town 9 m. SW. of Norwich, on the A11. Henry Peacham (1576?–1643?) was the Master of the Grammar School from 1617 to 1621. The last edition of his best-known work, *The Compleat Gentleman* (1622), was Johnson's source for the heraldic definitions in his dictionary. The school was held in the 12th-c. Becket's Chapel, now the county library.

Y

YAFFORTH, North Yorkshire. [5 Ec] Village on the Wiske and the B6271, 2 m. W. of Northallerton. Thomas Rymer was born (1641) at the Tudor Old Hall (altered). He was the author of *A Short View of Tragedy* (1692) and editor of fifteen volumes of historical documents, *Fœdera* (1704–35). The collection continued after his death (1713).

YARNTON, Oxon. [1 Bb] Village off the A34, 5 m. N. of Oxford. A. E. Coppard's poem 'The Sapling' commemorates the acacia he gave Agnes Evans for the garden of her new house (built 1907 by Ashbee and now called Byways) where he stayed and set the title story of *Adam and Eve and Pinch Me* (1921). In *It's me, O Lord* (1957) he regrets that the acacia, chosen because it was William Cobbett's favourite tree, didn't thrive.

YARROW WATER, Selkirks. (Borders). [6 Fd] River that rises above St. Mary's Loch (q.v.) and flows through splendid scenery in the once wild and wooded Ettrick Forest to join the Tweed 3 m. NE. of Selkirk (q.v.). It had a strong appeal for

Wordsworth even before he saw it, and he celebrated it three times in poems. The first poem, 'Yarrow Unvisited', was written in the autumn of 1803 after he and Dorothy and Coleridge had made a 6-weeks' tour of Scotland, during which they met Scott at Lasswade and stayed in his company at Melrose later. They came near to the Yarrow but left without seeing it and the poem expresses the sensation of a delight to be treasured for later enjoyment. It is also closely associated with the Wordsworths' new-found friendship with Scott. The second poem, 'Yarrow Visited', was written in 1814 after Wordsworth's second tour of Scotland, this time with his wife, Mary, their son John (aged 11), and Mary's sister, Sara. They met James Hogg, who became their guide, taking them to the source of the Yarrow and back by St. Mary's Loch and Newark Castle. The third poem, 'Yarrow Revisited', was written in the autumn of 1831, a few days after Wordsworth's second visit to the Yarrow, when he and his daughter, Dora, were staying with Scott at Abbotsford (q.v.). Scott, now frail and ageing, accompanied Wordsworth to Newark Castle and, in spite of the sadness that this was almost certain to be their last meeting, Wordsworth recollected the occasion as a 'day of happy hours'.

YATTENDON, Berks. [1 Cc] A village of quiet charm, off the B4009, 6 m. SW. of Streatley. Robert Bridges, Poet Laureate 1913–30, lived in the Manor House 1882–1904. His work of this period includes the long narrative poem *Eros and Psyche* (1885) and the 'Yattendon Hymnal' (1899), produced in collaboration with H. Ellis Woodbridge and printed by the Oxford University Press. Bridges is buried in the churchyard and has a memorial tablet in the church.

YEALMPTON (pr. Yampton), Devon. [2 Df] Village 7 m. SE. of Plymouth, on the A379. 'Mother Hubbard's Cottage' (now a café) on the main road is said to have belonged to the original of the nursery rhyme, a housekeeper at Kitley, 1 m. W., which was the home of the Pollexfens in Henry VIII's day, and later of the Pollexfen Bastards. The house, situated in a large park and not visible from the road, has been considerably altered and rebuilt. The library contains the only known copy of the first edition of the *Mother Hubbard* rhyme (1805), which was written by Sarah Martin (1768–1826), who lived here for a time with her sister, who had married Squire Bastard.

YORK, North Yorkshire. [5 Fd] Cathedral town on the A19 and the A54, the Roman Eboracum. Alcuin, author of metrical annals and philosophical works, was born (735) in the city and educated at the Cathedral School of which he became Master (778). He was later archbishop here but, after meeting Charlemagne, settled on the Continent.

The hero of Scott's *Ivanhoe* (1819), home from the Crusades, is helped by Isaac the Jew, who lived in Castlegate where Ivanhoe is nursed by Rebecca. The Poet Laureate Laurence Eusden was educated (c. 1700) at St. Peter's, now in Clifton on the NW., but whose traditions stem from Alcuin's school in the cloister.

Defoe, who makes York the birthplace of Robinson Crusoe, describes the city in *A Tour through the Whole Island of Great Britain*

(1724–7). Elizabeth Robinson, who as Mrs. Montagu presided over a fashionable literary salon in London, was born (1720) at the Great House, now the Treasurer's House.[1] Sterne, who married her cousin Elizabeth Lumley after a 2-year courtship, also sometimes stayed there, as he was made prebend of the cathedral in the same year (1741). Later he lodged in Stonegate where his inamorata, Miss Fourmantelle, was also staying. *Tristram Shandy* (1760–7), published in Stonegate, though generally popular, was disapproved of in York, as many of the characters, including Dr. Slop, were recognized as local people.

The Museum,[2] in the old prison, has the condemned cell where in 1739 Dick Turpin, a leading character in Ainsworth's *Rookwood* (1834), and 20 years later Eugene Aram, subject of a novel by Lytton, spent their last nights before being hanged. In 1811 Shelley, then just married to Harriet Westbrook, stayed with his friend Hogg at 20 Coney St., while trying without success to reconcile his father to the marriage. W. H. Auden, poet, dramatist, and critic, was born in 1907 at 54 Bootham.

[1] Open Apr.–Oct.: daily 11 a.m.–6 p.m.
[2] Open daily 9.30 a.m.–7.30 p.m. Earlier closing in winter.

YOUGHAL (pr. Yooall), Cork. [9 Ee] Old market town and port on the W. side of the Blackwater estuary, on the T12. Sir Walter Ralegh, who was a commander in Queen Elizabeth's army in Munster, was granted 42,000 acres of land in the counties of Cork and Waterford, which included the town of Youghal. He was appointed mayor, 1588–9, and lived for a time at Myrtle Grove, an Elizabethan gabled house standing in private grounds to the N. of St. Mary's Church. It is possible that Spenser, who had been writing *The Faerie Queene* at Kilcolman, near Doneraile (q.v.), visited Ralegh here and discussed the poem with him. In 1602 Ralegh sold Myrtle Grove, among his other estates, to Richard Boyle, later Earl of Cork.

William Congreve lived in Youghal as a child and probably received his first schooling here. His father had obtained a commission as lieutenant in the infantry and was stationed with the garrison of what was then a thriving seaport from 1674 to 1678, when he was transferred to Carrickfergus (q.v.).

Z

ZENNOR, Cornwall. [2 Af] Small village 4 m. W. of St. Ives, on the B3306. W. H. Hudson stayed here in December and January 1906–7 while gathering material for his book *The Land's End: a naturalist's impressions in West Cornwall* (1908). A plaque on the top of the hill near the old quarry commemorates the place where he used to sit and watch the sea-birds and wild-life around him.

D. H. Lawrence came here in 1916 with his wife Frieda and stayed at the Tinners' Arms while looking for a cottage to rent. They found Higher Tregerthen, one of a pair of small cottages in farm land near the sea, down a stony lane *c*. $1\frac{1}{2}$ m. NE. of the village, and moved there in March, for an annual rent of £5. They asked Katherine Mansfield and John Middleton Murry to come and live in the other cottage, with the object of forming 'a tiny settlement', but though the two did come they found the place uncongenial (Katherine was haunted by the crying of the gulls) and soon left. Lawrence stayed on, working on the sequel to *The Rainbow* (1915), published later as *Women in Love* (1921), but gradually he and Frieda—the bearded anti-war intellectual and his German wife—became objects of suspicion to the local people and on 12 October 1917 their cottage was searched by the police and they were told to leave (see his *Collected Letters*, ed. H. T. Moore, 1962). The bitterness of this experience is recorded in 'The Nightmare' chapter of the semi-autobiographical novel *Kangaroo* (1923).

INDEX OF AUTHORS

All places referred to have entries in the main text. References to titles of works are indicated by page numbers and columns (a *and* b) in parentheses.

1848, including 'All things bright and beautiful', 'There is a green hill far away', 'Once in Royal David's city' (313b), *Narrative Hymns for Village Schools* 1853, including 'Jesus calls us o'er the tumult' (53b), *The Sunday Book of Poetry* (ed.) 1864 (313b).

Alexander, William, Earl of Stirling (*c.* 1567–1640), poet and dramatist: lives in Stirling from 1632; d. in London (Covent Garden). *Aurora* 1604, *Recreations with the Muses* 1637 (311a).

Alfred (849–901), King of the West Saxons, Latin scholar and translator: b. Wantage; commemorated in Wantage, Winchester, and Stourhead. *Cura Pastoralis* (trans.) (332a), *Historia adversus Paganos* (trans.), *Anglo-Saxon Chronicle* (332b).

Allingham, William (1824–89), poet: b. and educ. Ballyshannon; customs officer in Killybegs *c.* 1849, in Lymington 1863–70; lives in Witley *c.* 1881; buried in Ballyshannon. 'The Fairies' (146b), *Laurence Bloomfield in Ireland* 1864, *The Ballad Book* (ed.) 1864 (233a), *Fraser's Magazine* (ed.) 1874–9 (14b), *Diary*, ed. H. Allingham and D. Radford, 1907 (233a).

Anderson, Alexander ('Surfaceman') (1845–1909), poet: b. and lives in Kirkconnel; assistant librarian 1880–3 and 1886–1909 in Edinburgh (University); buried in Kirkconnel. *A Song of Labour and other Poems* 1873 (148b).

Anderson, Robert (1770–1833), poet and pattern drawer: b. and educ. Carlisle; visits London (Vauxhall Gardens) 1794, Dumfries 1808; works in Belfast 1808–18; d. and is buried in Carlisle. 'Lucy Gray', *Cumbrian Ballads* 1805 (52b), 'The Mountain Boy', 'The Vale of Elva' (90a), *Poems on Various Subjects* 1810, contributions to *Belfast News-Letter* and *Commercial Chronicle* (20b), *Poetical Works* 1820 (52b).

Andrewes, Lancelot (1555–1626), theologian and classical scholar and translator of the A.V.: educ. Cambridge (Pembroke Hall); head of college at Cambridge (Pembroke Hall) 1589–1605; lives in London (Southwark: Winchester Palace); buried in London (Southwark Cathedral).

Angus, Marion (1866–1946), poet: b. Arbroath; lives in Aberdeen; meets W. H. Auden at Helensburgh 1931; d. Arbroath. 'Mary's Song', *The Lilt and Other Verses* 1922 (2a), *Tinker's Road* 1924, *Sun and Candlelight* 1927, *Lost Country and Other Verses* 1937 (2b), *Selected Poems* 1950 (9b).

Anstey, Christopher (1724–1805), poet:

b. Brinkley; educ. Eton and Cambridge (King's College); lives in Bath 1770–1805, buried in St. Swithin's, Bath. *The New Bath Guide* 1766 (16a).

Arbuthnot, Dr. John (1667–1734), satirist and physician: b. Arbuthnott; educ. Aberdeen and St. Andrews; physician to Queen Anne in London (St. James's: St. James's Palace) 1709–14; lives in London (Mayfair: Dover St.) 1714–21; visits Bath 1721, 1724, London (Twickenham); buried in London (St. James's). *John Bull* 1712 (10a).

Archer, William (1856–1924), journalist and translator of Ibsen: b. Perth; educ. Edinburgh (University); lives in London (Bloomsbury: Fitzroy Sq.).

Arlen, Michael (Dikrān Kouyoumdjian) (1895–1956), Bulgarian-born novelist: educ. Great Malvern; lives in Southport 1901– ; visits Padstow 1916. *The Green Hat* 1924 (307a).

Arnold, Sir Edwin (1831–1904), poet: educ. King's College, London (Strand: The Strand) and Oxford (University College); lives in Southend-on-Sea, in London (Kensington: Bolton Gdns.). *The Light of Asia* 1879 (199a, 306b).

Arnold, Matthew (1822–88), poet and critic: b. Laleham; spends holidays at Ambleside from 1834; educ. Winchester, Rugby, and Oxford (Balliol College); Fellow at Oxford (Oriel College) 1845–7; visits Douglas and Rydal; Dover 1851, Haworth 1852, and Llandudno 1864; lives in London (Belgravia: Chester Sq.) 1858–68, (Harrow on the Hill: Byron Hill) 1868–73, in Cobham 1873–88; d. Liverpool; buried in Laleham. 'Dover Beach' 1851 (79a), 'To a Gipsy Child by the Sea Shore' (78a), 'The Scholar-Gipsy' 1853 (13a, 270a), 'Haworth Churchyard' 1855 (7b, 131b), *On the Study of Celtic Literature* 1864 (162a), *Essays in Criticism* 1865 (270a), *New Poems* 1867 (166a, 270a), *Schools and Universities on the Continent* 1868 (166a), 'Rugby Chapel' (166a, 290a), 'Thyrsis' (166a, 270a).

Ashford, Daisy (*née* **Margaret**) (1881–1968), author of *The Young Visiters* and short stories: educ. Haywards Heath; visits J. M. Barrie in London (Adelphi) 1919; lives in Norwich. *The Young Visiters* 1919 (132a, 164b–165a), *Love and Marriage* (253a).

Asser (d. 909?), theologian and chronicler: abbot of Amesbury; bishop of Sherborne. *Life of Alfred c.* 893 (299a, b).

Aubrey, John (1626–97), antiquary: b. Kington St. Michael; educ. Oxford (Trinity

College); enters the Middle Temple, London (City: Temple) 1646; visits Epsom; lives in Broad Chalke; d. Oxford; memorials in Kington St. Michael and Oxford. *Topographical Collections of Wiltshire 1659–70* (148a), *Brief Lives* 1813 (176b, 184b, 272a).

Auden, Wystan Hugh (1907–73), poet and critic: b. York; educ. Holt and Oxford (Christ Church); teaches in Helensburgh; Professor of Poetry at Oxford 1956–61; lives in Oxford 1972–3; memorial in London (Westminster Abbey). *Oxford Poetry* (ed.) 1926, 1927, *Poems* 1928 (264b).

Austen, Jane (1775–1817), novelist: b. and lives in Steventon 1775–1801; educ. Oxford and Reading; visits Allington (Wilts.), Goodnestone, Godmersham, Great Bookham, and London (Lambeth); lives in Bath 1801–6; visits Teignmouth and Dawlish 1802, Ramsgate 1803, Dartford, Lyme Regis, and Adlestrop 1806; lives in Southampton 1806–9, in Chawton 1809–17; visits London (Covent Garden: Henrietta St.) 1813, and Box Hill; d. and buried in Winchester, memorial in Lyme Regis 1975. *Lady Susan* written *c.* 1805, ed. R. W. Chapman 1925, *The Watsons* written *c.* 1805, ed. R. W. Chapman 1927 (17a), *Sense and Sensibility* 1811 (75a, 222a, 310b), *Pride and Prejudice* 1813 (126a, 285a, 310b), *Mansfield Park* 1814 (17a, 126a, 258b, 283a, 285a), *Emma* 1816 (30a, 121a, 124a, 167b–168a, 202b, 306b), *Sanditon* written 1817, ed. R. W. Chapman 1925 (129b), *Northanger Abbey* 1818 (17a, 36b, 37a, 226b, 258b, 310b), *Persuasion* 1818 (17a, 232b–233a), *Letters*, ed. R. W. Chapman, 1952 (120b, 121a, 124a, 232b), 'Venta' 1817 (339a, b).

Austin, Alfred (1835–1913), Poet Laureate: educ. Whalley; lives in Hothfield, 1867–1913. *National Review* (ed.) 1883–94, *The Garden that I love* 1894 (136b).

Aytoun, Sir Robert (1570–1638), poet: educ. St. Andrews. 'Old Long Syne' (292b).

Aytoun, William Edmondstone (1813–65), poet and humorist: b. and educ. Edinburgh; Professor of Belles-Lettres, Edinburgh 1845. *Bon Gaultier Ballads* 1845 (100a), 'Widow of Glencoe' (119a), *Firmilian, or the Student of Badajoz* 1854 (118a).

Bacon, Sir Francis, Baron Verulam and Viscount St. Albans (1561–1626), essayist, philosopher, and statesman: b. London (Strand: The Strand), baptized in St. Martin-in-the-Fields (Strand: Trafalgar Sq.); educ. Cambridge (Trinity College);

enters Gray's Inn, London (Holborn) 1576, becomes Bencher 1586 and treasurer 1608; M.P. for Liverpool 1588–92; lives in London (Twickenham) 1595–1605; m. in London (Marylebone Parish Church) 1606; lives in St. Albans 1621–6; d. London (Highgate: Arundel House); is buried and has a memorial in St. Albans. *Essays* 1597 (224b, 291b–292a).

Bacon, Roger ('Doctor Mirabilis') (*c.* 1214–94), philosopher and scientist: b. Ilchester; lives in Oxford *c.* 1250–*c.* 1257; experiments at Sunningwell *c.* 1250; d. and is buried in Oxford.

Bagehot, Walter (1826–77), critic, economist, and political scientist: b. and lives in Langport; lives in London (Belgravia: Upper Belgrave St.). *The Economist* (ed.) 1860–77, *Literary Studies* 1879 (152b, 166b).

Bailey, Philip James (1816–1902), poet of the 'Spasmodic School': b. and lives in Nottingham. *Festus* 1839 (253b).

Baillie, Joanna (1762–1851), poet and dramatist: b. Bothwell; educ. and lives in Glasgow 1772–8; lives in London (Hampstead: Bolton House) 1806–51; buried in Hampstead Parish Church. *Fugitive Verses* 1790, *Plays on the Passions* 1798, *The Family Legend* 1810, *Metrical Legends* 1821 (189b).

Bale, John (1494–1563), theologian, historian, and dramatist: educ. Norwich; prebend of Canterbury *c.* 1558. *King John* 1548 (51b).

Ballantyne, Robert Michael (1825–94), novelist: b. and lives in Edinburgh; visits Ramsgate 1864, 1870, London (Mayfair: Regent St.) 1867, Botallack 1868, Inchcape Rock 1868; lives in London (Harrow on the Hill: Mount Park Rd.) 1880–93. *The Young Fur Traders* 1855 (100b), *Coral Island* 1858, *The Lifeboat* 1864 (285a), *The Lighthouse* 1865 (140a), *Fighting the Flames* 1867 (208a), *Deep Down* 1868 (28a), *The Floating Light of the Goodwin Sands* 1870 (285a).

Banim, John (1798–1842), novelist, dramatist and poet: b. Kilkenny. *The Fetches* 1825, *Tales by the O'Hara Family* (with Michael Banim) 1825 (145a).

Banim, Michael (1796–1874), novelist: b. Kilkenny. *Tales by the O'Hara Family* (with John Banim) 1825 (145a).

Barbauld, Mrs. Anna Letitia (1743–1825), poet and writer of children's tales: runs a school in Palgrave 1774–85; lives in Dorking 1796; visits Burford Bridge 1796; lives in London (Stoke Newington) 1802–25. *Hymns in Prose for Children*

1781 (276a), 'Lines on Burford Bridge' 1796 (40b, 78a), *Evenings at Home* 1794 (276a).

Barber, Margaret Fairless ('Michael Fairless') (1869–1901), essayist: lives in London (Chelsea: Cheyne Walk), in Torquay, and in Shermanbury; buried in Ashurst, nr. Shermanbury. *The Roadmender* 1901 (172a, 300a).

Barclay, Alexander (1475?–1552), theologian and poet: priest in Ottery St. Mary *c.* 1509; monk in Ely *c.* 1515–21; in Canterbury until 1552; rector of All Hallows, London (City: Lombard St.) 1552. *The Ship of Fools* (trans.) 1509 (257b), *Eclogues c.* 1515–21 (104b), *Life of St. Thomas* 1520 (51b), *Life of St. George* (trans.) (104b).

Barclay, Florence Louisa (*née* **Charlesworth**) (1862–1921), novelist: b. and buried in Limpsfield. *The Rosary* 1909 (157b).

Baretti, Giuseppe Marc Antonio (1719–89), Italian lexicographer and travel writer: tutor in London (Streatham) 1773–6. *Italian and English Dictionary* 1760 (223b).

Barham, Richard Harris (1788–1845), poet: b. Canterbury; educ. London (City: St. Paul's School) and Oxford (Brasenose College); curate of Warehorne; minor canon of St. Paul's Cathedral, London (City) 1821; lives in London (Holborn: Great Queen St.) 1821–4, (City: St. Paul's Churchyard) 1824–45; visits Bristol (Hotwells) 1845; d. London (City: St. Paul's Churchyard); commemorated in St. Martin-within-Ludgate (City: Ludgate Hill) and St. Paul's Cathedral. *The Ingoldsby Legends* 1840–7 (3a, 52a, 75b, 109a, 180b, 242b, 302b, 318b), 'As I lay a thinking' 1845 (180b).

Baring-Gould, Sabine (1834–1924), folklorist, antiquarian, hymn-writer, theologian, and novelist: b. Exeter; rector of East Mersea 1870–81; rector and squire of Lew Trenchard 1881–1924; buried in Lew Trenchard. *Mehalah* 1880 (94a), *The Gaverocks: A Tale of the Cornish Coast* 1887, *A Book of the West* 1889 (156a), *In the Roar of the Sea* 1892 (293a, b), *A Book of Dartmoor* 1900, 'Onward, Christian Soldiers' (156a).

Barnes, Barnabe (1569?–1609), poet: educ. Oxford (Brasenose College); lives in Durham; buried in Durham. *Parthenophil and Parthenope* 1593 (91b, 262a, b), *The Devil's Charter* 1607 (91b).

Barnes, William (1800–86), poet, schoolmaster, and clergyman: b. Rush-hay; educ. Sturminster Newton; teaches in Mere 1823–35, in Dorchester; a 'ten-year-man' at Cambridge (St. John's) 1838–48, B.D. 1850; writes of Beaminster; rector of Whitcombe and Winterborne Came (see Came) 1862–86; buried in Winterborne Came; statue in Dorchester.

Barrett, Elizabeth, see Browning, Elizabeth Barrett.

Barrie, Sir James Matthew (1860–1937), journalist, short-story writer, and playwright; b. Kirriemuir; educ. Dumfries and Edinburgh; lives in London (Kensington: Gloucester Rd.) 1895–8, (Bayswater: Bayswater Rd.) 1902–9, (Adelphi: Robert St.) 1909–37; visits Meredith in Mickleham; stays in Amhuinnsuidhe 1912; country cottage in Farnham; commemorated in London (Kensington Gdns.). *Auld Licht Idylls* 1888, *A Window in Thrums* 1889, *The Little Minister* 1891 (149a), *Sentimental Tommy* 1896 (9b, 149a, 200a), *Margaret Ogilvy* 1896 (149a, 200a), *Peter Pan* 1904 (110a, 165b, 200b), *What Every Woman Knows* 1908 (165b), *Mary Rose* 1920 (7b–8a).

Barton, Bernard (1784–1849), poet: lives in Woodbridge. *Poems* 1849 (342b).

Basse (or Bas), William (1583?–1653), poet: lives in Moreton (Oxon.). *Sword and Buckler, or Serving Man's Defence* 1602, *Three Pastoral Elegies* 1602, 'Epitaph on Shakespeare', 'Angler's Song' (243b).

Bates, Herbert Ernest ('Flying Officer X') (1905–74), novelist and short-story writer: b. Rushden; educ. Kettering; frequents Higham Ferrars; lives in Little Chart 1931–74; in R.A.F. at Oakington 1941, at Tangmere 1942. *The Two Sisters* 1926 (290a), *The Fallow Land* 1932, *The Poacher* 1935 (159a, 290a), *Fair Stood the Wind for France* 1944 (159a, 318a), *The Purple Plain* 1947 (159a), *The Jacaranda Tree* 1949 (159a), 'It's Just the Way it is', 'The Sun Rises Twice' (255a), *Love for Lydia* 1952 (159a, 290a), *The Sleepless Moon* 1956, 'The Hessian Prisoner' (133b), *The Vanished World* 1969 (133b, 145a, 159a), *The Blossoming World* 1971 (159a), *The World in Ripeness* 1972 (159a, 255a), the Larkin Family stories (159a).

Baxter, Richard (1615–91), Presbyterian minister: b. Rowton; assistant minister in Bridgnorth; minister in Kidderminster 1641; devises rules for the academy in Sheriffhales; lives in retirement in Melbourne; imprisoned in London (Southwark: King's Bench) 1685–6; commemorated by a statue in Kidderminster. *Aphorisms of Justification* 1649 (145a),

and theologian: b. Dysart Castle; educ. Kilkenny and Dublin (Trinity College); Dean of Londonderry 1724.

Berners, Gerald Hugh Tyrwhitt-Wilson, 14th Baron (1883–1950), novelist, musician, and painter: educ. Eton; lives in Faringdon 1931–50. *First Childhood* 1934, *The Camel* 1936, *Far From the Madding War* 1941 (109a), *A Distant Prospect* 1945 (106b, 109a).

Besant, Sir Walter (1836–1901), novelist and historian: b. Portsmouth; educ. King's College, London (Strand: The Strand) and Cambridge (Christ's College) 1856–9; lives in London (Hampstead: Frognal Gdns.) 1896–1901; memorial in London (City: St. Paul's Cathedral). *By Celia's Arbour* 1878 (282b–283a), *The Chaplain of the Fleet* 1881 (176a).

Betham-Edwards, Matilda (1838–1919), novelist: lives in Hastings. *Kitty* 1870 (130a).

Bierce, Ambrose Gwinnett (1842–1914), American journalist: lives in Bristol 1872, in Leamington Spa 1874. *The Fiend's Delight* 1873, *Nuggets and Dust* 1873 (36a), *The Lantern* 1874 (155a).

Binyon, Laurence (1869–1943), poet: b. Lancaster; educ. London (City: St. Paul's School) and Oxford (Trinity College); works in the British Museum (Bloomsbury) 1893–1933. *Lyric Poems* 1894 (273a), 'For the Fallen' 1914 (152a, 167b), *Collected Poems* 1931 (167b).

Birmingham, George A. See Hannay, Canon James Owen.

Black, William (1841–98), novelist: b. and educ. Glasgow; works in Glasgow until 1864. *James Merle* 1864, *A Daughter of Heth* 1871 (117b).

Blackmore, Richard Doddridge (1825–1900), novelist and poet: b. Longworth; spends boyhood at Newton Nottage and Elsfield; lives in Culmstock from 1831; educ. Tiverton and Oxford (Exeter College) 1844–7; spends holidays in Charles and Oare; teaches classics in London (Twickenham: Hampton Rd.) 1853–60; lives in London (Teddington: Doone Cl.) 1860–1900; buried in London (Teddington); memorials in Exeter and Oare. *Poems by Melanter* 1853, *Epullia* 1853 (225b), *Craddock Nowell* 1866 (224a), *Lorna Doone* 1869 (224a, 255a, 282b, 323b), *The Maid of Sker* 1872 (150b), *Cripps the Carrier* 1876 (104a, 224a, b), *Christowell: a Dartmoor Tale* 1881 (74b).

Blackwood, Algernon (1869–1951), short-story writer and novelist: b. London (Crayford). *John Silence* 1908, *Tales of the Uncanny and Supernatural* 1949 (185b).

Blair, Eric ('George Orwell') (1903–50), essayist and satirical novelist: educ. Eastbourne and Eton; spends childhood in Shiplake; goes hop-picking in Wateringbury 1931; lives in London (Hampstead: South End Green) 1934–5; visits Liverpool 1935; lives in London (Hampstead: Mortimer Cres.) 1943–4; lives on Jura 1946–9; buried in Sutton Courtenay. *A Clergyman's Daughter* 1935 (333b), *Keep the Aspidistra Flying* 1936 (191b), *The Road to Wigan Pier* 1937 (161b), *Animal Farm* 1945 (191a), *Nineteen Eighty-Four* 1949 (142b), 'Such, such were the Joys' 1952 (93b), 'Hop Picking' (333b).

Blake, George (1893–1961), novelist and editor of the *Glasgow Evening News*: settles in Helensburgh 1932. *Down to the Sea* 1937 (132b).

Blake, William (1757–1827), poet and engraver: b. London (Soho: Broadwick St.); serves apprenticeship in London (Holborn: Great Queen St.) 1771–8; m. in London (Battersea) 1772; lives in London (Soho: Poland St.) 1785–91, in Felpham 1800–4; tried for high treason at Chichester 1804; lives in London (Mayfair: South Molton St.) 1804–21; exhibits engravings in London (Soho: Carnaby St.) 1810; lives in London (Strand: The Strand: Fountain Ct.) 1821–7; visits John Linnell in London (Hampstead Garden Suburb) 1824–30, and Samuel Palmer in Shoreham 1826; buried in London (Finsbury: Bunhill Fields); memorials in London (City: St. Paul's Cathedral and Westminster Abbey). *Songs of Innocence* 1789, *The Book of Thel* 1789, *Tiriel* 1789, *The Marriage of Heaven and Hell* 1790 (217b), *Milton* 1804 (111a, 208b), *Jerusalem* 1804 (111a).

Blessington, Marguerite Gardiner (*née* Power), **Countess of** (1789–1849), b. Knockbrit; spends childhood in Clonmel; lives in Dublin; in London (Kensington: Kensington Gore) 1836–49. *Grace Cassidy, or the Repealers* 1833, *Conversations with Lord Byron* 1834, *The Belle of the Season* 1840, *The Keepsake* (ed.) 1841–51 (200b).

Bloomfield, Robert (1766–1823), poet: b. Honington; spends boyhood in Euston and Sapiston; works and lives in London (City: Telegraph St.) 1781; visits Chepstow, Ross-on-Wye 1807; lives in Shefford from 1814; buried in Campton. *The Farmer's Boy* 1800 (107a, 181a, 296a), 'A Visit to Ranelagh' (172b), 'On visiting the place of my nativity' (136a), *The Banks of Wye* 1811 (58a).

Blunden, Edmund Charles (1896–1974), poet and critic: educ. Christ's Hospital, and Oxford (The Queen's College); Fellow at Oxford (Merton College) 1931–44; lives in Long Melford 1965–74; buried in Long Melford. *Poems* 1914, *Poems translated from the French* 1914 (61a), *Poems 1930–40* 1940, *Shells by a Stream* 1944 (268b).

Blunt, Wilfrid Scawen (1840–1922), poet, diplomat, and traveller: educ. Stonyhurst College, Whalley; inherits estate in Worth 1872; imprisoned in Galway 1887; lives in Southwater 1895–1922. *Sonnets and Songs of Proteus* 1875 (345a), *In Vinculis* 1889 (115a), *Esther* 1892 (345a), *Collected Poems* 1914 (307b), *My Diaries* 1920 (307a).

Bodley, Sir Thomas (1545–1613), diplomat and scholar: b. Exeter; educ. Oxford (Magdalen College); Fellow at Oxford (Merton College) 1564; refounds the University Library in 1602 (see Oxford: Bodleian Library); buried in Oxford (Merton College).

Borrow, George (1803–81), novelist and traveller: b. Dumpling Green or East Dereham; educ. Edinburgh, Clonmel, and Norwich; lives in Stafford 1825, Oulton 1840–66, Great Yarmouth 1853–5, 1856–9; visits Llandovery, Llangollen, and Ponterwyd 1854; lives in London (Kensington: Hereford Sq.) 1860–74, in Oulton 1874–81; buried in London (Kensington: Brompton Cemetery); memorials in Glyn Ceiriog and Oulton. *The Bible in Spain* 1843 (257b), *Lavengro* 1851 (100a, 179b, 253a, 257b), *Romany Rye* 1857 (253a), *Wild Wales* 1862 (120b, 162a, 200a, 282a).

Boswell, James (1740–95), biographer of Dr. Johnson, barrister, and author of journals: b. and educ. Edinburgh; lives in Auchinleck; lodges in London (Westminster: Downing St.), frequents Somerset Coffee House (Strand: The Strand), and first meets Dr. Johnson (Covent Garden) 1763; visits Cullen, Slains Castle, Aberdeen, Glenshiel, Skye, Mull, Oban, Inveraray, Alexandria, Laurencekirk, and Glasgow on his tour of the Hebrides with Dr. Johnson in 1773; enters Inner Temple, London (City: Temple) 1775; lives in London (Marylebone: Queen Anne St.), frequents Mitre Tavern (City: Fleet St.), Ye Olde Cheshire Cheese (City: Fleet St.); visits Chester 1779; Ilam 1779; spends last years and d. in London (Marylebone:

Gt. Portland St.); buried in Auchinleck; statue at Lichfield; private papers found in Malahide Castle. *The Journal of a Tour of the Hebrides* 1774 (154a), *The Life of Samuel Johnson* 1791 (204b, 205b), *Boswell's London Journal 1762–1763* (204a, 227b).

Boucicault, Dionysius ('Dion') Lardner (c. 1820–90), playwright: b. Dublin. *London Assurance* 1841, *The Colleen Bawn* 1860, *Arrah-na-Pogue* 1864, *The Shaughraun* 1874 (83b).

Bowdler, Dr. Thomas (1754–1825), editor of Shakespeare: buried in Oystermouth. *Family Shakespeare* 1818 (274b).

Bowen, Elizabeth Dorothea Cole (1899–1973), novelist and short-story writer: lives in Oxford 1923– ; inherits Bowen's Court 1928; lives in London (Regent's Park: Clarence Ter.) 1935–52; honoured at Oxford 1957; sells Bowen's Court 1960. *Encounters* 1923, *Joining Charles* 1929 (260a), *The House in Paris* 1935, *The Death of the Heart* 1938, *Look at All Those Roses* 1941 (210a), *Bowen's Court* 1942 (29b), *The Demon Lover* 1945, *The Heat of the Day* 1949 (210a), *Eva Trout* 1969 (39a).

Bowles, William Lisle (1762–1850), poet: educ. Oxford (Trinity College); vicar of Bremhill 1804–50; visits Bristol (Hotwells) 1789, Bath 1795, Gloucester 1835, Bromham, Netley Abbey. 'Elegiac Stanzas' 1795 (16b), 'Elegy' (37b), 'Sonnet to Netley Abbey' (248a), 'On Hearing the Messiah Performed in Gloucester Cathedral' 1835 (120a).

Boyle, John, 5th Earl of Orrery (1707–62), friend of Swift, Pope, and Johnson: educ. Oxford (Christ Church). *Remarks on the Life and Writings of Dr. Jonathan Swift* 1751 (263b–264a).

Braddon, Mary Elizabeth (1837–1915), novelist: lives in London (Richmond: Sheen Rd.); buried in London (Richmond Parish Church). *Lady Audley's Secret* 1862 (211b), *The Conflict* 1903 (212a).

Bradley, Andrew Cecil (1851–1935), Shakespearian scholar: educ. Cheltenham and Oxford (Balliol College); Fellow at Oxford (Balliol College) 1874; Professor of Literature and History, Liverpool 1882–9; Professor of English at Glasgow 1890–1900; Professor of Poetry at Oxford (Balliol College) 1901. *Shakespearean Tragedy* 1904, *Oxford Lectures* 1909 (261b).

Bradley, Edward ('Cuthbert Bede') (1827–89), novelist and poet: educ. Durham 1843–7; lives in Oxford c. 1849. *The Adventures of Mr. Verdant Green, an Oxford Freshman* 1853–7 (92a, 258b–259a, 263a).

Brown, Thomas (1663–1704), satirist: b. Shifnal; educ. Newport (Salop) and Oxford (Christ Church). 'I do not love you, Dr. Fell' (263b).

Brown, Thomas Edward (1830–97), poet: b. Douglas; educ. King William's College, I.O.M., Oxford (Christ Church); Fellow at Oxford (Oriel College) 1853–8; m. in Maughold 1858; Vice-Principal at King William's College 1858–61; headmaster in Gloucester 1861–3; housemaster in Bristol (Clifton) 1864–93; retires to Maughold 1893; d. and is buried in Bristol (Clifton). *Betsy Lee* 1873 (36b), *Fo'c's'le Yarns* 1881 (36b, 78b), *Collected Poems* 1900 (120a), 'Clifton' (36b), 'Epistola ad Daykins' (37a), 'Braddan Vicarage' (78b), 'An Oxford Idyll' (267a).

Browne, Charles Farrar ('Artemus Ward') (1834–67), American humorous writer: d. and is commemorated in Southampton.

Browne, Sir Thomas (1605–82), physician and philosopher: educ. Winchester and Oxford (Pembroke College); settled in Norwich 1637–82; knighted in Norwich 1671; d. and is buried in Norwich; commemorated by a statue in Norwich. *Religio Medici* 1643 (252b).

Browne, William (1591–1645), poet: b. Tavistock; educ. Tavistock and Oxford (Exeter College); enters Inner Temple, London (City: Temple) 1611; frequents Mermaid Tavern (City: Bread St.); lives in Wilton; writes epitaph for the Countess of Pembroke in Salisbury. *Britannia's Pastorals* Bks. I 1613, II 1616, III 1852 (319b).

Browning, Mrs. Elizabeth Barrett (*née* **Barrett**) (1806–61), poet: b. Kelloe; lives in Hope End 1809–32, in Sidmouth 1832–5, in London (Marylebone: Gloucester Pl.) 1835–8, (Marylebone: Wimpole St.) 1838–46; stays in Torquay 1839–40; m. in London (Marylebone Parish Church) 1846; visits London (Marylebone: Welbeck St.) 1852, (Marylebone: Dorset St.) 1855. *Battle of Marathon* 1820, 'The Lost Bower' (136b), *Prometheus Bound* (trans.) and *Miscellaneous Poems* 1833 (206a, 302b), *Aurora Leigh* 1857 (203b), *Diary* 1969 (136b).

Browning, Robert (1812–89), poet: b. and lives in London (Camberwell); dines with Miss Mitford in London (Bloomsbury: Russell Sq.) 1836; m. in London (Marylebone Parish Church) 1846; visits London (Marylebone: Welbeck St.) 1852, (Marylebone: Dorset St.) 1855; lives in London (Paddington: Warwick Cres.) 1861–87; visits George Eliot in London (Regent's

Park: Lodge Rd.), Llangollen 1886, Llantysilio 1886; lives in London (Kensington: De Vere Gdns.) 1888–9; buried in London (Westminster Abbey). *The Ring and the Book*, 4 vols. 1868–9 (209a).

Bryant, William Cullen (1794–1878), American poet and editor of the New York *Evening Post*: visits London (Strand: The Strand) 1850.

Brydges, Sir Samuel Egerton (1762–1837), bibliographer, poet, and novelist: b. Denton; lives in Steventon 1886–8; visits Ramsgate; lives in Denton, in Littlebourne 1810–18. *Censura Literaria* 1805 (75b), *The British Bibliographer* 1810–14, *Restituta* 1814–16 (158b), *Autobiography* 1834 (310b).

Buchan, Anna ('O. Douglas') (d. 1948), novelist: b. Kirkcaldy; educ. and lives in Glasgow; spends holidays in Broughton; lives in Peebles. *Penny Plain* 1913 (40a), *The Setons* 1917, *Priorsford* 1932 (277a), *Unforgettable, Unforgotten* 1943 (148b, 277a).

Buchan, John, 1st Baron Tweedsmuir (1875–1940), novelist and statesman: b. Perth; educ. Glasgow and Oxford (Brasenose College); spends holidays in Broughton; lives in London (Marylebone: Portland Pl.) 1913–19, in Elsfield 1919–35; buried in Elsfield. *John Burnet of Barns* 1898 (15b), *The Thirty-nine Steps* 1914 (205b), *Midwinter* 1923 (104a), *Witch Wood* 1927 (40a), *Memory Hold the Door* 1940 (104a, 263a).

Buchanan, Robert Williams (1841–1901), critic, poet, and novelist: educ. and lives in Glasgow; lives in Oban 1866–74. *The North Coast and Other Poems* 1868, 'The Fleshly School of Poetry' 1871 (255b).

Bunyan, John (1628–88), Nonconformist preacher and writer: b. nr. Elstow; baptized in Elstow; preaches and is imprisoned in Bedford; his pulpit preserved in Breachwood Green; preaches in Wain Wood and Hitchin; buried in London (Finsbury: Bunhill Fields), and commemorated in Westminster Abbey. *Grace Abounding* 1666 (19b), *The Pilgrim's Progress* 1678 (8a, 19b–20a, 104b), *The Holy War* 1682 (104b).

Burgoyne, Sir John (1722–92), General and playwright: educ. London (Westminster School); lives in London (Mayfair: Hertford St.). *The Maid of the Oaks* 1774, *The Heiress* 1776 (207b).

Burke, Edmund (1729–97), statesman and orator: b. Dublin; educ. Ballitore and Dublin; enters Middle Temple, London (City: Temple) 1750; visits Bath 1756;

frequents Dr. Johnson's literary club, London (Soho: Gerrard St.); buys estate in Beaconsfield 1768; lives in London (Soho: Gerrard St.); elected M.P. for Bristol 1774; stays in Bristol (Henbury); buried in Beaconsfield; commemorated by statue in Bristol.

Burnand, Sir Francis Cowley (1836–1917), editor of *Punch* 1880–1906: educ. Cambridge (Trinity College).

Burnett, Mrs. Frances Eliza Hodgson (*née* Hodgson) (1849–1924), novelist: b. Manchester; lives in Rolvenden 1880–1901. *Little Lord Fauntleroy* 1886 (237a), *The Secret Garden* 1911 (288a).

Burney, Frances (Fanny) (Mme D'Arblay) (1752–1840), novelist: b. King's Lynn; visits Bristol (Hotwells) 1767; educ. and lives in London (Holborn: Queen's Sq.) 1770–4, (Soho: St. Martin's St.) 1774–86; visits Brighton and London (Chessington) 1770s, Tunbridge Wells, Devizes 1780, Batheaston; Teignmouth 1773, 1778, 1793; lives in Windsor and in London (Kew) 1786–91; visits Nuneham Courtenay 1786, Cheltenham 1788, Weymouth 1789, Saltram House 1789; m. in Mickleham 1793; lives in Great Bookham 1793–6, Mickleham 1796–1802, Bath 1815–18, London (Mayfair: Bolton St.) 1818–28; buried in Bath. *Evelina* 1778 reprinted 1962 (172a, 173b, 217b), *Cecilia* 1782 (217b), *Camilla* 1796 reprinted 1972 (30a, 124a, 327b), *Diary and Letters* 1778–1840, 1842–6 (30a, 147b, 255a, 327b, 336b).

Burns, Robert (1759–96), poet: b. and lives in Alloway; baptized and educ. in Ayr; studies in Kirkoswald 1775; lives in Lochlea 1777–84; studies in Irvine 1781–2; frequents Tarbolton and Mauchline; lives in Mossgiel 1784–9; visits Failford 1786, Kilmarnock 1786, Edinburgh 1786, Aberfeldy 1787, Falls of Bruar 1787, Jedburgh 1787, Stirling 1787, Selkirk 1787 and Dalswinton; lives in Ellisland 1789–91; visits Kirroughtree 1794 and 1795; lives 1791–6 and is buried in Dumfries; commemorated in Failford, Stirling, Irvine, Edinburgh, and London (Westminster Abbey). *Poems Chiefly in the Scottish Dialect* 1786 (146b, 164a, 244a), 'The Jolly Beggars' (239b–240a), 'The Holy Fair' (240a), 'The Ordination' (146b–147a), 'Epistle to Willie Creech' (297b), 'Ae fond kiss' (98a), 'Epitaph on William Muir', 'Death and Dr. Hornbook' (319a), 'Highland Mary' (91a, 125b, 319a), 'The Birks of Aberfeldy' (2b), 'Humble Petition of Bruar Water'

(108a, b), 'Tam o' Shanter' (5b–6a, 13b, 103b, 149a), 'To Mary in Heaven' (91a, 103b), 'A Red, Red Rose', 'Auld Lang Syne' (104a), *Scots Musical Museum* (98a, 103b–104a), 'Heron Election Ballads' (149b).

Burton, Sir Richard Francis (1821–90), Arabic scholar and traveller: prob. b. Torquay; educ. London (Richmond: Little Green) and Oxford (Trinity College); buried in London (Richmond). *Pilgrimage to Mecca* 1855–6 (325a), *The Lusiads* (trans.) 1880–4 (211a), *The Arabian Nights, or The Thousand and One Nights* (trans.) 1885–8 (211a, 325a), *Pentamerone* (trans.) (211a).

Burton, Robert (1577–1640), theologian: b. Lindley; educ. Nuneaton and Oxford (Brasenose College) 1593–9; Fellow and rector at Oxford (Christ Church) 1599–1640; rector of Seagrave 1632–40; buried and has a memorial in Oxford (Christ Church). *Anatomy of Melancholy* 1621–51 (263b, 297a).

Butler, Samuel (1612–80), satirist and poet: b. Strensham; educ. Worcester; lives in Wrest Park, in Ludlow 1661–2; in London (Covent Garden: Rose St.), frequents Will's Coffee House in Bow St. (Covent Garden); commemorated in Westminster Abbey (Westminster). *Hudibras* (3 pts.) 1662–78 (232a).

Butler, Samuel (1835–1902), satirist and novelist: b. Langar; educ. Shrewsbury and Cambridge (St. John's College) 1854–9; lives in London (City: Clifford's Inn) 1864–1902; visits Downe 1872. *Erewhon* 1872 (175b), *Unconscious Memory* 1880 (79b), *Erewhon Revisited* 1901 (175b), *The Way of all Flesh* 1903 (152a, 175b).

Byng, Hon. John, 5th Viscount Torrington (1742–1813), diarist: educ. London (Westminster School); lives in London (Marylebone: Duke St.); visits Halesowen 1781, Welwyn 1789, Mereworth 1790, Chicksands 1791, Bibury 1794. *The Torrington Diaries* 1934, reprinted 1970 (22a, 127b, 204a, 241a, 334a).

Byrom, John (1692–1763), Jacobite poet and hymn-writer: b. Manchester; educ. Merchant Taylors' School, London (City: Suffolk Lane); lives in and is buried in Manchester. 'Christians awake', 'To an Officer in the Army' (235b).

Byron, George Gordon, 6th Baron (1788–1824), poet: b. and baptized in London (Marylebone: Holles St. and St. Marylebone Parish Church); educ. Aberdeen, London (Harrow on the Hill) 1801–5,

memorial in Shaugh Prior. 'Dartmoor' (74a, b), *Teignmouth, Dawlish and Torquay Guide* 1810 (281a).

Carroll, Lewis. See Dodgson, Charles Lutwidge.

Carswell, Catherine Roxburgh (1879–1941), novelist and critic: b. and lives in Glasgow. *Robert Burns* 1930, *The Savage Pilgrimage* 1932, *Lying Awake* 1950 (118b).

Carter, Elizabeth (1717–1806), poet and letter-writer: b. and lives in Deal; visits Bath 1778; buried in London (Mayfair: South Audley St.). *Epictetus* (trans.) 1758 (75a).

Cartwright, William (1611–43), poet and dramatist: educ. London (Westminster School) and Oxford (Christ Church); d. Oxford. *The Royal Slave* 1636 (263b).

Cary, Arthur Joyce Lunel (1888–1957), novelist: b. Londonderry; educ. Bristol (Clifton) and Oxford (Trinity College); lives in Oxford 1920–57; papers and manuscripts in Oxford (Bodleian Library). *Aissa Saved* 1932, *The African Witch* 1936, *Mr. Johnson* 1939, *Charley is my Darling* 1940, *The Horse's Mouth* 1944, *Not Honour More* 1955 (273a).

Caxton, William (1422–91?), printer and translator: buried in London (St. Margaret's, Westminster).

Chambers, Robert (1802–71), publisher, editor, and miscellaneous writer: b. Peebles; stays at Tibbie Shiel's Inn 1820s; founds publishing firm in Edinburgh with his brother William; becomes Lord Provost of Edinburgh 1865–9. *Picture of Scotland* 1827 (322a), *Chambers's Edinburgh Journal* 1832, *Chambers's Encyclopaedia* 1859–68 (100a).

Chambers, William (1800–83), publisher, editor, and miscellaneous writer: b. Peebles; founds publishing firm in Edinburgh with his brother Robert. *Chambers's Edinburgh Journal* 1832, *Chambers's Encyclopaedia* 1859–68 (100a).

Chapman, George (1559?–1634), dramatist, translator, and poet: b. in or near Hitchin; lives in Hitchin; imprisoned in Old Marshalsea, London (Southwark: Borough High St., Mermaid Court) 1605; buried in London (Bloomsbury: St. Giles-in-the-Fields). *Eastward Hoe* 1605 (218b), translation of Homer (219b).

Chapone, Mrs. Hester (*née* Mulso) (1727–1801), writer of verses and letters: b. Twywell; frequents Mrs. Delany's house in London (St. James's: St. James's Pl.). 'The Loves of Amoret and Melissa' 1736, *Letters on the Improvement of the Mind* 1774 (328b).

Chateaubriand, François-René de (1768–1848), French académicien and diplomat: stays in Beccles and Bungay 1794; entertained in Dover 1822.

Chatterton, Thomas (1752–70), poet: b. and educ. Bristol; works in Bristol 1768–70; lives in London (Holborn: Brooke St.); frequents the Chapter Coffee House (City: Paternoster Row); d. Brooke St. (Holborn). *Rowley Poems* 1777 (34b–35a), *Collected Works* 1803 (35a).

Chaucer, Geoffrey (1345?–1400), poet: b. London (City: Upper Thames St.); stays in Canterbury 1360–1; believed to have stayed in Woodstock; lives in London (City: Aldgate High St.) 1374–86; may have visited Ewelme; buried in London (Westminster Abbey). *The Boke of the Duchesse* 1369–70 (222a), *Troylus and Cryseyde* ?between 1374 and 1386 (174a), *The Canterbury Tales c.* 1387–1400: 'Prologue (the Shipman)' (74b), 'Prologue (the Doctor of Physic)' (159a), 'Prologue (Wife of Bath)' (16a), 'Prologue (the Reeve)' (18a), 'The Miller's Tale' (258a), 'The Reeve's Tale' (13a, b, 44b, 48b), 'The Wife of Bath's Prologue' (124a), 'The Prioress's Tale' (157b).

Chénier, André (1762–94), French poet: visits London (Marylebone: Portman Sq. and St. James's: Pall Mall). *Bucoliques* (205b).

Chesterton, Gilbert Keith (1874–1936), essayist, novelist, and poet: b. London (Kensington: Sheffield Ter.); educ. London (City: St. Paul's School); lives in London (Kensington: Warwick Gdns.) 1879–99; in Beaconsfield 1909–35; buried in Beaconsfield. *The Wild Knight* 1900 (201b), *Thackeray* 1910, *Bernard Shaw* 1909, 1935, *Collected Poems* 1915 (18b).

Chudleigh, Lady Mary (1656–1710), poet and essayist: lives and is buried in Ashton. *The Ladies' Defence* 1701, *Poems on Several Occasions* 1703, *Essays upon several Subjects* 1710 (11b).

Church, Richard (1893–1972), poet and novelist: lives in Limpsfield 1916–28; meets T. S. Eliot in London (Soho: Frith St.) 1921; lives in Curtisden Green 1939–65; d. Sissinghurst Castle. *Oliver's Daughter* 1930 (157b), *The Solitary Man and other poems* 1941, *Over the Bridge* 1955, *The Golden Sovereign* 1957, *Kent* (a guidebook) 1948 (72b).

Churchill, Charles (1731–64), satirist: b. London (Westminster: Smith Sq.); educ. London (Westminster School) and Cambridge (St. John's College); makes a Fleet marriage in London (City: Farringdon

Collier, Jeremy (1650–1726), pamphleteer: educ. Ipswich; rector of Ampton 1679–84.

Collins, William (1721–59), poet: b. Chichester; educ. Winchester and Oxford (The Queen's College and Magdalen College); lives in Winchester; lives in London (Soho: Queen St.) 1744–9; frequents Bedford Coffee House (Covent Garden), visits James Thomson (Richmond: Kew Foot Lane); lives in Chichester 1749–59; buried in Chichester. *Persian Eclogues* 1742 (340a).

Collins, William Wilkie (1824–89), novelist: lives in London (Marylebone: Blandford Sq.) 1840s–1850, (Regent's Park: Hanover Ter.) 1850–9; spends holidays in Botallack 1851, Dover 1852; acts in Dickens's theatricals in London (Bloomsbury: Tavistock Sq.) 1850s; visits Clovelly 1861; holiday in Aldeburgh 1862; lives in London (Marylebone: Melcombe Pl.) 1864–7, (Marylebone: Gloucester Pl.) 1867–88; last months in London (Marylebone; Wimpole St.); buried in London (Kensal Green). *Antonina* 1850 (203b), *Rambles beyond Railways* 1851 (28a), 'A Terribly Strange Bed', *The Woman in White* 1860 (210a), 'A Message from the Sea' (with Dickens) 1861 (64a), *No Name* 1862 (4b), *Armadale* 1866 (205a), *The Moonstone* 1868 (204a).

Colman, George, the Elder (1732–94), dramatist and editor: educ. London (Westminster School) and Oxford (Christ Church); lives in London (Richmond: The Vineyard). *The Clandestine Marriage* (with Garrick) 1766 (212a).

Colman, George, the Younger (1762–1836), dramatist: educ. London (Westminster School) and Oxford (Christ Church).

Colum, Padraic (1881–1972), Irish poet and playwright: spends honeymoon in Greatham 1912; visits Southwater; opens Thoor Ballylee at Gort 1965.

Combe, William (1741–1823), poet: b. and lives in Bristol (see Hotwells); imprisoned in King's Bench Prison, London (Southwark: Scovell Rd.). *The Philosopher in Bristol* 1775 (37b), Verses for 'Dr. Syntax' (219a, b).

Compton-Burnett, Dame Ivy (1884–1969), novelist: lives in Hove (see Brighton) 1892–1916, London (Bayswater: Leinster Sq.) 1916–29, (Kensington: Cornwall Gdns.) 1934–69. *Pastors and Masters* 1925, *Brothers and Sisters* 1929 (165b), *Daughters and Sons* 1937, *Parents and Children* 1941, *Mother and Son* 1955 (199b).

Congreve, William (1670–1729), dramatist:

lives in Youghal 1674–8, Carrickfergus 1678–81; educ. Kilkenny and Dublin (Trinity College); visits Stretton Hall 1689; enters Middle Temple, London (City: Temple) 1691; lives in London (Strand: Surrey St.); frequents Kit-Cat Club in London (Barnes and Hampstead: Heath St.) and Will's Coffee House (Covent Garden); visits Ilam 1692; spends summers in Stowe; stays in Walton-on-Thames 1717 and 1719; visits Bath 1721 and 1722; buried in London (Westminster Abbey). *The Old Bachelor* 1693 (139a, 315b), *Love for Love* 1695 (165a, 222a), *The Way of the World* 1700 (222a).

Connolly, Cyril Vernon (1903–74), critic and essayist: educ. Eastbourne, Eton, and Oxford (Balliol College); lives in London (Regent's Park: Sussex Pl.) 1950s, Eastbourne 1970–4. *Enemies of Promise* 1938 (93b, 106b), *Horizon* 1939–50 (210b), *A Romantic Friendship* 1975 (262a).

Conrad, Joseph (Teodor Josef Konrad Korzeniowski) (1857–1924), Polish-born novelist: arrives in Lowestoft 1878; lives in London (Pimlico: Bessborough Gdns.) 1889–90, (Victoria: Gillingham St.) 1893–6; lives in Stanford-le-Hope 1896–8; visits Limpsfield 1898; lives in Postling 1898–1907, Aldington 1909–10, Orlestone 1910–19, Bishopsbourne 1920–4; buried in Canterbury. *Almayer's Folly* 1895 (209a, 226b), *The Outcast of the Islands* 1896 (226b), *Lord Jim* 1900, *The Inheritors* (with F. M. Ford) 1901 (283b), *Youth, Heart of Darkness, and Typhoon* 1902 (123b, 283b), *Romance* (with F. M. Ford) 1903, *Nostromo* 1904, *The Mirror of the Sea* 1906 (283b), *The Secret Agent* 1907 (188a), *Under Western Eyes* 1909 (4b), *Chance* 1913, *Victory* 1915, 'A Smile of Fortune' (257a).

Conway, Hugh. See Fargus, Frederick John.

Cooper, Edith Emma ('Michael Field') (1862–1913), poet and dramatist, with K. M. Bradley: b. Kenilworth; lives in Bristol (Stoke Bishop) 1878, in Reigate 1888. *Bellerophon* 1881, *Callirrhoë* 1885 (38a).

Cooper, James Fenimore (1789–1851), American novelist: visits London (Kensington: Holland House); Dover. *The Last of the Mohicans* 1826, *England, with Sketches of Society in the Metropolis* 1837 (79a).

Coppard, Alfred Edgar (1878–1957), short-story writer and poet: b. Folkestone; lives in Brighton 1881–1907; m. in Brighton 1906; lives in Oxford 1907–19, Combe c. 1914, Stanton St. John 1919–22; frequents Binsey; visits Yarnton 1907; lives in Thaxted; memorial in Thaxted. *Adam and Eve and Pinch Me* 1921 (309b, 346a), *Hips and Haws* 1922 (309b), *Clorinda Walks in Heaven* 1922 (66a, 309b), 'Ninepenny Flute', 'Pomona's Babe' (33b), 'The Sapling' (346a), 'The Poor Man', 'Arabesque', 'The Quiet Woman' (259b), *It's Me, O Lord* 1957 (112a, 259b, 346a), 'Piffing Cap' (66a).

Corbett, Richard (1582–1635), poet: educ. London (Westminster School) and Oxford (Christ Church); visits Warwick, Newark on Trent 1619; Dean of Christ Church, Oxford 1620; Bishop of Oxford 1628; lives in Oxford; Bishop of Norwich 1632. *Certain Elegant Poems* 1647, 'The Fairy's Farewell' (263b), 'Iter Boreale' (248b, 263b, 333b).

Corelli, Marie. See Mackay, Mary.

Corkery, Daniel (1878–1964), dramatist and scholar: b. and lives in Cork; Professor of English Literature at Cork. *The Threshold of Quiet* 1917 (68b), *The Study of Irish Literature* and *The Hidden Ireland* 1925 (68a, b), *The Labour, The Yellow Bittern, Fohnam the Sculptor* (68a).

Cornford, Frances Crofts (*née* Darwin) (1886–1960), poet: lives in Cambridge; m. in Cambridge 1908. 'In the Backs' in *Travelling Home* 1948, 'To a Fat Lady Seen from a Train' in *Collected Poems* 1954 (44a).

Cornford, Rupert John (1915–36), poet: b. Cambridge.

Cornwall, Barry. See Procter, Bryan Waller.

Cory, William Johnson (formerly William Johnson) (1823–92), poet: b. Great Torrington; educ. Eton and Cambridge (King's College); assistant master at Eton 1845–72. Translation of Callimachus' epitaph to Heraclitus, *Letters and Journals* 1897 (106b).

Coryate, Thomas (1577–1617), travel writer and wit: b. Odcombe; educ. Winchester and Oxford (Worcester College); lives in London (St. James's: St. James's Palace) 1607; frequents Mermaid Tavern (City: Bread St.). *Coryate's Crudities* 1611 (255b).

Cottle, Joseph (1770–1853), bookseller and publisher: lives in Bristol; visits Clevedon 1795, Nether Stowey 1796, Wrington 1814. *Early Recollections of Southey and Coleridge* 1837 (247b).

Cotton, Charles (1630–87), poet and translator: b. and lives in Beresford Dale; m. in Nottingham 1656; fishes in Dovedale; frequents Ilam; d. and is buried in London (St. James's: St. James's Church). *The Compleat Angler* 1676, *Wonders of the*

Peak 1681, Montaigne's *Essays* (trans.) 1685 (22a).

Cotton, Sir Robert Bruce (1571–1631), antiquary and collector of manuscripts: educ. London (Westminster School); lives in Chester; collection presented to British Museum, London (Bloomsbury) 1702.

Coverdale, Miles (1488–1568), translator of the Bible: Bishop of Exeter 1551–3; rector of St. Magnus the Martyr, London (City: Lower Thames St.) 1563–6, and buried there; commemorated in Paignton.

Coward, Sir Noël Pierce (1899–1972), dramatist: lives in London (Belgravia: Gerald Rd.) mid 1930s–mid 1950s. *Cavalcade* 1931, *This Happy Breed* 1943, *Present Indicative* 1937, *Future Indefinite* 1954 (166b).

Cowley, Abraham (1618–67), poet: educ. in London (Westminster School) and Cambridge (Trinity College); moves to Oxford (St. John's College) 1644–6; lives in Chertsey, London (Barnes: Barn Elms Pk.) 1663–5; buried in London (Westminster Abbey). 'On the Death of Mr. William Harvey' (49a).

Cowley, Mrs. Hannah (*née* Parkhouse) (1743–1809), dramatist and poet: b. Tiverton; d. and buried in Tiverton. *The Runaway* 1776, *The Belle's Stratagem* 1780, *A Bold Stroke for a Husband* 1783 (323b).

Cowper, William (1731–1800), poet: b. Berkhamsted; educ. Markyate and London (Westminster School); childhood holidays in Catfield; enters Middle Temple, London (City: Temple) 1748; attends St. George-the-Martyr church (Holborn: Queen St.); lodges in London (Bloomsbury: Russell Sq.) early 1750s; in asylum in St. Albans 1763–5; lives in Huntingdon 1765, Olney 1767–86; visits Gayhurst 1779; lives in Weston Underwood 1786–95; visits Eartham 1792; lives in Little Dunham 1795, Mundesley and East Dereham 1795–1800; buried in East Dereham; memorials in London (Edmonton) and Olney. *Olney Hymns* (with Newton) 1779 (256a), *Poems* 1782 (256b), *John Gilpin* 1782 (186b, 256b, 332b), *The Task* 1784 (256b), *Letters* 1803 (256a), 'On Receipt of my Mother's Picture out of Norfolk' (239b), 'To Mary', 'The Yardley Oak' (335b).

Crabbe, George (1755–1832), poet: b. Aldeburgh; educ. Stowmarket, apprenticed in Wickhambrook 1768; visits Cheveley 1796; apprenticed in Woodbridge 1771; works in Aldeburgh 1775; visits Beaconsfield 1781; ordained in Norwich 1782; chaplain at Belvoir Castle 1782–8; rector of Frome St. Quintin 1783; m. in Beccles

1783; curate in Stathern 1785–9; lives in Muston 1789–92; visits Aldeburgh and Lowestoft 1790; lives in Parham 1792, Great Glemham 1796–1801, Rendham 1801–5, Muston 1805–14, Trowbridge 1814–32; visits London (St. James's: Bury St. and Kensington: Holland House) 1817, Edinburgh 1822, Longleat 1824, Bath 1826, Hastings 1830, Bristol 1831; d. Merton; buried in Trowbridge; commemorated in Aldeburgh. *Inebriety* 1775, *The Candidate* 1780 (4a), *The Village* 1783 (4a, 19a, 21a), *The Newspaper* 1785 (21a), *The Borough* 1810 (4a, b), *Tales of the Hall* 1819 (212b).

Craigie, Pearl Mary Teresa ('John Oliver Hobbes') (1867–1906), novelist and dramatist: lives in Ventnor. *Some Emotions and a Moral* 1891, *The Ambassador* 1898 (330a), *Robert Orange* 1902 (330a, b).

Craik, Mrs. Dinah Maria (*née* Mulock) (1826–87), novelist: b. Stoke-on-Trent; lives in Newcastle under Lyme 1831, London (Hampstead: North End) 1857, (Bromley) 1865–87; d. and buried in London (Bromley and Keston); memorial in Tewkesbury. *John Halifax, Gentleman* 1857 (191a, 311b, 320b).

Crane, Stephen (1871–1900), American novelist and poet: lives in Oxted 1897, Rye 1899. *The Red Badge of Courage* 1895 (145a, 274b), *The Open Boat* 1898, *The Monster* 1899 (274b).

Cranmer, Thomas (1489–1556), biblical scholar and Archbishop of Canterbury: Fellow at Cambridge (Jesus College) 1515; stands trial in Oxford (St. Mary the Virgin) 1554; burnt at the stake in Oxford (see Martyrs' Memorial) 1556.

Crashaw, Richard (1612?–49), poet: educ. London (City: Charterhouse) and Cambridge (Pembroke College); Fellow at Cambridge (Peterhouse College) 1637–43.

Crocker, Charles (1797–1861), poet: b. and lives in Chichester; apprenticed to a shoemaker; becomes sexton at cathedral 1845; buried in subdeanery graveyard.

Crockett, Samuel Rutherford (1860–1914), poet, novelist, and minister: b. nr. Laurieston; lives in Penicuik 1886–95; buried nr. Laurieston. *Dulce Cor* 1887, *The Stickit Minister* 1893 (277b), *The Raiders* 1894, *The Lilac Sunbonnet* 1894 (154a, 277b).

Croker, John Wilson (1780–1857), editor and essayist and a founder of the *Quarterly Review*: educ. Dublin (Trinity College).

Croker, Thomas Crofton (1798–1854), antiquarian and folklorist: b. Cork; lives in Cork until 1818. *Researches in the South of Ireland* 1824 (67b), *The Fairy Legends and Traditions of the South of Ireland* 1825, *Legends of the Lakes* 1829, republished as *A Guide to the Lakes* 1831, *Killarney Legends* 1876 (68a).

Croly, George (1780–1860), novelist, poet, and playwright: b. and educ. Dublin. *Catiline* 1822, *Salathiel* 1829 (82a).

Cumberland, Richard (1732–1811), dramatist and novelist: b. Cambridge (Trinity College); educ. in London (Westminster School) and Cambridge (Trinity College); Fellow at Cambridge (Trinity College); stays in Clonfert 1771, London (Marylebone: Queen Anne St.) *c.* 1771; settles in Tunbridge Wells. *The West Indian* 1771 (63a, 192a, 205b).

Cunningham, Allan (1784–1842), poet: b. and self-educated nr. Dalswinton. 'A Wet Sheet and a Flowing Sea' (73b).

Cunningham, Peter (d. 1805), poet: curate at Eyam. 'Britannia's Naval Triumph', 'Russian Prophecy' (108b).

Cunninghame Graham, Robert (1735–97), poet: b. Gartmore; inherits Ardoch 1772; returns to Gartmore 1777; buried in Gartmore. 'If doughty deeds my lady please' (116a).

Cunninghame Graham, Robert Bontine (1852–1936), educ. London (Harrow on the Hill); lives in Gartmore 1885–1903, Ardoch 1903; imprisoned in London (Islington: Pentonville) 1887; visits Limpsfield; attends Conrad's funeral in Canterbury; buried in Inchmahome. *Father Archangel of Scotland* 1896 (116a), 'Sursum Corda' in *Success* 1902 (198b), *Doughty Deeds* (10a), 'Inveni Portum' in *Redeemed* 1927 (52a, 307a).

Daniel, Samuel (1562–1619), poet and dramatist: b. probably nr. Taunton; educ. Oxford (Hertford College); tutor at Skipton, Wilton; visits Titchfield, London (Twickenham: Twickenham Park); lives in Beckington 1610–19; buried in Beckington.

Darley, George (1795–1846), poet, critic, and editor of plays of Beaumont and Fletcher: b. and educ. Dublin; leaves Dublin for London 1822; lives in London (Victoria: Grosvenor Gdns.) 1827, 1830–9. *Sylvia* 1827 (226b), *Thomas à Becket: A Dramatic Chronicle* 1840 (51b).

Darwin, Erasmus (1731–1802), physician and poet: b. Elston; lives in Lichfield 1756–81. *The Botanic Garden* 1789–91 (156b).

Daudet, Alphonse (1840–97), French

Denham, Sir John (1615–68), poet and playwright: b. Dublin; educ. Oxford (Trinity College); enters Lincoln's Inn, London (Holborn) 1634, called to the Bar 1639; lives in Egham; buried in London (Westminster Abbey). *Cooper's Hill* 1642 (103a).

De Quincey, Thomas (1785–1859), essayist: b. and spends early years in Manchester; educ. Bath, Manchester, and Oxford (Worcester College); lives in Bath 1796–9; visits Dublin and Westport 1800; stays in Liverpool 1801, Chester 1802, London (Soho: Greek St.) 1802, Liverpool 1803; visits Grasmere, Nab Farm, Bristol (Hotwells 1807; meets Coleridge in Bridgwater 1807; stays in Grasmere 1808–9; rents Dove Cottage, Grasmere 1809–34; m. in Grasmere (see Nab Farm) 1817; stays in London (Covent Garden: Tavistock St.) 1821; owns Nab Farm 1829–33; frequents Edinburgh 1822–59; settles in Lasswade 1840; rents rooms in Glasgow 1841–7; buried in Edinburgh. 'Vision of Sudden Death' (236a), *Confessions of an English Opium Eater* 1821–2 (185a), 'On Murder as one of the Fine Arts' (1827 (35b, 99a), *Suspiria de Profundis* 1847 (274a).

Dermody, Thomas (1775–1802), poet: b. Ennis; teaches classics at Ennis for some years from 1784. 'Monody on the Death of Chatterton', 'Enthusiast', in *The Harp of Erin* 1807 (104b–105a).

De Vere, Aubrey (1814–1902), poet: b. Curragh Chase; educ. Dublin (Trinity College); lives and dies in Curragh Chase; buried in Askeaton. *The Waldenses and other poems* 1842, *The Legends of St. Patrick* 1872, *Critical Essays* 1887–9, *Recollections* 1897 (72b).

Dibdin, Charles (1745–1814), dramatist and song-writer: b. and spends early years in Southampton; lives in London (Soho: Charlotte St.) 1805–10, (Camden Town: Arlington Row); memorial in Southampton. *History of the Stage* 1795, 'Tom Bowling' (170b, 305b), 'Poor Jack' (305b), 'The Round Robin' (170b).

Dickens, Charles (1812–70), novelist: b. Portsmouth; educ. and lives in Chatham 1817–21; lives in London (Camden Town: Bayham St.) 1823–4; works as clerk in London (Holborn: Gray's Inn) 1827; posts first story in London (City: Fleet St.); lives in London (Marylebone: Bentinck St.) 1833–4; m. in London (Chelsea: St. Luke's) 1836; honeymoons in Chalk 1836; frequents Rochester, Cobham (Kent); lives in London (Holborn: Holborn)

1834–7, (Holborn: Doughty St.) 1837–9, (Twickenham: Ailsa Park Villas) 1838–9, (Marylebone: Marylebone Rd.) 1839–51, (Belgravia: Chester Row); establishes his parents in Alphington 1839–43; visits London (Richmond) 1836, 1839, Manchester 1837, 1852, Brighton 1837, 1848, Bowes, Liverpool 1838 and later, Barnard Castle 1838, Bath 1840, Stafford 1840s, Bonchurch 1849, Bristol (Clifton) 1851, Dover 1852, Leamington Spa 1855, 1862, Bury St. Edmunds 1859, 1861, Clovelly 1861, Chertsey, Ipswich, Ross-on-Wye 1867; performs in plays at Knebworth 1850, 1851; lives in London (Bloomsbury: Tavistock Sq.) 1851–60; buys house in Gad's Hill 1856; lives in Gad's Hill 1860–70; lodges in London (Kensington: Hyde Park Gate) 1862, (Marylebone: Gloucester Pl.) 1865; d. in Gad's Hill; buried in London (Westminster Abbey). *Sketches by Boz* 1835–6, 1836–7 (184b, 202b, 203a, 216b), *The Pickwick Papers* 1836–7 (17b, 19a, b, 39a, 42b, 56b–57a, 64b, 107b, 141a, 175b–176a, 176a, 178a, 194b, 211b, 223a, 287b, 316a, 320b), *Oliver Twist* 1838 (58a, 194b, 211b), *Nicholas Nickleby* 1839 (15b, 30a, 39a, 75a, 161a, 194b, 211b, 216b, 225b, 236b), *Master Humphrey's Clock* 1840–1 (15b), *The Old Curiosity Shop* 1841 (17b, 39a, 205a, 300a, 324a), *Barnaby Rudge* 1841 (39a, 60b, 194b, 205a), *A Christmas Carol* 1843 (205a), *Martin Chuzzlewit* 1843–4 (58a, 161a, 181b, 198b, 205a), *The Chimes* 1844 (176b), *Dombey and Son* 1848 (33b, 154b–155a, 205a), *David Copperfield* 1850 (26a, 26b, 39a, 52a, 56b, 125b, 174b, 211b, 220b, 223a), *Bleak House* 1852–3 (17b, 79a, b, 170a, 196b), *Hard Times* 1854 (170a, 236b), *Little Dorrit* 1857 (112a, 170a, 219a), *A Tale of Two Cities* 1859 (170a, 216a), *Great Expectations* 1861 (26b–27a, 55b–56a, 67b, 114a, b, 170a, 287b), *Our Mutual Friend* 1865 (114b), *Edwin Drood* 1870 (114b, 287b), *Bentley's Miscellany* 1837–9 (ed.) (207b), *American Notes* 1842 (205a), *Household Words* 1850–9, *All the Year Round* 1859–70 (223b), *Mr. Nightingale's Diary* (a play, privately printed) 1851 (36b, 170a), 'A Plated Article' in *Household Words* reprinted 1858 (308a), *The Uncommercial Traveller* 1860 (57a, 114b, 161a, 287b), 'The Holly Tree' in *Christmas Stories* 1871 (56b), 'A Message from the Sea' in *Christmas Stories* (with Wilkie Collins) 1871 (64a), *Mudfog Papers* 1880 (287b), 'Bound for the Great Salt Lake' (214b).

Dickinson, Goldsworthy Lowes (1862–1932), pacifist and critic: educ. Cambridge (King's College), Fellow 1886–1920; lives in London (Kensington: Edwardes Sq.) and Cambridge (King's College).

Digby, Sir Kenelm (1603–65), writer and diplomat: b. Gayhurst; educ. Oxford (Worcester College); lives and d. in London (Covent Garden).

Disraeli, Benjamin, 1st Earl of Beaconsfield (1804–81), statesman and novelist: b. London (Holborn: Theobald's Rd.); enters Lincoln's Inn, London (Holborn) 1824–31; m. in London (Mayfair: St. George's, Hanover Sq.) 1839; lives in Hughenden 1848–81; visits Bournemouth 1874–5; d. in London (Mayfair: Curzon St.); buried in Hughenden. *Coningsby* 1844 (78a), *Tancred* 1847 (137b), *Lothair* 1870 (6b, 137b, 325b), *Endymion* 1880 (30a, 137b).

D'Israeli, Isaac (1766–1848), miscellaneous writer: lives in Bradenham. *Curiosities of Literature* 1791 (30a).

Dobell, Sydney Thompson (1824–74), poet: b. Cranbrook; lives in Hucclecote 1846–8, Cheltenham 1848–53; visits Edinburgh 1854, Tintern Abbey 1858, Great Malvern; spends last years nr. Painswick; buried in Painswick. *The Roman* 1850 (57b, 137a), *Balder* 1854 (57b), 'Sonnets on the War' (with Alexander Smith) 1855 (100b).

Dobson, Henry Austin (1840–1921), poet and critic, author of *Eighteenth Century Vignettes* (1892, 1894, 1896): b. Plymouth.

Dodgson, Charles Lutwidge ('Lewis Carroll') (1832–98), scholar and writer for children: b. Daresbury; lives in Croft-on-Tees 1843; educ. Richmond, Rugby, and Oxford (Christ Church); lives in Oxford (Christ Church); vacations in Llandudno 1864, Guildford from 1868, and Eastbourne 1877–87; d. Guildford. *Alice's Adventures in Wonderland* 1865 (73b, 110b, 162a, b, 233b, 264b), *Through the Looking Glass* 1872 (264b), 'The Three Sunsets' (73b).

Dolben, Digby Mackworth (1848–67), poet: educ. Eton. *Poems* 1915, ed. R. Bridges (106b).

Donn, Rob. See Mackay, Robert.

Donne, John (1571/2–1631), poet and divine: b. London (City: Bread St.); educ. Oxford (Hertford College); enters Lincoln's Inn, London (Holborn) 1592; secretary to Sir Thomas Egerton at York House in London (Strand: The Strand) 1596–1601; imprisoned in London (City: Farringdon St.) 1601; frequents Mermaid Tavern in London (City: Bread St.); lives in Pyrford 1601, London (Mitcham) 1606–10; visits in London (Twickenham: Twickenham Park) 1605–10, Polesworth, and Montgomery 1613; preaches annually at Knole 1616–31; Dean of St. Paul's, London (City) 1621–31; visits Blunham annually as rector 1622–31; rector in London (City: St. Dunstan-in-the-West, Fleet St.); preaches in London (Chelsea Old Church); buried in St. Paul's (London: City). *Pseudo-Martyr* 1610, *Biathanatos*, *Ignatius His Conclave* 1611 (208b), *An Anatomie of the World* 1611 (131b), 'Good Friday 1613 Riding Westward', 'The Primrose, being at Montgomery Castle' (243a).

Doughty, Charles Montague (1843–1926), travel writer and poet: b. Theberton; educ. Cambridge (Gonville and Caius). *Travels in Arabia Deserta* 1888, *Dawn in Britain* 1906 (321a).

Douglas, Gavin (or Gawain) (1474?–1522), poet: educ. St. Andrews; appointed provost of St. Giles, Edinburgh 1501; appointed archbishop of St. Andrews 1514 and later imprisoned; lives in Perth; buried in London (Strand: Savoy St.). *The Palice of Honour* 1553?, *King Hart* 1786, *Aeneid* (trans.) 1553 (96a).

Douglas, George. See Brown, George Douglas.

Douglas, Keith Castellain (1920–44), poet: educ. Christ's Hospital and Oxford (Merton College). Poems published in *Kingdom Come*, *Cherwell* (ed.), help with *Augury* (269a).

Douglas, Norman (1868–1952), novelist and essayist: b. Tilquillie Castle; educ. Uppingham. *South Wind* 1917, *Looking Back* 1932 (322b).

Douglas, O. See Buchan, Anna.

Dowden, Edward (1843–1913), poet and Shakespearian scholar: b. Cork; educ. Cork and Dublin (Trinity College); becomes Professor of English Literature at Dublin 1867; buried in Dublin (Mount Jerome Cemetery).

Dowson, Ernest Christopher (1867–1900), poet: b. London (Lee); frequents the Rhymers' Club in London (City: Fleet St.) and the Café Royal (Mayfair: Piccadilly Circus). 'I have been faithful to thee, Cynara! in my fashion' in *Poems* 1896 (202b).

Dowson, Margaret Fairless. See Barber, Margaret Fairless.

Doyle, Sir Arthur Conan (1859–1930), novelist: b. Edinburgh; educ. Stonyhurst College, Whalley, and Edinburgh University; practises as doctor at Portsmouth

O Primo Basilio 1878, *Cousin Bazilio* 1953 trans. Roy Campbell, *Os Maias* 1880, *The Maias* 1965, trans. P. M. Pinheiro and A. Stevens, *A Reliquia* 1887, *The Relic* 1954, trans. A. F. G. Bell, *Letters from England* 1970, trans. A. Stevens (38a).

Edgeworth, Maria (1768–1849), novelist: b. Black Bourton; educ. Derby; school holidays at Northchurch 1776–80; lives in Edgeworthstown 1782–1849; visits Bristol (Clifton) 1791, 1799, Edinburgh 1803, 1823, Abbotsford 1823; buried in Edgeworthstown. *The Parent's Assistant* 1796–1800 (36a, 95b), *Practical Education* 1798, *Castle Rackrent* 1800 (95b), *Moral Tales* 1806 (36a).

Edwards, Richard (1523?–66), poet and playwright: educ. Oxford (Corpus Christi College and Christ Church); enters Lincoln's Inn, London (Holborn) 1547. *Palamon and Arcite* 1566 (263a).

Eglinton, John. See Magee, William Kirkpatrick.

Eliot, George. See Evans, Mary Ann or Marian.

Eliot, Thomas Stearns (1888–1965), poet and critic of American birth: educ. Oxford (Merton College), becomes Hon. Fellow 1949; works in London (Bloomsbury: Russell Sq.; City: Lombard St.) 1919–22; visits Rodmell and Garsington 1920s; buried in East Coker; memorials in London (Westminster Abbey) and Little Gidding. *The Waste Land* 1922 (179a, 288a), *Murder in the Cathedral* 1935 (51b), *Four Quartets* 1944 (93b, 159b), 'Rannoch by Glencoe' (119a).

Elliot, Jane (or Jean) (1727–1805), poet: b. Minto. 'The Flowers of the Forest' (112a).

Elliott, Ebenezer ('the Corn-Law Rhymer') (1781–1849), poet: b. nr. Rotherham; sets up iron business in Sheffield 1821; buried in Darfield; statue in Sheffield. 'Vernal Walk' 1798 (289a), *Tales of the Night* 1818 (289a, 298b), *The Village Patriarch* 1829 (74a, 298b); *Corn-Law Rhymes* 1831 (298b).

Elwin, Whitwell (1816–1900), critic and editor: b. nr. Booton; rector of Booton 1849–1900. *Quarterly Review* (ed.) 1853–60 (27a).

Emerson, Ralph Waldo (1803–82), American philosopher and poet: stays in London (Bloomsbury: Russell Sq.) 1833, (Strand: The Strand) 1847, 1848, Coventry 1848; lectures in Liverpool 1848. *Representative Men* 1850 (160b).

Erasmus, Desiderius (c. 1466–1536), Dutch humanist: rector of Aldington 1511; lives

at Cambridge while Reader in Greek (Queens' College) 1511–14. New Testament, trans. from Greek to Latin 1522 (135a).

Eusden, Laurence (1688–1730), poet: educ. York and Cambridge (Trinity College); Fellow at Cambridge (Trinity College); rector of Coningsby 1725–30.

Evans, Mary Ann or Marian ('George Eliot') (1819–80), novelist: b. nr. Nuneaton; educ. nr. Nuneaton and at Coventry; lives in Coventry 1841–9; visits Wirksworth; stays in London (Strand: The Strand) 1851; lives in London (Pimlico: Cambridge St.) 1853–4, (Richmond: Clarence Row and Park St.) 1855–9; works with George Lewes (Strand: Wellington St.); visits the Scilly Isles 1857, Gainsborough 1859; lives in London (Wimbledon) 1859–60, (Marylebone: Blandford Sq.) 1860–3, (Regent's Park: Lodge Rd.) 1863–80; visits Cambridge (Trinity College) and Oxford (Magdalen College and Lincoln College) 1873; stays in Shottermill 1871, Witley 1877–80; m. in London (Mayfair: St. George's Hanover Sq.) 1880; d. in London (Chelsea: Cheyne Walk); buried in Highgate cemetery (Highgate). *Amos Barton* 1857 (211a), *Mr. Gilfil's Love-Story* 1857 (296b–297a), *Janet's Repentance* 1857 (254a), *Scenes of Clerical Life* 1858 (211a, 254a, 296b–297a), *Adam Bede* 1859 (78b, 203b, 211a, 254a, 341b), *The Mill on the Floss* 1860 (114b–115a, 230a, 254a), *Silas Marner* 1861, *Romola* 1863 (203b), *Felix Holt* 1866, *The Spanish Gypsy* 1868, *The Legend of Jubal* 1870 (210b), *Middlemarch* 1871–2 (210b, 301b), *Daniel Deronda* 1874–6 (210b), *Theophrastus Such* 1879 (342b).

Evelyn, John (1620–1706), diarist: b. Wotton; educ. Lewes and Oxford (Balliol College); enters Middle Temple, London (City: Temple) 1640; lives in Wotton, London (Deptford: Sayes Court) 1653; visits Oxford (All Souls College and Balliol College), Audley End, Bath, Bristol (Hotwells), Cambridge (King's College), Penshurst 1652, Groombridge 1654, Tunbridge Wells; visits Pepys in London (Clapham Common) 1670, Norwich 1671, London (Vauxhall Gardens and Wanstead) 1683; lives in Wotton 1694–1706; stays in London (Mayfair: Dover St.) and d. there; buried in Wotton. His *Diary* 1955, refers to all the places mentioned above.

Ewing, Mrs. Juliana Horatia (*née* Gatty) (1841–85), writer of books for children: b. and grows up in Ecclesfield; lives in

Bowdon 1877–9, Trull 1883–5; buried in Trull; commemorated in Ecclesfield and Trull. *Aunt Judy's Magazine for Children* 1866 (95a), *A Flat Iron for a Farthing* 1870–1, *Six to Sixteen* 1872, *Jan of the Windmill* 1876 (29b), *Mary's Meadow* 1883–4, *Letters from a Little Garden* 1884–5 (326b).

Faber, Frederick William (1814–63), author of devotional books and hymns: b. Calverley; educ. Shrewsbury; becomes first head of Brompton Oratory in London (Kensington) 1849. 'My God, how wonderful Thou art', 'Pilgrims of the Night' (302b).

Fairless, Michael. See Barber, Margaret Fairless.

Falconer, William (1732–69), sailor and poet: b. Edinburgh. *The Shipwreck* 1762, revised 1764 and 1769 (96b–97a), *Universal Marine Dictionary* 1769 (97a).

Falkner, John Meade (1858–1932), novelist: educ. Marlborough and Oxford (Hertford College); lives and d. in Durham; buried in Burford. *The Lost Stradivarius* 1895 (266a), *Moonfleet* 1898 (52b, 111b), *The Nebuly Coat* 1903 (92a).

Fargus, Frederick John ('Hugh Conway') (1847–85), song-writer and author of the novel *Called Back* (1885): b. Bristol.

Farquhar, George (1678–1707), actor and dramatist: b. Londonderry; educ. Londonderry, Kilkenny, and Dublin (Trinity College); visits Lichfield and Shrewsbury 1705; buried in St. Martin-in-the-Fields, London (Strand: Trafalgar Sq.). *The Recruiting Officer* 1706 (302a, 332b), *The Beaux' Stratagem* 1707 (156b).

Farrar, Frederic William (1831–1903), novelist: educ. King William's College, I.O.M., and Cambridge (Trinity College); assistant master at Marlborough 1854, master at Harrow (London) 1855–70, Master at Marlborough 1871–6; rector in London (Westminster: St. Margaret's) 1876–95. *Eric, or Little by Little* 1858 (148a, 193a), *Julian Home, A Tale of College Life* 1859 (50a, 193a), *Life of Christ* 1874 (228a).

Fell, Dr. John (1625–86), promoter of the Oxford University Press: b. Longworth; educ. Thame; Dean of Christ Church, Oxford 1660; Bishop of Oxford 1676.

Fenton, Elijah (1683–1730), poet: b. Stoke-on-Trent; buried in Easthampstead. *The Odyssey* (trans. with Pope) 1725–6 (94a, 311b).

Ferguson, Sir Samuel (1810–86), poet and antiquary: b. Belfast; educ. Dublin; called to the Bar 1838 and lives in Dublin, becomes Deputy Keeper of the Records

of Ireland 1867; lives in Howth; buried in Donegore. 'Aideen's Grave', 'The Cromlech of Howth' (137a).

Fergusson, Robert (1750–74), poet: b. Edinburgh; educ. Edinburgh, Dundee, and St. Andrews; lives and d. in Edinburgh. *Poems by Robert Fergusson* 1773 (97b).

Ferrar, Nicholas (1592–1637), theologian and friend of George Herbert: founds religious community at Little Gidding 1625; memorials in Little Gidding and Bemerton.

Ferrier, Susan Edmonstone (1782–1854), novelist: b. Edinburgh; lives and d. in Edinburgh. *Marriage* 1818, *The Inheritance* 1824, *Destiny* 1831 (99a).

Ferriter, Pierce (d. 1653), one of the Four Kerry Poets: lives in Smerwick; d. Killarney; memorials in Killarney and Muckross.

Field, Michael. See Bradley, Katharine, and Cooper, Edith Emma.

Fielding, Henry (1707–54), novelist: b. Sharpham; educ. Eton; brings his wife to East Stour 1734; studies at Middle Temple, London (City: Temple) and is called to the Bar 1740; officiates in London (Covent Garden: Bow St.), meets Arthur Murphy in London (Covent Garden); lives in London (Twickenham: Holly Rd.) 1743–8, (Barnes) 1748–53, (Strand: Essex St.); visits Widcombe 1748. *Joseph Andrews* 1742 (94b), *Tom Jones* 1749 (94b, 185a, 225a, 330a, 337b), *Amelia* 1751 (175b), *Covent Garden Journal* 1752 (184b, 185a).

Fiennes, Celia (1662–1741), diarist: b. Newton Toney; visits Bath 1687, Cambridge 1697, Chester, Fowey, Holywell 1698, Burghley House, Bury St. Edmunds *c.* 1700, Epsom, Nottingham, and Worcester. *The Journeys of Celia Fiennes*, ed. C. Morris, 1947 (16a, 41a, 43b, 58b, 105a, 113b, 135b, 253a, 344b).

Finch, Anne, Countess of Winchilsea (1660–1720), poet, author of *The Spleen* 1709: lives in Canterbury.

Firbank, Arthur Annesley Ronald (1886–1926), novelist: b. London (Mayfair: Clarges St.); educ. Uppingham and Cambridge (Trinity Hall); lives in London (Chislehurst) 1886; visits Newport (Gwent) *c.* 1904; frequents Café Royal in London (Mayfair: Piccadilly Circus) 1913–14; lives in Oxford 1914–18; presents memorial to his parents to St. Julian's Church, Newport 1925. *Lady Appledore's Mésalliance* 1907 (173b), *Inclinations* 1916, *Caprice* 1917, *Valmouth* 1919 (259b).

FitzGerald, Edward (1809–83), poet and translator: b. Bredfield; educ. Bury St. Edmunds and Cambridge (Trinity College); visits Ipswich; visits Tennyson in London (Twickenham: Montpelier Row) 1851–3; lives in Woodbridge 1860–83; visits Merton and d. there; buried nr. Bredfield. *Euphranor* 1851 (49b–50a), *The Rubáiyát of Omar Khayyám* 1859 (31b, 141b).

Flecker, James Elroy (1884–1915), poet and playwright; educ. Uppingham, Oxford (Trinity College), and Cambridge (Gonville and Caius); lives in Cheltenham 1886– ; in sanatorium at Painswick 1910; buried in Cheltenham. *The Best Man* 1906, *Bridge of Fire* 1907 (273a), 'November Eves' (57b), 'Oak and Olive' in *The Old Ships* 1915 (57b, 275a, b).

Fleming, Marjory (1803–11), child author: b. and lives in Kirkcaldy; stays in Edinburgh; buried nr. Kirkcaldy. *Pet Marjorie* 1858, *The Complete Marjory Fleming*, ed. F. Sidgwick, 1934 (148b).

Fletcher, Giles, the Elder (1549?–1611), poet: educ. Eton and Cambridge (King's College). *Licia, or Poemes of Love* 1593 (46a).

Fletcher, Giles, the Younger (1588?–1623), poet: possibly b. Cranbrook; educ. London (Westminster School) and Cambridge (Trinity College); rector of Alderton *c.* 1618–23; buried in Alderton.

Fletcher, John (1579–1625), playwright: b. Rye; educ. Cambridge (Corpus Christi College); frequents Mermaid Tavern in London (City: Bread St.); buried in London (Southwark Cathedral).

Fletcher, Phineas (1582–1650), poet: possibly b. Cranbrook; educ. Eton and Cambridge (King's College); rector of Hilgay 1621–50. *The Purple Island or the Isle of Man* 1633 (134b).

Florence of Worcester (d. 1118), Benedictine monk and author of *Chronicon ex Chronicis*: lives and d. in Worcester.

Florio, John (1553?–1625), Italian-born lexicographer and translator: educ. Oxford (Magdalen College); stays in Titchfield 1590–1. *Italian–English dictionary* 1598 (266b).

Flower, Robin Ernest William (1881–1946), scholar and poet. *The Western Island* 1944 (25b).

Foote, Samuel (1720–77), actor and dramatist: b. and grows up in Truro; educ. Worcester and Oxford (Worcester College); d. in Dover; memorial in London (Westminster Abbey).

Ford, Ford Madox (originally Hueffer) (1873–1939), novelist: lives in Aldington 1890s; meets Conrad at Limpsfield 1898; lives in London (Kensington: Holland Park Ave.) 1908–10, (Kensington: Campden Hill Rd.) *c.* 1912–15. *The Inheritors* (with Conrad) 1901, *Romance* (with Conrad) 1903 (283b), *English Review* 1908–9 (ed.) (200a), *The Half Moon* 1909, *Some Do Not* 1924 (291b).

Ford, John (1586?–1640?), dramatist: b. nr. Ilsington; baptized Ilsington; educ. Oxford (Exeter College); enters Middle Temple, London (City: Temple). *'Tis Pity She's a Whore* 1633, *The Broken Heart* 1633 (139b).

Forster, Edward Morgan (1879–1970), novelist and essayist: childhood home at Stevenage; educ. Tonbridge and Cambridge (King's College); lives in Abinger Hammer 1902–45; visits Grantchester 1909; lives in London (Bloomsbury: Brunswick Sq.) 1929–39; member of 'Bloomsbury Group' (Gordon Sq.); lives in Cambridge (King's College) 1946–70. *The Longest Journey* 1907 (46a, b), *Howards End* 1910, 'Ansell' (310a), *The Celestial Omnibus* 1914, *A Passage to India* 1924, *The Eternal Moment* 1928 (3a), *Goldsworthy Lowes Dickinson* 1934 (46b), *Abinger Harvest* 1936 (3a), *Marianne Thornton* 1956 (311a), 'My Wood' (3a).

Forster, John (1812–76), biographer and dramatic critic: b. Newcastle upon Tyne; educ. Newcastle; enters Inner Temple, London (City: Temple) 1828; lives in London (Holborn: Lincoln's Inn Fields) 1832, (Marylebone: Montagu Sq.) 1850s; buried in London (Kensal Green Cemetery). *Charles at Tunbridge* 1828 (249a, b), *Goldsmith* 1854, *Landor* 1869, *Dickens* 1872–4 (196b).

Fothergill, John Rowland (1876–1957), miscellaneous writer: innkeeper in Thame 1922–32. *An Innkeeper's Diary* 1931 (320b).

Foxe, John (1516–87), martyrologist: b. Boston; educ. Oxford (Magdalen College); tutor in Reigate *c.* 1547–53; Canon of Salisbury 1563; lives in Waltham Abbey 1565 onwards; buried in St. Giles Cripplegate, London (City: Fore St.). *Actes and Monuments* 1563 (266b).

Franklin, Benjamin (1706–90), American statesman and writer: stays in London (Strand: Craven St.) 1757–62, 1764–72 and works at printing press (Smithfield: St. Bartholomew-the-Great) 1757; visits Twyford 1771. *Autobiography* 1868 (220b, 328a).

Frazer, Sir James George (1854–1941), social anthropologist: educ. Cambridge (Trinity College), Fellow (Trinity College) 1879; Professor at Liverpool 1907–22; lives in Cambridge (Trinity College) 1922–41. *The Golden Bough*, 12 vols. 1890–1915 (50a, 161b).

Freeman, Richard Austin (1862–1943), detective-story writer and doctor: lives and is buried in Gravesend. *The Red Thumb Mark* 1907 (123b).

Frost, Robert Lee (1874–1963), American poet: visits Dymock 1914 and 1957.

Froude, James Anthony (1818–94), historian and novelist: b. Dartington; educ. London (Westminster School) and Oxford (Oriel College); Fellow at Oxford (Exeter College) 1842–9; visits Bath 1848; lives in London (Kensington: Onslow Gdns.) 1862–92; visits Lauragh 1867, 1869–70; Professor of Modern History at Oxford (Exeter) 1892; retires to Salcombe 1894 and is buried there. *The Nemesis of Faith* 1849 (265a), *The English in Ireland in the Eighteenth Century*, 3 vols. 1872–4, *The Two Chiefs of Dunboy* 1889 (153b).

Fuller, Thomas (1608–61), historian and theologian: b. Aldwinkle; educ. Cambridge (Queens' and Sidney Sussex Colleges); perpetual curate at Cambridge (Corpus Christi College) 1630; lectures in London (Strand: Savoy St.) 1642; comes to Exeter with Royalists 1643; perpetual curate in Waltham Abbey 1649–58; rector in London (Cranford) 1658; lectures in London (Strand: Savoy St.) 1660; d. and is buried in London (Covent Garden and Cranford). *History of the University of Cambridge* 1655 (47b), *Church History of Britain* 1655 (331b), *The Worthies of England* 1662 (107b, 185b, 331b).

Furness, Richard (1791–1857), poet: b. Eyam; lives in Eyam 1813–21 and is buried there. *Rag Bag* 1832, *Medicus-Magus* 1836 (108b).

Furnivall, Frederick James (1825–1910), scholar and founder of the Early English Text Society: b. Egham; educ. Cambridge (Trinity Hall).

Galsworthy, John (1867–1933), novelist and playwright: b. London (Kingston upon Thames); educ. Bournemouth, London (Harrow on the Hill), and Oxford (New College); called to the Bar from Lincoln's Inn, London (Holborn) 1890; m. in London (Mayfair: St. George's) 1904; spends summers at Manaton 1904–19; visits Limpsfield; lives in London (Adelphi: Adelphi Ter.) 1912–18; refuses knighthood in Littlehampton 1918; lives in London (Hampstead: Admiral's Walk) 1918–33; spends much time at his country house in Bury 1920–33; ashes scattered nr. Bury. *The Man of Property* 1906 (157b), *The Country House* 1907, *Fraternity* 1909 (235a), *Strife* 1911 (161b), *Saint's Progress* 1919 (159b), *The Forsyte Saga* 1922, *A Modern Comedy* 1929 (189b), *Life and Letters* by H. V. Marrot 1935 (235b).

Galt, John (1779–1839), novelist: b. Irvine; spends adolescence at Greenock; imprisoned in London (Southwark: Scovell Rd.) 1829; retires to Greenock 1834–9; buried in Greenock. *Annals of the Parish* 1821, reprinted 1967 (141b).

Garnett, Constance (1861–1946), translator of Russian classics: lives in Limpsfield from 1896.

Garnett, Richard (1835–1906), miscellaneous writer: b. Lichfield; official at the British Museum, London (Bloomsbury) 1875–99. *The Twilight of the Gods* 1888 (157a).

Garrod, Heathcote William (1878–1960), critic, scholar, and poet: Fellow and Professor of Poetry at Oxford (Merton College); buried in St. Cross churchyard, Oxford. *Oxford Poems* 1912 (268b).

Gascoigne, George (1525?–77), poet: educ. Cambridge (Trinity College); enters Gray's Inn, London (Holborn); accompanies Queen Elizabeth I to Kenilworth 1575. *The Princely Pleasures of the Court of Kenilworthe* 1575 (143b), *The Queen's Majestie's Entertainment at Woodstock* 1575 (343a).

Gaskell, Mrs. Elizabeth Cleghorn (*née* **Stevenson**) (1810–65), novelist and author of *The Life of Charlotte Brontë* (1857): b. London (Chelsea: Cheyne Walk); educ. Stratford-upon-Avon; lives and is m. in Knutsford 1832; lives in Manchester from 1832; meets Charlotte Brontë at Briery Close 1850; visits Ashbourne 1850s, Haworth 1853, Whitby 1859; lodges at Silverdale; buys house and d. at Holybourne; buried in Knutsford. Chapter on Stratford-upon-Avon in W. Howitt's *Visits to Remarkable Places* 1840 (314b–315a), *Mary Barton* 1848 (236a), *Ruth* 1853 (150b, 303a), *Cranford* 1853 (150b), *North and South* 1855 (236a, b), *Sylvia's Lovers* 1863 (337a), *Letters*, ed. J. A. V. Chapple and A. Pollard, 1966 (33a).

Gatty, Mrs. Margaret (1809–73), writer for children: lives in Ecclesfield. *Aunt Judy's Magazine* est. 1866, *Parables from Nature* 1855–71 (95a).

Gauden, Dr. John (1605–62), theologian: b. Mayland; educ. Oxford (Wadham College); incumbent of Bocking 1641–60; Bishop of Exeter 1660–2, of Worcester

1662; lives in Hartlebury 1662; buried in Worcester. *Eikon Basilike* 1649 (26a, 128b).

Gay, John (1685–1732), poet and dramatist: b. and educ. Barnstaple; secretary to the Duchess of Monmouth in London (Chelsea: Lawrence St.) *c.* 1714; visits Cirencester 1718, Bath 1721, 1724, Tunbridge Wells 1723, Amesbury 1728, Edinburgh 1729, Rousham; lives in London (Richmond); d. in London (Mayfair: Old Burlington St.) and buried in Westminster Abbey. *The Captives* 1724 (327b), *The Beggar's Opera* 1728 (7b, 96a), *Polly* 1729 (96a, 145b).

Geoffrey of Monmouth (1100?–54), theologian and chronicler: studies at Oxford *c.* 1129; Archdeacon of Llandaff *c.* 1140; d. Llandaff. *Historia Regum Britanniae* 1136, printed 1508 (53a, 118b–119a, 162a).

Gerard, John (1545–1612), herbalist and barber-surgeon: *Herball or generall Historie of Plantes* 1597 (308a).

Gibbings, Robert John (1889–1958), wood engraver and travel writer: lives and is buried in Long Wittenham. *Sweet Thames run Softly* 1940, *Till I End My Song* 1957 (230b).

Gibbon, Edward (1737–94), historian: b. London (Putney); educ. London (Westminster School) and Oxford (Magdalen College); lives in Buriton 1758–72; in the Militia at Cranbrook and Sissinghurst Castle 1760; lives in London (St. James's: Pall Mall) 1769, (Marylebone: Bentinck St.) 1773–83; visits Fletching 1793, Bath 1793; d. in London (St. James's: St. James's St.); buried in Fletching. *History of the Decline and Fall of the Roman Empire* 1776–88 (41a, b, 203a), *Memoirs of my Life and Writings* (*Autobiography*) 1796 (184b, 203a, 209b), *Miscellaneous Works* 1796 (111b).

Gibson, Wilfrid Wilson (1878–1962), poet: b. Hexham; lives in Dymock 1914, London (Hampstead: Nassington Rd.) 1934–9. 'The Old Nail Shop' (92b), *Collected Poems* (*1905–25*) 1926 (191a), *The Golden Room* 1928 (92b), *Within Four Walls* 1950 (191a).

Gifford, William (1756–1826), poet, critic, and classical scholar: author of *The Baviad* and *The Maeviad*: b. Ashburton; educ. Ashburton and Oxford (Exeter College); spends last years and d. in London (St. James's: Buckingham Gate); buried in Westminster Abbey. *Anti-Jacobin* (ed.) (212a), *Quarterly Review* (ed.) 1809–25 (206b, 212a).

Gilbert, Mrs. Joseph (*née* **Ann Taylor**) (1782–1866), author of rhymes and stories for children: spends childhood in Lavenham until 1796; lives in Colchester 1796–1811, Ongar 1811 until marriage 1814; lives in Nottingham and is buried there. *Original Poems for Infant Minds* 1804, *Rhymes for the Nursery* 1806, and *Hymns* 1810 (all with her sister, Jane) (65a).

Gilbert, Sir William Schwenck (1836–1911), poet and writer of comic operas: educ. London (Strand: King's College, The Strand); lives in London (Kensington: Harrington Gdns.) 1883–90, (Harrow Weald) 1890–1911, (Belgravia: Eaton Sq.) 1907–11; d. and is buried in London (Harrow Weald). *Princess Ida* 1884, *The Mikado* 1885, *Ruddigore* 1887, *The Yeomen of the Guard* 1888, and *The Gondoliers* 1889 (200a), *Fallen Fairies* 1909, *The Hooligans* 1911 (166a, b).

Gilpin, William (1724–1804), writer and illustrator of tours: b. Scaleby Castle; educ. Oxford (The Queen's College); vicar of Boldre 1777–1804; tours the Lake District; visits Nuneham Courtenay; buried in Boldre. *Latimer* 1755, *Wycliffe* 1765, and *Cranmer* 1784 (271a), *Remarks on Forest Scenery* 1791, *Picturesque Tours* 1882 (26b), *Guide to the Lakes* 1789 (151b).

Giraldus Cambrensis (Gerald de Barri) (1146?–1223?), travel writer and chronicler: b. Manorbier; rector of Tenby 1172–5; elected bishop of St. David's; buried in St. David's. *Itinerarium* (238a, 293a).

Gissing, George Robert (1857–1903), novelist: b. Wakefield; educ. Manchester; lives in London (Chelsea: Oakley Gdns.), (Bloomsbury: Colville Pl.) 1878, (Marylebone: Cornwall Residences) 1884–90; visits Meredith at Mickleham; lives in Exeter 1891, Dorking 1898. *The Unclassed* 1884, *Isabel Clarendon* 1886, *Demos: A Story of English Socialism* 1886, *Thyrza* 1887 (203b), *A Life's Morning* 1888 (203b, 331a), *The Nether World* 1889, *The Emancipated* 1890 (203b), *New Grub Street* 1891 (177b), *Born in Exile* 1892 (107b), *The Private Papers of Henry Ryecroft* 1903 (107b, 168a).

Glanvill, Joseph (1636–80), theologian: b. Plymouth; educ. Oxford (Exeter College); rector of the Abbey Church, Bath 1666; buried in Bath. *The Vanity of Dogmatizing* 1661 (265a), *Sadducismus Triumphatus* 1666 (16a).

Gleig, George Robert (1796–1888), novelist, essayist, and biographer: b. Stirling;

educ. Oxford (Magdalen Hall). *The Subaltern* 1826 (267b–268a).

Godley, Alfred Denis (1856–1925), poet and classical scholar: Fellow at Oxford (Magdalen College) 1883–1912, and Public Orator 1910–25. *Verses to Order* 1892, *Lyra Frivola* 1899, *Fifty Poems* 1927 (267b).

Godolphin, Sidney (1610–43), poet: b. Godolphin House; killed in Chagford.

Godwin, Mrs. Mary Wollstonecraft (*née* **Wollstonecraft**) (1759–97), writer on education and women's rights: keeps a school in London (Stoke Newington); buried in Bournemouth. *Thoughts on the Education of Daughters* 1787, *Original Stories from Real Life* 1788 (220a), *A Vindication of the Rights of Women* 1792 (29b).

Godwin, William (1756–1836), philosopher and novelist: b. Wisbech; attends Coleridge's lectures in London (City: Crane Court); buried in Bournemouth. *Enquiry concerning Political Justice* 1793 (29b).

Gogarty, Oliver St. John (1878–1957), poet, playwright, and surgeon: b. and educ. Dublin; entertains at Rinvyle. *As I was going down Sackville Street* 1937 (84b).

Golding, Louis (1895–1958), novelist: b. and educ. Manchester. *Magnolia Street* 1931, *Five Silver Daughters* 1934 (237b).

Goldsmith, Oliver (1730?–74), poet, playwright, and novelist: b. Pallas or Elphin; baptized in Forgney; lives when a boy in Lissoy and frequents Kilkenny West; educ. Lissoy, Edgeworthstown, and Dublin; spends night in Ardagh; studies medicine in Edinburgh (University) 1752–4; lives in London (City: Green Arbour Ct.) 1759–60, (City: Fleet St., Wine Office Ct.) 1760–2, (Islington: Canonbury Tower) 1762–7, and visits Smollett in Chelsea (Lawrence St.), and 'Don Saltero's' (Cheyne Walk); visits Easton Maudit; thought to have visited Nuneham Courtenay 1761; visits Bath 1762, 1771, Leverington; lives in and nr. London (City: Temple) 1767–74, (Kingsbury) 1771–4; buried in London (City: Temple Church), and commemorated in Westminster Abbey. *Enquiry into the present State of Polite Learning* 1759 (178a), *Memoirs of M. Voltaire* (177a), 'Chinese Letters', later *The Citizen of the World* 1762 (178a), *The Traveller* 1764 (181a, 198a), *The Vicar of Wakefield* 1766 (177a, 309a), *The Good Natur'd Man* 1768 (181a), 'The Revolution in Low Life' in *New Essays* 1927 (254a, b), *The Deserted Village* 1770 (145b, 158b, 181a, 254a, b), *The History of England* 1771

(202a), *She Stoops to Conquer, or The Mistakes of a Night* 1773 (10a, 155b, 202a), *History of the Earth and Animated Nature* 1774 (202a).

Gordon, Adam Lindsay (1833–70), Australian poet: commemorated in London (Westminster Abbey). *Bush Ballads and Galloping Rhymes* 1870 (229a).

Gosse, Sir Edmund (1849–1928), essayist, poet, and critic: introduces Mallarmé to Swinburne in London (Bloomsbury: Great James St.) 1875; lives in London (Regent's Park: Hanover Ter.) 1901–28. *Father and Son* 1907 (210a).

Gosson, Stephen (1554–1624), poet and dramatist: baptized in Canterbury; educ. Oxford (Corpus Christi College); rector of Great Wigborough 1591–1600, and of St. Botolph's in London (City: Crosby Sq.) 1600–24. *Schoole of Abuse* 1579 (125a).

Gould, Nathaniel (1857–1919), sporting novelist: b. Manchester; educ. Southport.

Gower, John (1325?–1408), poet and classical scholar: lives in London and is buried in Southwark Cathedral (Southwark: Borough High St.). *Speculum Meditantis, Confessio Amantis, Vox Clamantis* (218a, b).

Graham, Robert. See Cunninghame Graham, Robert.

Grahame, Kenneth (1859–1932), novelist: b. Edinburgh; lives in Cookham Dean 1864–6; educ. Oxford; works at Bank of England, London (City: Threadneedle St.) 1898–1908; visits Fowey 1899; m. there 1899; lives in London (Kensington: Phillimore Pl.) 1901–8, Cookham Dean 1908–10, Blewbury 1910–24, Pangbourne 1924–32; buried in Oxford. *The Golden Age* 1895 (67a, 101a), *Dream Days* 1898 (67a), *The Wind in the Willows* 1908 (67a, 113b, 201b, 262a, 276a).

Grant, Mrs. Anne (1755–1838), poet and essayist: lives in Laggan 1779–1808. *Letters from the Mountains* 1803, *Memoirs of an American Lady* 1808 (151a).

Graves, Alfred Perceval (1846–1931), ballad and song writer: b. and educ. Dublin; lives in Taunton 1882–95. 'Father O'Flynn' 1875 (84a), *Songs of Old Ireland* (319b).

Graves, Richard (1715–1804), poet and novelist: educ. Oxford (Pembroke College); rector of Claverton 1739–1804. *The Spiritual Quixote* 1772 (61b–62a, 79b, 270b), *Columella, or the Distressed Anchoret* 1776 (62a, 270b), *Eugenius or Anecdotes of the Golden Vale* 1785, *Plexippus or the Aspiring Plebian* 1790 (62a).

London (Adelphi: Adelphi Ter.) 1862–7; works in London (Strand: Clement's Inn) 1870; visits St. Juliot 1870; m. in London (Paddington: Elgin Ave.) 1874; lives in Sturminster Newton 1878, London (Tooting) 1878–81, Wimborne 1881–3, Dorchester 1885–1928; visits Bonchurch 1910, Plymouth 1913, Oxford (The Queen's College) 1920, 1922; buried in London (Westminster Abbey) and his heart buried in Stinsford. *Under the Greenwood Tree* 1872 (134a, 311a), *A Pair of Blue Eyes* 1873 (27b, 294a), *Far from the Madding Crowd* 1874 (134a, 284a, b), *The Return of the Native* 1878 (315b–316a), *The Trumpet-Major* 1880 (224b, 283b, 336b), *Two on a Tower* 1882 (338b), *The Mayor of Casterbridge* 1886 (77b), *The Woodlanders* 1887 (299b), *Tess of the d'Urbervilles* 1891 (21b, 29b, 316a, 340a, 343b), *A Group of Noble Dames* 1891 (299b), *Jude the Obscure* 1895 (110b, 259a, 297b), *The Well-Beloved* 1897 (94a, 282b), *The Dynasts* 1903–8 (271b), 'Domicilium' 1850s (134a), 'A Church Romance' 1835, 'Afternoon Service at Mellstock' 1850 (311a), 'To a Tree in London' 1870 (220b), 'Copying architecture in an old minster' (338b), 'A Singer Asleep' 1910 (27a), 'The West-of-Wessex Girl' 1913 (281b).

Harington, Sir John (1561–1612), poet and translator: educ. Eton and Cambridge (King's College); lives in Kelston. *Orlando Furioso* 1591 (143a), *Nugae Antiquae* 1769 (143b).

Harris, Frank (1856–1931), journalist and miscellaneous writer: b. Galway.

Harrison, William (1534–93), topographical writer: educ. London (Westminster School); rector of Radwinter 1559–93. *Description of England, Description of Scotland* (trans.), in Holinshed's *Chronicles* 1577 (285a).

Harrison, William (1665–1713), poet: educ. Oxford (New College), Fellow at Oxford (New College) 1706–13. 'Woodstock Park' (269a, 343b).

Harte, Francis Brett ('Bret Harte') (1836–1902), American novelist, author of *The Luck of Roaring Camp* (1870): Consul in Glasgow 1880–5; buried in Frimley.

Hartley, Leslie Poles (1895–1972), novelist: b. nr. Peterborough; educ. London (Harrow) and Oxford (Balliol College); spends youth in Peterborough; visits Oxford (Wadham College). *The Killing Bottle* 1932 (280a), *The Shrimp and the Anemone* 1944 (137b, 280a), *Eustace and Hilda* 1947 (137a), *The Go-Between* 1953, *The Brickfield* 1964 (280a).

Harvey, Gabriel (1545?–1630), poet and critic: b. Saffron Walden; educ. Cambridge (Christ's College); Fellow at Cambridge (Pembroke College) 1570; entertains Queen Elizabeth I at Audley End.

Hawker, Robert Stephen (1803–75), poet and antiquary: b. Plymouth; educ. Oxford (Pembroke and Magdalen Colleges); vicar of Morwenstow 1835–74; buried in Plymouth. 'Pompeii' 1827 (267a), *The Quest of the Sangraal* 1863 (244a), 'The Song of the Western Men' 1825 (244a, 267a).

Hawkins, Sir Anthony Hope ('Anthony Hope') (1863–1933), novelist: educ. Marlborough and Oxford (Balliol College); called to the Bar in Middle Temple, London (City: Temple) 1887; lives in London (Bloomsbury: Bedford Sq.) 1903–17; lives and d. in Walton on the Hill; buried in Leatherhead. *The Prisoner of Zenda* 1894 (181a), *Memories and Notes* 1927 (332a).

Hawthorne, Nathaniel (1804–64), American novelist: U.S. Consul in Liverpool 1853–7; lives in Rock Ferry 1853–6; visits Bath, Lichfield, Woodstock, Uttoxeter; lives in London (Blackheath) 1856, visits Green Arbour Ct. (City), Leamington 1858. *The Scarlet Letter* 1850 (167a), *Tanglewood Tales* 1853 (287b–288a), *Our Old Home* 1863, reprinted 1970 (155a, 157a, 160b, 167a, 330b), *Journal* in *Passages from the English Notebooks* 1870, reprinted 1962 (287b).

Haydon, Benjamin Robert (1786–1846), painter, friend of Keats, and author of *Lectures on Painting and Design* (1846): lives in London (Soho: Great Marlborough St.) 1808–17; stays in Hastings, Playford 1840, Walmer. *Autobiography* 1853 (216b, 331b).

Hayley, William (1745–1820), poet and biographer: b. Chichester; educ. Cambridge (Trinity Hall); enters Middle Temple, London (City: Temple) 1766; lives in London (Holborn: Great Queen St.) *c.* 1770, Eartham, Felpham; d. and is buried in Felpham. 'Ode on the Birth of the Prince of Wales' (50b), *Ballads founded on Anecdotes of Animals* 1805 (111a).

Hazlitt, William (1778–1830), critic and essayist: b. Maidstone; early years at Bandon and Wem; educ. London (Stoke Newington); frequents Shrewsbury; visits Liverpool 1790, Nether Stowey, Lynmouth 1797, Llangollen 1798; m. in London (Holborn Circus: St. Andrew's) 1808; lives in Winterslow from 1808; d. London (Soho: Frith St.) and buried in St. Anne's (Soho: Wardour St.). Letter to the *Shrewsbury Chronicle* 1791 (302a), *Memoirs of Thomas Holcroft* (ed.) 1816 (341b), 'Farewell to Essay Writing' (341a), *Winterslow* 1839 (341b), 'On Going a Journey' in *Table-Talk* 1821-2 (162b).

Hearne, Thomas (1678-1735), antiquary: educ. Oxford (St. Edmund Hall); visits Ditchley; buried in Oxford. *Reliquiae Bodleianae* 1703 (271b), *Remarks and Collections*, ed. C. E. Doble, D. W. Rannie, *et al.*, 11 vols. 1885-1921 (76b, 271b).

Heber, Reginald (1783-1826), hymn-writer: vicar of Hodnet 1807-23; his chair preserved at Bridgnorth. 'From Greenland's Icy Mountains' (135a).

Heine, Heinrich (1797-1856), German poet: visits London (Strand: Craven St.) 1827.

Hemans, Mrs. Felicia Dorothea (*née* Browne) (1793-1835), poet: b. and spends early years in Liverpool; lives in St. Asaph 1809-12, 1812-25; returns to Liverpool 1827-31; visits Ambleside 1829-31; lives in Dublin 1831-5; buried in Dublin. 'Casabianca' (292b), *The Forest Sanctuary* 1826 (160a).

Henley, William Ernest (1849-1903), poet and critic: b. and educ. Gloucester; lives in London (Muswell Hill) 1896-9; memorial in London (City: St. Paul's Cathedral).

Henryson (or Henderson), Robert (1430?-1506), Scottish poet: probably a founder of Glasgow University.

Henslowe, Philip (d. 1616), theatrical manager: manages theatres in London (Southwark: Bankside), (Finsbury: Fortune St.), (Dulwich). *Diary* 1592-1609 (186a, b, 187b, 218a).

Henty, George Alfred (1832-1902), writer of boys' stories and novelist: educ. London (Westminster School); lives in London (Battersea: Lavender Gdns.); d. Weymouth; buried in London (Kensington: Brompton cemetery). *With Clive in India* 1884, *With Moore at Corunna* 1898, *With Buller in Natal* 1901 (165b).

Herbert, George (1593-1633), poet: b. Montgomery; educ. London (Westminster School) and Cambridge (Trinity College); Fellow at Cambridge (Trinity College) 1616 and Public Orator 1619-27; prebend of Leighton Broomswold; visits Dauntsey; rector of Bemerton 1630-2; buried in Bemerton and commemorated in Little Gidding. *The Temple* 1634 (21b, 159b), 'The Elixir' (155b).

Herrick, Robert (1591-1674), poet: apprenticed to his uncle in London (City:

Wood St.) *c.* 1604-14; educ. Cambridge (St. John's College); vicar of Dean Prior 1629-47, 1662-74; buried in Dean Prior. *Noble Numbers* 1647, *Hesperides* 1648 (75a, b), *Poetical Works*, ed. L. C. Martin, 1956 (75b).

Hewlett, Maurice (1861-1923), novelist, poet, and essayist: lives and d. in Broad Chalke. *The Song of the Plow* 1916, *Wiltshire Essays* 1921 (38b).

Hickey, William (1749-1830), writer of memoirs: lives Beaconsfield from 1809. *The Memoirs of William Hickey* 1913-25, 1960, 1975 (18b).

Higden, Ranulf (d. 1364), chronicler: monk at Chester and buried in the cathedral. *Polychronicon c.* 1342 (58b, 108a).

Hill, Aaron (1685-1750), poet and dramatist: educ. London (Westminster School); lives in London (St. James's: Petty France); associated with Theatre Royal (Covent Garden: Catherine St.); buried in Westminster Abbey. *Rinaldo* libretto 1711, *Athelwold* 1732, *Zara* 1736 (213a).

Hobbes, John Oliver. See Craigie, Pearl Mary Teresa.

Hobbes, Thomas (1588-1679), philosopher: b. Malmesbury; educ. Oxford (Magdalen Hall); spends last years and is buried in Ault Hucknall. *Leviathan* 1651 (308a).

Hocking, Joseph (1860-1937), minister and novelist: b. St. Stephen.

Hocking, Silas Kitto (1850-1935), novelist: b. St. Stephen. *Alec Green* 1878 (294b).

Hodgson, Ralph (1871-1962), poet: b. Darlington. *The Last Blackbird and other Lines* 1907, *Poems* 1917, *The Skylark and Other Poems* 1958 (74a).

Hogg, James ('the Ettrick Shepherd') (1770-1835), poet and novelist: b. Ettrick; stays at Edinburgh 1803 and later; granted farm in Altrive Lake 1815, his main home for the rest of his life; frequents Tibbie Shiel's Inn; meets Scott at Gordon Arms; buried in Ettrick. 'The Forest Minstrel' 1810, *The Queen's Wake* 1813, *The Private Memoirs and Confessions of a Justified Sinner* 1824 (98b).

Hogg, Thomas Jefferson (1792-1862), friend and biographer of Shelley: b. Norton; educ. Durham and Oxford (University College). 'Posthumous Fragments of Margaret Nicholson' (with Shelley) (273a).

Holcroft, Thomas (1745-1809), actor and playwright: b. London (Soho: Leicester Sq.) and baptized at St. Martin-in-the-Fields (Strand: Trafalgar Sq.); works in Mayfair (South Audley St.) as a boy; lives in Marylebone (Marylebone St.) 1780s; d. in Marylebone (Clipstone St.) and buried at Marylebone Parish Church. *Le Mariage de Figaro* (trans.) 1784 (208a).

Holinshed, Raphael (d. 1580), chronicler: educ. Cambridge (Trinity Hall). *Chronicles* 1577 (110b, 285a).

Holtby, Winifred (1898–1935), novelist: b. Rudston; educ. Oxford (Somerville College); buried in Rudston. *The Land of Green Ginger* 1927, *Poor Caroline* 1931, *Virginia Woolf: A Critical Study* 1932 (272a), *South Riding* 1936 (272a, 289b).

Home, John (1722–1808), minister and author of the romantic tragedy *Douglas* (1756): imprisoned in Doune 1745–6.

Hood, Thomas (1799–1845), poet and journalist: b. London (City: Poultry); lives in London (Islington: Essex St.); convalesces in Dundee 1815–17; spends honeymoon in Hastings 1825; lives in London (Adelphi) 1827, (Winchmore Hill) 1829–32, (Wanstead) 1832–5, (St. John's Wood: Elm Tree Rd. and Finchley Rd.) 1841–5; buried in London (Kensal Green Cemetery). *The Bandit* (90b), *Comic Annual* 1830 (227b, 230a), *Eugene Aram* 1831 (147b), *Tylney Hall* 1834 (227b), *New Monthly* 1841–3, *Hood's Magazine* 1843–4 (214a), *The Song of the Shirt* 1843 (174b, 214a).

Hooker, Richard (1553/4?–1600), theologian: b. Exeter; educ. Oxford (Corpus Christi College); rector of Boscombe 1591–5, and of Bishopsbourne 1595–1600; buried in Bishopsbourne; memorial statue in Exeter. *Laws of Ecclesiastical Polity* 1594 (27b), 1597 (24a).

Hopkins, Gerard Manley (1844–89), priest and poet: educ. London (Highgate: see Highgate High St.) and Oxford (Balliol College); studies at Stonyhurst College, nr. Whalley 1870–1, at St. Beuno's College 1874–7; ordained priest 1877 and becomes bursar at Mount St. Mary's College 1877–8; curate in Oxford (see Balliol College) 1878; Professor of Classics at Dublin (University College) 1884–9; buried in Dublin (see University College); memorials in London (Westminster Abbey) and Haslemere. 'Duns Scotus's Oxford', 'Heaven-Haven' 1866 (261b), 'The Wreck of the Deutschland' 1876, 'The Windhover' 1877, 'Pied Beauty' 1877 (293a), 'The Loss of the Eurydice' 1878 (244b), 'Binsey Poplars felled' 1879 (23b, 261b), 'St. Winefride's Well' 1879 (136a), *The Journals and Papers of Gerard Manley Hopkins*, ed. H. House, 1959 (261b).

Houghton, William Stanley (1881–1913), playwright: b. Ashton-upon-Mersey; educ.

Manchester Grammar School. *The Dear Departed* 1908, *Hindle Wakes* 1912 (237b).

Housman, Alfred Edward (1859–1936), poet: b. Fockbury; lives in Bromsgrove 1860–73; educ. Bromsgrove and Oxford (St. John's College); lives in London (Highgate: North Rd.) 1886–1905, (Pinner) 1905–11; Professor of Latin at Cambridge and Fellow (Trinity College) 1911; buried in Ludlow; memorial in Cambridge (Trinity College). *A Shropshire Lad* 1896 (31b, 50b, 64a, 193b), *Last Poems* 1922, *The Name and Nature of Poetry* 1933 (50b), 'The vane on Hughley steeple' (137b), *More Poems* 1936 (50b).

Howitt, William (1792–1879), miscellaneous writer: lives with his wife, Mary (1799–1888), in Nottingham 1822–35, Esher 1835–70. *The Forest Minstrel* (with Mary Howitt) 1823 (253b), *Rural Life in England* 1836 (105b), *Visits to Remarkable Places* 1840, 1842 (105b, 314b).

Hudson, William Henry (1841–1922), naturalist and novelist of American birth: lives in London (Kensington: St. Luke's Rd.) 1886–1922; visits Limpsfield, Brockenhurst 1903, Zennor 1906–7; buried in Worthing; memorial in London (Hyde Park). *Birds in London* 1898, *Birds and Man* 1901 (197a), *Hampshire Days* 1903 (39a, b), *Green Mansions* 1904 (197b, 201b), *The Land's End: a naturalist's impressions in West Cornwall* 1908 (348a), *A Shepherd's Life* 1910 (341a), *Adventures among Birds* 1913 (197a, b).

Hueffer, Ford Madox. See Ford, Ford Madox.

Hughes, John Ceiriog (1832–87), lyric writer: b. Llanarmon Dyffryn Ceiriog; memorial in Glyn Ceiriog. *Owain Wyn* 1856, 'God Bless the Prince of Wales' (120b).

Hughes, Thomas (1822–96), novelist: b. Uffington; educ. Rugby and Oxford (Oriel College); enters Lincoln's Inn, London (Holborn) 1845, Inner Temple (City: Temple) 1848; revisits Uffington 1857; d. Brighton; memorial in Uffington. *Tom Brown's Schooldays* 1857 (290a, 328a, b), *The Scouring of the White Horse* 1859 (328b), *Tom Brown at Oxford* 1861 (270a).

Hugo, Victor (1802–85), French poet and novelist: lives in St. Luke's 1852–5, St. Peter Port 1855–70. *Les Châtiments* 1853 (294a), *Les Misérables* 1862, *Littérature et Philosophie Mêlées* 1864, *Chansons des Rues et des Bois* 1865, *Les Travailleurs de la Mer* 1866 (294b).

Hume, David (1711–76), historian and philosopher: b. and educ. Edinburgh; lives in Edinburgh and Keeper of the

Advocates' Library 1752; buried in Edinburgh. *Political Discourses* 1752, *History of Great Britain* 1754–61 (96b).

Hunt, James Henry Leigh (1784–1859), essayist and poet: b. London (Southgate); educ. Christ's Hospital (City: Newgate St.); visits Hastings 1812; imprisoned in Horsemonger Lane gaol, London (Southwark: Borough High St.) 1812–14; lives in Hampstead (Vale of Health) 1815, Marylebone (Lisson Grove) 1815–17; visits Marlow 1817; lives in London (Chelsea: Upper Cheyne Row) 1833–40, (Hammersmith: Rowan Rd.) 1853–9; buried in London (Kensal Green Cemetery). *The Story of Rimini* 1816 (129a).

Hurd, Richard (1720–1808), critic and divine: b. Congreve; educ. Cambridge (Emmanuel College); Bishop of Lichfield 1775–81, Bishop of Worcester 1781–1808; lives in Hartlebury 1781–1808. *The Polite Arts: or, a dissertation on poetry, painting, music, etc.* 1749 (45a), *Letters on Chivalry and Romance* 1762 (128b).

Hurdis, James (1763–1801), poet: b. Bishopstone (East Sussex): educ. Chichester and Oxford (Magdalen College); curate at Burwash 1785–9; Fellow of Magdalen College, Oxford 1786; vicar of Bishopstone 1791; meets Cowper at Eartham 1792; buried in Bishopstone (East Sussex). *The Village Curate* 1788 (41b, 267a), *The Favourite Village* 1800 (24b).

Hutchinson, Arthur Stuart Menteith (1879–1971), novelist: makes his last home at Crowborough. *If Winter Comes* 1920 (34a).

Huxley, Aldous Leonard (1894–1963), novelist and essayist: educ. Eton and Oxford (Balliol College); visits Garsington 1915; lives in London (Hampstead: Bracknell Gdns.) 1917; teaches at Eton 1917–19; lives in London (Hampstead: Hampstead Hill Gdns.) 1919–20. *Defeat of Youth* 1918 (189b), *Leda and other poems* 1920 (106b, 190a), *Limbo* 1920 (190a), *Crome Yellow* 1921 (19b, 116a, 320b), *Eyeless in Gaza* 1936 (261b).

Hyde, Douglas (1860–1949), poet, historian, and statesman: b. Frenchpark, and retires here after an academic life.

Hyde, Edward. See Clarendon, Edward Hyde, 1st Earl of.

Inchbald, Mrs. Elizabeth (*née* **Simpson**) (1753–1821), novelist, actress, and dramatist: acts in Bristol 1772; lives in London (Covent Garden: Russell St.) 1788, (Soho: Frith St.) 1791, (Soho: Leicester Sq.) 1790s–1803, (Strand: The Strand) *c.* 1805–9. *Such Things Are* 1788 (185a),

A Simple Story 1791 (216a), *Wives as they Were* 1797 (217b), *Lovers' Vows* 1798 (17a, 217b), prefaces to *The British Theatre* 1806–9 (222b).

Ingelow, Jean (1820–97), novelist and poet: b. Boston. 'High Tide on the Coast of Lincolnshire 1571' in *Poems* 1863 (28a).

Irving, Washington ('Geoffrey Crayon') (1783–1859), American essayist and historian: visits Stratford-upon-Avon, Bromham, London (Kensington: Holland House); suffers business failure in Liverpool 1818; visits Birmingham. 'Rip Van Winkle' in *The Sketch-Book* 1820 (23b–24a, 160a, b), *Bracebridge Hall* 1822 (23b–24a).

Jacob, Violet (*née* **Erskine**) (1863–1946), poet and novelist: b. and lives in Strathmore. 'The Lang Road' in *Songs of Angus* 1915, *The Northern Lights* 1927, *The Lairds of Dun* 1931 (315a).

Jacobs, William Wymark (1863–1943), short-story writer: lives in Loughton; visits Ewelme. *Many Cargoes* 1896, *Short Cruises* 1907, *Sea Whispers* 1926, 'The Monkey's Paw' (231a, b).

James I (1394–1437), King of Scotland and poet: imprisoned in London (City: The Tower), and Windsor Castle; assassinated in Perth. *The Kingis Quair* 1783 (256a, 279b, 340b–341a).

James, Henry (1843–1916), novelist of American birth: lives in London (Mayfair: Bolton St.) 1876–85; visits Oxford, Dunwich, Witley, Cambridge; lives and winters in London (Kensington: De Vere Gdns.) 1886–1902; visits Mickleham 1895; lives at Rye 1896–1916; winters in London (Chelsea: Cheyne Walk) 1912–16; memorials (Westminster Abbey and Chelsea Old Church). *A Passionate Pilgrim* 1875 (259a), *The Europeans* 1878, *Daisy Miller* 1879, *Washington Square* 1881, *The Portrait of a Lady* 1881 (207a), *Portraits of Places* 1883 (130a, 259a), *The Princess Casamassima* 1886 (207a), *The Bostonians* 1886 (79b), *The Spoils of Poynton* 1897, *The Wings of the Dove* 1902 (291a), *The Ambassadors* 1903 (59a, 291a), *The Golden Bowl* 1904 (291a), 'The Altar of the Dead' (259a), 'Sir Edmund Orme' (33b–34a).

James, Montague Rhodes (1862–1936), antiquary and short-story writer: b. Goodnestone; brought up at Great Livermere; educ. Cambridge (King's College), Director of Fitzwilliam Museum, Cambridge 1893–1908; initiates restoration of Abbey glass at Great Malvern 1910; Provost of King's College, Cambridge

1905; Provost of Eton 1918; visits Aldeburgh. *Ghost Stories of an Antiquary* 1905 (121b), *Collected Ghost Stories* 1931 (124b).

Jameson, Mrs. Anna Brownell (1794–1860), author of *Shakespeare's Heroines* (1832): b. and lives early years in Dublin.

Jefferies, Richard (1848–87), novelist and naturalist: b. Coate; lives in London (Surbiton) 1877–82, Brighton 1885, Crowborough 1884–6; d. at Goring-by-Sea; buried in Worthing; bust in Salisbury Cathedral. *Round about a Great Estate* 1880, *Bevis* 1882 (64b), *Nature Near London* 1883 (224a), *Field and Hedgerow* 1889 (71b), *The Old House at Coate* 1948 (64a).

Jeffrey, Francis, Lord Jeffrey (1773–1850), co-founder and editor of the *Edinburgh Review* (1802–29): b. and lives in Edinburgh; educ. Edinburgh High School and University.

Jerome, Jerome Klapka (1859–1927), novelist and playwright: b. Walsall; lives nr. Ewelme from 1887, in London (Chelsea: Chelsea Gdns.) *c.* 1888–9 (Bloomsbury: Tavistock Pl.) 1889; visits Clifton Hampden, Dunwich; d. Northampton; buried in Ewelme. *Three Men in a Boat* 1889 (62b–63a, 170a, 171a, 276a), *Idle Thoughts of an Idle Fellow* 1889, *The Passing of the Third Floor Back* 1907 (170a).

Jerrold, Douglas William (1803–57), dramatist and poet: b. London (Soho: Greek St.); buried in London (Kensal Green Cemetery). *Black Ey'd Susan* 1829, *The Bride of Ludgate* 1831, 'Mrs. Caudle's Curtain Lectures' in *Punch* 1845, *Lloyds Weekly Newspaper* (ed.) 1852–7 (217a).

Jessopp, Augustus (1823–1914), topographical writer: headmaster of Norwich Grammar School; rector of Scarning 1879–1911. *Arcady for Better for Worse* 1887 (296b).

Jewel, John (1522–71), bishop and author of *Apologia Ecclesia Anglicanae* (1562): b. Berrynarbor; rector of Sunningwell *c.* 1550–2.

Johnson, Lionel Pigot (1867–1902), poet: educ. Oxford (New College); lives in London and frequents the Rhymers' Club (City: Fleet St.). 'Oxford' in *Poems* 1895 (269b).

Johnson, Samuel (1709–84), lexicographer, critic, and poet: b. Lichfield; educ. Lichfield, Stourbridge, and Oxford (Pembroke College); lives in Birmingham *c.* 1734; m. in Derby 1735; runs private school in Edial 1735–7; lives in London (Hampstead: Frognal) 1745, (City: Gough Sq.) 1749–50, (Holborn: Staple Inn) 1759–60,

(City: Gough Sq., Johnson's Ct.) 1765–76; frequents clubs and coffee houses (Chelsea: Lawrence St. and Cheyne Walk), (Soho: Gerrard St.), (Strand: Essex St.), (City: Mitre Tavern, Fleet St.); visits Garrick (Adelphi), Goldsmith (Fleet St.: Wine Office Ct.); frequents the Thrales' home (Southwark: Park St.) 1763–82, (Streatham) 1763–84; tours Scotland 1773, visiting Edinburgh, Auchinleck, St. Andrews, Inveraray, Alexandria, Aberdeen, Slains Castle, Cullen, Oban, Skye, Mull, Glensheil, Iona, Laurencekirk, Glasgow; visits Ashbourne, Great Torrington, Langton by Spilsby, Tetford, Hagley, Brighton, Bath, Beaconsfield, Bristol, Saltram House, Tremeirchion, Henley, Oxford (Trinity and University Colleges), Ilam, Uttoxeter; d. London (City: Fleet St.); buried in Westminster Abbey; statues in St. Paul's Cathedral, at St. Clement Danes (Strand), and Lichfield. *Birmingham Journal* essays 1734–5, *Voyage to Abyssinia* (trans.) 1735 (23b), *The Vanity of Human Wishes* 1749 (190a), *The Rambler* (ed.) 1750–2, *A Dictionary of the English Language* 1755 (177b), *The Idler* (ed.) 1758–60 (177b, 226a), *Rasselas* 1759 (177b, 197a), *A Journey to the Western Islands of Scotland* 1775 (120a), *Lives of the English Poets* 1779–81 (33a, 219b).

Johnson, William. See Cory, William Johnson.

Johnston, Arthur ('the Scottish Ovid') (1587–1641), doctor and Latin poet: b. Inverurie; Rector of Aberdeen University 1637–41. *Musae Aulicae* 1637, *Delitiae Poetarum Scotorum* (ed.) 1637 (1a).

Jonson, Benjamin (1572–1637): b. London (possibly Strand: Northumberland St.); educ. London (Westminster School); writes masque for James I's queen at Althorp 1603; imprisoned in Old Marshalsea, London (Southwark: Borough High St., Mermaid Court) 1605; lives in London (City: Blackfriars) 1607–16; visits Hawthornden 1618; frequents Devil and Mitre taverns in London (City: Fleet St.); visits Penshurst Place, Twickenham Park, London (Twickenham); buried in London (Westminster Abbey). *Eastward Hoe* 1605 (218b), *Epicœne* 1609 (332b), 'To Penshurst' in *The Forest* 1612 (278b), *Bartholomew Fayre* 1614 (215b).

Joyce, James Augustine Aloysius (1882–1941), novelist: b. Dublin; educ. Clongoweswood College and Dublin; lives in Bray 1888–91; stays in Sandycove 1904. *Chamber Music* 1907, *Dubliners* 1914 (85b), *A Portrait of the Artist as a Young Man*

1914–15 (31a, 63a, 85b), *Ulysses* 1922 (85b, 296a), *Finnegans Wake* 1939 (56a).

Keats, John (1795–1821), poet: b. London (City: Moorgate); educ. London (Enfield: Southbury Rd.); articled to a surgeon in Edmonton (Keats Parade) 1811–15; visits Leigh Hunt in Hampstead (Vale of Health) and Benjamin Haydon in Soho (Great Marlborough St.); works at Guy's Hospital (Southwark: Borough High St. and Stainer St.) 1816; visits Carisbrooke, Margate, Hastings, Burford Bridge, Box Hill, and Oxford (Magdalen Hall) 1817; lives with his brothers in London (City: Cheapside) 1816–18; visits publishers in Fleet St. (City); lives in Hampstead (Well Walk and Keats Grove) 1818–20; visits Teignmouth, Mull, Ben Nevis, Dumfries 1818; stays in Chichester, Bedhampton, Shanklin, and Winchester 1819; attends opening of chapel in Stansted 1819; spends last night on English soil in Bedhampton; commemorated in London (Hampstead Parish Church and Westminster Abbey). 'Much have I travell'd in the realms of gold' (175a, 219b), *Poems* 1817 (175a), 'To a Lady seen for a few moments at Vauxhall' (226a), 'Lines on the Mermaid Tavern' (175a), 'On the Sea' (52b), *Endymion* 1818 (40b, 238a, b, 320a), 'In a drear-nighted December' (40b), 'Ode to a Nightingale' (190b), 'Ben Nevis' (21b), 'On visiting the tomb of Burns', 'Meg Merrilees' (90a), 'Great spirits now on earth are sojourning' (216b), 'Hush, hush! tread softly!' (59b), *Lamia* 1819, *Otho the Great* (with C. A. Brown) 1819 (298a), 'The Eve of St. Agnes' (59b–60a, 339b), 'Ode to Autumn' (339b), 'Ode on a Grecian Urn' (167b), *Letters*, ed. H. E. Rollins, 1958 (52b, 267b, 320a).

Keble, John (1792–1866), theologian and writer of religious verse: vicar of Hursley 1836–66; d. and commemorated in Bournemouth; buried in Hursley. *The Christian Year* 1827 (138b).

Kelly, Hugh (1739–77), dramatist: b. Killarney; left Killarney for London 1760. *False Delicacy* 1768, *A Word for the Wise* 1770, *The School for Wives* 1773 (145b–146a).

Kempe, Mrs. Margery (b. *c.* 1373), mystic and traveller: b. King's Lynn; visits Norwich. *The Book of Margery Kempe* (147b, 252a).

Kennedy, Margaret (1896–1967), novelist: educ. Cheltenham and Oxford (Somerville College). *The Constant Nymph* 1924 (272a).

Kennedy, Walter (1460?–1508?), poet: lives in Maybole. Poems in Dunbar's *The Flyting of Dunbar and Kennedy* 1508 (240a).

Kerry Poets, The Four. See Ferriter, Pierce; O'Donoghue, Geoffrey; O'Rahilly, Aodhgan; and O'Sullivan, Eoghan Ruadh.

Keyes, Sidney (1922–43), poet: b. Dartford; educ. Dartford, Tonbridge, and Oxford (The Queen's College). *Iron Laurel* 1942 (271b, 323b), *Cruel Solstice* 1943, *Collected Poems* 1945 (271b).

Kickham, Charles Joseph (1828–82), poet, novelist, and patriot: b. and lives in Mullinahone; buried in Mullinahone; commemorated at Tipperary. *Knocknagow* (245a, b).

Killigrew, Thomas, the Elder (1612–83), actor and dramatist, author of *The Parson's Wedding* (1664): lives in London (Covent Garden: Covent Garden), theatre manager in Covent Garden (Catherine St.); buried in Westminster Abbey.

Kilvert, Robert Francis (1840–79), diarist: curate of Clyro 1865–72, Langley Burrell 1872–6; visits Bournemouth 1875, Brinsop 1879; vicar of Bredwardine 1877–9; buried in Bredwardine. *Diary*, ed. W. Plomer, 1938–40, new edn. 1969 (31b, 34a, 64a, 152b).

Kinglake, Alexander William (1809–91), historian of the Crimean War and travel writer: b. Taunton; educ. Ottery St. Mary, Eton, and Cambridge (Trinity College). *Eōthen* 1844 (106b, 319a).

Kingsley, Charles (1819–75), historian and novelist: b. Holne; spends childhood in Barnack and Clovelly; educ. Bristol, King's College, London (Strand: The Strand), and Cambridge (Magdalene College); curate in London (Chelsea: St. Luke's Church); rector of Eversley 1844–75; visits Torquay, Bideford 1854, Bristol 1858, Malham Tarn; Professor of Modern History at Cambridge (Magdalene College) 1860–9; stays in London (Harrow on the Hill: London Rd.) 1873; buried in Eversley; commemorated in Bideford, Clovelly, and Eversley. 'O Mary go and call the cattle home' (276b), *Alton Locke* 1850 (46b, 276b), preface to *Theologica Germanica* 1854 (324b), *Westward Ho!* 1855 (22b, 64a, 304b), *The Water Babies* 1863 (107a, 234b), *Hereward the Wake* 1866 (71b), 'A New Forest Ballad' (233b).

Kingsley, Henry (1830–76), novelist: b. Barnack; educ. King's College, London (Strand: The Strand) and Oxford (Worcester College); lives, d., and is buried in Cuckfield. *Ravenshoe* 1861 (274b).

Kipling, Rudyard (1865-1936), poet and novelist: lives in Portsmouth 1874-7; educ. Portsmouth and Westward Ho!; spends holidays in London (Fulham: North End Cres.) and Rottingdean; lives in London (Strand: Villiers St.) 1889-91, Maidencombe 1896-7, Rottingdean 1897-1902, Burwash 1902-36; spends summer in Kessingland, 1914; stays at Brown's Hotel (Mayfair: Dover St.); buried in London (Westminster Abbey); commemorated in Rottingdean and Westward Ho! *The Light that Failed* 1890 (223b, 283a), *Life's Handicap* 1891, *Barrack-Room Ballads* 1892 (223b), 'Recessional' 1897 (289a), *Stalky & Co.* 1899 (234a, 289a, 336a, b), *Kim* 1901 (289a), *Just So Stories* 1902 (289a), *Puck of Pook's Hill* 1906, *Rewards and Fairies* 1910 (41b), *Something of Myself* 1937 (41b, 234a), 'Sussex' (42a), 'The House Surgeon' (234a).

Knowles, Herbert (1798-1817), poet: b. and lives in Gomersal; educ. Richmond; buried nr. Gomersal. 'The Three Tabernacles' 1816 (121a, 286b).

Knowles, James Sheridan (1784-1862), dramatist: b. Cork. *The Welsh Harper* (67b).

Knox, Ronald Arbuthnott (1888-1957), essayist and detective-story writer: educ. Eton and Oxford (Balliol College); Fellow and chaplain at Trinity College; Catholic chaplain to the University 1926-39. *Essays in Satire* 1928, *Let Dons Delight* 1939 (273a).

Kouyoumdjian, Dikrān. See Arlen, Michael.

Kyd (or Kid), Thomas (1558?-94?), dramatist, author of *The Spanish Tragedy*: baptized in London (City: King William St.); educ. Merchant Taylors' School (City: Suffolk Lane); works in theatres in Southwark (Bankside).

Lamb, Charles (1775-1834), essayist, poet, and critic, brother of Mary Lamb: b. and baptized in London (City: Temple); educ. and first meets Coleridge at Christ's Hospital (City: Newgate St.); childhood visits to Widford and Mackery End; clerk in South-Sea House, London (City: Threadneedle St.) 1792-5 and East India House (City: Lime St.) 1795-1825; lives in Little Queen St. (Holborn: Kingsway) 1795-6; visits Coleridge in Nether Stowey 1797 and Keswick 1802; holidays in Cowes 1803; attends Hazlitt's wedding at St. Andrew's, London (Holborn: Holborn Circus); visits Hazlitt in Winterslow 1809 and 1810; inherits Button Snap in Westmill 1812; visits Calne 1816; lives in London (Covent Garden: Russell St.)

1817-21; holidays in Brighton 1817, Oxford, and Cambridge 1820, Margate 1821, Hastings 1823; lives in London (Islington: Duncan Ter.) 1823-7; visits Thomas Hood at the Adelphi (Robert St.) 1827; lives in London (Enfield) 1827-33, (Edmonton) 1833-4; buried in Edmonton. *Tales from Shakespear* (with Mary Lamb) 1807 (220a), *Mrs. Leicester's School* (with Mary Lamb) 1808 (234a, 337b), 'The Old Margate Hoy' (238b), 'Mackery End' (234a), *Essays of Elia* 1823 (198a, b, 238b), *Last Essays of Elia* 1833 (186b, 187b), 'When maidens such as Hester die' (222a), 'On an Infant Dying as soon as Born' (164b), 'The Grandame', 'Blakesmoor in H—', 'Dream Children' (337b-338a), *Letters*, ed. E. V. Lucas, 3 vols. 1935 (70a, 187b, 198a).

Lamb, Mary (1764-1847), joint author with her brother Charles of *Tales from Shakespear* (1807) and *Mrs. Leicester's School* (1808): lives, visits, and holidays with Charles Lamb (q.v.); buried in Edmonton.

Landon, Letitia Elizabeth ('L. E. L.') (1802-38), poet and novelist: lives in London (Marylebone: Upper Berkeley St.). 'Rome' 1820, *The Fate of Adelaide* 1821, *Ethel Churchill* 1837, *Traits and Trials of Early Life* 1837 (260a).

Landor, Walter Savage (1775-1864), poet and essayist: b. Warwick; educ. Rugby and Oxford (Trinity College); visits Swansea; lives in Llanthony c. 1807-14; m. in Bath 1811; lives in Bath 1838-58; reads in the Bristol Library in Bristol; dines with Mary Russell Mitford in London (Bloomsbury: Russell Sq.) 1836; commemorated in Bishop's Tachbrook and Warwick. *Gebir* 1798, 'Rose Aylmer' (317b), *Imaginary Conversations* 1824-9 (69a, b).

Lang, Andrew (1844-1912), scholar and poet: b. Selkirk; educ. Selkirk, Edinburgh, St. Andrews, Glasgow, and Oxford (Balliol College); Fellow at Oxford (Merton College) 1868-75; settles in London (Kensington: Marloes Rd.) 1875; returns finally to St. Andrews and is buried there. *Blue Fairy Book*, etc. (268b), *Ballades in Blue China* 1880, *Helen of Troy* 1882, *Custom and Myth* 1884, *Letters to Dead Authors* 1886, *Books and Bookmen* 1887, *Life and Letters of J. G. Lockhart* 1896 (201a).

Langland, William (1330?-1400?), poet: b. nr. Great Malvern, or Cleobury Mortimer, or Ledbury; educ. Great Malvern or Cleobury Mortimer. *The Vision con-*

cerning *Piers the Plowman* 14th c. (13a, b, 62a, 124a).

Latimer, Hugh (1485?-1555), Protestant martyr: educ. and a Fellow at Cambridge (Clare College); stands trial in Oxford (St. Mary the Virgin) 1554; burnt at the stake in Oxford (Martyrs' Memorial) 1555.

Law, William (1686-1761), theologian: educ. and a Fellow at Cambridge (Emmanuel College). *A Serious Call to a Devout and Holy Life* 1729 (45a).

Lawrence, David Herbert (1885-1930), novelist and poet: b. Eastwood; educ. Eastwood and Nottingham; frequents Underwood, Cossall; teaches in London (Croydon) 1908 12; visits the Garnetts in Limpsfield; stays in Greatham 1915; visits Garsington 1915; lives in London (Hampstead: Vale of Health) 1915, Padstow 1915-16, Zennor 1916-17, Middleton-by-Wirksworth 1918-19. *The White Peacock* 1911 (95a, 161b, 185b, 329a), *Sons and Lovers* 1913 (94b-95a, 329a), *The Lost Girl* 1920 (94b), 'Whether or Not' (157b), *The Rainbow* 1915, suppressed, re-published 1921 (124b, 191b, 348b), *Women in Love* 1921 (69a, 94b, 116a, 275a, 348b), *England, My England* 1922 (124b), 'A Fragment of Stained Glass' (19a), *Studies in Classic American Literature* 1923 (242a), *Kangaroo* 1923 (348b), *Collected Letters*, ed. H. T. Moore, 1962 (242a, 329a, 348b).

Lawrence, Thomas Edward ('Lawrence of Arabia') (1888-1935), Arabic scholar and traveller: b. Tremadoc; educ. Oxford (Jesus College and Magdalen College); Fellow at Oxford (All Souls); lives in Clouds Hill 1923-35; buried in Moreton (Dorset); commemorated in Wareham and London (City: St. Paul's Cathedral). *Seven Pillars of Wisdom* 1926 (63b, 260b, 262a).

Layamon (or Lawemon) (fl. 1200), chronicler: priest at Areley Kings. *The Brut* (10b).

Lear, Edward (1812-88), artist and writer of nonsense verse: b. and spends early years in London (Holloway); stays at Knowsley Hall; lives in London (Marylebone: Seymour St.). *A Book of Nonsense* 1846 anon., enlarged 1861 (150a).

Lecky, William Edward Hartpole (1838-1903), historian: b. nr. Dublin; educ. and lives in Dublin; lives and d. in London (Kensington: Onslow Gdns.); buried in Dublin (Mount Jerome cemetery); commemorated in Trinity College, Dublin. *The History of England in the Eighteenth Century* 1878-90 (83b).

Ledwidge, Francis (1891-1917), poet: b. and works in Slane. *Songs of the Field* 1915, *Songs of Peace* 1916, *Complete Poems* 1919 (304a).

Lee, Harriet (1757-1851) and **Sophia** (1750-1824), novelists and dramatists: live and are buried in Bristol (Clifton). *The Canterbury Tales* 1797-1805 (36a, 52a).

Lee, Nathaniel (1653?-92), playwright, author of *The Rival Queens; or The Death of Alexander the Great*: educ. London (Westminster School) and Cambridge (Trinity College); buried in St. Clement Danes, London (Strand: The Strand).

Le Fanu, Joseph Sheridan (1814-73), novelist, short-story writer, and poet: b., lives, and d. in Dublin; buried in Dublin (Mount Jerome cemetery). *Shamus O'Brien* 1837 (83b), *The House by the Churchyard* 1863 (56a, 83b), *Uncle Silas* 1864, *In a Glass Darkly* 1872 (83b).

Le Gallienne, Richard (1866-1947), poet and essayist: b. Liverpool; frequents the Rhymers' Club in London (City: Fleet St.). *The Romantic Nineties* 1926 (177b).

Lemon, Mark (1809-70), co-founder and first editor of *Punch*: spends childhood in London (Hendon); youth in Boston; helps to inaugurate *Punch* in London (City: Crane Court and Bouveric St.); lives in Ifield 1858-70; buried and commemorated in Ifield. *Tom Moody's Tales* 1863 (28a, 193a).

Leofric (d. 1072), 1st Bishop of Exeter: founder in Exeter of the Cathedral Library.

Leslie, Sir John Randolph Shane (1885-1971), novelist and biographer; educ. Cambridge (King's College). *The Cantab* 1926 (46b).

Lever, Charles James (1806-72), novelist: b., educ., and lives in Dublin; physician in Portstewart 1832-7. *Harry Lorrequer* 1837 (83a, 283a).

Lewes, George Henry (1817-78), miscellaneous writer and critic: works in London (Strand: Wellington St.); meets Marian Evans (Strand: The Strand) 1851; lives in London (Richmond: Clarence Row and Park Shot) 1855-9; visits the Scilly Isles 1857; Gainsborough 1859; lives in London (Wimbledon) 1859-60, (Marylebone: Blandford Sq.) 1860-3, (Regent's Park: Lodge Rd.) 1863-78; stays in Shottermill 1871; buys house in Witley 1877-8; dies in London (Regent's Park: Lodge Rd.). *The Leader* 1850-66 (223b), *Seaside Studies at Ilfracombe, Tenby, The Scilly Isles, and Jersey* 1858 (296b-297a), contributions to the *Pall Mall Gazette*, *The Fortnightly* (ed.) (210b).

Lewis, Alun (1915–44), poet: b. Cwmaman; educ. Cwmaman and Aberystwyth. *The Wanderers* (3a).

Lewis, Clive Staples (1898–1963), critic and novelist: b. Belfast; educ. Great Malvern and Oxford (University College); Fellow at Oxford (Magdalen College) 1924–54; Professor at Cambridge (Magdalene College) 1954–63. *The Pilgrim's Regress* 1933, *The Allegory of Love: a Study in Medieval Tradition* 1936, *The Problem of Pain* 1940, *The Screwtape Letters* 1942, *That Hideous Strength* 1945, *The Lion, the Witch and the Wardrobe* 1950, *English Literature in the Sixteenth Century* 1954 (267b), *Surprised by Joy* 1955 (21a), *The Magician's Nephew* 1955 (46b–47a), *Studies in Words* 1960, *Experiment in Criticism* 1961 (47a).

Lewis, Harry Sinclair (1885–1951), American novelist: visits Bearsted 1921, London (St. James's: Bury St.) 1922, 1924, and 1927. *Babbit* 1922 (19a, 212b).

Lewis, Dr. Howell Elvet (1860–1953), Welsh poet and hymn-writer, winner of Bardic crown and chair: b., lives, and is buried near Cynwyl Elfet.

Lewis, Matthew Gregory ('Monk' Lewis) (1775–1818), novelist and playwright: educ. London (Westminster School) and Oxford (Christ Church); meets Scott in Inveraray 1798; lives in London (Barnes), (Mayfair: Albany) *c*. 1812–18. *The Monk* 1796, reprinted 1973 (140a, 165a), *Romantic Tales* 1808 (140b), *Journal of a West Indian Proprietor* 1834 (206b).

Lillo, George (1693–1739), author of the play *The London Merchant, or the History of George Barnwell* (1731): buried in London (Shoreditch: St. Leonard's). *Arden of Feversham* 1762 (110b).

Linacre, Thomas (1460?–1524), physician and classical scholar, author of *Rudimenta Grammatices*: educ. Canterbury and Oxford (Christ Church); rector of Aldington.

Lindsay (or Lyndsay), Sir David (1490–1555), poet and advisor to James V of Scotland, author of *The Dreme* (1528) and *Complaynt to the King* (1529): educ. St. Andrews.

Linklater, Eric (1899–1974), novelist, playwright, and biographer: b. Orkney Islands; educ. Aberdeen. *White Maa's Saga* 1929 (257a).

Locke, John (1632–1704), philosopher: b. Wrington; educ. London (Westminster School) and Oxford (Christ Church); visits Sutton Court; lives in London (Strand: The Strand); influences design of gardens at Stourhead and Stowe; lives in High Laver 1691–1704; buried in High Laver. *Essay concerning Human Understanding* 1690 (221b–222a).

Lockhart, John Gibson (1794–1854), novelist and biographer of Sir Walter Scott: educ. Glasgow and Oxford (Balliol College); lives in London (St. James's: Pall Mall) 1820–30; visits Llangollen 1825; buried at Dryburgh Abbey. *Some Passages in the Life of Adam Blair* 1822, *Ancient Scottish Ballads* 1823, *Life of Scott* 1837–8 (212b).

Lodge, Thomas (1558–1625), lyric poet; author of *A Defence of Plays* (1580) and *Phillis* (1593): educ. Merchant Taylors' School, London (City: Suffolk Lane) and Oxford (Trinity College); enters Lincoln's Inn, London (Holborn) 1576.

Longfellow, Henry Wadsworth (1807–82), American poet: stays in London (Marylebone: Langham Pl.), visits Dickens in Devonshire Ter. (Marylebone: Marylebone Rd.), and Landor in Bath 1842; visits Shanklin 1868. *Hiawatha* 1855, 'Paul Revere's Ride' in *Tales of a Wayside Inn* 1863 (298a).

Lovelace, Richard (1618–58), Cavalier poet: educ. London (City: Charterhouse) and Oxford (Worcester College); imprisoned in London (Westminster Abbey Gatehouse) 1642; lives in Canterbury; buried in St. Bride's Church, London (City: Fleet St.). 'Triumph of Philamore and Amoret' (253a), 'To Althea from Prison' (229a).

Lover, Samuel (1797–1868), novelist and writer of short sketches and songs: b. and lives in Dublin; buried in London (Kensal Green Cemetery); commemorated in Dublin (St. Patrick's Cathedral). *Rory O'More* 1836 (82b), *Songs and Ballads* 1839 (83a), *Handy Andy* 1842 (82b–83a).

Lowell, James Russell (1819–91), American poet and critic: lives in London (Kensington: Lowndes St. and Lowndes Sq.) 1880–5; visits Meredith in Mickleham.

Lowry, Clarence Malcolm (1909–57), novelist and short-story writer: lives in London (Blackheath: Woodville Rd.) 1928; educ. Cambridge (St. Catharine's College) 1929–32; vacations in Rye; is befriended in London (Hampstead: Parliament Hill) 1932; lives in Ripe 1956–7; buried in Ripe. *Ultramarine* 1933 (48a, 167a, 191b, 291b), *Under the Volcano* 1947, *October Ferry to Gabriola*, *Hear Us O Lord from Heaven Thy Dwelling Place* 1962 (287a).

Lubbock, Percy (1879–1965), historian and biographer: educ. Eton and Cambridge (King's College); spends childhood holidays at Earlham Hall; Fellow at Cambridge (Magdalene College). *Samuel Pepys*

Mackay, Robert ('Rob Donn') (1714–78), Gaelic poet: commemorated nr. Balnakeil Bay.

Mackenzie, Sir Compton (1883–1972), novelist: b. Hartlepool; educ. Oxford (Magdalen College); enters Middle Temple, London (City: Temple); stays in Beech 1896–1900; frequents Alton; stays in Burford; lives in Barra 1939–45, Edinburgh 1962–72; buried in Barra. *Sinister Street*, 2 vols. 1913–14 (267b), *Guy and Pauline* 1915 (40b), *The Altar Steps* 1921, *The Parson's Progress* 1922, *Buttercups and Daisies* 1931 (6b, 20a), 'Mabel in Queer Street' (6b), *Whisky Galore* 1947 (15b), *My Life and Times* 1963–71 (101a, b).

Mackenzie, Henry ('the Addison of the North') (1745–1831), novelist: b., educ., and buried in Edinburgh. *The Man of Feeling* 1771 (97a).

Maclaren, Ian. See Watson, John.

Macleod, Fiona. See Sharp, William.

MacNeice, Louis (1907–63), poet: b. Belfast; childhood in Carrickfergus; educ. Marlborough and Oxford (Merton College); frequents Binsey; lecturer in Birmingham 1930–5. *Blind Fireworks* 1929 (268b), *Poems* 1935 (24a), *Autumn Sequel* 1954 (268b), *The Strings are False* 1965 (53b, 268b).

Macpherson, James (1736–96), poet: educ. Aberdeen and Edinburgh (University); builds mansion in Balavil; lives in London (Westminster: Fludyer St.); buried in Westminster Abbey. *Fingal* 1762 (2a, 14a), *Temora* 1763 (14a).

Magee, William Kirkpatrick ('John Eglinton') (1868–1961), associate of the Irish Literary movement: lives in Bournemouth. *Irish Literary Portraits* 1935, *Letters of George Moore* (ed.) 1942, *A Memoir of A. E.* 1937 (29a).

Maginn, William ('Ensign O'Doherty') (1793–1842), poet: b. Cork; educ. Dublin (Trinity College); dines with the Fraserians in London (Mayfair: Regent St.); visits Harrison Ainsworth in Kensal Green; spends last years and is buried in Walton-on-Thames. Contributions to *Blackwood's Edinburgh Magazine* (67b), *Fraser's Magazine* (co-founder) (67b, 332a), 'Homeric Ballads' in *Fraser's Magazine* (67b).

Mahony, Francis Sylvester ('Father Prout') (1804–66), poet: b. Cork; educ. Clongoweswood College; stays in London (Mayfair: Regent St.), visits Harrison Ainsworth (Kensal Green), visits his publisher (St. James's: St. James's Sq.); buried in Cork. Contributions to *Fraser's Magazine* 1834–6 (68a, 208a), to *Bentley's*

Miscellany* 1837, 'The Bells of Shandon', *Reliques of Father Prout* 1836 (68a).

Mair (or Major), John (1469–1559), classical scholar and chronicler, 'the last of the schoolmen': at the university in St. Andrews 1522–5 and 1530–50. *History of Greater Britain* 1521 (292a).

Mallarmé, Stéphane (1842–98), French poet: stays in London (Kensington: Brompton Sq.) 1862–3, m. in Brompton Oratory (Kensington) 1863, visits Swinburne (Bloomsbury: Great James St.) 1875. Poe's *The Raven* (trans.) (169a).

Mallet (or Malloch), David (1705?–1765), poet: b. Crieff; educ. Edinburgh (University); buried in London (Mayfair: South Audley St.). 'William and Margaret' 1723 (208b).

Malone, Edmond (1741–1812), critic and Shakespearian scholar: b. and educ. Dublin; lives in London (Marylebone: Langham St.) 1779–1812. *Works of Shakespeare* (ed.) 1790 (204b).

Malory, Sir Thomas (d. 1471), author of *Le Morte Darthur*: imprisoned, d., and is buried in London (City: Newgate St.). *Le Morte Darthur* finished between 1469 and 1470, ed. Caxton 1485, published in *The Works of Sir Thomas Malory*, ed. E. Vinaver, 3 vols. 1947, 2nd edn. 1968 (43a, 118b–119a, 126b).

Mangan, James Clarence (1803–49), poet: b., lives, and d. in Dublin; commemorated in Dublin. Contributions to the *Dublin University Magazine* and The *Nation*, 'My Dark Rosaleen' (83a).

Mansfield, Katherine. See Murry, Kathleen Mansfield.

Map (or Mapes), Walter (fl. 1200), chronicler: archdeacon in Oxford 1197; canon in Lincoln and Hereford. *De Nugis Curialium* (157b).

Markham, Mrs. See Penrose, Elizabeth.

Marlowe, Christopher (1564–93), dramatist: b. and baptized in Canterbury; educ. Canterbury and Cambridge (Corpus Christi); frequents the Mermaid Tavern in London (City: Bread St.); killed and buried in London (Deptford); commemorated in Canterbury, Cambridge, and Deptford. *Tamburlaine* 1590, *Edward II* 1594, 'The Passionate Shepherd to his Love', beginning 'Come live with me and be my love' in *The Passionate Pilgrim* 1599, *The Tragedy of Dr. Faustus* 1604 (186a), *The Jew of Malta* 1633 (157b).

Marmion, Shakerley (1603–39), poet and playwright: b. Aynho; educ. Oxford (Wadham College); visits Dover's Hill for the Cotswold Games. *The Antiquary*

1641 (13a), contributions to *Annalia Dubrensia* (79b).

Marryat, Captain Frederick (1792–1848), novelist: educ. in London (Enfield); lives in London (Marylebone: Spanish Pl. and Wimbledon) 1839–43; lives for a time in Lymington, Langham 1843–8; d. and is commemorated in Langham. *Masterman Ready* 1841 (206a), *The Children of the New Forest* 1847 (233a).

Marston, John (1575?–1634), dramatist and poet, author of *The Dutch Courtezan* (1605) and *Sophonisba* (1606): educ. Oxford (Brasenose College) 1591–4; enters Middle Temple, London (City: Temple); imprisoned in Old Marshalsea (Southwark: Borough High St., Mermaid Court) c. 1605; rector of Christchurch (Dorset) 1616–31; buried in London (City: Temple Church). *Eastward Hoe* (with Jonson and Chapman) 1605 (218b).

Martin, Sir Theodore ('Bon Gaultier') (1816–1909), poet and humorist: b. and educ. Edinburgh; practises as solicitor in Edinburgh before leaving for London 1846. Contributions to *Tait's Magazine* and *Fraser's Magazine* (100a, b), *Bon Gaultier Ballads* (with W. E. Aytoun) 1845 (100a).

Martin, Thomas ('honest Tom Martin of Palgrave') (1697–1771), antiquary: lives in Palgrave 1723–71. *The History of Thetford* 1779 (275b–276a).

Martin, Violet Florence ('Martin Ross') (1862–1915), novelist with her cousin Edith Somerville, as 'Somerville and Ross': lives, d., and is commemorated in Castletownshend. *The Real Charlotte* 1894, *Some Experiences of an Irish R.M.* 1899, *Further Experiences of an Irish R.M.* 1908 (54a).

Martineau, Harriet (1802–76), novelist and political economist: b. Norwich; lives in Ambleside 1845–76; first meets Charlotte Brontë in London (Bayswater: Westbourne St.) 1849; buried in Birmingham. *Illustrations of Political Economy* 1832–4 (253a), *Deerbrook* 1839 (7b, 166a), *Complete Guide to the Lakes* 1855 (7b), *Autobiography* 1877 (166a).

Martyn, Edward (1859–1924), poet, playwright, and patron of the arts, author of *The Heather Field* (1899) and other plays: educ. Oxford (Christ Church); lives in Tullira; promotes the idea of the Irish national theatre at Durras House.

Marvell, Andrew (1621–78), poet: b. Winestead; educ. Kingston upon Hull and Cambridge (Trinity College) 1633–8; tutor in Appleton Roebuck 1650–2; lives in London (Highgate: Waterlow Park);

buried in London (Bloomsbury: St. Giles-in-the-Fields church). 'The Garden', 'Upon Appleton House' (9a).

Masefield, John (1878–1967), Poet Laureate and novelist: b. Ledbury: cadet in Liverpool 1891–4; lives in London (Hampstead: Well Walk) 1913–16; lives in Oxford 1920s, Sapperton; visits Coole Park; commemorated in London (Westminster Abbey). 'The Valediction (Liverpool Docks)' 1902, 'The Wanderer of Liverpool' 1930, 'A Masque of Liverpool' 1930, *New Chum* 1942 (161b), *Land Workers* 1942 (296a), *Collected Poems* 1946 (155b, 296a), *The Badon Parchments* 1948 (119a), 'All the land from Ludlow Town' (31b).

Mason, William (1724–97), poet and friend of Thomas Gray: b. Kingston upon Hull; educ. Cambridge (St. John's College); Fellow at Cambridge (Pembroke College); rector of Aston 1754–97; visits Nuneham Courtenay. *Isis* 1748 (272b), *The English Garden* 1772 (255b).

Massinger, Philip (1583–1640), dramatist, author of *The Duke of Milan* (1623) and *A New Way to pay old Debts* (1633): baptized in Salisbury; educ. Oxford (Merton College); boyhood in Wilton; writes for theatres in London (Southwark: Bankside); buried in Southwark Cathedral.

Maturin, Charles Robert (1782–1824), novelist: b., educ., and lives in Dublin. *The Fatal Revenge* 1807, *The Wild Irish Boy* 1808, *The Milesian Chief* 1811, *Bertram* 1816, *Melmoth the Wanderer* 1820 (82b).

Maugham, William Somerset (1874–1965), novelist, dramatist, and short-story writer: educ. Canterbury; lives in Whitstable, London (Westminster: Vincent Sq.) 1895. *Liza of Lambeth* 1897 (52a, 228a), *Of Human Bondage* 1915 (33b, 52a, 337b), *The Circle* 1921, *The Breadwinner* 1930 (207a), *Cakes and Ale* 1930 (337b), *Collected Plays*, 3 vols. 1931, *For Services Rendered* 1932 (207a), *Catalina* 1948 (52a), *Complete Short Stories*, 3 vols. 1951, *Far and Wide*, 2 vols. 1955 (207a).

Mavor, Osborne Henry ('James Bridie') (1888–1951), playwright: spends childhood, educ., and practises medicine in Glasgow; lives in Helensburgh. *The Anatomist* 1931, *Tobias and the Angel* 1931, *A Sleeping Clergyman* 1933, *One Way of Living* 1939 (118b), *Mr. Bolfry* 1943, *Daphne Laureola* 1949 (132b).

Melville, Herman (1819–91), American novelist: visits Liverpool 1837, 1856.

Redburn 1849 (160b), *Billy Budd* written c. 1890, published 1924 (4b).

Meredith, George (1828–1909), novelist and poet: b. Portsmouth; lives in London (Belgravia: Ebury St.) 1849, Shepperton 1853–8, London (Chelsea: Hobury St.) 1858–9, Esher 1859–67; stays in London (Chelsea: Cheyne Walk) 1861–2; lives in Mickleham 1867–1909; buried in Dorking. *The Ordeal of Richard Feverel* 1859 (172a), *Evan Harrington* 1860 (105b, 172a, 282b), *Poems of the English Roadside* 1862, *Modern Love* 1862 (105b), *Beauchamp's Career* 1874 (105b, 306b), *Diana of the Crossways* 1885 (241b), *Lord Ormont and his Aminta* 1894 (111a), *The Amazing Marriage* 1895 (241b).

Merriman (or Merryman), Brian (Brian Mac Giolla Meidhre) (c. 1749–1805), Irish poet: prob. b. Ennistymon; lives and is buried in Feakle. *The Midnight Court* (*Cúirt an mheádhon oídhche*) 1780 (111a).

Merriman, Henry Seton. See Scott, Hugh Stowell.

Meynell, Alice (1847–1922), poet: lives in London (Bayswater: Palace Ct.) 1890–1905; arranges care of Francis Thompson in Storrington. *The Rhythm of Life* 1893, *The Colour of Life* 1896, *The Spirit of Peace* 1898 (166a).

Mickle, William Julius (1735–88), poet and translator: b. Langholm; lives, m., and is buried in Forest Hill. *The Lusiads* (trans.) 1775 (113a), 'Cumnor Hall' 1784 (72a, 113a, 152b), 'There's Nae Luck aboot the Hoose' ('The Sailor's Wife') (125b, 152b).

Middleton, Thomas (1570–1627), poet and dramatist: educ. Oxford (The Queen's College); enters Gray's Inn, London (Holborn) 1593; lives in London (Newington) 1609–27; buried in Newington. *The Wisdom of Solomon Paraphrased* 1597, *Micro-Cynicon* 1599, *The Ghost of Lucrece* 1600 (271a), *A Chaste Maid in Cheapside* 1630, *Women beware Women* 1657 (208b).

Miller, Anna, Lady (1741–81), verse-writer and literary hostess: lives in Batheaston 1766–81; buried in Bath.

Milman, Henry Hart (1791–1868), poet and historian: educ. and a Fellow at Oxford (Brasenose College); Professor of Poetry at Oxford 1821; Dean of St. Paul's Cathedral, London (City) 1849–68 and commemorated there. 'Apollo Belvedere' 1812, *Fazio* 1815, *Samor, the Lord of the Bright City* 1818 (262b), *Annals of St. Paul's Cathedral* 1868 (180a).

Milnes, Richard Monckton, 1st Baron Houghton (1809–85), first biographer of Keats: educ. Cambridge (Trinity College); lives in London (St. James's: Pall Mall) from 1837. *Tribute* 1836, *Life and Letters of Keats* 1848 (212b).

Milton, John (1608–74), poet: b. London (City: Bread St.); educ. St. Paul's School (City) and Cambridge (Christ's College); lives in Horton 1632–40; visits Stowmarket, Langley, and London (Harefield); m. in Forest Hill; lives in London (St. James's: Petty France), (Finsbury: Bunhill Row) 1662–74; escapes from the plague to Chalfont St. Giles 1665–6; buried in St. Giles Cripplegate, London (City: Fore St.); commemorated in St. Margaret's (Westminster) and Westminster Abbey. 'Hymn on the Morning of Christ's Nativity' 1629, 'On Shakespeare' 1630 (44a), 'On the University Carrier' (45a), 'Il Penseroso' 1632 (44a, 136b), 'L'Allegro' 1632 (136b), 'Arcades' 1633 (192b), 'Now the Bright Morning-Star', 'O Nightingale' (136b), *Comus* 1637 (232a), 'On the Late Massacre in Piedmont', 'Lycidas' (44b, 136b, 276b), 'On his Blindness' (213a), *Paradise Lost* 1667 (55b, 127a, 187b, 213a), *Paradise Regained* 1671 (187b).

Mitchel, John (1818–75), Irish nationalist and journalist: b. nr. Dungiven; educ. Dublin (Trinity College); buried in Newry. *The Nation* (ed.), *Jail Journal, or Five Years in British Prisons* 1856 (250a).

Mitford, Mary Russell (1787–1855), essayist, poet, and dramatist: b. New Alresford; educ. and lives in Reading; lives in Three Mile Cross 1820–51; stays in London (Bloomsbury: Russell Sq.) 1836; visits Clare in Northampton; lives from 1851 and d. in Swallowfield. *Our Village* 1819, *Recollections of a Literary Life* 1852, 'The Visit' (251a, b, 317a).

Mitford, The Hon. Nancy Freeman (1904–73), novelist and biographer: lives and is buried in Swinbrook. *The Pursuit of Love* 1945 (109a, 318b).

Molesworth, Mrs. Mary Louisa (*née* Stewart) (1839–1921), writer of children's books: educ. and lives in Manchester; holidays in Fleetwood; lives in London (Chelsea: Sloane St.) 1901–21. *Little Miss Peggy* 1887 (236b), *The Rectory Children* 1889 (111b), *The Carved Lions* 1895 (236b).

Monro, Harold (1879–1932), poet and founder of *The Poetry Review*: runs the Poetry Bookshop in London (Bloomsbury: Great Russell St.) 1913–32.

Montagu, Mrs. Elizabeth (*née* Robinson) (1720–1800), poet and leader of the 'blue stockings': b. York; has a fashionable salon in London (Marylebone: Portman

1865–72, visits Rossetti (Chelsea: Cheyne Walk); buys house in Kelmscott 1871; lives in London (Hammersmith: Upper Mall) 1878–96; commemorated in London (Hammersmith: Upper Mall) and Lower Inglesham; buried in Kelmscott. 'Scenes from the Fall of Troy' (167a), *The Life and Death of Jason* 1867, *The Earthly Paradise* 1868–70 (196b), *News from Nowhere* 1891 (143a, 189a).

Morrison, Arthur (1863–1945), novelist and short-story writer: b. London (Poplar); lives in Loughton 1892–1913; visits Arthur Osborne Jay in London (Shoreditch: Old Nichol St.) 1894; lives in High Beech 1913–18. *Tales of Mean Streets* 1894 (209b, 215a), *A Child of the Jago* 1896 (215a, 231a), *To London Town* 1899, *Cunning Murrell* 1900, *The Hole in the Wall* 1902 (231a).

Morton, John Maddison (1811–91), dramatist: lives in Chertsey. *Box and Cox* 1847 (58b).

Motherwell, William (1797–1835), poet: b. Glasgow; educ. Edinburgh; lives in Paisley 1812–30, Glasgow 1830–5; buried in Glasgow. *Minstrelsy, Ancient and Modern* 1827 (275b), 'Jeanie Morrison' in *Poems, Narrative and Lyrical* 1832 (117b).

Muir, Edwin (1887–1959), poet and critic and, with his wife Willa, translator of Kafka: b. Orkney Islands; lives in Crowborough 1929–32, London (Hampstead: Downshire Hill), Swaffham Prior 1956–9; buried in Swaffham Prior; commemorated in Swanston. *The Castle* (trans.) 1930 (71b), *An Autobiography* 1954 (190a), *Collected Poems* 1960 (317a), *Selected Letters of Edwin Muir*, ed. P. H. Butter, 1974 (316b–317a).

Mulgan, John Alan Edward (1911–45), New Zealand novelist: educ. Oxford (Merton College) 1933–5; works in Oxford. *Poems of Freedom* (ed.) 1938, *Man Alone* 1939, *Report on Experience* 1947 (268b).

Mulock, Dinah Maria. See Craik, Mrs. Dinah Maria.

Mulso, Hester. See Chapone, Mrs. Hester.

Munro, Hector Hugh ('Saki') (1870–1916), short-story writer: lives in Pilton. 'Sredni Vashtar' in *Chronicles of Clovis* 1911, 'The Lumber-Room' in *Beasts and Super-Beasts* 1914, *The Square Egg* 1924 (280b).

Munro, Neil (1864–1930), novelist: b. Inveraray; lives in Glasgow 1918–27, Helensburgh 1927–30; commemorated near Inveraray. *John Splendid* 1898 (132a, 140b, 147a), *The Vital Spark* 1906 (132a), *The Clyde: River and Firth* 1907, *The Brave Days* 1931 (118b).

Murphy, Arthur (1727–1805), actor and playwright; author of *The Way to Keep Him* 1760: lodges in London (Strand: The Strand) 1744; works in Cork 1747; lives in Lincoln's Inn, London (Holborn) 1757–88; introduces the Thrales to Dr. Johnson (Southwark: Park St.), visits the Thrales (Streatham); visits Great Yarmouth; frequents the Bedford Coffee House in London (Covent Garden: Covent Garden) and St. George's Coffee House (Strand: The Strand); lives in London (Hammersmith: Hammersmith Ter.) 1795–9; buried in St. Paul's churchyard (Hammersmith).

Murray, John (1778–1843), publisher: founds the *Quarterly Review* in London (City: Fleet St.) 1809; moves publishing premises (Mayfair: Albemarle St.); refuses to publish Byron's memoirs (Mayfair: Albemarle St.) 1824.

Murry, John Middleton (1889–1957), critic: educ. Christ's Hospital and Oxford (Brasenose College); lives in London (St. John's Wood: Acacia Rd.) 1915; visits D. H. Lawrence in Zennor 1916; lives in Mylor 1916; visits Garsington; m. Katherine Mansfield and lives in London (Hampstead: East Heath Rd.) 1918. *Rhythm* 1911 (ed.), *Between Two Worlds* 1934 (263a).

Murry, Kathleen Mansfield (*née* Beauchamp, 'Katherine Mansfield') (1888–1923), author of *Bliss and Other Stories* (1920) and *The Garden Party* (1922): educ. and lives in London (Marylebone: Harley St.) 1903–6; lives in London (St. John's Wood: Acacia Rd.) 1915; visits Garsington; visits D. H. Lawrence in Zennor 1916; lives in Mylor 1916; m. John Middleton Murry and lives in London (Hampstead: East Heath Rd.) 1918. *The Signature* (214a), *Journal* 1927 (190a).

Myers, Frederic William Henry (1843–1901), poet and scholar: educ. Cambridge (Trinity College); Fellow at Cambridge (Trinity College) 1865; invites George Eliot to Cambridge (Trinity College).

Nairne, Lady Caroline (*née* **Oliphant**) (1766–1845), writer of ballads in *Lays from Strathearn* 1846: b. Gask House; returns as a widow and is buried there.

Nash (or Nashe), Thomas (1567–1601), poet and dramatist: b. Lowestoft; educ. Cambridge (St. John's College); visits Titchfield; imprisoned in London (City: Farringdon St.). *Strange Newes* 1593 (48a), *The Isle of Dogs* 1597 (176a), *Lenten Stuffe* 1599 (125a).

Opie, Amelia (1769–1853), novelist and poet: lives in Norwich; has her portrait painted in London (Marylebone: Lisson Grove). *Father and Daughter* 1801, *Poems* 1802, *Adeline Mowbray* 1804 (252b), *Illustrations of Political Economy* 1832–4 (253a).

O'Rahilly, Aodhgan (d. 1728), one of the Four Kerry Poets: memorials in Killarney and Muckross.

Orczy, Baroness Emmuska (Mrs. M. W. Barstow) (1865–1947), novelist: lives in Acol 1908–9. *The Scarlet Pimpernel* 1905 (223a), *Beau Brocade* 1908, *Nest of the Sparrowhawk* (3a), *Links in the Chain of Life* 1947 (223a).

Ó Reachtabhra, Antoine ('Blind Raftery') (1784–1834), poet: loves the miller's daughter nr. Thoor Ballylee, Gort; buried in Killeenen.

Orwell, George. See Blair, Eric.

Osborne, Dorothy (1627–95), letter-writer: lives at Chicksands (perhaps her birthplace) until 1654; meets William Temple and stays in Carisbrooke 1648; visits Moor Park, Herts.; m. 1654 and spends honeymoon at Moor Park, Herts. 1654–5; moves to Farnham 1680. *Letters*, ed. E. A. Parry, 1888, ed. G. C. Moore Smith, 1928 (52b, 60a, 104b).

Ossian (or Oisin) (?3rd c.), legendary Gaelic bard: said to have been born in Glen Coe; traditionally buried in Sma' Glen.

Ó Súilleabháin, Tadhg Gaelach (1715–95), Gaelic poet: lives in Kilmacthomas; buried in Ballylaneen.

O'Sullivan, Eoghan Ruadh (d. 1784), one of the Four Kerry Poets: frequents 'Court of Poetry' in Ráthluirc; memorials in Killarney and Muckross.

O'Sullivan, Maurice (1904–50), author of *Twenty Years A-Growing* (1953): b. and lives on the Blasket Islands.

Ó Tuama, Seán (1706–75), Gaelic poet: lives in Croom; frequents 'Court of Poetry' in Ráthluirc; holds his own 'Court' in Croom after 1754; buried in Croom.

Otway, Thomas (1652–85), dramatist: b. Milland; spends early years in Woolbeding; educ. Winchester and Oxford (Christ Church); buried in London (Strand: St. Clement Danes); commemorated nr. Milland.

Ouida. See Ramée, Marie Louise de la.

Owen, Wilfred (1893–1918), poet: b. Oswestry; meets Siegfried Sassoon in hospital in Edinburgh 1917.

Paine, Thomas (1737–1809), political writer: b. and educ. Thetford; m. and lives in Sandwich 1759; lives in Lewes before going to America in 1774; his bones disinterred from New York grave and brought to Liverpool 1819; perhaps reinterred in Normandy. *The Rights of Man* 1791–2 (321a).

Palgrave, Francis Turner (1824–97), poet and critic: boyhood home in London (Hampstead: New End Hospital); educ. London (City: Charterhouse) and Oxford (Balliol College); Fellow at Oxford (Exeter College) 1847; Vice-Principal of training college in London (Twickenham: Whitton) 1850–5; Professor of Poetry at Oxford (Exeter College) 1885–95. *The Golden Treasury of Songs and Lyrics* 1861, 1896 (224b, 265a).

Paris, Matthew (d. 1259), monk and historian: enters monastery at St. Albans 1217; chronicler there 1236–59.

Park, Mungo (1771–1806), surgeon, explorer, and travel-writer: b. Foulshiels; practises as surgeon in Peebles 1801–5; memorial and museum in Selkirk. *Travels in the Interior of Africa* 1799 (113b).

Parker, Eric (1870–1955), writer on country life and sport: educ. Eton. *Eton in the Eighties* 1914 (106b–107a), *Playing Fields* 1922 (107a).

Parnell, Thomas (1679–1718), poet and scholar: b. and educ. Dublin; Archdeacon of Clogher 1706–16; dies and is buried in Chester. *Poems on Several Occasions* 1722, 'Elegy to an Old Beauty' (63a).

Paston, John (1421–66), letter-writer: m. Margaret Mautby 1440; lives at Caister Castle, Norwich; buried in Bacton; tomb removed to Paston. *The Paston Letters and Papers of the Fifteenth Century*, ed. N. Davis, Part I 1971, Part II 1976 (13b, 43a, 242a, 252a, b, 274b, 277a).

Paston, Margaret (*née* Mautby) (d. 1484), letter-writer: lives in Mautby; m. John Paston 1440; lives at Caister Castle, Norwich; returns to Mautby as widow 1466; buried in Mautby. *Paston Letters*. See Paston, John.

Pater, Walter Horatio (1839–94), essayist and critic: educ. Oxford (The Queen's College); Fellow at Oxford (Brasenose College) 1864; lives many years in Oxford; buried in Oxford. 'Winckelmann' in *Studies in the History of the Renaissance* 1873, *Marius the Epicurean* 1885, *Imaginary Portraits* 1887, *Appreciations* 1889, *Gaston de Latour* 1896 (262b).

Patmore, Coventry Kersey Dighton (1823–96), poet: lives in London (Marylebone: Percy St.) 1848–62; lives at Temple Grove 1865–75, in Hastings 1875–91, Lymington 1891–6. *The Angel in the House* 1854–62 (205b, 320a).

Peacham, Henry (1576?–1643?), schoolmaster and miscellaneous writer: educ. Cambridge (Trinity College); tutor in Norwich 1613–14; Master of Grammar School, Wymondham 1617–21. *The Compleat Gentleman* 1622 (252b, 346b).

Peacock, Thomas Love (1785–1866), poet and satirical novelist: b. Weymouth; childhood in Chertsey; returns from London to Chertsey and meets Fanny Faulkner at Newark Priory 1807; visits Shelley in Bishopsgate 1815; lives in Marlow 1816–18; buys house in Shepperton 1823 and retires there 1856; buried in Shepperton. 'Remember Me' 1809, 'Al mio primiero amore' 1813 (249a), *Nightmare Abbey* 1818 (239a), *The Misfortunes of Elphin* 1829 (325b), *Crotchet Castle* 1831 (249a), *Recollections of Childhood* 1837 (58a), 'Revisiting Newark Abbey' 1842 (249a), *Memoirs of Shelley* 1858, *Gryll Grange* 1860 (299a).

Pearse, Patrick (Pádraig Mac Piarais) (1879–1916), schoolmaster and poet: b. Dublin; educ. Dublin (University College); establishes a school in Dublin for teaching Irish; executed after the Easter Rising in Dublin 1916.

Pecock, Reginald (1395?–1460?), theological writer: Bishop of Chichester 1450; retires to Thorney 1458. *The Repressor of over much blaming of the Clergy* 1455, *Book of Faith* 1456, *Provoker* (not extant) (59a).

Penrose, Elizabeth ('Mrs. Markham') (1780–1837), writer of histories for the young: lives and is buried in Lincoln.

Pepys, Samuel (1633–1703), diarist: b. London (City: Fleet St.); educ. Huntingdon, London (City: St. Paul's School), and Cambridge (Magdalene College); m. in London (Westminster: St. Margaret's) 1655; begins *Diary* in London (Westminster: Axe Yard); works at Navy Office in London and lives in Seething Lane 1659–73 (City: Tower); lives in Strand (Buckingham St.) 1697–1700, Clapham Common 1700–3; banquets in the City (Guildhall) 1663; buys music outside Temple Church (City); visits Vauxhall Gardens and Smithfield; visits Will's Coffee House in Bow St. (Covent Garden) 1668, Brampton, Bath, Bristol, Oxford, Cambridge, Salisbury, Audley End 1677, Tunbridge Wells, Stourhead. *Diary* 1970–6 (12a, 16a, 30b, 34a, 46b, 178a, 183a, 184a, 215b, 225b–226a, 227b, 258a, 295a).

Percy, Thomas (1729–1811), antiquary and poet: b. Bridgnorth; educ. Bridgnorth, Newport (Salop), and Oxford (Christ Church); discovers ancient manuscripts in Shifnal; vicar of Easton Maudit 1756–78; visits Goldsmith in London 1761; lodges in London (City: St. Martin's le Grand) 1760s–1770s; D.D. at Cambridge (Emmanuel College) 1770; Dean of Carlisle 1778–82; Bishop of Dromore 1782–1811; buried in Dromore. *Reliques of Ancient English Poetry* 1765 (94a, b, 157b, 300a), *The Northumberland Household Book of 1512* 1768 (180a), *Memoir of Goldsmith* 1801 (94b).

Philips, Ambrose ('Namby-Pamby') (1675?–1749), poet: quarrels with Pope at Button's Coffee House, London (Covent Garden: Russell St.); buried in London (Mayfair: South Audley St.). *Pastorals* 1710 (185a).

Philips, John (1676–1709), poet: educ. Winchester and Oxford (Christ Church). *The Splendid Shilling* 1705 (263b).

Phillpotts, Eden (1862–1960), novelist: lives in Torquay *c.* 1901–29; visits Ewelme; spends last years and d. in Broad Clyst. *Children of the Mist* 1898 (74b), *The Secret Woman* 1905 (74b, 324b), *The Thief of Virtue* 1910, *Widecombe Fair* 1912, *The Farmer's Wife* 1917 (324b), *Children of Men* 1923 (74b), *Yellow Sands* 1926, *From the angle of 88* 1951 (324b).

Pilkington, Letitia (1712–50), poet: comes to London from Dublin and sets up a bookshop (St. James's: St. James's St.). *Memoirs* 1748 (213b–214a).

Pindar, Peter. See Wolcot, John.

Pinero, Sir Arthur Wing (1855–1934), dramatist: lives in London (Marylebone: Harley St.). *The Second Mrs. Tanqueray* 1893, *Trelawny of the Wells* 1898 (204b).

Piozzi, Mrs. See Thrale, Mrs. Hester Lynch.

Pitt, Christopher (1699–1748), poet: rector of Pimperne 1722–48.

Poe, Edgar Allan (1809–49), American poet and story writer: comes to Scotland and attends school in Irvine 1815; at school in London (Chelsea: Sloane St.) 1816–17, (Stoke Newington) 1817–20. *The Raven* 1845 (169a).

Pollok, Robert (1795–1827), Scottish poet: d. Southampton and commemorated there. *The Course of Time* (10 books) 1827 (306a).

Pope, Alexander (1688–1744), poet: b. London (City: Plough Ct.); educ. Twyford and at home; lives in Binfield 1700–13, London (Chiswick) 1716–18, (Twickenham) 1718–44; visits West Grinstead

(Clifton), and Oxford (Trinity College); lecturer in classics at Oxford (Trinity College) 1886–7; Fellow and Professor of English Literature at Cambridge (Jesus College) 1912; lives in Fowey 1892–1944; memorials in Fowey and Truro. *The Astonishing History of Troy Town* 1888 (113b), *The Oxford Book of English Verse* (ed.) 1899 (113b, 273a), *Major Vigoureux* 1907 (297a), *The Oxford Book of Ballads* (ed.) 1910 (273a), *On the Art of Writing* 1916, *On the Art of Reading* 1920 (45b).

Radcliffe, Mrs. Ann (*née* **Ward**) (1764–1823), novelist: lives in London (Victoria: Bressendon Pl.) 1815–23; buried in London (Bayswater: Hyde Park Pl.). *Mysteries of Udolpho* 1794, reprinted 1970 (226b).

Ralegh, Sir Walter (1552?–1618), historian and poet: b. East Budleigh; educ. Oxford (Oriel College) and Middle Temple, London (City: Temple); frequents Gray's Inn, London (Holborn); in army in Ireland and entertained at Castlegregory 1580; reputed to have been in action at Smerwick 1580; holds court at Padstow 1585; lives at Youghal 1588–9; imprisoned in London (City: Tower) 1592; leases castle at Sherborne 1592, owns it 1599 and builds new one; establishes club at Mermaid Tavern, London (City: Bread St.) *c.* 1603; tried for treason and condemned to death at Winchester 1603; imprisoned in London (City: Tower) 1603–16; beheaded and buried in London (Westminster: nr. St. Margaret's) 1618. *History of the World* 1614, 1634 (308a, 338b), Poem to Queen Elizabeth (88a, b), Will 1597 (299b), Speech from the scaffold (339b).

Ramée, Marie Louise de la ('Ouida') (1839–1908), novelist: b. Bury St. Edmunds; lives in London (Hammersmith: Ravenscourt Sq.) 1857–66, (Marylebone: Welbeck St. and Langham Pl.) 1867–70. *Granville de Vigne* 1863, *Strathmore* 1865, *Under Two Flags* 1867 (189a).

Ramsay, Allan (1686–1758), poet: b. Leadhills; educ. Crawford; m. in Leadhills; wigmaker's apprentice in Edinburgh 1701; becomes bookseller 1718 and publisher 1720 in Edinburgh; buried in London (Marylebone: Marylebone High St.); memorials in Edinburgh and Penicuik. *Tea Table Miscellany* 1724–32, *The Gentle Shepherd* (96a).

Randolph, Thomas (1605–35), writer of English and Latin verse: educ. London (Westminster School) and Cambridge (Trinity College); Fellow at Cambridge (Trinity College) 1629–32; frequents Devil Tavern in London (City: Fleet St.); buried

in Blatherwycke. *Aristippus or the Jovial Philosopher* 1630 (49a), 'An Ode to Anthony Stafford to hasten him into the Country' (25b).

Ransome, Arthur (1884–1967), writer of stories for children: stays at Newby Bridge; lives in Lowick 1947–9; spends last years at Haverthwaite. *Swallows and Amazons* 1931 (249a).

Raspe, Rudolph Eric (1737–94), mineralogist and compiler of Baron Munchausen's stories: buried in Muckross. *Baron Munchausen's Narrative of his Marvellous Travels and Campaigns in Russia 1785* (244b).

Raverat, Gwen (*née* **Gwendolen Mary Darwin**) (1885–1957), writer and woodengraver: b. Cambridge (see Darwin College); spends holidays at Downe until 1896. *Period Piece* 1952 (45a, 79b).

Read, Sir Herbert (1893–1968), poet and critic: b. Muscoates; lives in Stonegrave. *The Green Child* 1935, *In Defence of Shelley* 1935, *Poetry and Anarchism* 1938 (312a), *Annals of Innocence and Experience* 1940 (245b, 312a).

Reade, Charles (1814–84), novelist and dramatist: b. Ipsden; educ. Oxford (Magdalen College); enters Lincoln's Inn, London (Holborn) 1835; Fellow at Oxford (Magdalen College) 1838; spends holidays in Crieff 1838–48; lives in London (Mayfair: Bolton Row) 1856–68, (Hyde Park: Albert Ter.) 1869–79, (Hammersmith: Uxbridge Rd.) 1882–4; memorial in London (City: St. Paul's Cathedral). *Peg Woffington* 1852 (267a), *Christie Johnson* 1853 (70b), *It is Never too Late to Mend* 1856 (207a), *The Cloister and the Hearth* 1861 (47b, 207a, 267a), *Hard Cash* 1863 (207a), *Griffith Gaunt* 1866 (197b, 207a), *A Terrible Temptation* 1871 (197b).

Reeve, Clara (1729–1807), author of *The Champion of Virtue, a Gothic Story* (1777), later called *The Old English Baron* (reprinted 1967): b. Ipswich.

Reid, Forrest (1875–1947), novelist, author of *Uncle Stephen* (1931) and *Young Tom* (1944): b. Belfast; educ. Belfast and Cambridge (Christ's College).

Reynolds, John Hamilton (1796–1852), poet and friend of Keats: b. Shrewsbury; educ. Shrewsbury and London (City: St. Paul's School); lives in London (Soho: Golden Sq.) 1832, (Soho: Great Marlborough St.) 1836–8; appointed clerk to County Court in Newport (I.O.W.) 1846; d. and is buried in Newport.

Rhys, Ernest (1859–1946), poet and novelist: lives in London (Hampstead: Vale of

Rossetti, Dante Gabriel (Gabriel Charles Dante) (1828–82), poet and painter: b. London (Marylebone: Hallam St.); lives in London (City: Victoria Embankment) 1852–62; stays in Hastings 1854; m. in Hastings 1860; lives in London (Chelsea: Cheyne Walk) 1862–82; visits Old Dailly 1868–9; shares tenancy with Morris in Kelmscott 1871–4; lives last months and is buried in Birchington; memorials in Birchington, Hastings, and London (Chelsea: Cheyne Walk). 'The King's Tragedy' in *Ballads and Sonnets* 1881 (279b).

Rousseau, Jean-Jacques (1712–78), French philosopher: stays in London (Chiswick) 1765–6, Wootton (Staffs.) 1766; visits Ellastone 1766; said to have stayed in Nuneham Courtenay 1767. *La Nouvelle Héloïse* 1761 (162b, 254b–255a), *Confessions* 1781, 1788 (344a).

Rowe, Nicholas (1674–1718), playwright and Poet Laureate: b. Little Barford; educ. London (Westminster School); enters Middle Temple, London (City: Temple); frequents the Cocoa Tree (St. James's: Pall Mall); buried in Westminster Abbey.

Ruskin, John (1819–1900), writer on art and social subjects: b. London (Holborn: Hunter St.); stays as a child in Keswick; spends holidays as a boy in Perth; educ. Oxford (Christ Church); lives in London (Holborn) 1819–23, (Herne Hill) 1823–42; stays in Leamington Spa 1841; lives in London (Denmark Hill) 1842–72; m. in Perth 1848; lives in London (Herne Hill) 1852–4; makes frequent visits to Wallington House 1850s; promotes building of University Museum in Oxford (see Christ Church) 1855–8; visits Winnington Hall 1859–68; Slade Professor of Art at Oxford 1869; lives in Abingdon and Oxford (Corpus Christi College) 1871; buys property in Brantwood 1871 and lives there 1871–1900; buys land in Sheffield for the Guild of St. George 1876; buried in Coniston; memorials in London (Westminster Abbey), Keswick, and Oxford. *The King of the Golden River* 1841 (154b), *Modern Painters* 1843, 1846–60, *The Stones of Venice* 1851–3 (185b–186a), *The Winnington Letters*, ed. V. A. Burd, 1969 (341a), *Fors Clavigera* 1871–84 (30b), *Praeterita* 1885–9 (30b, 185b, 193b).

Russell, George William ('AE' or 'Æ') (1867–1935), poet, journalist, and painter: b. Lurgan; educ. Dublin; lives in Dublin *c.* 1877–1932, Bournemouth in his last years; d. Bournemouth and is buried in Dublin (Mount Jerome Cemetery). *Homeward: Songs by the Way* 1894, *Deirdre* 1902, *The Irish Homestead* (merged with *The Irish Statesman* 1923) (ed.) (88a).

Rutherford, Mark. See White, William Hale.

Rymer, Thomas (1641–1713), critic and archaeologist: b. Yafforth; educ. Cambridge (Sidney Sussex College). *A Short View of Tragedy* 1692 (48b, 346a), *Fœdera* (ed.) 1704–35 (346a).

Sackville, Charles, Baron Buckhurst, 6th Earl of Dorset (1638–1706), poet and patron: lives at Knole; visits Epsom 1668; frequents the Cock Tavern in London (Covent Garden: Bow St.); buried in Withyham. 'To all you ladies now at land' in *Collection of Poems* by Charles Sackville and Charles Sedley, 1701 (342a).

Sackville, Thomas, Baron Buckhurst, 1st Earl of Dorset (1536–1608), poet and patron: b. Withyham; lives at Knole; buried in St. Bride's Church, London (City: Fleet St.). *Mirror for Magistrates* (with William Baldwin and George Ferrers) 1559, *Gorboduc* (with Thomas Norton) 1565 (150a).

Sackville-West, The Hon. Victoria Mary (1892–1962), poet and novelist: b. Knole; lives in London (Belgravia: Ebury St.) 1920s, Sissinghurst Castle 1930–62. *Knole and the Sackvilles* 1923, *The Edwardians* 1930 (150a), *The Dark Island* 1934, *Saint Joan of Arc* 1936, *Pepita* 1937 (303a).

Saintsbury, George Edward Bateman (1845–1933), literary historian, critic, and essayist: b. Southampton; educ. Oxford (Merton College); Professor at Edinburgh 1895–1915; hon. Fellow at Oxford (Merton College) from 1909; lives in Bath 1915–33; buried in Southampton. *History of Criticism* 1900–4, *Notes on a Cellar Book* 1920, *A Scrap Book* 1922 (18a).

Saki. See Munro, Hector Hugh.

Santayana, George (1863–1952), Spanish-born American Professor of Philosophy at Harvard: stays in Oxford during the First World War. *The Last Puritan* 1935, *My Host the World* 1953 (260a).

Sassoon, Siegfried Lorraine (1886–1967), poet and novelist: educ. Marlborough and Cambridge (Clare College); lives in Matfield; visits Garsington on leave from the Front 1916; meets Wilfred Owen while convalescing in Edinburgh 1917; lives and dies in Heytesbury. *Collected Poems 1908–1956* 1961 (44b, 133b), 'At the grave of Henry Vaughan' (163b).

Savage, Richard (1697?–1743), poet: imprisoned in London (City: Newgate St.) 1727; stays in Swansea 1739–40;

imprisoned, d., and buried in Bristol. *The Bastard* 1728, *The Wanderer* 1729 (317b).

Sayers, Dorothy Leigh (1893–1957), poet, classical scholar, and detective-story writer: b. and educ. Oxford (Somerville College); lives in Bluntisham 1898–1917, Christchurch (Cambs.), Witham 1929–57, London (Bloomsbury: Great James St.). *Op. 1* 1916, *Catholic Tales* 1918 (26a), *Oxford Poetry* (ed.) 1917–19 (272a), *The Nine Tailors* 1934 (60b, 342a), *Gaudy Night* 1935 (272a), *Busman's Honeymoon* 1936 (259b, 272a, 342a), *The Man Born to be King* 1942, Dante's *Inferno* (trans.) 1940, and *Purgatorio* (trans.) 1955 (342a).

Schreiner, Olive Emilie Albertina ('Ralph Iron') (1855–1920), novelist: lives in London (Hampstead: Downshire Hill) 1885, (Paddington: Portsea Pl.) 1885–7; winters in Hastings; stays in Bournemouth 1886. *The Story of an African Farm* 1883 (209a).

Scott, Hugh Stowell ('Henry Seton Merriman') (1862–1903), author of the historical novels *In Kedar's Tents* (1897) and *Barlasch of the Guard* (1902): b. Newcastle upon Tyne.

Scott, Sir Walter (1771–1832), poet and novelist: b. Edinburgh; convalesces in Smailholm; educ. Kelso and Edinburgh; lives in Edinburgh to 1830; meets Charlotte Carpenter in Gilsland 1797, m. her in Carlisle 1797; visits Anna Seward in Lichfield; visits the Black Dwarf's Cottage 1797; spends summers in Lasswade 1798–1804; frequents Jedburgh; stays in Clovenfords 1799; Ashiestiel 1804–12; Sheriff of Selkirk 1800–32; visits the Wordsworths at Coleorton Hall 1807; stays in Mudeford 1807, Greta Bridge 1809 and 1812, and Doune *c.* 1816; donates tombstone for the prototype of Jeanie Deans in Irongray; lives in Abbotsford 1812–32; visits Kenilworth 1821; attends Literary Club meetings in London (St. James's: St. James's St.) and visits Mrs. Mary Ann Hughes (City: St. Paul's Churchyard); tours Ireland, visiting Dublin, Cork, Killarney, Glendalough, Mallow, Edgeworthstown 1825; visits Windermere 1825, Llangollen 1825, Durham 1827, Tibbie Shiel's Inn; meets James Hogg at the Gordon Arms; views Abbotsford from Galashiels; d. Abbotsford; buried in Dryburgh Abbey; commemorated in Clovenfords, Selkirk, Smailholm, Edinburgh, and London (Westminster Abbey). *Scott's Minstrelsy of the Scottish Border*, 3 vols. 1802–3 (98a), 'Rosabelle' (148b, 288b) in *The Lay of the Last Minstrel* 1805

(11b, 142a), *Marmion, A Tale of Flodden Field* 1808 (11b, 112a, 126b, 245a, 251a, 294b, 304b, 318b), *The Lady of the Lake* 1810 (11b, 103b, 139b, 315b, 326a), 'A weary lot is thine, fair maid' and 'Brignal Banks' in *Rokeby* 1813 (126a), *The Lord of the Isles* 1815 (141a), 'Glenfinlas or Lord Ronald's Coronach' (119b), 'Glencoe' in Thomson's *Select Melodies* 1814 (119a), 'The Maid of Neidpath' (247a), *Waverley* 1814 (11b, 78b, 98a, 108b, 109b), *Guy Mannering* 1815 (92a, 117a), *The Antiquary* 1816 (9b, 307a), *The Black Dwarf* (25a) and *Old Mortality* 1816 (126b), first titles in the series *Tales of My Landlord* (153a, 206b), *Rob Roy* 1817 (2b, 14b, 326a), *The Heart of Midlothian* 1818 (102a, 211b), *A Legend of Montrose* 1819 (140b, 315b), *Ivanhoe* 1819 (11a, 66b, 347a), *The Abbot* 1820 (164a), *Kenilworth* 1821 (72a, 143b, 271b, 328b, 333b), *Peveril of the Peak* 1823 (183a, 277b, 323b), *St. Ronan's Well* 1823 (140a), *Redgauntlet* 1824 (76a), *The Betrothed* 1825 (64a), *Woodstock* 1826 (76b, 343b), *St. Valentine's Day, or The Fair Maid of Perth* 1828 (279b), *Anne of Geierstein* 1829 (47b), 'The Eve of St. John' (304b), contributions to the *Quarterly Review* (206b).

Scott, William Bell (1811–90), poet and painter: annual guest at Old Daily; paints murals at Wallington House; lives in London (Chelsea: Cheyne Walk); d. and is buried in Old Dailly. 'The Old Scottish Home', 'Outside the Temple', 'Lost Love' (256a), 'Bellevue House' (172a).

Sedley, Sir Charles (1639?–1701), poet, dramatist, and wit; author of 'The Mulberry Garden' acted in 1668 and 'Bellamira' acted in 1687: educ. Oxford (Wadham College) 1656; stays with Dryden in Charlton 1665–6; takes the waters with Charles Sackville and Nell Gwynne in Epsom 1668; frequents the Cock Tavern in London (Covent Garden: Bow St.); spends last years in London (Hampstead: Haverstock Hill).

Selden, John (1584–1654), jurist and antiquary, author of *Table Talk* (1689): b. nr. Worthing; educ. Chichester and Oxford (Hertford College); enters Clifford's Inn, London (City: Clifford's Inn) 1602; frequents the Mermaid Tavern (City: Bread St.); lives at Wrest Park; buried in London (City: Temple Church); bequeaths books and manuscripts to the Bodleian (Oxford: Bodleian Library). *Marmora Arundelliana* 1624 (345b).

Settle, Elkanah (1648–1724), dramatist: educ. London (Westminster School) and Oxford (Trinity College); appointed City poet, London (City: Guildhall) 1691; writes sketches for Bartholomew Fair (Smithfield); lives 1718–24 and is buried in the Charterhouse (City: Charterhouse Sq.). *Cambyses, King of Persia* 1666 (272b), *The Siege of Troy* 1707 (215b).

Seward, Anna ('the Swan of Lichfield') (1747–1809), poet and letter-writer; b. Eyam; lives in Lichfield 1754–1809; visits Bath, Cowslip Green 1791, Eartham 1792 and 1796; writes epitaphs on Lady Miller of Batheaston at Bath and on W. B. Stevens at Repton. *Louisa* 1782 (93a).

Sewell, Anna (1820–78), novelist: b. Great Yarmouth; spends childhood holidays in Buxton; lives in Norwich 1867–78; buried in Lamas; memorial in Norwich. *Black Beauty* 1877 (42b, 253a).

Sewell, Mrs. Mary (1797–1884), author of the verses *Homely Ballads* 1858, *Mother's Last Words* 1860, and *Our Father's Care* 1861: lives in Norwich 1867–84.

Shadwell, Thomas (1642?–92), dramatist and poet: educ. Cambridge (Gonville and Caius College) 1656; enters Middle Temple, London (City: Temple); buried in Chelsea Old Church (Chelsea: Cheyne Walk). *Epsom Wells* 1673 (105a).

Shakespeare, William ('the Swan of Avon') (1564–1616), actor, poet, and dramatist: b. Stratford-upon-Avon (see also Clifford Chambers); educ. and lives to *c.* 1585 in Stratford-upon-Avon; m. Anne Hathaway of Shottery (see also Worcester) 1582; poaches deer in Charlecote Park 1585; frequents Titchfield; visits Wilton 1603; frequents the Mitre Tavern and the Mermaid in London (City: Fleet St. and Bread St.), acts at the Theatre and the Curtain (Shoreditch: Curtain Rd.), at the Rose and the Globe (Southwark: Bankside), and at Blackfriars' Theatre (City: Blackfriars), ? lives in Silver St. (City: Aldermanbury); spends last years, d., and is buried in Stratford-upon-Avon; credited with the epitaph to Thomas Stanley in Tong; commemorated by a flower garden in Manchester; commemorated in London (City: Aldermanbury), (Southwark Cathedral), (Westminster Abbey), by the Royal Shakespeare Memorial Theatre in Stratford-upon-Avon. *2 Henry VI* 1592, printed 1594 (218b), *Venus and Adonis* printed 1593 (214b, 262a), *The Rape of Lucrece* printed 1594 (214b), *The Comedy of Errors* 1594, printed 1623 (195a), *King Richard III* 1594, printed 1597 (176a, 218a), *Love's Labour's Lost* 1595, printed 1598 (323a), *Romeo and Juliet* 1595, printed 1597 (323a, b), *A Midsummer Night's Dream* 1595 or 1596, printed 1600 (218a, 323b), *1 Henry IV* 1597, printed 1598 (18a, 114a), *The Passionate Pilgrim* 1599 (323a), *As You Like It* 1603, printed 1623 (218a, 338a), *Twelfth Night* 1600–1, printed 1623 (218a, 323b, 332b), *Hamlet* 1603 (218a), *King Lear* 1608 (79a, 218a), *Sonnets* 1609, *A Lover's Complaint* 1609 (323a), *Cymbeline* 1610, printed 1623 (174b), *Macbeth* 1623 (218a).

Sharp, William ('Fiona Macleod'), novelist and critic; author of *The Mountain Lovers* (1895) and *The Sin Eater* (1895): educ. and works in Glasgow.

Shaw, George Bernard (1856–1950), playwright and critic: b. and educ. Dublin; holidays in Dalkey 1866–74; lives in London (Bloomsbury: Fitzroy Sq.) 1887–98 and m. 1898, (Adelphi: Adelphi Ter.) 1899–1927, (Westminster: Whitehall Ct.) 1928–45, Ayot St. Lawrence 1906–50; visits Garinish Island 1923, Coole Park, Rinvyle, Limpsfield; frequents Old Wyldes in London (Hampstead Garden Suburb); his plays performed at the Royal Court Theatre in London (Chelsea: Sloane Sq.); commemorated in Dublin and Ayot St. Lawrence. *Widowers' Houses* (with William Archer) 1892, *Mrs. Warren's Profession* 1893, *Arms and the Man* 1894, *Candida* 1894 (168b), *The Devil's Disciple* 1900 (207b), *Man and Superman* 1903, *Major Barbara* 1905 (164b), *Pygmalion* 1916 (184b), *Saint Joan* 1924 (115b).

Sheehan, Patrick Augustine (1852–1913), novelist: b. Mallow; works in Exeter 1875–7; priest in Doneraile 1895–1913; commemorated in Mallow and Doneraile. *Luke Delmege, My New Curate* 1898, *Lisheen* 1907 (77a).

Shelley, Mary Wollstonecraft (née Godwin) (1797–1851), novelist: lives in Bishopsgate 1815; accompanies Shelley and Peacock on the river to Lechlade; lives in Bath 1816, Marlow 1817, last years in London (Belgravia: Chester Sq.); buried in Bournemouth. *Frankenstein, or the Modern Prometheus* 1818 (29b, 239a).

Shelley, Percy Bysshe (1792–1822), poet: b. Warnham; educ. Eton and Oxford (University College); lodges in London (Soho: Poland St.) 1811; stays in the Elan Valley 1811 and 1812; m. Harriet Westbrook in Edinburgh 1811; stays in York 1811, Keswick 1811–12; lodges in Lynmouth 1812, Tremadoc 1812–13;

(159b, 252a), *Why Come ye nat to Courte* *c.* 1542–6 (187b).

Skinner, John (1721–1807), historian and song-writer: educ. Aberdeen; minister in Longside 1742–1807; d. Aberdeen; buried in Longside. 'The Reel of Tullochgorum', 'Eire with the Crookit Horn', 'Tune your Fiddle' in Johnson's *Musical Museum, Songs and Poems* 1859 (230b).

Smart, Christopher (1722–71), poet: b. Shipbourne; educ. Durham and Cambridge (Pembroke College); Fellow at Cambridge (Pembroke College) 1745–55; imprisoned for debt in London (Southwark: Scovell Rd.) *c.* 1769–71; his songs sung at Ranelagh (Chelsea: Ranelagh Gardens). *A Trip to Cambridge* (47a), *Song to David* 1763 (47b).

Smith, Adam (1723–90), philosopher, economic theorist, and member of Dr. Johnson's Literary Club: b. Kirkcaldy; educ. Glasgow and Oxford (Balliol College); retires to Kirkcaldy 1766. *An Enquiry into the Nature and Causes of the Wealth of Nations* 1776 (117a, 148b).

Smith, Albert Richard (1816–60), writer of humorous sketches and friend of Dickens: b. Chertsey. *Blanche Heriot or the Chertsey Curfew* 1842 (58b).

Smith, Alexander (1830–67), poet, essayist, and novelist: b. Kilmarnock; lives in Glasgow and Edinburgh 1854–67; visits Skye, Inveraray; buried in Edinburgh. *A Life Drama and other poems* 1853 (118a), *Sonnets on the War* 1855 (100b), 'Glasgow' in *City Poems* 1857 (118a), *A Summer in Skye* 1865 (118a, 303b), *Alfred Hagart's Household* 1866 (118a, 147a).

Smith, Mrs. Charlotte (*née* Turner) (1749–1806), poet and novelist: spends childhood at Bignor Park; in debtors' prison in London (Southwark: Scovell Rd.) *c.* 1784; lives in Woolbeding *c.* 1786, Chichester *c.* 1787, Brighton *c.* 1791; frequents Eartham; last years and d. in Tilford; buried in Guildford. *Elegiac Sonnets* 1784 (33a, 344a), *Manon Lescaut* (trans.) 1785 (344a), 'Bignor Park' (22b), 'To the Arun' (10b, 22b), *The Old Manor House* 1793, reprinted 1969 (93a), *Beachy Head and Other Poems* 1807 (33a).

Smith, Florence Margaret ('Stevie Smith') (1902–71), novelist and poet: b. Kingston upon Hull; educ. and lives in London (Palmer's Green) 1907–71. *Novel on Yellow Paper* 1936, *Over the Frontier* 1938, *The Holiday* 1949, *Selected Poems* 1972, *Collected Poems* 1975 (209a).

Smith, Horace (1779–1849), novelist and parodist: clerk in London (City: Coleman St.); visits Gore House (Kensington: Kensington Gore); lives in London (Fulham: New King's Rd.) 1818–21, Brighton, last years and d. in Tunbridge Wells. *Rejected Addresses* (with his brother James) 1812 (175b), contributions to the *New Monthly Magazine* (33b).

Smith, James (1775–1839), parodist: educ. Chigwell; visits Gore House, London (Kensington: Kensington Gore); buried in St. Martin-in-the-Fields (Strand: Trafalgar Sq.). *Rejected Addresses* (with his brother Horace) 1812 (175b).

Smith, Logan Pearsall (1865–1946), American essayist and bibliophile: educ. Oxford (Balliol College). *The Unforgotten Years* 1938 (262a).

Smith, Sarah ('Hesba Stretton') (1832–1911), novelist and short-story writer: spends childhood in Church Stretton; lives and is buried in London (Ham); her story used by Shaw (Chelsea: Sloane Sq.); commemorated in Church Stretton. *Jessica's First Prayer* 1866 (61a, 188a, b), *The Children of Claverley* (61a).

Smith, Stevie. See Smith, Florence Margaret.

Smith, Sydney (1771–1845), essayist and wit: educ. Winchester and Oxford (New College); curate in Netheravon; promotes the *Edinburgh Review* on his stay in Edinburgh 1798–1803; lives in London (Holborn: Doughty St.) 1803–6, (Marylebone: Orchard St.) 1806–9; rector of Foston-le-Clay 1806–28; prebend of Bristol; rector of Combe Florey 1829–45; lives in London (City: St. Paul's Churchyard); frequents Holland House (Kensington: Holland House); lives and d. in London (Mayfair: Green St.) 1839–45; buried in Kensal Green Cemetery (Kensal Green); commemorated in Foston-le-Clay and Combe Florey. *Letters of Peter Plymley* 1807–8 (205b), *Letters*, ed. Nowell C. Smith, 2 vols. 1953 (35b, 66a).

Smollett, Tobias George (1721–71), novelist: b. and spends childhood nr. Alexandria; lives in London (Chelsea: Lawrence St.) 1750–62; visits Bath; imprisoned in London (Southwark: Scovell Rd.) 1759; stays in Edinburgh 1766; revisits family home and is commemorated nr. Alexandria. *The Adventures of Roderick Random* 1748 (335a), *Peregrine Pickle* 1751, *Ferdinand Count Fathom* 1753, *Sir Launcelot Greaves* 1760–2 (172b), *Humphry Clinker* 1771 (16b, 96b, 128b, 172b, 198a, 216b, 226a, 296b).

Somerville, Edith Œnone (1858–1949), novelist with her cousin Violet Martin, as 'Somerville and Ross': lives, d., and is commemorated in Castletownshend. *The Real Charlotte* 1894, *Some Experiences of an Irish R.M.* 1899, *Further Experiences of an Irish R.M.* 1908 (54a).

Somerville, William (1675–1742), poet: b. Colwich; educ. Winchester and Oxford (New College); Fellow at Oxford (New College) 1693; enters Middle Temple, London (City: Temple) 1696; lives nr. Wootton Wawen; commemorated in Wootton Wawen. *The Chace* 1735 (269a, 344a).

Sorley, Charles Hamilton (1895–1915), poet: educ. Marlborough. *Marlborough and other Poems* 1916, 'I have not brought my Odyssey' (239a).

Soutar, William (1898–1943), poet: b., lives, and d. in Perth. *Collected Poems* 1948, *Diaries of a Dying Man* 1954 (280a).

Southerne, Thomas (1660–1746), dramatist: b. and educ. Dublin; enters Middle Temple, London (City: Temple); frequents Pontacks (City: Lombard St.). *The Fatal Marriage* 1694 (81a), *Oroonoko* 1695 (81a, 346a).

Southey, Robert (1774–1843), poet: b. Bristol; educ. Corston, London (Westminster School), and Oxford (Balliol College) where he meets Coleridge 1794; spends youth and vacations in Bath; visits Lower Sapey 1793, Cheddar 1794; settles with Coleridge and m. (1795) in Bristol 1794–5; enters Gray's Inn, London (Holborn) 1797; lives in Burton 1797; visits Bournemouth and Mudeford; lives in Bristol (Westbury on Trym) 1798; visits Cowslip Green, Norwich 1798, Porlock 1799; lives in Keswick 1802–43; visits Llanthony and Llangollen 1811; second marriage in Boldre 1839; d. Keswick; buried in Crosthwaite; commemorated in London (Westminster Abbey). 'The Retrospect' 1793 (68b), *Joan of Arc* 1796 (261a), 'To A Dead Friend' (260b), *Minor Poems* 1797 (195a), *Letters from Spain and Portugal* 1797 (38a), *Thalaba the Destroyer*, 2 vols. 1801 (41b, 195a), *Madoc* 1805 (38a, 144b, 195a), 'The Holly Tree', 'Ebb Tide', 'Winter' (38a), 'The Inchcape Rock' (140a), *The Curse of Kehama* 1810, *Roderick the last of the Goths* 1814, *History of Brazil* 1810–19 (71b, 144b).

Spelman, Sir Henry (*c.* 1560/64–1641), antiquary: b. nr. and bequeaths his library to Swaffham.

Spence, Joseph (1699–1768), author of *Anecdotes* (1820), and friend of Pope: meets Pope in Oxford 1735; lives, d., and

is commemorated in Byfleet. *Observations, anecdotes and characters*, ed. S. W. Singer, 1820 (258b).

Spencer, Bernard (1909–63), poet: educ. Oxford (Corpus Christi College). *Oxford Poetry* (ed.) 1929–30, contributions to *New Verse* (265a).

Spencer, Herbert (1820–1903), philosopher: b., educ., and teaches in Derby; works in London (Strand: Wellington St.); d. Brighton.

Spenser, Edmund (1552?–99), poet: educ. Merchant Taylors' School, London (City: Suffolk Lane) and Cambridge (Pembroke College); spends boyhood and youth 1576–8 in Hurstwood; lives in London at Lord Leicester's house (Strand: Essex St.) 1578–80; secretary to Lord Deputy in Dublin 1580–6; is entertained in Castlegregory 1580; reputed to have been in action at Smerwick 1580; granted estate in Doneraile 1586; visited by Ralegh in Doneraile 1587; ?visits Ralegh in Youghal between 1588 and 1589; lives in Alton 1590; m. in Cork (or Youghal) 1594; lives in London (Strand: Essex St.) 1596–7; High Sheriff of Cork 1598; in London 1598–9 and d. (Westminster: King St.); buried in Westminster Abbey. *The Shepheards Calender* 1579 (47a, 139b, 221a), *Colin Clouts come home againe* 1595 (12b, 77a, 139b), *The Faerie Queene* 1590 (6b, 67b, 77a, 86a, 221a), *Complaints, containing sundrie small poems of the worlds vanitie* 1591 (6b), *Amoretti* 1595 (77a), *Epithalamion* 1595 (13a, 67b, 77a), *Prothalamion* 1596, *View of the Present State of Ireland* 1596 (221a), *Fowre Hymnes* 1596 containing 'Hymnes in honour of Love and Beauty' (47a).

Spring, Howard (1889–1965), novelist: journalist in Manchester 1915–31; lives in Mylor 1939–47, Falmouth 1947–65; buried in Mylor. *Shabby Tiger* 1934 (237a), *Fame is the Spur* 1940 (237a, 246b), *In the Meantime* 1942, *Hard Facts* 1944 (246b), *There is No Armour* 1948, *Winds of the Day* 1964 (108b).

Squire, Sir John Collings (1884–1958), poet and critic, founder and editor of *London Mercury* (1919–34): b. and educ. Plymouth.

Stacpoole, Henry de Vere (1863–1951), novelist and poet: lives and is buried in Bonchurch. *The Blue Lagoon* 1909, *In a Bonchurch Garden* 1937 (27a).

Staël-Holstein, Germaine Necker, baroness de (Mme de Staël) (1766–1817), woman of letters, author of *Considérations sur la Révolution française*: visits Mickleham 1793,

London (Soho: Argyll St.) 1813-14. *De l'Allemagne* 1810-13 (216a).

Stanyhurst, Richard (1547-1618), historian and translator of Virgil: b. Dublin; after studying law in England returns to Dublin until 1579. Contributions to Holinshed's *Chronicles* Vol. I, 1577, *Aeneid* (trans.) 1582 (81a).

Steele, Sir Richard (1672-1729), dramatist and essayist: b. Dublin; educ. London (City: Charterhouse) and Oxford (Christ Church and Merton College); lives in London (Hampton) 1707, (St. James's: Bury St.) 1707-12; frequents Don Saltero's Coffee House (Chelsea: Cheyne Walk), Will's Coffee House (Covent Garden: Bow St.), Dick's Coffee House (City: Fleet St.), White's and the Thatched House Tavern (St. James's: St. James's St.); rents a cottage (Hampstead: Haverstock Hill) 1712; lodges in London (St. James's: St. James's St.) 1714-16; lives in Carmarthen 1724 and Llangunnor; d. and is buried in Carmarthen; commemorated in Llangunnor. *Tatler* 1709-11 (172a, 176b, 196a, 212a, 213b), *Spectator* 1711-12 (212a), *Town Talk* 1715-16 (213b), *The Conscious Lovers* (34b, 163a).

Stephen, Sir Leslie (1832-1904), philosopher, biographer, and essayist: educ. Cambridge (Trinity Hall) 1850-4; Fellow at Cambridge (Trinity Hall) 1854-67; lives in London (Kensington: Hyde Park Gate) 1879-1904; buried in Highgate Cemetery (Highgate). *Dictionary of National Biography* (ed.) 1882-91 (200a), *Henry Fawcett* 1885 (50b).

Stephens, James (1882-1950), poet and novelist: b. and lives in Dublin; promotes the *Irish Review* in Dublin 1911. *Insurrections* 1909, *The Crock of Gold* 1912 (86a).

Sterne, Laurence (1713-68), novelist: b. Clonmel; is rescued at Annamoe 1721; educ. Cambridge (Jesus College) where he meets John Hall; vicar of Sutton-on-the-Forest 1738-68; prebendary of York 1741; visits Bath, Don Saltero's, and Smollett in London (Chelsea: Cheyne Walk and Lawrence St.); vicar of Coxwold 1760-8; buried in London (Bayswater: Hyde Park Pl.); reburied in Coxwold 1969. *The Life and Opinions of Tristram Shandy*, 9 vols. 1760-7 (70a, 316b, 347b), *A Sentimental Journey*, 2 vols. 1768 (70a), *Letters of Yorick to Eliza* 1775 (35b, 70a), *Memoirs of the Life and Family of the late Rev. Laurence Sterne* 1775 (8a).

Sternhold, Thomas (d. 1549), versifier, with J. Hopkins, of the psalms: lives and is buried in Hursley. *The Whole Book of Psalms* by Sternhold, Hopkins, and others 1562 (138b).

Stevens, George Alexander (1710-84), actor and song-writer; pioneer of the dramatic monologue; visits Bartholomew Fair, London (Smithfield). *Songs* 1772 (215b).

Stevens, William Bagshaw (1756-1800), poet: usher 1776, headmaster 1779-1800 at Repton; chaplain to Sir Robert Burdett in Foremark 1779-1800; d., buried, and commemorated in Repton. *Poems* 1782 (286b), *Journal of William Bagshaw Stevens 1756-1800* 1965 (113a, 286b).

Stevenson, Robert Louis (formerly Lewis Balfour) (1850-94), poet, essayist, and novelist: b. and educ. Edinburgh; holidays at Swanston 1867-81; visits Tibbie Shiel's Inn 1867, Glencourse Old Church; lodges in Anstruther 1868, Burford Bridge; visits Mickleham; lives in Bournemouth 1884-7; commemorated in Edinburgh and Bournemouth. 'Voces Fidelium' 1868 (9a), *The Body Snatchers* 1881 (119b), *The New Arabian Nights* 1882 (40b), *Treasure Island* 1883 (101a), *Prince Otto* 1885 (29a), *A Child's Garden of Verses* 1885 (29a, 100b), *More Arabian Nights* 1885 (29a), *The Strange Case of Dr. Jekyll and Mr. Hyde* 1886 (29a), *Kidnapped* 1886 (119a, 307a), *The Merry Men* 1887, *Underwoods* 1887 (29a), 'Random Memories' in *Across the Plains* 1892 (9a), *Catriona* 1893 (318b), *Vailima Letters* 1895 (65a), *Weir of Hermiston* 1896 (101a, 318b), 'The Skye Boat Song' in *Songs of Travel* 1896 (303b), *St. Ives* 1898 (101a, 318b).

Stoker, Abraham ('Bram') (1847-1912), Civil Servant and writer of horror stories: b. and lives in Dublin 1847-97; lives in London (Chelsea: Durham Pl.). *The Duties of Clerks of Petty Sessions* 1878, *Dracula* 1897 (84a).

Stow, John (1525-1605), chronicler and antiquary: buried and commemorated at St. Andrew Undershaft in London (City: Leadenhall St.). *The Annales of England*, Holinshed's *Chronicle* (ed.) 1585-7, *Survey of London* 1598 (178b).

Stowe, Mrs. Harriet Elizabeth Beecher (1811-96), American author of *Uncle Tom's Cabin* (1852): stays in Liverpool 1853; visits Mrs. Gaskell in Manchester 1853, Lady Byron and Lord John Russell in London (Richmond: Richmond Park) 1859.

Strachey, Giles Lytton (1880-1932), biographer: b. London (Clapham Common); lives in London (Bayswater: Lancaster Gate) 1884-1909; educ. Liverpool and Cambridge (Trinity College) 1899-1903;

visits Rupert Brooke in Grantchester, Lady Ottoline Morrell in Garsington; lives in London and becomes one of the Bloomsbury Group (Bloomsbury: Gordon Sq.) 1909–17; proposes to Virginia Stephen (Bloomsbury: Fitzroy Sq.); lives in Tidmarsh 1917–24, Ham 1924–32. *Eminent Victorians* 1918 (322a), *Queen Victoria* 1921 (169a, 322a), *Elizabeth and Essex* 1928, *Portraits in Miniature* 1931, *Characters and Commentaries* 1933 (128a).

Street, Arthur George (1892–1966), journalist and novelist: b. and farms nr. Wilton. *Farmer's Glory* 1932, *Strawberry Roan* 1932, *Ditchampton Farm* 1946 (338b).

Stretton, Hesba. See Smith, Sarah.

Strong, Leonard Alfred George (1896–1958), novelist: b. Plymouth; educ. and teaches in Oxford (Wadham College). *Dewer Rides* 1929 (273b, 281b).

Sturt, George ('George Bourne') (1863–1927), novelist and diarist: b., educ., works, and d. in Farnham. *The Bettesworth Book* 1901, *Memoirs of a Surrey Labourer* 1907, *The Wheelwright's Shop* 1923, *The Journals of George Sturt*, 2 vols. 1967 (110a).

Suckling, Sir John (1609–42), lyric poet and dramatist: b. London (Twickenham); educ. Cambridge (Trinity College); lives at Roos Hall and estate in Barsham. 'Why so pale and wan, fond lover?' (15b–16a).

Surrey, Henry Howard, Earl of (1517?–47), poet: b. Kenninghall; condemned to death for treason in London (City: Guild-Hall) 1547; buried and commemorated in Framlingham. *Songs and Sonnets*, ed. R. Tottel, 1557 (176b), *Aeneid* (trans.) (114a).

Surtees, Robert (1779–1834), antiquary and topographer: b. Durham. *History of Durham* 1816–40 (91b).

Surtees, Robert Smith (1803–64), writer of humorous sporting novels and founder of *The New Sporting Magazine*: educ. Durham; lives at Hamsterley Hall; High Sheriff of Durham 1856; d. Brighton; buried nr. Hamsterley Hall. *Hillingdon Hall* 1845 (128a).

Swain, Charles (1803–74), poet and engraver: b. Manchester; lives and is buried in Prestwich, nr. Manchester. 'When the Heart is Young', 'I cannot mind my wheel, mother', 'Dryburgh Abbey, a Poem on the Death of Sir Walter Scott' (236a).

Swift, Jonathan (1667–1745), satirist: b. Dublin; educ. Kilkenny and Dublin; secretary *c.* 1690–4 to Sir William Temple nr. Farnham; incumbent of Kil-

root 1695–6, of Laracor 1700–45; writes to 'Stella' from Parkgate and Chester 1710; lodges in London (St. James's: Bury St.) 1710, 1713, 1726, (Soho: Leicester Sq.) 1711; patronizes the Thatched House Tavern (St. James's: St. James's St.), and the Fountain Tavern (Strand: The Strand); spends summers in Virginia; Dean of St. Patrick's, Dublin 1713–45; visits Pope in London (Twickenham); visits Celbridge, Unionhall, and Castletownshend 1723, Cirencester 1726, Bibury and Markethill; d. and is buried in Dublin; commemorated in Dublin, Celbridge, and Markethill. *The Battle of the Books* 1704 (49b, 109b), *A Tale of a Tub* 1704 (109b, 147a), 'Cadenus and Vanessa' 1713 (55a), *The Drapier's Letters* 1724 (81b), *Gulliver's Travels* 1726 (81b, 330b), *Verses on the Death of Dr. Swift* 1731, *A Complete Collection of Polite and Ingenious Conversation* 1738 (81b), *Carberiae Rupes* (54a, 329b), *Journal to Stella*, ed. Harold Williams, 2 vols. 1948 (58b, 109b, 276b).

Swinburne, Algernon Charles (1837–1909), poet: b. London (Belgravia: Chester St.); spends youth in Bonchurch and at Capheaton Hall; visits Wordsworth in Rydal 1848; frequents Wallington House; educ. Eton and Oxford (Balliol College); is tutored in Navestock 1859; visits Meredith in Esher 1859; lives in London (Belgravia: Grosvenor Pl.) 1860–1, with Rossetti (Chelsea: Cheyne Walk) 1862–4; visits Tintagel 1864; stays with parents in Shiplake 1865–79; lives in London (Belgravia: Wilton Cres.) 1865, (Marylebone: Dorset St.) 1865–70; is visited by Mallarmé and lives in London 1872–5 and 1877–8 (Bloomsbury: Great James St.), visits Dunwich; lives in London (Putney) 1879–1909; buried in Bonchurch. *The Queen Mother. Rosamond. Two Plays* 1861 (166b, 246b, 261a), 'Queen Yseult' (261a), *Atalanta in Calydon* 1865 (166b, 322b), *Chastelard* 1865 (166b), 'Laus Veneris' (105b, 203b), 'A Song of Italy', 'Dolores', 'A Litany', in *Poems and Ballads* 1866 (203b), 'By the North Sea' in *Studies in Song* 1880 (91a), *Tristram in Lyonesse* 1882, 'On the Cliffs' (301a), *Letters*, ed. C. Y. Lang, 6 vols. 1959–62 (27a).

Symonds, John Addington (1840–93), poet, translator, essayist, and critic: b. Bristol (Clifton); educ. London (Harrow on the Hill) and Oxford (Balliol College); Fellow at Oxford (Magdalen College) 1862; m. 1864 and lives in Hastings; lives in

Bristol 1868–80; visits Sutton Court. 'Clifton and a Lad's Love' in *In the Key of Blue* 1893 (36b, 316a), *Letters* 1907 (36b).

Symonds, William Samuel (1818–87), novelist: rector of Pendock. *Malvern Chase* 1881, *Hanley Castle* 1883 (277b).

Synge, John Millington (1871–1909), dramatist: b., educ., lives, and d. in Dublin; visits Ashford (Wicklow) 1872, 1889, Aran Islands 1898–1902; buried in Dublin (Mount Jerome Cemetery). *In the Shadow of the Glen* 1903 (84b, 120a), *Riders to the Sea* 1904, *The Well of the Saints* 1905, *The Aran Islands* 1907, *The Playboy of the Western World* 1907 (84b).

Tagore, Sir Rabindranath (1861–1941), Indian poet and dramatist: lives in London (Hampstead: Vale of Health) 1912. *Gitanjali* 1912 (191b).

Taliesin (*fl.* 550), reputed Welsh bard: buried, according to tradition, at Tre-Taliesin. *Book of Taliesin* 14th c. (2b, 325b).

Tannahill, Robert (1774–1810), poet and song-writer: b. and lives in Paisley; frequents Gleniffer Braes; d. and buried in Paisley. *Poems and Songs* 1807 (275b), 'Keen blows the wind on the braes o' Gleniffer' (119b).

Tate, Nahum (1652–1715), dramatist and Poet Laureate: educ. Dublin (Trinity College); buried in London (Southwark: Borough High St., Church of St. George the Martyr).

Taylor, Ann. See Gilbert, Mrs. Joseph.

Taylor, Sir Henry (1800–86), dramatic poet: spends youth in Witton le Wear; lives in London (Marylebone: Blandford Sq.); visits Lady Ashburton nr. New Alresford. *Philip van Artevelde* 1834 (203b), 'The Cave of Ceada' and 'The Lynnburn' (342b).

Taylor, Isaac (1759–1829), dissenting minister and engraver: lives in Lavenham, Colchester 1796–1811, Ongar 1811–29. *Specimens of Gothic Ornaments Selected from the Parish Church of Lavenham* 1796 (154a).

Taylor, Jane (1783–1824), author of rhymes and stories for children: spends childhood in Lavenham until 1796; lives in Colchester 1796–1811, Ongar 1811–24; buried in Ongar. *Original Poems for Infant Minds* 1804, 'Twinkle, twinkle, little star' in *Rhymes for the Nursery* 1806, and *Hymns* 1810 (all with her sister, Ann) (65a), *Display, A Tale for Young People* 1815 (256b).

Taylor, Jeremy (1613–67), devotional writer and bishop: b. Cambridge; educ. Cam-

bridge (Gonville and Caius); Fellow at Cambridge (Gonville and Caius) 1633; Fellow at Oxford (All Souls) 1635 and preaches at the University Church; rector of Uppingham 1638–42; retires after imprisonment following Royalist defeat in Cardigan to Golden Grove 1645–58; preaches in Ballinderry while staying near by 1658–9; as Bishop of Down and Connor receives additional See of Dromore 1661 and rebuilds cathedral; lives in Lisburn 1661–7; buried in Dromore; memorials in Ballinderry and Lisburn. *Holy Living* and *Holy Dying* 1650–1, *The Golden Grove* 1655 (120b–121a), *Ductor Dubitantium* 1659 (14a).

Taylor, John ('the water-poet') (1580–1653), poet and traveller: b. and educ. Gloucester; lives in Oxford (Oriel College) 1625, 1645; visits Kingston upon Hull.

Taylor, William (1765–1836), man of letters and translator of German authors: educ. Palgrave; lives in Norwich. *Historic Survey of German Poetry* 1828–30, poems in *Annual Anthology*, ed. Southey, 1799–1800 (253a).

Tennant, William (1784–1848), poet and scholar: b. Anstruther; educ. St. Andrews; teaches in Anstruther; Professor of Oriental Languages in St. Andrews 1838–48; buried in Anstruther. 'Anster Fair' 1812 (9a).

Tennyson, Alfred, 1st Baron Tennyson (1809–92), poet: b. Somersby; educ. Louth, Somersby, and Cambridge (Trinity College); visits Harrington Hall 1834; lives in High Beech 1837–40; visits Torquay 1838; frequently stays in Shawell; visits Tealby, Curragh Chase 1848, Killarney 1848, New Alresford; m. in Shiplake 1850; visits Clevedon on honeymoon 1850; lives in London (Twickenham: Montpelier Row) 1851–3, Farringford from 1853 for many years; visits Swainston Hall, Caerleon, Shottermill, Woodbridge; builds Aldworth in Haslemere 1868, his home for the rest of his life; stays with Froude in Salcombe 1889; d. Haslemere; buried in London (Westminster Abbey); memorials in Haslemere and nr. Farringford. 'The Devil and the Lady', *Poems by Two Brothers* (with his brother Charles) 1827 (305a), 'Timbuctoo' 1829 (50a), *Poems Chiefly Lyrical* 1830, 'The Lotos-Eaters', 'Œnone', and 'Two Voices', in *Poems* 1833 (305a), 'The Lord of Burleigh' 1833 (41a), 'Love and Duty' c. 1840 (133b), 'Break, break, break' (62b), *In Memoriam* 1850 (50a, 57b, 62b, 300b), 'Ode on the Death of the

Brighton 1770s, Beaconsfield, Hagley, Holywell, Tremeirchion, and Ilam 1774; visits, with Fanny Burney, Devizes 1780, Bath, and Tunbridge Wells; lives 1783-4 and m. Gabriele Piozzi in Bath; settles in Tremeirchion 1795; lives in Bath 1814-20, Penzance 1820-1; last months at Bristol (Clifton); buried in Tremeirchion; commemorated in London on Dr. Johnson's monument at St. Clement Danes (Strand: The Strand), and Clink St. (Southwark: Park St.). Anecdotes of the late Samuel Johnson 1786, Letters of Samuel Johnson, with Mrs. Thrale's genuine letters to him 1788, ed. R. W. Chapman, 3 vols. 1952 (224a), Thraliana: the diary of Mrs. Thrale, 1776-1809, ed. K. C. Balderstone, 2 vols. 1942, 1951 (219b).

Thynne, William (d. 1546), editor of Chaucer's works: lives in London (Erith); buried in All Hallows Barking (City: The Tower of London); commemorated in Westminster Abbey.

Tickell, Thomas (1686-1740), poet: b. Bridekirk; educ. Oxford (The Queen's College); obtains post under Addison in Dublin 1710; elected Professor of Poetry, Oxford (The Queen's College) 1711; settles c. 1723, and is buried in Dublin. 'Oxford' 1707, On the Prospect of Peace 1712 (271a), 'On the Death of Mr. Addison' in Addison's Works (ed.), 4 vols. 1721 (86b).

Tobin, John (1770-1804), playwright, author of The Curfew (1807) and The School for Authors (1808): buried in Cobh. The Honey Moon 1805 (64b).

Tolkien, John Ronald Reuel (1892-1973), scholar and novelist: educ. and lives Oxford (Exeter College), Fellow and Professor of Anglo-Saxon (Pembroke College) 1926-45, Fellow and Professor of English Language and Literature (Merton College) 1945-59. The Hobbit 1937, Beowulf: the monsters and the critics 1936 (270b), The Lord of the Rings 1955 (269a).

Toplady, Augustus Montague (1740-78), author of Psalms and Hymns for Private Worship (1776): b. Farnham; educ. London (Westminster School); vicar of Broadhembury 1768-78; shelters from a storm in Burrington Combe. 'Rock of Ages, cleft for me' 1775 (41b).

Toynbee, Arnold Joseph (1889-1975), historian: Fellow at Oxford (Balliol College) 1912-15, hon. Fellow from 1957. A Study of History, 12 vols. 1934-61, Acquaintances 1967 (262a).

Traherne, Thomas (1638?-74), poet: b. Hereford; educ. Oxford (Brasenose College); rector of Credenhill 1657-67; chaplain to Sir Orlando Bridgeman 1669-74 and rector 1672-4 in London (Teddington), d. and is buried in Teddington. Centuries of Meditation 1674 (70b), Poems, ed. Dobell, 1903 (224a), Poems of Felicity 1910 (70b).

Train, Joseph (1779-1852), antiquary, poet, and friend of Sir Walter Scott: lives, is buried, and commemorated in Castle Douglas.

Trelawny, Edward John (1792-1881), friend of Shelley: lives in London (Belgravia: Eaton Sq.) 1838. Adventures of a Younger Son 1831, Records of Shelley, Byron, and the Author 1858 (166a).

Trevelyan, George Macaulay (1876-1962), historian: educ. London (Harrow on the Hill); Master of Trinity College, Cambridge 1927-40. English Social History 1942, illustrated edn., 4 vols. 1949-52 (50b).

Trollope, Anthony (1815-82), novelist: b. London (Bloomsbury: Keppel St.); educ. Winchester and London (Harrow on the Hill); Post Office official in Banagher 1841, Clonmel 1844-5, Mallow 1845-51, Belfast 1853-4; visits Salisbury; lives in Dublin 1854-9; lives in Waltham Cross 1859-70, London (Marylebone: Montagu Sq.) 1872-80, South Harting 1880-2; d. London (Marylebone: Welbeck St.); buried in London (Kensal Green Cemetery). The Macdermots of Ballycloran 1847, The Kellys and the O'Kellys 1848 (15a), The Warden 1855 (20b, 295b, 339b), Orley Farm 1862 (332a), The Claverings 1867, The Last Chronicle of Barset 1867 (331b), The Eustace Diamonds 1873 (205b), John Caldigate 1879 (43b), Autobiography 1883 (295b).

Tschiffely, Aimé Felix (1895-1950), travel-writer: visits Cunninghame Graham in Ardoch 1936. From Southern Cross to Pole Star 1933, later edns. called Tschiffely's Ride, Don Roberto 1937 (10a).

Turgenev, Ivan Sergeyevich (1818-83), Russian novelist: visits George Eliot in London (Regent's Park: Lodge Rd.) 1878.

Tusser, Thomas (1524?-80), poet: educ. Cambridge (Trinity Hall); farms in Cattawade; memorial in Manningtree nr. Cattawade. Hundreth Good Pointes of Husbandrie 1557 (54b), Stanzas 1580 (50b).

Twain, Mark. See Clemens, Samuel Langhorne.

Tyndale, William (d. 1536), translator of the Bible into English: preacher at St. Dunstan-in-the-West, London (City: Fleet

St.) 1523-4; commemorated in London (Westminster Abbey) and North Nibley.

Udall (or Uvedale), Nicholas (1505–56), dramatist and scholar: educ. Winchester and Oxford (Corpus Christi); headmaster of Eton 1534–41, Westminster School, London (Westminster) 1554–6; rector of Braintree 1537–44. *Ralph Roister Doister* 1566 (106a).

Urquhart (or Urchard), Sir Thomas (1611–60), translator of Rabelais: b. Cromarty; educ. Aberdeen *c*. 1628; lives in Cromarty 1645–50, 1652–3. 'Ekskubalauron' in *Collections of Miscellaneous Treatises* 1774, 1834 (71a).

Ussher, James (1581–1656), scholar and archbishop, author of the history *Annales Veteris et Novi Testamenti* (1650–4): educ. Dublin (Trinity College); buried in London (Westminster Abbey); bequeaths his books and manuscripts to Trinity College, Dublin.

Vachell, Horace Annesley (1861–1955), novelist and playwright: educ. London (Harrow on the Hill); lives in Widcombe 1927–52. *The Hill* 1905 (193a, 337b), *Quinneys* 1914, *Fellow Travellers* 1923, *Methuselah's Diary* 1950 (337b).

Vanbrugh, Sir John (1664–1726), playwright and architect, author of *The Relapse* and *The Provok'd Wife* (1697): designs Blenheim Palace in Woodstock 1705; suggests alterations at Audley End 1721; member of the Kit-Cat Club in London (Barnes: Barn Elms Park), (Hampstead: Heath Rd.); buried in St. Stephen Walbrook (City: Poultry). *The Country House* 1705, *The Confederacy* 1705 (343b).

Vaughan, Henry ('the Silurist') (1621–95), poet and physician, author of the poem 'They are all gone into the world of light': b. Llansantffraed; educ. Oxford (Jesus College); practises medicine, d., and is buried in Llansantffraed. *Silex Scintillans* 1650, 1655 (163b).

Verlaine, Paul (1844–96), French poet: lodges with Rimbaud in London (Soho: Howland St.) 1872–3, (Lambeth: Stamford St.) 1874; teaches in Stickney 1875–6, Bournemouth 1876–7. *Romances sans Paroles* 1874 (217a), *Sagesse* 1881 (29a, 310b), 'La Mer est plus belle' in *Amour* 1888, *Amour, Bonheur* 1891, *Liturges Intimes* 1892 (29a).

Voltaire (François Marie Arouet) (1694–1778), French dramatist, essayist, novelist, and poet, author of *Zaïre* (1732), *Essai sur les mœurs* (1756), and *Candide* (1759): visits Pope when in exile in London (Twickenham: Crossdeep) 1726–9; stays in Southampton between 1750 and 1755.

Waddell, Helen (1889–1965), medieval scholar and novelist: Research Fellow at Oxford (Somerville College) 1920–2. *Peter Abelard* 1933 (272a).

Waller, Edmund (1606–87), poet: b. Coleshill; educ. Cambridge (King's College) 1620–2; lives in Beaconsfield 1624–87; m. in London (Westminster: St. Margaret's) 1631); courts 'Sacharissa' at Penshurst Place; buried in Beaconsfield. 'On my Lady Dorothy Sidney's picture', 'At Penshurst', 'To the Servant of a Fair Lady' (278b).

Walmsley, Leo (1892–1966), novelist: lives in Robin Hood's Bay; frequents Whitby. *Three Fevers* 1932, *Foreigners* 1935, *Sally Lunn* 1937 (287b).

Walpole, Horace, 4th Earl of Orford (1717–97), poet, novelist, collector, and letter-writer: b. and lives in London (St. James's: Arlington St.) 1717–79; educ. Cambridge (King's College) 1735–9; lives at his country house, London (Twickenham) 1747–97, his town house (Mayfair: Berkeley Sq.) 1779–97; visits Ampthill, Hagley 1753, Bath and Batheaston 1766; Nuneham Courtenay, Rousham, Aston, London (Chelsea: Ranelagh Gardens), St. George's Coffee House (Strand: The Strand), Schomberg House (St. James's: Pall Mall); d. in London (Mayfair: Berkeley Sq.); buried nr. Houghton Hall. *The Castle of Otranto, a Gothic Story* 1765, *The Mysterious Mother* (225a), *Letters*, ed. Mrs. Paget Toynbee, 16 vols. 1903–5, Yale edition of *Correspondence*, *c.* 50 vols. 1937– (8a, 16a, 18a).

Walpole, Sir Hugh (1884–1941), novelist: educ. Canterbury and Cambridge (Emmanuel College) 1902–5; stays in St. Ives (Cornwall) and Esthwaite Lodge; spends last years and d. in Borrowdale; buried and commemorated in Keswick. *The Cathedral* 1922, *The Old Ladies* 1924, *Harmer John* 1926 (326b), *The Herries Chronicle: Rogue Herries* 1930 (27b), *Judith Paris* 1931 (27b, 106a), *The Fortress* 1932, *Vanessa* 1933 (27b).

Walsh, William (1663–1708), poet and critic: lives, d., and is buried in Abberley; M.P. for Worcester. 'The Despairing Lover' in *Poems* 1716 (1a).

Walton, Izaak (1593–1683), angler and biographer: b. and baptized in Stafford; lives in London (City: Fleet St.); m. in Canterbury 1626; attends Magdalen Herbert's funeral in Chelsea Old Church, London (Chelsea: Cheyne Walk); retires to Shallowford; lives in Hartlebury 1660–2; writes his wife's epitaph in

Wilson, Alexander (1766–1813), poet and ornithologist: b. and commemorated in Paisley. 'Watty and Meg' in *Poems* 1791, *The Foresters* 1805, *American Ornithology* 1808–14 (275b).

Wilson, John ('Christopher North') (1785–1854), poet, essayist, and critic: b. and educ. Paisley; lives in Windermere 1807–12, Edinburgh 1812–54; visits Tibbie Shiel's Inn; entertains Scott and Lockhart in Windermere 1825. *The Isle of Palms and other Poems* 1812 (340b), *Noctes Ambrosianae* in *Blackwood's Magazine* (99b, 322a, 340b).

Wilson, Margaret Oliphant. See Oliphant, Mrs. Margaret Oliphant.

Winchilsea, Countess of. See Finch, Anne.

Wingate, David (1828–92), poet: b., lives, d., and is buried in Glasgow. *Poems and Songs* 1862, *Annie Weir* 1866 (117b).

Wither, George (1588–1667), poet: b. Bentworth; educ. Bentworth and Oxford (Magdalen College); enters Lincoln's Inn, London (Holborn) 1606; imprisoned in the Old Marshalsea (Southwark: Borough High St., Mermaid Court) 1614 and 1621; Puritan commander in Farnham 1642; imprisoned in London (City: Newgate St.) 1660–3; d. and is buried in London (Strand: Savoy St.); commemorated nr. New Alresford. *Abuses Stript and Whipt* 1613, *Shepherd's Hunting* 1615, 'Shall I wasting in despair' in *Fidelia* 1615, *Wither's Motto* 1621 (218b), *Fair Virtue* 1622 (248b, 266b), 'A Love Sonnet' (266b), *Vox Vulgi* (179b), *De Defendendo* 1643 (109b).

Withers, James Reynolds (1812–92), poet: b. and educ. Weston Colville; works in Fordham from 1824; apprenticed in Weston Colville; d., is buried, and commemorated in Fordham. *Poems* 1854, 'Wicken Fen' (112b), 'My Native Village' (334b–335a) in *Collected Poems* 1863 (335a).

Wodehouse, Sir Pelham Grenville (1881–1975), humorous novelist: educ. London (Dulwich).

Wolcot, John ('Peter Pindar') (1738–1819), author of the satirical 'Lyric Odes to the Royal Academicians' and *The Lousiad* (1785): b. and educ. Kingsbridge; buried in St. Paul's Church, London (Covent Garden: Covent Garden).

Wolfe, Charles (1791–1823), poet: b. Clane; educ. Hyde Abbey School, Winchester, and Dublin (Trinity College); rector of Donaghmore 1818–21; buried in Cobh; commemorated in Dublin (St. Patrick's Cathedral). 'The Burial of Sir John Moore' 1817 (76b).

Wolfe, Thomas Clayton (1900–38), American novelist: lodges in London (Chelsea: Wellington Sq.) 1926; visits Oxford. *Look Homeward, Angel* 1929 (173b), *Of Time and the River* 1935 (260a).

Wollstonecraft, Mary. See Godwin, Mrs. Mary Wollstonecraft.

Wood, Anthony (later à Wood) (1632–95), antiquarian: b. Oxford (Merton College); educ. Thame and Oxford (Merton College); lives, d., is buried and commemorated in Oxford (Merton College). *Historia et Antiquitates Univ. Oxon.* 1674, *Athenae Oxonienses* 1691–2, *The Life and Times of Anthony Wood described by himself*, ed. A. Clark, 5 vols. 1889–99 (268a).

Wood, Mrs. Henry (*née* Ellen Price) (1814–87), author of *East Lynne* (1861) and *The Channings* (1862): b. Worcester; lives in Mallow; buried in London (Highgate Cemetery). *Mrs. Halliburton's Troubles* 1862 (344b).

Woodforde, James ('Parson Woodforde') (1740–1803), diarist: b. and curate in Ansford; educ. Oxford (New College) 1759–63; Fellow and Sub-Warden at Oxford (New College) 1773; rector of Weston Longville 1776–1803; visits East Tuddenham, Great Yarmouth, Honingham, Exeter Exchange, London (Strand: The Strand), Stourhead. *Diary of a Country Parson*, 5 vols. 1924–31 (9a, 125a, 136a, 239b, 313a, 335a).

Woolf, Virginia (*née* Stephen) (1882–1941), novelist and essayist: b. London (Kensington: Hyde Park Gate); spends childhood holidays in St. Ives (Cornwall); lives in London (Bloomsbury: Gordon Sq.) 1905–7; visits Grantchester; lives in London (Bloomsbury: Fitzroy Sq. 1907–11, Brunswick Sq. 1911–12); after marriage, lives in Asheham 1912–17; lives in London (Richmond: The Green) 1914–24; buys Monks House, Rodmell 1919; lives in London (Bloomsbury: Tavistock Sq. 1924–39, Mecklenburg Sq. 1939–40), dies 1939–41, d., and is buried in Rodmell. 'The Mark on The Wall' in *Two Stories* 1917, *Kew Gardens* 1919 (211a), *A Haunted House and other short stories* 1943 (11a), *To the Lighthouse* 1927 (293b), *Orlando: a Biography* 1928 (149b), *A Room of One's Own* 1929 (47a), *Flush: a Biography* 1933 (206b).

Wordsworth, Dorothy (1771–1855), diarist: b. Cockermouth; holidays with her brother William in Penrith; lives at Racedown Lodge 1795–7; visits Coleridge in Nether Stowey 1797; lives at Alfoxton Park

1797–8; visits Lynmouth, Porlock, Tintern Abbey; stays in Sockburn 1799 and later; lives in the Lake District 1799–1855, Grasmere 1799–1813; frequents Ambleside; visits London (Westminster Bridge) 1802, Bartholomew Fair with Lamb (Smithfield) 1802; accompanies William to Brompton-by-Sawdon October 1802; crosses the Hambleton Hills October 1802; visits Dumfries, Inversnaid, the Trossachs 1803; lives nr. Coleorton Hall 1806–7, Rydal 1813–50; visits Yarrow Water, Cambridge (Trinity College) 1820; in Bath for her niece's wedding 1841; visits Brinsop; buried in Grasmere. 'Alfoxden Journal' and 'Grasmere Journals' in *Journals of Dorothy Wordsworth*, ed. W. Knight, 1896, ed. Mary Moorman, 1971 (5a, 90a, 122b, 128a, 229b, 326a).

Wordsworth, William (1770–1850), poet: b. Cockermouth; lives with an uncle in Penrith; educ. Cockermouth, Hawkshead, and Cambridge (St. John's College); lodges in Colthouse 1779–87; frequents Grantchester; visits Brighton 1791; stays in Keswick 1794; first meets Coleridge in Bristol; lives at Racedown Lodge 1795–7; visits Coleridge in Nether Stowey 1797; rents Alfoxton Park 1797–8; visits Lynmouth, Porlock, Tintern Abbey; stays in Sockburn 1799 and later; lives in the Lake District 1799–1850; lives in Grasmere 1799–1813; frequents Ambleside; visits London (Westminster Bridge) 1802, Bartholomew Fair with Lamb (Smithfield) 1802; m. in Brompton-by-Sawdon 1802; crosses the Hambleton Hills 1802; visits Dumfries, Inversnaid, the Trossachs, Sma' Glen 1803; lives nr. Coleorton Hall 1806–7, in Rydal 1813–50; visits St. Mary's Loch, Yarrow Water 1814 and 1831, Oxford 1820, Souldern 1820, Cambridge (Trinity College) 1820, the Ladies of Llangollen 1824, Maria Edgeworth in Edgeworthstown 1829, Nottingham 1831, Douglas, I.O.M. 1833; dines with Miss Mitford in London (Bloomsbury: Russell Sq.) 1836; upset at his daughter's wedding in Bath 1841; visits Brinsop, Bishopstone (Hereford and Worcester), and Ledbury; d. Rydal; buried in Grasmere; commemorated in London (Westminster Abbey) and Grasmere. 'Salisbury Plain' 1796, *The Borderers* 1795–6, 'Lines Left upon a Seat in a Yewtree', 'The Ruined Cottage' (285a), 'Lines Composed a Few Miles above Tintern Abbey, on revisiting the Banks of the Wye during a Tour, July 13, 1798' (323a), *Lyrical Ballads* 1798 (5a, 123a, 233b, 323a), 'To the Cuckoo', 'My heart leaps up' (123a), 'Composed upon Westminster Bridge, September 3, 1802' (229a), 'Dark and more dark the shades of evening fell' 1802 (128a), 'The Trosachs' (326a), 'To a Highland Girl at Inversneyde', 'The Brownie' (140b), 'At the Grave of Burns' (90a, 304a), 'Yarrow Unvisited' 1803 (294b, 346b), 'Yarrow Visited' 1814, 'Yarrow Revisited' 1831 (346b), *Memorials of a Tour of Scotland* 1803 (294b), *Ode: Intimations of Immortality* (123a), *The Excursion* 1814 (123b), 'Character of a Happy Warrior', 'Elegiac Stanzas' (282b), *The White Doe of Rylstone* 1815 (26b, 290b, 291b, 305a), 'Recollection of the Portrait of King Henry the Eighth, Trinity Lodge, Cambridge' (49b), 'Inside of King's College Chapel, Cambridge' 1820 (46a), 'Oxford, May 30, 1820' (259a), 'On a parsonage in Oxfordshire' (305a), *The River Duddon* 1820 (90a), 'Persuasion' in *Ecclesiastical Sonnets* 1822 (142a), 'On Entering Douglas Bay, Isle of Man' 1833 (78a), 'Tynwald Hill' (328b), 'Roman Antiquities Discovered at Bishopstone' 1835 (24b), 'St. Catherine of Ledbury' 1835 (155b), *Guide through the Lakes* 1835 (151b), *The Prelude* 1850 (44b, 48b, 65a, 66a, 131a, 215b, 284b, 285a).

Wotton, Sir Henry (1568–1639), poet and ambassador: b. Boughton Malherbe; educ. Winchester and Oxford (New College and The Queen's College) 1584–6, friend of Donne (Hertford College); Provost of Eton 1624–39; visits Boughton Malherbe; buried at Eton. *Tancredo* (271a).

Wroth, Lady Mary (*née* **Sidney**) (*fl.* 1621), poet and patron: childhood and m. 1604 at Penshurst Place; lives in Loughton. *The Countesse of Mountgomerie's Urania* 1621 (231a).

Wyatt, Sir Thomas (1503?–42), poet and courtier: b. Allington (Kent); educ. Cambridge (St. John's College); imprisoned in London (City: the Tower of London) 1536 and 1540–1; d. and buried in Sherborne. *Songs and Sonnets* in *Tottel's Miscellany* 1557 (5b, 176b).

Wycherley, William (1640–1716), dramatist, author of *The Country Wife* (1675) and *The Plain Dealer* (1677): b. nr. Preston Brockhurst; educ. Oxford (The Queen's College); enters Inner Temple, London (City: Temple) 1659; frequents Will's Coffee House (Covent Garden: Bow St.); last years in London (Covent Garden: Bow St.), buried in London (Covent Garden: St. Paul's Church).

Wycliffe, John (1320?–84), instigator of

the first translation of the Gospels into English: Fellow, later Master, at Oxford (Balliol College); rector of Lutterworth 1374–8, d. and is buried in Lutterworth, his body exhumed and ashes cast into the Swift near by; memorial in Lutterworth.

Wynne, Elizabeth, Lady Fremantle (1779–1857), diarist: lives in Swanbourne. *The Wynne Diaries*, ed. A. Fremantle, 3 vols. 1935–40 (317a).

Wyntoun, Andrew of (1350?–1420?), historian: canon-regular in St. Andrews; Prior in St. Serf's Inch to ?1420. *The Orygynale Cronykil* 1795 (292a, 294b).

Yeats, William Butler (1865–1939), poet and dramatist: b. Dublin; educ. Godolphin Boys' School in London (Hammersmith: Iffley Rd.) and Dublin; lives in London (Chalk Farm: Fitzroy Rd.) 1867–74, (Kensington: Edith Rd.) 1874–6, (Chiswick: Woodstock Rd.) 1876–80; lives in Howth 1880; holidays in Sligo; founds the Rhymers' Club in London (City: Fleet St.) 1891; lives in London (Bloomsbury: Woburn Pl.) 1895–1919; rents cottage in Coleman's Hatch 1912–13; buys Thoor Ballylee nr. Gort 1917; lives in Oxford, Shillingford, and Thame 1921; visits Coole Park, Durras House, Tullira Castle, Rinvyle, Steyning, and Withyham; buried in Drumcliff. *The Wanderings of Oisin and other poems* 1889 (149b), 'Ballad of Father O'Hart' in *Crossways* 1889 (65b), *The Wind among the Reeds* 1899, *Cathleen ni Hoolihan* 1902, *On Baile's Strand* 1904, *Deirdre* 1907, *The Green Helmet and other poems* 1910 (170b), *Seven Poems and a Fragment* 1922 (300b), *The Wild Swans at Coole* 1919, 'Coole Park, 1929' (67a), *The Tower* 1928, *The Winding Stair* 1933 (121b), 'The Lake Isle of Innisfree', 'The Fiddler of Dooney' (140a), 'Meditations in Time of Civil War' (300b), 'Under Ben Bulben' (80b), 'Purgatory' in *Last Poems and two plays* 1940 (310b).

Yonge, Charlotte Mary (1823–1901), novelist: b., lives, and is buried in Otterbourne; commemorated in Winchester. *The Heir of Redclyffe* 1853 (257b).

Young, Arthur (1741–1820), agricultural theorist; author of *Tour in Ireland* (1780) and *Travels in France* (1792): lives in Bradfield Combust; visits Cork.

Young, Edward (1683–1765), poet: b. Upham; educ. Winchester; Fellow in Law at Oxford (All Souls College) 1708; rector of Welwyn 1730–65; frequents Tunbridge Wells; commemorated in Welwyn. *The Complaint, or Night Thoughts on Life, Death, and Immortality* 1742–5 (327b, 334a).

Young, Francis Brett (1884–1954), physician, novelist, and poet: b. Halesowen; practises medicine in Brixham 1907–14; spends summers at Esthwaite Lodge 1928–33; lives in Fladbury 1932–c. 1945; commemorated in Worcester and Halesowen. *Deep Sea* 1914, *The Dark Tower* 1914 (38b), *The House under the Water* 1932 (106a), *White Ladies* 1935 (111b).

Young, Robert ('Rabin Hill') (1811–1908), tailor and poet: b., lives, d., and is buried in Sturminster Newton. 'Rabin Hill's Visit to the Railway' 1861 (315b).

Zangwill, Israel (1864–1926), playwright and novelist: founder and first president of the International Jewish Territorial Organization: visits Ewelme; commemorated in London (Bethnal Green: Old Ford Rd.). *Children of the Ghetto* 1892 (107b, 166b), *The Melting Pot* 1908 (166b).

BOOKS FOR FURTHER READING

Austen-Leigh, R. A., *Jane Austen and Southampton*, 1949
Banks, F. R., *The Penguin Guide to London*, 1960
Barbeau, André, *Life and Letters at Bath in the XVIIIth Century*, 1904
Buchanan, David, *The Treasures of Auchinleck*, 1975
Byford-Jones, W., *The Shropshire Haunts of Mary Webb*, 1937
Cullen, Sara, *Books and Authors of Co. Cavan*, 1965
Draper, F. W. M., *Literary Associations of Hornsey*, 1948
Ellmann, R., *Ulysses on the Liffey*, 1972
Fletcher, Geoffrey, *Pocket Guide to Dickens' London*, 1976
Gill, Richard, *Happy Rural Seat*, 1972
Green, R. Lancelyn, *Authors and Places*, 1963
Hardwick, Michael and Mollie, *The Charles Dickens Encyclopaedia*, 1973
Hartley, Rachel, *Literary Guide to the City*, 1966
Keith, W. J., *The Rural Tradition*, 1975
Kirby, Sheelagh, *The Yeats Country*, 1962
Lillywhite, Bryant, *London Coffee Houses*, 1963
Magoun, Francis P., Jun., *A Chaucer Gazetteer*, 1961
Milward, Peter, S.J., and Schoder, Raymond, S.J., *Landscape and Inscape.*
  Vision and Inspiration in Hopkins's Poetry, 1975
Norrie, Ian, *Hampstead. A Short Guide*, 1973
— *Highgate and Kenwood. A Short Guide*, 1967
Pinion, F. B., *A Hardy Companion*, 1968
Scott, W. S., *Green Retreats*, 1955
Williams, George G., *Guide to Literary London*, 1973

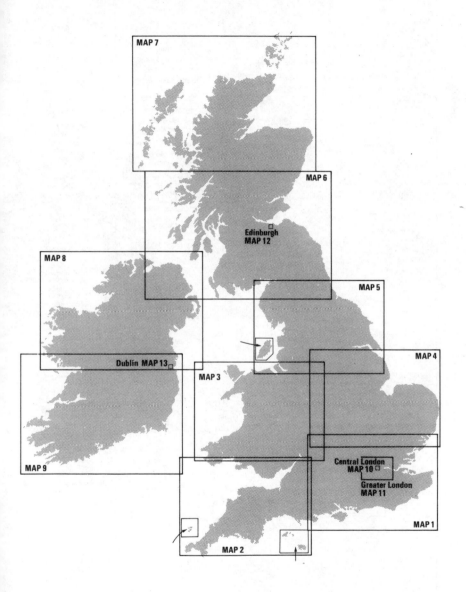

MAP 7

MAP 6

Edinburgh
MAP 12

MAP 8

MAP 5

Dublin MAP 13

MAP 4

MAP 3

MAP 9

Central London
MAP 10

Greater London
MAP 11

MAP 1

MAP 2

MAP 1

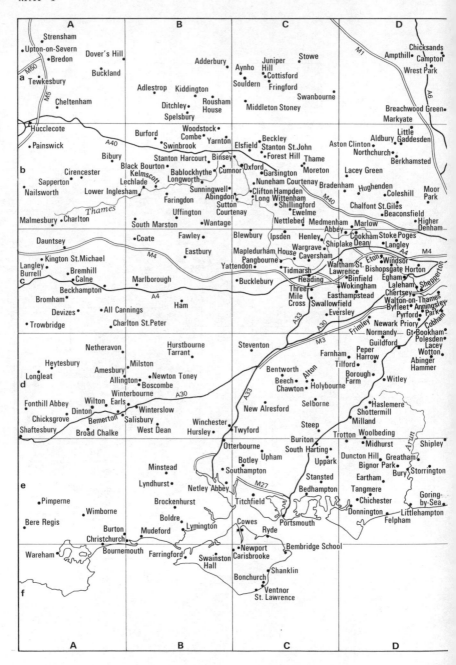

MAP 1

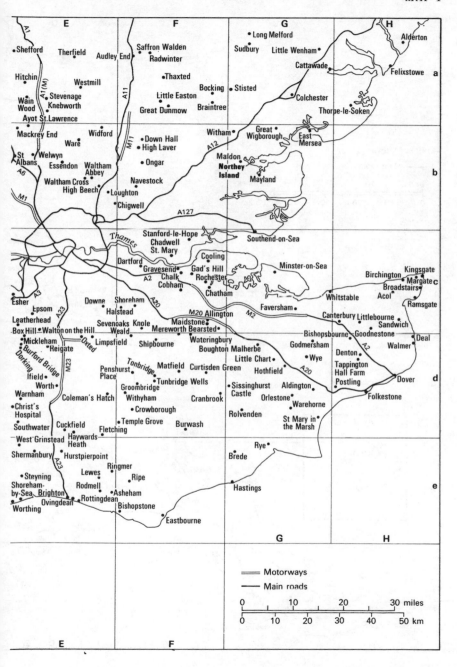

MAP 2

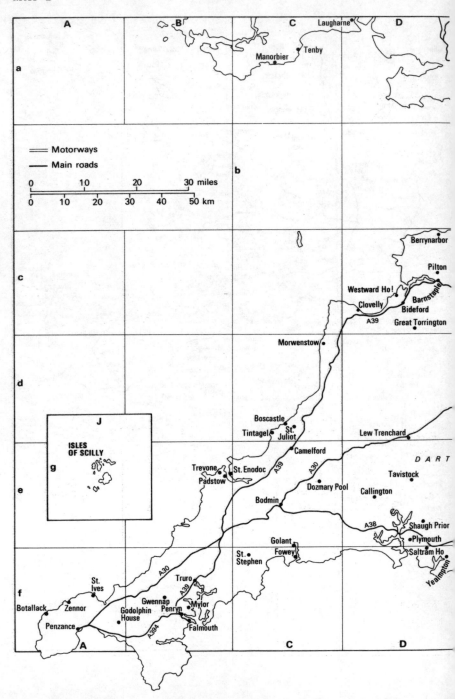

MAP 2

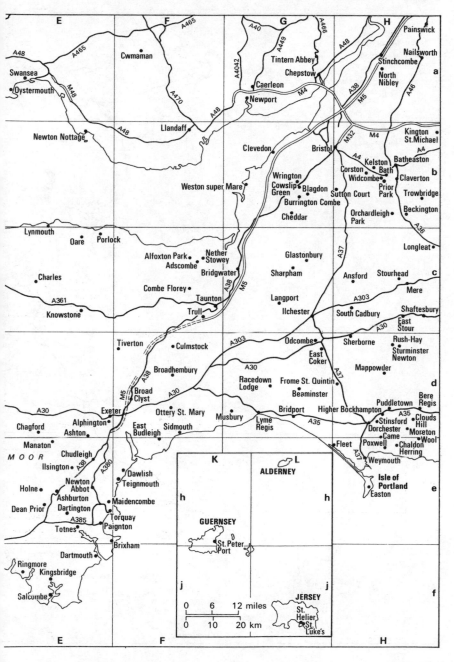

MAP 3

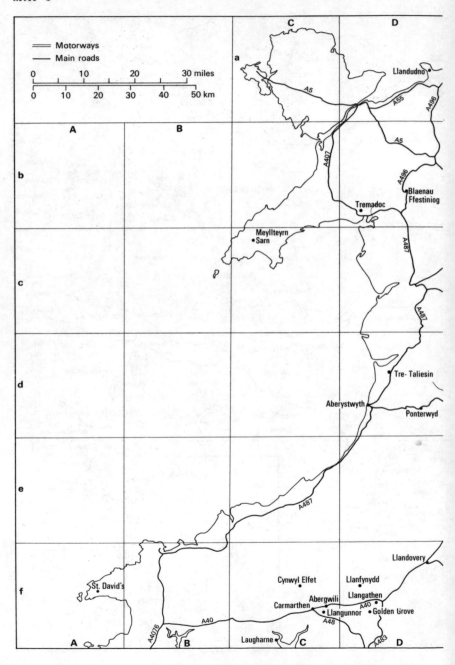

MAP 3

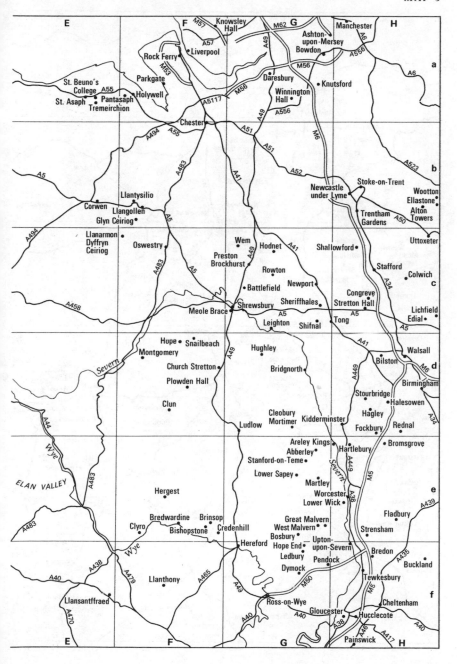

MAP 4

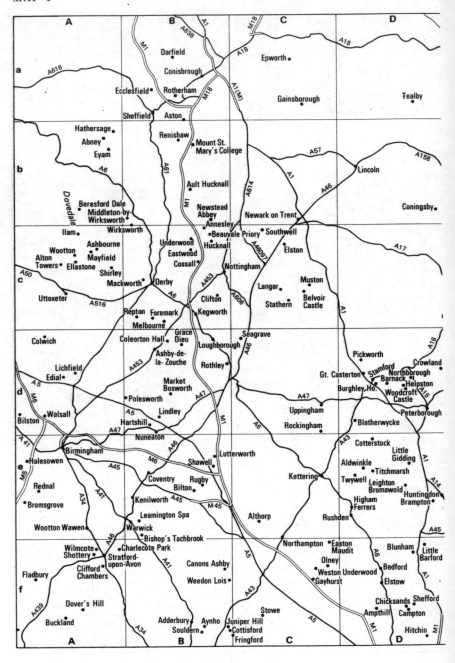

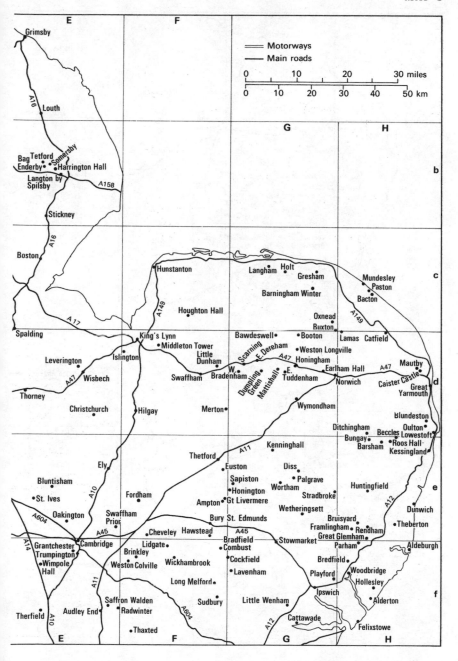

MAP 4

MAP 5

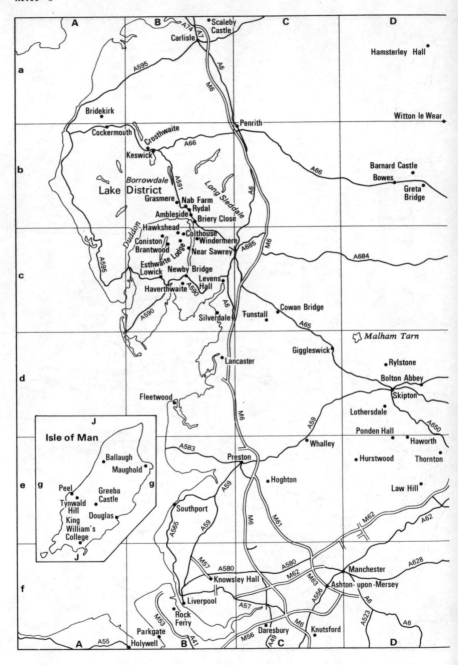

MAP 5

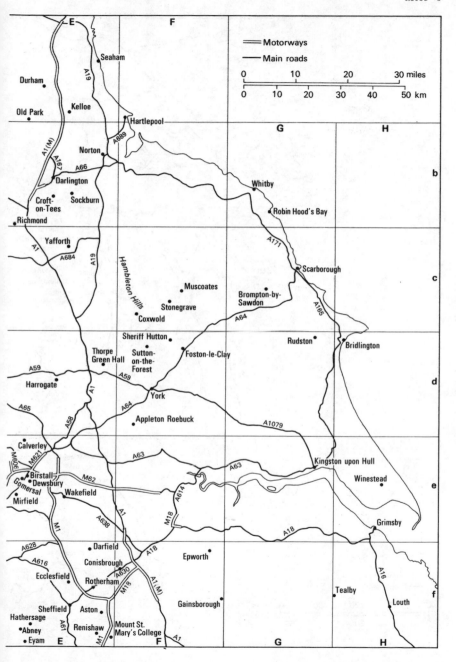

MAP 6

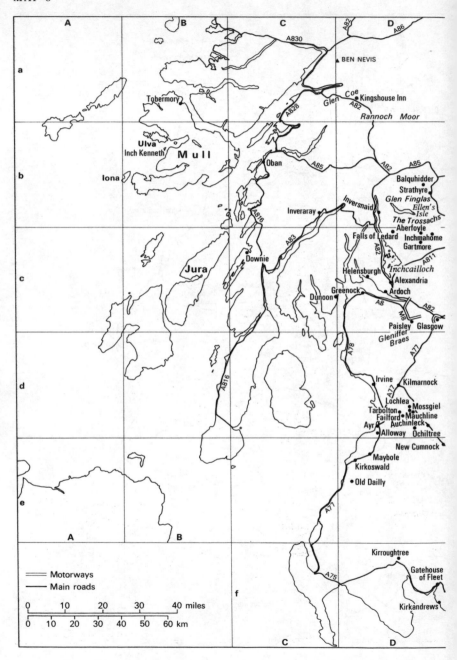

MAP 6

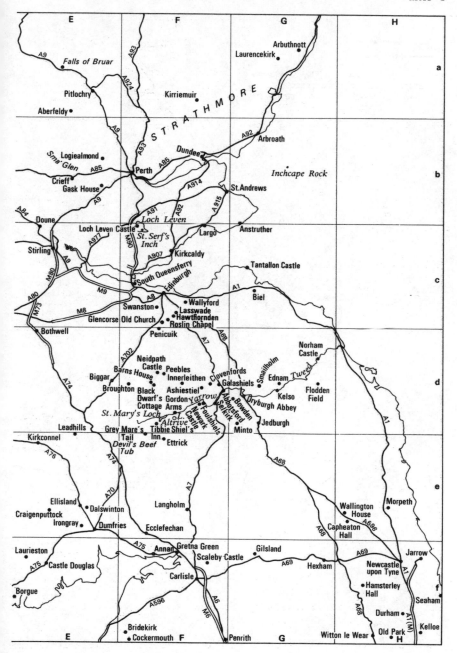

MAP 7

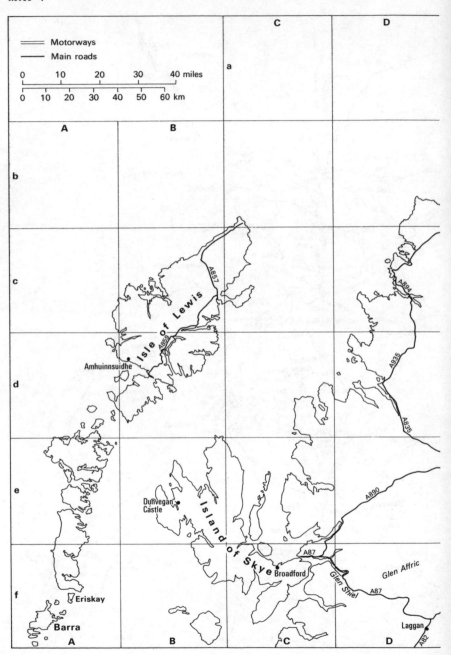

MAP 7

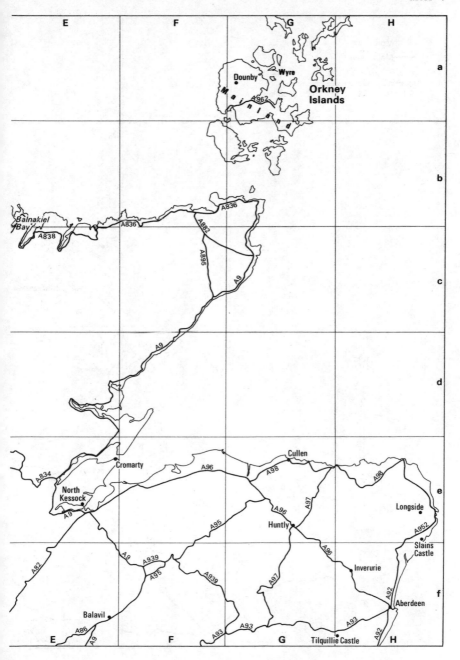

MAP 8

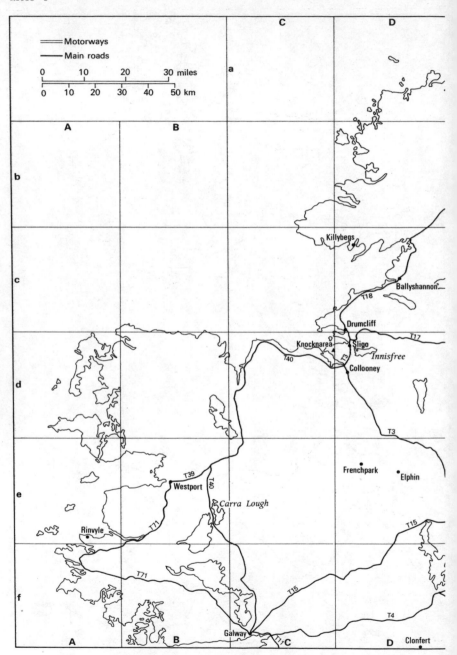

MAP 8

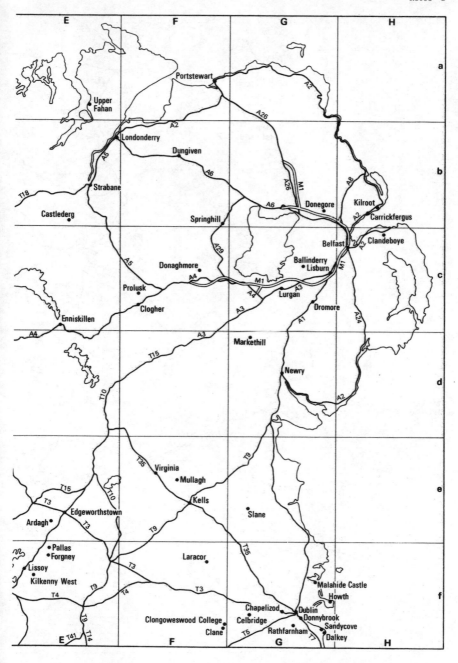

MAP 9

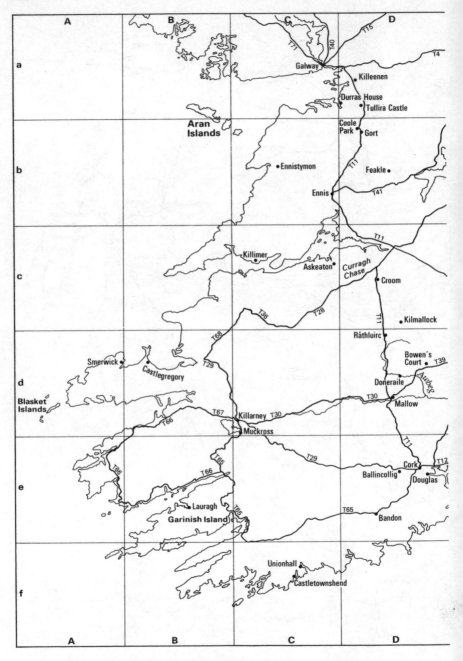

MAP 9

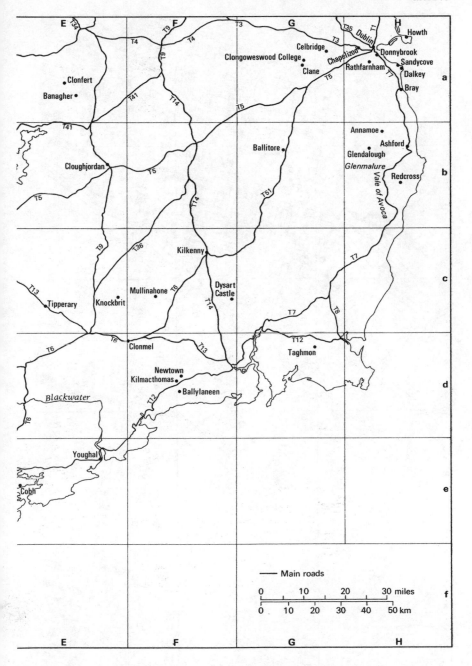

E   T34   T9   F   T4   T3   G   T35   Dublin   T1   H   Howth

T4   T9   T4   Celbridge   T3   Donnybrook

Clongoweswood College   Chapelizod   Sandycove

Clane   Rathfarnham   Dalkey   a

Clonfert   T5   Bray

Banagher •   T41   T14   T5

T41   Annamoe •

Ballitore •   Ashford

Glendalough   b

Cloughjordan   T5   Glenmalure

T5   T14   T51   Redcross

Vale of Avoca

T9   T36   Kilkenny   T7   c

T13   Mullinahone   T6   Dysart Castle

Tipperary   Knockbrit   T14   T8

T7   T7

T6   T6   Clonmel   T13   T12   Taghmon

Newtown   d

Kilmacthomas •   Blackwater   T12   • Ballylaneen

T6   Youghal

Cobh •   e

Main roads

0   10   20   30 miles

0   10   20   30   40   50 km   f

E   F   G   H

MAP 10   CENTRAL LONDON

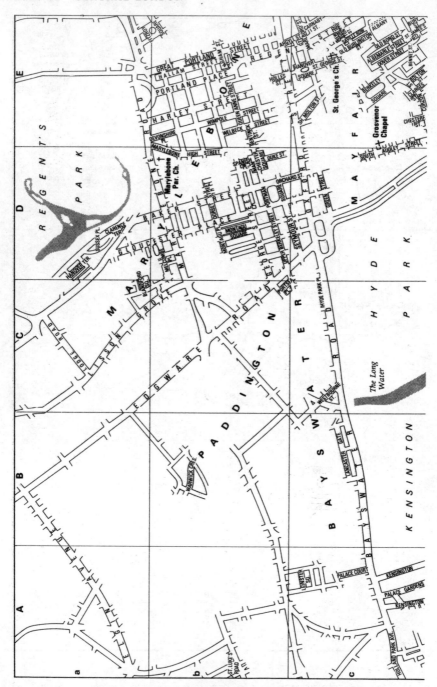

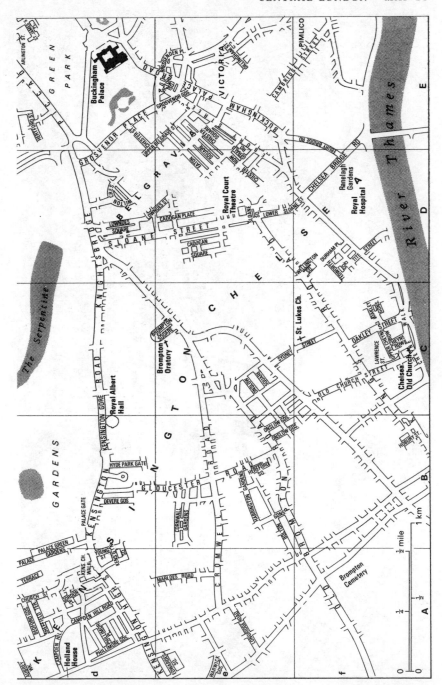

MAP 10   CENTRAL LONDON

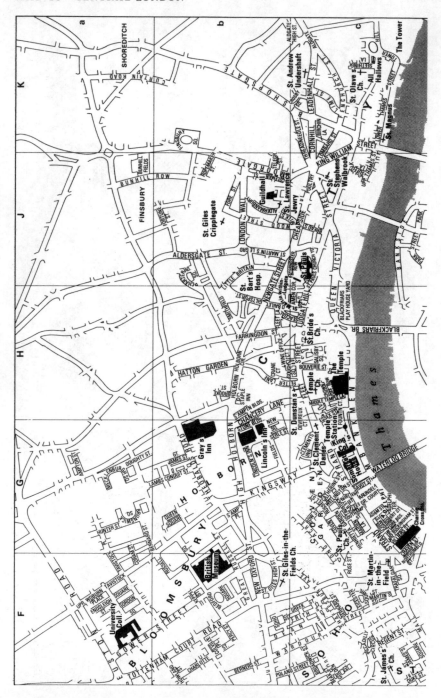

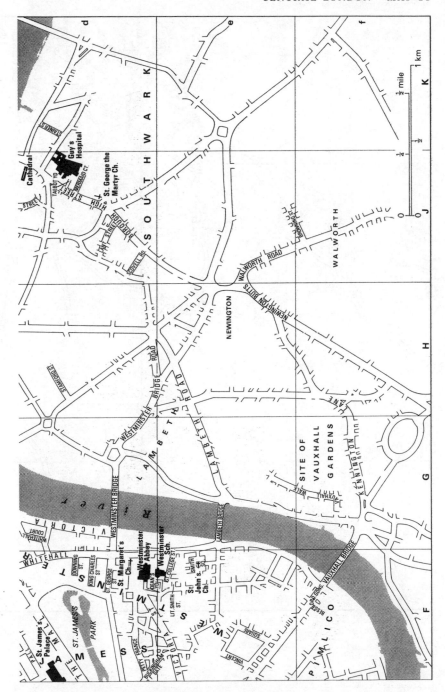

MAP 11   GREATER LONDON

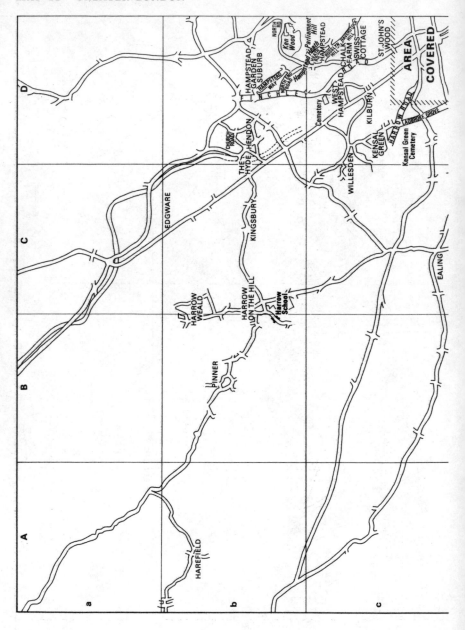

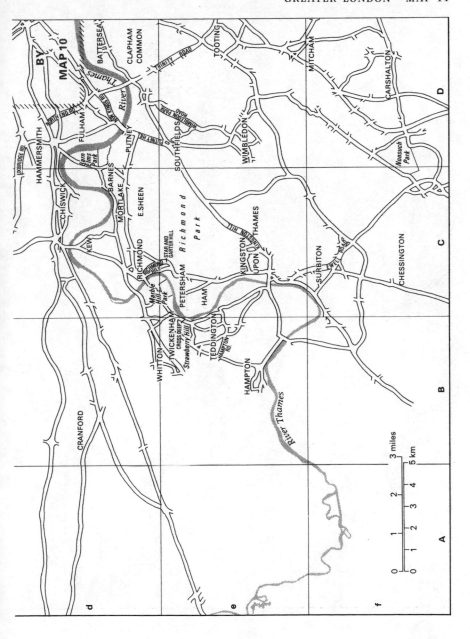

MAP 11   GREATER LONDON

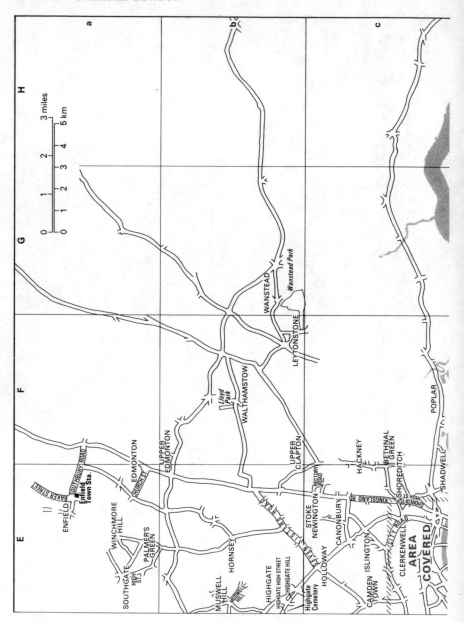

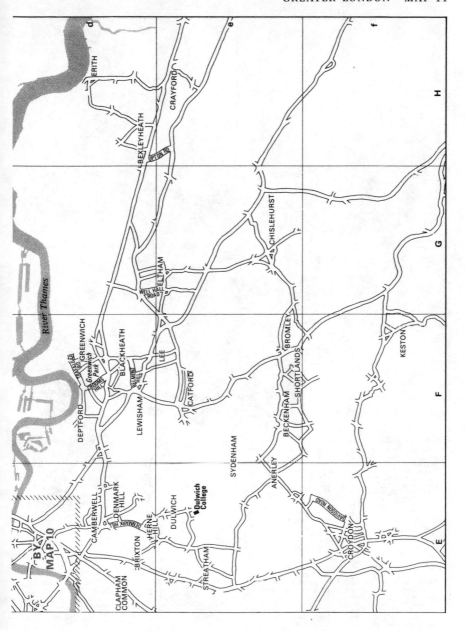

MAP 12   EDINBURGH

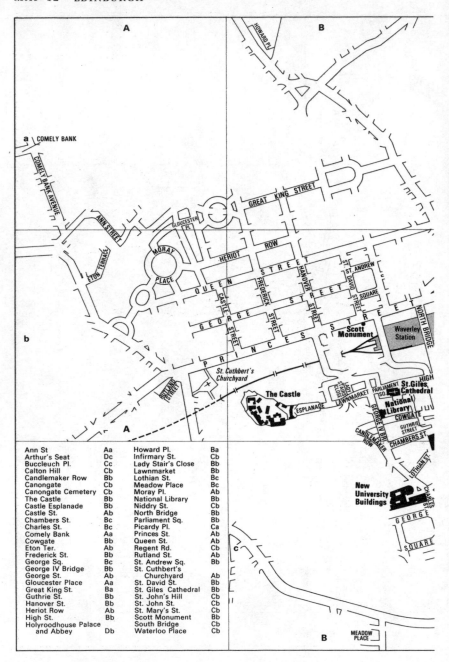

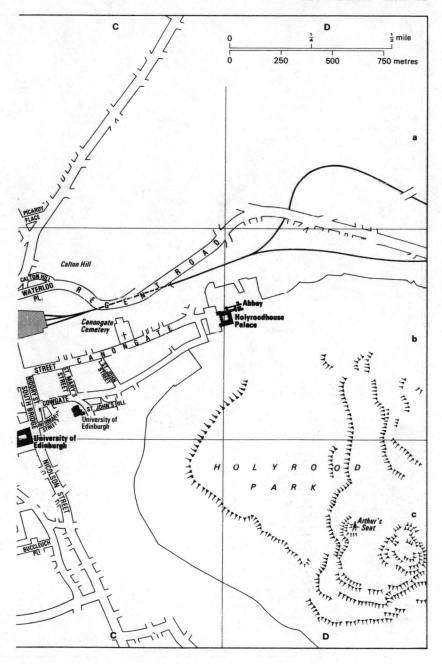

C

D

$\frac{1}{4}$

$\frac{1}{2}$ mile

0   250   500   750 metres

a

PICARDY
PLACE

Calton Hill

CALTON HILL

WATERLOO
PL.

R E G E N T   R O A D

Canongate
Cemetery

C A N O N G A T E

Abbey

Holyroodhouse
Palace

b

STREET

ST. MARY'S
STREET

ST. JOHN
STREET

NIDERY ST.

SOUTH BRIDGE

COWGATE

ST. JOHN'S HILL

INFIRMARY
STREET

University of
Edinburgh

University of
Edinburgh

NICOLSON   STREET

H O L Y R O O D

P A R K

BUCCLEUCH
PL.

Arthur's
Seat

c

C

D

MAP 13 · DUBLIN

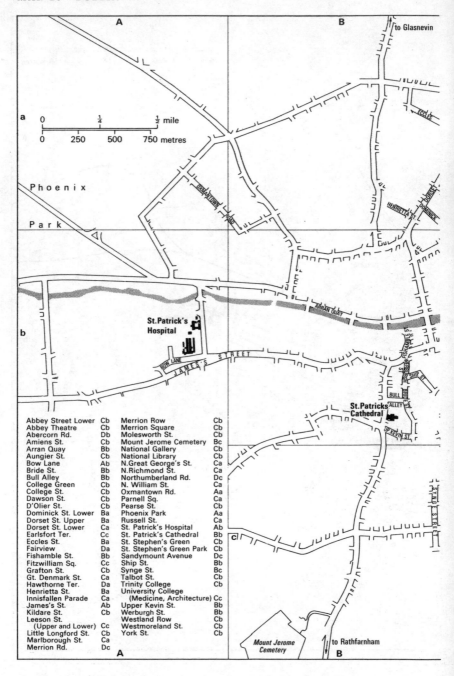

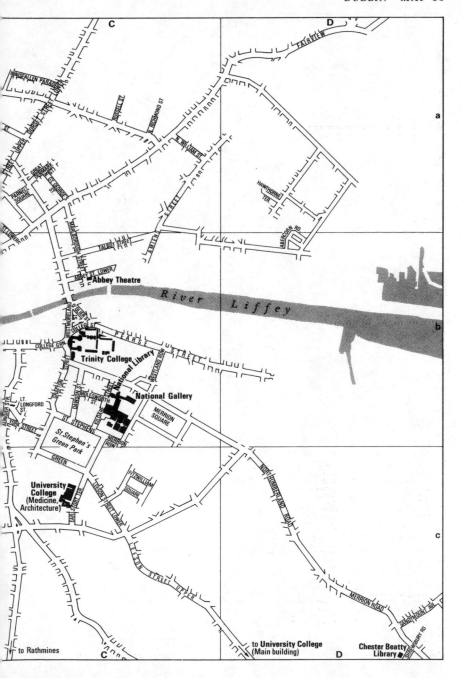

C

D

FAIRVIEW

a

INNISFALLEN PARADE

ST.

LOWER

PARNELL SQUARE

GREAT DENMARK ST.

GARDINER ST.

RUSSELL ST.

N. RICHMOND ST.

N. WILLIAM ST.

HAWTHORNE TER.

ABERCORN RD.

STREET

GARDINER STREET

TALBOT STREET

AMIEN STREET

ABBEY ST. LOWER

Abbey Theatre

River Liffey

b

WESTMORELAND ST.

D'OLIER ST.

COLLEGE ST.

PEARSE STREET

COLLEGE GRN.

WESTLAND ROW

Trinity College

National Library

DAWSON ST.

KILDARE ST.

MOLESWORTH ST.

National Gallery

LT. LONGFORD ST.

AUNGIER ST.

YORK STREET

ST. STEPHENS

GREEN

MERRION SQUARE

MERRION ROW

St. Stephen's Green Park

FITZWILLIAM SQUARE

LESSON STREET LOWER

EARLSFORT TER.

University College (Medicine, Architecture)

NORTHUMBERLAND ROAD

c

LESSON STREET UPPER

MERRION ROAD

SANDYMOUNT AVE.

SHREWSBURY RD.

to Rathmines

C

to **University College** (Main building)

D

Chester Beatty Library

NOTES

NOTES

NOTES